Tomas Casas-Klett

Towards an Elite Theory of Economic Development

Tomas Casas-Klett

Towards an Elite Theory of Economic Development

An Inquiry into Sustainable Value Creation

DE GRUYTER

ISBN 978-3-11-073890-2
e-ISBN (PDF) 978-3-11-073463-8
e-ISBN (EPUB) 978-3-11-073487-4
DOI https://doi.org/10.1515/9783110734638

Library of Congress Control Number: 2023944759

Bibliographic information published by the Deutsche Nationalbibliothek
The Deutsche Nationalbibliothek lists this publication in the Deutsche Nationalbibliografie; detailed bibliographic data are available on the internet at http://dnb.dnb.de.

Cover image: miakievy/DigitalVision Vectors/Getty Images
Typesetting: Integra Software Services Pvt. Ltd.

www.degruyterbrill.com
Questions about General Product Safety Regulation:
productsafety@degruyterbrill.com

Acknowledgments

This theoretical work is the result of a multitude of exceptional intellectual exchanges and the support of many extraordinary friends and colleagues, a few of which are acknowledged here.

The University of St.Gallen and its School of Management (SoM-HSG) has been my academic home during the creative and execution phases of this work and my gratitude first goes to the institution for allowing me the freedom to engage in research outside of the conventional social science boundaries. The operationalization and empirical research of elite quality would not have been possible without Professor Guido Cozzi, co-editor of the annual Elite Quality Report (EQx) and an expert in eliciting disciplined imagination, and Professor Martin Nerlinger, co-editor of the Value Creation Rating Report (VCr) and intent on resolving the tradeoffs in allocating capital between sustainability and profit. Both have been scholarly pillars in their commitment to sustainable value creation – of nations and firms respectively. The fantastically supportive team of researchers at the HSG includes the brilliant Dr. Celine Diebold and the extraordinarily efficient Alex Tonn, as well as the energetic Camile Zeller, Nils Unell, and Elia Mueller. All have played instrumental roles in completing this work. In addition, this research has received valuable inputs and inspiration from Professor Zhang Jun at Fudan University, Dr. Sam Shi at Fudan Development Institute, Dr. Christian Erk, Professor Etsuro Shioji at Chuo University, Professor Óscar Afonso at Universidade do Porto, Professor Dimitrios Georgakakis at the University of Leeds, Professor Huang Zhengkai at Tsinghua University, and Professor Shi Weilei at CKGSB.

The foundations for this work were laid by scholars to whom I am grateful as a lateral entrant into the world of academia, starting with the late Professor Jean-Pierre Lehmann at IMD, Professor Rui Minjie at Fudan University, as well as Professor Martin Hilb, Professor Winfried Ruigrok and Professor Gudrun Sanders at the HSG. Inspiration from the project has come from many corners of practice and memorable conversations with Joachim Schoss, Dr. Lee Howell, and Professor Michael Hilb.

The realization of the manuscript would not have been possible without the efforts of John Stuart, formally this book's copy-editor, but in truth a wise, generous, and infinitely patient counselor in matters of readability and coherence who most importantly challenged each and every paragraph for its sense-making and elegance. The many visuals in the book were expertly rendered by Massimo and Gina Rodríguez to make many of its abstract notions into appealing and clear figures that should help the reader apprehend its logic and language. The precise indexing work of Ellie Blair, Heinz Gabathuler, and Patrick Ziltener is also acknowledged.

Finally, I would like to thank André Horn, Steve Hardman, and Lucy Jarman at De Gruyter Brill for their professional support and expertise in publishing this book.

als meus pares
imaijo

Contents

List of Figures

https://doi.org/10.1515/9783110734638-204

Chapter 7

Chapter 8

Epilogue

Appendices

List of Tables

https://doi.org/10.1515/9783110734638-205

Epilogue

Appendices

Preface
The conceptual and exploratory nature of this inquiry

> The complicated analyses which economists endeavour to carry through are not mere gymnastic. They are instruments for the bettering of human life. The misery and squalor that surround us, the injurious luxury of some wealthy families, the terrible uncertainty overshadowing many families of the poor—these are evils too plain to be ignored. By the knowledge that our science seeks it is possible that they may be restrained. Out of the darkness light! (Pigou, 1920/1932, Preface, p. vii).

Elites are the fundamental force that shapes societies. The agency of elite coalitions characterizes the political economy and determines economic and human trajectories. Yet it remains the case that elites are not duly articulated as a conceptual element in mainstream economic theory. Rather, academia and the public discourse associates elites with fallacies, and systematic attempts are rarely made to understand elite business models and link these to institutional change, ascertain their impact in terms of sustainable value creation, develop economic policy, and deliver targeted structural reform. Elite agency is only considered reactively or in exceptional times, as is the case with The International Military Tribunal at Nuremberg, the West's sanctions on Russian elites in response to the invasion of Ukraine (Bertrand, 2022), or the ascendance of the so-called 'tech bros' at the onset of the second Trump Administration (see Epilogue). Otherwise, elite agency is either obfuscated by unsystematic narratives or overlooked by most development research agendas that fail to methodically model its inclusive and extractive effects.

Human societies evolve, and our 10,000 years of social advancement is undeniable. Yet, developmental outcomes vary wildly across political economies in time and space; a diversity that is primarily due to the creation and transfer of value and risk driven by domestic elite agency. About a century ago, Pigou, in the above-cited preface to *The Economics of Welfare*, explained that the objective of developing political economy knowledge is to help constrain processes that are contrary to societal welfare. This work has been conceived to further such insights.

The theory this book promulgates is that the value creation of elite business models determines the fate of nations. Business models based on first-order productive activities create value not only for the organizations and individuals performing them—they benefit us all. On the other hand, there are also extractive business models based on all forms of theft, including inflation, under/overregulation, substance abuse, monopolies, discrimination, war, and trade barriers. These enrich a few winners while impoverishing the rest creating a net loss that stymies overall economic growth. The elite business models of dominant coalitions like corporations, civil servants, financial houses, the foreign policy establishment, billionaires, or labor unions have the potential to do both good and bad. This whole inquiry rests on a simple but foundational ontological as-

https://doi.org/10.1515/9783110734638-001

sumption: 'value is created or transferred'. Societies are therefore characterized by value creation to the degree that second-order transfers from one subset of society to another are limited.

Development is the result of continuous elite transformational leadership to consolidate sustainable value creation business models that reject value and risk transfers. However, even the fairest of political economies—capitalizing on robust intra-elite contests, a comprehensive elite separation of powers and strong elite cohesion—see elite agency short-circuited by new tests and temptations, from the growing climate crisis to artificial intelligence (AI). Society requires capable elites committed to the relentless pursuit of institutional change and structural reform that is weighted and targeted, both in terms of the incentives that are provided and the restraints that are placed on business models.

This work references theories on elites to build a conceptual architecture that links elite agency to economic and social outcomes. Elites are examined objectively on the back of rich and diverse philosophical, sociological, and economic traditions that leverage the notions of Aristotle, Frédéric Bastiat, Karl Marx, Joseph Schumpeter, Vilfredo Pareto, Gaetano Mosca, Robert Michels, Mancur Olson, C. Wright Mills, Gordon Tullock, Robert Tollison, Anne Krueger, James Buchanan, George Stigler, William Baumol, Douglass North, Francis Fukuyama, Alice Amsden, Daron Acemoglu, James Robinson, David Brady, Michael Spence, Stefan Dercon, Peter Turchin, and many others. The ideas of Adam Smith, Arthur Schopenhauer, Friedrich Nietzche, Carl Menger, Arthur Pigou, Frank Knight, Erwin Schrödinger, Oliver Williamson, Ronald Coase, Erich Fromm, Hannah Arendt, Friedrich Hayek, Harry Markowitz, Amartya Sen, Adam Brandenburger, Nassim Taleb, Ruth Aguilera, Roberto Garcia-Castro, Eliezer Yudkowsky, and Marc Andreessen are not about elites *per se*, yet they inform key aspects of this work's conceptualization of elite agency. To this inquiry, elites are the conceptual element that best explains socio-economic reality, a unifying force that brings together diverse areas of the social sciences and is of the highest order of impact.

The value creation-appropriation (VCA) framework is applied to division of value strategies to elucidate how elite agency, aggregated at the national elite system level, generates variances in economic and human development outcomes. The importance of 'elite quality'—defined as the aggregate amount of value creation in relation to value extraction in an elite system—is especially topical in light of ever more rapid technological disruptions or systemic shocks like pandemics or wars. In some nations, elites are poised to increase the *size* of the economic pie (e.g., through innovation), while in others they will focus on increasing their *share* of the economic pie (e.g., through government handouts), thus shrinking it overall. At the same time, we have been witnessing growing non-elite discontent—and even an attempted insurrection in the US—since the 2008 Great Recession and its aftermath, with the fatidic 2020s characterized by increasingly bitter intra-elite contests, a lack of elite leadership, and the erosion of social cohesion in all its forms. These destabilizing events are happening across the planet, begging the question of where humanity is heading. The elite theory of economic development (hereinafter also referred to as the ETED) that this inquiry develops posits parsimoniously that everything, including non-elite discontent, depends on the scale of extractive value and risk transfer activities and the amount of rent seeking prevalent in the economy. Political economies with inclusive elite business models and high rates of value creation and risk origination, regardless of their ideological persuasion, cultural background, or institutional trajectories will be best positioned to deliver better futures for their citizens.

To achieve its purpose, this inquiry takes an integrative interdisciplinary approach towards whole and grand theorizing in the social sciences. Such a unifying "systematic" project must acknowledge Mill's critique of "a theory of history" and "a theory of 'the nature of man and society'" (1959, pp. 22, 23) "in the name of imagination" (Skinner, 1990, p. 3) and contend with both the post-modernist and positivist aversions to general theory that Fukuyama (2016) articulates, while attempting to craft a coherent system inspired by intellectual traditions as diverse as McGilchrist (2021) or Taleb's *Incerto* (2020, pp. iv–v). However unorthodox this approach might be it seems justified by the requirements of practice, as any undertaking that wishes to have constructive impact in the social sphere cannot be split up and corseted by the silos of academia. Although this book's approach will justly be deemed to be speculative according to the benchmarks by which research is currently judged, it seeks to be a reference for study in fields such as economics or finance. At the micro-level, the sustainable value creation premise supplies frameworks and measurements for managerial decision-making, capital allocation, and regulatory processes. The financial 'quantifiability of value transfers' assumption encourages action in line with the 'weight and offset value transfers' implication for principal-stakeholder relationships (see Figure A5.4a). A further applied challenge of this work is to address the political process; to nudge grassroots movements and the demands of citizens (referred to as 'non-elites' throughout this work) towards responding to the *qui generat valorem* ('who create value') question by allying themselves with high quality elites while resolutely opposing rent seekers across the board.

Evidently, a key requirement for such a multi-level, interdisciplinary, and exploratory undertaking is a clear structure.[1] Part I (Propositions) presents and refutes three popular fallacies about elites before launching the broad inquiry into the subject with a series of 20 propositions spread across three chapters. These propositions are specific theoretical positions developed from a review of the extant multidisciplin-

---

1 In this book, the development of discrete ideas often occurs not sequentially but progressively (and often somewhat haphazardly) across different sections and chapters. This is the result of their broad scope, the cross-disciplinary approach, and the incremental inputs required for their advancement. For instance, firm-level sustainable value creation is first introduced Chapter 2, further steps for the conceptualization and operationalization of value transfers are described in Section 5.3.1, and the all-important metrics are discussed in Section 6.6.1. To articulate the implicit structure while orientating the reader, all chapters have introductions and summaries, while pointers to the ideas that crisscross the text are provided by detailed cross-references.

ary literature on elites; taken together they constitute the foundation for an integrated theory of economic and social development. Conjectures are also advanced throughout the book, some of which are quite bold and controversial, many based on intuition and lacking substantive evidence as yet. While provisional, all are designed to be testable assertions. Conceptual elements and their definitions are also submitted. These ultimately flow into the development of a logic for elite agency (Chapter 1), elite business models, the sustainable value creation of which can be established with firm-level measurements like the Value Creation Rating (VCr) (Chapter 2), and ultimately the meso-level national elite system (Chapter 3).

In Part II (Integration) the structure that binds the propositions, conjectures, and conceptual elements together is tightened with an examination of how elite agency is both constrained and enabled by (bargaining) power and institutions (Chapter 4). The emerging system is then articulated through a comprehensive account of how the economy works, and a proposal for the elite theory of economic development (ETED) grounded on sustainable value creation elite business models is presented (Chapter 5).

Part III (Implications) takes the ETED, now a refutable grand social science elite theory of economic (and human) development, and operationalizes its cardinal ideas and principles through the existing comparative measure of elite value creation—the global 'Elite Quality Index' ('EQx') (Chapter 6). The inquiry, having suggested multiple measurements to test the theory, then proceeds by considering the research implications of the ETED to the fields of management science, finance, or international relations, while providing applied frameworks for decision-making. In terms of public policy, the emphasis is on seeking targeted and weighted structural reform to adjust the economy's long-run incentive system rather than relying on mainstream broad fiscal and monetary approaches (Chapter 7). In closing, this study gleans a socio-economic structure that is used to advance the applied notion of transformational elite leadership. Non-elite interests are central, and the required freedoms to realize these are implicit in a set of ethical principles that animate the ETED and are derived from the maxim, *To the creators the value created* (Chapter 8). The final chapter wraps up the work by affirming the speculative and pragmatic philosophies that anchor the elite theory paradigm and its applied transformational leadership positions.

As a conceptual work focused on developing a falsifiable elite theory of economic development, this inquiry suggests "new relationships among constructs", specifically through the original interpretation of extant research to "provide an integration of literatures, offer an integrated framework, provide value added, and highlight directions for future inquiry" (Gilson & Goldberg, 2015, p. 127). The starting point for this endeavor is the determination, selection, and classification of conceptual elements or variables from a wide range of sources in economics, management science, finance, sociology, political science, international relations, and philosophy. When applying the ETED's integrative logic and language to this diverse set of disciplines, discretionary judgments are made to establish their contributions to a system grounded in premises that would conventionally run up against the walls of academic silos. This approach has led, for instance, to understanding elite agency in terms of value creation and appropriation business models functioning as the transmission mechanism between micro-level activities and macro-level social outcomes. The relationships proposed between diverse conceptual elements are formalized in the propositions and conjectures—such as connecting intra-elite contests with value creation and risk origination (or extractive value and risk transfers)—and add up to an internally consistent whole. The epistemology of this inquiry is recognizable in the project overview. Figure P.1 depicts how conceptual elements from multiple disciplines are integrated into an overarching system with a particular language and narrative that seeks operationalization through sustainable value creation (SVC) measurements to facilitate tangible outputs in research and transformational action in practice.

This work on elite agency implicitly and explicitly responds to five of Whetten's seven questions in "What Constitutes a Theoretical Contribution?" (1989): (a) What's new? (b) So what? (c) Why so? (f) Why now? (g) Who cares?[2] Regarding the latter, situating intra-elite contests at the origin of institutional change might re-energize debates on the impact of political economy arrangements and incentives for society at large. The unconventional and systematic attempt at explaining the interrelationships between variables in economics, management, and political science through the lens of elite agency results in theory that provides latitude for human agency in its applied aims. This motivates the incipient and growing international research and practitioner community engaged in the construction, interpretation, and statistical validation of a comparative measurement of elite quality (Casas-Klett, Cozzi, Diebold, & Zeller, 2020; Diebold, 2022) and micro-level sustainable value creation measurements (Casas-Klett & Nerlinger, 2023), while since its 2020 pilot, five annual *Elite Quality Index* reports have been published (Casas-Klett & Cozzi, 2021, 2022, 2023, 2024, 2025). A key aim of the sustainable value creation measurements proposed in this work is to enrich established formal models (of economic forecasting, equity valuations or credit ratings) in an effort to enhance their realism and utility. In the process, the EQx (which aggregates elite quality at the elite system meso-level) and the VCr (which operationalizes value creation and risk origination and extractive transfers at the firm micro-level) will either validate or refute the elements, logic, and language of the ETED. Where successful, the value creation locus of this work will inform the evolving conversations on sustainability and environmental, social, and governance (ESG) concerns.

The wide remit and ambition of this work expose it to criticism. So does its reliance on intuition and imagination, two of McGilchrist's "four main pathways to the truth" (2019, p. xxvi). Another challenge is its likeness to the "tradition of the *essai*" (May, 2017, p. 415) with "numerous digressions" and assertions that are left to further research and empirical validation. The inquiry itself is also bereft of specific method-

2 The additional two questions: (d) "Well done?" (e) "Done well?" can only be addressed by the reader.

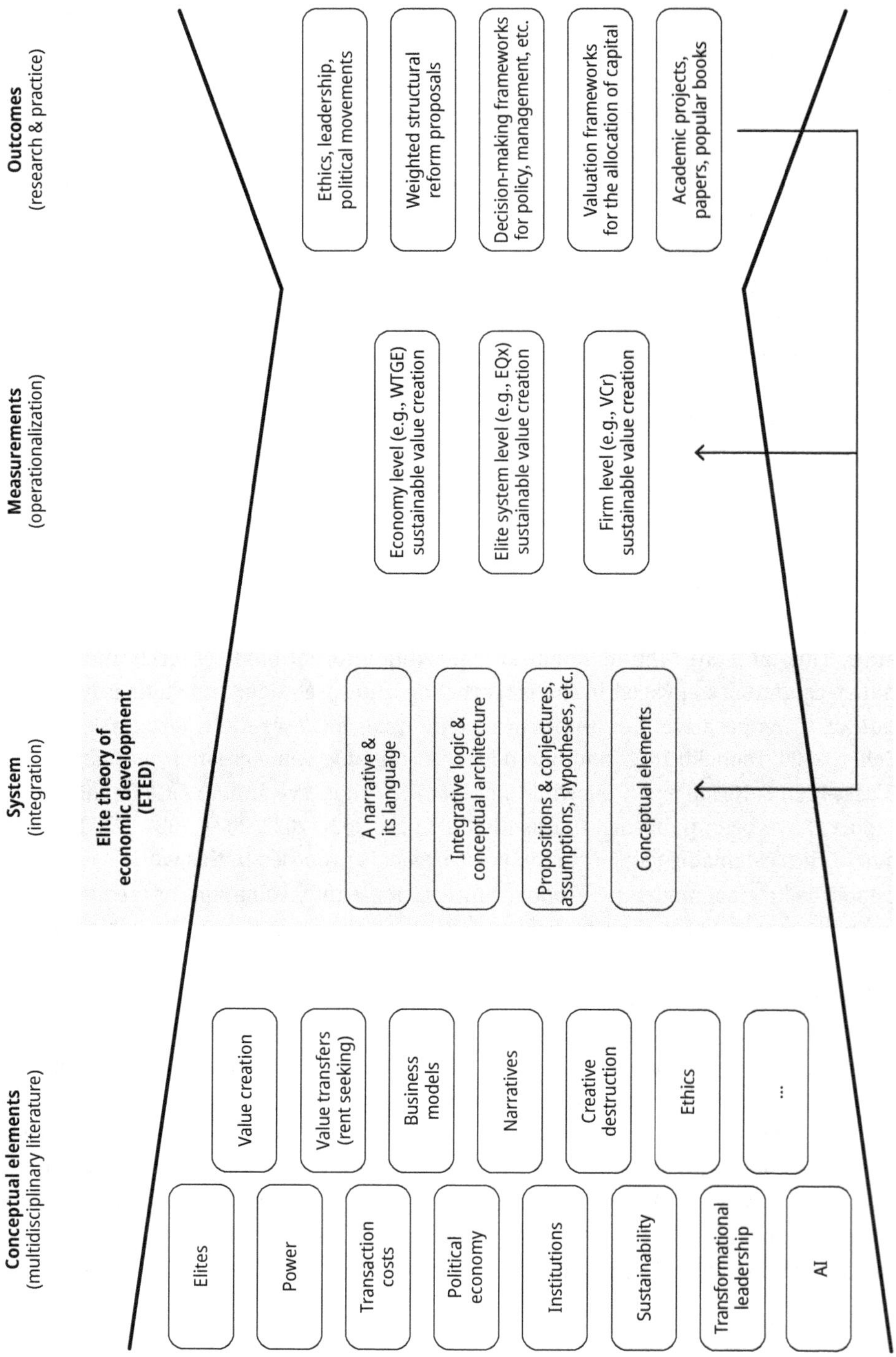

Figure P.1: The elite theory of economic development: Project overview.

ologies other than "disciplined imagination" (Weick, 1989), in the pursuit of conceptual integration, and so the proposed theoretical framework is perplexing in its scope. Moreover, the title of this book starts with the preposition "towards", indicating that the study merely aims to start a dialogue on economic development centered on elite agency, albeit one with an unambiguous normative destination—a political economy that minimizes value extraction. The final proviso is the association with Isaiah Berlin's figurative application of Archilochus' metaphor of the 'fox' to a type of thinkers:

> those who pursue many ends, often unrelated and even contradictory, connected, if at all, only in some de facto way, for some psychological or physiological cause, related to no moral or aesthetic principle. These last lead lives, perform acts and entertain ideas that are centrifugal rather than centripetal; their thought is scattered or diffused, moving on many levels, seizing upon the essence of a vast variety of experiences and objects for what they are in themselves, without, consciously or unconsciously, seeking to fit them into, or exclude them from, any one unchanging, all-embracing, sometimes self-contradictory and incomplete, at times fanatical, unitary inner vision. (Berlin, 2013, p. 2)

The problem that the 'centrifugal' approach of this work aims to contribute to is that of economic growth and human development. There is, though, a 'unitary vision': the sustainable value creation of elite agency. To the degree that the elite theory advances toward the relevant 'truth' in human relationships—value transfers and their optima —it functions as a 'theory of everything' in society.

The title of this book could have been an 'elite theory', an 'elite theory of development' or, more specifically, an 'elite business model theory of economic and social development'. The longer title is more precise, while the shorter ones are more appealing to those disinclined to put the spotlight on micro-level business phenomena to decipher macro-level economic and social advancement. Given the focus on economic development and the primacy of economic concepts (e.g., value, institutions or rent seeking), this inquiry settles nonetheless on the 'elite theory of economic development' (ETED). Ultimately, this is a work of transformational leadership and not a treatise on economics: the foundation of its vision is the 'inextinguishable value creation option of elites' to engage in first-order productive and sustainable value creation activities, understood in terms of value appropriation.

Part I: **Propositions**

Part I of this book, 'Propositions', starts with a discussion on three elite fallacies, before moving on to the core 20 propositions presented over its three chapters. These address elite agency (Chapter 1), elite business models (Chapter 2), and the national elite system (Chapter 3). A cogent theoretical structure emerges to describe the relationship between elites and economic development. The conceptual elements, propositions, and conjectures introduced here suggest a persistent logic that operates at the abstract level in *all* societies.

The propositions in this first part of the book are declarative statements meant to be testable, many with roots in diverse academic fields. Additionally, and throughout this work, conjectures are also advanced (they are compiled in Table A1.3) in the Popperian spirit of having "the definite intention of testing a theory" (1962, p. 46); bold assertions that are imaginatively put forth (see Weick, 1989; McGilchrist, 2019) to falsify the diverse components of this work's attempt at grand theory (Skinner, 1990). Conjectures support theorizing by addressing narrow questions, while the 20 propositions connect the conceptual elements of this work and provide the foundation for the theoretical integration in Part II.

https://doi.org/10.1515/9783110734638-002

Chapter 1
Towards a logic of elite agency

The inquiry into the nature of elites begins by delineating what elites are and what they are not. To this end, we will first discuss two fallacies that have hampered clear reasoning on the subject: the elite denial fallacy and the elite populist fallacy (1.1). These set the stage for consideration of a third; the non-elite rule fallacy, discussed later in this work. In the subsequent section, a wide-ranging literature review supplies ideas and context for a working definition of elites and associated conceptual elements (1.2). This inquiry evaluates and takes positions on *anacyclosis*, Marxist thought, power elite theory from sociology, elite theories from political science, and economic theories such as classical elite theory and collective action logic. This exercise facilitates the development of three basic propositions on the logic of elite agency in the closing section (1.3) and serves as the basis for the conceptual link between elite business models and value creation/extraction that is advanced in Chapter 2.

1.1 Denial and populism: Elite fallacies

The study of elites is conditioned by two widespread fallacies. The elite denial fallacy ('elites don't exist') negates the agency of elites and the idea that they are a discrete, high-impact social phenomenon. At times this fallacy is advanced to deflect social scrutiny and even academic inquiry into the subject of elites, often as a response to the elite populist fallacy ('elites are bad'). This second fallacy takes the opposite position—elites do exist—and suggests that they are a root cause of most socio-economic ills. Elite agency ('what elites do') is taken to be overwhelmingly detrimental for society in this second fallacy (which is a recurring point in many narratives designed to court the favor of non-elites). The elite denial fallacy is rejected at the beginning of this book and additional arguments are subsequently offered to refute it throughout this work. The elite populist fallacy is also addressed throughout this inquiry with theoretical and empirical evidence, and especially so in the discussion of elite quality (in Chapter 6). A third fallacy, amply referenced later in this work (see Sections 3.3.3 or 8.1.3)—the non-elite rule fallacy ('people power')—mirrors the logic of the first fallacy and constitutes an aspirational twist of the second (see the summary of all three fallacies in Table A4.1).

The elite denial fallacy is exemplified by the position of Berle (1968, p. 202), an official in the Roosevelt Administration, who dismissed the idea that the "elite exercises power or that any 'class' governs or rules". Members of UK elite coalitions surveyed by Reeves and Friedman (2024) find the narrative of a closed access, self-perpetuating elite distasteful and attribute their own high positions in society to meritocratic hard work and talent. There are also the pluralist versions of the elite denial fallacy such as those that recognize "community power" where "rarely could a single elite be discovered im-

https://doi.org/10.1515/9783110734638-003

posing itself in each area of decision, policy, and conflict" (Merelman, 1968, p. 451). Cryptocurrencies claim that elites should not exist and Bitcoin is characterized in its foundational white paper as having "no central authority" (Nakamoto, 2008, p. 4). Whether in Washington or in cyberspace, the embrace of the denial fallacy is often a reaction to the elite populist fallacy, encapsulated in Mills' "power elite" (1956) or Domhoff's "governing class" in *Who Rules America* (1967) and *The Higher Circles* (1970). These theories link to a tradition in American political thought harking back to founding father and second President, John Adams, who feared "the tendency of the elite few to undermine both popular representation and effective government" (Mayville, 2015, p. 5). Berle considered negative characterizations of elites to be neo-Marxist "fallacious piece[s] of propaganda" bent on liquidating a "selfish oligarchy" (1968, p. 202). The literature review in Section 1.2 confronts the denial fallacy through wide-ranging descriptions of the dominant agency of elites that are consistent with a realistic theory of the political economy and society. The elite relationship to power (e.g., see Sections 4.4 and 4.5) and measurements of the actual power that elite coalitions and the elite system hold (see the EQx 'power' sub-index in Chapter 6) are discussed to shed light on a question that has long been a matter of contention: "From the earliest writings in social science there have been lively debates over the extent to which societies are dominated by elites" (Kerbo & Della Fave, 1979, p. 5).

The elite denial fallacy is also substantiated by a different class of arguments that posit the theoretical irrelevance of elites: elites may exist, yet they are not pertinent as a discrete socio-economic concept since they are not required to explain variance in political economy outcomes. For instance, in relation to free markets and perfect competition, "the marginal rates of substitution between any two commodities or factors must be the same in all their different uses" (Hayek, 1945, p. 519). Any differences in wealth, power, or coordination capacity are temporal because, "above cost payments to any entrepreneurs or resource owners must attract other profit rent seekers to enter identical or closely related employments" (Buchanan, 1980, p. 5). Under classical economic assumptions, elites form but remain in a fragile or transient state, their ascent and consolidation irremediably blocked by the logic of competition that preempts lasting privilege and influence. New market entrants, who constantly propose substitutes that embody better ideas or new knowledge, place overwhelming pressure on the profit margins and residual incomes of incumbent elite business models. While the management strategy literature emphasizes differentiation and entry barriers to competitors to sustain profitability (see Porter, 1980), *de facto* strengthening market power, the theory of competition under maximalist free-entry assumptions precludes market dominance and the sizable value appropriation by business models associated with elites.

To what extent does the persistence of high residual income (profit) generating elite business models point to elite agency, challenging classical and Hayekian assumptions? Perhaps elite power short-circuits the free market? As a matter of fact, elites running business models that are not challenged by other profit-seekers for protracted periods of time are described across ages and geographies in their full splendor; from Popes, rulers of Caliphates, and political mavericks such as Otto von Bismarck, to contemporary high-tech entrepreneurs like Pony Ma, the five miners that control Bitcoin's network operations (Kharif, 2020a) or Elon Musk. The "personal biography approach" towards studying elites developed by Krcmaric, Nelson and Roberts (2020) is, however, not the direction taken by this work. The focus is rather on how elites play determinant roles in the historical and economic trajectories of nations.

Fukuyama (2011, p. 336) explains the fate of the French *Ancien Régime* elite system through its "ultimate weakness and inability to tax or control its own elites". Kerbo and McKinstry, in the book *Who Rules Japan?* (1995), analyze the country through the lens of an elite imbued with Shintoistic values, dominating the country since the end of World War II and achieving—at least until the late 1980s—impressive economic performance. On the other side of the Pacific, the early promise of America was visible in the turnover dynamics of elites whose merchant business models amassed fortunes as they evolved in synchronicity with new technologies from one century to the next:

> "urban merchant capitalists . . . were the wealthiest, best informed, and most powerful segment of early American society" (1971, p. 6). These all-purpose merchants nevertheless gave way to specialized merchants early in the 19th century; such merchants then became "the most important men in the economy" (1971, p. 8). Yet specialized merchants in turn found their functions sharply cut back by the rise late in the 1800s of integrated manufacturers: "The long reign of the merchant had finally come to a close. [. . .] A new economy dominated by the modern, integrated manufacturing enterprise had arisen" (1971, p. 12). (Porter & Livesay, 1971, as cited in Williamson, 1981, p. 561)

The natural sciences also provide arguments to debunk the elite denial fallacy, as for instance does the idea of pervasive hierarchy articulated by Bejan (2020, p. 26): "Hierarchies are everywhere [in the lung, the river basin, and the forest], including where it matters to us the most, in society".[3] A still more audacious connection could be made to thermodynamics, the fundamental laws of physics relevant to all natural sciences. The under-

3 Bejan intriguingly writes that certain hierarchies "are invisible to most, and known only to a few. In the field of social dynamics, [these] are known as dark networks and mafias" (2020, p. 26), while Lingelbach and Rodríguez Guerra note that oligarchs "are secretive and stealthy, flying under the radar for as long as possible" (2023, p. 195). Note that Auguste Kerckhoffs' design principle (from cryptography) for systems, rejects "security through obscurity" as illusive (see Swire, 2004), and emphasizes their safety when all about them is public, and "the enemy knows the system" (Shannon, 1949, p. 662). Secrecy makes elite coalitions and their systems fragile and unsustainable. Conversely, when antagonistic elites and non-elites know who the established elites are, these are institutionally secure in their positions. The ETED claims that elite protection is also augmented by the existence of barriers such as the exclusive access to institutional change mechanisms and the opacity of elite business model rule formation (see the 'elite vs non-elite knowledge gap' hypothesis of Section 2.2). As a contemporary illustration, AI elites are known to everybody, but this is not necessarily the case for the rules by which their power and residual income are enabled and accumulated, see Section 5.2.2). The ETED's inquiring focus is on the residual income of the business model, while elites atop hierarchies are a visible reality. In sum, secure elites are clearly discernable (see the definition of elites in Section 1.2.4) and through the use of cross-disciplinary political economy analysis, so are their business models.

standing of energy and entropy is offered as a framework to appreciate the social sciences:

> thermal energy of a uniform temperature cannot be converted into work. As Lord Kelvin observed long ago, it is not possible for ships to sail by using the energy of ocean waters, immense though that energy is; for some depth, that energy is of uniform temperature. (Georgescu-Roegen, 1986, p. 5)

Taking a page from "the nature of nature" (Brown, Gupta, Li, Milne, Restrepo, & West, 2002), elites are but a manifestation of power laws in the realm of society (see "social fractals" in O'Brien et al., 2023, p. 1452). This inquiry will suggest that in the political economy, development is impossible without elites and their power (energy) differentials expressed as hierarchies. As for the extensive track record of elites at the top of the socio-economic pyramid, organic chemistry supplies empirical evidence in ways that the social sciences and the humanities cannot. For example, DNA evidence confirms the existence of "first-degree incestuous union", in turn found to associate with being on the long end of dietary and fine-scale haplotypic structure variance, all of which indicate the historical existence in Ireland of a closed elite. The *Nature* study in question, demonstrating how elites and non-elites differ in terms of privilege is aptly titled: "A Dynastic Elite in Monumental Neolithic Society" (Cassidy et al., 2020, p. 384). Carles Lalueza-Fox's *Inequality: A Genetic History* (2022) shows how DNA sequencing technologies reveal genetic marks associated to migratory movements or funerary practices that prove the existence of socio-economic pyramids and elite agency throughout history.

Whether in Neolithic Ireland or Silicon Valley, the conspicuousness of elite privilege and power ushers forth the elite populist fallacy ('elites are bad'). In modern times, this tradition harks back to Marx and Engels' writing on the class struggle (1848/1969) and has strong roots in 20th century sociology, especially in the works of Mills (1956) and Domhoff (1967, 1970). Debunking the populist fallacy requires both a theoretical basis and empirical evidence linking elites to positive human and economic development outcomes. The problem in doing so faces a different challenge: while elites are a recurring and observable phenomenon and elite power shapes the political economy, elite agency is not integrated as a conceptual element into mainstream economic theory, nor is it operationalized in economic models. That necessitates the use of research on elites across diverse disciplines and that becomes a most compelling and indispensable resource for this inquiry (see, for example, elite conceptualizations in the literature review in Section 1.2 below). Still, in the prevailing economic paradigm, while elites are not necessarily negated, their agency remains at the margins, outside established macroeconomic models and seldom targeted by policymaking. Any elite theory of economic development that addresses unexplained variance in growth or other outcomes will, by virtue of linking elites to positive developmental outcomes, debunk the second fallacy.

1.2 Towards a definition of elites: A multidisciplinary literature review

It is often pointed out that "the process of social development is in reality a multidimensional one, whose different elements interact with one another in complex ways" and so, for instance, new institutional theory recognizes that economic growth requires the study of politics (Fukuyama, 2016, p. 208). To provide a realistic understanding of economic development, this first survey of the literature on elites is multidisciplinary, and a stepping-stone towards the integrative logic of diverse domains (see Figure P.1).

Elites were first theorized about very early on in history. They are the central construct in Aristotle's *Politics*, and still figure in modern political science theory (e.g., Best & Higley, 2018; Pakulski, 2018). Elites are also seen as critical drivers in the field of history, for example, in the Marxist view where "the history of all hitherto existing society is the history of class struggles" (Marx & Engels, 1848/1969), or in historical interpretations of national development (such as Fukuyama, 2011). Brezis and Temin emphasize the importance of elites in economic history and point to the works of Cassis (1997), Crouzet (1999), and Lachmann (2002), while in reviewing the "literature that analyzes the effects of the elite on economics" ascertain the non-mainstream nature of such writing "that departs from pure economics" and strays into the fields of "psychology, political science and sociology" (2007, p. 5). In economics, elites have also been theoretically discussed (e.g., Pareto, 1968/1991; Mosca, 1939; Michels, 1962/1999; Olson, 1965/1971, 1982; North, Wallis, & Weingast, 2006; Acemoglu, 2006; Robinson, 2010) albeit, as mentioned above, the concept is rarely formalized or operationalized and remains outside of the mainstream. Sociology is lucid about elites as a conceptual element that is "a convenient way to designate categories standing at the apex of societies" (Daloz, 2010, p. 1). Mills' much-debated *The Power Elite* (1956), led to specific contentions that might appear far-fetched, such as the existence of a global ruling class (Robinson & Harris, 2000), or the so-called "transnational capitalist class" (Sklair, 2002). Management science examines elites too, but at the micro-level of firms, where it singles out "dominant coalitions" (March & Simon, 1958; Thompson & McEwen, 1958; Cyert & March, 1963) with elite members distinct from "non-members" (Pearce, 1995, p. 1075). Upper echelons theory links their agency, often determined by their background characteristics, to organizational outcomes (Hambrick & Mason, 1984).

Many of the elite theories and conceptualizations reviewed next are sorted by analysis level and perspective in the classification matrix presented in Figure A5.2. The analysis level—macro to micro—ranges from the large-scale (e.g., elites as a factor in the last 10,000 years of social development, in North, Wallis, and Weingast, 2006) to the small-scale (e.g., the characteristics and decisions of top management teams shaping organizational behavior, in Hambrick and Mason, 1984). The analytical perspective—particularism to universalism—ranges from context-specific (e.g., Japan's "iron triangle", in Kerbo and McKinstry, 1995) to context-transcending theorizing (e.g., collective action logic, in Olson, 1982).

For reference purposes, a summary of each of the conceptualizations reviewed in this section is available in the Appendix (see Table A1.1), outlining both their working assumptions and the position this work takes in terms of adopting, adjusting, or rejecting the associated ideas.

1.2.1 Grand socio-political conceptualizations of elites

This sub-section discusses two cardinal socio-political conceptualizations of elites: the ancient Greek *anacyclosis* theory of elite rule, and Marxist class theory (1867/1959b), both of which still inform certain contemporary conceptions of elites and their agency.

The *anacyclosis* theory of cyclical elite rule. Aristotle, in his hierarchical classification of regimes (*Politics*, 1912, Book III) and Polybius (*Histories*, 1889, Book VI) suggests a cyclical theory of political development: *anacyclosis* (or 'eternal revolutions'). States, as this notion is explained by Podes (1991), undergo different types of rule by elites (of one, of the few) as well as by non-elites (of the many), in sequence. Each of these forms of government oscillates between benign and perverted versions. History starts with primitive monarchy (benign rule by one), which, after a series of (mostly violent) rule transitions, culminates in anarchy (perverted rule by the many). Machiavelli (1517/1883, 1.2) later refers to this idea of recurrence "for this is the circle revolving" in the *Discourses on the First Decade of Titus Livius*, although his cycles have patterns that are distinct from Polybian ones: his focus is on how to prevent political "degeneration" and the devastations of political transitions and intra-elite contests for which he suggests a "mixed constitution" that optimally combines different forms of government (Gagné, 2011). This focus on intra-elite contest rules followed in the footsteps of Cicero (*The Republic*, 1829/2017) who emphasized that while constitutional solutions are desirable, they will not withstand the "corruption of the ruling classes" (Atkins, Harrison, & Lane, 2000, p. 477) suggesting that elites are more powerful than the institutions designed to constrain them.

In the original conceptualization of *anacyclosis*, benign rule by the few *aristoi*—"the best" or aristocracy—is possible where "the economic elites are acting out of virtue and for the sake of the general welfare" (Neil, 2011, p. 28). Aristocracy is in dialectical opposition to oligarchy, which Plato and Aristotle describe as "the rule of the rich" (Bradshaw, 2011, p. 140) where narrow economic elites' "rule out of self-interest" (Neill, 2011, p. 28). Proudhon (1851/1971, p. 84), however, embraces the elite populist fallacy and does not see the ruling few as capable of being virtuous: their plunder and theft sows the seeds for violent leveling revolutions which then provide the conditions for reaction and counter-democratic revolutions, "and so on, and again and again" (Koivukoski, 2011, p. 180). To this day, cyclical conceptualizations of the political economy centered on elites are advanced, at times in pursuit of purported social agendas. For instance, Strauss and Howe's *Fourth Turning: An American prophecy - what the cycles of history tell us about America's next rendezvous with destiny (1997)* frames (American) history as cycles that end "when the nation's institutions become unfit to serve the interests of anyone other than the elite" (Barrett, 2017). The key message in Rubio's *Decades of Decadence: How our Spoiled Elites Blew America's Inheritance of Liberty, Security, and Prosperity* (2023) is clear. Such ideas incorporate calls for action: for example, they informed Steve Bannon's anti-elite narratives ("drain the swamp"), which he leveraged in his capacity as CEO of Donald Trump's 2016 presidential campaign (Guilford & Sonnad, 2017). Turchin (2023) argues that the rhythm by which the elite turns on and off the "wealth pump", which is designed to suck non-elite wealth up to the top, determines the phases of prosperity and collapse of nations.

Marx's class theory. The theoretical version of Marxist thought in *Capital: A Critique of Political Economy* (1867/1959b) and Marx and Engels' applied version in the *Manifesto of the Communist Party* (1848/1969) saw revolutionary "class struggle" (even if 'class' was never explicitly defined) in a Hegelian (1812/2010) framework around the elite business models of industrial production. The conceptualization of "exploiters vs exploited" echoes concerns about extraction, with the necessary tension between the upper/rich vs lower/poor classes defining both the course of history and the political economy (Andrew, 1975, p. 458). Specifically, the 19th century version of this conflict pitted the narrow property-owning class against the proletariat or the industrial working class. Marxism emphasizes classes rather than institutions as the organizing powers in society (Barrow, 2007, p. 403). The Marxist solution—a "vision of a classless society"—is considered unrealistic and naïve by classical elite theory (see Section 1.2.3), which conceives the elite with its "circulations and struggles" as being an "eternal" feature of social systems (Higley & Pakulski, 2012, p. 321).

1.2.2 Contemporary conceptualizations of elites

The 20th century saw the emergence of several descriptions of elites in the fields of sociology and political science, with some having an impact in economics and even management science. Below, some of the most salient contemporary conceptualizations of elites are discussed.

Power elite theory. The connections between elites and institutions are central to Mills' power elite theory with "institutions the necessary bases of power, of wealth, and of prestige" (Mills, 1956, p. 9). Mills developed power elite theory in the context of post-World War II America. He saw leadership positions in business, political administration, and the military as "an intricate set of overlapping cliques", with shared values and interests making joint "decisions having at least national consequences" (as cited in Bell, 1958, p. 239). Along similar argumentative lines, Domhoff's (1967, 1970) "governing class" model "attempts to show that one of the most important means of upper-class dominance is through holding key institutional positions in the society" (Kerbo & Della Fave, 1979, p. 6). Such power structures also operate at the local community level as is recounted by Hunter (1953). Cousin, Khan, and Mears (2018) recount how the study of elites in sociology is often anchored in the Bourdieusian approach to elites and social domination—as, for instance in Bourdieu's *The State Nobility: Elite Schools in the Field of Power* (1996). This broader theoretical trajectory, at times not far from Marxism and redolent of the elite populist fallacy, has the interlocked elite capturing government policy through its dominance of institutions.

Specific conceptualizations of a power elite. Notions akin to or originating from power elite theory maintain the institutional emphasis while accentuating distinct elements. For instance, iron triangle notions have (rather closed) elite coalitions composed of business interests, the legislative body, and the civil service, coordinating to influence policymaking in countries as distinct as the US or Japan (Adams, 1981; Gais, Peterson, & Walker, 1984; Kerbo & McKinstry, 1995). Some power elite derivations transcend borders. Elites conceived in political power terms have also been formalized in economic theories of regulation (e.g., Stigler, 1971).

Transnational elite constructs. In the age of globalization, the scope of action for power elite coalitions broadens accordingly and constructs such as a global power elite "superclass" (Rothkopf, 2008) or "cosmopolitan capital" (Bühlmann, David, & Mach, 2012) have been developed to characterize the new elite reality. The transnational capitalist class (TCC) is theorized as consisting of four factions: the major multinational enterprises, as well as "globalizing bureaucrats and politicians, globalizing professionals, and consumerist elites" (Sklair, 2012, p. 144). The integration of Europe is viewed in this vein as a top-down "elite project" (Best, Lengyel, & Verzichelli, 2012). In a rather critical view of globalization, anchored by neo-Gramscian perspectives on hegemony (Cox, 1983; Bieler & Morton, 2004), political economies are no longer bound by the nation state.[4] This raises the issue of the accountability of global elites (Hoffmann-Lange, 2012) and of institutional arbitrage and its consequences. Can elite business models manage to escape the control of local institutions if transnational institutions like the World Bank, the WHO, NATO or the EU become their anchor, as Jönsson and Tallberg (2010) suggest? The elite coalitions running these business models are likely to have converted their strong bargaining positions over local domestic institutions into a supranational "transnational state apparatus" that primarily serves their interests (Robinson & Harris, 2000). Nonetheless, the concept of transnational elites and their connection to decisive attendant transnational institutions is by no means generally accepted. For instance, Hartmann (2017) emphasizes the national character of elites and dismisses concepts such as "cosmopolitan elites" or that elite business schools are institutions implicated in the formation of transnational elites as a "myth".

Elites as the custodians of narratives. Diverse authors directly or indirectly connect narratives to elites and power—from Plato's "the noble lie" (Dombrowski, 1997) or

4 In the ETED, borders matter greatly, and so the relevant institutional context for elite coalitions and their elite business models is found in the political economy of the nation state. This informs the analysis of cross-border elite business models (see Sections 7.3.2 and 7.3.3).

Gramsci's cultural "hegemony" of the "dominant group" (Hoare & Nowell Smith, 1999, p. 145) to Beckert's (2016) "fictional expectations"—a link that is amplified and theorized about in this work. The advocacy coalition framework (ACF) is a specific "causal theory of the policy process" that explains policy decisions in political sub-systems, where the gravitational force of shared beliefs matters as much as specific interests (Jenkins-Smith & Sabatier, 1993). The idea that narratives are a coordinating force in elite formation and agency is central to the ACF view and also critical to the ETED (and first discussed in Section 1.3.2, see Figure 1.2). The ACF framework shows how narratives anchor the formation of elites (i.e., elite business models) that exist across the political spectrum from Left to Right. It also illustrates that dominant elite coalitions need not be narrow. Broad, extensive groups such as issue networks (gun owners, environmental activists, supporters of abortion rights), or professions (lawyers, government consultants, civil servants) are narrower than society at large and can be as effective as business elites in furthering their business model interests.

The technocratic ideal view. *Exodus* 19:6 (King James Bible, 1769/2017) exhorts a technocracy based on morality: "And ye shall be unto me a kingdom of priests, and an holy nation". Political elites have been theorized in terms of their agency ("to rule") and normatively ("to rule well") as far back as Plato's (1969) philosopher kings in the "beautiful city" of Kallipolis (*The Republic*, Book VI). A normative modern version of the philosopher king notion proposes elites as rational technocrats, an idea first espoused by Saint-Simon (1952, p. 72–75, as cited in Putnam, 1977, p. 384). A technocracy and the industrial state "could be directed by man's rationality to bring about a social reformation where poverty, injustice, superstition, and class conflict would be abolished" (Akin, 1977, p. 1). The assumption is that rationalization of the economic order, with the required "separation of politics from administration" would have as elites "scientific experts and problem solvers" (Crane, 2008, p. 1162). Is a modern Veblenian technical aristocracy tasked with "the construction of a new industrial order devoted to maximum production" (Elliott, 1978, p. 94) a feasible political economy project unlike earlier failed Platonic experiments?

Despite its age, the notion of a technocracy has not come to the fore and its theoretical bases are untested. It faces suspicion in the West where it is often viewed as "less responsive, more remote, less sensitive to the needs of disadvantaged groups" (Putnam, 1977, pp. 383, 408). In Asia, on the other hand, core elite coalitions (see Figure 8.1) have turned (often Confucian) technocracy narratives into tangible and rather successful socio-political realities that are quite responsive and sensitive to non-elite needs (e.g., Singapore following the vision of founding father, Lee Kwan Yew). Under the precepts of the ETED, a modern version of technocracy would result from an elite settlement, pact or bargain (Burton & Higley, 1987; O'Donnell & Schmitter, 1986; Khan, 2010; Dercon, 2022) where the core coalition promotes elite cohesion around institutional change associated with specific sustainable value creation elite business models and economic development goals (even when these conflict with the interests of other coalitions in the elite system).[5] Technocratic and reductionist elite agency, along the lines of Morozov's "technocratic solutionism" (2019), is considered in the context of the AI in the final chapter.

Elite research in political science. Sociology has long anchored the study of elites, and Savage (2024, p. 361) highlights its ability "to champion rich and powerful ways of doing descriptive work", thus disrupting conceptual frameworks and enriching paradigms beyond the discipline. Vibrant enquiry was undertaken in the second half of the twentieth century on political elites, including the development of power elite theory and the comparative work of Putman (1976). Noteworthy recent examples of the political elite perspective are found in Vogel, Gebauer and Salheiser's (2019) *The Contested Status of Political Elites* or Best and Higley's (2018) *The Palgrave Handbook of Political Elites*. These contributions, many from European authors, constitute a coherent research platform, able to deliver insights on a multitude of specific issues such as the changing attitude of Italian political elites towards the EU as a result of the financial crisis and the wider implications of this shift (Conti, Cotta, & Verzichelli, 2016). The connection between political power and economic elites is natural, as the latter shape institutional change (e.g., Paniagua & Vogler, 2022). Lobbying theories are a specific and important part of political science, actualizing what Best calls "the symbiosis between political and economic elites" which is so necessary for "modern capitalism" and the Weberian "rational state" (2018a, p. 333). They are discussed in more detail next.

Lobbying theories. Lobbying activity has foundations in public choice theory and rent-seeking theory (e.g., Tollison, 2012) and concerns itself with "the application of economic reasoning to nonmarket decision making" (Ostrom, 1975, p. 848). According to Hall and Deardorff: "lobbying is primarily a form of legislative *subsidy* [. . .] to the enterprises of strategically selected legislators" (2006, p. 69) that serves the profit maximization aims of corporate interests (Hillman, Keim, & Schuler, 2004; Mellahi, Frynas, Sun, & Siegel, 2016). This and similar conceptualizations situate political elites in the role of supplier stakeholders to business principals. For context it should be pointed out that, as per Gilens and Page (2014) and their taxonomy, not all theories of politics (in America) fall into the "economic-elite domination" category that have business interest groups at the center: there are also notions such as "majoritarian electoral democracy" (citizens at the center) or "majoritarian pluralism" (a balance of interest groups). Yet since Beard's (1913) take that the US Constitution is the result of the agency of the economic elite, there is an influential body of thought that sees non-elite rule as fallacious (see Table A4.1) and posits that the economic elite has ascendance over its political counterparts. This view is shared by the aforementioned Mills (1956) and more recently by authors such as Bartels in *Unequal Democracy*

5 The advent of artificial general intelligence (AGI) is expected to disrupt many aspects of the political economy, including policymaking and governance. Could a fair, value-optimizing form of superintelligence reinvigorate the arguments for technocracy? The Epilogue explores this question.

(2008), Winters' *Oligarchy* (2012), and Nader's *Unstoppable* (2014), that sought to elicit joint opposition by a left-right alliance to the emergence of a corporate state, as well as by Holcombe's *Political Capitalism* (2018). Lobbying, as a political process studied in economics, is a prime avenue for institutional capture (e.g., Stigler, 1971; Laffont & Tirole, 1991) and rent seeking (e.g., Tollison, 2012; Tullock, 1967). To researchers it is an essential fact of the political economy that issues the licenses to operate necessary for the "very survival" of interest organizations given the "severe policy threats" these invariably face (see Lowery, 2007, p. 39). While the aim of this book is general theorizing that goes beyond the US context, and the focus is on sustainable value creation by elite business models at the meso- and micro-aggregate levels, these conceptualizations of elites triggering institutional change through power accumulation processes are relevant references.

Dominant coalitions in organizations. Michels' (1962/1999) theory of organization saw elites in hierarchies and bureaucracies as a natural and rational response to management challenges. Pettigrew calls for the "contextual and processual analysis of managerial elites" (1992, p. 163). The dominant coalition concept from the micro-organizational perspective was conceived by Cyert and March (1963) and later coined by Thompson (1967). According to this theory, groups interact and coordinate based on compatible interests. Thompson's notion gained ascendancy with the emphasis on the "political processes in organizations" (Stevenson, Pearce, & Porter, 1985, p. 258). A given group can project influence and enforce its preferences within an organization as it achieves dominant coalition status (Scott & Davis, 2017; Pearce, 1995). Scholars who disagree that Michels' (1962/1999) iron law of oligarchy applies to organizations and "make the theoretical case for truly democratic organizations", still admit that in practice "oligarchy-free" firms not run by dominant coalitions are a rarity (Diefenbach, 2019, p. 558).

Coalitions at the firm-level have been conceived of as shifting entities: as a result of bargaining processes, their agency is often unstable in terms of decision-making, goal-setting, and problem-solving processes, which might lead to ill-defined outcomes (Cyert & March, 1963 as cited in Stevenson, Pearce, & Porter, 1985, p. 257). Importantly, the characteristics of the dominant coalition in a firm have also been found to impact organizational performance (Hambrick & Mason, 1984). This work is premised on elite agency being an essential feature of all economic, social, and organizational phenomena, impacting performance at all levels, from the micro to the macro.

1.2.3 Conceptualizations of elites relevant to economics

Classical elite theory (Italian school of elitism). The three Italian classical elite theorists, Pareto (1968/1991), Mosca (1939), and Michels (1962/1999)—the first two of which have been labeled as "neo-Machiavellians" (Denord, Palme, & Réau, 2020, p. 3)—posit that elites rule all societies. They further specify that such elites are always minorities. Pareto's ideas are derived from the sociological premises of Rousseau and Marx

(Mayhew & Schollaert, 1980). Classical elite theory has its foundations in the early intellectual legacies of Machiavelli (1513/1998) and Hobbes (1651/2002), while the three Italian thinkers also benefited from the "critical and skeptical" influences of Weber, Schumpeter and Ortega y Gasset (all European liberals active between 1890–1940); their "anti-utopian" positions were based on "a political and methodological realism" which implied leadership where "effective governance depends upon talented and skilled leaders imbued with political will, confidence, and foresight" (Pakulski, 2018, p. 9). Their "views of social change" are in "obvious proximity" to Weber's (Pakulski, 2012, p. 38), while Hartmann sees them as "an important ideological basis" for fascism and "authoritarian leadership" (2007a, pp. 2, 3). Yet classical elite theory "sought to ride no political horse" (Higley & Pakulski, 2012, p. 321). Zetterberg (1991, p. 8) pronounces the 'elite' used in Pareto's work "as a value-free term", and the three Italians "describe political behavior as it was, not as it ought to be" (Lerner, Nagai, & Rothman, 1996, p. 3).

Pareto supplies an unambiguous definition of the subject: "The part of the group or class which tries to ensure hegemony over its own group or its own class, or also over all groups and all classes, is called the élite" (Busino, 2000, p. 225).[6] Classical elite theory is consistent with contemporary conceptualizations in economics where the elite is the "small, dominant group that enjoys the power of decision in the various sectors of the economic and social organization of a state" (Brezis & Temin, 2007, p. 1). Elites are "those who score highest on scales measuring any social value or commodity ('utility'), such as riches, power, knowledge," and while elites are recognized in the fields of arts or ethics (i.e., "the most artistic", "the most virtuous"), the classical theorists' emphasis is on "elites within the economy and the body politic" (Zetterberg, 1991, p. 8). Controversially, they imply a "conceptual pairing of elites and non-elites" (Pakulski, 2018, p. 9) where elites concentrate power as unified and efficient rulers, while non-elites are powerless and unqualified to govern themselves. Caveats notwithstanding, classical elite theory's sociological and economic foundations inform this inquiry and Table A1.1 lists the various elements of classical elite theory that the ETED adopts or adjusts. As a side note, while Michels (1962/1999) delved into the psychological features of elite leadership, this work also discusses the topic but from a variety of different perspectives (see, for instance, the 'inextinguishable value creation option of elites', transformational leadership, and the code of ethics in Chapters 7 and 8, Table 7.2, and Figure 8.7).

Theory of groups. *The Logic of Collective Action: Public Goods and the Theory of Groups* (Olson, 1965/1971) posits that large groups have high costs when organizing for collective action and thus see less successful collective action per capita. This chimes with Higley's insight that: "Elites derive from a fundamental and universal fact of

---

6 This two-level distinction between elites is expounded on in Section 8.1.1 (including Figure 8.1) where a conceptual differentiation is made between (1) elites in general and (1.1) the core elite coalition. Note, however, that in the ETED, the focus is not on "hegemony" but on elite business models, the principal beneficiaries of which are members of elite coalitions.

social life, namely, the absence in any large collectivity of a robust common interest" (2010, p. 162). Small elite groups face relatively low coordination and transaction costs and are more effective, with Olson admitting to the counterintuitive nature of his conclusion: the "surprising tendency for the 'exploitation' of the great by the small" (1965/1971, p. 3). A problematic aspect of these special interest groups, or "distributional coalitions", is described in *The Rise and Decline of Nations: Economic Growth, Stagflation, and Social Rigidities* (Olson, 1982) and later works by the same author (Olson, 1996): they tend to flourish over time on the back of redistribution that transfers value away from certain subgroups of society to themselves, and nations so encumbered descend into institutional decay and economic malaise.

Research has provided empirical backing for Olson's thesis that elites ("powerful special interest groups") hamper growth (see McCallum & Blais, 1987, p. 17), while his "theory of institutional sclerosis is generally but certainly not universally supported" (Heckelman, 2007, p. 18). At the same time, scholars suggest mechanisms through which dominant elites are able to extract. For instance, the embedded view of 'social structure' (Granovetter, 2005) is consistent with a "dichotomous society . . . with cooperators prospering in a close-knit, strongly bound elite, and defectors earning low payoffs in a weakly connected periphery" (Gallo, Riyanto, Teh, & Roy, 2019). Olson's ideas are essential to the ETED, as his collective action logic provides an explanation for elite coalition formation and consolidation, while also advancing the link between elites and economic performance.

Institutions as constraints on elites. "The elite—the group in power" (Acemoglu, 2006, p. 516) and its agency is limited by institutional arrangements, and these are essential for economic development (Acemoglu & Robinson, 2013b, 2019a). The implicit normative assumption is that elite agency must be constrained. New institutionalist perspectives see the role of institutions as fundamental in both constraining and enabling elites. As a result of this understanding of the nature of the relationship between institutions and elites, the concentration of power in the hands of narrow elites is seen as the consequence of extractive political institutions (Acemoglu & Robinson, 2019a), not vice versa. The idea that elites shape institutions is implied by Cicero (Atkins, Harrison, & Lane, 2000), argued by the research just discussed on lobbying, found in the literature on institutional capture (e.g., Stigler, 1971; Laffont & Tirole, 1991) or rent seeking (e.g., Tullock, 1967, Tollison, 2012). The two-way causal relationship between elites and institutions is central to the later chapters this book (see, for instance, Figure 4.2).

Social order as an outcome of elite agency. Hobbes' social contract theory (1651/2002) is fundamental to the general understanding of social order, but non-elites may have little or no agency in its formation. Elites create social order, with stratification achieved and maintained through various means, including rituals such as human sacrifice (Watts, Sheehan, Atkinson, Bulbulia, & Gray, 2016). Rooted in the institutional perspective and integrating politics and economics, North, Wallis, and Weingast (2006) develop the open/limited access theory of social order covering the entirety of human history and part of its pre-history (the last 10,000 years). Elite agency establishes social orders with "limited access" that manage to rein in overall violence and create the conditions for specialization and exchange. Presented as a quid pro quo, elites erect barriers to economic entry and benefit from the ensuing rents. Social orders work via highly scalable elite business models, the earliest being that of grain.[7] Farmers, without options to move up socially, paid to their lords or the state a tribute of up to a "fifth of the harvest" (any more would compromise their survival), a *de facto* "rent that elites appropriated for their own subsistence and display" (Scott, 2017, p. 123). Insights into transitions away from limited access, the natural state in traditional societies founded on pre-modern (elite) personal relationships, to "open access" social orders characterized by competition in the political and economic realms "is the holy grail, for it is the process of modern social development" (North, Wallis, & Weingast, 2006, p. 7).

In Olsonian terms (1993, 2000), "stationary bandits" are elites that invest in sustainable social orders and provide public goods on their own terms, in contrast to the comparatively more extractive and short-term oriented "roving bandits". The agency of the former sows the long-term seeds for development and value creation. The value creation of stationary bandits and open access elite systems informs this inquiry throughout.[8] Yet it is extraordinarily hard for elites to become stationary (think of plutocrats parking their wealth outside of the jurisdictions where it was created) and thereafter to move towards openness. The reason, according to North, Wallis, and Weingast, is that these transitions are premised on institutional change that will be made only if they can "potentially make most elites better off as access opens" (2006, p. 64).

1.2.4 Working definitions of elites and elite agency

This inquiry references the ideas surveyed above and adopts, rejects, or qualifies many of their key tenets, at times by suggesting extensions (see the precise positions taken in Table A1.1). Two working definitions—or first signposts—are now proposed for the elite and elite agency conceptual elements that are fundamental to the elite theory paradigm concerning itself with economics.

7 "The key to the nexus between grains and states lies, I believe, in the fact that only the cereal grains can serve as a basis for taxation: visible, divisible, assessable, storable, transportable, and 'rationable.' Other crops—legumes, tubers, and starch plants—have some of these desirable state-adapted qualities, but none has all of these advantages. To appreciate the unique advantages of the cereal grains, it helps to place yourself in the sandals of an ancient tax-collection official interested, above all, in the ease and efficiency of appropriation" (Scott, 2017, p. 129).

8 Since principal-stakeholder bargaining power differentials (see Proposition 8) are a feature of all economic systems, open access is a matter of degree and never complete—even stationary bandits never completely refrain from extraction. In the ETED, the transformation towards ever-greater degrees of openness that is so critical for development will be chiefly attributed to the dynamics (e.g., intra-elite contests, bargaining power) within the elite system, rather than to non-elite preferences or Hobbesian bilateral elite/non-elite arrangements.

The definition of 'elite agency' has its foundations in the ideas that have been reviewed and incorporates notions that will be discussed and developed in subsequent sections:

> Elite agency is 'what elites do' in relation to their elite business model as the principals in a coalition of economic, political, and knowledge interests that is narrower than the stakeholders with whom it has a direct or indirect exchange relationship and that exercises leadership to successfully turn the coalition's lower transaction costs, higher levels of trust, and superior coordination capacity into (bargaining) power that is then converted into society's largest streams of residual income via value creation or extractive value transfers.

Given the importance of 'residual income' to this work, it should be noted that the notion is used in the manner of the value chain (Porter, 1985) in the value creation and appropriation (VCA) framework (e.g., Brandenburger & Stuart, 1996; Coff, 1999; Amit & Zott, 2001; Lepak, Smith, & Taylor, 2007; Di Gregorio, 2013; Garcia-Castro & Aguilera, 2015). Garcia-Castro and Aguilera (2015, p. 139) state: "Traditional corporate metrics of value creation use simple measures such as net income or profit ratios, which can easily be compared across competitors. There are other more refined metrics such as economic added value (Davis & Kay, 1990), which estimates economic profit deducting the firm's costs of capital". 'Residual income'—also variously referred to as profit, earnings, or net income—is used in this work to describe the 'bottom line' income left over for the principal beneficiaries of the business model (e.g., the equity holders or owners) from the revenues generated after all expenses, costs, depreciations, amortization, and taxes are paid. That is, prices minus costs. Note that costs also include all the obligations to non-equity capital suppliers (debt holders). While technically both terms are not equivalent, most of this work's applied frameworks equate residual income with profits (see Figures 7.2, 7.3, and A5.7). 'Revenue', on the other hand, refers to the 'top line' in the profit and loss (P&L) statement of the organization or business model, generated by the sales of goods or services. The firm-level value chain perspective will employ the terms 'revenue adjusted' and 'residual income' to refer to the terms 'revenue' and 'profits' that are used in statutory financial statements. Both pairs of terms have a close correspondence to each other (for further details see Chapter 2 and the equations in Table 2.4).

Elite agency is inexorably linked to organizations, and hence to the micro-level notion of leadership which is discussed in Chapter 7 (see the elite leadership typology in Table 7.2). The gravitational force that holds the elite coalition together is the elite business model (historically ranging from grain to algorithm ownership), which is distinct from regular business models on account of its high value creation and/or appropriation capacity and hence its high levels of residual income, which in turn facilitate elite wealth accumulation. Notwithstanding more detailed descriptions provided later (see Table 4.1), a succinct definition of the 'elite' conceptual element would be:

> An elite is a coalition operating society's leading value creation and appropriation business models that generate the highest quantities of economic activity and/or residual income.

Organizationally, an elite is therefore a business model that has secured from institutions—through wins in the political economy's market, non-market, and narrative market arenas (see Figure 1.2)—the limited rights that afford value appropriation advantages and, in consequence, operates at a discrete sustainable value creation position. Analytically, elites both create and extract value (see Table A4.2).

1.3 Basic propositions on the logic of elite agency

The above overview of the conceptualizations of elites points to the wide-ranging, multifaceted, and diverse nature of the subject: historical and contemporary, sociological and economic, and part of the ideologies of both the Right and the Left on the political spectrum. While some elite coalitions are extremely narrow and concentrated (and all are narrower than their counterparties), many are surprisingly broad and extensive. Evidence-based and realist notions of elites abound, as do populist and idealist conceptualizations, with many of the latter clearly non-falsifiable. This inquiry now proceeds to develop a set of 20 intendedly testable propositions—some unfolding into subsets, conjectures, or new conceptual elements—on elites. Taken together, the first four propositions advanced in this chapter establish the logic of elite agency (i.e., 'what elites do'). These propositions are on: the elite dominance iron law (Proposition 1); the multi-dimensional elite circulation process (Proposition 2); how the mode of elite circulation affects development (Proposition 3); and on the coordination capacity of elites from a transaction cost perspective (Proposition 4).

1.3.1 Proposition 1: The elite dominance iron law is structural to society

> The majority is thus permanently incapable of self-government. [. . .] the majority of human beings, in a condition of eternal tutelage, are predestined by tragic necessity to submit to the dominion of a small minority, and must be content to constitute the pedestal of an oligarchy. (Michels, 1962/1999, p. 334)

The three Italian classical elite theorists (first Michels, then Mosca and Pareto) coincide in their agreement that there is an "iron law" of oligarchy, an idea that is not exempt from controversy on account of its elitism and "anti-democratic" nature (Nye, 1977), a criticism associated with the elite populist fallacy ('elites are bad'). The elite theory of power is steadfast that a minority—whether termed as an elite, dominant coalition, oligarchy, establishment, aristocracy, plutocracy, special interest group, ruling class, or hegemonic group—sits atop all societies. The controlling ruling elite of Mosca (1939) is made up of those who, according to Pareto (1968/1991), have superior qualities. Michels (1962/1999) expounds on the qualitative divisions between leaders and followers and his "assumptions concerning the 'incompetence of the masses' corresponded greatly with those of Lenin" (Lipset, 1999, p. 33). The Italian elitist perspective claims to constitute a "realistic" elite theory that is, however, non-Marxist (Blondel & Müller-Rommel, 2007, p. 3), even when referenced by Marxist elite sociologists such as Bottomore (1993). Other thinkers, including Olson (1965/1971, 1982) or North, Wallis and Weingast (2006) arrive at conclusions similar to the Italians, albeit via different analytical paths.

What about revolutions from below? Should a movement of the masses come to power, Mosca argued that the emerging narrow coalitions would quickly become new elites, a notion that essentially conforms to the precepts of the elite dominance iron law. The waning or wholesale replacement of an elite does not result in non-elite dominance, but rather, the rise of a new elite:

> Even when the discontent of the masses culminates in a successful attempt to deprive the bourgeoisie of power, this is after all, so Mosca contends, effected only in appearance; always and necessarily there springs from the masses a new organized minority which raises itself to the rank of a governing class. (Michels, 1962/1999, p. 334)

This expression of the iron law can be emphasized through the following example, set out by Milovan Djilas, the Yugoslav former deputy to Tito:

> the Communist revolution, conducted in the name of doing away with classes, has resulted in the most complete authority of any single new class. Everything else is sham and an illusion. (Djilas, 1957, p. 36, as cited in Lipset, 1999, p. 33)

Based on the claim that the masses are not qualified to rule and that elites have superior qualities, Mosca (1939) developed a normative position that advocated for elite rule (Blondel & Müller-Rommel, 2007, p. 5). While the iron law is accepted in this work, this parallel classical elitist idea that elites have superior qualities must obviously be questioned. Any elite theory of economic development cannot assume that the superior qualities of elites are, as Pareto claimed: "the strongest, the most energetic, and the most capable—for good as well as evil" (1968/1991, p. 32). The casual observer can see that in many societies, while many brilliant individuals occupy the top echelons, so will their less capable descendants, the lucky, the brutish, or the well-connected but inept. The essential problem for development is that extractive elite business models can endure over time despite their inability to create value because elite power maintains extractive institutions. Interestingly, Pareto realized the necessity of value creation at the apex: "It is particularly important that an elite predominantly composed of consolidators admit intelligent innovators in its stratum. Failure to pursue this policy leads to difficulties, even revolutions" (Zetterberg, 1991, p. 10). Only in a frictionless, highly competitive, and idealized political economy would extractive activities fall by the wayside and elites be superior due to the higher value creation of their business models. Superior or not, elite dominance is the definitive constant in societies.

1.3.2 Proposition 2: Elite circulation is multi-dimensional and characterizes society

Occupancy at the top is subject to change, and Pareto's theory of the circulation of elites (1968/1991, p. 36) stresses that "the history of man is the history of the continuous replacement of certain elites: as one ascends, another declines". According to Zetterberg, this idea "both resembles and modifies Marx' dictum of history" (1991, p. 16). The notion of elite circulation is distinguished from elite replacement: both see elite business model transitions, but the former preserves the elite system to a degree that the latter does not. Elite circulation is conceptually tightened here by examining its various dimensions, which include: its progressive or regressive qualities; its drivers; its speed; the startling role played by narrative markets; the varying degrees of elite replacement; and its uncertain substance.

The process of elite circulation and replacement has frequently been construed in the literature as being progressive. In Marxism, where elites are representatives of the dominant class, their replacement is related to changes in the economic system's mode of production. So, in 19th century European states, the bourgeoise replaced the nobility and critically introduced business models that monetized the technologies of the industrial age. Technological shifts and innovation have been theorized as a cause for economic cycles, see medium-run (7–11 year) fixed-investment Juglar (1862) waves, and long-run (45–60 year) technological Kondratieff (1925/1935) waves. Schumpeter (1939) incorporated the Juglar and Kondratieff waves into his theory of business cycles and research has since shown that upswings, rather than recessions, usher forth creative destruction by entrepreneurs (Legrand & Hagemann, 2017, p. 253). The ETED conceives of such emerging elites as surfers, catching and riding technological waves to their full potential. Elite circulation or replacement under this premise is progressive and creates value.

'Progressive elite circulation' is discernible and understood. Specific instances include the automotive industry replacing the horse and buggy industry; Amazon's e-commerce and WeChat's social commerce models superseding traditional offline retail; and the Russian post-1990 oligarchs operating assets at higher efficiencies than their Soviet predecessors. Under progressive elite circulation, emerging elites rise to the top on the back of innovative, higher value creation elite business models. Yet the relationship between elite circulation and increasing value creation is anything but universal. At times, elites might even be replaced while the old elite business models linger on. This was the case for imperial Chinese dynasties adopting the extractive taxation agriculture model of their predecessors, a 2,600 year-old model only discontinued in 2006.[9] It gets worse when emerging elites turn out to be more extractive than their predecessors. The Yuan replacing the Southern Song Dynasty after the naval battle of Yashan in 1279 pro-

9 China's elite business model of taxing farmers (imperial grain and state taxes, *huangliang guoshui*) is probably the longest in the human historical record (594 BC – 2006). The origins of agricultural tax are attributed to a reform in the pre-imperial state of Lu, *chu shui mu* (i.e., land is taxed for the first time based on acreage) which is recounted in the *Xuan Gong Shi Wu Nian* section of the *Zuo Zhuan*. The Xinhua News Agency stated on December 30, 2005 that: "China's 2,600-year-old agricultural tax

vides an example of 'regressive elite circulation', since the racist four-class system of the Mongols was particularly extractive towards the Chinese Han and Southerners, especially during the early stages of their rule. Other examples of regressive elite circulation readily come to mind in contemporary regime changes in Libya, Venezuela, or Afghanistan. A concrete and painfully regressive business model replacement occurred in Medellín when Pablo Escobar's organization and peers supplanted "the textile sector (elites) flourishing before the appearance of the drug industry", blighting "the strong entrepreneurship mentality that characterizes Colombia's second city" (Naef, 2018, p. 12).[10]

Elite circulation occurs in specific areas of the political economy and within unique contexts through intra-elite contests, usually between established and emerging elites, but also sometimes between rival incumbents. Incumbent replacement might be self-inflicted through incompetence, excessive and unsustainable rent seeking, or ineffective elite coalition cohesion. Christensen (1997) suggests that established organizations are comparatively less adept at innovation and catching the waves of disruptive technologies. Henry Ford realized the possibilities of the assembly line in 1913, earlier than his older American, German, or French competitors, while Tesla seized the climate change narrative far sooner than the now aged Ford Motor Company. Emerging elites must be innovative as they seek ways to neutralize the formidable incumbency advantage, for instance, by offering better visions for how the future ought to unfold or by delivering greater value to customers. At times, rather than facing incumbents head on, it might be more effective to lay low, consolidate power in peripheral arenas and then, at the opportune moment, strike. The 1980 licensing contract between IBM and Microsoft for the operating system of personal computers, the importance of which was famously missed by IBM's top brass, launched one of history's most progressive elite circulations. Still, in the majority of cases incumbent power prevails: YouTube, Instagram, and ChatGPT all had the potential to spur elite circulation or even replacement but were instead incorporated into existing models (respectively by Google in 2006, Facebook in 2012, and Microsoft in 2023).

Elite circulation processes, if successful, always beg the same question: will the winning elites create more value than the incumbents they supersede? Even innovation can

---

will be rescinded as of Jan. 1, 2006, after China's top legislature voted on Thursday to adopt a motion on the regulations revoking the agricultural tax. [. . .] Wan Baorui, former vice minister of agriculture and vice chairman of the Agriculture and Rural Affairs Committee of National People's Congress told Xinhua that the abolition of the agricultural tax demonstrates that [China] ushers into a new era of 'industry subsidizing agriculture'. [. . .] During the more than 2,000 years, agricultural tax was always the main source of the country's coffer". Anecdotical conversations with Chinese farmers 15 years after the reform reveal a deep awareness and gratitude to the People's Republic of China (PRC) then leaders President Hu Jintao and Premier Wen Jiabao for the momentous decision to reverse the direction of value transfers between government and agriculture that had spanned across three millennia.

10 Baumol's framework in "Entrepreneurship: Productive, Unproductive, and Destructive" (1990) provides insight on why individuals such as Escobar (and Julius Caesar, see Section 7.3.2)—entrepreneurs of the unproductive and destructive type—are a feature of certain societies.

be hypothetically regressive if it is associated with value transfers in the service of extractive elite business models. Elite circulation in Medellín was regressive in this way and started with the dollar inflows to drug cartels from instigating the explosion in demand for cocaine in the US (Lee, 1988), a notionally innovative consumer product that enjoyed both the witting and unwitting support of American knowledge elites driving the groundbreaking cultural transformations of the time. On the other hand, the emergence of new technologies and ideas in society are opportunities for progressive elite circulation.

Besides innovation, circulation and replacement might also be driven by other exogenous events such as pandemics. While the bubonic plague of 1350 weakened the English feudal system (as labor became more valuable), neither elite circulation nor replacement materialized (the Peasant Revolts were eventually defeated). On the other hand, typhoid ended the siege of Athens in 430 BC and led to Sparta's victory in the Peloponnesian War which saw the winning elite wielding comparatively more extractive business models. In the case of elite circulation, and regardless of whether its origin is caused by bacteria (see Dartnell, 2023) or technological disruption, any factor outside of the elite system will have endogenized when kick-starting the process—external events become intrinsic to the political economy and can only materialize through intra-elite contests in the elite system. In the 1990s, France was ahead of every other country in e-commerce through France Telecom's Minitel service,[11] a lead that was squandered due to a lack of intra-elite contests and circulation. The way that the French establishment endogenized the breakthrough technology, e.g., through inadequate telecommunication regulation reforms, meant that the related value creation potential was realized by elite business models based in the US and China.

The replacement of sectoral elites as well as a nation's core elite coalition occurs through the combined wins of emerging elite coalitions in the market, non-market, and narrative market arenas. Narratives merit special attention and are as germane to Tesla as they were in Paris in 1789. In 1788, drought and the ensuing harvest failure drove the French revolutionary narrative synthesized in the tripartite motto *liberté, égalité, fraternité*. The old narrative of the *Ancien Régime* did not withstand this revolutionary challenge in the non-market political contest arena. This was due in great part to the incumbent elite system failing to address concerns arising from the royal business model such as a regressive tax system and increased inequality.

When narrative markets trade in new ideas, beliefs, and ideologies, they can become a natural starting point for discontinuous elite replacement processes. Emergent coalitions might introduce new narratives, sometimes as localized foreign transplants, that become overwhelming challengers to the status quo in their domestic political economy arenas. The achievements of such coalitions can be astonishing, as the might

---

11 The Organization for Economic Co-operation and Development (OECD) calculated that: "In 1994, 1.2 million [French] households used the Minitel to buy a product, whereas in the same year, only 800 000 US households used the Internet to carry out at least one commercial transaction" (1999, p. 116).

of an emergent elite increases in proportion to the virality of its narrative. In July 1921, the Communist Party of China (CPC) was founded by just 13 delegates in Shanghai; less than three decades later, in 1949, the new narrative had enabled complete outsiders to form a powerful modern Chinese state, a yearned for yet elusive goal since the Opium Wars of the 19th century. Similarly, Ilya Repin's (1903) masterpiece, *Ceremonial Sitting of the State Council on 7 May 1901 Marking the Centenary of its Foundation*, is a premonitory portrayal of the keepers of the reactionary, paralyzing, and ineffective Romanov narrative and its closed access elite system, foreshadowing a counter-narrative that would bring about its downfall. The first such challenge, the February 1917 Bourgeoise Democratic Revolution, did not consolidate the elite replacement bid, but the Bolsheviks succeeded in the October 1917 Revolution. As a result of their handling of World War I, Tsar Nicholas II and then Alexander Kerensky lost decisive battles in the narrative market arena, followed by their respective forfeiture of the throne and the short-lived Russian Republic. Soviet Marxist-Leninist socioeconomic thought, on the other hand, was the driving force for elite replacement, a bloody process that became irreversible after the Russian Civil War victory in 1923.

The historical expansion of Islam, divinely inspired and possibly history's largest and most extensive elite circulation process, occurred in territories as diverse as the Levant, Mesopotamia, North Africa, Iberia, Transoxania, Sindh, Bactria, and the Caucasus. It rested on revamped elite business models like "an increased money supply" (Shatzmiller, 2013, p. 305), while its nature was more nuanced than the Bolshevik revolution and included varying degrees of elite replacement. In one instance, "non-Muslim indigenous élites levied taxes for a small Muslim/Arab ruling class claiming the exclusive right of sovereignty", but their "star began to decline at the tail-end of that century, particularly as Arabisation and Islamicisation took hold" (Robinson, 2000, p. 90). That is, the tax farming business model of the emergent elites required the collaboration of the old elites, but only temporally. In another instance, after the final collapse of the Neo-Persian Empire's exhausted Sassanid Dynasty in 651, many members of the upper classes managed to conserve their elite status by converting to Islam. In doing so, the old elite not only avoided paying the poll tax to the Arabs, but also even received the state stipends allocated to aristocrats (Morony, 1976, p. 54).[12] Muslim conquest related elite business model replacement could, however, also be revolutionary and absolute, as the Hispano-Gothic aristocracy, most of whom did not convert to Islam, discovered in 711 when Tariq ibn Ziyad's North African Umayyad troops overwhelmed Iberia. As these examples show, the degree of completeness in elite replacement processes has varied widely throughout history.

This discussion has illustrated the multi-dimensional characteristics of elite circulation and replacement processes: they can be either progressive or regressive in value

12 Interestingly and in domino fashion, some of the refugee Sassanid aristocrats became elites in Central Asian kingdoms and even as far as China. Narsieh, the grandson of the last Sassanian emperor, Yazdegerd III, famously rose to become the commander of Tang Emperor Gaozong's imperial guards.

creation terms; the variety of the underlying drivers impacting intra-elite contests and effecting circulation is considerable, with technology now becoming ever more central; the forces that catalyze elite circulation frequently arise in narrative markets; and the degree of completeness of the process can differ greatly. This is also the case for the speed of the process, as elite circulation may sometimes not happen at all, stop midway through, occur at a glacial pace, or come with revolutionary fervor almost overnight. This all implies deep uncertainty. Following the complex system logic of "randomness with direction" (Gleick, 1987, p. 314), once the vagaries of elite circulation see new business models arrive at the apex of the political economy, predictions about economic development can be made by examining the aggregate sustainable value creation of elite business models at the meso-level of the elite system (see Proposition 17).

Normatively speaking, elite circulation and replacement driven by technological advances and innovation is progressive and desirable from a developmental perspective on the assumption that the outcome is value creation. For instance, digitalization and the rise of the electric vehicle are associated *a priori* with enormous new value creation. A connected question here is the role of the circulation process and whether (and to what extent) both the leading incumbents and emerging contestants realize the value creation opportunities afforded by waves of technological disruption. Will the top global automotive firms of Germany, the US, and Japan be replaced by the likes of Tesla, Rivian, and Lucid Motors or by Chinese challengers such as BYD Auto, NIO, and XPeng Motors? The newcomers' ultimate market share matters less than whether the size of the pie grows overall. To the ETED, the elite circulation dimensions that characterize society are relevant in terms of their association to value creation.

1.3.3 Proposition 3: The mode of elite circulation affects economic development

Proposition 3 proposes a framework for how elite circulation affects economic development based on two elite system properties: social order access (see North, Wallis and Weingast, 2006); and aggregate value creation, i.e., elite quality (the measurement of which is described in Chapter 6). These two properties reflect many of the dimensions of the circulation process expounded on in Proposition 2 and result in four modes, each associated with differing growth trajectories. These are depicted in The Elite Circulation Matrix (Figure 1.1).

Elite circulation modes have been a topic of discussion in the literature. Pareto identified slow infiltration replacement processes (Michels, 1962/1999, p. 167) alongside more sudden and violent revolutionary changes (Pareto, 1968/1991). Michels articulated an intermediate elite circulation mode characterized by admixture:

> Pareto's *théorie de la circulation des élites* must, however, be accepted with considerable reserve, for in most cases there is not a simple replacement of one group of *élites* by another, but a continuous process of intermixture, the old elements incessantly attracting, absorbing, and assimilating the new. (Michels, 1962/1999, p. 326)

Elite preservation strategies are often put in place to either preempt or weaken elite circulation and are then reflected in the mode that this process takes. Busino (2000, p. 225) articulates Pareto's sociology in this regard: "there are two ways of maintaining stability and social continuity: eliminating those who contest and therefore jeopardize the social order and the existence of the élite, and/or absorbing the elements of the governed class who may be useful or usable." Pareto and Michels reflected on the elite system's openness, and while they did not formalize a typology of elite circulation modes, Figure 1.1 incorporates their concerns by conceptualizing elite circulation in terms of social order access and elite quality. These two factors associated to elite circulation are deemed to have the most wide-ranging impact on economic and human development outcomes.

Elite circulation is short-circuited by revolutions and by wars when these are not intra-elite contests *per se*. The result in such cases is discontinuous replacements that degrade or destroy the incumbent elite system along with its knowledge, networks, and coordination capacity. Elite replacements, such as 'liberation' processes, that are mostly exogenous to the incumbent elite system do not constitute circulation (the analysis of revolutionary tipping points and the violent replacement of elites is deferred until Proposition 19 considers the options available to non-elites). Endogenous elite circulation processes can, however, also be beset by intra-elite violence. No greater calamity can befall a society than deinstitutionalized intra-elite conflict, a situation much more frequent than revolutions, and equally destructive. Once the fog of narratives (often designed to enlist non-elite groups) clears, it becomes evident that the cause of most of the suffering throughout history is intra-elite conflict resulting from elite system failure (i.e., the breakdown of the elite separation of powers and elite cohesion, see Figure 5.2). From this perspective, wars are deinstitutionalized cross-border intra-elite contests for division of value, many of which have their origins in domestic intra-elite rivalry. Elite replacements do occur as a result of the vagaries of war, but such transitions do not constitute an elite circulation mode within the social order. Nations revert to discrete endogenous elite circulation modes after exogenous shocks with clear pre- and post-war/pre- and post-revolution social orders. These orders are characterized by institutionalized intra-elite conflicts that do not compromise the existing knowledge, networks, and coordination capacity of elites. The Elite Circulation Matrix concerns itself with circulation modes that occur endogenously, within the reigning social order.

The four modes of elite circulation in the political economy are: 'admixture' (quadrant 1), which refers to the active integration of new value creation elites into the system and is reflected by vigorous social mobility; 'blockage' (quadrant 3), when elite circulation grinds to a halt leading to developmental regression; 'infiltration' (quadrant 2); and 'endosmosis' (quadrant 4), both of which denote unsatisfactory and stunted forms of elite circulation. In the ETED, admixture, which has been a hallmark of the US system for over two centuries, is associated with sustainable development, while infiltration and endosmosis result in haphazard, temporary,

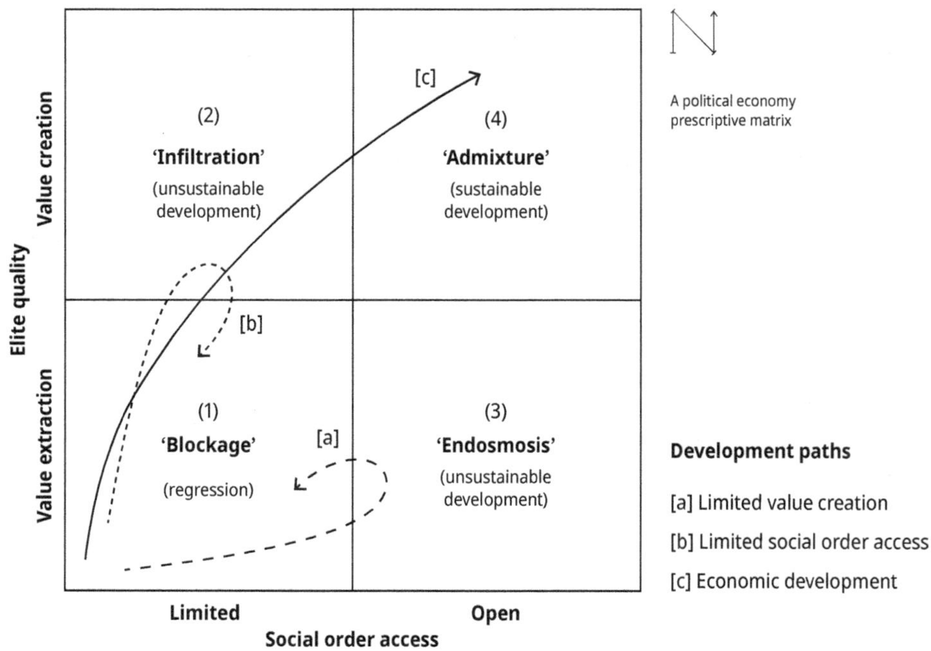

Figure 1.1: The Elite Circulation Matrix.[13]

unsustainable growth that soon loses steam. With infiltration, new value creation elite business models force their way into the elite but in insufficient numbers to transform the existing dominant models, thus remaining marginal forces in the elite system. With endosmosis, those who enter the elite system do so with extractive business models.

Each of the four modes is examined in some detail, starting with endosmosis (quadrant 4). The metaphor is based on the inward diffusion of water stopping when the concentration is the same inside and outside the membrane. Applied to The Elite Circulation Matrix, outsiders enter the system on the premise of higher value extraction. That is, the system is open to competitive and innovative outsider business models based on extractive value transfers and rents. Emergent rent seekers, or criminal organizations, can be assumed to simply be more efficient or ruthless than the incumbents they join or replace.[14] Since the elite system does not gain value creation capac-

13 Based in part on the social order access notion of North, Wallis, and Weingast, 2006.

14 The intra-elite contest dynamic in this mode of circulation is institutionalized, and even its violence follows recognizable patterns. For example, it has been noted that "the effects of mafias on the relationship between political power and the social order" result in situations where the "actors in power, legal and illegal, maintain agreements on the modes of social regulation" while at the same time incumbent elites (e.g., those controlling the state apparatus) and emerging ones (e.g., drug traffickers) appear at odds with each other (Duncan, 2014, pp. 18, 19).

ity when the extractive incumbents traverse the membrane, the economic vitality contributed by the new entrants is haphazard and unsustainable. For instance, opening the social order to democratization processes (see Section 8.1.4) often brings hopes of growth, but if such changes are not associated with higher elite quality levels the developmental trajectory (see path [a] in Figure 1.1) will end in a cul-de-sac.

In the infiltration mode of elite circulation (quadrant 2), the limited social order access similarly results in only temporary development. Newcomers with value creation business models are only exceptionally able to join the ranks of the elite and so lack the critical mass to meaningfully agglomerate and affect elite quality levels in the system. Moreover, emergent elites who *contra-natura* push through rare openings in the barriers that keep social divisions in place (e.g., thanks to exceptional creative energy and wealth accumulation powers) will regress their business models and become extractive. Once inside the system, the new elites essentially become undistinguishable from the old in terms of value creation. The reason behind such unsustainable development (see path [b] in Figure 1.1) is simple: it is cost-effective for elite coalitions admitted into the system to leverage their newly-found embeddedness to mimic insider rent-seeking behavior, soon losing any incentive to invest in value creation. For development to occur, there is a need for a critical agglomeration of newcomer value creation elites (see Section 4.3.5) with the power and desire to affect institutional change.

A particularly dismal scenario for human and economic development, one characteristic of most pre-modern social orders, is blockage (quadrant 3): extractive low elite quality systems with limited social access are hopelessly mired in regression with virtually no elite circulation. The large amounts of value creation needed to keep modern societies dynamic requires an ever-higher degree of openness and elite quality, with rapid elite circulation in the admixture mode (quadrant 1) for sustainable economic and social development. Admixture allows newcomers with value creation business models to quickly ascend within the system, a combination that results in the robust business model transformation of the economy and society (see path [c] in Figure 1.1).[15] An optimum speed for a type of admixture that maximizes aggregate value creation and economic development might exist. The ETED, however, suggests a simpler 'minimum elite circulation velocity' conjecture that relates the speed of elite circulation within the national elite system to the rate of development (the higher the velocity, the more development), conditioned by the emergence of new technologies (that elite business models then absorb and adopt).

---

15 For example, in 19th century Russia or Spain, emerging elites might include industrialists or talented state officials who, once established, ran business models based on proximity to the court and its related privileges. In contrast to the infiltration of St. Petersburg or Madrid, England and parts of Germany saw admixture. The admixture mode of elite circulation has a bidirectional absorptive quality across the old and the new. In England, a section of the established aristocracy committed their resources and coordination capacity to industrialization or its finance, while today, established Wall Street firms are heavily invested in Silicon Valley.

The minimum elite circulation velocity would also have to take into consideration Knight's supply of uncertainty-undertaking self-confident individuals: "the rashness or timidity of entrepreneurs (actual and potential)" that place business bets (1921/2002, p. 283) in order to have a chance of rising to elite status. The aggregate agency of those that are willing to respond to value creation incentives and expose themselves to risk by undertaking uncertainty is a significant determinant of economic outcomes. While the primary concerns of the ETED might appear to be at the meso- and macro-level aggregates (e.g., elite quality, economic growth), the single individual—the leader at the helm of a start-up, an established firm, a state-owned enterprise, or government project—matters greatly to economic development. Can the single individual's agency in Carlyle's (1840/2008) Great Man Theory of history (or leadership) have a parallel with and be of relevance to economic development in the context of elite circulation? A 'hero orthodoxy' already exists in the development literature and stresses the roles of "individual leaders" (Jones & Olken, 2005, p. 835), of "influential high-level leaders", as well as "of leadership in change processes" (Andrews, 2013, pp. 2, 5), and even of unsavory "economically benevolent dictators" (Gilson & Milhaupt, 2011). These "stories", when tested, however, "have not held up well in the contemporary empirical growth literature" (Easterly, 2011, p. 1, also see Easterly & Pennings, 2020). The edited work, *Leadership and Growth*, by the Commission on Growth and Development at the World Bank emphasizes this and provides some nuance:

> There is no one style of leadership that covers all the high-growth economies. Nor is leadership the only input. At best one can venture that effective leadership involves seizing opportunities created by the political-economy dynamics to institute change in strategy, structure, and direction. (Brady & Spence, 2010, p. 4)

To the ETED, change and transformational leadership in all of its forms is the critical input (see the typology of elite leadership types in Table 7.2) and substantiates 'the great elite coalition for development' conjecture. Members of an enlightened elite coalition have a decisive impact on development outcomes—through both macro-level structural reforms and new or revamped micro-level business models—when they support sustainable value creation. This is a notion and ethical position that is further developed in the final chapters of this work. Any elite system running business models that increase value creation is, to quote Carlyle, "great", even when elite agency is narrowly focused on specific domains or sectors. This is what makes the mode and velocity of elite circulation (Figure 1.1) so important: when admixture occurs at an optimal pace there is a far greater likelihood of 'great' elite agency, both in incumbent and emerging elite coalitions.

This section on the modes of elite circulation and their associated economic development outcomes closes with an example of admixture that epitomizes both elite circulation and the decisive impact of 'great' individual leadership in the elite coalition. America would be a noticeably different economy absent the imagination and amazingly innovative value creation agency of Steve Jobs. Without admixture, incumbents such as IBM, Sony, or Motorola might be in rather better shape than is currently the case, yet without the powerful elite coalition that brought the Mac, iPhone, and App-Store ecosystem into existence, the global economy's production function would be considerably diminished.

1.3.4 Proposition 4: Elites in the abstract are coordination capacity enabled by low transaction costs

The elite dominance iron law is, as discussed earlier, a rebuke of the elite denial fallacy ('elites don't exist'). Elites are a mathematical certainty, but by what logic? Michels' theory of the organization put the emphasis on the efficiency of hierarchies and massive organizations that "give their officers a near monopoly of power" (Lipset, 1999, p. 17). Bejan's idea of economies of scale links the social and physical world around the idea of hierarchies with few at the top:

> Economies of scale is the common observation that [sic] is easier and more efficient to move a unit of something along with other units (in bulk) than to move it alone. All flow systems (with power, movement, and freedom to morph) tend to unite and organize for this reason. In every such system, the resulting organization is a hierarchy of few large and many small, which is the antithesis to the one-size design with identical movers, and without organization. (Bejan, 2020, p. 13)

Hierarchy is omnipresent in natural and social systems and is realized in the political economy through the organizing force of the elite system. What theoretical perspectives best explain elite dominance? To the transaction cost perspective, the transaction is "the basic unit of analysis" for the economic system (Commons, 1924; Williamson, 1981, pp. 548, 549). Williamson further explains that "transaction cost economics is the means by which to breathe operational content into governance and organization" emphasizing "contractual relations from a transaction cost economizing perspective" (2010, pp. 673, 687). Olson's (1965/1971, 1982) collective action logic rests on an economic rationale consistent with the transaction cost advantages at the origin of elite dominance. The efficiency imperative, which requires hierarchy and organization, gives Olsonian small groups with concentrated interests a collective action advantage over distributed and larger groups, improving their chances of gaining positions at the top of hierarchies. The lower transaction costs of cohesive coalitions with a narrow membership underlie Olson's logic of collective action and theory of groups.

In addition to size, the transaction cost advantages of elite coalitions also rest on network effects and trust. Social networks are a powerful conceptual element, "a tool for linking micro and macro levels of sociological theory" (Granovetter, 1973, p. 1360), and a key component of the social structure impacting economic outcomes (Granovetter, 2005, p. 33). Elite networks are more effective because they are posited to possess higher levels of trust than non-elite networks. Trust is social capital (Fukuyama, 1995) and a valuable product of social elite networks (Morck & Yeung, 2004). As a manifestation of the relational dimension of social interaction, trust is germane to the success of any human endeavor; for instance, at the intrafirm level, it can bring about product innovation gains (Tsai & Ghoshal, 1998). Even "impersonal elite exchange" (North, Wallis, & Weingast, 2006, pp. 63–64) will be more scalable and efficient than impersonal exchange between non-elites. In short, small groups with lower transaction costs and higher levels of trust move to the central positions of social networks and to the top of hierarchies, making elites the largest repositories of coordination capacity—and power—in society.[16] The enormity of contemporary elite coordination capacity, i.e., applied power, is astounding, and exemplified by Apple's 2.4 million US job footprint, China's railway system managing more than 4 billion passenger trips per year, or the 2.5 billion monthly active users on YouTube.[17]

Elites in the abstract are but a manifestation of coordination capacity. This power, one which any social system affords to its apex (as per Proposition 1), seems disproportional to the coordination capacity of non-elites, especially when it manifests itself in terms of income disparities. While one may easily apprehend that elites have certain transaction cost advantages (by virtue of being in a small coalition benefiting from network effects and high levels of trust), it is incomprehensible that these are magnified out of all proportion in terms of power and coordination capacity differentials. A key facet of political economy systems is that even if elites enjoy only a small transaction cost advantage over non-elite stakeholders, this gap widens exponentially as transactions and time pass by. There is therefore an evident leverage effect associated with hierarchies and power. This lever technically works like credit creation in fractional reserve banking or the mechanics of economic multipliers (Lange, 1943). The functioning of 'the power multiplier' is conceptually akin to the

16 "We have proposed a system for electronic transactions without relying on trust" (Nakamoto, 2008, p. 8). This first sentence of the conclusion in the foundational Bitcoin white paper suggests a future where trust might no longer be needed and is replaced with "cryptographic proof instead of trust" (Nakamoto, 2008, p. 1). If the trust advantage of elites shrinks, the comparative bargaining power advantage and role of elites in the economy will correspondingly diminish. A testable hypothesis for the obsolescence of trust in cryptocurrency business models is whether their elites (e.g., founders, miners, the producers of $BTC blocks, exchanges) are less powerful and decentralized (and less rich) in their domains than elites in established sectors such as traditional finance. Knowing what percentage of wallets own how much Bitcoin would address the question of the distribution power (i.e., applied coordination capacity) which emanates from the trust and networks of small groups: if 2% of "whales" own 95% of Bitcoin (as claimed by Kharif, 2020b), Nakamoto's ideal is nowhere near to realization. This is precisely why Bitcoin seems to be holding its value when other digital assets are not, as trust is a key feature of any successful blockchain project. The trust existing among members of the narrow elite coalition is the reason why stakeholders trust that coalition's elite business model with their resources and assets. Hence, another test about whether cryptographic proof or another model has really replaced trust is what happens when outsiders cannot trust that elite coalition members trust each other, as was the case with Luna or FTX.

17 See: https://www.apple.com/newsroom/2019/08/apples-us-job-footprint-grows-to-two-point-four-million/; https://www.globaltimes.cn/page/202412/1324320.shtml; https://backlinko.com/youtube-users.

"force multiplier" of military affairs with its generation of "fighting power" which in turn is the result of factors like "doctrine" (Sloan, 2012) or even religion (Hassner, 2016). A precise description of 'the power multiplier' can be found in *A Book of Five Rings*, the Japanese classic on strategy, *kenjustsu*, and philosophy, where Miyamoto Musashi (1645/1974, pp. 46–47) writes:

> If he attains the virtue of the long sword, one man can beat ten men. Just as one man can beat ten, so a hundred men can beat a thousand, and a thousand can beat ten thousand. In my strategy, one man is the same as ten thousand, so this strategy is the complete warrior's craft.

A multiplier of 10,000 might appear modest compared to the ratios implicit in the levers of Steve Jobs with his products, the Apostle Paul with his epistles, or Vladimir Putin with his security apparatus. When the multiplier effect generates power that is completely out of proportion with the differentials normal in regular social relationships, the elite coalition is said to wield 'the extraordinary lever' in its sector of the political economy (see the visualization in Figure A5.3a). That is, modest transaction cost advantages in bilateral principal-stakeholder relationships magnify across the length of the value chain, creating enormous power differentials that are perfect for value appropriation for those at the top. Once accumulated, this power (a topic that is the exclusive focus of Section 4.3), becomes applied coordination capacity and a key for human development. When applied inclusively, it explains, for instance, why a maverick entrepreneur builds reusable rockets that the space agency of the national state with the largest economy will not. Power, the applied coordination capacity afforded by 'the extraordinary lever', can likewise be extractive, as is evident when a monopolist raises prices in a narrow market segment that it dominates or a president unilaterally decides to invade a neighbor, initiating a war that most of its elites and non-elites did not want or expect. The differences between inclusive and extractive elite coalitions can be traced back to the characteristics of the elite system including the comprehensiveness of the elite separation of powers, a matter amply discussed later in this work (see Figure 3.7 and Table 3.2).

Elites are master coordinators, but how do they accumulate power? Through wins in the three contest arenas of the political economy: the political non-market (where elites gain an institutionally sanctioned license to operate); the economy's market (where elites gain residual income); and society's narrative market (where elites gain sway over hearts and minds and thus the legitimacy for their license to operate). 'Elite coordination leadership' facilitates wins in the economy's market arena that result in 'money' (i.e., power in the economy); wins in the political non-market arena that result in 'might' (i.e., power in politics); and wins in society's narrative market arena that result in 'mind' (i.e., power in society). Effective elite coordination leadership wins in these three contested arenas provides elite agency with its first objective: the accumulation of power (see Figure 1.2). Power accumulation secures 'the extraordinary lever', the effectiveness of which is boosted across the value

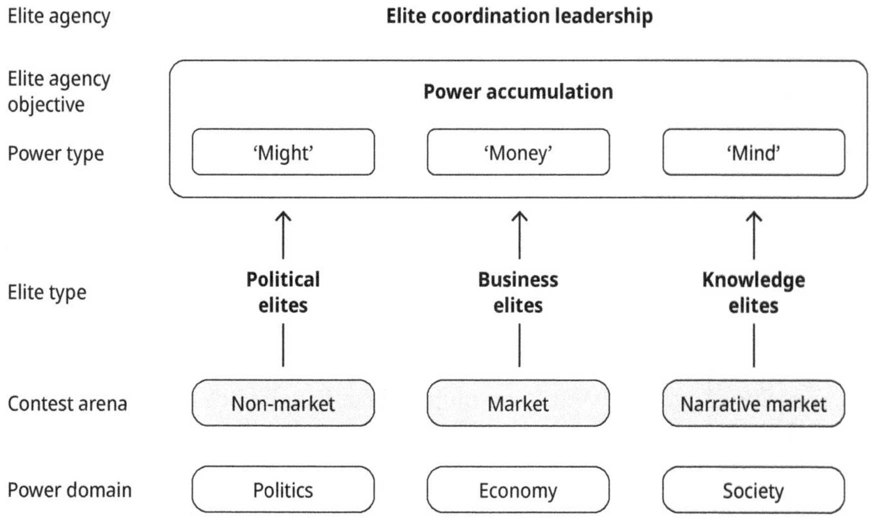

Figure 1.2: Elite coordination leadership: Power accumulation in the three political economy contest arenas.

chain (*de facto* structured as a hierarchy) of cascading principal-stakeholder relationships.[18] Power must be an essential component of the elite theory paradigm and is later examined in theoretical detail and duly incorporated into the ETED architecture (see Sections 4.4 and 4.5), as is the process that further converts this power into residual income (see Figure 4.4).

Beyond the theoretical, one might ask what does the concrete practice of elite coordination leadership entail? In the *The Art of the Deal* (1987, 1:39), Donald Trump stresses the importance of his 50–100 calls and a dozen meetings per day. The biggest shareholder of the world's foremost commodities trader, Ivan Glasenberg, paradigmatically has a talent for power accumulation—characteristic of leaders since time immemorial—as is vividly captured by *The Financial Times*:

> Rivals and colleagues say he is constantly on the phone, gathering intelligence or cementing relationships, and supposedly always ready to jump on the plane and smooth a deal, whether by visiting a chief executive or head of state. (Blas, 2011)

18 Leaving constraining institutions aside and *ceteris paribus*, the more complex and technologically sophisticated a business model is, the greater the hierarchical relationship with its stakeholders. Hence, business models based on data have more leverage over their stakeholders than predecessor models based on the factors of production such as land, labor and capital. The rapid advance of artificial intelligence ups the ante even further in this regard. Generally speaking, elite coordination leadership will always strive to minimize friction across the hierarchical levels (the power transmission mechanism is made up of local small levers between one level and the next) so that 'the power multiplier' (again, applied coordination capacity) is not lost. Data reduces friction and transaction costs and so preserves 'the extraordinary lever', a specific aim of elites that is also achieved through enabling institutions.

In a zero transaction cost world, accumulated (bargaining) power would be irrelevant (North, 1990, p. 16), as would the insights of standard economics (Williamson, 2010, p. 687). Moreover there would be no fulcrum for 'the extraordinary lever'. By applying the Coase theorem (Coase, 1960; Medema, 1994), government would also be superfluous and, as Marciano (2011, p. 4) recounts, "in the absence of transaction costs, externalities are internalized, that is private and social costs coincide and, in addition, legal rules do not matter" for the purpose of resource allocation. Crucially for the ETED, in a world with no transaction costs, elites would also be irrelevant and unnecessary, since elite coordination capacity or high levels of trust would offer no advantage in political economy contests. However, in the absence of such a brave new world (that still may emerge with the singularity),[19] low transaction costs and trust-producing networks facilitate wins by elites in the contest arenas of the political economy. Transaction cost economics supports "positive political economy" analysis because it recognizes a relationship, one that will later be critical in this work, between regulatory institutions and the "goals of political agents" (Weingast & Marshall, 1988, as cited in Joskow, 1995, p. 256). In the market, non-market, and narrative market arenas, the transaction cost reduction roles of elites facilitate the formation and maintenance of elite business models and explain 'the power multiplier'. The role of elites in reducing transaction-cost mechanisms matter to development because of their magnitude: North (1984, p. 7) estimated these costs to be "as much as 50 percent of GNP" and hence they "have determined the output of political/economic systems throughout history".

19 In a world where only knowledge matters and transaction costs are the result of knowledge asymmetries, the advent of a superintelligence or AGI where the "the marginal cost of intelligence" becomes insignificant (Hoffman, 2022) might, all else being equal, turn off 'the power multiplier' altogether, meaning that elite agency would cease to work as described in this work (see the various hypotheses on the possible effects of AI on the political economy in Table A4.6).

Summary of Chapter 1

Towards a logic of elite agency

Chapter 1 launches the inquiry towards an elite theory of economic development (ETED) with four propositions on elite agency ('what elites do'). To prepare the conceptual terrain for these propositions, Section 1.1 embarks on a discussion of two elite fallacies—the elite denial fallacy ('elites don't exist') and the elite populist fallacy ('elites are bad'). In Section 1.2, a multidisciplinary elite literature review eventually leads to a working definition of elites (1.2.4) that is grounded in an examination of grand socio-political conceptualizations of elites (1.2.1), contemporary conceptualizations of elites (1.2.2), and conceptualizations of elites relevant to economics (1.2.3), all of which is summarized in Table A1.1 and organized by analysis level (micro to macro) and perspective (particularism to universalism) in the classification framework of Figure A5.2. A third elite fallacy that is derived from the first two—the non-elite rule fallacy ('people power')—is also introduced.

Section 1.3 covers four initial propositions on the logic of elite agency. Proposition 1, 'The elite dominance iron law is structural to society' (1.3.1), is controversial, but here is deemed to be undeniable and self-explanatory, with its roots in sociological traditions. Proposition 2, 'Elite circulation is multi-dimensional and characterizes society' (1.3.2), clarifies some of the characteristics of elite replacement processes such as their progressive or regressive qualities or the role played by narrative markets. Proposition 3, 'The mode of elite circulation affects economic development' (1.3.3), stresses two properties of the elite system that associate with elite circulation and affect developmental outcomes: social order access and elite quality, i.e., the aggregate sustainable value creation of elite business models. A suggested framework, The Elite Circulation Matrix (Figure 1.1), has four discrete modes and provides an original description of a political economy while also facilitating the tracing of development trajectories. Relatedly, the 'minimum elite circulation velocity' conjecture is submitted and posits that circulation velocity should be in sync with technological cycles (the image is that of emerging and incumbent elites 'catching' and then 'surfing' Kondratieff waves).

Proposition 4 closes the chapter by integrating the first three conjectures and laying out the economic rationale underlying the iron law, 'Elites in the abstract are coordination capacity enabled by low transaction costs' (1.3.4). Low transaction costs result from Olsonian small groups organized as high-trust networks. Elite coordination leadership enables power accumulation—the necessary first objective of elite agency. As coalitions reach the top of social hierarchies, they realize the benefits of 'the power multiplier', since elite agency is inseparable from 'the extraordinary lever'. That is, elite coordination capacity becomes applied, a process that is essential to growth as it correlates with the reservoir of coordination capacity in society at large. At the root of this is the transaction cost advantage that a coalition has over stakeholders with which it has direct relationships (as depicted in Figure A5.3a). Power augments in hierarchies along each level of the value chain. The three political economy contest arenas for the accumulation of power endowments: market, non-market, and narrative market (in the respective power domains of the economy, politics, and society) are then introduced for the first time (and visualized in Figure 1.2). With this suggested foundational schema for elite agency, the inquiry moves to the elite business model and its value creation and appropriation logic.

Chapter 2
Towards a value creation and appropriation logic for elite business models

Having reviewed the literature and determined what elites are and 'what elites do', we will now examine the central focus of elite agency—the elite business model—through the development of seven more propositions (5 to 11). The first two of these, relating respectively to elite rationality and income maximization, establish the behavioral logic of elites (2.1). This is followed by an in-depth look at a central set of three propositions on the elite business model (2.2). A business model has principals and stakeholders, both producers and claimants of value. Their interactions are understood within the value creation-appropriation (VCA) framework, which has been advanced in the strategic management literature (e.g., by Brandenburger & Stuart, 1996; Amit & Zott, 2001; Lepak, Smith, & Taylor, 2007; Di Gregorio, 2013; Garcia-Castro & Aguilera, 2015). The VCA, with its stakeholder view of strategy (Freeman, 1984; Donaldson & Preston, 1995), is fundamental to this work and is used to elucidate the elite business model. Bargaining power endowments (Coff, 1999; MacDonald & Ryall, 2004; Moatti, Ren, Anand, & Dussauge, 2015) are a key analytical device in this regard. The closing section (2.3) first presents a proposition to contextualize value appropriation and then initiates the operationalization of this work's conceptual elements into sustainable value creation (SVC) measurements (see the equations in Table 2.4) by asserting, for instance, that elite business models operate at measurable positions on a conceptual 'business model value creation spectrum' ranging from value creation to value extraction.

2.1 Propositions on the behavioral logic of elite agency

Elite behavior is modeled on the basis of neoclassical insights (Proposition 5), which leads to the residual income maximizing elite business model as the defining aspect of elite identity (Proposition 6).

2.1.1 Proposition 5: Elite behavior maximizes utility and is potentially sustainable

Under neoclassical assumptions (e.g., Becker, 1993) of rational choice theory (RCT), which are congruent with the ideas of utilitarian political economists like Bentham (1781/1970) and Mill (1863/2001), agents in the economy have an orderly and stable hierarchy of preferences and are premised to maximize utility. Critically assessed as the "default mode of social theorizing" (Williams, 2000), "rational choice consists simply of selecting that alternative whose consequences rank highest in the payoff function"

https://doi.org/10.1515/9783110734638-004

(Allison & Zelikow, 1999, p. 18). The 'elite utility function' has also been conceived in RCT terms, specifically as income maximization and consistent with the "elite's lifetime income maximization problem" of Wang (2021). The value creation-appropriation (VCA) framework (Brandenburger & Stuart, 1996; Coff, 1999; Amit & Zott, 2001; Lepak, Smith, & Taylor, 2007; Di Gregorio, 2013; Garcia-Castro & Aguilera, 2015) provides a theoretical foundation for elite agency that is consistent with RCT, as bargaining power differentials enable utility maximizing value appropriation. Residual income (a form taken by appropriated value) and power are therefore interchangeable (at conversion rates determined by the elite business model). Bargaining power enables elite income maximization.

Elite agency in the ETED is characterized by a utility function where residual income is the highest ranked preference (because agency is no longer *elite* the moment that significant residual income flows cease to accrue). This position has specific theoretical bearing. The agency versus structure debate in organization studies is pivotal to this inquiry (see Chapter 3) as the residual income maximization utility function of elites is posited to be a cause of institutional change (effected through the dynamics of intra-elite contests, see Propositions 16 or 20).

In Chapter 4, the microfoundational framework of institutional theory and embedded agency will be discussed in the context of institutional change by elite agency. Williamson (2000), using the four levels of the social analysis framework for the economics of institutions (see Figure 3.1), proposes neoclassical marginal analysis for the micro-level of the firm (level 4). In the ETED, the micro-level analysis is applied to the elite business model (as a firm is a bundle of business model activities), not to individual members of the elite (even when the agency of specific elite individuals is indistinguishable from that of their firm or its business model). It is a *leitmotif* of this work that elite business models appropriate both the value that they create and the value they do not in pursuit of residual income. The latter is known as rent seeking in economics, and is referred to in this inquiry as either value extraction or second-order transfer activity (see Table 2.3); technically value (turned into residual income or revenue) that is transferred *into* a business model. This 'value appropriated but *not* created' is operationalized as 'value transfer-IN', mirrored by an offsetting value 'transfer-OUT' from the counterparty, i.e., 'value created but *not* appropriated'. The residual income maximization utility function of elites drives behavior (elite agency) in the context of elite business models that is tractable under RCT assumptions.

This leads to the question of whether elite agency conceived on a RCT footing can be consistent with sustainability? The answer references Olson (1993, 2000) and his bandit metaphor, since, consistent with the RCT premise, elites can inherently make the transition from "roving bandit" to "stationary bandit" if they adjust their temporal perspective when they seek to maximize income. On this journey, the business model, driven by the elite utility function, is transformed by the sustainability notion.

The income maximization utility function of elites must be qualified by the applicable temporal perspective, which is derived from circumstance, conditions in the political economy, and personal choice. Acemoglu and Robinson (2006) suggest that secure elites, such as those in 19th century Prussia or contemporary China, will modernize and increase their country's production function in order to extract more in the future. In contrast to the Olsonian "roving bandit", the "stationary bandit" (elite coalition members anchored in a given political economy whose business models have restricted mobility) will not maximize income with a short-term fixation on appropriating all extractable value (from stakeholders, including non-elites), because non-elite stakeholder value creation needs to occur for future value appropriation to be feasible. Borrowing Dercon's notion in *Gambling on Development* (2022), this type of "elite bargain" would be both rational and long-term. Clearly, not all elites are stationary or have the cohesion, ability, or appetite to realize such bargains; much has been made of Latin American, African, or Eastern European potentates who fit Olson's description of the roving bandit, earning fortunes in their countries of origin while transferring that wealth to their bases in Miami, Paris or London. The more stationary (and secure) an elite is, the less short-term the income maximization horizon will be and the greater the incentive to self-constrain present extraction and transfer-IN from non-elites. In short:

> If the stationary bandit successfully monopolizes the theft in his domain, then his victims do not need to worry about theft by others. [. . .] With the rational monopolization of theft—in contrast to uncoordinated competitive theft—the victims of the theft can expect to retain whatever capital they accumulate out of after-tax income and therefore also have an incentive to save and to invest, thereby increasing future income and tax receipts. (Olson, 1993, p. 568)

In summary, residual income maximization atop the hierarchy of preferences in the elite utility function optimizes a trade-off between two variables, each associated with a discrete time horizon: firstly, short-term residual income flows (that serve, among other purposes, the satisfaction of present consumption); and secondly, long-term wealth stocks (that generate income flows over time and are consistent with investments to secure elite status across generations). Elites that are unwilling or incapable of creating value will give precedence to immediate income. To augment the stock of wealth (i.e., accumulated residual income flows), the model stationary bandit must, on the other hand, restrain excessive extractive short-term transfer-IN from stakeholders and non-elites (to avoid these opting for 'exit' or other unsustainable responses, see Table 5.1). The long-term thus requires both a degree of value creation through business models that enhance the economy's production function and limits to the amount of transfer-IN from stakeholders (i.e., value extraction below the level that bargaining power differentials may allow). Given that such transformational agency will comprise inclusive transfer-OUT from elites to non-elites, positive externalities, and the creation of public goods, do stationary elites deserve the 'bandit' moniker at all? Rational utility maximizing elite agency with a long-term orientation makes the political economy sustainable.

The RCT foundation of this inquiry introduces the key notion of sustainability. The ETED purports that elite income maximization and long horizons are associated to sustainability, a position that is consistent with the historical roots of the notion. The "term was first coined several hundred years ago by a German forester, Hans Carl von Carlowitz, in his 1712 text *Sylvicultura Oeconomica*, to prescribe how forests should be managed on a long-term basis" (Scoones, 2007, p. 590). From these origins in addressing a narrow business model (forestry), the concept eventually gained widespread attention through Gro Harlem Brundtland's milestone report for the United Nations, *Our Common Future*. The now generally accepted definition of sustainability focuses, like the elite coalitions seeking to maximize wealth through value creation and risk origination, on the long term: "Sustainable development is development that meets the needs of the present without compromising the ability of future generations to meet their own needs" (Brundtland, 1987).

2.1.2 Proposition 6: Elite identity is driven by residual income

Proposition 6 tests the RCT premises put forward in Proposition 5 to address elite identity. Williamson's social analysis framework alluded to, but did not further pursue, a "level zero [. . .] the level in which the mechanisms of the mind take shape" (Williamson, 2000, p. 600). However, if "psychology and sociology of identity" was the decisive "economic model of behavior" (Akerlof & Kranton, 2000, p. 715), to what extent is elite psychological and sociological identity a behavioral driver distinct from mere RCT income maximization? Does non-economic identity, possibly fueled by attendant narratives, figure in elite utility functions? Does it, for instance, inform Maslowian human needs (1943) like reputation, prestige, and recognition from others—all part and parcel of the leading theories of human motivation? Why do status threats and the fear of losing power condition the rational decision-making of elites (Renshon, 2015)?

In *The Prince* (1513/1998), Machiavelli asserted that in the political arena the "acquisition and maintenance of power" is as important as its seizure (Spackman, 1990, p. 144). More specifically, in the case of Japan's elites, researchers note: "The primary goals of [*keiretsu*] are power, wealth, and status, and [*keiretsu*]-building for prestige is an ongoing preoccupation of the elite in Japan. A focus all the rich and powerful everywhere try to practice" (Kim, 1996, p. 342). Elite behavior to preserve acquired or inherited elite status tends to manifest itself as a "whatever it takes" response in all three of the contest arenas of the political economy. The relevant question though is whether elite status is motivated by psychological and sociological identity, or whether the core of individual or family elite identity is instead economic, revolving mainly around the residual income generating elite business model. In other words, can elite agency be conceived of beyond residual income maximization and include non-economic identity elements? If not, then "status" at the macro level (Piazza & Castellucci, 2014) and Machiavelli's power are simply instrumental means for the elite business model (and not objectives *per se*), while identity and the "mechanisms that shape the mind"—Williamson's (2000) "level zero"—can be safely ignored for theorizing about elite agency.

Notwithstanding psychological and sociological factors or deeply anchored personal and family narratives (e.g., a common genealogy, a religious ideal) the ETED posits that elite identity is primarily driven by the residual income generating elite business model. This assertion has equivalence with Winters' (2011) claim that the prime concern of oligarchs is to engage in "wealth defense". This conjecture is confirmed if elites, when presented with a dichotomy between their non-economic identity and residual income maximization, choose the latter (controlling for non-elites facing equivalent choices). That is, if the elite utility function preference for income maximization is ranked higher than alternative preferences associated with the psychological and sociological integrity of elite identity and its original narrative. A series of historical examples are offered below: members of communist elite families becoming business owners, former slaves transforming themselves into slaveholding elites, and Calvinist elites converting to Catholicism.

A selection bias operates against elites endeavoring to preserve identity and the related narrative integrity that is associated with expired (i.e., bereft of residual income generation potential) elite business models. Loyalty to the narrative that propelled coalitions or families to elite status leads to them being captives of the past, trapped in an existential *cul de sac*. Thus, communist cadres in Vietnam's state sector leveraged their centrality in political economy networks to become entrepreneurs and leaders of listed firms (Fujita, 2020). Since Liberia's independence in 1847, the descendants of the freed and repatriated African slaves (the Americo-Liberians) "completely dominated all the country's institutions" (from 1847 until their violent overthrow in 1980), creating an elite identity around freedom but utilizing elite business models that brutally focused on residual income maximization even as these evolved—from slaveholding (until the 1920s) to wage repression (Robinson, 2010, p. 7–8). The Good King Henry of Navarra (Henry IV of France) converted to Catholicism because "Paris is well worth a Mass", swiftly overcoming "religious convictions, promises of fidelity to Calvinism, and reluctance to yield to the demands of others" (Dickerman, 1977, p. 2). Apparently, running the royal business model was the elite identity that trumped the supposedly non-negotiable Calvinist narrative.

2.2 Propositions on the logic of elite business models

The inquiry has now proposed a residual income maximization driven elite utility function (Proposition 5), where the elite business model defines elite identity ahead of any other psychological and sociological considerations (Proposition 6). Residual income maximization and the optimization of short- and long-term perspectives occurs in all elite business models that are now examined in detail as being central to elite agency (Proposition 7). Their capacity to generate all-important residual income is explored through the value creation-appropriation (VCA) framework (Propositions 8 and 9), a process that will enable the measurement of sustainable value creation and extractive transfers at the micro-level, and serve as the foundation for aggregate measurements of the meso-level elite system (such as elite quality) that impact the macro-economy and affect economic development.

2.2.1 Proposition 7: The elite business model is the locus of elite agency

Proposition 7 places the elite business model at the center of elite agency. Such a position would appear to address concerns that elite theory has "turned away from an emphasis on material power" (Winters, 2011, p. 31). Yet wealth is not the business model, the conceptual element that theoretically grounds the sustainable value creation of elites at the micro-level. Drucker (1994) introduces the concept of "what a business will and won't do" and while he never defined "business model" *per se* in his theory of business it is understood to be "assumptions about what a company gets paid for" (Ovans, 2015). A business model is the engine of residual income generation (and eventually wealth stocks), while at the same time "a useful representation of how the organization creates value through transforming and transferring matter" (Arend, 2013, p. 391), and "a template that depicts the way a firm conducts its business" (Zott & Amitt, 2013, p. 404). More granular conceptualizations include the role of the principal and the principal's counterparts—the stakeholders (Coff, 1999; Brandenburger, 2002; Zott & Amitt, 2013; Garcia-Castro & Aguilera, 2015). The concept of stakeholders (Freeman, 1984; Donaldson & Preston, 1995) is necessary to link the business model to value creation and value extraction.

The principal-stakeholder perspective of the business model describes the system of interdependent activities that are performed by the firm and its partners and the mechanisms that connect these activities to each other (Zott & Amit, 2010). Zott and Amitt further specify that "business models center on the logic of how value is created for *all* stakeholders, not just how it is captured by the focal firm", i.e., the principal (2013, p. 404). By combining these ideas on business models with the reviewed literature on elites, the elite business model conceptual element is defined for the purpose of this inquiry:

> Elite business models are the largest residual income and reward business models in the economy and constitute a system of interdependent activities that are performed by a particular principal, as part of an elite coalition, in relation to its stakeholders. An elite business model describes *how* the principal and the stakeholders respectively create and appropriate value through division of value strategies to generate proprietary residual income, and associates with discrete sustainable value creation.

If elite business models are the locus of elite agency, what makes them feasible and successful? Elite business models first require 'elite coordination leadership' to accumulate power (see Figure 1.2) and subsequently 'elite business model leadership' to convert this power into residual income (see Figure 2.1) that is generated through successful value appropriation activities (also conceptualized as applied coordination capacity, see

Figure A5.3a). Some of the value appropriated is created, while some is extracted as a transfer-IN from the original value creators (value appropriated but *not* created). How elites create, appropriate, and transfer value is illustrated through a rather extravagant case study depicting the interdependent activities of an elite business model: Coca-Cola's operations in Libya during the period prior to the ousting of Colonel Gaddafi in 2011 (based on Fritschle, 2006; Hosenball, 2011).

In WikiLeaks one reads that the Libyan ruler "speaks out publicly against government corruption, but the politically-connected elite has direct access to lucrative business deals. Qadhafi son Mohammed heads the Libyan Olympic Committee that now owns 40% of the Libyan Beverage Company, currently the Libyan joint venture Coca-Cola franchisee" (Fritschle, 2006). This particular elite business model required effective elite coordination leadership to manage multiple stakeholders and elite business model leadership across disparate activities to convert power into income. The latter form of leadership was visible in market arena wins that included the production of the bottled drinks according to Coca-Cola standards and their effective distribution and marketing. Elite coordination leadership, on the other hand, entailed wins in the non-Libyan narrative market arena: the bottling deal had to somehow be acceptable to Coca-Cola, the US Embassy in Libya, and the International Olympic Committee. Wins in the domestic political non-market arena were equally crucial, and meant that the heart of Colonel Gaddafi had to be won over (and here, in a reversal of fortune, Muhammad Muammar eventually lost out to his brother, Mutassim, in a dramatic showdown that will be presented as an example of intra-elite contests in Section 3.3.1).

The Libyan Coca-Cola case brings about a more sophisticated analytical perspective introduced through Acemoglu and Robinson (2000, p. 129) who develop plausible models to explain "why landed elites in Russia and Austria-Hungary, but not Britain and Germany, decided to block innovations and the railroads". Their examples not only raise questions about elite business model leadership but about leadership at the elite system level (expounded on in Section 7.2.4) and what happens when elite business models fail to transform. The authors' explanation for the lack of transformation in Russia and Austria-Hungary is "the threat that industrialization posed to political power, not to economic rents" (Acemoglu and Robinson, 2000, p. 129). This inquiry argues that if these elites had invested in and transformed their business models, new sources of power would have more than compensated for the erosion of their original political power bases caused by the new institutional arrangements necessary for industrialization. Political power is instrumental and hence secondary; it can be gained, lost, and regained with residual income. The Romanov and Habsburg elite systems retained their out-of-date extractive transfer models because they lacked transformational leadership (a conceptual element that is developed in Section 7.2.4) and obviated that knowledge also affords bargaining power. The comparative developmental and geopolitical fate of the two empires demonstrates that if incumbent elites can't or won't surf fixed-investment (medium-run Juglar) waves and technological (long-run Kondratieff) waves, then rival emerging domestic or foreign elites will do so and make them obsolete.

Political power is meaningful inasmuch as the non-market contest arena contributes to the overall power endowment at the disposal of elite business model leadership. Elite business models rely on power in all its forms (again, see Figure 1.2): the economy power domain ('money') works in close combination with the politics power domain ('might') and the society power domain ('mind'). Market arena wins (in the economy) are complemented by wins in the non-market arena (in politics) and narrative market arena (in society). Successful elite business model leadership has bases in all three of these power domains (economy, politics, and society), secured in the respective contest arenas (market, non-market, and narrative market). Ultimately and as depicted in Figure 2.1, the accumulated power is converted into its most fungible form, residual income/profits or 'money', which can be disposed of at the pleasure of elite business beneficiaries and is the primary local entropy reduction mechanism in the modern world.

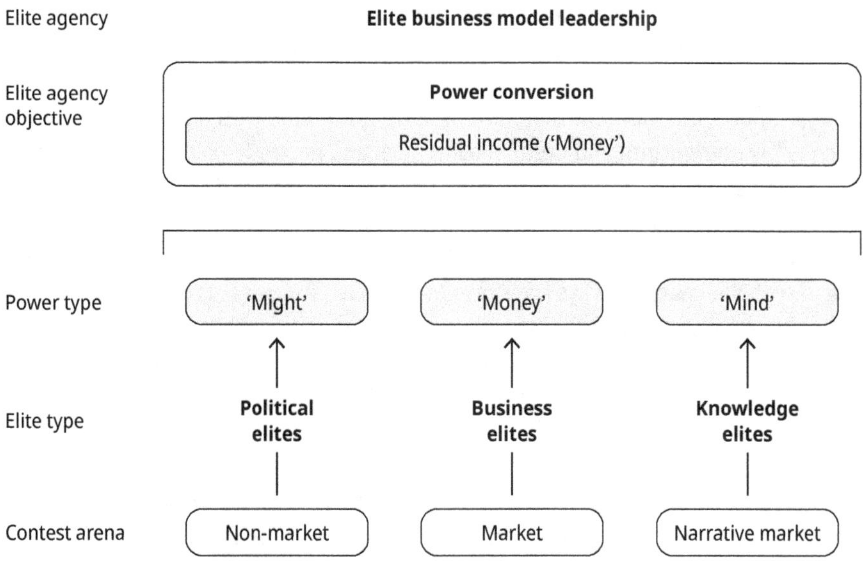

Figure 2.1: Elite business model leadership: Converting power into residual income.

For Mills (1956, p. 9) "the elite are simply those who have the most of what there is to have, which is generally held to include money, power, and prestige—as well as all the ways of life to which these lead". The ETED's suggested tripartite power structure for elite contests takes no position on which power type reigns supreme: whether economic 'money', political 'might', or social 'mind', the decisive power type depends on the business model and the given political economy context (as depicted in the overview of elite agency in Figure A5.1). A headline in *The Wall Street Journal* provides material for analysis of a specific intra-elite contest (later dissected in Table 3.1), "Keystone XL Oil Project Pledges Zero Carbon Emissions: Controversial pipeline would be powered by renewables, built by union labor in bid to avoid ax [sic] from Biden" (Puko, 2021). Eventually, the anticipated win in the narrative market (in the citation, the sustainability and labor stakeholder narratives) did not materialize, and there was no win in the political non-market (the Biden Administration cancelled the project) that would then have led to the ultimate business win in the market for energy transportation (i.e., an efficient pipeline to dislodge the established oil-by-rail model). In this case, the power domain of politics was the decisive arbiter. However, in principle, elite coordination leadership needs combined wins in all three of the power domains (economy, politics, and society), even if for some models one of the three corresponding contest arenas is more relevant than the others. For example, society's narrative market arena is more relevant for the Vatican, the political non-market arena for labor unions, and the economy's market arena for smart phone manufacturers. Whatever the primary domain, power eventually needs to be converted into residual income (profits). 'Money', not as power but as a freely disposable residual, is the final objective of elite business model leadership.

Successful elite agency includes leadership to accumulate power and then convert it into income through a business model that both creates and appropriates value. Some elite business models are comparatively more competitive and innovative and so are able to generate more value, including for stakeholders (e.g., by having customers with a higher willingness to pay). The 19th century British and German elites mustered the leadership to transform and run the elite business models of industrialization, while the Russian and Austrian aristocratic elites did not and continued to operate less profitable and more extractive pre-industrial and agricultural empire models. The 'inextinguishable value creation option of elites' is the (leadership) premise that elites can always transform business models towards ever more sustainable value creation positions (and forgo value appropriated but *not* created). The discussion on business models now proceeds with an examination of the key enabler of value appropriation, the all-important strategic management notion of bargaining power.

2.2.2 Proposition 8: The elite business model is characterized by principal-stakeholder bargaining power differentials required for value appropriation

Proposition 8 is a lengthy disquisition with new conceptual elements and logical leaps. After a brief literature review that stresses collaborative value creation, the starting point is the definition of value. Then the principal-stakeholder relationships—including between a principal and 'nature'—turn value into prices in a process that is mediated by an effective division of value strategies. Value appropriation relies on bargaining power and its differentials. Two discrete sources of bargaining power ('knowledge' and 'political economy know-how') are then established with their respective links to development. Specific applied challenges for economic growth are also articulated through the 'the Amazon dilemma' of the political economy and its hypothesized constituents, the 'elite vs non-elite knowledge gap' and the 'elite power vs value creation gap'.

The ultimate source of residual income is 'value', which has been discussed earlier in the context of the business model but not precisely defined. Clarity about what value actually constitutes is essential. Properly answering this question would require inputs from a wide range of disciplines, from anthropologists to neurobiologists (Arend, 2013, p. 398). An ethical perspective would suggest that: "A practical inference framework sees value creation as a creative process of practical reasoning guided by values" (Donaldson, 2021, p. 21). Identifying "real value creators" is not straightforward and to some, productive and unproductive activities in the economy cannot easily be ascertained if price is the only measurement criteria, making judgments (and measurements) on value subjective (Mazzucato, 2018, 2019). At the same time, helpful perspectives on value figure notably in early economic discussions. Adam Smith "gave quite a prominent place to value in his system [with a] significant portion of Book I of *The Wealth of Nations* [devoted] exclusively to this subject", but while he focused on its measurement he did "not offer a general theory" of value (Gupta, 1960, p. 105).

Smith's "so-called *additive* theory of value [. . .] argues that value of a commodity is determined by adding up independently determined wages, profits and rent", a notion which has been assessed critically (Sinha, 2010, p. 29). For instance, Schumpeter termed it "a cost-of-production theory" (Henry, 2000, p. 1). Stanley Jevons' marginalist approach highlights that "value depends solely on the final degree of utility" or "upon the number of persons who find it useful" (1871, pp. 159, 160) and hence is subjective. The same is true of Menger's theory of value where "value does not exist outside the consciousness of men" (1871/2007, p. 121). Smith's "rejection of utility as determinant of value" is critically viewed in many quarters (Douglas, 1927, p. 53). Utilitarianism remains central to the "current understandings of 'value'" with its roots in the work of Jeremy Bentham (1781/1970) and J. S. Mill (1863/2001). The former had a "focus on value as measured by specific aggregate measurements of pleasure and pain"; for the latter, value followed the "greatest happiness" principle (Harrison & Wicks, 2013, pp. 99, 100). Further to the above criticisms, others assert that Smith's theory is simply incomplete (e.g., Mazzucato, 2018). Yet Smith's understanding of rent as "price in excess of the cost of production" led to Ricardian rent, "a surplus in the form of a differential", and eventually to Henry George (1898), who closed the classical position by conceiving of rent as an "unearned increment" (Lackman, 1976, p. 287).

The classical rent theory "forged the concept of costless surplus, which then meant returns earned above another's return without an increase in 'real' cost. Later, the surplus was defined in terms of opportunity cost analysis" (Lackman, 1976, p. 298). This starkly contrasts with Sen (1987, 1999b) who suggests social and individual perspectives of value "beyond aggregate utility" including "the creation of capabilities essential to development and living a good or happy life" (Harrison & Wicks, 2013, p. 100). The contemporary Left variously argues that in its present form, the neoclassical, marginalist, utilitarian, price-centric understanding of value has led to shareholder-centric reductionism and a variety of financial capitalism that dangerously overlooks society's real productive forces (Mazzucato, 2018).

Marx's theory of value (1867/1959b) has a "classical residue" but is distinct, positing that the "exchange value" of all commodities should be reduced to labor, their common property (Itoh, 1976, pp. 307, 308). While undoubtedly also being a reductionist over-abstraction, the Marxist edifice emphasizes labor value appropriated but *not* created by capitalist principals as an unearned distributional rent—or "exploitation" (Shelby, 2002). Cohen (1979, p. 342) lays out the "Traditional Marxian Argument" as follows:

(5) Labor and labor alone creates value.
(6) The laborer receives the value of his labor power.
(7) The value of the product is greater than the value of his labor power.
∴ (8) The laborer receives less value than he creates.
(9) The capitalist receives the remaining value.
∴ (10) The laborer is exploited by the capitalist.

Non-orthodox approaches to value also exist, even if they end up referencing utility. Beinhocker (2006, p. 303) takes the ideas of Nicholas Georgescu-Roegen (1971, 1986) to advocate an understanding of value creation based on economic transformations and transactions under three combined conditions: that they are thermodynamically irreversible; that they reduce local entropy (disorder) in the economic system (though entropy increases globally); and lastly, that the newly high-ordered complexity is fit and useful for the purposes of humans. Notwithstanding the discussions of classical, Marxist, and other economists and their takes on value, labor, rent, exploitation, distribution, costless surpluses, or unearned increments, the analysis and subsequent operationalization of value for the purposes of this inquiry now references the strategic management literature because this has conceptualized value in a manner that is most tractable when the business model is the prime object of analysis.

One might start with two images derived from Porter's (1980) model of "the whole vertical chain of economic activity": first, a "value pie" created by firms together with their buyers and suppliers, and subsequently the "pie's slices", as value is divided up among the different players (Brandenburger, 2002, p. 58). The principal-stakeholder perspective is also important to consider, with value defined here by Harrison and Wicks (2013, pp. 100–101) "broadly as anything that has the potential to be of worth to stakeholders". Value is determined by market prices, but the idea of worth must also include non-economic dimensions as is pointed out by Aspers and Beckert (2011). Garcia-Castro and Aguilera's generic notion of value explains what the pie is made up of: "the sum of the consumer and the producer surpluses" (2015, p. 137). Evidently, value may consist of new surpluses such as those generated by activities associated with productivity gains. The streamlined elucidation of the 'value' conceptual element for the purposes of the ETED then becomes:

> Value is everything that humans determine is worth appropriating.

Value appropriation (the pie's slices) at the firm (the elite business model) level will be scrutinized in Proposition 9 through the value creation-appropriation (VCA) framework, as described by Garcia-Castro and Aguilera (2015, p. 137–138). Value is claimed at the negotiating table (Bazerman, 2001, p. 116) and business models that fail to appropriate enough value (a sufficiently large slice of the pie) will not generate the expected or necessary (for survival) positive residual income (profits) for their principal (a particular firm or elite). The VCA framework becomes pivotal to this inquiry because of its fundamental focus on the principal-stakeholder perspective and division of value strategies (Brandenburger & Stuart, 1996; Brandenburger, 2002; MacDonald & Ryall, 2004). It should be noted that value creation and appropriation are "intertwined" (Di Gregorio, 2013, p. 40). This inquiry exposes the contradictions of their association in the political economy and how mismatches can affect development.

To Brandenburger and Stuart (1996), the stakeholders of a principal's business model consist of two types: suppliers who sell inputs, and customers or buyers who pay for the principal's business model's outputs. For Mazzucato (2018), value creation is a "collective process" of stakeholders. For Brandenburger (2002, p. 58), the principal (the organization running the business model) and both stakeholder types (again, suppliers and customers) jointly create Porter's value pie. Table 2.1 illustrates joint value creation by describing the four types of agents: the principal, the two habitual stakeholder types—customers and suppliers—as well as the 'nature' stakeholder.[20] Their division of value strategies and their respective value creation and appropriation objectives are detailed in relation to each other.

Including nature as a stakeholder requires clarification, as this is uncommon in the strategic management literature. Nature obviously has, exceptions aside, no legal agency *per se* in the economic system. Can the agency of a nature stakeholder therefore be included in principal-stakeholder analysis within the VCA framework? Such a question parallels that of Starik, who asked: "Should Trees Have Managerial Standing?" and contended "that the non-human natural environment can be integrated into the stakeholder management concept" (1995, p. 2007). Laine (2011) argues that the natural environment should simply be included as a stakeholder. It is beyond evident that nature offers value and ecological resources to the principal, while also providing the material reality for all economic and human activity. Just as governments receive taxes as a quid pro quo for the valuable services they provide to firms, it can be argued that firms ought to pay nature for the even more fundamental and valuable services they receive in the form of air, water, soil, or life forms—and a sufficient amount to at least ensure their full regeneration. Principals need "environmental services" (Swallow et al., 2009) from nature to function. The extension of the VCA logic also means that nature (or its custodian entity in the legal system) should appropriate value from the relationship in return for its services, just as any other stakeholder does in division of value processes.

The 'nature stakeholder' assumption is thus introduced to the ETED in the context of the VCA framework and will be operationalized in the same way as other principal-

20 Professor Martin Nerlinger, University of St.Gallen School of Finance and Swiss Finance Institute, reviewed the sustainable value creation conceptual element applied to the firm and provided guidance on its operationalization, such as suggesting that nature be integrated as a discrete stakeholder type in the division of value strategies analysis and linking the theory to specific literatures like welfare economics. His inputs on the formalization of the sustainable value creation equations (see Table 2.4) consolidate these for the purposes of finance and provide a foundation for forthcoming research and applied projects.

stakeholder relationships. For example, if a principal keeps its greenhouse gas emissions below zero by using carbon capture and storage technologies (CCS), the nature stakeholder has in this instance realized its value appropriation objective. As ecological resources increase their alternative uses (e.g., through institutional changes such as carbon pricing initiatives) the value allocated to the nature stakeholder will increase and facilitate regeneration. Increasing alternative uses is a standard division of value strategy (as in Brandenburger, 2002), so extending it to the nature stakeholder (technically its custodian) mirrors the strategies of other suppliers of inputs to principals. Again, value is always jointly created, but the task of attributing its proportions to the parties involved in its creation is computationally overwhelming. Nonetheless, once created, value must and will be divided—and will likely be priced—with both principal and stakeholders seeking to appropriate as large an amount as possible. While the business model enables the principal and stakeholders to both create and appropriate value, its monetization—value appropriation—generates the residual income flows. Division of value strategies between the principal and stakeholders underpin value appropriation objectives realized in the context of competition between the different claimants (MacDonald & Ryall, 2004), with the analytical focus here being bargaining power (Coff, 1999). For Di Gregorio (2013, p. 43), "market-based bargaining power" is one of the sources of value appropriation and works "by harnessing market forces to establish unilateral dependence" with firm stakeholders in inter-organizational settings by utilizing strategies such as cost switching, replacement cost advantages, scarcity, or information asymmetries.

The value creation and appropriation logic of the division of value strategies in Table 2.1 applies to all business models. However, as has repeatedly been noted, elite business models are distinct due to their size. To recap, elite business models have transaction cost advantages that enable them to convert potential coordination capacity over factors of production such as land, labor, capital, or data into the largest streams of residual income in the economy, which in turn accumulate into the largest pools of wealth in society. This quantitative differential understanding again alludes to Mills (1956, p. 9) who associated elites with "the most of what there is to have". The specific cut-off point between an elite and non-elite business model in terms of size is an empirical matter left for later inquiry as it is contingent on the case-by-case context of a country or industry. However, in all cases, power characterizes the elite business model because it underpins its bargaining position and makes strategies to achieve value appropriation objectives feasible. The bargaining power of an elite business model emanates from wins in the three contest arenas of the political economy (see Figures 1.2 and 2.1). Value appropriated by one party is limited by the balance between its own bargaining power and that of the counterparties, consistent with Coff's (1999) examination of the impact of bargaining power on value (rent) appropriation.

A business model is a complex network of relationships with a range of external and internal stakeholders that go far beyond suppliers and customers to encompass employees, trade unions, governments, investors, creditors, business partners, nature, communities, or taxpayers. The VCA framework implies that residual income is, most

Table 2.1: Principal and stakeholder division of value strategies.[21]

	Agent	Objective	Bargaining power application
Principal [p]	Runs the business model, creates outputs (uses as inputs supplier's outputs)	Generation of residual income (= price of outputs – costs of inputs) (see equation 1, Table 2.4); Cost of capital (= its opportunity cost) below return on equity	Decrease alternative uses of inputs (resources bought from supplier) Decrease substitutes for outputs (products bought by customer)
Supplier stakeholder [s]	Supplies outputs to principal (principal's inputs)	Price of resources (= cost of inputs to principal) below own opportunity costs	Increase alternative uses of resources
Customer stakeholder [cu]	Buys products from principal (principal's outputs)	Cost of product (= price of output by principal) below own willingness to pay	Increase substitutes for products
Nature stakeholder [n]	Supplies ecology, the fundamental material reality, to principal (principal's inputs)	Price of ecological resources (= cost of ecological inputs to principal) below nature's own regeneration opportunity costs	Increase alternative uses of ecological resources

crucially, not just dependent on the value created but also on the bargaining power differential between the principal and the stakeholders. Relative bargaining power determines strategic discretion and the viability of a particular division of value strategy. In his renowned work on competitive strategy, Porter (1980) proposes five competitive forces, two of which explicitly refer to bargaining power (the bargaining power of buyers and the bargaining power of suppliers). His model also stresses that increasing bargaining power is a general strategic objective that enables value appropriation. Moatti, Ren, Anand, and Dussauge (2015, pp. 746–747) assert that "bargaining power measures the economic clout at the firm level" and explain how M&A activity extends this power given its positive association "with size versus competitors, suppliers and customers" as well as, of course, with most other stakeholders. M&A strategies are avidly pursued by management because they may potentially improve firm performance in two ways that correspond to two theoretical perspectives on firm size: greater "bargaining power with respect to suppliers and customers, and operating efficiency arising from scale economies" (Moatti, Ren, Anand, & Dussauge, 2015, p. 745). 'Size' alone leads to advantages in the non-market arena while 'efficiency' is associated with knowledge, a source of bargaining power that is especially relevant in the market arena.

21 This table summarizes and extends Figure 1 (Explaining the Five Forces Model) in Brandenburger (2002, p. 59) with nature added as a stakeholder in the analysis (see Starik, 1995 or Laine, 2011).

It must be re-emphasized that bargaining power, in Olsonian fashion, originates from the ability of acting in concert, "as a cohesive bargaining unit", a unit that is "capable of unified action" (Coff, 1999, pp. 122, 124). Consistent with the earlier discussion on coordination capacity and lower transaction costs (Proposition 4) and by referencing the principal-stakeholder perspective, elite business models amass the greatest bargaining power endowments in the economy through their grip of 'the extraordinary lever' in their particular sector. In the abstract, elite coalitions are coordination capacity; in the concrete, applied coordination capacity is the power of their business models to benefit from both value created and appropriated as well as value appropriated and *not* created.

In sum, value is all that which humans determine is worth appropriating, while all ongoing business models exist as mechanisms to appropriate value. Is it possible for a business model to appropriate more value than it creates, or to create no value while still appropriating value (from its stakeholders)? Yes, contingent on it having sufficient bargaining power. This notion is at the center of this inquiry as business models might at times destroy significant amounts of value in the process of forcing through value transfers. One obvious example is the collateral damage caused by criminal business models based on coercion. Extractive business models can also be entirely legal as is demonstrated by the varieties of institutionalized "theft" considered in the work of Tullock (1967) and Olson (1993) and the extensive rent-seeking literature (reviewed in Section 5.2). Overall, economies and societies advance because a majority of their business models—including elite business models—mostly rely on value created and appropriated rather than on value appropriated but *not* created. Then, stakeholders such as suppliers, customers, or governments participating in the principal business model have an incentive to create value since they can also *a priori* appropriate a substantial part of that value for themselves, and through that appropriation generate their own residual income.

Coalitions with comparatively small amounts of bargaining power in the overall political economy, such as air traffic controller associations, might nonetheless be able to concentrate these modest endowments in a narrow sector and thereby manage to appropriate more value than they create (sometimes even in a relationship with a more powerful but dispersed principal). Extractive narrow elites that possess 'the extraordinary lever' in their specific niche latch their transfer models not only onto weaker stakeholders, but also onto powerful elite business model principals. From an economic development perspective, the proliferation of such small extractive models in the nooks and crannies of the economy can accumulate into a very severe problem.

Power will appropriate value, which when not created by the appropriating principal (or the appropriating stakeholder) constitutes a value transfer-IN from the counterpart. When counterparties enjoy similar amounts of bargaining power, transfer-IN/OUT (value taken away from stakeholders/principals) is unlikely to occur. From a price perspective, this is the equilibrium brought about by equalized bargaining power. This situation is termed the 'equalized bargaining power equilibrium prices' condition and will become a theoretical cornerstone of this inquiry.

Under the premise that power is supreme in principal-stakeholder relationships, dissimilar levels of bargaining power can lead to maximum transfer-IN. In labor markets, that would correspond to Marx's (1844/1959a, p. 3) depiction in the "Wages of Labour":

> The lowest and the only necessary wage rate is that providing for the subsistence of the worker for the duration of his work and as much more as is necessary for him to support a family and for the race of labourers not to die out. The ordinary wage, according to Smith, is the lowest compatible with common humanity, that is, with cattle-like existence.

Workers (stakeholders supplying labor) in most of the economies of today do not receive Marxist subsistence wages. Why? Because they have increased their bargaining power thanks to 'political economy know-how' (power in the political non-market and narrative market arenas) by forming political movements or trade unions, and relevant 'knowledge' (power in the market arena) by acquiring, for instance, valuable skills and increasing the demand for their services in labor markets.

Transfer-IN/OUT needs to be understood as a matter of degree. For the two counterparties in a relationship, positive residual income (and positive value appropriation) is possible within a price corridor that "arises when the maximum that the buyers will pay (their willingness to pay) exceeds the minimum that the suppliers will accept (their opportunity cost)" (Brandenburger, 2002, p. 58). Within such an acceptable price range when does the price point reflect an extractive transfer? Whether the price point is closer to one end or the other of the range depends on the respective bargaining power endowments of the principal and stakeholders (see Figures 2.2 or 2.6). Extraction (transfer-IN/OUT) is conjectured as actual prices that differ from an 'equalized bargaining power equilibrium price' counterfactual. A theoretical—and obviously practical—problem arises when the price point (the reflection of a large bargaining power differential) sees stakeholders receiving untenable amounts of residual income (e.g., laborers with Marxist subsistence levels, suppliers whose margins are squeezed almost to breaking point by principals, indebted governments that fail to collect sufficient taxes or, conversely, governments that excessively tax their businesses and citizens).

Figure 2.2 illustrates actual price points determined by the respective bargaining power of the counterparties in the principal-stakeholder relationship (the arrows signify bargaining power endowments that push prices in the direction of a counterparty's value appropriation). Effective elites or businesspeople are adept at accumulating and augmenting bargaining power in various ways (for instance, by creating the perception of decreased alternative uses for stakeholder resources in the market arena, as was indicated in Table 2.1). Price equilibria in the real economy are never the result of equalized bargaining power endowments, but neither are they the sole result of objective bargaining power differentials. Rather, prices are the outcome of these power differentials (see elite coordination leadership, Figure 1.2) *and* of division of value strategies (see elite business model leadership, Figure 2.1). The starting point of strategic management is therefore the maximization of bargaining power and how it is applied to stakeholder relationships.

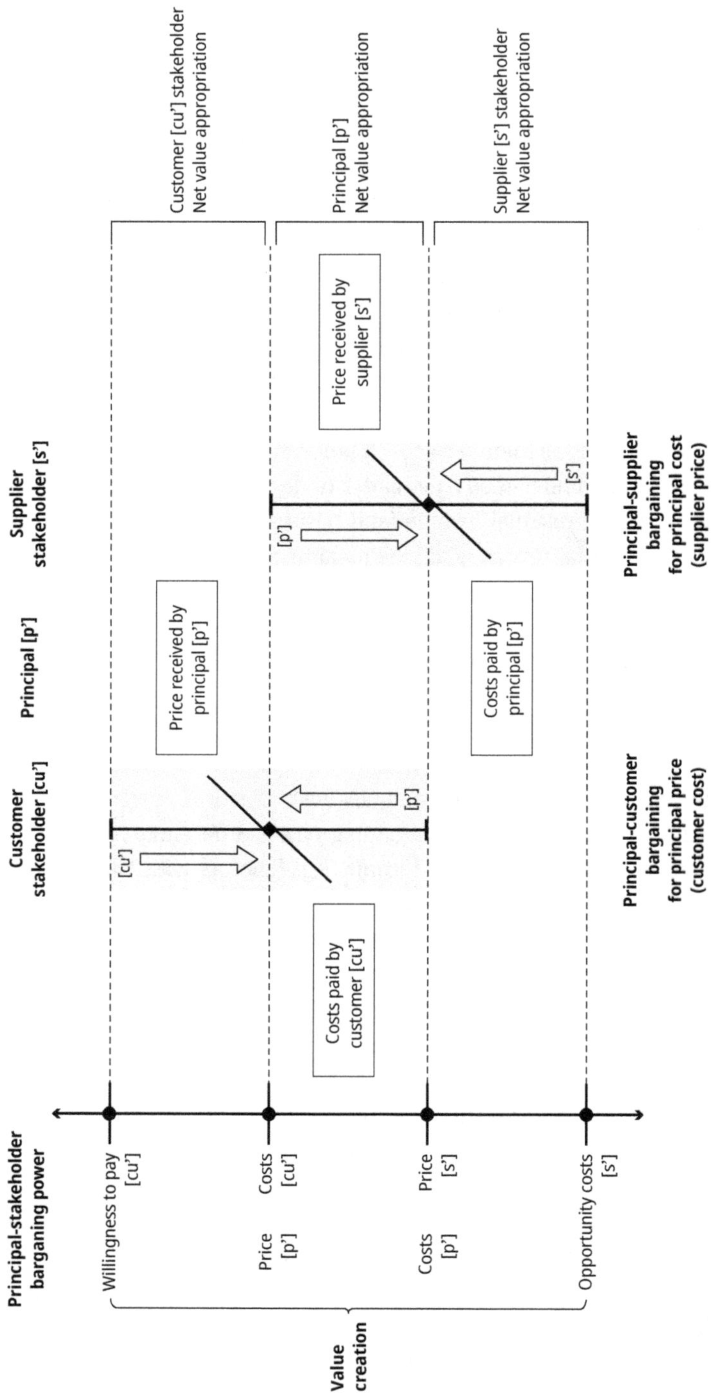

Figure 2.2: Bargaining power as a determinant of the division of value in principal-stakeholder relationships.[22]

The ultimate role of inclusive institutions (in politics), fair narratives (in society), or free markets (in the economy) might well be to enable value creators to appropriate a commensurate share of their created value and so receive residual income flows. This entails building conditions that approximate 'equalized bargaining power equilibrium prices', as opposed to prices and costs resulting from political economy-determined accumulations of bargaining power. The normative economic and human development optimum can, however, hardly be the full rebalancing of bargaining power when some of this power is the result of 'knowledge' (of markets, production, R&D, etc.). 'Knowledge' creates value and yields bargaining power. Yet here, a vital applied challenge of the political economy arises: 'the Amazon dilemma', that rests on two components. An 'elite vs non-elite knowledge gap' hypothesis has elite models that boast an overwhelming and irrevocable 'knowledge' generation advantage. In the past, this was achieved by creating deliberate barriers to alphabetization (Goody & Watt, 1963), while today the gap exists due to business model rules that magnify the "economic properties of data and the monopolistic tendencies of data economy" (Cheng, 2020), or, as a result of AI's large language models (LLMs), the trained neural networks which appear set to lower the cost of intelligence to nearly zero (Hoffman, 2022). In parallel, the 'elite power vs value creation gap' hypothesis posits that the growth of elite (bargaining) power will surpass that of value creation, meaning that 'the extraordinary lever' gains even more leverage (thus driving 'The Elite Business Model Lifecycle', see Section 4.3, Figure 4.5). Jointly, and when confirmed, these two hypotheses set forth the conditions for extractive value transfers by value creators that jeopardize development even in light of technological progress.[23]

Generally speaking, the appropriation of uncreated value is associated with well-known allocative efficiency problems, such as distortions in incentive structures or the integrity of what is known as the Hayekian 'information-processing system' (Bowles, Kirman, & Sethi, 2017, p. 217). These complications encumber economic growth and general human welfare potential. However, from an economic perspective, the optimal transfer amount is not a linear 'the less, the better'. This inquiry provokingly asks whether extractive value transfers could go hand in hand with or even be a precondition for value creation (see Proposition 10 or Section 8.2 on acceptable redistribution). Measurement difficulties notwithstanding, if value creation and ap-

---

22 This figure extends and adapts Figure 2 (on the division of value) in Brandenburger and Stuart (1996, p.10) with the addition of bargaining power.

23 Amazon's unprecedented 'knowledge' creation, management powers, and enormous scale have led to immense value creation along with the growth of its (bargaining) power. Whether (i) Amazon has opened an unsurmountable knowledge gap with lesser existing and emerging competitors; (ii) its bargaining power growth has been higher than the growth of its value creation, and (iii) this alleged power vs value growth differential has resulted in value appropriated but *not* created from stakeholders are three testable questions. Suggested approaches to elucidate these start here with sustainable value measurements like the Value Creation Position (VCp), introduced later in this chapter.

propriation are quantifiable, new prescriptive avenues might be opened for economic policymakers and transformational elite business model leadership. To complete this sub-section's discussion on bargaining power, a conceptual look at its sources is essential.

The German automotive industry is used as an example as it is known globally for its principals, with leading companies such as Volkswagen AG Wolfsburg, Daimler AG Stuttgart, Bayerische Motoren Werke AG Munich, Robert Bosch GmbH Gerlingen and thyssenkrupp AG Essen. Their elite business models have diverse stakeholder relationships with highly skilled workforces, sophisticated supplier networks, a professional class of engineers and managers, as well as the German government and taxpayers at large. In this value chain, all parties engage in value creation and value appropriation while pursuing a variety of power accumulation and value division strategies to generate a residual income in the form of profits, decent salaries, and taxes. The appropriation of the portions of the pie by each stakeholder depends on their respective bargaining power and how they use it. A part of this power invariably emanates from sheer competitiveness resting on (Hayekian "differentiating", 1948/1958, p. 96; Bowles, Kirman and Sethi, 2017, p. 219) activities in engineering, marketing or production, many of which are quite innovative ('knowledge' in Figure 2.3). Exercising influence over German institutions such as labor laws or the tax code and leveraging the existing correlation of political forces, popular sentiment, and the cyclical strengths of certain narratives for advantage, are all part of the activities (resting on Hayekian "personal relationships", 1948/1958, pp. 96–97; Bowles, Kirman and Sethi, 2017, p. 219) that top managers and shareholders engage in with legislators, media influencers, or civil servants ('political economy know-how' in Figure 2.3). Every principal and stakeholder will seek to combine the two sources of bargaining power that jointly enable degrees of value appropriation. Eventually, the principal and each stakeholder, such as the IG Metall (the German metalworkers' union), settle on price points (e.g., for wages). The two discrete sources of bargaining power ('knowledge' and 'political economy know-how') and the underlying competencies in the strategic management context that support power accumulation and the division of value strategies for the objective of value appropriation—and ultimately the generation of residual income flows—are depicted next.

The two sources of bargaining power in Figure 2.3 reference Hayek's interpretation in "The Meaning of Competition" (1948/1958). Also, 'political economy know-how' would be associated with the dimension of ownership that Monteiro and Miranda (2023) call "institutional competence", while 'knowledge' would align with what Foss, Klein, Lien, Zellweger, and Zenger (2021) conceive as "ownership competence". Because they underpin bargaining power differentials, they are constitutive of price disequilibria as opposed to competitive equilibrium prices. Again, unequal power endowments determine principal-stakeholder prices and hence the prospects for value appropriated but *not* created. This inquiry suggests that a counterfactual price equilibrium under the assumption of freedom is a benchmark for the appropriateness of the appropriation and

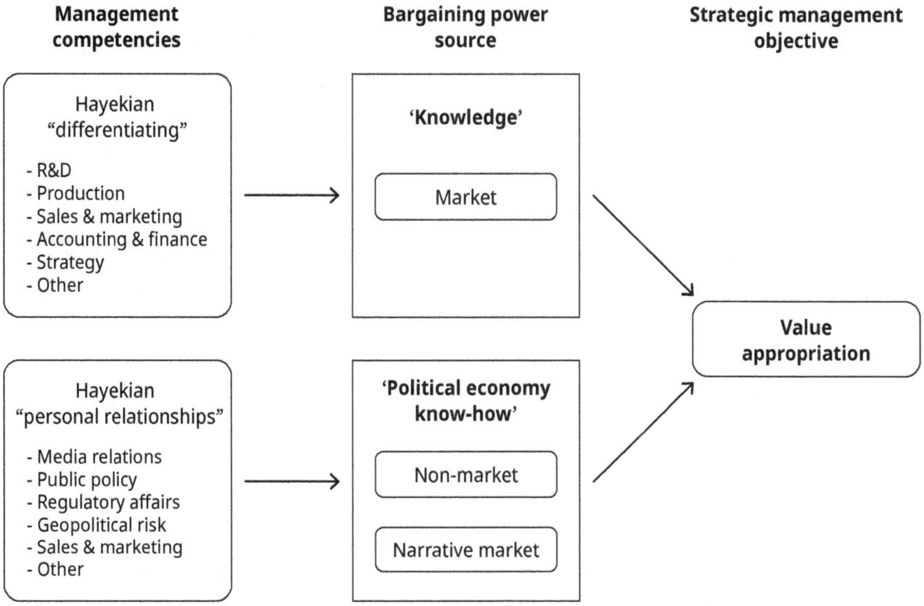

Figure 2.3: The 'knowledge' and 'political economy know-how' sources of business model bargaining power.

is relevant from an economic development perspective. The ETED suggests three freedoms that balance bargaining power in the final chapter of this book (Section 8.3), but these do not work in equal measure on the two sources of power. As is expounded next, development is consistent with bargaining power differentials that result from 'knowledge', a resource that has the property, from a political economy perspective, of being perishable.

Why are bargaining power differentials that originate from 'knowledge' sourced in the market arena preferable to those derived from 'political economy know-how' sourced in the non-market and narrative market arenas? The power emanating from 'knowledge' is essentially related to value, must prove its mettle in the more competitive market arena, and is relatively less stable than power sourced from the political non-market and narrative market arenas. This is so because 'knowledge' incessantly evolves and is developed outside of the purview of incumbent elites, away from established models and organizations (see Schumpeter, 1911/2003; Christensen, 1997). Elite business model bargaining power emanating mainly from 'knowledge' will quickly erode and be rebalanced by new market entrants, thus being more temporary and thereby preempting continued value transfers. This all leads to an approximation of Hayekian equilibrium pricing, the improvement of offerings (Hayekian "differentiating") and to development.

A caveat must be raised here: to the extent that the 'elite vs non-elite knowledge gap' hypothesis is correct, the elite will retain the bargaining power originally sourced from 'knowledge' longer than is theoretically warranted. "When we had slavery in America, the white masters adopted laws to make it unlawful to instruct even freed Negroes", the universal principle being that "masters try to keep the people whom they rule in a state of ignorance" (Roucek, 1967, p. 483). As part of elite preservation strategies, non-elites are insulated from relevant and cutting-edge knowledge through deliberate and methodically erected barriers and hence impaired from constructively challenging elite business models (as emergent entrepreneurs, politicians, intellectuals). This has been the case since time immemorial,[24] while today, opaque algorithms (e.g., in social networks)[25] or "closed" access to the "resources needed to build AI from scratch, and to deploy large AI systems at scale" (Widder, West, & Whittaker, 2023) further a state of ignorance that has similar effects on bargaining power differentials.

In a further twist, even when non-elites do have access to knowledge, the bargaining power distance between elites and non-elites is exacerbated by the combination of the elite business model 'knowledge' advantage and 'political economy know-how'. That is why this work would predict that the Microsoft-backed Open AI will triumph over open source AI projects even if the latter are "faster, more customizable, more private, and pound-for-pound more capable" (Patel & Ahmad, 2023). The technologist investor Marc Andreessen (2023a) criticizes "the drive for AI regulation right now" because it benefits the extractive forces ("bootleggers") of the political economy. Fundamentally, 'the Amazon dilemma' associates with extractive value transfers when the 'elite vs non-elite knowledge gap' hypothesis combines with the 'elite power vs value creation gap' hypothesis. While new knowledge is notionally liberating, when the two hypotheses come together in business model reality the result is that 'knowledge' is at the root of extractive value transfers (Section 8.2.4 and the Epilogue whether and how the AI and non-elites, augmented with superintelligence at their fingertips, could address this issue).

Notwithstanding 'the Amazon dilemma', 'knowledge' is, for the policymaker and everyone concerned about sustainable value creation and inclusive prosperity, the fa-

24 It must be stressed that since the emergence of civilization, the central role of knowledge elites (besides knowledge creation) is to artificially erect knowledge gaps that serve as moats to preserve elite business models. In early Egypt, Mesopotamia, or China "a literate elite of religious, administrative and commercial experts emerged and maintained itself as a centralized governing bureaucracy on rather similar lines. Their various social and intellectual achievements were, of course, enormous; but as regards the participation of society as a whole in the written culture, a wide gap existed between the esoteric literary culture and the exoteric oral one, a gap that the literate were interested in maintaining. Among the Sumerians and Akkadians, writing was the pursuit of scribes and preserved as a 'mystery', a 'secret treasure'" (Goody & Watt, 1963, p. 314). On exactly the same principle, a "leaked internal Google document" shows that its technologists, the main knowledge elites of Big Tech coalitions, are raising alarm bells about the lack of a knowledge gap with non-elites (in relation to open source AI projects): "But the uncomfortable truth is, we aren't positioned to win this arms race and neither is OpenAI. While we've been squabbling, a third faction has been quietly eating our lunch. I'm talking, of course, about open source. Plainly put, they are lapping us" (Patel & Ahmad, 2023).

25 A point made by *The Wall Street Journal* (2021) video investigation, *Inside TikTok's Highly Secretive Algorithm*, that "reveals how the video-centric social network is so good at figuring out interests you never expressly tell it".

vored source of bargaining power in the economy. This is so because 'knowledge' is valuable in itself, and *a priori* more distributed and temporal. In contrast, the differentials and disequilibria resulting from 'political economy know-how' (wins in the non-market and narrative market arenas) are purported to be more stable and require much longer time horizons to reverse. Therefore, and because of their respective impact on the economy, the bargaining power sources behind value appropriation are essential to the ETED and possess prescriptive and ethical implications.

This section's extended discussion started by defining value as everything that humans determine is worth appropriating. Value appropriation is a manifestation of an accumulation of bargaining power (via elite coordination leadership) and the specific division of value strategies (of successful elite business model leadership). Bargaining power differentials end up determining the residual incomes of principals and stakeholders alike. To maximize residual income, all business models seek to create and then appropriate value, including value *not* created. However, the latter approach is far less available to non-elite business models given their lower bargaining power endowments. Non-elite models do, at times, have an advantage over incumbent elite models in terms of 'knowledge' (by being more agile and innovative, see Schumpeter, 1911/2003; Christensen, 1997) but are at an irremediable disadvantage in terms of 'political economy know-how'. Proposition 8 asserts that the elite business model is characterized by bargaining power differentials vis-à-vis its stakeholders which enable value appropriation (including uncreated value) and so generate the economy's main residual income flows. Price equilibria that approximate hypothetical equalized bargaining power—'equalized bargaining power equilibrium prices'—describe the incentive structure that maximizes value creation. For economic development and policy purposes, the source of elite business model bargaining power to be prioritized is 'knowledge'.

2.2.3 Proposition 9: Value creation-appropriation (VCA) is the framework best suited to understand elite business models' division of value strategies

The previous section delved into bargaining power, identifying its sources while providing the general framework for price setting in principal-stakeholder relationships. The focus now moves to the strategic management objective of value appropriation, i.e., how bargaining power is converted into residual income via division of value strategies. This process is explained with the VCA framework, which analyzes the business model recognizing the discrete relationships between the elite principal and the multiple stakeholders. Each principal-stakeholder relationship has its own bargaining power accumulation reality and division of value strategies. Table 2.2 illustrates through the VCA analytical framework (as a continuation of Table 2.1) a set of specific division of value instances between the business model principal and diverse stakeholders (see the visualization in Figure A5.13a). As established in Proposition 8, for elite business models, the elite principal's bargaining power advantage has a bearing on the viability of division of value strategies and value appropriation outcomes.

Table 2.2: Division of value strategies and outcomes.

Ref.	Principal and stakeholder	Relationship	Outcomes
[s] [p]	Supplier stakeholder vs Firm principal	Suppliers of necessary inputs (e.g., rare earth elements and semiconductors) enjoy a near monopoly. As a result, suppliers enjoy a bargaining power advantage and set prices above the levels that would prevail in a competitive market under the conditions of 'equalized bargaining power equilibrium prices'.	Supplier stakeholder(s): Includes value appropriated but *not* created, i.e., value transfer-IN. Firm principal: Includes value created but *not* appropriated, i.e., value transfer-OUT.
[m] [p]	Top management stakeholder vs Firm principal	Stage 1: The executive pay of the incoming top management team is below industry standards. The top management stakeholder goes on to deliver exceptional above average performance. Stage 2: The firm's top management leverages its newly acquired bargaining power (the source of which is 'knowledge') to renegotiate terms. Executive pay is adjusted to match industry standards and accurately reflect performance.	Top management stakeholder: Includes value created but *not* appropriated, i.e., value transfer-OUT. Firm principal: Includes value appropriated but *not* created, i.e., value transfer-IN. Stage 2: Transfer-IN/OUT ceases with both counterparties benefiting from value created and appropriated.
[g] [p]	Government stakeholder vs Firm principal	The principal uses political connections and effective lobbying to gain an uncommon tax break as well as the transfer of intellectual property (IP) at no cost from an expensive government-funded research project.	Government stakeholder: Value created but *not* appropriated, i.e., value transfer-OUT. Firm principal: Value appropriated but *not* created, i.e., value transfer-IN (taxpayers pay for the tax breaks and the subsidized technology).
[l] 1/2 [p]	*Scenario 1/2* Employee stakeholder (labor) vs Firm principal (Visualized in Figure 2.4)	The principal has a monopsony position, and *a priori* bargaining power is such that the firm can force lower wage conditions onto labor. However, the firm principal refrains from doing this and offers wages comparable to those prevalent in neighboring labor markets which are competitively set and a valid productivity reference.	Employee stakeholder: Value created and appropriated. Firm principal: Value created and appropriated (transformational leadership to forfeit the option of leveraging bargaining power for value appropriation purposes. See also the set of ethical principles, Chapter 8).

Table 2.2 (continued)

Ref.	Principal and stakeholder	Relationship	Outcomes
[l] 2/2 [p]	*Scenario 2/2* Employee stakeholder (labor) vs Firm principal (Visualized in Figure 2.4)	Relationship: Organized labor leverages bargaining power differentials in the political non-market and societal narrative market arenas to force institutional change that brings regulation where wages are above market clearing equilibrium levels.	Employee stakeholder: Includes value appropriated but *not* created, i.e., value transfer-IN (from principal, plus from the workers whose jobs disappear due to declines in the demand for labor, triggered by labor costs above market equilibrium prices). Firm principal: Includes value created but *not* appropriated, i.e., value transfer-OUT.
[p] [k]	Firm principal vs Creditor stakeholder	A creditor financial institution issues a loan with a market-based risk-adjusted interest rate that is repaid on agreed terms.	Firm principal: Value created and appropriated. Creditor stakeholder: Value created and appropriated.
[p] [p]	Firm principal vs Firm principal (shareholder)	After paying interest to a creditor, the principal shareholder of the firm appropriates whatever income remains as residual income.	Firm principal (shareholder): Returns on capital derived from residual income (profits), the sum of the residuals of all stakeholder relationships in the business model—the net value appropriation (see Table 2.4, equation 1.3). Residual income (profits) is also the difference between revenue (the customer prices) and all the costs (see Table 2.4, equation 1.1).
[cu] [p]	Customer stakeholders vs Firm principal	The firm is innovative and its customers' willingness to pay for its products is above the firm's costs. Moreover, prices are higher than those of competing products. The product price premium is a fraction of the innovation value to the customer, so the customer appropriates sizable value. The firm's 'knowledge' is the source of extraordinary value creation and transactions occur in a free, competitive market.	Customer stakeholder: Includes value appropriated but *not* created (consistent with instances where the customer is a joint participant in the value creation process). Firm principal: Includes value created but *not* appropriated.

Table 2.2 (continued)

Ref.	Principal and stakeholder	Relationship	Outcomes
[n] 1/2 vs [d]	*Scenario 1/2* Nature stakeholder vs Firm principal (Visualized in Figure 2.5)	The principal implements ESG principles and has a carbon neutral footprint having undergone ISO 14064–1 greenhouse gas emissions verification.	Nature stakeholder: Value created and appropriated (nature's ability to deliver ecosystem services is preserved). Firm principal: Value created and appropriated, (transformational leadership to forfeit the option of value appropriation from nature absent the legal requirement to have a carbon neutral footprint. See also the set of ethical principles, Chapter 8).
[n] 2/2 vs [p]	*Scenario 2/2* Nature stakeholder vs Firm principal (Visualized in Figure 2.5)	A polluting firm has a large carbon footprint from its business activities that it does not offset with carbon credits.	Nature stakeholder: Includes value created but *not* appropriated, i.e., value transfer-OUT (by principal). Firm principal: Includes value appropriated but *not* created, i.e., value transfer-IN (from the nature stakeholder by not paying for the usage of ecosystem services, and from society at large, both of whom suffer from the effects of climate change).

The two scenarios for the firm vs employee (principal-stakeholder) relationship detailed in Table 2.2 are now visualized in Figure 2.4. In the first scenario 1/2, the firm vs employee relationship (described in [l] scenario 1/2, Table 2.2) is balanced and hence there is no transfer-IN/OUT i.e., the value created equals the value appropriated. Then there are situations where "powerful unions sometimes cripple firms by forcing them to pay higher wages than the market would otherwise command" (Harrison, Bosse, & Phillips, 2010, p. 70). Scenario 2/2 represents such a firm vs employee (principal-stakeholder) relationship (described in [l] scenario 2/2, Table 2.2) where employees are beneficiaries of value appropriated but *not* created (i.e., political non-market arena sourced bargaining power is used to push wages above market equilibrium levels).[26]

26 That wages above equilibrium are associated with elites is counterintuitive because the single worker benefiting from this extractive transfer model receives monetary rents that cannot possibly be compared in terms of their size with the incomes of the individuals running, for instance, corporate business models. The personal incomes of union leaders (at least those in advanced economies), even when 'the extraordinary lever' and their considerable bargaining power differentials (sourced

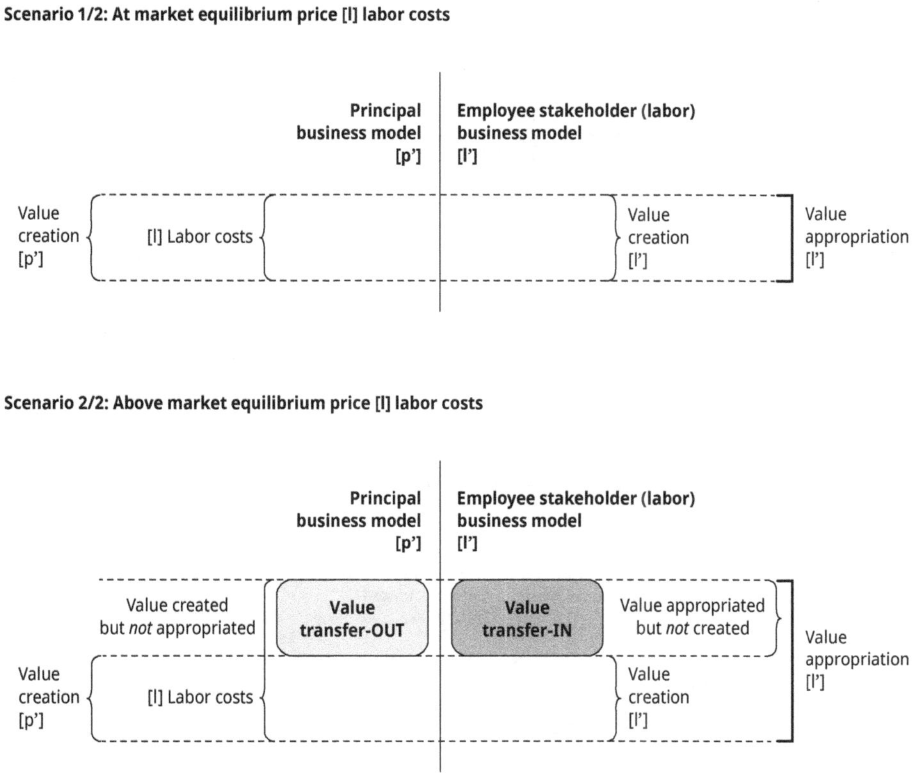

Figure 2.4: Division of value in the firm-employee (principal-stakeholder) relationship: Scenario 1/2, labor costs at market equilibrium; scenario 2/2, labor costs above market equilibrium.

Next, the two scenarios for the firm vs nature (principal-stakeholder) relationship outlined in Table 2.2 are depicted in Figure 2.5, where the nature stakeholder is the hypothetical aggregate of all of nature's services relevant to the principal under the 'nature stakeholder' assumption. Laine (2011) argues that the natural environment should be visualized in any stakeholder network and Starik suggests that "organizations which begin to treat non-human nature as one or more stakeholders will be perceiving a more realistic, if more complex, picture of their respective business environments" (1995, p. 216). Such a realistic visualization is presented in Figure 2.5 through the VCA

through 'political economy know-how') allow them to implement aggressive minimum wage policies, would hardly endow them with a wealth stock that qualifies them as 'elites' in the commonly understood sense of the term. Yet, on aggregate, the minimum wage business model has an impact on economic development (in terms of residual income transfers, sapping the incentive system or creating joblessness, especially youth unemployment) that is as significant as that of any other extractive elite business model. From the developmental perspective, labor unions that succeed in setting minimum wages above equilibrium *de facto* run transfer elite business models.

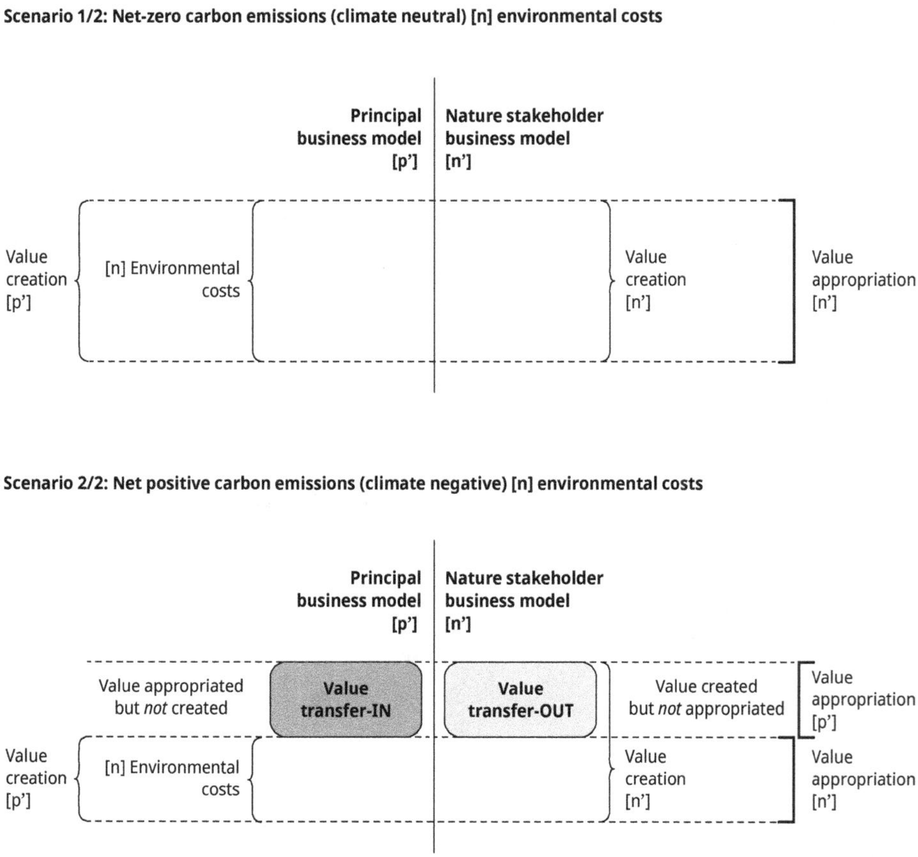

Figure 2.5: Division of value in the firm-nature (principal-stakeholder) relationship: Scenario 1/2, Net zero carbon footprint; scenario 2/2, high carbon emissions.

framework applied to the ETED. First, in scenario 1/2, the firm vs nature relationship (described in [n] scenario 1/2, Table 2.2) is balanced; the firm has a validated carbon neutral position and so there is no transfer-IN/OUT, meaning that the value created equals the value appropriated for both counterparties. In Scenario 2/2 on the other hand, the firm vs nature (principal-stakeholder) relationship (described in [n] scenario 2/2, Table 2.2) sees the firm underpay for the ecological services it receives from nature, deriving a cost advantage from being a polluter and thus benefiting from value appropriated but *not* created. The surplus carbon balance is climate negative and permitted under applicable law (politically sourced bargaining power by the principal that is converted into residual income by not paying the price to offset emissions).

The two sources of bargaining power discussed in the previous section (and portrayed in Figure 2.3) not only facilitate value appropriation (by labor from the firm and by the firm from nature in Figures 2.4 and 2.5 respectively), but also provide an indication on whether the party appropriating value has also created it or there has been a value transfer. How can this inquiry then ascertain value creation of the 'knowledge' type through the use of the VCA framework?

To do so, we must again reference Garcia-Castro and Aguilera's (2015, p. 137) decrease of opportunity costs and the increase in prices (willingness to pay). Zott and Amitt (2013, p. 408) similarly circumscribe the process by which value is created: "Value is created by activities that (i) reduce buyer costs or (ii) raise buyer performance through product differentiation". That is, the pie is enlarged. Value creation resulting from 'knowledge' is reflected by a higher willingness to pay and lower opportunity costs materialized as residual income in the business model value chain (as in Figures 2.2 or 2.6). With value thus created, the larger value pie is divided via prices between the principal and stakeholders as per their respective (division of value) strategies backed by bargaining power. In contrast, bargaining power attained through 'political economy know-how' does not result in better performance or reduced costs (i.e., in a higher willingness to pay and lower opportunity costs), yet the party wielding the increased power can capture a bigger slice of the existing (or shrinking) pie (i.e., transfer-IN, value appropriated but *not* created, as is seen in Figure 2.4, scenario 2/2 and Figure 2.5, scenario 2/2).

Equations for residual income (1/9)

The various VCA-derived conceptual elements that have been discussed are next described as equations for the operationalization purposes of this inquiry. The first equation refers to the ultimate strategic objective of any business model, residual income (profits). From the revenue amount received from sales (the prices customer stakeholders pay) applicable costs are subtracted (see Figures 2.6, 2.7, or 2.9) to arrive at the residual income (note that debt holder interests are considered to be costs). All of the equations that follow (see the full list in Table 2.4) are presented in two equivalent versions: the first is an intuitive text version, while the second (where the equations are followed by an 'a', 'b', or 'c' suffix) use the notational conventions of finance. The first equation (1.1) is part of a set that describes residual income (RI),[27] for both principals and stakeholders:

$$\text{residual income} = \text{revenue adjusted} - \text{costs} \tag{1.1}$$

$$RI_t = R'_{x,t} - c_t \tag{1.1a}$$

The VCA framework holds that all business models are but a bundle of principal-stakeholder relationships. Due to lower transaction costs and a larger coordination capacity (consistent with both 'knowledge' and 'political economy know-how') elite business model principals are especially adept at appropriating and possibly creating value. Bargaining power enables the appropriation of a significant part of the value created in the principal-stakeholder relationship, including value appropriated but

27 For financial statement profits the rendition of equation (1.1) is: profits = revenue – costs.

not created (value transfer-IN). As a result, elites generate the largest flows of residual income, which over time accumulate into the largest stocks of wealth in the economy.

Under the hypothetical conditions of 'equalized bargaining power equilibrium prices', residual income equals value creation. Yet as business practice moves away from these conditions, equation (1.1) becomes too elementary and therefore inadequate. We have already discussed how, with asymmetric bargaining power levels, the party holding the power advantage can and will leverage their power differential to maximize residual income (by reducing the value appropriation of the counterparty). Value transfer-IN accrues to the residual income of the principal. Therefore, and in the context of sustainable value creation, the residual income (of the principal and the stakeholders) will account for 'net value extraction'—which is in turn later described in equation (3.3) as transfer-IN minus transfer-OUT. This amount (regardless of whether the net of transfer-IN/OUT is positive or negative) is added to (or, if negative, offset against) the amount of (principal and stakeholder) 'net value creation'—described in equation (2.3) as value appropriation minus transfer-IN. Further, and referencing VCA language, residual income (profits) is deemed to be 'net value appropriation'—formulated in equation (3.4) as 'net value extraction' plus 'net value creation'. The residual income expressions referencing the VCA framework follow:

$$\text{residual income} = \text{net value creation} + \text{net value extraction} \tag{1.2}$$

$$RI_t = NVc_t + NVe_t \tag{1.2a}$$

$$\text{residual income} = \text{net value appropriation} \tag{1.3}$$

$$RI_t = NVa_t \tag{1.3a}$$

Figure 2.6 backs up the above discussion and visually renders equations (1.1), (1.2) and (1.3) and their conceptual elements.

Theoretically, a principal with power can extract value from a stakeholder up to marginal subsistence levels (in reference to Marxist wages). In situations approaching this hypothetical limit (as illustrated in Figure 2.7 below), the value appropriation of the principal increases (the slice of the pie) while that of the other stakeholders (in this case the supplier) correspondingly decreases. The supplier stakeholder's value created but *not* appropriated is so large that value appropriation tends towards zero and could even be negative, below Marx's "cattle-like existence" level (see the responses to extraction outlined in Table 5.1). On the other side, the principal's value appropriated but *not* created (value transfer-IN) increases residual income when it exceeds value created but *not* appropriated (value transfer-OUT). The difference between the two is net value extraction; technically the net of value transfers, see equation (3.3). This line of reasoning implies that hefty residual incomes and extraordinary profiteering (due to all forms of transfer activities, from pollution to share buybacks) are evidence of a political economy landscape with uneven accumulations of bargaining power sourced through 'political economy know-how' and characterized by price levels far removed from 'equalized

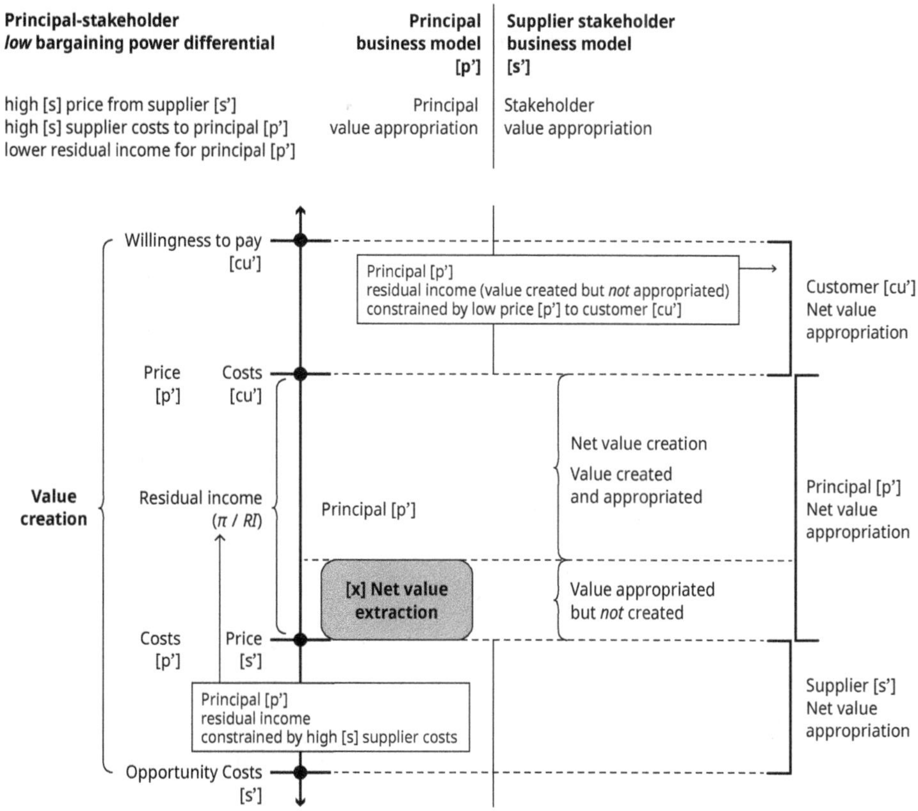

Figure 2.6: Visual representation of residual income conceptualization: Principal business model.[28]

bargaining power equilibrium prices'. That is, it provides evidence of a market arena bereft of robust contests and operating far from Hayek's interpretation of competition.

Equations for value creation (2/9)

Value creation by the business model sees a "value pie" cooperatively created by the principal and all stakeholders as a "collective process" (Porter 1980; Brandenburger, 2002; Mazzucato, 2018). Value jointly created is often jointly appropriated: "Although not directly observable in the firm's accounting statements, the returns to other stakeholders are also significant in terms of, for example, employees' increased salaries or consumers' reduced prices" (Garcia-Castro & Aguilera, 2015, p. 139). Nonetheless, value shared does not imply that value is appropriated in proportion to one's contribution and hence does not preclude

28 Conceptual extension based on Figure 2 in Brandenburger and Stuart (1996, p. 10) and a modification of Figure 1 in Garcia-Castro and Aguilera (2015, p. 139). Debt holder interests are assumed to be part of the costs.

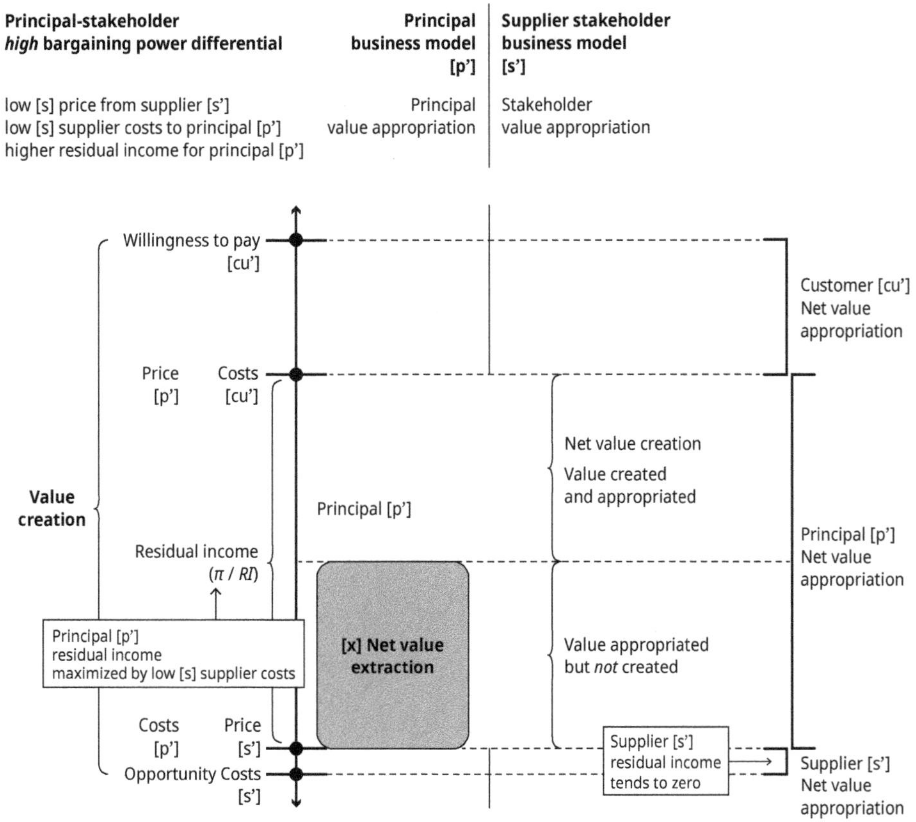

Figure 2.7: Bargaining power differential: Principal maximizes value appropriation.

transfer-OUT (value created but *not* appropriated), which occurs as long as stakeholders exist at the short end of bargaining power differentials. This is the case when salaries are higher than industry standards for comparable work and so the firm suffers transfer-OUT which equals lost residual income (as in scenario 1/2, Figure 2.5). Transfer-OUT is thus still part of a firm's value creation—the part not appropriated. In this sense, the respective descriptions of value creation by the principal, or by any stakeholders, are:

$$\begin{aligned}\text{value creation(principal)} &= \text{net value creation(principal)}\\ &\quad+\text{transfer-OUT(principal)}\end{aligned} \tag{2.1}$$

$$Vc_{t,principal} = NVc_{t,principal} + Vt^{out}_{t,principal} \tag{2.1a}$$

$$\begin{aligned}\text{value creation(stakeholder)} &= \text{net value creation(stakeholder)}\\ &\quad+\text{transfer-OUT(stakeholder)}\end{aligned} \tag{2.1'}$$

$$Vc_{t,stakeholder} = NVc_{t,stakeholder} + Vt^{out}_{t,stakeholder} \tag{2.1b}$$

The value creation of a business model is therefore the sum of all value creation components by the principal and the stakeholders in equation (2.2). The premise is that value jointly created can be computationally disentangled in discrete components, each attributed to one or the other party (see the discussion on redistribution and AI in Section 8.2.5). Conceptually, one could add to this amount the net value extraction by the principal and all stakeholders as is set out in equation (2.2'). Yet the addition of this component would be of no material consequence because the sum of all net value extraction in a chain of value equals zero. The positive/negative net value extraction amounts—net value extraction equals transfer-IN minus transfer-OUT, see equation (3.3)—of all principals and stakeholders in a business model offset each other and hence the addition of this term in equation (2.2') is a zero-sum.

$$\text{value creation(business model)} = \Sigma\,[\text{value creation(principal), value creation(stakeholders)}] \tag{2.2}$$

$$Vc_{t,business\ model} = \sum Vc_{t,principal}, Vc_{t,stakeholder} \tag{2.2a}$$

$$\text{value creation(business model)} = \Sigma[\text{value creation(principal), value creation(stakeholders)}] + \Sigma[\text{net value extraction(principal), net value extraction(stakeholders)}] \tag{2.2'}$$

$$Vc_{t,\ business\ model} = \sum Vc_{t,principal}, Vc_{t,stakeholder} + \sum NVe_{t,principal}, NVe_{t,stakeholder} \tag{2.2b}$$

Net value creation is the first-order productive activity (by any party) that is appropriated. One calculation method for this is value creation minus the value created but *not* appropriated and lost to counterparties as value transfer-OUT. This is described in equation (2.3) below:

$$\text{net value creation} = \text{value creation} - \text{transfer-OUT} \tag{2.3}$$

$$NVc_t = Vc_t - Vt_t^{out} \tag{2.3a}$$

An alternative method to establish net value creation is through the value appropriation (rather than value creation) approach. The value transfer-IN (value appropriated but *not* created and taken from counterparties) must be subtracted from value appropriation to reach net value creation amounts, as in equation (2.3'). Equation (2.3") swaps value appropriation for revenue adjusted, with the formulation below later used for the operationalization of sustainable value creation measurements (e.g., VCp/VCr):

$$\text{net value creation} = \text{value appropriation} - \text{transfer-IN} \tag{2.3'}$$

$$NVc_t = Va_t - Vt_t^{in} \tag{2.3b}$$

$$\text{net value creation} = \text{revenue adjusted} - \text{transfer-IN} \tag{2.3''}$$

$$NVc_t = R'_t - Vt_t^{in} \tag{2.3c}$$

Equations for value appropriation and transfers (3/9)

Value appropriation is evidently an ultimate strategic management objective for those in charge of organizations or running business models. The equations for value appropriation are now formalized. The first equation (3.1) is a tautology where the VCA framework notion of value appropriation corresponds to revenue. However, to differentiate this revenue from generally accepted accounting notions, it is termed 'revenue adjusted'. Just as residual income denotes the (net) profit on the statutory P&L statement in the previous equations, revenue adjusted (R') closely mirrors and is derived from revenue, albeit with a technical adjustment[29] for the purpose of establishing value appropriation:

$$\text{value appropriation} = \text{revenue adjusted} \tag{3.1}$$

$$Va_t = R' \tag{3.1a}$$

Revenue adjusted is revenue associated with net value creation and transfer-IN, meaning that revenue not associated with these two elements is not to be included in R'. Value appropriation (which might differ from statutory revenue in the P&L statement) is the revenue that an organization generates adjusted for value and is conceptualized in the next equations (3.2) and (3.2') as the sum of 'net value creation' (which is value creation minus the value transfer-OUT) and value transfer-IN (value appropriated but *not* created).

$$\begin{aligned}\text{value appropriation(principal)} &= \text{net value creation(principal)}\\ &\quad + \text{transfer-IN(principal)}\end{aligned} \tag{3.2}$$

$$Va_{t,principal} = NVc_{t,principal} + Vt^{in}_{t,\,principal} \tag{3.2a}$$

$$\begin{aligned}\text{value appropriation(stakeholder)} &= \text{net value creation(stakeholder)}\\ &\quad + \text{transfer-IN(stakeholder)}\end{aligned} \tag{3.2'}$$

$$Va_{t,stakeholder} = NVc_{t,stakeholder} + Vt^{in}_{t,stakeholder} \tag{3.2b}$$

Value appropriation equations obviously do not account for value transfer-OUT, as this is value created but *not* appropriated and not included in the P&L. Such transfer-OUT

29 The adjustment factor calculation is left for further research. Nerlinger (in various conversations with the author in 2022) suggests borrowing from the "net value added" (NVA) approach (from value added reporting literature and practice) to craft a formulation of revenue adjusted (R') conceptually consistent with the theoretical disquisition of this chapter. Value added reporting, "a type of social reporting model based on conventional accounting, which is focused on how companies create value and how that value is distributed among each category of stakeholders" is a tool suitable for sustainability (Aldama & Zicari, 2012). Conceptual problems (Rutherford, 1977) are also being addressed in the field of finance to make it fit for "integrated reporting" (Haller & van Staden, 2014). Note that in economics, 'NVA' is distinctly defined from the field's own perspective: "Net value added is the value of output less the values of both intermediate consumption and consumption of fixed capital" (United Nations Statistics Division, n.d).

amounts do matter to the sustainable value creation of the business model even if they are missed or forfeited revenue (revenue adjusted) and residual income (profits). Therefore, value transfer-OUT is included in the 'net value extraction' equation (3.3) as a mathematical negative set against the positive transfer-IN amount. Net value extraction has already been conceptually discussed as the net of all the (extractive/inclusive) value transfer-IN/OUT amounts in the business model. The net value extraction amount is usually positive for elite business model principals, while for non-elite stakeholders it is usually negative. The notion represents a party's extractive value transfer-IN (value appropriated but *not* created from counterparties) set against the inclusive value transfer-OUT (value created but *not* appropriated by all the counterparties), where:

$$\text{net value extraction} = \text{transfer-IN} - \text{transfer-OUT} \tag{3.3}$$

$$NVe_t = Vt_t^{in} - Vt_t^{out} \tag{3.3a}$$

When the value chain perspective is applied to the profits recorded in the P&L statement these are termed in this inquiry as residual income, which also requires them to be adjusted (mirroring the earlier discussion on revenue/revenue adjusted). In VCA framework terms, residual income is net value appropriation, which is linked to the notions of net value creation and net value extraction. Net value appropriation refers to all the value the business model has been able to appropriate, and that includes reckoning the sum of the value transfer-IN/OUT amounts from all the counterparties (net value extraction) plus the sum of the model's own value created *and* appropriated (net value creation). Unpacking the two constitutive variables of the net value appropriation equation (3.4) lets it be expressed as equation (3.4'), and then as the more elegant, though at first sight possibly less intuitive, equation (3.4") that subtracts value transfer-OUT from value appropriation:

$$\text{net value appropriation} = \text{net value creation} + \text{net value extraction} \tag{3.4}$$

$$NVa_t = NVc_t + NVe_t \tag{3.4a}$$

$$\begin{aligned}\text{net value appropriation} = {} & [\text{value appropriation} - \text{transfer-IN}] \\ & + [\text{transfer-IN} - \text{transfer-OUT}]\end{aligned} \tag{3.4'}$$

$$NVa_t = (Va_t - Vt_t^{in}) + (Vt_t^{in} - Vt_t^{out}) \tag{3.4b}$$

$$\text{net value appropriation} = \text{value appropriation} - \text{transfer-OUT} \tag{3.4"}$$

$$NVa_t = Va_t - Vt_t^{out} \tag{3.4c}$$

As discussed, the P&L statement notion of revenue (R) can be used to derive revenue adjusted (R') in the value chain perspective that in turn matches value appropriation (Va); the P&L statement notion of profits (π) parallels the value notion to residual income (RI) which here corresponds to net value appropriation (NVa). The appropriation perspective fully closes a circle by reverting to equation (1.3) where net value appropriation equals residual income. The net value appropriation equation (3.4) hence makes residual income (profits) equivalent to the sum of net value creation plus net value extraction.

Note that the 'value creation' annotation in the value chain schema of Figures 2.4–2.7 depicts joint value creation. A visualization schema referencing the VCA framework and emphasizing the key conceptual business model elements in the value chain, for both the principal and stakeholders, is provided in Figure 2.8 and includes: value creation, value appropriation (revenue/revenue adjusted), transfer-IN/OUT and the resulting net value extraction, as well as the net value appropriation (profits/residual income). It should also be noted that both the principal and the stakeholder manage transfer-IN (at the cost of the counterparty's transfer-OUT). How so? To illustrate the multi-layered and complex nature of even a single principal-stakeholder relationship one might imagine a firm (principal) and its national government (stakeholder). The firm benefits from government subsidies not provided to its competitors (transfer-IN), while at the same time delivering social services for underprivileged citizens traditionally supplied by the government (transfer-OUT) that cost it less than the subsidies it receives.

Both principals and stakeholders need to appropriate value—first in the form of revenue—and then generate profits (by maximizing prices, including via transfer-IN, by minimizing costs, including via transfer-OUT) to sustain operations. This self-evident principle applies to all business models including those with principal-stakeholder relationships beyond the traditional types depicted in Table 2.2 and Figures 2.4–2.7 (i.e., suppliers, customers, employees, etc.). For instance, one might think of the unconventional stakeholders of non-fungible token (NFT) business models identified by Wilson, Karg and Ghaderi (2021): individual creators (originators of audio, art, or metadata), content owners with vested ownership rights (art dealers, media companies, or sport agencies), core intermediaries (such as the Ethereum Foundation providing the infrastructure), technical non-core intermediaries (such as the developers of proprietary ecosystems like Dapper Labs), related business non-core intermediaries (such as OpenSea marketplace), and stakeholders claiming ownership to the digital record (including consumers, collectors, investors, or speculators). Of course, in the case of NFTs, the value chain roles of the elite principal and the non-elite stakeholder business models are evolving as different parties seek to realize their division of value strategies. Eventually, and if the "asset pricing bubble" (Barbon & Ranaldo, 2023) does not kill off NFTs, an elite will invariably emerge as the party that manages to accumulate the most bargaining power and appropriate the largest amounts of transfer-IN while minimizing its own transfer-OUT.[30]

30 Whether Ethereum would then become the principal of the NFT business model in the way that Microsoft is the chief orchestrator and value appropriator of personal and office computing value chains is also anybody's guess. Despite narratives of decentralization, the elite dominance iron law is structural to society (see Proposition 1) and applies to any blockchain project in the same way that it does to software or petroleum.

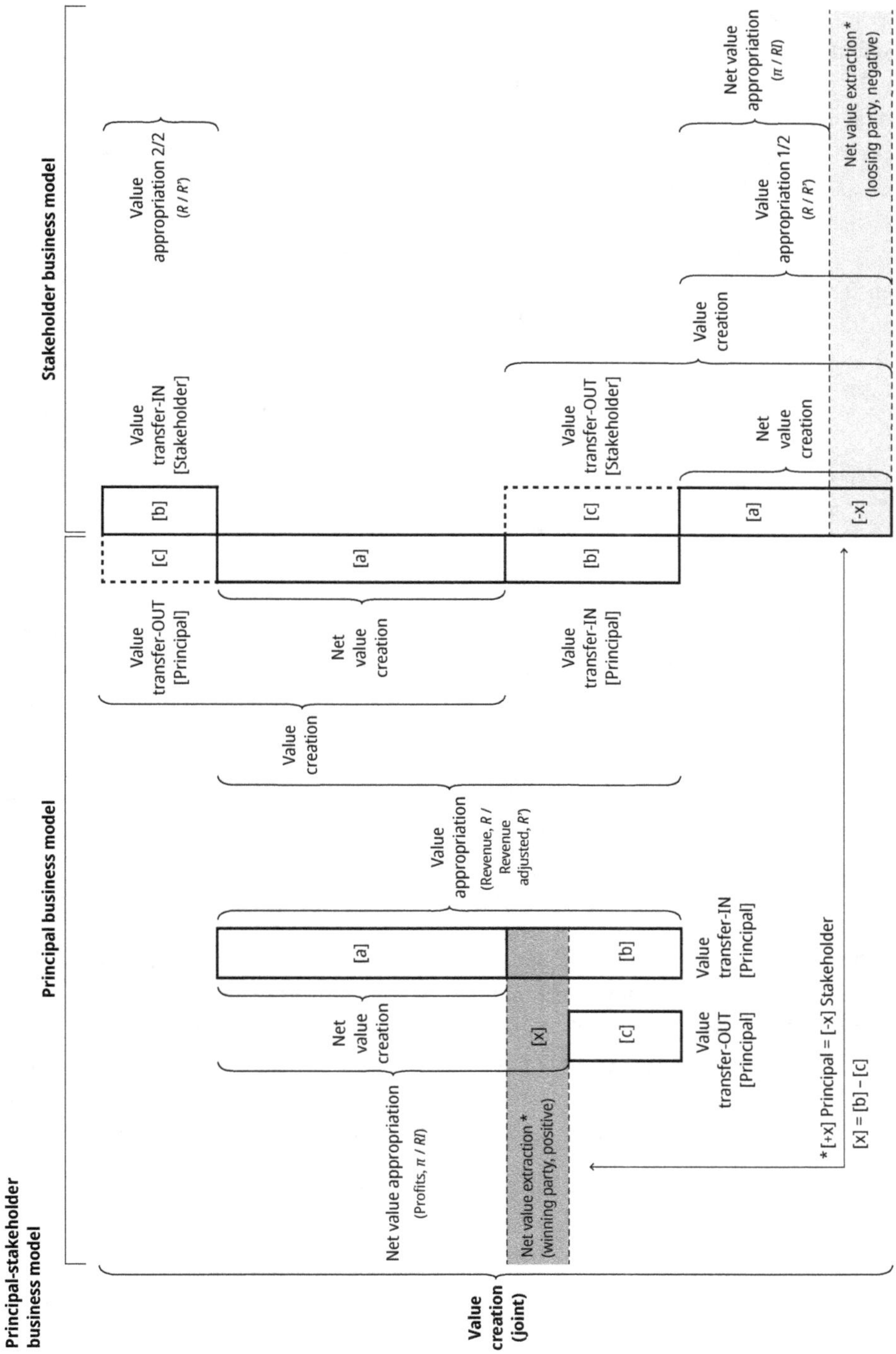

Figure 2.8: Selected conceptual elements of the business model based on the VCA framework and adjusted for the ETED.

As was pointed out when introducing equation (2.2'), the net value extraction across the economy is zero-sum. Assuming frictionless transfers, all value transfer-OUT and transfer-IN amounts offset each other across business models because one party's business model value transfer-IN is the counterparty's business model value transfer-OUT. This is so even when some of the specific value transfer-OUT amount that benefits stakeholders, such as a positive externality, is almost impossible to price, quantify, and attribute. This is also the case when second-order value transfers (associated with transfer-IN) are conceptually speaking diametrically distinct from first-order value creation (which includes transfer-OUT) (see Table 2.3 or the discussion of rent-seeking theory in Section 5.2). The transfer-IN/OUT argument yields the identities:

$$\text{transfer-IN(principal)} = \text{transfer-OUT(stakeholder)} \tag{3.5}$$

$$Vt^{in}_{t,principal} = Vt^{out}_{t,stakeholder} \tag{3.5a}$$

The reverse perspective is:

$$\text{value transfer-IN(stakeholder)} = \text{value transfer-OUT(principal)} \tag{3.5'}$$

$$Vt^{in}_{t,stakeholder} = Vt^{out}_{t,principal} \tag{3.5b}$$

Finally, for a given principal, the total amount of transfer-IN is the sum of the transfer-IN from all principal-related stakeholders, which corresponds to the sum of the transfer-OUT from all stakeholders with whom the principal has a relationship, as is described in equation (3.6):

$$\begin{aligned}\text{transfer-IN(principal)} &= \Sigma\,(\text{principal value transfer-IN from n stakeholders})\\ &= \Sigma\,(\text{n stakeholders transfer-OUT to principal})\end{aligned} \tag{3.6}$$

$$Vt^{in}_{t,principal} = \sum_{n}^{N} Vt^{in}_{t,principal\ of\ stakeholder_n} = \sum_{n}^{N} Vt^{out}_{t,stakeholder_n} \tag{3.6a}$$

For sustainable value creation operationalization purposes, transfer-IN and transfer-OUT amounts are calculated from constituent sustainable value creation (SVC) metrics (see Section 6.6.1). As per equations (3.7) and (3.8) below, the transfer-IN of a firm (whether principal or stakeholder) is the sum of the entire transfer-IN amounts for all the available SVC metrics used to operationalize sustainable value creation; likewise, the transfer-OUT of a firm is the sum of the entire transfer-OUT amounts for all the SVC metrics.

$$\text{transfer-IN(firm)} = \Sigma\,(\text{n transfer-IN metrics}) \tag{3.7}$$

$$Vt^{in}_{t,principal} = \sum_{n}^{N} Vt^{in}_{t,metrics_n} \tag{3.7a}$$

$$\text{transfer-OUT(firm)} = \Sigma\,(\text{n transfer-OUT metrics}) \tag{3.8}$$

$$Vt^{out}_{t,principal} = \sum_{n}^{N} Vt^{out}_{t,metrics_n} \tag{3.8a}$$

The analytical framework developed to establish elite business models' division of value strategies in Proposition 9 is rendered graphically for the entire business model (see Table 2.2) with the template provided by Garcia-Castro and Aguilera's "Value creation and appropriation with multiple stakeholders" and its "vertical chain of value decomposition" (2015, pp. 138, 140, Figure 2). The principal business model of Figure 2.9 articulates for all stakeholder relationships value creation and value transfers, with the latter including value appropriated but *not* created (i.e., transfer-IN by the principal in the form of low labor costs from the labor stakeholder) and value created but *not* appropriated (i.e., transfer-OUT from the principal in the form of higher costs of materials and services from the supplier stakeholder).

To close this section, it should be highlighted once more that extractive activities might occur on either side of the principal-stakeholder relationship (see the examples in Table 2.2); a positive net value extraction balance is, after all, the aspiration of every single division of value strategy (including those of non-elites). Success necessitates the securing of sources of bargaining power (see Figure 2.3). The field of strategic management concerned with firm performance examines strategies for both value creation and appropriation (also referred to as "capture", e.g., Brandenburger, 2002; Lepak, Smith, & Taylor, 2007; Garcia-Castro & Aguilera, 2015). The ETED, with its concern for economic development, emphasizes value appropriated but *not* created (transfer-IN) given its perverse impact on the incentive system.

Alesina and Rodrik (1994, p. 465) wrote: "A crude distinction between economics and politics would be that economics is concerned with expanding the pie while politics is about distributing it". A world free from bargaining power differentials, and with zero transaction costs in the sense of Coase (1960; Medema, 1994), would have value appropriation equal value creation. Value transfers would tend to zero and only be permissible under certain ethical principles and logics like the 'alternating value extraction and value creation' conjecture (discussed next in Section 2.3.1). Distributional games would largely be irrelevant residues of the past with energies instead being intensely focused on 'expanding the pie' and putting economic and human development on an ascending trajectory running on autopilot. In such a world, maybe that of an omniscient, omnipotent and technocratic superintelligence (see the discussion on AI in Chapter 8), the "politics" described by Alesina and Rodrik would simply not exist. Yet reality is such that value transfers and redistribution away from value creators are a principal avenue to residual income flows and wealth stocks. As a result, division of value strategies must for now rely on power differentials accrued in the contest arenas of the political economy.

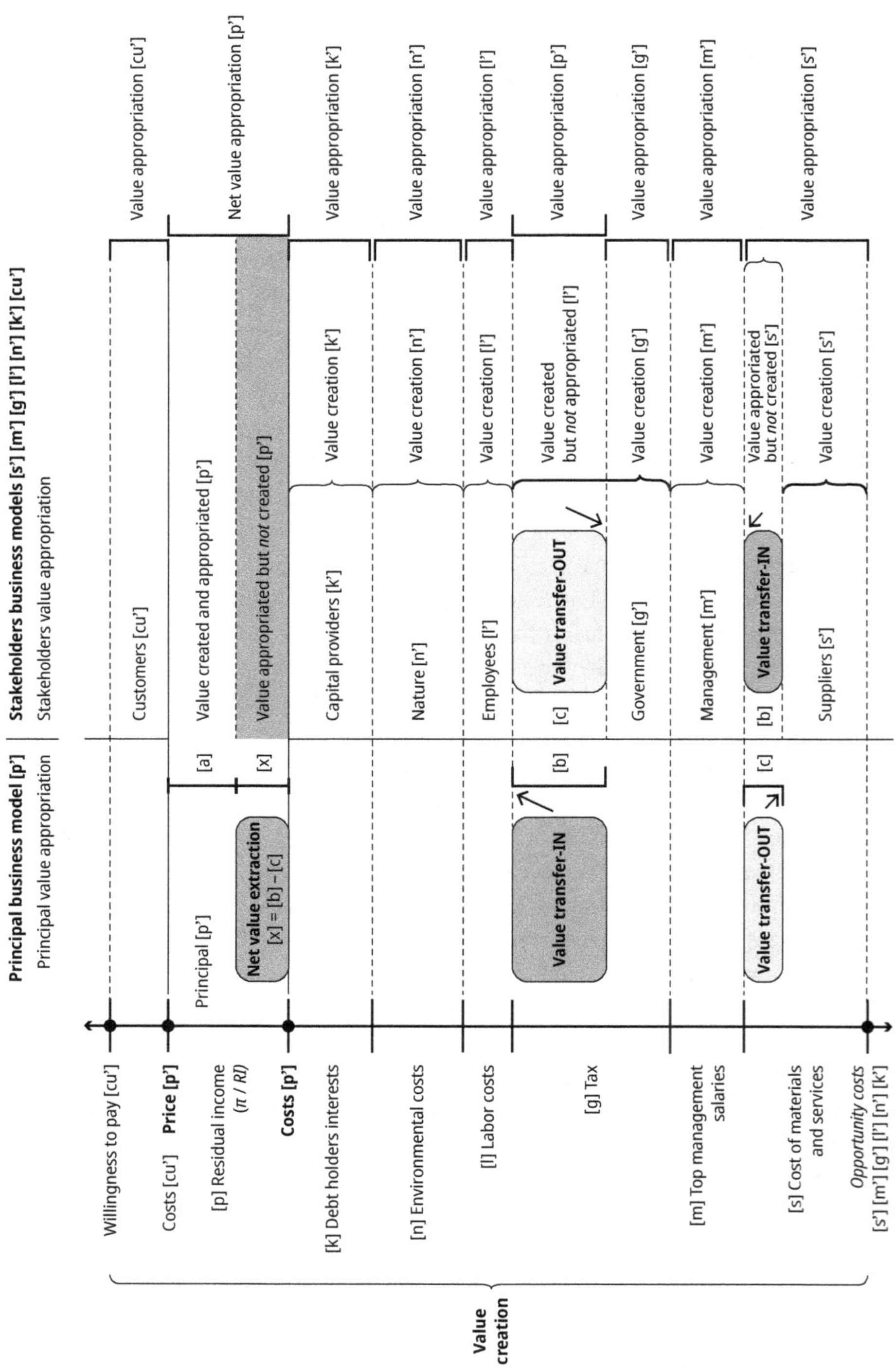

Figure 2.9: Principal and stakeholder business models across the value chain.[31]

2.3 Propositions on value creation and value transfers as extraction

The importance of bargaining power differentials was discussed in relation to value appropriation (Proposition 8), while the VCA framework was employed to provide the foundation for the division of value strategies (Proposition 9). This section goes a conceptual step further. First, Proposition 10 describes actual value creation in practice by differentiating between first-order productive and risk origination activities and second-order value and risk transfer activities on the basis of the 'value is created or transferred' ontological assumption of the ETED. Development occurs when first-order productive activities (value creation) preponderate over second-order transfer activities (value extraction), certain caveats, such the conjectured 'alternating value extraction and value creation' and its 'extractive push' dilemma notwithstanding. Next, Proposition 11 asserts that all elite business models have a position on a spectrum that ranges between the extremes of absolute value creation (all activities are first-order productive activities) and absolute value extraction (all activities are second-order transfer activities). This is the 'business model value creation spectrum' (hereinafter also referred to as the 'value spectrum'), a conceptual element that, together with others proposed in the ETED, advances the firm-level sustainable value creation measurements: the Value Creation Position (VCp) and Value Creation Rating (VCr). These measurements, along with all of the equations developed in this work, are summarized at the end of this section in Table 2.4.

2.3.1 Proposition 10: Sustainable value creation results from the proportion of first-order productive activities (value creation) relative to second-order transfer activities (value extraction)

> (. . .) the operators of two dams, one upstream of the other, sued one another repeatedly at least from the second half of the thirteenth century until the beginning of the fifteenth, when the downstream dam finally succeeded in driving the other out of business as the latter ran out of money to pay the court fees. (Gimpel, 1976, p. 17–20, as cited in Baumol, 1990, p. 907)

Value appropriated but *not* created (value transfer-IN) moves value away from the original value creators. This leads us onto the ontological foundation of the ETED, now made explicit (see also Figure A5.4a). Ontology "is concerned with 'what is', with the nature of existence, with the structure of reality as such" (Crotty, 2003, p. 10). This work holds—adhering to the principle of parsimony—that the nature of socio-economic relations and activity is that 'value is created or transferred'. A large body of literature exists in economics on value transfers and rent seeking and is examined in Section 5.2.1. To the business model,

31 Conceptual extension based on Figure 2 in Garcia-Castro and Aguilera (2015, p. 140). Note that (as pointed out in Section 1.2.4) in order to determine residual income, creditors (debt holders) interests are assumed to be costs. That is, creditors are stakeholders whose value appropriation claims are not substantially different from those of other stakeholders.

any income-generating value transfer activity, like the wins from the litigation in the above example, is 'second-order', while the direct value creation, the provision of water management services, is 'first-order'. This sequential logic helps to establish extractive value transfers (the beneficiary's transfer-IN) in the principal-stakeholder relationship. A classification schema that builds on the dualism of the ontological assumption of the ETED and assesses which activities cause or constitute second-order value transfers away from the original value creators is essential (and attempted in Table 2.3). This dichotomous separation and understanding of business model activity highlights a vexing developmental (and ethical) problem since value that is jointly created in a collaborative fashion by the principal and stakeholders is not appropriated according to the respective contributions made and is often transferred away from one party to the other. Under the hypothetical condition of 'equalized bargaining power equilibrium prices' (Section 2.2.2) no such value transfers may occur, and, as a result, all activities are first-order productive.

Economic life starts with value creation (see the definitions of value in Section 2.2.2 and value creation in Section 2.2.3). Millennia ago in *The Arthashastra*, Kautilya (1992, pp. 13, 15) stressed that *artha* (or wealth in the sense of *The Wealth of Nations*) is "the source of the livelihood of men", urging kings to engage in "economically productive activity" on the premise that first-order value creation is the material foundation for everything else in the state. That includes the fruitful activities of economic agents which in the widest sense include farmers, workers, soldiers, professionals, researchers, micro-enterprises, corporations, banks, NGOs, governments, and the vitally important Smithian "productive powers of labour" (1776/1904, p. 5). A key test for value creation is whether there is 'skin in the game', a given in fields such as "plumbing, dentistry, surgery, engineering, activities where operators are evaluated by tangible results or subjected to ruin and bankruptcy" (Taleb, 2020, p. 13). Productive value creation is termed a first-order activity because it can exist on its own terms, while second-order value transfer activities cannot exist without the presence of first-order activities. Value creation activities are also quite self-evident and include agriculture, manufacturing, trading, innovation, financial and other services, the building of something (often from nothing), and the origination and bearing of risk. Value extraction activities, on the other hand, are transfers that occur only because of value creation and risk origination (and bearing) elsewhere in society; they represent the appropriation by one economic agent of value previously created by another party. Many examples of second-order transfers are provided throughout this work, an extreme one being the Troubled Asset Relief Program (TARP), the bailout of the financial system under the Emergency Economic Stabilization Act of 2008, which saw US taxpayers relieving the risk originators from their massive losses. More commonplace instances include the excessive taxation of SMEs to support an unproductive civil service or any number of white elephant projects. In this work, second-order value and risk transfers are seen as the principal cause of regressive economic development. First-order value creation activities are, on the other hand, invariably positive and the *condicio sine qua non* for all economic and human development. It will be argued that the mechanisms that enable value transfers—the second-order activities—*are* the political economy.

It is necessary to stress that a most important form of value creation and transfer relates to risk and the coupling or decoupling of its origination and bearing. Whether one considers a current transition to fusion energy or to iron in Bronze Age societies, elites "either delay or accelerate the speed of spread of the innovation" on account of their strategic willingness to undertake, often massive, investment risks (Kim, 2001, pp. 472–473). As a rule, all business activities and value creation are associated with levels of risk. Since Markowitz (1952), the formalized relationship between risk and return has been a tenet of finance. Investing in potentially high value creation projects generally means exposure to high levels of risk. The "reckless" bets of the uncertainty undertaker can create value that leads, as long as new value is appropriated, to "wild success":

> Elon Musk illustrates [that] solid financial success is largely the result of skills, hard work, and wisdom. But wild success (in the far tail) is more likely to be the result of reckless betting, extreme luck, & the opposite of wisdom: folly. [. . .] Go back and check the numerous times when Tesla was on the brink of going bust. (Taleb, 2022)

Value creation and risk origination, including its 'wildest' form, are interchangeable and equivalent in the financial sense. Risk bearing, especially as a consequence of undertaking Knightian uncertainty, is essential for value creation, as is evident in Damodaran's (2005) firm valuation frameworks. Rent seeking therefore includes value appropriation without the commensurate exposure to risk, as well as its opposite, the "transfer of harm", a notion developed by the polemicist Nassim Taleb in *Skin in the Game* (2018) where "one does not bear the full risks and negative consequences of one's actions" (p. 244). In short, all references to 'value creation' in the ETED must also be understood in terms of 'risk origination', *and* the bearing of risk. Value creation requires those operating the business model to have skin in the game. Those that do not should not appropriate value.

Wins in the political non-market and societal narrative market arenas attained through 'political economy know-how' (see Figure 2.3) become problematic from a sustainable development perspective if they lead to institutionally sanctioned value and risk transfers. Such wins provide *de jure* or *de facto* institutional cover for activities such as price ceilings, exclusive licenses, cartels, exchange restrictions (such as non-tariff trade barriers), litigation, taxation, subsidies, guarantees, bailouts, and even theft. Value and risk transfer activities are examined in further theoretical detail in the literature review of rent seeking (Section 5.2), Bastiat (1845/1996, pp. 8–9), and here Buchanan (1980, p. 9) provides a preview of their economic nature: "Governmental licenses, quotas, permits, authorizations, approvals, franchise assignments—each of these closely related terms implies arbitrary and/or artificial scarcity created by government". Turchin's "wealth pumps" (2023) is an apt metaphor for such value transfer models. Table 2.3 reflects the dualist ontological assumption that 'value is created or transferred' and accordingly lists business model activities categorized into two fundamental types:

Table 2.3: A typology of business model activities referencing value.

Business model activity	
Value creation *First-order productive activity*	**Value extraction** *Second-order transfer activity*
– 'Sustainable risk origination' that bears the associated risk exposure (of actual and potential losses)	– 'Unsustainable risk origination' that transfers risk, transfers harm, hides risk, and benefits from the risk origination of others
– The Smithian "productive powers of labour"	– Trade and exchange restrictions Incl. tariffs, non-tariff barriers, quotas
– Skilled and unskilled trades, the professions	– Regulation, licenses, patents, and bureaucratism
– Intrapreneurship, entrepreneurship	– Price floors and ceilings
– Productivity growth, incremental innovation	– Taxes, confiscations, and subsidies
– Handicrafts, industrial production and other manufacturing sectors	– Discrimination, bigotry, favoritism in all of its forms
– Agriculture and food production activities	– Clientelism, client politics, patronage
– Services, trade and exchange	– Corruption Incl. bribery, embezzlement, nepotism
– Finance Incl. hedge funds, risk and venture capital, private equity and debt, Swiss private banks with partner liability (i.e., until the shift to corporate partnership structures on January 1, 2014)	– Monopolies, oligopolies, and cartels Incl. market dominance, "too big to fail" (TBTF) and "too big to jail"
– Radical innovation	– Monetary policies Incl. inflation, negative interest rates
– Art, in all of its forms	– Litigation aimed at certain transfers
– Specialization	– Environmental destruction
– Human capital development	– Criminal activity Incl. unlawful theft, extortion, murder
– Networks and value co-creation Incl. e-commerce, social media platforms, cloud computing, crowdsourcing	– Negative externalities Incl. antibiotic resistance, AI misalignment
– Positive externalities Incl. knowledge spillovers, vaccinations	

first-order productive activities (i.e., value creation and risk origination and bearing) and second-order transfer activities (i.e., value extraction and risk transfer).[32]

The distinction between 'first-order productive activities' and 'second-order transfer activities' in Table 2.3 is essential for the inquiry into micro-level (firm) and macro-level (the economy) sustainable value creation. The two activity types are separated by the

32 A key limitation of Table 2.3 is that the activities listed are only broad brushstroke indications of value creation and extraction. They should also not be confused with the business model *per se*, which in itself is a complex bundle of activities. For instance, an agricultural model might produce valuable crops (classified here as a first-order productive activity) while employing unsustainable farming practices that overly rely on chemical pesticides and fertilizers that deplete the soil and constitute extraction by *de facto* impeding future value creation (classified here as a second-order transfer activity). Sustainable value creation measurements (like the VCp/VCr) must provide a transparent view of these two types of activities in their respective proportions.

'revenue is value creation unless value transfer is proven' (constructive) implication, itself an application of a 'bona fide value appropriation' (positive) assumption (see Figure A5.4b) where all the revenue (and profit) of a business model is deemed in good faith to be net value creation. This rule is integral to the ETED and its operationalization as this inquiry advances the concept of sustainable value creation on the basis of a distinction between first-order productive and second-order transfer activities. Sustainable value creation at the business model level is the proportion of each class of these activities (measured by metrics, which in this work are aggregated into firm-level VCp/VCr scores, see Section 6.6.1). At the macro-economy level, sustainable value creation refers to the proportion of first-order productive and second-order transfer activities on aggregate, i.e., for all elite business models in society (measured, for instance, by the EQx in international comparative terms for the elite systems of nations). Again, sustainable value creation is consistent with both the sustainable development concept of the *Report of the World Commission on Environment and Development: Our Common Future* (1987), with its emphasis on the needs of future generations, and the focus of von Carlowitz (1712/2022) on the business model (see Section 2.1.1, Proposition 5).

It is important to dwell further on value transfers as these come with conceptual issues of their own. First, they are omnipresent and figure in all socio-economic relations. Every business model in society includes activities designed to transfer value away from original value creators, albeit to varying degrees. Second, establishing whether a value 'transfer' happens (or does not) is technically not always a clear-cut exercise and requires a valid framework. For instance, Baumol (1990, 2010) takes to task litigation and corporate takeovers in their rent-seeking modes while both activities can also clearly lead to value creation. Third, certain value transfers intend—as 'third-order' transfers, one might say —to reverse or compensate for previous second-order transfers (see Section 8.2.4 on redistribution). Litigation or green energy subsidies fit this description: a court sentence might result, for example, in a compensatory transfer from an offender back to the aggrieved party, while the tax credits for electric vehicles under the Inflation Reduction Act (2022) aim to mitigate inter-generational transfers of ecological resources from future generations to the present. Fourth, the literature on welfare economics and its analysis of positive/negative externalities (Pigou, 1920/1932; Coase, 1960; Buchanan & Stubblebine, 1962; Baumol, 1972; Bueno de Mesquita, 2016) addresses both value (and risk) creation and transfers (transfer-IN/OUT) and provides an important reference for the calculation of sustainable value creation (SVC) measurements (see Section 5.3.1). Fifth, certain first-order productive value creation activities are, due to their nature, inseparable from and inevitably bundled with second-order value transfer activities. Does innovation not require the grant of exclusivity—patents—that produce rents for the patent holders at the expense of technology users?

The fact that value extraction—again, second-order value transfers away from first-order producers—is sometimes a prerequisite for subsequent sustainable value creation is formalized in the 'alternating value extraction and creation' conjecture. Examples abound, with taxation probably being the most salient of these. Without such second-order transfers there are no state investments in public infrastructure, health, or education that enable individuals and organizations to create value. Additional reasons for transfers are described in the ample literature and illustrate how they address market failures in the provision of public goods (e.g., Comes & Sandler, 1996). The most sweeping examples of such transfers are related to violence and its suppression. North, Wallis, and Weingast race through the historical landscape from the Neolithic revolution 10,000 years ago onwards, with a conceptual framework that explains elites and how their value extraction is linked to its creation:

> limited access orders solve the problem of containing violence by political manipulation of the economic system to generate rents by limiting entry to provide social stability and order. (North, Wallis, & Weingast, 2006, p. 4)

Similarly, the 'extractive push' dilemma is faced by countries as they transition from one economic development stage to the next. That is, the extractive Leviathan of Hobbes' social contract theory (1651/2002) is the beneficiary of second-order transfers (e.g., taxes, corvée labor) received as a quid pro quo for providing public goods (e.g., social order that halts "the war of all against all") indispensable for subsequent value creation. What if violence becomes the premise for value creation? This inquiry begs to disagree with Turchin (2016) that the centralized elite business model of war is what "made humans the greatest cooperators on earth" (do commerce or religion not provide more effective forms of collaboration than war?). The 'alternating value extraction and creation' conjecture does, nonetheless, present some predicaments.

The dilemma can be illustrated through the decades-long industrial policies to support Korean 'wealth cliques' or *chaebol* (industrial conglomerates). Without second-order transfer activities like state-sanctioned privileged access to banking funds, there would have been no "Miracle on the Han River" (Gemici, 2013) in the 1960s, nor the Samsung Galaxy of today. Without the human capital and nation building legacy of Israel's post-independence "centrally controlled socialist" system—what Sharkansky (1997) called "a cumbersome giant"—with its kibbutzim and dominant state-owned enterprises, the phenomenal value creation of the "start-up nation" of today (Senor & Singer, 2009) would not exist. This dilemma entails policy decisions with regard to which elite coalition should be favored. Countries that have successfully transitioned to the digital economy have accepted Big Tech national champions and their associated extractive monopolies, initially gained thanks to a 'knowledge' advantage that played out in the market arena. The dilemma, with its deep ethical implications, includes considerations of when to grant the 'license to steal', to whom, and, most critically, when to take it away (an issue that is prescriptively addressed later in this book, see, for instance, A Transfer Constraints Framework for policy formulation, Table 8.2). The assumption is that there will be no kick-start or transition to a higher phase of development without a given, optimal amount of extractive value transfer activities by elite business models.

2.3.2 Proposition 11: All elite business models have a measurable value creation position on a 'value spectrum'

The 'alternating value extraction and creation' conjecture not only applies to the macro-level; it also operates at the level of the firm, as has been shown by 'the Amazon dilemma'. Having established the types of business model activities more likely to correspond to value creation and risk origination (first-order productive activities) and value extraction and risk transfer (second-order transfer activities), the aim is now to operationalize these ideas by establishing sustainable value creation measurements for firm-level business models. An initial proposal is a conceptual spectrum that ranges from absolute value creation (hypothetical business models with only first-order productive activities) to absolute value extraction (those with only second-order transfer activities). Every business model in the economy (and every national elite system) is a combination of both value creation and value extraction activities. This combination is first articulated through a 'value creation position' (VCp) measurement, based on an assessment of revenue (value appropriation) and the value transfer-IN that is singular to the business model. These two assessments yield the VCp and are schematically represented in the 'value spectrum' of Figure 2.10, along with the implicit net value creation and value transfer-OUT (which is relevant to other measurements).

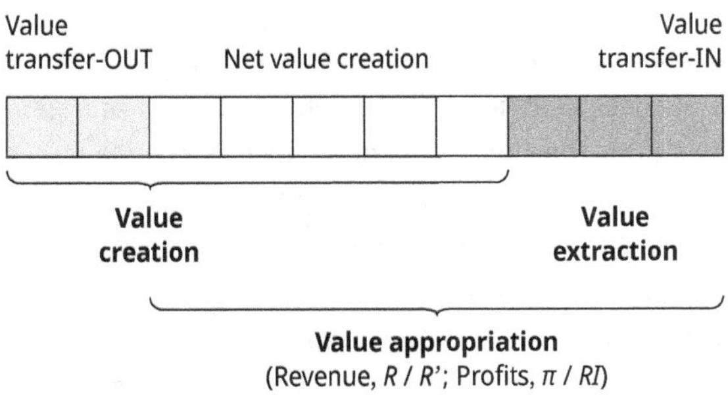

Figure 2.10: The 'value spectrum' (also referred to as the 'business model value creation spectrum').

Equations for sustainable value creation (SVC) measurements (4/9)

How can the sustainable value creation of a particular business model—for either the (elite) principal or a stakeholder—be determined? Two conceptual elements in the form of measurements are advanced for this purpose: the just examined Value Creation Position (VCp) and the Value Creation Rating (VCr). Both associate with the firm's P&L statements since they are based on revenue or profits, and require the assessment of one of the two components related to value extraction: transfer-IN and transfer-OUT (again, both are derived from the VCA framework). The VCp/VCr measurements are designed to provide a micro-foundation to elucidate the economic development question. At the same time, any such firm-level sustainable value creation measurements must directly connect to practice and be relevant for the organization and its leadership, as well as for third parties like providers of capital and regulators.

In the literature, Garcia-Castro and Aguilera's work (2015, pp. 138, 140–143) opened the path for these measurements on the premise of joint value creation (irrespective of whether value is positive or negative), conceiving of "elastic" and "inelastic" value appropriation where the "VCA elasticity" notion "captures the relationship between the value appropriated by a stakeholder and the total value created in a period of time". On the back of successful division of value strategies, value distribution occurs between the principal and stakeholders. For instance, under "elastic" appropriation, Toyota's sustained productivity increases in the 1980s and 1990s created value that was captured by both labor stakeholders and the principal owners. Under "inelastic" appropriation—or excessive value appropriation—General Motors (suffering from generalized "low total value creation") saw a specific stakeholder group appropriate incremental value; that is, employees enjoying higher salaries at the expense of shareholders who suffered negative capital gains (Lieberman, Garcia-Castro, & Balasubramanian, 2017).

The Value Creation Position (VCp), the first ETED sustainable value creation (SVC) measurement at the firm level, assesses the sustainability of the business model by initially benchmarking P&L statement data like revenue or profits. The VCp equation establishes the proportion of all value appropriated or firm revenue (revenue adjusted) that is derived from net value creation. Since value appropriated is net value creation plus extractive value transfer-IN, it is essential that the latter is assessed. Value transfer-IN (value appropriated but *not* created), while not specifically identified, is obviously part and parcel of financial statements and impacts both the top and bottom lines. Yet since value transfer-IN is not explicitly defined as such in the P&L, determining transfer-IN amounts associated to firm revenue and profits (i.e., to the corresponding revenue adjusted or residual income) is the key methodological challenge for calculating the VCp (see Sections 5.3.1 and 6.5 on how to determine it with recourse to its component metrics).

The VCp formulation, which can be seen as an alternative way of implementing Garcia-Castro and Aguilera's notion of "VCA elasticity" (2015, p. 138), is presented in the text version of equations (4.1) and (4.1') in terms of 'revenue' and 'profit'; and in the financial version of equations (4.1a) and (4.2b) in terms of 'revenue adjusted' and 'residual income'. In either case, and for all these amounts, there must be a corresponding forensic attribution to transfer-IN activities, which in turn are quantified through an appropriate set of metrics.

In the text notations of the following equations, the VCp/VCr are annotated with the P&L statement terms 'profits' or 'revenue', as in VCp(revenue) or VCp(profits). In the mathematical notations of the equations, the VCp/VCr are annotated with the value creation terms 'revenue adjusted' (R') or 'residual income' (RI), as in $VCp_t^{R'}$ and VCp_t^{RI}. The firm VCp results are expected to differ depending on whether revenue (revenue adjusted) or profits (residual income) are used as a basis for the calculations. Any such differences will shed important light on division of value strategies as well as on the 'knowledge' and 'political economy know-how' of the firm. Lastly, equation (4.1") depicts the understanding of VCp as the proportion of net value creation in relation to overall value appropriation:

$$\text{Value Creation Position, VCp(revenue)} = [\text{revenue} - \text{transfer-IN(revenue)}] / \text{revenue} \qquad (4.1)$$

$$VCp_t^{R'} = \frac{R_t' - Vt_t^{R'\ in}}{R_t'} \qquad (4.1a)$$

$$\text{Value Creation Position, VCp(profits)} = [\text{profits} - \text{transfer-IN(profits)}] / \text{profits} \qquad (4.1')$$

$$VCp_t^{RI} = \frac{RI_t - Vt_t^{RI\ in}}{RI} \qquad (4.1b)$$

$$\text{Value Creation Position, VCp} = \text{net value creation} / \text{value appropriation} \qquad (4.1")$$

$$VCp_t^{RI} = \frac{NVc_t}{Va_t} \qquad (4.1c)$$

The VCp that is obtained from the above equations is presented as a percentage that ranges from 0 to 100 in order to make easier comparisons across firms. A result of 0% means that all revenue adjusted/residual income derives from transfer-IN and value appropriated but *not* created. A result of 100% means that transfer-IN is null, and all revenue adjusted/residual income derives from the value creation of the business model. A VCp (revenue) of 70% would mean that 70% of the firm's revenue is generated from business model activities associated with value creation, while 30% of the revenue is generated from value appropriated from counterparties, i.e., from extractive transfer-IN. The higher the VCp percentage score, the more sustainable the firm and its business model are viewed under the ETED's notion of sustainable value creation. In such a case, the dependency of the firm and business model on the non-market and narrative market arenas of the political economy is likely to be lower. VCp assessments are industry dependent and must also be controlled for country, firm size, firm age, and possibly even for the cultural context (Choi and Storr, 2019, found that rent seeking is also cultural), along with other applicable variables.

The second SVC measurement, the Value Creation Rating (VCr), is more comprehensive and assesses the overall value contribution of a business model to the economy and society at large. Unlike the VCp, the VCr does consider inclusive value transfer-OUT (value created but *not* appropriated) and must take a view on the total transfer-OUT amounts that accrue to counterparties and assorted stakeholders such as suppliers, technical non-core intermediaries, customers, governments, or to society at large. While transfer-IN is assessed with reference to the financial statement, data on transfer-OUT cannot be dealt with in this way and has to be obtained from a range of distinct sources including (at times subjective) assessments that might be made without direct reference to the firm's financials (e.g., innovation spillovers or noise pollution). The complex methodological and practical challenges of assessing the constituent datasets—the metrics—for transfer-IN/OUT are tackled in later chapters. Refer to the 'quantifiability of value transfers' (finance) assumption for socio-economic relations of Section 5.3.1; the discussion in Section 6.6.1 on metrics; the examples offered in Table 6.2 on the contributions of individual SVC metrics to the sum of transfer-IN/OUT; and to Figure A5.5 on the three-stage calculation process to establish SVC measurements.

In common with the VCp, the VCr can also be determined based on 'revenue' and 'profits' as in the text version equations (4.2) and (4.2'), and 'revenue adjusted' and 'residual income' in the financial version equations (4.2a) and (4.2b). The last equation (4.2") depicts the understanding of VCr as an ultimate ratio: the proportion of all value creation relative to all value appropriation:

$$\text{Value Creation Rating, VCr(revenue)} \\ = [\text{revenue} - \text{transfer-IN(revenue)} + \text{transfer-OUT(revenue)}] / \text{revenue} \tag{4.2}$$

$$VCr_t^{R'} = \frac{R'_t - Vt_t^{R'in} + Vt_t^{R'out}}{R'_t} \tag{4.2a}$$

$$\text{Value Creation Rating, VCr(profits)} \\ = [\text{profits} - \text{transfer-IN(profits)} + \text{transfer-OUT(profits)}] / \text{profits} \tag{4.2'}$$

$$VCr_t^{RI} = \frac{RI_t - Vt_t^{RI\ in} + Vt_t^{RI\ out}}{RI_t} \tag{4.2b}$$

$$\text{Value Creation Rating, VCr} = \text{value creation} / \text{value appropriation} \tag{4.2"}$$

$$VCr_t = \frac{Vc_t}{Va_t} \tag{4.2c}$$

The firm in a perfectly 'balanced' value relationship vis-à-vis all of its stakeholders (where transfer-IN equals transfer-OUT) has a VCr of 1.00. A business model relying on extractive activities will have a VCr trending below 1.00; that is, extractive transfer-IN exceeds inclusive transfer-OUT (net value extraction is positive). A firm with a sustainable value creation business model that contributes to the economy and society at large (willingly or unwittingly) with substantial inclusive transfer-OUT will have a VCr above 1.00; that is, inclusive transfer-OUT exceeds extractive transfer-IN.

Expressed as equation sets (4.1) and (4.2), the VCp and the VCr are the two fundamental SVC measurements suggested in this work. Both are designed for a variety of constituencies such as management, regulators, capital providers, or the general public and seek diverse practical applications. The measurements offer insights on the relative amount of value creation and sustainability of a firm business model, whether elite or non-elite (see the 'The Sustainable Valuations Matrix', depicted in Figure A5.7, which applies to any firm whether elite or non-elite). These micro-level measurements, if obtained for a majority of the leading elite business models in an economy, could also be employed to derive the meso-level, aggregate elite quality measurement of a country on a non-comparative basis. Such an approach— a 'bottom-up' (micro-to-meso level) rating of a national elite system based on the value creation of its leading elite business models to derive a notional 'Elite Quality Rating' ('EQr')—is discussed (in Section 6.5.2) as a complement to the established and internationally comparative Elite Quality Index (EQx, see Chapter 6).

Besides being central for the ETED's theoretical advancement (as elite agency is the transmission mechanism between the micro- and macro-levels), the VCp/VCr measurements supply the basis for sustainable value creation assessments and the classification of any business model. In that capacity the measurements have potentially powerful practical applications. For elite business models, the most evident is that they can support business model transformation (see the varieties of transformational leadership in Table 7.2) by providing rigorous financial benchmarks. Policymakers and political elites interested in pursuing targeted structural reforms and institutional change will also be supported by references to the sustainable value creation measurements of elite business models in specific sectors of the economy. A further application is for the financial markets: the VCr is designed and intended to adjust equity, debt, and firm valuations (see Table 5.2) in the SVC valuation frameworks (see Figures A5.6a, A5.6b, and A5.6c). The aim of such adjustments is the allocation of capital on the basis of the degree to which a company's business model creates value or benefits from value appropriated but *not* created. Finally, knowledge elites in the media, entertainment, or academic fields can support transformational initiatives by referencing the VCr/VCp when producing evidence-based narratives.

Figure 2.11, an extension of Figure 2.10, renders a final conceptual summary on the discussion and depicts the VCp of a specific principal business model on the 'value spectrum' based on revenue (for a profits-based rendition, see Figure A5.5a). To that end, and in addition to revenue (adjusted), the visualization clearly shows the three discrete business model value categories derived from the VCA framework that are applied to the ETED—net value creation, transfer-IN and transfer-OUT.[33]

As already discussed, at the micro-level and in the context of strategic management, competitive advantage is not necessarily associated with value creation, but rather with the success or failure of a firm to appropriate the value it creates (Coff, 1999, p. 119). Pointedly, Brandenburger and Stuart (1996, p. 6) note: "How much value can that player be expected to capture? This is a central question in business strategy". Not being able to appropriate value created is of great interest to practitioners such as top management, consultants, investors, or potential acquirers and private equity firms. Having control of 'the extraordinary lever' as a result of lower transaction costs, higher trust levels, and, ultimately, bargaining power differentials from wins in the political economy's contest arenas, elites appropriate most of the value their models create (and potentially even more than that).[34] The possibility of value appropri-

---

33 Incidentally, referencing the annotations of Figures 2.8, 2.9, and 2.11 and obviating revenue/revenue adjusted, the Value Creation Position would be expressed as VCp = [a]/([a]+[c]), and the Value Creation Rating as VCr = ([a]+[b])/([a]+[c]).

34 On account of their power, elite business models will not be at the receiving end of value transfer-OUT, yet their transfer-IN is bound to vary across countries (or industries within a country) due to, for instance, the particular constraints of intra-elite competition rules (as elite business models face both constraints against extraction and incentives to contribute to specific non-elite subsets of society). A related research question, to elucidate the micro- to macro-level transmission mechanism's relevance

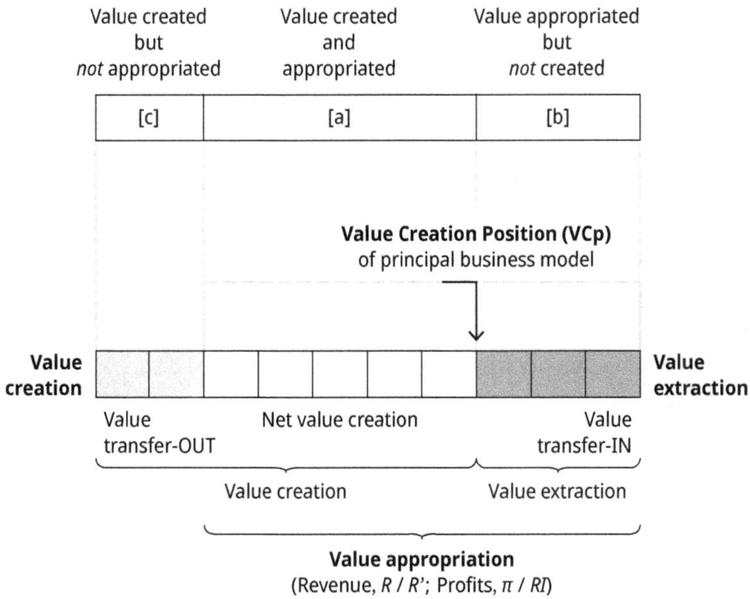

Figure 2.11: The 'value spectrum' (for revenue) and the business model Value Creation Position (VCp).

ated but *not* created is implicit in the VCA model, as incremental value is created and distributed depending on the negotiations between the business model's stakeholders (Garcia-Castro & Aguilera, 2015, pp. 139–141), but rent seeking has not been systematically addressed in terms of organizational behavior, conceptually connecting the economics, strategic management, and sustainability literatures. A central question for macro-level economic growth suggested by this work is the size, direction, and effect on the incentive system of value transfer-IN activities in the economy.

Elites are defined (see the overview in Table 4.1) as operating the economy's highest impact value creation and value extraction business models. At the same time, and while elite membership is exclusive (Olson, 1965/1971; Pareto, 1968/1991; Busino, 2000; North, Wallis, & Weingast, 2006), elite agency can be deemed to be inclusive if the revenues and residual income of elite models do not rely on excessive extractive transfer-IN activities. This is the conceptual basis for 'high' elite quality and the empirical work of the comparative EQx global index (Casas-Klett & Cozzi, 2020, 2021, 2022, 2023, 2024). The VCp and VCr open new transformational possibilities for elites, bring transparency to society, and contribute to debunking the elite populist fallacy ('elites are bad') by ascertaining the value creation contributions of specific firms and elite business models.

to economic development, is the relationship between elite power levels (e.g., as measured by the EQx or EQr) and the favored transfer-IN practices (institutionalized as monopolies, trade barriers, subsidies, war, etc.) of a country's elite business models.

Table 2.4: Equations for micro-level sustainable value creation and related SVC measurements referencing the VCA framework.

Ref.	Equation set	Description
1/9	**Equations for residual income**	
1.1	residual income = revenue adjusted – costs (profits = revenue – costs)	Residual income (akin to P&L profits) is earned revenue adjusted (derived from P&L revenue and based on prices received) minus all costs paid (including debt holders' claims).
1.1a	$RI_t = R'_{x,t} - c_t$	
1.2	residual income = net value creation + net value extraction	Residual income (profits) is the sum of net value created and net value extracted.
1.2a	$RI_t = NVc_t + NVe_t$	
1.3	residual income = net value appropriation	Residual income (profits) is net value appropriation.
1.3a	$RI_t = NVa_t$	
2/9	**Equations for value creation**	
2.1	value creation(principal) = net value creation(principal) + transfer-OUT (principal)	Value creation is the value from first-order productive activities of a business model (principal or stakeholder) and is described as [a] net value creation plus [c] transfer-OUT.
2.1a	$Vc_{t,principal} = NVc_{t,principal} + Vt^{out}_{t,principal}$	
2.1'	value creation(stakeholder) = net value creation (stakeholder) + transfer-OUT(stakeholder)	
2.1b	$Vc_{t,stakeholder} = NVc_{t,stakeholder} + Vt^{out}_{t,stakeholder}$	
2.2	value creation(business model) = Σ [value creation(principal), value creation(stakeholders)]	The value creation of the business model is cooperative and collective, i.e., the sum of the value creation of all stakeholders, including the principal.
2.2a	$Vc_{t,business\ model} = \sum Vc_{t,principal}, Vc_{t,stakeholder}$	
2.2'	value creation(business model) = Σ [value creation(principal), value creation(stakeholders)] + Σ [net value extraction(principal), net value extraction(stakeholders)]	In the business model, value transfer-IN and -OUT cancel each other out, so the sum of all net value extraction in the business model is zero.
2.2b	$Vc_{t,business\ model} = \sum Vc_{t,principal}, Vc_{t,stakeholder} + \sum NVe_{t,principal}, NVe_{t,stakeholder}$	

Table 2.4 (continued)

Ref.	Equation set	Description
2.3	net value creation = value creation – transfer-OUT	Net value creation refers to [a] 'value created and appropriated'. It can be calculated in three ways: firstly by deducting from value creation the amount of the [b] 'value created but *not* appropriated', i.e., transfer-OUT; and secondly by deducting from the total value appropriation the amount of the [c] 'value appropriated but *not* created', i.e., transfer-IN. Thirdly, and as in VCp/ VCr calculations, revenue adjusted is used for value appropriation (from which transfer-IN is also deducted).
2.3a	$NVc_t = Vc_t - Vt_t^{out}$	
2.3'	net value creation = value appropriation – transfer-IN	
2.3b	$NVc_t = Va_t - Vt_t^{in}$	
2.3"	net value creation = revenue adjusted – transfer-IN	
2.3c	$NVc_t = R'_t - Vt_t^{in}$	
3/9	**Equations for value appropriation and transfers**	
3.1	value appropriation = revenue adjusted	Value appropriation is 'revenue adjusted', which is derived from 'revenue' used for statutory and accounting purposes. Value appropriation can also be understood in terms of 'residual income' (profits).
3.1a	$Va_t = R'$	
3.2'	value appropriation(principal) = net value creation(principal) + transfer-IN(principal)	Value appropriation is conceptualized as the sum of [a] the 'value created and appropriated' i.e., net value creation plus the [c] 'value appropriated but *not* created', i.e., value transfer-IN.
3.2a	$Va_{t,principal} = NVc_{t,principal} + Vt^{in}_{t,principal}$	
3.2"	value appropriation(stakeholder) = net value creation stakeholder) + transfer-IN(stakeholder)	
3.2b	$Va_{t,stakeholder} = NVc_{t,stakeholder} + Vt^{in}_{t,stakeholder}$	
3.3	net value extraction = transfer-IN – transfer-OUT	Net value extraction by the business model is all the [c] 'value appropriated but *not* created' i.e., value transfer-IN, minus all the value lost to stakeholders, the [b] 'value created but *not* appropriated' i.e., value transfer-OUT.
3.3a	$NVe_t = Vt_t^{in} - Vt_t^{out}$	

Table 2.4 (continued)

Ref.	Equation set	Description
3.4	net value appropriation = net value creation + net value extraction	Net value appropriation conceptually refers to all the value the business model has been able to appropriate and retain, i.e., net value creation plus net value extraction. Equations for alternative formulations are also presented, including value appropriation minus transfer-OUT. Note that net value appropriation is equivalent to residual income (profits) in equation (1.3).
3.4a	$NVa_t = NVc_t + NVe_t$	
3.4'	net value appropriation = [value appropriation – transfer-IN] + [transfer-IN – transfer-OUT]	
3.4b	$NVa_t = (Va_t - Vt_t^{in}) + (Vt_t^{in} - Vt_t^{out})$	
3.4"	net value appropriation = value appropriation – transfer-OUT	
3.4c	$NVa_t = Va_t - Vt_t^{out}$	
3.5	transfer-IN(principal) = transfer-OUT(stakeholder)	Value transfer-OUT and value transfer-IN amounts offset each other across business models, as one party's value transfer-IN is another counterparty's value transfer-OUT.
3.5a	$Vt_{t,principal}^{in} = Vt_{t,stakeholder}^{out}$	
3.5'	transfer-IN(stakeholder) = transfer-OUT(principal)	
3.5b	$Vt_{t,stakeholder}^{in} = Vt_{t,principal}^{out}$	
3.6	transfer-IN(principal) = sum(principal transfer-IN from n stakeholders) = sum(n stakeholders transfer-OUT to principal)	A principal's total amount of transfer-IN is established as the sum of transfer-IN from all its stakeholders, which corresponds to the sum of the transfer-OUT endured by all the principal-related stakeholders.
3.6a	$Vt_{t,principal}^{in} = \sum_{n}^{N} Vt_{t,principal\ of\ stakeholder_n}^{in} = \sum_{n}^{N} Vt_{t,stakeholder_n}^{out}$	
3.7	transfer-IN(principal) = sum(transfer-IN metrics)	Transfer-IN for a firm is the sum of all transfer-IN amounts derived from the metrics used to measure its sustainable first-order value creation.
3.7a	$Vt_{t,principal}^{in} = \sum_{n}^{N} Vt_{t,metrics_n}^{in}$	
3.8	transfer-OUT(principal) = sum(transfer-OUT metrics)	Transfer-OUT for a firm is the sum of all transfer-OUT amounts derived from the metrics used to measure its sustainable – but non-appropriated – value creation (i.e., value transfers benefiting the counterparty).
3.8a	$Vt_{t,principal}^{out} = \sum_{n}^{N} Vt_{t,metrics_n}^{out}$	

Table 2.4 (continued)

Ref.	Equation set	Description
4/9	**Equations for sustainable value creation (SVC) measurements**	
4.1	Value Creation Position, VCp(revenue) = [revenue – transfer-IN(revenue)] / revenue	The VCp is a measurement of the sustainability of a firm. It requires the referencing of revenue/profits and establishing the second-order [c] 'value appropriated but *not* created' transfers i.e., 'value transfer-IN' that benefits the business model. The VCp is conceptualized on a 'value spectrum' with one segment for [a] 'value created and appropriated' i.e., 'net value creation', and the opposing one for [c] 'value appropriated but *not* created', i.e., 'transfer-IN'. The latter is quantified through metrics. The VCp score is a percentage that represents [a] 'value created and appropriated', i.e., 'net value creation', over all 'value appropriation' [a+c], i.e., revenue/profits (revenue adjusted/residual income).
4.1a	$VCp_t^{R'} = \frac{R_t^{'} - Vt_t^{R'\ in}}{R_t^{'}}$	
4.1'	Value Creation Position, VCp(profits) = [profits – transfer-IN(profits)] / profits	
4.1b	$VCp_t^{RI} = \frac{RI_t - Vt_t^{RI\ in}}{RI_t}$	
4.1"	VCp = net value creation / value appropriation	
4.1c	$VCp_t^{R} = \frac{NVc_t}{Va_t}$	
4.2	Value Creation Rating, VCr(revenue) = [revenue – transfer-IN(revenue) + transfer-OUT(revenue)] / revenue	The VCr is a comprehensive measurement of the sustainability of a firm. It requires the referencing of revenue/profits and establishing second-order [c] 'value appropriated but *not* created' transfers i.e., 'transfer-IN', as well as [b] first-order 'value created but *not* appropriated' transfers i.e., 'transfer-OUT'. Both are quantified through metrics. The VCr is provided as a score with two decimal points that describes the proportion of all 'value creation' [a+b] in relation to all 'value appropriation' [a+c] i.e., revenue/profits (revenue adjusted/residual income). The VCr operationalizes the relationship between a firm and society by assessing all second-order value transfers, both the extractive (transfer-IN) and the inclusive (transfer-OUT).
4.2a	$VCr_t^{R'} = \frac{R_t^{'} - Vt_t^{R'in} + Vt_t^{R'out}}{R_t^{'}}$	
4.2'	Value Creation Rating, VCr(profits) = [profits – transfer-IN(profits) + transfer-OUT (profits)] / profits	
4.2b	$VCr_t^{RI} = \frac{RI_t - Vt_t^{RI\ in} + Vt_t^{RI\ out}}{RI_t}$	
4.2"	VCr = value creation / value appropriation	
4.2c	$VCr_t = \frac{Vc_t}{Va_t}$	

The main formulas related to the calculation of sustainable value creation (SVC) measurements anchored in the VCA framework are summarized in Table 2.4. All have been reviewed in this chapter. A final series of equations (5/9 to 9//9) for the valuation of debt, equity, and the firm—based on SVC measurements—are addressed at a later stage (Section 5.3.1, see also Figures 5.4 and A5.6, and Tables 5.2, 5.3 and A3.3 for a detailed overview of the valuation frameworks).

Now that value creation and value extraction have been operationalized, the relationship of elite agency to bargaining power in value transfers is conceptually revisited to interpret transfer-IN/OUT in the VCp/VCr measurements. The transfer-OUT from agents *with* power (powerful elites parting with value despite having power) is assumed to be an inclusive transfer; transfer-OUT from agents *without* power (powerless non-elites parting with value) is assumed to be an extractive transfer.

When the beneficiary of value appropriated but *not* created has low bargaining power and the value transfer-OUT comes from a party with higher bargaining power (a principal, an elite), it is deemed to be inclusive, an uncoerced accepted contribution, a positive externality, and a public good (such as innovation spillovers, circular production processes, fair trade prices). The beneficiaries are political economy agents (non-elites) who would not otherwise have the means and leverage to demand and appropriate such value.

On the other hand, when the beneficiary of value appropriated but *not* created has high bargaining power (usually a principal, an elite) and the value transfer-OUT comes from a party with lower bargaining power, it is deemed to be a coerced extraction, an involuntary tax, a negative externality, and a public bad (again, monopoly rents, depleted soil, inflation). The beneficiaries are political economy agents (elites) with the means and leverage to demand and appropriate such value.

Section 6.6.1 discusses the data building blocks that describe transfer-OUT—the metrics that establish the VCr. These do not provide information about whether the transfer-OUT is by high/low power agents. Transfer-OUT is simply classified as value creation. As such, value created but *not* appropriated is accounted for as a first-order productive activity, whether it comes from elite or non-elite business models. Transfer-OUT is value creation by both the conscientious firm sequestering more carbon than it emits and by the exploited worker at the short end of monopsony power. Transfer-IN is, on the other hand, always accounted for as a second-order transfer activity. As pointed out by equation (3.5), total transfer-OUT in an economy equals total transfer-IN if no value leakage occurs between the counterparties when value appropriated but *not* created is secured (though deadweight losses, social losses, and resource misallocations—see Harberger, 1964; Tullock, 1967; Tollison 1982—are actually severe). Note that one component of the transfer-IN of 'value appropriated but *not* created' is 'cost created but *not* borne', i.e., transfer-COST. The 'extractive' transfer-COST has a 'destructive' shadow counterpart (that is not part of transfer-IN): '*negative* value created but *not* appropriated'. Both types of transfer-COST are expounded on in subsequent chapters, including a case study on the opioid crisis in Section 8.2.1 (the 'extractive' and 'destructive' transfer-COSTS are also depicted in the 'value spectrum' of Figure A5.5a and in The Value Creation and Appropriation Matrix of Figure 6.7).

Moving forward, a recurring rationale informs this inquiry. Economies that see 'the extraordinary lever' and associated bargaining power differentials invested in business models characterized by extractive value transfer-IN and rent-seeking activities will witness suboptimal resource allocation, skewed incentives, and broken information systems, along with friction, higher transaction costs, and a *de facto* tax levied on the majority. In such societies, a substantial chunk of the total value created is transferred from one subset of society to another via mechanisms activated with 'political economy know-how' (in the non-market and narrative market arenas). On the other hand, there are inclusive countries where elites do not immediately appropriate the full value their applied coordination capacity allows. Such elites are less reliant on extractive transfer-IN from their stakeholders, are less distracted by political economy considerations, and have a sharper focus on the market arena where 'knowledge' generates the residual income and the wealth stock required for their status. A *leitmotif* of this inquiry is that when non-extractive business models prevail in society, the majority of the economy's stakeholders, both high and low, unencumbered, free, and able to keep the value they produce, are posited to produce more. High value creation elite business models are in themselves the strongest incentive system for productive work and inclusive prosperity. The two main firm-level sustainable value creation measurements of the ETED—the VCr and VCp—are meant to assess the sustainability of elite business models and, when aggregated, the sustainability of the political economies in which they operate.

Figure 2.12 closes this chapter with a summary of the two measurements and their two variants —firm revenue and profits. Note that throughout this work revenue (R) and profits (π) are also described as residual income (RI) and revenue adjusted (R'). The two nomenclatures are meant to respectively reflect the P&L statement perspective (revenue/profits) and the value chain (VCA) perspective (revenue adjusted/residual income). For instance, Figure 2.11 depicts the 'value spectrum' for a business model based on revenue, while Figure A5.5a does so for profits. While conceptually very close to being interchangeable, the two concepts are technically (in accounting terms) not equivalent. The two perspectives join when transfer-IN/OUT—the value chain perspective—is matched against revenue/profits—the financial statement perspective—in the operationalization of sustainable value creation (SVC) measurements (VCp/VCr). When addressing economic development—in disquisitions about institutional change, power, or elite quality—this work favors the term 'residual income' over 'profits'.

	Revenue (Revenue adjusted, R')*	**Profits** (Residual income, RI)*
Transfer-IN	(1) **Value Creation Position VCp(revenue)** = [revenue – transfer-IN(revenue)] / revenue. Equation (4.1a) $VCp_t^{R'} = \frac{R_t' - Vt_t^{R'\,in}}{R_t'}$	(2) **Value Creation Position VCp(profits)** = [profits – value transfer-IN(profits)] / profits. Equation (4.1b) $VCp_t^{RI} = \frac{RI_t - Vt_t^{RI\,in}}{RI_t}$

- VCp calculations require: value transfer-IN; revenue or profits.
- Transfer-IN amount is calculated from component metrics, the conceptually indivisible, discrete data sources that represent firm-level quantifiable value and risk transfers.
- Graphical representation of the VCp measurement referencing relevant concepts and figures:

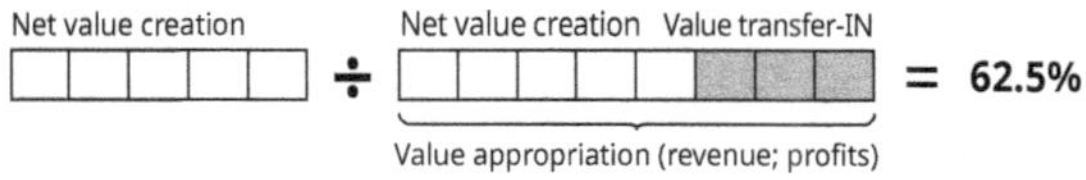

- The VCp measurement is provided as a percentage (with one decimal point).
- A score of 100% indicates that a firm's revenue/profits are entirely attributable to first-order value creation; a score of 0% indicates that these are entirely attributable to second-order extractive value transfers (transfer-IN).

Transfer-IN & Transfer-OUT	(3) **Value Creation Rating VCr(revenue)** = [revenue – value transfer-IN(revenue) + value transfer-OUT(revenue)] / revenue. Equation (4.2a) $VCr_t^{R'} = \frac{R_t' - Vt_t^{R'in} + Vt_t^{R'out}}{R_t'}$	(4) **Value Creation Rating VCr(profits)** = [profits – value transfer-IN(profits) + value transfer-OUT(profits)] / profits. Equation (4.2b) $VCr_t^{RI} = \frac{RI_t - Vt_t^{RI\,in} + Vt_t^{RI\,out}}{RI_t}$

- VCr calculations require: value transfer-IN; value transfer-OUT; revenue or profits.
- Transfer-IN and transfer-OUT amounts are calculated from component metrics, the conceptually indivisible, discrete data sources that represent firm-level quantifiable value and risk transfers.
- Graphical representation of the VCr measurement referencing relevant concepts and figures:

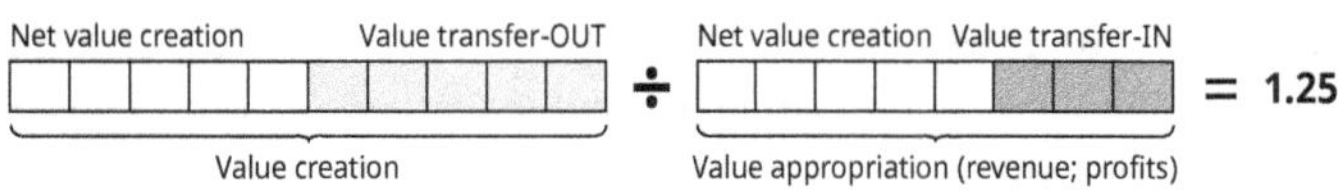

- The VCr is provided as a score, its first digit (mostly zero or one) is followed by two decimal points.
- A score of 1.00 indicates that a firm's overall value creation and value appropriation (revenue/profits) are equal and in balance; a score over/below 1.00 indicates that a firm has a net positive/negative relationship with its stakeholders and society at large, with inclusive second-order value transfers (transfer-OUT) higher/lower than extractive second-order value transfers (transfer-IN).

* Note: In the text notation of the equations the financial statement perspective is used for 'revenue' and 'profits'; in the mathematical notion of the equations the value creation perspective is used, respectively 'revenue adjusted' (R') and 'residual income' (RI).

Figure 2.12: Sustainable value creation measurements: An overview of the VCp and the VCr.

Summary of Chapter 2

Towards a value creation and appropriation logic for elite business models

Chapter 2 establishes sustainable value creation in the overall architecture of this work as the micro-level foundation for the macro-level economic theorizing of subsequent chapters. The elite business model is made the locus of elite agency in seven related propositions (Propositions 5–11), developed over three sections. The chapter begins with Section 2.1 on the behavioral logic of elites.

Proposition 5, 'Elite behavior maximizes utility and is potentially sustainable' (2.1.1), uses neoclassical assumptions of rationality for elite behavior to posit an income maximization 'elite utility function' driven by the optimization of short-term income flows and long-term wealth stocks. This position situates the sustainability perspective of this book. Elite agency, conceived on RCT tenets, is consistent with Olson's (1993, 2000) stationary bandit, for whom the pursuit of wealth is best served by a long horizon. Proposition 6, 'Elite identity is driven by residual income' (2.1.2), tests and reinforces the utilitarian perspective by claiming that elite identity, while evolutionary and often obfuscated by the meta-level of narratives, is always about status-enabling residual income. As the utility function requires that elites appropriate value, it introduces two of the most critical elements of this work: extractive 'value transfer-IN' ('value appropriated but *not* created'), and its counterpart, inclusive 'value transfer-OUT' ('value created but *not* appropriated').

The logic of the elite business model informs the three propositions in Section 2.2. First, Proposition 7, 'The elite business model is the locus of elite agency' (2.2.1), examines the mechanism of residual income maximization that is central to elite agency. Elite business model leadership is posited to support this objective of elite agency by joining and converting the different power types into revenue and profits (see Figure 2.1). Then, by employing the bargaining power concept as an analytical cornerstone, Proposition 8, 'The elite business model is characterized by principal-stakeholder bargaining power differentials required for value appropriation' (2.2.2), begins with a review of the wide range of ideas on value from Smith (1776/1904) to Marx (1867/1959b) and concludes by suggesting that value is everything that humans deem worth appropriating, while its creation is a collective process by principals and stakeholders. Consistent with the previous notion of 'the extraordinary lever', the business model is then characterized vis-à-vis its stakeholders by the bargaining power differentials required for value appropriation. The sources of power enabling the value appropriation of business models are 'knowledge' and 'political economy know-how' (see Figure 2.3), and their respective proportions not only typify a given business model but also impact economic development. This understanding leads to 'the Amazon dilemma' of the political economy, which consists of the hypothesized 'elite vs non-elite knowledge gap' and the 'elite power vs value creation gap'. In Proposition 9, 'Value creation-appropriation (VCA) is proposed as the analytical framework best suited to understand elite business models' division of value strategies' (2.2.3). The strategic management perspective and principal-stakeholder prices and costs (within the opportunity cost to willingness to pay corridor) in the vertical chain of value (see Figure 2.6) become a primary analytical device of this work. Various sets of equations are then presented as a preliminary step to operationalize sustainable value creation. Both Propositions 8 and 9 lay the foundations for the subsequent links made between prices, power, profits, leadership, and ethics (see Sections 7.2, 8.2, and 8.3).

Section 2.3 closes the chapter with two propositions on value creation and value transfers as extraction. Proposition 10, 'Sustainable value creation results from the proportion of first-order productive activities (value creation) relative to second-order transfer activities (value extraction)' (2.3.1), provides a twist as it not only identifies and distinguishes extractive second-order value transfers from first-order productive value creation, but also posits that the former might be necessary at certain critical stages of economic development for value creation to reach scale. The insights are captured by the 'alternating value extraction and creation' conjecture and the somewhat problematic 'extractive push' dilemma that points to value transfers as a precondition for development. Lastly, Proposition 11, 'All elite business models have a measurable value creation position on a 'value spectrum'' (2.3.2), delves into the various concepts developed through the VCA framework—such as 'net value creation', 'value transfer-IN' or 'value transfer-OUT'—configured into equations (see Table 2.4), an important step for the operationalization of the ETED. The Value Creation Position (VCp) and Value Creation Rating (VCr)—equations (4.1) and (4.2) respectively—are presented as two ways of measuring the sustainability of a business model, while the latter will also become the critical input for the SVC adjustments to equity, debt, and firm valuations (see Table 5.2 for an overview of the valuation frameworks and Figure 5.3 for the relationship between SVC measurements and SVC valuation frameworks).

The view espoused is that while the subject of business models falls under the purview of strategic management, the degree of inclusive value creation and the extractive value transfers of micro-level business models transition into and impact the highest levels of the political economy system and hence society at large. Sustainable value creation aggregates, such as elite quality, are advanced as being germane to economic development and growth.

Chapter 3
Towards a logic for the elite system

This chapter completes the development of the ETED system's architecture with nine further propositions organized into three sections, designed to describe the logic under which a national elite system operates. The first set of propositions (3.1) identifies the theoretical perspectives that inform elite agency in the elite system. The second section (3.2) offers a theoretical grounding of the meso-level elite system with its component elite coalitions. In micro-meso-macro complex structures, the meso-level refers to intermediate conceptions (such as regional knowledge clusters, inter-firm industrial organization, and national innovation systems) that are "bigger than micro, but smaller than macro" (Dopfer, Foster, & Potts, 2004, p. 268). In the ETED, the elite system is the key meso building block of the economic system at large (see Figure 3.8). Moreover, it is a transmission mechanism with measurable emergent properties (like elite quality) that connects the micro-level elite business model to aggregate macroeconomic outcomes. The chapter closes (3.3) with a discussion of intra-elite contests, the chief dynamic in the elite system that determines distributional outcomes in the political economy and, consequently, the fate of non-elites and the trajectory of human and economic development.

3.1 Propositions on the theoretical perspectives that inform elite agency

> I go still further. When *plunder* has become a way of life for a group of men living together in society, they create for themselves in the course of time a legal system that authorizes it and a moral code that glorifies it. (Bastiat, 1845/1996, p. 130)

The inquiry changes gear in this section to make explicit the three theoretical perspectives that anchor the ETED to elite agency: new institutional economics (Proposition 12), political economy analysis (Proposition 13), and narrative economics (Proposition 14). The roots planted in the propositions of this section address Bastiat's legal system and moral code and facilitate the theoretical tractability of the ETED in Part II ('Integration') and throughout this work going forward.

https://doi.org/10.1515/9783110734638-005

3.1.1 Proposition 12: Elite agency is the principal microfoundation of institutional change

> Hence, competing institutional logics are not fixed in some structural order but are continuously and flexibly instantiated in the momentary processes by which individuals adjust to any given situation. (Smets, Jarzabkowski, Burke, & Spee, 2015, p. 937)

Olson stressed the importance of "microeconomic incentives" for macroecnomic performance (1984), while North described how institutions are society's "rules of the game" (1990, p. 3, 1991a, p. 98), essentially the constraints and transaction-cost-reducing mechanisms of the economy (1984, 1991). To the ETED, elites are the *de facto* primary transaction-cost-reduction mechanisms of the economy by virtue of employing 'the extraordinary lever' to secure institutional approval for their business models to persevere over time. Institutional change is instantiated by the principals of elite business models who seek licenses to operate and desire that the various stakeholders with whom they interact have their value appropriation behavior (and bargaining power) curtailed by rules when residual income is divided up.[35] In this work, elite agency links up with the notion of individual behavior as the microfoundation of institutions and institutional change (e.g., DiMaggio & Powell, 1991; Powell & Colyvas, 2008) in relation to its practice and behavioral variant (Giddens, 1984; Smets, Jarzabkowski, Burke, & Spee, 2015).

To further place and understand elite agency and the elite system within the context of institutions we draw on Williamson's (2000, pp. 596-597) four levels of social analysis. These are: level 1, "embeddedness" (informal norms); level 2, "institutional environment" (formal rules); level 3, "governance" (playing the game); and level 4, "resource allocation" (prices and quantities). New institutional economics focuses on levels 2 and 3 of this analysis, the space where elite agency also operates. It should be noted that Seo and Creed's solution to the "paradox of embedded agency" (see Section 4.2.3) is facilitated by conceptualizing the "larger whole" as being "composed of multiple, interpenetrating social structures operating at multiple levels" (2002, p. 225).

Figure 3.1 situates elite agency within Williamson's 'Economics of Institutions' framework (as in his original rendition, the solid arrows between levels signify constraints, while the dotted arrows signify feedback). Elite agency is neatly and simplistically separated and rendered as elite coordination and elite business model leadership (see its five types in Table 7.2). It is then first softly bound by tradition or culture—Williamson's "embeddedness" (level 1)—since business models can successfully negotiate

35 Elites seeking institutional change will argue that the alternative, bilateral principal-stakeholder *ad hoc* negotiation, especially under equalized bargaining power, would be prohibitively expensive (and usher forth an array of problems such as a lack of incentives for long-term investments or risk-taking). Conversely, the normative idea of 'equalized bargaining power equilibrium prices', introduced in Section 2.2.2, provides benchmarks and has implications that reverberate through various parts of this work up until the final Section 8.3 and the Epilogue. The introduction of the freedom to *exit* (Figure 8.5) also rebalances bargaining power differentials and qualifies the advocacy of power differentials.

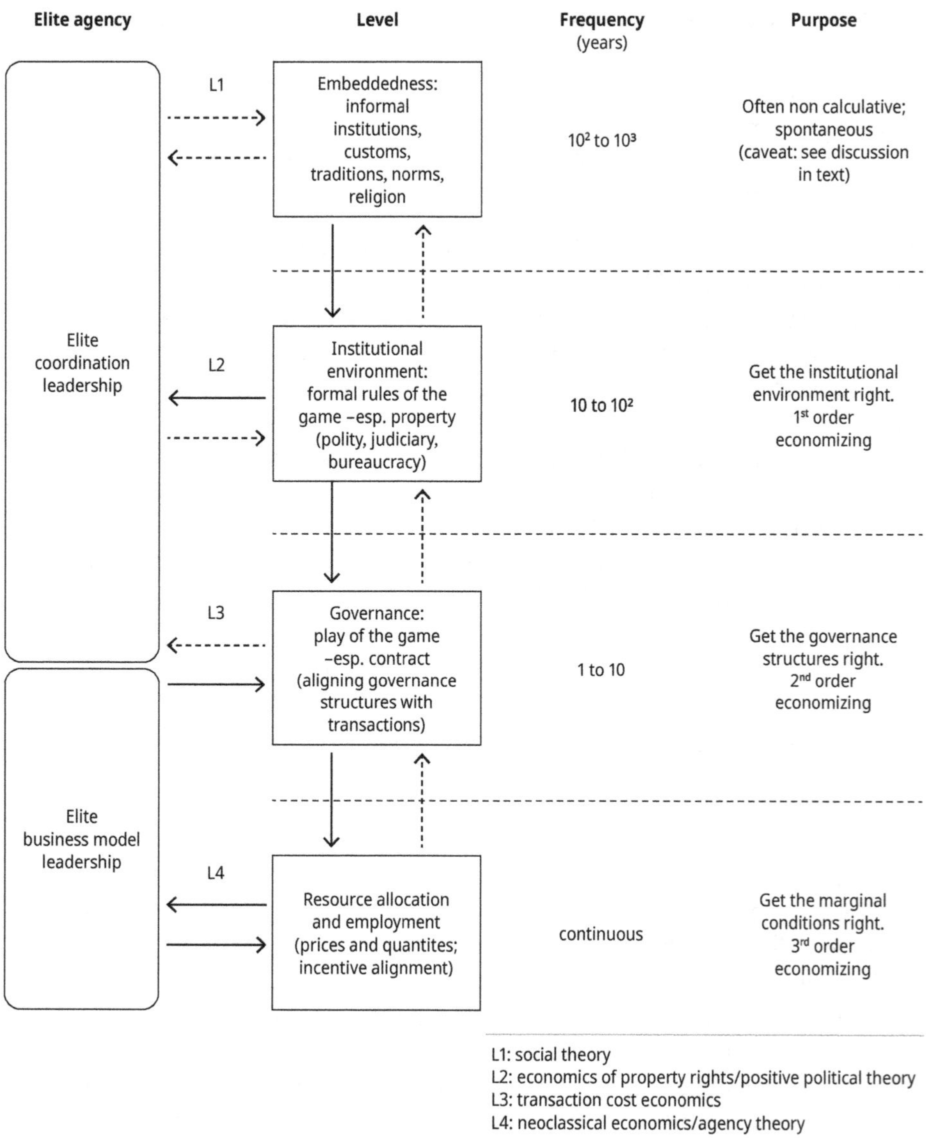

Figure 3.1: The role of elite agency in the 'Economics of Institutions'.[36]

most such limitations, for instance, by managing the narratives that interpret and evolve culture. The individual elite coalition is more strongly constrained by its "institutional environment" (level 2), but, underpinned by its agency, emits powerful feedback on its preferences regarding the fundamental institutional make-up of the country. In

36 Based on and adapted from Figure 1 in Williamson (2000, p. 597).

terms of "governance" (level 3) and the alignment of structure with transactions, elite agency is the more significant force and plays a constraining role. Elite agency in the institutional environment (level 2) relies on coordination capacity to advance specific elite business model rules and intra-elite contest rules (see Figure 4.3 for a typology of institutional change), yet in practice it is more compelling in governance (level 3) as elites "play the game" through business model leadership. As for "resource allocation" (level 4) applicable to the day-to-day running of their business models, elites, through business model leadership, strive to impose their preferences and create interim constraints on stakeholders while at the same time being bound themselves by the business rules implemented by more powerful rival elite coalitions.

Further to the earlier discussion on value appropriation (Propositions 8-11), business model rules enable both value creation and its extraction (i.e., value appropriated but *not* created). Baumol saw value extraction as a problem created by institutions when specific "changes in the rules" allocate entrepreneurial resources that are conducive "to acts of 'unproductive entrepreneurship'" and of "questionable value to society" (1990, pp. 897, 916). Buchanan's analysis of extractive rent seeking deems it "institutional economics in a very real sense" (1980, p. 14). What is at the source of such institutional failures that result in reallocations (transfers) "between productive activities such as innovation and largely unproductive activities such as rent seeking or organized crime" (Baumol, 1990, p. 893)? Olson dwells on "institutional sclerosis" (Olson, 1982; Heckelman, 2007) that he sees as a factor in the "decline of nations". What then are the causes of sclerotic institutions and how do institutional arrangements form that lead to rent seeking? Economists reference the political non-market arena and identify both government interventions and non-interventions with market inefficiencies, externalities, the absence of public goods, or changes to incentives that leave everyone worse off and that have been studied in the context of economic development (e.g., Krueger, 1990). Such (non)interventions are even thematized in textbooks on general economic principles (Mrozek, 1999). What theoretical perspectives best explain the institutional context that permits government action or inaction to occur?

The authors cited in this section convincingly address these questions on the origins of institutional formation and change processes. The explanation this work offers for unproductive entrepreneurship, institutional sclerosis, or sub-optimal government (non)intervention is unequivocal: having positioned elite agency as a precursor in Williamson's institutional framework of economics, it follows that an understanding of value creation and extractive transfers should be based on the elite agency microfoundations of institutional change, as is schematized in Figure 3.2. That is, elite preferences are the main force shaping the rules of the economy, but are also constrained by their function as an incentive in a two-way relationship. Preferences include the absence of rules to incentivize value creation (e.g., de-institutionalized contexts, grey areas, deregulation) as well as an excess of rules that incentivize extractive value transfers (e.g., over-institutionalized contexts, onerous regulation).

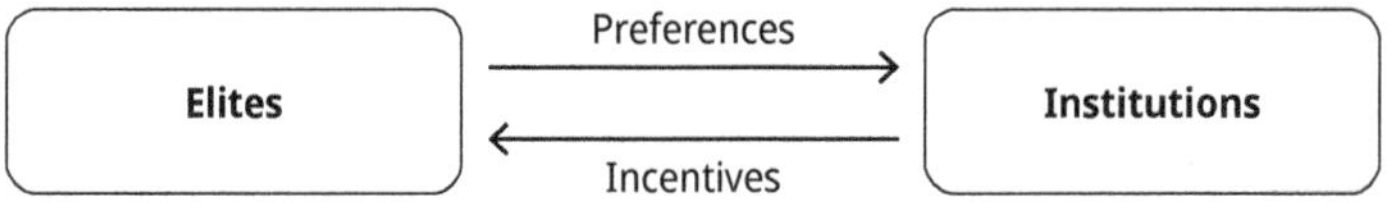

Figure 3.2: The elite agency microfoundations of institutional change model.

A central perspective for this inquiry is new institutionalism, with elite agency explicitly added to the theory to elucidate Arrow's "traditional questions of economics—resource allocation and the degree of utilization" and "new questions, why economic institutions emerged the way they did and not otherwise" (1987, p. 734, as cited in Williamson, 2000, p. 596). In the two-way causal effect relationship between elites and institutions depicted in Figure 3.2, the latter is both determined by *and* emergent from the deliberate agency of the former as it imposes its preferences. Resource allocation and utilization is first and foremost a matter of elite business model preferences incorporated in the incentive system and embodied in institutions. This inquiry also applies the microfoundations of new institutional economics (e.g., Giddens, 1984; DiMaggio & Powell, 1991; Powell & Colyvas, 2008; Smets, Jarzabkowski, Burke, & Spee, 2015) to economic development to posit that elite behavior is the driver of institutional change. North was unambiguous when he claimed that: "formal rules are created to serve the interests of those with the bargaining power to devise new rules" (1990, p. 16). Similarly, Streeck and Thelen's theoretical perspective on "institutions as regimes" has "rule makers" and "rule takers" (2005, p. 13); as posited in Proposition 13, the former are the winning elites and the latter the losers. Other authors also see elite preferences as shaping institutional change (Bourguignon & Verdier, 2010; Acemoglu & Johnson, 2005; Acemoglu & Robinson, 2008; Brezis & Temin, 2007; Robinson, 2010; contributors to Amsden, DiCaprio, & Robinson's *The Role of Elites in Economic Development*, 2014). As will be further discussed (in Section 4.2.2) and consistent with Proposition 7, the locus of elite agency engagement with institutions is the elite business model. Every business model operates on a value position, operationalized by sustainable value creation (SVC) measurements like the VCp or VCr (see the equations in Table 2.4), and so contributes to institutional quality.

Elite wins in all three of the contest arenas of the political economy (furthering bargaining power differentials vs other stakeholders) shape institutions (see Section 4.3 on power and elite agency). In the "visible hand" model of Chandler (1977), "the institutions of competitive capitalism were replaced by large-scale corporate enterprise" (Kirby, 1992, p. 638). While Chandler's powerful corporate visible hand sets the rules of the game, the relationship between specific elites and institutions must always be recognized as a two-way street: elites are also rule takers and subject to institutional constraints once these are formed or changed (as is indicated by the arrows of levels 2 and 4 in Figure 3.1). Of critical importance in the elite theory's calibration of institutional economics is that such rule changes, while formally emanating from institutions, mostly occur due to the agency of rival elites (see Section 3.3). When elites encounter rules that are unfavorable to their business model interests, these are likely to be favorable to competing elites in the elite system. Intra-elite contests renegotiate or settle the outcomes of such situations. These, and the nature, direction, and strength of the relationship between institutions and value creation and transfers are primary concerns of this inquiry.

3.1.2 Proposition 13: Elite agency determines distributional outcomes—the winners and losers in the political economy

Political economy analysis is concerned with the interaction of political and economic processes in society responsible for distributional outcomes; the "central political question" of "who gets what?" (Kelly, 2005, p. 865), or how winners win and losers lose (see a range of literature from Bastiat, 1845/1996, to Alesina & Rodrik, 1994). There is now a call to integrate political economy and institutional perspectives and so, for instance, new institutional economics has been asked "to expand its domain to include a more complete analysis of the causes as well as the consequences of government regulation" with frameworks that introduce "distributional considerations as well as efficiency considerations into the analysis" (Joskow, 1995, p. 256). Alesina and Perotti (1994, p. 351) further state that: "economic policy is the result of political struggle within an institutional structure". Lobbying, initially discussed in Section 1.2.2, is a means to that end (Hall & Deardorff, 2006), while Lowery notes that theories of lobbying "begin with the simplifying assumption that [the] prime purpose is to influence public policy", while also stressing that "interest organizations are motivated actors whose primary purpose is to survive" (2007, p. 29). Successful lobbying (see Brown, 2018; Bhagwati & Srinivasan, 1982) also aims at what economists refer to as "regulatory capture" (Stigler, 1971; Laffont & Tirole, 1991). Since business models must endure, elite agency seeks influence over public policy, regulatory capture and, in the final analysis, institutional change. It can then be argued that theories of the political economy are those that explain the institutional interactions by which elites become winners, i.e., successfully attain and retain their residual income streams.

When discussing elites and their micro-level agency, political economy performance is understood as the successful appropriation (or not) of value (created and not created) that is ultimately materialized as residual income (profits). The value appropriation capability of business models—amply discussed in Chapter 2—produces the winners and losers in the political economy. The centrality of elite business models is consistent with the work of Commons (1950), namely the idea that "the dominant organizational forms of collective action are corporations, labor unions, and political parties" (Elliott, 1978, p. 103). In fact, the list is not limited to just these three groups but is vastly more extensive and contingent on social, cultural, or historical contexts. Dominant organizational forms or coalitions might comprise a certain class of civil servants such as Britain's "treasury-dominated civil service elite obsessed with macroeconomic issues" (Kirby, 1992, p. 637), or artists like the beneficiaries of the Spanish

Society of Authors and Publishers (*Sociedad General de Autores y Editores*, SGAE). These elite coalitions need not dominate society, just the fractal nooks and crannies of the political economy associated with their substantial residual income flows (see Figure E.2); and they need not be particularly narrow, just narrower than their counterparts in the principal-stakeholder relationship. What elites then require are the bargaining power differentials to work out the specific rules of their particular game in order to appropriate value (including value appropriated but *not* created, value transfer-IN) through their business model activities.

What are the concrete institutional benefits sought by elites for their business models in political economy contests? Consistent with Table 2.2, these include licenses to operate financial intermediation (e.g., to fund highly uncertain bets on technology or issue mortgage-backed securities), free trade or trade barriers (e.g., steel tariffs), or the grant of royalties (to protect the value of creative work or transfers). The diversity of these aims determines national development. For instance, the Spanish daily *El Mundo* (2013) reports that SGAE had the audacity, until public pressure forced it to recant, to demand that a local village hand over 10% of the ticket sale receipts from their amateur performance of the beloved play *Fuenteovejuna* written by Lope de Vega in 1610. A germane point here is that institutional change that originally yielded new value creation will eventually result in extractive transfers, as the example below illustrates.

> The Internet Tax Freedom Act (ITFA; P.L. 105-277), enacted in 1998, implemented a three-year moratorium preventing state and local governments from taxing Internet access, or imposing multiple or discriminatory taxes on electronic commerce. [. . .] The original three-year moratorium had been extended eight times before being converted to a permanent statute (though the passage of the Trade Facilitation and Trade Enforcement Act of 2015 (P.L. 114-125)). (Stupak, 2016)

Institutional change driven by elite agency determines which elites and their counterparty stakeholder groups in society win and lose (and to what degree). That is, they establish the institutionally sanctioned terms—the business model rules—for value creation and value appropriation (including transfer-IN/OUT) regimes. Given that institutionally sanctioned elite business models habitually result in winners and losers, the question for development is whether the winners are value creators or value extractors. Ricardo's *On the Principles of Political Economy and Taxation* (1817/1999), eventually contributed to the repeal of the protectionist Corn Laws (1815-1846), resulting in victory for the Manchester industrialists over aristocratic London-based absentee landowners championing trade barriers on grain (a tax on bread). The extractive transfer-IN agricultural landowner business models gave way to the comparatively more inclusive higher value creation models of the industrialists.

In short, all elites strive to advance their preferences (rules supportive of their business models) upon institutions, while institutions in turn provide incentives consistent with specific elite business model preferences. The process by which losing elites are constrained by the very incentives that benefit winning elites is visualized in Figure 3.3. This extension of the elite agency microfoundations of institutional change model (Figure 3.2) emphasizes the role of elite agency, which when positive brings about the desired division of value and political economy distributional outcomes.

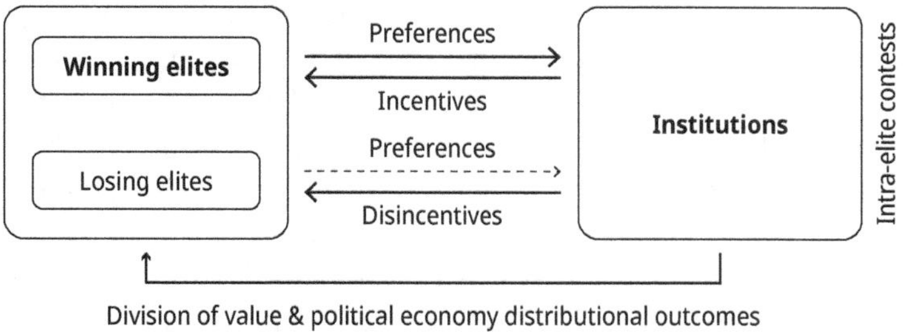

Figure 3.3: Distributional outcomes of the political economy in the elite agency microfoundations of institutional change model.

To end this sub-section on an economic development note, Laffont and Tirole alarmingly demonstrate that elite power increases "when its interest lies in inefficient rather than efficient regulation", inefficiency being "measured by the degree of informational asymmetry between the regulated industry and the political principal" (1991, p. 1089). The economic problem of positive performance at the micro-level and negative performance at the macro-level that this work addresses is brilliantly exhibited below in an article that portrays the perverse logic by which the winners of intra-elite contests in the political non-market arena are so often the losers in value creation terms:

> Governments frequently intervene to support domestic industries, but a surprising amount of this support goes to ailing sectors. We explain this with a lobbying model that allows for entry and sunk costs. Specifically, policy is influenced by pressure groups that incur lobbying expenses to create rents. In expanding industries, entry tends to erode such rents, but in declining industries, sunk costs rule out entry as long as the rents are not too high. This asymmetric appropriability of rents means losers lobby harder. Thus it is not that government policy picks losers, it is that losers pick government policy. (Baldwin & Robert-Nicoud, 2007, p. 1064)

3.1.3 Proposition 14: Elite agency effects institutional change through the political economy's narrative market

> As a public policy, the moratorium on taxing Internet access has economic and fairness implications. The policy likely improves lower income individuals' ability to purchase Internet access, which has economic benefits, but the blanket nature of the moratorium likely results in some economic waste. (Stupak, 2016)

There is a cynical intellectual tradition to conceive of narratives as a product of elite agency that function as a narcotic, fostering non-elite 'acceptance' responses to extractive business models (e.g., Marx, 1844/1959a). For instance, smart and sophisticated narratives are crafted by legal knowledge elites such as those in finance industry coalitions, with Pistor (2019) poignantly explaining in *The Code of Capital* "how the law creates wealth" as well as "inequality". Elites have a commonly unnoticed advantage in the narrative market: their own narratives do not have to occupy their own affective bandwidth; it suffices if they work on the cognitive plane. That is, elites enjoy the privilege of not having to believe in their own narratives and can just focus on how these support the residual income of their business models. Hence, when judging elites by their actions, one will frequently notice how religious leaders don't live by their faith, politicians don't honor their pledges, or corporations don't stick to their mission statements. For non-elites, the connection between narratives and residual incomes is much more tenuous and so their relationship with them is through affect, emotion, and sentiment. The utility function of the elite is aligned with elite identity (Section 2.1.2) and firmly anchored by the business model, and hence can be best represented with RCT tenets (Section 2.1.1). In contrast, non-elites are permanently unclear about where their residual income interests are. This problem is accentuated by the fact that they are at both the long and short-end of multiple and narrow models and narratives (as employees, taxpayers, energy consumers, interest rate payees, and even as direct or indirect participants in wars). Through this dispersion, non-elites are not positioned to discern whether a given narrative provides them with an advantage, thus naturally embracing narratives by their affective qualities at the expense of objective and rational merits that are to them mostly unforeseeable and *de facto* unknowable.

Regardless of whether one concurs with this Olsonian and economic logic (that helps to explain the resilience of non-elite faith and the Marxist opium metaphor), narrative markets are of great consequence in most political economies. They are also the very reason why diverse knowledge elites—with specializations ranging from the law to entertainment—are underscored in this work as one of the three discrete elite types (see Figure 1.2). What then are narratives?

Narratives *per se* are open-ended stories that communicate values, invite participation, and "spark action" (Denning 2006, p. 44); they can go viral and in so doing impact human behavior and economic reality (Shiller, 2017; Hagel, 2011) including the very value of a business (Damodaran, 2017). Of interest here is that many narratives—e.g., the blanket policy not to tax Internet access that "improves lower income individuals' ability to purchase Internet access" (Stupak, 2016), articulated as a "fairness" narrative—are launched in political economy contests to effect division of value strategies and hence the distributional outcomes desired by elite coalitions (see also, Alesina, Cozzi, & Mantovan, 2012). Narratives are essential to any elite theory and are not a construct that has slipped through the empirical grasp. To Abell (2004, p. 287), narrative explanations can be taken as "an alternative to the better established variable-centered explanations".

Moreover, narratives and institutions are not always “clearly distinguishable” (Beckert, 2016, p. 153) which one may posit is due to a property that they have in common with elite agency, namely transaction cost reduction. In fact, no matter how well-endowed institutions are—think of the US dollar or China’s Belt and Road Initiative (BRI)—all need to be sheathed in a winning narrative to be sustainable (Casas-Klett & Li, 2021). Narratives have “the power of pull” (Hagel, Brown, & Davison, 2010) and capture affective and cognitive bandwidth, which addresses the collective action dilemma by overcoming individual interests and allowing forms of cooperation that make everybody better off (Shiller, 2017; Casas-Klett & Buckup, 2018). Narrative markets have such an impact that when Yuval Noah Harari makes the claim “that AI has hacked the operating system of human civilization” it follows that “storytelling computers will change the course of human history” (*The Economist*, 2023a). Narrative pull is what Donaldson (2021, p. 5) terms “practical inference”; narratives ultimately package ideas and “Ideas make for actions. Ideas serve both as motivators and justifications for action”.

Narratives compete against each other for the contested power of ‘mind’ (see Figure 1.2). Winning power in society’s narrative market arena is a strategic objective for elite agency since it facilitates the desired institutional change. Moreover, wins for the power type of ‘mind’ enable intra-elite alignment in the context of a given coalition (e.g., renewable energy entrepreneurs with venture capitalists, legislators, or scientists). Narratives conjure the full coordination capacity of shared “sensemaking” thus tightening the “loose [. . .] correspondence between concepts and observables” (Gergen, 1986, as cited in Weick, 1989, p. 519) and as such, they are a device for both intra-elite and elite/non-elite cohesion. Critically, however, when viewed through the analytical lens of this inquiry, narratives can be a device for extraction, as is the case when the “fairness” supposedly intrinsic to the Internet Tax Freedom Act “likely results in some economic waste” (Stupak, 2016), distorting income flows in favor of elites whose models stand to benefit from tax privileges. Because of their coordination effect, narratives, the primary products of knowledge elites, “set changes and transformations in motion that have impacts on the big picture” (Boje, 2008, p. 13); for the ETED, they do so by first granting and then confirming the licenses to operate elite business models in society.[37]

Narratives are dynamic and evolve. As an instrumental power type, they are subject to lifecycles, and are especially relevant in times of disruption “when environmental contexts change in a way that leaves actors without an ontologically complicit

37 In fact, to some philosophers, ‘the big picture’ means that narratives influence—or are even—the totality of “reality”, as in Bruner’s claims that “narrative organizes the structure of human experience” (1991, p. 21), or in the Foucauldian hypothesis: “that in every society the production of discourse is at once controlled, selected, organised and redistributed by a certain number of procedures whose role is to ward off its powers and dangers, to gain mastery over its chance events, to evade its ponderous, formidable materiality” (Foucault, 1981).

relationship to institutions as scaffolds of action" (Strand & Lizardo, 2017, p. 164). Just as there is no institutional determinism (Seo & Creed, 2002), there is no narrative determinism. Narratives constantly need refreshing and adjusting to both social and business model realities. It is not old narratives, but the "practical belief" contained in new narratives that will "orient action in an effective way because it is formed in relation to objective probabilities" (Strand & Lizardo, 2017, p. 188). Purchasing behavior is one such action and so firms invest in their brands with particular, contained narratives that give their owners or handlers bargaining power, notably in the form of pricing.

Linking an organization with winning narratives is a unique strategic management capability that is consistent with Lyotard's (1979) *petits récits*—"localized" narratives—in this case those focused on a particular business model. Leading corporations have associated themselves with or adopted the Black Lives Matter (BLM) narrative, a trail blazed by Nike with its 'Dream Crazy' spot featuring NFL quarterback Colin Kaepernick for the 30th anniversary of its 'Just Do It' campaign (Buckup & Casas-Klett, 2018). Narratives are created, captured, refined, and maintained through the agency of highly specialized knowledge elites within business models that strive for advantage in the political economy. The fate of individual narratives is highly uncertain and dynamic, as the rise of BLM or Bitcoin from marginal to mainstream illustrates. Some narratives may triumph in arenas material to elites and thus garner substantial impact while remaining marginal to the public discourse (e.g., TESCREAL narratives[38]). A majority of narratives remain stillborn, while others go viral (Shiller, 2017), sometimes unexpectedly, to then either suddenly collapse (e.g., FTX in November, 2022) or evolve to score continued wins in narrative markets sometimes for centuries (e.g., religious sects that go on to become established faiths). Narratives form in the spaces of knowledge elites that are specific to each society: academia, religion, publishing, traditional and new media, film and TV production, the justice and legal systems, art and literature, conferences and events, or on digital platforms where influencers and key opinion leaders ply their trade.

Like narrative market outcomes, their capture by business models is often unintended (e.g., Buddhism becoming an establishment religion in East Asia rather than South Asia) to the point of disappointment (e.g., Bitcoin becoming a significant means of payment for illicit activities in Darknets[39]), especially for the knowledge elites that

---

38 TESCREAL is an acronym for transhumanism, extropianism, singularitarianism, cosmism, rationalism, effective altruism, and longtermism, with some claiming that these narratives have "become immensely influential in the world today—especially in Silicon Valley", with Musk, Thiel, Page, Andreessen, or Altman taking action and making investments that fit its precepts, meaning that "one cannot make sense of the AGI race without some understanding of this bundle" (Torres, 2023).

39 Europol articulates the gap between a narrative and its actual application. Darknets, the networks, their tools, and crypto forms of payment "are designed and intended to protect users from traffic analysis, which 'threatens personal freedom and privacy, confidential business activities and relation-

created the narratives in the first place. Equally disappointing to their creators are narratives that are adopted as mechanisms to preempt the institutional changes they advocate from being implemented. This is precisely what is happening in the case of the United Nations' (UN) Sustainable Development Goals (SDGs) as evidenced by more than 3,000 published scientific studies:

> Our findings suggest that the goals have had some political impact on institutions and policies, from local to global governance. This impact has been largely discursive, affecting the way actors understand and communicate about sustainable development. More profound normative and institutional impact, from legislative action to changing resource allocation, remains rare. We conclude that the scientific evidence suggests only limited transformative political impact of the Sustainable Development Goals thus far. (Biermann et al., 2022, p. 795)

However, not all narratives are captured part way through their lifecycles, domesticated[40], and then put into the discursive service of business models.

Some 'localized' narratives are born with highly intentional aims and the product of a specific elite coalition that consistently nurtures their growth (e.g., the modern Olympic Games). Narratives hatched on a grand scale by core elite coalitions, such as post-World War II liberal democracy, resulted in massive political economy reforms. Once this narrative became viral and spread across the globe, its associated institutions supported an array of specific elite business models and brought about unprecedented new value creation. After the extractive catastrophes of the first half of the 20th century, this narrative champion—a *de facto* sophisticated concerted bet on value creation—was further buttressed by diverse elite coalitions with contributors coming from all three types of elites: business, political, and knowledge. Narratives endure in the 'mind' (and heart). Nonetheless, what really matters is their relationship with the hard reality of value appropriation. Meanwhile, some narratives, like the unintelligible Q-Anon, also go viral, and while their original purpose remains opaque, it is hard to see how they will result in anything other than value extraction. Wins of the power type of 'mind' are unceasingly converted into residual income whether the narratives are initiated or later captured by business models. A well-forged narrative provides cover for elites across every conceivable nook and cranny of the economy, in every single market niche:

---

ships, and state security' (Tor, https://torproject.org/), they are also used by criminals operating online to protect their own freedom—by frustrating law enforcement attempts to identify and arrest them". See: https://www.europol.europa.eu/iocta/2016/darknets.html

40 The process of domesticating narratives can include the culling of its primary components. One might assert that this is what transpired when Archbishop Athanasius of Alexandria proclaimed the four Christian canonical Gospels in the year of 367, as he "sent an order to purge all 'apocryphal books' with 'heretical' tendencies", the vast corpus of Gnostic and other texts (see Pagels, 1979, p. 120). More recently, in *Elite Capture* (2022), Olúfẹ́mi Táíwò discusses the take-over of identity narratives ("and everything else") by "the powerful".

> This "consumer welfare" theory of antitrust was the poison dart that plunged trustbusting into a 40-year coma. Bork and his cronies at the University of Chicago School of Economics – the cradle of neoliberalism – set up a sweet side-hustle, building complex mathematical models that only they understood.
>
> These models were used to prove that every monopoly was untouchable under consumer welfare enforcement standards – even if a company bought all its competitors and then increased prices 1,000% (as Luxottica-Essilor did for eyeglasses, after buying nearly every eyeglass brand, retailer, insurer and lens-maker), it was still untouchable. (Doctorow, 2022)

The "influence on doctrine, policy debate in the United States" of Robert Bork's narrative in *The Antitrust Paradox* (1978) "is unequalled. No scholar has left such a durable imprint on the U.S. antitrust system" (Kovacic, 2014, p. 855). In short, incumbent or emerging elite business models pursue a variety of narrative strategies to attain the power over 'mind'. These include starting-up and cultivating a specific narrative (e.g., Tesla's high end electric vehicles combat climate change), or piggybacking on it as it grows (e.g., Daimler or Ford signing the COP26 pledge to sell only zero-emissions vehicles by 2040). Strategic management also entails discarding narratives at their peak or as they become tarnished (e.g., investors disposing of "algorithmic stablecoins" after the TerraUSD sell-off in May, 2022). While they hold claim on cognitive and affective bandwidth, narratives are used for desired institutional change. The success of legal scholar Robert Bork's "consumer welfare" narrative is evident from its positive transition into legal doctrine to defang anti-trust legislation, the value appropriation services it provides to countless elite business models such as Luxottica-Essilor, and the all-out defense of the narrative by its beneficiaries against reforms such as those proposed by Lina Khan, President Biden's Chair of the Federal Trade Commission (FTC).[41]

The narrative market, like the two other political economy arenas, might be conceptualized as a mediator—and an especially effective one—of the relationship between elites and institutions. The strength of the mediation role of narratives is due in part to the intra-elite and elite/non-elite cohesion effect they possess. To the theoretical architecture of the ETED, it is important that the narrativized preferences embodied in winning narratives shape the rules that determine the winners (and losers) in political economies. Frequently, the narrative market is the defining arena in intra-elite business model contests. A case in point is found in the complex political economy of Indonesia: "elite competition turned to religious and then to ethnic identity politics when district executives encountered both the enrichment possibilities of decentralizing governance and the risks of newly competitive, more democratic, elections" (Aragon, 2007, p. 39). To the earlier discussion of Ricardo's free trade narrative (1817/1999) in support of modern industrial elite coalitions, we can add Mokyr and

41 See: https://instituteforlegalreform.com/blog/robert-h-bork-jr-joe-bidens-antitrust-paradox-wheres-the-consumer-welfare/

Nye's (2007, p. 50) insight in attributing the transformation of the terms of the debate around the political economy to the Scottish enlightenment's ideological changes, "so that gainers from industrialization could compensate or overcome traditional interests". Gramsci's theory of cultural hegemony, articulated in his *Prison Notebooks*, specifically places narratives at the center of society and links them to elite agency:

> The basic premise of the theory of hegemony is one with which few would disagree: that man is not ruled by force alone, but also by ideas. "The foundation of a ruling class" he wrote "is equivalent to the creation of a *Weltanschauung.*" (Gramsci, 1948/1966, p. 75, as cited in Bates, 1975, p. 351)

Whether termed "the ideologies and belief systems [that] underlie the choices humans make" (North, 1994, p. 363), or the "neo-Marxist variation of the upper-class thesis" that Lerner, Nagai and Rothman (1996, p. 2) and others (see Bieler & Morton, 2004) label "neo-Gramscian", social order is not maintained through hard power alone: "class rule exists because the cultural, political, ethical, and intellectual elite articulates a worldview that everyone, ruling and ruled, comes to uphold". The notion that "culture has been captured", as Giblin and Doctorow contentiously assert (2022, p. 2), should therefore come as no surprise. Social order, or in more farfetched versions a "world order" (Cox, 1983), is invariably constituted of the winning narrativized preferences of specific elites and their business models. Alesina, Cozzi, and Mantovan specifically show how "beliefs about fairness"—here taken to become functional as narrativized preferences (e.g., for redistributive policies)—"can keep two otherwise identical countries on different development paths for a very long time" and hence affect growth (2012, p. 1244). Wins in the narrative market explain a key mechanism that underpins the relationship between elites and institutional change. Figure 3.4 illustrates the function of the narrative market as a mediator between elites and institutions.

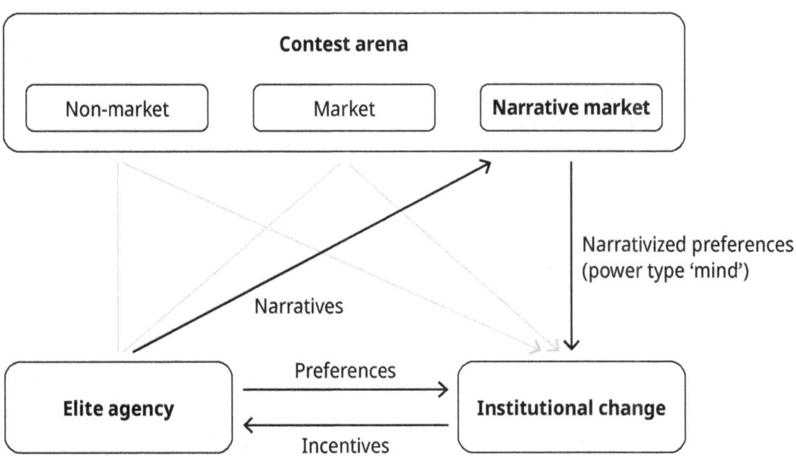

Figure 3.4: The narrative market as a mediator in the elite agency microfoundations of institutional change model.

As implied by the discussion above, narratives are enormously challenging to manage. As outcomes of complex adaptive systems, their emergence, power-law distributions, virality, and trajectory are unpredictable, curious, and often paradoxical, thriving in reversal and surprise. And yet the narrative market supplies elites with potentially stable, highly effective, and low-cost bargaining power endowments, and as a result hosts some of the most sophisticated, persistent, and high impact intra-elite contests. These include the contests that determine the core elite coalition and its role in a political economy (see Figure 8.1, Section 8.1.2). All elite coalitions will strategically select and develop, co-opt, domesticate, handle, and nourish narratives from the non-elite public domain as they seek to use them to align institutional change with their business model preferences. At times it is hard to tell whether narratives are being repurposed by elite agency (and by which coalition) or have escaped their purview, genuinely taking on a life of their own. A narrative's journey might also start with a specific application in an intra-elite contest, only to reappear later in the service of unrelated business models. An example of the travails of one such resilient narrative—seemingly operating on its own terms—is the *Magna Carta Libertatum*.

The first version of the Magna Carta dates from 1215, a narrative that resolved the intra-elite power struggle between two competing elite business models: the model of the King of England and the model of the barons (a dispute that revolved around payments to the Crown). Centuries later, the Magna Carta narrative had evolved to support very different kinds of interests. An emergent elite coalition, the American colonists, used it "no longer as an anti-royal instrument so much as a check upon the powers of an over-mighty parliament" (Vincent, 2018, p. 36), a struggle that led directly to the 1776 *United States Declaration of Independence*. American liberation meant the establishment of institutions more advantageous to the business models of local elites. Further down the line, there are even "echoes" of some of the clauses from the Magna Carta in the 1948 *United Nations Universal Declaration of Human Rights* (Vincent, 2018, p. 32). It might even be argued that the Magna Carta narrative, now broadly repositioned in terms of human rights and liberty, has at last freed itself from its instrumental role in supporting specific elite business models.

Interestingly, narratives can also be a unique avenue for non-elites to effect institutional change, on the condition that elites support and incorporate non-elite narrativized preferences into their business models. Google and Nike are just two of the elite business models that have associated their brands not only with BLM in general, but also with its non-elite narrative of social justice, ostensibly in a win-win fashion. Rules and policies on business models that impact the appropriation of value creation by non-elites like college loan guarantees, wars, or universal healthcare are regularly updated by political elites and often occur on the back of non-elite narratives (whether and to what extent they ultimately realize the diverse interests of non-elites in value creation terms is a separate matter). A common tension in such alignments is the betrayal felt by non-elites when they ally with elites that then dilute or even reverse their original narratives, as when "ex-Google workers sue company, saying it betrayed 'Don't Be Evil' motto" (Allyn, 2021). More dramatically, from the non-elite standpoint (a perspective further advanced in Chapter 8) the wrong battles are won when victories elevate elites that then devise business models that conflict with the value creation interests extolled by the narratives that forged the original alliances and grounded elite/non-elite cohesion. For instance, religious and secular values, ethics, ideologies, and philosophies emerge and gain traction as a non-elite reaction to value extraction and, once preeminent, are taken up by elites to legitimize both inclusive and extractive institutions. Expensive theocracies and value transfer models run by extractive priestly castes represent a reversal of non-elite narrativized preferences. Many of the non-elites that helped bring the Chavez-Maduro regime to power in Venezuela assert the same thing. A further twist occurs when non-elites support narratives that clearly disadvantage them, as many would claim is the case with key elements of the Trump Administration's original MAGA policy package, such as the "sabotage" (Thompson, 2020) of the Affordable Care Act of 2010 (Obamacare). Non-elite narrative confusion over where their real interests and narrative preferences ought to lie is facilitated by elite/non-elite knowledge asymmetries. This brings about business models that see non-elites happily being extracted on the back of narratives, as is evident in debates on trade, monetary policy, or immigration. While Pareto does not address narratives directly, he provides keen observations on the messiness of their journeys and reversals after originally emerging to serve non-elites:

> From the day when Jesus preached love and peace in Galilee to the day when warlike prelates donned armor over their stoles and went out to kill in the name of the divine master, a good many centuries have gone by. But only a few years passed between the day on which the German Marx announced the glad tidings to the proletariat and the day on which some German socialists substituted for the motto: Proletarians Unite, the motto: Proletarians Kill Each Other. (Pareto, 1968/1991, p. 55)

Despite these treacherous waters, the narrative market, as described in Figure 3.5 below, is where non-elite interests can most readily gain ascendancy and impact the narrative preferences of elites to effect inclusive institutional change. This route can be used strategically—though it is usually not—to nudge elites towards transformation and sustainable value creation (i.e., better VCp/VCr scores) in high-impact business models where broad swathes of non-elites are major stakeholders. Later in this inquiry, a more explicit non-market role within the elite theory's system is outlined for non-elites to advance more inclusive political economies, for instance, via active non-elite participation in intra-elite contests (see the political options for non-elites to advance their interests in the context of the elite/non-elite relationship in Figure 8.2).

In the reviewed literature, the link between narratives and elites is emphasized and richly formulated. From Gramsci's (1948/1966; see also Hoare & Nowell Smith, 1999) macro-level theory of hegemony and "political ideologies as means of getting

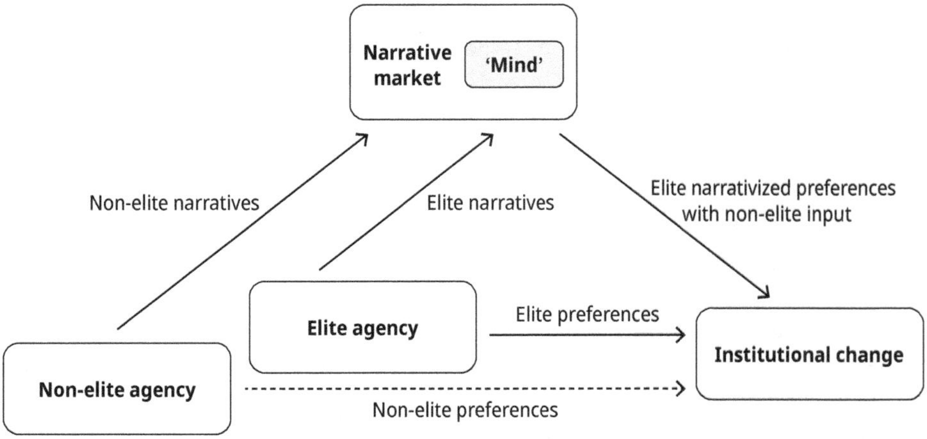

Figure 3.5: The narrative market as a mediator in the institutional change model incorporating non-elite narratives.

votes" (Downs, 1957, p. 96) to Zingales (2017, p. 115) "'political theory' of the firm", where two out of the six "nonmarket factors" relate to narratives, i.e., the media market and the dominant ideology. The fact of the matter is that the narrative market arena, despite the abstraction levels of some narratives, yields very tangible opportunities for practical institutional change and transformational leadership. Again, narratives can be effective tools even for elite coalitions active in the most recondite of niches. For example, not three days had elapsed since the coup d'état against the State Counsellor of Myanmar, Aung San Suu Kyi, in February 2021, before Spanish rice farmers lobbied Brussels—utilizing the human rights narrative—for the annulment of trade agreements with Myanmar to benefit their interests (Vigario, 2021). Any analysis of the distributional outcomes in the political economy requires a theoretical prime of place for narratives.

As notions and theories of narratives (Abell, 2004; Denning, 2006; Hagel, 2011) enter economics and are enriched by the behavioral sciences (Shiller, 2017), the linkages to elite agency are likely to be further explored and modeled. Without the coordination capacity and the power over 'mind' (understood as a piece of the cognitive and affective bandwidth of others) that narratives afford, knowledge elites would be relegated by 'might' (political elites) and 'money' (business elites) to the sidelines of the political economy. A precise understanding of the role of narratives in the political economy's distributional contests; how they emerge and evolve, how they can be quantified, how elite business models narrativize preferences, how narrativized preferences impact institutional change and motivate leadership, and how novel AI-concocted narratives influence the narrative market (again, see Harari in *The Economist*, 2023a) must all be part and parcel of a comprehensive theory on the subject of elites.

3.2 Propositions on the national elite system

Elite agency is the force that fuses economics and sociology together, defying the lack of a unified social science. According to Fukuyama (2016, p. 208), this absence is due to a post-modernist impossibility of general theory and to the exaggeratedly positivistic and theoretical nature of economics. This situation is galling, as Parsons, the leading pundit on Weber, aimed for economics to be "conceived as standing within some sort of theoretical matrix in which sociological theory also was included" (1970, p. 828). His book, *The Social System* (1951/1991), provides an integrated, interdisciplinary social science that combines economics, sociology, political science, as well as the family. Should a theory of economic development that potentially affects the welfare of all participants in society not also aim for such integration? The next three propositions move this inquiry in the direction of such a general theory and introduce a systems perspective. The first applies systems theory to the elite system and elite coalitions (Proposition 15). The next develops the key integrative property of the elite system, the Three-tier Set of Intra-elite Checks and Balances (Proposition 16). Finally, the elite system is situated squarely at the meso-level of the political economy (Proposition 17).

3.2.1 Proposition 15: Elite coalitions are the constitutive elements of national elite systems

Aristotle's notion (1912, 5.8) that "the whole and all the parts together are large, though made up of small parts", grounded Von Bertalanffy's (1972, p. 407) general systems theory, where a system is a cohesive aggregate of interdependent components possessing emergent behaviors. This proposition postulates the existence of a cohesive elite system as a component of every single political economy, the interdependent, constitutive components of which are elite coalitions characterized by their elite business models.

The "scientific exploration of 'wholes' and 'wholeness'" (Von Bertalanffy, 1972, p. 415) can be applied to the study of elites as components in a system, an understanding that fits with the positions of Parsons (1951/1991), Simon (1962) or Hayek (1964/1967). The system's component elite coalitions should in turn also be understood as a system, albeit a sub-system of the whole. Earlier, this work reviewed Mills' (1956) "power elite", Domhoff's (1967, 1970) "governing class", Jenkins-Smith and Sabatier's (1993) work on advocacy coalitions, and Sklair's (2012) "transnational capitalist class" (TCC), all of which portray how various elite types and actors complement each other, jointly functioning like a system. Zingales (2017, p. 114) pinpoints the systemic nature of elite coalitions with a historical metaphor; the "Medici vicious circle", where "economic and political power reinforce each other" (to which this theory adds knowledge elites, see Figure 1.2). Applying systems theory to elite agency means, for instance, that analysis of the Princely House of Thurn und Taxis elite coalition and its courier business model is not viable without considering the Hapsburg political economy system and its imperial narrative. Hall and Deardorff's theory of lobbying is also consistent with the idea of coalitions as sub-systems since the objective "is not to change legislators' minds but to assist natural allies in achieving their own, coincident objectives" (2006, p. 69).

In every coalition, 'interdependent' member elites coalesce around a preferred business model. Amazon would not be possible without the support of knowledge elites behind the 'fair', tax-free Internet access narrative, political elites like US lawmakers, and business elites on Wall Street. In turn, at the national elite system level, the different elite coalitions and their business models 'reinforce each other' as sub-systems of a larger whole irrespective of their varying degrees of elite cohesion or "horizontal integration" (see Best, 2018a). In times of international crises, American elite coalitions and their separate business models—e.g., the US military-industrial complex, Big Tech, The White House Office of Science and Technology Policy (OSTP), the foreign policy establishment's knowledge elites at The Council on Foreign Relations (CFR), or Princeton's Woodrow Wilson School of Public and International Affairs—cohere in an unmatched fashion.

In essence, the analysis of elite agency is strengthened by systems theory applied at two levels: the elite system, and the elite coalition (see Figure 3.8). The higher of these (at the meso-level, see Proposition 17) is the national elite system (technically also a sub-system of the political economy system) whose component parts are elite coalitions (at the micro-level). Elite coalitions are hence systems too (technically sub-systems of the national elite system) that bind together diverse individual elite members, each proficient at winning intra-elite contests in their respective political economy areas for their elite business model. The operation of the elite coalition business model must be considered as a whole, even when the constituent elites may run their own independent residual income generating concerns that can be analyzed separately (in the previous example, Amazon, the 'fair access' narrative, academic and media elites, legislators, the investment banks and, of course, Jeff Bezos).

Different types of elites within the coalitions in the elite system have been variously theorized about and empirically identified in the literature: economic, political, financial, legal, intellectual, intelligence, military, civic, media, artistic, etc. Elite research in political science, reviewed in Section 1.2.2, concentrates on their differences, finding for instance "that the political elite were different from other elite groups" (Blondel & Müller-Rommel, 2007). This work proposes that the at times dazzling repertoire of elite types identified across time and space (from military and religious to banking and corporate) be simplified and conceptually typified based on the three arenas in which elites carry out their principal contests. To recap, this suggested tripartite elite typology of the ETED (see Figures 1.2 and 2.1) is comprised of business elites (the winners of contests for the power of 'money' in the market arena of the economy), political elites (the winners of contests for the power of 'might' in the nonmarket arena of politics), and knowledge elites (the winners of contests for the power of 'mind' in the narrative market arena of society). Elite coalition business models integrate these three elite types and combine their respective wins and the power this affords through elite coordination leadership (see Figures 1.2, 4.1, or 4.4). Elite business model leadership of the coalition then converts this power via division of value strategies into residual income for its diverse members (see Figures 2.1, 4.1, or 4.4).

Pareto's (1968/1991) hierarchy of elites distinguished between the governing and non-governing elite by political power. In the ETED, the elite hierarchy is the result of two leadership types. Elite business model leadership is exercised—sub-system by sub-system—at the elite coalition level. Elite system leadership (discussed in Section 7.2.4) is exercised by the 'core elite coalition' (see Section 8.1.2; Figure 8.1, the socio-economic structure pyramid) at the elite system level. Their concerns include setting the rules for intra-elite contests, national development, and gaining advantage over foreign elites (see Table 7.2 on the varieties of leadership). Elite system leadership of the core elite coalition, what Sebudubudu and Molutsi (2011) call "grand coalition" in their study of Botswana, institutionalizes intra-elite contests. Elite business model leadership, on the other hand, is a key focus of this section and primarily concerned with generating and maintaining residual income flows and influencing institutional change relevant to the coalition's business model. As such, the leadership exercised by the many independent coalitions around their models is the fundamental organizing dynamic in national elite systems and figures prominently in the conceptualization of the elite coalition shown in Figure 3.6.

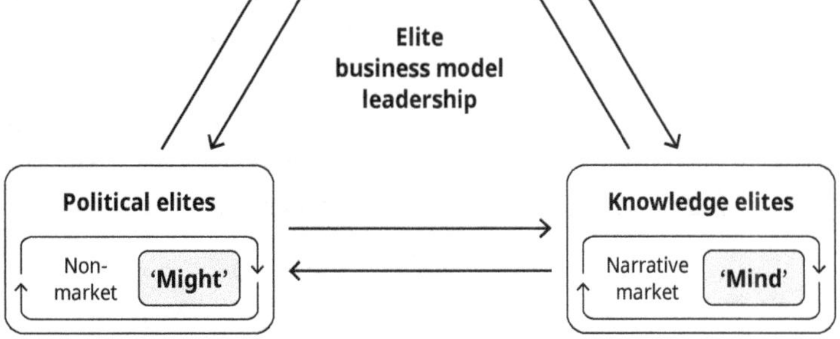

Figure 3.6: The elite coalition as a sub-system of the elite system held together by elite business model leadership.

Consistent with the systems approach, Figure 3.6 shows that members of all three elite types participate in elite coalitions, sub-systems in the elite system that are held together by the gravitational force of elite business model leadership. Note that the principal of an elite business model is seldom a single firm but a collection of interdependent organizations benefiting from the model's power differentials, each receiving their own discrete residual income flows (and not suffering from degrees of extraction in the way that non-beneficiary stakeholders might). The foremost beneficiaries of elite business models within the coalition (i.e., those who appropriate the largest shares of residual income) are usually those that supply the highest coordination capacity and then apply it to manage the conversion of power into residual income. The members of the coalition that do not lead the elite business model still have their own activities embedded within it and are beneficiaries, taking a share of the residual income derived from value appropriation (including income derived from transfer-IN activities). The ancillary models of coalition members might include high-end service providers such as the partners in white-shoe law firms or lobbyists, highly differentiated suppliers in industrial value chains, or individual members of old boy networks of retired politicians and top civil servants (such as the Japanese *amakudari*, literally those who 'descend from heaven').[42]

To thrive (or survive), elite coalition leadership must deliver a degree of integration into the national elite system for its coalition sub-system. Integration is especially relevant for emerging elite coalitions regardless of whether they are undergoing endosmosis, infiltration, or admixture (see the modes of elite circulation in Figure 1.1). Returning to the emerging elites of crypto and to illustrate their integration into the elite system, *The Wall Street Journal* articulates the headline "Crypto Aims to Boost Influence With Washington Hires" (Kiernan & Michaels, 2022),[43] while *The Financial Times* highlights the case of Sam Bankman-Fried, the now imprisoned "FTX entrepreneur" who just a few months before his arrest and extradition "emerged as the second-biggest donor to liberal groups after George Soros" (Palma, Weaver, & Gilbert, 2022). Ultimately, the destiny of specific elite coalitions and their business models is inseparable from the elite system in which these become embedded components (see Section 4.2.3). To further describe the concept of the elite coalition within the system let us consider the cases of Facebook or Google.

The success of any coalition is attributable to effective elite coordination and business model leadership realized in all three of the system's contest arenas. Specifically, Internet firms not having to pay "for the content they carry from publishers"

42 The typical "old boy" *amakudari* standing "at the apex of power" is the "former government official who after retirement from civil service (*amakudari*), is re-employed in politics or the private or quasi-private sector and begins a second career in which he draws heavily on the expertise and personal relationships he accumulated in his former profession as a bureaucrat" (Schaede, 1995, p. 29, as quoted in Schmidt 2004, p. 80).

43 The recruits now "working for or advising cryptocurrency firms or investment funds include three former chairs of the Securities and Exchange Commission, three former chairs of the Commodity Futures Trading Commission, three former U.S. senators, and at least one former White House chief of staff, former Treasury secretary and former chair of the Federal Deposit Insurance Corporation" (Kiernan & Michaels, 2022).

(Ingram, 2020) might profit from value appropriated but *not* created, riding on wins in the political non-market arena. Such wins (see the discussion on the microfoundations of institutional formation and change in Section 4.2) are often preceded by wins in the narrative market (see Proposition 14), in this case from the doctrine that open technology platforms are not publishers. Here, a critical contribution to the success of Internet coalitions has been provided by knowledge elites in the media, law, and academia. Reflecting 'political economy know-how', the narrative market and political non-market arenas wins support, and are supported by, income streams derived from online traffic i.e., wins in the (advertising) market arena, thanks to superior management, sales techniques, and technology, i.e., 'knowledge'. In contrast, the inconsequence of the Facebook and Google coalitions in the Chinese market illustrates the role and importance of the *national* elite system and, in this case, their disinterest or inability to integrate (unlike the Apple or Tesla coalitions, both of which have booming elite business models in China). It also highlights the interdependencies that exist across the three contest arenas: a loss in the political non-market arena (here in Beijing, but potentially in Delhi, Brussels, or, as was the case with Huawei, in Washington DC) can *ipso facto* nullify wins in the local market and narrative market arenas. The extent to which the remedies that will follow US federal judge Mehta's 286-page decision (United States District Court for the District of Columbia, 2024) that Google is a "monopolist" interfere with the gravitational pull of its massive residual income generation capacity is yet to unfold.

Not all elite systems exhibit the same degree of cohesion (a conceptual element further harnessed in Section 5.3.3 and linked to a discussion on leadership in Section 7.2.4). Here, and further to Proposition 14 on institutional change effected via narrative markets, special emphasis must be placed on the role of narratives in creating the elite system cohesion that connects the overall system with the single coalition. Elite coalitions are atomized by vocation (and literally split from each other by nature) because while their sole desire is to maintain their own residual income and the elite status of their members, in practice they are also integrated and dependent subsystems of the wider elite system. That means that an agricultural elite business model might be extremely focused on sugar production and marketing, but to make significant returns from cane production is not possible in the US—unless one is part of an elite coalition profoundly embedded in the system. So, when "the U.S. spends $4 billion a year subsidizing 'Stalinist-style' domestic sugar production", the coalition's specific residual income recipe of 'sugar production (market) + farm bill (non-market) + US farm protectionism (narrative market)' can be explained as follows:

> The program, which dates back to the 1981 farm bill, generates over $1 billion a year in profits for growers, or an average of more than $200,000 per grower, according to the [American Enterprise Institute] report. One Florida family that plays a dominant role in cane production is estimated to benefit to the tune of between $150 million and $200 million a year.

> No wonder the U.S. Sugar Alliance, the major lobbying arm for U.S. sugar growers, is extremely well funded and uses its resources to maintain a highly protectionist, trade-distorting program that costs a family of four between about $44 and nearly $50 a year in subsidies. (Smith, 2018)

Since subsidies (a prevalent second-order value transfer activity) are not paid directly by consumers, sugar is comparatively cheap, leading to higher sugar consumption and thus to other known negative externalities such as obesity,[44] which in effect constitute additional extractive value transfer-OUT from stakeholders. Another "agricultural lobby", one that "is powerful in the Knesset and organizes quickly", invests its non-market and narrative market wins in a different transfer model type:

> "In Israel, not only do we have a lot of protections for the agricultural sector, we have a very peculiar way of protecting it [. . .] protections come not in the form of subsidies (although there are some) but rather in allowing the farmers to form legal cartels."
>
> There is a cartel of eggs. There is a cartel of vegetables. There's a cartel of milk. For each one of these agricultural products, there is a cartel. And they don't have to compete with imports because imports are very restricted. Of course, this increases the price of food. (Sarel, 2022)

This section's emphasis has been on the constitutive elements of the elite system, as the goals of each individual elite member can only be realized as part of an elite coalition, which in itself is a complex system "made up of a large number of parts that interact in a nonsimple way" (Simon, 1962, p. 468). Individual members of the elite coalition not only interact with each other but also with members of other coalitions (as is the case in intra-elite contests). An elite coalition, in a top-down analysis, is a sub-system nested within—and an integral part of—a national elite system that is itself a sub-system nested within the political economy, together creating the complex whole. This is so even when the national system is characterized by low elite cohesion and barely institutionalized intra-elite conflicts (across different tiers, see Proposition 16). Short of system collapse, antagonistic interests face off with each other in the political economy's contest arenas where the outcomes enshrine their conflicting business model preferences in institutional change processes.

---

44 Recognizing the effects of this particular negative externality, i.e., the social costs are not paid by the originators of the problem (a transfer-COST), a knowledge elite, the Wolfson Institute of Population Health at Queen Mary University of London, is "successfully working to reach a consensus with the food industry [the elite business model principals] and Government over the harmful effects of a high sugar diet, and bring about a reduction in the amount of sugar in processed foods". See: www.actiononsugar.org.

3.2.2 Proposition 16: The elite system operates on a multi-tier set of checks and balances

It has been shown in Proposition 15 that elite business model leadership requires that the three types of elites in a coalition (business, political, and knowledge) work in concert to generate residual income. At the same time, different coalitions compete with each other for advantage in the political economy. The Keystone XL project, referenced earlier, now serves as a case study for how intra-elite coalition competition dynamics play out, setting the stage for an extension of checks and balances theory. Cancelled on the Biden Administration's very first day in office, the constituent members of the winning and losing elite coalitions of the Keystone XL presidential ruling are outlined in Table 3.1.

Table 3.1: Keystone XL intra-elite contest with winning and losing elite coalitions and their constituent business, political, and knowledge elites.

Winning elite coalition	Losing elite coalition
Business elite coalition members	
– Oil-by-rail. Includes Berkshire Hathaway Inc.'s subsidiary, Burlington Northern Santa Fe (BNSF) Railway Co., which has the capability to haul Canadian oil to the US by rail (Efstathiou, 2012). "US energy expert Anas Alhajji posted on Twitter: 'With rail, money goes to the richest of the rich, who happen to be large donors and supporters of Obama/Biden'" (Staples, 2021). – Middle East oil suppliers. The *Edmonton Journal* winning coalition analysis identifies: "Dictator oil producers: Winners. Along with oil-by-rail, Texas will tanker in more oil. 'Middle Eastern heavy crude grades win in this situation', said Montreal energy analyst, Tracy Shuchart of Capital Benoit" (Staples, 2021).	– The pipeline's promoter. Calgary's TC Energy Corp. – Labor unions. Teamsters General President Jim Hoffa issued the statement: "The Teamsters strongly oppose yesterday's decision, and we would urge the administration to reconsider it. This executive order doesn't just affect US Teamsters; it hurts our Canadian brothers and sisters as well who work on this project. It will reduce good-paying union jobs that allow workers to provide a middle-class standard of living to their families" (Hoffa, 2021). – The US oil industry. US firms associated with the construction and operation of the pipeline.
Political elite coalition members	
– The Biden Administration. – The US Democratic Party. – The Rosebud Sioux Tribe and the Fort Belknap Indian Community. Indian tribes filed the lawsuit Rosebud Sioux Tribe v. Dep't of Interior, No. CV-20-109-GF-BMM-JTJ (D. Mont.) (Harvard Environmental and Energy Law Program, 2021).	– The liberal federal government of Canada under Prime Minister Justin Trudeau. – The Trump Administration. – The US Republican Party. – The Government of Alberta. Made an investment of C$ 1.5 billion to jump start pipeline construction (Gibillini, 2020).

Table 3.1 (continued)

Winning elite coalition	Losing elite coalition
Knowledge elite coalition members	
– A majority of the US environmental movement. – Academic platforms. Includes the Harvard Law School's Environmental and Energy Law Program that provided a voice to the opponents of Keystone XL focusing on "the construction's impact on wildlife. The pipeline's route and associated power lines would span the majority of endangered whooping cranes' southern migration route to Texas from Canada. It would also cross the remaining habitats of other threatened species such as piping plovers, sage grouse, and swift fox. The pipeline's route crosses over 50 streams, increasing the risk that oil spills would affect pallid sturgeon habitats".	– *The Wall Street Journal*. Promotes the jobs narrative evident from its editorial board headline: "Biden's Keystone Pipeline Kill: On his first day he insults Canada and ends thousands of jobs" (*The Wall Street Journal* Editorial Board, 2021) – *Edmonton Journal*. Articulates a narrative of localism and value for non-elites: "Losers: Albertans. The pipeline would have created good jobs, taxes and higher oil prices" (Staples, 2021).

Table 3.1 illustrates how two elite coalitions, each with its members sorted by elite type and gravitationally connected by the elite business model, are in fierce competition with each other for their institutional change preferences. While the dynamics of intra-elite rivalries can compromise elite system cohesion, institutionalized contests are posited in this elite theory to show the strength of a political economy, irrespective of which side's business models create more value. A priority for human and economic development is an elite separation of powers that is characterized by open, intense, but civil competition between elite coalitions. Under this premise, the previously referenced current winning streak of US Big Tech in almost all of the material contest arenas of Western political economies might at some time in the future reverse because of rules-based intra-elite competition. After all, America's elite system since the Civil War has been characterized by fierce intra-elite contests, extractive business models that become diluted by inclusive institutional change instigated by emergent elites, as well as incumbents on the wane that regroup to fight another day by transforming their business models (see AT&T, which despite its breakup, remains a potent force in telecommunications and employs over 200,000 people). At present, the settlement of the 'tap-and-go' antitrust probe of Apple by the EU (Espinoza, 2024b), the coalition of 33 US states suing Meta Platforms for "addictive features" that are ushering in "a mental health crisis" (Wilowski, 2023), or "tech antitrust crusader" Lina Khan's FTC (see Hatmaker, 2021) seem unlikely harbingers of decisive elite business model rule changes. Yet it is not unconceivable that America's elite circulation dynamics and multi-tier set of checks and balances eventually give rise to transformational elite and elite system leadership. Should the opposite scenario transpire, the absence of authentic intra-elite competition and the subsequent retardation of

elite circulation velocity would signal—to repurpose Fukuyama's (1992) concept—the beginning of the 'end of history' for America.

Intra-elite contests pave the way for elite circulation and replacement and play out in the three tiers of intra-elite checks and balances that ought to forge and characterize every elite system. Figure 3.7 depicts The Three-tier Set of Intra-elite Checks and Balances: 'within-arena' ('Tier 1'); 'across-arena' ('Tier 2'); and 'within-system' ('Tier 3'). The resulting seven intra-elite power relations are later discussed in detail (see Table 3.2). Conceived on the basis of the three elite types (business, political, and knowledge), The Seven Intra-elite Power Relations and The Three-tier Set of Intra-elite Checks and Balances that mediate them are at the core of the ETED's conception of a separation of powers in the political economy. Although the normative purpose of this conception is the same as Montesquieu's tripartite separation of the political realm, or Madison's federal Constitution, it is evidently a more extensive analytical tool. When applied to elite agency, the diverse relationships described (both when in or out of balance) point to the value creation and extractive transfer possibilities ensuing from intra-elite contests

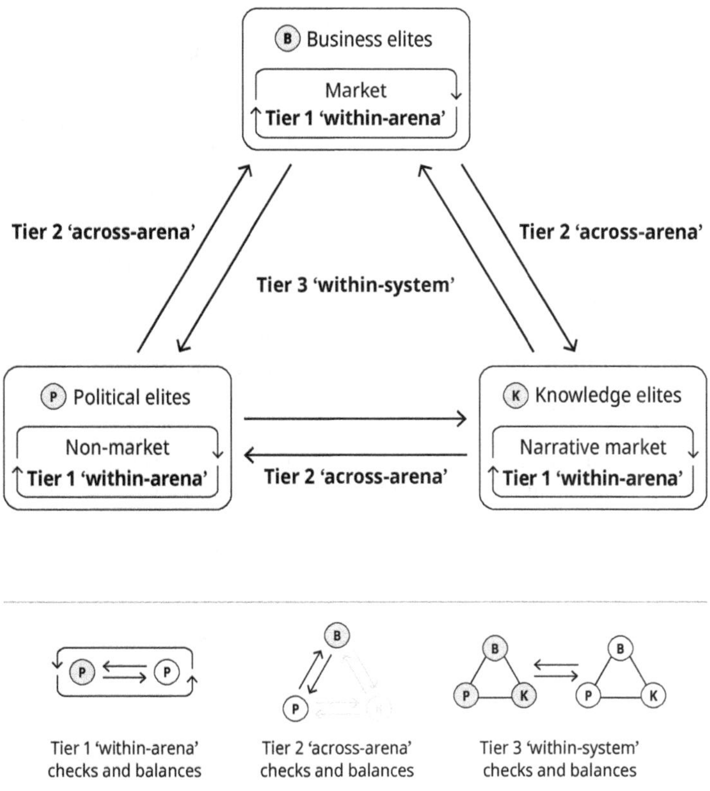

Figure 3.7: The Three-tier Set of Intra-elite Checks and Balances in the elite separation of powers.

and hence provide an expedient framework to anticipate outcomes in human and economic development.

There are three central tiers of intra-elite checks and balances in the separation of powers theory of the ETED (note that two additional tiers moored to the core elite coalition and foreign coalitions are later formulated, see Figure A5.11b). Tier 3 'within-system' checks and balances see the highest impact contests as the business models of different elite coalitions directly vie for residual income streams and institutional advantage. At the highest analytical level, the Corn Laws or Keystone XL examples already presented illustrate how Tier 3 'within-system' checks and balances between rival elite coalitions play out.

The elite separation of powers next materializes in 'across-arena' Tier 2 checks and balances. The different elite types—business, political, and knowledge—balance each other across the market, non-market, and narrative market arenas with their respective 'money', 'might', and 'mind' power endowments. To illustrate this, we can again reference the example of the revocation of the Corn Laws in 1846: Prime Minister Sir Robert Peel, with parliamentary support (political elites), leveraged Ricardo's (1817/1999) free trade narrative (knowledge elites) to the benefit of Manchester industrialists (winning business elites) and to the detriment of large landholders and their protected grain elite business model (losing business elites). While the two coalitions were competing 'within-system' (Tier 3), the key to the outcome was the dynamic English Tier 2 'across-arena' checks and balances. That is, the checks operating in the power relations that balance knowledge elites against both business and political elites. This balance, essential for sustainable value creation, is enabled by intra-elite contest rules such as the all-important freedom of speech, lucidly articulated in the *Universal Declaration of Human Rights*.[45] The following passage describes business elites teaming up with vocal knowledge elites beyond David Ricardo to align with the interests of non-elites that through "agitation" led the march to an inclusive victory over the established political elites:

> In the late (eighteen hundred) thirties and early forties, manufacturers in Manchester founded an Anti-Corn Law League to move the whole country for their repeal. They poured into that League the wealth which the Industrial Revolution had brought, and the force and ability that had produced it. They gained as leader Richard Cobden, one of the most effective economic controversialists of that day, and recruited John Bright, one of its greatest orators, and they developed an agitation which in its mixture of violence of language and piety of sentiment, middle-class leadership and popular organization, was a portent in our history. (Clark, 1951, p. 2)

45 Article 19 reads: "Everyone has the right to freedom of opinion and expression; this right includes freedom to hold opinions without interference and to seek, receive and impart information and ideas through any media and regardless of frontiers". See: https://www.un.org/en/about-us/universal-declaration-of-human-rights

Finally, Tier 1 checks and balances are those that occur 'within-arena'. Here, in each of the three contest arenas, same-type (business, political, or knowledge) elites, some of which are established and some of which are emerging, contend with each other. In the market arena, rival firms evidently vie for customers' willingness to pay. In narrative markets, different ideas, religious doctrines, and media (e.g., CNN vs Fox News vs Tucker Carlson) fiercely compete with each other as they seek power over 'mind', the cognitive and affective bandwidth of elites and non-elites alike. Narratives may well achieve domination, pausing competition and stymieing the checks and balances in the power domain of society that then ceases to contribute to the separation of power dynamics. In Tier 1 within-arena contests, rivalries evolve and alliances are formed and reconstituted on the logic of elite coalitions (which also give meaning to competitions in Tiers 2 and 3). At times, the alliances within a coalition seem *contra natura*; in the political non-market arena, Prime Minister Peel was supported by the liberal Whigs in Parliament and opposed by his own conservative Tory Party.[46] The overview of the multi-tier set of checks and balances that manifested around the Corn Laws is synopsized in Figure A5.11.

The Tier 1 'within-arena' checks and balances most heavily institutionalized and emphasized in constitutional democracies are the executive, legislative, and judicial branches of the political non-market arena. These are also the focus of the separation of powers theory of Montesquieu (1748/1949). However, on paper, nothing prevents a system of political checks and balances to be split along alternative lines, for instance, between the emperor, the Inner Court's (*Nei Ting*) eunuchs, and the mandarinate in Imperial China. In the People's Republic of China of today, the checks and balances of the political system include an array of elements and constituencies: the CPC front door (talent identification and nurturing); the CPC's back door (anti-corruption); the dual-leadership setup (party and state administration); "the subgroups in the decision-making circle"; the judicial system; the United Front ("democratic parties"); and the civil affairs offices.[47] In modern Japan, the system's checks and balances occur between Nagatachô, the location of the Diet and its *zokugiin* clique members, and Kasumigaseki, the location of the ministries and the 'old boy' *amakudari* networks of ministerial bureaucrats (Schmidt, 2004, pp. 79-81). Political elites are important given their direct hand in institutional change processes, but the role of political 'within-arena' contests in the overall schema of the elite system should not be overly emphasized. Today, Montesquieu's checks and balances across government branches or Madison's federal Constitution (1787/1977) to balance 'factions', while still being relevant, are inadequate frameworks for a separation of powers that prevents extraction by the sophisticated elite business models associated with 21st century technologies.

---

46 Prime Minister Peel's leadership availed itself of the 'inextinguishable value creation option of elites' to cause business model transformation (see Section 2.2.1 and Figure A5.4c), in this case by repealing an extractive law.

47 Based on communication with Professor Ray Di, 18th March, 2021.

Proposition 18 will set forth the notion that the key driver of institutional change is intra-elite contests. It is hypothesized that the more competitive that intra-elite power relations are, the lower the bargaining power differentials found in society and the greater the likelihood that value creation elite business models will, along with supporting institutions and narratives, emerge from 'knowledge' and prevail in the economy. The analytical and normative emphasis is therefore not on institutional quality (the perspective of a diverse research stream that includes works from Jung, 2020, or Glaeser, La Porta, Lopez-de-Silanes, & Shleifer, 2004), but on the sources of accumulated institutional change: the diversity, quantity, and sophistication of intra-elite contests. The premise for these contests is that they should be numerous and carried out across all of The Seven Intra-elite Power Relations (see Table 3.2) derived from The Three-tier Set of Intra-elite Checks and Balances discussed in this subsection (Figure 3.7). A comprehensive and functioning separation of powers is in turn enabled by adherence to intra-elite contest rules and elite system cohesion (as detailed in Figure 5.2 on the dialectical relationship between elite cohesion and the separation of powers as a precondition for development). Winners that thus emerge from robust intra-elite contests held under a comprehensive system of checks and balances are more likely to be operating at high value creation positions on the 'value spectrum' (see Figures 2.10, 2.11, and SVC measurements like the VCp, VCr, or 360-VCz).

3.2.3 Proposition 17: The national elite system is situated at the meso-level

This work has proposed that elite coalitions are the constitutive components of a national elite system (Proposition 15). This begs the question of how the elite system should be theoretically described in relation to the macro-level political economy system. The system of national elites fits Dopfer's meso-level proposal (2012, p. 145) because it "explain[s] generic structure and processes" in the economy, and it is both an idea (i.e., the aggregate of individual elite agency) as well as an observable reality (i.e., elites in the system run residual income generating elite business models, literally "matter-energy that is actualized in time and space"). The key consideration is that the meso-level "is made of complex other things (micro) and is an element in higher order things (macro) [. . .] in the specific sense of identifying and conceptualizing the dynamical building blocks of an economic system" (Dopfer, Foster, & Potts, 2004, p. 268). The micro-level 'complex other things' are elite coalitions (sub-systems of the elite system, as discussed in Section 3.2.1 and visualized in Figure 3.6), activated through elite business models and their associated leadership. The elite system is itself a sub-system of the macro-level political economy system. In this theory, the elite system is posited to be the critical meso-level sub-system able to shape the political economy system's outcomes and performance in a far more profound way than other meso-level sub-systems (such as innovation or financial systems).

In short, the ETED holds that elites constitute a system (in the sense used by Von Bertalanffy, 1969/2003, 1972) that is coherent (in its discrete degrees of cohesion), and that the elite system and its emergent properties (see Anderson, 1972; O'Connor, 1994) such as inequality or this work's emphasis on elite quality, is theoretically apt for consideration at the meso-level as a sub-system of the macro-level political economy system. The connections between analytical levels are the scientifically relevant "emergent phenomena", understood by Bedau as "somehow constituted by, and generated from, underlying processes" while also "somehow autonomous" from these (1997, p. 375). Chalmers (2006) points out that "a high-level phenomenon is *strongly emergent* with respect to a low-level domain when the high-level phenomenon arises from the low-level domain, but truths concerning that phenomenon are not *deducible* even in principle from truths in the low-level domain". Such a clear-cut ontological partition between the macro- meso- and micro-levels would imply that elite quality is not reducible to micro-level elite business models and that the macro-level political economy is unexplainable by the elite system's characteristics. This can "raise the specter of illegitimately getting something from nothing" (Bedau, 1997, p. 376). With "weak emergence" on the other hand, "the high-level phenomenon arises from the low-level domain, but truths concerning that phenomenon are *unexpected* given the principles governing the low-level domain" (Chalmers, 2006). In other words, meso-level emergent properties like elite quality arise from micro-level constituent parts like elite business models and can be explained, understood, and measured, even when they cannot be predicted.

Figure 3.8 describes the micro- meso- and macro-levels of analysis for this theory and situates elite coalitions at the conceptual center. It also depicts the relationship between the three levels, the meso-level having the all-important intermediate transmission mechanism function that connects the micro to the macro.

The establishment of the elite system as a meso-level sub-system of the political economy stresses the latter's complexity. The national elite system has been theoretically anchored and contextualized as a conceptual element in this section with the aim of better understanding the relationship between its emergent states (e.g., social order access, elite quality, economic and human development) and the political economy. As the ETED becomes further grounded in the terrain of systems theory, the logic of complex adaptive systems comes to the fore. McDaniel, Lanham and Anderson (2009, p. 4) here identify "five key characteristics" from the organizational studies literature (Beinhocker, 2006; Cilliers, 1998; Maguire, McKelvey, Mirabeau, & Oztas, 2006; Waldrop, 1992): "(a) diverse agents that learn, (b) nonlinear interdependencies, (c) self-organization, (d) emergence, and (e) coevolution". Evolutionary approaches can be seen as constituting "a generic framework for understanding social change", specifically one that "directs our attention to the processes of variation, selection, retention, and struggle that jointly produce patterned change in evolving systems" (Aldrich, 1979/2008, pp. xv–xvi), including those described by power-law distributions that account for the rise of elite business models and how they circulate.

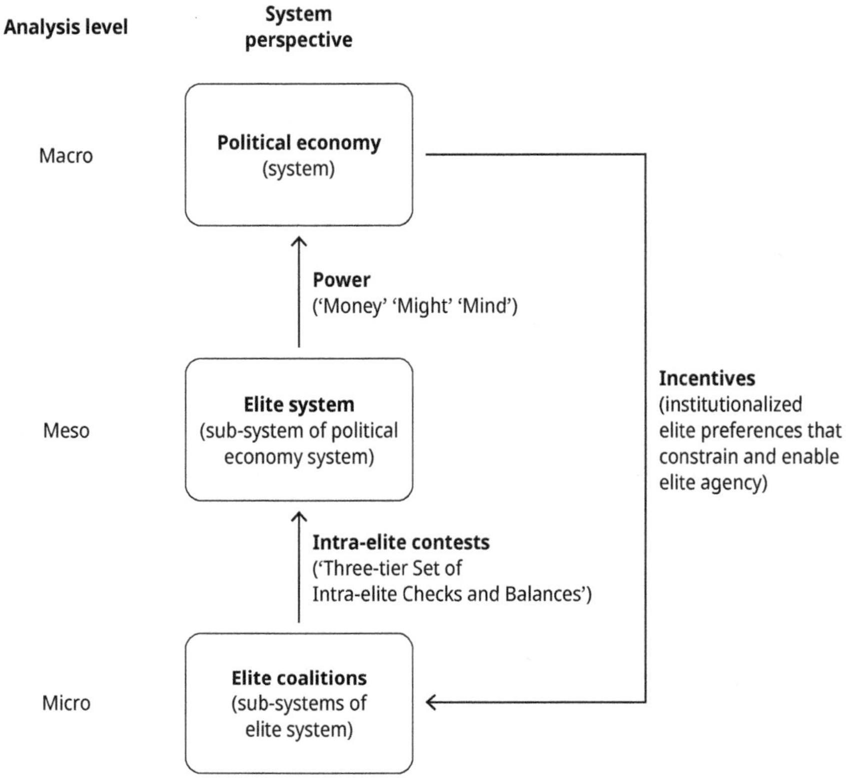

Figure 3.8: The meso-level elite system: The transition mechanism between the micro- and macro-levels.

This inquiry's focus on the meso-level accentuates chaos, initial states not determining future states, (weak) emergence and evolution, and the breakdown of periodicity as the non-repeating patterns of one sustainable value creation national state morphs into the next (see the acumens of Von Bertalanffy, 1969/2003; Parsons, 1951/1991; Hayek, 1964/1967; Simon, 1962; Anderson, 1972; Gleick, 1987; O'Connor, 1994). Nonlinear interactions result in learning by agents giving rise to "self-organization" and "coevolution" (Camazine, Deneuborg, Franks, Sneyd, Theraulaz, & Bonabeau, 2001, as cited in McDaniel, Lanham, & Anderson, 2009, p. 3) and are the medium in which intra-elite contests evolve, thereby defining the properties of the autonomous elite system. Another notable viewpoint is important when looking at complex elite systems—fractal patterns:

> A fractal is a object [sic] in space that has an ever larger number of ever smaller pieces. It is self-similar, meaning that the smaller pieces are reduced copies of the larger pieces. For some fractals, the smaller pieces are exact copies of the larger pieces. For most fractals in nature, the smaller pieces are kind-of-like the larger pieces. A tree is such a fractal. It has an ever larger number of ever smaller branches. A fractal can also be a process in time. (Liebovitch & Scheurle, 2000, p. 34)

From an elite business model perspective, the political economy system is fractal—like other systems in nature (see Mandelbrot, 1989; Brown, Gupta, Li, Milne, Restrepo, & West, 2002)—especially where it counts: the spaces where value is created and transferred. While the core coalition holds 'the extraordinary lever' (see Figures 8.1, A5.3a, and A5.3b), elite agency functions at lesser levers in an analogous manner, upholding bargaining power differentials and residual income logic across every nook and cranny of the economy (see the implications in Sections 7.1.4 or 7.1.5). Inequality can reflect such patterns (see Cozzi & Privileggi, 2009). Econometric models of the economy (see Section 7.1.1), particularly when rendered as games (see Figure set A5.14), must aim to describe the fractal nature of the economic landscape and its business spaces, limits, and the micro to macro transmission mechanisms of the system's emerging properties, as agents at different scales create and transfer value across principal-stakeholder relationships. Power law distributions in society, as the statistical signatures of fractality, are adept at representing the skewed distributions in society such as the power endowments of the political economy (the most relevant manifestation of which is elite agency).

As a final point, the phenomenological uncertainty associated with the understanding of complex adaptive systems means that when examining the elite system one must (as would also be the case with financial markets, policy networks, or health care organizations) "anticipate, but not try to predict, change [. . .] The focus is on preparation for inevitable surprise rather than prediction of events" (McDaniel, Lanham, & Anderson, 2009, p. 5). That is, insights into economic development are comparatively more feasible when the objective is to ascertain meso-level elite quality, the emergent aggregate sustainable value creation of elite business models. Much less predictable is how to determine *who* at the micro-level—the specific disaggregated individuals, firms, and models—will attain or lose the 'extraordinary lever' in a fractal field and thus a residual income position in the overall elite system as a result of intra-elite contests. Here, the exercise of leadership, in all its varieties and despite all of its vagaries, will be shown to be the key insight and determinant (see Section 7.2.4 or the Epilogue to this book), even if this variable exists chiefly in retrospect to the observer. While transformational leadership in pursuit of sustainable value creation cannot be predicted at the micro-level, its appearance can be incentivized at the meso-level to contribute to macro-level economic and human development.

3.3 Propositions for the logic of intra-elite contests in the elite system

Since intra-elite contests are central to the ETED, they must be viewed from all vantage points. This section first completes the previous discussion on elite contests as the primary shaper of institutions (Proposition 18). Then, the inquiry transitions to how non-elite participation in intra-elite contests might constrain value extraction (Proposition 19). The final proposition reaffirms the importance of a sophisticated elite separation of powers, not just for economic growth, but also to garner inclusive political economy outcomes for non-elites (Proposition 20).

3.3.1 Proposition 18: Elites shape institutions primarily through intra-elite contests

From Marxist class struggle to anti-colonialist discourse (e.g., Said, 1993), but also in the fringe anti-elite intellectual positions taken by the likes of Steve Bannon (Guilford & Sonnad, 2017), non-elite vs elite struggle often takes center stage in the analysis of political economy contests. Morck and Yeung (2004, p. 392) describe "political rent seeking" by elite families who benefit in Olsonian fashion from the "high level of trust between members of a small elite" and collude to the detriment of the non-elites. Their evidence backs the notion of "political rent seeking as a cooperative game among members of the elite and a non-cooperative game between the elite and the rest of society". At the same time, Acemoglu conceives a non-elite middle-class struggle against elites as follows: "middle-class profits reduce the elite's political power and endanger their future rents. The elite will then want to tax the middle class in order to impoverish them and consolidate their political power" (2006, pp. 516-517).[48] As the authors cited in this paragraph imply, elite business models often rely on value transfer-IN from non-elite stakeholders. However, what if the institutions that enable value appropriation are not the result of non-elite vs elite (including the middle-class) struggle, but rather the outcome of intra-elite contests? It has also been lucidly argued that "features of a nation's mass culture have a strong imprint on elite characteristics" and are "a powerful social force in shaping the quality of elites" (Welzel, 2002, p. 275). One must be vigilant here against the non-elite rule fallacy ('people power') as it muddies understanding of institutional change, of the sustainable value creation impact of non-elite culture, and of the fact that inclusive transformations are generally brought about by elite coalitions (winning contests for inclusive institutional change against their more extractive peers). Proof for such a conjecture would come from evidence that institutions are primarily designed for intra-elite contests.

Forsdyke's study of ancient Greece (2005) relies on theories from anthropology to argue that everything from sanctuaries and re-settlement to laws and citizen armies, even state formation itself, is the result of intra-elite competition. So are wars. Taking

48 The middle-class, like all socio-economic non-elite categories, is not a coherent whole but split into many specific non-elite groupings. The relevant agency options of each of these groups are limited and based on the possibilities to tilt the balance of intra-elite contests (a dynamic detailed in Section 8.1.3; see Figure 8.2 on the political options for non-elite groups to advance their interests and overcome the 'low non-elite cohesion' problem). The relevant question in political economy analysis is *which* non-elite groups ally with *which* elite coalitions to extract from *which* other non-elite groups. Such analyses must transcend the general elite vs non-elite (or elite vs middle-class) dichotomy, even in light of non-elite extraction.

this assertion one step further and in qualified contrast to the non-elite vs elite struggle model, the key political economy contests affecting institutional change that are relevant to the welfare of non-elites take place between elites (see Table 3.2). Intra-elite competition is usually very visible and provides much inspiring material for the humanities. For example, the war between Octavian and Antony in the Shakespearean tragedy that narrates an epic conflict ending at the Battle of Actium and Cleopatra's suicide ultimately led to the transition from republic to empire, a dramatic instance of institutional change. Yet such heady narratives often obfuscate the more sober central point. Whether "intra-elite rivalry" is fueled by slush funds in Indonesia (Dick & Mulholland, 2011), the highly codified but often violent Archaic Athens intra-elite competition, or elections in contemporary America, the structure for this inquiry is that beneath intra-elite rivalry and contests lie disparate elite business model interests that operate at discrete degrees of sustainable value creation, and that these differences hold the keys for economic development.

Intra-elite contests become relevant for non-elite interests (and economic development) when the sustainable value creation of contesting elite business models are dissimilar. After Actium, even though Octavian became Caesar Augustus, the formidable builder of empire and the *Pax Romana*, his elite business model of conquer and tax may have been more secure and institutionalized but was essentially no different to that of his rivals for the laurel wreath. In other conflicts however, the extraction from non-elites by the business models of the contending parties markedly diverge. For example, compared to its opponent in the American Revolutionary War, Great Britain clearly fielded the more extractive model (to defray the costs of the Seven Years War, London had implemented grating institutional changes like the Stamp Act of 1765, or the Townshend Acts passed during 1767 and 1768).[49]

Institutions are predominantly an expression of the outcomes of intra-elite contests rather than non-elite vs elite struggles. To suggest otherwise—e.g., that "you and I", non-elites, "are fully in charge" in the context of the institutional change necessary to control AI, as suggested by the technologist and thought leader Gawdat (2021)—is at best but another ingenuous manifestation of the non-elite rule fallacy. The institutions

49 It is noteworthy that elites and non-elites that cohere on account of sharing the same nationality, narrative, or geographical origin—even after independence struggles with foreign powers—does not necessary associate with comparatively less transfer-IN from non-elites. Foreign elites, for instance, might rely more on elite/non-elite cooperative arrangements than the new local elites that replace them. In the case of Eritrea, many who fought for freedom in the long and painful Eritrean War of Independence (1961–1991) wonder whether the business models of today's native elites are truly less extractive and create more value than those that were run by Ethiopia as foreign occupying power. The general point is that empires can notionally be less extractive than the smaller polities or nation states that emerge in their wake, partially on account of maintaining narrower and less costly elite systems than those of successor local elites. It has been argued, not without controversy, that extraction from non-elites by new post-imperial elites increased after the termination of the Spanish and Ottoman Empires (see the discussion of cross-border elite business models in Section 7.3.1 and 7.3.3).

of ancient Greece, as remains the case for any institutional arrangement today, were designed for the intra-elite contests that secure business model rules: "institutions and written law have been interpreted as unsystematic ad hoc arrangements designed to defuse conflict within the elite and to protect its position" (Hölkeskamp, 1992, as cited in Ma, 2016, p. 403). On the other hand, the lack of sophistication and recourse to violence in intra-elite contests is problematic for value creation and economic development. The earlier example involving the local residual income streams of Coca-Cola's international business in Libya demonstrates the problems associated with haphazard and non-institutionalized intra-elite contests. A Reuters' journalist sheds further light on this case based on access to Wikileaks cables:

> Then, on December 28, 2005—two weeks after the Tripoli plant began turning out locally-bottled batches of Coke—"two military cars carrying armed personnel without clear identification illegally broke into the facility, asked the employees to leave the premises and shut down the plant" [. . .]
>
> The US mission in Libya learned from other sources that the troops were loyal to Mutassim Gaddafi [. . .] According to the State Department cable, Mutassim bore a grudge against his brother [. . .] Sporadic violent incidents continued to erupt in the weeks after Mutassim's forces occupied the bottling plant. [. . .] The Libyan leader, according to the cable, "declined to get involved personally" yet urged plant owners to do "everything within (their) power to resolve the matter according to Libyan law." [. . .]
>
> The State Department cable describes the Coca-Cola conflict as a "case study in the involvement of Qadhafi (sic) family members directly influencing the flow, pace, and nature of economic activity. Family members squabble over personal financial interest with little regard to the possible impact on foreign investors or international public opinion." (Hosenball, 2011)

Various reasons might explain why elite systems underinvest in the rules and institutional arrangements of intra-elite contests. Some relate to overconfidence or short-sighted calculations of increased value appropriation possibilities if contests remain non-institutionalized. Regardless, in the absence or low quality of institutions, intra-elite contests escalate and become personal, unrestrained, and bring increased dangers and uncertainty, often also to the winning elites. Moreover, there is always the possibility that fractures in the elite system cause society itself to fragment and descend into violent conflict centered on elite personalities (clientelism in its basic form) or narratives (ideological, religious, or based on identity). Many coalitions in the elite system lose (think of purges in authoritarian systems or of Roman proscriptions), while in addition to extraction, the collateral damage for non-elites is often catastrophic (think of contemporary Lebanon or of any civil war).

Of particular interest to economic development are the conditions that result in the setting of intra-elite contest rules to establish institutionalized and therefore more restrained forms of intra-elite contests. That is, intra-elite contest rule regimes—whether in 19th century Manchester or in 21st century Shenzhen—where high elite circulation velocity and the rapid adjustment of business model rules incentivize emergent players to operate at increasingly higher degrees of value creation (e.g., VCr) and thus attain elite status. Succession planning forms a part of such rules and is particularly relevant in core coalitions (Section 8.1.2), even more so "in any personal dictatorship or tyranny [where] one thing is certain: some day there will be a succession crisis" (Rush, 1962, p. 259). Desirable intra-elite contest rules also include those that facilitate alliances between emergent and incumbent elite coalitions and result in win-win outcomes. For instance, President Reagan's 'Star Wars' initiative saw the military-industrial complex embrace Silicon Valley via the Strategic Defense Initiative anti-ballistic missile program. Even better for development are cases where emerging elites advance without the need for alliances or offering a cut to the establishment, manage to effect institutional change, and eventually appropriate the growth portions of the enlarged pie as well as parts of the slices held previously by less innovative incumbents. One might consider to what degree the contests between Tesla and traditional automotive manufacturers, between Amazon and traditional retailers, or between Netflix, Amazon (who acquired MGM in 2021) and the Hollywood studios fit such a pattern.

Intra-elite contests might intensify and habitually de-institutionalize in situations where the overall economic pie shrinks and dominant coalitions exhibit a bias towards retaining the 'same size of the slice' for themselves. The incumbent vs incumbent elite scenario is especially vicious when it becomes clear that not all elite business models and players can survive a crisis. Johnson (2009) discusses this in the context of IMF rescue packages where loan facilities are limited and only a fraction of a country's elite models can possibly be saved, leaving those who don't receive assistance to go under. The optimal decision criterion for the core elite coalition and the enlightened position of independent political and knowledge elites is often to downsize or selectively cull an elite system where the value creation engine is stalling, thus preempting decades of stagnation or mayhem down the road. In such instances, the institutionalized approach is to support elite coalitions with business models that possess the highest levels of value creation (measured by VCp, VCr, or 360-VCz) and decisively weed out all of those that don't make the cut, as was done in the 1997-98 Korean financial crisis (see Kim, 2006)[50]. This general principle, reflected in the normative aspects of this work (e.g., the constraints in A Transfer Constraints Framework for policy formulation, Table 8.2), becomes all the more relevant in deep economic downturns, armed conflicts, pandemics, or other black swan events.

Underlying the feasibility of constructive responses by the elite system, whether in normal times or times of crisis, are institutionalized intra-elite contest rules that include a robust elite separation of powers together with elite system cohesion (see Section 5.3.3, Figure 5.2). Both factors, the former being paradoxically the cause of the latter, make intra-elite contest rules resistant to institutional decay. After all, intra-elite contests may

50 How severe the prescriptive cuts ought to be is shown by the example of Korean merchant banks where 22 licenses were revoked and whose sum "was reduced from 30 at the end of 1997 to only three by June 2003" (Ahn & Cha, 2004, as cited in Kim, 2006, p. 15).

also bring about de-institutionalization and, alongside it, the escalation of value transfers, especially when violence is a factor. Nothing ushers in national decline (and non-elite suffering) and exposes a country to unrest or extraction (also by foreign elites, see the discussion on cross-border elite business models in Section 7.3) like a polarized or fractionalized elite system reneging on its intra-elite contest rules.

3.3.2 Proposition 19: Non-elite agency can constrain value extraction through participation in intra-elite contests

> Kant famously denied the right to revolution, whereas Marx thought revolution so necessary that the normative question concerning its acceptability did not even bear direct asking. (Ypi, 2014, p. 263)

Residual-income-maximizing elites incessantly develop novel elite business models and pursue institutional change. Problems for non-elites—and for development—arise when new models are based on increased value extraction from those engaged in first-order productive activities (as is the case with monopolies, monopsonies, wars, subsidies, negative interest rates, inflation, particular regulations, or onerous taxation rates, see Table 2.3). Value transfer models, Clark's economic "friction" (1899/1908) facilitated by power differentials or "force" (1903), preempt non-elites from appropriating the value they have created through their business models as workers, business owners, farmers, the professional class, and other roles. What responses to extractive practices are then in their best interests? To the ETED, non-elite interests are best served by the full or significant appropriation of value created, i.e., minimal extractive value transfers. The individual non-elite responses to extraction are deemed to be 'acceptance', 'exit', 'informality', and 'challenge' (as expanded upon in Section 5.2.3 and outlined in Table 5.1). At the political aggregate level, the options for non-elites to advance their interests exist in two broad categories: 'confrontation', specifically direct 'non-elite vs elite struggle', and the more constructive 'cooperation', which includes options for the passive 'trust in elites' and the active 'tactical' and 'strategic participation' in intra-elite contests (as expanded upon in Section 8.1.3 and detailed in Figure 8.2).

When individual 'challenge' responses swell into organized political 'non-elite vs elite struggle', the violence can be either sporadic or of continued revolutionary ferocity. The legacy of such confrontation and its impact on development requires that this option be well understood in both theoretical and practical terms. The final paragraph of the *Manifesto of the Communist Party* exhorts the "forcible overthrow of all existing social conditions. Let the ruling classes tremble at the Communist revolution"; for Marx and Engels, institutional change is "to be attained through recourse to violence" (Schaff, 1973, p. 263). Earlier, Hegel[51] had presciently "imagined that the no-

51 Marx, both profoundly influenced by and fervidly opposed to Hegel (1807/2018; 1812/2010), had advocated for the physical destruction of elites and even for the terror that Hegel critically disputed.

tion of an absolutely free will as conceived by Rousseau was responsible both for inaugurating the French Revolution in its overthrow of the ancien regime [sic] and subsequently for producing the Terror" (Wokler, 1998, p. 35). Lenin's pragmatic take on Marxist ideology[52] centered on professional revolutionaries engaging in forceful struggle to bring about a dictatorship of the proletariat.

Non-elite "misery and squalor" (as in Pigou, 1920/1932) has always been evidently real, but so is a widely recognized fact: "Revolt is only one of several paths that may be taken by the oppressed" (Goldstone, 1982, p. 187). The ETED argues that the path of revolutionary or social violence is counterproductive because it escalates uncontrollably, is unlikely to succeed, destroys 'knowledge', and mostly results in regressive elite circulation (see Section 1.3.2). The effectiveness of violence in reversing extractive models and fostering inclusive institutional change is, however, often viewed as an empirical question. Acemoglu and Robinson (2006) see constitutional change towards lesser extraction (democracy) on the back of threats of non-elite violence. So, what if violence is the only means to compel elites to reduce extraction and, for instance, cast aside their 'same size of the slice' bias? Is the union of political liberation frameworks with the noble instincts of "people's bandits" such as Salvatore Giuliani (Hobsbawm, 1969/2000) the progressive way forward for societies? While violence, or even its insinuation, will make a complex system more uncertain and chaotic, the consequentialist point of sincere revolutionaries is that the suffering it brings is a price worth paying to attain the political power necessary for a more inclusive society.

The first problem with this argument is that non-elites usually end up losing such conflicts at great personal cost. This is because they generally have limited coordination capacity and are capable of organized violence only non-strategically, sporadically, or in moments of crisis. On the opposing side, the incumbency advantage of 'the extraordinary lever' is reflected by elites that are specialists in effectively protecting their models in all the three contest arenas of the political economy. Moreover, the costs of a violent challenge are primarily and poignantly borne by non-elites because the struggle reduces the size of the total pie more than the slices possessed by elites. The uneven reduction of residual incomes in times of trouble favors elites in such contests and ought to be a strategic consideration in non-elite vs elite struggle. With conflict, non-elite business models are the first to dry up or generate lower incomes. In sum, non-elites can usually ill-afford protracted political conflict and so most struggles breed misery and failure. Narratives can induce non-elites to willingly engage in

---

Marx was Editor-in-Chief of the revolutionary newspaper *Neue Rheinische Zeitung* (1849/1994, p. 1) that, in its final issue in May 1849, proclaimed: "We have no compassion and we ask no compassion from you. When our turn comes, we shall not make excuses for the terror."

52 Referring to Engels, Lenin writes (1918, p. 15) that: "the 'special coercive force' for the suppression of the proletariat by the bourgeoisie, of millions of working people by handfuls of the rich, must be replaced by a 'special coercive force' for the suppression of the bourgeoisie by the proletariat (the dictatorship of the proletariat)".

radical sacrifice, self-extraction, and terror (as, for example, in the case of Ho Chi Minh's Viet Minh and Viet Cong and their nationalist non-elite challenges against various incumbent elite coalitions and their respective Japanese, French, and ultimately, American partners).

Revolutionary movements often edge forward on pyrrhic victories while the decisive revolutionary triumph never arrives. The rare historical overthrows of an elite system show that besides luck, timing and decisive action is essential. If non-elites have not managed to cause elite replacement through successes on the battlefield, they will be outmaneuvered in any subsequent deals. At the height of the Peasant's Revolt of 1381, King Richard II agreed to the rebels' charters of freedom that abolished serfdom and conceded free land, yet reneged as soon as he had Wat Tyler and other leaders killed. Once the opportunity for violence passes and non-elites have failed to accumulate the decisive power endowments, what are the incentives for elites to honor promises for institutional change or reform and phase out extractive business models? Sometimes, elites may tactically acquiesce to reforms to divide and weaken non-elite resistance and defuse the political struggle. In other cases, even in the midst of societal upheavals, cool-headed elites opportunistically ride on the back of non-elite movements and incorporate non-elite narratives to strengthen their own positions against rivals in intra-elite contests. This chimes with Blok's criticism that "Hobsbawm's comparative treatment of banditry over-emphasizes the element of social protest and obscures the significance of the links which bandits maintain with established power-holders" (1972, p. 502). Either way, once non-elite coordination capacity loses momentum and the threat is over, or the intra-elite contest is resolved, many elite playbooks will discard self-restraint and double down on value appropriation and extractive repression.

A second consideration that has already been implied is that violent confrontation may result in regressive elite circulation (Section 1.3.2). When sincere revolutions succeed, does "sham and illusion", as described by Milovan Djilas (see Section 1.3.1) invariably await, or are the new elites that emerge from the midst of non-elites able to run inclusive business models? On occasion, revolutions do end with positive outcomes for non-elites. While by no means costless, the American Revolution is an example of new elites emerging from revolutionary processes that then went on to implement less extractive elite business models that were clearly beneficial to non-elites (though not all: Native Americans had good reason to ally with the British since the Proclamation of 1763 had banned colonist expansion west of the Appalachian Mountains). With successful violent revolutionary processes, history is remade along with society's cardinal narratives, but the key question remains: are the more inclusive models of the American republic an accurate representation of post-revolutionary business models?

The rural non-elite Maccabees revolt, started in 167 BC by Mattathias the Hasmonean, eventually replaced the yoke of Antiochus IV and the Seleucid line of despots. The French Revolution extinguished the *Ancien Régime* elite system and led to Emperor Napoleon I (1804-14/15), the Bourbon Restoration (1814-30), the July Revolution with Louis-Philippe's July Monarchy (1830-48), and ultimately consolidated the bourgeoise and its elite business models. Chairman Mao's communists ushered in New China and established a new elite system that rid the nation of its creative industrialists as well as the opium business model and extractive foreign powers, and whose progeny and successors in the 21st century have delivered comparatively high elite quality, especially if adjusted for GDP per capita (see Casas-Klett & Cozzi, 2023, p. 5), and might be on target to make China's economy the largest in the world in nominal terms. Every one of those long (taking decades to complete) revolutionary elite circulations—each consisting of a two-fold process of struggle to first consolidate power and then implement elite business models—saw untold extraction from non-elites. The Great Leap Forward and the Cultural Revolution led to famine and despondency; so did Robespierre's Committee of Public Safety and the Terror's program of revolutionary trials; while the destruction of Jewish Hellenized temple elites, including those represented by Menelaus, the notorious High Priest in Jerusalem, shattered valuable economic networks.

As with its precursors, the ultimate 20th century revolution appeared to have legitimacy in its aim to redress the fundamental value transfer inequities of imperial Russia. The Czarist elite system had been too sluggish in the transformation of its business models, finding its cohesion through an outdated narrative, lacking a robust separation of powers, and running intra-elite contests that led to perverse outcomes. For instance, the landed gentry sidelined Prime Minister Count Witte despite his success as Minister of Ways and Communications (making Russian railroads extremely efficient), and as a modernizing Minister of Finance, recognized by Alexander III as his most able minister. Another transformational member of the elite, Prime Minister Stolypin, who had succeeded in enacting land reform and drastically increasing the Empire's agricultural production, was likewise sidelined by the same elite system (he was assassinated in 1911). In France too, the *Ancien Régime* could have formed stronger links with the bourgeoise and incentivized their value creation models. Such failures meant that in both the French and Russian examples, the ever-latent and seldom actualized might of non-elites was unleashed through the coordination device of choice: the respective narratives of *liberté, égalité, fraternité* and "Peace, Land, Bread!"

Once victorious, revolutions face an impasse akin to that captured in the film *The Candidate* (Ritchie, 1972), and encapsulated in Robert Redford's closing line to his campaign manager after his election victory: "Marvin, what do we do now?" While the French and Russian revolutionaries might have had a blueprint of what to do, they also had the fatal bias that characterizes most winning non-elite movements: overly abstract narratives. When concrete, these narratives generally aim at redistribution, obviating practical incentives to foster first-order value creation activities such as agriculture, industry, or innovation. Equally absent are systematic and applied proposals to lift the productivity of capital, and so the new elites, unable to receive guidance from their narratives, are unlikely to implement superior value creation elite business models. Bastiat went as far as linking religion with plunder when stating that: "Theocracy diverts many energies toward childish or injurious ends" (1845/1996, p. 131). If the blatant extractive transfers of previous incumbent elites is discontinued then that is a positive, but it is only half the battle.

The origin of non-elite struggle against an elite system is usually discontent at being on the short end of abusive value transfer-OUT. Therefore, non-elites are susceptible participants in contests for the 'mind' and become attracted by narratives that promise to eliminate or limit the degree of extraction. Those that support such narratives, including the authors, seldom understand business, risk, or management and so, bereft of 'knowledge', commit the cardinal sin of obviating the underlying mechanisms of the extractive elite business model, including its value creation components. Instead, all energies are indiscriminately aimed at the demolition of the old system. This failure becomes painfully visible when the revolutionary elite takes over and its elite business models do not deliver the aspired for growth. Revolutionary narratives are, almost by design, destructive rather than constructive (Marxism included). Ignorant of the intricacies of elite business models, such narratives are rudimentary, unrealistic, and offer scant detail on meaningful elite business model transformation. The success of the system of 'socialism with Chinese characteristics' since the 1980s is due to it being more Chinese than theoretically Marxist.

But was not the French Revolution's "momentous impact" across Europe inclusive as it dismantled "the legal and economic barriers that had protected the nobility, clergy, guilds, and urban oligarchies" (Acemoglu, Cantoni, Johnson, & Robinson, 2009)? Do "economies grow faster after coups and revolutions due to the destruction of existing special-interest organizations" as Heckelman and Whaples (2006, p. 36) ask? Are uprisings only a problem insofar that revolutionary narratives lack the components for elite business model transformation? Where such a deficit occurs, the new elites will likely end up adopting the business models of the system that they sought to vanquish. There are thus fundamental reasons for incoming elite coalitions being less effective value creators than their predecessors over longer horizons. Again, one explanation for failed post-revolutionary societies is that the knowledge elites of the new system are specialists in revolt and non-elite mobilization during the struggle phase, not in the mundane 'knowledge' (of the law, technology, finance, etc.) or the competitive processes associated with first-order productive activities. Once victorious, and given the personal risks that they undertook, the last thing on the minds of the new ruling class is the all-important development of a multi-tier set of checks and balances and intra-elite contest rules that are essential to foster the continuous 'knowledge' generation that enables value creation business models. Instead, the legacy of "violent struggle" is the increasingly stale and barren narrative used to secure elite cohesion and "authoritarian durability" in times of crisis, as explained by Levitsky and Way (2012) in the case of post-Cold War Africa. In other instances, as the phrase attributed to revolutionary leader Georges Danton, "La révolution dévore ses enfants"[53] shows, the violence used to affect the initial elite replacement trumps a separation of powers becoming the governance tool of choice for the new elite system.

Long after it is over, the original violent struggle phase still casts its long shadow, diminishing the likelihood that elite business models pursue value creation activities. Again, 'knowledge' is eroded and potential transformational leadership alienated, as is shown by Franck and Michalopoulos (2017) in their analysis of emigration following the French Revolution. On their own, the empowered newcomers will face an impossibly steep learning curve in developing sustainable value creation businesses at the micro-level. Even in a best-case scenario where victorious revolutionaries open up the political economy contest arenas to competition, building the necessary coordination capacity to run the meso-level elite system on more inclusive terms is a challenge that requires more than one generation to master, as a managerial, technical, and creative class (see Section 8.1.1, Figure 8.2) cannot be formed overnight. In another instance, if the current situation is any indication, few would claim that most of the warring, unconsolidated elite coalitions succeeding the Gaddafi regime after 2011 have either the inclination or the 'knowledge' to eventually be less extractive than the vanquished despot: "Executions, torture and slave markets persist in Libya: U.N" (Nebehay, 2018). The general principle is that besides eradicating the monsters, 'draining the swamp' also drains accumulated 'knowledge', thus being detrimental to the economy and often fatal in terms of human development:

> Despite decades of human rights violations, Gaddafi's regime upheld one of the more comprehensive and effective health care systems in the Arab World. Funded by oil exports, the government offered free, quality health care to all citizens. [. . .] Seventeen hospitals have been closed, while only four of Libya's 97 health care facilities are functioning above 80 percent of their normal capacity. The remaining hospitals are overcrowded, struggling to perform basic procedures as medicines and supplies are often depleted and many health care providers have fled the country. (Dunphey, 2019)

Such bleak pictures of the outcomes from non-elite confrontation and struggle do not attempt to exonerate the incumbent elite coalitions caught up in revolutionary processes. They are the proximate cause of revolutionary mayhem and their own worst enemies, having fueled the flames of discontent by failing to engage in the transformation of their elite business models before non-elite pain reaches the tipping point.

For most of the non-elites that survive revolutions, the sacrifice will not have been worthwhile. But what are the prospects for their descendants? In the French

53 The origin of this phrase might be an analogy to Saturn according to Mallet du Pan (1793, p. 63) who describes how the struggles that followed the post-revolutionary fragmentation of power ("The *ensemble formidable* that united all its parts and directed its movements is now dissolved") led to new disputes and counter-revolutions within the revolution ("the Convention and its factions are working to concentrate power within themselves; but before they can achieve this, they must reduce the rebellious departments and cities, defeat the victorious royalists in the West, prevent systematic coalitions, and suppress the dangerous example of effective resistance").

case, Hobsbawm (1990) and Acemoglu, Cantoni, Johnson, and Robinson (2009) see progressive consequences in the long historical process. Industrial and commercial elite business models replaced those of the aristocracy via policies effecting land redistribution, increased equality, a streamlined legal system and the elimination of barriers and fiscal obstacles protecting oligarchic arrangements. More controversially, in the Russian case, Allen (2003), who never contemplates the Tsarist elite system transitioning to a liberal system, assesses the Soviet industrial revolution transformation from "farm to factory" in positive developmental light. One wonders whether the full extent of the chaos and suffering caused by Napoleon and Stalin are truly factored into these positive assessments. Plausibly, for non-elites and elites able to stomach the human cost of political violence, a new payoff structure in the economy (using the language of Baumol, 1990, p. 899) with more inclusive institutions geared towards higher levels of value creation may justify revolution. But such outcomes do not happen in the near-term and even in the best-case scenario only come to pass during the lifetimes of their children and grandchildren.

Given the unpredictable outcomes of violent non-elite vs elite political confrontation and the travails of the victorious new elites in their efforts to consolidate coordination capacity, by what general principle should non-elites effectively advance their interests? In the context of the elite/non-elite relationship a range of options for collaboration and confrontation have been suggested, but this inquiry posits that the optimal non-elite response is to take sides and participate in intra-elite contests. While the nuances of each option are delved into later (in Section 8.1.3 on how elites can best serve non-elite interests), the premise is that non-elites should strategically and systematically ally with elite coalitions whose business models generate residual income with comparatively greater value creation (and minimize net value extraction from non-elite stakeholders). In the tradition exemplified by Ricardo (1817/1999), *The Economist*, and Cobden and Bright, knowledge elites (see Figure A5.11) should be instrumental in such processes, reaching out to non-elites who usually lack the necessary insight into the intricacies of elite business models.

Intra-elite contests are constant and of great consequence to non-elites, as one or the other of the contending elite business models will invariably offer more sustainable value creation (manifested, for instance, by a higher VCr). Still, this is not always easy to discern. For example, which of Apple or Meta is the less extractive based on *The Wall Street Journal* headline below?

> Apple, Facebook Trade Barbs Over Privacy-Focused Business Models: Tim Cook criticizes app-tracking tools a day after Mark Zuckerberg accused Apple of interfering with how Facebook apps work. (Higgins, 2021b)

While for Mark Zuckerberg, the extraction his firm suffers from Apple is "soul crushing" and an incentive for his AI open source approach (Cheung, 2024, 0:07), a society is in crisis when knowledge elites cannot differentiate between the actual and potential sustainable value creation of competing models and are co-opted by one or the other to peddle their narratives. That is, a society where the 'elite vs non-elite knowledge gap' hypothesis holds and is not addressed (as part of what has been termed 'the Amazon dilemma' in Section 2.2.2). Of course, there are genuine technical and research challenges at play here too, especially with the emergence of ever more complex supply chains, technologies, and business models where the degree and direction of transfer-IN/OUT is extremely difficult to determine. Another factor is the disinterest, cynicism, and venality of knowledge elites in elucidating non-elite interests, meaning that non-elites are *de facto* impeded in taking a stance consistent with their self-interest. Instead, white noise and false flags are purposely produced to increase knowledge asymmetries. This is even more galling when elite/non-elite alliances to effect institutional change end up heading in the wrong direction. Examples of misguided non-elite choices abound. Numerous automotive workers voted for Brexit only to subsequently lose their livelihoods (pointedly, the day before the UK's separation from the EU, 66,032 jobs had been destroyed in that sector according to the *Brexit Job Loss Index*).[54] The media, academics, religious leaders, and other knowledge elites often fall into the trap of supporting facile and populist narrative designs of all persuasions that wittingly or unwittingly sabotage non-elite interests.

Well-meaning knowledge elites today are unable to solve the Gordian knot of asymmetries in the 'elite vs non-elite knowledge gap', one that is possibly intractable with the prevailing elite separation of powers. Are privacy narratives a distraction once data becomes the key factor of production? Is not the relevant issue how much value is appropriated but *not* created by technology firms or the main owners of LLMs from their consumers and other stakeholders?[55] Answers to these or the earlier Apple vs Facebook question are impossible to arrive at without changes in intra-elite contest rules to ensure algorithm and, more importantly, business model transparency, along with generally established sustainable value creation frameworks and measurements. Doctorow (2024b) documents the "small cartels" hidden in the "payments system" cranny of the American economy that extract "2-5% out of virtually every dollar exchange"; thanks to "MEGO" ("My Eyes Glaze Over"), there is currently a zero probability that such "performative complexity" will be institutionally challenged. Will this generation of knowledge and political elites ever be able to fully assess the value creation and transfers of elite business models and then act on minimizing the latter?

Unless the answer is positive, non-elites will lose the political options to tactically or strategically side with the higher quality elite and tilt intra-elite contests (as is

---

54 See the statistics at: https://smallbusinessprices.co.uk/brexit-index/

55 Since metadata and content are so effective at modeling and influencing human behavior, advocacy groups like ProPublica could try to assess value appropriated but *not* created and quantify sustainable value creation in conjunction with their commendable efforts to shed light on "privacy" (see: https://www.propublica.org/article/how-facebook-undermines-privacy-protections-for-its-2-billion-whatsapp-users).

shown in the discussion of Figure 8.2). It has been argued that culture determines elite quality (Welzel, 2002, p. 275) and this is true insofar that culture affects the motivation for transformational leadership at the top (see Section 5.3, Table 7.2). Elites are in a permanent state of competition against other elites, not against non-elites, and both sides of the intra-elite contest have access to the same mass culture to craft narratives in support of their business models and subsequently impact cultural dynamics. Narrative markets are fortified by knowledge elites that connect mass culture with sustainable value creation (e.g., regarding emerging technologies) and from there with wider social and political movements (Figure A5.12a). They may well be the political economy's most important route to further non-elite interests, as one elite can nudge or pressure the rent-seeking business model of another towards inclusive transformation.

As non-elites can hardly force elites to undertake transformation, the constructive impetus must come from *inside* the elite system. Having tentatively rejected the path of non-elite vs elite confrontation—and especially revolutionary violence—in favor of political options that invoke taking cooperative positions and making informed alliances in intra-elite contests, this theory argues in the final Proposition 20 that both economic development and non-elite interests are critically served by an elite separation of powers realized in all of the elite power relations implicit in The Three-tier Set of Intra-elite Checks and Balances (see Figure 3.7).

3.3.3 Proposition 20: Non-elite interests are served by a comprehensive elite separation of powers

Proposition 20 closes the loop on the non-elite perspective by tying together the various bases for economic development developed in previous propositions and conjectures. It also completes the circle started in Proposition 1 by providing a normative benchmark for institutions that incorporates the elite dominance iron law. Fundamental to all of this is the rejection of the earlier non-elite rule fallacy ('people power') that references democratic ideals or the notion of polyarchy, as, for example, in *Who Governs?*, where Dahl sees an America where elites compromise because of "long-run changes from oligarchy to pluralism" (1961/2005, p. 223). The reasons for elite dominance due to the existence of 'the extraordinary lever' are comprehensively discussed throughout this work, but the Olsonian coordination capacity advantage of elites as articulated in the theory of groups should be reiterated: "concentrated interests will be overrepresented, relative to diffuse interests, in the policymaking process" (Bueno de Mesquita, 2016, p. 109).

The Wall Street Journal highlighted that "Bitcoin Fans Are Suddenly a Political Force" (Rudegeair & Bykowicz, 2021), while a follow-up article focused on the influence that crypto has gained in Washington by enlisting former high-level officials like Mary Jo White, Lawrence Summers, Christopher Giancarlo, and Brian Brooks (Kiernan & Michaels, 2022) or by "polluting the US election" in their support of candidate Trump (Kelly, 2024). Crypto elite coalitions have suffered setbacks, but those that survive increasingly do so on account of their elite coordination leadership over the institutions that regulate finance. Despite their anti-establishment appeal and grassroots support, these emergent elite coalitions (often led by rather unconventional knowledge elite members such as technologists and blockchain specialists) have risen not by tapping into the power of non-elites, but rather by establishing an intra-elite bargain through which the emergent coalitions integrate with part of the financial establishment and are blessed by political power (see the quote above, the eight figure political campaign contributions by Sam Bankman-Fried in the 2022 US midterm elections, or the Epilogue discussing Trump's coalition). Such intra-elite alliances are certainly perplexing when they support decentralized finance "DeFi" narratives that purportedly encapsulate non-elite preferences. Nonetheless, crypto coalitions have already successfully admixed into the elite system: "The growth in professional investors underscores the rapid mainstreaming of cryptocurrencies in recent years", with 80% of the 300 institutional investors surveyed by State Street having rules that permit "exposure to cryptocurrencies" (Vigna, 2022). The best may yet still be to come for the institutional entrepreneurs of crypto as indicated by price rises (Yaffe-Bellany, 2023) on expectations that the Securities and Exchange Commission (SEC) was about to continue to clear the path for exchange-traded funds like the Invesco Bitcoin Strategy ETF, an investment product based on "futures contracts on bitcoin [. . .] traded on commodity exchanges registered with the Commodity Futures Trading Commission".[56]

While the inclusion of non-elite voices hardly matters when it comes to the nitty-gritty of institutional change associated with elite business models, the sustainable value creation premise of this work stresses that elite and non-elite interests are *not* zero-sum or exist in contradiction (e.g., as in Marxism), nor are they invariably non-cooperative and adversarial as implied in some economic models (e.g., Acemoglu, 2006). The ETED holds that non-elite interests are symbiotic with those of value creating inclusive elites, while evidently incompatible with rent seekers and extractive elites (the relevant question for academics, policymakers, or the non-elites in the earlier example is which DeFi models—if any—create more value than they extract).

As previously emphasized, non-elite interests are best served by the full appropriation of the value they create and the minimization of being at the receiving end of transfer-IN. The likelihood of inclusive elite business models advancing in the political economy increases with a more robust and comprehensive elite separation of powers along all possible relationships in 'The Three-tier Set of Intra-elite Checks and Balances' (Figure 3.7, also see Table 3.2). Such a separation of powers provides more opportunities for non-elites to throw in their lot with elites that are running or promising

56 From the 'From N-1A' Registration Statement filed with the SEC by the registrant and available at: https://www.sec.gov/Archives/edgar/data/1418144/000119312521236682/d209327d485apos.htm

less extractive elite business models. The elite separation of powers requires that there is elite system cohesion and institutionalized intra-elite contest rules. Two of the various mechanisms at work in the practical realization of Proposition 20 are now explained.

First, a robust separation of powers encourages greater competition and demands overcoming knowledge asymmetries and adding transparency about the value creation positions of elite business models. Knowledge elites will have more chance of finding a protective home in one of the many elite coalitions, thereby being less dependent on and less likely to be captured by (the more extractive) dominant coalitions, notionally enabling them to articulate narratives and analyses that emphasize sustainable value creation and reflect the non-elite perspective. Second, and perhaps more fundamentally, the separation of powers means a lower bargaining power differential handicap for emergent value creation elites in their rise to the top. As a result, they—and the narratives that they bring with them—will be more numerous, while the incumbent gatekeepers they encounter on their journey will be less reactionary under the open access social order that such competitive conditions presuppose. That is, the value creation 'knowledge' advantage will more readily convert into power.

According to the 'value creation by elite separation of powers' conjecture, national elite systems with power distributed across many coalitions, institutionalized intra-elite contest rules, and numerous vibrant contests for elite business model standing, increase the likelihood that sustainable value creation elites will emerge to serve non-elite interests. In the meantime, conceptualizations of non-elite dominance, such as co-rule, post-revolutionary paradises, or genuine democracy, are misleading and risk being a distraction to the advancement of value creation elite business models and achieving inclusive societies. Does this conjecture imply that non-elites have no role at all to play? Quite the contrary, as the discussion of the case of Rosa Parks will show later in this section (and as is argued in Proposition 19 and depicted in Figure 8.2). Guiding principles for non-elites include not to fall prey to populism and to be vigilant against divisive narratives that selectively address extractive transfer models (and benefit certain non-elites rather than most non-elites). Non-elites should also be cautious about winner-take-all monolithic narratives that impoverish the elite separation of powers. At the other extreme—and equally problematic—the waters of the political economy become muddied if an array of weak and chaotic narratives proliferate and churn into irreconcilably opposed positions, triggering the de-institutionalization of intra-elite contests and impairing elite system cohesion. Since the mid-2010s, US politics has seemingly been on a rendezvous with this extreme, leading to the key empirical question of whether such shrill polarization results in increased or decreased value transfers away from non-elites via extractive business models in such hotly debated areas as health care, inflation, immigration, data and AI, abortion, industrial subsidies, public safety, or even war.

When elites with high value creation positions win institutionalized intra-elite contests, they grow the pie, and their models are more likely to enable both the principals and non-elite stakeholders to appropriate the value they create. The case of the Corn Laws of 1815 is further expounded upon because it provides a textbook example of the limited, supporting role of non-elites as allies of value creation elites in economic and human development. The narrativized preferences of non-elites and agitation by the Anti-Corn Law League played a part in the rise of the industrialist elite. They had very good reasons to strategically collaborate as the new package meant more jobs in the factory system, as well as cheaper bread on the back of the repeal of the grain tariffs (at the expense of the old elite landed aristocracy model). After all, "grain formed a very large part of the standard of living of the working classes (perhaps one-third of total expenditures)" (Stigler, 1952, p. 200). Still, it must be stressed that the repeal of the Corn Laws in 1846 was not effected by non-elite agency or elite agency for the sake of non-elites. Rather, it was due to the effective mobilization of the industrialist elite coalition against its rival in a majestic decades-long institutionalized 'within-system' (Tier 3) contest, a characteristic of Great Britain that predates its modern history.

Upon accumulating the power of 'might' in the political arena, in part thanks to having the power of 'mind' in society's narrative arena to which non-elite inputs contributed (Figure 3.5), the Manchester industrialists were able to pay lower subsistence wages to their non-elite labor thanks to cheaper grain imports. As Marx and Engels insistently recounted, even after the repeal of the tariffs, life for the working classes continued to be harsh. Nonetheless, it is indisputable that without the existence of a vigorous and comprehensive British elite separation of powers, elite system transformation toward higher sustainable value creation positions (and higher elite quality) would have been more difficult or even impossible. Overall, the development journey after this critical juncture produced positive outcomes such as a higher quality of life over the following two centuries (life expectancy in the UK went on to more than double from 35 years of age in 1770). What is essential to the ETED is that the development process was kick-started on the back of manifold institutionalized intra-elite contests operating on the foundation of a robust elite separation of powers balanced by elite cohesion. This was in contrast to Junker Prussia, where excessive cohesion nullified checks and balances and blocked attempts at an elite transformation away from protectionist models (also for grain). While German life expectancy grew in a similar way to that of Britain, the stymied intra-elite competition in the political economy had far-reaching and devastating consequences for Europe and humanity at large (Gerschenkron, 1943/1966; discussed in the Epilogue of this work). Notably, elites need not be altruistic; rather, in pursuing their self-interest and to maintain their status they must be ready for open and fair (i.e., institutionalized) fights for ascendancy against their peers.

The Three-tier Set of Intra-elite Checks and Balances is the ultimate protective mechanism for non-elites against extractive elite business models. Moreover, the elite separation of powers opens the portal for non-elites to participate in and help determine the outcomes of intra-elite contests that result in inclusive business models and institutional change. In this regard, the non-elite strategic collaboration with elites is important, as the case of Rosa Parks demonstrates. Non-elites have roles to play in all three political economy arenas, particularly in market arena contests, for instance, by activating their bargaining power as consumers in the Montgomery bus boycott. Again, the 'value creation by elite separation of powers' conjecture posits that the more comprehensive and robust the intra-elite set of checks and balances are, the more numerous are the avenues that open up for tactical and strategic non-elite participation in intra-elite contests and the higher the likelihood that value creation elite business models prevail in the political economy. In the decades prior to Parks' stand in 1955-56, the key problem was that America had few elites of any type (business, political or knowledge) ready to contest the business models of incumbent racist elites, with most staying on the sidelines instead of supporting the demands of African American non-elites to end extractive transfers. The ability of non-elite preferences to pressure and effect institutional change to advance their interests rests on alliances with elites and on the roles that non-elites can take as arbiters in the intra-elite contests of the political economy.

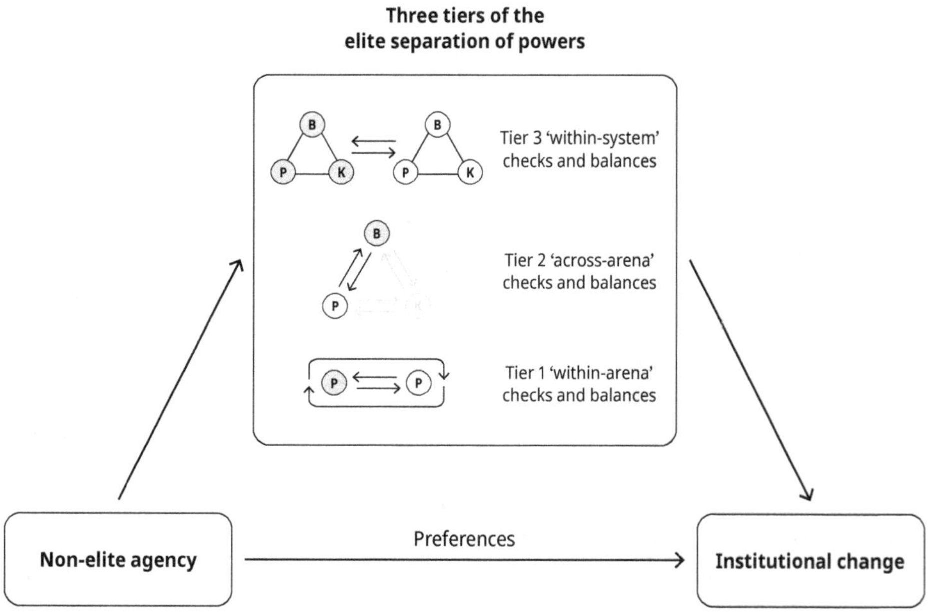

Figure 3.9: Three tiers of the elite separation of powers mediating the relationship between non-elite agency and institutional change.

Figure 3.9 shows that non-elite interests are considered and advanced as preferences for institutional change during intra-elite contests through a robust elite separation of powers which functions as a mediating variable (that explains the mechanism by which the non-elite agency independent variable affects the institutional change dependent variable). Political systems can be analyzed through the lens of The Three-tier Set of Intra-elite Checks and Balances to ascertain the degree to which different elite types (i.e., political vs business vs knowledge, but also incumbent vs emergent or domestic vs foreign) effectively balance each other. Checks and balances are a feature of intra-elite power relations in sophisticated and inclusive modern political economies. As discussed in Proposition 16, elites compete in parallel 'within-arena' (checks and balances within one of the three arenas, Tier 1); 'across-arena' (checks and balances between any two arenas, Tier 2); and, most critically, 'within-system' (checks and balances between coalitions in a system, Tier 3) to maximize residual income. An additional two tiers, 'across-system' ('Tier 4') describing foreign elite agency (Section 7.3.1) and 'from-core' ('Tier 5') describing the role of the core elite coalition (Section 8.1.2), are examined later (see the five tiers of Figures 3.10 or A5.11b).

In practice, the array of institutionalized checks and balances denotes the degree to which there is an open access social order. In Popper's "open society, many members strive to take the place of other members" (1947, p. 153) and succeed in doing so. The "theory of the double balance", proposed by North, Wallis, and Weingast (2006, p. 6), suggests that the economic and political spheres are jointly either open or limited access. In the ETED, the elite power domains of politics and the economy are complemented by the addition of society (see Figure 1.2), and the actual co-variations of emergent properties (Anderson, 1972; O'Connor, 1994) such as elite quality, inequality (Epstein & Axtell, 1996), including its polarized and fractal emanations (Cozzi & Privileggi, 2009), or open access in each of the three domains, are a vital matter for empirical inquiry. This is so because political economies are, at the level of institutions, defined by the discrete configuration of checks and balances across all the intra-elite power relations (of Table 3.2) that usher forth the characteristic intra-elite contests of a country that then heighten its levels of elite quality and associated economic development.

Two important points need to be emphasized about the relationship between non-elites and elite business models. First, the apparent contradiction in a situation where non-elite groups are regular beneficiaries of value appropriated but *not* created via elite business models (e.g., the bounty goes to soldiers of fortune as much as to the elite military contractors) that are extractive of other non-elite segments (in this case, the victims of war). Second, and as discussed earlier (e.g., Section 3.1.2), it must be stressed that a non-elite business model may acquire elite-like agency when it becomes "narrower than the stakeholders with whom it has a direct or indirect exchange relationship", thus generating some of the highest residual incomes in society (see the definition of elites in Section 1.2.4, Proposition 13, or Table 4.1). Such extensive coalitions include labor unions, civil servants, anarchist groups, air traffic controllers, lawyers, or farmers associations and are, for all purposes, sub-systems of the elite system. In short, non-elite agency becomes elite, even if the beneficiaries of residual income are very numerous, when it is supported by important bargaining power endowments and capable of both value creation and extraction activities. Extractive transfers are enabled by power, a quality that is dynamic and always on the lookout for new masters.[57]

The idea of dividing power has deep roots in the West. Aristotle, in *Politics* (1912, 4.14), conceived of a separate legislature (the general assembly), administration (the public officials), and judicial establishment, which in practice was never separate from the assembly and also had executive privileges (Fairlie, 1923, pp. 393-394). In *Histories* (Book IV), Polybius goes beyond his anacyclosis finding (see Section 1.2.1) to suggest a "mixed constitution" based on "several distinct organs, each set off against the others by the constitution, in which the cooperation of these different organs is essential, and therefore where one of them by withholding it may check and obstruct the action of the rest" (McIlwain, 1932, pp. 100-101, as cited in Hexter, 1956, p. 80). Modern China had similar concerns about the concentration of power (see Walker, 1947) and

57 It is important to stress ahead of the discussion of ethics in Chapter 8 that non-elites and elites—the poor and the rich—can all be conceived as utility maximizing agents, and as such are *a priori* morally equivalent when it comes to value appropriation. If the Kardashian-Jenner family and their one and a half billion Instagram followers mirror non-elite aspirations then value appropriation is ingrained in mass culture. The only difference between elites and non-elites is that the latter have not accumulated power and so fail to reap any significant amount of value appropriated but *not* created. Yet human nature and behavior is such that when circumstances allow non-elites to acquire even the smallest bargaining power differential advantage (over other non-elites), the lever need not be extraordinary at all; such advantages will be mercilessly squeezed for whatever value can be appropriated from another. The lesser magnitude of value appropriation aside, the non-elite propensity to exercise an 'inextinguishable value creation option of elites' (Section 2.2.1, Figure A5.4c) equivalent and pursue transformational leadership in their modest domains must, for theorizing purposes, be set to equal that of elites. Elite status does not undermine an individual's ethical fiber any more than possessing non-elite status makes one morally superior (see the discussion of non-elite quality in the Epilogue). Aristotle preferred aristocracy to democracy and Madison's "main fear" was "too much direct democracy" (Winters, 2011, p. 30). The perpetrators of some of the 20th century's most heinous crimes provide evidence of non-elite moral predispositions when a twist of fate places 'the extraordinary lever' in their hands. For instance, the methods of the most notorious leaders of the Tsar's Okhrana (elite born) pale in comparison to those of "the bloody dwarf" Yezhov and others at the NKVD (mostly non-elite born). Again, in terms of social life and personal utility maximization, all humans are *a priori* assumed to be equal, i.e., to possess a similar propensity for value appropriated but *not* created. The 'universal value extraction propensity of humans' (socio-economic) premise, rooted in the basic constraint of the human condition (Figure 8.6), is a notion that has not gone unnoticed by philosophers like Nietzsche, whose Zarathustra states: "and even in the will of the serving I found the will to be master" (1883/2006, p. 89). Xunzi, "the second great representative of the Confucian tradition [. . .] recognized that human nature needed to be restrained not only to protect one human being from another but also to protect Nature from being destroyed by unregulated human exploitation" (Ivanhoe, 1991, p. 309). Both elites and non-elites will extract from other non-elite groups to the extent that their power differentials permit. Finally, given this understanding, a multitude of testable hypotheses might be formulated for economic development such as which institutions (including those that are *de facto* embedded in cultures) most effectively constrain which second-order value transfers across each and every socio-economic level (see the visualization in Figure A5.14).

likewise developed solutions for its separation such as the *The Five-Power Constitution* conceived by its first president, Sun Yat-sen:

> Western countries have practiced the separation of legislative, judicial, and executive powers for only a little over a century. However, if we now want to combine the best from China and the best from other countries and guard against all kinds of abuse, we must take the three Western governmental powers—the executive, legislative, and judicial—add to them the Chinese powers of examination and censorate and make a perfect government of five powers.[58] (Sun Yat-sen, 1946, adapted from *Zhongshan quanshu,* as cited in de Bary & Lufrano, 2000, p. 326)

At its core, the modern democratic ideal, like the narratives of most political philosophy systems, seeks restraints on elite rent seeking. Democracy's chief utility to non-elites is not so much in the purported access to institutional arrangements that were once only privy to traditional elites, such as all-important guarantees on property rights and freedom. Modern democracies come with an explicit form of the elite separation of powers to preempt extraction—intra-elite contest rules that protect some rights and freedoms. Their focus is mainly on the political non-market arena, following the signposts provided by Montesquieu and the *Constitution of the United States of America* (1788) which, as Levi (1976, p. 373) recounts, was inspired by Gibbon's first volume of *The Decline and Fall of the Roman Empire* (1776/2001), Voltaire, Rousseau, and Adam Smith's *Wealth of Nations* (1776/1904), with the latter "emphasizing the economic vitality of separating functions". The legislative, executive, and judicial separation of powers, more so than voting, opens the avenues mentioned earlier for non-elites to affect intra-elite contests and so realize their own interests. Democracies have also adopted other balancing political mechanisms to stop the abuse of power.

To Madison, the larger political union balances different interest groups that otherwise would go unchecked. His opening sentence in *Federalist No. 10* (1787/1977) is unambiguous: "Among the numerous advantages promised by a well constructed union, none deserves to be more accurately developed than its tendency to break and control the violence of faction". He goes on to expound how if such "factions"—here understood as elite coalitions—are unrestrained, they will extract value from the majority. He argues that a union under a federal Constitution will act to check and balance local "factions" for the "common good" before they are able to engage in what he saw as extractive activities:

> A rage for paper money, for an abolition of debts, for an equal division of property, or for any other improper or wicked project, will be less apt to pervade the whole body of the union, than a

58 The power of examination refers to the meritocratic selection of government officials through tests, while the power of the Censorate refers to the institutions that control the effectiveness and integrity of government officials. Note that: "The Censorate was included among the five independent powers [in Sun Yat-sen's theory] because tradition marked it as a good old institution, and because under a system of separation of powers it was felt that an independent organ was needed to check on the other governmental organs to keep them within their scope of authority" (Ch'ien, 1936, p. 337, cited in Walker, 1947, p. 3).

> particular member of it; in the same proportion as such a malady is more likely to taint a particular county or district, than an entire state. (Madison, 1787/1977, *Federalist No. 10*)

For all the vision and thoughtfulness of this 18th century thinker, the separation of powers in a democracy and constitution is hardly fit for the purpose of dealing with the social and technological changes and increased complexity of the 21st century, especially given the onset of the "fourth industrial revolution" (as framed by Schwab, 2016) and its novel intelligent technologies and data-driven elite business models. The problem is not that the checks and balances in the political non-market arena—whether within the democratic legislature or the federal union—do not work. These arrangements have simply been superseded by the manner and speed of how power is now amassed and monetized, and by the very nature of intra-elite contests. The connection between centuries-old checks and balances and present-day business model rules in practice is distant and tenuous, as is evident in business areas such as AI, Big Pharma, or ride hailing. The headline for the *Uber Files*: "How Uber won access to world leaders, deceived investigators and exploited violence against its drivers in battle for global dominance"[59] makes clear that formulations for a separation of powers cannot rely on the precedents of Montesquieu, Madison, or any other ideas that overstate the politics power domain. Rather, a checks and balances theory must be comprehensive, transcend the political non-market arena, systematically address the first three tiers ('within-arena', 'across-arena', and 'within-system'), incorporate as many coalitions as possible—especially knowledge elites from the society power domain (in the Uber case, note the role of the International Consortium of Investigative Journalists)—while at the same time fostering intra-elite competition (in this case driven by business elites such as incumbent taxi coalitions or fast-rising start-ups) to curtail extractive models.

Hypothetically, could illiberal polities be comparatively more inclusive and have higher sustainable value creation, even if constitutional checks and balances in the political non-market arena are deficient? That is, if they offer a stronger overall elite separation of powers across The Seven Intra-elite Power Relations, the framework described in Table 3.2 below and based on The Three-tier Set of Intra-elite Checks and Balances (depicted earlier in Figure 3.7). This possibility is evaluated in Section 8.1.5 in considering which political system best serves non-elite interests (see also the sustainability test for political and business systems described in Figure 8.3). To assess the inclusiveness of a political system and its ability to deliver value for non-elites, *all* seven power relations must be examined to ascertain the degree to which those holding the three types of power endowments ('money', 'might', and 'mind') are in balance and able to check each other. Such a detailed analysis provides a basis for predicting sustainable value creation in an economy. For instance, the study of intra-elite power relations 4 and 5 would assess whether the power endowments of business elites respectively capture or sideline political and knowledge elites (or vice versa).

59 See *Uber Files* at: https://www.icij.org/investigations/uber-files/

Table 3.2: The Seven Intra-elite Power Relations in The Three-tier Set of Intra-elite Checks and Balances.

Intra-elite power relations (numbered)		Checks and balances in intra-elite contests	Separation of powers tier
1 Business vs Business	Market 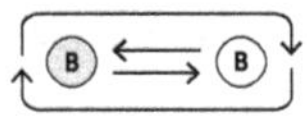	Rival business elites check and balance each other in contests for 'money' (economic power) in the market arena	
2 Political vs Political	Non-market 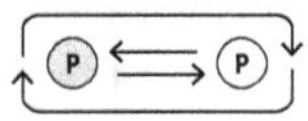	Rival political elites check and balance each other in contests for 'might' (political power) in the non-market arena	**Tier 1** 'within-arena'
3 Knowledge vs Knowledge	Narrative market 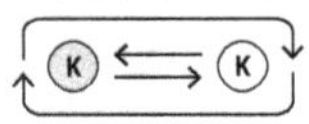	Rival knowledge elites check and balance each other in contests for 'mind' (social power) in the narrative market arena	
4 Business vs Political	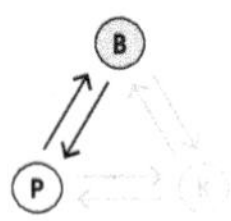	Business elites and political elites check and balance each other in contests between 'money' and 'might' (economic and political power)	
5 Business vs Knowledge	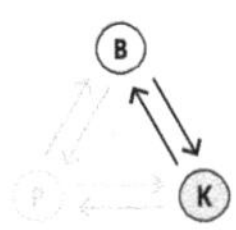	Business elites and knowledge elites check and balance each other in contests between 'money' and 'mind' (economic and social power)	**Tier 2** 'across-arena'
6 Political vs Knowledge	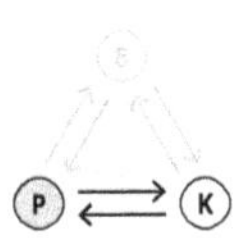	Political elites and knowledge elites check and balance each other in contests between 'might' and 'mind' (political and social power)	
7 Elite coalition vs Elite coalition	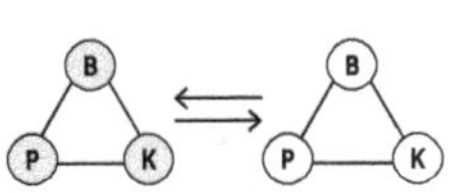	Elite coalitions check and balance each other in contests for power (the aggregate of economic, political, and social forms of 'money', 'might', and mind') in all three political economy arenas (market, non-market, narrative market)	**Tier 3** 'within-system'

To this elite theory, "institutional sclerosis" (Olson, 1982) or "institutional failure" (Baumol, 1990; Acemoglu, Johnson, & Robinson, 2005) are representative of a failed and ossified system of checks and balances across The Seven Intra-elite Power Relations. The lower the intra-elite competition in these intra-elite power relations, the higher the likelihood of extractive transfer-IN. Elites transform their models towards higher value creation positions because new elite business model rules (brought about by institutional change) emerge from civil and vigorous intra-elite contests that are mediated by intra-elite contest rules (Figure 3.9) in the context of strong elite cohesion that is often mediated by narratives (see "Evangelicals in the Power Elite" in Lindsay, 2008; "ideological integration" in Gulbrandsen, 2012). Regressive elite business model transitions towards increased extraction results from the deinstitutionalization of intra-elite contests and is regularly associated with low elite system cohesion—the opposite of transformational leadership (Table 7.2). A key problem for economic development occurs when extractive elites do not transform their models and remain unchallenged in polities that lack an effective and comprehensive elite separation of powers. Sokoloff and Engerman (2000) illustrate the problem through their description of the glacial rates of elite circulation characteristic of the sugar plantation elite systems in colonial and post-colonial Latin America. The concentration of power, the lack of intra-elite contests, and excessive elite cohesion (see the discussion in Section 5.3.3 and Figure 5.2 on the 'intra-elite quality contest' dilemma) preserves extractive models (for generations).

Swiss direct democracy, on the other hand, generates such high levels of prosperity because it is conducive to vigorous intra-elite contests that play out referenda by referenda. It fosters the ideal where political sustainable value creation—the effective supply of public goods—is "determined by demand (i.e., by citizens' willingness to pay) rather than by supply factors, in particular by the politicians' and bureaucrats' own interests" (Frey, 1994, p. 341). That means that Swiss elite business models actively compete with each other for public expenditure and licenses to operate while robust intra-elite contest rules based on the separation of powers facilitate an elite/non-elite cooperative game for institutional change at the ballot box. As a result, elites check and balance each other across many of The Seven Intra-elite Power Relations and their residual income flows are more sustainable, as their models strategically take into account a wide array of non-elite (voter) interests and narrativized preferences (Figure 3.4).

The Seven Intra-elite Power Relations is a framework that can be applied and empirically tested relationship-by-relationship to elucidate different aspects of society and the political economy. For instance, Paniagua and Vogler (2022, pp. 47-48) have conceived a geological resource diversity construct and show that the greater the diversity of such resources, the higher the level of competition between business elites (intra-elite power relation 2) is likely to be. The fact that the Brahmin priestly caste (a knowledge elite) is superior to the ruler, administrator, and warrior Kshatriya caste (a political elite) reveals much about traditional Indian power structures and the limits to 'across-arena' (intra-elite power relations 5 and 6) contests among elites. In present day America, when Mearsheimer makes the following contentious statement, he is also referring to the state of checks and balances (in intra-elite power relation 6) between political and knowledge elites:

> The American mainstream media is basically toothless, you young people in the audience can't appreciate it because you don't remember when the American mainstream media actually had some bite, but I can assure you it is toothless now and presidents manipulate it with great ease (The University of Chicago, 2012, 58:50)

The intra-elite power relations framework is also useful for comparative purposes. For instance, let us consider the Korean *chaebol* and the Japanese *keiretsu* national elite systems over the last three decades. In many of The Seven Intra-elite Power Relations, Korea displays more vibrant elite rivalry. Specifically, in intra-elite power relation 4, Korea is constantly rocked by scandals that bring to light attempts by the business elite to capture the political elite, while in Japan, the "iron triangle" (Kerbo & McKinstry, 1995; Schmidt, 2004) remains nearly unassailable as a rather pliant media causes any controversies to lead at most to cosmetic change. In intra-elite power relation 1, Korea has the more diverse political landscape—at the cost of eroding elite cohesion—with successive presidents hailing from alternating parties, while post-World War II Japan has been ruled almost exclusively by the Liberal Democratic Party (LDP) since the establishment of the electoral system in 1955, apart from a 10-month pause between 1993 and 1994 (Krauss & Pekkanen, 2011). Taking the 'across-system' (Tier 4) perspective on intra-elite power relation 2, Korea is the more open economy (imports plus exports account for about 97% of GDP, while in Japan the figure is just 47%).[60] Korean elite business models have thus done the unthinkable and caught up with or surpassed Japan in sectors ranging from LNG shipbuilding to semiconductors. The ETED framework suggests that growth and prosperity have been achieved in Korea through the centrality of intra-elite contests (Proposition 18), supported by a well-functioning three-tier set of intra-elite checks and balances.

An elite system tempered by a separation of powers that is materialized in a sophisticated three-tier intra-elite set of checks and balances should be a central aim for non-elite agency and a factor in non-elite narrativized preferences, but is likewise in the best interest of elites. Paniagua and Vogler (2022, p. 47) provide a logic for why elites have "incentives to establish and to commit to the maintenance of power-sharing mechanisms", i.e., intra-elite contest rules, namely the "threat that elites face from other elite groups' unconstrained political authority". Members of the non-elite strata, which regularly become elites in modern and open societies, might in principle have an additional motivation afforded by their personal stories. Once at the top, these former non-elite individuals ought to widen the paths of opportunity that led them to elite status, rather than pulling up the ladder on which they ascended. There is likely no greater contribution to society than fortifying the elite separation of powers and quickening elite circulation with the resources provided by sustainable value creation business models.

60 Data on exports as percentage of GDP show Japan at 21.5% and Korea at 48.3%, while imports for Japan are at 25.3% and for Korea at 48.5% for 2022 (The World Bank, n.d.-a; The World Bank, n.d.-b).

Summary of Chapter 3

Towards a logic for the elite system

Chapter 3 starts with a theoretical dissection of elite agency, before Propositions 12-20 transition the inquiry from a micro- to meso-level understanding that refines the elite system logic and consolidates this work's theoretical architecture.

Section 3.1 proposes three theoretical bases for elite agency, each with their respective anchor propositions. These are the institutional perspective outlined in Proposition 12, 'Elite agency is the principal microfoundation of institutional change' (3.1.1), where elite agency is posited to be the independent variable of institutional change in the theory's microfoundations of institutional change model (Figure 3.2). Proposition 13, 'Elite agency determines distributional outcomes—the winners and losers in the political economy' (3.1.2), recounts how institutions enable winning elites and constrain the losers in the elite agency microfoundations of institutional change model (Figure 3.3). Narrative economics anchors Proposition 14, 'Elite agency effects institutional change through the political economy's narrative market' (3.1.3), which stresses the mediating role of the narrative market in the elite agency microfoundations of institutional change model (Figure 3.4). All three propositions theoretically ground the ETED and are further developed in Chapter 4 and beyond.

Section 3.2 focuses on the system of national elites and in Proposition 15, 'Elite coalitions are the constitutive elements of national elite systems' (3.2.1), conceives an elite system wholly constructed upon interdependent elite coalitions. Systems theory is applied here to strengthen the analysis of elite agency at two levels: the meso-level national elite system and micro-level elite coalitions. The latter, sub-systems of the former, come into full existence by exercising business model leadership at the micro-level (its gravitational force is depicted in Figure 3.6). Proposition 16, 'The elite system operates on a multi-tier set of checks and balances' (3.2.2), expounds on the functioning of the elite system, emphasizes intra-elite contests, and proposes The Three-tier Set of Intra-elite Checks and Balances ('Tier 1' is 'within-arena', 'Tier 2' is 'across-arena', and 'Tier 3' is 'within-system', as in Figure 3.7). These enable and constrain the agency of one elite coalition with the agency of another and thus account for how elite coalitions become winners or losers in the political economy. The elite system is then validated as a meso-level conceptual element in Proposition 17, 'The national elite system is situated at the meso-level' (3.2.3), as it is constituted by other elements (micro-level elite coalitions) and is itself part of a higher order system (the macro-level economy). This theory's hierarchy places micro-level elite coalitions at the bottom, the higher meso-level elite system in which these coalitions are embedded in the middle, and the macro-level political economy system that hosts the elite system—the preeminent level from an economic development perspective—at the top (see Figure 3.8). Here, the complex systems perspective, including uncertainty, emergent properties (such as elite quality), and non-linear dynamics (for economic development trajectories) become relevant to this inquiry.

Section 3.3 closes the loop on the idea that elites are constrained by other elites, rather than by institutions, by positing that institutional change is the result of accumulated intra-elite contests. The significance of elite rivalry is laid out in Proposition 18, 'Elites shape institutions primarily through intra-elite contests' (3.3.1), linking institutional change to winning coalitions and stressing that nothing stunts development like a fractionalized elite system reneging on its intra-elite contest rules. Proposition 19, 'Non-elite agency can constrain value extraction through participation in intra-elite contests' (3.3.2), reviews the non-elite perspective and suggests two basic political options for non-elite agency to further its interests: 'confrontation', through violent 'non-elite vs elite struggle'; or 'cooperation', through active 'tactical' and 'strategic participation' in intra-elite contests or the more passive 'trust in elites'. The use of any type of violence is rejected because the destruction of value during the revolutionary and post-revolutionary phases first and foremost harms non-elites. Proposition 20, 'Non-elite interests are primarily served by a comprehensive elite separation of powers' (3.3.3) is central to this inquiry, prescriptive, and equally applies to elites. The three tier elite separation of powers explains the political economy's distributional outcomes and mediates the relationship between non-elite agency and institutional change (Figure 3.9) and is best understood through The Seven Intra-elite Power Relations (Table 3.2), derived from the Three-tier Set of Intra-elite Checks and Balances (of Figure 3.7).

The ETED is a theory that relies on the separation of powers, but its set of checks and balances seeks to extend those put forward by Montesquieu, Madison, or the US Constitution. In subsequent chapters this is taken two steps further as an expanded elite separation of powers is advanced that includes an international tier to recognize the endogenized agency of foreign elites ('Tier 4' is 'across-system') and the distinct agency of the core coalition ('Tier 5' is 'from-core') as is depicted in Figure 3.10 below.

The logic of the elite system yields conceptual frameworks that are tools for analyzing the critical intra-elite contests. These can be used for purposes such as assessing the stability and health of a political system, structural reform, or the prospects for human development. Vigorous and open elite competition, if balanced with elite cohesion and governed by intra-elite contest rules, offer non-elites the best option to further their interests by allying with high quality elites to nudge elite business model transformation and inclusive institutional change applied to elite business model rules. The ensuing sustainable value creation of elite business models postulates economic growth, with non-elites more likely to appropriate the value they create.

'Towards a logic for the elite system' is the last of the three chapters that comprise Part I ('Propositions') of this inquiry. Together with those put forward in Chapter 1, 'Towards a logic of elite agency' and Chapter 2, 'Towards a value creation and appropriation logic for elite business models', a total of 20 propositions have been developed on elite agency (a summary is provided in Table A1.2 of the Appendix). These, and the positions taken on existing elite and other theories; their key ideas, conceptual elements, and assumptions (presented in Table A1.1 of the Appendix), set out the diverse foundations for this paradigm of economic development. Given the specific language and the expansive theoretical architecture advanced to posit that growth is caused by elite agency, Part II of this work, 'Integration', will further stitch together the ideas set forth so far and tighten the overall structure of the system to facilitate the next theorizing steps. In addition, it sets the stage for the theory and its constituent ideas to be relevant for practice—both at the firm level and in macro-level policymaking—by making proposals for SVC measurements and frameworks for decision-making.

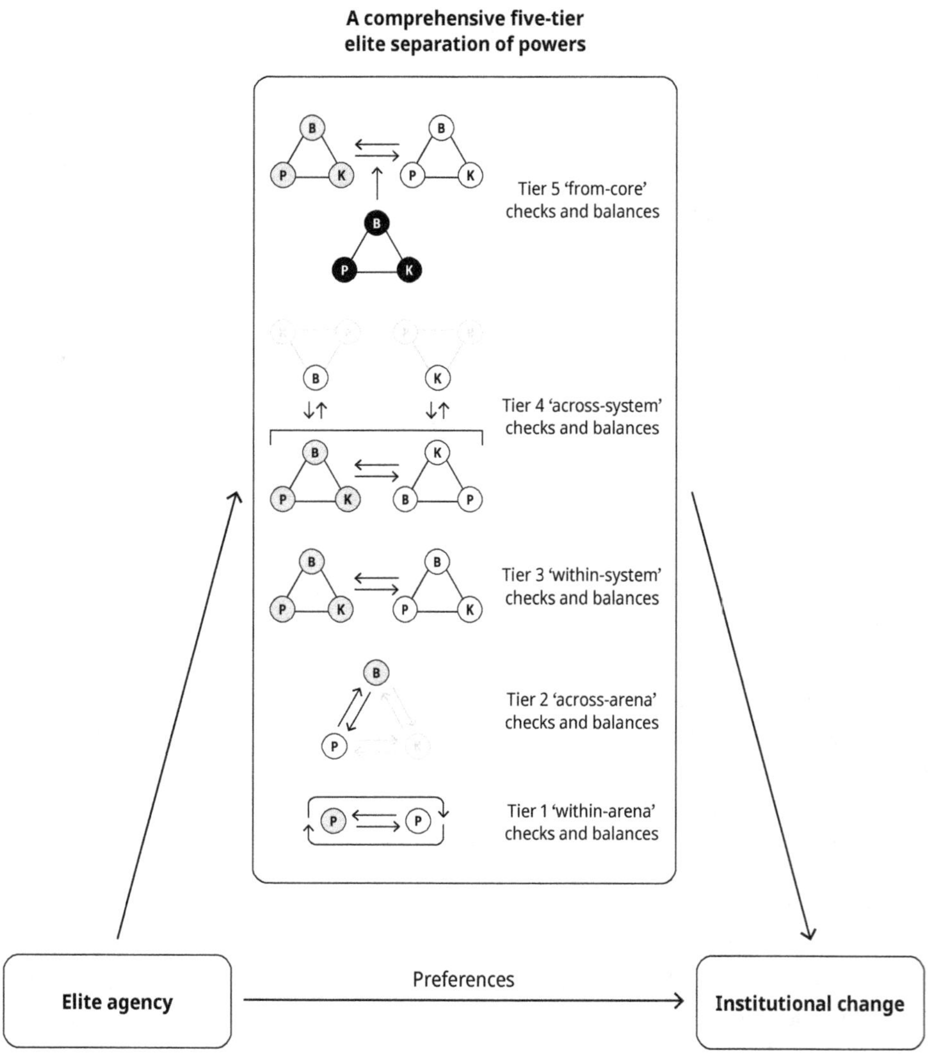

Figure 3.10: A comprehensive five-tier elite separation of powers mediating the relationship between elite agency and institutional change as analytical tools for intra-elite contests.

Part II: **Integration**

In ‘Propositions’, Part I of this inquiry, the first three chapters put forward 20 propositions that form the conceptual core of elite agency and set the stage for the ETED. Part II now builds on this work with two chapters that have an integrative theory consolidation function. In Chapter 4, ‘Towards elite agency constrained and enabled by power and institutions’ the all-important construct of elite agency is further amplified through consideration of its role as the microfoundation of institutions and its relationship to power. Elite leadership is developed as a natural extension of the discussion and the seeds are planted for the applied realization of this work’s core idea of sustainable value creation. These, and previously developed ideas, come together in Chapter 5, ‘Towards the elite theory of economic development (ETED)’, in another step towards the formalization of this book’s overarching system. Like all theories of economic development, this inquiry seeks to explain and predict economic growth, the impediments to growth, and suggest policy directions for inclusive human advancement.

https://doi.org/10.1515/9783110734638-006

Chapter 4
Towards elite agency constrained and enabled by power and institutions

> Another moral is that macroeconomics, like microeconomics, must go beyond Keynesian and monetarist formulas and analyze the structure of the incentives [. . .] Macroeconomic evils, like other social and economic phenomena, would not persist unless they brought gains to some. (Olson, 1984, p. 644)

This cross-disciplinary chapter on institutions focuses on the incentive system and takes specific positions in relation to the literature. For instance, this inquiry concurs with North (1994, p. 364) when he states that: "Incentives embodied in belief systems as expressed in institutions determine economic performance through time," but adds an emphasis derived from the opening quote above: institutions express incentives yet these incentives—the relevant incremental change stored as institutional arrangements—are manifested in business models to a much greater degree than belief systems and the "cumulative experience of past generations that is embodied in culture".

Institutional change is understood as the adjustment of the incentive system. This chapter starts by reinforcing the conceptual scaffolding of elite agency in the political economy (4.1). The ideas reviewed from the literature on the political economy and studies of power in sociology coalesce into the new institutional economics framework in line with North's grand theorizing as outlined by Telles (2024), thereby further consolidating the notion that elites are the microfoundation of institutional formation and change and hence of incentive structures (4.2). The chapter closes with a critical examination of the relationship between elite power and leadership (4.3).

4.1 Conceptual elements for elite agency in the political economy

This brief introductory section reexamines the building blocks of elite agency with an emphasis on leadership (4.1.1), before pausing to revisit the conceptual elements from Chapter 3 that support theorizing on elites in the political economy (4.1.2). On these bases the inquiry proceeds to a theoretical discussion of the elite as the agency that moves and advances all that is relevant in society.

https://doi.org/10.1515/9783110734638-007

4.1.1 Elite agency as leadership

> This difficulty in identifying individual leader effects should prompt policy makers and commentators alike to be cautious when opining that particular leaders are good or bad for growth. (Easterly & Pennings, 2020, p. 6)

This work takes the position that the two fundamental varieties of business model leadership (see Figures 1.2, 2.1, and 4.1) are part and parcel of elite agency, and that additional transformational varieties (Table 7.2) are necessary for growth. Leadership is deployed in the service of the coalition's elite business model. Elite agency is understood to be the cardinal and most decisive type of agency in the political economy. Elite agency is 'what elites do' and is realized through leadership that succeeds at attaining and then maintaining elite status (through power) while maximizing the utility function of the coalition (through residual income, see Propositions 5 and 6). Elite leadership thus necessitates the articulation of visions in the three discrete contest arenas of the political economy to accumulate (bargaining) power and convert these power endowments into residual income gains. Effective leadership relies on 'political economy know-how' and 'knowledge' (see Figure 2.3). Leadership—"one of the most comprehensively researched social influence processes in the behavioral sciences"—is described in Parris and Peachey's literature review:

> the success of all economic, political, and organizational systems depends on the effective and efficient guidance of the leaders of these systems (Barrow, 1977). A critical factor to understanding the success of an organization, then, is to study its leaders. [. . .] Great leaders create a vision for an organization, articulate the vision to the followers, build a shared vision, craft a path to achieve the vision, and guide their organizations into new directions (Banutu-Gomez & Banutu-Gomez, 2007; Kotter, 2001). [. . .] Leadership theories attempt to explain and organize the complexity of the nature of leadership and its consequences (Bass & Bass, 2008). Over the years, some leadership scholars have called attention to the implicit connection between ethics and leadership. (Parris & Peachey, 2013, p. 377)

Elite leadership introduces the conceptual element of micro-level leadership into analysis of the political economy. Elite agency requires an understanding of the processes by which the proximate power accumulation objective fulfills the distal, ultimate objective of elites—the generation of sustainable residual income streams. The difference between elite and non-elite business model leadership is the degree to which the former succeeds in accumulating power and then utilizing the 'extraordinary lever' to interact with institutions in pursuit of institutional formation and change (see Figure 4.4). Effective elite agency is carried out at the elite business model level through the two discrete forms of elite leadership: elite coordination leadership, which requires 'political economy know-how', the objective of which is power (see Figure 1.2), and elite business model leadership, which requires 'knowledge', the objective of which is residual income (see Figure 2.1), ultimately accumulated into wealth. These two fundamental leadership varieties are depicted in Figure 4.1.

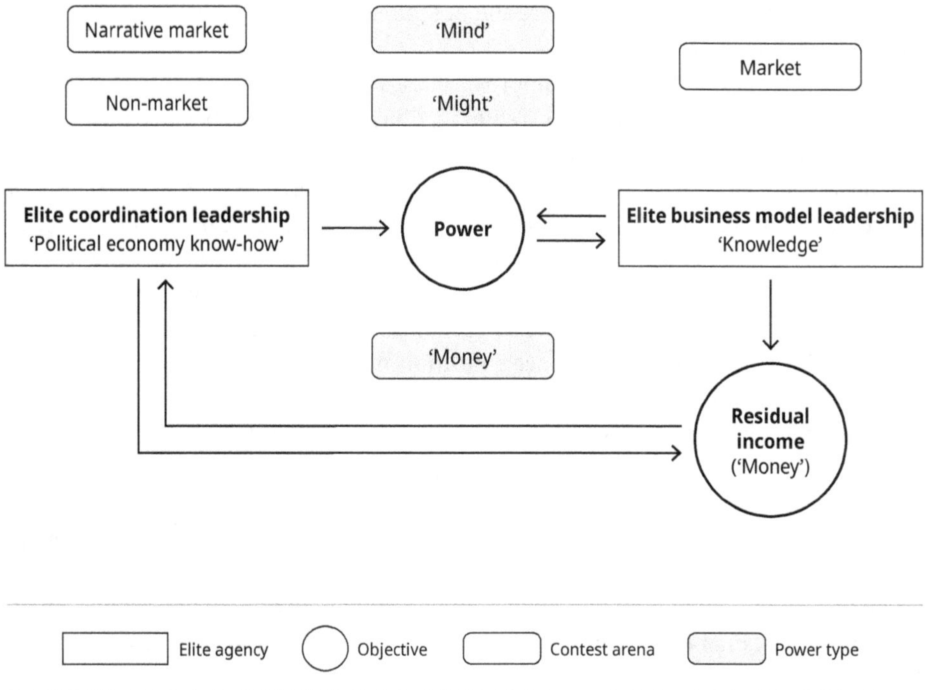

Figure 4.1: The two fundamental elite agency leadership varieties and their power and residual income objectives.

The study of elite business models necessarily brings the subjects of strategic management and leadership into contact with institutionalism. Elite coordination leadership accumulates power in the political economy (in the three contest arenas) to obtain a license to operate within the general institutional set up to legitimately scale power endowments and residual income flows. It is self-evident that elite business model leadership requires 'knowledge', exemplified in an array of management capabilities, as 'political economy know-how' alone is an insufficient condition to prevail in the market arena and effectively convert power into residual income.[61] The two-way conversion process between accumulated residual income (wealth) and power that is intrinsic to Figure 4.1 is a widely known and understood relationship (see the examples of oligarchs from El Salvador to South Africa detailed in Lingelbach and Rodríguez

61 An issue that is often overlooked by political elites at the center of elite coalitions is that the power types of 'might' and 'mind' alone do not guarantee sustainable residual income flows. The performance of Petróleos de Venezuela, S.A. (PDVSA) is an example of how powerful and institutionally privileged business models with ample 'political economy know-how' and bargaining power, but bereft of 'knowledge', can deteriorate into chronic underperformance, generating far less 'money' than it should given its munificent resources.

Guerra, 2023). Residual income generation at scale is a necessary but insufficient condition for economic development.

Transformational leadership, amply discussed later and essential to this work's normative positions (see Section 5.3, Table 7.2, Chapters 7 and 8), is leadership that is oriented towards implementing and incentivizing the higher sustainable value creation elite business models that lead to development. This is where leadership and the set of ethical principles of the ETED (see Chapter 8) explicitly connect and can inform social and political movements and initiatives (for further details on this logic see Figure A5.12a). Easterly (2011), Easterly and Pennings (2020), and other works that minimize the impact of leadership on the political economy, discount elite agency. Instead, this inquiry adheres to Brady and Spence's position that by "making basic choices and building consensus without which the economic dynamics cannot get off the ground", and by many other means, "leadership plays a role in generating sustained growth" (2010, p. 4). This aligns with 'the great elite coalition for development' conjecture, derived from Carlyle's (1840/2008) Great Man Theory of history (Section 1.3.3), where the leadership choices of eminent individual elites drive human and economic development (see the reflections on elite judgment that close this book in Chapter 8). It is also consistent with "a micro-level approach to understand what drives successful change", connecting "sustainability change agents" with business leadership and asking: "how, then, do we create heroic leaders?" (Walls, Salaiz, & Chiu, 2021, pp. 499, 503).

4.1.2 Central conceptual elements for a theory of elites

> From Adam Smith's *Wealth of Nations* in 1776 (or perhaps the Physiocrats even earlier) until at least John Stuart Mill's *Principles of Political Economy* in 1848, what we now call "economics" was in fact generally referred to as "political economy". (Drazen, 2000, p. 3)

There was an early awareness that the economy does not operate on the logic of mechanistic equilibrium but on the rules of a distributional game. This is in accordance with today's generally accepted understanding of the political economy: "The study of production and trade and their relations with law, custom and government; and with the distribution of national income and wealth".[62] This definition, on the website of the Department of Economics at Harvard University, references "law, custom, and government", i.e., institutions, while "production and trade" points to value creation and the "distribution of national income and wealth" to the value transfers that ultimately result in the economic winners and losers (see Proposition 13 on elite agency performance). Ultimately, analysis of the political economy in this inquiry is analysis of the value creation and extractive value transfer possibilities and actualities (transfer-IN/OUT) enabled by a society's business model rules. The sustainable

62 See: https://economics.harvard.edu

value creation (SVC) framework elucidates the long-term development trajectories of nations, a subject which becomes especially gripping in comparative terms: for example, refer to the divergent paths between the UK and Germany from the second half of the 19th century until 1945 (see Ricardo, 1817/1999; Gerschenkron, 1943/1966); the US or Argentina in the early 20th century; or China and India in the late 20th century and early 21st. Any appraisal of a country's future cannot overlook political economy distributional outcomes in the elite agency microfoundations of institutional change model (see Figure 3.3), the mechanisms by which winning elites win and losers lose, the quantities of transfers and the ensuing sustainable value creation of winning elite business models, how these agglomerate at the meso-level of the elite system and are reflected in elite quality, and consequently impact the economy and development.

Analyses based on the sustainable value creation and value and risk transfers (i.e., rent seeking) of specific elite business models are marginal to mainstream economic theory (as in the neoclassical syntheses of Hicks, 1937; Samuelson, 1947), seldom find application in policymaking, and are often also missing from public discussion forums unless, like inflation, war, or gun rights, they have major social effects. Even then, the models and debates are not framed in terms of value creation or quantified with measurements (like the VCr, through the use of precise extractive/inclusive transfer-IN/OUT SVC metrics). For instance, whether one examines the public discourse on the low interest rates introduced after the 2008 Great Recession or the COVID-19 fiscal support packages, the link between micro-level elite coalition business models enabled by the politics of institutional and policy changes and the aggregate value creation capacity of the elite system and society as a whole is rarely considered systematically, even when there is abundant relevant knowledge (see, for instance, the analysis of political economy responses to the recent pandemic by Coyne, Duncan, and Hall, 2021).

Key conceptual elements developed in the inquiry to address this gap are presented in Table 4.1. They provide a basis for an elite-based analysis of the political economy and institutional change and are the conceptual building blocks for the ETED. Elite agency is the central behavioral force in the political economy, the decisive micro-driver of macroeconomic development trajectories. The elite system is made up of elite coalitions in competition and subject to the checks and balances of their competitors as they procure institutional change consistent with their business model preferences. Through lower transaction costs and higher levels of trust, elites are more effective at collective action and so accumulate power (elite coordination leadership). Then, the capable hands of leaders, often managing 'knowledge', convert (bargaining) power into residual income (elite business model leadership). The critical issue for society and the economy essentially becomes one of transformational leadership: do elites increasingly generate their residual income through value creation or extractive value transfers and, if the latter seem to be more typical than the former, how can leaders transition their business models to higher levels of sustainable value creation?

The elite system, made up of a nation's elite business models, is the meso-level construct that integrates all value and risk creation and extractive value transfers. Elite quality is the aggregate emergent conceptual element that characterizes the functioning of the elite system as the transition mechanism between firms at the micro-level and macro-level economic outcomes. Conceptually, it is a description of 'GDP origination', the proportion of national income that emanates from first-order productive value creation activities vs second-order value transfer activities. The corollary is that the degree of sustainable value creation of elites in particular (measured by SVC measurements like the VCr) jointly adds up to the overall wealth of a nation. It is normatively consequential to incentivize those *qui generat valorem* ('who create value'). Foundational conceptual elements related to the ETED view of the political economy, along with the respective levels of analysis, are presented in Table 4.1.

Table 4.1: Definitions of key ETED conceptual elements and the analysis level used.

Analysis level	Conceptual element (Section reference)	Definition
Micro	Elite business model (Section 2.2.1, Proposition 7)	Elite business models are the largest residual income and reward business models in the economy and constitute a system of interdependent activities that are performed by a particular principal, as part of an elite coalition, in relation to its stakeholders. An elite business model describes *how* the principal and the stakeholders respectively create and appropriate value through division of value strategies to generate proprietary residual income, and associates with discrete sustainable value creation.
Micro	Elite (Section 1.2.4)	An elite is a coalition operating society's leading value creation and appropriation business models that generate the largest quantities of economic activity and residual income. Organizationally, and thus for analytical purposes, an elite is a business model that a coalition has secured from institutions—through wins in the political economy's market, non-market, and narrative market arenas—with limited rights that afford value appropriation advantages and, in consequence, a license to operate at a discrete sustainable value creation position.
Micro	Elite agency (Section 1.2.4)	Elite agency is 'what elites do' in relation to their elite business model as principals in a coalition (of economic, political, and knowledge interests) that creates value jointly with stakeholders in formal and informal exchange relationships, exercising leadership to successfully leverage lower transaction costs, higher levels of trust, and superior coordination capacity into (bargaining) power that is then converted into society's largest streams of residual income via first-order value creation or second-order value transfers.

Table 4.1 (continued)

Analysis level	Conceptual element (Section reference)	Definition
Micro	Value (Section 2.2.2, Proposition 8)	Value is everything that humans determine is worth appropriating. The creation of value is via first-order productive activities.[63]
Meso	Elite system (Section 3.2.3, Proposition 17)	The elite system is a meso-level generic structure constituted by elite coalitions and characterized by their business models. It is a high-impact sub-system of the macro-level economic system whose emerging properties play an outsized role in a nation's economic development.
Meso	Elite quality (Chapters 4, 5 and 6)	Elite quality is the meso-level emergent property of the elite system that describes the relative proportion of first-order productive value creation and second-order extractive value transfers of all elite business models in a political economy. This sustainable value creation aggregate has a purported independent variable relationship with human development and economic growth. A comparative global measurement of elite quality is the Elite Quality Index (EQx).
Micro, meso, macro	Sustainable value creation (Section 2.3.2, Proposition 11, see Table 2.3)	A conception of sustainability based on the business model where value is appropriated from first-order activities rather than transferred from the first-order value creation activities of third parties. Value is everything that humans determine is worth appropriating and business models based on 'value appropriated but *not* created' are non-sustainable. The relative proportion between first-order value creation and second-order value transfers at the business model level is operationalized by measurements such as the Value Creation Rating (VCr) and Value Creation Position (VCp).

The first two entries in Table 4.1 are 'elite business model' and 'elite'. While the distinction between the two conceptual elements has already been made (see Section 2.2),

63 Value can be understood in alternative terms, for instance, by using an analogy to the second law of thermodynamics with its focus on energy and its dispersion (positive entropy occurs in an isolated system as energy naturally disperses). In a socio-economic system, value is consumed or decays, becoming increasingly obsolete to humans, and so also tending to disperse (i.e., there is nothing of value worth appropriating) unless new value is created. The creation of value is therefore the human agentic mechanism by which entropy is locally reduced in the human domain (i.e., value that is worth appropriating expands). In contrast, the friction and inhibiting ramifications of second-order transfers of value locally hasten the increase of entropy. That is, elements that would otherwise be arranged in valuable configurations become disordered. The zone of the social habitat where the value creation vital to economic development—the high order (negative entropy)—that human beings require to advance and flourish occurs is the elite system of the political economy. See also footnote 169 and Sections 7.2.3, 8.1.6, and 8.3.3.

it is now further detailed with reference to social network theory, its structuralist perspective, and the notion of elite agency (Section 1.3). Social networks are defined in Mitchell as "a specific set of linkages among a defined set of persons, with the additional property that the characteristics of these linkages as a whole may be used to interpret the social behavior of the persons involved" (1969, p. 2, as cited in Tichy, Tushman, & Fombrun, 1979, p. 507).

Based on the above understanding, social network analysis (SNA) emerges as a method "to identify central individuals and key decision-makers" (Kostiuchenko, 2011, p. 195). Scott stresses SNA's "origins in classical sociology and its more recent formulation in social scientific and mathematical work" (1988, p. 127), while Mizruchi (1994 p. 339) emphasizes that "not only can network analysis be employed in conjunction with institutional theory but it is compatible with and capable of extending the population ecology and transaction cost models as well" which is consistent with the embeddedness of Granovetter (1985) and its focus on the transaction. Since the "social network provides a powerful model for social structure" it is employed in a variety of fields such as "studies of kinship structure, social mobility, science citations, contacts among members of deviant groups, corporate power, international trade exploitation, class structure, and many other areas" (Scott, 1988, p. 127). Past reviews noted that "network analysis represents an underutilized framework for analyzing and conceptualizing organizations" (Tichy, Tushman, & Fombrun, 1979, p. 516), while Coles (2001) chided criminologists for not using SNA to study organized crime. Today, the approach unlocks the boundless possibilities of data, not only in criminology but in fields such as risk management, innovation management, or knowledge management, where studies showcase the extent and "practical use of SNA in business and management research" (Anugerah, Muttaqin, & Trinarningsih, 2022, p. 1). By capitalizing on the embeddedness notion of Granovetter (1985), SNA even reveals performance where, for instance, "individuals' positions within social networks confer advantages" in the organization (Sparrowe, Liden, Wayne, & Kraimer, 2001, p. 316). At the political economy level, SNA elucidates "the interlocking ties of corporations and states" (Wellman, 1983, p. 179), or "the structure of an elite network in major American institutions" (Moore, 1979, p. 689). This method primarily identifies elite individuals, which seems vital "when interest groups and friendship networks become the basis for the creation of an internally circulating 'ruling class' whose members periodically seize key positions in different institutions and collectively capture the decision-making process at the state level" as Kostiuchenko analyzed for Ukraine (2011, pp. 195–196). Yet while the chief analytical focus of SNA is on individuals, this inquiry positions the elite business model—with its value and financial flows across stakeholder relationships—as the central conceptual element.

Social network analysis is relevant to the ETED insofar as it elucidates principal-stakeholder relationships that have residual income implications across and within organizations, and is of particular interest in instances when there is a lack of clarity (e.g., criminal organizations; the "secretive and stealthy" oligarchs of Lingelbach & Rodríguez

Guerra, 2024). However, simply determining an 'elite' within a network, whether using SNA or any other method, does not imply the identification of the elite business model or the individuals that will capture most of the value. Siegel (2009, p. 137) notes how "the impact of highly connected individuals" will be constrained by rivals in intra-elite contests and by the effectiveness of their agency (especially elite business model leadership, Figure 4.1), while the network position or the "number of connections", even when elites in the abstract are coordination capacity enabled by low transaction costs (Proposition 4, Section 1.3.4), does not reveal the business model, much less its all-important sustainable value creation. In this work, elites and the business model (with its certainly elite) beneficiaries are deliberately separated for the purpose of analysis, as the latter is relevant for development (see Table A4.2 for diverse perspectives on the 'elite' conceptual element) and is best ascertained with recourse to plain economic and financial analysis (see footnote 3). The social network diagram for the single individual (such as Musk or an autocrat in an emerging market) will commonly differ from that of the elite business model with its array of stakeholder relationships—the locus of elite agency—from which members of the elite coalition collect residual income.

To distinguish the basic conceptual elements of this theory a final point is needed. When individual elites are connected to their legacies, institutions are often portrayed as the most salient element. Thus, as Ralph Waldo Emerson writes:

> An institution is the lengthened shadow of one man; as Monachism, of the hermit Antony; the Reformation, of Luther; Quakerism, of Fox; Methodism, of Wesley; Abolition, of Clarkson. Scipio, Milton called "the height of Rome"; and all history resolves itself very easily into the biography of a few stout and earnest persons. (Emerson, 2005, para. 8)

Whether one considers the leadership of Scipio in the non-market arena or of Luther in the narrative market arena, the "lengthened shadow" that they cast are their business models; institutions, no matter how worthy and inclusive, are simply their instruments.

4.2 Elites as the microfoundations of institutional formation and change

The original use of the term "institutional economics", employed by Hamilton in "The Institutional Approach to Economic Theory" asserts that "economic theory should unify economic science" (1919, p. 312), and invites a holistic conceptualization of the economy (Rutherford, 2001) that is compatible with Parsons (1951/1991). This inquiry's system represents an effort in that direction, one that Fukuyama (2016, p. 213) would term an "attempt to return to macro theorizing" where the purpose is "to explain long-term institutional development in an integrative fashion". This holistic institutional perspective builds on Proposition 12 that posits elite agency as the chief microfoundation of institutional change.

In the initial sub-section, background research is presented to support the notion of institutions as the incentive structure that is at the root of residual income flows resulting from division of value strategies, and thus of variances in economic and development outcomes (4.2.1). The next sub-section presents the modest but pointed research on the causal relationship between elite agency and institutional variance (4.2.2). The elite agency microfoundations of institutional change model is updated with the specification that the institutional preferences of elites are for business model rules (Figure 4.2). This is followed by a review of elite embeddedness and the paradox of agency that is both constrained and enabled by institutional structures (4.2.3). The 'room' metaphor of Giddens (1984) is appropriated and adapted to explain institutional change driven by elite business models. Discrete elite conceptualizations of embeddedness for business model and intra-elite contest rules are respectively proposed and the relationship between the two is expounded on (see Figure 4.3). Finally, the early institutionalist debate around spontaneous and deliberate institutional formation and change is discussed to explain elites as the microfoundation of institutionalism and further bolster the bedrock for this work's grand macro theorizing (4.2.4).

4.2.1 Institutional theory links incentive structures with division of value strategies and economic outcomes

> In political bargaining over institutional change, the positions taken by individual parties are determined by their expected net gains from the new arrangement. Those net gains are a function of both the anticipated aggregate benefits from modifying [institutions such as] property rights and the associated share formula for distributing those benefits. (Libecap, 1989, p. 7)

From an economic development perspective, the decisive institutions are those that North (1991a, p. 97) notes determine "the profitability and feasibility of engaging in economic activity". That is, the rules that act as a *de facto* incentive structure and lead to action (Nee & Swedberg, 2008), or, in Baumol's celebrated phrase, provide "the reward structure in the economy" (1990, p. 894). Olson also makes the same connection in his journal article: "Microeconomic Incentives and Macroeconomic Decline" (1984). Economic rewards will accrue to those whose business models align with institutions. More precisely, these rewards—in the form of power and, ultimately, residual income—go to those who can effect institutional change, or "hack" institutions (see Schneier, 2023), i.e., in both cases adjust the incentive system in favor of their business models. Elite agency secures the preferred division of value strategies in the principal-stakeholder relationship to appropriate value created, as well as value *not* created (see the application of the VCA analytical framework at the firm level, Section 2.2.3). Power and residual income (or profits) are resources that in turn enable their beneficiaries to further advance institutional change for incentive system adjustments consistent with their business model preferences. The process has a circular quality (as depicted in Figure 4.1), since elite coordination leadership and elite business model leadership on the one hand, and their outcomes (power and residual income) on the other, are mutually reinforcing. Power enables institutional change that in turn clears the path for more power and residual income accumulation (i.e., wealth) to facilitate further institutional change and incentive system adjustment (as is later depicted in Figure 4.4).

Veblen (1899/1924, 1904/1975), an early exponent of institutionalism, viewed institutions as "constraints" and "generally accepted ways of thinking and behaving" that were "due both to the inertia inherent in any established scheme and to the defensive activities of vested interests", all of which were deemed potentially problematic when these were "out of step with new technological means and with the economic issues and social problems they generated" (Rutherford, 2001, p. 174). In other words, the proto-institutionalism of Veblen already conceived of the links between elites (vested interests) and institutions and implied the existence of extraction (including by elites who fail to innovate by maintaining business models that do not keep up with progress). Another early institutionalist, Commons, shared the logic of elites effecting institutional change, pointing to "customary rules that are initially produced from below and later sanctioned from above" (Chavance, 2012, p. 33). Moreover, in *Legal Foundations of Capitalism* (1924), the approach of Commons "was built on his notions of the pervasiveness of distributional conflicts, of legislatures and courts as attempting to resolve conflicts (at least between those interest groups with representation), and of the evolution of the law as the outcome of these ongoing processes of conflict resolution" (Rutherford, 2001, p. 176). In short, an early theoretical foundation exists to support the idea that elite business model preferences and elite agency drive institutional change (as is reflected in the elite agency microfoundations of institutional change model, Figure 3.2) and, more specifically, the shaping of intra-elite contest rules.

Despite its promising progress in the interwar period, after 1945, institutional economics failed to advance out of the long shadow of neoclassical theory, was squarely outside of the mainstream, and was "banished to the ill-regarded discipline of sociology" (Rutherford, 2001, p. 186). Recovery came when variations of institutional theory leveraged some (not all) of the cardinal assumptions of neoclassical economics, including scarcity and competition: "Douglass North, along with Ronald Coase, Elinor Ostrom, and Oliver Williamson, transformed the early intuitions of new institutional economics into powerful conceptual and analytical tools that spawned a robust base of empirical research" (Ménard & Shirley, 2014, p. 3). Mainstream economic theory then "took over those aspects of institutionalism amenable to 'model analysis'" (Copeland, 1951, p. 59, as cited in Rutherford, 2001, p. 184), such as labor economics and industrial organization. Yet, as the re-born institutional approach managed to plug an important gap in neoclassical economics, it did not articulate a specific role for elites in its revamped discourse. Institutions, however, have entered the realm of development economics.

Hall and Jones (1999) argue that institutions (which they conceive of as social infrastructure) account for the differences in capital endowments and productivity and hence for long-term growth in line with research by Glaeser, La Porta, Lopez-de-Silanes, and Shleifer (2004). Djankov, McLiesh, and Ramalho demonstrate how the World Bank's *Doing Business Report* database is a measure of institutional quality (understood as the "burden of business regulations") and hence "an important determinant of growth" (2006, p. 399). The literature on varieties of capitalism recognizes the relationships among institutions, politics, and the economy and the impact of those relationships on economic outcomes (Hall, 2015, p. 1). Acemoglu and Johnson (2005) unbundle institutions and identify those that have "a first order impact on long-run economic growth", i.e., the "property rights institutions" that "protect citizens against expropriation by the government and powerful elites", contrasting these with "contracting institutions" that are found to matter less (2005, p. 949). Rodrik, Subramanian, and Trebbi (2004), start their seminal paper, "Institutions Rule", by citing Smith's *Wealth of Nations* ("Commerce and manufactures, in short, can seldom flourish in any state in which there is not a certain degree of confidence in the justice of government") and go on to show how institutions are more relevant than geography or trade in determining income levels around the world. Robinson, in the spirit of Hamilton's "general concern" of economics (1919, p. 318), describes the centrality of institutions in terms of both incentives and the division of value:

> Economic institutions matter for economic growth because they shape the incentives of key economic actors in society, in particular, they influence investments in physical and human capital and technology, and the organization of production. Economic institutions not only determine the aggregate economic growth potential of the economy, but also the distribution of resources in the future. (Robinson, 2010, p. 3)

4.2.2 Elite business model variance drives institutional variance

> Institutions are the rules of the game in a society or, more formally, are the humanly devised constraints that shape human interaction. In consequence they structure incentives in human exchange, whether political, social, or economic. Institutional change shapes the way societies evolve through time and hence is the key to understanding historical change. (North, 1990, p. 3)

Rules exist as such, but they also manifest as "formal organizational structures [that] arise as reflections of rationalized institutional rules" (Meyer & Rowan, 1977, p. 340). The rules that organized entities like government bodies, political parties, law enforcement agencies, courts, central banks, stock exchanges, research institutes, educational institutions, churches, NGOs, museums, and sports federations put in place address specific functions in society. There is a consensus that institutions are a key determinant of economic outcomes and development.[64] Does it then matter how institutions—those "humanly devised constraints"—arise in the first place?

64 Institutions and policies are two constants of this work. Both conceptual elements overlap since, according to Khan (2018, p. 640), they "have an effect on economic, social or political outcomes" and

Hall and Jones (1999) argue that institutions are endogenously determined by history (they are even partially captured in language) while Greif and Laitin (2004) build on repeated game theory to offer a dynamic theory of endogenous institutional change and stability. Sachs (2003) or Easterly and Levine (2003) identify geography as a determinant factor while Rodrik, Subramanian and Trebbi (2004, p. 135) nuance its "significant effect on the quality of institutions". State capacity accounts for the quality of institutions in the work of Bourguignon and Verdier (2010) as well as in Acemoglu and Johnson (2005), Rodrik, Subramanian, and Trebbi (2004), and Zhang (2022). Alexander and Welzel affirm the scholarly consensus "that state failure in the enforcement of rule of law is the key factor separating effective from ineffective democracies" (2011, p. 271). Leaning on Proposition 12 ('Elite agency is the principal microfoundation of institutional change') and foundational to this inquiry are the works of Bourguignon and Verdier (2010, pp. 1, 2), who point to institutional change brought about by elites, as well as Acemoglu and Johnson (2005), Acemoglu and Robinson (2008), Brezis and Temin (2007), "The Elite as a Critical Factor in National Development", a case study on Botswana by Sebudubudu and Molutsi (2011), and especially Robinson (2010), and various contributions to Amsden, DiCaprio, and Robinson's *The Role of Elites in Economic Development* (2014). Khan (2018, p. 636) offers a coherent causality argument: "Institutions and policies describe rules that in turn determine resource allocation, and these can affect different types of organizations in very different ways. Organizations can be expected to support, resist or distort particular institutions or policies depending on their interests and capabilities."

To Robinson (2010, p. 3) "a crucial factor in explaining the persistence of institutions is how elites form around sets of institutions and how elites persist and reproduce over time". In this articulation, the direction of development is from institutions to elites, yet, at the same time, the elite agency of winning elites accounts for institutional persistence. For instance, one could consider the effects of French revolutionary reforms to abolish the seigneurial regime and establish free (labor) markets on the German guild system. The first takeaway from this example is that institutional differences lead to divergent economic outcomes. Specifically, the institutional differences associated with the application (or not) of the *Code Napoléon* resulted in dissimilar value creation incentives and hence divergent growth trajectories:

> Acemoglu, Cantoni, Johnson and Robinson (2009) show that parts of Europe that were reformed by the French between 1792 and 1815 experienced significantly more rapid economic growth and increases in urbanization in the 19th century compared to those parts which were not reformed. (Robinson, 2010, p. 17)

"change the distribution of benefits in society". Their distinction in this work follows his articulation: "Policies can be defined as rules that are generally easier to change than institutions".

A second and critical takeaway is that an accumulation of institutional change results from elite agency (or the lack thereof):

> After 1815 (Congress of Vienna), the reforms implemented by the French persisted in precisely those areas where old elites were unable to return. (Robinson, 2010, p. 17)

As previously stated, the ability of elites to apply their preferences on institutions—elite coordination leadership—rests on 'the extraordinary lever' of elite coalitions and their lower transaction costs and higher trust levels compared to distributed larger non-elite groups (see Proposition 4; Figure A5.3a). Power can be used for value extraction, as is illustrated by Acemoglu's (2006, p. 515) words: "elite preferences over inefficient policies translate into inefficient economic institutions". As stressed by Khan (2010, p. 25), "the 'rent-seeking' activities of powerful groups result in the creation of both formal and informal institutions". On the other hand (and consistent with elite business models as the locus of this theory), elites running business models with high levels of sustainable value creation (measured by VCp/VCr) lobby for efficient institutions and bring about higher degrees of long-term economic and human development. One might think of the factory business model of the industrial revolution that combined division of labor, sizable capital outlays, and management to cost-efficiently mass-manufacture standardized products. Elite institutional preferences emerge from elite business models with varying degrees of sustainable value creation and lead to inclusive/extractive institutions—in the terms of Acemoglu and Robinson (2013a)—through accumulated institutional change (which can also be imagined on an extractive to inclusive conceptual continuum that parallels the business model 'value spectrum' in Figure 2.10). Elite agency, actualized through effective elite coordination leadership and elite business model leadership, develops business models while advancing rules on taxation, subsidies, technology, trade, environment, safety, labor, intellectual property, privacy, transportation, data, consumer protection, energy, public health, zoning and land use, immigration, telecommunications, cybersecurity, securities markets, bankruptcy, etc. for their advantage. By promoting the optimal set of laws (binding statutes established by government bodies) and regulations (actionable and enforceable guidelines derived from laws and policy) as the rules for their business models in the political economy, elites become the determinant factor of institutional change and incentive setting (again, both inclusive and extractive). Figure 4.2 provides additional granularity to the elite agency microfoundations of institutional change model (Figure 3.2) by highlighting that the relationship between elites and institutions is anchored by the preferences that matter most to the residual income of elites—the business model rules.

Of all agents in the economy, it is the principals of elite business models that have the strongest motivation to amass and wield the full power of their agency to enable their preferences and remove institutional constraints. Elite coalitions reap the highest returns (or losses) from business model rules that align with (or deviate from) their business model logic and so have rather more at stake than broader or non-elite coalitions. These narrower coalitions have less dispersed interests that they are more

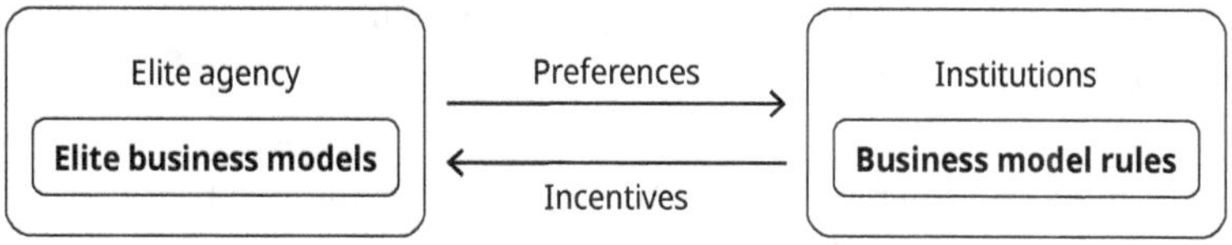

Figure 4.2: Elite institutional preferences as business model rules in the elite agency microfoundations of institutional change model.

adept at defending. Consistent with Proposition 18 ('Elites shape institutions primarily through intra-elite contests'), the major constraints for elites are not institutions (e.g., the returning old elites in Germany scrapped elements of the *Code Napoléon*), but rival elite coalitions (e.g., new elites in Germany that preserved the Napoleonic institutional change and encumbered the return of old elites). Do the power differentials exhibited in intra-elite contests to secure business model rules constrain elite agency more than the intra-elite contest rules? The latter provide a more stable framework for development if there is elite cohesion and a comprehensive separation of powers. Yet any law or its *de facto* impact (see Figure 4.3 which distinguishes between business model rules and intra-elite contest rules) is amendable if there are sufficient power differentials, sometimes employed midway through an intra-elite contest through lawsuits, novel legal interpretations, *ad hoc* regulations and ordinances, presidential decrees, and various forms of rule *by* law rather than the rule *of* law (see the discussion in Section 4.3.2 on meta-institutions and the rules that change institutions).

Business model rules function to constrain non-elites and their value appropriation options. Intra-elite contest rules function to constrain losing elites. The applicable business model rules are an expression of intra-elite contest outcomes. A simple 'follow the money' heuristic to identify the causes of institutional change would suggest that *cui bono* ('who benefits') from institutional change has likely instigated it. For instance, Janet Yellen conceding that "she was 'wrong' about inflation threat" (Politi, 2022) is misleading, as business model rules (interest rate changes are *de facto* such a rule) are not amended by error or accident if elites have agency. Wherever there are significant residual income flows, investments by a business model in changes to the political economy rules have channeled these. To understand inflation or any other inclusive or extractive phenomena in the economy, it is important to 'follow the money' and determine who benefits. The *cui bono* analysis of the political economy likewise applies to institutional change that originates in the narrative market arena (e.g., tariffs and sanctions, diversity, equity, and inclusion (DEI), universal healthcare). After all, the human beings of North's "humanly devised constraints" are elites. Normatively, the *cui bono* agents that succeed in effecting both inclusive and extractive institutional change would be those *qui generat valorem* (consistent with the maxim, *To the creators the value created*, see the set of ethical principles in Chapter 8 as well as 'A Weighted Structural Reform Framework' for policy in Table 7.1).

4.2.3 Discrete conceptualizations of elite embeddedness for elite business model rules and intra-elite contest rules

Elites as the central agents of the economy are posited to be at the deepest level of what Seo and Creed (2002) refer to as the "paradox of embedded agency". This paradox is important, and two formulations follow:

> How can actors change institutions if their actions, intentions, and rationality are all conditioned by the very institution they wish to change? (Holm, 1995, p. 398)

> If institutions are, by definition, firmly rooted in taken-for-granted rules, norms, and routines, and if those institutions are so powerful that organizations and individuals are apt to automatically conform to them, then how are new institutions created or existing ones changed over time (DiMaggio & Powell, 1991)? (Seo & Creed, 2002, p. 222)

The paradox of institutional change is theoretically not easy to handle, and neither are the accounts that seek to explain it:

> In neo-institutional theory, changes to institutions are usually explained by disruptions to the institutional order. [. . .] Therefore, explaining an institutional change in situations that lack disruption of the institutional order or exhibit institutional plurality and complexity appears to be valuable. (Goldenstein & Walgenbach, 2019, p. 136)

In early neo-institutionalism, agents were "implicitly assumed to have a limited degree of agency" and so complied with institutional pressures (Battilana & D'Aunno, 2009, p. 31). Such institutional determinism is obviously problematic when evaluating institutional change in support of a new business model. Another original weakness of such neo-institutionalist conceptions of institutional formation and change is its inconsequence for practice, as articulated by Hodgson (2000, p. 318): "Although institutional economists are keen to give their theories practical relevance, institutionalism itself is not defined in terms of any policy proposals". This position shifted because of ambitious visions for the field exemplified in works like "Institutions as the Fundamental Cause of Long-Run Growth" (Acemoglu, Johnson, & Robinson, 2005) and progress in the understanding of specific phenomena like poverty traps. Theoretically, and in dialectical fashion, Seo and Creed (2002, p. 240) eschew neo-institutionalism's agents "as passive recipients of institutional frameworks", but also as the "unconstrained" utility-maximizing agents of North (1991b) using the proactive manipulation strategies of Oliver (1991). They then settle between these "extreme positions" on a middle-way that sees institutional change and human agency conceptualized "as praxis", action that is "conditioned but not determined by existing social arrangements" (Seo & Creed, 2002, p. 240).

The metaphorical 'room' of Giddens (1984) is also an intermediate approach: the agent is within "the walls of a room from which an individual cannot escape (signifying 'embeddedness'), but inside of which s/he can move around at whim (signifying 'agency')" (Lok & Willmott, 2019, p. 470). The idea here is that "the relation between structure and agency is understood as mutually constitutive; or, as Bourdieu and Wacquant (1992, p. 20) incisively put it, as 'ontologically complicit'" (Lok & Willmott, 2019, p. 470). Cardinale (2018, p. 132) proposes an approach to set the microfoundations for institutional theory where "structure not only constrains and enables action but also actively orients it toward some possibilities over others". While he claims that such an approach will "bridge long-standing divides within institutional theory", he is taken to task by Lok and Willmott (2019) on account of his two-level conceptualization of embeddedness, the desire to connect structure and agency (which to them are not partially autonomous juxtaposed forces but "mutually constitutive" with action shaped by structural conditions). In practical and theoretical terms, is agency enabled and constrained "by" (Cardinale, 2018) or "through" (Lok & Willmott, 2019) structure and institutions? Given the elite theory's integration with practice, elite agency is deemed to happen "through" structure rather than being acted upon "by" structure, in alignment with Gidden's theory of structuration (1984, p. 25) where the "constitution of agents and structures are not two independently given sets of phenomena, a dualism, but represent a duality".

This elite theory is expeditious in its conceptualization of the relationship between (elite) agency and institutions. Clearly, Giddens' room and its features are the accumulated institutional changes brought about by previous generations of elites (driven by their business model preferences). Yet there is an area surrounding the room that is of great interest for general development purposes. Emergent or rival elites with sufficient power from their wins in the political economy's three arenas (market, non-market, and narrative market) creatively force their way through the room's walls or ply their trade outside, notably in the adjacent spaces opened up by technological shifts or narrative possibilities. Institutionally, these are self-similar offshoots, sometimes a reduced version of the original, but in cases when new technological advances allow, a scaled-up version of the original fractal patterns—normatively, value creation patterns ought to take precedence. In time, however, emerging elites erect a roof over the fresh walls of their new domain and fervently protect it while accumulating power (Figure 4.5 describes the lifecycle of elite business models). As far as the bargaining power differentials permit, and when incumbent elites fail to reinforce the existing barriers, lock the exits, or shrink the space, the newcomers either take over or simply dismantle the old structures. In this work, institutions are the rules that constrain elite agency insomuch as there are power differentials between elites in the context of intra-elite rivalry. Institutions are the accumulated change layers of temporally resolved intra-elite contests—they "are both the medium and outcome" (as in "the duality of structure" outlined by Giddens, 1994, p. 25) of the winners. The constraining effects of institutions matter in terms of value appropriation, but in the main these apply to non-elites and elites that are on the losing side of intra-elite contests. A different and more significant constraint on winning elites, though far from airtight, is the set of rules that govern intra-elite contests, such as elections or the budgeting processes of a state.

Lobbying (see Hall & Deardorff, 2006; Lowery, 2007; Baldwin & Robert-Nicoud, 2007; Smith, 2018) by organized interests "to affect what the government does" (Nownes, 2006, p. 5) is sometimes the visible hand of agency driving institutional change and has long been recognized as such: "Adam Smith [. . .] offered trenchant discussion of the activities and effects of mercantile interest groups" (Tollison, 2012, p. 74). Lobbying has become so visible, institutionalized, and sophisticated that the management literature now employs the more extensive term of corporate political activity (CPA). CPA encompasses and distinguishes between discrete activities like political action committees (PACs) and contributions or donations to electoral campaigns (Hillman, Keim, & Schuler, 2004), where the "nonmarket strategy refers to a firm's concerted pattern of actions to improve its performance by managing the institutional or societal context of economic competition" (Baron, 1995; Lux, Crook, & Woehr, 2011, as cited in Mellahi, Frynas, Sun, & Siegel, 2016, p. 144). When successfully carried out via elite coordination leadership, the direct agency of a coalition's political elites in the non-market political arena, supported by more indirect agency in the narrative market arena, brings forth the institutional changes required for its business model's residual income objective. Acemoglu, Johnson, and Robinson (2005, pp. 406–407) note that: "Bad institutions are therefore kept in place, clearly not for the benefit of society as a whole, but for the benefit of the ruling elite, and this is a pattern we encounter in most cases of institutional failure". Institutional failure is therefore cumulative institutional change in support of extractive elite business models (or its failure to support inclusive models). Lobbying activities (a prime manifestation of 'political economy know-how', see Figure 2.3), have been linked to rent seeking in work by Tullock (1967) and Buchanan (1980, p. 14) who see non-market interactions working side-by-side with Smithian competitive markets (requiring 'knowledge') to shape institutional formation and change. The subtlety of institutional change achieved through lobbying varies, as documented by the US Senate Special Committee to Investigate the National Defense Program in the context of WWII:

> Such corporate executives in high official roles were too inclined to make decisions for the benefit of their corporations. "They have their own business at heart", [Senator] Truman remarked. The report called them lobbyists "in a very real sense", because their presence inevitably meant favoritism, "human nature being what it is". (McCullough, 1992, p. 265, as cited in Williamson, 1993, p. 81)

Despite the critical assessment above, lobbying, which plays out as part of the set of checks and balances between business and political elites (see Table 3.2; intra-elite power relation 4), can lead to sustainable value creation—though this depends on the elite business model that is being advanced. The ETED's general position is that institutional change, including inclusive change, is caused by elite business model preferences. As elite business models backed by bargaining power differentials materialize, elite agency fashions new institutional layers. Institutions are the embodiment of cumulative elite preferences for rule formation and their change. At the same time, the analysis of institutions as constraints benefits from their separation into the two categories considered earlier—and now depicted in Figure 4.3—subject to a discrete examination of their formation and change: business model rules and intra-elite contest rules.

Mahoney (2000, p. 507) notes that "path dependence characterizes specifically those historical sequences in which contingent events set into motion institutional patterns or event chains that have deterministic properties". Libecap (2011, p. 64) discusses "institu-

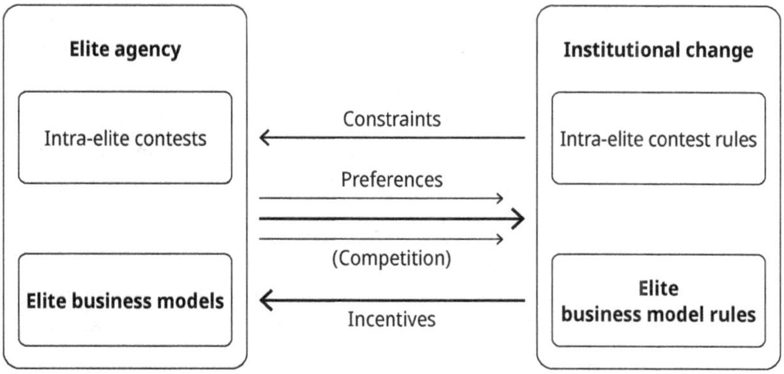

Figure 4.3: Elite business model rules and intra-elite contest rules in the elite agency microfoundations of institutional change model.

tional path dependence" and elucidates how "past arrangements to meet conditions of the time constrain contemporary economic opportunities. They cannot be easily significantly modified or replaced ex post". In theorizing the 'elite business model critical junctures' conjecture (Sections 4.3.4 and 5.1.1), the ETED's view of institutional change articulates the importance of such inflection points but does not obviate institutional stickiness or momentum. Rather, 'elite business model agglomeration' underlies Libecap's assertion that institutions "cannot be easily significantly modified or replaced ex post". Surely, while institutional inertia and structuralist traps are real, these can be counterbalanced by the 'inextinguishable value creation option of elites' (Figure A5.4c) or other less edifying expressions of their agency. Business model transformation or new forms of extraction are always possible, as are switches in the institutional path associated with business model rules (see Section 2.2.1). The latter, requiring enormously strong elite transformational leadership (see Table 7.2) to counter the agency of rival elites are, when inclusive, activated via the rules of intra-elite contests or by the use of naked power (see the role of power as a meta-contest resolution mechanism, Section 4.3.2).

Elites are primarily subject to peer constraints in political economy contests, but to a lesser extent are also affected by non-deliberate rules, including tradition or extra-legal self-organization (see Section 4.2.4). The rules of intra-elite contests, which approximate the concept of meta-institutions put forward by Mokyr and Nye (2007)[65], ought to mediate how competing elite preferences succeed in changing the business model rules, relative power notwithstanding. Cumulative institutional changes affected by previous generations of elites set such rules and these weigh heavier on elites than any other constraints (again, it is eas-

65 The construct as used in the ETED does not reference Stepan's (2001) advancement of the term, but rather approaches Lorini's (2014) "'meta-institutional concepts'" [which] are concepts that are conditions of possibility of institutions", and so constitute a "new level of the structure of institutional reality" (Polyakova, Nesterenko, & Sverdlikova, 2019, p. 140).

ier to change business model rules). Still, the elite coalitions with a profitable business model and enough power can break through most accumulated institutional constraints. For example, the institutions of central banking in the West lived up to their mandates for price stability to successfully mollify inflation for nearly four decades, yet this painfully extractive business model was suddenly and effortlessly reactivated by elite agency in 2021.

The integrity of the intra-elite contest rules in the political economy (e.g., a functioning justice system) is crucial, as it is often the backstop against overly extractive models. These rules require a degree of elite cohesion to be in place and are maintained in circular fashion by the elite separation of powers this instigates. Elite cohesion possesses cultural bases, and the "two-way causal effect between culture and institutions" theorized by Alesina and Giuliano (2015, p. 898) has a discrete impact on intra-elite contest rules. Inclusive institutional change then results from a powerful coalition set on elite business model transformation and a degree of consensus among elite coalitions that are otherwise competing and at odds with each other, i.e., a modicum of elite cohesion (the core elite coalition has an important role to play here, see Table 7.2). Stable intra-elite contest rules in turn support elite cohesion and consolidate a culture of robust intra-elite contests and the legitimacy of separation of powers arrangements. The delicate balancing act needed for these conditions to be met (see the 'intra-elite quality contest' dilemma, Figure 5.2) and the capricious nature of intra-elite contests make it highly difficult *ex ante* for a single coalition to predict rule changes and how these will affect its business model. Coalitions in the elite system will have agency but still need to deal with the complexity, non-linearity, emergence, evolution, and non-repeating patterns described in systems theory (see Section 3.2.3, and Von Bertalanffy, 1969/2003; Parsons, 1951/1991; Gleick, 1987; or O'Connor, 1994). *Ex post*, however, all rule changes emanate from the agency of identifiable elites.

A mandate of elite system transformational leadership (discussed in detail in Sections 6.3.2 and 7.2.4) is securing intra-elite contest rules that act as incentives for competitive intra-elite contests and minimize the negative externalities of such contests. For example, such conditions are evident in Swiss referenda, the "Elections Clause" of the US Constitution (Article I, Section 4, Clause 1) that specifies the respective powers of Congress and the states regarding "The Times, Places and Manner of holding Elections for Senators and Representatives", or the Hatch Act of 1939, which constrains the political activities of federal civil servants. In the mid-1990s, the new elite coalitions that had emerged under President Boris Yeltsin in Moscow took a step consistent with such leadership by deciding on a *de facto* rule for intra-elite contests that included an injunction against violence as a means of solving their business disputes.[66] It is, nonetheless, busi-

---

66 The deinstitutionalization of intra-elite contests now seems more prevalent, as the analysis of events at the "Amazon of Russia" in *The Moscow Times* illustrates: "The bullets flying at Moscow's Wildberries HQ last week are a chilling sign that Russia's wild 1990s are back with a vengeance. [. . .] In a deadly shootout straight out of a mobster's playbook, the violent chaos that once ruled the streets has returned to the Moscow boardroom, leaving two dead and the nation wondering whether Russia's ruthless past ever really went away" (Corcoran, 2024).

ness model rules that have the more direct and tangible impact on positive economic development. These are determined by the interactions between competing elite preferences within the constraints of intra-elite contest rules on an ongoing basis.

In short, the focus of this discussion has been on the two types of institutional rules relevant to an elite theory of economic development—intra-elite contest rules and business model rules—and their respective conceptualizations of embeddedness. The former are fundamental, comparatively constraining, and stable, while the latter are more bound by immediate elite agency and ought to be in flux in a dynamic economy characterized by technological and social progress.

4.2.4 Additional support for institutional formation and change by elite agency

Which existing theoretical positions best explain the formation of institutions considering their heterogeneity in practice (Ostrom, 2005), and which of these are consistent with the proposed explanation of elite agency as a key driver? Early on, Menger (1883/1985) suggested two modes of institutional formation: deliberate/pragmatic and spontaneous/organic, both of which later underwent further development (Chavance, 2012, p. 43). That is, some theories "emphasize the deliberate creation of institutions through the political process, while others emphasize the spontaneous emergence of institutions through evolutionary processes" (Kingston & Caballero, 2009, p. 151).

The theoretical position of this work discussed above aligns with Commons' emphasis on the former mode for both the formation and change—deliberate, by elite agency—of institutions, while deemphasizing the Veblenian, Hayekian, and Austrian stress on spontaneous formation and structuralist leanings. For instance, this elite theory qualifies the stance of Hayek, who "opposed the view that institutions were 'deliberate contrivances', arguing instead that they emerged through trial and error across generations" (Bowles, Kirman, & Sethi, 2017, p. 216), by emphasizing the strategies and resources behind the 'trials' and the systematic learning in intra-elite contests, including the corrective measures made by elite coalitions to 'errors' and the confirmatory actions taken as a result of wins. This position is held even in light of the critique against Commons' "failure to give sufficient emphasis to extra-legal institutions, extra-legal self-organization, or spontaneous orders that do not involve legal rules" (Hodgson, 2003, p. 547), and despite the emphasis on purported "cultural norms" behind "responsive and inclusive elites" (Welzel, 2002, p. 269). Elite agency is agile, employs surprise, arbitrages institutions, leverages institutional voids, builds on culture, and improvises. Moreover, without its fundamental pursuit of self-interest (elite business model preferences), the formal *and* informal institutions (of business model rules) are purposeless, conflicted, and messy, or of scant relevance for economic development. Institutional evolution, even with its cycles of Hayekian trial and error, haphazard appearance, and unpredictability is always driven by elite agency, as is posited in the 'follow the money' heuristic, the *cui bono* of institutional change. This notion also extends to deregulation and deinstitutionalization, "the processes by which institutions weaken and disappear" (Scott, 2001, p. 182). One such interesting instance is the successful effort by Wall Street investment banks to liberalize the financial markets by lobbying for the Clinton Administration's Financial Services Modernization Act of 1999 (also known as the Gramm-Leach-Bliley Act) that signified the repeal of the Glass Steagall Act of 1933, the regulatory framework that constrained the speculative activities that had caused the 1929 crash. It was Allan Greenspan and his Federal Reserve Board (FRB) that opened the floodgates for this by exploiting a temporary loophole in the anti-affiliation constraints of the Bank Holding Company Act of 1956 to license and concoct the first universal bank since the Great Depression, the merger of Travelers with Citicorp, thus creating what was then America's largest bank. While the new Citigroup soon span the Travelers unit off in 2002, the approval of the merger paved the way for the US Congress to destroy President Franklin D. Roosevelt's legacy of nearly seven decades of financial stability and constraints on value transfers. For human and economic development, the institutions that really have impact are those associated with the rules for the value creation and transfers of elite business models. These, or their absence, are the 'deliberate contrivances' that matter. In the example above, Clinton's institutional change for 'modernization' in the finance industry triggered a surge of transfer activity and created the conditions for the Great Recession in the pivotal period between 2007 and 2009.

Can these deliberate contrivances be irrational and thus support structuralist arguments and the spontaneous formation of institutions? For instance, in the field of ESG, Edmans notes that: "irrational sustainability involves pursuing a project, investment, or certification just because it is viewed as sustainable" (2024, p. 13). In fact, behavioral economists have long identified many institutional inconsistencies: "legal statutes are less tolerant of carcinogens in our food than in our drinking water or our air" (Fischhoff, Lichtenstein, Slovic, Keeney, & Derby, 1980, p. 2); "In the United Kingdom, 2,500 times more money per life saved is spent on safety measures in the pharmaceutical industry than in agriculture (Sinclair, Marstrand, & Newick, 1972, as cited in Fischhoff, Lichtenstein, Slovic, Keeney, & Derby, 1980, p. 2); "According to some calculations, U.S. society spends about $140,000 in highway construction to save one life and $5 million to save a person from death due to radiation exposure (Howard, Matheson, & Owen, 1978, as cited in Fischhoff, Lichtenstein, Slovic, Keeney, & Derby, 1980, pp. 2–3)". In light of such evidence, behavioral economics could claim "incoherent policies save fewer lives at greater costs than other possible policies" (Messick & Bazerman, 2001, pp. 220–221). Yet to this inquiry, the ensuing prescriptions would seem naïve: "We can protect ourselves from such errors by improving the judgments of managers in the private and public sectors" (Bazerman, 2001, p. 43). Theoretically, mainstream economics and the RCT paradigm (Allison & Zelikow, 1999) are admittedly hard pressed to handle irrationality or even build "Rational Models of Irrational Behavior" (Akerlof & Yellen, 1987), while "bounded rationality" (Simon, 1957) acknowledges imperfect information and cognitive limitations, and behaviorism relies on biases and heuristics to explain judgments made under uncertainty in the economy (Tversky & Kahneman, 1974; Kahneman & Lovallo, 1993). It is true that inconsistent rules are the "failure to explicitly deal with risk tradeoffs" (Messick & Bazerman, 2001, p. 221) and it is therefore essential to systematically weight and offset these in policymaking. Yet this can only be done in a political economy that recognizes elite agency. This work's theory contends that institutional anomalies, whether they are the residual leftovers of anachronistic political processes or genuine errors of judgment, are best dealt with through the lens of elite agency and the *cui bono* analysis.

For instance, "Bork used the institutional irrationality theme to drive home his case for change" with a "depiction of a powerful regulatory system gone mad", describing "the U.S. antitrust system as prone to erratic swings in policy" (Kovacic, 2014, p. 858). If antitrust law, or any other business model rule—irrational or not— is harmful to powerful elite interests, it will be contested. The sweeping victory of Bork's narrative controverts his position by demonstrating that elite agency will fix any irrationality when the interests of a sufficiently powerful business model are at stake. Rules that support any remaining anomalies are simply irrelevant or subordinated in the face of the force of elite coordination leadership. Lastly, and returning to safety legislation, there is technically no way to disagree with: "By using a consistent value of life for all products, one minimizes the total chance of death from all products" (Owen, 1981, p. 715). In the political economy, inconsistencies characterize the value of life through eminently straightforward *cui bono* explanations. Institutions are deliberate.

Hall and Thelen (2009, p. 9) emphasize that a "sophisticated understanding of institutional change" is "not incompatible with dynamic views of the political economy". This can be affirmed in even stronger terms: the political economy is a distributional game with winners and losers; the feasibility of distribution of value strategies are determined by institutional formation and cumulative institutional change driven by elite agency. This idea is now cemented with some illustrative examples.

Smartphone ride-hailing is demonstrative of how institutions (and non-elite stakeholder positions) are shaped by elite agency in support of its models. In their intra-elite contests with traditional taxi firms, Uber (see the *Uber Files* reference in Section 3.3.3) and Lyft gained ride-hailing licenses from institutions "municipality upon municipality" with few exceptions (Brail, 2018, pp. 52, 55). When, in 2003, Taobao offered a "custodial transactions" feature without a proper license and was warned of the legal consequences, Jack Ma's response was "If someone has to go to jail, I'll go" (Wu, 2019). His boldest move into Internet finance came in 2013 with the launch of *Yu'ebao*, a money market fund "for the masses" retailing "through PayPal-like Alipay" (Mu, 2014), even though Alibaba still lacked a banking license (which was only granted by the China Banking Regulatory Commission the following year, in 2014). As a result of such institutional arbitrage, by 2020, Ma's Ant Financial empire had successfully re-shaped Chinese industry with a business model valued at US$ 225 billion (Xie & Yang, 2020). Yet, in a reversal that made international headlines, the political elite checked the business elite (see Figure 3.2; intra-elite power relation 4) as Ant

Financial's public offering, the world's largest-ever, was suspended on November 5, 2020, a few days before its expected trading debut to the relief of incumbent banking elites who would have been at the receiving end of data asymmetries. What Jack Ma had dared do, Jeff Bezos or Mark Zuckerberg would not.[67] Thereafter, China's market regulator got generally tougher on Big Tech and its perceived market dominance-driven extractive value transfers, and China's State Administration for Market Regulation noted:

> Antitrust complaints against platforms are increasing by the day, and make clear that the development of the online economy has come with some risks for competition. (Yang, 2020)

Is this sequence of institutional changes, first driven by the will to create and appropriate value and then by a counterresponse from the system's core coalition to purportedly curb the power of monopolies and prevent transfer-IN from non-elites, a desirable approach to revitalize competition and support emerging elites and elite circulation, while placing a proper political power check on economic power? Structural reform questions such as these are essential to economic development. From Veblen (1904/1975) to Acemoglu and Robinson (2013b), institutions and their incentive structures are posited to constrain elites. Every time a model is institutionally sanctioned, the winning elites, Streeck and Thelen's (2005) "rule makers", force the losing elites to become "rule takers", at least until the next round of the contest. Ant Financial did not prevail in the political economy's non-market contest arena (see Figure 3.6), and institutional change was implemented against its preferences to the benefit of competing elites, especially rival financial institutions, including state owned ones. While still a formidable elite business model, Ant Financial accepted the new rules that now constrain and diminish it.

The above does not mean that non-deliberate, spontaneous, and organic factors have no influence on institutional formation and change. Accidents, traps, and traditions matter, and Knightian uncertainty is pointedly relevant to the single elite coalition's agency. The emergence of viral 'orphan' narratives, devoid of elite godfathers, also causes degrees of both inclusive and extractive institutional change (e.g., cryptocurrencies, BLM, or even anti-vaccination narratives in some countries). But like any contingency or custom they end up being captured and integrated, as this is part of the mandate of capable elite leadership. Institutions, like narratives, can have a logic, life, and an inertia of their own—at least for a while—even if they all eventually end up in the service of one elite business model or another.

Elite agency as a microfoundation of institutional formation and change places elite business models (and their aggregate agency) at the center of society and the

---

67 In the US, Silicon Valley and Wall Street harness their synergies, yet the current technological shift might skew the power equilibrium vis-à-vis political elites. Pundits like Aschenbrenner propose the "AGI government project" (2024, pp. 145, 153) that, while using a geopolitical rationale, aims to *de facto* restore a classical balance in intra-elite power relation 4.

economy due to their outsized impact on the inclusive or extractive nature of national institutions. Sustainable value creation measurements (such as the VCp/VCr) of elite business models then predict economic and human development to a degree that this inquiry suggests no other variable does. Uncompetitive manufacturers explain tariffs, competitive exporters explain free trade, and the interests of trade unions explain minimum wages above the equilibrium and inflexible labor laws (even in the face of excessive levels of youth unemployment in countries such as Spain or Argentina). Since the work of Coase, North, and new institutional economics, institutional arrangements have been widely recognized as being as important for macroeconomic performance as fiscal or monetary policy. Yet the intimate links between institutions and elite business models, and the value creation implications that the latter have on society, are manifestly underrepresented in policy agendas, econometric models, or the public discourse. To address this deficit, frameworks for policymaking are advanced (from Chapter 6 onwards) on the premise that elite business models are antecedents of institutional change (or the lack thereof), and thus the definitive drivers of economic and human development.

Elites, due to lower transaction costs, high levels of trust, and concentrated (business model) interests, secure 'the extraordinary lever' in their particular fields as they consolidate wins in the political economy's three contest arenas that emanate from their coordination leadership. Victories against rival elites lead to the accumulation of power and then to institutional change in the form of rules favorable to their business models. A deeper dive into the nature of power is the focus of the next section before the chapter concludes the discussion on institutional change by establishing its endogenous nature (Section 4.3.5).

4.3 Power and elite agency

Ample research has documented how agency impacts institutions. DiMaggio (1988) brought "agency and interests directly into the relationship between power and institutions", but the analytical links between institutions and power in organizational fields still remain immature (Lawrence & Buchanan, 2017, p. 477). Proposition 8 addressed this issue by linking bargaining power differentials to elite business models, through the lens of the VCA framework. 'The extraordinary lever' that power (applied coordination capacity, see Figures A5.3a or A5.3b) confers to those atop social hierarchies is further elucidated in subsequent sub-sections to scrutinize the relationship between elite agency and power. These begin with an examination of power's coordination function in society (4.3.1), and continue with the assertion that power serves as a meta-contest resolution mechanism (4.3.2). Since power differentials are the ultimate movers of institutions and the economy (4.3.3), it is the power of elite business models that resolves critical junctures (4.3.4). In the final sub-section of Chapter 4 these diverse reflections on power are brought together by an affirmation of the endogenous nature of elite business model driven institutional change (4.3.5).

4.3.1 The omniscience of power and the formation of a common will

Denord, Palme, and Réau's comprehensive study of elite research theory and methods focuses on the concept of power (2020), while Hoffmann-Lange is unambiguous: "Power and elites are universal social phenomena" (2007, p. 910). Power was earlier examined from a management science perspective in terms of the role it plays during bargaining for value appropriation (in the form of revenue and profits) in principal-stakeholder relationships. But what is the general, deeper nature of power? Foucault (1982, pp. 778, 791) claims that: "Power is everywhere; not because it embraces everything, but because it comes from everywhere" and as a result, "to live in society is to live in such a way that action upon other actions is possible—and in fact ongoing. A society without power relations can only be an abstraction". Pareto is more specific, defining power as the ability to coordinate and control (Powers, 1981, p. 104). Consistent with Proposition 4 on coordination capacity and lower transaction costs, one source of power are the "positions in a network of relations" and specifically network centrality (van der Eijk, 2018, p. 99), while "the power of social elites depends strongly on the structure of the network in which they reside" and having control of a network is "power to effect change" (Siegel, 2009, p. 123). Nonetheless, and as discussed in Section 4.1.2, a structuralist SNA analysis is insufficient to explain power, since elite agency in all its leadership varieties comes into being against the backdrop of uncertain intra-elite contest dynamics. Powerful figures certainly benefit from 'the power multiplier' effect underlying 'the extraordinary lever', but this construct is built by their deliberate agency. Its amplification mechanism leverages social hierarchies, network effects, and the successive principal-stakeholder relationships along the economic value chain (Section 1.3.4, see also Figure A5.3a).

Habermas and McCarthy (1977) contrast two notions of power: first, Max Weber's (1925, pp. 1:16, 2:1, as cited in Habermas & McCarthy, 1977, p. 4), where "power means every chance within a social relationship to assert one's will even against opposition", i.e., social coercive agency (*Zwang*); and second, Hannah Arendt's communicative action model that goes beyond power as force (*Gewalt*) and is especially relevant for this theory's understanding of elite business models and elites. To Parsons, power is "a facility for the performance of function in and on behalf of the society as a system" (1957, p. 139), while Arendt's communicative action model also places power at the collective level relates it with coordination capacity:

> Power corresponds to the human ability not just to act but to act in concert. Power is never the property of an individual; it belongs to a group and remains in existence only so long as the group keeps together. When we say of somebody that he is "in power" we actually refer to his being empowered by a certain number of people to act in their name. (Arendt, 1970, p. 44, as cited in Habermas & McCarthy, 1977, p. 4)

Powerful principals 'acting in the name of others' may or may not act in the interest of the stakeholders from which their power emanates. Power has often been conceptualized dualistically in both its repressive or productive employment (Hörnqvist, 2010). Foucault underscores non-elite animadversion against elite dominance but acknowledges that "the exercise of power can produce as much acceptance as may be wished for: it can pile up the dead and shelter itself behind whatever threats it can imagine", while also accepting that "every relationship of power puts into operation differentiations" which encompass "differences in know-how and competence" (1982, pp. 789, 792, 795). Power can be used for both value creation and extraction. After all, power "has collective as well as distributive functions" (Parsons, 1957, p. 139) and resolves value appropriation outcomes (see bargaining power in Proposition 8). Its appropriative nature is illustrated by the following example:

> In the US South, even though political institutions changed in such a way as to redistribute de jure political power away from the white elites, the elite was still very cohesive as a group. As a consequence, they were able to compensate for the change in political institutions through the use of de facto power. It is perhaps not surprising that the plantation elites had such a relative advantage over the newly freed slaves in terms of their ability to act collectively. In consequence, they maintained their political control. (Robinson 2010, p. 10)

The plantation business model persevered *de facto* if not *de jure* because Southern elites excelled at providing value to their customers; elite business models generally endure as long as elite networks retain their lower transaction costs and cohesion and exercise effective elite coordination leadership. New power sources across all three of the power domains (economy, politics, and society, see Figure 1.2) are obtained to compensate for any circumstantial losses and setbacks and rebuild 'the extraordinary lever'. The plantation owners forfeited power in the non-market arena ('might' in the politics power domain) during the Civil War, but after the Reconstruction era (1865–1877), the material institutional arrangements stayed in place (e.g., plantations were not expropriated). In the market arena ('money' in the economy power domain), wins could then be netted (e.g., from demand for cotton and tobacco). Even in the narrative market arena ('mind' in the society power domain), the once defeated Southern elites experienced quite a comeback, manifested in works such as D.W. Griffith's *The Birth of a Nation* (1915). These wins in turn led them to recover much of their pre-Civil War power in the political non-market arena (as evidenced by Jim Crow legislation, or Black Codes). These examples of arbitrage across power domains showcase how 'might' is directly converted into 'money' (i.e., wages were below 'equalized bargaining power equilibrium prices' see Section 2.2.2).

Narratives are the form of power (see Proposition 14) most resilient to the test of time. The power of narratives ('mind') in the society power domain has something of the miraculous, in both positively inspirational and far less edifying ways. As long as they are not forgotten, narratives can overturn institutional arrangements (as was the case with the elites in the Southern US states after 1877), allow a people to persevere in the cruelest of circumstances (Sephardic Jews blossomed in Amsterdam after the expulsions of 1492 and 1497), and even cheat death (the tragic Smolensk air disaster that killed Polish President Lech Kaczyński and many members of the Polish elite on April 10, 2010 did not dent their Law and Justice party, and its narrative has continued to thrive). It is easy to overlook that in each of the preceding examples, the elite coalition narrative competed against rivals in the narrative market arena, and narrative wins typically facilitate power accumulation in the fiercely contested non-market and market political economy arenas.

The amassing of power in one domain needs to be followed by wins in the other two. How these three power domains—each with their own contest arenas—synergistically work together for a coalition is demonstrated by a historical elite business model critical juncture. This is the case of an emerging elite trying to break free just as much from a narrative that supported the notion of 'purgatory' borne out of Parisian theology (Vincent, 2002), as from one specific elite business model activity that this doctrine sustained: papal indulgences. Martin Luther's Reformation challenge to the extractive business model of the Catholic Church started with his new Protestant elite coalition winning an important share of 'mind' in German narrative market arenas by disputing that sins could be atoned for by payments to Rome. But power also had to be won by Protestant elite coalitions in the political domain's non-market arena—the bloody battlefields of the Thirty Years War and its 8 million dead (Wilson, 2008, p. 554). The newfound power ('might') attained by enduring in the wars against stronger incumbent forces gave wings to the Germanic princely elite business models that, no longer 'taxed' by the Vatican, added economic power ('money') to their endowments. With the Protestant and "German liberties" narratives at the forefront, local elites replaced the Vatican and its extractive institutional arrangements in many areas of Western Europe.[68]

Elon Musk at Tesla—before jumping on the Trump bandwagon and the subsequent "showstopping breakup" (Schwartz & Maidenberg, 2025) notwithstanding—serves as a contemporary illustration of successful business model leadership that has attained bargaining power endowment differentials across principal-stakeholder relationships in the three power domains of economy, politics, and society. A very skillful operator of narratives, Musk's elite coordination leadership enlisted both elites and non-elites to score wins for its electric vehicle (EV) business model (positioned in opposition to the traditional combustion engine automotive). News agencies reported on the institutional

---

68 This is not to say that Martin Luther's Reformation was devoid of extractive elements. Quite the opposite, as he "fought for the subjugation of the Jewish people" (Kaufmann, 2019, p. 46), and in the *Bauernkrieg* (War of the Peasants, 1524–1526), "He rejected outright the peasants' protests against serfdom on the basis of biblical injunctions. He insisted Scriptures accepted the fact of human slavery" (Kuenning, 1987, p. 313). To cap it all and in tune with the unenlightened times, "he could not perceive women as learned in any way. Women do not write books, he claimed, and women are men's servants" (Classen & Settle, 1991, p. 235).

change that Musk's narrative market wins in the society power domain ('mind') brought about in politics power domains across the world ('might'); twin wins that eventually led to further victories in the economy power arena ('money'), with all three power types eventually converting into residual income, profits, and more 'money'[69]:

> In the US where "the federal government is subsidizing electric cars with a $7,500 consumer tax break"; in Norway where "the country government exempted battery-powered vehicles from the 25% value-added tax imposed on petrol and diesel engines"; and in China with a "generous five-year subsidy program for so-called new energy vehicles". (Reuters, 2020)

Whether Weber's assertion of will against opposition (as cited in Habermas and Mc-Carthy, 1977), Parsons' (1957) "collective" and "distributive" functions within a system, Arendt's (1970) notion of power as an "act in concert" with the "formation of a common will", Coff's (1999) capacity for "unified action", or Musk's applied EV narrative; in political economy terms, all power gains further leverage by moving institutions and bringing about the implementation of preferred elite business model rules. Mills articulates the relationship between power and institutions as follows:

> By the powerful we mean, of course, those who are able to realize their will, even if others resist it. No one, accordingly, can be truly powerful unless he has access to the command of major institutions, for it is over these institutional means of power that the truly powerful are, in the first instance, powerful. [. . .] Not all power, it is true, is anchored in and exercised by means of such institutions, but only within and through them can power be more or less continuous and important. (Mills, 1956, p. 9)

The power obtained in the domains of politics, the economy, and society to fuel elite agency is ultimately manifested as collective action at the coalition (micro), elite system (meso), and political economy (macro) levels through elite coordination leadership. Power is eventually converted into residual income (also 'money') via elite business model leadership. Institutional change is a nexus between the two forms of leadership. Power in all three domains is the outcome of elite coordination leadership and a necessary input for, and one of the outcomes of, elite business model leadership (as represented in Figures 4.1, 4.4, and A5.3). Power is now examined from an intra-elite contest resolution perspective to further discern its functional equivalence to institutions.

69 Residual income or profits are also 'money', but of the freely disposable variety. Profits and their aggregation as wealth can be employed beyond the power accumulation purposes of the business model and be used for disparate investments (e.g., Musk taking Twitter private at a cost of US$ 44 billion in October, 2022), conspicuous consumption, or philanthropy.

4.3.2 Power is a meta-contest resolution mechanism that bests institutional processes

> What I want particularly to stress is that the solution is essentially the transformation of the *conflict* from a political *problem* to an economic transaction. An economic *transaction* is a solved political problem. Economics has gained the title of queen of the social sciences by choosing *solved* political problems as its domain. (Lerner, 1972, p. 259)

Why are economic transactions solved political conflicts? Because of the workings and nature of institutions, power, or both. Institutions are the low-cost dispute resolution mechanism par excellence. The dispute resolution view of institutions proposed by Commons (1950) was summarized by van de Ven (1993) and articulated by Williamson (1993, p. 78) as "a response to scarcity and conflicts of interest" with the "transaction as the basic unit of analysis". DiMaggio's critique of institutional change appreciates "conflict-laden processes that define fields and set them upon trajectories that eventually appear as 'natural' developments to participants and observers alike" (1991, p. 268 as cited in Scott, 2008, p. 437). Commons further argues that: "the negotiational, organizational political economy is the way contemporary collective capitalism works" (Elliott, 1978, p. 105). Institutions solve transactional conflicts in a cost-efficient manner by providing the framework for negotiation. Bargaining power is also important in such negotiations and can be the decisive factor in solving conflicts. It might even do so at low cost by directly nudging the transaction into the spaces where institutions are either missing or not able to complete the task by themselves.

Institutions might be deficient in a political economy but power is always present in socio-economic relations (see Foucault, 1982) and from the economic standpoint, it is ready to address conflicts and conclude any given transaction. The first way that power contributes to the transaction is through its direct application by one party upon the other. It must be noted that the power differential is of theoretical interest for development economics as a mechanism to solve conflicts about rules (obviously business model rules, but also intra-elite contest rules) rather than just as a facilitator of specific transactions. Here, bargaining power is the ultimate solution of the non-transaction as it tackles meta-contests, i.e., conflicts about how conflicts are resolved. Conflicts about institutions rely on meta-institutions, i.e., institutions "that wrote the rules by which other institutions changed" (Mokyr & Nye, 2007, p. 55), which are basically intra-elite contest rules (see also the "meta-institutional concepts" of Lorini, 2014, as cited in in Polyakova, Nesterenko, & Sverdlikova, 2019, p. 140). In short, instead of submitting to meta-institutions to unscramble conflicts, including those around institutional change, the second and more expeditious way to conclude the transaction is by leveraging the power differentials across elite coalitions.

In the end, elite agency as leadership is not about closing the transaction, but about securing the business model rules that govern how they are conducted. These include licenses to operate—from monopoly grants to securing property over asset classes like real estate, data, or the electromagnetic spectrum—and rights over scarce economic resources. Elite business models acquire these scarce licenses by winning not just intra-elite contests (to set 'business model rules' that determine 'who gets what') but also intra-elite meta-contests (contests about the 'intra-elite contest rules' that decide *how* 'who gets what'). Through exercising their power in the political economy, elites are therefore able not just to ink a transaction on favorable terms but also to win the meta-contests that determine standards and intra-elite contest wins. Elite agency seeks to enable value creation and appropriation and so the neoclassical notion of scarcity (applied to rules) explains the recourse to power in all intra-elite contest types. That is, power is also a meta-contest resolution mechanism that functions in parallel with but independently of institutional processes as it shapes the fundamental arrangements that govern the rules of institutional change.

As examined in Proposition 8, high levels of bargaining power are visible in (higher) prices received or (lower) costs paid (Figure 2.2). All power domains—politics ('might'), economy ('money'), and society ('mind')—resolve transactions at the principal-stakeholder level. More strategically, the power of elites resolves meta-contests about the rules that govern institutional change, for instance, those that determine the allocation of rights, whether for natural resource concessions, the setting of minimum wages, oligopoly rents, agricultural and interest rate subsidies, and, of course, any of the so called 'licenses to steal'. Power is, in summary, a key allocative criterion that resolves scarcity (or artificially creates it, as Bastiat explains in *Economic Sophisms*, 1845/1996) in its capacity as a meta-contest resolution mechanism. For Foucault, power trumps institutions as: "one must analyze institutions from the standpoint of power relations, rather than vice versa" (1982, p. 791). As a result, power will work directly in a specific transaction but is far more essential as a shaper of meta-institutions and intra-elite contest rules, since it seeks to determine the business model rules that enable the appropriation of residual income.

4.3.3 Power differentials move institutions and the economy

This sub-section distils the essence of the discussion on power up to this point and stresses its significance for development. Power, with its meta-contest resolution capabilities, is first treated as a value-free outcome of elite coordination and business model leadership in the employ of elite business models and their respective sustainable value creation positions. Hence, the notion that elites necessarily "control" institutions (Mills, as cited in Bell, 1958, p. 239) through the capacity afforded by 'the extraordinary lever' is immaterial and perilously close to the elite populist fallacy ('elites are bad'). The relevant 'power question' for the ETED is *how* elite business models (e.g., those of the East India Company, John D. Rockefeller, the House of Saud, the *chaebol* or OpenAI) accumulate power to defeat rivals in intra-elite contests. Special attention is merited when power relations may be about to be radically altered:

> My work at OpenAI reminds me every day about the magnitude of the socioeconomic change that is coming sooner than most people believe. Software that can think and learn will do more and more of the work that people now do. Even more power will shift from labor to capital. If public policy doesn't adapt accordingly, most people will end up worse off than they are today. (Altman, 2021)

The key point that Sam Altman makes—the acceleration of the shift of power from labor to capital—is a non-issue for elite coalitions, and despite being in the public eye is rarely addressed in advanced political economies with actual institutional change (though Gates proposes the taxing of robots, see Michel, 2023).[70] The ultimate consequence of an AI-induced rebalancing of power from *multiple* elite coalitions to just *one* goes far beyond the displacement of labor and has massive implications. This novel redistribution of power is depicted in 'the absolute lever' of the AI (see Figures A5.3c and A5.3d and the discussion in Sections 8.1.3, 8.1.6, and the Epilogue). Whether or not the once powerful elites of the automotive industry or the military-industrial complex would have to outsource much of their decision-making and operations to the superior intelligence, their value appropriation models would become reliant on the "software that can think" and the terms of service of the AI coalitions. The notion of 'the extraordinary lever' transitions from power belonging to a few in each of the many nooks and crannies of the economy, to 'the absolute lever', held by only a few in the entire political economy. Practitioners know that "technology" is power that affords the "ability to coordinate in groups of unrestricted size" (Suleyman & Bhaskar, 2023, p. 96). More concretely, it also explains why RentPage's "algorithms and artificial intelligence" have succeeded in coordinating price-fixing by large landlords and "changed market structures across the economy" causing rents to increase by 30% in just two years (Stoller, 2024). Later in this inquiry, the capacity of technology to bring the Will to Power that is intrinsic to life and development to a radical ultimate realization is reviewed.

Previous sections have made clear that the accumulation of elite power is a pursuit for preferred institutional change that is more intentional, purposeful, and concentrated than the agency of non-elites (which is a factor in conceptualizing elite agency as antecedent of institutional change). The realization of the Will to Power (the *Wille zur Macht* element in the first principles of the speculative philosophy of this work's paradigm, see Section 8.3.3, Figure 8.6) in all of its Nietzschean force invariably emerges in elites because business model rules enabled by institutions are

70 The elite agency of organized labor has decayed in most advanced economies. For many decades it has shortsightedly focused on concerns like wage levels rather than on strategic approaches to the relevant intra-elite contests of the age. Meanwhile, in value creation terms, the ever-more capable managerial, technical, and creative class (see Figure 8.1) has benefited from its service and closeness to elite business models, while ceding its own autonomous voice and agency in the political economy. AI could reveal this to be a fatal flaw if it ends up delivering a blow to the value creation and appropriation prospects of this class (e.g., see Eloundou, Manning, Mishkin, & Rock, 2023).

existential to them: the rules of the game determine the flows of residual income and the very preservation of elite status (see Proposition 6 on elite identity). Agency with concentrated Olsonian preferences can be assumed to have the stronger action bias over both pragmatic institutions (which represent interests that are more diluted) and organic institutions (anchored in tradition or history), both with unclear ownership and thus more liable to 'capture' (in reference to Stigler, 1971). How power differentials lead to institutional change is described below:

> There will be a conflict of interest over the choice of economic institutions. In such a situation it will be the distribution of political power in society that determines what institutions are chosen. The group with more political power will tend to secure the set of economic institutions that it prefers. (Robinson 2010, pp. 5–6)

The distribution of power in the economy (and its consequences) is an extremely intricate and granular affair with highly uncertain system outcomes. It is hard to determine for the observer or even those deep in the thick of intra-elite contests like Altman, who despite seemingly being ahead of his rivals will need exceptional elite business model leadership skills[71] to ultimately prevail. Since the distribution of power resulting from such leadership determines the terms of principal-stakeholder value appropriation, it can be inferred *post facto*, and serves to inform economic analysis. What is clear is that quantifying the power associated with discrete elite coalitions and the impact that it has requires sophisticated approaches. One such approach is the analysis undertaken by Cozzi and Galli (2014, p. 184) on the bargaining power positions of basic researchers vs applied researchers (or developers) in the US after the early 1980s which "show that an increase in the relative bargaining power of basic researchers [upstream innovators] has harmful short-run consequences for economic growth, even though it could be conducive to higher growth in the longer term". At this point, it is useful to revisit the counterfactual world with no power differentials, one that is the opposite of the AI scenario described above (see Table E.2, hypothesis AI_H1), a world where 'the extraordinary lever' is moot.

Going back to Lord Kelvin's energy analogy of an ocean devoid of temperature differentials, the absence of bargaining power differentials sees no movement, no coordination, and no economic and human development. Intriguingly, power is sometimes treated as a dilemma: "the elites must choose between consolidation of their personal power by continuing to resist change or beginning to make necessary sacrifices for their nation at the expense of their own privilege and prestige" (Kim, 1996, p. 342). This quote implies that there is a trade-off for elites between the retention of

71 Altman's remarkable elite coordination leadership skills were spectacularly displayed in a critical few days of November, 2023 when he triumphantly returned to the helm of his coalition as CEO after his board carried out a "secret plan" to "ambush Sam and remove him from power for the good of humanity" (Huet, 2024, 5:26). Challenged by Musk and Meta (Robison, 2024), Trump's second election victory will further test his mettle.

power and elite system transformation. However, this is a false dichotomy. How elites choose the levels of sustainable value creation for their business models is independent from power accumulation. While there are calls for the power of technology elites to be constrained (from academics like Acemoglu & Johnson, 2023, and pundits like Varoufakis, 2021), the innovation and the benefits that they bring scale with power. Again, all power ('money', might', and 'mind') is instrumental for elites to realize their business model preferences, and when they do so these power types associate with one of the two institutional arrangements that Acemoglu and Robinson (2019b, p. 16) describe: "inclusive economic institutions, which create broad-based economic incentives and opportunities, and extractive economic institutions, which do not". Power must be treated as a quantum-like potentiality on institutions—maybe inclusive, maybe extractive—until it associates with the actual sustainable value creation of business models.

This inquiry basically classifies elite systems by how its coalitions employ power on aggregate. In 'The State of the Elite System Framework' for the political economy, national elite systems characterized by high power can be 'enlightened' or 'rentier', while systems with low power are described as being 'competitive' or 'striving' (on account of their respective high or low 'value', see Figure 6.5). Elite power should not be associated with the repression or absence of sustainable value creation. Yet does this inquiry not advocate for equalized bargaining power, and for competitive intra-elite contests under the conditions of a strong elite separation of powers by using The Three-tier Set of Intra-elite Checks and Balances as a premise for inclusive institutional change?

The ETED calls *ceteris paribus* for a high velocity of elite circulation (see Section 1.3.3), meaning that power endowments ought to mirror 'knowledge', the favored Hayekian advantage in intra-elite contests. Knowledge-based power differentials enable elite coalitions with sustainable value creation business models to enact inclusive institutional change. Power is applied coordination capacity (see Figure 5.3) and is as essential for value appropriation as it is for value creation. Moreover, new elites can only overcome the inertia advantage and reactionary challenges from extractive incumbents with power. Power differentials should exist in order for 'the extraordinary lever' to do its job across the value chain, but these ought to be as short lived as the superiority of 'knowledge' is in competitive markets (see Section 2.2.2).

To recap, power, like elites, must circulate and be used in the right way. This goes to the crux of the eternal and formidable balancing act of the political economy: power must quickly dissipate from particular hands, while its accumulation by a coalition—especially if based on 'knowledge'—should be ironed out of the system at the right time: not too soon (an unusual challenge, but real in polities where the elite populist fallacy holds some sway, such as in Germany or even China), or (more commonly) too late. Once in possession of 'the extraordinary lever', elite business model leadership will take risks—at the very minimum as institutional entrepreneurs in intra-elite contests—to amass and then convert the scarce resource of power into residual income by advancing its preferences for laws and regulations. This power conversion process is the lifeblood of the political economy: without power differentials there are no states, no technology, no social evolution, no civilization, no modernity, and the world is bereft of coordination capacity. Elite coordination leadership accumulates that power in the first place by structuring a coalition of business, political, and knowledge elites, each contributing their power type ('money', 'might', and 'mind') to the business model with wins in their respective contest arenas of the political economy. At the end of the process, accumulated power is converted into residual income/profits—in its most fungible form, 'money'—and can be used beyond the business model at the discretion of its beneficiaries. A supplementary graphic rendition of the overarching role of power in the elite agency microfoundations of institutional change model (building upon Figures 2.1 and 3.2) is provided in Figure 4.4.

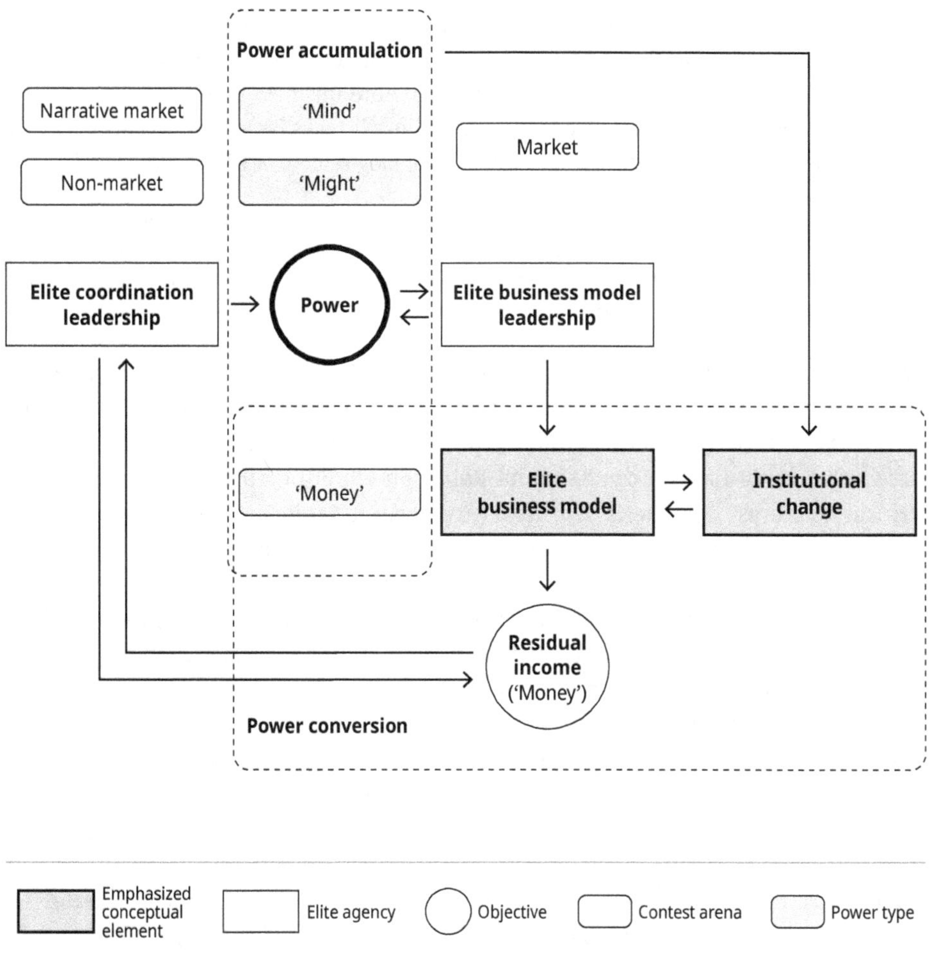

Figure 4.4: The role of power in the elite agency microfoundations of institutional change model.

4.3.4 Power consolidates at elite business model critical junctures

Elite agency is 'institutional entrepreneurship' in the sense that intra-elite contest risks are taken in order to convert power into institutional change consistent with the preferences of specific elite business models (see Figures 3.2, 3.3, and 4.5). As has been discussed, however, the relationship between institutions and elites is often conceived in reverse. That is, institutions and their incentive structures constrain elites. Acemoglu and Robinson (2013a) argue in *Why Nations Fail: The Origins of Power, Prosperity, and Poverty* that the business models of Bill Gates and Carlos Slim (Mexico's telecoms magnate and wealthiest individual) are a consequence of their country's institutions. The elite theory maintains that Gates, in his antitrust case (United States v. Microsoft Corporation, 253 F.3d 34, D.C. Cir. 2001), and Slim, in building alliances with political elites (Presidents José López Portillo and Miguel de la Madrid), essentially amassed the power endowments to effect institutional change (i.e., to overcome constraints or maintain the propitious non-constraints) put in place by previous elites (on occasion heeding non-elite narrativized preferences). Again, whether in Mexico or the US, institutions are the consequence of elite business models that have won intra-elite contests, rather than vice-versa. Gates himself takes issue with the determinant role of inclusive/extractive institutions in his critical blog review of *Why Nations Fail*:

> The authors [Acemoglu & Robinson, 2013a] believe that political "inclusiveness" must come first, before growth is achievable. Yet, most examples of economic growth in the last 50 years—the Asian miracles of Hong Kong, Korea, Taiwan, and Singapore—took place when their political [sic] tended more toward exclusiveness. (Gates, 2013)

Acemoglu, Johnson, Robinson and Yared (2009) dispute the modernization hypothesis (Lipset, 1959; see Section 5.1.1.) where per capita income gains cause increased democracy, more inclusive institutions, and the prosperity that is correlated with it. In their terse response to Gates, Acemoglu and Robinson (2013b) emphasize an alternative "critical junctures" hypothesis of growth (Acemoglu & Robinson, 2013a), and note that "extractive growth doesn't automatically lead to more inclusive institutions", especially when such growth is the consequence of "leaders and dominant elites' belief in their relative security". Their main corollary is "that ambitious entrepreneurs like Gates or Slim will do good for society if inclusive institutions constrain them, and that they will mostly serve their own interests otherwise".

What then happens if the critical juncture sees an intra-elite contest regulated by inclusive institutions with teeth? Lizzeri and Persico demonstrate that during Britain's "Age of Reform", institutionalized "divisions within the elite" led to the democratic "model of voluntary franchise extension" which materialized in "public education" and "urban public goods, particularly public health infrastructure such as sewerage, waterworks, and paved roads" (2004, pp. 736, 737, 755), ultimately contributing to development and the rising incomes of the industrial revolution. In the decision of US federal judge Mehta, Google was found to be in violation of US antitrust law (for instance, for using "distribution contracts" that are "exclusionary") to the detriment of Gates' firm that "has invested

$100 billion in search in the last two decades" to earn a paltry US$ 12 billion in revenue (compared to Google's US$ 146 billion) as the "perpetual scale and quality deficit means that Microsoft has no genuine hope of displacing Google" (United States District Court for the District of Columbia, 2024, pp. 6, 207, 236). The court's final remedies and penalties could set in motion a critical juncture affecting Big Tech's monopolistic positions beyond the online search and search advertising industry and constitute proof that the US is a 'competitive' rather than a 'rentier elite system' (Figure 6.5) where institutions are used by inclusive coalitions to constrain value transfers.

Normatively, the need for constraints parallels 'The Elite Business Model Lifecycle' rendered in Figure 4.5 below. This conceptual element references the management life cycle theory of the firm (Mueller, 1972) and incorporates political economy power in order to derive the 'value transfers replace value creation at maturity' conjecture and visualize the 'elite power vs value creation gap' hypothesis (see its normative opposite, the 'equalized bargaining power equilibrium prices' situation in Figure A5.9c). In his seminal work on "The Nature of the Firm", Coase states that: "a firm will tend to expand until the costs of organising an extra transaction within the firm become equal to the costs of carrying out the same transaction by means of an exchange on the open market or the costs of organising in another firm" (1937, p. 395). The ETED claims that a firm grows to the degree that its political economy power enables value appropriated but *not* created (i.e., allows it to rent-seek), doubtlessly a different kind of efficiency.

The sequence inherent to elite agency starts with emerging models that possess little power, their residual incomes originating from pure value creation. As value is created, power is also amassed, but at a slower temporal pace, meaning that these new sustainable business models (with high VCr scores) are inclusive, contributing substantial transfer-OUT to society. Then, as the new elites become embedded in the national system, their bargaining power grows, increasingly breaking free from institutional constraints. The pace of the increase in their power at this point surpasses that of their value creation. All models, organizations, and people age, and as this happens value creation declines and eventually approaches zero. Elite business models in the latter stages of this lifecycle prevail because they have switched to maximizing transfer-IN and become vested interests that have institutionally consolidated (see lobbying, Section 1.2.2). All elite business models, whether operating in the fields of coalmining, arms, railways, pharma, or search engines, will follow this natural value creation lifecycle and gradually cease creating value irrespective of how much they generated in their heyday. Cory Doctorow (2024a) conceives of "enshittification": "first, platforms are good to their users. Then they abuse their users to make things better for their business customers. Finally, they abuse those business customers to claw back all the value for themselves. Then, there is a fourth stage: they die." The problem is that elite business models don't die or easily go bankrupt when their time has come. Instead, they are able to conserve power even with extremely low sustainable value creation positions and general mismanagement when the elite system fails to engage in weighted structural reforms (see the renditions of The Elite Business Model Lifecycle in Figure A5.9a). The 'elite vs non-elite knowledge creation gap' hypothesis may also kick in as part of 'the Amazon dilemma' outlined in Section 2.2.2.[72] If it does not, it is more probable that the natural cycle of life dictates that these models gently slip away or are creatively destroyed in Schumpeterian fashion, opening the door for more innovative new entrants. Still, in some cases, the granting of power within the political economy, usually in the non-market and narrative market arenas, enables zombie models to resist (Fernandez & Rodrik, 1991), sucking negative entropy and continuing to appropriate value from the living long after they have ceased to create it.

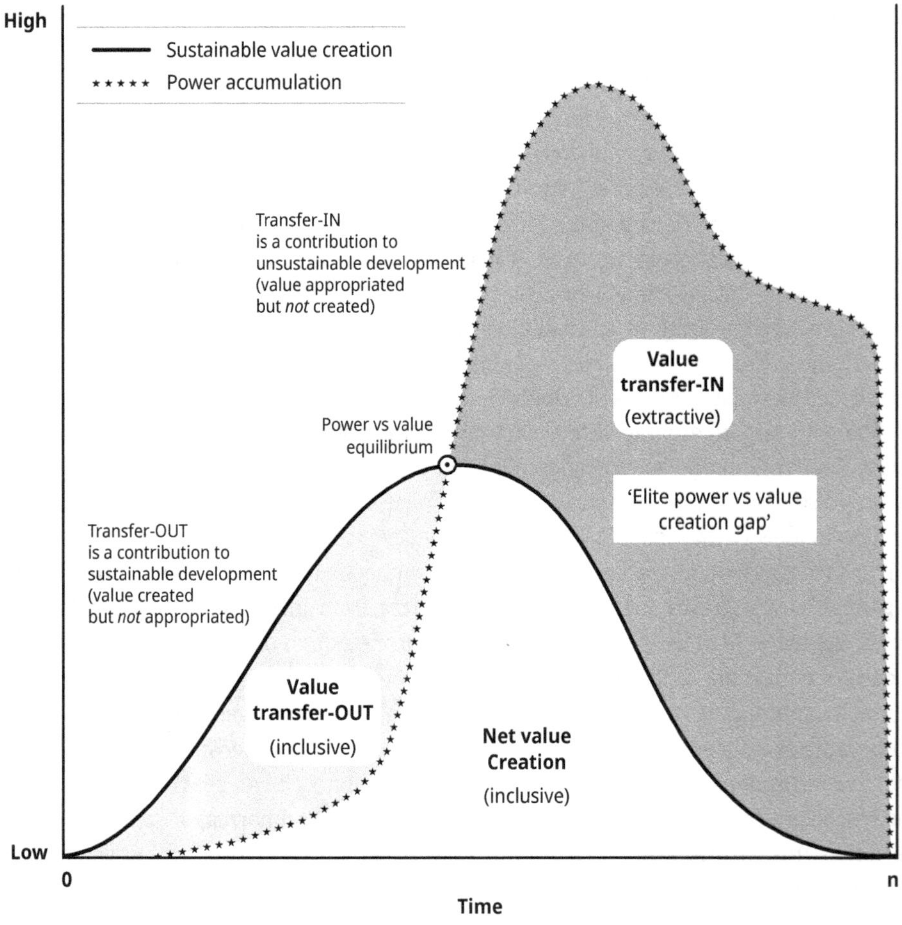

Figure 4.5: The Elite Business Model Lifecycle: The 'value transfers replace value creation at maturity' conjecture and the 'elite power vs value creation gap' hypothesis.

72 Judge Mehta's findings that "In truth, Google's penchant for innovation is consistent with the behavior of a monopolist" provide an apt explanation of 'the Amazon dilemma' which in essence causes a "perpetual scale and quality deficit" (United States District Court for the District of Columbia, 2024, pp. 236, 251) for the totality of stakeholders in society.

The liability of value transfer models cannot be tackled wholesale but must be politically and institutionally targeted and weighted on a case-by-case basis. When extraction becomes unbearable for one set of stakeholders, the business model finds itself at a turning point: it can continue to pursue extraction or instigate a transformation process. The 'value transfers replace value creation at maturity' conjecture means that if an excessive number of zombie elite models agglomerate in the final stages of their lifecycles (as in Figure 4.5), the political economy will itself enter a critical juncture. The depiction of the political economy referencing Elite Business Model Lifecycle scenarios in Figure A5.9a shows two possible paths at such a critical juncture: (a) weighted structural reform with elite bargains that (i) incentivize value and (ii) equalize bargaining power differentials resulting in recovery and increased sustainable value creation; and (b) failed reform or inaction with the consequent collapse of first-order productive activities and ultimately of accumulated power. As elite models agglomerate, the critical juncture reform dilemma applies both to industries and, consequentially, to nations. Failed structural reform (the inability to change elite business model rules) is a turning point where institutions are left to ossify and their constraints become moot, while intra-elite contests degrade and a regressive development path is *de facto* embarked on (both domestically, and, in the case of great powers, with cross-border impacts, see Section 7.3.3). Transformational leadership by individual principals inside the system notwithstanding, elite system leadership (see Table 7.2) must—through interventions in intra-elite contests—implement weighted structural reforms to incentivize value creation and equalize power and value levels (resulting in the pattern of Figure A5.9b).

This chapter has already spent time considering the constraints on elites (i.e., other elites), and now delves deeper into critical junctures. David sees path dependency where "one damn thing follows another", and it is "historical accidents" and remote "chance elements rather than systematic forces" that cause economic change (1985, p. 332). Acemoglu's "directed technical change" and "state dependence" (2002) narrowly deals with the locking-in effects of technology and investment choices on economic outcomes. The scope of historical institutionalism departs from earlier "structural explanations of historical outcomes" and is usually broader, advancing "critical junctures in which actors chose between institutional alternatives, which in turn led to path dependence" (Weyland, 2008, p. 281). What is clear is that "Junctures are 'critical' because they place institutional arrangements on paths or trajectories, which are then very difficult to alter" (Pierson, 2004, p. 135, cited in Capoccia & Kelemen, 2007, p. 342). Libecap's notion of "institutional path dependence" (2011) and the critical junctures hypothesis both see "historical factors" behind the "divergent political and economic development paths of various societies" (Acemoglu, Johnson, Robinson & Yared, 2009, p. 1057). Be as this may, to this inquiry what changes before and after a critical juncture is the amount of power needed by elites to effect institutional change, i.e., how the balance of power between the contestants—often the old and the new—has shifted.

Analysis of the "circumstances under which institutions are—and are not—subject to self-reinforcing 'lock-in'" (Mahoney & Thelen, 2010, p. 3) has not emphasized elite business models. While Pierson injects an economic rationale to path dependency, his "basic logic of increasing returns processes" is technically a combination of volition and decision rules with accident and randomness in Pólya urn fashion (2000, p. 253) more than the concentrated agency of elite business models. The ETED, as discussed, sees elites constrained by the agency of other elites materializing into cumulative institutional change. At the same time, a critical junctures hypothesis where one-off power differentials between elite contestants lead to developmental tipping points is a further reference for a theory of elites.

This work proposes that long-range developmental critical junctures result from a critical mass of wins in intra-elite contests by a coalition or an alliance of coalitions made possible by their attainment of a power differential during a singular window in time. As winning elite business models subsequently agglomerate, they not only contribute to cumulative institutional change but also, due to their augmented power, cause tipping point institutional change that yields path dependency. Examples of powerful elite coalitions that determined the development paths of nations are numerous: the Soviet Union's military-industrial complex, Germany's automotive industry and its stellar small and medium-sized enterprise (SME) ecosystems, America's private equity (PE), venture capital (VC) and finance industries, Cameroon's Customs Administration (Cantens, 2010), Spain's tourism and construction sectors, and Brazil's agribusiness. At elite business model critical junctures, new dominant coalitions regularly emerge from an elite bargain. In Indonesia, "Soeharto's New Order regime clearly brought considerable material benefits to the majority of the population", with Madame Tien Soeharto promoting specific business models that brought growth and poverty reduction while at the same time receiving a slice of state contracts and thus earning the moniker, "Madam Ten Percent"[73] (McLeod, 2000, pp. 99, 101; Dercon, 2022).

The critical junctures hypothesis in this work suggests that turning points can often be traced to the time when specific business models became those of the core elite coalition as a result of an intra-elite contest (see Figure 8.1). Moreover, because of the weight that they have in the economy, the sustainable value creation positions that they hold have a disproportionate effect on the quality of institutions and the economic and human developmental path of the nation. Which coalition amasses the most power and prevails in a critical juncture might be random (as suggested by David, 1985, and partially by Pierson, 2000), but once 'the extraordinary lever' is in

73 In contrast, the wealth and power amassed by Asif Zardari in Pakistan, also given the "Mr. Ten Percent" nickname by his political opponents (Lingelbach & Rodríguez Guerra, 2023), was not part of an elite bargain for growth with the government led by his late wife, Benazir Bhutto (the country's only female prime minister), or the one he presided over after her assassination. The presence or absence of bargains and inclusive tipping points in fractionalized elite systems explains divergent economic trajectories, in this case between the two most populous Muslim countries. Despite being at similar levels at the turn of the century, Indonesia's GDP per capita is now close to USD 5,000, over three times that of Pakistan (The World Bank, n.d.-c).

the hands of the winner, the subsequent growth trajectory is not (i.e., what follows after the juncture point is 'less' random, while there is *always* elite agency and the potential for transformational leadership). The developmental trajectories of nations consolidate as power trickles down in support of the preeminent models to ever-smaller nooks and crannies in the political economy on the back of institutional change caused by winning coalitions. In parallel to the development paths of nations, emerging core elite coalitions affect the development trajectories of specific industries as the example below illustrates:

> Tesla's no-dealership model now is being adopted by other electric-vehicle startups such as Rivian Automotive and Lucid Group Inc. These fledgling firms, backed by heavyweights such as Amazon.com Inc., are lobbying to change dealer-franchise laws in many states so they also can sell vehicles directly to shoppers. (Naughton, 2021)

In summary, the "composition of de facto and de jure power in society will determine which economic institutions arise" (Robinson, 2010, p. 6). In the ETED, power accrues from intra-elite contests, and the power of rivals is a greater constraint on elites than either institutions or the agency of non-elites. It is the degree of sustainable value creation by the elite coalitions driving critical junctures that determines whether institutional change will be inclusive or extractive. Winning elites will later employ their power differentials to maintain institutional arrangements (a form of institutional change) and preserve their business models, thereby causing development paths to persist. This was the case in 19th century Austria, in post-colonial Latin American states, or, more contemporaneously, in Germany (see Keese, 2017). The 'elite business model critical junctures' conjecture refers to a traceable point in time where a critical mass of power was attained by one or more elite coalitions that achieved economies of agglomeration[74] around certain business models, typically including the 'national business model' that is often run by the core coalition and its constituents.[75] At the

---

74 The term "agglomeration economies" comes from economic geography, and has been linked to wage premiums or productivity boosts, "where cities and clusters of activity boost the productivity of firms located within them" (Duranton & Kerr, 2015, p. 2). It is not to be confused with 'elite business model agglomeration' as used in this theory. Here, agglomeration refers to the clustering of specific elite business models, the impact of which is only positive if it associates with high sustainable value creation.

75 Firms are characterized by their choice of business models. The patterns that are available to them are recounted in Gassmann, Frankenberger, and Sauer (2016). Likewise, at the macro level, the elite systems of polities and nations, both ancient and modern, are a recombination of business model patterns whose dominant expressions are often easily recognizable by the layperson: the conquer and tax model of the Roman Empire; the theft model of "young Mexican shepherds to tend the vast herds of horses they had also stolen" from American Southwest Comanches (Cameron, 2016, p. 7); what *The Financial Times* has designated as contemporary Germany's "broken business model" of high quality manufacturing exports, a cheap euro, energy imports, and dependency on China and Russia (Chazan & Nilsson, 2022); Russia's oil and gas business model (van den Beukel & van Geuns, 2021), unendurable for large nations aspiring to advanced economy status; the Swiss model of free trade and investment,

'juncture', some models become preeminent, while others invariably become disadvantaged, with the winners able to double down on their institutional preferences and so determine the grand development trajectory of the nation, elite circulation notwithstanding. The conjecture is further explored from an economic development perspective in Section 5.1.1.

4.3.5 Elite business model driven institutional change is endogenous

Chapter 4 closes with a required final disquisition on institutionalism and the endogeneity of power-supported, elite-driven institutional change that extends the ideas developed in Section 4.2.4. Romer's seminal paper on endogenous technological change premises its appearance to the "intentional actions taken by people who respond to market incentives" (1990, p. S72). Kingston and Caballero (2009, p. 166) refer to Ayres' position on "exogenous technological progress as the main driver of institutional change: technological development forces change upon the institutional structure by changing the material setting in which it operates (1944, p. 187)". Technological or otherwise, the nature of the source of institutional change—whether it is endogenous or exogenous—is at the core of a theoretical debate:

> On one hand, the bread-and-butter theorem of neo-institutionalists—the "punctuated equilibrium" (Krasner 1984, p. 226) of path dependency and critical juncture (Arthur 1994; Capoccia & Kelemen 2007; Collier & Collier 1991; Pierson 2000)—emphasize sudden and exogenously induced change. On the other hand, a powerful recent critique of this approach to understanding change has taken a markedly different perspective by outlining gradual processes that slowly undermine institutional substance. The main drivers for this type of change are not seen as exogenous shocks but rather in terms of incremental endogenous developments (Bernhard 2015; Mahoney & Thelen 2010; Weyland 2008). These two poles of exogenous rupture versus endogenous gradual change dominate current research and mark opposite ends of a continuum in explaining institutional change. (Gerschewski, 2021, p. 218)

Let us address the endogenous vs exogenous question and its attendant disruptive vs continuous implication with an example that refers to the earlier discussion on critical junctures. Spain's development path was not marked by the loss of the institutions of democracy after the Civil War (1936–39), but the new regime's technocratic *desar-*

a strong currency, and MNEs coupled with competitive SMEs; the model of the US dollar "as an international public good" and the ensuing trade (and fiscal) deficits of "Triffin's dilemma" (Bordo & McCauley, 2017) coupled with the innovation leadership of post-WWII America. The 'national business model' refers to the value creation and appropriation patterns, i.e., the "recombination of patterns" (again, like firms, as in Gassmann, Frankenberger, & Sauer, 2016, p. 19) found in the agglomerated elite models of dominant industries, along with their specific set of institutional, economic, political, and social characteristics. From an economic development perspective, the degree of sustainable value creation embedded in the patterns of the national business model is its critical feature.

rollismo bets on industry, tourism, and infrastructure in the 1960s. The critical juncture, or most institutional change for that matter, is not "sudden and exogenously induced" (Gerschewski, 2021, p. 218). It is instead endogenous, and either gradual, where institutional change accumulates driven by elite business model preferences until a critical mass—a point of no return—is reached, or sudden, where transformational (or regressive) leadership comes to the fore (the inscrutable and creative decision-making of leaders accounts for unpredictability and uncertainty in the political economy). Eventually, even suddenly materializing inflection points result in elite models that agglomerate and consolidate, setting the country on long development trajectories of one kind or the other.

In a similar vein, should the credit for Korea's prosperity go the inclusive political institutions that emerged from the 1987 democracy protests, or to the business models of the *chaebol* and their attendant rules endogenously developed during General Park's tenure? Likewise, the extent to which the country's development trajectory was inclusively adjusted by the advent of democracy and the painful IMF reforms a decade later that penalized the family business conglomerates that had become unsustainable value destroyers remains a matter of debate. Transformational leadership was nonetheless evident during the 1997–98 Korean financial crisis when the "massive corporate failures served as credible signals that the government's implicit guarantee regime had indeed ended". As a result, 14 out of the 30 largest *chaebols* basically went "bankrupt or entered into out-of-court workouts by the end of 1999" (Kim, 2006, p. 17) and the country continued with its economic ascent.

The exceptional emergence of Kim Beom-soo ("Born to parents who did not study beyond elementary school, Mr Kim grew up in poverty", Song, 2015), the founder of KakaoTalk and KakaoBank and once "the country's richest man with a fortune of about $13.5bn [. . .] richer than Samsung's jailed leader Lee Jae-yong, whose net worth is $12.6bn" (Song, 2021) may, despite his subsequent arrest and partial downfall (Song, 2024), constitute elite circulation of the admixture type (see Figure 1.1, The Elite Circulation Matrix). Nations benefit when new elites rise up within the system by endogenously amassing power (in the form of 'money', 'might', or 'mind') through novel business models that, as they agglomerate, reconfigure the economy on new trajectories. Certain leaders appear at times to lead this process either with a new business model or by destroying an existing one—sometimes even their previously inclusive own—for its lack of sustainable value creation. In the latter case, in *The Man Who Broke Capitalism*, Gelles (2022) discusses the 1980s and 1990s corporate business model in the US that was allegedly undone by the drive for financialization, outsourcing, and M&As by General Electric's celebrity CEO, Jack Welch. Some concrete turning points in an area of the economy, when magnified by the agency of other coalitions, become elite business model critical junctures that alter the path of economic development. There are also events that are sudden and trigger a track change, as is inclusively exemplified by the Korean financial crash of 1997–98, but are these not exogenous?

Evidently, exogenous shocks such as financial crises, wars, breakthrough discoveries, unexpected political non-market outcomes, or pandemics, are game changers. However, as they occur, time-honored mechanisms usually kick-in and the shocks are absorbed and endogenized (sometimes calmly and smartly, sometimes not) by the current elites while they are invariably integrated into the system. Exogenous shock absorption in the political economy occurs via existing intra-elite contests, endogenous institutional change and, at times, elite circulation. Exogenous events are a factor in on-going intra-elite contests with the winners proving themselves to be more adept at aligning their interests and business model rule preferences with the ramifications of the particular (and ultimately, from an elite perspective, not so shocking) shock. The emergence of applied AI with the launch of the ChatGPT 3.5 model in November, 2022, the Russian war in Ukraine, COVID-19, Trump's November 2016 election victory, and the 2008 Great Recession are all decidedly unexpected exogenous shocks that have been duly endogenized by capable elite coalitions, i.e., digested and integrated into their business models. It is very rare for the elite system and its absorptive mechanisms to collapse, and only in extreme cases, such as the second Taliban takeover of Afghanistan, the October Russian Revolution, or the conquest of the Aztec Empire following the Spanish-Aztec War (1519–21) is institutional change exogenous. The power grabs of the Nazi political elites in Germany and the military elites in Japan were quickly endogenized, with the offending elements extirpated by the victors and local elites in the successful post-World War II development trajectories of post-Nuremberg Germany and post-MacArthur Japan. Selective purges of individual elite members and changes to the dominance enjoyed by specific elite coalitions were a part of this process:

> In Germany, Hitler had done away with independent unions as well as all other dissenting groups, whereas the Allies, through measures such as the decartelization decrees of 1947 and denazification programs, had emasculated cartels and organizations with right-wing backgrounds. In Japan, the militaristic regime had kept down left-wing organizations, and the Supreme Commander of the Allied Power imposed the antimonopoly law of 1947 and purged many hundreds of officers of zaibatsu and other organizations for their wartime activities. (Olson, 1982, p. 76)

The two successive shocks that both countries underwent preserved the elite system but led to the elite business model reconfigurations recounted above, all seemingly exogenous. All four of them (including Hitler's horrific *Machtergreifung* and the meteoric rise of some of his henchmen from non-elite to elite status),[76] point to the endogeneity of the

76 "The alliance of Junkers and industrialists with Brown fascism" led to admixture elite circulation as was obvious to clear-eyed observers like Brown (1934, p. 670), a stance validated, Reichswerke Hermann Göring aside, by the fact that there were "hardly any nationalizations of private firms during the Third Reich" (Buchheim & Scherner, 2006, p. 391). Yet even in admixture mode, new elites can bring their non-elite input, now embedded in winning narratives (see Figure 3.5) to bear. While the 'universal propensity to extraction' assumption (Section 3.3.3) places the morality of elites and non-elites on the same plane, the criminal excesses of the new elites of non-elite extraction in the Third Reich or Stalin's Soviet Union would seem to align with Aristotle's normative position that elites

processes at play and to the absorptive capacity of the system's elite circulation (see Proposition 2).[77] Especially revealing of the endogenization of the exogenous is the rapid post-war economic success of the two countries as a result of exogenous institutional change: many of the incumbent elite coalitions survived and drove inclusive elite business models and genuine elite system transformation.

Established elites, even if defeated in war, usually possess higher accumulated power endowments and coordination capacity in their political economy than alternative coalitions. The Japanese and German miracles are not about Sony or Kyocera, but about the successful transformation of incumbents like the Mitsubishi Group or Panasonic Corporation; not about Otto Verlag or SAP, but about the transformation of BMW or Thyssenkrupp. In The Elite Circulation Matrix terms (Figure 1.1), Japan and Germany saw an exemplary post-war admixture elite circulation mode where relatively high value creation elite business models combined with a respectable level of social order access. However, over the ensuing decades, circulation slowed down, social mobility at the top stalled, and without critical junctures driven by elite agglomeration around innovative new development trajectories (such as the one started by the breakup of AT&T in the US, see Sections 1.3.2 and 7.1.3), opportunities were missed. The once prosperous incumbent models created less and less value and resulted, from the 1990s onwards, in the two countries becoming increasingly detached from the global technology frontier.

Political economies where the speed of business model transformation is not higher than the rate of institutional change see few emerging elite coalitions pushing for the opening up of the novel institutional spaces enabled by technological breakthroughs. Elite business models can be more persistent than elites in the flesh. Exogenous events like new technologies can result in new business models *and* coalitions, but inertia-breaking dynamics necessitate rigorous transformational leadership. Portions of elite power and the coordination capacity of incumbent coalitions must dissolve. Korea's bounce back from the 1997–98 crisis entailed eliminating half of its *chaebol* and, as Johnson (2009) coldly notes, "If the IMF's staff could speak freely about the U.S., it would tell us what it tells all countries in this situation: recovery will fail unless we break the financial oligarchy that is blocking essential reform". The elite system is preserved while its power endowments are reshuffled. Wholesale exogeneous elite replacement processes do take place (e.g., in many post-Soviet states),

---

should be born and trained to take on this role, as is the case with an aristocracy or Pareto's "best". It is worth reemphasizing that throughout history non-elites have shown that they can more than outdo their previous masters when it comes to the worst forms of value extraction.

77 For Germany, details are provided in DeJong's *Nazi Billionaires: The Dark History of Germany's Wealthiest Dynasties* (2022). For Japan, note the following citation and its nuance: "The Zaibatsu have steadily built their power and have revived. No, more than that. Before the war, the Zaibatsu had to share their hegemony with large landowners and were under the Emperor and the militarists, but now there are no militarists or large landowners. The Emperor, too, has become an accessory. The power of Japan now rests squarely in the hands of the Zaibatsu, the sponsors of the Conservative Party" (Nagasu, 1959, p. 118, as cited in Yamamura, 1964, p. 539).

but occurrences where the elite system and most elite coalition sub-systems disappear are rare (as discussed in Section 3.3.2). The ideal admixture elite circulation mode suggested throughout this work (e.g., Wall Street's handholding of loss-making Amazon on its path to core elite coalition status) is fundamentally endogenous.

This section has surmised about the endogenous nature of elite business model driven institutional change. In economic models, the distinction between endogenous and exogenous variables is critical, but by establishing the endogenization of the exogenous, this distinction loses relevance. Furthermore, such a distinction is already redundant if endogenous events are embedded in a complex system and characterized by their randomness, non-linearity, emergence, and evolution, as in systems theory (see Section 3.2.3): endogenous and exogenous events might receive a different mathematical treatment in models, but their properties and patterns resemble each other in a complex system. The infection and fatality rates of a novel virus' mutations, or a foreign leader's decision to start a war, are exogenous events, yet there is minimal practical difference between their impact on elite business models and the similarly unpredictable and endogenous emergence of the AI or which firms will win the intra-elite race for its value appropriation. The most consequential variables in the economy for the purposes of growth are not so on account of whether they originate inside or outside the system, but rather because of their non-repeating, unpredictable, emergent, chaotic, and high-impact nature. Grasping the patterns and behaviors of such variables as they come into existence requires modeling the complex adaptive elite system from which they emerge. This is then not a problem of determining the exogenous or endogenous factors or of projection. Rather, it one of estimating the "range of reasonable possibilities" coupled with the awareness that "forecasts are better viewed as distributions of probabilities than as exact predictions" (Beinhocker, 2006; Liebovitch, 1998; Prigogine, 1996, all cited in McDaniel, Lanham, & Anderson, 2009, pp. 4, 6). The kinds of probabilities that this theory sets out are those associated with inclusive institutional states where sustainable value creation elites have outcompeted their rivals in the arenas of the political economy whose business models lean more extensively on value transfers.

In closing this chapter, a further reflection on the role of power is required. Power is a strategic capability that provides value appropriation options for those that hold it—the elites. Obviously, it can also be used to accomplish much more than simply maintaining extractive transfer-IN models against resistance. Power is considered misused, for instance, when incumbent elites refrain from taking risks, are unable to innovate, and fail to transform their business models to match the speed of general social and technological progress. Power is what provides elites with the options for successful transformation and the absorption of exogenous shocks. If applied effectively it will prevent a solid business model from decaying (à la General Electric) or fading into oblivion (à la Kodak) through new value creation. At the national level, the power and cohesion of the core elite coalition (see Figure 8.1) is the ultimate backstop to prevent a political economy from sinking into an extractive free-for-all that takes a country and its elites down. Such a free-for-all endogenous extractive degeneration characterized China's early Republican fragmented elites and feuding warlords after the Xinhai Revolution in 1911–1912, as well as the imperial ruling Confucian narrative-imbued Manchu elite of the late Qing Dynasty. Both powerless and excessively powerful elites can lead to the state of affairs described by Lu Xun, who delved into the analogy of cannibalism in his masterpiece, *A Madman's Diary* (1918/1985).[78]

There is no determinism in power and its use. For instance, powerful elites that have fallen behind their peers in terms of the value creation of their business model can strategically leverage their existing coordination capacity through alliances with new, emerging, and value creating elite coalitions. At the country level, this is what the CPC elites did under Deng when launching their "Socialism with Chinese characteristics" economic reforms on December 18, 1978, or what US elites did in the 1990s by seizing the possibilities of the Internet revolution. This admixture, facilitated, even if not actively promoted by all incumbents, is one of the desirable outcomes enabled by power. One must never forget that degrees of power, like degrees of extraction (see the 'alternating value extraction and creation' conjecture), are necessary for value creation. This appears to fly in the face of 'equalized bargaining power equilibrium prices' (see Section 2.2.2), a contradiction that lingers throughout this inquiry.

Faced with an exogenous or endogenous event with tipping point potential, i.e., able to affect power transitions, how can sustainable and productive admixture prevail over vicious intra-elite contests and civil strife? One might consider the powerful US finance industry and its legally codified rules for venture capital (Armour & Cumming, 2006) that provide the incentive structure for innovation and drive the Bay Area's immense value creation. Such institutional change is in essence a win-win partnership between incumbent and emerging elite coalitions kick-starting new development trajectories that boost economic and human development. It is of little concern to the enlightened self-interest of the establishment that the rising elites they support become wealthier and eventually accumulate more power than their original sponsor. Members of Silicon Valley elite coalitions have now circulated to the apex and bested those of Wall Street[79] by realizing the potential of technology to unlock novel forms of value appropriation, using 'the extraordinary lever' to endogenously double down on institutional change as necessary. These transformations have also been highly advantageous to the legacy coalitions in their role as investors.

78 "It has only just dawned on me that all these years I have been living in a place where for four thousand years human flesh has been eaten". In this poignant passage, Lu Xun (1918/1985, p. 51) points to an extractive terminus, a low point free-for-all where the practice of value extraction has spread to elites and non-elites alike and imbues both culture and institutions.

79 The profits for US Fortune 500 companies in the technology sector reached US$ 306 billion for the fiscal year ending March 31, 2023, while those in the financial sector were less than half of this (US$ 139 billion). See: https://www.growandconvert.com/research/most-profitable-fortune-500-companies-in-2023/

Summary of Chapter 4

Towards elite agency constrained and enabled by power and institutions

Part II of this book ('Integration') seeks to bind its diverse conceptual elements into a coherent theoretical system. This work begins with Chapter 4's exploration of how elite agency is both constrained and enabled by power and institutions. The initial Section 4.1 hones in on the basic building blocks of elite agency in the political economy, the first of these being the leadership required for its success. This behavioral construct is a *leitmotif* of the ETED and the examination details its two fundamental varieties: elite coordination leadership and business model leadership (4.1.1). They respectively relate to the attainment of the two objectives of elite agency in the political economy, power and residual income (see Figure 4.1). Here, the discussions briefly reconvene and (in Table 4.1) the chief conceptual elements for a political economy theory of elites (4.1.2) are recounted.

Section 4.2 consolidates elite agency as the microfoundation of institutional formation and change, a recurring theoretical meeting place in this inquiry. Aiming at the development of a comprehensive institutional perspective (anchored by Proposition 12), the focus of the first sub-section (4.2.1) is on the incentive structures that make specific division of value strategies feasible, thus enabling and constraining residual income and economic growth. A step back is taken in the next sub-section (4.2.2) to explore elite agency through the 'follow the money' *cui bono* heuristic of institutional change. The theory now tightens the connection between these insights to strengthen the idea that the immediate elite preferences for institutional change concern business model rules (see Figure 4.2) with their discrete potential for sustainable value creation. As a result, these rules contain signals of future economic and human development (note the link to the elite quality discussion in Chapter 6). Further grounding for elite agency is then provided (4.2.3) through a review of elite embeddedness, the paradox of agency, and how limitedly structure constrains elites; in reality they are mainly constrained by their peers (or by structures maintained by their peers). Discrete elite conceptualizations of embeddedness for business model and intra-elite contest rules are respectively proposed and the relationship between the two rule types is expounded on (see Figure 4.3). The closing sub-section (4.2.4) then canvasses additional theoretical support and provides historical examples of elite agency by focusing on the differences between spontaneous and deliberate institutional formation and change. The inquiry emphasizes deliberate elite agency that strives to adjust the incentive system in consistency with its business model preferences.

Section 4.3 focuses on power and elite agency. Institutional change is feasible with the accumulation of power through wins in the political economy's three power domains (economy, politics, society) and its associated contest arenas (market, nonmarket, and narrative market) that emanate from elite coordination leadership. The first sub-section (4.3.1) reviews the notion of 'power' and posits that it is everywhere, inescapable, and, as a facilitator for the formation of a common will and the ability to project it, resolves value appropriation in society. The next sub-section (4.3.2) reviews power as a mechanism for the meta-contest resolution of conflicts and explains how power differentials supersede meta-institutions—basically intra-elite contest rules—at effecting institutional change. Power differentials are essential to move institutions and the economy and the next sub-section (4.3.3) provides a synthesis (Figure 4.5) that considers countervailing emphases like circulation velocity and 'knowledge' as the key source of power. The 'elite business model critical junctures' conjecture, an extension of the critical junctures hypothesis, is then introduced to explain the development trajectories of nations on account of 'elite business model agglomeration' (4.3.4). The underlying logic of The Elite Business Model Lifecycle is rendered in Figure 4.5. Finally, the closing sub-section (4.3.5) takes a position on the critical question of whether institutional change is exogenous or endogenous and stresses the preeminence of endogenization.

There is an unambiguous principle of the political economy: value transfers require power. Extractive political institutions reflect extractive elite business model preferences that are realized through control of 'the extraordinary lever'. As a critical conceptual element of this inquiry's paradigm, power is measured (e.g., it is one of the main components in operationalizing elite quality, see Sections 6.2.2 and 6.2.4). It should also be recalled that power is functional to elite agency. It is not pursued for subtle psychological motives but to generate residual income (see Proposition 6 on elite identity). Yet Arendt's understanding that power is a mechanism to act on behalf of others also stresses its deep ethical quality and potential: it is extant and necessary in society and provides options for inclusive elite business model and elite system transformation on the back of discrete types of leadership.

Having tightened the links around the key theoretical bases, Chapter 5 now aims to establish the first approximation of an elite theory of economic development.

Chapter 5
Towards the elite theory of economic development (ETED)

> Economics is the body of substantive generalizations on the workings of economic systems. (Stigler, 1952, p. 206)

Chapter 5 ties together the previously developed micro- and meso-level ideas about elite agency and begins the process of transitioning these to the macro-level with implications for general economic performance. The macro discussion of economic development emphasizes sustainable value creation and rent-seeking phenomena in matching parallel to the first-order value creation and risk origination and second-order transfer activities of elite business models in relation to their stakeholders. The aggregate value creation of elites at the meso elite system level is consolidated as the conceptual cornerstone of this elite theory of economics. Analogous to the study of elite business models, elite agency is further understood in terms of its influence on macro-level development. Hence, in Section 5.1, existing theory is leveraged to further reveal the theoretical links and transmission mechanisms between firm-level value creation and macroeconomic development through the advancement of elements like the 'elite business model critical junctures' conjecture. Section 5.2 takes a similar approach but hones in on firm-level extractive value transfers and negative macroeconomic development by advancing elements like the typology of individual non-elite responses to value transfers. Section 5.3 further consolidates the ETED system conceptually through the advancement of sustainable value creation (SVC) measurements and the development of conceptual elements like elite cohesion and the 'extractive escalation dynamic'.

5.1 Theoretical support for value creation as the microfoundation of economic development

Value creation refers to first-order "productive" activities (see the examples listed in Table 2.1), as in Bhagwati (1982, p. 989): "To produce goods or services that enter a utility function directly or indirectly via increased production or availability to the economy of goods that enter a utility function". "Unproductive" activities, on the other hand, are second-order transfers where "direct output is simply zero in terms of the flow of goods and services entering a conventional utility function" or DUP ("directly unproductive, profit-seeking") which "can be pronounced 'dupe' activities, coming close to the spirit in which economists must view these activities!" (Bhagwati, 1982, p. 990). Whether Marx's stages theory of economic development, structural change theory focusing on urbanization, or neoclassical theories advocating unim-

https://doi.org/10.1515/9783110734638-008

peded free markets, many thought systems that seek to explicate desirable economic development stress value creation as a first-order productive economic activity. To the ETED, incentivizing micro-level transformation towards sustainable value creation is the most demanding challenge for policymakers because it requires political leadership to overcome the resistance of extractive vested interests (e.g., *The Contest for Japan's Economic Future: Entrepreneurs vs Corporate Giants*, Katz, 2024), a deep understanding of business models and their links to society, the impact of laws and regulations, as well as knowledge elites able to discern all of this and design effective structural reform with the attendant winning narratives.

The first section of Chapter 5 concerns itself once more with value creation business models and the nature of productive activities. It starts with a brief review of economic development theories and then tightens the conceptual link between development and the 'elite business model critical junctures' conjecture by offering specific examples (5.1.1). Next, innovation activities are appraised as a central tenet of economic and human development (5.1.2). The section closes by suggesting that all sustainable value creation can be ascertained, whether on- or off-balance sheet, because quantifying value transfers from one sub-set of society to another is possible (5.1.3).

5.1.1 Elite business model critical junctures for economic development

Theories of economic development vary significantly. Marx saw the sequential stages of feudalism, capitalism, and socialism in terms of extraction and the broad brushstrokes of class struggle, but did not comprehensively delve into the specifics of elite business models. Neither does the modernization theory of Lipset (1959) that links a transition from traditional to modern social practices with democracy and economic development, or Rostow's *The Stages of Economic Growth* (1960), a "non-Communist" structuralist blueprint for modernization theory with its linear (six) stages of growth. Such economic development models see development occur in a mandatory sequence based on capital accumulation facilitated by international and domestic savings. Modernization theory has been criticized for being simplistic, as has international dependence theory that arose in the 1970s. The latter is an alternative left-leaning development theory that sees dependence as "a situation in which the economy of certain countries is conditioned by the development and expansion of another economy to which the former is subjected" (Dos Santos, 1970, p. 231), and is centered on denunciations of imperialism, neocolonialism, and external impediments as the causes of a failure to develop. Prebisch, one of its earliest exponents, complains of Latin America's role at "the periphery of the world economic system", and of an "out-dated schema of the international division of labour" devised to reduce underdeveloped countries to "producing food and raw materials for the great industrial centres" (1950, p. 1). Conveniently, dependency theory underemphasizes domestic factors, such as the extractive practices of local elite business models, which are central to the ETED.

The Smithian free market model focuses on exchange to achieve full value creation potential and realize "any potential value that resides in an economic system [. . .] facilitating the continual reallocation of resources to their more productive uses [. . .] and reorders the set of resources that are available for new combinations" (Moran & Ghoshal, 1996, p. 42). The Keynesian Harrod-Domar model of economic growth focuses on savings and capital investments with a coefficient that acts as a multiplier or accelerator for long-run growth (Solow, 1956, pp. 65–66). When fixed proportions are assumed for the factors of production (population/labor and savings/capital), one is stuck in a constant returns to scale function that eventually hits diminishing returns or, even worse, is very unstable and "balanced on a knife-edge of equilibrium growth" (Sato, 1964, p. 380). By modeling capital accumulation (stock) per head dynamics, the economic exogeneous growth model, independently developed by Solow (1956) and Swan (1956), aims at the long run, with no rigidities or fixed factor proportions in the fashion of the neoclassical tradition in which it is embedded. Critically, in the Solow-Swan model, capital and labor production factor constraints break free through technological advances and productivity increases. Technological change—like labor force increases—is also conveniently assumed to be an exogenous variable in the model. From the 1980s, the neoclassical paradigm associated with Solovian steady growth and sustained equilibrium became ascendant over structuralist, linear stage models, both in the theory and policy arenas. The endogenous growth models that followed (Romer, 1986 and 1990; Lucas, 1988), and Schumpeterian growth theories and models (Aghion & Howitt, 1992) with a focus on the inner dynamics of the political economy, such as technology adoption rates, will be touched upon in the next section.

Institutionalists agree with the basics of neoclassical economics but view the theory as "unable to account for economic growth since it is only concerned with the operation of markets, not with the way markets develop overtime" (North, 1996, p. 342, as cited in Faundez, 2016, p. 386). The critical junctures hypothesis, an important contribution to development theory, references path dependency (David, 1985) of the institutional kind (Libecap, 2011): "institutional change which affects both economic and political development is initiated by differences during a certain critical historical juncture" (Acemoglu, Johnson, Robinson, & Yared, 2009, p. 1043). The 'elite business model critical junctures' conjecture (see Section 4.3.3) maintains that institutional change is endogenous. When inclusive, institutions are brought about by new elite business models, often those of Schumpeterian newcomers (such as the Manchester industrialists, Tesla, or BYD Auto), shaking up the system of established dominant coalitions (such as the London landowners or the internal combustion engine) and resulting in an admixture of new and old elites. Moreover, as previously discussed, this elite theory posits that the discrete development paths of the nations of the world accrue from the variance of the value creation positions of the business models in their national elite systems. Elites gravitate towards, come together, and agglomerate around specific elite business models that, once a threshold is reached, consolidate as a critical development juncture in a theoretical transition from the micro- to the macro-level through the meso-level elite system.

At critical junctures, elite business models in possession of 'the extraordinary lever' assert dominance and so chart a nation's path, affecting long-term developmental performance through the degree of their sustainable value creation and extractive transfers and how that adjusts over time. Given the inexorable pace of technological and social progress, without business model transformation, today's inclusive elites will become tomorrow's extractors. Returning to the example of the combustion engine, in Germany (despite the inventions of Karl Benz in the 1870s, the over 80 auto companies existing in the 1920s, and the *Motorisierung* policies of the 1930s), the business model only took off in the postwar era and today remains the chief pillar of Germany's political economy, even though its days now seem numbered. Japan's slowly eroding *keiretsu* main bank model is rooted in the Meiji Restoration of the late 19th century. The developmental consequences of the Soviet Union's Dutch disease, a model based on the discoveries of Ural oil in West Siberia and Tyumen in the 1970s, are expounded on in a Carnegie Endowment for International Peace report:

> Between the end of World War II and the mid-1960s, the Soviet Union's economy was one of the most vibrant in the world. The country had successfully launched the first man into space and was competing with the United States in developing cutting-edge military technology. However, by the end of the 1980s, the economy was in a miserable state. (Ermolaev, 2017)

In the earlier example of Spain (Section 4.3.5), the decisive critical juncture came about in the 1960s through the innocuous policies of *desarrollismo* that ushered in the elite business models (and the subsequent incremental institutional change) of regulated energy and utilities, construction and tourism, and banking finance. Under the precepts of the paradigm of this work, these elite business models and supporting rules have further agglomerated via endogenous gradual reinforcement and insufficient transformation, negatively impacting on modern Spain's comparative prosperity in Western Europe. One might argue that the impact of elite business models is always greater than more visible, high-order institutional change, in this case the restoration of democracy in 1977 or accession to the EU in 1986. For instance, like Kim Beom-soo, Amancio Ortega, the founder of Inditex—the world's largest fashion group—has origins far from Spain's Madrid elite. Both have created immense value, but unlike his Korean peer, Ortega's amazing value creation journey is not a native Spanish story: the phenomenal success of Inditex has nothing to do with Spanish institutions—it happened despite its elite system—and everything to do with the institutions of globalization. Moreover, the company will make no contribution to an elite business model critical juncture in Spain and so the impact on economic development of Ortega[80] is currently not comparable to

80 A distinguished new figure in the Spanish establishment, the personal wealth of Ortega is deployed in the time-honored fashion of his incumbent elite peers and consistent with the country's path depen-

that of Kim: the Spaniard has built the world's most efficient and innovative fashion company, while the Korean endogenously nudges the national elite system and its institutional make-up towards higher value creation positions spurred by the evolution of technology.

The above discussion adds nuance and brings to life the 'elite business model critical juncture' conjecture. Value creation results from activities such as production and exchange (see the full list in Table 2.3) and includes, according to Baumol (1990, p. 893), "productive activities such as innovation". To have relevance for economic development, however, the waves of innovative value creation models must agglomerate and materialize in institutional change. Baumol's emphasis moves us to Schumpeter's (1911/2003) perspective and his comprehensive placement of innovation as the central theoretical foundation for value creation.

5.1.2 Innovation as the central value creation activity for economic development

The innovation dynamics of capitalism emanate from intra-elite contests, the most important of which take place between incumbent and emerging elites. This is actually the view of Marx and Engels in their *Manifesto of the Communist Party*:

> The bourgeoisie cannot exist without constantly revolutionizing the instruments of production, and thereby the relations of production, and with them the whole relations of society. [. . .] Constant revolutionizing of production, uninterrupted disturbance of all social conditions, everlasting uncertainty and agitation distinguish the bourgeois epoch from all earlier ones. All fixed, fast-frozen relations, with their train of ancient and venerable prejudices and opinions, are swept away, all new-formed ones become antiquated before they can ossify. (Marx & Engels, 1848/1969, p. 16)

In economics, innovation is understood as Solow's (1957, p. 312) formalization of technical change: "variations in output per head [not due] to changes in the available capital per head". Abramovitz (1993, pp. 217–218) was quick to point to empirical findings (like Solow's own) where labor and capital account for only 10% of growth, while technical change, or total factor productivity (TFP), accounts for 90%; due to its residual nature, innovation "hogs the whole show", yet is also a "grab bag" as well as "some sort of measure of ignorance". Degrees of ignorance, however, have receded as innovation has been incorporated into models as an endogenous variable. Technological changes provide increasing returns over time (Romer, 1986), where "vertical innovations, generated by a competitive research sector, constitute the underlying source of growth" (Aghion & Howitt, 1992, p. 323). The government's pivotal role in education

dent institutional make-up: real estate and regulated sectors (as suggested by Chamizo, 2021). This would suggest that Spain's elite circulation mode is one of 'infiltration' (see The Elite Circulation Matrix, Figure 1.1).

and research means that policymakers must ask "what are the best institutional arrangements for encouraging the production and use of new knowledge?" (Romer, 1994, p. 21). Moreover, economic productivity growth's relationship to innovation has also been probed (Aghion, Bloom, Blundell, Griffith, & Howitt. 2005), as have its institutional causes: the model of Chu, Cozzi, and Galli (2012, p. 742) puts the accent on "the asymmetric effects of patent rights on different types of innovation and the potentially different policy implications on economic growth and social welfare".

At the micro-level, innovation has been associated with investment in human capital. Dewar and Dutton (1986) point out that "extensive knowledge depth" embodied in human capital is essential for the two innovation types expressed in many value creation business models: incremental innovation (requiring moderate degrees of new knowledge) and radical innovation (requiring high degrees of new knowledge). Innovation must play a central role at firms (Christensen, 1997), especially when, as Moran and Ghoshal (1996, p. 41) claim, "all firms are not equal in their prospects for innovating or for exploiting the innovations of others" and in conceiving strategy as value creation and value appropriation for the long term. For Porter (1991, p. 111), innovation gives firms "considerable latitude in both influencing their environment and responding to it". Kirzner, and consistent with the alignment of this elite theory with fundamental aspects of the Austrian School, connects innovation with human agency as he rejects the RCT paradigm:

> At the individual level Austrians have taken sharp exception to the manner in which neoclassical theory has portrayed the individual decision as a mechanical exercise in constrained maximization. Such a portrayal robs human choice of its essentially open-ended character, in which imagination and boldness must inevitably play central roles. (Kirzner, 1997, p. 64)

In a similar vein, Damodaran addresses a fallacy of risk at the firm level:

> Risk management has to be defined far more broadly to include actions that are taken by firms to *exploit uncertainty*. In fact, risk management may involve increasing, rather than decreasing, exposure to at least some types of risks when a firm believes that increasing the risk will give it an advantage over its competitors. (Damodaran, 2005, p. 38)

Open-endedness, imagination, and boldness by decision makers undertaking uncertainty (Knight, 1921/2002) rather than optimizing positions along the lower reaches of the risk/return efficiency frontier (Markowitz, 1952; Sharpe, 1964) by prioritizing low risk exposure and moderate returns are the essence of innovative business models. Such are the business model leadership approaches that account for new resource combinations (Schumpeter, 1911/2003; Buchanan, 1980). Who then are the agents of innovation-based value creation?

Nicholas (2003, p. 1023) recounts how Schumpeter saw two types of organizations driving innovation: the proverbial "small entrepreneurial ventures as seedbeds of technological discovery" of *The Theory of Economic Development* (1911/2003) and "large firms with market power [that] accelerate the rate of innovation" in *Capitalism,*

Socialism and Democracy (1942/2000). Innovation by incumbent and emerging elites is the focal point of value creation by "creative destruction"[81], ushering in:

> the great economic and social process by which business, individual positions, forms of life, cultural values and ideals, sink in the social scale and finally disappear [seeing] the continual emergence of new economic and social forms and of continually raising real incomes of all social strata. (Schumpeter, 1911/2003, p. 255)

That is, development. "Creative Destruction" is Schumpeter's "essential fact about capitalism" (1942/2000, p. 83), and so "over the long run, the process of creative destruction accounts for over 50 percent of productivity growth" (Caballero, 2008, p. 1). The disruptive entrepreneurs of Schumpeter (1911/2003) and the "alert" ones of Kirzner (1997)—in this work seen as potential, emerging, or future elites—connect micro-level entrepreneurship with macro-level outcomes such as economic growth (Hoselitz, 1952; Aghion & Howitt, 1992; Holcombe, 1998; Acs & Szerb, 2007). Some of the intermediate linkages that have been identified include knowledge externalities and spillovers (Audretsch, 2007; Audretsch & Keilbach, 2008) given that entrepreneurship "serves as the vehicle of innovation and change" (Carree & Thurik, 2010, p. 588), and competition (Wennekers & Thurik, 1999, p. 30, Figure 1). This dynamic is not necessarily kind to incumbents since development that is based on innovation is an ever-unfolding process of disruption:

> when one firm gains some advantage over others, that advantage becomes a target for all other firms to emulate [and] begins to erode with competition. In time, no firm is any better off, relative to the others, than when it started and the search for new advantages must begin again (if it ever ceased in the first place). As a result, yet another phase in this Schumpeterian cycle of creative destruction that accounts for the progress of most economic systems, is initiated. (Moran & Ghoshal, 1996, pp. 44–45)

Irrespective of whether they are the result of recent entrepreneurial entrants or long serving incumbents, innovative elite business models create so much value that their stakeholders can, in most cases, appropriate a significant amount without compromising the elite status of the principal. This is another reason why innovation brings about sustainable and inclusive economic development. Of course, to establish the *overall* sustainable value creation of an organization, one must also consider the other side of the coin and measure extractive value transfers.

---

81 Despite being popularized by and associated with Schumpeter, "the idea of 'creative destruction' enters the social sciences by way of Friedrich Nietzsche [as in "Whoever must be a creator always annihilates", see 1883/2006, p. 43]. The term itself was first used by German economist Werner Sombart, who openly acknowledges the influence of Nietzsche on his own economic theory. The roots of creative destruction are traced back to Indian philosophy, from where the idea entered the German literary and philosophical tradition" (Reinert & Reinert, 2006, p. 55).

5.1.3 Ascertaining sustainable value creation with value transfers

> Suppose that, instead of discovering a new commodity or service or production process, an innovating entrepreneur discovers a way to convince the government that he "deserves" to be granted a monopoly right, and that government will enforce such a right by keeping out all potential entrants. No value is created in the process; indeed, the monopolization involves a net destruction of value. The rents secured reflect a diversion of value from consumers generally to the favored rent seeker, with a net loss of value in the process. (Buchanan, 1980, p. 7)

It has been shown that value creation occurs via first-order productive activities (see the list in Table 2.3) such as agriculture, manufacturing, exchange, finance, and, as just discussed, innovation in any of its many forms such as incremental product improvements. At the micro-level of firms these activities are readily identifiable and pursued by competent management teams characterized by their 'knowledge'. Yet, as in the ETED's ontological 'value is created or transferred' assumption (see Figure A5.4a; also described in the 'value spectrum', see Figures 2.10, 2.11), value creation and extraction always go hand in hand. The hideous slave plantation system produced valuable cotton along with immense value extraction that was borne by labor—the compulsory stakeholder-victims prevented from exit. However, for many 21st century business models there is far less clarity on the value appropriated but *not* created. A technology monopolist may be innovative, but if the prices charged are higher than would be the case with the existence of competition and counterfactual 'equalized bargaining power equilibrium prices' (see Section 2.2.2), then extraction is also an intrinsic part of the model and the principal's residual income. Contemporary institutions are, however, either technically incapable or largely unconcerned about quantifying and addressing the value extraction question unless it becomes material in an intra-elite contest. As a result, what Bastiat (1845/1996) calls "plunder" and Olson (1993) and Tullock (1967) term "theft" is essentially legalized. Apple's initial "resounding victory" in the landmark antitrust case brought by Epic Games Inc. included the preservation of the tech giant's "restrictions for third-party software" because:

> "While the court finds that Apple enjoys considerable market share of over 55% and extraordinarily high profit margins, these factors alone do not show antitrust conduct," the judge wrote. "Success is not illegal." (Higgins, 2021b)

Apple's original win in this intra-elite contest begs the question of whether it benefits from value appropriated but *not* created; what Elon Musk calls Apple's "secret 30% tax".[82] The implication here is that the world's most valuable firm appropriates a chunk of the value created by app developers in its store (such as Epic or X Premium). As the "Success is not illegal" opinion suggests, such extraction logic does not figure in legal doctrine. For rent seeking to be a decision-making factor for leaders involved in

82 See: https://x.com/elonmusk/status/1597301968208556032

intra-elite contests, and especially for it to become a technically feasible consideration in policymaking, it needs a strong conceptual applied framework; one that can extend the theoretical understanding of rent seeking, negative externalities, or extractive economic institutions into the realm of the law. “Microsoft’s stunning courtroom victory over US regulators trying to block its acquisition” of Activision (Waters & Palma, 2023) is another recent example of a legal system’s obliviousness to the potential and actual distortions of bargaining power differentials, value extraction, and the realities behind President Biden’s remark that: “what we’ve seen over the past few decades is less competition and more concentration that holds our economy back. We see it in big agriculture, in big tech, in big pharma. The list goes on” (The White House, 2023). In tandem with suitable sustainable value creation frameworks, it is essential that SVC measurements are developed that can stand up in court on account of using standardized methodologies for collecting constituent data and interpreting the evidence (as is aimed at in Section 5.3). In order to disentangle value creation from extraction, the spotlight must be on quantifying tangible transfers from stakeholders to principals. As will be discussed in detail (see Section 5.3.1), the business model SVC measurements (VCp/VCr) presented in Table 2.4 are only feasible if transfer-IN (and transfer-OUT) amounts can be established as part of (and in relation to) P&L statement revenue and profits.

Value extraction, for the purposes of this theory and its application, occurs through value transfers. That is, transfers from one individual to another, from one stakeholder to a principal, from one subset of society to another (see a tentative rendition of the set of value transfer relationships in the political economy, Figure A5.14). These transfers were earlier conceptualized as value appropriated but *not* created (transfer-IN) and its opposite, value created but *not* appropriated (transfer-OUT) by business models with the micro-level value creation-appropriation (VCA) framework (see Chapter 2). By establishing value transfers, value creation can be ascertained. The constructive, positive assumption used in operationalizing sustainable value creation measurements at the micro-level is that the revenue/profits of a business model are *a priori* considered full first-order productive value creation and not a value transfer. That is, in the ‘bona fide value appropriation’ (positive) assumption, the starting point is that value appropriated *is* value created; and its practical implication is that ‘revenue is value creation unless value transfer is proven’ (see Figure A5.4a). That means that the burden of proof rests on establishing value transfers, which must be confirmed both conceptually and in monetary terms by empirical evidence of transfer-IN to the business model (see the process for the establishment of SVC metrics, Section 6.6.1). The theoretical bases of such extractive value transfers, how these are accounted for at the macro-level, and their impact on national development are further considered next.

5.2 Theoretical support for value transfers and responses to extraction

The second part of this section completes the literature review on rent seeking by first examining the theoretical foundations of why it matters (5.2.1). Yet the overarching purpose is to understand the structural and psychological factors of why value extraction exists at all. This is done by first examining the 'acceptance' responses of stakeholders that suffer from extractive transfers (5.2.2). The full range of responses to value extraction—including the 'exit' response—are then reviewed (5.2.3). This analysis of causes goes a long way towards explaining the economic development consequences of value transfers, a key theme of this work.

5.2.1 Why do rent seeking and value transfers matter both theoretically and in practice?

> It is the purpose of this work to show that the distribution of the income of society is controlled by a natural law, and that this law, if it worked without friction, would give to every agent of production the amount of wealth which that agent creates. (Clark, 1899/1908, p. 3)

In practice "friction", essentially the result of power, i.e., "force", on both "the employer's side" and "on the worker's side" (Clark, 1903, p. 612) annuls the "natural law":

> What we must admit, however, is that the principle of monopoly is a bad one, and that in the business world it is becoming too nearly dominant. Trusts are seeking to create monopolies of products, and trade unions are trying to establish monopolies of labor. (Clark, 1903, p. 599)

Rent seeking matters because it disrupts the path to economic and human development. John Bates Clark correctly qualifies inclusive development outcomes to the absence of this "friction". However, a political economy is characterized by deliberately introduced friction, typified by the manner and degree to which rent seeking occurs. In Tullock's quantitative examination of rent seeking, he outlines the costs, transfers, and redistributions "from losers to winners in activities such as regulation and monopolization" (Tollison, 2012, p. 73). The breadth of the distortions presented is astounding and their logic stunning.

Firms that are regulated are more likely to obtain government aid (Zingales, 2012). Rent seeking is akin to interventions that cause costs beyond the already onerous deadweight losses—see "The Measurement of Waste" (Harberger, 1964)—associated with price floors, price caps or quotas in Harberger triangles where a wedge is driven between the prices received by producers and the prices paid by consumers. Tollison (2012, p. 74) articulates the implications of "expenditures made to capture a transfer" such as lobbying: each of these expenditures is but a misallocation that "diverts resources away from positive-sum activities into zero- and even negative-sum efforts to capture transfers, resulting in social costs". Consistent with sector-specific research that confirms "large sums of money [are spent] on lobbying and campaign contributions to influence legislative and election outcomes" (Wouters, 2020, p. 696) and other findings (e.g., Bhagwati & Srinivasan, 1982; Baldwin & Robert-Nicoud, 2007), "the resources spent in the pursuit of a transfer are *wasted* from society's point of view. These expenditures add nothing to social product (they are zero-sum at best), and their opportunity cost constitutes lost production to society" (Tollison, 1982, p. 576). Economists concur that extractive rent seeking results in resource misallocation, deadweight losses, allocative inefficiencies, and, to top it all off, will cause "socially undesirable consequences" (Buchanan, 1980, p. 8). This inquiry's firm-level SVC measurements (e.g., VCr) incorporate these costs—'cost created but *not* borne'—in their operationalization as the 'extractive' transfer-COST part of value transfer-IN (see Section 8.2.1 and Figures A5.5a and 6.7, the latter visualizing the framework for the classification logic for SVC metrics). Many of the primary constituent SVC metrics capture expenditures associated to transfers that are borne by third parties (i.e., deadweight losses, waste, negative externalities), thus recognizing the importance of this most unsustainable practice to development (such as elite business models based on pollution, opioid addiction, war). It should be remembered here that such value extraction—and any economic outcome for that matter—is primarily the result of the incentive system (Olson, 1984; North, 1990, 1994; Robinson, 2010) in the form of the license to operate.

Rent seeking is an expedient conceptual element because it is theoretically separable from value creation. The rent-seeking literature underpins the distinction between first-order productive activities (value creation) and second-order transfer activities (value extraction) outlined in Table 2.3 (providing a dualist typology of business model activities referencing value, consistent with this theory's ontological assumption). Tullock (1967), Krueger (1974), Buchanan (1980), Bhagwati (1982), and Baumol (1990) distinguish unproductive, value destroying, resource wasting, rent-seeking activities from profit-seeking ones such as "entrepreneurship in the competitive model", which "creates value such as new products and the allocation of resources to higher valued uses" (Tollison, 2012, p. 74). Unproductive activities, such as Bhagwati's (1982) "'dupe' activities" ("directly unproductive, profit-seeking"), see a minority, mostly comprised of the elite, profiting at the expense of general welfare (Olson, 1965/1971). In these situations, the minority exploits the majority. The societal costs in the US of the American Sugar Alliance were shown earlier, while Hufbauer and Elliott (1994) calculated the annual cost to consumers of "special" trade protections to be between US$ 100,000 and US$ 1 million per job saved. The Trump Administration's 25% tariff on steel imports implemented in March 2018 represented a consumer and producer cost of US$ 900,000 per job saved, 13 times the average steelworkers salary (Long, 2019).

To ascertain the value extraction of trade barriers is straightforward, but what about the impact of other extractive activities that are stealthier but just as pervasive, such as Taleb's hiding of risk (2018) or the setting of standards? Michael Sarel, Head of the Kohelet Economic Forum, airs a very specific complaint: "Do you know that we have a standard for tea bags in Israel different from Lipton? It's ridiculous [. . .] The only reason is because that was exactly the barrier [The Wissotzky Tea Company] needed. They created a standard for Wissotzky" (Isaac, 2022). Stigler, in "The Pleasures and Pains of Modern Capitalism", recounts the multiplicity of value and risk transfers sought in each nook and cranny of the economy, making it clear how businesses avoid market dynamics and instead focus on the political non-market arena to earn their profits:

> And so we face an embarrassing problem if we wish to return to a freer, more traditionally liberal society: the business community does not wish to be released from the public interventions to which it is subject. The merchant marine does not want unregulated, unsubsidized cargo ships; the steel industry does not want free imports; the construction industry does not want competitive interest rates. Each industry will agree on the desirability of making other industries freer and more competitive, but will assert that its own industry would become disorganized and perhaps even non-viable if the state withdrew. (Stigler, 1996, p. 139)

Rent seeking theory developed following Tullock's seminal paper: "The Welfare Costs of Tariffs, Monopolies, and Theft" (1967), while Krueger (1974) in "The Political Economy of the Rent-seeking Society" made explicit the political connection between institutions and value transfers. Murphy, Schleifer, and Vishny (1993, p. 409), in echoing Tullock, provide a precise understanding of rent seeking as "any redistributive activity that takes up resources", or, in political economy terms, as redistributive transfers that require wins in the non-market and narrative market contest arenas. Rent-seeking theory has been taken up by the ETED and linked to micro-level value appropriation through the VCA framework (see Chapter 2).

As discussed in Chapter 2, at the micro-level, every specific elite business model is a bundle of value creation and extractive transfer activities, the proportions of which are quantifiable (by the VCr). For instance, hardwood from the Amazon creates value when it is transformed into furniture, but cutting down a primeval rainforest leads to the irrecoverable loss of unique assets for the nature stakeholder (and is a forced transfer of value from future generations to the present one). Tesla's unproductive, second-order value transfer rent-seeking activity seems as audacious as its first-order value creation:

> Taleb accidentally bought $4,333 in software and got in touch with Tesla to get a refund. According to the author, it was due to a "butt dial." He could not ask for a refund on the app in which the purchase inadvertently happened. When he went to a Tesla office to ask for a refund, Taleb had to wait eight days to get an answer. And it was "no." Well, a little worse than a simple no.
>
> [In its reply, CustomerSpport@tesla.com noted:] This would be similar to the situation of paying for an addition to a house, deciding you don't like it, and then requesting a refund from the contractor. [. . .] The features received from the software that was purchased are listed in your Tesla and maybe of significant use to yourself. [. . .] Thank you for helping us accelerate the world's transition to sustainable energy."[83] (Ruffo, 2020)

83 For the full story of the X exchange between a customer stakeholder (Nassim Taleb) and the supplier principal (Elon Musk), reflecting Tesla's bargaining power differential advantages enabled by data and elite business model rules, see: https://insideevs.com/news/393102/nassim-taleb-tweets-elon-musk-replies/

After Taleb revealed the conversation, Musk resolved the matter and tweeted. The general point is that on account of the rich theoretical foundations for a myriad of rent-seeking practices, it becomes essential to assess the monetary amounts of the value transfers of elite business models relative to their value creation. This is because these are integrated into a national elite system and become the meso-level aggregate reflection of transfer-IN/OUT activities carried out in an economy. For the assessment of a single elite business model at the micro-level, and eventually for the elite system at the meso-level, value transfers (transfer-IN) must be established as per the 'quantifiability of value transfers' (finance) assumption (Figure A5.4a). For value creation this process is at first straightforward as per the 'bona fide value appropriation' (positive) assumption—all value appropriation (revenue/profits) is treated as value creation at the outset. Moreover, value created but *not* appropriated (transfer-OUT) is then added. However, while making judgments based only on transfers is a natural impulse for the public, pundits, or politicians that are concerned about a sustainable future, a more balanced analysis is needed, as is typified by Yergin's appraisal of Rockefeller and the robber barons:

> Yet, whereas many of the other robber barons amassed their wealth by speculation, stock and financial manipulation, and outright fraud—cheating their stockholders—Rockefeller built his fortune by taking on a youthful, wild, unpredictable, and unreliable industry, and relentlessly transforming it according to his own logic into a highly organized, far-flung business that satisfied the basic hunger for light around the world. (Yergin, 1991/2009, p. 39)

Because of the impact of rent seeking and the solid theoretical ground upon which it rests, it can be empirically ascertained at both the micro- and aggregate meso-level to support balanced estimates of the proportions of value creation and transfers, weighted normative action, and predictions of economic and human development. Estimating the sustainable value creation (through the VCr) of models as diverse as The Standard Oil Trust or ChatGPT is important and must be done in a balanced way. In the case of the former company, this means balancing the provision of light to humanity (value creation) against its 90% domination of the US refined oil market (an extractive value transfer). For the purposes of macro-level economic performance, the aim is to ascertain a meso-level (elite system) aggregate (of all elite business models). In the historical example above, that would entail ascertaining the value transfer-IN/OUT of the totality of Rockefeller interests, of other contemporary trusts in America like meat or steel, as well as those of the robber barons. The ensuing set of VCr data would then be combined and weighted with that of all other elite business models in that particular economy to yield the Elite Quality Rating (EQr), the 'bottom-up' (micro-to-meso level) elite quality measurement that complements the 'top-down' (macro-to-meso level) EQx (see Sections 6.2 and 6.3 as well as the overview of SVC measurements in Table 7.8).

In parallel, and just as important in establishing value transfer measurements is understanding the dynamics that can bring about the cessation of transfers in the context of the political economy (see the implications of the elite theory for the incentive system, Chapter 7). John D. Rockefeller's organization was first challenged by the anti-monopoly Sherman Antitrust Act of 1890, and two decades later, in 1911, it was broken up because of the Supreme Court's ruling on *Standard Oil Co. of New Jersey v. United States*. The stakeholders at the short end of extraction had successfully engaged in a drawn out intra-elite contest (i.e., intra-elite power relation 4 in The Seven Intra-elite Power Relations, Table 3.2) ushering in inclusive institutional change.

Transformational institutional change can theoretically have a forward-looking quality in terms of preventing future extraction, as attested by the non-market checks and balances of the US Constitution of 1787 (elite power relation 2). Political economy foresight can also be the subject of fiction, as in Asimov's three "fundamental Rules of Robotics". These were meant as a call for preemptive institutional change to avoid extraction from the human race as a whole, and have recently reemerged into the public discourse with the realization that the AI is becoming ever more intelligent and capable.[84] With the introduction of the fourth law ("Zeroth Law"), this fictive proposal for preemptive institutional change became an "inspiration for many real-world roboticists and AI scientists like Joseph Engelberger and Marvin Minsky" (UNESCO & COMEST, 2017, p. 13). It remains to be seen to what degree the Rules of Robotics are translated into regulations and hard coded into, for instance, Anthropic's Claude or unmanned aerial vehicle (UAV) military aircraft. In fact, Asimov's rules are already deemed partially obsolete and insufficient and so new sets of increasingly specific laws have been proposed to constrain the AI in exercises that might not be all that suppositional if autonomous non-human AI elite agency ever arises (see hypothesis AI_H2 in Table E.2).[85]

The advent of the hypothetical extractive AI notwithstanding, the very real question of why transfers persist as a chronic feature of the economy and institutional change is now addressed from another key perspective: non-elite responses to extraction.

5.2.2 The non-elite 'acceptance' response to value transfers and its causes

Extraction should theoretically not exist under Smithian/Hayekian free markets, Fromm's assumptions on freedom (1994), or Biden's advocacy of a "competitive econ-

84 Asimov's three "fundamental Rules of Robotics" are: "One, a robot may not injure a human being under any conditions—and, as a corollary, must not permit a human being to be injured because of inaction on his part. [. . .] Two, [. . .] a robot must follow all orders given by qualified human beings as long as they do not conflict with Rule 1. [. . .] Three: a robot must protect his own existence, as long as that does not conflict with Rules 1 and 2." (Asimov, 1942, p. 100). To these, Asimov (1985) added a "Zeroth Law" which takes precedence over the original three: "A robot may not harm humanity, or, by inaction, allow humanity to come to harm".

85 Tegmark's (2023) suggestions include: "Don't teach it to code [. . . ;] Don't connect it to the internet [. . . ;] Don't give it a public API [. . . ;] Don't start an arms race".

omy" (The White House, 2023), yet it evidently does. Where exactly do these assumptions go wrong, or is the competitive free society nothing more than a mostly hollow narrative in practice, even in the 'Land of the Free'?

Inequality has been a historical constant (Scheidel, 2017) and being at the short-end of extractive transfer-IN is still an unceasing reality for many classes of stakeholders. These might include farmers, SMEs, savers, entrepreneurs of last resort, opioid addicts, certain EV owners, as well as taxpayers and, in some political economies, even bankers or mega entrepreneurs. The prevalence of extractive activities is not just a reflection of a given incentive system (Olson, 1984; North, 1990, 1994; Robinson, 2010), but in itself a further disincentive to value creation activities, especially those that involve risk taking (Figure 6.9) and innovation. For instance, subsidized electricity in Colombia deters the development of a modern power infrastructure (McRae, 2015). The theoretical puzzle is not why elites persevere with their extractive models; they are residual income maximizers, so even the shortsighted Olsonian stationary bandits that do not think in terms of sustainability or longer-term time horizons are rational agents given their (one might say misguided) preferences. It is tenable for principals to amass power and preserve or change institutions to implement value transfers away from value creators. The question is why their counterparts, suffering from extraction in a business model relationship, do not simply opt out.

Why do workers, firms, taxpayers, and all other stakeholders subjected to extractive transfers accept such practices? No matter what the power differentials are in a relationship, no one should rationally stick with a situation that makes one worse off. To understand this predicament, we must examine the 'impossible exit' conjecture, which exposes a critical rigidity of the economy and society. Why is it the case that stakeholders accept unfavorable or mere subsistence-level prices? Why are stakeholder relationships 'sticky', even in presumably free societies and markets? To address these questions, we will examine four causes of 'acceptance' that individually and jointly attempt to explain the stickiness of the extraction problem.

In 1649, the *Ulozhenie* law code, in effect until the 19th century, closed the main door to exit from extraction for Russian peasants with the application of state power and violence. This critical juncture, an "absolutist, interventionist [. . .] basis for state building", abolished the "statute of limitations on runaway peasants" who through their hereditary bondage could now, upon escape, be recovered by their owners, *de facto* an institutional change that "established complete enserfment in Russia" (Kivelson, 1993, pp. 735, 741, 750). Paths to compulsory *resignation* and *embrace* 'acceptance' responses are certainly less ruthless today, but are similar bargaining power differentials and value transfer proportions essentially still at play? Can a transportation company cease to fill its trucks with gas if exorbitant prices are determined by the OPEC+ oil cartel? Can Australia afford life without Google in a situation where "Google has threatened to close its search engine in Australia if the government proceeds with a plan to force Big Tech groups to pay news providers for their content" (Ruehl, 2021)? To what extent can Colombian governments stop subsidizing electricity? When one receives the new Microsoft Services Agreement e-mail, is there truly a choice to "not agree" and "choose to discontinue using the products and services, and close your Microsoft account before these terms become effective"?[86] Could the Bush and Obama Administrations have chosen *not* to develop and support the US$ 700 billion TARP to buy and insure distressed assets to stabilize the financial sector?

The primary cause for the first individual non-elite response to transfers and the persistence of extractive models—(i) 'acceptance'—is the lack of other options. The less powerful party whose value creation is appropriated in the context of the principal-stakeholder relationship may have no viable alternative. Opting out is simply not a choice and *resignation* the only way to go on with business or life. This situation applies to stakeholders in many markets such as Internet search engines, rare earth minerals, energy, medicines, or fast fashion sweatshops. It is a state of affairs where power differentials and business model rules successfully eliminate substitutes. Violence, or its threat, establishes bargaining power differentials that remove alternatives, as the example of hereditary Russian serfdom or "forced or, more generally, of compulsory labor", defined by the International Labour Organization (ILO) as "all work or service which is exacted from any person under the menace of any penalty and for which the said person has not offered himself voluntarily" (International Labour Organization, 1930). Nassim Taleb got redress from Tesla because of his power in the narrative market, but the situation is different for those without a massive X (formerly known as Twitter) following. The extractive party sources the necessary bargaining power advantages via 'political economy know-how' and/or 'knowledge' (see Figure 2.3), while the ensuing value transfers are evidenced by prices (including wages) significantly deviating from the counterfactual competitive 'equalized bargaining power equilibrium prices'.

A second cause for the 'acceptance' of extractive transfers is that the aggrieved parties expect to gain from transfer-IN in another of their relationships; value appropriated but *not* created elsewhere in the business model might match or exceed the value of the forced transfer-OUT in the specific loss-making relationship. The perverse reckoning behind accepting extraction through such an *embrace* is premised on positive 'net value extraction'.[87] Ultimately, the stakeholder is ahead because larger transfer-IN value is appropriated from third parties than is coerced away though extractive transfer-OUT from the principal. That is, 'compensatory' transfer-IN is imposed on others. For instance, a transportation company boss might calculate that while gas prices are excessive, the taxpayers subsidize freeways and many of his employees

---

86 Reddit user 'deepasleep' writes: "That's why they've been so aggressively pushing to make everything a subscription. You will own nothing and be forced to pay them in perpetuity to access your data." See: https://www.reddit.com/r/privacy/comments/1f0tq5a/microsoft_your_services_agreement_made_clearer_if/

87 See Table 2.4, equation (3.3): net value extraction = value transfer-IN – value transfer-OUT; $NVe_t = Vt_t^{in} + Vt_t^{out}$.

loading the trucks are low-wage illegal immigrants whose passports he holds and to whom he pays below equilibrium wages. That is, when deconstructing the value chain, some economic agents suffering transfer-OUT by an elite business model might expect to come out ahead, thereby becoming positive net value extractors. Again, and consistent with the 'universal extraction propensity of life' law of nature upon which the socio-economic 'universal value extraction propensity of humans' premise sits (see Figure A5.4c), transfers are a goal of elite and non-elite business models alike.

A third and more extreme cause of acceptance is when stakeholders remain in a negative net value extraction relationship because of an amalgamation of psychological factors, such as the expectation of receiving better residual income in the future. In the extreme case of slavery, labor is brutally extracted. Indeed, everything is taken away through such coercion other than life itself (and possibly the lives of other family members). Not all slaves opt out, try to escape, or commit suicide[88] (although many do). Clearly, slavery still tragically persists as a business model in the 21st century. *The Global Slavery Index* reported that "an estimated 50 million people were living in modern slavery on any given day in 2021" (Walk Free, 2023), while an earlier edition stressed that "it exists in every corner of the world yet is seemingly invisible to most people" (The Minderoo Foundation, 2018). Those on the receiving end of such punishing value transfers might be coerced (through outright violence), but often endure it in *resignation* in the hope that circumstances will change for them or their offspring. That is, some of the surplus value that they create will not be extracted away and be theirs to keep at some point in the future. The psychology of hope is formidable. There are also other psychological and behavioral-based reasons for 'acceptance' in its *resignation* and *embrace* variants, but in all cases, the extractive transfer-IN that today exists in fast fashion workshops, cocoa plantations, or on high seas fishing boats, constitutes a residual income transfer mechanism from the stakeholders (the workers) to the elite (and non-elite) business model principals.

A fourth cause of 'acceptance' is ignorance. For principals, preempting or overcoming resistance responses (such as 'exit', 'informality', or 'challenge', see the explanations in Section 5.2.3) is expensive. A more efficient strategy is making the business model value transfer mechanisms opaque (the identity of the beneficiaries need not be secret at all). That is, by not articulating extraction in the first place and circumventing narratives that would make it all too explicit. Marx (1844/2009) claims in the introduction to *A Contribution to the Critique of Hegel's Philosophy of Right* that: "Religion is the sigh of the oppressed creature, the heart of a heartless world, and the soul of soulless conditions. It is the *opium* of the people." Whether out of *resignation* or in sincere *embrace*, the 'acceptance' of transfers is discerned in terms of a narra-

88 Can moral positions on suicide be linked to the elite value appropriation perspective? In both Jewish and Christian traditions "suicide is implicitly condemned in the commandment not to commit murder (Exodus 20:13)", while the "Qur'an is more explicit in its injunction against suicide (Surah 4:29)" (Cook, 2014, pp. 254–255).

tive-induced sleep where incognizance is mixed with other psychological factors like the abstract anticipation of hypothetical or metaphysical events beyond the present reality of the political economy.

Opacity also results from limited cognitive bandwidth, exemplified by the Tesla users who inadvertently buy software and will never know that they did not notice. Buchanan (1980, p. 9) explains another cognitive bias surrounding value transfers: "Few questions will be raised concerning the emergence of rent seeking when governmental action creates and supports monopoly positions and effectively prevents entry". Paradoxically, these biases, or the narrative-induced slumber, preserve value as it is being transferred. If the extracted are unaware that value extraction is taking place, the total social loss is reduced: "A successful bank robbery will inspire potential thieves to greater efforts, lead to the installation of improved protective equipment in other banks, and perhaps result in the hiring of additional policemen. These are its social costs, and they can be very sizable" (Tullock, 1967, p. 231).

Efficient capital allocation processes are central to economic development. A topical illustration of the resigned 'acceptance' response is the business model of negative interest rates. Fischer records that the European Central Bank (ECB) "lowered its deposit rate into negative territory three times since June 2014, most recently to minus 0.30 percent in December" (2016, p. 40). Any analysis of the negative interest rate elite business model must start with Hicks' elemental observation:

> If the costs of holding money can be neglected, it will always be profitable to hold money rather than lend it out, if the rate of interest is not greater than zero. Consequently the rate of interest must always be positive. (Hicks, 1937, pp. 154–155)

What is the explanation for the 'acceptance' of a model that widely and negatively impacts nearly everybody in society and that in theory ought not to exist (below-zero interest rates)? Fischer lists the factors that have been cited for the "decline in the long-run equilibrium real rate":

> The first is persistent weakness in aggregate demand. A second is the slowdown of productivity growth. A third is demographic trends. A fourth is high saving rates in many emerging market countries, coupled with a lack of domestic investment opportunities in those countries the global savings glut hypothesis advanced by Ben Bernanke (2005) about a decade ago. (Fischer, 2016, p. 39)

The ETED explanation for the real, and even nominal, negative and ultra-low interest rates that persisted in many parts of the advanced world from 2008 until 2022 lies elsewhere; at the intersection between the political economy, institutional change, and an unprecedented elite business model that obscured value transfers through the mainstream economics narrative of the need for lower borrowing costs to enable recovery. There are clearly distributional effects associated with low or negative interest rates. If one was to 'follow the money' (*cui bono*), who were the winners? Firstly, elite business models that rely on rising asset prices, such as real estate or cryptocurrencies. Secondly and thirdly, heavily indebted governments benefit, as do "zombie" firms (Caballero, Hoshi, & Kashyap, 2008; Banerjee & Hofmann, 2018). Fourthly, one would have to include the financial institutions living off subsidized money, like those in Japan that overindulged in risk on the back of an artificially enlarged credit supply (Hong & Kandrac, 2018), as well as their counterparts elsewhere such as Silicon Valley Bank or Credit Suisse who, buoyed by access to cheap financial resources, abdicated their responsibility to diligently price risk. Who then were the losers? When the overall economic pie does not increase and elites prioritize the 'same size of the slice' bias, all those in society who are not beneficiaries of the business model residual income streams lose out. The redistributive effects of negative interest rates in the years following 2008, and the ensuing misallocation of capital, resulted in massive transfers away from the asset-poor young and elderly pensioners to the asset-rich old. These transfer business models continued even when the consequences caused by mispriced money and risk—the initially hidden and subsequently exploding levels of inflation and resurgent asset bubbles—were apparent. Fischer's factors for the downward trend in interest rates all have impeccable academic merit, but does he miss the forest for the trees?

Once interest rates rose with the post-COVID advent of inflation, the financial institutions with a strong franchise and market power concocted a novel form of transfer: "lenders got higher yields for their deposits at the Fed but kept rates lower for many savers, the review of Federal Deposit Insurance Corporation data showed" (Gandel & Franklin, 2024). What is the exact amount of value appropriated but *not* created in this case? According to the same authors, "US banks made a $1tn windfall from the Federal Reserve's two-and-a-half-year era of high interest rates, an analysis of official data by the Financial Times has found".

The ability to resist extraction is critically limited by ignorance and opacity, implying the failure of knowledge elites to shed timely light on the transfers at hand. *The Financial Times* piece cited in the above paragraph is essentially two years too late. The 'value transfers replace value creation at maturity' conjecture (associated with the 'elite power vs value creation gap' hypothesis, see Figure 4.5) is largely enabled by the shortcomings of knowledge elites. The elite business model of negative interest rates creates both winners and losers but is a negative-sum game that does not enlarge the pie. The general point is that obliviousness, associated with knowledge asymmetries abetted by feeble or venal knowledge elites, is often the necessary condition for the establishment and continuation of extractive business models and institutions (i.e., the undermining of checks and balances where these play a role, see intra-elite power relations 5 and 6 in Table 3.2). When the 'acceptance' response to extraction by non-elite individuals and firms happens in *resignation*, it is mostly outside the context of elite/non-elite dialectics and reflects an unsettling quietness in the relationship; when it happens in *embrace*, it proceeds with trust in the elite that could be reciprocal (see the paternalistic 'elite agency on behalf of non-elites' political option in Section 8.1.3, Figure A5.8). With a better understanding and popularization of extraction mechanisms on the other hand, individuals and firm stakeholders will be better equipped to realize either the 'exit' and 'informality' responses, or to resist and choose individual 'challenge' responses to their loss of hard-earned value and income (the *struggle* and *participation* variants of the latter response can aggregate into discrete and constructive non-elite political options, see Section 8.1.3). Without question, and as in Tullock's example, responses other than 'acceptance' would intensify if non-elites apprehended these transfers (aided by knowledge elites) as a form of "robbery".

5.2.3 The full range of individual non-elite responses to value transfers

Faced with transfer-IN as an institutionally sanctioned form of robbery, the response of those trapped in sticky business model stakeholder relationships is not always (i) 'acceptance' and to endure at the margins of a business model in survival mode. Three additional individual micro-level response types associated with variations of the 'impossible exit' conjecture are now discussed: (ii) 'exit', (iii) 'informality', and (iv) 'challenge'. These four responses to extraction are summarized in Table 5.1 and visualized in Figure A5.8.

'Exit' can mean making a fresh *new start*, for example, by quitting a job and becoming a freelancer or going into personal or business bankruptcy. The latter avenue becomes likelier with shorter statutes of limitations on debts. 'Exit' might also mean emigration; America has grown from these individual responses to extraction, from the arrival of the Mayflower in 1620 to the caravans arriving at the Mexico-US border today. The elite theory has worked on the assumption of neoclassical utility maximization for elite agency. But a part of the edifice so far constructed in this inquiry would collapse if the RCT paradigm and the freedom to *exit* (see Section 8.2) cannot be assumed to exist for non-elite stakeholders suffering from extractive transfers. Neoclassical utility does not extend to such stakeholders if they cannot simply opt out in pursuit of their own utility maximization. Instead, the conjectured 'impossible exit' has *a priori* the non-accepting counterparties of elite business models acquiescing to extraction. That is, 'acceptance', an unproductive response steeped in exploitation, even potentially in a tragic *resignation*, in lieu of the pursuit of alternative avenues to maximize utility. The absence of institutional arrangements to enable an escape—a *new start*—in many political economies, coupled with continued extractive business models causes liberal, free market, free exit assumptions to be untenable. Moreover, without a sanctioned freedom to *exit* (see Section 8.2.1), when a productive *new start* is unavailable, a non-institutionalized form of 'exit' emerges: *withdrawal*.

History has been shaped by those realizing a *new start*, and not only in the case of America. Cossack ethnogenesis has been constructed as starting with militarized peasants who established self-governing communities in the steppe hinterlands of the Caspian and Black Seas to escape serfdom in Russia or Poland. Lattimore discusses peasants escaping the statist business model of grain and, as a consequence, "wavering between devolution toward the economy of the steppe and evolution toward the economy of China" (1937, pp. 543, 548). Exit from the state taxation of agriculture is described in James Scott's *Against the Grain: A Deep History of the Earliest States* and explains "secondary primitivism" (Clastres, 1974), or "going over to the barbarians" which "is far more common than any of the standard civilizational narratives allow for [. . .] far from being seen as regrettable backsliding and privation, it may well have been experienced as a marked improvement in safety, nutrition, and social order. Becoming a barbarian was often a bid to improve one's lot" (2017, p. 232). In this light, Beckwith recounts a relevant swath of human history:

> There was a constant drain of peoples escaping from China to the realms of the eastern steppe, where they did not hesitate to proclaim the superiority of the nomad lifestyle. Similarly, many Greeks and Romans joined the Huns and other Central Eurasian peoples, where they lived better and were treated better than they had been back home. (Beckwith, 2009, p. 76, as cited in Scott, 2017, pp. 232–233)

A modern form of Clastres' "secondary primitivism" is the *withdrawal* 'exit' response of Japan's over one million "being confined" *hikikomori* (1.2% of its population according to Rooksby, McLeod, and Furuhashi, 2020) or China's "lying flat" *tang ping*. The mindset of "lying down instead of being a productive member of society" is further portrayed below:

> Luo explained how he was living a low-desire, zero-pressure lifestyle without stable employment, while staying with his parents in Zhejiang province. When he was feeling up for it, he would travel three hours to Dongyang, Zhejiang, where the world's largest film studio is located. He found work there that he considered perfect – acting as a dead body in movies. (Ji, He, & Peach, 2021)

In other cases, 'exit' is the more extreme form of *withdrawal* and involves a hard and sometimes deadly departure from the social order. In many countries, despair at the unbearable levels of extractive transfers is often reflected in economic distress, substance abuse (see the opioid epidemic in Section 8.2.1) or, when cultural and religious norms fail, suicide. Case and Deaton's *Deaths of Despair and the Future of Capitalism* (2021) and the official US Congress Joint Economic Committee's *Long-Term Trends in Deaths of Despair* (2019), document this awful and pervasive phenomenon among middle-aged non-Hispanic whites that is responsible for the unprecedented shortening of life expectancy in the US. This is currently at its lowest level since 1996 and, for the first time in history, it has fallen below China's (see Arias, Tejada-Vera, Kochanek, & Ahmad, 2022; The World Bank, n.d.-d). The antinatalism stance on procreation "that we should not produce any more lives that are bad (quality of life) or can be bad (risk)" (Häyry & Sukenick, 2024, p. 238) and "that it would be preferable for our species to die out" (Benatar, 1997, p. 353), is a radical and absolute form of 'exit' for non-elites (partially arising form not being able to 'exit' extraction in the here and now) that would also wreck and hence deny 'the extraordinary lever' to elites (many of whom, such as Pope Francis or Elon Musk, publicly counter this pessimistic position). However, not everybody decides on such absolute forms of 'exit' and the instinct for self-preservation and the urge to preserve one's lineage keeps most people in 'acceptance' and at the short end of extraction.

A third individual response to extraction is also problematic: to hide value creation activities through the informal economy. The (iii) 'informality' response has value creators devise strategies to avoid being taxed or otherwise penalized at the losing end of transfer-IN by extractive elite business models. Legitimate activities go underground (De Soto, 1989). This is a reversal of the earlier scenario on knowledge asymmetries as non-elite value creators keep their value appropriation activities (and even their value creation models) opaque and elites are left ignorant. This is often more *efficient* than the extractive alternatives. Obviously, one is better off if the thieves don't know that there is something of value to steal in the first place. Hart (1970) is credited with starting the study of informality with his analysis of small-scale entrepreneurs in Ghana that conceived them not as parasites but as legitimate and productive value creators. Pisani and Ovando Rivarola (2019), in their lucid analysis of the determinants of the informal economy in Paraguay, reference the research of Portes and colleagues, differentiating value creation from value extraction and pointing out how legal institutions are circumvented to prevent transfer-OUT:

> Portes distinguishes between licit and illicit processes and transactions in determining informality. In essence, the informal economy consists of market transactions that avoid government regulation, oversight, and/or taxation, though these same transactions may be conducted legally under the full auspices of government monitoring (Portes, Castells, & Benton, 1989). So, informal transactions are technically illegal. Yet, informal transactions and work activity is not said to be criminal since the product (good or service) or work itself is legal, but it is generally undertaken outside the scrutiny and legal bounds of government mandated regulation and legislation (Portes & Schauffler, 1993). Hence, such everyday products and activities as food and street vending, automotive and tire repair, personal and domestic services are common and informal nearly everywhere. (Pisani & Ovando Rivarola, 2019, p. 28)

Pisani and Ovando Rivarola (2019, pp. 30–33) supply the perspectives on 'informality' that emerge from the literature, including: neo-Marxist (capitalism is the problem), structuralist (the problem is endemic to emerging markets, growth is the solution), practitioner (micro-interventions in the economy are the solution), and legalist (the state is the problem). The development problem is both immense and quantifiable. For instance, in Williams and Youssef's (2014) study of Latin America, economies are at best semi-formal (i.e., 40% informal employment) while many countries exhibit outright informal economies (with over 70% of employment underground). Pisani and Patrick (2002) nonetheless qualify such findings when assessing 'informality' as a "bright spot" in Central America as, for instance, in the way that the underground economy liberates entrepreneurs, many of last resort, in their quest to create value. However, far from being the exclusive domain of emerging economies, 'informality' is a non-elite response to value transfers everywhere: for example, the boom in cryptocurrencies is a reaction to the low interest rates and growing inflation rates of extractive monetary policies:

> [A 2% inflation rate] means the organised loss of all value in about 30 years, coincidentally the time of the long government bond. If this is all they can do, why do we still have them? Even cryptocurrencies may prove better stores of value. No wonder they are doing all right. (Dalhuisen, 2021)

The above reflection points as much to extraction as it does to the elite capture of a non-elite narrative (decentralized finance). The intrinsic danger with 'informality' is that many participants—whether they are workers, SMEs, or investors—become beholden to non-state elites (i.e., where business elites are unchecked by political elites as per intra-elite power relation 4), some of which are plainly criminal organizations. Leaving aside the stealth and flexibility advantages for the value creating individual or firm that 'informality' provides, informal transactions and grey markets are always precarious and more *inefficient* than their institutionally sanctioned counterparts (as cryptocurrency exchanges illustrate). Property is also less protected (as the fate of numerous crypto projects shows). Thus, the informal economy lacks incentives for long-term investments and does not allow value creators to scale (unless they engage in institutional arbitrage or create parallel institutional arrangements, using blockchain, for instance). The amount of potential value creation not realized because of 'informality' in its *inefficient* variant is a social tragedy. So are, to different degrees, all of the responses to extractive value transfers and their consequences (summarized in Table 5.1) other than the constructive variants of the fourth response to extraction, the 'challenge' response.

In the 'challenge' response, while the principal-stakeholder relationship may be accepted, the extractive transfers are not. As discussed in Proposition 19 ('Non-elite agency can constrain value extraction through participation in intra-elite contests'), when a critical mass of individual (iv) non-elite discontent 'challenge' responses of the political *struggle* variety pile up, these might trigger the onset of overt 'non-elite vs elite struggle'. More constructively, individual 'challenge' responses might be channeled into political *participation* variants where non-elites take sides in intra-elite contests, for instance, through shared narratives. In this scenario, non-elite groups might cooperate tactically (i.e., consider only the interests of their own group), or strategically (i.e., seek to instigate generally inclusive institutional change or advance value creation narratives). How the 'challenge' responses of individuals accumulate and provide political options in the elite/non-elite dialectics of the political economy is discussed through the lens of non-elite interests in Section 8.1.3.[89] The *struggle* variant, especially when violently manifested through insurrections or rebellions, is deemed to be comparatively riskier for non-elites and commonly ineffective. Individual 'challenge' responses that lead to diverse variants of political *participation* in intra-elite contests are usually more productive, though they require elite transformational leadership on the opposing side.

---

89 Note that with individual (ii) 'exit' and (iii) 'informality' responses the elite/non-elite relationship ceases to exist, basically precluding Hegelian (1812/2010) synthesis or resolution.

Table 5.1: A typology of individual non-elite responses to extractive value transfers by elite business models.

Non-elite individual response types	**Description of non-elite individual responses to extractive value transfers**	**Individual responses: evidence**
(i) 'Acceptance'	The 'acceptance' response is mostly one of (a) *resignation* to extraction. Based on the 'impossible exit' conjecture it is primarily premised on a trap-like lack of alternatives. At times 'acceptance' is facilitated by compensation considerations where transfer-IN from other stakeholders exceeds the coerced transfer-OUT affected by the principal. Psychological factors such as the survival instinct, knowledge asymmetries, and ignorance may play an important part, as do narratives and religion. Non-elites might also (b) *embrace* extraction and place their trust in elites as in the 'elite agency on behalf of non-elites' assumption (Section 8.1.3) when they perceive extraction to be limited or legitimate.	(a) *Resignation*: subsistence business models; inequality; general but contained discontent; high supervision costs for demotivated labor. (b) *Embrace*: stability in stagnation or decline; loyal subjects; narrative believers. Note: The (i) 'acceptance' response may morph into any of the other three alternative individual responses to extraction and even become (ii) 'exit' as the 'impossible exit' restraint weakens.
(ii) 'Exit'	The 'exit' response is the cessation of the elite/non-elite relationship by the stakeholders suffering extraction. It ranges from the problematic (a) *withdrawal* from productive activity, including a hard departure from the social order, with behavior aimed at self-destruction or the destruction of others, to the positive (b) *new start* under different business model rules (which requires the enabling freedom to *exit*, Section 8.2.1).	(a) *Withdrawal*: Leisure; videogame addiction; voluntary unemployment; suicide; crime; substance abuse; emigration (e.g., from Syria). (b) *New start*: Job departure; entrepreneurship; debt forgiveness; bankruptcy; immigration (e.g., to America).
(iii) 'Informality'	The 'informality' response type is associated with the underground informal economy and reverse knowledge asymmetries that hide non-elite value creation activity and so protect the creators from extraction by elites. It ranges from (a) *efficient* to (b) *inefficient*, and might resemble a partial 'exit response' where value creation continues to be pursued outside of the institutional framework.	(a) *Efficient*: low transaction cost, semi-scalable and fragmented markets for labor, goods and services, and capital. (b) *Inefficient*: high transaction cost, non-scalable markets for labor, goods and services, and capital hampered and diminished by *ad hoc* deinstitutionalized arrangements.

Table 5.1 (continued)

Non-elite individual response types	Description of non-elite individual responses to extractive value transfers	Individual responses: evidence
(iv) 'Challenge'	The 'challenge' response has non-elites assertively confronting elites. To have inclusive impact, it requires non-elite coordination leadership with clear proposals benefiting from knowledge elite input for institutional change that constrains extraction by elite business models. It ranges from (a) destructive political *struggle*, escalating to overt 'non-elite vs elite struggle', to (b) constructive *participation*, including shared narratives and other initiatives seeking strategic and tactical participation in intra-elite contests via the political process to induce inclusive institutional change (for the political options available to non-elites, see Figure 8.2).	(a) *Struggle*: degrees of violence including insurrection, revolution, terrorism; political impasses and polarization; non-elite suffering, even in the absence of violence, such as declining life expectancy. (b) *Participation*: strategic and tactical participation in intra-elite contests is evidenced by shared narratives; inclusive institutional change; economic growth; and human development.

The discussion of non-elite political options to extraction in Section 8.2 shows how the (b) *embrace* variant of (i) 'acceptance' and the two (iv) 'challenge' variants of (a) *struggle* and (b) *participation* aggregate into non-elite political agency. All of the other individual responses do not. These are: the (a) *resignation* variant of (i) the 'acceptance' response; the (a) *withdrawal* and (b) *new start* variants of (ii) the 'exit' response; and the (a) *efficient* and (b) *inefficient* variants of (iii) the 'informality' response (see Figure A5.8). While 'informality' is the most ingenious of the four individual responses and has a low transaction cost *efficient* form, 'acceptance' through *resignation* is the most common and goes a long way to explain the feasibility and prevalence of extractive elite business models as well as suboptimal economic development outcomes.[90] The 'exit' response is most constructive through the (b) *new start* option when there is an institutionally sanctioned freedom to *exit* (see Section 8.2) from forced transfers, but is also a most destructive route for economic development when there is not, leading to (a) *withdrawal*. This enabling freedom to *exit* will be shown to be critical (Figure 8.5), as it steers individuals away from the hard *withdrawal* 'exit' option. It also deactivates the trap-like 'impossible exit' rigid-

90 The non-elite "hope for a better life in the hereafter or for deliverance in a messianic future" (Cohn, 1970, cited in Goldstone, 1982, p. 188) is an *embrace* response, although many will consider it *resignation*.

ity of the economy by increasing the bargaining power of non-elite value creators, thereby facilitating their rejection of extractive arrangements.

At present, the US government is at pains to explain the skyrocketing "deaths of despair" trend (United States Congress Joint Economic Committee, 2019, p. 10). Any solution is conceptually simple: first, recognize the underlying economic reality of extractive value transfers which requires a modicum of elite soul searching (i.e., transformational leadership at the elite system level with significant inputs from knowledge elites) and elite cohesion; second, reform laws and regulations (i.e., institutional change) to facilitate low-cost 'exit' responses by non-elites trapped in extractive relationships such as pay-day lending,[91] low-paying jobs in monopsony labor markets, subpar access to healthcare with no viable alternatives, recourse mortgages, or student loans[92]. Note that these models need not necessarily be made illicit, but the essential freedom to *exit* must be granted to their non-elite stakeholders. Rather than taxpayer-funded bailouts this might require measures like jubilee debt cancelations, certainly not a novel solution, as "for thousands of years, economic polarization was reversed by cancelling debts and restoring land tenure to smallholders who cultivated the land" (Hudson & Goodhart, 2018, p. 7), as is expounded on in Section 8.2.4. Without the path to a *new start*, countless more citizens bereft of the *exit* option will continue to despair about their lot and *withdraw* from productive life.

5.3 Additional conceptual elements for the consolidation of the ETED system

The closing section of this chapter develops a series of heterogenous auxiliary insights and requisite tools for this inquiry's theory making. It starts with a key section that revisits the sustainable value creation (SVC) measurements of the business model to further hone in on the conceptualization and operationalization of extractive value transfers (5.3.1). Hence, the inquiry next moves into the applied realm of capital allocation as the VCp/VCr become the original inputs for 'The Five Sustainable Value Creation (SVC) Valuation Frameworks' (5.3.2). Two frameworks are proposed for equity (Figure A5.6a), two for debt (Figure A5.6b), and a fifth for firms (Figure A5.6c). These are derived from the SVC functions (with their VCp/VCr inputs) to produce SVC out-

---

91 The Pew Charitable Trusts makes inclusive "recommendations for regulations and product designs" for payday loans, see: https://www.pewtrusts.org/en/research-and-analysis/articles/2023/06/07/what-does-the-research-say-about-payday-loans

92 On the 'trap' of student loans, The Education Data Initiative at *EducationData.org* finds that "11% of new graduates default in the first 12 months of repayment", a problem that "affects 9 million borrowers and their families"; with every passing year an additional million default, all of who will have tanked credit scores and so "may not be eligible to receive other types of loans, such as home and auto loans. It can take years to undo the damage" (Hanson, 2022).

puts (such as SVC cost of equity, SVC cost of debt, SVC credit risk spread) to be applied in line with the central approaches of finance practice (such as the Capital Asset Pricing Model (CAPM), the Weighted Average Cost of Capital (WACC), and the credit agencies' methodologies for credit rating).

The subsequent sub-sections shift gear, firstly with a focus on the elaboration of the elite cohesion conceptual element that is established as a precondition for development, but only if it exists in conjunction with its antithesis, the elite separation of powers (5.3.3). The balance of these two conceptual elements is the core of the 'intra-elite quality contest' dilemma. In the spirit of the conceptual consolidation of this chapter, SVC measurements provide signals for elites to engage in elite system transformational leadership that are consistent with the endogenous institutional change position that reform must come from inside the elite system and leverage intra-elite contests. Without transformation towards increased value creation, the 'extractive escalation dynamic' takes root in society and induces negative development (5.3.4). In closing, links are drawn between the theory of capitalism, its present incantation, and the potential of any type of business or political system for value creation (5.3.5).

5.3.1 Further steps in the conceptualization and operationalization of value transfers

To recap, Proposition 11 posited that elite business models operate at measurable sustainable value creation positions on a conceptual 'value spectrum' (Figure 2.10) which is operationalized by the Value Creation Position (VCp), an SVC measurement that also provides the basis for the enhanced Value Creation Rating (VCr). The VCp assesses the relative proportion of revenue (or profits) associated to net value creation and extractive value transfers (transfer-IN) of a business model. The chief measurement challenge for the VCp is the assessment of revenue (or profits) attributable to extractive value transfer-IN (value appropriated but *not* created). Inclusive value transfer-OUT (value created but *not* appropriated), which unlike transfer-IN is not captured by financial statements, is not considered for the VCp, but is the differential element of the VCr. The latter is thus a more comprehensive sustainability measurement, as it establishes the overall value contribution of a business model, including uncaptured value, to the economy and society at large. For both the VCp and VCr measurements the value transfer-IN of the principal business model must be ascertained.

As was discussed in Section 2.3.2, it matters if the party that sees value created but *not* appropriated (transfer-OUT) has higher/lower bargaining power than the counterparty benefiting from said transfer. If the party with higher bargaining power (e.g., the principal, an elite) is at the receiving end of value created but *not* appropriated, then the transfer-OUT is deemed to be inclusive, an uncoerced contribution, a positive externality, and a public good (such as innovation spillovers, circular production processes, or fair trade prices). If, on the other hand, the party experiencing transfer-OUT is the one with lower bargaining power (e.g., a stakeholder to the principal, a rival elite), the value transfer to the beneficiary transferee (benefiting from transfer-IN) is deemed to be extractive, coerced, an involuntary tax, a negative externality, and a public bad (such as monopoly rents, depleted soil, or inflation). Hence, as far as the transferor is concerned, transfer-OUT is always inclusive value created but *not* appropriated, while if one takes the beneficiary transferee perspective, it can either be inclusive (e.g., society benefiting from valuable innovation spillovers) or extractive (e.g., higher prices benefiting cartels). In any event, the counterparty of a transfer-OUT technically has an equivalent transfer-IN and vice versa. In this inquiry, this is important for operationalizing and classifying value transfer SVC metrics. For inclusive (where the transferee has higher bargaining power) value transfers in the principal-stakeholder relationship this is framed as transfer-OUT; for extractive transfers (where the transferee has lower bargaining power) it is framed as transfer-IN.

It must be re-emphasized that despite the ETED's criticisms of rent seeking and extraction as roadblocks to development and its calls for the quantification of extractive transfer-IN, both the theory and operationalization of SVC measurements are constructive, as is seen in the underlying assumptions for socio-economic relations, the implications for financial analysis, and even in the understanding of how value constrains and links to human behavior (refer to in Figures A5.4b and A5.4c). First, this is because by necessitating the quantifiability of all transfers (see the discussion later in this subsection), specific transfer-IN activities at a firm are properly weighted and counterbalanced against value creation (net value creation and value transfer-OUT). Transfer-IN (including the 'extractive' type of 'cost created but *not* borne', the transfer-COST expounded on in Section 8.2.1, Figure A5.5a) does not preclude the existence of proportionally greater amounts of value creation activities at present (captured both on/off-P&L) or in the future (captured in firm valuations). Secondly, and in the longer run, the 'alternating value extraction and creation' conjecture (see Section 2.3.1) allows second-order value transfers today when they are a precondition for value creation tomorrow. Thirdly, the 'bona fide value appropriation' (positive) assumption (see Figure A5.4a) holds that all activity registered in a firm's financials is value creation (net value creation) until proven otherwise (i.e., as evidenced by transfer-IN). Thus, under the derived 'revenue is value creation unless value transfer is proven' (constructive) implication, in the absence of extractive value transfer-IN activity, all P&L statement revenue (or profits) is deemed to be first-order value creation (again, net value creation). Fourthly, there is the basic injunction to establish the value creation amounts not accounted for in the P&L by quantifying inclusive transfer-OUT contributions that are central to the most comprehensive firm-level SVC measurement (VCr).

This work has repeatedly stressed that both value creation and extraction activities go hand in hand, play out in specific business models, and can be measured. When the valuation of Apple topped a scarcely believable $3 trillion, *The Wall Street Journal* headline read: "Apple at $3 Trillion Isn't All About Apple" (Gallagher, 2022). Clearly, the elite business model of Apple reaps benefits from its extraordinary value creation (from Apple silicon to *Ted Lasso*), but also from monetary policy, a non-neutral carbon footprint (at least until 2030), and especially the monopolistic power of its App Store platform that allows a "secret 30% tax". To what proportion is Apple inclusive and extractive? That is the fundamental micro-level sustainable value creation question of this theory, addressed firm-by-firm and metric-by-metric by assessments of transfer-IN/OUT as inputs for the VCp and VCr measurements.

How much value do principals create and how much value is appropriated from key stakeholders (including the nature stakeholder) as it is converted into revenue/profits ('money')? A specific case, of the manufacturer U.S. Steel, is now used to illustrate the SVC measurement assessment process (further elaborated on in Section 6.1.1). At the outset, the goal is to establish the proportion of the firm's revenue or profits that is verifiably attributable to transfer-IN activities (a process that will first yield a proportion as depicted in the business model 'value spectrum' of Figure 2.11 for revenue, and in Figure A5.5a for profits). For U.S. Steel, the import tariffs placed on foreign competitors and the incremental revenues generated from related price increases in the American market are critically profitable second-order transfer activities. That is, additional revenue is transferred from a very specific group of stakeholders: customers. Tariff-induced higher steel prices constitute value appropriated but *not* created by the steelmaker. Far from a theoretical disquisition, calculating such transfers using a SVC metric is straightforward and can be done by accountants, business valuation and finance specialists, credit rating professionals, or sustainability analysts. *S&P Global Market Intelligence* assessed the spectacularly positive impact that tariffs had on the bottom line of U.S. Steel, which:

> made a net loss of $1.64 billion [in 2015] and hemorrhaged a further $440 million in 2016, [but then came] Trump's tariffs that truly sparked the revival. A profit of $1.12 billion in 2018 marked the company's best performance since the end of the commodity super cycle in 2008. (Brennan, 2019)

U.S. Steel's business model, like that of any firm, engages in first-order value creation *and* in second-order extractive value transfer activities, both of which are in principle independently quantifiable with the appropriate framework and measurements. The full impact of tariffs, calculated in dollar terms, would be captured by a 'gains from import tariffs' SVC metric to conceptually determine the transfer-IN phenomena (and unbundle it from related business model activities). Multiple metrics are required for the SVC measurements, each quantifying extractive transfer activities such as 'subsidies' (transfer-IN) or inclusive transfers such as 'capital expenditures as a percentage of revenue' (transfer-OUT). Metrics that establish value transfers are also discussed in Section 6.6.1 (see also Figure 6.6 on the calculation process for sustainable value creation measurements) with ten examples provided in Tables 6.1 and 6.2. Upon the quantification of the material value transfer-IN amounts of a firm, expressed by a comprehensive set of conceptually relevant metrics, the VCp can be calculated, see Table 2.4, equation (4.1).

Again, for U.S steel, import tariffs might be the main but not the only form of transfer-IN (there might also be direct subsidies or a failure to fully offset its carbon emissions exposure). The approximation of a principal's total amount of transfer-IN is the sum of all discrete transfer-IN amounts, each captured by a unique SVC metric, that is always attributable to specific stakeholders—the counterparties suffering extractive transfer-OUT (in this case, customers, taxpayers, and nature). U.S. Steel's business model will certainly also include activities where value is created but *not* appropriated, creating transfer-OUT in the form of innovation spillovers, supply chain resilience, and well-paying union jobs (in this case, the stakeholder beneficiaries are society at large, customers, and labor). This logic is articulated in equation (3.6), while the transfer-IN/OUT amounts are in turn the aggregation of the firm metrics as per equations (3.7) and (3.8). Upon the quantification of all the value transfer-IN and transfer-OUT amounts of a firm, and on the basis of respectively constituent metrics, the VCr can likewise be calculated, see Table 2.4, equation (4.2). The calculation procedure to transform the transfer-IN/OUT SVC metrics inputs into SVC measurement outputs (VCp/VCr) is basically a three-stage process (set out in Figure 6.6).

SVC metrics are assessed by referencing financial statements, third-party suppliers of metrics, set calculations, survey responses, and other sources. For instance, the actual amount of the 'gains from import tariffs' for U.S. Steel (again, a transfer-IN) is inferable from set calculations based on diverse data such as assessments of stakeholders at the receiving end (the coerced transfer-OUT from the counterparties). *Reuters* refers to this transfer amount in the headline: "Trump metals tariffs will cost Ford $1 billion in profits, CEO says" (Carey & Shepardson, 2018). This illustrates that putting a figure on a transfer-OUT (from the stakeholder, Ford) that equals the transfer-IN (to the principal, U.S. Steel) in the context of specific principal-stakeholder transactions is feasible (see the mirroring in Figure 2.9). In this case, the actual steel purchases made by Ford (costs) from U.S. Steel (revenues) form the basis to determine the specific amount of transfer-IN that U.S. Steel has extracted from Ford because of the first Trump Administration's tariffs (the total transfer-IN of the 'gains from import tariffs' metric would also encompass the other customers of U.S. Steel). In addition to considering the customer stakeholders (Ford and others), equation (3.6) requires that the complete bundle of transfer-IN/OUT principal-stakeholder relationships be reviewed (Figures 2.9 and A5.13a render business model stakeholders across the value chain). In the earlier example of Apple, such an analysis would uncover inclusive transfer-OUT from its very substantial technology spillovers (to the benefit of employee stakeholders who receive training or customer stakeholders whose efficiency increases above and beyond the prices they pay for the devices) or increased valuations (to shareholders profiting from above market returns on their investment). The flip side, which is incorporated into both the VCp and VCr, are Apple's extractive transfer-IN amounts such as carbon emissions (from the nature stakeholder) or monopolistic activities (from supplier stakeholders via the App Store).

A key methodological issue is the quantification in monetary terms of the SVC metrics reflecting all material transfer-IN/OUT in principal-stakeholder relationships. This, the *de facto* pricing of everything, is essential for conceptually addressing sustainability, as all businesses in a society are ultimately interconnected. Nicolai Tangen, the CEO of Norges Bank Investment Management, responsible for running the Norwegian Sovereign Wealth Fund, is in a position to take a comprehensive view and states: "If you have one part of the portfolio that is polluting and destroying the environment, you're going to be hit in another part of the portfolio" (Milne, 2022). In short, extractive transfer-IN activities in one sector of the economy reverberate across many other sectors. This work suggests that such interconnectedness and unity is best addressed by establishing quantifiable monetary equivalence brought about by prices to support managerial, investment, and policy-making decisions for sustainable value creation and ultimately transformational leadership (see Figure A5.4a).

In addition to the fundamental (i) 'value is created or transferred' (ontological) assumption and the (iii) 'bona fide value appropriation' (positive) assumption, a further vital piece is now advanced to complete the pragmatic understanding of socio-economic relations in this theory: the (ii) 'quantifiability of value transfers' (financial) assumption (see Figure A5.4a). Prices are the means to quantification (for example, by using a cap-and-trade system for carbon credits) and the necessary standard to feasibly assess value transfers and cut across the diversity of principal-stakeholder relationships (overriding the objection that value cannot truly be measured by prices, e.g., Mazzucato, 2018). The bundle of relevant transfer-IN/OUT activities of a business model need to be determined and expressed in prices, whether these are determined by third-party suppliers of data and commercial metrics (see Table 6.1 and Figure 6.6), or self-reported by boards through self-assessment surveys (see Sections 6.6.1, 6.6.3, and Table A3.6). Once value is converted into monetary terms, Tangen's interconnections across business model activities can be made explicit. Most prescient for decision-making, once calibrated and weighted (Figure 6.6), these can be offset as one sustainability objective is traded-off for another. This core and holistic implication (Figure A5.4b) results from the three assumptions advanced for socio-economic relations (Figure A5.4a) and is necessary for the conceptualization and operationalization of sustainable value creation and transformational leadership. In short, the (ii) 'quantifiability of value transfers' assumption and the (c) 'weight and offset value transfers' implication are not just applicable for decision-making at investment houses or sovereign wealth funds, but also become the master key for transformational business, political, and knowledge elites, as well as for the concerned public wishing to influence intra-elite contests. As a result, sustainable value creation becomes a tractable optimization problem.

The paramount conceptual element of offsetting, which resembles applied consequentialist cost-benefit analysis (see Frank, 2000), is utilized in this inquiry to solve the practical aspects of the optimization problem and is rooted in the reality of economic trade-offs. In Campbell and Kelly's words (1994, p. 422):

> Trade-offs are central to economics, as they are to life. They are at the heart of economics because neither the decision-maker nor society can have everything it wants. We look at the trade-offs that must be made when the criteria that are used to govern social decisions cannot all be fully satisfied.

In this work's paradigm, offsets establish trade-offs between the activities of business models based on their monetary quantification (e.g., the proactive linking of monopoly rents and CO_2 emissions, as in next paragraph). Taken in isolation, the single value creation/transfer activity that is part of the business model bundle cannot coherently be maximized (the prescriptive position for value creation activities) or minimized (the prescriptive position for value transfer activities). Instead, a totality perspective is taken[93]. Firm activities are thus offset using strategic decision-making (keeping an eye on long-term risks and valuations) in line with institutional requirements, based on the activities' respective pricing and the ensuing monetary amounts (heeding the 'quantifiability of value transfers' finance assumption). At times, the process of offsetting requires negotiated (elite) bargains. The transformational leadership needed for offsetting is viable thanks to the set of SVC metrics used to assess a business model. Again, a metric is the basic indivisible unit of a business model that signifies and quantifies a particular value creation and transfer activity. Upon the aggregation of the SVC metrics, the entirety of a model's impact (on development) is deducible. The counterbalancing offsetting mechanisms—implemented from outside the model by policy or from the inside by transformational leadership—constructively acknowledge and address the negative aspects of trade-offs by optimizing the sustainable value creation of the model as a whole.

Consequently, questions such as "how many carbon offsets are required to compensate monopoly rents?" or "what price ought tobacco firms pay for each cigarette butt liable to pollute Spanish beaches"[94] or "how large should technology spillovers be to make up for monopoly rents?" have numeric answers that can be deduced for the purposes of practice. *The Financial Times'* article, "City Investors Putting UK Security at Risk over ESG, Ministers Warn", points out that "Andrew Griffith, the City minister, and James Cartlidge, the defence procurement minister, said it is 'perverse' for institutions to be shunning or divesting from defence and security companies at a time of war in Europe" which "risks starving the industry of capital at competitive valuations" (Pfeifer, 2023). As security is an inclusive transfer, should military hardware not be included and priced as a positive contribution in current ESG frameworks? Evidently, managers, investors, scholars, and citizens might raise a multitude

93 This matches Edmans' proposal (2024, p. 13) for "rational sustainability" that factors in "diminishing returns and trade-offs" and "recognizes that sustainability factors are subject to the same laws of gravity as everything else. It encourages us to look at the big picture – rather than getting engrossed with the benefits, to step back and consider the costs."

94 See Spanish legislation, *Ley 7/ 2022, de 8 de abril, de residuos y suelos contaminados para una economía circular* (BOE, 2022, p. 66).

of analogous questions about the micro- and macro-level impacts and trade-offs of multiple business activities just as policymakers do in the context of weighted structural reforms (see Section 7.1.1). Pigouvian tax/subsidies (Pigou 1920/1932) use prices to address the internalization of specific negative/positive externalities, and they can likewise be used to offset transfer-IN/OUT. The pricing of value (and risk) transfers implicit in specific business model activities in relation to counterparty stakeholders is a feasible approach to ultimately attain generalized sustainable value creation. From an economic and human development perspective, SVC measurements (such as the VCr) based on quantifiable transfer-IN/OUT metrics are designed to benchmark elite (business model) transformational leadership (see Table 7.2) and guide structural reforms aimed at an economy's incentive system (Section 7.1.4).

To have impact, SVC measurements and their related tools and frameworks must be intuitive. As discussed in Chapter 2, the value creation position (VCp) is operationalized (and normalized on a notionally common scale) using a percentage range. A putative 0% represents full value transfer-IN (i.e., all the firm's revenue or residual income is derived from transfers and value appropriated but *not* created), while 100% represents full value creation by the principal with no transfer-IN (i.e., absolutely no value appropriated but *not* created is taken from any stakeholder). On the 'value spectrum', it is easy to see where a firm, elite, or non-elite sits between the two extremes of 0 and 100 (total value extraction or pure value creation by firms is rare).[95] The four scores estimated in Figure 5.1a provide a conceptual rendition of the VCp and VCr SVC measurements. They are rendered for a second time in Figure 5.1b to provide a clearer grasp by adding their respective equations (4.1a) and (4.2a). The top rows (a) visualize an inclusive business model (with high degrees of value creation), while the bottom rows (b) set out an extractive business model (with high degrees of extractive transfers). For each of these two models, the VCp scores are provided (in the left column), as are the VCr scores (in the right column). Net value creation and value transfer-IN (jointly accounting for revenue), as well as value transfer-OUT, are visually depicted for each of the four renditions to facilitate understanding of these two SVC measurements.

The two depictions of VCp on the left of Figures 5.1a and 5.1b (with their respective scores of 80% and 40%) describe prototypical inclusive and extractive firms, with the business model respectively relying on value creation (top left) and on extractive

95 This operationalization, both anchored and constrained by the P&L statement, limits total value extraction (transfer-IN) to the amount of revenue (or profits), a restriction that all too often does not bear out in practice when, for instance, value is destroyed and the costs borne by the third parties exceed the revenue appropriated from them (see Figure A5.5a and Figure A5.5b, as well as the Purdue Pharma case in Section 8.2.1). Expanded details on this matter are provided from Section 6.6.1 onwards.

transfers (bottom left).[96] The two depictions of VCr on the right side of both figures (with their respective scores of 1.20 and 0.70) describe the same inclusive (top right) and extractive (bottom right) prototypical firms. The important conceptual distinction between the VCp and VCr scores is that for the latter the transfer-OUT amounts from SVC metrics have been ascertained and added into the calculations as inputs. The VCr is thus distinct from the VCp on account of requiring an assessment of the principal's transfer-OUT amounts.[97] Transfer-OUT metrics must quantify value in monetary terms, and price value creation that is not monetized (or monetizable) by the business model (as it is off-P&L and not reflected in any financial statement). Thus, transfer-OUT makes value created but *not* appropriated explicit. To do so, price equivalencies must be rendered and corresponding judgments made. For instance, for offsetting carbon emissions, for paying wages that exceed standard market rates, for generating innovation spillovers, and for a plethora of other value benefits provided to stakeholders—including to society at large—often conceptualized as positive externalities (see Buchanan & Stubblebine, 1962; Bresnahan, 1986; Ayres & Levitt, 1998).

It helps to imagine the beneficial spillover effects of value creation as positive externalities, like municipal parks. Again, externalities, one of the keys to economic and human development, are "situations in which one person's actions directly affect another person's welfare" and that "affect the overall size of the utility pie" (Bueno de Mesquita, 2016, p. 100). The question of externalities, part of theoretical welfare economics (Pigou 1920/1932; Coase, 1960; Buchanan & Stubblebine, 1962; Baumol, 1972), is integrated into this inquiry through elite business model positive externalities operationalized as inclusive transfer-OUT (where the principal transferors of value created but *not* appropriated are emitters of value and stakeholders are its recipients) and negative externalities operationalized as extractive transfer-IN (where the principal transferees of value appropriated but *not* created are absorbers of value, while stakeholders are the transferors who pay). Of particular interest are positive externalities that are widely spread or otherwise appear elusive. The classical example is that of high-speed computers as a positive externality representing "a very large social gain to computerization that was not captured by manufacturers of computers" (Bresnahan, 1986, p. 742). The same is true for innovations as diverse as Wikipedia or penicillin and may also be the case for rapidly evolving AI. On the other hand, the consummate firm that captures and stores more carbon and other greenhouse gases than it

96 Table 2.4 explains the VCp equation (4.1): VCp(revenue) = [revenue – transfer-IN(revenue)] / revenue; $VCp_t^{R'} = \frac{R'_t - Vt_t^{R'\,in}}{R'_t}$. To reconcile Figure 5.1a with equation (4.1), use the following formulation of equation (2.3"): revenue = net value creation + transfer-IN(revenue).

97 Table 2.4 explains the VCr equation (4.2): VCr(revenue) = [revenue – transfer-IN(revenue) + transfer-OUT(revenue)] / revenue; $VCr_t^{R'} = \frac{R'_t - Vt_t^{R'in} + Vt_t^{R'out}}{R'_t}$. To reconcile Figure 5.1a with equation (4.2), use equation (2.3"): net value creation = revenue – transfer-IN(revenue).

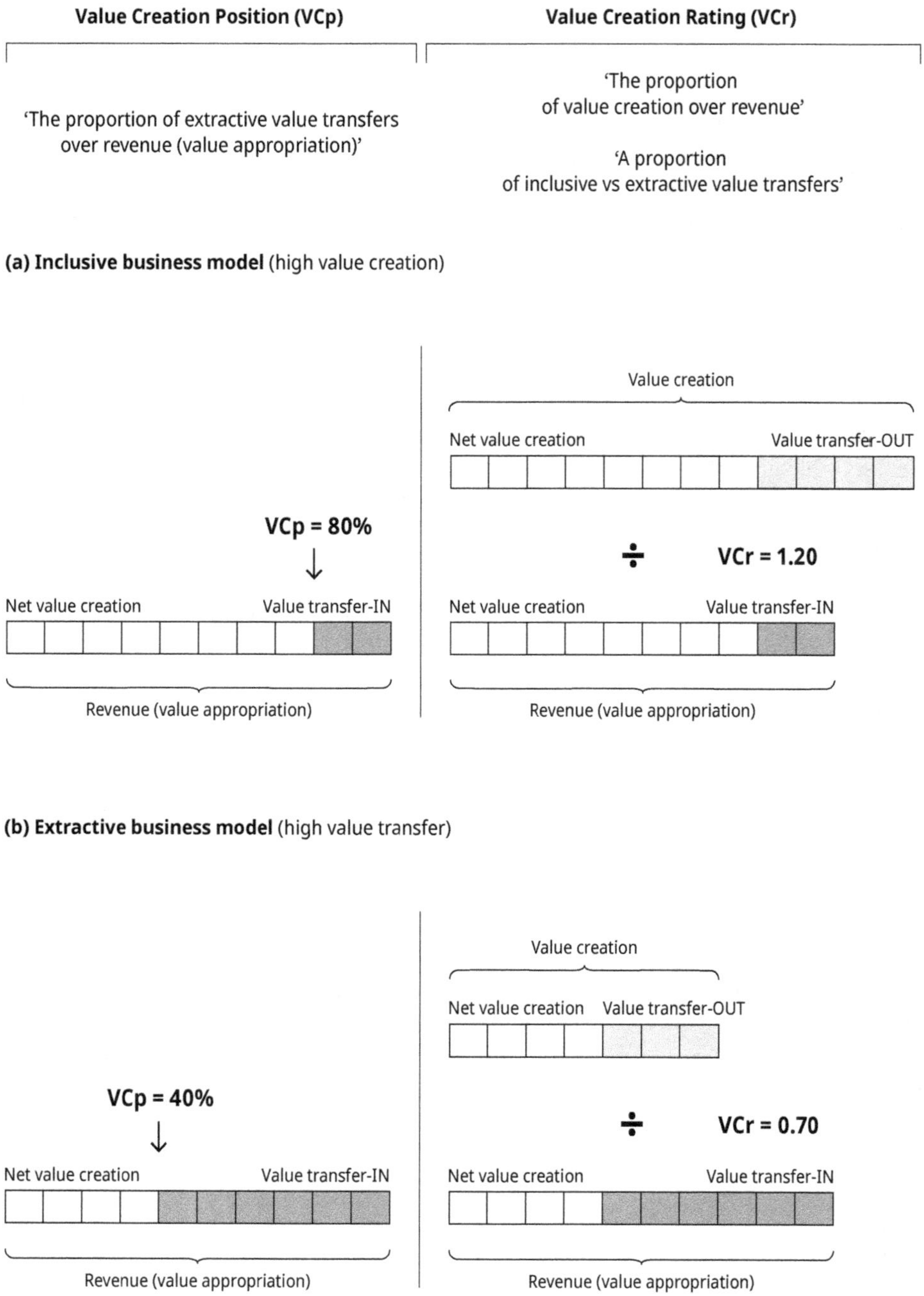

Figure 5.1a: A conceptual rendition of value creation and value extraction business models with their respective Value Creation Position (VCp) and Value Creation Rating (VCr) scores.

Value Creation Position (VCp) equation

$$VCp_t^{R'} = \frac{R'_t - Vt_t^{R'in}}{R'_t}$$

Value Creation Rating (VCr) equation

$$VCr_t^{R'} = \frac{R'_t - Vt_t^{R'in} + Vt_t^{R'out}}{R'_t}$$

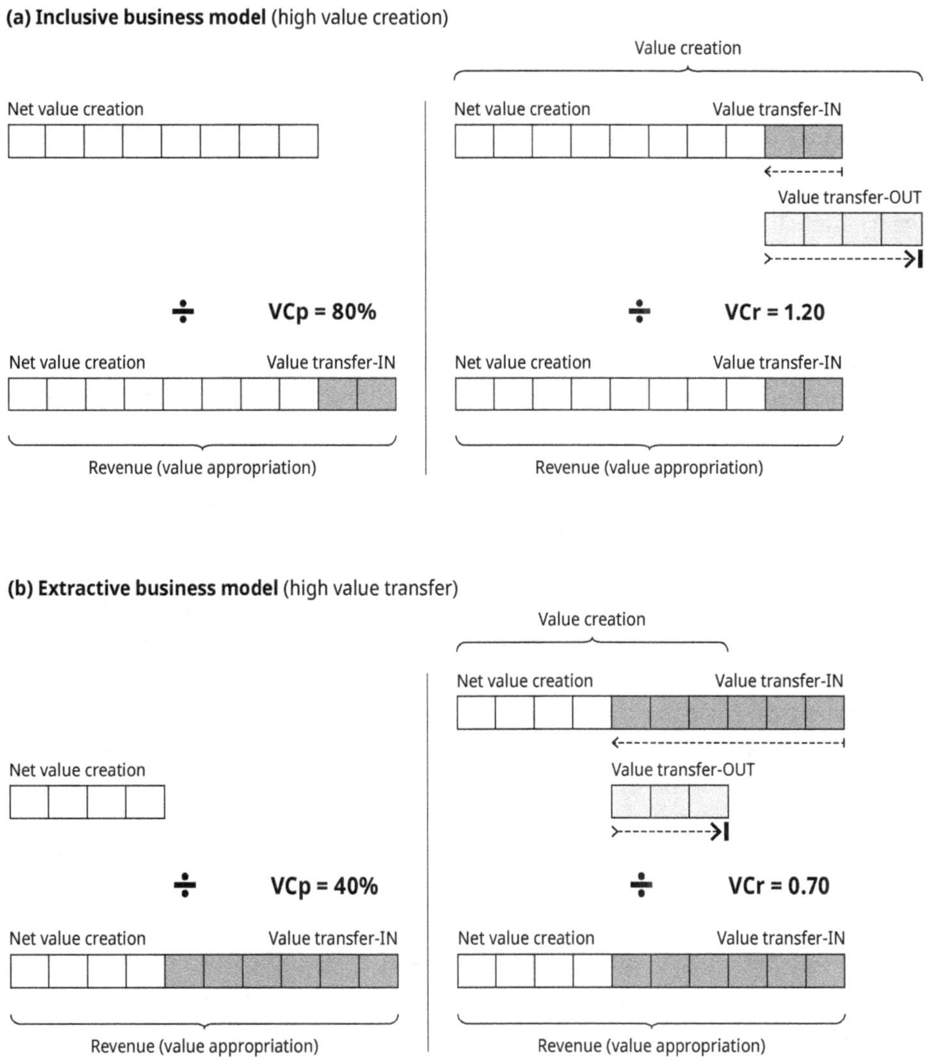

Figure 5.1b: An equation-based conceptual rendition of value creation and value extraction business models with their respective Value Creation Position (VCp) and Value Creation Rating (VCr) scores.

emits, receives ISO 14064-1 certification, and then sells carbon credits through the European Union Emissions Trading System (EU ETS), possesses the hard evidence for a quantifiable metric that attests to the positive externality that it generates.

From a value creation-appropriation (VCA) framework perspective, positive externalities are value transfer-OUT and represent value captured by stakeholders that are often contractual parties to the elite business model. The sizable amount of inclusive transfer-OUT is a central reason why value creation business models are so essential to progressive economic and societal development. Conceivably, the more value that a business model creates, the higher the likelihood of value transfer-OUT:

> Value creation, rather than value appropriation, lies at the heart of effective firm strategies. Strategies that focus on creating new value undoubtedly led to some of that value spilling over to other firms and to society as a whole. (Moran & Ghoshal, 1996, p. 45)

The transfer-OUT process is deemed to be inclusive when the transferor enjoys a power differential advantage over the transferee (see earlier in this sub-section and Section 2.3.2). But why is there inclusive transfer-OUT at all by elites given their skewed bargaining power differential advantage over non-elite stakeholders? One answer to this question is that some positive externalities might be impossible to capture while others may leak unintentionally. The prices of Big Tech's products and services have over the years not come close to the value they deliver to many customers. This could mean continued price increases if these business models decide to double down on monetization rather than sustain their transfer-OUT. In other cases, transfer-OUT is part of a rational strategy aimed at the consolidation of positions in the market, non-market, or narrative market arenas for intra-elite contest purposes. The reckoning here could be that the inclusive transfer-OUT strengthens elite/non-elite cohesion, or a particular business model that becomes a source of power for an elite and provides residual income for a non-elite group. For instance, the value spillovers of staging the Olympics sees construction companies in tactical partnerships with sports enthusiasts and their clubs when preparing a city's candidacy. Hence, transfer-OUT amounts might be conscientiously left on the table by elite principals for a variety of reasons consistent with their power and residual income interests. Yet there are evidently also genuinely non-coerced, altruistic, and deliberate non-utility maximization motivations—at times anchored in ethics or religion—that run counter to Proposition 5's assertion that elite behavior is rational and predominantly driven by a residual income maximization utility function. In an era where massive amounts of rent seeking occurs in the educational sector (as evidenced by defaulting student loans in the US, see Brennan & Magness, 2019; Hanson, 2022), consider Germany's social contract for its vaunted dual-track vocational training system (Euler, 2013) where most of the value created remains in the hands of the less powerful, broad non-elite constituencies—apprentices and participating firms, many of them SMEs. Elite coalitions that constrain their own value appropriation, even when motivated by minimizing their risks and creating a sustainable future for their models, are consistent with the 'inextinguishable value creation option of elites' (Section 2.2.1 and Figure 5.4c) and with the set of ethical principles associated with the normative aspects of the ETED (Chapter 8).

Establishing the transfer-IN/OUT and eventually the VCr of elite business models supports legal and economic reform and judgment on macro policy, for instance, by shedding light on whether 'progressive elite circulation' is occurring (see Section 1.3.2). The relevance of such discernments, vital for elite system transformational leadership (Table 7.2), becomes evident in the review of Russia's post-Soviet elite below:

> Some consider the oligarchs to be the engine of Russia's economic recovery and institutional reform since 1999 (Boone & Rodionov, 2002; Aslund, 2004). As oligarchs are the only currently feasible counterweight to the predatory and corrupt Russian bureaucracy, they are a unique constituency that is both willing and able to lobby for development of market institutions. They are also the only Russian owners who can afford to invest and restructure Russian industries in a very hostile business environment. To others, the oligarchs have weakened Russia's economy by stripping assets from Russian firms and sending money abroad and also by bringing the ideas of private property and corporation into disrepute. In addition, the oligarchs have also arguably weakened Russia's democratic institutions, by causing tremendous inequality and through their capture of federal and state politics (Stiglitz, 2002; Goldman, 2004; Hoff and Stiglitz, 2004). (Guriev & Rachinsky, 2005, p. 131)

As a result of their comprehensive examination, Guriev and Rachinsky (2005, p. 149) conclude that: "Both negative and positive stereotypes about Russian oligarchs are true", conceding that they might "run their empires more efficiently than other Russian owners" or the former Soviet elites. By using a systematic quantification of the conceptual transfer-IN/OUT criteria (the SVC metrics the authors conceptually suggest are 'efficiency' or 'investments' as transfer-OUT and 'capital flight' or 'institutional capture' as transfer-IN) a VCr is estimable, thus providing prescriptive possibilities for policymaking and weighted structural reforms (see Table 7.1).

Clearly, political economies where elite business models engage in excessive amounts of extractive transfer-IN stunt economic development. The costs and risks generated by the principals of these models are transferred to stakeholders via their activities, at times by higher prices and on other occasions as negative externalities. If a principal's P&L benefits from transfer-IN revenue/profit, this inquiry's imperative calls for the incremental gain (and risk reduction) to be established and operationalized with an appropriate metric. Admittedly, some of these amounts might be unquantifiable by metrics for a variety of reasons: association with market failures, conceptual elusiveness resulting in data unavailability, the intentional hiding of some activities (see Taleb, 2018, on hiding risks), or implicit principal-stakeholder relationships that are not direct or contractual. Quantifying Baumol's (1972, pp. 310–311) "laundry whose output is damaged by smoky air" is relatively easy in comparison. Hidden or not, a complicating *leitmotiv* of this inquiry's paradigm is that such extractive transfer-IN activities are often indispensable, both for the business model's overall performance and general human development. Still, the essential fact of development is the different degrees to which elite business models rely on extractive practices or leave part of the value they create on the table for non-elite appropriation.

The inclusive economic development problem is therefore first one of measurement, which the Pigouvian tax/subsidies approach to resolving externalities considers key (Buchanan & Stubblebine, 1962; Baumol, 1972). The journey starts here by ascertaining the irreducible elements of firm-level value creation/extraction, i.e., the SVC metrics. The challenge becomes how to incorporate into the standardized SVC measurements most of the material extractive/inclusive transfer-IN/OUT activities that constitute a business model, even when many corresponding metrics are by nature hard to pinpoint (as many negative/positive externalities or public goods are). If successful in estimating these (the methods are further expounded on in Section 6.6.1), SVC measurements like the VCr or VCp will fairly reflect sustainable value creation as theorized in this work. By approximating the actual value creation and value transfers of business models, the inclusive/extractive factors that many ESG measurements obviate (such as trade barrier gains, regulatory protections, innovation spillovers, subsidies, competitive markets, or monopoly power) will be addressed. As all of these elements are systematically applied, it becomes possible to understand the full impact of a firm on the economy, while the resultant measurements can also be used to optimize capital allocation processes for sustainable development through novel valuations of equity, debt, and firms as is discussed next.

5.3.2 Five valuation frameworks for sustainable capital allocation

> Similarly, question 12 of the specimen exam for the CFA UK Level 4 Certificate in ESG Investing is "What impact will a high ESG rating have on a company's cost of capital?" The answer key gives the correct response as "A: A lower cost of capital". (Edmans, 2023, p. 20)

'The Five Sustainable Value Creation (SVC) Valuation Frameworks' for finance introduced in this section are a set of decision-making tools for the allocation of capital. Two of these are aimed at enterprise value and equity; two are aimed at debt; and the fifth is intended for firm valuations using WACC. All five rely on generally accepted methods of finance to compute different aspects of an SVC firm valuation. An 'SVC valuation' is thus an adjusted price of a private enterprise or publicly traded equity, a rated or non-rated debt, or of a firm, which can be applied to an asset, project, liability, or financial instrument to expresses the inclusive value creation and extractive value transfers of the underlying business model. Bancel, Glavas, and Karolyi (2023) show that "the discount rate is the key parameter adjusted in valuations based on the discounted cash flow approach". This sub-section might also remind the reader of the Nordhaus-Stern discount rates for sustainability controversy regarding climate policies, government projects, and economic modeling[98] (see Dasgupta, 2007; Schoenmaker & Schramade, 2024). Edmans position is clear when he states that it is a "myth" that "Sustainability Risks Increase the Cost of Capital (*No, sustainability risks lower expected cash flows*)" (2023, p. 17) and clarifies his stance further:

> Remember that a project's cost of capital depends only on market risk. Diversifiable events can affect project cash flows but they do not increase the cost of capital [. . .] Don't give in to the temptation to add fudge factors to the discount rate to offset things that could go wrong with the proposed investment [. . .] Adjust cashflow forecasts instead (Brealey, Myers, Allen, & Edmans, 2022, cited in Edmans, 2023, p. 14).

On the other hand, this inquiry's more assertive position is that cash flow reductions are best (and *a priori* can only be) addressed with the sustainable value creation risk factor with which they associate. The premise is that the risks associated with extractive value transfers (as measured by the VCr) are company-specific but non-diversifiable (just like market risk is non-diversifiable) and therefore firms engaged in sustainable value creation will enjoy lower costs of capital.

The original input to the valuation frameworks is the VCr, and this chief firm-level SVC measurement adjusts the discount rate. The discrete calibrated and weighted metrics that make up the VCr ought to cover all materially relevant value (and risk) creation and transfer activities of a business model (Section 6.6.1 is devoted to the SVC metrics that establish value transfers). Figure 5.3 in this chapter's summary illustrates the relationship between the VCr and the five sustainable value creation valuation frameworks (SVC valuations).

The five SVC valuation frameworks and their pertinent equations, logic, and enabling conceptual elements are summarized in Table 5.2 before being further specified. Readers may also refer to the appendices for the corresponding graphical overviews: the two sustainable value creation valuation frameworks for enterprise value are presented in Figure A5.6a; the two for debt are depicted in Figure A5.6b; and the framework for firms, based on SVC costs of capital and debt, is visualized in Figure A5.6c.

98 Nordhaus' (1994) high discount rate (of 4.3%) and Stern's (2006) low discount rate (of 1.4%) have discrete ramifications for policies on climate change: Nordhaus "rationalises postponing necessary climate investments" while Sir Nicholas Stern's *The Review of Economics on Climate Change* argues that a "lower discount rate makes the far future look more important today, and supports greater future-oriented investment" (Schoenmaker & Schramade, 2024, p. 1). The non-technical, judgmental nature of establishing such discount rates points to them being "ethical and political issues more than economic ones" (Godard, 2008, p. 39), as is articulated by Dasgupta's criticism of the Stern Reviews' conclusion as containing particular *"views on intergenerational equity; it isn't driven so much by the new climatic facts the authors have stressed"* (2007, p. 4). As Schoenmaker & Schramade (2024, p. 6) note: "Measurement and valuation of social and environmental impacts is work-in-progress. Not all impacts can (yet) be measured and put in monetary terms in a reliable way."

Table 5.2: Summary of 'The Five Sustainable Value Creation (SVC) Valuation Frameworks' for equity, debt and firms.

Sustainable value creation (SVC) valuation framework	Purpose	Description of calculation approach	Conceptual elements Equations
(SVC-VF.1) 'The SVC-adjusted enterprise valuation framework' for private firms	Compute the 'VCr revenue multiple adjustment' (VCr^m) and the 'VCr enterprise value adjustment' (VCr^{EV}) to establish the 'SVC enterprise valuation' for private firms (EVm'; EV').	The 'VCr enterprise value adjustment functions' ($fVCr^m$ / $fVCr^{EV}$) have the VCr as their input and the 'VCr multiple adjustment' (VCr^m) and 'VCr enterprise value adjustment' (VCr^{EV}) as their outputs. These then become the inputs of the revenue multiple-based enterprise value (*EVm*) and the enterprise value (*EV*) equations for the two SVC-adjusted enterprise valuation approaches (EVm'; EV').	- 'VCr enterprise value adjustment functions': $fVCr^m / fVCr^{EV}$ - 'VCr revenue multiple adjustment': VCr^m - 'VCr enterprise value adjustment': VCr^{EV} --- - Equation (5.1a) 'SVC revenue multiple-based enterprise value': $EVm' = Revenue * (Revenue\ Multiple * VCr^m)$ - Equation (5.2a) 'SVC-adjusted enterprise value': $EV' = (Equity\ Value * VCr^{EV}) + Net\ Debt$
(SVC-VF.2) 'The SVC cost of equity valuation framework' for public firms	Compute the 'SVC cost of equity' (k_E') to establish the 'SVC equity valuation' for public firms (SVC_E')	The 'SVC risk premium function' for equity has the VCr as its input and the 'SVC risk premium' (r_{svc}) as its output, which then becomes an added input to CAPM; the resulting 'SVC cost of equity' rate (k_E') becomes the discount rate for the DCF-based 'SVC equity valuation' (SVC_E'), a net present value (NPV) of equity.	- 'SVC risk premium function' for equity: fr_{SVC} - 'SVC risk premium': r_{SVC} - 'SVC cost of equity': k_E' - 'SVC equity valuation': SVC_E' --- - Equation (6.1a) 'SVC cost of equity': $k_E' = r_f + \beta_E * (r_m - r_f) + r_{SVC}$ - Equation (6.2a) 'SVC equity valuation': $SVC_E' = \frac{CF_1}{(1+k_E')^1} + ... + + \frac{CF_n}{(1+k_E')^n}$

Table 5.2 (continued)

Sustainable value creation (SVC) valuation framework	Purpose	Description of calculation approach	Conceptual elements Equations
(SVC-VF.3) 'The SVC-adjusted credit rating valuation framework' for credit-rated debtors	Compute the 'SVC risk premium for credit rating' ($r^{cr}_{SVC,D}$) to establish the 'SVC debt valuation' for rated debtors ($SVC^{cr'}_{D}$)	The 'SVC risk premium function for credit rating' ($fr^{cr}_{SVC,D}$) has the VCr as its input and the 'SVC risk premium for credit rating' ($r^{cr}_{SVC,D}$) as its output, which is then applied to the credit rating cost of debt to produce the 'SVC-adjusted credit rating cost of debt' ($k^{cr'}_{D}$). This cost of debt becomes the discount rate of debt cash flows resulting in the 'SVC-adjusted credit rating debt valuation' ($SVC^{cr'}_{D}$), i.e., the NPV of debt.	– 'SVC risk premium function for credit rating': $fr^{cr}_{SVC,D}$ – 'SVC risk premium for credit rating': $r^{cr}_{SVC,D}$ – 'Credit rating spread': CS^{cr}_{i} – 'SVC-adjusted credit rating cost of debt': $k^{cr'}_{D}$ – 'SVC-adjusted credit rating debt valuation': $SVC^{cr'}_{D}$ – Equation (7.1a), 'SVC-adjusted credit rating cost of debt': $k^{cr'}_{D} = r_f + CS^{cr}_{i} + r^{cr}_{SVC,D}$ – Equation (7.2a), 'SVC-adjusted credit rating valuation': $SVC^{cr'}_{D} = \frac{CF_1}{\left(1+k^{cr'}_{D}\right)^1} + \ldots + \frac{CF_n}{\left(1+k^{cr'}_{D}\right)^n}$
(SVC-VF.4) 'The SVC cost of debt valuation framework' for debtors	Compute the 'SVC cost of debt' (k'_D) to establish the 'SVC debt valuation' for debtors (SVC'_D)	The 'SVC risk premium function for debt' ($fr_{SVC,D}$) has the VCr as its input and the 'SVC risk premium for debt' ($r_{SVC,D}$) as its output. This is then added to the standard cost of debt formula. The resulting 'SVC cost of debt' rate (k'_D) becomes the discount rate for the DCF-based 'SVC debt valuation' (SVC'_D), an NPV of debt.	– 'SVC risk premium function for debt': $fr_{SVC,D}$ – 'SVC risk premium for debt': $r_{SVC,D}$ – 'Credit rating spread': CS_i – 'SVC cost of debt': k'_D – 'SVC debt valuation': SVC'_D – Equation (8.1a), 'SVC cost of debt': $k'_D = r_f + CS_i + r_{SVC,D}$ – Equation (8.2a), 'SVC debt valuation': $SVC'_D = \frac{CF_1}{(1+k'_D)^1} + \ldots + \frac{CF_n}{(1+k'_D)^n}$

Table 5.2 (continued)

Sustainable value creation (SVC) valuation framework	Purpose	Description of calculation approach	Conceptual elements Equations
(SVC-VF.5) 'The WACC-based valuation framework' for firms	Compute the 'SVC WACC' ($WACC''$) to establish the 'SVC firm valuation' for firms (SVC'')	The 'SVC cost of equity' rate (k_E') and the 'SVC cost of debt' rate (k_D') (or alternatively, the 'SVC-adjusted credit rating cost of debt', $k_D^{cr'}$), are used to calculate the weighted discount rate ($WACC''$) for the 'SVC firm valuation' (SVC''), i.e. the full sustainable value creation adjusted NPV of the firm.	– 'SVC WACC': $WACC''$ – 'SVC firm valuation': SVC'' ——— – Equation (9.1a), 'SVC WACC': $WACC'' = \left(\frac{E}{V} * k_E'\right) + \left(\frac{D}{V} * k_D^{cr'} \vert k_D'\right)$ – Equation (9.2a), 'SVC firm valuation': $SVC'' = \frac{CF_1}{(1 + WACC'')^1} + \ldots + \frac{CF_n}{(1 + WACC'')^n}$

Further to the summary above, the logic, conceptual elements and their operationalization as the equations of the five valuation frameworks are now further stipulated. The starting point for all the SVC valuation frameworks is the VCr. This measurement is the primary input to the functions whose outputs are SVC adjustments that in turn become the original inputs to established valuation methods. Hence, this inquiry's conceptual element of sustainable value creation is, via its VCr measurement and its focus on extractive value transfer-IN and inclusive value transfer OUT, incorporated into existing financial valuation frameworks.

The process of linking sustainable value creation and financial valuations starts with conceptual elements that are fit for purpose and then moves on to their operationalization. The SVC functions are central to the implementation of SVC valuations because the outputs are introduced to standard valuation methods and ultimately yield SVC-adjusted valuations. That process, and the functions themselves, must be transparent, a requirement that includes revealing their underlying weighting and algorithms.[99]

99 The calculations for the VCr—the primary input to SVC valuations—are based on extractive/inclusive transfer-IN/OUT metrics that are likewise subject to weighting (see Table 6.2, Section 6.6.1, and Table 6.6) and, as a resource and incentive for transformational leadership, must likewise be transparent and open to scrutiny.

As part of 'The SVC-adjusted enterprise valuation framework' for private firms (SVC-VF.1) there are two 'VCr enterprise value adjustment functions' ($fVCr^{EVm}/fVCr^{EV}$); one produces the input for a revenue multiple-based adjustment to the enterprise value, while the other one produces an adjustment of the equity value, from which the enterprise value can be derived by adding net debt. 'The SVC-adjusted credit rating valuation framework' for credit-rated debtors (SVC-VF.3) has the 'SVC risk premium function for credit rating' ($f\,r^{CR}_{SVC,D}$), the output of which will affect the credit rating cost of debt. These three functions will undergo an interactive development process with either a simple linear weighting or more sophisticated non-linear configurations.

The 'SVC risk premium function' for equity (fr_{SVC}) of 'The SVC cost of equity valuation framework' for public firms (SVC-VF.2), and the 'SVC risk premium function for debt' ($fr_{SVC,D}$) for 'The SVC cost of debt valuation framework' for debtors (SVC-VF.4) will also undergo cycles for their development and the calibration of premia and are expected to become more complex, multi-factor, and non-linear. This might entail weighting them with factor models that reflect a certain conceptual understanding or even the underlying data structures (e.g., of publicly listed firms) to best model sustainable value creation. That is, the (endogenous) empirical determination of SVC risk premia (for equity and debt, respectively r_{SVC} and $r_{SVC,D}$) rather than an explicit (exogenous) determination. Computational approach options here include the Fama-MacBeth regression (Fama & MacBeth, 1973); the Fama and French (2015) factor model; Merton's interest rate risk structure (1974) for debt valuation; and even machine learning for function approximation using neural networks.

Further to the introduction of their cornerstone functions, the five valuation frameworks are reviewed by referencing their respective equations (grouped into five sets, 5/9 to 9/9, following the nomenclature of the equations in Table 2.4).

Equations for enterprise valuation (5/9)

'The SVC-adjusted enterprise valuation framework' for private firms (SVC-VF.1)—see the overview in Figure A5.6a—offers two routes for valuing enterprises: one based on the revenue multiple (it could be EBITDA or industry-specific multiples, such as the number of subscribers); and the second based on the standard equity value plus the net debt equation. These two routes respectively become the 'SVC revenue multiple-based enterprise value' equation (5.1), and the 'SVC-adjusted enterprise value' equation (5.2). The SVC-adjusted equations have as their inputs the 'VCr revenue multiple adjustment' (VCr^{m}) and the 'VCr enterprise value adjustment' (VCr^{EV}), which are the outputs of two versions of the 'VCr enterprise value adjustment functions' ($fVCr^{m}/fVCr^{EV}$). The VCr^{m} is in turn applied to derive enterprise value in the 'SVC revenue multiple-based enterprise value' in equation (5.1), and the 'VCr^{EV} to do so in the 'SVC-adjusted enterprise value' equation (5.2). The revenue and other multiples for the practice of private firm valuations are derived from the average trading multiples of listed comparable firms in the same industry and country and of similar size, as well as from multiples in recent

M&A transactions. These two equations (5.1) and (5.2) respectively yield two valuations (*EVḿ*; *EV'*) that represent two routes to ascertain the sustainable value creation of enterprises. The two valuation approaches are intended to be used for private firms and though both can also be used for publicly traded firms, the next valuation framework for equity (SVC-VF.2) is deemed to be more suitable for these.

Equations for cost of equity valuation (6/9)

The second valuation framework for equity is 'The SVC cost of equity valuation framework' for public firms (SVC-VF.2)—the overview is also provided in Figure A5.6a—and introduces a novel conceptual element: the 'SVC risk premium' for equity. This 'SVC risk premium' (r_{SVC}) is added to the CAPM (Capital Asset Pricing Model) equation to yield the 'SVC cost of equity' rate (k_E'). The CAPM is a method that has solved (see Treynor, 1961; Sharpe, 1964) a "fundamental question in finance" i.e., "how the risk of an investment should affect its expected return" (Perold, 2004, p. 4). The cost of capital or the expected return is established on the basis of non-diversifiable risk (also called market risk or systematic risk) that is represented by 'beta' (β). The beta coefficient is thus a risk adjustment that reflects the sensitivity of a firm, investment, or asset (i.e., the return) to market risk (i.e., the overall market return) and hence is the ultimate determinant of the cost of equity (and capital). In a standard CAPM formulation, the cost of equity (and also the expected return required by equity investors) equals the risk-free rate (r_f) plus the beta coefficient multiplied by the market risk premium. The market risk premium is the expected market return minus the risk-free rate ($r_m - r_f$).[100] The 'SVC risk premium' (r_{SVC}) for equity results from the 'SVC risk premium function' for equity (fr_{SVC}). In a simple version, this key function could derive a multiplier factor from a cubic function or other with min/max limits, and apply it to the risk-free rate.[101] As has already been mentioned, a desirable and more sophisticated version would reference underlying data structures (as in Fama & MacBeth, 1973; Merton, 1974; Fama & French, 2015). The 'SVC cost of equity' (k_E') adds the 'SVC risk premium' (r_{SVC}) to CAPM as depicted in equation (6.1):

$$\text{'SVC cost of equity'} = \text{risk} - \text{free rate} + \text{beta(market risk)} * \text{market risk premium} + \text{'SVC risk premium'} \tag{6.1}$$

$$k_E' = r_f + \beta_E * (r_m - r_f) + r_{SVC} \tag{6.1a}$$

100 CAPM equation for reference: $k_E = r_f + \beta_E * (r_m - r_f)$

101 Possibilities include a linear formula such as *Linear* $r_{SVC} = r_f * \min\{\max[1 - 0.9 * VC_r; -0.8]; 1\}$ or a cubic formula *Cubic* $r_{SVC} = r_f * \min\{\max[(1 - VC_r)^3; -0.8]; 1\}$. The latter might be more appropriate if it succeeds in incentivizing transformational leadership on account of the acceleration effects brought about by the increasing marginal rate premium/discount.

The 'SVC risk premium' for equity (r_{SVC}) and its inclusion in the calculation of the cost of capital is the link between capital allocation processes and economic development. Its realization in practice will involve alignment with the institutions whose mandate is to incentivize growth and human development and who have their eyes on the efficient allocation of capital, such as the SEC, the European Financial Reporting Advisory Group (EFRAG), or the BIS (Bank for International Settlements) and its Basel Committee on Banking Supervision (BCBS). Alignment is likewise necessary with institutions that focus on sustainability (see Section 7.2.5), such as the sustainability disclosure standards of the International Sustainability Standards Board (ISSB) that operate under the umbrella of the International Financial Reporting Standards (IFRS) Foundation and complement the IFRS standards of the International Accounting Standards Board (IASB).

The 'SVC cost of equity' (k_E') derived from the 'SVC risk premium' is the rate used to compute the sustainable value creation valuation of equity, i.e., the 'SVC equity valuation' (*SVC'*). Following in the steps of Irving Fisher, valuation methods have concentrated on establishing present value: "The value of any property, or rights to wealth, is its value *as a source of income* and is found by discounting that expected income" (1930/1961, p. 12). Except for the first SVC valuation framework (SVC-VF.1), all of the other four rely on discounting cash flows to achieve the present value of sustainable value creation and transfers. They thus employ the standard discounted cash flow (DCF)[102] valuation methods (Williams, 1938; Gordon, 1959) of finance. The 'SVC equity valuation' (SVC_E') is a DCF method that obtains the present value of cash flows by discounting these with the 'SVC cost of equity' (k_E') rate obtained as is described by equation (6.2):

$$\text{'SVC equity valuation'} = \text{cash flow year } 1/(1+\text{'SVC cos to fequity'})^\wedge \text{year } 1 + \ldots + \text{cash flow year n} / (1+\text{'SVC cost of equity'})^\wedge \text{year n} \quad (6.2)$$

$$SVC' = \frac{CF_1}{(1+k_E')^1} + \frac{CF_2}{(1+k_E')^2} + \ldots + \frac{CF_n}{(1+k_E')^n} \quad (6.2a)$$

To sum up, the non-debt valuation frameworks proposed in this inquiry—'The SVC-adjusted enterprise valuation framework' for private firms (SVC-VF.1) and the 'The SVC cost of equity valuation framework' for public firms (SVC-VF.2)—are designed to establish sustainable value creation for private and public firms. By doing so, these valuations can inform the capital allocation processes in finance. Next, the two SVC valuation frameworks for debt are explained.

102 Standard discounted cash flow (DCF) valuation method for reference: $DCF = \frac{CF_1}{(1+k_E)^1} + \frac{CF_2}{(1+k_E)^2} + \ldots + \frac{CF_n}{(1+k_E)^n}$

Equations for credit rating cost of debt valuation (7/9)

Further to the first two valuation frameworks aimed at the sustainable value creation of private and public enterprises, the third framework (of Table 5.2) targets the SVC valuation of debt. 'The SVC-adjusted credit rating valuation framework' for credit-rated debtors (SVC-VF.3)—an overview of which is provided in Figure A5.6b—rests on the 'SVC risk premium for credit rating' ($r^{cr}_{SVC,D}$). It complements 'The SVC cost of debt valuation framework' for debtors described in the fourth valuation framework (SVC-VF.4) which has a different basis, the 'SVC risk premium for debt' ($r_{SVC,D}$).[103]

Credit ratings calibrate the market risk premium of debt instruments that impact the cost of debt, i.e., the interest rate on new debt (before tax) implicit in any debt instrument. To the SEC, credit ratings are "an assessment of an entity's ability to pay its financial obligations [that applies] to debt securities like bonds, notes, and other debt instruments [and] also are assigned to companies and governments [but not] to equity securities like common stock" (SEC, 2017). The 'SVC risk premium function for credit rating' ($f\,r^{cr}_{SVC,D}$) has the VCr as its input and the 'SVC risk premium for credit rating' ($r^{cr}_{SVC,D}$) as its output. This is then introduced into the 'credit rating cost of debt' equation ($k^{cr}_D = r_f + CS^{cr}_i$) that uses a credit rating spread (CS^{cr}_i)[104] to reflect the credit rating. The credit ratings of the agencies are based on their methodologies and issued on a scale that grades going up or down by notches as the discrete sustainability assessment of a debtor's probability of default.

The rating agencies, including the three leaders—Standard & Poor's (S&P), Moody's Investor Services, and Fitch Ratings—"use broadly similar methodologies in arriving at their credit rating determination" with their analysis honing in on "business risk" and "financial risk" (Santos, n.d., pp. 45–46). These credit ratings are widely used[105] and based on sophisticated methodologies and models with appended credit-

103 Collaboration with credit rating agencies will determine how distinct the 'SVC risk premium function for credit rating' ($fr^{cr}_{SVC,D}$) and 'SVC risk premium function for debt' ($fr_{SVC,D}$) functions are in practice and hence if there are any differences between the two SVC risk premia for debt ($r^{cr}_{SVC,D}|r_{SVC,D}$).

104 Since firms have only one cost of debt, the credit spreads CS^{cr}_i and CS_i should be the same. A common example where one would try to estimate the CS^{cr}_i is when trying to compute the cost of debt of a rated firm with no traded bonds. In such a case, no yield to maturity (YTM) can be computed, and so one can instead estimate a credit spread CS^{cr}_i for that rated firm based on the actual spreads CS_i of comparable companies with the same rating. This widely used technique implies that CS^{cr}_i and CS_i should be identical (see Damodaran, 2012, p. 211). Given that the risk-free rate (r_f) and cost of debt should be identical in the two equations 7.1a ($k^{cr'}_D$) and 8.1a (k'_D), the two risk premia should also be equal in theory. However, as the CS^{cr}_i is an estimation of the CS_i of the firm, it will not equal the actual CS_i. The main reason for this is that credit ratings do not dynamically fluctuate based on market sentiment but are periodically reviewed and updated by professionals. Therefore, in practice, the rating of a firm might not always be up to date and thus, in such a case, the CS^{cr}_i would not equal the actual CS_i of the firm one is trying to value (based on commentary by Nils Unell, January, 2024).

105 Deloitte Touche Tohmatsu Limited use credit ratings in their private debt valuation practice, see: https://www2.deloitte.com/content/dam/Deloitte/lu/Documents/financial-advisory/lu_deloitte-vluation-conference_private-debt-valuation_032016.pdf

relevant quantitative and qualitative factors[106, 107]. These additional factors (different agencies use terms like “modifier” or “consideration”) are applied at discrete stages of the various rating methodologies, modifying intermediate results and ultimately the credit ratings themselves by incrementing or decrementing these with notches. The credit rating, the output of such rating agency models, becomes the basis for the ‘credit rating spread’ (CS_i^{cr}). Credit spreads are important elements in finance used to determine the cost of debt, which is the risk-free rate plus the credit spread.[108] The extent to which “credit ratings correlate negatively with the cost of debt” can be empirically ascertained, as was done in “The Cost of a Notch” (Vazza, Kraemer, & Gurwitz, 2019). In the application of ‘The SVC-adjusted credit rating valuation framework’ for credit-rated debtors (SVC-VF.3), the ‘SVC-adjusted credit rating cost of debt’ ($k_D^{cr'}$) will differ from the credit rating cost of debt (k_D^{cr}), even as the agency's credit rating spread for debt (CS_i^{cr}) is maintained, because of the addition of the ‘SVC risk premium for credit rating’ ($r_{SVC,D}^{cr}$). The ‘SVC-adjusted credit rating cost of debt’ is described in equation (7.1):

$$\begin{aligned}\text{‘SVC – adjusted credit rating cost of debt’} &= \text{risk – free rate} + \text{‘credit rating spread’} \\ &\quad + \text{‘SVC risk premium for credit rating’}\end{aligned} \tag{7.1}$$

$$k_D^{cr'} = r_f + CS_i^{cr} + r_{SVC,D}^{cr} \tag{7.1a}$$

The ‘SVC-adjusted credit rating valuation for debt’ ($SVC_D^{cr'}$) utilizes a DCF method described in equation (7.2). The rate to discount cash flows it uses to reach the net present value (NPV) is the ‘SVC-adjusted credit rating cost of debt’ ($k_D^{cr'}$) rate obtained from equation (7.1)[109]. Potential users of this third valuation framework include rated firms

106 For examples of Moody's Investor Services and Fitch Ratings' use of modifiers and factors in their rating methodologies see: https://www.fitchratings.com/research/sovereigns/fitch-ratings-publishes-exposure-draft-for-sovereign-rating-criteria-08-06-2022; https://www.moodys.com/sites/products/ProductAttachments/Exhibit2.pdf

107 Modifiers based on ETED conceptual elements, such as an elite quality modifier for country risk derived from the EQr or EQx, could possibly be integrated into the Corporate Industry and Country Risk Assessment (CICRA) section of S&P's business risk methodology or as an appended factor in Moody's methodology (as per Unell, 2023).

108 Cost of debt equation for reference: $k_D = r_f + CS_i$

109 An alternative to the ‘SVC-adjusted credit rating cost of debt’ approach would be the ‘SVC-modified credit rating cost of debt’, though this would require cooperation with rating agencies and access to credit rating models. An ‘SVC modifier for credit rating function’ ($fVCr^{CRx}$) would have, as its output, an ‘SVC-modifier for credit rating’ (VCr^{CRx}) that would be introduced into the credit rating models to yield an ‘SVC-modified credit rating’ ($CR^{\times}$). Based on the agencies' methodologies, the ‘SVC-modified credit rating’ would then be converted into a new credit rating spread, the ‘SVC-modified credit rating spread’ (CS_i^{crx}). Lastly, this spread would be plugged into the standard cost of debt formula ($k_D^{crx} = r_f + CS_i^{crx}$) for the ‘SVC-modified credit rating cost of debt’.

that do not have traded bonds (a rating might help them to meet regulatory requirements),[110] or firms that have neither traded bonds nor are rated by credit rating agencies but construct synthetic ratings to compute the cost of debt (Damodaran, 2012) or are rated by banks.[111] 'The SVC-adjusted credit rating valuation framework' for credit-rated debtors (SVC-VF.3) does, in consistency with the credit rating methodologies that it uses as baseline, provide new and relevant information on the 'likelihood of default' of a debt instrument. The assumption here is that the risk of insolvency associates with the amount of sustainable value creation and unsustainable value transfers inherent in the business model activities that underlie a firm's cash flows.

Equations for cost of debt valuation (8/9)

'The SVC cost of debt valuation framework' for debtors (SVC-VF.4)—an overview of which is also provided in Figure A5.6b—also renders the SVC debt valuation. Its mechanics start by applying the 'SVC risk premium function for debt' ($fr_{SVC,D}$), where the VCr is the input and the 'SVC risk premium for debt' ($r_{SVC,D}$) is the output. This output is then added to the standard cost of debt formula based on the risk-free rate plus a credit spread (CS_i) which is the additional rate investors require to be compensated for to cover the risk of default of the particular debtor. These additions yield the 'SVC cost of debt' rate (k_D'), as per equation (8.1):

$$\text{'SVC cost of debt'} = \text{risk} - \text{free rate} + \text{credit spread} + \text{'SVC risk premium for debt')} \tag{8.1}$$

$$k_D' = r_f + CS_i + r_{SVC,D} \tag{8.1a}$$

The 'SVC debt valuation' (SVC_D) is also a DCF method and described in equation (8.2), see Table 5.2. The rate to discount cash flows it uses to reach the present value is the 'SVC cost of debt' rate, previously obtained from the 'SVC cost of debt' equation (8.1).

In short, the third and fourth (SVC-VF.3 and SVC-VF.4) valuation frameworks arrive at the SVC debt valuation via two discrete costs of debt approaches ($k_D^{cr'}$ and k_D'). These are respectively based on the 'SVC-adjusted risk premium for credit rating' ($r_{SVC,D}^{cr}$) and the 'SVC risk premium for debt' ($r_{SVC,D}$) adjustments. Either one of the two costs of debt can then be used to discount debt cash flows with the standard DCF method to respectively obtain the SVC debt valuation as the 'SVC-adjusted credit rating debt valuation' ($SVC_D^{cr'}$) or the 'SVC debt valuation' (SVC_D'). In practice, at any given point in time, and notwithstanding the two discrete costs of debt approaches presented here, there is a *de facto* single current cost of debt for the firm that is established at the time of the credit agreement negotiation with the particular creditor

110 See: https://www.finma.ch/en/authorisation/rating-agencies/

111 See Credit Suisse's ratings overview of Swiss firms: https://www.credit-suisse.com/media/assets/corporate/docs/about-us/media/media-release/2014/08/000000022792.pdf

with whom the firm incurs the liability. These liabilities assume the form of loans or bonds, the latter being a debt security. For the single liability, the cost of debt will depend on market conditions like maturity dates, market sentiment, political events, tax benefits and, critically, central bank policy rates like the ECB's Refinance Rate, the People's Bank of China (PBOC) Medium-term Lending Facility (MLF), or the Fed's Federal Funds Rate (FFR). Once the debt securities are publicly traded, the cost of debt is the computed yield to maturity (YTM) of these securities. The legal covenants used in debt instruments affect their perceived risk and hence determine the cost of debt. They include collateral requirements, restrictions on further debt or dividends issuance, negative pledge clauses, or change of control provisions. The respective discrete implications of SVC valuation adjustments for firms with debt securities[112] and firms with only non-negotiable financial instruments, is an item for further analysis.[113]

Either two of the approaches outlined here; the addition of an 'SVC risk premium for credit rating' ($r^{cr}_{SVC,D}$) or an 'SVC risk premium for debt' ($r_{SVC,D}$), might be used to establish the cost of debt for the financial liability at hand.[114] The actual approach and the ensuing cost of debt would be determined with the creditor based on the market conditions that affect valuations and are subject to the provisions of the legal covenants negotiated. In the same fashion as the SVC valuation frameworks for enterprise and equity (SVC-VF.1 and SVC-VF.2), the two SVC valuation frameworks for debt (SVC-VF.3 and SVC-VF.4) keep their sight firmly on the economic and human development imperative of this inquiry by providing benchmarks for the allocation of capital

112 See IMF definition: https://www.elibrary.imf.org/display/book/9781475510102/ch002.xml

113 The market value for debt securities—and hence the YTM—are in a state of continuous change and so the cost of debt constantly fluctuates (similar to the cost of equity due to evolving beta coefficients). On the other hand, some firms without debt securities borrow through non-traded, non-negotiable financial instruments (such as bank loans). Since their debt is not subject to dynamic market pricing, their debt YTM is much more stable and equals the weighted interest rates on the firm's loans (the private firm loan YTM is only known to those with access to the credit agreement terms). The interest rates on non-traded debt, generally structured as base rate plus margin, usually only change under two circumstances during a loan's tenure: when the base rate (a benchmark like the Swiss Average Rate Overnight, SARON) varies; or if the stipulated leverage thresholds (for example, based on the net debt to EBITDA ratio) are reached as outlined in the credit agreements. Since the cost of debt for firms without debt securities is not dynamically priced (notwithstanding base rate movements), market sentiment and external factors only impact it when new debt is raised (based on exchanges with Nils Unell in January, 2024).

114 The formulas for the cost of debt presuppose the availability of firm credit spreads (CS_i). In the case of firms with traded debt securities, which are typically rated, the CS_i is easy to compute (the YTM of the bonds). Non-rated traded bonds are uncommon and usually either non-investment grade or issued by small municipalities. Computing the credit spreads (CS_i), and thus the cost of debt for non-rated debtors without traded bonds is comparatively more complicated. Current methods include analyzing past borrowing history or estimating a synthetic credit rating from the firm's financial ratios (as in Damodaran, 2012).

based on sustainable value creation (via its primary input, the VCr measurement and its constituent SVC metrics).

Equations for firm valuation (9/9)

In the Modigliani and Miller theorem, "the average cost of capital to any firm is completely independent of its capital structure" (1958, pp. 268–269), which articulates the relationship between firm value and its financing. Firm financing can be through equity or debt and its cost of capital is the weighted average cost of capital (WACC), a generally accepted method of finance widely applied in academia and pervasive in practice. The conceptual elements used for the SVC valuation of debt and equity are here supplemented by the WACC formula in the 'The SVC WACC-based valuation framework' for firms (SVC-VF.5), an overview of which is provided in Figure A5.6c.

The cost of equity input in the 'SVC-WACC' equation ($WACC''$) is the 'SVC cost of equity' (k'_E). The CAPM approach automatically aligns the calculation of the cost of equity to real-time market conditions, as it is sensitive to volatility, risk premiums, and expected returns. This is different for the cost of debt. Firms issue multiple bonds and take out multiple loans over the years. Their cost of debt is the effective weighted interest rate paid for all the debts, and so one can imagine the entire list of borrowed funds in both of their forms—as loans and bonds. For SVC valuation purposes, each liability has either the 'SVC risk premium for credit rating' ($r^{cr}_{SVC,D}$) or the 'SVC risk premium for debt' ($r_{SVC,D}$) adjustments applied. The choice made here will be informed by the original cost of debt determination approach and must take into account current market dynamics. For instance, the original credit rating assessment would need to be updated to reflect upgrades or downgrades in accordance with the firm's actual financial situation. The SVC debt valuation is straightforward in the sense that for whichever cost of debt determination approach the firm uses, the 'SVC-adjusted credit rating cost of debt' ($k^{cr'}_D$) or the 'SVC cost of debt' (k'_D) is added.

Jointly, the sustainable value creation cost of equity and debt rates—which conceptually account for the weighted value creation and transfer-IN/OUT of the business model on account of the primary input, the VCr— yield the new cost of capital of firms, the 'SVC WACC' ($WACC''$), the output of equation (9.1):

$$\text{'SVC} - \text{WACC'} = [(\text{equity / value}) * \text{'SVC cost of equity'}] + [(\text{debit/value}) * \text{'SVC} - \text{adjusted credit rating cost of debt' (or) 'SVC cost of debt'}] \tag{9.1}$$

$$WACC'' = \left(\frac{E}{V} * k'_E\right) + \left(\frac{D}{V} * k^{cr'}_D | k'_D\right) \tag{9.1a}$$

The WACC rate is the average cost of the diverse sources of equity and debt for financing that a firm uses to fund itself. The $WACC''$ represents a firm's expected average cost of financing itself, i.e., the blended sustainable value creation rate that a firm pays to its capital providers. Used in the DCF financial modeling method, WACC establishes the NPV of estimated future cash flows. The 'SVC firm valuation' (SVC'') is derived from applying to the firm's cash flows the $WACC''$ rate of equation (9.1) analogously to what is done with the other DCF-based equations (6.2), (7.3), and (8.2) as per equation (9.2):

$$\text{'SVC firm valuation'} = \text{cash flow year } 1/(1+\text{'SVC WACC'})^\wedge \text{year } 1 + \ldots + \text{cash flow year } n/(1+\text{'SVC WACC'})^\wedge \text{year } n \quad (9.2)$$

$$SVC'' = \frac{CF_1}{(1+WACC'')^1} + \frac{CF_1}{(1+WACC'')^2} + \ldots + \frac{CF_n}{(1+WACC'')^n} \quad (9.2a)$$

Table 5.2 summarized the five valuation frameworks for the sustainable value creation of enterprise and equity, debt, and the firm. Table 5.3 now lists and describes them (in the format of the SVC measurements used in Table 2.4).

Table 5.3: Equations for 'The Sustainable Value Creation (SVC) Valuation Frameworks' for equity, debt, and firms (a continuation of the equation set of Table 2.4).

Ref.	Equation set	Description
5/9	**Equations for 'The SVC-adjusted enterprise valuation framework' for private firms (SVC-VF.1)**	
5.1	'SVC revenue multiple-based enterprise value' = Revenue * (Revenue Multiple * 'VCr revenue multiple adjustment')	The 'SVC revenue multiple-based enterprise value' approach employs the conventional enterprise value equation based on multiples (e.g., of revenue) that reference, in the form of a ratio, similar firms. The multiple undergoes a VCr-based adjustment that is the output of the 'VCr enterprise value adjustment function' ($fVCr^m$).
5.1a	$EVm' = Revenue^* \left(Revenue\ Multiple^*\ VCr^m\right)$	
5.2	'SVC-adjusted enterprise value' = (Equity value * 'VCr enterprise value adjustment') + Net Debt	The 'SVC-adjusted enterprise value' employs the conventional enterprise value approach based on equity value and net debt (debt minus cash and equivalents). The equity component undergoes a VCr-based adjustment that is the output of the 'VCr enterprise value adjustment function' ($fVCr^{EV}$).
5.2a	$EV' = (Equity\ Value\ * VCr^{EV}) + Net\ Debt$	

Table 5.3 (continued)

Ref.	Equation set	Description
6/9	**Equations for 'The SVC cost of equity valuation framework' for public firms (SVC-VF.2)**	
6.1	'SVC cost of equity' = risk-free rate + beta(market risk) * market risk premium + 'SVC risk premium'	The 'SVC cost of equity' (k_E') is the cost of equity rate adjusted for sustainable value creation and is based on CAPM, to which an additional return is appended, the 'SVC risk premium' for equity (r_{SVC}), making equity financing more expensive (or more affordable). The 'SVC risk premium' (r_{svc}) rate is the output of the VCr-based 'SVC risk premium function' for equity (fr_{svc}). The standard CAPM cost of equity equation is: $k_E = r_f + \beta_E * (r_m - r_f)$
6.1a	$k_E' = r_f + \beta_E * (r_m - r_f) + r_{svc}$	
6.2	'SVC equity valuation' = cash flow year 1 / (1 + 'SVC cost of equity') ^ year 1 + . . . + cash flow year n / (1 + 'SVC cost of equity') ^ year n	The present value of equity adjusted for sustainable value creation, the 'SVC equity valuation' (SVC_E') is derived from applying the discounted cash flow (DCF) method to equity cash flows. The 'SVC cost of equity' (k_E') is the discount rate, which in turn is derived from adding the 'SVC risk premium' for equity (r_{SVC}) to the standard cost of equity formula. The standard discounted cash flow (DCF) valuation method is: $DCF = \frac{CF_1}{(1+k_E)^1} + \frac{CF_2}{(1+k_E)^2} + \ldots + \frac{CF_n}{(1+k_E)^n}$
6.2a	$SVC_E' = \frac{CF_1}{(1+k_E')^1} + \frac{CF_2}{(1+k_E')^2} + \ldots + \frac{CF_n}{(1+k_E')^n}$	
7/9	**Equations for 'The SVC-adjusted credit rating valuation framework' for credit-rated debtors (SVC-VF.3)**	
7.1	'SVC-adjusted credit rating cost of debt' = risk-free rate + 'SVC risk premium for credit rating'	The 'SVC-adjusted credit rating cost of debt' ($k_D^{cr'}$) is the cost of debt rate adjusted for sustainable value creation and is based on the cost of debt formula to which an additional yield is appended, the 'SVC risk premium for credit rating' ($r_{SVC,D}^{cr}$) (if negative it is a negative yield), making debt financing more expensive (or more affordable). The 'SVC risk premium for credit rating' ($r_{SVC,D}^{cr}$) is the output of the 'SVC risk premium function for credit rating' ($fr_{SVC,D}^{cr}$) based on the VCr. The standard cost of debt formula is: $k_D = r_f + CS_i$
7.1a	$k_D^{cr'} = r_f + CS_i^{cr} + r_{SVC,D}^{cr}$	

Table 5.3 (continued)

Ref.	Equation set	Description
7.2	'SVC-adjusted credit rating debt valuation' = cash flow year 1 / (1 + 'SVC-adjusted credit rating cost of debt') ^ year 1 + . . . + cash flow year n / (1 + 'SVC-adjusted credit rating cost of debt') ^ year n	The 'SVC-adjusted credit rating debt valuation' ($SVC_D^{cr'}$) is the present value of debt adjusted for sustainable value creation and is derived from applying the DCF method to debt cash flows using the 'SVC-adjusted credit rating cost of debt' ($k_D^{cr'}$) discount rate, which in turn is derived from adding to the standard cost of debt formula, the 'SVC risk premium for credit rating' ($r_{SVC,D}^{cr}$).
7.2a	$SVC_D^{cr'} = \frac{CF_1}{\left(1+k_D^{cr'}\right)^1} + \frac{CF_2}{\left(1+k_D^{cr'}\right)^2} + \ldots + \frac{CF_n}{\left(1+k_D^{cr'}\right)^n}$	
8/9	**Equations for 'The SVC cost of debt valuation framework' for debtors (SVC-VF.4)**	
8.1	'SVC cost of debt' = risk-free rate + credit spread + 'SVC risk premium for debt'	The 'SVC cost of debt' (k_D') is the cost of debt rate adjusted for sustainable value creation and is based on the standard cost of debt formula, to which an additional yield is appended, the 'SVC risk premium for debt' ($r_{SVC,D}$) (if negative it is a negative yield), making debt financing more expensive (or more affordable). The 'SVC risk premium for debt' ($r_{SVC,D}$) is the output of the 'SVC risk premium function for debt' ($fr_{SVC,D}$) based on the VCr.
8.1a	$k_D' = r_f + CS_i + r_{SVC,D}$	
8.2	'SVC debt valuation' = cash flow year 1 / (1 + 'SVC cost of debt') ^ year 1 + . . . + cash flow year n / (1 + 'SVC cost of debt') ^ year n	The 'SVC debt valuation' (SVC_D') is the present value of debt adjusted for sustainable value creation and is derived from applying the DCF method to debt cash flows using the 'SVC cost of debt' (k_D') discount rate, which in turn is derived from adding to the standard cost of debt formula, the 'SVC risk premium for debt' ($r_{SVC,D}$).
8.2	$SVC_D' = \frac{CF_1}{(1+k_D')^1} + \frac{CF_2}{(1+k_D')^2} + \ldots + \frac{CF_n}{(1+k_D')^n}$	
9/9	**Equations for 'The SVC WACC-based valuation framework' for firms (SVC-VF.5)**	
9.1	'SVC WACC' = [(equity / value) * 'SVC cost of equity'] + [(debt / value) * 'SVC-adjusted credit rating cost of debt' (or) 'SVC cost of debt']	The 'SVC WACC' ($WACC''$) is the weighted average cost of capital adjusted for sustainable value creation based on the standard WACC formula: the proportion of firm equity to firm value is multiplied by the 'SVC cost of equity' (k_E'); and the proportion of firm debt to firm value is multiplied by the 'SVC cost of debt' (k_D') or alternatively by the 'SVC-adjusted credit rating cost of debt' ($k_D^{cr'}$). The standard weighted average cost of capital formula is: $WACC = \left(\frac{E}{V} * k_E\right) + \left(\frac{D}{V} * k_D\right)$
9.1a	$WACC'' = \left(\frac{E}{V} * k_E'\right) + \left(\frac{D}{V} * k_D^{cr\times} \mid k_D'\right)$	

Table 5.3 (continued)

Ref.	Equation set	Description
9.2	'SVC firm valuation' = cash flow year 1 / (1 + 'SVC WACC') ^ year 1 + . . . + cash flow year n / (1 + 'SVC WACC) ^ year n	The present value of a firm adjusted for sustainable value creation (SVC'') is derived from applying the DCF method to firm cash flows. The 'SVC WACC' ($WACC''$) is the discount rate, which in turn is derived from the 'SVC cost of equity' (k_E'), and, for the cost of debt, from either the 'SVC cost of debt' (k_D') or the 'SVC-adjusted credit rating cost of debt' ($k_D^{cr'}$).
9.2a	$SVC'' = \frac{CF_1}{(1+WACC'')^1} + \ldots + \frac{CF_n}{(1+WACC'')^n}$	

The discussion of the five SVC valuation frameworks, each with their attendant equations, underlines the main objective of the SVC measurements in general and the VCr in particular: practical impact on economic and human development. Organizations and their executives, owners, and investors might reference and integrate these valuations into their financial toolset to achieve both their sustainability objectives and a more competitive cost of capital, including efficiently priced debt. The five SVC valuation frameworks, all originating from the VCr and with functions deriving adjustments and risk premia, seek to provide a fair and feasible expression of value and risk rooted in the ontological assumption of the nature of socio-economic relations in this work that 'value is created or transferred'. In consequence, they express the weighted value transfers inherent in value appropriation. The valuation frameworks complement existing decision-making tools such as credit ratings, while also being linked to decision-making frameworks (e.g., see the set in Figure A5.6).

The SVC measurements (in Table 2.4) and the SVC valuation frameworks (see Tables 5.2 and 5.3 in this sub-section) operate at the micro-level and must now be taken up at the meso-level from an elite system perspective in order to return to this work's economic development mandate. This begins with an examination of a coincidence of opposites, where two antagonistic conceptual elements that are characteristic of the elite system shape the inclusive/extractive proportions and nature of elite business models: the cohesion of the elite system and its separation of powers.

5.3.3 The conceptualization of elite system cohesion balanced with the separation of powers as a precondition for development

> For instance, many of the leaders married their classmates or friends of their sisters, brothers and cousins, invited one another into political parties, formed community-based organizations together, recruited one another into the public service and even formed private business investment agencies as friends, colleagues and inter-ethnic/racial elite groups. [. . .] a broad-based schoolmate camaraderie evolved which later enabled easy networking relationships. In this way,

> education was a key factor and underpinned the coalitions that emerged later, and contributed to Botswana's development [. . .] Familiarity with each other enabled the emerging Botswana national elite to form a successful "grand coalition" which in turn contributed to political, social and economic stability. The 'grand coalition' has become a critical success factor in Botswana and stands in sharp contrast with countries such as Burundi, Ethiopia, Kenya, Lesotho, Malawi, Rwanda, Somalia, Sudan, Zambia, Zimbabwe, and many other African countries, where ethnic and racial conflict and in-fighting created unstable governments and hampered development. (Sebudubudu & Molutsi, 2011, p. 11)

Elite cohesion is paramount for the general development of countries as diverse as Botswana or Switzerland. The quote above explains the reason for unity in the former while the latter "continues to be characterized by a cohesive elite whose members simultaneously occupy political and economic positions" (Bühlmann, David, & Mach, 2012, p. 727), a finding confirmed despite "a strongly decentralized system and a particularly internationalized economy" (Rossier, Ellersgaard, Larsen, & Lunding, 2022, p. 316). Cohesion is essential to the objectives of the core coalition or knowledge elite coalitions, as is portrayed by Putnam (1977, p. 409): "The prospects for technocracy also depend in part on the cohesiveness of technocrats". During its Golden Age (between 1915 and 1960), the Hollywood elite business model—like the military—mirrored the reigning elite cohesion while also prompting social cohesion, with business and knowledge elites conjoined by political institutions as movie-going became one of "the most central American civic rituals" (Decherney, 2005, p. 22). On other occasions, an "elite settlement" is crafted *ad hoc* to deliberately usher forth the "fundamental transformation of elite structure from the condition of disunity to that of consensual unity" (Burton & Higley, 1987, p. 306). In "Causes of Revolution", Gottschalk examines the weakness of elite groups "which may be caused by disputes among themselves" (1944, p. 1). A lack of elite cohesion and deinstitutionalized intra-elite conflicts are also problematic for Goldstone, who sees them as "the ingredients for a full-scale revolution" (1982, p. 200). However, cohesion can also be excessive and stifling if it is not in a productive balance with a comprehensive separation of powers. Its workings are also put to the test when elite systems face existential threats, as two historical examples illustrate.

The first is the French Revolution, the origins of which can be traced not to non-elite agency but rather to the revolt of the 144 "notables" of Louis XVI against their very own royal absolutist system. This elite coalition demanded broader representation on financial matters, and while their refusal to support the king's fiscal reform and tax levies was indeed a "reactionary defense of privilege", it also supplied arguments such as "no taxation without representation" that led to the system's demise (Gruder, 1982, p. 263). A fatidic intra-elite contest ensued and escalated, leading to a state that Higley (2021) terms "disunified elites", and eventually cracked the elite system open to the madness of Robespierre and others. The second example illustrates the opposite and showcases the preservation of elite cohesion in the German Revolution of 1848–1849. Despite considerable popular non-elite pressure and the efforts of incipient elite coalitions famously represented by the 809 delegates to the Frankfurt

National Assembly at the *Paulskirche*, the Prussian king, Friedrich Wilhelm IV, was able to reject the imperial crown offered to him (with democratic strings attached) by the National Assembly's *Kaiserdeputation* on April 3, 1849. This was possible because the Prussian system had stayed intact and retained its elite coordination leadership. As a result, at this critical juncture in (world) history, incumbent elites preempted emerging elites from realizing the narrativized preferences they shared with non-elites (see Figure 3.5) for German unification and democracy through a constitutional monarchy, the *Frankfurter Reichsverfassung*. In France, the elite system of Louis XVI lost cohesion as a result of his inclusive transformation attempts and so collapsed. The elite system of Friedrich Wilhelm IV and local princes elsewhere in Germany retained cohesion and rejected transformational demands, emerging from the confrontation even more powerful.

Hobsbawm (1962/1996) analyzes how narratives that are more in tune with changing social and economic realities drive revolution. Davies' theory on revolutions contends that these "are most likely to occur when a prolonged period of objective economic and social development is followed by a short period of sharp reversal" (1962, p. 5). Yet, when facing a situation of objective or subjective discontent before an approaching tipping point, cohesive elites can avoid turmoil by dialing down or even temporarily turning off their value extraction pumps and letting the storm of non-elite anger pass. Today, excessively extractive elite business models remain a recognized social and political economy problem and are subjected to criticism in the public discourse. Part of the quandary is when value transfers erode elite cohesion, not to mention all other forms of social cohesion. In his column for *The Financial Times*, Wolf (2018) condemns rents as "rewards over and above those required to induce the desired supply of goods, services, land, and labor". In *Forbes*, Marotta (2013) defines rents in Tullock's (1967) theft terms as ownership of "someone else's surplus in the end". *The Economist* (2014) looks at the macro picture—the economic pie—and uses Porter's imagery to typify rent seeking as "grabbing a bigger slice of the pie rather than making the pie bigger". Mazzucato's work (2018, 2019) distinguishes between the "earned income" of "makers", derived from real value creation activities like innovation, and the "unearned income" appropriated by "takers". Value extraction is repudiated because 'takers' create two types of losers: the stakeholders that unwillingly suffer direct transfer-OUT, and society at large through the decline of the production function. Counterproductive responses to extraction such as 'informality' (reviewed in Table 5.1) then combine with the misallocation of resources and perverse incentive structures, leading to value destruction and the absence of its creation (see Section 5.2.1).

Discontent about rent seeking and extractive business models also emanates from narrative dissonance, a deep two-pronged sense of wrong: losers should not have lost (why should value creators be unable to appropriate the value they have created, or pay for the risks they have not taken); and development that is below potential (why should all members of society not have higher incomes or a better quality of life). The Council of Europe (2007) has a "social cohesion strategy" that provides a set of indicators, the underlying aspiration being "the capacity of a society to ensure the welfare of all its members, minimising disparities and avoiding polarisation". The concentrated focus of this elite theory is on extractive transfers that spill over tolerable thresholds—both objective and subjective—as these erode social cohesion. Such transfers are seen as the root cause of intensified unproductive individual non-elite responses and the related aggregate political options that these foster (see Sections 5.2.2, 8.1.3, and 8.2.4 on sustainable redistribution) with detrimental consequences for development and competitiveness.

Public sentiment becomes increasingly confused and strained when reality runs counter to the narratives of fairness upon which most societies are founded. As a result, elite/non-elite cohesion is damaged, a crucial construct that together with elite cohesion and non-elite cohesion constitutes this inquiry's conceptualization of 'social cohesion'; what Stanley refers to as "the willingness of members of a society to cooperate with each other in order to survive and prosper" (2003, p. 5), and Chan, To, and Chan define as "a state of affairs concerning both the vertical and the horizontal interactions among members of society" (2006, p. 298). The deterioration of elite/non-elite cohesion entails systemic risk if, and only if, it erodes intra-elite contest rules and leads to the questioning of the legitimacy of business model rules at the elite system level. Consistent with the earlier historical examples of Louis XVI and Friedrich Wilhelm IV, the general truism pointed out by Brown's study of Southeast Asian nations (1993) is that "political stability depends primarily upon the effectiveness with which élite cohesion is maintained" (1993, p. 111). Polarization, even in present-day America and Europe, is not primarily an elite vs non-elite matter but an intra-elite issue. Divisions within the elite are what stoke rifts and create discord in the non-elite. A key question is whether non-elite political options of the confrontation type (Figure A5.8), which also reflect fractures in elite cohesion, end up strengthening or weakening the elite system. If the latter, the outcome is increased transaction costs for elites and eroded intra-elite trust, while the overall coordination capacity of the nation can fall precipitously.

The predicament is thus as follows: terminating extractive elite business models requires elite transformational leadership, that when undertaken, even when fueled by non-elite discontent (see Louis XVI), can short-circuit elite cohesion. The transmission mechanism by which all of this occurs is the stress, and even the existential challenge, to which intra-elite contests subject many elite coalitions. Some emerging elites sense an opportunity in growing discontent to advance their interests and take shortcuts to amass power, including by stirring up non-elites, while others calculate that since the pie is shrinking, whatever is needed to reduce the number of elite coalitions is welcome, from declarations by the IMF (Johnson, 2009) to contemporary equivalents of Roman-style proscriptions. In the worst-case scenario, the door opens for an intra-elite free for all where elite identity is at stake and the contest becomes one of survival for specific elite coalitions and their individual members. Intra-elite contest rules cease to apply and there are no power differentials in the elite system—there is no longer a core coalition—able to substitute for institutions when power becomes so fragmented. With the deinstitutionalization of the political economy's intra-elite contests, the elite separation of powers becomes anarchic along with the existing three-tier set of intra-elite checks and balances. To make matters worse, sensing the breakdown of the elite system, a plethora of emergent elite coalitions with great drive and little to lose join the fray literally out of nowhere. This leads to the intensification of conflict, which can only be stopped when elite system leadership rebuilds cohesion and the primacy of intra-elite contest rules.

"Elite overproduction" is a state deemed by Turchin as "inherently destabilizing" where "more elites and elite aspirants than the society can provide positions for" results in a "frustrated" and "radicalized" class of "counter-elites" (2013, p. 244). Technically, such would-be elites are not surplus elites but rather members of the managerial, technical, and creative class (see Figure 8.1). The numbers in this stratum (the priest aiming for the cardinal robe, the zealous military officer, the start-up founder, the Ivy League graduate in a Wall Street firm dreaming to be inducted a partner) have always exceeded by a large margin the membership slots in elite business model coalitions. Also of relevance is that the agency of value creation elites produces new elite positions. However, the game is zero-sum and results in *End Times* (Turchin, 2023) when intra-elite contests revolve around transfer business models that abscond first-order value creation and focus on the non-market and narrative market arenas. Competition for extractive rents is the primary reason for the deinstitutionalization of intra-elite contests rules and diminished elite cohesion.

Regardless of the causes, when elite cohesion fractures and the political system fragments or dramatically polarizes, the consequences can be grave, though events like the second fall of Afghanistan to the Taliban, the US Civil War, or the collapse of the Louis XVI system are rare. Elites are usually keenly aware of what is at stake in a non-cooperative game. One might recall the modest impact on the Putin elite system's functional cohesion caused by the Wagner Group's failed insurrection in June 2023. On the other hand, elite systems can suddenly lose unity and collapse. For over two decades, the challenges to the Qing Dynasty by Chen Tianhua, Sun Yat-sen, and other republican visionaries were foiled. Yet, as Rhoads (2000) recounts, in October 1911, the modest Wuchang Uprising sparked the Xinhai Revolution, and within four months China's two-thousand-year-old imperial system ended with the deposition of the Xuantong child emperor (Puyi) and the founding of Asia's first republic on 12 February, 1912.

Elite cohesion is a precondition that lies at the heart of institutional order. It is likewise critical for established and emergent elite coalitions seeking transformation. Jewish elites across Europe achieved newfound cohesion around the modern political Zionism narrative, articulated for instance by Theodore Herzl in the pamphlet *Der Judenstaat* (1896). Vall-Prat (2022) explains the elite split in Spain that saw the formation of a specific regional elite in Catalonia at the end of the 19th century around the business model of industrialization. However, the lack of subsequent elite cohesion, coupled with a notorious lack of elite system leadership and deinstitutionalized intra-elite contests explains why Catalonia, despite the national trauma narrative of its September 11 (the 1714 defeat in the Siege of Barcelona, with the attendant loss of centuries-old institutions and the corroboration that the beloved Catalan language would be stateless and exposed to the vagaries of Madrid) that galvanizes a significant proportion of its elites and non-elites, has consistently failed to attain statehood despite the unremitting attempts of one generation after another over the last three centuries. When faced with the formidable leadership and cohesion (at least on this issue) of the Spanish elite system, the Catalan elites are amateurs with meager chances of success.

Elites retain their coordination capacity and transaction cost advantages for as long as no major coalition reneges (for too long) on the system's intra-elite contest rules. If the system fails to swiftly deal with reticent non-cooperative elite players after they break ranks, then serious problems will promptly follow. Coup d'états in political and other arenas (e.g., the events at OpenAI and Microsoft in November, 2023) are the culmination of non-institutionalized contests aiming to reshuffle the membership of a coalition or the elite system itself, at times seeking the replacement of the core elite coalition. But even then, as long as elites remain united and genuine defectors are few or conflicted, the incumbent arrangements prevail. The establishment will also override most non-elite challenges, including opportunistic moves from defecting elite coalitions, some of whom may try to leverage social conflict and discontent. Elite cohesion requires the maintenance of generally accepted intra-elite contest rules (see Figure 4.3) and effective elite system leadership (see Table 7.2). The latter is critical, as a separation of powers without elite cohesion leads to situations like "vetocracy" which, in the case of the US, Fukuyama defines as a "situation in which it was easier to stop government from doing things than it was to use government to promote the common good" (2016, p. 58). Institutions are essential, but they don't function well without elite cohesion. The bleakest scenario for failing elite cohesion is civil war, an extreme form of deinstitutionalized intra-elite conflict, almost never the direct result of non-elite demands (even if narratives might disingenuously frame the conflict as the realization of non-elite aspirations, as in many a *Kulturkampf*).

In short, elites that circle the wagons will prevail, no matter how shrewd the dissenting elite's conspiracy or obstinate the non-elite resistance. The 'elite cohesion underpins social order' conjecture posits that the social order necessary for development will be maintained for as long as elites preserve their natural coordination capacity advantage in the face of internal elite system or non-elite challenges and discontent.[115] Moreover, it also implies that the cohesion of the elite is more important for economic and human development than other forms of social cohesion. One reason for this is the hypothesis

115 National elite cohesion is at times desired and influenced by outsiders that have a relationship with the country. This is obvious in the provision of financial facilities by the IMF or World Bank, or by Western military support to Ukraine that would have been difficult if President Zelenskyy did not have the support of the country's cohered elite. Cohesion can also be fleeting and tactical as in the case of the elite pact to install Mario Draghi as Italian Prime Minister in 2021, an interim state of elite cohesion that was driven, at least in part, by EU funding considerations.

that elite cohesion precedes, and will usher in, elite/non-elite and non-elite cohesion. Of course, if viewed through an economic development lens this can be highly unsatisfactory: as long as the elite system perseveres the political economy will endure, even if it is with a dwindling and suboptimal production function punctuated by social mayhem. For instance, elite homogeneity, which fosters cohesion, is found by Hartmann (2007b) to associate with inequality in Europe. Still, while a nation may be mired in troubles, when its elite system collapses everything gets worse. Elites know this very well and cynically play the 'me or the flood' card to sustain the status quo.

Given the primacy of elite cohesion, should we conclude that elites are able to ride roughshod over non-elite challenges, with no incentive to end extractive micro-level elite business models? The answer to this question is a resounding no. The costs of maintaining extractive elite business models, especially over the long run, are inordinate: lower levels of human and economic development, stagnation or regression, waves of emigration (by dispossessed non-elites or the expert class), the displacement of many elites (their wealth mostly intact but their status gone), and the weakening of the nation in the international system (as well as being potentially reviled by the objective mantle of history, which might be of concern to some elites). Olsonian stationarity does then matter, but not all elites are thus capable, as is evident if one contrasts the fates of elite dynasties in China, Russia, or Iran over the last century with those of the US, Japan, or France. Consistent with endogenous institutional change (see Section 4.3.5), the sustainability of the system is in the interests of elites and is achieved by engaging in elite transformational leadership while the core elite coalition pushes 'from-core' (see Tier 5, Figure A5.11b) for elite system transformational leadership (see Table 7.2 for the varieties of leadership; Figures A5.12a and A5.12b). Every single business model invariably contains both value creation and extractive transfer activities: the stronger that those with a higher proportion of the former are (as reflected in the VCr) the greater the elite quality, the institutional quality, and the overall economic, social, and human development of a nation. Incentives for inclusive business model rules must originate from within the elite system, i.e., be instigated by business model insiders in competition with rivals. But how do these drivers of positive change emerge and succeed?

The preconditions for an inclusive political economy are elite cohesion (as discussed in this sub-section) *and* a comprehensive (five-tier) elite separation of powers (illustrated in Figure 3.10). Both of these seemingly irreconcilable elements must go hand in hand. Resolving this dilemma requires the creative tension that comes with a union of the opposites, akin to the balance that is found in *coincidentia oppositorum* as philosophically articulated in McGilchrist (2021). Figure 5.2 depicts what is referred to here as the 'intra-elite quality contest' dilemma: elite quality emerges from intra-elite contests framed by a robust elite separation of powers (here, the simplified three tier rendition) that is bound together rather than stymied by the right levels of elite cohesion.

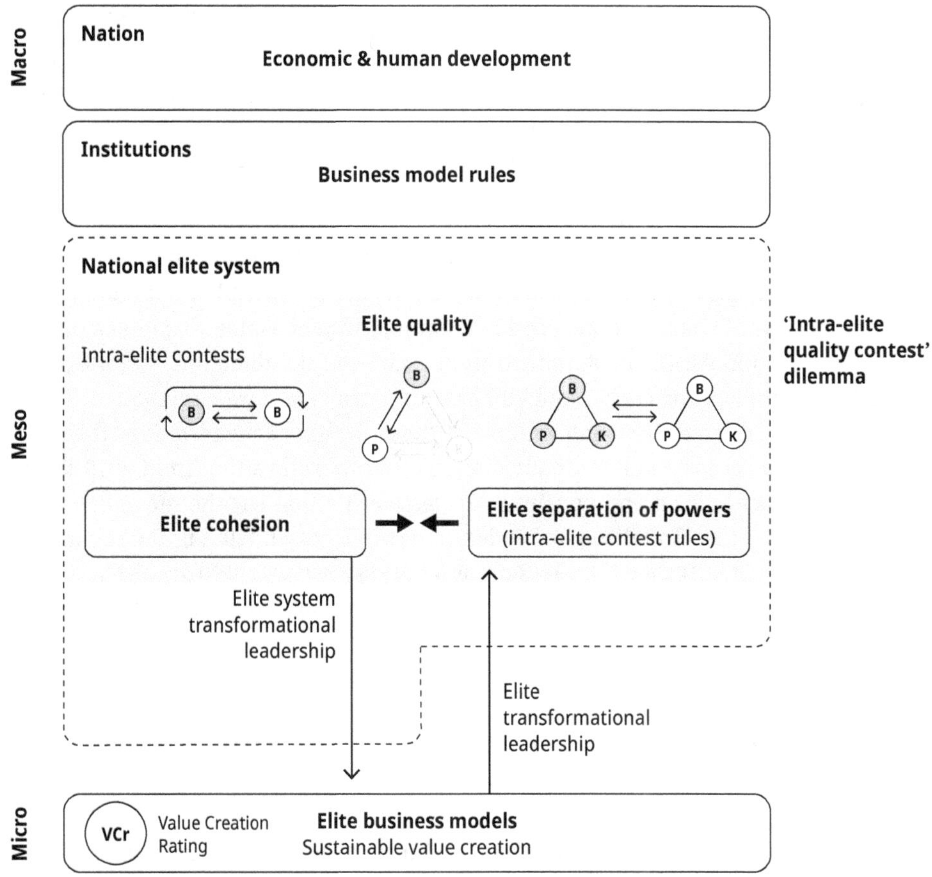

Figure 5.2: The 'intra-elite quality contest' dilemma: Elite cohesion and the separation of powers as joint preconditions in opposition to and in balance with each other for development.

An illustration of how one 'intra-elite quality contest' dilemma was mastered is the Great Depression critical juncture. President Roosevelt had long been deeply embedded in the US elite system when he responded to the aftermath of the 1929 financial crash with the 1933 Glass-Steagall legislation and the 1935 Banking Act amendments that decisively reformed the elite business model rules of finance. Winthrop Aldrich, the president of Chase Bank, was the US President's point man in Wall Street. He was the consummate insider and started an intense intra-elite conflict within the parameters of intra-elite rules. Despite the high stakes and the stress placed on elite coalitions, the system retained elite cohesion and institutional change was affected within the intra-elite contest rules. Tabarrok (1998, p. 8) describes this effective example of elite transformational leadership of the business model:

> Aldrich denounced the connection of investment banking and commercial banking as "almost inevitably leading to abuses." He threw his support behind the Glass bill to separate commercial

> banks and their security affiliates, but he argued that the bill did not go far enough. [. . .] The New York Times made Aldrich's announcement front page news on March 9 with the headline "Aldrich Hits at Private Bankers in Sweeping Plan for Reforms." The Times noted that Aldrich, "who is a representative of the John D. Rockefeller interests," was attacking "some of Wall Street's most powerful figures and their particular interests." More than anyone else, the Aldrich program "strikes directly at the position of J.P. Morgan and Company."

President Obama, on the other hand, was an elite system outsider who, when faced with an analogous financial crash, did not work towards FDR-like deep-seated institutional change aimed at reforming elite business model rules while maintaining elite cohesion (this would have undone President Clinton's financial liberalization a decade earlier, see Section 4.2.4). His administration eschewed the dilemma, took no risks, and did not reinforce the checks and balances (in intra-elite power relations 1, 4, and 5) to articulate an intra-elite contest to make space for elite transformational leadership. The response to the 2008 financial crisis was therefore the timid 2010 Dodd-Frank Wall Street Reform and Consumer Protection Act that left the incumbent elite business model intact. To Silicon Valley luminary Andreessen (2023a), the separation of powers went missing as the lawmaking process "was coopted by the [. . .] big banks. The result is that the same banks that were 'too big to fail' in 2008 are much, much larger now".

5.3.4 The conceptualization of the 'extractive escalation dynamic' conjecture as the end of development

Having established the transition mechanism function of the meso-level elite system for sustainable value creation, the processes by which micro-level transfer-IN elite business models impact and reverberate throughout the economy are now considered. The attractive returns from any single extractive elite business model are hugely detrimental to an economy as it quickly engenders an avalanche of similar requests. The pursuit of rents then eventually characterizes the contests across the political economy and, through its impact on a nation's culture, the non-elite predisposition for value creation (see Epilogue).

Further to the discussion on agglomeration, "an increase in rent-seeking activity may make rent-seeking more (rather than less) attractive relative to productive activity" resulting in an equilibria that the economy settles on (Murphy, Schleifer, & Vishny, 1993, p. 409). The grants of rights, licenses, regulations, barriers, subsidies, and the like (see Table 2.3) are keenly sought after the signal is sent that a value extraction model is institutionally feasible and legitimate. Baumol's (1990) "unproductive, and destructive" entrepreneurial energies and investments will flow into the political non-market and narrative market arenas. As the race to the bottom towards an 'extractive end point' gathers pace, narratives and institutional change in support of extractive models proliferate. Compensation is a preferred theme for such narratives, and quite effective in fostering institutional change:

> The political process often compensates the losers from technical change or international competition in an economically inefficient way, namely by subsidizing or protecting declining industries instead of encouraging the movement of resources to other more productive uses. (Dixit & Londregan, 1995, p. 856)

How extractive elite business models multiply and spread throughout the body of the economy is well illustrated by the earlier example of the Trump Administration's tariffs on steel imports. As a result of this protectionist move, the American Keg Company could not price its products competitively in its domestic market as German and Mexican importers were able to use cheaper steel to produce their products. It therefore lobbied for tariffs on kegs and although it failed—unlike the American "nails and bumpers" sector whose lobbying bagged the tariff—made-in-America kegs still "got protection under a different US trade law called antidumping" (Bown, 2020).

Such 'cascading protection' is a version of the 'extractive escalation dynamic', a conjectured general political economy trap. These extractive sub-optimal equilibria see value transfer business models agglomerate around them and carve out a path dependency (see Section 5.1.1, the 'elite business model critical junctures' conjecture) that once in place is hard to reverse. Elites, especially risk-averse coalitions, become markedly less capable in terms of 'knowledge' and attach their business models to the societal narratives of the day rather than to value creation while resisting all transformation. With pervasive rent seeking, no coalition will rock the boat; elite cohesion becomes excessive (see Section 5.3.3) and is maintained on the back of 'political economy know-how', resulting in economic paralysis and deep if ultimately fruitless social discontent. In Lebanon, even after "Beirut's Deadly Blast Reignites Anger Against Lebanon's Ruling Elite" (Collard, 2020), nothing changed. Acemoglu and Robinson (2019b, p. 23) describe "feedback loops", where extractive/inclusive economic and political institutions bring about vicious/virtuous cycles.

Inclusive, virtuous escalations of value creation models are likewise possible and evidently desirable, as the example of China's special economic zones (SEZs) at the end of the last century demonstrates. In this case, a policy of experimentation was implemented by both top-down measures from political elites and bottom-up efforts from emerging business elites, with institutional arrangements that evolved as market signals were relayed to receptive government ears (Zeng, 2012, pp. 5–7). As a result, a chain reaction of value creation transformed Shenzhen, the inconsequential fishing village of yore, as described in *Forbes*:

> It is said that 90 percent of the world's electronics are made in Shenzhen. With tens of thousands of factories, 5,000 product integrators, and thousands of design houses, this city has become a one-stop-shop for anything consisting of circuits, chips, LEDs, and touchscreens. Shenzhen is also home to 20% of China's P.h.Ds, has the country's highest rate of business owners, and has pro-

> duced more billionaires than anywhere else in China. In 2014, *The Economist* declared Shenzhen to be the best place in the world for a hardware innovator to be. (Shepard, 2016)

A core insight of the ETED is that an 'inclusive escalation dynamic' occurs in nations where preferences in the elite system are inclined towards value creation business models, ushering in economic growth and human development. Conversely, political economies stagnate at sub-optimal equilibria when emerging elites seek to emulate the dominant extractive elite business models of incumbents (see the endosmosis mode of elite circulation in Figure 1.1) and make no attempt at transforming them towards higher sustainable value creation. The allocation of incentives and resources away from value creators marginalizes their activities and diminishes their potential contribution to society (see the unproductive individual responses to extractive value transfers in Table 5.1). In extreme cases, political economies will even manage to jettison the informal underground economy (e.g., Tunisia's notorious attempts to stop street vending). With no value creation opportunities at home, citizens increasingly look for 'exit' responses, including migration, which further aggravate the decline of the production function.

Acemoglu (2006, p. 515) has modeled an economy where "groups with political power, the elite, choose policies to increase their income and to directly or indirectly transfer resources from the rest of society to them". Such an 'extractive escalation dynamic' will eventually hit a dead end, as did the Medici vicious circle. Even the sublime artworks that the Florentine potentates commissioned must have been little consolation to the non-elites and elites alike that were caught in a spiral of economic and human development underperformance: Florence went "from one of the most industrialized and powerful cities in Europe to a marginal province of a foreign empire" (Zingales, 2017, p. 120). Innovation, as discussed in Section 5.1.2, is one of the value and risk creation activities most affected by extractive transfer-IN. Innovation activities "are typically long-term and involve slow accumulation of capital" and will disappear first when rent seekers are given "plenty of opportunities for future expropriation" because value creators are then put in an impossible bind: "for if a project succeeds, the returns are expropriated, whereas if it fails, the innovator bears the cost" (Murphy, Schleifer, & Vishny, 1993, p. 413). Beinhocker highlights the complexity economics perspective where the idealized version of the market rests on an "evolutionary search mechanism that incentivizes deductive-tinkering leading to differentiation and then provides a fitness function on which economic selection can than act" (2006, p. 294). The extractive practices of elite business models require institutions and incentive structures that simply short-circuit such an evolution that stops innovation in its tracks.

The end game of value extraction is a materially impoverished, demoralized society where non-elites and elites alike are disincentivized from creating value and undertaking risk. Tullock (1967, p. 239) describes the generalized exit response in such a scenario: "One way of minimizing loss by theft is to have little or nothing to steal. In a world in which theft and plunder were legal we could expect this fact to lead to a reduction in productive activities and a great expansion in leisure". *Ad absurdum,* extractive cascading dynamics reach a point where economies slide into situations where literally nobody attempts to create value and everybody attempts to steal from the other. Referring once more to Lu Xun's analogy: "Wanting to eat men, at the same time afraid of being eaten themselves, they all eye each other with the deepest suspicion" (1918/1985, p. 47). The Chinese author here masterfully describes the psychological state of a society at the 'extractive end point'.

However, despite massive extractive transfers, most societies do not collapse because the 'extractive end point' is seldom reached due to the remnants of elite cohesion (see Section 5.3.3) and the individual non-elite responses of 'acceptance' and 'informality' (rather than 'exit' or the destructive 'challenge' forms of *struggle,* see Table 5.1). David Pilling, the Africa editor at *The Financial Times* (2023), describes an example of such sub-optimal equilibrium: "Eskom is a study in miniature of what has gone wrong with South Africa. A power utility that cannot keep the lights on, it is gradually draining the country's economy of its lifeblood. It is riddled with corruption, desperately inefficient and daily losing expertise". Surely, even extractive elite agency of the lowest quality can deploy high quality narratives, the opium that ensures a minimum supply of genuine value creators. Otherwise, and without these non-elite contributors, a society of thieves will soon end up with nothing to steal. The cannibalistic society of Lu Xun is in contradiction with itself: everybody might aspire to "eat men" but obviously not everybody can be a cannibal. Narratives opposing such cannibalism constrain the 'universal value extraction propensity of humans' at the non-elite level (see Figure A5.4c) and preserve the social order. Of course, another way to maintain the domestic order is to eat men from other polities through cross-border extractive business models (such as war or colonialism, a discussion that is expanded on in Section 7.3 on elite agency in the international context). In any event, an equilibrium hovering just above the 'extractive end point' should not be an aspiration or be at all confused with development.

A political economy approximating society's 'extractive end point'—a society of thieves—is characterized by elites enjoying the value transfer-IN and transfer-COST of captured rents, while lower down the ladder, non-elites engage in unproductive or leisure activities and seek their own rents in socially wasteful appropriation contests between themselves. The latter includes competition for limited civil service jobs handed out in nepotistic fashion, small businesses that survive on patronage and the clientelistic practices of "asymmetric but mutually beneficial relationships of power and exchange" (Roniger, 2004, p. 353), or job markets distorted by labor unions with links to criminal enterprises (see the labor racketeering discussed in Jacobs & Peters, 2003). Even further down the ladder, one finds pervasive petty and not-so-petty criminality that redistributes from the very poor to the moderately poor (and a few rich bosses), emigration,[116] 'informality' of last resort, possibly a modicum of welfare and charity, and other non-elite responses that keep the system from imploding. As extractive escalation dynamics fester, the ramifications on culture endure over time to the degree that non-elites may come to detest value creation.[117] Nearly everyone in society is hurt in one way or another in a society subsumed by extractive agency. Many coalitions in the elite system also lose when their peers persevere with extraction. Others squander their own value creation potential (e.g., the East German *Sozialistische Einheitspartei Deutschlands* ruling party cadres, Habsburg aristocrats, or even the banks that benefited from loose monetary policy), distracted by pouring their energies and wits into capturing extractive rents.

The extractive escalation dynamic will come to a rest at a given sub-optimal equilibrium point. As discussed, most systems settle on stability slightly before social disintegration—the hypothetical 'extraction end point'—with most wishful rent seekers unable to realize theft and plunder becoming resigned to a *modus vivendi* characterized by marginal value creation and value created but *not* appropriated. This is the definition of underdevelopment, and it is endogenous. As a matter of course, any society, no matter how dysfunctional, must have productive first-order value creation lest it revert to the conditions of primitivism. For any value transfers to occur, the stakeholders of elite business models and non-elite groups must first, through their labor, have engaged in productive activities, no matter how modest. This is the value that will then, to different degrees contingent on elite power and reflecting the development momentum of a particular country, be extracted away. Such extracted groups include entrepreneurs of last resort like the 26-year-old Tarek el-Tayeb Mohamed Bouazizi, the Tunisian street vendor who self-immolated on December 17, 2010, unable to bear the extractive escalation dynamic that materialized in the confiscation of his small wheelbarrow of produce by the police. His tragic 'exit' response was the spark that ignited the futile Arab Spring.

---

116 Emigration is a gift to the extractive elites in the country of origin, the very people that cause this 'exit' response. Individual non-elite 'challenge' responses become less likely, as do both the political confrontation and cooperation options (on aggregate), including the participation of non-elites in intra-elite contests (see Figure A5.8). As a result, the pressure on extractive elites to reform loses steam and salience. On the other side of the phenomenon, immigration is likewise a gift to elites in the recipient country as it increases the supply and reduces the cost of many types of labor, often at the expense of the most vulnerable and less skilled of local non-elites.

117 Welzel theorizes on the "cultural norms toward greater emphasis on responsive and inclusive elites" (2002, p. 269). Conversely, elites steeped in sustainable value creation can foster non-elite cultural transformations towards imaginative value creation and *Lebensfreude*-filled mindsets. Singapore is the quintessential example of a successful elite-guided cultural transformation that has been gently and systematically instilled over generations centered on the notion of a "social national identity" where previously there was none: "Singaporeans desired opportunities to make a good living and realise their potential, regardless of their background", a longing that was first sparked and then actualized in top-down fashion by enlightened elites stressing social cohesion. See: https://www.sg101.gov.sg/social-national-identity/sharedidentity/

5.3.5 Understanding capitalism and its derivations and alternatives through the lens of the ETED

For advanced economies, the World Economic Forum proposes what is essentially a path out of value extraction practices through the notion of stakeholder capitalism, where "long-term value is most effectively created by serving the interests of all stakeholders" (Moynihan & Schwab, 2020, p. 3). Joining together the terms 'stakeholder' and 'capitalism' implicitly points to capitalism being associated—at least in the mind of the public—with extraction from stakeholders. We have already examined how elite business models generate residual income through their value creation and appropriation activities, including through value appropriated but *not* created (transfer-IN). Such second-order value (and risk) transfers include subsidies, regulations, tariffs, monopolies, repressed interest rates, and political-bureaucratic jobs with compensation and privileges above equivalent alternatives (see Table 2.3). Bastiat (1845/1996), Tullock (1967), and Olson's (1993) loaded "plunder" and "theft" notions perfectly fit the description of various extractive rent-seeking modalities. Meanwhile, capitalism's theoretical and idealized version has no rents, no plunder, no theft, and no extractive activities, and the market process "ensures that any economic rents that appear will be dissipated by the forces of competitive entry" (Buchanan, 1980, pp. 8–9). In other words, stakeholder capitalism addresses the fact that real world capitalist economies do not fit capitalism's original paradigm (Bartels, 2008; Stockman, 2013; Nader, 2014, Reich, 2015; Standing, 2016; Holcombe, 2018; Tepper, 2018; Williams & Khanna, 2020; Sharma, 2024b); what we generally refer to as capitalism is clearly not capitalism as it was originally conceived. Varoufakis asserts that "capitalism today is being toppled by a new economic mode: techno-feudalism" (2021). Giblin and Doctorow introduce the concept of "chokepoint capitalism" where elite business models "lock in suppliers and customers and lock out competitors" through a whole "bestiary" of laws (2022, p. 200). So, to what extent are purportedly capitalist political economies still capitalist? This puzzling situation is of concern to academia as is lucidly described in the abstract of the article "Capitalism, Cronyism, and Management Scholarship: A Call for Clarity" (Klein, Holmes, Foss, Terjesen, & Pepe, 2021):

> Capitalism, characterized by private ownership, coordination through markets, and decentralization, is blamed for a variety of economic, environmental, and social ills. These critiques often confuse capitalism with cronyism, a system of government favoritism toward particular firms. We show how this confusion harms management research, teaching, and practice.

Sharma's reflection on "Where Capitalism is Working" (2024a) sees Switzerland, Taiwan, and Vietnam as systems that "show that giving people more economic freedom is still humanity's best hope for economic and social progress". Would a return to the theoretical roots and freedoms of capitalism solve the many complications of economic and human development by reining in the dominance of transfer-IN models that rely on second-order value extraction activities? In the value-free inquiry that characterizes this work's paradigm and looks at the world 'as it is', a system that organizes productive activities and allocates capital and data must primarily be assessed not in relation to its foundational narrative but strictly in terms of its tolerance for rent seeking. That is, the strength of the extractive embrace evidenced by value transfers that are afforded by power; a system is inclusive, capitalist or not, to the degree that it limits extraction and transfer-OUT away from its value creation stakeholders and non-elites (see the test for political and business systems from a non-elite standpoint in Figure 8.3).

The various conceptual refinements in this chapter have tightened the theoretical system of the ETED while establishing a normative development model independent of whether an economy is capitalist, communist, socialist, Catholic, Protestant, Islamic, Confucian, or is best described by any of the world's classified business systems (Hall & Soskice, 2001; Hall & Gingerich, 2009; Witt, Kabbach-Castro, Amaeshi, Mahroum, Bohle, & Saez, 2018). As a result, the world's business and political systems will be scrutinized in Section 8.1.5 through the optics of elite quality by employing the dialectical device of contraposing democracy with authoritarianism, the *leitmotiv* of this inquiry being that all variations are *a priori* valid to the elite theory on the condition that the elite system operates on the long-run premise of sustainable value creation business models. The ensuing operationalization of elite quality in Chapter 6 paves the way for falsifiable hypotheses on matters of human and economic development.

Summary of Chapter 5

Towards the elite theory of economic development (ETED)

Part II of this book supplies a further approximation of the elite theory of economic development from two different angles. While Chapter 4 focused on elite agency constrained and enabled by power and institutions, Chapter 5 is an integrative effort designed to fill lacunae in the inquiry and tighten the overall discourse.

Section 5.1 starts the chapter by considering various aspects of the value creation of elite business models as the micro-level source of economic and human development. It begins with a foundational conjecture for economic development theory, a derivation of the critical junctures hypothesis centered on the elite business model (5.1.1). Innovation activities are then reviewed as the engines of value creation and essential to economic and human development (5.1.2). The section closes by asserting that value can be ascertained as it is moved from one sub-set of society to another, and that measuring such value transfers is not only conceptually feasible and technically manageable, but a necessary task (5.1.3). The starting point here is the 'bona fide value appropriation' (positive) assumption (see Figure A5.4a), with the derived 'revenue is value creation unless value transfer is proven' implication implying that in order to discern the amount of sustainable value creation, value transfers must be ascertained.

Section 5.2 poses three questions to interrogate the theoretical basis of value extraction as the micro-level source of negative economic and human development. The first dips into the extensive theory of rent seeking in economics and asks why it matters (5.2.1). The second seeks to find an answer to the raison d'être for extractive activities, which is possible by gaining an understanding of the underlying causes of non-elite 'acceptance' responses to extraction in the context of the 'impossible exit' conjecture (5.2.2). This is then complemented and nuanced with a discussion on the full range of non-elite responses to being on the receiving end of extractive transfer-IN (5.2.3). A typology of responses to value transfer-OUT by non-elites is proposed with four categories: 'acceptance', 'exit', 'informality', and 'challenge' (summarized in Table 5.1).

Section 5.3 elaborates on the transition from micro-level value appropriation to macro-level performance. Earlier, this work asserted that all elite business models sit on a 'value spectrum' (Proposition 11; Figure 2.10). Section 5.3 starts by further specifying the fundamental conceptual elements that allow the calculation of the two main sustainable value creation (SVC) measurements: the Value Creation Position (VCp) and the Value Creation Rating (VCr) (5.3.1). These include the notions of negative and positive externalities, which are respectively operationalized through transfer-IN/OUT based on the 'quantifiability of value transfers' (finance) assumption. Critically, decision-makers can weight and then offset against each other different value creation and transfer activities (see the implications in Figure A5.4a). As a result, the capital allocation process SVC measurements—with the VCr as the input—can be used to derive 'The Sustainable Value Creation (SVC) Valuation Frameworks' for equity, debt and firms (Table 5.2) with a supporting set of equations (Table 5.3). Risks associated with extractive value transfers are company-specific but non-diversifiable (just like market risk) and hence their minimization is deemed to lead to a lower cost of capital. The subsequent sub-section makes a thematic leap to address another base: the meso-level conceptualization of elite cohesion at the elite system level in relation to the separation of powers (5.3.3). The 'elite cohesion underpins social order' conjecture is tempered by the idea that elite cohesion must exist in balance with a robust elite separation of powers. These two seemingly incompatible elements provide the creative tension for vibrant intra-elite contests to escape stasis or even more regressive outcomes (as is described in Figure 5.2 illustrating the 'intra-elite quality contest' dilemma). In the next sub-section, the 'extractive escalation dynamic' conjecture consolidates an understanding of the micro to macro transition mechanism and explains social and economic decay, as well as its opposite: virtuous, self-reinforcing development achieved through the 'inclusive escalation dynamic' (5.3.4). The closing sub-section continues to consolidate the theory system of this chapter and advances a *leitmotif*: capitalism, or any other business and political system, needs to be judged by the sustainable value creation agency of its elite agency (5.3.5).

To summarize, the two chapters of Part II ('Integration') worked on the idea that elites create and appropriate value through business models that enjoy a bargaining power advantage attained through wins in the market, non-market, and narrative market arenas. Elite business models are in essence but a bundle of value and risk creation and extractive transfer activities. The relative proportions of creation and extraction determine development outcomes. No elite business model is pristine. All benefit from value appropriated but *not* created (transfer-IN) and these amounts (part of revenue/profits) are captured by the VCp measurement (see Figure 5.1a). The extended VCr counterpart additionally accounts for value created but *not* appropriated (transfer-OUT). Taken together, the two are the ETED's proposed micro-level sustainable value creation measurements, and, as such, a key building block of this inquiry. For instance, as the theory enters the field of finance, the VCr is the primary input for 'The Sustainable Value Creation (SVC) Valuation Frameworks' (described in Table 5.2).

Figure 5.3 illustrates the applied arc between the SVC measurements and the SVC valuation frameworks that should act as incentives for the allocation of capital. Both the SVC measurements (conceptualized and operationalized from Chapter 2 onwards), and the SVC valuation frameworks (that now take a central applied role), are tightly coupled with this theory's three assumptions for socio-economic relations and their implications for financial analysis (see Figure A5.4b) and both toolsets are designed to support micro-level decision-making. In the next chapters, additional SVC measurements are introduced to further the quest for macro-level development.

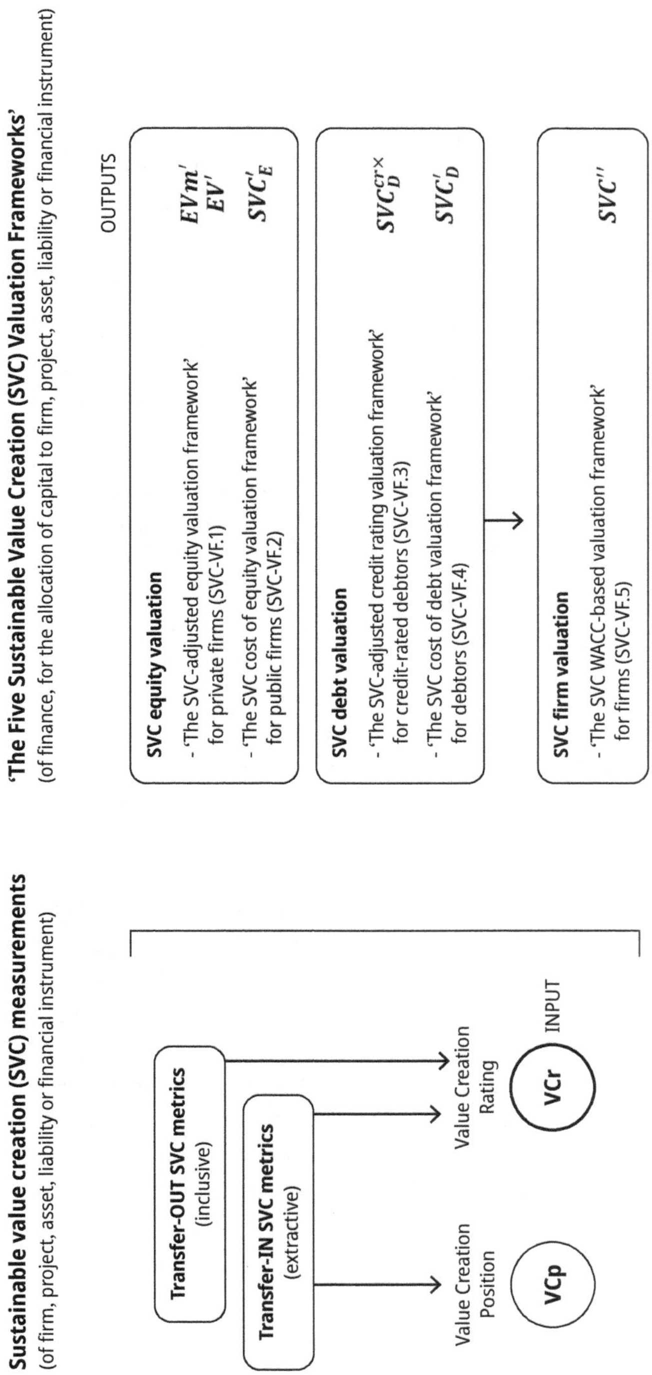

Figure 5.3: The relationship between sustainable value creation (SVC) measurements and sustainable value creation (SVC) valuation frameworks.

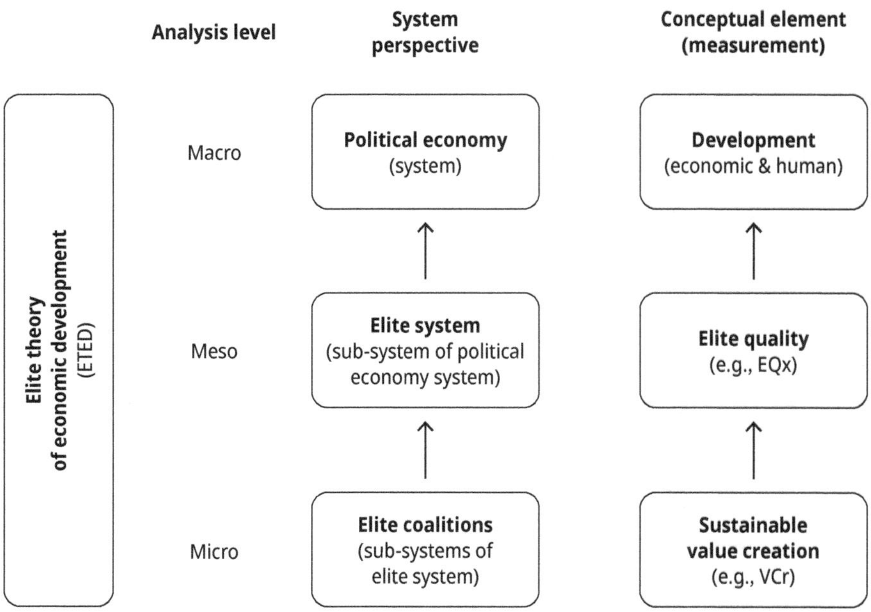

Figure 5.4: The systems perspective of the ETED.

The political economy system, its sub-systems, and their respective levels of analysis, as well as the key conceptual elements and associated measurements are now presented in Figure 5.4 as a summary of the theoretical efforts made in the first two parts of this book. Jointly these outline a general systems framework for elite agency that selectively integrates an eclectic literature.

The inquiry proceeds in Part III by comprehensively considering the 'Implications' of the elite theory that are relevant for policymaking, including measurements and frameworks that aim to quantify and incentivize the aggregate value creation of a given economy's elite business models. The applicability of the ETED to the problems of the real world stem from its central working hypothesis that the sustainable value creation of both firms and an economy can be ascertained. Given its connection to institutional quality, elite quality at the elite system level becomes an essential concern. The inquiry therefore turns to elite quality measurements (starting with the EQx) that are posited to be portals through which it becomes possible to both envisage and steer the prospects for mid- to long-term economic growth and human development.

Part III: **Implications**

The falsifiability of the conceptual elements, propositions, and conjectures introduced in this book, along with the robustness of its theoretical edifice, are open matters. The concern of the final part, 'Implications', shifts to their validation, putative relevance, and implications.

The three chapters of Part III take the theoretical discussion into the realms of the measurable but also to the actionable and the normative. Chapter 6 focuses on measuring sustainable value creation, first at the meso-level through the global and comparative Elite Quality Index (EQx), and then through advances in the operationalization of the parallel micro-level sustainable value creation (SVC) measurements for firms. Chapter 7 considers the various implications of the ETED for research in fields ranging from management science to international relations. The focus of Chapter 8 is on the judgment that is needed for elite leadership, a notion that in its transformational variant impacts society and non-elites and represents the ethical context that knits this work together.

https://doi.org/10.1515/9783110734638-009

Chapter 6
Towards measurements for an elite theory of economic development

The preceding chapters have proposed new relationships between conceptual elements related to the phenomena of elites in line with what conceptual work should be, as per Gilson and Goldberg (2015). These relationships are both grounded in and crafted from the integration of disparate literatures and constitute a general framework that hones in on elite agency. The discrete conceptual elements are integrated into a system, but their refutability necessitates that they are operationalized as measurements to support both research and practice (see Figure P.1). The fundamental idea, relevant for society at large and with practical applications for policymaking and firm strategy, is the primacy of value creation. Yet, as has been repeatably stressed in this book and formalized in the 'all elite agency creates and transfers value' (realist) inference (see Figure 8.7), first-order value creation and second-order value transfers co-exist in every (elite and non-elite) business model (the impulse from Chapter 2 onwards has been to quantify the proportion of value transfer-IN/OUT). Eccles (2024) notes that: "Almost all companies produce negative externalities, even those that have both strong ESG performance and a positive impact on the world". In aggregating value creation and value transfers as fundamental inputs at the elite system level, the balance between the two becomes germane to economic and human development.

To ascertain the overall development potential of a nation and the impact of the national elite system—the central sub-system of a political economy (see Figure 3.8)—requires that elite quality, the critical emergent property, be operationalized. The initial measurement choice is a global comparative composite index of elite quality. This chapter therefore advances the theoretical foundations for nation-level sustainable value creation (SVC) measurements and starts with a review of a comparative index—the Elite Quality Index (EQx)—designed to capture the aggregate micro-level agency of individual elites, the eventual objective being its empirical validation. This index, if robust (OECD, 2008; Santeramo, 2017; Casas, Cozzi, Diebold, & Zeller, 2020; Diebold, 2022), will together with other SVC measurements be reflective of the current state of meso-level national elite systems, a heuristic relevant to international macro-level analysis and, once validated, possibly an input for the econometric approaches used in economic forecasting and macroeconomic modeling.

Section 6.1 opens this chapter by establishing the existence of an elite quality measurement gap. The impact that elite business models have on institutions and development (Figure 4.2) requires an SVC measurement for nations. Section 6.2 presents the operationalization of the meso-level index based on the EQx2024 version, reviewing its architecture and constituent elements, including the indivisible *indicators* that signify and quantify inclusive value creation and extractive value transfers in the politi-

https://doi.org/10.1515/9783110734638-010

cal economy. Narratives and frameworks to interpret the globally comparative EQx are offered in in Section 6.3, while Section 6.4 considers the limitations of the EQx measurement. Section 6.5 presents additional elite quality measurements that are both complimentary and go beyond the EQx, including the meso-level 'Perceptions of Elites Survey' ('PEz') for both elites and non-elites, and the country-specific Elite Quality Rating (EQr). Section 6.6 changes the analytical perspective to advance and operationalize firm-level SVC measurements (like the VCr, see Chapter 2) that mirror elite quality by establishing its constituent elements, the indivisible *metrics* that express and quantify the extractive and inclusive value transfers of the business model. Micro-level 'SVC Metrics Self-assessment Survey' instruments for firms: the 'Self-assessment Value Creation Position' ('self-VCp'), the 'Self-assessment Value Creation Rating' ('self-VCr'), and the 360-degree principal and stakeholder 'Perceptions of Value Creation Survey' ('360-VCz') complete the measurement toolbox. Finally, it is stressed that risk origination and risk transfers are critical for all of the SVC measurements suggested for the ETED.

6.1 Is there a measurement gap?

Preceding chapters have developed the link between institutional change and elite agency. Institutions are already being measured at different levels of aggregation, often for policy-making purposes. Kunčič (2014, p. 135) identified over "30 established institutional indicators" categorized into three groups—legal, political, and economic—to describe "the complete formal institutional environment of a country". The *Ease of Doing Business Index* (The World Bank, 2020) became "a major resource for academics, journalists, and policymakers", and "has passed from being a data source and research tool to playing a role in the political economy of development policy" (Besley, 2015, pp. 99–100). In the same vein, a "World Institutional Quality Ranking" would establish "whether a country is improving or worsening its relative institutional environment" (Kunčič, 2014, p. 135). Specific institutional quality variables are extensively collected and widely used in economic reports and analysis by governments, central banks, and the finance industry. Core statistics on economic growth, inflation, or employment, are often complemented by other measurements describing the political economy or its sub-systems, including indices on economic competitiveness, such as *The Global Competitiveness Report* produced by The World Economic Forum (Schwab & Zahidi, 2020), or on innovation, such as the output pillars of *The Global Innovation Index* produced by the World Intellectual Property Organization (WIPO, 2021).

This work's overarching 'sustainable value creation' framework, with its focus on the business model, requires that elite agency, the microfoundation of institutional formation and change (see Section 4.2), be quantified and aggregated. This connects with the literature on institutional quality as a leading cause of human and economic development (e.g., Acemoglu & Robinson, 2013a). Consistent with the view of this inquiry that elite agency is paramount, Brezis and Temin (2007, p. 5) note in their literature review that: "this small group called the elite has numerous effects on the world economy". What attempts have then been made to operationalize "the elite"? The answer is relatively few given its importance, and the emphasis is usually on institutional aspects. For example, the "Weberianness Scale" (Evans & Rauch, 1999, p. 748) measures the "meritocratic recruitment" of state elites, claiming that elite Weberian characteristics, especially in East Asia, "significantly enhance prospects for economic growth, even when we control for initial levels of GDP per capita and human capital". Such meritocratic determination of elite status is consistent with North, Wallis, and Weingast's (2006) open access social orders,[118] brings Schumpeterian creative destruction to politics, while describing the value creation possibilities in the political economy. Overall, progress has been made in developing data sets that link theory to measurements of elites and their agency since Kerbo and Della Fave (1979, p. 5) observed that while "empirical data have been considered for elite backgrounds, elite interlock, elite unity, and elite influence on public policy [the] interpretation of the data continue to be problematic". For instance, the Swiss elite observatory database "has more than 40,000 entries about political, economic, administrative and academic elites in the 20th and 21st century"[119] and has been used to ascertain transitions of elite coordination models (Bühlmann, Beetschen, David, Ginalski, & Mach, 2017). The *World Elite Database* (WED) is "an international consortium of 70 social scientists founded in 2022" that goes a step further by studying populations "to systematically describe, compare and explain national economic power structures" (Bühlmann et al, 2025, p. 2).

The elite business model perspective central to this inquiry is, however, seldom central to global comparative measurements of institutions and elites. Some notable exceptions do exist, such as *The Crony-Capitalism Index* produced by *The Economist,* which drew from the ideas of Gandhi and Walton (2012) and measured the national aggregate wealth of billionaires active in "rent-heavy industries" (such as casinos, timber, oil, steel, real-estate, defense, or telecoms services) that are "vulnerable to monopoly or that involve licensing or heavy state involvement" (*The Economist*, 2014). As an invaluable—albeit narrow—proxy for the sustainable value creation of national elite systems, the measurement could have been expanded, for instance, by comparing self-made vs inherited billionaires (the former more likely to be value creators) or self-made female vs male billionaires (again, the former are the more probable value creators). Crony capitalism is "an ideology supporting substantial state interference in the allocation of resources; institutions and practices that facilitate rent-seeking" (Klein, Holmes, Foss, Terjesen, & Pepe, 2021, p. 9) that requires

118 The design of educational institutions for meritocratic elite recruitment is a mark of open social order, but might end up achieving the opposite if an institution is captured by incumbent elites. When the French President circulated the idea to close the Ecole Nationale d'Administration (ENA) it appeared consistent with public perceptions of entrenched, unimaginative, and extractives elites. See *The Financial Times* article: "Macron to close training school of French elite" (Abboud, 2021).

119 See the Swiss Elite Database website: https://www2.unil.ch/elitessuisses

"collusion among elites" (Pei, 2016, p. 21). It is an omnipresent risk for all political economies—from China to the most advanced capitalist countries—and it is not unusual for the rentier elite coalitions to be broad-based with non-elite beneficiaries such as local professions, alcohol distributors, or taxicab syndicates (see Mellor and Carpenter's *Bottleneckers*, 2016). Gandhi and Walton's proposal to operationalize the concept in order to address the danger it presents to the economic and social fabric (e.g., Stockman, 2013; Holcombe & Castillo, 2013; Klein, Holmes, Foss, Terjesen, & Pepe, 2021) ought to be a component of any measurement of elite quality.[120]

Despite its discontinuation after just two iterations, it is worth reflecting on the findings, interpretations, and practical implications of the initial *Crony-Capitalism Index*. The closer to a score of 100, the worse the levels of crony capitalism were deemed to be in a country. In its first edition, in 2014, the worst performer (i.e., the economy most prone to crony capitalism) was the Hong Kong Special Administration Region (SAR), with a score nearing 80 out of 100. That score was drastically worse than second-worst placed Russia, with a score close to 20 (the fifth-worst placed territory was Singapore with a score close to 15). Interestingly, in the second edition (*The Economist*, 2016), Hong Kong was purged from the list altogether and the SAR data merged with China's, resulting in that country's ranking falling from being the 4th best to a middling 11th position. The discontinuance by the World Bank of its *Ease of Doing Business Index* due to data manipulation allegations sent shock waves across the world, with Jeffrey Sachs (2021) blaming it on "Anti-China hysteria" and Joseph Stiglitz (2021) calling the affair a "hatchet job" of a geopolitical nature. These developments point to how global indices irritate some and ruffle feathers. They also reveal that the international political economy of measurements often overshadows the political economy measurements themselves.

The dearth of elite agency measurements that can then be linked to development is due to a variety of reasons such as the cross-disciplinary nature of the concept, weak theoretical foundations, and elite fallacies (see Table A4.1) associated with public controversy. The first two chapters of this book partially address these issues by defining elites in terms of elite business models and elite agency in terms of value creation and value transfers (in reference to this work's ontological assumption). Elites operate the highest residual income generating business models that produce varying degrees of sustainable value creation (as in the VCr). The novel claim that this inquiry makes is that the value creation and transfers of micro-level elite business models is directly and indirectly observable, computable, and, when aggregated at the meso-level as elite quality (as in the EQx), sheds light on the prospects for development.

120 The Crony-Capitalism Index, based on Gandhi and Walton's methodology, lives on as the 'CRO', one of the 146 indicators used for the EQx2024 (Casas-Klett & Cozzi, 2024, p. 141). See: https://papers.ssrn.com/sol3/papers.cfm?abstract_id=4779686

The elite quality of an elite system is an essential independent factor at the beginning of a causal chain that leads to degrees of economic and human development performance. Essentially, elite quality is derived from the rent-seeking literature (see Section 5.2.1) and conceptually close to constructs like Turchin's "wealth pump" (2023).[121] Importantly, elite quality as a 'phenomenon' at the system level has a nature that precisely conforms to O'Connor's understanding of emergence since it "is at once grounded in and yet emergent from the underlying material structure with which it is associated" (1994, p. 91). Elite quality emerges from the sustainable value creation of elite business models seeking to maximize profit. Elite business models, which are neither uniform nor homogenous but are all embedded in the complex national elite system, interact with each other and co-evolve. Elite quality then emerges as an antecedent of institutional quality. In this theoretical paradigm, institutional quality refers to the inclusive/extractive rules (for business models and intra-elite contests) that enable or constrain elite business models. The premise is that elite agency causes institutional change (see Proposition 14) and is thus ultimately responsible for the definitive dependent variables in the economy, those describing human and economic development. This reasoning is depicted in Figure 6.1.

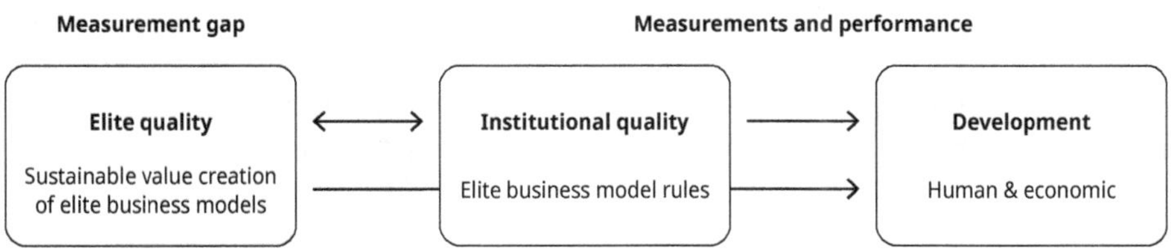

Figure 6.1: The relationship between elite quality (independent variable), institutional quality, and development performance (dependent variables).

The initial SVC measurement of elite quality is a synthetic composite index (Freudenberg, 2003; Ivaldi, Bonatti, & Soliani, 2016) similar to indices measuring other discrete economic phenomena such as the previously cited examples of competitiveness or innovation. The EQx is a global comparative ranking that highlights the relative elite quality

121 Technically, the various extractive activities of a business model consolidate into a single "wealth pump". Business models are the analytically relevant object at the micro-level from both the VCA and the macro-level economic development perspectives. When an examination of the political economy takes the general non-elite viewpoint, one might think of a single wealth pump for a nation, which is what the elite quality conceptual element does. When the sum of all pumps is conceived of as such an outsized device, the inimical effects of transfers on general welfare become more apparent. While distinct from the 'national business model', elite individuals can be beneficiaries of multiple business models and hence derive their residual income from multiple pumps. The 'net value extraction' component of the value chain (see Figure 2.7) can be considered an operationalization of a given organization's wealth pump.

of a specific country (in relation to other countries), while a longitudinal dataset, the 'Panel-EQx' ('PEQx', see Casas-Klett, Cozzi, Diebold, & Tonn, 2024, pp. 32–35)[122] highlights its evolution. A composite or "aggregated index comprising individual indicators" (Nardo, Saisana, Saltelli, & Tarantola, 2005, p. 4) aims to provide insights for both research and practice and is beneficial due to its "ability to integrate large amounts of information into easily understood formats and are valued as a communication and political tool" (Freudenberg, 2003, p. 2). The benefits of such a measurement also emanate from the fact that "rankings are seen as a form of information intermediation, as comparative orderings, or as a means for surveillance and control" (Rindova, Martins, Srinivas, & Chandler, 2018, p. 2175). An index that describes the sustainable value creation of elites will invite debate, as "measurements are not neutral: they affect behavior and vice versa" (Mazzucato, 2019), an assertion that is in the vein of the ETED.

The annual EQx, first released in 2020, has been undergoing comprehensive development and validation (Diebold, 2022). Based on relevant literature, the preparatory and initial steps described here (following the index construction methodology of the OECD, 2008) have established the conceptual index architecture that operationalizes many of the ideas associated with elite agency, sustainable value creation, and elite quality presented in this inquiry. Finally, it must be emphasized that the EQx is a meso-level measurement that uses macro-level data series (indicators) as proxies for elite agency. More intricate and refined bottom-up micro-to-meso approaches for computing elite quality that use consolidated micro-level SVC measurements based on firm data (metrics) are also proposed later in this chapter (Section 6.5.2).

6.2 The EQx operationalization of elite quality: A four-level conceptual architecture

This section discusses the Elite Quality Index (EQx), the comparative SVC measurement for the 'sustainable value creation of nations' in both conceptual and methodological terms, starting with the two sub-indices (6.2.1) and the two index dimensions (6.2.2). It then takes a step back to present the overall index architecture (6.2.3) before delving into the four index areas and the 12 pillars, each of which have their own indicators (6.2.4). Finally, the weighting methodology is discussed (6.2.5). Each subsection introduces specific EQx terms, a vocabulary that is summarized in Table A3.2.

A composite index is built on its multiple data sources. These are conceptually indivisible discrete indicators that jointly make up the index. For the EQx, each of these indicators must represent a quantifiable phenomenon in the political economy that provides evidence of first-order value creation or extraction (i.e., second-order

122 Data, featuring country comparison webtools, available at: https://www.unisg.ch/en/research/research-in-focus/elite-quality-index/

value transfers). An EQx indicator is a data set reflecting the relative positions of nations and their relevant elite business models along a conceptual 'elite system value spectrum' (paralleling the firm-level value spectrum set out in Figure 2.10) that ranges from absolute value creation to absolute value extraction (transfers). When aggregated (see the initial methodology paper by Casas-Klett, Cozzi, Diebold, & Zeller, 2020), these indictors specify in global comparative terms the value creation of the meso-level elite system. Venture capital, school life expectancy, and free trade policies all constitute evidence of sustainable value creation by elite business models. Monopolies, trade barriers, or the existence of modern-day slavery are extractive transfers and proof of the contrary. These six examples point to the diversity and dynamism of elite business models and how they are manifested in society, as well as to the need for clear conceptual categories and a logical structure to meaningfully arrange indicator datasets in the index.

6.2.1 Two sub-indices: 'Power' and 'Value'

The operationalization of elite quality requires an architecture that sorts and logically organizes diverse component indicators. Based on the preceding theoretical discussion and the centrality of sustainable value creation, the key foundational element in this endeavor is 'value' which is expressed as two sub-indices: 'power' and 'value'. The data that directly measures present value (its creation or extraction/transfer) is incorporated into the 'value' sub-index. Given the forward-looking nature of the index, potential future value (its creation or extraction/transfer) is then measured in the 'power' sub-index. Our earlier review of power led to the conjecture that power represents future potential (in probabilistic terms) value transfers, i.e., extraction (see Section 4.5). It is commonly accepted that both political and economic power enable elites to "extract a great deal of such rent from everybody else" (see Wolf, 2019); hence, the 'power as potential future value extraction' assumption of the ETED. Power is a predictor of extractive value transfers because it is a pre-condition for 'value appropriated but *not* created', one that—and this is critical and relates to the leadership notion of this work—is not necessarily deployed by elites for extractive purposes even if it is abundantly possessed.[123] Therefore, in the weighting schema of the index, the 'power' sub-index has a lower weight than the 'value' sub-index (see Section 6.2.5). Since power is *conditio sine qua non* for extraction, the 'power' sub-index is referred to as sub-index I. The 'value' sub-index is referred to as sub-index II.

---

123 Relatedly see the 'inextinguishable value creation option of elites' assumption, Section 2.2.1.

6.2.2 Two index dimensions: 'Political' and 'Economic'

Each dataset or indicator incorporated in the index belongs to one of two dimensions: 'political' or 'economic' (measuring the respective agency of political and economic elites). The 'value' sub-index (measuring value creation at present) and the 'power' sub-index (measuring probable value creation in the future) in conjunction with the two dimensions, 'political' and 'economic', produce a 2x2 matrix (Figure 6.2) with four index areas or sectors. All indicators in the EQx are allocated to one of these index areas: 'political power', 'economic power', 'political value', or 'economic value' as is represented in the 'The Political Economy Power and Value Matrix' of Figure 6.2.

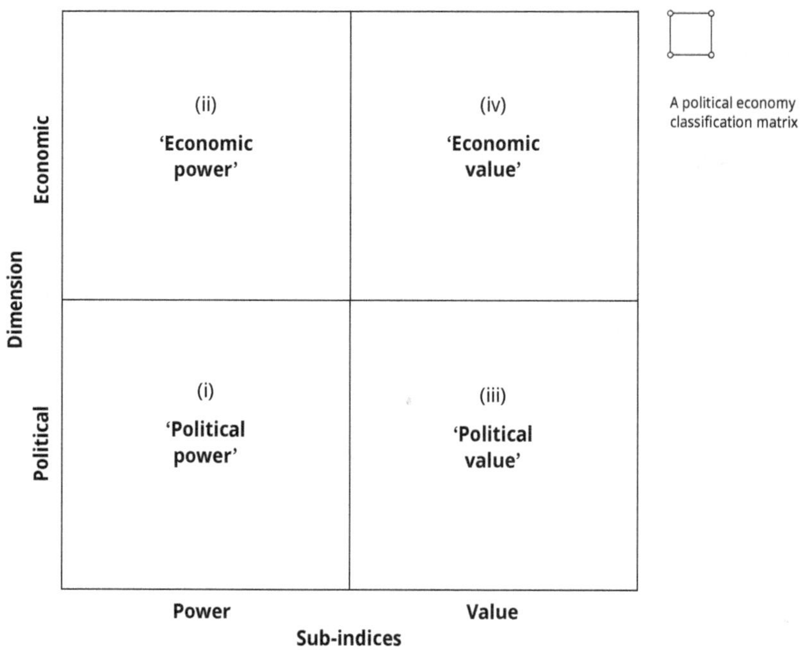

Figure 6.2: The Political Economy Power and Value Matrix.[124]

6.2.3 Index architecture

The index is constructed in four levels. The higher three levels of the index are the result of data that has been normalized, aggregated, and weighted as methodologically appropriate. The EQx aggregate score is given at level 1. The two sub-indices

124 Note that the quadrants of Figures 6.2 and 6.4 use roman numerals that are consistent with the EQx architecture's annotation standards.

('power' and 'value') are combined with the two dimensions ('political' and 'economic') yielding the four index areas discussed in the previous sub-section (see Figure 6.2), all of which are structurally set at level 2. The structure becomes more granular with the level 3 categories. Each of the four index areas has 3 pillars (resulting in a total of 12 pillars at level 3). Each pillar embodies a clear and academically grounded idea that conceptually fits with one of the four index areas of level 2. Each pillar at level 3 then in turn becomes the conceptual home for the level 4 indicators. These indivisible indicators have their origin in datasets taken from multiple sources. Each dataset has a rationale for its materiality in terms of value creation/extraction (see Casas-Klett & Cozzi, 2024, pp. 136–172; Section 6.4.1) and a value creation optima is determined (Section 6.4.2) as the data undergoes methodological refinement to be used as an indicator by the index. EQx indicators constitute fundamental evidence of meso-level value creation/extraction and represent phenomena emanating from elite business models that are relevant for the macro aggregate level. Each indicator is allocated to one of the 12 pillars based on conceptual proximity (this allocation may involve judgment calls as some indicators have a conceptual affinity to more than one pillar). The 12 proposed pillars (3 for each index area) are identified and situated within the architecture in Figure 6.3.

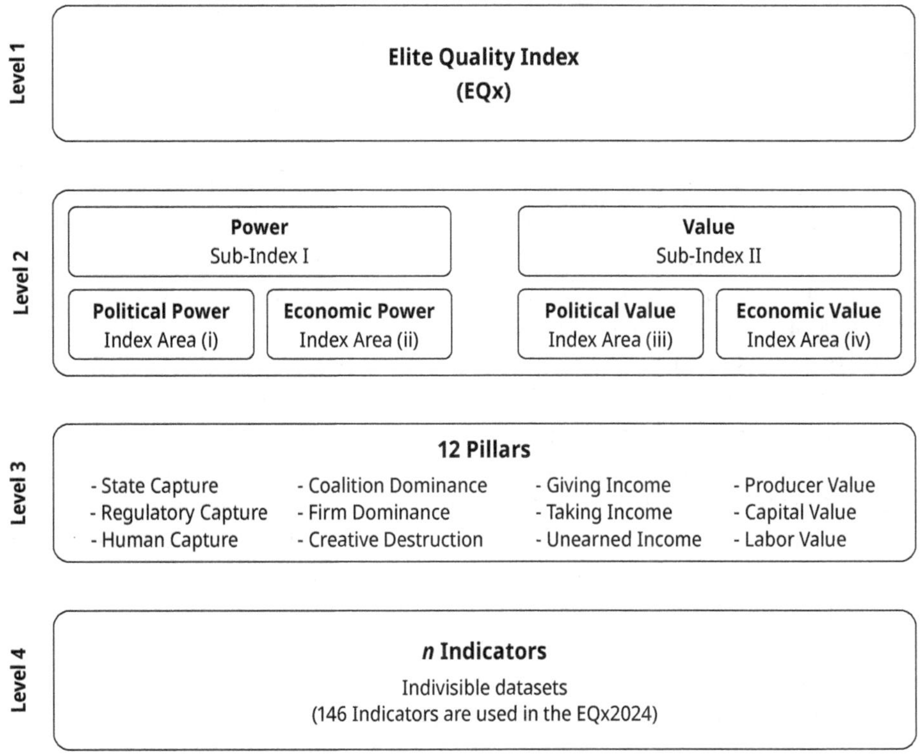

Figure 6.3: The four-level architecture of the Elite Quality Index (EQx).

6.2.4 Index area pillars and exemplar indicators

This section introduces and discusses all 12 of the EQx pillars in the four index areas and provides exemplar indicators for illustration purposes (for actual EQx indicators, see the global elite quality reports, Casas-Klett & Cozzi, 2020, 2021, 2022, 2023, 2024).

Power (sub-index I) is the theme of the first two index areas, representing the ability of elites to realize their preferences (see Section 4.2), and has been conceptualized in this work (see Figure A5.1) as 'money', 'might', and 'mind', the result of wins in the three political economy contest arenas (market, non-market, and narrative market). Once elite coordination leadership secures the "common will" (Arendt, 1970) and 'the extraordinary lever' (see Figures A5.3a and A5.3b), underlying power is converted through elite business model leadership into residual income (the flow is described in Figures 4.1 and 4.4). The 'political' and 'economic' dimensions of the index mean that power is measured through both of these lenses.

The first index area is (i) political power, and its grounding idea, one that clearly lends itself well to operationalization, is the notion of 'capture'. Associated with the work of Stigler (1971), or Laffont and Tirole (1991), the concept of capture emerges from theories on regulation. Regulation has been viewed as "simply an arena in which special interests contend for the right to use government power for narrow advantage" (Levine & Forrence, 1990, p. 167). Using this notion, the first two pillars are proposed. Datasets that provide evidence of the capture of state apparatus, including the government, are assigned to the 'state capture' pillar (i.1). "Elites organize" state capture whose "essence lies in a distinct network structure in which corrupt actors cluster around parts of the state allowing them to act collectively in pursuance of their private goals to the detriment of the public good" (Fazekas & Tóth, 2016, pp. 320–321). Mazzucato and Collington (2023) have created a polemic by arguing that state capture is at present organized by knowledge elites such as McKinsey, Boston Consulting Group, Bain & Company, PwC, Deloitte, KPMG, and EY. This pillar includes indicators such as political turnover, social mobility or corruption. The second pillar is the 'regulatory capture' pillar (i.2) that directly addresses the aforementioned capture by zeroing in on the enabling rules. Its indicators include measures of overall institutional quality such as expropriation risk, but also power phenomena associated with institutional change, such as permitting crony capitalism (see Section 6.1). Lastly in the political power index area, the 'human capture' pillar (i.3) concerns itself with the power of elite business models over the agency of people. Its component indicators measure diverse facets of power applied in an extractive way over humans through business models that, for example, lack gender inclusiveness, absent academic freedom, or add to modern-day slavery.

For the economic power index area (ii), the constitutive concept is 'dominance'; that is, a phenomenon that is an anathema to free markets and Smithian competitive processes, and to capitalism as originally described. Concentrations of economic power are obviously expected in non-capitalistic and authoritarian regimes but are also amply found in ostensibly capitalistic and democratic systems (Wedel, 2009; Zingales, 2012; Standing, 2016; Tepper, 2018; Streeck, 2016). The relevance of these is underscored by empirical "evidence that competition, as measured by increased numbers of competitors or by lower levels of rents, is associated with a significantly higher rate of total factor productivity growth" (Nickell, 1996, p. 724), now a generally accepted understanding (see the work of Geroski, 1989; Lever & Nieuwenhuijsen, 1999). Thus, the economic power index area (ii) first puts forth an Olsonian 'coalition dominance' pillar (ii.4) focusing on the influence of agglomerated business models on the power of groups in specific industries or labor market domains. The power of individual organizations is then ascertained with the 'firm dominance' pillar (ii.5). The coalition dominance pillar measures economic complexity, unionization rates, or the economic output of top industries as a percentage of GDP, while the firm dominance pillar includes indicators on the profitability of leading firms, such as the prevalence of SMEs, or the relative economic power of billionaires (including self-made billionaires) in an economy. The third pillar in the economic power index area is the opposite of both the above: the anti-dominance Schumpeterian notion of 'creative destruction' (ii.6). Evidence of unimpeded Hayekian markets and of the free realization of humanity's creative and innovative potential is represented here through indicators that measure firm entry and exit ratios, and facets of entrepreneurship such as government support or access to venture capital.

The third and fourth index areas—'political value' and 'economic value'—are concerned with the theme of sub-index II, value, and its creation and transfer. Again, value represents the ability to create something that humans determine is worth appropriating. The political value index area (iii) has three pillars all grounded by the concept of income. The first two pillars focus on income 'given' (value created by a political principal benefiting a stakeholder) and income 'taken' (value transferred to a political principal that is appropriated from a stakeholder). Transfers are a direct result of intra-elite contests in the non-market arena (through the agency of political elites), and, more indirectly, via narrative market arena outcomes (through the agency of knowledge elites). Indicators therefore conceptually measure how power endowments attained in the power domains of politics and society are utilized for either value creation or value transfers, i.e., extraction.

The first pillar in the political value index area (iii) is termed 'giving income' (iii.7) and the analytical emphasis is on political giving i.e., political principal value creation (benefiting non-elite stakeholders). Of importance are the sizes of the underlying transfer amounts and, most critically, what happens to the income allocated in the political sphere from a value creation perspective and in comparative terms. Thus, this pillar measures the positive impact of income transfers and whether these enable further value creation by including indicators on education, Internet infrastructure, or health. Also incorporated are indicators that potentially reflect extractive transfer business models like subsidies, regional redistribution, or expenditure on general public services as a deviation from an optimum. The second pillar is 'taking income' (iii.8) and the analytical emphasis here is on non-elite stakeholders that, as a result of power differentials, have to transfer their value (i.e., in SVC measurement terms, their value transfer-OUT to a principal's transfer-IN). This pillar's indicators measure the size and burden of the transfers away from first-order 'producers' that are implemented—or permitted—by elites in the political sphere in delivering or not delivering on their public (giving) mandates. Thus the 'taking income' pillar measures transfers away from those generating value and includes indicators on taxation, such as the delta between capital gains tax and income tax. Datasets on criminal activity such as the homicide rate or the prevalence of substance abuse disorders are also included since it is the responsibility of every state and political elite to eliminate such onerous transfer business models and the elites that benefit from them. The third political value pillar focuses on 'unearned income' (iii.9) and is comprised of indicators pointing to income that the principal beneficiaries have 'not earned' as the value cannot be attributed to their first-order productive agency, but instead secured from transfers facilitated by wins in the non-market and narrative market arenas. Indicators for this pillar include state monopolies and evidence of specific intergenerational transfer phenomena (the beneficiaries of transfer-IN from the current generation at the expense of the next, see Galloway, 2024; Rüdiger & Casas-Klett, 2022; Krznaric, 2020; Stern, 2006), such as debt, and most crucially, environmental degradation.[125]

The fourth and final index area is economic value (iv), which is articulated by market arena concepts. Value is created or extracted in the three markets of the economy: goods and services, capital, and labor. Indicators in these pillars measure both positive value creation and extractive transfer activities in all three markets. The 'producer value' pillar (iv.10) examines the market of goods and services. It includes indicators such as globalization, as well as trade freedom and its opposite, discriminatory or liberalizing "state interventions affecting trade in goods and services, foreign investment and labor force migration" as, for instance, is monitored by the *Global Trade Alert*.[126] Other indicators in this pillar function on the premise that optima can be developed, such as the optimum size of a given industry in the economy (e.g., real estate, military, or healthcare as a percentage of GDP, where both excesses and deficits point to rent seeking). The 'capital value' pillar (iv.11) addresses capital markets. It

125 ETED micro-level sustainable value creation (SVC) measurements (such as the VCp or VCr) incorporate metrics that reflect the 'nature stakeholder' assumption (see Section 2.2.2, Figure 2.5), as do measurements of aggregate sustainable value creation at the meso-level such as elite quality. Elite business models that take unearned environmental resources (such as healthy and fertile soil) engage in extractive intergenerational transfers if they deplete these (turning fertile soil into unproductive dirt through industrial agricultural practices that sap its microbiome). The impact of all these activities on society is stressed by models of stochastic growth on the technological evolution of humankind, with the more extreme of these positing a 90% likelihood of the self-destruction hypothesis within the next 20–40 years, meaning the "catastrophic collapse in human population, due to resource consumption" (Bologna & Aquino, 2020, p. 8).

126 See: https://www.globaltradealert.org

includes indicators that reflect the valuable services that capital markets provide in the economy, such as unicorns hatched or financial inclusiveness, as well as evidence of capital rents such as when non-market mechanisms determine the price of money (e.g., deviation from a neutral interest rate). Phenomena associated with 'unemployed capital' such as share buybacks (where "companies now buy back more stock [. . .] than they issue" Roosevelt Institute, 2019) or ballooning reserve balances with Federal Reserve Banks (Board of Governors of the Federal Reserve System, 2024)[127] point to transfers as damaging to non-elites as unemployed labor. Finally, the 'labor value' pillar (iv.12) relates to the labor markets. It includes indicators that describe labor value creation as well as value transfers, such as the gender wage gap, youth unemployment, or the delta between real wages and productivity increases.

The four index areas are presented in Figure 6.4, each with their own conceptual logic that is consistent with the underlying ideas of the index's architecture.

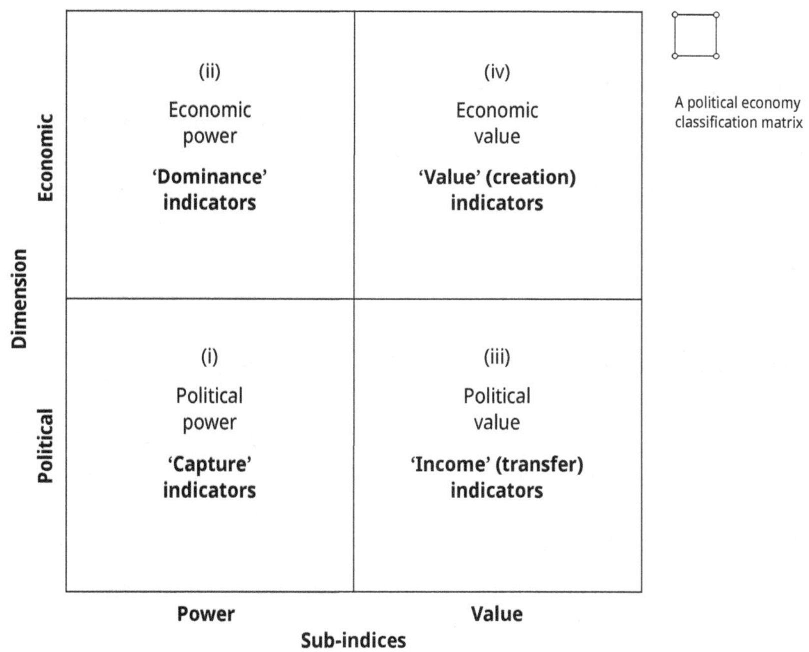

Figure 6.4: The classification logic for elite quality indicators.

The architecture of the EQx can be summarized as follows. Its foundational, indivisible elements are the indicators (level 4), each reflecting a specific value creation or

127 The amounts that depositary institutions park at the US central bank have grown exponentially as a result of 2008 monetary policy, from weekly averages of around US$ 10 billion to balances well above US$ 3 trillion. See: https://fred.stlouisfed.org/series/WRESBAL

extractive transfer phenomenon associated with the elite business models of the political economy and consistent with the ontological assumption of this work that 'value is created or transferred' (Figure A5.4c). Every indicator has a conceptual fit within one of the 12 pillars (level 3). Each of the 12 pillars in turn belong to one of the four index areas which result from combining the two 'political' and 'economic' dimensions with the two sub-indices of 'power' and 'value' (level 2). The two sub-indices of 'power' and 'value' then aggregate up to the final EQx index (level 1). Level 3 pillars receive data from the level 4 indicators; level 2 sub-indices and index areas in turn receive data from the level 3 pillars and; the level 1 index is informed by the level 2 sub-indices and index areas. Given that the EQx is designed for policy action and targets weighted structural reform (see Table 7.1), the number of indicators that could be used for the index could potentially grow from the present total of over a hundred to many hundreds on the condition that every dataset reflects a discrete value creation/extraction phenomena in the political economy and does so with a consistent methodology across the countries it covers. In fact, for the EQx to remain meaningful and relevant over time, its constructors must identify and collect data on as many value creation and transfer phenomena as possible. That includes evidence of emerging elite business model realities brought about by fundamental economic shifts (e.g., technology or demographics) and exogenous shocks (e.g., pandemics or wars). However, not all indicators have an equal impact in economic and human development terms, and this leads us to consider a key step in the construction of the index: the weighting methodology.

6.2.5 Conceptual positions on index weighting and methodology

Consistent with the OECD (2008) and as expounded in the EQx methodology paper (Casas-Klett, Cozzi, Diebold, & Zeller, 2020), the weighting of index components is well served by a combination of the budget allocation process (BAP) and the more stable conceptual deliberation method. "The main advantages of BAP are its transparent and relatively straightforward nature and short duration" where experts, ideally "representing a wide spectrum of knowledge and experience to ensure that a proper weighting system", allocate a "budget" of points "based on their experience and subjective judgment of the relative importance of the respective indicators" (OECD, 2008, p. 96). The BAP is suited for indices where indicators are added (and withdrawn) depending on shifts in reality and the availability of data, as is the case with the EQx. The EQx weighting is discussed in detail the aforementioned paper and in the elite quality reports (Casas-Klett & Cozzi, 2020, 2021, 2022, 2023, 2024), where it is noted that the BAP is used for the weighting of pillars (pillar weights within each index area) and indicators (indicator weights within each pillar).

Conceptual deliberation is a method that has been employed in global comparative indices to establish weighting. For instance, the *Global Peace Index* gives a 60%

weighting for internal peace and a 40% weighting for external peace on the basis that internal peace is correlated with external conflict (Institute for Economics & Peace, 2019, p. 86). In the EQx, conceptual deliberation is used for weighting 'power' sub-index I vs 'value' sub-index II (conceptual deliberation 1); for weighting the 'political power' index area (i) vs the 'economic power' index area (ii) (conceptual deliberation 2); and finally, for weighting the 'political value' index area (iii) vs the 'economic value' index area (iv) (conceptual deliberation 3).

Conceptual deliberation 1 assigns weights to 'power' and 'value'. While power is a pre-condition for value transfers, it is here conceived in terms of potential future value extraction and the 'present doubles future' assumption is made. Thus, the 'power' sub-index is discounted to half the level of the 'value' sub-index, at a 1/3:2/3 weighting (rounded to 33% and 67%). Conceptual deliberations 2 and 3 relate to the split between the 'political' and 'economic' dimensions and their respective weightings within the 'power' and 'value' sub-indices. The rationale for this judgment call is partially like conceptual deliberation 1; elite business models in the 'political' dimension are deemed to eventually consolidate and grow into the 'economic' dimension. Critically, however, the economic sphere has a higher impact on general value creation and the 'economics doubles politics' assumption is made. Hence, for conceptual deliberations 2 and 3, the 'political' dimension is given half the consequence of the 'economic' dimension (for consistency, the 33% and 67% weightings are again applied). Finally, and when there is a strong theoretical case to stress a specific value creation or extraction phenomena, conceptual deliberation weightings for specific indicators (or even pillars) could also be assigned (e.g., for entrepreneurship or risk capital indicators in the creative destruction pillar in light of Schumpeterian theory).

The conceptual deliberation weightings described were established for the original iterations of the Elite Quality Index, are consistent with the logic of the ETED, and will be revisited as necessary. With regard to the BAP weightings, the constructors of the index must periodically confirm or update indicator weightings and so adjust the balance between consequence, data availability, and consistency over time. The addition of specific domain experts to the BAP panel, such as those with specialized knowledge in key areas like labor, innovation, tax, education, or diversity and inclusion, is essential to keep the EQx relevant. Other aspects of the index construction methodology add precision to the measurement and to its conceptual development (see Casas-Klett, Cozzi, Diebold, & Zeller, 2020; and Diebold 2022 for aggregation methods, the normalization process, the imputation of missing data, robustness tests, or detail on the index construction steps).

6.3 Interpreting elite quality: Narratives and frameworks

The EQx provides a position on elite quality for 151 country scores that jointly make up the global ranking. This section discusses how to interpret SVC measurements for nations. The anchor is the sustainable value creation elite perspective of the political economy that, as a paradigm that diverges from mainstream economics, necessitates discrete analytical tools. This is evident from the narratives and economic prospects for countries that emerge as researchers and pundits interpret EQx scores and connect the four levels of the index architecture (indicators, pillars, index areas/sub-indices, and ultimately, the index itself). Each data point reveals, in global comparative terms, aspects of elite business models that reflect actual or potential future value creation and extraction. The big picture analysis is the fulcrum for institutional change and social and political movements (see Figure A5.12a) that center on elite and elite system transformational leadership (see Table 7.2). New narratives are essential for the advancement of sustainable value creation via the agency of elite business model principals and beneficiaries that materialize in institutional and (de)regulatory measures in the context of weighted structural reform (see Section 7.1.5, Figure 7.1). Critically, the analysis must link the SVC measurements, including the EQx, to ongoing intra-elite contests and the contending models in order to select the right policy options for reform and ground visions of desirable institutional change in winning grand narratives (6.3.1). The State of the Elite System Framework for the political economy is a tool for this purpose (6.3.2).

6.3.1 The EQx supports the analysis of narratives and a big picture view

The postmodern distrust of *metarécits*, or "metanarratives" (Lyotard, 1979) is misguided; grand narratives do matter and are extremely useful in supporting elite business models (see Proposition 14 on institutional change and the narrative market). The EQx can contribute to the benchmarking of such big pictures with its scores in the 'power' and 'value' sub-indices. "Economic and political institutions (and ideas) serve essentially facilitative, adaptive, obstructive, or destructive roles in economic and social change" (Elliott, 1978, p. 93). Change is often initiated by narratives and their embedded ideas (Figure 3.5) and is overdue if one believes blunt views like "today we have the most unfree market system ever created. It is deeply corrupt because its leaders claim it is the opposite of what it is becoming" (Standing, 2016, p. 1). Welzel suggests that non-elites embracing "emancipative values are readily prepared to measure their elites by the rankings, scores, and evaluations" (2002, p. 292, see also Sections 3.3.2 and 8.1.3), while this inquiry contends that transformation occurs when elites appraise themselves.

The interpretation of elite quality measurements can trigger fundamental political economy questions that may prove overly broad, strategic, and certainly distracting to the politician preparing for the next election, the treasury official dealing with financial upheavals, or the analyst working with newly released economic data. However, far from being impractical, the concrete demonstration of value creation or extraction (transfer-IN/OUT) by elite agency and its location in the political economy landscape—often under the cover of narratives—is meant to support policymakers focus on the right nooks and crannies of the economy. The fact that a measurement of elite quality can pierce through aggregates and shine a light on micro-level phenomena provides direct connections with the actual experiences and challenges faced by society's diverse stakeholders. Understanding the political economy structures keeping the big picture in place, and how these are driven by specific business models, adds texture and insight to large-scale social or historical analyses. It also supplies the bases for specific legal, (de)regulatory, and institutional changes that flow from this work's applied frameworks for policy (e.g., see Table A4.4). Narratives have the uncanny ability to enter and shape intra-elite contests that determine new business model rules (see Figures 4.3 and A5.12b).

Policymakers, investors, CEOs, and journalists consider longer horizons and require a broad perspective. Elite quality widens the lens and sharpens the focus as its measurements suggest whether an economic system enjoys an "ordered market" of capitalism, or whether "non-market decision-making" based on power and resulting in extraction has become prevalent, as Buchanan (1980, p. 14) once claimed. How much Hayekian competition (1948/1958) is still left in the political economies of capitalist societies, or how much non-elite value creation is found in communist regimes, is inferable from an analysis of the EQx 'power' sub-index and its components. In times of uncertainty—whether caused by inflation, war, or AI—original frameworks and measurements that facilitate a view of the overall direction that a society is heading are helpful for crafting new visions.

The ETED has the Popperian obligation to make its logic falsifiable and, in this vein, it is *a priori* agnostic regarding the grand narratives that materialize in the world's political systems (recounted by Almond, 1956; Hall, 1993) and business systems (see Hall & Soskice 2001; Hall & Gingerich, 2009; Witt, Kabbach-Castro, Amaeshi, Mahroum, Bohle, & Saez, 2018) and the contributions that they make to value creation or transfers. Instead, the approach is to focus on empirical validation through refutable comparative tests of political and business systems (see Figure 8.3) that leverage EQx scores (as well as alternative SVC country-based measurements such as the bottom-up micro-to-meso level Elite Quality Rating, see Table A3.1a). Establishing the degree to which elite value creation and development performance correlates with business and political systems may eventually lead to across-systems learning, but the more immediate and practical objective of the EQx's interpretative work is to provide big picture clarity about key shifts and patterns in the political economy by highlighting putative critical junctures where elite quality (or power, or creative destruction) improves or worsens, along with the incentives responsible for such ascendant or declining trajectories, thus locating the areas of the economy where inclusive reforms would yield the most gains.

6.3.2 The EQx supports the construction of frameworks for the analysis of the political economy

The EQx annually updates its scores and rankings across its four architecture levels, thereby offering opportunities for political and knowledge elites to construct dynamic, responsive policy frameworks to address weaknesses. As a starting point, this inquiry proposes The State of the Elite System Framework for the political economy, a comparative classification system of national elite systems for domestic reform purposes. Here, the two cardinal properties of the political economy, the two EQx sub-indices, are visualized as a matrix: 'power' (potential future value extraction) and 'value' are placed on the x-axis and y-axis respectively to describe a given political economy in terms of the sustainable value creation of its elite system via four distinct quadrants:

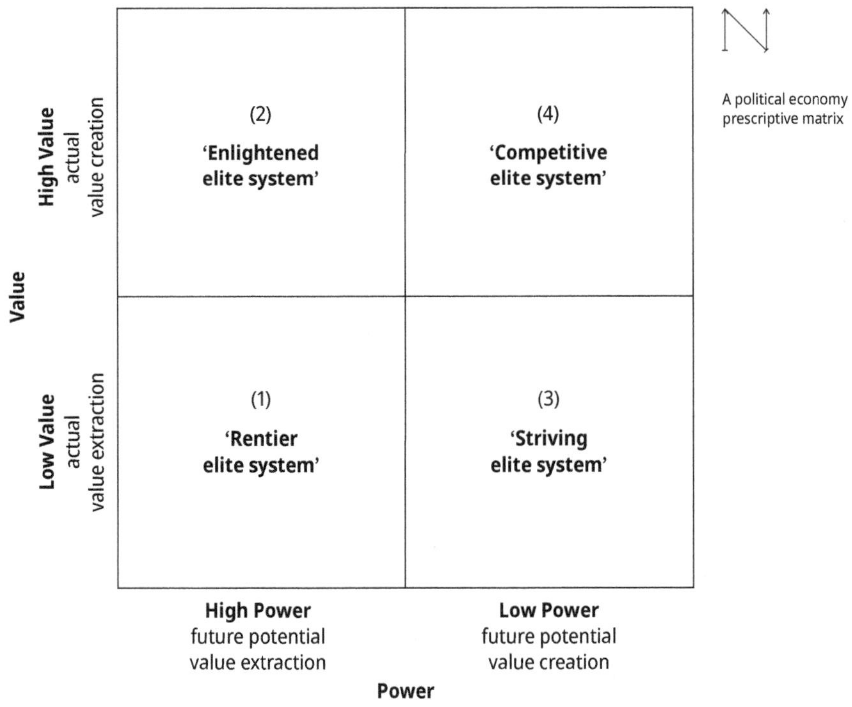

Figure 6.5: The State of the Elite System Framework for the political economy.

Nations whose EQx sub-index scores denote an elite system that is characterized by high levels of value extraction combined with low dominance are deemed to possess a 'striving elite system' (quadrant 3). This type of system is found during state formation (e.g., Japan during the Meiji Restoration) or follows state failure (e.g., Libya post-Gaddafi). More positively, the competition for primacy among low-power striving elite business models can incentivize differentiation, innovation, and the adoption of disruptive technologies (e.g., the beginnings of the industrial revolution or China's rapid growth phase during the 1980s). This is a rare system because of its unstable nature and propensity to chaos due to deinstitutionalized intra-elite contests, even though these might at times foster development and free up value creation potential. If the winners are extractive elite coalitions that manage to consolidate through 'political economy know-how' and use power to secure their value appropriation models, what ensues is regression to a 'rentier elite system' (quadrant 1). That is, countries whose economies are characterized by powerful elites that have legitimized value transfers.

In some nations, highly dominant winners refrain from rent seeking and value extraction models (at least initially) despite their potential ability to implement such practices. This situation typifies the 'enlightened elite system' (quadrant 2) depicted at the top left of Figure 6.5. Singapore, the country that topped the EQx rankings for four out of its first five years can be characterized in such terms in relation to other advanced economies. The 'enlightened elite system' is clearly a desirable human and economic development scenario, with powerful elites investing their coordination capacity and 'the extraordinary lever' into productive activities and value creation business models. Another such positive configuration is the 'competitive elite system' of quadrant 4.

The 'competitive elite system' (quadrant 4) most closely resembles the free market, with Hayekian decentralization and Schumpeterian entrepreneurs emerging and waning in waves on the back of creative destruction processes and elite circulation. At times, such a state also emerges from the productive chaos of a 'striving elite system' (quadrant 3). The system is characterized by an important proportion of new elite business models (e.g., China after its market-oriented reforms and opening-up) or by incumbents whose business models are pushed by newcomers and switch to value creation activities (e.g., the Silicon Valley effect on America Inc.). The 'competitive elite system' scenario is therefore distinguished by the admixture mode of elite circulation (see Figure 1.1), with market-based intra-elite contests utilizing 'knowledge' bargaining power sources, thereby engendering highly productive elite coalitions that trade places in quick succession, all managing to amass wealth from munificent residual income flows during their sustainable value creation tenures. Here, intra-elite competition is institutionalized and in creative tension with elite cohesion as evidenced by a plethora of public goods, positive externalities, and bountiful transfer-OUT by key elite business models. Non-elites also drive sustainable development as they retain the value they create and thus have the incentive to create even more. From a strict economic perspective, long-term growth is maximized and is only limited by human imagination and the capacity to innovate, which, to optimists, is limitless.

The two EQx sub-index scores place each country within one of the four categories of The State of the Elite System Framework for the political economy. It is then the task of the political analyst or scholar to assess the implications of this classification for a country and formulate development options and outcomes. Transformational elite leadership (Table 7.2) drives the elite system via structural reforms aimed at elite business model rules that bolster the two upper quadrants (2) and (4).

The EQx is a meso-level aggregate that does not measure the agency of specific elite coalitions. Nonetheless, interpretative analysis can utilize the results across the four index architecture levels to establish the elite coalition landscape and identify specific business models, including the national models (Section 8.1.2), that account for the scores of various index components. Some authors place responsibility for economic outcomes such as stagnation or inequality on the shoulders of the political elite because they determine "the growth process of the economy" (Bourguignon & Verdier, 2000, p. 287), or because "within the Japanese leadership groups, the position of the political elite is central" (Schmidt, 2004, p. 82). Assessments of this kind are too general and do not account for the 'follow the money' heuristic of institutional change (i.e., trace the beneficiaries of residual income). Macro-level analyses, informed by the elite theory and meso-level quantifications of the elite system such as the EQx, must seek connections to micro-level business models assessed for sustainable value creation with measurements like the VCr (see Figure 7.8) for the purposes of designing structural reform that is weighted for value creation and transfers (see Table 7.1). By consulting the architecture (see Figure 6.3) and leveraging data using different levels of abstraction, it becomes possible to map the sustainable value creation landscape of a society. On this basis, an evidence-based understanding of the specificities of elite agency emerges that can be used to build accurate descriptions for a given political economy and potentially model its growth prospects.

6.4 Limitations of the Elite Quality Index

The Achilles heel of any index is the necessary usage of subjective judgments. Various aspects of the operationalization of the index and its methodology are based on such judgment calls (Casas-Klett, Cozzi, Diebold, & Zeller, 2020), including the important weighting procedures just reviewed. Subjective judgments invite controversy and even nomenclature decisions can have an impact on understanding. For instance, the 'Getting Credit indicator' used in the World Bank's *The Ease of Doing Business Index* was criticized for being "named in a potentially misleading way" (Besley, 2015, p. 111). This section now systematically sheds light on the most important limitations of the EQx. These include the controvertible evidence of value creation (6.4.1); the establishment of value creation optima (6.4.2); splitting an elite business model across indicators (6.4.3); and the existence of blind value creation and extraction spots in an economy (6.4.4).

6.4.1 Controvertible evidence of value creation and transfers

For every indicator incorporated in the EQx, a value creation/transfer position is articulated. Each of these positions can be subject to perennial debate about whether the phenomenon captured by the specific indicator actually measures (in the case of the 'value' sub-index) or leads (in the case of the 'power' sub-index) to value extraction (or to its opposite, value creation). For instance, there has been a raging theoretical controversy over whether competition or monopolies (and the antitrust rules to prevent them) result in higher levels of innovation, as is depicted in the two viewpoints below:

> Antitrust enforcement surely keeps prices low and output high, but is it good for innovation? The question arises because the relationship between competition and innovation is the subject of a familiar controversy in economics. One view, often associated with Joseph Schumpeter, argues that monopolies favor innovation. An opposite view, often associated with Kenneth Arrow, argues that competition favors innovation. (Baker, 2007, p. 575)

The EQx puts a value creation premium on competition and considers monopolies to be a form of power and hence a precursor to potential second-order value transfers. These, and all other forms of dominance, are categorized as extraction in the coalition dominance pillar (ii.4). Relatedly, antitrust regulation would reduce monopolistic power and increase competition: in the institutional capture pillar (i.2) this institutional arrangement type is assessed positively. Baker would concur, since "the benefits of antitrust rules and enforcement extend beyond lower prices, greater output, and higher product quality; they also include increased innovation" (2007, p. 602). Yet here, as well as in other indicators, the prescriptive implications directly derived from this theory and hence the EQx's ontological position—dividing the world into value creation and transfers—are by no means met with universal agreement, as the following reference makes evident:

> The lesson for policymakers is that antitrust intervention in product markets may disturb the very incentive structures that lead to rapid technological change. (Nicholas, 2003, p. 1055)

6.4.2 Value creation optima

After a position is taken on whether an indicator's dataset measures value creation or extractive value transfers, the next question that habitually arises is the degree to which the quantitative manifestations of indicator scores express that position. In this respect, some EQx indicators require the establishment of non-linear optima, ideally anchored in research. For instance, and referencing the discussion in the previous subsection, what is the optimum level for competition in an industry given Aghion, Bloom, Blundell, Griffith, and Howitt's (2005) inverted-U relationship between competition and innovation? If one were to employ the Herfindahl-Hirschman Index (HHI), a measure used by the US Justice Department's Antitrust Division for market concentration, one would settle on a specific number or range between zero and 10,000. Yet, given the HHI measure's "sensitivity to asymmetry" (Calkins, 1983, p. 404), this is by no means straightforward. In another example, whether in Japan (Johnson, 1982), Africa (Herbst, 2000) or China (Zhang, 2022), the point must be found where state capacity contributes to "long-run economic growth" (Dincecco & Katz, 2014, p. 189) and development and where it does not—as in "extreme cases of unproductive spending" by public administrations (Tanzi, 1997, p. 22) once the target of Musk's Department of Government Efficiency (DOGE). Frye and Shleifer, for instance, associate the "helping hand" of state capacity with "organized corruption" (1997, p. 355). When describing the "predatory state", Evans finds that "the efficacy of the developmental state depends on a meritocratic bureaucracy with a strong sense of corporate identity and a dense set of institutionalized links to private elites" (1989, p. 561), meaning that factors like the separation of powers (power relation 4, see Table 3.2) might also have to be quantified and incorporated. State capacity and its funding mechanisms are associated with both value creation and extractive elite business models that rely on transfer-IN. Given these nuances and that both excessive and insufficient state capacity is suboptimal, can an optimal degree of public activities (vs private ones) be established? The EQx researchers must make difficult judgments on the optimum levels of value creation for indicators like taxation, fiscal decentralization, or, more controversially, for equality, with many probably adjusted for factors like income levels.

Whether the decision is on the optimal number of years that patents should be protected for, unionization rates, acceptable inflation ranges, or income and capital tax levels, the impossibility of reaching a scholarly consensus is immediately obvious. The value creation optima judgments are therefore both a necessity and a lasting limitation of the index. The often irreconcilable and diverse viewpoints mean that the EQx will need to be transparent with its epistemological positions on an indicator-by-indicator basis, both as expressions of elite business models and in terms of the value creation and transfer impact described by their quantitative manifestations.

6.4.3 Multiple indicators describe one elite business model's impact on the elite system

A large number of metrics are required to fully describe an individual business model in terms of its sustainable value creation and extractive transfers (for instance, to deduce its VCp/VCr measurements, see Sections 5.3.1, 6.6.1). Likewise, incorporating a particular elite business model into aggregate elite quality might require various indicators that fully capture the impact of its diverse value creation and extractive transfer activities on the political economy and society at large. For example, the business model of policing would be denoted by indicators of police spending as a percentage of GDP (financed by taxes, a transfer) as well as by indicators that convey whether this spending is effective in terms of reducing the homicide rate or organized crime levels. In the EQx2022, nine indicators point to the multi-faceted phenomena of entrepreneurship: 'Women self-made billionaires' ('human capture', pillar i.3); 'Entrepreneurship', 'Venture capital finance', 'Billionaire's creative destruction', 'Index of Women Entrepreneurs', 'Venture capital availability', and 'Government support to entrepreneurship' ('creative destruction', pillar ii.6); 'Unicorns per 1 million people' and 'Billionaires self-made as % of total billionaires' (capital value, pillar iv.11). Each indicator conveys a unique perspective (e.g., is there a glass ceiling in entrepreneurship?) that provides an opportunity for reform and transformational leadership. The need to include various indicators to express the sustainable value creation impact of elite business models at the meso-level elite system level parallels the firm-level 'value spectrum' conceptual element (Figure 2.10) where both value creation and extraction activities invariably combine in every single business model. This links to the most uncomfortable paradox of the political economy: that value creation often necessitates value extraction, as is articulated in the 'alternating value extraction and creation' conjecture (Section 2.3.1, Proposition 10) and in the 'all elite agency creates and transfers value' realist inference of this work's pragmatic philosophy (Figure A5.4a).

Once multiple indicators have been established for a specific elite business model, isn't the task of weighting these to ascertain a 'fair' meso-level impact almost futile? Healthcare is a paradigmatic example of a treasured public service that enables non-elites to engage in sustainable value creation. Yet, at the same time, public health provision is multifaceted as the healthcare industry's business model is paid for by extraction from value creators through taxes, regulations, and onerous entry barriers. The US National Health Expenditure Accounts (NHEA) calculated 2021 American health care spending to be $4.3 trillion, $12,914 per person, or 18.3 percent of GDP.[128] That is the annual cost of between four and five US militaries, begging the question of whether and to what extent there is rent-seeking transfer-IN by principals like regional hospital monopolies. Combining multiple indicators to describe a single business model (in this case, health quality rankings and healthcare industry spending as a percentage of GDP), and their respective weights in the index, implies a multivariable function. How accurately can such functions reflect the proportion of value creation and extractive transfers? The multiple data sources chosen, the conceptual determination of the indicators, and the judgments made on their relative weighting invites impossible debates even when encouraging further research.

128 See: https://www.cms.gov/research-statistics-data-and-systems/statistics-trends-and-reports/nationalhealthexpenddata/nationalhealthaccountshistorical

6.4.4 Blind spot value creation and transfer phenomena

Another limitation of the EQx relates to high-impact elite agency responsible for value creation and extractive transfer phenomena that are only partially described or remain completely unaccounted for. The challenges here might be conceptual and of measurement, as is the case for business models premised on risk transfers that benefit from being "too big to fail" or "too big to jail" (see Hardouin, 2017). A related cause for this first blind spot of the EQx is identifying indicators that can quantify the impact of extractive transfers when these are attributable to legitimate, tax-paying business models, even when these exceed the damage done by criminal enterprises. For example, during the first Trump Administration, the Oval Office established that ultra-extractive opioid elite business models—not all run by illicit enterprises—cost an astounding 2.8% of US GDP (Council of Economic Advisers, 2017). The number of deaths—over 33,000 Americans—has since more than tripled on the back of synthetic opioids like fentanyl. Such complex business models, especially those where principals have a license to operate, are incompletely captured in the index using current indicators (such as 'Death rate from substance abuse disorders' in the 'taking income' pillar iii.8).

Similarly, while the next two examples are well documented, they are illustrative of the problems in satisfactorily quantifying impact in terms of comparative economic and human development. First, the Hong Kong SAR suffers, as reported in *The Crony-Capitalism Index* (*The Economist*, 2014), from rent seeking that the *China Daily* suggests can be traced to a single business model: "HK is the 'Least Affordable Housing Market' for the 10th Year Running" (Lu, 2020). The territory's Housing Affordability Index score of 20 and over has for years been almost double that of the other most expensive cities in the world. The fact that value is extracted from the young seeking to join the housing ladder is even more galling considering that the Research Office of the Legislative Council Secretariat (2016) reports that 76% of the territory is "non-built-up land". In 2024, the EQx added the 'Housing Affordability Index' indicator ('producer value', pillar iv.10), but this does not address the notable price variations across cities in countries like China or the US. A final example comes from the squatter's paradise of Spain, where the most basic institution, that of property rights, has deteriorated to such an extent that housing ownership is left unprotected by the legal system against extractive transfers by the *okupa*, even if these are *de jure* illegal. Anarchist networks actually operate as elite coalitions that are narrower than their counterparts, the more than 87,000 defenseless owners whose properties they have seized (Institut Cerdà, 2017), as Spanish courts *de facto* side with the occupiers.

A second blind spot is that many key elite business models are localized and thus cannot be represented by the EQx in comparative terms. The three particularly extractive phenomena described above—the opium epidemic in the US, exorbitant real estate prices in Hong Kong, and property taken from its owners by squatters in Spain—are country-specific extractive elite business models that weigh much more heavily on the US, HK SAR, and Spanish economies than elsewhere. Hence, even if data is available for a sufficiently large number of countries, the weighting of an indicator is problematic since the elite business model does not have the same impact on value creation/extraction across polities (i.e., a housing affordability indicator would have to carry much more weight in Hong Kong than elsewhere). A solution to this problem might be the inclusion of a 'critical impact indicator' category in the EQx, possibly to be weighted equally across countries and reserved for the highest value creation/transfer impact elite business model(s) in an economy.

A third and different type of blind spot relates to knowledge elites. At present, the EQx has only two dimensions, 'political' and 'economic' (see Figure 6.2), and so the specific sustainable value creation agency of knowledge elites is included in the 'political power' and 'political value' index areas. A more evolved EQx architecture would possess a third dimension referencing the power domain of society, with indicators that describe the sustainable value creation agency of knowledge elites. The resultant six index areas would then mirror the tripartite elite typology of this theory (see their depiction in Figures 2.1 and A5.1). Obviously, knowledge elites and their agency in the narrative market have a discrete impact on value creation/transfer: "To govern, to rule, or to exercise power at all requires an institution or coordinated institutions, organized under and held together by an idea-system, vesting power in and allocating it among stated individuals, for tacitly agreed or overtly stated purposes" (Berle, 1968, p. 202). The idea-system, the "myths" of institutions (Meyer & Rowan, 1977), the "role of ideas" (Hall, 1993, p. 289), the collective consciousness of Hegel's *Geist* (1807/2018), "ideas" Donaldson (2021), Plato's "noble lie" (Dombrowski, 1997), the "belief systems" (North, 1994) or simply "beliefs" (Alesina, Cozzi, & Mantovan, 2012), the charisma behind "mobilizational power" (Winters, 2011), Gramsci's "worldview" (Cox, 1983), Foucauldian discourse and the "narrative construction of reality" (Bruner, 1991), "fictions" and "stories" (Harari, 2015), culture capture (Giblin & Doctorow, 2022, p. 2), "doctrine" (Moore, 1958), or narratives (Abell, 2004; Denning, 2006; Hagel, 2011) legitimize both value creation and extractive value transfer models (see also Proposition 14 on the impact of elite agency on institutional change through narrative markets). Political economy narratives could be addressed in the EQx by first ascertaining their existence (as in Shiller, 2017), and then by assessing the 'power' and 'value' of the elite business models they enable. Nonetheless, this blind spot is currently left unaddressed and therefore constitutes another evident limitation of the current version of the EQx.

6.5 The development of additional elite quality measurements

The EQx is the flagship measurement of elite quality found in the meso-level elite systems of 151 countries, with five annual reports (see Casas-Klett & Cozzi, 2024) published to date. At the same time, and given the limitations of the EQx, the elite quality conceptual element would benefit from alternative approaches to how it is measured.

In the social sciences, triangulation refers to "the combination of methodologies in the study of the same phenomenon" (Denzin 1978, p. 291, as cited in Jick, 1979, p. 602), that "enhances our belief that the results are valid and not a methodological artifact" (Bouchard, 1976, p. 268, as cited in Jick, 1979, p. 602). Two different measurement approaches are now proposed to overcome some of the limitations of the EQx outlined in the previous section and to enhance the validity of the elite quality conceptual element. The more straightforward of these additional SVC measurements is a survey instrument, the Perceptions of Elites Survey (PEz), which aims to determine non-elite and elite perceptions of elite quality (6.5.1). The second will be the outcome of a large-scale project: the country-specific Elite Quality Rating (EQr), that will aggregate the VCr measurements for available elite business models (6.5.2).

6.5.1 The Perceptions of Elites Survey (PEz)

The first alternative suggested method to measure elite quality is a perceptions survey designed for both elite and non-elite respondents. Tried and tested bases in the academic literature exist for perception surveys; some are experiments that assess perceptions of both public and private performance (see Hvidman & Andersen, 2016), while others determine economic expectations as in how "Americans perceive their near-term futures" (Dominitz & Manski, 1997, p. 261). Governments and their affiliated institutions conduct perception surveys on policy matters as described by the OECD's (2012b) *Measuring Regulatory Performance: A Practitioner's Guide to Perception Surveys*. Such research can be very specific, such as the Danish Business Authority's "burden hunter methodology" which "is an integral part of the Danish better regulation effort", the findings of which enable "the authorities to focus on simplifying the regulation that businesses perceive as the most costly and burdensome".[129] A highly refined survey research industry led by companies such as Nielsen, IQVIA, Kantar, Gartner, Ipsos, Circana, Dynata, Westat, or Intage has for decades assessed public opinion, brand perceptions, and often very specific questions such as physician's perceptions about a given product.

Elites are also surveyed in academia for their "Europeanness" (Best, Lengyel, & Verzichelli, 2012), on their attitudes (Scholte, Verhaegen, & Tallberg, 2021), for questions of strategic management (Bednar & Westphal, 2006), to gain various insights through interviews and observation (Rodríguez-Teruel & Daloz, 2018), by comparing them across countries (Walgrave & Joly, 2018), or even by using experiments on them (Kertzer & Renshon, 2022). For the purposes of practice, McKinsey Global Surveys run "research with global executives on the pressing business, economic, and manage-

129 See: https://danishbusinessauthority.dk/burden-hunter-hunting-administrative-burdens-and-red-tape

ment issues they face".[130] Indices such as World Economic Forum's *Global Competitiveness Report* also reference surveys that essentially gauge elite perceptions (see, for instance, "The Executive Opinion Survey: The Voice of the Business Community" by Browne, Di Battista, Geiger, and Gutknecht, 2014).

However, most available surveys on elites do not focus on the value creation and appropriation of their business models. Both the 'Non-elite Questionnaire' (1/2) and the 'Elite Questionnaire' (2/2) of the Perceptions of Elites Survey (PEz) are designed to precisely address this matter (refer to Tables A3.4a and A3.4b for extracts of the sample questionnaires, each of which feature 10 questions). The PEz project will provide discrete questions for both elite and non-elite respondents, since "the distinction between elites and non-elites is therefore an important aspect of social analysis" (Hoffmann-Lange, 2007, p. 910). Proper "elite identification" can leverage approaches including "the reputational method, the decisional method, and the positional method" (Parry 2005; Putnam 1976, p. 15 ff. as cited in Hoffmann-Lange, 2007, p. 912). Whether using web-based elite expert surveys (see Dahlberg, 2007) or the face-to-face mode (see Maestas, Neeley, & Richardson, 2003), open or closed question types or how to solicit participation, the survey questionnaire design must adhere to best practices for conducting quantitative research, such as those detailed by Vis and Stolwijk (2021) for political elites. As for the conceptual structure, both the elite and non-elite questionnaires used in the survey will adhere to the four-level EQx architecture. In this way, the elite perceptions survey may enhance the ability to refute hypotheses built upon this book's conceptual elements. With a rigorous design, the avoidance of biases, and caution about interpretation (see Iarossi, 2006), survey findings might prompt political economy debates and stimulate public engagement. Particularly noteworthy are the differences that are likely to arise from employing discrete empirical methods and tools to establish the sustainable value creation of elites. For instance, any divergence in the perceptions of elite and non-elite respondents with regard to elite quality should provide comparative insights and complement the EQx.

The PEz survey's Non-Elite Questionnaire (1/2) and Elite Questionnaire (2/2) will both garner inputs not readily available in conventional economic data sets on a timelier basis, including, for instance, shifts about whether non-elites perceive value extraction by elites to be on the rise or in decline, even in relation to unfolding events. This would make signs of discontent as exemplified by headlines such as "Biden's Economy Is Great Everywhere Except in the Polls" (Yglesias, 2023) less perplexing. The PEz will also be able to address different and narrower research questions than the EQx and do so in an international context by dealing with cross-cultural issues (Harkness, van de Vijver, & Mohler, 2003) deemed by the survey designers to be relevant to both the non-elite perceptions of elites and the self-perceptions of elites. At the same time, it can transcend the particular comparative angle of the EQx which, as currently

130 See: https://www.mckinsey.com/featured-insights/mckinsey-global-surveys

conceived, finds it difficult to assess country-specific matters such as the functioning of the elite separation of powers, specific dynamics in The Seven Intra-elite Power Relations, or the extremely important fluctuations in elite cohesion for a given economy (see Table 3.2). The PEz will also allow the testing of questions related to certain conjectures and propositions put forward in the ETED. For example, the survey might be used to probe perceptions on the degree of elite cohesion or elite/non-elite cohesion, reveal awareness of value creation and the pain points of value transfer activities, pinpoint the connections between the dominant narratives in society by how their relationship to the value creation/extraction of elite business models is regarded, and even link such findings to economic development outcomes. Beyond being a service to the public, the PEz will be a tool for political reformers while academics will be able to tackle and test novel hypotheses. This alternative measurement method will be a step towards triangulation and increases the validity and meaningfulness of elite quality and related constructs for research and for policy purposes.

6.5.2 The country-specific Elite Quality Rating (EQr)

Another noteworthy contribution to the study of the sustainable value creation of nations is the impending Elite Quality Rating (EQr), premised on the sustainable value creation of firms. This highly sophisticated country-specific SVC measurement is meant to be both complementary and an alternative to the EQx index and the PEz survey. Characterized by a 'bottom-up' micro-to-meso approach, this assessment method will aggregate the value creation and transfers of elite business models measured by the VCr (rather than the effects of their agency evidenced at the macro-level, as is the case with the 'top-down' macro-to-meso level indicators used for the EQx). The meso-level aggregate EQr measurement will rely on the sustainable value creation (VCr) of selected elite firms, therefore incorporating the sums of all their value appropriated but *not* created (transfer-IN) and their value created but *not* appropriated (transfer-OUT).[131] As a result, it will offer a comprehensive view of the contribution of elite business models to an economy and society. It will be expressed (like the VCr scores that constitute it) as a digit with two decimal points, where 1.00 reveals that the total value creation and extraction effected by elites is in balance. A score

131 A suggested 'Elite Quality Position' ('EQp') measurement would conceptually describe a position on the meso-level 'elite system value spectrum'. That would be the weighted average of the 'value spectrum' positions of the pertinent micro-level organizations that represent the elite. Such a meso-level aggregate SVC measurement for nations would narrowly focus on extractive transfer-IN and ignore inclusive transfer-OUT (and is left to further inquiry). Its usefulness for both research and as a tool for economists resides in its potential to highlight macro-level aggregate transfer-IN vs transfer-OUT patterns. The EQp would thus be a weighted average of all the VCp scores in the system, or the sum of the transfer-IN amounts of elite models as a proportion of their total revenues.

over/below 1.00 will manifest an elite system with a net positive/*negative* value relationship with society at large, where inclusive second-order value transfers (transfer-OUT) are higher/lower than extractive second-order value transfers (transfer-IN). In addition to being industry specific (see Section 6.6.4), the EQr will also be country specific, and so the results would not be valid for international comparison purposes without adjustment.

The actual elite system EQr measurement will be derived from the elite business models that are representative of the sustainable value creation of a nation (though ideally all models would be incorporated in this selection) by aggregating and weighting their associated VCr scores. It will be possible for the aggregate VCr components—derived from the sums of transfer-IN/OUT metrics organized into scorecard categories and mirroring the four-level EQx architecture (see Figure 6.8)—that are implicit in an EQr score to be made explicit (e.g., 'power', 'creative destruction', 'producer value'). Once specified, all of the discrete conceptual elements of the EQr would be linked to the value creation/extraction phenomena captured and deduced from the EQx. The establishment of causality between concrete elite business models and general value transfers observed in various areas of the economy and society is an ultimate macroeconomic value creation modeling aim in the context of the institutional change imperative of the ETED (see 'weighted transfers modeling' in Figure 7.1 and its application in Table 7.1).[132]

For the purposes of the EQr calculation, the selection of representative elite business models material to the sustainable value creation of a country's elite system will follow financial criteria such as profits and revenue size, but also the (estimated) monetary impact (e.g., via budget size) of elite coalitions that are not organized as firms such as civil servants, religious establishments, or the military. Each political economy and society has its own specific coalitions. For instance, in Germany, high-impact models include the automotive industry, the banking sector, and the labor unions; in India, the conglomerate models of the traditional business houses exemplified by Reliance Industries, the Tata Group, or the emergent Adani Group,[133] the civil service, and the political parties; in the US, the health care industry, Big Tech, Big Oil, Wall Street, and possibly the military-industrial complex; in China, the upper echelons of the CPC, the administrative system, the centrally controlled SOEs in oligopolistic markets and in competitive markets, and to a lesser extent the leading private coalitions in technology or industrial sectors. Each country's particular elite business mod-

132 Perfect 'weighted transfers general equilibrium' (WTGE) macroeconomic models (see how 'WTGE' relates to the SVC measurements in Figure 7.8) require novel and massive data sets such as electronic payments, social commerce transactions, and even the weights of neural networks in LLMs that control the magnitude of one neurons effect on another, or the movements and exchanges of the future metaverse (see Section 7.1.1 and the speculative discussion in the Epilogue).

133 Even as a relative newcomer, the Adani Group is not free of controversy, having been described by pundits in the Indian media as "the center of India's shift to oligarchy" (Kant, 2021).

els, including its national business model (see Section 8.1.2), create value and risk to discrete degrees and, as noted above, can range from publicly listed firms, to family dynasties in a patrimonial state, to the custodians of belief systems. In this regard, the EQr could address the country-specific business model blind spot problem expounded on in Section 6.4.4.

Once categorized as 'elite' and selected for inclusion in the EQr, the diverse business models in an economy—each with their own VCr—will be assigned respective weights. As suggested, the default approach is a financial size weighting based on the relative magnitude of a business model's revenue, profit, or budget. Alternative judgments could also be made, such as weightings that adjust for peculiarly inclusive or extractive impacts not captured by the VCr. For instance, in the case of SMEs, one might increase their weighting given the positive impact they have on local communities; in the case of the legal opioid models, one might increase the weighting in line with lives lost to account for the exceptionally high and unquantified 'cost created but *not* borne' (see 'destructive' transfer-COST, Figure A5.5b, and Section 8.2.1). On the premise that the VCr's for elite models are available, weighting—whether based on financial size or adjusted for impact—will not be a fundamental methodological challenge for the EQr, as even the default financial size weighting approach is capable of accounting for the shifting dynamics of political economies. That matters, since intra-elite contests bring about the emergence and decline of elite business models—some surging due to AI, inflation, or hosting the Olympic games; others falling behind due to globalization, financial securitization, or war—with such shifts sometimes occurring rapidly due to factors (many exogenous, though rapidly endogenized, see Section 4.3.5) like new technologies, policy choices, narratives with non-elite input, the natural environment, or fluctuating geopolitical realities.

As has already been expounded upon, in order to perform the aggregation, normalization, and weighting of business models to garner a country's EQr, the VCr for the selected models will need to have been established. Its theoretical foundations, conceptualization, and derived equations have already been examined (see Chapter 2, Section 5.3.1), while the detailed procedural steps for the calculation of its component transfer-IN/OUT metrics are described in the next section.

6.6 Advancing the firm-level sustainable value creation (SVC) measurements that underlie elite quality

The next five sub-sections deal with the inherent causes of elite quality, turning away from the elite system and returning to the firm level. That is, to the SVC measurements and their operationalization, thereby building on the foundations of Chapter 2. Paralleling the indivisible macro-level indicator datasets, the first and pivotal sub-section describes the method for establishing value transfers through the utilization of the indivisible constituent SVC metrics for the essential VCp and VCr firm-level SVC measurements (6.6.1). Next, four additional SVC measurements based on survey instruments are presented (6.6.2). Three of these are currently at a testing stage and utilize the SVC Metrics Self-assessment Survey instrument to yield the self-VCp, the self-VCr, and, from a subset of the latter's metrics, a discrete measurement for international business, the 'International Business Self-assessment Value Creation Rating' ('IB-self-VCr'). These three measurements mirror the VCp, the VCr, and the IB-VCr (see Section 7.3.1). The fourth measurement is the planned Perceptions of Value Creation Survey (360-VCz), employing the comprehensive two-tier 'Firm Stakeholder Questionnaire' (1/2) and 'Firm Principal Questionnaire' (2/2). Tables A3.5a and A3.5b present extracts of the sample questionnaires, each featuring 12 questions. The subsequent sub-section explains how the EQx architecture is referenced to propose the Business Model Sustainable Value Scorecard, which supports the conceptual determination and weighting of the SVC metrics used to calculate the firm-level SVC measurements (6.6.3). The fifth additional SVC measurement advanced is the 'Sector Value Creation Rating' ('sector-VCr'). This provides benchmarks that enable industry-specific materiality considerations and meaningful comparisons between same-sector firms, as well as pointers for subsequent practical investment or policy action (6.6.4). The fifth and final sub-section calls for risk origination, uncertainty undertaking, and risk transfer metrics to be featured systematically in all SVC measurements (6.6.5).

6.6.1 Value transfers as SVC metrics and inputs for firm-level SVC measurements

This inquiry develops an elite theory of economic development by positing that elite agency, aggregated at the meso-level elite system level, is the transmission mechanism between micro- and macro-perspectives. The EQx that has been described in this chapter is the initial comparative aggregate measurement at the meso-level of the elite system designed to test the relationship between elite quality and developmental outcomes on the premise that elite agency is the endogenous microfoundation of institutional change. The index is based on macro-level *indicators* that provide evidence of aggregate value creation/extraction by elite business models. The sustainable value creation of these business models is evaluated through SVC measurements like the VCr that are based on firm-level *metrics* representing evidence of value creation/extraction by the individual firm. How are these metrics (I) conceptually determined, how are they (II) quantified (to realize the 'quantifiability of value transfers' assumption), and what is the (III) process to incorporate them into the equations for the SVC measurements? Figure 6.6 provides a visual rendition of this three-stage process to establish firm-level SVC measurements and their metrics.

As described in Section 5.3.1 on the conceptualization and operationalization of value transfers, and consistent with the implications resulting from the three assumptions for socio-economic relations (Figure A5.4a), SVC measurements directly or indirectly reference P&L financial statements and so each of their constituent SVC metrics

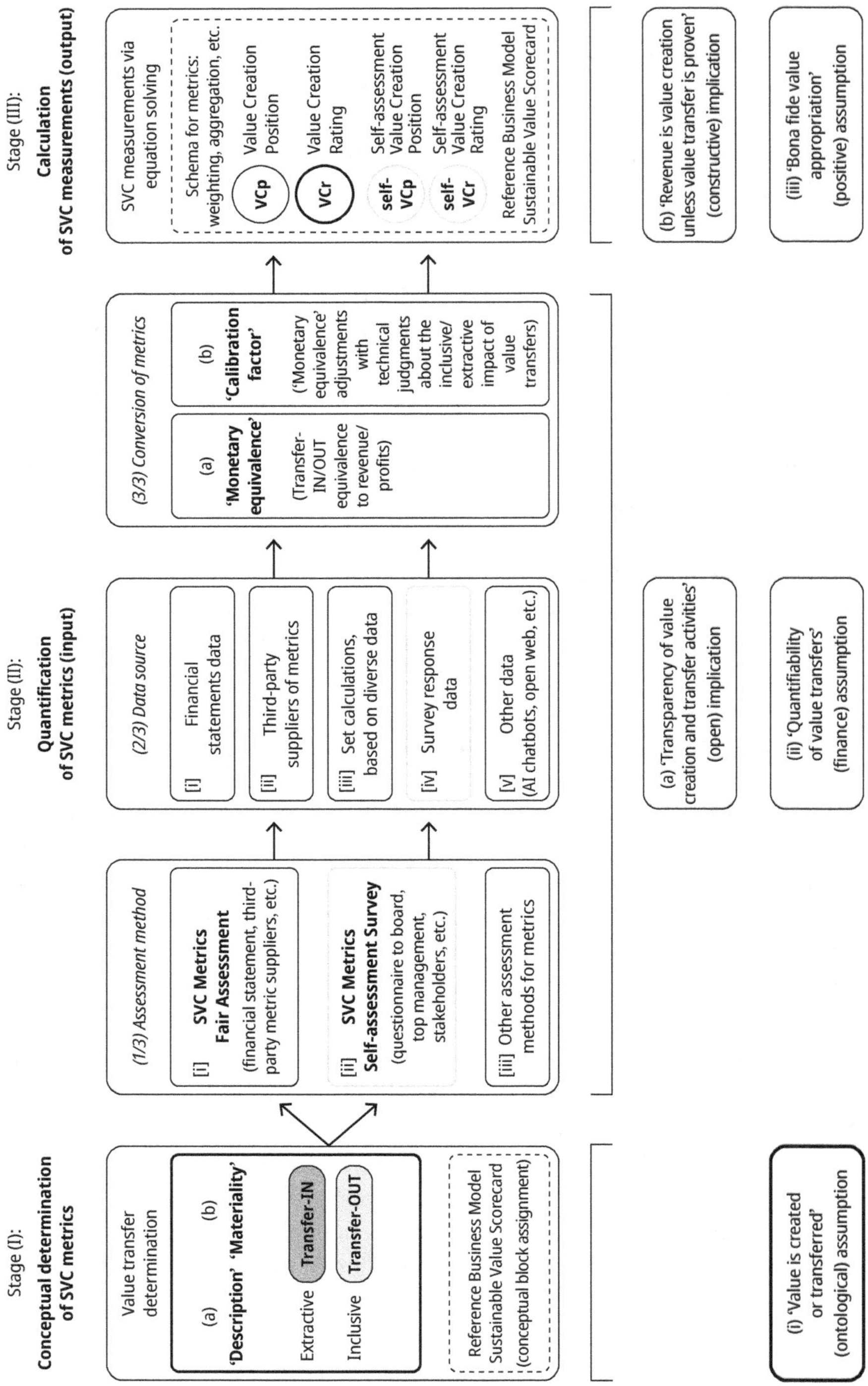

Figure 6.6: The three-stage process to establish firm-level SVC measurements and their metrics.

must do the same. As noted throughout, for transfer-IN (value appropriated but *not* created) it is easier to determine the revenue from value created by stakeholders than it is to determine the savings from 'cost created but *not* borne' (even the 'extractive' transfer-COST, see Figure A5.5a) that have such an impact on profits (facilitated by negative externalities and activities such as creating pollution that transfer costs away from the principal). As with the transfer-OUT (value created but *not* appropriated) amounts, these costs are also off-book. Transparency is universally understood as the foundation of financial institutions, generates trust in capital markets, and underpins accountability (Kaufmann & Weber, 2010). Hence, in pursuit of the 'transparency of value creation and transfer activities' (open) implication for financial analysis (see Figure A5.4b), and after ascertaining that both transfer-IN—including the 'extractive' transfer-COST—and transfer-OUT activities have conceptual integrity, are material, and can be described by SVC metrics, the aim must be to quantify and express them all as exact amounts directly derived from (transfer-IN) or indirectly matched (transfer-OUT) with the revenue/profits of the P&L statement.[134] On this premise, both types of metrics (transfer-IN/OUT) serve as the primary inputs for the four SVC measurements. For the VCp and the VCr the process commences with the 'SVC Metrics Fair Assessment'; for the self-VCp and the self-VCr it begins with the 'SVC Metrics Self-assessment Survey'. The next paragraphs describe creating the SVC measurements as a three-stage process: (I) the *conceptual determination of SVC metrics* in accordance with the six categories of The Value Creation and Appropriation Matrix, see Figure 6.7; (II) the *quantification of SVC metrics (input)* in order for them to be integrated as inputs into the SVC measurements, see Tables 6.1 and 6.2 and; (III) the *calculation of SVC measurements (output)*. Figure 6.6 serves a guide going forward, with its numbering and notational logic alluded to throughout this sub-section.

The classification of SVC metrics provided in Figure 6.7 summarizes the value transfer arguments made so far (the second, third, and fourth sextants follow the logic established in Chapter 2, see Figure 2.11) or still to come (the fifth sextant is covered in Section 8.2 on ethics, see also Figure A5.5a) employing a (2x3) matrix that is based on the notions of value creation (on the x-axis) and value appropriation (on the y-axis).

134 The 'destructive' transfer-COST (the '*negative* value created and *not* appropriated' in Figure 6.7) of, for instance, legal opioids or the banned (since The Hague Convention) hollow-point bullets ("bullets which expand or flatten easily in the human body", International Peace Conference, 1899), are indelibly associated with the profits of their respective business models. Yet, unless this cost is institutionalized *per se* as a statutory part of an income statement category (i.e., as an expense incurred through legally mandated penalties for undertaking these activities), its value destruction is not considered a transfer-IN amount and does not function as an input to SVC measurements. The treatment of these negative off-P&L costs therefore contrasts with positive value transfer-OUT amounts where SVC metrics are also off-P&L but *are* incorporated in the VCr. Nonetheless, documenting and quantifying 'destructive' transfer-COST metrics as far as is practicable will be undertaken to support 'value destruction ratio' calculations (see Sections 8.2.1 and 8.2.2 and Figure A5.5b) and is also of relevance to researchers, investors, or policy initiatives.

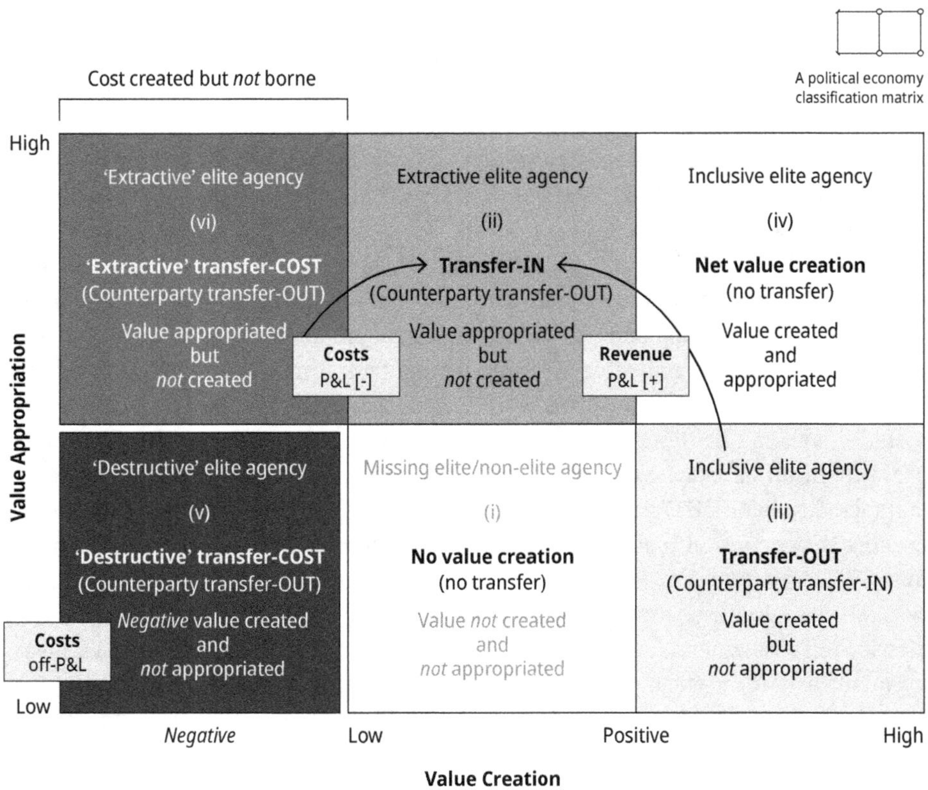

Figure 6.7: The Value Creation and Appropriation Matrix: A framework for the classification logic of SVC metrics.

The operationalization of sustainability through transfer-IN/OUT metrics, including the transfer-COST metrics ('cost created but *not* borne' is further elaborated on in Sections 8.2.1, 8.2.2 and Figure A5.5a), bolsters the assertion that SVC measurements facilitate firm valuations and decision-making that point towards more inclusive futures. For instance, Damodaran highlights the importance of "*strong barriers to entry*", including those of a legal nature, because barriers "create more value when new entrants can be kept out of the business" (2005, p. 43). The pertinent question that the transfer-IN/OUT approach addresses is whether such value is truly a first-order productive activity or should rather be classified as a second-order extractive value transfer (see Table 2.3). Barriers clearly increase value appropriation and hence, in Damodaran's view, the valuation of firms. This is equally the case for all other conventional valuation methods and is encouraged in practice by frameworks like the Morningstar Economic Moat Rating.[135] The open issue is whether barriers or moats (or competitive monopolies,

135 See: https://www.morningstar.com/investing-definitions/economic-moat

subsidies, and market concentration) are sustainable if they result in value transfer-IN? The valuation frameworks for sustainable value creation—'The Five Sustainable Value Creation (SVC) Valuation Frameworks'—are able to account for extractive/inclusive transfer-IN/OUT because the primary input of their functions is the VCr (see the Figure set A5.6). Hence, the conceptual determination of the transfer-IN/OUT metrics that underlie and subsequently quantify SVC measurements like the VCr is integral to business model decision-making when SVC valuations become determinants in capital allocation processes (see Section 5.3.2). That means, for instance, that powerful firms currently benefiting from barriers to entry will, contrary to the stances taken by Damodaran and Morningstar, see diminished SVC valuations because of the effects of transfer-IN metrics. Again, the transfer-IN/OUT SVC metrics classification is in accordance with the logic of The Value Creation and Appropriation Matrix (Figure 6.7).

The first of the three stages (I) to establish SVC measurements is the *conceptual determination of SVC metrics* and hinges on the value transfer materiality of the constituent metrics. SVC metrics are, as per Eccles and Stroehle's "insights from a sociology of quantification and knowledge construction" for ESG data (2018, p. 1), grounded in "Social Origins". The raison d'être of each metric underlying SVC measurements is the economic and human development impact imperative that, on account of the ETED's operating premises, resolves the value creation and value transfer dichotomy. The dualistic (i) 'value is created or transferred' (ontological) assumption, the (ii) 'quantifiability of value transfers' (finance) assumption, and the (iii) 'bona fide value appropriation' (positive) assumption set out in Figure A5.4a, jointly constitute a call for a conceptually clear and evidence-based discernment of value transfers and their all-important materiality. Single materiality primarily looks at how sustainability (ESG) factors affect profits and are material to investors seeking to maximize these. Double materiality, with its "two dimensions namely: *impact materiality* and *financial materiality*" [emphases in original] where impact materiality takes the principal-stakeholder perspective and looks at extended "*business relationships*" which "include those in the undertaking's upstream and downstream *value chain* [emphases in original] and are not limited to direct contractual relationships" (European Commission, 2023, Annex I, 3.3, 3.4)

In practice, this statutory position means to Schoenmaker and Schramade (2023, pp. vi, 28) that management ought to "focus on integrated value (which integrates financial, social and environmental value) rather than just financial value" and as a result the "*Responsible company* [emphasis in original] manages and balances profit (financial value) and impact (social and environmental value)". In line with the earlier discussion, the dual materiality framework of this elite theory of economic development comprehends 'impact' as 'value transfers'. Such transfers are both extractive (the negative value transfer-IN) and inclusive (the positive value transfer-OUT), and their operationalization starts with the lowest indivisible constituents, the SVC metrics, before proceeding upwards to firms, sectors, and the overall elite system. So, what transfers are then material? Hicks (1964, p. 158) provides the decision criteria: "In essence, 'materiality' means simply this: if it doesn't really matter, don't bother with it."

Can this theory's approach to materiality address a critical issue that Pazienza, de Jong, and Schoenmaker (2023, pp. 19–20) identify: "The lack of linkage between the 'how' to measure and 'what' to measure is a primary cause for missing a tested and applicable methodology for measuring corporate sustainability". This is especially prescient given that the institutional backdrop allows considerable discretion. For instance, the European Sustainability Reporting Standards (ESRS):

> do not mandate how the materiality assessment process shall be designed or conducted by an undertaking. This is because no one process would suit all types of economic activity, organisational structure, location of operations or upstream and downstream value chains of all undertakings applying the ESRS. [. . .] In any case, an undertaking shall consider the full scope of environmental, social and governance matters (i.e., sustainability matters) [. . .] material from an entity-specific perspective (EFRAG, 2024, p. 19).

That is, while the "full scope" is to be tackled, including "positive impacts" (European Commission, 2023, Annex I, 3.4), the mandate remains ambiguous regarding the process for the "materiality assessment". For instance, how quantifiable are the thresholds for the materiality of potential impacts based on "likelihood" and "severity" criteria (EFRAG, 2024, p. 31)? De Cristofaro and Gulluscio argue that evaluations of actual corporate non-financial reports "highlight variety in both double materiality assessments and adoption disclosures, as well as related criticalities" and caution that "this foreshadows a fragmented landscape of materiality analysis disclosure over the next few years that presently requires great attention and increased operational guidance by the international standard setters involved" (2023, p. 1). In contrast, the value transfers conceptual element that underpins SVC measurements, while likewise striving for "the full scope", seeks hard quantification and monetary equivalence (with revenue or profits) as described in this sub-section and in Figure 6.6, Stage (III).

The unpacking and determination of business model activities as material transfer IN/OUT launches the process of establishing firm-level sustainability measurements. The Business Model Sustainable Value Scorecard (see Section 6.6.3), which parallels the EQx architecture in using conceptual elements like 'power', 'market value' or 'creative destruction', aids the selection and classification of metrics into 'pillars' to support their weighting adjustments at the final equation solving stage (III) of the process. Table 6.1 shows how in the first stage (I) value transfer SVC metrics are conceptually determined via their (a) 'description', and their sustainable value creation (b) 'materiality' to ascertain their extractive transfer-IN and inclusive transfer-OUT using the classification logic of The Value Creation and Appropriation Matrix (Figure 6.7).

This initial stage (I) to establish SVC measurements—the *conceptual determination of SVC metrics*—is completed once the value transfer determination for a sufficient and relevant set of metrics (the number of metrics will likely be in the dozens, though over a hundred will be needed for higher precision SVC measurements) for a specific sector (see Lydenberg, Rogers, & Wood, 2010; Eccles, Krzus, Rogers, & Serafeim, 2012) or set of firms (e.g., from listed firms in Switzerland to poverty alleviation retail start-ups in emerging markets).

Table 6.1: (continues in Table 6.2): Stage (I) conceptual determination of 10 selected SVC metrics and their transfer-IN/OUT in the three-stage process to establish firm-level SVC measurements (based on Casas-Klett & Nerlinger, 2023, Table 3, pp. 43–45).

Metric		Stage (I): Conceptual determination of SVC metrics	
Ref.	(1) *Name* (2) Identifier (ID) (3) Category (pillar) (b') Value transfer type	(a) Metric description	(b) Metric materiality
01	(1) *Lobbying* (2) VCr_rc.LOC (3) Regulatory Capture [i.2] (b') Transfer-IN	Lobbying, the "variety of methods to influence government policies" (de Figueiredo & Richter, 2014, p. 164), is a firm expense designed to convert into revenue (and profits).	Lobbying is the exercise of power in the political arena; it can skew competition, lead to regulatory capture and stymie effective public policies. Hence it is potential transfer-IN.
02	(1) *Gender wage gap* (2) VCr_hc.GWG (3) Human Capture [i.3] (b') Transfer-IN (transfer-COST)	The gender wage gap is the difference between male and female median wages, divided by the male median wage.	The long-term objective for this metric is a value of 0 (as per the ambition of UN SDG 5). A deviation is a cost reduction, a transfer-IN from and a transfer-COST to female (or, rarely, male) employees.
03	(1) *Market concentration* (2) VCr_fd.HHI (3) Firm Dominance [ii.5] (b') Transfer-IN	In the theory of industrial organization (e.g., Tirole, 1988), market concentration is when a small number of firms control large market shares and is commonly measured by the Herfindahl-Hirschman Index (HHI).	Market concentration affects market competition and reflects market power, which "is a firm having the ability to influence the price at which it sells its product(s)" (Syverson, 2019, p. 25).
04	(1) *R&D expenses as percentage of revenue* (2) VCr_RDE_x (3) Creative Destruction [ii.6] (b') Transfer-OUT	Research and development (R&D) expenses represent all direct and indirect costs related to the creation and development of new processes, techniques, applications, and products with commercial possibilities.	R&D is one of the means for future firm growth and competitive advantage. It generates innovation spillovers (Griliches, 1992) and hence is an inclusive transfer-OUT.

Table 6.1 (continued)

Metric		Stage (I): Conceptual determination of SVC metrics	
05	(1) *Subsidies* (2) VCr_ti.SUB (3) Taking Income [i.8] (b') Transfer-IN	"A subsidy is defined as a 'financial contribution' by a government which provides a benefit" (WTO, 1994b).[136]	Subsidies are a transfer-IN from the government (taxpayer) stakeholder and can be "particularly harmful" (WTO, 1994b).
06	(1) *Effective tax rate compared to peers* (2) VCr_ti.ETR (3) Giving Income (iii.7) (b') Transfer-OUT	The effective tax rate is defined as the percentage of income at which an individual or corporation is taxed (in comparison to its peers).	Taxes are an important link between firms and the society that surrounds them. A firm paying less/more taxes than its peers is engaged in transfer-IN/OUT.
07	(1) *Carbon exposure* (2) VCr_ul.CEX (3) Unearned Income (iii.9) (c) Transfer-IN (transfer-COST)	Companies that reduce their emissions to (below) zero are deemed to be sustainable. The Carbon (emissions) exposure is defined as CO_2 and CO_2-equivalent emissions (Scope 1) in tonnes (1 ton is equal to 1000 kgs of carbon dioxide) multiplied by the latest carbon price and divided by revenue.	At least since the 2015 Paris Agreement, carbon emissions from public companies have come under increasing scrutiny. Carbon emissions over zero are a transfer-COST to the nature stakeholder as well as a cost to future generations.
08	(1) *Capital expenditures as percentage of revenue* (2) VCr_cv.KEX (3) Capital Value (iv.11) (b') Transfer-OUT	CapEx divided by revenue.	CapEx are long-term investments that generate transfer-OUT as financial returns, benefit stakeholders such as workers or communities, and have multiplier effects as part of the economy's investment function.[137]

136 The rules in the Agreement on Subsidies and Countervailing Measures (SCM Agreement) of the WTO (1994b) reference US law (Title VII of the Tariff Act of 1930) and detail the various forms that a subsidy can take: (a) "a direct transfer of funds (e.g., a grant, loan, or infusion of equity)"; (b) "a potential transfer of funds or liabilities (e.g., a loan guarantee)"; (c) "foregone government revenue (e.g., a tax credit)"; or (d) "the purchase of goods, or the provision of goods or services (other than general infrastructure)" (International Trade Administration, U.S. Department of Commerce, n.d.). See: https://www.trade.gov/trade-guide-wto-subsidies

137 Limits to this rationale might apply to shareholders. See research pointing to "the negative abnormal capital investment/return relation" (Titman, Wei, & Xie, 2004, p. 677).

Table 6.1 (continued)

Metric		Stage (I): Conceptual determination of SVC metrics	
09	(1) *Capital expenditures as percentage of debt* (2) VCr_cv.KED (3) Capital Value (iv.11) (b') Transfer-IN	CapEx divided by total debt.	Debt is first a transfer-IN of value from the future to the present associated with the risk of not realizing returns on capital (e.g., because of malinvestments).[138]
10	(1) *Human Rights Score* (2) VCr_lv.HRS (3) Labor Value (iv.12) (b') Transfer-IN (transfer-COST)	The human rights score measures a company's effectiveness in respecting fundamental human rights conventions.	Not respecting human rights reduces costs but is an intolerable form of transfer-IN by firm principals from vulnerable stakeholders such as disenfranchised workers.

The second stage (II)—the *quantification of SVC metrics (input)*—is itself a three-step process that revolves around the data needed to quantify the metrics. It begins with a fundamental choice: the (1/3) *assessment method*. Available methods are currently [i] the SVC Metrics Fair Assessment and [ii] the SVC Metrics Self-assessment Survey, though [iii] 'other assessment methods for metrics' such as utilizing AI might be pertinent and feasible in the future. Regardless of the assessment choice, each metric is matched with numerical data to expresses in quantifiable terms the specific aspect of the business activity it describes in value transfer-IN/OUT terms. The 'quantifiability of value transfers' (finance) assumption (Figure A5.4b) comes to life during the second choice to be made at this stage: the (2/3) *data source*.

In the case of fair assessment, the data sources will either originate from [i] audited 'financial statement data', [ii] 'third-party suppliers of metrics'[139], or [iii] 'set calculations based on diverse data such as public data, financial statements, non-financial information included in integrated reports (Eccles & Spiesshofer, 2015), industry associations, or global institutions like the IMF. In the case of self-assessments

138 Limits to this rationale exist, such as taking on excessive debt to finance "empire building" by management (Titman, Wei, & Xie, 2004).

139 These include ESG products from MSCI, ISS (Governance and ESG), LSEG (Data & Analytics and FTSE Russell), Bloomberg, S&P Global (Global Market Intelligence and Trucost), CDP, and Morningstar Sustainalytics.

(see the discussion in next section), the sources are [iv] 'survey response data' from questionnaires. The raw survey responses are obtained from company executives, directors, or other business insiders that complete these for the purposes of strategizing, public outreach, board reviews, or even executive education (see the discussion in Section 6.6.2 and a sample of the SVC Metrics Self-assessment Survey for firms in Table A3.6). These raw responses are ultimately also converted via data transformation rules applied at the (3/3) *conversion of metrics* step into monetary amounts. Thirdly, there might be metrics that rely on [v] 'other data', such as generative AI or open web data.

Table 3.6 shows sample questions for the SVC Metrics Self-assessment Survey. For example, responses to the question 'Estimate the percentage of the firm's revenues gained from cartel agreements' are used to establish the 'cartel power' metric; responses to the question 'Is the firm's effective tax rate above (+) or below (-) the industry average and what does this tax advantage/disadvantage represent as a percentage of firm revenue?' are used to establish the 'effective tax rate in comparison to peers' metric; and responses to the question 'Estimate the firm's R&D expenses as a percentage of revenue' serve to establish the 'R&D expenses as a percentage of revenue' metric. Table 6.2 illustrates the diverse data sources used for the SVC Metrics Fair Assessment. For example, ESG datasets from third-party commercial suppliers inform the 'gender wage gap' metric; set calculations with data from various sources yield the 'carbon emissions exposure' metric; and data in the financial statement is used to establish the 'R&D expenses as a percentage of revenue' metric. Note that the quantification of the metrics derived from the SVC Metrics Self-assessment Survey conducted to establish the self-VCp/self-VCr will differ from those derived from the SVC Metrics Fair Assessment conducted to establish the VCp/VCr, as the latter rely on independent third-party suppliers and set calculations (the invariable divergences between the two versions will be an instructive subject for reflection and analysis).

Once this second step—(2/3) *data source*—to establish firm-level SVC measurements has produced sufficient data pertinent to a minimum set of relevant metrics, the all-important third step—(3/3) *conversion of metrics*—is undertaken. This step requires: (a) establishing 'monetary equivalence' and (b) the application of a 'calibration factor' based on technical judgments to account for the extractive/inclusive impact of an SVC transfer-IN/OUT metric.

Examples of implementing the conversion of metrics to establish 'monetary equivalence' and the 'calibration factor' for transfer-IN/OUT are detailed in Table 6.2. For the 'gender wage gap', the 'monetary equivalence' is arrived at by ascertaining the labor cost savings from lower wages as a percentage of P&L revenue (e.g., 2%), while the 'calibration factor' is set at 110% to account for the full cost savings effect plus a punitive component (10%) of this transfer-IN to account for gender discrimination;[140] for the 'R&D expenses as percentage of revenue' metric, the 'monetary equivalence' is straightforward as R&D expenses are a line item in the P&L (e.g., 12%), while the 'calibration factor' is set at a high rate of 200% to account for the positive spillover effects of the transfer-OUT; for the 'carbon emissions exposure' metric, the 'monetary equivalence' is arrived at by ascertaining the cost savings achieved for not paying the national carbon price for x metric tons of carbon discharges as a percentage of P&L revenue (e.g., 6%), while the 'calibration factor' is set at 100% to account for the full transfer-IN as the price of the carbon offsets needed to reach carbon neutrality. As the three examples reveal, establishing (a) 'monetary equivalence' is a daunting data-driven task in the *conversion of metrics* (3/3), and is followed by the need for equally formidable judgments to set the (b) 'calibration factor'. As Hicks (1964, p. 171) highlights, even accountants must exercise judgments on materiality, while in the case of setting sector-specific indicators, the expert also "relies on subjective judgments" (Lydenberg, Rogers, and Wood (2010, p. 22).

Not applying a judgment for a 'calibration factor' would mean that the 'monetary equivalence' amount of a given metric is final, thus establishing (with an implicit 'calibration factor' of 100%) the transfer-IN/OUT amounts that will be directly set against the firm's revenue/profits. When a 'calibration factor' is utilized it must be consistent across the selected firms in a set (in an industry, a country, or a business model type). As described in the examples above, the factor choices are informed by the sustainable value creation impact of the particular metrics and utilize approaches such as evidence-based conceptual deliberation, or *ad hoc* criteria. For instance, in the case of the 'R&D expenses as percentage of revenue' metric, theoretical and empirical evidence of innovation spillovers, economic growth, higher productivity-driven value creation (as suggested by Romer, 1990) and purported multiplier effects, lead to the judgment to double the impact (i.e., a 'calibration factor' of 200%). Table 6.2 provides ten instances of the (3/3) *conversion of metrics* on the basis of a metric's (a) 'monetary

---

140 Systematic investigation is needed for a full understanding of the facts surrounding a metric in order establish transfer-IN/OUT amounts. For instance, discrimination must underlie the setting of the 'calibration factor' for the gender pay gap. In a "gig" economy business model "with no gender discrimination and highly flexible labor markets", a gender earnings gap should in principle not exist. Consequently, for any gender wage gap detected as a result of discrimination, the fixed 'calibration factor' percentage applied to 'monetary equivalence' in order to establish the transfer-IN just described would apply (i.e., 110%: the full cost savings for the firm plus a punitive uplift of 10% for discrimination, see Table 6.2). However, when a gender pay gap is detected—to the tune of 7% in the case of Uber—it "can be entirely attributed to three factors: experience on the platform (learning-by-doing), preferences and constraints over where to work (driven largely by where drivers live and, to a lesser extent, safety), and preferences for driving speed", the conclusion being that the 7% gap is in fact not "gender discrimination" (Cook, Diamond, Hall, List, & Oyer, 2020). Does this research therefore suggest that an optimum gender earnings gap of 7% should be universally applied for the "gig" economy with the 'calibration factor' of 100% applicable in a non-linear fashion, that is, only for gaps that are above or deviate from this benchmark?

equivalence' and (b) a 'calibration factor' that is judged to correspond to fair impact. The conversion of metrics is the last step of stage (II) and provides in monetary terms the raw material for the equation solving in stage (III)—the *calculation of SVC measurements (output)*, based on the equation set in Table 2.4—that completes the three-stage process to establish the sustainable value creation of firms.

Table 6.2: (continuation of Table 6.1): Stage (II) quantification of 10 selected SVC metrics in the three-stage process to establish firm-level SVC measurements (based on Casas-Klett & Nerlinger, 2023, Table 3, pp. 43–45).[141]

Metric	**Stage (II): Calculation of SVC metrics (input)**			
	(1/3) Assessment method	***(2/3) Data source***	***(3/3) Conversion of metrics***	
Ref. (1) *Name* (b') Value transfer type	[i] SVC Metrics Fair Assessment [ii] SVC Metrics Self-assessment Survey [iii] Other assessment methods for metrics	[i] Financial statements [ii] Third-party suppliers of metrics [iii] Set calculations [iv] Survey response data [v] Other data	(a) 'Monetary equivalence' (the criteria to derive revenue/profits equivalence)	(b) 'Calibration factor' (a percentage that adjusts monetary equivalence)

141 These 10 metrics are representative of transfer-IN/OUT business model activities and are for the most part used in the *Value Creation Ratings Pilot Report 2024: The Sustainable Value Creation of Firms* (Casas-Klett & Nerlinger, 2024), establishing the VCr (and VCp) for approximately one hundred publicly listed firms. They are also appropriate for the questionnaire used for the SVC Metrics Self-assessment Survey to establish the self-VCp/self-VCr (and the IB-self-VCr subset) of participating firms. Setting the 'monetary equivalence' and the 'calibration factor' for metrics is crucial for the determination of VCp/VCr and self-VCp/self-VCr scores.

Table 6.2 (continued)

	Metric	Stage (II): Calculation of SVC metrics (input)			
		(1/3) Assessment method	*(2/3) Data source*	*(3/3) Conversion of metrics*	
01	(1) *Lobbying* (b') Transfer-IN	[i] SVC Metrics Fair Assessment [ii] SVC Metrics Self-assessment Survey	[iv] Survey response data [iii] Set calculations (e.g., from the US, Center for Responsive Politics data)	A lobbying expenses multiplier[142] (e.g., 3x)	50% (half of revenue generated by lobbying is transfer-IN)
02	(1) *Gender wage gap* (b') Transfer-IN (transfer-COST)	[i] SVC Metrics Fair Assessment [ii] SVC Metrics Self-assessment Survey	[ii] Third-party suppliers of metrics (e.g., Sustainalytics; MSCI social scores; LSEG Data & Analytics, SODODP016) [iv] Survey response data	Cost savings due to lower wages (e.g., 2% lower labor costs)	110% (full cost savings from lower female wages is a discriminatory transfer-IN)
03	(1) *Market concentration* (b') Transfer-IN	[i] SVC Metrics Fair Assessment [ii] SVC Metrics Self-assessment Survey	[iii] Set calculations [ii] Third-party suppliers (e.g., Product Segment 1 Sales, LSEG Data & Analytics, WC19501)[143] [iv] Survey response data	Price premium vs competitive market price counterfactual (e.g., 10% higher prices)	150% (full price uplift plus an additional 50% to account for transfer-IN due to long-term market distortion effects)

142 While "a large number of papers show lobbying has positive returns", isolating the effects of lobbying and quantifying these (and answering questions like "when do the marginal benefits of spending an extra dollar on lobbying begin to be outweighed by the marginal costs?") requires transaction-related data, natural experiments, and other methodologies, along with advances in theory (de Figueiredo & Richter, 2014, pp. 169, 177, 178, 179). While most pundits "take for granted that the more money an interest group has, the more likely it is to get what it wants", McKay advocated caution and the need for "further research on the effects of money in policymaking" (2012, p. 908). The ultimate research insight from a transfer-IN perspective is how much revenue each dollar, euro, or yuan spent on lobbying generates for the organization.

143 A reference point for the establishment of the HHI for US public firms using third-party data from Compustat can be found in Grullon, Larkin, and Michaely (2019).

Table 6.2 (continued)

Metric		Stage (II): Calculation of SVC metrics (input)			
		(1/3) Assessment method	*(2/3) Data source*	*(3/3) Conversion of metrics*	
04	(1) R&D expenses as percentage of revenue (c) Transfer-OUT	[i] SVC Metrics Fair Assessment [ii] SVC Metrics Self-assessment Survey	[i] Financial statement	R&D expenses (e.g., 12%)	200% (double the R&D expenses are a transfer-OUT to account for spillover effects)
05	(1) *Subsidies* (b') Transfer-IN	[i] SVC Metrics Fair Assessment [ii] SVC Metrics Self-assessment Survey	[iii] Set calculations (e.g., data from WTO, OECD, government records) [v] Other (open web)	Sum of received government subsidies, SCM Agreement definition (e.g., 15%)	67% (1/3 of full monetary equivalence is discounted in deference to rationale for government grant)
06	(1) *Effective tax rate compared to peers* (b') Transfer-OUT	[i] SVC Metrics Fair Assessment [ii] SVC Metrics Self-assessment Survey	[i] Financial statements [ii] Third-party (Income Taxes, LSEG Data & Analytics, WC01451) [iii] Set calculations[144]	Extra tax expenses/ tax savings due to lower/ higher effective rate (e.g., +/-3%)	120% (full 100% for extra tax/tax savings plus 20% for social cohesion gain/loss assumption)
07	(1) *Carbon emissions exposure* (c) Transfer-IN (transfer-COST)	[i] SVC Metrics Fair Assessment [ii] SVC Metrics Self-assessment Survey	[ii] Third-party suppliers (e.g., CDP) [iii] Set calculations	Cost savings, based on national carbon price (e.g., 6% of revenue)	100% (full 100% for carbon offsets required)

144 Set calculations could consist of the combination of Bureau van Dijk Orbis data on income tax expenses for companies and OECD benchmarks (see: https://stats.oecd.org/index.aspx?DataSetCode=CTS_ETR).

Table 6.2 (continued)

Metric		Stage (II): Calculation of SVC metrics (input)			
		(1/3) Assessment method	***(2/3) Data source***	***(3/3) Conversion of metrics***	
08	(1) *Capital expenditures as a percentage of revenue* (b') Transfer-OUT	[i] SVC Metrics Fair Assessment [ii] SVC Metrics Self-assessment Survey	[i] Financial statements	CapEx (e.g., 18% of revenue)	150% (full 100% plus 50% for positive effects on employment, growth, innovation, etc.)
09	(1) *Capital expenditures as percentage of debt* (b') Transfer-IN	[i] SVC Metrics Fair Assessment	[i] Financial statements [iii] Set calculations	CapEx (e.g., 10% of revenue) times likelihood (e.g., 20%) of overinvestment due to debt financing (e.g., 2% of revenue)	40% (discount on full monetary equivalence based on technical approach adjusting for confidence in overinvestment likelihood estimate)
10	(1) *Human Rights Score* (b') Transfer-IN (transfer-COST)	[i] SVC Metrics Fair Assessment [iii] Other assessment	[ii] Third-party suppliers (e.g., LSEG Data & Analytics, TRESGSOHRS) [v] Other (open web)	Cost savings from disregarding human rights (e.g., 1.5% of revenue)	100% (full 100% cost saving is transfer-IN)

The calculations for the third stage (III) of the process brings the many SVC metrics together—like the indicators in the meso-level EQx counterpart—and requires technical decisions regarding the aggregation schema, the type of normalization required, and, most critically, various judgments about weighting. Such weightings concern the comparative significance of each metric relative to others and must be made both within a metric category and across categories of metrics. The 12 pillars of The Business Model Sustainable Value Scorecard (see Section 6.6.3 and Figure 6.8) constitute such metric categories. In order to model sustainable value creation as accurately as possible, and just as with the discussion on the functions underlying SVC valuations (in Section 5.3.2), current weighting could be superseded at a later stage by factor models that embody conceptual insights or the fundamental data architecture. These would be functions based on empirically ascertaining the underlying data structures of publicly listed firms that reflect *de facto* weightings of a SVC metric based on market performance across the selected firm set. The weighting functions would mirror CAPM formulas, with the estimated beta (the sensitivity measure based on the regression of stock returns) linked to specific transfer-IN/OUT SVC metrics to enable a weighting that references market performance. Further approaches in this regard include the application of the Fama-MacBeth (1973) regression used to assess risk factor premia in order to explain asset returns, and the use of Principal Component Analysis (PCA) to identify and preserve the most important features or patterns of multiple metrics.

The 'bona fide value appropriation' (positive) assumption and the derived 'revenue is value creation unless value transfer is proven' (constructive) implication (see Figure A5.4b) considers all revenue/profits of a business model to be net value creation until the moment that the transfer-IN sum is ascertained (or that the costs shifted to stakeholders are confirmed). With the aggregation of the transfer-IN amounts from all constituent metrics, a firm's revenue/profits can be split and allotted to the two value categories necessary for VCp (and self-VCp) calculations: net value creation and transfer-IN. Note that the transfer-IN metrics utilized will include those that represent and quantify 'extractive' transfer-COST, as this is the value appropriated but *not* created form of 'cost created but *not* borne' (as in Figure 6.7 that sets out the framework for the classification logic of SVC metrics). While these unrealized costs have technically no bearing on revenue, they are essential to profits. In order to achieve inclusive neutrality, a firm would need to generate additional revenue equal to the amount of these costs to offset the extraction. Hence, in the context of SVC metrics, any cost *not* borne that can be linked to the P&L is deemed to be 'extractive' and thus equated to a revenue amount that is fit for transfer-IN quantification purposes (metrics that capture 'destructive' costs, or '*negative* value created and *not* appropriated', can certainly be calculated, but as they are off-P&L are not currently inputs for SVC measurements). The sum of all transfer-IN metrics, when matched against the P&L statement and deducted from revenue (or profits, depending on the value appropriation criteria), yields net value creation (see Figure 2.9 and equation (2.3″)).[145]

The sum of all transfer-OUT metrics is necessary for the VCr (and self-VCr) calculations. The SVC metrics representing value created but *not* appropriated are all off-P&L and as such rely as much on data as on judgment for their conversion into monetary terms and impact assessment. This differs from their value appropriated but *not* created transfer-IN counterparts where off-P&L metrics are not considered, even when the amounts sadly exceed revenues, as when non-institutionalized 'destructive' transfer-COST is shifted to stakeholders (e.g., business models with severe pollution externalities such as those caused by fertilizers and pesticides, or Purdue Pharma's

---

145 The visualization provided in Figure 2.8 and the equation (2.3′) in Table 2.4 defines 'net value creation' as 'value appropriation' minus 'value transfer-IN'. In contrast, to derive the full 'value creation' amount, the transfer-OUT sum is added to 'net value creation' as in equation (2.1).

induced opioid addiction business model with its hundreds of thousands of lost or destroyed lives, see Section 8.2.1).[146] The judgments for inclusive transfer-OUT metrics, on the other hand, are rendered to estimate off-P&L value to society at the (3/3) *conversion of metrics* step: (a) 'monetary equivalence' is ascertained before amounts are adjusted up or down with the (b) 'calibration factor'. While always in relation to a firm's revenue/profits, particularly sustainable firms may well exceed these amounts since the transfer-OUT value created but *not* appropriated can be boundless (e.g., the effects on long-term employment caused by the growth of capital expenditures, or the value spillovers in terms of lives saved from Penicillin or the mRNA vaccines developed by Moderna and BioNTech).

The VCr, advanced in this book as the main firm-level sustainability measurement (this sub-section extends the discussions in Chapter 2 and Section 5.3.1), as well as the VCp, are calculated for an organization in stage (III)—*calculation of SVC measurements (output)*—upon the completion of the two initial stages of the three-stage process (depicted in Figure 6.6). That is, once conceptually suitable transfer-IN/OUT SVC metrics (see examples in Table 6.1) have been determined in stage (I) and quantified in stage (II) through a three-step process (see examples in Table 6.2), stage (III) consolidates these into SVC measurements through the application of normalization, aggregation, and weighting schema. The ensuing transfer-IN/OUT aggregates enable the calculation of the SVC measurements based on equation sets (4.1) and (4.2). Note that some of the SVC metrics used for the VCr relate to the international interests of a firm and are the constituent elements of the 'International Business Value Creation Rating' (IB-VCr). This VCr-derived measurement is designed to address matters that are specific to organizations engaged in international business (as is discussed in Section 7.3.1, for instance).

The SVC metrics based output scores of the VCr and other allied measurements, including the IB-VCr or the 'Sector Value Creation Rating' ('sector-VCr') discussed in

146 Since the value amount of transfer-OUT can be practically unlimited (e.g., penicillin), there is no upper limit to the magnitude of a VCr score. On the other hand, as is recounted in the examples provided in Section 5.3.1, the present calculation of the VCp/VCr limits transfer-IN to a maximum amount equivalent to revenue/profits, meaning that the lowest possible respective VCp/VCr scores are technically set at 0.00 and 0%. It was noted earlier that this is an incorrect reflection of practice and can be a gross underestimation of impact, as the size of the 'destructive' transfer-COST (Figure A5.5a) created by the principal and borne by stakeholders can be immense, as the examples adduced in the text illustrate (e.g., legal opioids). An alternative approach would be a quantification that assigns the full 'monetary equivalence' and a fair 'calibration factor' to incorporate as transfer-IN any 'destructive' transfer-COST metrics (*negative* value created but *not* appropriated) in order to account for all the 'cost created but *not* borne' by principals and loaded onto stakeholders. When the transfer-IN sum exceeds revenue/profits, the VCp enters negative (percentage) territory. Such an unconstrained transfer-IN approach also impacts the VCr, since when the transfer-IN exceeds revenue/profits the VCr score will likewise be pushed down towards zero and potentially turn negative (unless it is compensated for by an equivalent transfer-OUT sum).

Section 6.6.5, constitute this inquiry's intended sustainability benchmarks for investors (such as asset managers, mutual funds, or insurance companies), issuers (such as corporations or municipalities), intermediaries (such as investment banks), social activists (such as NGOs), political parties (from across the spectrum), institutions and the law (such as politicians and regulators), decision-makers active in the international arena (such as officials in multilateral organizations and MNE executives) and, most importantly, for the transformational leadership of elite business owners and their top executives (discussed in detail in Section 7.2.4 and in the review of the main frameworks for management, policy, and finance in the concluding Chapter 8).

The first global report on the sustainable value creation of firms is the *Value Creation Ratings Pilot Report 2024: The Sustainable Value Creation of Firms* (Casas-Klett & Nerlinger, 2024). Also referred to as the pilot VCr2024, it is an initial exploratory attempt to deliver VCr and VCp scores for over a hundred leading corporations from the world's major economies. The process of preparing the pilot report addressed technical issues such as monetary equivalence weighting, particularly in stages II and III of the three-stage process described in Figure 6.6. The conceptual and empirical micro-meso-macro connection between sustainable value creation at the micro firm-level (e.g., as measured by the VCr) and elite quality at the macroeconomic via meso-level (e.g., as measured by the EQx) is a *leitmotif* of this work (refer to Figure 5.4): elite business models that exhibit sustainable value and risk creation bring about a higher degree of elite quality at the meso-level elite system level and *ceteris paribus* boost the prospects for economic and human development.

6.6.2 Survey-based firm-level SVC measurements

This sub-section delves into the four survey-based SVC measurements and their two respective survey instruments. The SVC Metrics Self-assessment Survey, discussed as part of the SVC metrics data transformation process (Figure 6.6), yields the first Self-assessment Value Creation Position (self-VCp) measurement and the second Self-assessment Value Creation Rating (self-VCr) measurement. A subset of the latter becomes the third measurement, the International Business Self-assessment Value Creation Rating (IB-self-VCr), which is specific to international business. In addition, the Perceptions of Value Creation Survey (360-VCz), a fourth planned firm-level SVC measurement (that does not rely on value transfer-IN/OUT metrics) will be based on a two-tiered instrument made up of the Firm Stakeholder Questionnaire (1/2) tailored to stakeholder type (e.g., employees, suppliers, governments), and the Firm Principal Questionnaire (2/2) aimed at the residual income beneficiaries (e.g., owners, executives, directors).

The SVC Metrics Self-assessment Survey for the firm is a self-audit method to calculate the self-VCp/self-VCr—the VCp/VCr's rudimentary twins—by asking questions to the top management team (but can be extended and adjusted for other principals such as the board or large investors). The survey response data is converted into quantifiable amounts of value and risk (transfer-IN/OUT) for each of the metrics assessed (see a draft questionnaire in Appendix A3.6). While some questions will seem similar to those of the 360-VCz survey's Firm Principal Questionnaire (2/2) introduced shortly, their aim is not to gauge perceptions but rather to establish hard monetary equivalences because the quantified metrics are devised in relation to P&L revenue/profits. Respondents must come fully prepared to the self-assessment session and conceptually understand each SVC metric. They can answer the surveys either individually or collectively, the latter being appropriate when a team is jointly responsible for the business model and its performance. Again, as most metric questions reference revenue or profits, respondents require recourse to financial statements, internal information, and other third-party data to guide their answers, even though the examination is not as thorough and the self-VCp/self-VCr 'monetary equivalence' not as precise a conversion as the SVC Metrics Fair Assessment used for the VCp/VCr (refer to Figure 6.6).

One motivation to obtain self-VCp/self-VCr scores is to contrast them with their rigorous hard-data VCr/VCp counterparts produced through the SVC Metrics Fair Assessment (meant for external stakeholders such as investors or regulators) and ascertain any divergence between the two SVC assessment methods and the causes of this. The purpose of these more informal self-assessments is primarily internal: to support strategic planning, elicit reflections on transformational leadership, and to provide orientation for actual decision-making on sustainability. While the survey questions are based on metrics and the self-audit process is compact, systematic, and documented, the resulting self-VCp/self-VCr measurements are quick, subjective, and preliminary—somewhat akin to a VCp/VCr heuristic.

As with the SVC metrics of the VCr that produce the IB-VCr (see Section 6.6.1), a sub-set of the self-VCr survey contains discrete questions related to the international business of the organization and specifically inquires about cross-border stakeholder relationships to ascertain value (and risk) creation and transfers. In line with the other self-VCr questions, conversion rules will be applied to the responses to attain 'monetary equivalence' with firm revenue/profits. This sub-set of the survey, the International Business Self-assessment Value Creation Rating (IB-self-VCr) will be designed to address matters specific to international management and governance, including entities like subsidiaries or foreign suppliers, and serve as a preliminary self-assessment for international business sustainable value creation measurements (see the discussion of the IB-VCr in Section 7.3.1).

The fourth and final firm-level survey-based SVC measurement will be generated from a second and somewhat different type of questionnaire: the Perceptions of Value Creation Survey (360-VCz). This multi-rater comprehensive feedback instrument will be comprised of the Firm Stakeholder Questionnaire (1/2) for the different types of external stakeholders and the Firm Principal Questionnaire (2/2) for top decision-makers and beneficiaries of the firm's residual income (see sample extracts in Tables A3.5a and A3.5b respectively). Stakeholders can include customers, suppliers, debt-holders, dataholders and intelligence providers, media, taxpayers, government, regulators, NGOs, employees, management, and others. Principals include the different types of beneficiaries (see ownership types in Boss, Connelly, Hoskisson, & Tihanyi, 2013) as well as those agents (Jensen & Meckling, 1976) tasked with decision-making on behalf of owners such as board directors and top executives. As a genuine appraisal of perceptions, this questionnaire will not directly draw on or require data from the financial statement's revenue/profits (unlike the VCr/VCr with its signaling and external orientation, or the self-VCp/self-VCr with its strategic reflection and internal orientation). Since the survey is being designed for use by both principals and stakeholders it actualizes the ideas of the 360-degree performance feedback interventions (DeNisi & Kluger, 2000) that it references. Questions in the 360-VCz might be more straightforward and unstructured than those in the self-VCp/self-VCr as it strives to be an intuitive snapshot of sentiments and diverse perspectives that does not require supporting documents. Yet, despite resting on veritable perceptions rather than metrics' data, the results will have a similar purpose: to support leaders in reflecting on their organization's sustainable value creation impacts while taking stakeholder perspectives into account. In the spirit of consistency, this micro-level tool will have parallels with the Perceptions of Elites Survey (PEz) introduced earlier in this section and primarily focusing on the elite system. The survey questionnaire categories will patently adhere to the EQx architecture and the 12 pillars of the Business Model Value Scorecard (Figure 6.8), and still reference VCr metrics and EQx indicators where necessary. The 360-VCz will therefore serve as a practical addition to the transformational leadership toolset and, as such, will be suitable for use in several contexts, including engagements with boards of directors or in executive education.

6.6.3 A supporting tool for the determination and weighting of SVC metrics

Firm-level metrics reflecting value creation and risk origination and transfers are the data inputs for producing SVC measurements. Can the prior conceptual determination and the subsequent weighting of these metrics be made for the assessment of VCp/VCr and self-VCp/self-VCr with a logic that parallels that of the elite quality measurements?

As is denoted by the adoption of the EQx 'pillar' categories in Table 6.1 to facilitate the conceptual determination of a metric, the answer to this question is yes. The ETED's sustainable value creation elements aim to be conceptually consistent across the micro- and meso-levels, as is the operationalization of the respective measurements. Therefore, the two EQx sub-indices become the two 'sub-ratings' of (I) 'power' and (II) 'value' and remain unchanged; the 'political' and 'economic' dimensions are now termed as 'market' and 'non-market' to articulate the firm perspective and have four associated 'rating areas': (i) 'non-market power'; (ii) 'market power'; (iii) 'non-market value'; and (iv) 'market value'. As the 12-pillar architecture becomes a 12-pillar structure, the nomenclature used for the EQx pillars remains intact. As discussed in

Section 6.6.1, the transfer-IN/OUT quantities of the micro-level metrics are based on 'monetary equivalence' and a 'calibration factor' referencing firm revenue (or profits). Borrowing from practice-oriented literature on business models, "a visual model or artifact" is purposed "to assist strategic managers in thinking about how they can act" (Simonse, 2014, p. 67). The scorecard's four 'rating areas' and 12 'pillars' presented in Figure 6.8 is such a visual model, an applied tool designed to support the determination and the weighting of metrics that comprise the SVC measurements at the firm level (the VCp/VCr and self-VCp/self-VCr). This artifact is essentially also a representation of a firm's agency in the political economy.

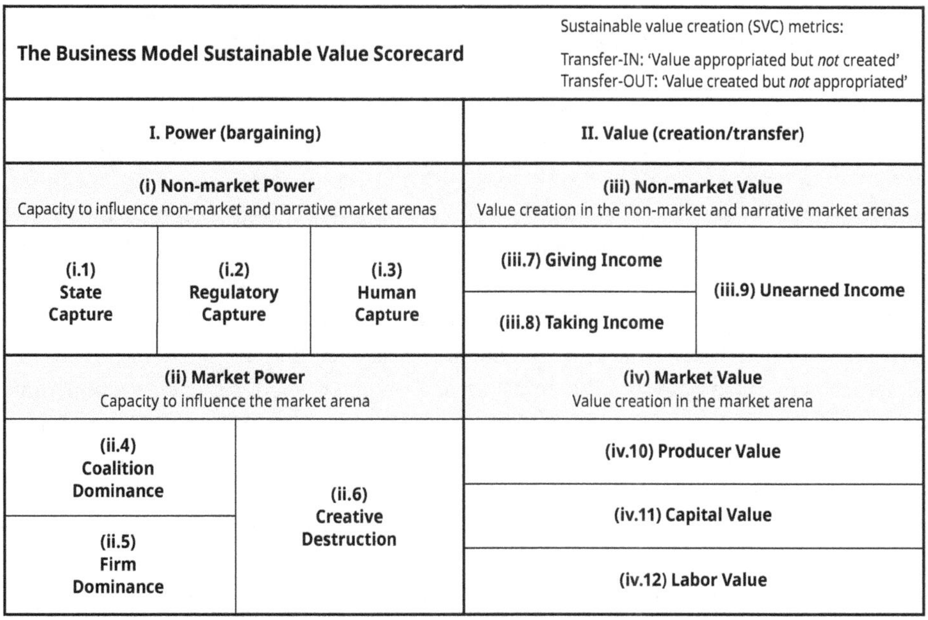

Figure 6.8: The Business Model Sustainable Value Scorecard with its four rating areas and 12 pillars.

The Business Model Sustainable Value Scorecard supports the conceptual determination and classification of SVC metrics, as well as the judgments for their relative weights in SVC measurements after their 'monetary equivalence' and 'calibration factors' have been established. That is, the scorecard is used in stages (I) and (III) of the three-stage process to calculate firm-level SVC measurements (see Figure 6.6). The 12 pillars of the scorecard facilitate both the organization and the aggregation of a firm's transfer-IN (including transfer-COST) and transfer-OUT sums, and by doing so establish their relative proportions which become determinant in the VCp/VCr/self-VCp/self-VCr equations.

Besides organizing the SVC metrics—and equally significant—the scorecard offers a wide range of analytical and interpretative opportunities; for instance, by aggregating pillars of firms at the industry level (see the discussion in the next sub-section). This is also a framework to support practice in various ways; for instance, by assisting credit rating agencies that assess the probabilities of debt default, or for financial institutions that provide valuations for equity. The final sub-section of this chapter (6.6.5) focuses on the relationship between sustainable value creation and risk. The aggregation of SVC metrics in the pillars of the scorecard that express risk provide novel information to policymakers aware that risk origination is also the creation of value, while its transfer is exceedingly detrimental to human and economic development.

6.6.4 A sector-specific SVC measurement for industry benchmarking and policy

The VCp and VCr measure value creation relative to value transfers in absolute terms. But when it comes to interpretation, how much sense does it make to compare firms across industries or to a national average? The carbon footprint of the machine-building industry relying on extensive metal welding and mechanical operations that require signifiant energy consumption is certainly higher than that of the largely digital software industry. But in the VCr calculation, machine builders will offset such extractive transfer-IN with rich transfer-OUT in terms innovation spillovers and future blue-collar employment. That is not so much the case for the producers of cement; all of which will invariably exhibit low VCr scores given their massive carbon footprints.[147] Comparing the VCr scores of firms across industries could therefore be nonsensical. The sustainable value creation solution (note that at the macro policy level, offsets are possible across industries, while at the firm level this happens across the activities of the business model) is to compare cement producer against cement producer. To benchmark such comparisons, the 'Sector Value Creation Rating' ('sector-VCr'), positioned between the micro and meso levels (see Figure 7.8) and based on sector-specific SVC metrics, is proposed. In the prior example, firms that are more invested in producing green cement composites (Wen, Wang, Dai, Shi, Jin, Wang, & Jiang, 2023) will receive scores higher than the sector-VCr that could be an average, a median, or, in stricter versions, set at or above the 51st percentile (for instance, at the 70th percentile). What matters from the elevated double materiality perspective is that firms that score above the median will lift their overall industry benchmark and *de facto* improve the incentive system for the industry. The sector-VCr thus serves as an important reference for narratives that drive transformational leadership at both the elite system and firm levels, as illustrated in Figure A5.12b.

147 The case of the cement industry points to the need for baselines, to the intricacies of setting these across sectors, and to the conceptual determination and weighting of metrics, especially as according to Smil (2022), cement is one of "the four pillars of modern civilization" (the other three being steel, plastics, and ammonia).

"The Need for Sector-specific Materiality and Sustainability Reporting Standards" is persuasively advocated by Eccles, Krzus, Rogers, and Serafeim (2012, pp. 65, 70) on various grounds such as standardization ("By holding industry constant, one would expect less variation") or data availability ("if one company can provide quantitative metrics, it should be possible, at least in theory, for the others to do so"), and so "developing sector-specific guidelines on what sustainability issues are material to that sector [. . .] would significantly improve the ability of companies to report on their ESG performance". The Global Reporting Initiative (GRI) multi-stakeholder approach for sustainability reporting encompasses the GRI Sector Program to "develop standards for 40 sectors, starting with those that have the highest impact".[148] Khan, Serafeim, and Yoon (2016, p. 10) detail the massive effort behind how SASB (Sustainability Accounting Standards Board) "produced guidance for six sectors (out of a total of 10) that include 45 industries" with standards developed "via a multi-stakeholder process consisting of research supported by Bloomberg technology, data and analytical tools; balanced, multi-stakeholder industry working groups; a public comment period; and review by an independent Standards Council comprised of experts in standards development, securities law, environmental law, metrics and accounting". Methods to "Create a tailored set of key performance indicators for the most material issues for each sector" have also been proposed (see, for instance, Lydenberg, Rogers, & Wood, 2010, p. 18). The sector-VCr will reference existing industry and sector classifications and utilize them to determine sector-specific SVC metrics.

In short, the sector-VCr will primarily fulfill two functions. First, to assess and benchmark firms within a given sector on the basis of a set of SVC metrics that is material to that industry. These metrics will be established in Stage (I) during the conceptual determination (see Figure 6.6) while also referencing existing practice given that "consensus within an industry" regarding materiality is necessary (Eccles, Krzus, Rogers, and Serafeim, 2012, p. 70). What matters is whether a firm's VCr is above or below the sector-VCr benchmark (and by what distance). To evaluate firms in relation to others in an industry is valuable to many stakeholders, especially asset managers or policymakers.

Second, and from the macro vantage point, the sector-VCr will assist the formulation of policy, including decision-making on which industries a nation ought to favor or discourage. The measurement could be used to support or to phase out an entire industry as in the cases of the CHIPS (Creating Helpful Incentives to Produce Semiconductors) and Science Act of 2022 (The White House, 2022) or China's "National Sword" reform of 2018. The latter policy "banned the import of most plastics and other materials headed for that nation's recycling processors, which had handled nearly half of the world's recyclable waste for the past quarter century" and because of this "effort to halt a deluge of soiled and contaminated materials [its] plastics imports have plummeted by 99 percent" (Katz, 2019). To China's government, it was immaterial whether

148 See: https://www.globalreporting.org/standards/sector-program/

recycling processor A or recycling processor B had a higher VCr. The industry's general extraction was deemed substantial—its sector-VCr would have been low—so the plastic waste import elite business models were eliminated.

6.6.5 Incorporating risk origination and risk transfers in all SVC measurements

> Corporations that embrace market mechanisms and decry government intervention in the good times should not change the rules when times turn tough. Privatizing profits while socializing risks isn't capitalism: It's rigged roulette. (Williams & Khanna, 2020)

Materiality considerations include sustainability risks (Eccles, Krzus, Rogers, and Serafeim, 2012; Lydenberg, Rogers, & Wood, 2010) and so taking account of sustainability frameworks is a form of risk management and "provides an 'insurance-like' benefit" (Godfrey, Merrill, & Hansen, 2009, p. 425). To this inquiry, the most material sustainability risks are those associated with the transfer of risk. 'Sustainable risk origination' is as important as value creation. Yet a number of elite business models are deemed to be unsustainable because they are based on risk transfers, such as the bailouts implied above. Given the importance of first-order risk origination and the pervasiveness second-order risk transfers—and the enormous adverse impacts that the latter have on development—'The Sustainable Risk Framework' for society is now proposed to think through the risk origination and transfer question. This is also a call for the systematic operationalization of risk origination and transfers, both as metrics for SVC measurements and as indicators for elite quality measurements (the EQx implicitly measures risk, for instance, in the creative destruction pillar). The matrix framework depicted in Figure 6.9 is based on two variables: risk origination on the x-axis (which is a form of value creation and can be either low or high) and value appropriation on the y-axis (also low to high). Taleb places the blame for the 2008 financial crisis on "bankers, master risk transferors" (2018, p. 12) and, in the example provided in the opening quote of this sub-section, the socialization of risks often on the back of bailout culture and ongoing state interevention (Sharma, 2024b) consolidated in narrative markets, equates to 'unsustainable risk origination' (quadrant 3). That is, those that undertake risk do not bear the downside (i.e., *negative* value) when their bets do not pay off.

Political economies where risk-takers see no downside when their bets turn sour are characterized by elites that recklessly raise the stakes and so intensify second-order risk transfers. Consequently, genuine first-order risk creators will abscond, and those members of society undertaking little risk and expecting to appropriate the value they create (as workers, farmers, savers, taxpayers, etc.) will see their modest but honestly earned present and future value sucked away to cover the losses of wealthy gamblers who, when their wagers are fruitful, benefit from the fully private gains. Does this mean that risk origination is morally hazardous and ought to be avoided or that the high profits of uncertain bets should be socialized?

Quite the contrary; the nature of risk is such that small amounts of *positive*—and *negative*—value accrue from taking moderate risks, while large amounts of value—along with losses—ensue from "aggressively seeking out and exploiting risk" (Damodaran, 2005, p. 38), large exposure to risk (Markowitz, 1952; Sharpe, 1964), and the undertaking of Knightian uncertainty, no matter how well managed. Without the daring bets of first-order risk-takers engaging in highly uncertain projects in pursuit of new and novel business models there is scant technological, social, or economic development. Without risk there would be none of the value creation underpinning "the best-performing 4% of listed companies [that] explain the net gain for the entire US stock market since 1926" (Bessembinder, 2018, p. 440). 'Sustainable risk origination' (quadrant 4) occurs when risky undertakings are successful, value materializes, and the risk-takers reap the residual income associated with value creation. Such an incentive structure supports economic development. Counterintuitively, 'sustainable risk origination' also occurs when risky projects fail, because success and failure are two sides of the same coin, two states of a single reality that are joined—not separated—by their respective probabilities. There is no shame in undertaking risky projects and not succeeding, as long as the risk creator bears the losses. Incentives for bearing the brunt of failure insure against reckless gambling and excessive risk origination, sharpen the mind, and activate the ingenuity that liquidates moral hazard. Risk to value conversion is thus bound to increase. Smart and well-managed (Damodaran, 2005) risk-taking by elite business models explains why the US and China have grown faster than Germany and Japan in recent decades.

At the firm level—and referencing Markowitz's risk/return efficient frontier (1952)—there can be no large profits without large risk exposure unless, of course, the political economy is a "rigged roulette". A system with 'unsustainable no-risk origination' (quadrant 2) has agents that eschew uncertainty yet reap the profits from the risk-taking of others, mostly society at large. For instance, rent seeking, sclerotic bureaucracies, landowners in economies growing on account of social transformations not of their making (e.g., the rapid-growth industrialization phase) that see rapid real estate price rises, or the executives and shareholders of state-owned enterprises or private corporations that benefit from taxpayer-funded risk origination in university and science establishments. Finally, there is the 'null risk origination' scenario where there is simply no risk origination and hence no value creation, only stagnation (quadrant 1). This is the case in early social development phases, both at the beginning and the dreaded 'end of history'. In the context of "rational sustainability", Edmans spotlights the irrationality of the "'zero-risk bias,' which leads people to seek the complete elimination of a risk" (2024, p. 14). This behavioral trait—so fatal for development—has an association with the incentive structure of the political economy (and its freedoms, see Section 8.3) and bureaucratism. Regression paths to zero risk might also occur when 'unsustainable no-risk origination' ('risk *not* originated but *positive* value appropriated') and 'unsustainable risk origination' ('risk originated but *negative* value *not* appropriated') in extractive political economies gravitate towards 'null risk origination' (risk *not* created *no* value to appropriate) as is indicated by the paths of arrows [a] and [b] in Figure 6.9 (emanating from quadrants 3 and 2 towards quadrant 1). The path of arrow [a] sees countries where too much 'unsustainable no-risk origination' kills animal spirits and paralyzes economic activity, especially non-elite agency. The path of arrow [b] sees countries with too many elite business models engaged in 'unsustainable risk origination' experience a proliferation of unsophisticated and hazardous bets. Both routes lead to the gradual disappearance of genuine risk takers. In other words, a state of affairs where risk is not risky and risky projects have no risk-takers, meaning that value cannot be created—the risk version of the 'extractive escalation dynamic'.

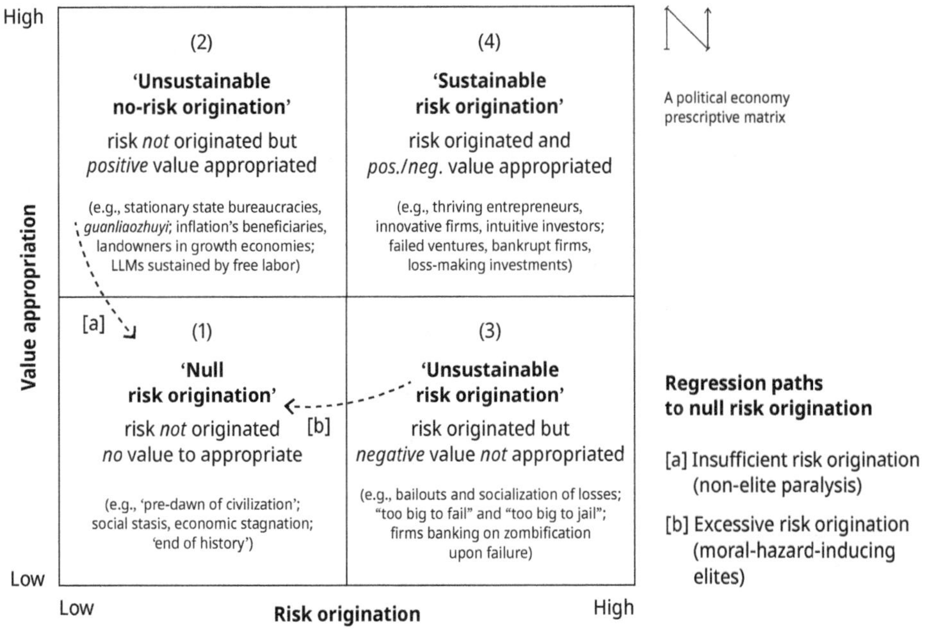

Figure 6.9: The Sustainable Risk Framework for society.

As mentioned in Section 2.3.1 and stressed again here, value and risk are equivalent and represent two sides of the same business reality. While all of the proposals to operationalize elite quality and sustainable value creation discussed so far have focused on measuring value from a revenue and residual income perspective, any SVC measurement that does not explicitly account for risk origination (which is always inclusive) and risk transfer (which is extractive) is incomplete. Damodaran (2005, pp. 38, 39) conveys this idea in discussing valuation frameworks that encourage firms to "*exploit uncertainty*", since "risk management is about using risk to advantage". This inquiry wholeheartedly embraces this position and argues that the undertaking of uncertainty and risk origination activities of elite business models must be understood by policymakers as contributing to sustainable value creation. Uncertainty undertaking and risk origination activities are to be conceptually determined and operationalized as transfer-OUT metric constituents of the VCr. This position is coherent with Knight's uncertainty (1921/2002), Schumpeter's innovation activities (1911/2003), Markowitz's risk/return (1952), Damodaran's exploitation of uncertainty (2005) or Taleb's "transfer of harm" and "skin in the game" (2018, 2020), and are classed as 'sustainable risk origination' in (quadrant 4). In this state, risk is created and the ensuing *positive* or *negative* value is fully appropriated by the creators. This is the case in the "the decentralized hedge fund space" where "owner-operators have at least half of their net worth in the funds, making them relatively more exposed than any of their customers, and they personally go down with the ship" (Taleb, 2018, p. 13).

Ultimately, 'sustainable risk origination' (value creation) as well as 'unsustainable risk origination' and 'unsustainable no-risk origination' (the latter two constituting value transfers) must be part of elite quality meso-level SVC measurements (EQx/EQr and PEz) and their firm-level counterparts (VCp/VCr and self-VCp/self-VCr/360-VCz). Comprehensive, accurate, and theoretically grounded methodologies to operationalize risk, the creation of uncertainty, and their transfer are a precondition to test the ETED and the robustness of its system. A most consequential aspect of the further research agenda is therefore to identify and select the SVC metrics (at the firm level) and indicators (at the elite system level) that best capture and reflect risk origination and transfers.

Summary of Chapter 6

Towards measurements for an elite theory of economic development

Chapter 6 is the first of the three chapters in Part III of this book that focuses on the 'Implications' of the ETED. The conceptual development and abstract foundations of the theory are brought into the realm of practice through several measurements. The first meso-level measurement, the Elite Quality Index (EQx), is discussed in depth to prepare the terrain for economic development policy ideas at the macro-level. Other meso- and micro-level measurements and their implications are then proposed, while the operationalization of sustainable value creation (SVC) measurements for firms is advanced with the discussion of their constituent SVC metrics.

The chapter starts in Section 6.1 by affirmatively answering the question about whether there is an elite agency measurement gap that this work should address. Having established the need for an elite quality measurement—even a simple heuristic would provide novel insights—Section 6.2 proceeds to introduce the initial actualization of aggregate value creation in a national elite system. The EQx is a global comparative measurement tool with a four-level architecture. The index (level 1) and the two sub-indices of 'power' and 'value' (level 2) are discussed (6.2.1), and the two index dimensions, 'political' and 'economic' are then explained (6.2.2). These elements form a matrix, 'The Political Economy Power and Value Matrix' (Figure 6.2), with four index areas that, taken together, conceptually anchor the architecture of the EQx (6.2.3). The next sub-section (6.2.4) explains the 12 EQx pillars (level 3), provides exemplar indicators (level 4), and synthesizes the conceptual logic for the classification of indicators into the four index areas and their constituent three pillars (Figure 6.4). The indicators of the (i) 'political power' index area follow the logic of 'capture'; those of (ii) 'economic power', the logic of 'dominance'; those of (iii) 'political value', the logic of 'income (transfer)'; and those of (iv) 'economic value', the logic of 'value' creation. The section closes by expounding on the weighting methodology used in the EQx (6.2.5).

Section 6.3 discusses the interpretation of the results of the EQx through the elite agency sustainable value creation perspective of the political economy. First, the big picture possibilities (6.3.1) that are important for crafting narratives distinct from those offered by existing macroeconomic models are considered. 'The State of the Elite System Framework' for the political economy (Figure 6.5) is then proposed to classify national elite systems (6.3.2). The purpose of this interpretation is to support elite system transformational leadership.

Section 6.4 then considers some of the limitations of the EQx. These include the fact that in the absence of scholarly consensus, the EQx will need to take positions one way or the other on the value creation/extraction of certain phenomena such as monopolies, surely inviting controversy (6.4.1); the establishment of value creation optima (6.4.2); the need for multiple indicators to fairly account for the value creation/

extraction impact at the meso-level of elite business models (6.4.3); and blind spots in a global comparative index where value creation/extraction phenomena remain unaccounted for—a vital issue when high-impact country-specific business models such as opioids in the US or natural resource extraction in Russia flourish (6.4.4). The inclusion of 'critical impact indicators' is suggested to duly capture the consequences of such influential elite business models.

Section 6.5 then adds proposals to advance sustainable value creation measurements beyond the EQx. These are firstly, the 'Perceptions of Elites Survey' (PEz), with a 'Non-Elite Questionnaire' (1/2) and an 'Elite Questionnaire (2/2)' designed to (self-)assess elite quality (6.5.1), and secondly, the country-specific 'Elite Quality Rating' (EQr), a sophisticated 'bottom-up' (micro-to-meso level) measurement arrived at by aggregating the VCr's of the elite system's material business models (6.5.2).

Section 6.6 closes the chapter by returning to underlying development at the micro-level. The extended first sub-section (6.6.1) describes the three-stage process (Figure 6.6) to establish SVC measurements and their SVC metrics, and which stands on the three assumptions for socio-economic relations (Figure A5.4a). The first stage is the conceptual determination of the constitutive metrics of SVC measurements that parallel the EQx indicator datasets expressing value creation and extractive transfers. The second stage is the quantification of these value transfer-IN/OUT metrics. In the final third stage, the SVC measurements are calculated by applying, weighting, and using other statistical schema on the calibrated SVC metrics. Tables 6.1 and 6.2 use ten exemplar metrics for VCp/VCr to illustrate how transfer-IN/OUT activities are ascertained, with data that emphasize the materiality needed for their conceptual determination, assessment method—such as the 'SVC Metrics Fair Assessment' or the 'SVC Metrics Self-assessment Survey'—and conversion process, with its 'monetary equivalence' and 'calibration factor'.

The self-assessment of metrics approach yields two SVC measurements that mirror the VCp/VCr: the 'Self-assessment Value Creation Position' ('self-VCp') and the 'Self-assessment Value Creation Rating' ('self-VCr'). Both depend on a questionnaire, the SVC Metrics Self-assessment Survey, designed for top management and business insiders with access to firm information to gather the data that will establish monetary equivalence between a metric and the P&L revenue/profit. A subset of this questionnaire is the 'International Business Self-assessment Value Creation Rating' ('IB-self-VCr'), which is relevant in the context of international business. Together these self-assessments provide management and boards with a quick, subjective, and tentative indication of sustainable value creation. A second approach will leverage the 'Firm Stakeholder Questionnaire' (1/2) and the 'Firm Principal Questionnaire' (2/2), for a fourth firm-level survey-based SVC measurement, the 'Perceptions of Value Creation Survey' ('360-VCz'), to gain a comprehensive view by including the thoughts and opinions of firm stakeholders (6.6.2). The four firm-level survey-based SVC measurements (self-VCp, self-VCr, IB-self-VCr, and 360-VCz) form a toolkit to help leaders reflect on sustainability trade-offs, and hence the impact and purpose of their organizations.

'The Business Model Sustainable Value Scorecard' (Figure 6.8), with its two 'sub-ratings', four 'rating areas' and 12 'pillars', mirrors the EQx architecture to support the conceptual determination and weighting of the SVC metrics that comprise the SVC firm measurements (6.6.3). The 'Sector Value Creation Rating' ('sector-VCr') is then introduced to benchmark firms in a particular industry and inform industrial policy (6.6.4). Finally, specific importance is placed on the impact of risk origination and transfers and a recommendation is made that all such activities should be captured by suitable SVC metrics (6.6.5). 'The Sustainable Risk Framework' for society matches risk origination and value appropriation and is presented (Figure 6.9) to serve as an essential framework for development policies.

This chapter's extensive proposals for the various SVC measurements lead us into Chapter 7 which, on the premise that the elite business model establishes the incentive system of the political economy, discusses the implications of this book's theory for research and the practical endeavors of policymakers, managers, boards, and investors before ultimately widening its purview to consider international perspectives.

Chapter 7
The implications of the ETED for incentive systems

> Perhaps no idea has been so influential on economics as the idea that outcomes depend crucially on the structure of incentives facing the participants in an economy. If tariffs, tax rates, subsidies, or property laws change, the economist normally predicts that a different outcome or allocation of resources will occur. [. . .] Economists have also been relatively successful in providing parsimonious explanations of economic behavior with theories built upon the assumption that the individuals and firms in an economy respond to the incentives with which they are confronted. Certainly there is no other system of thought in the social sciences with anything like the same explanatory power. (Olson, 1984, p. 644)

The fundamental tenet of an elite theory of economic development is that elite agency explains growth and progress by shaping incentives. Elite business models, formed as a result of endogenous institutional change and intra-elite contests, both constitute and reflect the principal incentive structure of the economy. In the ETED, the level of economic and human development results from variations in the degree of value creation delivered by these models. This extensive chapter begins by examining the policy implications of this position on development, emphasizes the need to weight and offset value transfers, and then links this work to diverse fields—including practice—while proposing new directions for research. All of this includes the need to test conjectures and to develop falsifiable hypotheses for the gainful utilization of the proposed sustainable value creation (SVC) measurements, such as the Elite Quality Index (EQx) at the macro level and the Value Creation Rating (VCr) at the firm level.

Elite business models depend on intra-elite contest victories in the market, nonmarket, and narrative market arenas of the political economy. Winning elite coalitions convert power into institutional change that is consistent with the preferences of their elite business models and ultimately into residual income (as depicted in Figures 3.3 and 4.4). Elite business models are by no means in contradiction with the common good; indeed, to this theory, high quality elites are conceivably a nation's greatest development asset. Olson (1982, p. 74) contemplates this in recognizing that elites "have some incentive to make the society in which they operate more prosperous". Schumpeter (1911/2003, p. 255) notes that if the upper echelons of society are creative and competitive, the results are "continually raising real incomes of all social strata". For example, while causing a Dutch disease of sorts with an influx of foreign currency, a higher krone, and lower interest rates, Novo Nordisk's innovative weight loss drugs Ozempic and Wegovy bolster the welfare of Danish society through larger tax payments, high-quality jobs, the growing assets of the country's pension funds, the activities of the grant recipients of its foundation,[149] and the vibrant local pharma eco-

149 "The Novo Nordisk Foundation is the world's wealthiest grant maker, with more than $114 billion in assets." (Stiffman, 2023).

https://doi.org/10.1515/9783110734638-011

system. In the latter realm, vital inclusive transfer-OUT includes the world-class output by the Center for Protein Research at the University of Copenhagen in the field of proteomics, or, as a *Nature* piece sums up, "building on the success of blockbuster drugs, the country's focus on reinvestment is feeding a stream of discovery" (Nogrady, 2023, p. S16).

This chapter will discuss how countries with inclusive elites that excel at first-order productive activities such as innovation reap an array of benefits, including a higher likelihood that they will prevail in international relations and so preempt extractive transfers from both their elites and non-elites by the elites of foreign powers. It examines the main implications of this inquiry's exhortations for sustainable value creation that emanate from the ontological, finance, and positive assumptions incorporated in its measurements: to holistically 'weight and offset value transfers' against value creation activities (Figure A5.4b). The examination starts with the macro-level implications for policymaking (7.1), before continuing at the micro-level with management, board, and investor perspectives (7.2). Subsequently, an extensive review of international perspectives and the wider implications of cross-border elite business models—from geopolitics to international business—is undertaken (7.3).

7.1 The macro-level policy implications of sustainable value creation

> In summary, the organization of economic activity through voluntary exchange presumes that we have provided, through government, for the maintenance of law and order to prevent coercion of one individual by another, the enforcement of contracts voluntarily entered into, the definition of the meaning of property rights, the interpretation and enforcement of such rights, and the provision of a monetary framework. (Friedman, 1962/2002, p. 27)

None of Friedman's assumptions in *Capitalism and Freedom* can possibly hold true with the existence of bargaining power differentials. One must only consider the adjudication of rights to monetize the current most important factor of production—data, from which intelligence emerges—or the fact that negative interest rates and inflation are realities in even the most advanced societies. At the same time, Friedman implicitly acknowledged elite agency as the microfoundation of institutional change: a dominant coalition might run an extractive labor union or a monopoly that "generally, arises from government support or from collusive agreements among individuals" (Friedman, 1962/2002, p. 28). While economists recognize these distortions, their econometric models do not make them explicit, specify their economic quantitates, or systematically attribute (elite) business models' profits to extractive transfers and value creation. Yet the political economy never witnesses "capitalism and freedom", but is rather characterized by varying degrees of rent seeking and value transfers across the socio-economic landscape enabled by power. Extractive elite agency, like its value creation counterpart, is opportunistic, ever present, independent of belief systems, and realized without exception by all sides of the political narrative spectrum and in all cultural contexts.

Elites necessarily source political power in the non-market arena (see Figures 1.2 and 2.1) to secure transfers. For instance, the nationalization of the Big Four British railway companies into British Railways/Rail (1948–1997) led to electrification in the 1960s and general modernization, as well as falling passenger demand and substantial losses; the subsequent Hayek and Friedman-inspired privatization by Margaret Thatcher resulted in increased passenger numbers and higher freight ton-miles with lower operating costs, but also growing public dissatisfaction and more reliance on public financial assistance (Welsby & Nichols, 1999; Dixon & Joyner, 2000; Pollitt & Smith, 2002). As the years went on, the disastrous Hatfield crash and the reversal of privatization's initial efficiency gains led researchers to conclude that: "poor productivity appears to have resulted in increases in subsidy" (Cowie, 2009, p. 102). In short, whether they are state-owned or private, elite business models are alike in that they strive to collude to reduce competition, secure subsidies, and otherwise add value transfer-IN to their income statement to maximize residual income. This is the natural and expected state of affairs, is not objectionable, and is what businesses must do, transformational leadership notwithstanding.

Neoclassical premises about markets are an unrealistic idealization, as are policies that recall the putative primeval free market of the brewer, the butcher, and the baker. The bargaining power differentials of today, typified by the data and intelligence powered expansion of 'the extraordinary lever' in every field (see the four variations in Figure A5.3) make this even more of a chimera. The focus of growth policy ought not to be on fiscal and monetary measures (optimizing the former or targeting prices for the latter, as Friedman would have it) but a constant push for proactive, informed, weighted and targeted structural reform that perennially adjusts the economy's incentive system to induce value creation business models and dismantle the sterile and potentially destructive value transfers persistently designed by the lower quality elites in the system. The first sub-section (7.1.1) examines the general implications of the ETED for the economic policy mix. This is followed by a discussion of its implications for both emerging economies (7.1.2) and advanced economies (7.1.3). Next, selected implications for academic work aimed at policy impact are considered (7.1.4). Finally, policymakers are addressed with a discussion on implementing weighted and targeted structural reform with a long run view (7.1.5).

7.1.1 General implications for the economic policy mix

The discussion in Section 5.3.1 on the conceptualization and operationalization of value transfers was presented as being crucial in addressing questions such as "how many carbon offsets are required to compensate monopoly rents?". Society is such that value creation and transfers are two states of a single reality that are joined—

never separated—by how they are respectively weighted (in the 'sustainable risk origination' discussion of Section 6.6.5, success and failure are two realities joined together by 'probabilities'). This dichotomous typology of business model activities, referencing value on the basis of the binary 'value is created or transferred' ontological assumption (Section 2.3.1), is later worked into the set of ethical principles of Chapter 8 and now addressed in terms of policymaking.

SVC measurements, which are themselves constituted by weighted metrics or indicators, are designed for the weighting of diverse business model activities and the myriad of elite business models in an economy, each with discrete extractive value transfer positions. Since all systems have value transfers, the imperative is to maximize value creation to the best extent possible. This work explicitly advocates structural reform because value transfers are already weighted and offset as a matter of course in all decision-making, implicitly (but also overtly) by elite agency in every domain of the political economy from consumer safety to geopolitics. For instance, legal reforms introduced mandatory seat belts because "seat belt use significantly reduces fatalities among car occupants" (Cohen & Einav, 2003, p. 828). In the midst of World War I, John Bates Clark wrote that:

> Some of the effects of this burden in fettering and crushing the life of the future will transcend all economic measurements, much as do the killing, maiming, and general ravaging that have already gone on. Only the purely economic effects lend themselves to measurement, and a few principles applying to these are what this paper will attempt to state (1916, p. 85).

Given the accumulation of rent seeking and its impact on human and economic development, the ambition of the SVC measurements is to quantify most of these effects and make weighting, already occurring inadvertently and on an inherent and partial basis, explicit. Any limitations to this aim lie not in the theory or its conceptual elements, but with the elite system and the technical feasibility.

The indicators for elite quality and the metrics for the SVC measurements of firms ultimately pursue monetary equivalence (in terms of national GDP origination or firm revenue) for all value creation and extraction activities (from carbon emissions to the value of statistical life for policies that reflect people's mortality rates). Structural reform is aimed at the underlying *de facto* existing structure of weighting and offsetting in the political economy. The pragmatic and technocratic policy slant of this section aspires to overcome the effects of narratives and other forms of power that cause society to experience excessive value transfers. The first implication that emerges from the three assumptions for socio-economic relations (Figure A5.4a) is that weighting must be transparent and consequently deliberate, systematic, targeted, and ultimately transformational. In the interest of development, the weighting and offsetting of transfers should not be left to arbitrary processes, social inertia, or culture, and much less so to winning narratives and their associated biases, blind spots, and the likelihood that they are captured by extractive business models.

This inquiry calls for a novel set of analytical tools and related measurements to underpin and augment policymaking options that are premised on the centrality of business model transformation in a two-way causal relationship between elites and institutions (Figure 3.2). The elite theory sharpens business, societal, and economic understanding to derive actionable prescriptions. More specifically, the intent is a paradigm shift that supplies the conceptual groundwork for effective micro-interventions on institutions that are aimed at intra-elite contests and the long run. The spotlight must be directed on those that associate with business model rules such as the regulation of commerce, central banking policies, or government budgets that provide incentives for value creation or transfers. Advances in economics regularly offer new analytical possibilities, often thanks to new measurements, although these do not always translate into policy. For instance, on the premise that economic complexity leads to growth, Hidalgo, Hausmann, and Dasgupta (2009, p. 10575) suggest development strategies that create incentives that will "encourage the further coevolution of new products and capabilities", and on such a basis, Hausmann et al. (2013) proposed the Economic Complexity Index (ECI). *The Ease of Doing Business Index* was, despite its turbulent history, a benchmark for structural reform and had been publicly endorsed by many leaders capable of shaping institutions, including the Prime Minister of India and the President of Russia (Besley, 2015, pp. 99–100). It is important to stress here that even with new theoretical insights and measurements at hand, adjustments to the incentive system take time, for reasons ranging from cognitive dissonance (Kuhn, 1962) to the resistance against a loss of privileges (Fernandez & Rodrik, 1991). However, contrary to short run and more immediately implemented fiscal and monetary policies, structural reform is carried out with a long view and so reformers who, for instance, wish to encourage entrepreneurship must "start enterprise development policies early" (Acs & Szerb, 2007, p. 109).

SVC measurements seek to serve as variables in the macroeconometric approaches employed for macroeconomic models on the premise that they reflect the critical reality of the elite system: value transfers. The signals that they capture connect to the prospects for development and provide policymakers and society at large with forewarning of specific sectors of the economy that are becoming either problematic or promising because of their abnormal value transfer-IN/OUT patterns. They may even anticipate critical junctures, including the dreaded descent into the 'extractive escalation dynamic' that is a hardly reversible trap—even over the course of a generation. By affording timely transparency on the micro-level analytical perspective, the measurements open windows of opportunity to redress unsustainable rent seeking and preempt the consequent incarnations of the political economy. On the other hand, for countries that are enjoying an inclusive and ascendant economic path, there is a need for clarity and understanding about which elites are contributing most to development so that there is a legitimate rationale to strengthen the incentives in the political economy that support their agglomeration (see Section 4.3.5) when they engage in intra-elite contests. Figure 7.1 depicts the aspirations of the ETED

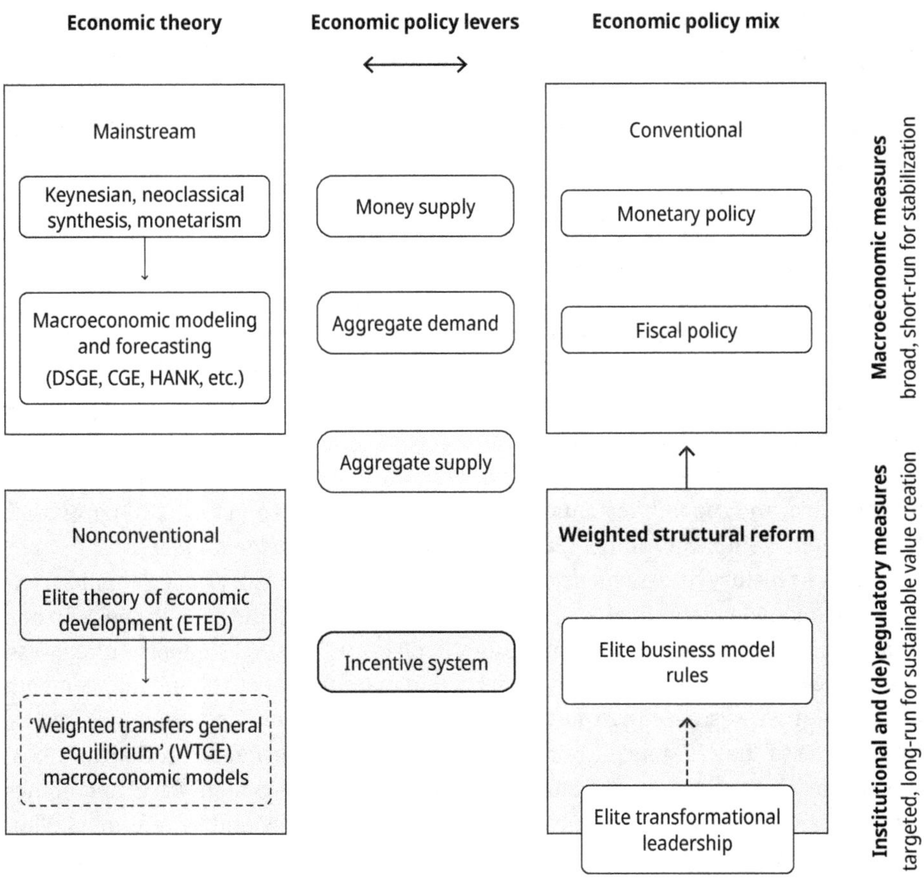

Figure 7.1: The ETED in the economic policy mix: A weighted structural reform approach for the incentive system.

in the economic policy mix: boosting the incentive system for elite business model transformation towards higher sustainable value creation.

The economic policy mix based on the premise of sustainable value creation necessitates the systematic identification of first-order productive activities (value creation), and second-order transfer activities (value extraction) in the economy (see Table 2.3). It can then focus on weighted and targeted policy initiatives for the long run rather than on broad short-run monetary and fiscal measures (as in Figure 7.1). That is, the emphasis should be on narrow institutional change and modifications to specific business model rules that indirectly shape aggregate supply, rather than comprehensive or sweeping interventions that adjust monetary mass or government expenditure to modulate aggregate supply and demand.

Singapore regularly places first in the EQx's ranking of elite quality in 151 countries, excelling in continuous targeted reform. The "roadmaps" for the Industry Transformation Programme of Singapore's Ministry of Trade and Industry (n.d.) are "developed for 23 industries to address issues within each industry". State capacity is key to success and feasible through measurements like the "Smart Industry Readiness Index", an assessment to support firms "initiating their I4.0 [Industry 4.0 digital] transformation journey spanning across organisation, process and technology" (TÜV SÜD, 2024). Reform also requires creative destruction, possibly including replacing capital before it depreciates. While Young suggested "that Singapore is a victim of its own targeting policies, which are increasingly driving the economy ahead of its learning maturity into the production of goods in which it has lower and lower productivity" (1992, p. 16), the government has been proven right time and time again, as putting pressure on elite business models to upgrade is *de facto* a key to development.

In this inquiry, 'reform' starts with an impact assessment where value creation and transfers are attributed metric-by-metric to the stakeholder relationships of principals of elite (and also non-elite) business models and then quantified. In the subsequent policy formulation step, new weightings for these activities are proposed. As the entanglements and links of transfers to other economic variables are determined, nonconventional econometric modeling ensues. That is, scenarios are produced to describe and contrast extant and implicit weighting with normative and explicit weighting benchmarks that maximize long-run value creation. The conceptual element of weighting brings the elite theory into the realm of practice. Weighting as currently realized by conventional measures is seldom explicit, but mostly utilized implicitly and in comparative terms for domains across the economy (leading to erratic institutional arrangements like the inconsistent principles that inform safety measures for pharma vs agriculture vs radiation exposure, etc., as cited in Fischhoff, Lichtenstein, Slovic, Keeney, & Derby, 1980). Rules and regulations directly result from bargaining power differentials that deviate from the counterfactual 'equalized bargaining power equilibrium prices'. The implicit weighting of transfer activities reflects the large/small power endowments of business models that consequently appropriate more/less value than otherwise would be the case. Weighting is universal and emergent, but under transformational leadership and reform scenarios, the pricing of second-order transfer activities becomes explicit, institutions are more likely to result from deliberate action beyond the beneficiary coalition's priorities, and efficient offsets become feasible. Essentially, the implicit weighting will undergo a 're-weighting'. Econometrically, such an approach, here referred to as the 'weighted transfers general equilibrium' macroeconomic model (also, the 'WTGE' model or, more generically, 'weighted transfers modeling'), seeks to stand on its own distinctive qualities while drawing from the conventional toolset for fiscal and monetary macroeconomic measures such as dynamic stochastic general equilibrium (DSGE) models, time series modeling, computable general equilibrium (CGE) models, or Heterogeneous Agent New Keynesian (HANK) models.

Kydland and Prescott's (1982) DSGE is informed by growth and real business cycle theory (RBC), a model of the economy that aims to explain fluctuations and incorporate period sequences that ultimately "mimics the world along a carefully specified set of dimensions" (Kydland & Prescott, 1996, p. 69). Such models' representations of reality have become indispensable policy analysis tools in areas ranging from central banking to the corporate boardroom. One such model, Smets and Wouters' DGSE, estimated "business cycle fluctuation in the euro area" and incorporates features like sticky prices, habit formation, and variable capacity utilization, as well as "ten orthogonal structural shocks" from productivity to monetary policy (2003, p. 1123). DSGE models provide a faithful rendition of the economy (e.g., by eschewing price rigidities). Of high relevance to the elite theory are attempts like those of Costa Junior and Garcia-Cintado to derive the time series of the "unobservable variable" of rent seeking "in an otherwise standard open-economy DSGE model" (2021, p. 1). Time series modeling (Box & Jenkins, 1976) supplies insights into upcoming shifts, anticipating vulnerabilities in specific sectors, while its forecasts also enable macro stabilization and the formulation of policies to optimally stimulate demand. CGE models are also useful in their capacity to assess the impact of specific institutional change, such as environmental regulation (even if only partially, see Jorgenson & Wilcoxen, 1990). HANK models deal with market incompleteness and emphasize "(i) precautionary savings and cyclical uninsurable risk [and] (ii) marginal propensity to consume (MPC) heterogeneity and the sensitivity of high-MPC households' income to the business cycle" (Acharya & Dogra, 2020, pp. 1113–1114). However, while being based on microfoundations, neither of these models comprehensively quantify high impact phenomena such as rent seeking, the bargaining power differentials that characterize elite business models, or the extractive transfer-IN and transfer-COST, and the inclusive transfer-OUT, much less their respective impacts (weights) to permit offsets. As such, to the ETED, and for all their remarkable utility, these are tools with finite competence to extrapolate long-term human and economic development trajectories.

All macroeconometric models (see Fair, 2018) aim to analyze the economy, and mostly employ a model construction methodology that traces back to the "Cowles Commission approach" anchored by Tinbergen (1939). Attendant econometric techniques and computational methods have since evolved to include Bayesian inference (Geweke, 1989) and nonlinear optimization algorithms. As noted, 'weighted transfers modeling' would extend existing macroeconomic models by incorporating value transfers as its discrete microfoundation, working with SVC measurements as available (see the full set in Figure 7.8 and Table A3.1a). When converted into variables suitable for modeling, these could contribute to estimated stochastic equations (e.g., to the investment function along with the existing interest rate, output, and other explanatory variables) and be part of identities (e.g., in 'output = consumption + investment + government spending + net exports', ascribing a discrete weight for each component to denote the relative amount of the value transfer). SVC measurements operationalize the 'value is created or transferred' ontology via conceptual elements like elite quality, elite power, extractive and inclusive firm-level transfers, 'cost created but *not* borne', creative destruction, or labor value. As such, they add nuance or insight to the estimated equations for investment, exchange rates, the level of exports, the level of domestic prices, inequality, and, all the way down to their indivisible indicators and metrics, can be plausibly plugged into macroeconometric models and associated equations as variables. The regressions for sustainable growth linked to elite quality would reference work like Acemoglu, Johnson, and Robinson (2005), Durlauf, Johnson, and Temple (2005), and Rodrik (2012). A pivotal concern is how regressions that are extended by adding SVC measurements to standard variables enhance predictive power. Is it conceivable that elite quality turns out to be an explanatory variable (with highly significant coefficient estimates) in the estimated investment equation, vying for importance with the interest rate? Clearly, any extension of the existing "large-scale statistical macroeconomic models", testable with "strategies of econometric analysis", require "a connection between these models and reality" (Sims, 1980, p. 1) at the construction stage. Moreover, "one way to test a theory is to determine whether model economies constructed according to the instructions of that theory mimic certain aspects of reality" (Kydland & Prescott, 1996, p. 83). The ETED's claims of predictability, and the dependability of its policy toolbox, rest on the empirical validation of the relationships between variables that are conjectured throughout this work.

In their most ambitious and ideal form, WTGE macroeconomic models and econometric approaches address optimization problems like the 'alternating value extraction and creation' conjecture by first weighting the impact and then offsetting value creation and value transfers. Their efficacy would in part be contingent on the exactitude with which some of the key insights of Proposition 17 ('The national elite system is situated at the meso-level', Section 3.2.3) can be described. These include the fractal patterns that characterize the emerging properties at the meso level (e.g., elite quality or power endowments) and make up the micro to macro transmission mechanisms and, relatedly, the nonlinear scaling that organizes the nooks and crannies across the economy and governs principal-stakeholder relationships. Hard to capture actualities such as principal-stakeholder bargaining power differentials would be derived from prices, as would the counterfactual prices of zero bargaining power differentials (see approximation of Figure A5.9c). Support for such an exercise would come from theory; for instance, in identifying the stage of The Elite Business Model Lifecycle and the size of the 'elite power vs value creation gap' (Figure 4.5) in specific firms and sectors, as well as the degree to which their bargaining power differentials emanate from 'knowledge' or 'political economy know-how' (Figure 3.2). In the Coase theorem, if "transaction costs are zero, voluntary bargaining between agents will lead to an efficient (and invariant, according to Coase at the time) outcome, regardless of how rights are initially assigned" (Medema, 1993, p. 209). The zero bargaining power differential cum zero transaction cost world is an impossibility (and undesirable) due to the assertions on elite agency made throughout this work, yet models that use this notion to benchmark and establish the deviations and implicit weightings of transfer activities might still capture vital slices of political economy reality. Thus, cognizant of departures from hypothetical optima, while cautiously approximating the conditions of 'equalized bargaining power equilibrium prices', the models would run simulations under varying offsetting scenarios. Incentives to rebalance power differentials and establish explicit new weightings for value transfers, such as (de)regulatory measures or even Pigouvian remedies to align private costs with social costs (with transfers like taxes, subsidies, or tradable permits), would address negative externalities and rent seeking. Macroeconomic models incorporating insights on issues such as bargaining power would reveal counterfactual pricing, levels of value appropriated but *not* created, and ultimately market inefficiencies.

The estimated coefficients for the new variables in econometric models are crucial because extractive transfers can be both efficient and inefficient. As a result, they become benchmarks for the formulation of weighted policy and legal reforms in areas like M&As or IP. In other words, the models are intended to quantify this qualitative sequence in monetary terms:

> From 2003 onward, Google rolled up much of the online intermediary world. It bought YouTube, Applied Semantics, Keyhole, Admob, Urchin, Android, Neotonic, and hundreds of other firms. Though Google portrayed itself as innovative, in fact, most of its products, from Maps to Gmail, came from acquisitions. By 2014, Google was no longer just a search engine; if you bought advertising, sold advertising, brokered advertising, tracked advertising, etc., you were doing it on Google tools. It tied its products togethers [sic] so you couldn't get access to Google search data or YouTube ad inventory unless you used Google ad software, which killed rivals in the market. (Stoller, 2022)

Simply put, WTGE models establish the impact of an M&A on market dominance, then on consumer and supplier prices, and ultimately on growth and economic development. They become prescriptive when calculating discrete optimal timeframes for IP protection in each industry. Better still, these models offer estimates of the probability of a cigarette butt polluting a Spanish beach to justly tax tobacco firms (see BOE, 2022) for this particular 'cost created but *not* borne' (transfer-COST), thereby ensuring polite beachgoers do not pay for the uncivil behavior associated with smoking. The number of linkages and the underlying variables associated with value creation and value transfers that can be worked on and adjusted is evidently immense. To enable weighting and offsetting, WTGE models would need to theoretically formalize transmission mechanisms, for instance, to explain the relationship between various copyright protection timeframes and inclusive/exclusive transfers like innovation spillovers (transfer-OUT) or higher prices (transfer-IN). The set of dynamic equations capturing the effects of the incentive structures to be fine-tuned by policy, and relating these to economic performance, requires quantitative, structural, and micro-founded macroeconomic modeling of high complexity, all the more so when the specific numerical representations aim to reflect innate knowledge of value creation and transfers that falsification processes have observationally validated.

In a world where all material transactions are available as data, possibly on a blockchain, ascertained for their value creation by a LLM or similar, the relevant principal-stakeholder transactions in the political economy could also be mapped out. Econometric models would thus simulate the impacts of institutional change, structural reforms, new laws, (de)regulatory measures, and fiscal budgets and monetary policies on business model principal-stakeholder relationships to anticipate economic growth and human development. WTGE models processing econometric scenarios that weight and offset transfers to establish *qui generat valorem* through the lens of value optimization are akin to players prompting structural reforms in a 'weighted transfers game' (WT-Game), the large-scale, comprehensive simulation of transfers in all socio-economic relations (see Table A3.1b). Its rich data inputs could include SVC measurements of elite business models pertaining to the analytical mapping of coalition social networks across market, non-market, and narrative-market arenas, in relation to institutional change—as generated by political economy AI services (expanded versions of the 'chatbotEQx', Chen, Lu, Scherl, & Sutter, 2025). That is, an intelligent and interactive digital twin of the national economy, a *de facto* dynamic registry of all first-order value (and risk) creation and second-order value (and risk) transfers embedded in the principal-stakeholder relationships of a national economy. The game would capture the seemingly endless combinatorial political economy possibilities emerging from applying 'value is created or transferred' or the even more complexity-inducing 'all elite agency creates and transfers value' onto stakeholder relationships. At the start of the project, and to handle the profusion of weights and offsets, there would need to be a relatively high materiality cutoff threshold (in terms of revenues/profits) for the elite business models described in the game. A progressively higher-fidelity digital rendition of the political economy based on the transferors and transferees of value (or game equivalents such as money or energy) would become a benchmark for real-life elite and elite system transformational leadership (Table 7.2). The identification of inclusive value creators (with entropy reduction agency in the game) would yield proposals to incentivize these via the reform of elite business model rules. It is even conceivable that the scope of 'weighted transfers modeling' could scale internationally. A 'global weighted transfers general equilibrium' macroeconomic model ('G-WTGE') would, on the understanding that transnational elite agency is limited (Section 1.2.1), describe cross-border elite business models with significant impacts (Section 7.3.1), link diverse national elite systems, and incorporate variables expressing the value creation and transfers in international principal-stakeholder relationships. This addition would be the bedrock for the even more comprehensive and demanding 'global weighted transfers game' ('GWT-Game') and stretch the value creation/extraction map to cover the stakeholders of cross-border business models in the global economy.

Gamers already employ their collective intelligence to solve political economy problems akin to those that could be optimized in a 'weighted transfers game'. For instance, in the *SimCity* series, players manage taxation, budgeting, and resource management; in *Anno 1800*, players deal with industrialization, including the lives of factory workers, city-building projects, and colonial trade; in the *EVE Online* massively multiplayer online role-playing game (MMORPG), players interact with futuristic in-game professions like mining, manufacturing, and trading; in the *Capitalism Lab* business simulation, the decision-makers seek optimal production, effective marketing, and growth for their virtual company; and, in the *Tropico* series, players are themselves the elite—the "El Presidente" of the Caribbean island country—and deal with election fraud, offshore bank accounts, and powerful foreign elites such as Fruitas Ltd (seemingly inspired by a real company, United Fruit). Still, a WT-Game as conceived here, with its econometric formulas, SVC measurements, and computational requirements, seems hardly feasible without the advent of a powerful AI in support of players' decisions and sweeping access to transactional data (see Epilogue). Nonetheless, and while such a game might seem a speculative exploration that scarcely merits any purpose beyond amusement, it is suggested as a research avenue analogous to a quest for 'political economy omniscience' (Figure A5.10 and Table A3.1b depict it in relation to other SVC measurements). Relatedly, and perhaps in the context of a plausible gaming service, Figure set A5.14 provides wireframes that outline the flows of value creation and transfers across business model principal-stakeholder relationships that explicitly connect society's diverse socio-economic groups. The fact that value transfers matter along income distribution percentiles is stressed (in Figure A5.14a), albeit not in an accurate fractal manner (that would require a more nuanced visualization, making explicit the relationships for the percentiles within the top 1 percent, the percentiles within the top 0.1 percent and so on, until one reached the leading elite coalitions at the top as well as the most unfortunate individuals at the bottom). These value creation/transfer relationships constitute the core statements of the gameplay. In using such interactive entertainment platforms, committed and ethically motivated gamers, such as those of Minecraft (see Faber, 2025) could, using human and other intelligence, establish weights that play out as optimal general development. For instance, weighting would include benchmarks for 'alternating value extraction and creation' in each industry or region of the world, thus transitioning across the fractal depths of the political economy while setting 'calibration factors' for value transfer-IN/OUT metrics, weighting them for SVC measurements (see Figure 6.6), and *creatively* proposing offsets. Besides recreation, the applied aim of such a game would be for users to computationally unravel the value creation relationships in the economy and validate elite business models, laws, and institutions that maximize economic and human development.

In summary, a more profound understanding of the micro-meso-macro transmission mechanisms and the linkages between them, possibly through the use of 'weighted transfers modeling' (based on systematically identifying, quantifying, and factoring in value transfers), means that the all-important incentive structure variously described in the literature (see Olson, 1984; North, 1990, 1994; Holmstrom & Milgrom, 1994; Nicholas, 2003; Robinson, 2010) can be more precisely targeted and adjusted. When top-down institutional change and bottom-up elite leadership at the firm level are mutually reinforcing they foster effective elite business model transformation towards sustainable value creation (Figure 7.1). Weighted structural reforms contribute to this end by restraining business models based on transfers that diminish the production function and short-circuit economic and human development. Reforms that strive to constrain extraction are pointedly relevant to advanced economies that rely on innovation, while those that aim to enable novel business models are particularly pertinent to emerging economies that rely on investment.

7.1.2 Implications for emerging economies

"A crucial element of economic growth is that the recruited elite be of the highest quality" (Brezis & Temin, 2007, p. 4). In terms of the ETED, 'highest quality' is understood to be when the leaders of elite coalitions are—relative to their predecessors—running sustainable value creation business models. Technically, it suffices if only a bare majority of elites (e.g., business models representing just 51% of total output) create more sustainable value today than they created yesterday. These patterns explain the continual advances made by some countries (e.g., China or Israel) while others stagnate in the middle-income trap (e.g., Argentina or the Philippines) or seem to plateau at higher income levels (e.g., Japan or Spain). The basic development corollary of this theory for policymaking is continuous structural reform to incentivize value creation elite business models (as measured by their VCr) leveraging intra-elite contests. This eventually results in higher elite quality (as measured in international comparative terms by the EQx and in domestic terms by the EQr). Yet the realities of growth stages require nuance; elite quality is postulated to have differing significance for emerging and advanced economies. According to the neo-classical theory of economic growth, as economies develop, they experience diminishing returns on increasing capital and labor inputs and must therefore transition to productivity and innovation-based growth (Krugman, 1994). This has led to discrete policy recommendations; for instance, on the types of entrepreneurship best suited for the factor-driven stage, the in-between efficiency-driven stage, or the innovation-driven stage (Acs, Desai, & Hessels, 2008). On such a basis, optimal extractive transfer weights specific to each development stage can be determined, while the space for rent-seeking elite business models inexorably narrows as GDP per capita surges (as is later discussed in the 'advanced economies have a higher sensitivity to elite quality' conjecture).

The neo-classical theory of economic growth views emerging economies as not yet at the point of reaching diminishing returns for capital- and labor-based growth (Solow, 1957). Capital- and labor-based business models with comparatively lower levels of elite quality (thereby reducing institutional quality) can nonetheless deliver growth. The establishment of the optimal elite quality levels for discrete stages of social and economic development is an important question for further empirical inquiry (how much rent seeking is permissible?). At the same time, for economic growth rates to approximate their potential, elite quality needs to run ahead of income levels (which would be reflected, for instance, by a country's EQx score being higher than that of countries with comparable GDP per capita, see Casas-Klett & Cozzi, 2024, pp. 2, 3). While extractive elites in developing nations might controversially be given some temporary slack, this inquiry's interpretation of the middle-income trap stresses that work on raising elite quality cannot be postponed indefinitely. Notwithstanding this, it is important to delve into the logic behind why extractive models (such as monopolies, subsidies, or nepotism) can have positive effects on development over a limited time horizon.

In political economies with low levels of economic activity and weak institutions, having a business model, even if it is extractive, might be better than having none at all. An extensive analysis of the effectiveness of Chinese overseas aid by Dreher, Fuchs, Hodler, Parks, Raschky, and Tierney "suggests that a 10% increase in Chinese funding leads to a 1.3% increase in per-capita light output [. . .] which corresponds to an increase in subnational GDP of around 0.39%" (2019, p. 13), meaning that the economic growth and inclusive socioeconomic development benefits are real even when these business models associate with extractive transfers such as environmental costs or political favoritism (Dreher, Fuchs, Parks, Strange, & Tierney, 2022).[150] Moral conundrums immediately arise from such implicit weightings: is it preferable to have low-wage employment in textile factories (sweatshops) in South Asia and an inefficient, subsidized, and monopolistic electricity system in Latin America than to have no jobs or no power at all? For instance, in many developing countries, electricity and water are subsidized, benefiting both low-income households and, even more so, the business model principals, usually rent seekers taking advantage of a monopoly. How could such a "misallocation of resources" (Harberger, 1954) ever be acceptable? The answer lies in the fact that in the early stages of development the logic of the 'alternating value extraction and creation' conjecture requires longer transfer phases, as with the 'extractive push' dilemma (see Section 2.3.1, and Proposition 10).[151]

The 19th century elite renovations in Britain or Germany saw land-owning aristocrats transforming into innovative industrialists and investors through inclusive business models with positive externalities such as trade expansion, urbanization, and other forms of transfer-OUT. These investments in industry were financed by both the precursor extractive elite models (that enabled land and human capital accumulation) and the new models' extractive components (for example, the monopsonist lowering of wages for displaced peasants). That leads to a conceptualization of development where one set of extractive elite models evolves to another extractive set that is, however, less extractive than its predecessor, with higher value creation offsetting (part or most of)

150 For further details, see AidData's Global Chinese Development Finance Dataset, Version 2.0 (Custer et al. 2021), which "captures 13,427 projects worth $843 billion financed by more than 300 Chinese government institutions and state-owned entities across 165 countries in every major region of the world" (see: https://www.aiddata.org/data/aiddatas-global-chinese-development-finance-dataset-version-2-0).

151 Specific policies can be derived from this argument on issues such as patent law, because "without the possibility of monopoly, society could not progress" (Machlup & Penrose, 1950, p. 8). Yet under the 'advanced economies have a higher sensitivity to elite quality' conjecture, if England's first patent law, the Statute of Monopolies of 1623, which granted a limited 14-year term "or less" (section VI) was an optimal transfer limitation given the speed of technological progress at the time, then the 20-year term included in article 70 of The Patent Law of the WTO is too long a monopoly for the contemporary elite business models of advanced economies in light of today's rapid pace of technological change. See: https://www.legislation.gov.uk/aep/Ja1/21/3/section/VI, and https://www.wto.org/english/thewto_e/acc_e/cgr_e/wtacccgr27a3_leg_9.pdf

its own extraction. This weighted and gradual approach to development is unsavory as it invariably involves significant transfer-IN from models characterized by value appropriated but *not* created (e.g., from industrial workers, through protectionist tariffs, etc.).

A key consideration for development is the need to incrementally intensify elite system intra-elite contests and the elite business model transformation dynamic as a nation becomes richer. That is, to reach the point where running water does not generate any transfer-IN for an elite coalition on account of the existence of competition, effective institutions, sustainable pricing, and the spread of knowledge in the sector, thus removing the justification for subsidies on development grounds. It can be argued that robust checks and balances should intensify in tandem with elite business models that augment their coordination capacity through means such as capital or data accumulation.

Returning to the Republic of Korea, Amsden (2001, p. 11) notes how "a lucrative license to establish a general trading company depended on exports meeting criteria related to value, geographical diversity, and product complexity". The *chaebol* are the textbook example of elite business models relying on extraction before transforming towards increased value creation (from the ships of Samsung Heavy Industries to the semiconductors of Samsung Galaxy devices) in step with and powering up the development of a nation. Eventually, and after various cycles of elite business model transformation, the 'alternating value extraction and creation' conjecture results in lower levels of extraction, while the 'extractive push' dilemma becomes less of a predicament: shorter periods of rent transfers to elites suffice in achieving economic growth and transitioning through the stages of development. This corresponds with more inclusive institutions (and improved intra-elite contest rules) that further support growth models based on sustainable value creation. For instance, while it literally took decades of backing Samsung and selected *chaebol* to kick start and then consolidate the competitiveness of Korea Inc. in export markets abroad, on the back of its second five-year plan (described in Adelman, 1969), the tacit institutional support for Alibaba to develop domestically and then emerge as an internationally recognized platform can be measured in mere years (from 2013 to November 2020, see the earlier reference to Ant Financial in Section 4.2.4). The normative implications of the 'alternating value extraction and creation' and the 'advanced economies have a higher sensitivity to elite quality' conjectures require a note of caution with regard to time horizons: value extraction models should have explicit and irreversible expiration dates (as in A Transfer Constraints Framework for policy formulation, Figure 8.2).

Elite agency's impact on development in emerging economies can be illustrated by the classic juxtaposition of Korea's *chaebol* with Argentina's Peronist coalitions over the last six decades.[152] Yet the Miracle on the Han River was initially all but pre-

152 In 1962, the GDP per capita of Korea was US$ 106, about 1/11th of Argentina's US$ 1,155. Six decades later, in 2022, Korea's GDP per capita was US$ 32,255, over three times that of Argentina's US$ 13,686 (The World Bank, n.d.-e).

mised on a robust balance between political elites and business elites (see intra-elite power relation 4, Table 3.2): President "Park Chung Hee provided protection and rents to the *chaebol* in return for economic performance" (Gemici, 2013, pp. 183–184; Kim & Park, 2011). Over time, however, and on the back of domestic value transfers converted into success in the global market arena, checks and balances evolved and the *chaebol* became more powerful than Korea's political (e.g., democratically elected governments, a lenient judiciary) and knowledge (e.g., a compliant media) elites. Some would say that the family-owned industry-spanning conglomerates have become too dominant, and their extractive business model practices have faced bouts of heightened scrutiny. Park (2021) identifies a litany of second-order transfer activities including monopsony, exclusive supply chains, price squeezing, sub-optimal investments, or "IP extortion when bargaining with its suppliers", and thus advocates for "fundamental changes in the country's economic structure and policies. Chaebol reform is the key to these indispensable changes". As will be discussed in the next section, Korea is now at a point where it has less leeway and so its intra-elite contests must progressively squeeze out extractive transfer activities from its economy. Comparing this energetic Asian tiger to Argentina is no longer meaningful.

In the case of Colombia, the subsidized electricity elite business models remain in place despite having been found by McRae to cause "unreliable supply, [and] deter investment to modernize infrastructure" (2015, p. 35). What might once have been a comparatively sustainable value creation model (despite its extractive components) for electricity to kick start economic development (when there was no electricity or even any demand for power) is no longer effective in later development stages after the economic system has acquired knowledge and an appetite for electricity and stable demand exists. As economies develop, the sustainable becomes non-sustainable and structural reform to disincentivize anachronistic elite business models that have outlived their original usefulness is essential wherever they exist. Both the core elite coalition and other beneficiary elites must engage in transformation. In the particular case of Colombia, escaping McRae's "subsidy trap" might involve both the break-up of local monopolies and increasing competition, and "replacing consumption subsidies with capital investment subsidies" for upgrades of "precarious distribution networks" and infrastructure, thus economizing on state outlays (2015, pp. 35, 65).

For policymakers, the main takeaway of this elite theory's emphasis on weighting is that extractive models are unavoidable and even necessary in the early stages of development. Subsequently, however, continuous bursts of structural reform need to recalibrate the weightings to ensure the feasibility of offsets and realign the incentives for continued elite business model transformation towards high value creation positions. Such policies will be facilitated by increasing the elite separation of powers in the context of ever-sharper competition under munificent elite cohesion overseeing stable intra-elite contest rules (see the dilemma of Figure 5.2).

7.1.3 Implications for advanced economies

In advanced economies, value extraction must be progressively met with zero tolerance, notwithstanding this inquiry's caveat: business model exceptions in the context of the 'alternating value extraction and creation' conjecture. This was done, for example, through the Internet Tax Freedom Act of 1998 three-year moratorium that disallowed state and local governments from taxing Internet access (though extending it eight times and then making it a permanent statute is, at the very least, a subpar approach to the 'extractive push' dilemma and questionable from an economic development perspective). The higher relative importance of elite quality for advanced economies is a core implication of this work and has previously been formulated as the 'advanced economies have a higher sensitivity to elite quality' conjecture.

This conjecture links the accepted dictum that the more advanced an economy, the higher its dependencies on innovation for growth (Solow, 1957; Krugman, 1994). Innovation, a key component of elite business models, demands longer-term investments (relative to the intensified capital or labor input models typical of early development stages) and so is comparatively more sensitive to extractive institutions (as discussed earlier, also see Murphy, Schleifer, & Vishny, 1993, p. 413). Rent seeking by elite business models, including 'risk *not* created but value appropriated' (see Figure 6.9), compromises innovation ecosystems by reducing the incentives to undertake sustained investments (entrepreneurial, human capital, etc.) and uncertainty. Less knowledge is therefore created. Emerging economies might import knowledge from elsewhere, but advanced economies must produce new knowledge by themselves.

To Krugman's position (1994) that development represents a move from an inputs-based growth model to productivity-based growth, we must add the rationale of elite agency. As economies develop, they need higher elite quality, since the higher the demand for specialized knowledge inputs there is, less leeway remains for tolerating extractive activities. Veering off of an inclusive pathway when a nation's GDP per capita is ascending will result in economic reversal and regression. The space and timeline for the 'extractive push' dilemma drastically shrinks with the 'advanced economies have a higher sensitivity to elite quality' conjecture. The prevalence of value transfers in a political economy (reflected by elite quality SVC measurements) matters to emerging and advanced economies alike, but the negative impact is relatively higher for the latter. *Ceteris paribus*, the proportion of value transfers explains the "divergence" in the economic trajectories of Europe and China that have shaped their distinct paths to modernity (complementing the analysis by Pomeranz, 2000) and also accounts for the discrete growth rates of leading economies, for instance, between the US and Japan at the cusp of the 21st century.[153] The paralysis of Japan's elite

153 The US and Japan were, in nominal GDP terms, the two largest economies in the world from the late 1960s to 2010 when the latter was overtaken by China. Data from The World Bank (n.d.-f) shows

business models, anchored by the inertia of the "iron triangle" or the bureaucratic *keiretsu* bereft of family ownership (see Grabowiecki, 2006, p. 26), is the root cause of the nation's lost three decades. Japan's stagnation during this period contrasts with Korea's rise, powered by its family-run conglomerates, or the radical economic regeneration in the US, driven by elite circulation of the admixture type with transformational elite leadership in sectors as diverse as software, finance, and energy.

The more advanced and closer to the technological frontier an economy is, the higher the elite quality that is required for sustained growth. The indolent elite systems of advanced economies whose elites eschew sustainable value creation see diminishing VCr scores for their leading business models and slip away from the cutting edge of innovation. Exogenous technological shocks will not be seized as opportunities when they are endogenized, but instead result in relative decline. Whether the ossification of Voslensky's (1984) Soviet nomenklatura, the failed strategies of Japan's Ministry of International Trade and Industry (MITI) for the semiconductor industry that saw the country's global market share fall from 50% in the 1980s to 10% today (Suzuki et al., 2023), or the glacial responses to digitalization by the Eastman Kodak Company and Matsushita Electric Industrial Co. Ltd. (now Panasonic Corporation), the more advanced the economy or firm, the higher the cost of resisting transformation towards higher value creation models consistent with the technological state of the art. On the other hand, when elite coalitions engage in business model transformation, some of them will succeed and general economic growth will follow. In the early 1980s, pundits still reeling from the difficult and stagflation-infused 1970s claimed that in the US, institutions had "moved away from ordered markets toward the near chaos of direct political allocation; rent seeking has emerged as a significant social phenomenon" (Buchanan, 1980, p. 4). Institutional decline was at this juncture deemed to be the bedfellow of endemically extractive elite business models. Yet, this was precisely at a time when the seeds for a reversal were planted in a key sector through the outcome of an intra-elite contest—the anti-trust breakup of AT&T in 1984.

New spaces for dynamic intra-elite contests were opened in the market arena (i.e., intra-elite power relation 2, see Table 3.2) ushering in an American technological revolution with global impact. In virtuous cycle fashion, the US elite system and the Federal Communications Commission (FCC) steered institutional change in the 1990s in line with the possibilities of the evolving innovation frontier. The landmark US Telecommunications Act of 1996 was lauded as "the most comprehensive revision of the nation's communications laws in over sixty years" even if it came under criticism from those advocating even deeper structural institutional reforms (May, 2004, p. 1308). The combination of newly enabled elite coalitions with a revamp of the regu-

that in 1995, the GDP per capita of Japan was US$ 44,198, about one third higher than America's US$ 28,691. By 2023, the tables had turned, with the latter at US$ 81,695 and the former at US$ 33,834. American's GDP per capita has close to tripled while in dollar terms Japan's has shrunk by about a quarter. There are reasons to argue, however, that Japan might have reached the bottom and, in accordance with a sequential elite quality pattern, is now plausibly poised to rebound (see Shioji, 2024).

latory regime made America the world's foremost value creator, leaving Japan and the EU in its wake as its ascendant business models surfed the Internet wave. Not only was the once dominant AT&T coalition overtaken, so were its Baby Bell successors. Out of nowhere, innovation-based entrepreneurs predicated on value creation took center stage (see the early stages of The Elite Business Model Lifecycle, Figure 4.5) and became today's Big Tech, admixing into the US elite system and replacing some of its incumbents. For a century and a half, the leadership choices made in the American elite system for structural reform and elite business model transformation, affirming elite circulation and bolstered by a comparatively robust elite separation of powers imbued with cohesion, has seen elites and non-elites alike profit from a sustained burst of innovation that powers the country to this day.

According to Porter: "Innovation and entrepreneurship are at the heart of national advantage" (1990, p. 125). Innovation-based entrepreneurship is central to the ETED because it is the preferred mechanism of elite circulation through which new elites emerge in advanced economies. It also supports the all-important 'minimum elite circulation velocity' conjecture (see Section 1.3.3). As noted in Section 5.1.2, substantial research links the influence of firm founders and Schumpeter's (1911/2003) creative destroyers with economic growth (Aghion & Howitt, 1992; Wennekers & Thurik, 1999; Audretsch, 2007; Carree & Thurik, 2010; Chen, 2014). While postulating conditions for entrepreneurship at the individual, firm, and macro levels, such as "business culture incentives" or institutions, "little is known, either on how entrepreneurship can best be promoted or on how entrepreneurship influences economic performance" (Wennekers & Thurik, 1999, p. 51). Still, Holcombe suggests "the incorporation of entrepreneurship into the framework of economic growth [will lead to] more promising economic policy recommendations for fostering economic growth" (1998, p. 60). Concrete policy reform measures should clearly utilize existing academic insights into entrepreneurship.

Scholarly work has sought to provide a foundation for the formulation of initiatives for the policy mix (see descriptions in Figure 7.1 and Table 7.1). The implications of the finding that "the size of government is negatively correlated and sound money is positively correlated with entrepreneurial activity" (Bjørnskov & Foss, 2008, p. 307) are straightforward. Post-secondary entrepreneurial education appears to matter in high-income nations in "quite specific ways" (Levie & Autio, 2008, p. 253), an observation that is easily implementable as research agendas are reviewed (Nabi, Liñán, Fayolle, Krueger, & Walmsley, 2017) and realized. Carree, van Stel, Thurik, and Wennekers identify a "low barrier to entry and exit" as "vital for a sound economic development" and thus a matter for policymakers to address (2002, p. 271). Diverse authors also champion measures to "directly stimulate entrepreneurship" (Chen, 2014, p. 73), and initiatives to promote economic growth by incentivizing the accumulation of "entrepreneurial capital" (Audretsch, 2007) and reach the verdict that "any policy recommendation on economic development should be based on an analysis that incorporates entrepreneurship, the engine of economic growth" (Yu, 1998, p. 906). In this regard, Caballero's analysis (2008, p. 2) of creative destruction ups the ante because it leads to specific proposals to stimulate international competition, lower market entry regulations (as per Klapper, Laeven, and Rajan, 2004), ensure "well-functioning financial institutions and markets" (as per Caballero, Hoshi, & Kashyap, 2008), or undertake reforms that encourage "job flows" (as per Davis, Haltiwanger, & Schuh, 1996), where a tenth of the jobs destroyed or created per annum is a reallocation that increases productivity (as per Foster, Haltiwanger, & Krizan, 2001), meaning that "within narrowly defined sectors" these dynamics become "an integral part of the process by which an economy upgrades its technology".

The policy possibilities described above represent an incentive structure to transform the economy towards sustainable value creation. The time lag between business model transformation and technological change determines the competitive edge of firms and, at the aggregate level, national advantage. When the speed of elite business model transformation, a process that relies on newcomers and the admixture mode of elite circulation (Figure 1.1), trails technological change, growth tapers off. Elites that persevere with their models create less value and become less competitive in international comparative terms. Further illustrations include the long relative declines of the once sprawling Daimler-Benz AG, the former leading mobile devices manufacturer, Motorola, Inc., or the diminished (though still vast) Mitsubishi Group *keiretsu*. The prosperity of entire countries is at stake when the largest elite coalitions respond to crises by consolidating their domestic power in the face of technological change (as in The Elite Business Model Lifecycle with its 'elite power vs value creation gap' and the possibility that 'value transfers replace value creation at maturity', see Figure 4.5). In healthy political economies this is an unworkable stratagem. Motorola, in ideal Schumpeterian fashion, was essentially creatively destroyed when taken over by Google in 2012, but the Japanese and German examples have long maintained commanding positions in their particular fields to the detriment, one could argue, of the prosperity of their respective nations.

Complacent leadership, management inertia, a dearth of the joined-up thinking emblematic of creative elites, or a lack of appetite for risk-taking all trigger suboptimal responses to change. However, the key cause is the ease and viability of doubling down on extractive transfers thanks to institutional arrangements and bargaining power differentials in the political economy. These decision-making reflexes enabled by institutional arrangements are termed here as 'automatic destabilizers' because they increase downward economic turbulence in contrast to the automatic stabilizers (i.e., the "automatic rules" designed into the "tax-and-transfer systems" of "most countries" as moderators of economic fluctuations, see McKay & Reis, 2016, p. 141). Concrete examples include Japan's "highly inefficient, debt-ridden" zombie firms (Ahearne & Shinada, 2005) and zombie banks (Caballero, Hoshi, & Kashyap, 2008) pushing for low interest rates, subsidized capital, lax regulation, or the huge financial inflation-inducing 'lifelines' offered during the COVID-19 pandemic in the EU and the US, stunning details of which are provided by Coyne, Duncan and Hall (2021, p. 1127):

> Examples of rent seeking in the COVID-19 pandemic abound (see Vogel, 2020). Consider, for instance, the Coronavirus Aid, Relief, and Economic Security Act, or CARES Act, a $2.2 trillion relief package passed by Congress and signed by President Trump in late March 2020. With more than 1,500 entities reporting lobbying activity related to the legislation, the bill became the second most lobbied bill in U.S. history (Evers-Hillstrom, 2020). Public Citizen, a nonprofit watchdog group, found that 40 lobbyists with ties to the Trump administration were able to secure more than $10 billion in coronavirus aid (Tanglis & Lincoln, 2020). Several members of Congress also secured funding for their businesses, with little transparency, through the Paycheck Protection Program they helped to institute, including the Chrysler Dodge Jeep dealership owned by Rep. Roger Williams, who is one of Congress's wealthiest members (Ferris et al., 2020).

When these types of handouts (and transfers in general) multiply and compound in advanced countries, often automatically, the resultant extraction is felt by taxpayers, those at the bottom—and even in the middle—of the socio-economic pyramid (e.g., via inflation or debt that needs to be repaid later), and particularly by the young (see Galloway, 2024). Development and growth are compromised due to a variety of mechanisms such as the leakage of value (see Okun's "leaky buckets", 1975/2015) or the fact that the transfers from the bottom and the middle classes to the top go to inefficient "losers" (Baldwin & Robert-Nicoud, 2007; see also Section 8.2.4 on redistribution). Ricochet effects include eroded social cohesion, non-adoption of new technologies, and the destabilization of complex industry and business systems (high dependencies signify fragility and diminishing engagement with the innovation frontier). Japan's two-generation stagnation is by no means a worst-case scenario; contrary to expectations and for nations facing decline, the island nation is a touchstone of sorts. First, particular elite coalitions or their individual members have not disproportionally appropriated sizable value transfer amounts (at least until the yen started weakening in 2022). Second, while its elite culture sincerely values equality, 'acceptance' has been the chief non-elite response to extraction (Table 5.1) and 'trust in elites' the preferred aggregate non-elite political option (Figure 8.2). In contrast, in Western polities, non-elite responses to similar circumstances are less likely to be based on faith in the elite and veer more towards 'challenge' of the less constructive kind. America and Europe will also see a greater proportion of the more sterile *withdrawal* forms of non-elite 'exit' (as typified by their diverse varieties of addiction) than Japan and its pliant *hikikomori* (Figure A5.8; Section 5.2.3). Elite systems might be inclined to respond to the shrinking pie, for instance, when facing a "polycrisis" (World Economic Forum, 2023) or a "polytransition" (Casas-Klett & Zhang, 2024), with the 'same size of the slice' bias and double down on transfers. Social polarization and radicalization will reflect such perceptions in election results. On a more positive note, every single elite business model transformation towards a higher value creation position grows the pie for all. Political and knowledge elites also play their part in fostering institutional change and implementing structural reforms that tilt the balance in intra-elite contests in favor of the value creation elites. Progressive and targeted reform proposals weight and offset value transfers, on a sector-by-sector (and even firm-by-firm) basis, as is stressed in the next sections.

7.1.4 Implications for research with relevance for policy

The elite theory aims to produce research insights relevant for practitioners, including policymakers. The obvious first suggestion is to test elite quality as an independent variable fit for econometric models that forecast beyond the mid-term (Casas-Klett & Cozzi, 2020, p. 62). Besides growth, elite quality might also relate to other economic phenomena such as innovation or inequality. What falsifiable hypotheses ought to be explored for the applied purposes of the elite theory?

One might posit that the more extractive a nation's elites are (as reflected in low EQx or EQr scores), the less likely the country is to engage in international trade. Levchenko conceives of the "institutional content of trade", where "institutional differences are an important determinant of trade flows" (2007, p. 791). More specifically, the gravity equation in international trade,[154] one of economics' most robust empirical discoveries (Anderson, 2011; Frankel & Romer, 1999), might be extended and adjusted for elite quality. This could be done using the template of the gravity equation's revision for institutional quality; findings show that the "omission of indices of institutional quality biases the estimates of typical gravity models" (Anderson & Marcouiller, 2002, p. 342). A testable hypothesis is whether bilateral trade between two countries is proportional to GDP, inversely proportional to the geographic distance between them, and proportional to an elite quality distance/proximity factor (to each other or to an elite quality benchmark). Such a factor could be derived from existing elite quality measurements and theoretically advanced and operationalized to indicate the distance in elite quality between countries in a bilateral relationship. Similarly, this 'Elite Quality Distance' ('EQ-dist') SVC measurement could be used to model foreign direct investment (FDI) patterns. Will elite quality (as per EQx/EQr scores) or the proximity patterns between home and host countries (EQ-dist) help to explain bilateral FDI flows? The rationale for such hypotheses is discussed in more detail in Section 7.3.6. Their falsifiability matters to structural reform policymaking since the incentives for elite business model transformation towards sustainable value creation would then support trade and investment flows.

As already discussed, unweighted policy responses to economic problems are especially problematic when, however well meaning, they cause extractive transfers (e.g., inflation as a consequence of fiscal measures to reverse COVID's temporary effects on aggregate demand). Could the trap-like situation described in the 'extractive escalation dynamic' conjecture and other elements of the elite theory explain economic phenomena and structural impasses in a different light and so contribute to policy debates? For instance, secular stagnation, conceptualized as lower productivity

154 The gravity equation holds that bilateral trade is proportional to the GDP (economic size) of the two states in question, and inversely proportional to the (geographical) distance by which they are separated.

growth (after having taken "all the low-hanging fruit of modern history" as per Cowen, 2011), and linked to "the decline of real interest rates since 1980" (Eichengreen, 2015, p. 66), has been understood as a major economic challenge for many decades (see Higgins, 1950). BlackRock founder Larry Fink relates "The collapse of productivity" to inflation (Masters, 2023).[155] Rachel and Summers (2019, p. 1) "argue that the economy of the industrialized world, taken as a whole, is currently—and for the foreseeable future will remain—highly prone to secular stagnation" attributable to "changes in saving and investment propensities". But what if the critical factor in secular stagnation is not savings and investments but the lowering of elite quality and the increase in the proportion of extractive rent-seeking and transfer activities by the elite business models of the economy? We discussed Buchanan's concerns earlier: "Behaviorally, rent seeking has become more important because institutional changes have opened up opportunities that did not exist in the nineteenth and early twentieth centuries" (1980, p. 3). Technological advances, from electricity to data, also provide opportunities for rent seeking and, as Glode and Ordoñez explain, "the recent decoupling between information technology and economic progress" (2023, p. 28). Modeling and predicting extractive escalation rounds and linking their impact to growth and economic variables and phenomena relevant to development (like secular stagnation) are worthy areas of research with implications for policy.

An understanding of the microfoundations of increased extractive transfers and economic decline entails investigation in disciplines beyond economics. For instance, political science might shed light on faulty intra-elite competition or on deficiencies in the elite separation of powers; cultural studies might be useful in probing elite system cohesion; sociology in explaining social cohesion; management science might make plain the activities and strategies of value appropriation in excess of value creation at the firm level; philosophy and religious studies might illuminate narratives that nudge elites towards transformational leadership or in the opposite direction; and interactions between psychology and ethics might be the only way to decipher individual transformational leadership. The inclusion of any such insights to the broad fiscal and monetary policy mix of mainstream economics requires theory work and refutable hypotheses followed by a detailed mapping of the legal and other incentive systems to understand their particular effects on value transfers, one business model and business model rule at a time. Rent seeking (transfer-IN and the attendant transfer-COST) is analogous to dark matter that subdues the economy and prevents it from expanding to its full potential. The levers of the incentive system need to shift viewpoints, downplay the macro-level aggregates and instead zero in on each nook and cranny in every business and industrial sector. Even if they are *a priori* less accessible

155 The reader "Diego Velasquez", sardonically commenting on this piece in *The Financial Times*, supplied an alternative interpretation: "Fink says productivity gap caused inflation - maybe 12 years of money printing that enabled Blackrock [sic] to use free money to buy houses and other assets without creating new value had something to do with it?"

to policymakers, the low hanging fruits to boost growth lie in the often-overlooked fractal corners of the economic landscape.

How much respect and momentum could knowledge elites gain in the elite system if they referenced and formulated evidence-based, theoretically grounded, precisely targeted and weighted structural reform proposals for sustainable value creation in the existing political economy, for instance in its fast-emerging spaces like AI, renewable energy, or crypto? Academics, journalists, legal scholars, judges, consultants, religious leaders, movie producers, influencers, and other knowledge elites will naturally find allies in high quality elite coalitions and might even be welcomed as members. These coalitions are inherently predisposed to support inclusive policy interventions, burdened as they are by uncompetitive extractive peers that distort the incentive system and allocative processes with their unproductive political non-market and narrative market arena wins. One can safely presuppose that *The Wall Street Journal* headline "Who Won in Afghanistan? Private Contractors" (Nissenbaum, Donati, & Cullison, 2021) is part of a (losing) narrative launched by particular elite coalitions wishing to neuter the perceivably extractive business model of war. New, competitive, and well-crafted narratives with an aesthetic pull tacitly suggest structural reforms and intensify institutionalized intra-elite contests (across many of The Seven Intra-elite Power Relations, see Table 3.2) while protecting the optimal state of elite cohesion that sparks elite circulation and novel coalition configurations around value creation business models.

Economic models and research within the elite theory will yield policy proposals that make value transfers explicit and propose weightings for them that aim to nudge institutions towards inclusive change by tipping the scales toward the higher value creation elite coalitions in intra-elite contests. Narratives for the weighted structural reform of elite business models that are targeted, designed for the long run, and academically refutable can, when disseminated by knowledge elites, also be packaged for non-elites, going viral as memes on social networks or contributing to the programs of political movements (see their narrative bases in Figure A5.12a). The resultant increased awareness of where their interests lie will enable non-elites to better play the tactical or strategic role of the referee (see Section 3.3.2, Figure 8.2) in political processes where elite coalitions face-off against each other.

7.1.5 Implications for targeted and weighted structural reform by policymakers

> This makes it all the more puzzling that most of the explanations of macroeconomic and monetary problems that economists offer are not systematically derived from an analysis of the incentives facing the participants in the economy. (Olson, 1984, p. 644)

The above inconsistency is still a fact of life despite the undisputed understanding that the incentives embedded within institutions are critical to economic development and that these can only be adjusted with consequential structural reforms. Lewis (1954, p. 155) sought insight into the mechanism, critical to development, by which nations save more (e.g., from 4–5% to 12–15% of GDP), while Laitner (2000, p. 545) affirmed that increases in savings rates are due to the "structural change accompanying growth". Surging incomes are indelibly associated with structural reforms that are highly visible, for instance, in resource reallocations from primary sectors to the manufacturing industries (Kaldor, 1970). One aim of deliberate reform is "inducing firms to improve their efficiency and competitiveness to international levels and thus helping them to export" (Cuervo-Cazurra & Dau, 2009, p. 480). However, structural reforms will always face challenges by incumbent players. The degree to which these are overcome account for the "divergent reform experience of Eastern Europe, the Former Soviet Union, and China" (Sachs & Woo, 1994, p. 103). To be sustainable, structural reform must conscientiously adjust the incentives for elite business models, especially in terms of their rules (see Figure 4.3). At the same time, in any country, dominant coalitions uncertain about how structural reform will affect them will hunker down, resist, and defend their residual income flows (Fernandez & Rodrik, 1991). In this situation, the core elite coalition, and other elite coalitions, must show leadership to create a consensus in the elite system to address the structural impediments to development, weight and offset extractive transfers, and push through a reform agenda for the incentive system. A systematic way of achieving this is now proposed in 'A Weighted Structural Reform Framework' for policy.

Table 7.1: A Weighted Structural Reform Framework for policy.

	Weighted structural reform	Description
(i)	**Impact assessment: Value transfers** (Business and knowledge elite transformational leadership)	(a) Assess elite business models and weight their inclusive/ extractive value transfers (e.g., with the VCr and other micro-level SVC measurements).
		(b) Assess the impact that the value transfers of specific elite business models (e.g., with SVC measurements) have on economic growth and human development variables (e.g., with 'weighted transfers modeling', see also WTGE). Integrate into macroeconomic models a map of elite business model principal-stakeholder value transfers and devise an estimable formulation of the relationship between elite agency at the micro-level (e.g., VCr), the meso-level elite system (e.g., EQr), and macro-level for economic development outcomes (e.g., growth, innovation, inequality).

Table 7.1 (continued)

	Weighted structural reform	Description
(ii)	**Formulation: Institutional and (de)regulatory measures** (Knowledge elite transformational leadership)	(a) Formulate targeted long-run *institutional and (de)regulatory measures* for enhanced sustainable value creation by improving the incentive system, i.e., business model rules, laws, etc., to stimulate value creation, constrain power, and offset value transfers by elite business models.
		(b) Formulate broad short-run regulations for *macroeconomic measures* (both monetary and fiscal) aimed at economic stabilization by managing both aggregate supply and demand along with controlling money supply to support long-run *institutional and (de)regulatory measures*.
(iii)	**Elite transformational leadership: 'Elite institutional change bargain'** (Political and knowledge elite transformational leadership)	(a) Utilize elite transformational leadership to resolve intra-elite contests via elite bargains (that include offsets) to implement institutional and (de)regulatory measures for the incentive system (particularly business model rules) and for the regulations governing (monetary, fiscal) macroeconomic measures to *constrain* value transfers; secure the execution of the elite bargains.
		(b) Utilize elite transformational leadership to resolve intra-elite contests via elite bargains (that include offsets) to implement institutional and (de)regulatory measures for the incentive system (particularly business model rules) and for the regulations governing (monetary, fiscal) macroeconomic measures to *enable* value creation; secure the execution of the elite bargains.

The ETED's main policy theme is that value creation models should replace those of value extraction, and so A Weighted Structural Reform Framework for policy (Table 7.1) aims to address Olson's complaint about perverse incentives. A key focus is on identifying, weighting, and offsetting extractive transfers, while phasing out as many of these as possible. What about incentivizing value creation? While also evidently desirable, policymakers must tread carefully here given the baked in knowledge asymmetries. It is very hard for those not in the business arena, for those not facing uncertainty, to know, much less to grasp *a priori*, the source of value—where and by whose agency it will emerge. This includes the need for making a meticulous distinction between the rationales for regulation and deregulation and when they create or transfer value.

In *Over Ruled: The Human Toll of Too Much Law* (2024), Supreme Court Justice Neil Gorsuch, alongside Janie Nitze, illustrate how legal complexity strains the lives of ordinary citizens. Stigler's theory of regulation considers "the potential uses of public resources and powers to improve the economic status of economic groups" (1971, p. 3), pointing to elite preferences for value transfers through the reduction of competition. As a result, over-regulation explains falls in productivity growth, "a matter of great concern to policymakers, associated as it is with inflation, unemployment, and declining real wage growth" (Gray, 1987, p. 998). In such scenarios, deregulation is a policy choice that benefits both the public (Winston, 1993, p. 1284) as well as many of the incumbents that at one time had sought regulatory rents only for these to dissipate (Peltzman, Levine, & Noll, 1989). Nevertheless, in a complex adaptive system nothing is straightforward and both power-law distributions and reversals are the norm, as is exemplified by the case of the US airline industry. After the Airline Deregulation Act of 1978, competition rose and prices fell, spectacularly so for a time (much to the chagrin of Thiel and Masters, critical of average ticket prices of US$ 178 yielding only 37 cents profits for carriers, 2014, p. 23). Some companies experienced hardships, and in the longer run, mergers resulted in oligopolistic consolidation (i.e., American, United, Delta, and Southwest controlling 80% of the market), market dominance that is viewed by some as being positive "monopolistic competition" (Wolla & Backus, 2018; see the origin of the concept in Chamberlin, 1933/1949). Conversely, in some other cases, deregulation has quickly led to business models that drastically harm consumer welfare as well as overall economic efficiency:

> Compared to utilities in states that stayed regulated, deregulated utilities realized higher prices but lower average and marginal costs. Overall, markups increased substantially. Our findings are consistent with the exercise of market power in deregulated markets. Generation facilities were able to charge prices at substantial markups above costs, and the vertical separation of generation and retail allowed for additional price increases due to double marginalization. (MacKay & Mercadal, (2022, p. 43)

While shifting elite preferences about regulation are explained by the elite circulation dynamics that emerge from elite intra-competition and division of value strategies, policymakers must transcend these considerations and rigorously assess the value creation and transfers associated with each specific piece of regulation or deregulation. One the one hand, their calculations must factor in the administrative and bureaucratic costs of regulation (see Gray, 1987, or the farming protests against "overbearing EU regulations", Cokelaere & Brzeziński, 2024). On the other hand, when considering anti-trust regulations and faced with the theory of "contestable markets" and other neoliberal arguments (such as the "domination of many industries by a few giants with very high profits" comes from "the success of the few firms that were the most efficient ones in the industry which grew and displaced their less efficient rivals", Kotz, 2015, p. 12), their decisions must factor in power's ability to convert 'political economy know-how' into profits (see Figure 4.1); The Elite Business Model Lifecycle and its 'value transfers replace value creation at maturity' conjecture; and the 'elite power vs value creation gap' hypothesis (see Figure 4.5). In brief, either regulation or deregulation may create value and policymakers must recognize and make judgments on which value creation/transfer paradigm applies in each case.

Once there is evidence of value creation for a specific business model or industry, policymakers should jump in and provide institutional support through (de)regulation, eliminating (or establishing) barriers to entry, limited and targeted transfers like subsidies or state procurement, or even by involving the narrative market. Policies work when they strive to make an impact in the context of intra-elite contests (Sections 3.3.1 and 3.3.2). The two subsequent frameworks in the weighted policymaking set (Table 8.2 and Table 8.3) respectively focus on the limits of that support and emphasize the constraints required for sustainable transfers and redistribution. It should be borne in mind that the gravitational center of leadership in the political economy shifts during the structural reform process, but that knowledge elites play a central role throughout, from assessment to formulation and even in the implementation stages, especially in their technical and legitimizing roles realized as constituent members of elite coalitions. Top-down institutional change implementation, even when driven by the core coalition and endorsed by the winning narratives, must be met with a modicum of bottom-up micro-to-meso elite transformational leadership at the business model level (see elite leadership varieties, Table 7.2) which, in line with the two-way causal effect model of the relationship between elites and institutions (Figure 3.2), is more probable under the pressure of competitive intra-elite contests.

The framework (in Table 7.1) starts with the (i) *impact assessment of value transfers*, identifying and weighting both sustainable and unsustainable transfers by using SVC measurements[156] and then capturing these dynamics, possibly via 'weighted transfers modeling' (Section 7.1.1). The methods used must ascribe value creation and transfers to elite business models in as many principal-stakeholder relationships as possible in the economy, specifying the transferees and transferors (the winners and losers) and projecting the probable developmental outcomes. The intellectual challenge here is considerable as is confirmed by a review of the business model of private equity. In their European Bank for Reconstruction and Development (EBRD) working paper, Biesinger, Bircan, and Ljungqvist "open up the black box of value creation in private equity with the help of confidential information on value creation plans and their implementation" and determine that "portfolio companies significantly improve operations (increasing employment, wages, labor productivity, and capital intensity), boost their top-line (increasing sales and market share while reducing price markups), engage in financial engineering (reducing their effective tax rate as they take advantage of tax shields by increasing leverage, and reducing the interest rate they pay on their debt), and reduce their working capital needs" (2020, pp. 5, 31).

156 A vast literature supports social or socio-economic impact assessments (SIA), "a hybrid" where social science meets "the policy-making process" by traversing "the usual disciplinary boundaries" to ascertain a "broad range of social consequences" in a "generally anticipatory" manner (Freudenburg, 1986, p. 451). The Structural Reform Framework for policy starts by assessing sustainable value impacts before formulating structural reforms and their implementation to target institutional change.

Conversely, in *These Are the Plunderers*, Morgenson and Rosner aim to demonstrate "how private equity runs—and wrecks—America" (2023).

The general understanding is that "interest groups affect both microeconomic and macroeconomic outcomes" (Coates, Heckelman, & Wilson, 2007, p. 377) via their agency in specific sectors such as finance (see Rajan & Zingales, 2003); the normative position is the *selection* of elites whose business models are most likely to bring about positive growth outcomes if offered incentives. Here, one cannot obviate a reference to Lewis (1954) on the "overwhelming evidence of spatial and sectoral disparities within countries" (Gollin, 2014, p. 86), to stress the requirement that the (ii) *formulation of institutional and (de)regulatory measures* discretely target every nook and cranny of the economy, including the governance of macroeconomic measures (both monetary and fiscal). Addressing a particular space of the economy means targeting its specific elite business models when their reliance on value transfers is excessive. Real world examples of measures that incentivize value creation are those that favor venture capital (see Armour & Cumming, 2006), freedom (see Friedman, 1962/2002), or trade (see Ricardo, 1817/1999), while measures that constrain bargaining power differentials might address monopolists (see Doctorow, 2022), "bottleneckers" in the professions (see Mellor & Carpenter, 2016), or crony capitalism (see Klein, Holmes, Foss, Terjesen, & Pepe, 2021). Once more, the strengthening of sustainable value creation occurs through the intra-elite dynamics (see Section 3.1) that shape the incentive system. Macroeconomic stabilization policies are also a robust incentive mechanism (especially during financial crises, election campaigns, or pandemics) and so those designing monetary and fiscal measures and their regulations, guidelines, and protocols should be thoroughly aware of their rent-seeking potential.

Finally, the impact assessment and policy formulation lead to action with (iii) *elite transformational leadership for the 'elite institutional change bargain'* to reform the incentive system. Here, elites will settle on narrowly targeted micro-policy interventions that nudge a set of elite business models towards higher value creation positions by deactivating their extractive transfers, and on sector-specific rules that incentivize value creation. While fiscal and monetary measures are minimized as policy tools, the bargain would include regulations and guidelines governing these to rid the political economy of the detritus of ingrained value transfers from Keynesian and monetary measures. Leadership in policymaking means instigating inclusive institutional change by resolving intra-elite contests through the 'elite institutional change bargain' mechanism. To be effective, such bargains must be predicated on the 'weight and offset value transfers' (holistic) implication that is derived from the three assumptions for socio-economic relations in this theory (set out in Figure A5.4a) and be cognizant of the political economy dynamics of particular firms and industries in relation to The Elite Business Model Lifecycle (see Figure A5.9a). Ideally weighted structural reforms are continuous, occur bargain by bargain, and, when successful (as shown in the outcome on the left side of Figure A5.9b), the elite business model lifecycle dynamic that emerges resembles the one depicted in Figure A5.9c. Here, the lines of trajectory that represent sustainable value creation and power accumulation move concurrently, while the extractive transfers facilitated by the 'elite power vs value creation gap' (Section 2.2.2) remain modest.

The conceptual and technical aspects of integrating the SVC measurements of elite business models (such as the VCr) and the elite system (such as the EQr) into a working 'weighted transfers general equilibrium' macroeconomic model (WTGE) able to provide the necessary insight for the targeted and weighted structural reform of the incentive system aimed at the long run are remarkably difficult. Given the unpredictable nature of a complex adaptive system, this is the case because structural reforms can badly misfire. For instance, Palma (2014, p. 7) reviews "'premature' de-industrialisation, a phenomenon that has characterized Latin America since the beginning of the neo-liberal economic and political reforms, and conclude-[s] that it contains important components of policy-induced 'uncreative destruction'". Reforms can get entangled in narratives as well as in cultural preferences and shifts. For instance, "Sephora Kids" is both a cultural and business phenomenon where girls at "the tender age of 11" develop a desire for high-end cosmetics and skincare products that their "favourite content creators, like Alix Earle or Meredith Duxbury, have used in their 'Get Ready With Me' videos" (Clark, 2024). Should policymakers consider this a value transfer requiring regulatory intervention? Also, for structural reform initiatives to overcome resistance (Fernandez & Rodrik, 1991; Tompson, 2002; Katz, 2024) and effect inclusive transformations or Schumpeterian creative destruction they require narrative packages around laws and rules crafted by knowledge elites that are evidence-based and properly weighted to truly optimize sustainable value creation. *The Financial Times* article, "Tencent Rocked by New Chinese Online Gaming Restrictions", describes a push to reform a business model that is considered extractive (again, of youth), resulting in the firm's shares (and those of its competitor, NetEase) to suffer "the sharpest one-day drop" in a decade and a half as the company's "promotions to reward consumers for consecutive days of play and account top-ups, [are] features which appear to have been directly targeted by the regulator" (White & Lockett, 2023). This micro-intervention denotes a clear assessment of the existence of extractive transfers by political and knowledge elites in China that is in line with Haidt's (2024) assertions of 'destructive' transfer-COST in *The Anxious Generation: How the Great Rewiring of Childhood is Causing an Epidemic of Mental Illness.*

Political economies are constituted around elite settlements (Khan, 2018)[157], pacts (Burton & Higley, 1987; O'Donnell & Schmitter, 1986), or bargains, that, as Dercon (2022) points out, are often not articulated but must be deduced. All of these affect

157 These three notions as used indistinctively for this work's purposes, but as Khan (2018, pp. 635, 653) points out, there are particular variations amongst them, with the political settlement framework focusing on "the distribution of organizational power" in the political economy, while the elite pact focusing on cohesion has become "the definition of choice for researchers trying to analyze transitions from conflict to peace and the sustainability of a social order".

macro-level and developmental outcomes (Burton & Higley, 1987; Khan, 2010). If lucidly spelled out, along with the winners and losers and their respective payoffs, policymakers, members of the elite, as well as non-elites, might join calls in the narrative market for transformation towards sustainable value creation models through institutional change on a bargain-by-bargain basis. Constructive public debates put the onus on articulating and incentivizing value creation, phasing out transfers, equalizing bargaining power, and strengthening both intra-elite contests and social cohesion. Still, in the end, bargains are explicitly weighted and will contain compromises on value transfers and possibly on the scale of structural reform. The coordination capacity requirements of structural policy processes can be daunting. Nassif, Feijó, and Araújo provide an illustration:

> the Brazilian government could use the state's purchasing policy, for example, to boost and construct dynamic comparative advantages in industries such as shipbuilding, machinery and equipment for extracting oil, machinery and equipment associated with paper and cellulose, petrochemicals, pharmaceutical products, etc. [. . .] (i) policies of supply-side stimuli should be balanced by demand-side ones; and (ii) long-term policies, such as industrial and technological policies, infrastructure, education, etc., will not perform well if they are not well coordinated with other economic institutions, notably short-term macroeconomic policies. (2015, p. 1328)

Amsden (2001, pp. 289, 293) shows the importance of "getting the institutions 'right'" and the limits of standardized economic development policies that focus on "getting the prices 'right'". Still, and as stressed in A Weighted Structural Reform Framework for policy (Table 7.1), a vital point for policymaking is that broad fiscal and monetary policies are short-run fixes that can distort or even destroy pricing and other incentive structures for value creation, end up diminishing the production function, and, when overstressed, are incompatible with long-term, sustainable economic growth. Broad and sweeping interventions that adjust monetary mass and government expenditure to stimulate or dampen aggregate supply and demand and master fluctuations are shortsighted if they conceptually neglect—particularly if they intellectually belittle the role of risk and the undertaking of uncertainty in development—how value is created and why transfers are extractive. Given the superior bargaining power of elites in the political economy, productive non-elites in both the middle and lower classes regularly foot the bill for such fiscal and monetary transfers.

Arguably, because it constitutes (in reference to Kuhn, 1962) "the reigning paradigm" (Nickles, 2002, p. 2), mainstream monetary and fiscal policy is now consistently misused and should be in the crosshairs of any elite theory of economic development. As is explained by Kalecki (1942), it has long been understood that government spending increases business profits, often at the expense of present and future taxpayers. The quandary of applying the orthodox economic toolkit with its emphasis on fiscal measures is articulated in *The Financial Times* headline: "The EU Faces Brutal Choices Over Coronavirus Corporate Rescue Money: Member States Will Need to Decide Which Companies to Support and Which to Allow to Fail" (Fleming & Espinoza, 2021).

Since handouts are *de facto* rewards for specific elite business models paid for by the unrewarded, they alter the incentive system. As such, at the very least they should be narrow and provided on the condition of targeted structural adjustments that support value creators in the long run, enabling economies to not only withstand economic downturns but to emerge from them in a stronger state. Indiscriminate payments or helicopter money, on the other hand, will invariably culminate in rent seeking (again, the COVID-19 'lifeline' details provided by Coyne, Duncan, and Hall, 2021, are revealing) and are often simply assorted types of extraction from non-elites. In the context of "America's war on the young", Scott Galloway (2024) enumerates the transfers to older "cohorts" (already the beneficiaries of "the extraordinary post-war economic boom of the 20th century"), who "have pulled the ladder up behind them", thus leaving the increasingly impoverished non-elite young to foot the bill for items such as rising debt repayments and inflation.[158] There is a need for think tanks, universities, public intellectuals, and other dedicated knowledge elites to engage in the task of understanding the nuts and bolts of elite business models that use value transfers, especially those associated with mainstream policies. Only when their implicit weighting is clear can explicitly weighted policies (based on SVC or other measurements) provide the right incentives for the right elite business models—targeted micro-policy measures that liberate for the long run the forces of sustainable value creation held back by extractive models commanding 'the extraordinary lever' in a particular nook and cranny of the economy. While data, intelligence, and knowledge asymmetries are obstacles to this task, quality work already exists that is available to policymakers and political elites.

For instance, the journalists from Africa Uncensored "investigate, expose and empower" with their goal "to show Africa as it really is".[159] The SOAS Anti-Corruption Evidence (ACE) research consortium at the University of London produces work "to help policymakers, business and civil society adopt new, feasible, high-impact strategies to tackle corruption"[160]. The fourteen academics at Credit Slips "blog on all things about credit, bankruptcy, consumers, and financial institutions" and "discuss and debate issues not just for specialists but for anyone who cares about creating good policies in these areas".[161] At RemedyFest, hosted by Bloomberg Beta and run by Y Combinator, "a wide range of leaders, thinkers, and doers" mull over "what should the responses be to Big Tech's dominance".[162] The Electronic Frontier Foundation, with its

158 In this regard, the 'Next Generation Value Creation Barometer' has been "jointly designed by the St.Gallen Symposium and the EQx team to provide insights on key dimensions of intergenerational equity (beyond climate change, as in Stern, 2006) and how the value creation business models of different countries compare in this regard. The Barometer uses five equally weighted categories, comprising a total of [33] component Indicators [. . .] as measurements to highlight intergenerational relationships, both in terms of value creation and extractive transfers" (Rüdiger & Casas-Klett, 2022, p. 5).

159 See: https://africauncensored.online

160 See: https://ace.soas.ac.uk/what-is-ace/

161 See: https://www.creditslips.org/creditslips/

162 See: https://www.ycombinator.com/blog/content/files/2024/06/RemedyFest-Final-Report.pdf

mandate for "digital privacy, free speech, and innovation", applauded when Slack launched a "best-practice privacy and security" product feature that provided "free workspace admins the option to automatically delete all messages older than 90 days".[163] Further removed from the structures of the status quo one finds "The American Economic Liberties Project launched in February 2020 to help translate the intellectual victories of the anti-monopoly movement into momentum towards concrete, wide-ranging policy changes that begin to address today's crisis of concentrated economic power."[164] Truly engaged knowledge elites supply the understanding necessary to design incentives that tilt intra-elite contests to benefit value creation models. Of high relevance now is the need for algorithm transparency that shines light on the "black box society" (Pasquale, 2015) and contributes to the rebalancing of the power differential between elite AI algorithm owners and the stakeholder users that supply the data (see hypothesis AI_H1, 'AI augments non-elite power and causes the end of elites', Table E.2).

A highly effective course of action is for business elites themselves (with 'money') to drive narratives (and garner the power of 'mind') for political engagement (that provides 'might') and negotiations with institutions for structural reforms. For instance, John Arnold, a Texas billionaire, has "antagonized public-employee unions and pharmaceutical firms with campaigns to reform government-funded pensions and bring down high drug prices" and now "has a new foe: big-hospital monopolies" with *The Wall Street Journal* recounting how he is funding Fairmark Partners LLP, a law firm leading lawsuits that eventually seek to stop extractive value transfers effected by market power:

> Hospital systems with facilities that dominate one or more local markets gain power to raise prices across all their markets—even where there is competition—by insisting on terms with insurance companies to include every market or none, economists say. Such terms are known as all-or-nothing. Insurers, which negotiate prices on behalf of consumers, can't balk because they need multiple hospital markets to be included under health plans sold to employers with workers scattered across wide areas. (Evans, 2022)

As is repeatedly emphasized in this work, great elite coalitions (see the conjecture on development in Section 1.3.3) running sustainable value creation business models (with high VCr scores) are critical in driving inclusive and weighted structural reforms, as only establishment players possess inside knowledge of the practices that should be targeted to bring about the cessation of extractive transfers.

Structural reform policies that target elite business model rules to boost growth and development must address the numerous sectors of the economy and do so across geographies. The early proponents of structural change recognized this (Kaldor, 1970) and focused on the importance of regional policies. All in all, reforms require heavy investments in data and knowledge to first produce the impact assessments of value

163 See: https://www.eff.org/deeplinks/2022/09/victory-slack-offers-retention-settings-free-workspaces
164 See: https://www.economicliberties.us/about/#

transfers (with SVC measurements, plausible WTGE models), and then establish a creative brain trust to formulate credible institutional change proposals (see Table 7.1). The political elite eventually plays a decisive role here; the state capacity it controls is deemed essential for development (Besley & Persson, 2010; Zhang, 2022) because it facilitates assessment and policy formulation work, acts as a balance to business elites, and is the agency that implements the targeted interventions to realize policy actions aiming at the long run. As Evans notes, "aspiration without the requisite state capacity can lead to bungling that undercuts even the existing bases of comparative advantage" (1995, p. 10). Acemoglu, García-Jimeno, and Robinson (2015) discuss the positive links between state capacity and development, an idea latent in Hobbes (1651/2002) and "Weberian rational bureaucracy" that came to the fore with the "East Asian Miracle" (Johnson, 1982) and that has since been further strengthened (e.g., by Herbst, 2000; Centeno, 2002; Michalopoulos & Papaioannou, 2013); they then show the importance of focusing on the nooks and crannies since "local state presence is indeed a first-order determinant of current prosperity" along with related "network effects" (2015, pp. 2364, 2405). In the case of China, Aghion, Dewatripont, Du, Harrison, and Legros (2015, p. 1) demonstrate "that industrial policies allocated to competitive sectors or that foster competition in a sector increase productivity growth", while Amsden shows that even the "early industrializers", with Britain at the forefront, relied on "government intervention" (2001, p. 285).

Because mainstream fiscal and monetary policies do not resolve but more often than not intensify problems such as secular stagnation, market dominance, and uncontrolled pork and subsidies that bake in inefficiencies, the time would seem ripe for a paradigm shift in policymaking. Does China's tight grip on the competition rules for Internet firms provide a touchstone for how to weight value transfers? Angela Zhang, an expert on Chinese antitrust legislation at the University of Hong Kong, highlights the practices targeted by these measures: "false advertising, fraudulent online reviews, unfair competition, interoperability issues, data protection and consumer privacy issues" (Shepherd, 2021). Any such top-down reforms of the incentive system—even if targeted—smack of industrial policy, an approach that carries negative connotations in so many quarters that the OECD has published articles like "Industrial Policy: Not a Bad Word" (Primi, 2015). After all, List's (1841/2011) anti-laissez-faire interventionism (see Levi-Faur, 1997) was considered unorthodox by many economists. Today, sector-specific "industrial policy is experiencing a global resurgence" (Mazzucato & Rodrik, 2023), and, according to *The Harvard Business Review*, "The New Era of Industrial Policy Is Here" (Shih, 2023), as the paradigm started to be embraced in earnest by the Biden and Trump Administrations in something of a volte-face for the US. The EU Commission has also relaxed its rules for state aid, and since March 2022, approximately euro 650 billion has been handed out for "the manufacturing of strategic equipment" such as solar panels or batteries, with about 50% of the subsidized firms being German and about 30% French (Chan, 2023 as cited in Blake, 2023, p. 85). Nonetheless, political elites in countries with a continuous and strong structural reform tradition grounded in state capacity like Korea or Singapore have an experience advantage when designing policies that address elite business model value creation and constrain sterile transfers. What matters to the elite theory is, for instance, the extent to which a Chinese *Five-Year Plan for National Economic and Social Development*, the 15th of which will run from 2026–2030,[165] is informed by sustainable value creation. More generally, and obliquely referencing Milo's understanding of natural and social systems in *Good Enough: The Tolerance of Mediocrity in Nature and Society* (2019), how does the elite system handle business models that are simply '*not* good enough' in sustainable value creation terms?

Since transfers compromise general welfare, weighting and offsetting necessitates transformational leadership that firmly confronts reactionary elites and *contra natura* rejects prudent mediocrity to decisively boost inclusive economic development. This means structural reforms based on elite bargains that utilize intra-elite contests to cull extractive rent seeking and incentivize firm-level sustainable value creation.

7.2 Firm-level implications of sustainable value creation

The ETED holds that elite business models antecede institutional change in the two-way causal effect relationship between elites and institutions (Figure 3.2). That implies, for instance, that both the transformational 1979 Employee Retirement Income Security Act's (ERISA) "prudent man", known for an "unprecedented increase in money flowing into the venture capital sector" (Gompers, 1994, p. 2; see also Gompers, Lerner, Blair, & Hellmann, 1998), and the US Telecommunications Act of 1996 had to be driven by 'Silicon Valley', once a minor emergent elite coalition in the American national elite system. The coalition added members from business, political, and knowledge elites: technology visionaries and entrepreneurs, venture capitalists and Wall Street bankers, higher-education leaders in California, officials in the President's cabinet, regulatory agency chiefs, the military-industrial complex, and others poised to benefit from the value creation and appropriation associated with the business models enabled by such institutional change. Elite coordination leadership is complemented by business model leadership to monetize the new technologies and tilt the power balance accordingly within the coalition towards those that have an action and imagination advantage—the business elites in this case. This work argues that it is in the interest of all elite business model beneficiaries and stakeholders to make the advantages brought about by such leadership sustainable in the long run in terms of value and risk creation, meaning that there should be strategic restraint on 'value appropriated but *not* created' (Figure 2.11), 'cost created but *not* borne' (Figure A5.5a),

165 Note a version of the official declaration: "the economic planner will revolve around significant theoretical and practical issues concerning promoting the Chinese modernization to carry out intensive and in-depth research work, explore new concepts and measures, focus on solving major bottleneck [sic], and identify key tasks that will be significant for the overall planning in the 2026-2030 period" (Xinhua, 2023).

'risk originated but *negative* value *not* appropriated', and 'risk *not* originated but value appropriated' (Figure 6.9).

This section on the firm-level implications of the inquiry relies on a series of management frameworks primarily designed to elucidate the practice of sustainable value creation. "A management framework (like the Business Model Canvas or SWOT) is a combination of interlinked items that support a particular approach to a specific objective" (Budler & Trkman, 2023, p. 173). 'The Sustainable Value Matrix' and 'The Sustainable Finance Matrix' (Figures 7.2 and 7.3) are frameworks for managers and investors respectively. Ultimately, their aim is to support both elite and all other types of business model transformation.

The starting point is a consideration of the sustainability implications of value creation in the organization, the first focus being on management (7.2.1), and the second on corporate boards and governance (7.2.2). The small social unit, including at the intra-firm level, is then assessed for internal 'producers' and 'takers' based on the value creation and transfer ontology (7.2.3). An important discussion then follows on sustainable elite leadership with the introduction of a typology on the different varieties included in this work (7.2.4). The practical implications for investors are next considered (7.2.5), before the section ends by accounting for the value creation strategies of the principal vs stakeholders (7.2.6). Underlying all of the ideas discussed is the premise that sustainable value creation is a discrete factor that helps to explain organizational behavior, business strategy, and firm performance, and is even mirrored in the smallest social units like the community or the family.

7.2.1 Implications of sustainable value creation for management

This inquiry's emphasis on economic development focuses its attention on the aggregate meso-level elite system, the transmission channel that integrates the micro-level firm into macro-level economic analysis (see Figure 3.8). In Chapter 6, several SVC measurements were advanced. The EQx is the operationalization of meso-level sustainable value creation, with elite quality being relevant to macro-level performance. In parallel, the claim was made that any business model can be assessed at the micro-level by using equivalent measurements like the VCr. Signaling theory is used in the management literature to understand how organizations convey information to their various stakeholders (Connelly, Certo, Ireland, & Reutzel, 2011). In Bitektine's "theory of social judgments of organizations", organizational legitimacy, reputation, and status are "organizational resources" (2011, p. 151) and he references literature that shows how firms gain legitimacy through "discursive means", i.e., narratives (e.g., Golant & Sillince, 2007; Suddaby & Greenwood, 2005). This section, and the next on corporate governance, are anchored by aspects of signaling and legitimacy theory to further embed the micro-level facets of the ETED within the orbit of corporate social responsibility (CSR), and environmental, social, and governance (ESG).

CSR and lobbying, the latter also sometimes referred to as corporate political activity (CPA), are analytically joined in the strategic management literature using a synthesis known as "nonmarket strategy research" (Mellahi, Frynas, Sun, & Siegel, 2016). Strategic agency in the non-market and narrative market arenas of the political economy requires establishing legitimacy, a process that is never straightforward for management. Accordingly, ESG initiatives also include non-financial data and sustainability KPIs for "Powering financial markets to deliver a sustainable future" (see, www.esgbook.com). As is detailed later in this chapter, when academics examine these claims there can be unpleasant surprises—in the case of Refinitiv (now LSEG Data & Analytics), a leading ESG ratings supplier, an "(un)predictable past" (Berg, Fabisik, & Sautner, 2021) refers to inconsistent and duplicitous data. These and other issues led Glenn Hegar, the Texas comptroller of public accounts, to complain that "the ESG movement has produced an opaque and perverse system in which some financial companies no longer make decisions in the best interests of their shareholders or their clients" (Temple-West & Masters, 2022). Signal failure, delegitimization, and a plethora of other negative issues associated with ESG and CSR are identified in the literature and further expanded upon in the next section on corporate governance. Such weaknesses have resulted in novel, compelling, and conceptually refined proposals like Edmans' "Rational Sustainability" that "includes everything that improves long-term value" (2024, p. 15). For this elite theory, it is critical that existing ESG efforts and improved sustainability initiatives theoretically address the larger economic development perspective.

For instance, how does a privileged elite business model signal the weighting and hence the legitimacy of the extractive stage of an 'alternating value extraction and creation' cycle in an industry that is poised to create great value for all through future positive externalities? Like the discussion of value creation optima in the EQx (Section 6.4.2) or the formulation of structural reform policies (Section 7.1.5), weighting to properly articulate offsets must be sought for such models, as without extractive rents (such as those enabled by monopolies, subsidies, or regulations) firms might not have the resources or financial slack to invest in value creation (see, for example, the U-shaped relationship between slack and innovation in Nohria & Gulati, 1996). At times, a firm first develops an innovative technology (value creation), files patents or otherwise secures a monopoly on its business model, and thereafter prices the technology significantly higher than under the premises of free entry and competition. This is the logic behind the observation that "data-opolies can extract wealth by getting personal data without having to pay for the data's fair market value" (Stucke, 2018). Silicon Valley's Big Tech is highly adept at winning battles in the non-market arena (e.g., the 2001 settlement of the antitrust case that nullified the District Court's mandate to breakup Microsoft, thus permitting it to remain intact as a single entity) and the narrative market (e.g., the doctrine of "dynamic competition" articulated by Petit and Teece, 2021) to legitimize their oligopolistic positions and the ensuing value transfers, and is now poised to repeat the feat in the mother of all intra-elite contests that is playing out over AI. Considering the above and since every successful business model in the real economy incorporates both value creation and extractive transfer-IN (as is graphically represented by the 'value spectrum', see Figures 2.10, 2.11, and A5.5a), how should a sustainable value creation framework for management be modeled? Does Edmans' observation that "rational sustainability is about value creation, not politics" (2024, p. 9) obviate the reality of the license to operate; and is not every business model anchored in institutional constraints that require political non-market agency, with the more elite requiring legally sanctioned permissions for value transfers given their association with value creation (see the realist inference, Figure 8.7)? Should Mazzucato's (2019) "value of everything" actually be weighted and signaled? The SVC measurements (see equations 4.1 and 4.2 in Table 2.4) are designed to provide the basic elements to address these quantification issues.

Value Creation Position (VCp) scores include two of the three main value categories discussed: value created and appropriated (net value creation); and value appropriated but *not* created (extractive value transfer-IN). Value Creation Rating (VCr) scores add and quantify the third value category: value created but *not* appropriated (transfer-OUT). When the more comprehensive VCr sustainable value measurement scores are matched against P&L performance benchmarks like profits (residual income), fresh perspectives materialize. A performance framework for management at the firm level is operationalized here as The Sustainable Value Matrix (presented in Figure 7.2). The matrix has two constituent variables that represent firm performance and sustainable value creation, in this case, the VCr (on the x-axis) and profits (on the y-axis).

The management framework provides a classification schema for the purposes of understanding and analyzing the relationship between performance and sustainability at the firm level. If sustainable value creation is high *and* the firm is profitable, the principal qualifies as a 'sustainable' firm (quadrant 1). The Sustainable Value Matrix places a firm that creates value (as reflected by a high VCr) but is unprofitable (due to the inability of the model to appropriate at least part of the significant value it creates) in the 'naïve' firm category (quadrant 2) of the framework. Business models with low sustainable value creation are extractive, but if adept at value appropriation, especially from stakeholders (value transfer-IN), and hence profitable, they belong in the 'rentier' category (quadrant 3). Firms that are both extractive and unprofitable are 'living-dead'[166] firms (quadrant 4) that are in the business of destroying financial capital and value and will not prevail.[167]

Investors and consultants can support firms that are 'naïve' and "(un-)capturing sustainable value" (see Wagner & Kabalska, 2023) by upgrading their appropriation ca-

---

166 Note that the research on "zombie" organizations plagued by debt and inefficiencies (Ahearne & Shinada, 2005; Caballero, Hoshi, & Kashyap, 2008) referenced earlier solely considers firm performance (profits)—not sustainability or sustainable value creation.

167 Note that the 'destructive' off-P&L transfer-COST (see Figures 6.7 and A5.5a) is currently not part of the SVC measurements and hence The Sustainable Value Matrix does not fully capture the consequences of value destruction in its quadrants.

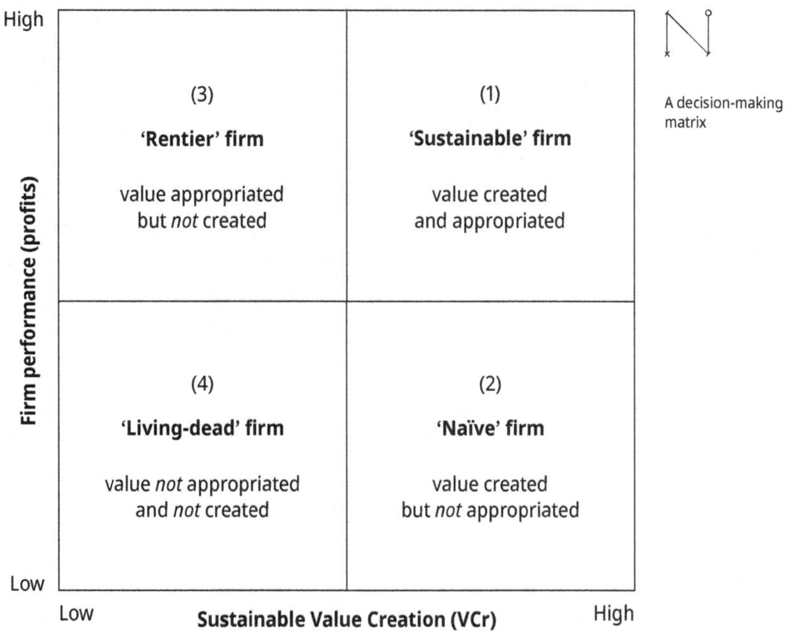

Figure 7.2: The Sustainable Value Matrix: A performance framework for management.[168]

pabilities (value created but *not* appropriated might be a political economy non-market issue that is fixable with lobbying) and transforming them into 'sustainable' firms. They can also assist 'rentier' firms in a journey towards increased sustainable value creation. Backing a 'living-dead' firm across two parallel journeys—to profits *and* to sustainability—is, however, a tall order. How The Sustainable Value Matrix (Figure 7.2) is extended to support the analysis of investments is explored in Section 7.2.5 and visualized in The Sustainable Finance Matrix (Figure 7.3). For a debt and equity valuation perspective, refer to The Sustainable Valuations Matrix framework for investors and sustainable finance, and to the explanations at the end of Section 7.2.5 (see also Figure A5.7).

168 Out of the thirteen (13) matrix frameworks in this inquiry, the nine (9) that describe the political economy or its states have the quadrant annotated as (1)/(i) placed in the lower left and quadrant (4)/(iv) in the upper right. Out of these, four (4) are 'political economy classification' matrices and use Roman numerals—as in Figures 6.2, 6.4, 6.8, and A5.2—to depict their quadrants. Further to these descriptive classifications are five (5) 'political economy prescriptive' matrices that express a desirable development path—as in Figures 1.1, 6.5, 6.8, 7.5, and 8.4—and use Arabic numerals where quadrant (1) indicates the less desirable state, one which can evolve and culminate in the ideal quadrant (4) with transformational elite leadership. There are also four (4) matrix frameworks—Figures 7.2, 7.3, 7.4, and A5.7—designed to be used for 'elite decision-making'. Due to their micro-level prescriptive quality (for strategy, investment, etc.) their quadrant numbering follows a reverse order: quadrant (1) is placed in the upper right of the matrix as the normative benchmark, while quadrant (4) indicates the least desirable state and is placed in the lower left.

Milton Friedman's famous op-ed for *The New York Times* was entitled "The Social Responsibility of Business is to Increase its Profits" (1970). The value creation-appropriation (VCA) framework and bargaining power differentials in the political economy (see Chapter 2) strongly qualify this view. In this work, firms, especially those running elite business models, contribute to society both through value appropriation (evidenced by profits) and sustainable value creation (evidenced by SVC measurements). Many firms are both profitable and 'sustainable' (quadrant 1), providing returns to shareholders while offering higher wages, innovation spillovers, economic growth, net zero carbon footprints, and an array of other positive externalities and forms of value for their stakeholders. This is consistent with Friedman's position that 'sustainable' firms and their principals (including elites) require sufficient profits (and some transfer-IN that will be weighted and offset) to compensate for risks taken and to continue investing in value creation. However, not all profitable firms offset their extraction and are thus sustainable; those in the 'rentier' category (quadrant 3) hinder economic development through their disproportionate transfer-IN (which also includes 'extractive' transfer-COST, see the 'value spectrum' of Figure A5.5a and the discussion in Section 8.2.1) and distort the incentive system.

Residual income (profits) generated through the 'knowledge' bargaining power source (see Figure 2.3) best aligns sustainability, social responsibility, and inclusivity concerns with capital allocation and investor perspectives (see Section 7.2.5). Signaling theory can be helpful in reducing information asymmetries (Spence, 1973) and allowing management to convey to the market and multiple stakeholders (Connelly, Certo, Ireland, & Reutzel, 2011) their sustainability commitments (Bae, Masud, & Kim, 2018). With The Sustainable Value Matrix, management signals to shareholders and stakeholders its sustainable value creation in relation to profits, potentially a prime source of legitimacy for the organization.

7.2.2 Implications of sustainable value creation for governance

By being relevant to stakeholders such as investors or regulators, the operationalization of sustainable value creation at the firm level (e.g., the VCr), which parallels elite quality at the meso-level, invariably moves this inquiry into the realms of corporate governance, further strengthening the links to CSR and ESG considerations. The underlying mandate is for boards to consider value creation along with the maximization of shareholder value (a variety of proposals already exist, e.g., Thomsen, 2020). Consistent with the signaling perspective reviewed above on "social judgments of organizations" (Bitektine, 2011) and "legitimacy as a social judgement" (Ashforth & Gibbs, 1990, p. 177), a foundation for the CSR/ESG discourse is crystalized in Bénabou and Tirole's words: "Society's demands for individual and corporate social responsibility as alternative responses to market and distributive failures are becoming increasingly prominent" (2010, p. 1). While management can position the firm in The

Sustainable Value Matrix (Figure 7.2), the ultimate responsibility of a firm in many key matters related to sustainability resides with its board and corporate governance structure, "the system by which companies are directed and controlled" (Cadbury, 1992, p. 14). One might posit that generally speaking, organizational CSR/ESG responses to political and social demands for legitimacy are a matter primarily addressed by top managers, with board support forthcoming in the non-market and narrative market arenas, the latter being particularly relevant in the context of intra-elite contests.

A driving notion behind the CSR/ESG literature is to achieve an alignment between what is good for the firm (principals) with what is good for society (stakeholders). At the same time, boards are sensitive to the criticism and uncertainty that surrounds existing corporate governance, CSR, and ESG theory and its practice frameworks and metrics. Many of the charges leveled against the field are of material concern. Is sustainability practice substantive or symbolic (Ashforth & Gibbs, 1990) and simply discursive (Biermann et al., 2022)? Edmans (2020) notes that sustainability is a bland label, a generic term containing no information and simply signifying the long term, making all firms that persevere, no matter how successfully, somewhat 'sustainable'. There is a barrage of criticism concerning the ineffectiveness of these approaches during global crises, their failure to deliver on grand challenges, of being a device for greenwashing, of oversimplifying social problems, of being inconsistent, of embodying conflicts of interest, of lacking comprehensiveness, and of being unrelated to actual performance (Deakin & Konzelmann, 2003; Letza, Sun, & Kirkbride, 2004; Williams, 2004; Yeoh, 2010; Clarke, 2010; Liang & Renneboog, 2017; Eccles & Stroehle, 2018 (for an overview of the issues, see Casas-Klett & Nerlinger, 2023, pp. 35–36). Perhaps most controversial is the lack of integrity associated with ESG ratings exemplified by the retroactive rewriting of scores via "unannounced data modifications" so that "rankings and classifications of firms into ESG quantiles change significantly" (Berg, Fabisik, & Sautner, 2021, p. 22).

This inquiry gives voice to an issue, one that is usually—and often intendedly—not on the radar screens of boards: value transfers as determinants of economic and human development. Are such transfers truly of secondary importance to corporate governance and, if so, how critical a blind spot are they in current CSR/ESG practice? This can be illustrated with a case provided by Acemoglu and Robinson (2019b, p. 19) who reference an OECD report on the costs (transfer-IN from society) of Mexico's telecommunications monopoly (an SVC metric): US$ 129.2 billion from 2005–2009 (about 1.8% of the country's annual GDP). What amount of ESG, CSR, or philanthropy can ever compensate for what some economists (Tullock, 1967; Tollison, 1982) have termed net social losses, resource misallocations, or the deadweight of value extractive elite business models? In contrast, business models that create value without resorting to transfers might be conceived of as executing the 'ultimate' form of sustainability, to the point where compensatory or charitable engagements become redundant. For one of the greatest individual value creators in history "there is no public record of Mr. Jobs giving money to charity", as this was seen as a "distraction" to the Apple founder with a "single-minded focus on work over philanthropy" (Sorkin, 2011). Sustainable value creation requires, provides for, *and* weights and qualifies Friedman's profits (1970). Any board supplying evidence of high sustainable value creation can stop all charitable giving in good conscience as it is overseeing a business model that represents philanthropy of the highest caliber by taking the human and economic development perspective into account. As is depicted in Figure A5.4b, this elite theory and its core assumptions views sustainability and sustainable governance holistically (as in the 'value is created or transferred' ontological assumption and the holistic 'weight and offset value transfers' implication) and constructively (as in the 'bona fide value appropriation' positive assumption and the 'revenue is value creation unless value transfer is proven' constructive implication) because of its business model focus on *how* organizations generate residual income (profits).

Bénabou and Tirole, ask: "who, among the state, stakeholders and firms, is best placed to address market failures and inequality?" (2010, p. 16). Given the examined endogenous nature of institutional change and the bargaining power differentials of elites, this inquiry provides the means to answer this *who* question. For instance, it places the primary responsibility for elite system transformational leadership on the core elite coalition. The beneficiaries of elite coalitions then have ownership over inclusive transformations in the nooks and crannies of the economic landscape in which they operate. In practical, prescriptive terms, transformational leadership is within the purview of board directors who can provide guidance to management on performance objectives consistent with sustainable value creation. For board directors concerned about legitimacy and positive social behavior that take a view on general development beyond mainstream CSR/ESG frameworks and metrics, the way forward is unambiguous: direct the firm towards maximizing residual income generation (Friedman's profits) through value creation and risk origination business model activities that do not rely on power and extraction (value transfer-IN), and ideally generate munificent positive externalities (value transfer-OUT). Then, aggressively signal high sustainable value creation positions and ratings to the public, customers, shareholders, regulators, and all other stakeholders.

7.2.3 Implications of sustainable value creation inside firms and other micro-level social units

All elite systems contain an assortment of coalitions of both high and low quality, running extractive and inclusive value creation elite business models. This variance also holds true inside any social unit and is intuitive to anyone who looks at their own family: some members are 'producers' while others are 'takers', living out their existence at different degrees of parasitism on the back of a family unit. Works of literature take on this theme, Dostoyevsky's *Crime and Punishment* (1866/1917) being a notable example: Semyon Zakharovitch Marmeladov trades his clerical government job for the bottle, while his wife Katerina Ivanovna is forced to raise her three children without income, all of which leads her eldest 18-year-old daughter, Sonya, into prostitution to bring food to the family table. Of course, ascertaining who is a 'producer' and who is a 'taker'—and in what proportion—is not always straightforward.

Was F.C. Barcelona's Leo Messi a value 'producer', with his record number of goals and trophies, or did he become a 'taker', due to his exorbitant compensation and style of play that forced his teammates to adapt to a system that allowed his genius to flourish, perhaps preempting the development of the next generation of players from *La Masia*? The reasons for Barça's current state of financial distress and potential ruin that became evident after Messi's departure in 2021 are multiple and well understood by many supporters and those who follow the business of football. In another example, Musk decided to slash about 85% of the workforce because: "Twitter had a 'lot of people doing things that didn't seem to have a lot of value'" (Dean, 2023). Additionally, "more than 100,000 tech jobs across more than 360 companies have been cut in 2024 so far, with tech layoffs showing no signs of abating" (Hughes, 2024). Is this phenomenon due to owners' particular positions on moderation and diversity, a more general trend towards AI replacement, or initiatives to tackle rent-seeking coalitions of employees inside firms now that surveillance technology allows for better assessments of productivity? The takeaway is that establishing and weighting value creation, while challenging at the firm level (see the SVC metrics in Section 6.6.5), is even more complex at the intra-organizational level and inside the micro units of society.

The value creation (first-order 'producer') and value extraction (second-order 'taker') dualism is universal, reflected at the macro-level of a national economy, in the meso-level elite system, in the micro-level single organization, and existing in even smaller constituent units of society like the family, the social club, or a group of friends.[169] Further to Proposition 8 on bargaining power differentials (Section 2.2.2,

169 The ontological position that informs this work seems reductionist and Manichean, dividing socio-economic relations into first-order 'producer' and second-order 'taker' behaviors. In continuity, the 'universal value extraction propensity of humans' is the premise for social and economic ties and is applicable to human elites and non-elites alike (see Figure A5.4c). It transcends the human order considering that it is also a universal feature of the relationships between all living things and thus of life itself (see the 'universal extraction propensity of life' law of nature, Figure 8.6). This general principle of life is, for instance, evident in phagocytosis, an early evolutionary process by which certain cells, the phagocytes, enjoy value appropriated but *not* created through the ingestion of other living cells. From a different analytical vantage point, Schrödinger's *What is Life?* reflects on "negative entropy", stating that: "the device by which an organism maintains itself stationary at a fairly high level of orderliness (= fairly low level of entropy) really consists in continually sucking orderliness from its environment" (1944/2013, p. 73). The universal propensity for such extractive "sucking" is, for the purposes of this work, not tempered by purported research claims that life does not "always feed on negative entropy" as in microbial realms where "entropy-neutral, entropy-driven, and entropy-retarded growth exist" (von Stockar & Liu, 1999, p. 1412). There certainly are conceptions of life based on symbiotic mutualism, such as the microbiome in the human gut or the processes in natural ecosystems. In fact, "symbionts play a pivotal role in shaping biodiversity at ecological and evolutionary scales" (Chomicki, Beinart, Prada, Ritchie, & Weber, 2022). Moreover, the co-evolution of animals and plants with

see Figure 2.3), the inquiry has centered on principal-stakeholder relationships in an inter-organizational setting by reducing the analytical scope to division of value strategies. If we examine the intra-organizational perspective more granularly there is no escaping the logic of power that owners, managers, or workers have over their colleagues as a result of "existing relations and associated resources (e.g., status, prestige, legitimacy)" emanating, for instance, from being "uniquely positioned to broker intra-organizational knowledge flows by virtue of maintaining unparalleled social ties within the firm and by possessing tacit knowledge concerning organizational routines" (Di Gregorio, 2013, pp. 43, 44). Within companies, value is also divided, as some executives and workers appropriate more value than they create for the organization ('takers'), while others create more than they appropriate ('producers').

The particular proportion of 'producers' and 'takers' that an organization employs is a critical factor in its performance. 'Takers' increase costs in so many ways that they should in theory not exist at all in a firm that maximizes profit, but perhaps by being adept at office politics (and intrigue), they often thrive. Despite being a hindrance to organizational objectives, 'takers' persevere because they either gain formal authority or develop connections to leaders that rise to the top based on coordination leadership and an ability to amass power. As for company leaders, although some of these are also clearly 'takers', it is a cliché that those at the top benefit from the producers at the bottom. All the greater grounds for top executives, along with mid-level managers and workers, to be subject to assessments through the lens of sustainable value creation, maybe by an 'Individual Value Creation Rating' ('ind-VCr').

The HR departments of most organizations are premised on carrying out explicit assessments of employees and managers. However, the higher up the ladder one goes, the greater the ambiguity becomes on how value creation is attributed (see Zajac & Westphal, 1995, on CEO compensation) or misattributed (Sánchez-Marín, Baixauli-Soler, & Lucas-Pérez, 2010). While research suggests that when "a shirking CEO causes underperformance and harms shareholder wealth" he or she is "more likely to be replaced, especially when the CEO is early in their tenure" and if "board independence" is high (Biggerstaff, Cicero, & Puckett, 2016), Jensen and Murphy hypothesize in their

microbes points to "strong, persistent symbiotic associations" now set to shape the understanding of "all subdisciplines of biology' (McFall-Ngai, 2024), with *de facto* exchanges based on relatively equalized bargaining power a defining property of nature. Nonetheless, the 'value appropriation demand of humans' basic constraint of the human condition is deemed to be foundational to this work and 'value appropriated but *not* created' is recognized as being inescapable in the 'all elite agency creates and transfer value' (realist) inference where its pragmatic philosophy plays out. Interestingly, it is tempered in public life and provided with inclusive expression in societies everywhere by religion, ethics, customs, and narrative restraints. Chapter 8 suggests ethical principles for curbing these extractive tendencies in order to maximize development. Are these ethical principles pertinent only in the context of *intra-human* relationships? Section 8.1.6 on the ethical boundaries in a political economy examines their application to relationships across species and life forms, such as in factory farming or the rapidly evolving interactions between humans and post-biological superintelligence.

seminal paper "that public and private political forces impose constraints that reduce the pay-performance sensitivity", while shareholders and their representatives on the board lack the "complete information regarding the CEO's activities and the firm's investment opportunities" (1990, pp. 225, 226). At the upper echelons of a firm, the default narrative is that individual performance equates to organizational performance adjusted for risk. Effective checks and balances and effective governance notwithstanding, those with internal bargaining power differentials that sit atop the hierarchy and benefit from "status" (Piazza & Castellucci, 2014) need not self-assess and can easily attribute the collective value creation and residual income of what they manage, fairly or not, to themselves (and even diverting the responsibility for losses to others). Theoretically, extractive internal value transfers (from one sub-set of firm members to another) are associated with the agency of dominant coalitions and their power inside the firm (March & Simon, 1958; Thompson & McEwen, 1958; Cyert & March, 1963). Their influence might be ascertained through measures derived from social network analysis methods that leverage key organizational datasets (see the embeddedness of Granovetter, 1985; Sparrowe, Liden, Wayne, & Kraimer, 2001; Siegel, 2009; and Section 4.1.2). But to reiterate, power can create value and not be used for extraction. Overall, the value creation position and performance of a firm is conjectured as being severely impacted by the internal relative (bargaining) power weights of its 'producers' and 'takers'.

At the same time, it must be pointed out an organization led or populated by 'takers' throughout its higher ranks might well be profitable. The relationship of such organizations with their external stakeholders is the chief determinant of their financial performance (see the discussions on the VCA framework in Chapter 2). Residual income levels are high because of extractive transfer-IN from external stakeholders (see the 'rentier' firm quadrant, Figure 7.2) as is the case for the inefficient but profitable monopolist, or a bloated civil service supported by taxpayers. Evidently, in the intra-organizational context, the negative weight and impact of 'takers' on performance is theorized to matter less in business models that are based on value extraction, since these can afford in-house inefficiencies and excess burdens due to value appropriated but *not* created from stakeholders outside of the firm.

In sum, from a management and sustainability perspective, the distribution of 'producers' and 'takers' within an organization is critical. In many instances, tacit knowledge already exists about who the 'producers' and 'takers' are and of their relative contributions to the collective success or failure of an organization. Scholars have established the deadweight that incompetent executives and workers represent, especially in competitive markets, and the literature has identified many of the roots of intra-firm value extraction: wage growth over productivity or its opposite (see Economic Policy Institute, 2024; and mandated wages above equilibrium in Table 2.2 and Figure 2.4); executive bonuses not associated with performance (Jensen & Murphy, 1990); worker rents through membership in unions, and managerial rents through investments in firm-specific human capital (Sørensen, 2000). The organizational lifecycle might also be a factor (much like the lifecycle postulated for elite business models, Figure 4.5) and, over time, extractive rent-seeking activity by internal associates accumulates. Unsurprisingly, research also confirms significant destruction of extractive rents thanks to corporate restructuring, though interestingly this is less true for managers than for workers because, according to Dencker and Fang (2016), relatively more open and market-based contracts are already imposed on the latter.

7.2.4 Implications of sustainable value creation for leadership

That elite agency is realized through leadership was established in Section 4.1.1. In the context of this theory, leadership is about amassing and wielding power and having a functional "influence on organizational activity", which Stogdill (1950, p. 1) conceived of as a process or act informed by objectives and the will to achieve these. Simply put, leadership is about obtaining and wielding 'the extraordinary lever' of power. Two forms of micro-level leadership in the context of elite agency, each associated with the performance of their own discrete objectives, have so far been advanced in this work: (a) 'elite coordination leadership', where the objective is power accumulation (see Figure 1.2); and (b) 'elite business model leadership', where the objective is residual income maximization (see Figure 2.1). To complete a fundamental understanding of elite leadership, a third form, the meso-level (c) 'elite system leadership' is now advanced and will eventually become theoretically embedded in the framework of institutionalized intra-elite contest rules and the elite separation of powers. The objective of this type of leadership is to increase elite cohesion (see the 'elite cohesion underpins social order' conjecture) and the bargaining power and residual income (i.e., value appropriation) of elites as a socio-economic category (see Figure 8.1). This work considers these three types of leadership to be 'fundamental' leadership varieties found in any elite system and its coalitions (independently of whether the system boasts high or low elite quality, as per its EQx or EQr scores). They are supplemented by two other vital types of leadership, jointly referred to in this work as 'transformational' leadership varieties on account of their normative and disruptive nature and their main objective: enhancing sustainable value creation.

The two varieties of transformational leadership are: (d) 'elite transformational leadership', and (e) 'elite system transformational leadership'. Transformations occur through the practice of self-restraint, such as a "voluntary power handover" (Boucekkine, Piacquadio, & Prieur, 2019), on taking a long-term perspective (Olson, 1993), on "enlightened self-interest" at the top (Mizruchi, 2017), and on self-critically recognizing the "wealth pump" (Turchin, 2023) and its benefits and then weighting, offsetting, and even suspending its flows. These two leadership varieties weight and offset transfers to move organizations and the elite system towards greater sustainable value creation and thereby contribute to higher degrees of national elite quality and, ultimately, to economic development. For organizations, and for nation states, such leadership addresses and resolves an optimization problem since the value (and risk) creation and transfers of different activities can be set against each other (as is implicit in the 'quantifiability of value transfers' assumption, see Section 5.3.1 and Figure A5.4a). The presence or absence of 'elite system transformational leadership' is hypothesized to be the most important determinant of national non-elite welfare and the driver of historical processes and cycles. An overview of the five varieties of leadership that concern the ETED is provided in Table 7.2.

Table 7.2: A Typology of The Five Varieties of Elite Leadership.

Elite leadership variety [analysis level]	**Objective [elite agency]**	**Definition**
(i) Fundamental leadership varieties		
(a) Elite coordination leadership [micro-level]	Bargaining power [elite coalitions]	Elite coalition leadership at the business model level that leverages accumulated coordination capacity and uses it for maximum bargaining power differentials over stakeholders (see Figures 1.2, 3.6, 4.1, A5.3a).
(b) Elite business model leadership [micro-level]	Residual income [elite coalitions]	Elite coalition leadership at the business model level that converts bargaining power differentials over stakeholders into maximum residual income (see Figures 2.1, 4.1, A5.3a).
(c) Elite system leadership [meso-level]	Elite cohesion; bargaining power; residual income [core elite coalition]	Leadership at the elite system level, usually by the core elite coalition, to increase elite cohesion for the maximization of elite bargaining power and residual income.
(ii) Transformational leadership varieties		
(d) Elite transformational leadership [micro-level]	Sustainable value creation; residual income [elite coalitions]	Elite coalition leadership at the business model level that converts bargaining power differentials over stakeholders into maximum residual income that is, nonetheless, self-constrained by the minimization of value (and risk) transfers and the maximization of value (and risk) creation. This transformational leadership variety has an ethical anchor, necessitates a long-run temporal perspective, requires purposeful and continuous business

Table 7.2 (continued)

Elite leadership variety [analysis level]	**Objective [elite agency]**	**Definition**
		model transformation (e.g., in consistency with social and technological changes), accrues legitimacy on account of signaling, and technically requires the weighting and offsetting of value creation (including transfer-OUT) against value transfer (transfer-IN) activities (see Figures 5.2, 8.3, A5.12).
(e) Elite system transformational leadership [meso-level]	Elite quality; sustainable value creation; a sustainable elite system; economic development; elite/non-elite cohesion; bargaining power in the international system [core elite coalition]	Leadership at the elite system level by the core elite coalition that utilizes elite cohesion and the elite separation of powers (see Figure 5.2) to raise elite quality by constraining extractive value (and risk) transfers and engaging in structural reform to incentivize sustainable value creation. Such leadership is driven by a set of ethical principles, relies on individual elite judgment, accrues legitimacy on account of signaling, and technically requires the weighting and offsetting of value creation (including the sum of transfer-OUT) against value transfers (the sum of transfer-IN) in the political economy as it seeks a sustainable elite system via economic and human development that furthers elite/non-elite cohesion and bargaining power advantages in the international system (see Figures 5.2, 8.3, A5.12).

The implications that this typology of the varieties of elite leadership have for economic development are more numerous than can be covered in this work, and the theoretical path from the leadership literature to the political economy needs to advance further, as is suggested by the work of Jones and Olken (2005) or Brady and Spence (2010). The assertion of this inquiry is that the two transformational varieties of leadership link to sustainability because they require elite judgments to constrain value and risk transfers in the pursuit of residual income to move the needle in a less extractive direction.

It is important to stress that this work's conceptual element of elite transformational leadership should not be conflated with 'transformational leadership' as presented in the extant literature, even though both aim at positive change. The latter, like the "4 I's of transformational leadership" comprised of "idealized influence, inspirational motivation, intellectual stimulation, and individualized consideration" (Avolio, Waldman, & Yammarino, 1991, as cited in Bass & Avolio, 1993, p. 112), focus on followers, their "values and ideals" (Piccolo & Colquitt, 2006, p. 327), and is often contrasted with, although also seen as complementary to, transactional leadership, with its rewards and punishments resting on "exchanges or agreements" between leaders and the led (Bass & Avolio, 1993, p. 112). Elite transformational leadership, on the other hand, is specific to elite agency and its business models. Hence, it has discrete properties, including an association with decision-making that entails risk, such as a CEO who is responsible to shareholders and whose commitment to new value creation does not immediately make up for the lost residual profits derived from the cessation of extractive transfer-IN activities.

Relatedly, it must be emphasized that the higher the degree of transformational leadership, the greater the courage and exposure that is required. The effects of organizational "empowerment", or the processes "by which leaders become change agents" and "heroic leaders" (Walls, Salaiz, & Chiu 2021, pp. 502, 504) lose significance—transformational leadership cannot simply be manufactured. Elites are made of power and the ethical positions they take on sustainable value creation are self-driven, unconstrained, and intrinsic, linked to their internal Will to Live and Will to Power (Figure 8.7) manifestations. As such, the root of their transformational agency transcends current incentive structures. Non-elites, including the second stratum's managerial, technical, and creative class, while often driven by intrinsic motivation, do respond to incentives. Elite principals concerned about low quality stakeholder agency that wish to incentivize non-elite sustainable value creation can refer to the virtuous feedback loops that transpire when non-elites see transformational leadership at the top. For instance, research on authentic leadership shows that there is impact "on followers' ethical and pro-social behaviors" and a positive relationship with moral courage (Hannah, Avolio, & Walumbwa, 2011, p. 555).

Leadership can be theoretically at odds with the conceptualization of transformation in complex adaptive systems (see Section 3.2.3). In contrast, "to person-centered accounts", Aldrich's evolutionary approach "using an aggregate as opposed to an individual level of analysis" and the population ecology model accentuates "the nature and distribution of resources in organizations' environments, rather than on internal leadership or participation in decision making" and so, for instance, "selection derives from the consequences of action, not the intentions of actors" which "can seem maddeningly indirect and impersonal" (Aldrich, 2008, pp. xxi, xxviii). The elite theory obviously minimizes "forces exogenous" and "environmental forces treated as unchangeable by managers and organizations (Aldrich, 2008, as cited in Aldrich & Yang, 2014, p. 77) and is closer to "organization theories using an evolutionary approach

[that] today treat environments as subject to manipulation and transformation" (Aldrich & Ruef, 2006, as cited in Aldrich & Yang, 2014, p. 77). The emphasis is on elite agency to explain change in complex evolutionary systems for all of Aldrich's stages of variation, selection, retention, and struggle. Leadership during variation and selection rests on individual creativity and the Will to Power; retention demands the courage to oppose the forces of reaction; and struggle relates to personal survival and the Will to Live.

In practice, the crux of the matter for top management, boards, or investors is whether a successfully transformed 'sustainable' firm can really perform better financially than a 'rentier' firm (see The Sustainable Value Matrix, Figure 7.2, and the discussion on the implications for investors in Section 7.2.5). This critical topic has produced a diverse and vibrant academic literature that lacks consensus and is not immune to the controversies that surround sustainability in society (e.g., Hart & Ahuja, 1996; Friede, Busch, & Bassen, 2015; Billio, Costola, Hristova, Latino, & Pelizzon, 2020; Berg, Kölbel, & Rigobon, 2022; *The Economist* (2022). Regardless of any actual and potential trade-offs between profitability and CSR/ESG, in many elite quarters there is a push for sustainability to control the related "financial risk", as articulated by Tangen (FT Film, 2024, 1:55). Transitioning to higher sustainable value creation business models is also consistent with a variety of existing ideas (such as stakeholder capitalism, see Fink, 2020; Moynihan & Schwab, 2020) and regulations (see the discussion in Section 7.2.5). However, transformational leadership will still be exposed to the elements and require heavy ethical anchors bolstered by courage and boldness (see Chapter 8). A putative link might then exist with leadership theories relevant to the organization, such as the burgeoning research field of servant leadership, characterized by its concern for ethics, virtues, and morality (Graham 1991; Lanctot & Irving 2010; Parolini, Patterson, & Winston, 2009; Russell, 2001; Whetstone, 2002, as cited in Parris & Peachey, 2013, pp. 377, 378).

The transformational varieties of elite leadership in this work ultimately link to ethical positions on economic development. Yet single elite coalitions that are intent on prevailing cannot be expected to not be extractive if intra-elite contest dynamics and business model rules are overly sympathetic to transfer-IN business models. For the most part, elites in pursuit of the residual income maximization aspect of the utility function (see Section 2.1.1) will apply high discount rates to future income flows and not self-constrain on account of ethical, moral, or religious beliefs; on the contrary, righteous narratives will be used as a cloak to appropriate value. There are striking historical illustrations to support this point. For instance, Martin Luther's support for enslaving fellow Germans in the context of the *Bauernkrieg* (1524–1526), or the brutality of the Castilian conquest under the aegis of evangelization that totally vanquished Native American paternal Y-chromosome lineages (in striking contrast, Native American DNA still contributes to 33% of maternal lineages in Cuba, Mendizabal et al., 2008). Behavior more sensitive to economic and human development in 16th century Germany or New Spain would have run up against then permissible value appropriation. On the other hand, there is often virtue and long-term wealth to be gained when elites transform their business models and limit residual income (profits) under their own volition (see the 'inextinguishable value creation option of elites' assumption in Section 2.2.1 and Figure 8.7). Such inspiring examples of elite transformational leadership abound. For instance, "many big and successful corporations started out as social businesses, with, for example, Henri Nestlé providing baby-food to help mothers who were unable to breastfeed and William Lever, a founding father of Unilever, helping to make cleanliness, hygiene, and health common place in Victorian England" (Dylick & Muff, 2015, pp. 15–16). Wikipedia, with its enormous and well-known externalities (transfer-OUT) and modest value appropriation (from donations) can certainly be placed in the 'naïve' firm category (Figure 7.2) and will see its value promptly transferred to LLMs, despite the fact that Jimmy Wales and Larry Sanger were moved by high ideals consistent with the ethics of sustainable value creation. Then there is the case of Sir Alexander Fleming who:

> is revered not just because of his discovery of penicillin – the antibiotic that has saved millions of lives – but also due to his efforts to ensure that it was freely available to as much of the world's population as possible. Fleming could have become a hugely wealthy man if he had decided to control and license the substance, but he understood that penicillin's potential to overcome diseases such as syphilis, gangrene and tuberculosis meant it had to be released into the world to serve the greater good. (Ablott, 2011)

However, it is understandable that most elite coalitions will, and for reasons related to the very survival of their elite identity, behave as game-theoretical models require. They do not self-constrain, as their advantage would then move to a rival elite coalition that does not reject the institutionally sanctioned value appropriated but *not* created that is afforded by power. Again, ethical considerations are both deeply personal and need to originate at the elite system level before becoming institutionalized and operative through the incentive structure of the political economy.

Core elite coalitions (see their theoretical and applied role in Section 8.1.2 and their socio-economic position in Figure 8.1) are exceptionally placed to rise above narrow utility maximization logic and, as the most powerful coalition (and likely the most stationary of Olsonian bandits, see Section 2.2.1), pursue long-run objectives at the elite system level that reject value and risk transfers and advance structural efficiency to further a nation's economic and human development and its strength on the international stage. Here, the *coincidentia oppositorum* between elite cohesion and the separation of powers (see Figure 5.2) is a precondition for intra-elite contest outcomes that move institutions towards more inclusive business model rules. According to Evans, "comparative evidence suggests that the efficacy of the developmental state depends on a meritocratic bureaucracy with a strong sense of corporate identity and a dense set of institutionalized links to private elites" (1989, p. 561). One may take the "dense" and "institutionalized links" across political and business elites to describe mastery of the 'intra-elite quality contest' dilemma (Figure 5.2). Even if it is often discordant, a "symbiosis" exists between business and political elites (Best, 2019), with the corporatist model of Fascism (see Pinto, 2017) exemplifying its most intensified form. Decades ago, research showed "that considerable integration exists among elites in all major sectors of American society" (Moore, 1979, p. 689) but Mizruchi argues in *The Fracturing of the American Corporate Elite* (2013) that such conditions no longer exist—corporate elites and CEOs are unable to act collectively as they compete, and have absconded from their positions of responsibility with nefarious consequences for society. Without cohesion, elite system transformational leadership is not feasible. That is, sustainable business models will see their value appropriated by elites, as no constraints are placed on value appropriated but *not* created (transfer-IN). The successful course of elite system transformational leadership pursued by Lee Kwan Yew, the founding father of Singapore, is not the haphazard sustainability journey of Larry Fink, the CEO of the world's largest money manager, BlackRock; these contrasting paths are partially attributable to the discrete degrees of elite cohesion in the two countries. Piecemeal institutional change, as is suggested by A Weighted Structural Reform Framework for policy (see Table 7.1), as well as any inclusive winner in an intra-elite contest, positively contribute to development. The core elite coalition's systematic participation in intra-elite contests, even when these are unrelated to their own members' business model interests, is of far-reaching consequence. On the other hand, cohesion makes elite system transformational leadership easier to materialize as an emerging property; contests are won by high quality elites and new rules of the game for generating residual income are established. Moreover, regular elite business models faced with a novel incentive structure become more likely to join the flow and seek to transform toward higher sustainable value creation positions.

The transformational leadership of political elites (generals, emperors, popes, presidents, or secretary-generals) and knowledge elites (leading religious figures, writers, philosophers, scientists, or artists) is widely admired. Business elites, in contrast, elicit little such praise when their names are recalled: the transformational leadership and value creation contributions of Lü Buwei, Mayer Amschel Rothschild, Thomas Lipton, Minomura Rizaemon, Friedrich Krupp, King Camp Gillette, Eric Schmidt, and Jensen Huang, to name but a few, are seldom given their due or are tainted by other considerations (e.g., their personalities,[170] their philanthropy, their errors). Within their coalition or at the elite system level, transformational leaders might hail from any of the three power domains of the economy, politics, or society. Their agency might leverage the power of 'money', 'might', or 'mind' to achieve institutional change in the business model rules that underpin their value creation and

170 Leaders that effect transformational leadership are bound to psychologically deviate from conventional norms of human behavior and accepted standards of elite conduct. As they creatively destroy resistance, they face and generate enormous amounts of uncertainty. Their very business models also tax their mental coping mechanisms because painful extraction from third parties is required, even when these transfers are more than offset by larger amounts of value creation (see the 'all elite agency creates and transfer value' realist inference, Figure 8.7).

appropriation, entailing desirable transfer-OUT spillovers and public goods like security, innovation, and human development. It is through the lens of sustainable value creation—at both the elite business model and elite system levels—that history ought to assess the accomplishments of the powerful and influential.[171]

To sum up, elite business models are the ultimate target of elite system transformational leadership, which consequently becomes a momentous force that opens up the whole gamut of *homo sapiens*' choices for what Wengrow and Graeber term "social creativity" (2015, p. 613), thus affecting the fundamental configurations of the political economy. The two anthropologists "propose an alternative to the characterization of Palaeolithic societies in binary terms ('complex' versus 'simple', 'hierarchical' versus 'egalitarian') [a model where] Pleistocene hunter-gatherers alternated – consciously and deliberately – between contrasting modes of social organization" (2015, p. 599). In the context of this inquiry, non-elite agency cannot compete with 'the extraordinary lever' which, when consciously and deliberately held by elites and imbued with the spirit of transformational leadership, engenders sustainable and egalitarian societies.

171 'The great elite coalition for development' conjecture was advanced in Section 1.3.3 by referencing Carlyle's (1840/2008) Great Man Theory of history and leadership. Moreover, "heroic leaders" that "transform their companies into business beyond usual" can perhaps be developed (Walls, Salaiz, & Chiu, 2021, p. 494). Yet by what standard should posterity judge the individual? The theoretical focus of this theory of economic development is the elite business model, and hence any historical or contemporary figure of note (whether a business, political, or knowledge elite) can thus be appraised. Judgments passed on the likes of Hippocrates of Kos, Elizabeth I of England, Thomas Paine, Karl Marx, Milton Friedman, Deng Xiaoping, Chuck Feeney, Narendra Modi, Oprah Winfrey, or Dario and Daniela Amodei would revolve around their roles *as* inspirators, originators, or leaders of business model coalitions associated with discrete sustainable value creation positions. The suggested 'Individual Value Creation Rating' (ind-VCr) assessments refer to the nature of leadership and the impact of individuals on society, organizations, and teams and hence will invariably be conflicted. Think of a fugitive commodity trader's extractive practices, but whose agency also created enormous value in driving the "rising prosperity of the resource-rich developing world, the growth of commodity markets and the capacity of producers to profit from them" (Breiding, 2013). The academic question, referencing *The Financial Times* headline: "Yes, He Played Dirty—but Marc Rich also Changed the World", is to what proportion? This SVC measurement would include quantifiable metrics on the individual's relationships with his/her direct and indirect stakeholders across all related business models (which could well evolve into primary data inputs for their characters in the 'weighted transfers game', Figures A5.10 and A5.14b). In some cases, the family (e.g., the Marmeladovs), would be treated as a business model and its members rated as 'producers' (e.g., Sonya) or 'takers' (e.g., Semyon); in other cases, the business model of the individual would extend to stakeholders in the wider community or at the national level and be computable for any individual (whether Rich, Messi, or Modi). The notion of sustainable value creation at the individual level to complement country and firm level measurements was inspired by the entrepreneur and philanthropist, Joachim Schoss, during various exchanges with the author in Spring of 2023. Data availability notwithstanding, he has encouraged its realization as a ranking and believes that its laudatory and shaming effects would nudge elite agency in constructive directions.

7.2.5 Implications of sustainable value creation for investors

With Larry Fink's celebrated *2020 Letter to CEOs*, sustainability became a more consequential part of the narratives and products of the finance industry even if much of that enthusiasm has now subsided.[172] Robert Eccles (2024), the founding chairman of the SASB, notes that in the US "shareholder proposals, both pro- and anti-ESG, have reached the front lines of the culture wars", and while it remains unclear "what it means to be a responsible business" he welcomes "that the acronym ESG will eventually fade entirely". Traction within the space is being lost in part due to the confusion caused by the sprawl of sustainability frameworks, metrics and assessment systems, and standard setting organizations. In addition to the problematic CSR/ESG issues identified by academia (and discussed in Section 7.2.2), this multiplicity translates at the practical level into overwhelming possibilities that result in "an unholy mess", flanked by "missionary creep" and "false marketing" (*The Economist*, 2022) in line with a lack of conceptual consistency and suspicious datasets. Hence, "these days, some like to joke that if you want a better ESG rating all you need to do is change your rating provider" (Murray, 2021). Third-party providers are known to recycle metrics from each other that at times are impromptu and lack a solid academic foundation. In response, investors and consumers of sustainability assessments have developed their own proprietary evaluation systems (e.g., State Street Global Advisors has the 'Responsibility Factor' scoring system to guide investors and support the ESG practices of firms; TPG developed 'The Impact Multiple of Money' for its impact investing The Rise Fund).

The bedrock of any sustainability assessment is the underlying conceptual framework and derived data processing standards. Here, academia is contributing to conceptual clarity (e.g., Walls, Phan, & Berrone, 2011) and developing models (e.g., Elkington, 1997, and his "Triple Bottom Line" for "people, planet, and profit"), while the 'big' global ESG voluntary framework and standard-setting organizations have done important and impactful work. These include the GRI, the CDP (formerly the Carbon Disclosure Project), the Climate Disclosure Standards Board (CDSB), the International Integrated Reporting Council (IIRC), the UN's Global Investors for Sustainable Development alliance (GISD), and SASB. The latter's standards currently "identify the sustainability-related issues most relevant to investor decision-making in 77 industries" (IFRS Foundation, n.d.). While the concept of "integrated reporting" has been advanced to include financial information (for shareholders) and nonfinancial information (for stakeholders) to engage "significant audiences" (Eccles & Spiesshofer, 2015, p. 3), a particular focus of institu-

172 From 2023, Fink started to backpedal on ESG in response to novel dynamics in the narrative market, claiming that "attacks are now personal. They're trying to demonize the issues", while Elon Musk, surely a beneficiary of the 'E' element in ESG narratives "tweeted earlier that the S in ESG stands for 'Satanic'". See: https://www.swissinfo.ch/eng/bloomberg/larry-fink-says-esg-narrative-has-become-ugly–personal/48210604

tional change is now double materiality. In this vein, "a growing number of so-called benefit corporations (with B Corporation certification) are aiming for profit and impact" (Schoenmaker & Schramade, 2024, p. 6).

Most critically, the overarching framework of the European Commission's Corporate Sustainability Reporting Directive (CSRD) 2022/2464, that incorporates the European Sustainability Reporting Standards (ESRS), expands the scope of the earlier Non-Financial Reporting Directive (NFRD) 2014/95/EU and emphasizes the concept of double materiality for sustainability reports in the EU.[173] To advance the institutionalization of this notion "the responsibility for further developing the concept of double materiality and providing guidelines for its practical application is transferred to the EFRAG, as an organization that will set standards in the field of European Sustainability Reporting Standards in the future", meaning that ultimately "companies must respond to the increased demand for sustainability information from their stakeholders" (Baumüller, & Sopp, 2022, pp. 20, 23). The GRI notes that: "The materiality assessment process enhances investment decision making" (Adams, Alhamood, He, Tian, Wang, & Wang, 2021, p. 5). Through the legal lens, Mezzanotte (2023, p. 633) "recommends (1) that a sound legal strategy guide the company stakeholders interaction regarding external impacts, (2) that enforcement strategies be designed to accommodate unintentional greenwashing, and (3) that assurance practices for sustainability reporting be expeditiously implemented".

This is all of consequence to the field of accounting far beyond European borders. Disclosure requirements are now being further advanced globally through the International Sustainability Standards Board (ISSB) that develops and approves the International Financial Reporting Standards (IFRS) via the IFRS S1 (General Requirements for Disclosure of Sustainability-related Financial Information) and IFRS S2 (Climate-related Disclosures),[174] even though these rely on single (financial) materiality. The ISSB's IFRS initiative is supported by the International Organization of Securities Commissions (IOSCO), an umbrella association comprised of the world's securities and futures market regulators. Standards are based on frameworks such as the Financial Stability Board's (FSB) Task Force on Climate-related Financial Disclosures (TCFD), which advances climate-related financial reporting. The World Economic Forum's 2020 White Paper (Moynihan & Schwab, 2020), written in collaboration with Deloitte, EY, KPMG, and PwC, reviews frameworks to advocate "common metrics" and "consistent reporting of sustainable value creation". A key milestone in the institutionalization of sustainable finance was reached in 2019 when the EU adopted the Sustainable Finance Disclosure Regulation (SFDR) 2019/2088, that (now working in tandem with the CSRD):

---

173 Mezzanotte (2023, p. 634) specifies that the CSRD "Entered into force on 5 January 2023. Members States will have 18 months to transpose this legislation into their national legal regimes".

174 See: https://www.ifrs.org/issued-standards/ifrs-sustainability-standards-navigator/ifrs-s1-general-requirements/; and https://www.ifrs.org/issued-standards/ifrs-sustainability-standards-navigator/ifrs-s2-climate-related-disclosures/

> lays down sustainability disclosure obligations for manufacturers of financial products and financial advisers toward end-investors. It does so in relation to the integration of sustainability risks by financial market participants (i.e. asset managers, institutional investors, insurance companies, pension funds, etc., all entities offering financial products where they manage clients' money) and financial advisers in all investment processes and for financial products that pursue the objective of sustainable investment. (European Commission, 2019)

The ETED's SVC measurements may have a role to play in development economics or strategic decision-making, but can a business model centered conceptualization of sustainability become a reference for capital allocation? This question was positively answered in this work in Section 5.3.2—contrasting with the position of Edmans (2023) while referencing the findings of Bancel, Glavas, and Karolyi (2023)—with Figure 5.3 detailing the relationship between SVC measurements and SVC valuation frameworks. These technical frameworks (aimed at enterprise and equity, debt, and firm valuations) rely on SVC metrics and conceptually describe how business models generate profits, with each resting on a theoretical foundation that references the VCA framework and principal-stakeholder relationships, bargaining power differentials, and the notion of value creation and its extractive transfers, and hence link to economic development theory. Very importantly in terms of agency, all value (and risk) creation and extractive transfer activities correspond with prices on the back of the 'quantifiability of value transfers' (finance) assumption and its 'transparency of value creation and transfer activities' (open) implication for financial analysis (see Section 5.3.1 and Figure A5.4b). The ultimate practical consequence is to 'weight and offset value transfers' against value creation activities, the holistic implication of this theory[175] where business model activities can be traded against each other (see Figure A5.4b), meaning that sustainable value creation is a tractable optimization problem.[176]

175 Pazienza, de Jong, and Schoenmaker (2023, p. 19) complain that existing methodologies to assess sustainability "fail to provide a holistic measure which can be applied across firms and sectors consistently".

176 Without SVC measurements, the trade-offs between value transfer activities can hardly be conceived, optimization can hardly be approximated, and offsets can hardly be implemented. This is the case because the decisions concerning two or more interrelated activities with sustainable value creation trade-offs are often separate and independent. Some offset possibilities approach the dire or can seem impossible to formulate such as: how many human lives is a panda bear worth? Still, questions not that dissimilar are common as is evident in the case of pandemics or in the trade-off between violent hostilities and environmental protection, where the business model of war is in many instances beneficial to the nature stakeholder. For example, in the case of Colombia, Clerici et al. find that "the presence of armed conflict may ultimately prevent [logging, habitat conversion and illegal activities] to a greater extent than the absence of conflict", and that in the cases of Rwanda, Liberia, and Peru, "post-conflict development results in higher threats to forested ecosystems than conflict itself" (2020, p. 1). In short, the weighting and offsetting implications of SVC measurements reach their applied limits in extreme real-world situations when human lives are valued in acres of rainforest, or when freedom of movement is curtailed as part of public health policies during certain stages of a

Further to the previous discussions on sustainable governance (Section 7.2.2) and SVC valuations, investors will want to know to what extent a firm is optimizing sustainable value creation over profitability (or sacrificing one for the other) when funding a business. To this end, 'The Sustainable Finance Matrix' for investments (Figure 7.3), which mirrors the format of 'The Sustainable Value Matrix' for management (Figure 7.2), is now introduced. The focus here is on discrete investment categories with the decision layer applying to each of the four quadrants.

In The Sustainable Finance Matrix, firms are assigned an investment category based on two variables: sustainable value creation (VCr) on the x-axis, and firm performance (profits) on the y-axis. The first quadrant of the matrix defines the 'sustainable' investment category (quadrant 1) as being applicable to firms that are characterized by high profits and a high VCr (or an alternative SVC measurement). Financing this category is an obvious choice for investors, all else being equal in terms of valuation and risk. But are such firms too good to be true? *The Economist* (2022) declares that: "It's a myth that ESG investments inevitably outperform. You can't have it all."

Research findings are split. While it has been found that ESG "has no impact on financial performances [sic]" (e.g., Billio, Costola, Hristova, Latino, & Pelizzon, 2020, p. 1), another plane of analysis "surprisingly shows that ESG controversies are associated with greater firm value", while yet another reveals that these "have no direct effect on firm value" (Aouadi & Marsat, 2018, p. 1027). On the other hand, Hart and Ahuja argued almost thirty years ago "that efforts to prevent pollution and reduce emissions drop to the 'bottom line' within one to two years of initiation" (1996, p. 30). In this vein, meta-studies have shown that the business case for ESG investing is empirically very well founded. Roughly 90% of studies find a non-negative ESG-CFP (corporate financial performance) relationship (Friede, Busch, & Bassen, 2015, p. 210). A wide-ranging investigation of "22,527 firm-year observations from 62 countries" established "that the value-enhancing effect of CSR is prevalent in the non-competitive industries" (Gupta & Krishnamurti, 2021, p. 1). At the same time, identified "associations between corporate governance and environmental performance" can be "in directions not predicted by extant theories" (Walls, Berrone, & Phan, 2012, p. 900) or even "find that CSR has a neutral impact on financial performance" (McWilliams & Siegel, 2000, p. 603). The nature of the hypothetical trade-off between performance and sustainability will remain elusive as long as there is theoretical incompleteness, the profusion of frameworks noted earlier prevails, and, as Billio, Costola, Hristova, Latino, & Pelizzon stress: "ratings differ considerably across the providers" (2020, p. 11). In the face of "the rater effect", some scholars suggest that "regulators could address the issue of ESG rating divergence" by forcing disclosures about the ESG definitions used, increasing the transparency of measurement methodologies, and trying to understand

pandemic (see also the discussion on the weighting and relativization of evil in value transfers and destruction in Section 8.2.1).

"the rater effect to avoid potential biases" (Berg, Kölbel, & Rigobon, 2022, p. 29). In sum, and despite the normative ideal of inclusive businesses transferring value to society while still making profits (e.g., Dylick & Muff, 2015, p. 16), the financial performance of sustainable investments, while obviously vital to investors, can be expected to remain an unresolved and open issue in academia. This aligns with the understanding that causal outcomes for entities in complex systems such as the economy and the financial markets are notoriously hard to determine given their inherent uncertainty, emergent properties, and non-linear dynamics (see Section 3.2.3). Investor agency, however, has a clear role to play to [a] make sustainable but unprofitable firms profitable, and to [b] make profitable but unsustainable firms sustainable, as is implied by the arrows representing the transformational paths in Figure 7.3.

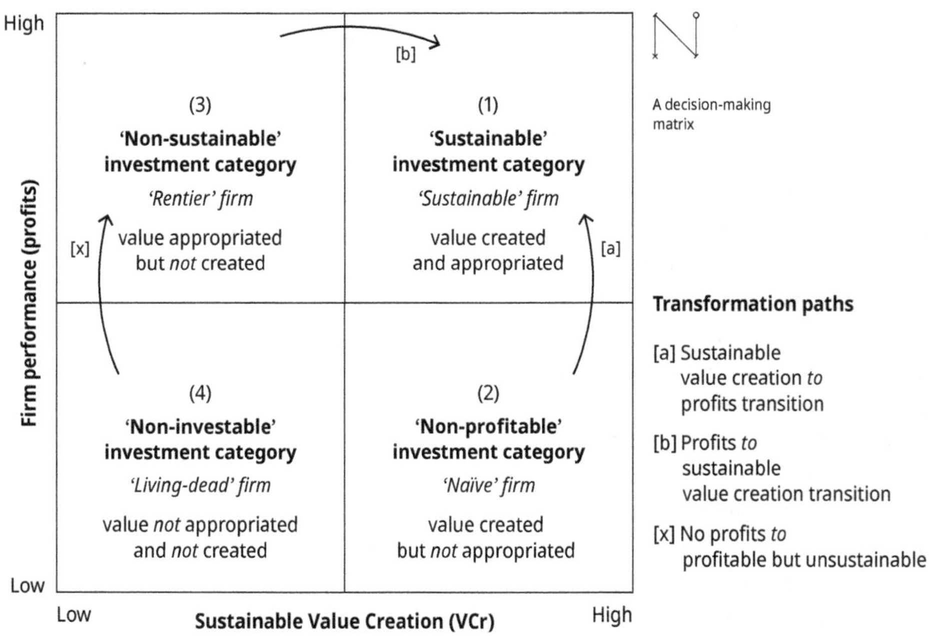

Figure 7.3: The Sustainable Finance Matrix: A framework for investments.

Firms that are not profitable but create large amounts of value have long been the targets of activist investors, as in the transformational path marked by arrow [a]. Less edifying would be the transitioning of extractive firms from the unprofitable to the 'non-sustainable' but profitable, as in arrow [x]. Many loss-making firms belong in the 'non-profitable' investment category (quadrant 2) yet are sustainable. As such, suppliers of capital could support management in developing strategies and operations so that their business models leave less money on the table and instead develop the capability to appropriate a greater slice of the value they create. Activist shareholders, hedge funds, private equity funds, or private debt funds often use shareholder resolutions, proxy fights, litigation, divestment threats, or short selling to lead firms through their value appropriation transformational journeys to reduce the amount of value created but *not* appropriated. Past exponents of such investment approaches include Nelson Peltz's Trian Fund Management in transforming the fast-food chain, Wendy's, and Bill Ackman's Pershing Square Capital Management and its transformation of Canadian Pacific Railway. While such deal-making has so far focused on the monetization of general value creation and rarely revolved around sustainability and CSR/ESG concerns, corporate M&As are a tested route for investor-led transformations, specifically targeting firms rating high on conventional sustainability but showing little profit. Examples include Tesla's acquisition of energy services provider SolarCity Corporation, and Unilever Plc's acquisition of the eco-friendly home care products company, Seventh Generation Inc.

Investors can also influence another inclusive type of transformation, depicted by arrow [b]. Already profitable firms in the 'non-sustainable' investment category (quadrant 3) are prompted to become increasingly sustainable without renouncing value appropriation. These were the hopes when in 2021, "Engine No. 1, a San Francisco-based activist hedge fund stunned the corporate world by landing three of its eco-conscious nominees on Exxon's board", although two years later *The New York Times* reassessed the event and concluded that there was scant evidence of transformation (Sorkin et al., 2023). This approach is incipient, yet many, including *The Economist* (2023b), still see opportunities for ESG shareholder activism. Lastly, 'living-dead' business models that have low residual income streams and low sustainable value creation scores are termed 'non-investable' (quadrant 4), a self-explanatory category in The Sustainable Finance Matrix.

No investors in the 'non-profitable' investment category (quadrant 2) will refrain from seeking or expecting transformation. However, this is not the case for investors in the 'non-sustainable' investment category (quadrant 3), where many are attracted precisely by the firm's rents and impervious to questions about whether these are associated with extractive value transfers, at least while the existing institutional arrangements remain in place. For instance, while a market concentration SVC metric (see VCr_fd.HHI in Table 6.1) is deemed an extractive transfer-IN, Grullon, Larkin, and Michaely determine "that over the last two decades the Herfindahl–Hirschman index (HHI) has systematically increased in more than 75% of US industries, and the average increase in concentration levels has reached 90%", while "the higher profit margins associated with an increase in concentration are reflected in higher returns to shareholders" (2019, pp. 697, 698). On the other hand, investors backing unsustainable strategies for the sake of higher returns might find out that they also forfeit the profits. Boeing's sobering counter transformational path is akin to the [b] arrow in reverse—moving from being a 'sustainable' firm (quadrant 1) to a 'rentier' firm (quadrant 3)—carried out through an aggressive division of value strategies vs its stakeholders including workers and engineers, suppliers, and taxpayers. Exemplified by moving its headquarters first from Seattle to Chicago (2001), and then to Arlington, near the US capital (2022), it is proving to be unsustainable in terms of product quality, market share, profits, stock price, and even end-user perceptions of aircraft that few now look forward to flying in.

Evidently, the returns from 'rentier' business models (quadrant 3) are tempting and though they may eventually be phased out by the dynamics of the political economy, they have a negative impact on economic and human development. Rather problematically, the time horizon for effecting institutional change and transitioning away from non-sustainable models might be extremely lengthy. For example, slavery in North America lasted a quarter of a millennium from 1619 to the 1862 *Emancipation Proclamation*. Opioids in the US produced substantial returns for principals for over two decades and even after recent lawsuits and restrictions, many members of the elite coalition and their investors have managed to retain most of these gains (see the discussion in Section 8.2.1). Despite being associated with nefarious costs and destructive for society at large, there will always be investment opportunities in rent-seeking and value transfer activities that are lawful. The normative role of elite transformational leadership and elite system transformational leadership is to develop and support the value creators in intra-elite contests. Investors and their capital allocation decisions have an essential role to play in nudging such transitions forward.

As has been repeatedly emphasized since Section 5.3.2, a precise goal of the proposed SVC measurements and applied frameworks is that they function as tools to adjust the equity and debt valuations of firms. For a perspective on the investment strategy impact of SVC valuations in the analysis of asset allocation in portfolio management, refer to 'The Sustainable Valuations Matrix' for investors (see Figure A5.7). It has the same two dimensions—sustainable value creation (VCr) on the x-axis and firm performance (profits) on the y-axis—and the quadrant logic of The Sustainable Finance Matrix (Figure 7.3).[177] The impact matrix for investors associates the investment category quadrants with equity and debt valuations and aims to augment the sustainable investor toolset. The hypothetical impact of investment strategies on equity and debt valuations, pending empirical validation, is now speculatively deduced.

In The Sustainable Valuations Matrix (Figure A5.7), the 'sustainable' investment category (quadrant 1) sees both equity and debt valuations trend *upward*. For the 'non-investable' category (quadrant 4), the *downward* opposite will be the case. For the 'non-profitable' and 'non-sustainable' investment categories (quadrants 2 and 3) the equity valuations will move in dissimilar directions as per a rationale akin to that stipulated in the 'SVC risk premium function' for equity (fr_{SVC}), referred to in equations 6/9 in Table 5.3. That is, equity valuations will trend *upward* for 'non-profitable' category (quadrant 2) firms with high sustainable value creation on the grounds of increased value appropriation (including via transformational journeys along arrow

177 Adding the VCp as a variable to the matrix would make it three-dimensional (and accordingly, result in eight quadrant spaces). This enhanced version of The Sustainable Valuations Matrix would establish the discrete relative impact of value transfer-IN on firm valuations backed by the logic and categories of The Value Transfer Strategy Matrix (Figure 7.4).

[a] in Figure 7.3); and *downward* for 'non-sustainable' (quadrant 3) investment category firms on the grounds that the market will price results from untenable profit levels in the long run (there is the possibility to increase a valuation if a firm's VCr evolves along arrow [b] in Figure 7.3). On the other hand, the valuation of debt for firms in both categories (quadrants 2 and 3) is taken to be in a stable *range-bound* trend as per a rationale akin to that stipulated in the 'SVC risk premium for credit rating function' ($fr^{cr}_{SVC,D}$) and the 'SVC risk premium for debt function' ($fr_{SVC,D}$), referred to in equations 7/9 and 8/9 in Table 5.3. For a 'non-profitable' investment category firm, this rests on the notion that current high sustainable value creation would be monetized should an insolvency event be near; for a 'non-sustainable' category firm, it rests on the notion that current high profits, while comparatively insecure and eroding, safeguard solvency in the foreseeable future barring negative institutional change or major market events.

7.2.6 Implications of sustainable value creation strategies for principals and key stakeholders

In the context of sustainable value creation, strategy is about achieving a balance between inclusive value creation (net value creation, i.e., 'value created and appropriated' as revenue/profits and transfer-OUT, i.e., 'value created but *not* appropriated') and extractive value transfers (transfer-IN, i.e., 'value appropriated but *not* created', including transfer-COST, i.e., 'cost created but *not* borne'). By taking into account the practical primacy of value transfers that is articulated in the 'revenue is value creation unless value transfer is proven' implication (see Figure A5.4a) and the two basic firm-level SVC measurements—the VCp and the VCr—a matrix is proposed to provide what is analytically one of the conceptually most exigent 2x2 sustainability frameworks in this work: 'The Value Transfer Strategy Matrix' framework for principal-stakeholder relationships, visualized in Figure 7.4. This allows the principal and key stakeholders—management, capital suppliers, and the government—to formulate strategies with a 360-degree overview of a business model's sustainable value creation relationships.

The VCp and VCr scores provide the two dimensions of the matrix and describe a firms relationships with stakeholders based on the value transfer-IN/OUT sums of its component SVC metrics. Value transfer-IN and -OUT are, even when related or part of an intertemporal sequence, epistemologically two independent realities that constitute the two axes of the Value Transfer Strategy Matrix. On the VCr x-axis, the conceptual emphasis is on transfer-OUT relative to transfer-IN, with inclusive agency reflected in a high score. Strategy is here placed on a range from 'keeper' (the firm keeps a part of the value appropriated as transfer-IN since it is not compensated for by transfer-OUT) to 'giver' (the firm creates and transfers more value to stakeholders than it extracts from them). On the VCp y-axis, the conceptual emphasis is on transfer-IN, with extractive agency reflected in a low score. Strategy is therefore here placed on a range from 'inclusive' (no extraction) to 'extractive' (extraction occurs). The ensuing typology of principal vs stakeholders strategy is based on inclusive/extractive transfer levels and value-keeping/value-giving to become an applied sustainability framework for boards, top management teams, or investors. It is actionable when principals drill down to consider the dozens of SVC metrics in their stakeholder relationships that nudge the firm in one direction or another within the confines of the matrix. Moreover, given the large residual incomes of elite business models, the framework is potentially a highly revealing tool for policymakers. Next, the four quadrants of the Value Transfer Strategy Matrix are described and examples of the types of firms that fit their conceptual descriptions are provided.

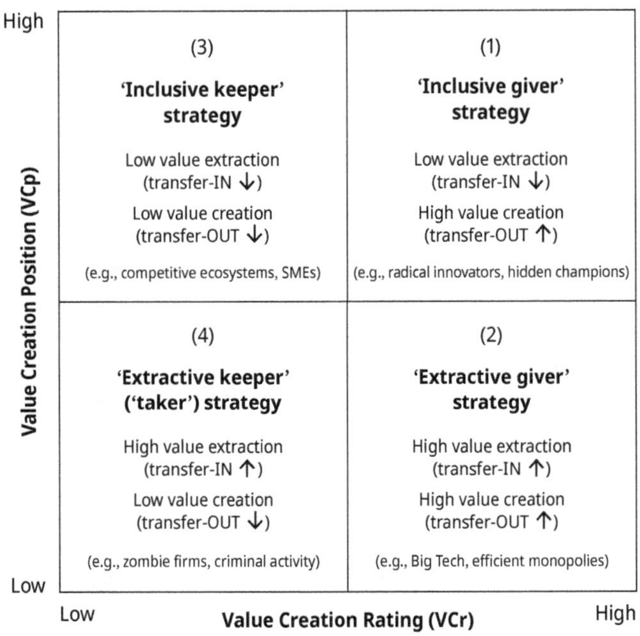

A decision-making matrix

Figure 7.4: The Value Transfer Strategy Matrix: A sustainability framework for principal-stakeholder relationships.

The strategies of the 'inclusive giver' (quadrant 1) do not extract (low transfer-IN) from stakeholders (hence 'inclusive') while generating value spillovers (high transfer-OUT) for stakeholders (hence 'giver'). Firms with such strategies include leading innovators and hidden champions, often very profitable and with no need to extract. Some firms and individual members of elite coalitions in this category are so powerful that they could easily affect institutional change and increase their profits with transfer-IN, but might have a worldview infused by the ethics of transformational leadership or the restraint of Olsonian stationary bandits. They are the drivers of economic and human development and include the Wikipedia Foundation, or radical innovators like Apple or Alibaba prior to any monetization of their monopoly power. Using power in such a manner spells a departure from this category, a path represented in The Elite Business Model Lifecycle of Figure A5.9a when power accumulation levels overtake value creation (compare this to Figure A5.9c where the 'elite power vs value creation gap' is almost non-existent). Once firms become too powerful and in the absence of robust intra-elite contests, transformational elite system leadership, and elite cohesion, the temptation for them to extract is incessant, and so their sojourn as 'inclusive givers' is likely to halt as they leverage their power into residual income and 'extractive giver' strategies.

'Extractive giver' strategies (quadrant 2) result in successful rent seeking and extraction (high transfer-IN) from stakeholders (hence 'extractive'), but such firms are also highly efficient, innovative, and otherwise generate positive externalities (high transfer-OUT) for stakeholders (hence 'giver'). These firms ought to be encouraged with policy incentives, while at the same time the power that they derive from 'political economy know-how' in the politics and society power domains should be carefully curtailed (to limit value appropriated but *not* created) by diligent policy weighting and offsetting, but not eliminated (since an optimal power differential is necessary for value creation and general development). Firms in this category include leading players in the Big Tech, Big Finance, Big Pharma, and Big Oil sectors, as well as efficient public monopolies and prospering state-owned enterprises. Organizations whose strategies place them in the 'extractive giver' quadrant ought to be nudged by the core elite coalition and non-elites to engage in transformational leadership of their own accord, as they have sufficient resources to do so. Is that what occurred with Alibaba but is not happening with Amazon? At any rate, the crafting of constructive and duly weighted non-elite narratives that acknowledge power differentials and extraction optima in the elite/non-elite strategic collaboration context (see Figure 8.2) is essential.

'Inclusive keeper' strategies (quadrant 3) do not extract excessively (low transfer-IN) from stakeholders (hence they are 'inclusive'), but do not generate value or many positive externalities (comparatively low transfer-OUT) either, so their VCr scores will be modest at best. This category includes SMEs or firms in highly competitive industries without bargaining power differentials in their favor. These firms are not a burden on development and do not harm other participants in the economy. On the contrary, their self-centered and narrow agency can create very efficient ecosystems where transfer-OUT happens at the system aggregate level. Even if they are not significant individual contributors to economic growth, they provide stability and jobs to society and should by no means be penalized. Becoming profitable and scaling can associate here with a transition from 'keeper' to 'giver'[178] if not preyed upon by pow-

178 The enhanced three-dimensional matrix (see preceding footnote), would add profits as the third parameter in The Value Transfer Strategy Matrix and thereby provide new analytical spaces for strategy (in eight quadrants) for both principals and stakeholders.

erful elites and their institutions (see the discussion on responses to extraction such as 'informality' in Section 5.2.3). Hence, 'inclusive keeper' firms, likely with low power endowments (evidenced by low transfer-IN), need support (and protection) from the state or other elite coalitions. This should include incentives for them to upgrade their value creation and appropriation capabilities.

'Extractive keeper' (quadrant 4) strategies—or, more concisely, 'taker' strategies—are detrimental to development since the chief firm asset is the power to extract (high transfer-IN) from stakeholders, while offering no quid pro quo, as might be evidenced by few positive externalities or spillovers (low transfer-OUT). Firms in this quadrant with business models based on 'political economic know-how' are poisonous, or even "parasitic" if one uses "a naturalistic conception of exploitation over a moralized one" (Shelby, 2002, p. 383), to the economy and society. Notwithstanding the resistance fueled by the attractive profits of many 'rentier' firms (explored in Section 7.2.5), policymakers should deactivate such agency via intra-elite contests by weakening the power endowments of rentiers and phasing out the legal frameworks that enable *contra natura* the 'extractive keeper' strategies of 'takers' in the first place.

7.3 International implications: Cross-border value creation and appropriation

Whether through the *dirigiste* policies of Colbert (1661–1683/1863) and 17th and 18th century European mercantilism, or the highly regulated economy of China's militarist-physiocratic empire exemplified by the first emperor, Qin Shi Huang, and the early Han Empire (von Glahn, 2022), the state has had a long tradition as *the* core elite coalition in resolving intra-elite contests. However, the state also exists in relation to other states, as "the idea that there is a sovereign authority within the single community involves the corollary that this authority is one among other authorities which are ruling other communities in the same sovereign way" (Hinsley, 1967, p. 242). Thus, if the state revolves around its national business models domestically, international relations are precisely shaped by cross-border elite business model preferences and value appropriation. In this section, the international implications of the ETED, centered on the conceptual element of cross-border elite business models, are discussed in relation to their potential relevance for the theoretical understanding of international relations (7.3.1). The analysis transitions into practical applications by studying the interaction between cross-border elite business models and international relations through the VCA framework (7.3.2). The all-important implications of elite system leadership are subsequently considered (7.3.3), with many previously discussed conceptual elements applied to the case of Europe's underdeveloped or even non-existent elite system (7.3.4) and the global tragedy of the commons brought about by AI (7.3.5). Finally, the implications for scholars in the field of international business are discussed (7.3.6).

7.3.1 Implications of cross-border elite business models for understanding international relations

> An international system is established for the same reason that any social or political system is created; actors enter social relations and create social structures in order to advance particular sets of political, economic, or other types of interests. (Gilpin, 1981, p. 9)

This section posits that the core rationale of international relations—both in theory and in practice—lies in cross-border elite business models, while the construct that bridges the field to economics and management is power. Morgenthau (1948) advanced the comprehensive contemporary international relations (IR) theory as a "science of international politics", whose basic premise is the unsentimental pursuit of power. According to realist IR theories, states will ensure their security by accumulating as much relative power as possible: "Only a misguided state would pass up an opportunity to be the hegemon in the system because it thought it already had sufficient power to survive" (Mearsheimer, 2001, p. 35). The criticism has long been levied that despite its claims to be "a more scientific approach to the study of international relations" (Korab-Karpowicz, 2018), realism and "the 'scientific' approach to the study of international relations appears to work no better, in forecasting the future, than do the old-fashioned methods it set out long ago to replace" (Gaddis, 1992, p. 56). No matter, even if realism is just another constructed narrative to understand history (as set out in Reisch, 1991), it informs the foreign policy of political and other elites whose objective is the power of the state and so: "Great powers do not compete with each other as if international politics were merely an economic marketplace. Political competition among states is a much more dangerous business than mere economic intercourse; the former can lead to war" (Mearsheimer, 2001, pp. 32–33).

The ever-present possibility of violence, wars, and even invasions, as the tragedies in Ukraine or Yemen illustrate, makes security emanating from state power a public good that matters to all coalitions in the elite system. Undoubtedly, the national security objectives of power-maximizing realist IR theory form the narrative foundation for the defense elite coalition (what Eisenhower termed the "military-industrial complex" in his 1961 Farewell Address).[179] However, beyond ensuring one's physical existence, to many other elite coalitions in the elite system, national power is also an asset for the purpose of forging ahead with their cross-border business preferences. So, can this elite (cross-border) business model-centric understanding accommodate hypotheses such as the "sleepwalk" into war, as in the analysis of how World War I broke out (Clark, 2012)? National power and military readiness take inordinate

179 The President's statement is an admonition for checks and balances against an elite coalition's power and its extractive potential: "In the councils of government, we must guard against the acquisition of unwarranted influence, whether sought or unsought, by the military-industrial complex. The potential for the disastrous rise of misplaced power exists and will persist." See the speech transcript: https://millercenter.org/the-presidency/presidential-speeches/january-17-1961-farewell-address

amounts of effort and agency to accumulate. Like bargaining power in the domestic context, this is functional as it shapes the international rules of the game, i.e., the international *de jure* and *de facto* institutions that enable elite business models to obtain residual income, in this case, across borders. A state might find itself at war due to a miscalculation, but it will not sleepwalk into one.

How do the alternative theories to realist IR, especially those that are closer to being full narrative explanations, relate to the ETED? At the outset, liberal IR theory sits opposite to realism's fixation with power: "The Kantian triad of democracy, trade, and international institutions analytically linked to outcomes of peace and prosperity has been and remains the foundation of IR theory" (Sterling-Folker, 2015, p. 43). Yet Keohane and Nye's (2012) liberal framework of "complex interdependence", with its nuanced and contingent understanding of hierarchies, explicitly acknowledges that power is fundamental. Generally speaking then, what role does liberalism, with its emphasis on cooperation and international institutions, suggest for residual income generating international elite business models? What about constructivist perspectives that are even further removed from realism? The conventional variant of constructivist IR theory has its focus on "communities of intersubjectivity in world politics, domains within which actors share understandings of themselves and each other, yielding predictable and replicable patterns of action within a specific context" (Hopf, 1998, p. 199). To this inquiry, which at the micro-level theoretically relies on bargaining power to foster value appropriation (see Chapter 2), the liberal and constructivist approaches are chiefly alternative mechanisms to attain and consolidate state power. That is, to bolster 'might' in the global political non-market arena and ascendance over 'mind' in the global narrative market arena. Eventually and unceremoniously, all approaches to power translate into institutional change relevant to cross-border elite business models (as in Figures 3.4 or 4.4). Simply put, this elite theory coalesces the relative primacy of power in realist IR—transformational leadership notwithstanding—with a supporting role for the institutional and cooperation focus of liberal IR theory and some consideration for the narrative basis of constructivist IR theory. Accordingly, the guiding forces in international relations are domestic elite preferences for (international) institutional change that is advantageous to elite business models seeking international business opportunities. Most coalitions in a national elite system will assess their state's power through the sober optic of whether changes in international institutions further their cross-border residual income flows.

The embedding of elite agency in IR theory, with a preferential weight given to realist IR, might still be consistent with the synthesis between realism and liberalism in Moravcsik's theory (1992) and Putnam's two-level game theory (1988) that places a spotlight on domestic interest groups. The latter author quotes Robert Strauss' now classic observation on the GATT Tokyo Round trade negotiations:

> During my tenure as Special Trade Representative, I spent as much time negotiating with domestic constituents (both industry and labor) and members of the U.S. Congress as I did negotiating with our foreign trading partners. (Twiggs, 1987, p. vii, as cited in Putnam, 1988, p. 433)

While there is more to interstate relations than trade and residual income generated from cross-border business models (such as security), the obvious domestic filters to reach the international negotiation table mean that internal elite business models are always prominently represented. Under the premises of this inquiry, cross-border elite business models operate under the value creation-appropriation (VCA) logic and the value transfer-IN imperative, which by its existential logic (see Proposition 6 on elite identity, Section 2.1.2, and the behavioral 'universal value extraction propensity of humans', Figure A5.4c) applies not only within but also across political economies. An international and *de facto* fourth separation of powers tier—Tier 4 'across-system'—of intra-elite checks and balances (that moderates to varying degrees—as in Figure A5.11b—the three basic tiers detailed in Figure 3.7) can justifiably be extended to include foreign elite coalitions. Raw power and institutional arrangements like regional free trade agreements, international investment agreements,[180] the World Trade Organization's (WTO) Agreement on the Trade-Related Aspects of Intellectual Property Rights (TRIPS Agreement; WTO 1994a), or the WTO's Agreement on Subsidies and Countervailing Measures (WTO 1994b), whether attained through realist or liberal principles, become germane to the elite coalitions of a nation state in two ways. First, they are important internationally, in support of the cross-border ambitions of their business models[181] (or, conversely, to the detriment of elites that find themselves at the extractive receiving end of aggressive foreign elite coalitions). Second (and relatedly), as foreign elites become members of coalitions in the local elite system, they enrich intra-elite contests and become an additional factor in the checks and balances of the political economy. This point must be understood from the perspective that the security of the residual income flows and interests of elites in a foreign system is supported by the international relations power of their home state. Elite business models seek to realize value created and appropriated, and value appropriated but *not* created, both within and across borders, and so strive for gainful international institutional change (such as trade rules, security regimes, and tax rules for digital services). As with the domestic political economy, the parsimonious position is that the bargaining power of elite agency leverages the state for international institutional change.

To reiterate the points already made, nations jockey for relative power advantages in the international system, an activity that is driven by national elite coalitions that employ internationalization as a strategy to expand residual income streams. So, what does state power accumulated in the international relations arena exactly mean for a nation's elites? First and foremost, it enables value appropriation across borders.

180 See the United Nations Conference on Trade and Development (UNCTAD) Investment Policy Hub's International Investment Agreements Navigator: https://investmentpolicy.unctad.org/international-investment-agreements

181 The "trade-based approach to intellectual property protection" narrative was enterprisingly advanced in the US by Edmund Pratt, the CEO of Pfizer (Braithwaite & Drahos, 2000, p. 62).

This understanding informs 'The Global Influence of the Elite System Framework' for international relations (Figure 7.5) that takes domestic elite quality (as captured by the EQx or the EQr) as its x-axis, while the y-axis represents the aggregate value creation (vs extractive transfers) of a given country's domestic elites in relation to their foreign cross-border stakeholders as they engage in international business. This therefore suggests the concept of 'cross-border elite agency', operationalized at the aggregate level with an international measurement: the 'Cross-border Elite Quality Rating' ('cb-EQr'). The cb-EQr assesses 'country A vs the world', while a second measurement, the 'Bilateral Elite Quality Rating' ('bl-EQr') is a narrower assessment for 'country A vs country B'[182] (see the overview of all SVC measurements in Figure 7.8 and Table A3.1). The cb-EQr is hypothesized to impact economic and human development and, as an aggregate of all a nations' cross-border (elite) business models, is material to policymakers. The same is true of its firm-level counterpart, the International Business Value Creation Rating (IB-VCr), an SVC measurement that hones in on stakeholder relationships outside a given principal's home jurisdiction (with overseas subsidiaries, joint ventures, suppliers, customers, and governments).

To illustrate the above points, the PRC's 1978 Open-Door policy saw Western firms with high IB-VCr scores such as Volkswagen, Schindler, and Apple make contributions to China's development, including transfer-OUT like "technological and international market access spill-over benefits for Chinese firms" (Buckley, Clegg, & Wang, 2002, p. 637). Moving forward, Musk's contention "that the Chinese car companies are the most competitive car companies in the world" (Walz, 2024) implies that without the massive 2019 Gigafactory investment in Shanghai, Tesla would be less competitive internationally. In another example—and further to all its other ills—colonialism is a retardant to development when foreign elites run low IB-VCr extractive transfer busi-

182 The 'cb-EQr' expresses the relative amounts of value (and risk) creation and extractive value (and risk) transfer of cross-border business models on aggregate for a given country. That is, the sustainable value creation relationship of a particular state in relation to the rest of the world. Conceptually, it a 'bottom-up' (micro-to-meso level) SVC measurement, determined from the international business value creation (IB-VCr) of the most significant elite cross-border elite business models of a national state (e.g., its 10 or 100 largest MNEs or exporters). Note that a country's cb-EQr can be broken down into the cross-border elite quality of each of its bilateral relationships. That is, a rating for 'bilateral elite quality', actualized as the 'bl-EQr' to describe the sustainable value creation relationship of country A based on the cross-border value creation/extraction of the elite coalitions that conduct international business in country B. Given the two-way nature of bilateral relationships, two bl-EQr scores would be needed to reveal the full picture (from which would emerge distance and value creation balances akin to the bilateral measurements of trade and investment flows). The cb-EQr and bl-EQr ultimately result from business models and hence emanate from the SVC metrics that a nation's elites maintain with their domestic and foreign stakeholders. The cb-EQr measurements would be a useful input for a 'global weighted transfers general equilibrium' macroeconomic model (G-WTGE). However, its proper conceptualization and operationalization is an intricate endeavor at the intersection of international business and the international political economy, and so despite being amply referenced throughout this chapter, it is set aside for further research.

ness models (see the examples of Rome and Britain, but not Roman Britain, in Sections 7.3.2 and 7.3.3).[183] Also, "in Korea, gambling by Korean citizens is considered unlawful, and citizens who breach the law face severe penalties [. . .] The government adopted this move to boost the gambling economy and tourism in South Korea while protecting the citizens from its ill effects", as any form of gambling is a low sustainable value creation (VCr) business model (a transfer away from the foolish or the poor, a regressive tax[184]). The East Asian nation's "roughly 18 actual casinos that are designed only for foreign tourists" (Anyaa, 2023) represent a poor IB-VCr model.

Conceptually, The Global Influence of the Elite System Framework for international relations of Figure 7.5 describes the nature of international relations by examining state power (its global 'money', 'might', and 'mind') in terms of cross-border value appropriation—both of value created and value *not* created. International institutional change is pursued and leveraged to permit both the value creation and extractive value transfers of domestic cross-border business models. Every nation has a meso-level degree of aggregate elite quality (operationalized by the EQx or EQr), as was discussed in Chapter 6. Now it is suggested that every state also has an aggregate degree of cross-border elite quality (operationalized by the cb-EQr, or, bilaterally, by the bl-EQr) as its elites go global and conduct international business. The combination of these SVC measurements, both variables anchored in the sustainable value creation agency of business models, is posited to be a main determinant that characterizes the behavior of a state and its relationships with other states in the international system.

The quadrants of The Global Influence of the Elite System Framework for international relations that characterize IR are quite self-explanatory. The prototypical 'global public goods' elite system (quadrant 4), with high domestic and cross-border elite quality, is exemplified by post-World War II America and its domestic prosperity, open trade system, and security guarantees, where US elite coalitions largely advanced inclusive business models abroad (especially in Western Europe, Japan, and South Korea) based on capital investments and knowledge transfers. The notion of a 'global subsidizer' elite system (quadrant 2), with low domestic elite quality but comparatively high cross-border elite quality, might be counterintuitive, and given the premises of utility maximization ought not to exist. Yet it links to concepts like "overstretch" (Kennedy, 1987) and is explained by the existence of a domestic elite coalition

---

183 Refer to Fleming's *The Material Fall of Roman Britain, 300-525 CE* (2021) and to Gilley's highly divisive analysis that expounds on the "objective cost/benefit approach [that] identifies a certain need of human flourishing—development, security, governance, rights, etc.—and asks whether colonialism improved or worsened the objective provision of that need. One main challenge of this research is to properly enumerate the things that matter and then to assign them weights" (2018, p. 169).

184 This intuition, at the root of gambling prohibitions to safeguard the public such as those instituted in Korea or at state and federal levels in the US prior to 1950 (Blakey, 1984), is reflected in popular culture, as in the celebrated lyrics of the song in Henry Fielding's *The Lottery: A Farce* (1732): "A Lottery is a Taxation, Upon all the Fools in Creation", see also: https://coulditbeyou.co.uk/history-general/lotteries-a-tax-on-the-stupid/

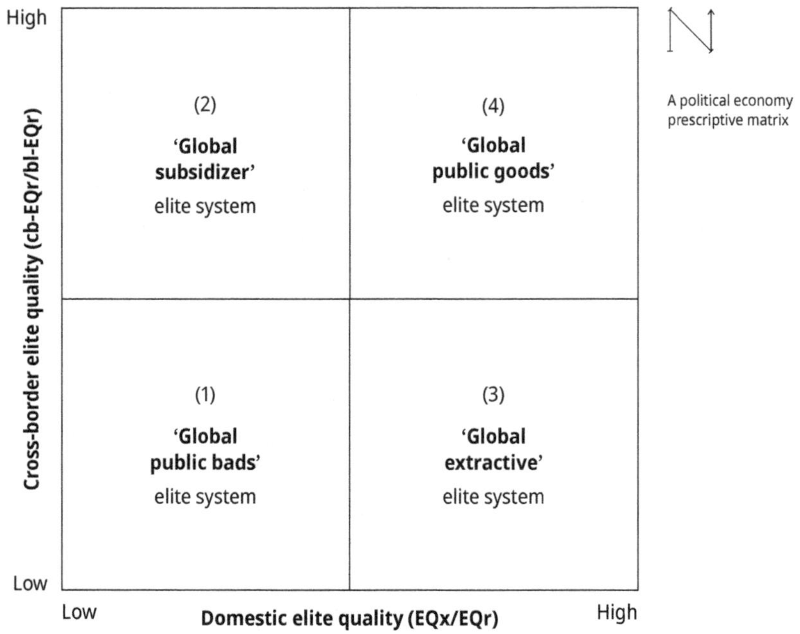

Figure 7.5: The Global Influence of the Elite System Framework for international relations.

benefiting from its 'generosity' to overseas stakeholders at the expense of stakeholders in its home country. The category might apply to the post-WWII Soviet Union if, in parts of its empire (e.g., certain Central Asian republics) and spheres of influence (e.g., Cuba), its extractive low quality domestic elite system ran business models that transferred, certainly on ideological or security grounds, value to the periphery (including knowledge and investments in infrastructure and social development such as women's rights) while refraining from the full value appropriation that its power differential advantages could have afforded. Most problematic are the 'global public bads' elite systems (quadrant 1) that have both low EQx and cb-EQr scores for models that are extractive both domestically and internationally. If the elites of the Soviet,[185] Spanish, or British empires were extractive of their peripheral subjects (in Ukraine, Latin America, or India) as well as of their domestic non-elites, they would fit this description. All three empires might, on the other hand, have had 'global extractive' elite systems (quadrant 3) with high EQx and low cb-EQr scores on the assumption that their elites did not run extractive business models domestically. The Cross-border Value

185 The Soviet Union illustrates the added insight that an international SVC measurement on bilateral relationships could provide. The bl-EQr, detailed in footnote 182, might show extremely extractive relationships with Poland and the German Democratic Republic (i.e., very low bl-EQr), but significant value creation relationships (i.e., higher bl-EQr) with Vietnam and Cuba, where the costs of providing security services and development aid had no proportional quid pro quo at the time.

Transfers Matrix analytical framework is now put to use to shed light on the Spanish empire's elite system business model and its contribution to development.

The first Europeans that saw Tenochtitlan described the capital of the Aztec Empire and today's Mexico City "as the greatest city they had ever laid eyes on. Built in the midst of the waters of a series of connected lakes, the city far exceeded Spain's largest cities in size and was a cosmopolitan hub" (Caplan, 2013, p. 334). What cross-border elite business models did the Castilian Crown implement upon its conquest? The starting point was the mining model based on "structured labor systems, including mass corvees, slavery, and incipient wage labor. It fueled settlement and urbanization. [. . .] Mining in sum, was a key agent in the early modern transformation of the societies we now know as Latin America" (Studnicki-Gizbert & Schecter, 2010, p. 110). Even though purported instances of value creation (e.g., urbanization) are cited, silver was an extractive transfer-IN model, not just from labor stakeholders, but also from the nature stakeholder (see Section 2.2.2). So much wood consumption for fuel was required that even the Viceroy, Antonio de Mendoza, in Olsonian stationary bandit fashion advocated for environmental protection:

> [He] was forced to issue what were possibly the first colonial ordinances limiting forest clearing in the Americas – these were for the mines of Taxco in 1542. Some years later the viceroy explained why: "In just a few years a large area of forest was destroyed," he wrote, "and it was feared that the woods would be finished sooner than the ore." (de Mendoza, 1965, p. 288, as cited in Studnicki-Gizbert & Schecter, 2010, p. 94)

Not all attempts by the Castilians to impose elite business models based on forced transfer-OUT from their colonial subjects succeeded. The non-elite Mexicas positively resisted the business model of fiat money as Fray Juan de Torquemada described:

> in 1544, the Mexicas (or Aztecs) dumped massive numbers of two and four maravedí copper and low-denomination silver coins into Lake Texcoco. By 1552, the official coinage of copper ceased, not to be resumed for two hundred and fifty years. In the absence of small denomination coins, cacao was used as a currency into the nineteenth century. Previous scholars have attributed the Mexicas' actions to spontaneous negative reactions to the coins. However, analysis of notes from the Spanish *cabildo* suggests that the Mexicas were working to remove from circulation coins that threatened to replace indigenous commodity currencies. Cacao's survival as a currency was the result of this successful undertaking. (Caplan, 2013, p. 333)

Overall, while the extractive business model of fiat money lost out to cacao, the essential Conquistador elite business model of mining was secured by power differentials sourced in the non-market arena (the 'might' of arms) and in the narrative market arena (the power of 'mind', activated by European knowledge elites, the Catholic priesthood). In terms of the effects of this business model on development and in order to reach a cb-EQr score, how should one weight the outright extraction and negative externalities (value transfer-IN) against inclusive agency (value transfer-OUT)?

> As the forests of the New Spanish mining belt disappeared, so too did many of the communities that depended upon them. [. . .] Bands of the many peoples of highland and northern Mexico –

> Guachichiles, Tecuanes, Tepehuanes, Pames, Raramuri, and others – were settled on missions, converted, and set to work in the fields and mines. They were pacified, as the Spanish put it, and molded into a new class of subjected and sedentarized Indians. (Studnicki-Gizbert & Schecter, 2010, p. 111)

If one connects the dots and benchmarks value of statistical life accounting (VSL), the figures are stunning: "The population of Latin America was about 40 to 60 million people before 1492, with some estimates as high as 100 million (Denevan, 1992, p. 370). After a century of genocide, slavery, and disease, that figure was reduced to 4 million (Brea, 2003, p. 5)." In what quadrant of The Global Influence of the Elite System Framework for international relations does the Spanish state then belong? Scholars debate whether there was a "Destrucción de las Indias", as famously denounced by Fray Bartolomé de las Casas in *A Short Account of the Destruction of the Indies* (1552/1821), or whether the emphasis ought to be on "the construction of colonial Spanish America?" (Lafaye & Lockhart, 1992, p. 315).

Assuming the examples and evidence provided above are reliable and representative of the *La Conquista* model, the cb-EQr is low. Research focusing on the institutions of the "mercantilist model" (Lange, Mahoney, & vom Hau, 2006, p. 1416) also finds that the "path-dependent legacy of Spanish colonialism" means that centuries later "territories that constituted the centers of the Spanish colonial empire tended to become the region's least developed countries" and those least exposed to the Castilian elites "tended to become the most developed countries (Mahoney, 2003, p. 50). Moreover, if the Spanish elites also managed to extract from large segments of their own population in Iberia, such as from landless peasants in Andalusian *Reconquista latifundia*, or the Soviet Union extracted as much from Russians as it did from subjects in the Baltics or in Eastern Europe, their elite agency would be 'global public bads' (quadrant 1). However, counter arguments in the vein of Gilley (2018) are also made for cross-border value creation through models relying on the introduction of new technologies, urbanization, or, in the case of *El Descubrimiento*, the elimination of human sacrifice practices in Mesoamerica. Spaniards "built or rebuilt all of the cities in New Spain, they created the legislation of the Indies and New Spain, and they established its economy" (Lafaye & Lockhart, 1992, p. 319). If such elite agency and associated institutions resulted in an acceptable cb-EQr and if domestic elite quality was high after all, a totally different assessment would be reached, one that is consistent with the position of some academics and the swathes of Spanish public opinion that espouse the Black Legend hypothesis (a narrative that rejects overly negative interpretations of Spanish colonial history as part of a distorted myth, see Marías, 1985/2014). In this scenario, the Spanish Empire was a 'global public goods' elite system (quadrant 4). Irrespective of which metrics and indicators are used, their conceptual determination, and whatever weighting or assessments are finally made, this inquiry reduces complex international relations—and even civilizational interactions—to elite business models and the sustainable value creation that is embedded in the exchanges. As these aggregate into cross-border elite quality, the history of the world unfolds.

Two additional points are stressed in concluding this sub-section. First, the cross-border business models of 'global extractive' elite systems (quadrant 3) might well include distinctive elite models with a high IB-VCr. Likewise, 'global public goods' elite systems (quadrant 4) will include extractive models based on transfer-IN (with a low IB-VCr). This echoes the contentious 'alternating value extraction and creation' conjecture, and places it in the international context. The weighting and the relativization of cross-border elite business models whose power differentials rest on coercion associate with the "enormous controversy" elicited by the publication of Gilley's "The Case for Colonialism" in *Third World Quarterly*, where "serious threats of violence against the editor led the journal to withdraw the article" (2018, p. 168). Earlier, Grier had claimed "that colonies that were held for longer periods of time than other countries tend to perform better, on average, after independence", also because of higher education levels (1999, p. 317), while Chaudhuri's *The Autobiography of an Unknown Indian* (1951/1989, p. v) was dedicated to "the British Empire in India",[186] echoing Olson's stationary bandit. It is important to recognize the sustainable value creation differences relevant to the economic and human development of great powers; for example, between the 20th century American and Soviet hegemons or the 19th century British Empire and its earlier Iberian rival.

The collapse of the Soviet Union in 1991 and the rush of its satellites to join Western institutions settled the comparison with the US. In the case of Britain, historians like Gilpin (1981) argue that the Empire supported public goods like stability and prosperity with institutional arrangements that facilitated international trade, maritime routes safeguarded by a dominant navy, a global monetary system with the British pound sterling at its core, and, above all, the industrial revolution with its enormous and lasting knowledge spillovers. But how does one weight the costs? By considering excess mortality rates, Sullivan and Hickel calculate that in India "some 50 million people lost their lives under the aegis of British capitalism" (2023, p. 12). In the case of Spain, those who do not consider the Black Legend to be a myth will stress that the Spanish genetically replaced the male lineages of entire populations (Mendizabal et al., 2008) and oversaw extractive models in Latin America with profits flowing back to a Madrid-centered aristocratic elite that invested these not in innovative institutions for economic development but on the construction of monumental places of worship, royal palaces, and endless wars in European theaters. According to the new institutional economics perspectives of Sokoloff and Engerman (2000), Easterly and Levine (2003a), Rodrik, Subramanian, and Trebbi (2004), or Acemoglu and Robinson (2013a), such practices benefited neither party. Again, these assessments remain a matter of contention in both Spain and Latin America, as does the question of which empire—Spanish or British—was the greater or lesser good or evil.

186 The full dedication is: "To the memory of the British Empire in India which conferred subjecthood on us but withheld citizenship; to which yet every one of us threw out the challenge: 'Civis Britannicus sum' because all that was good and living within us was made, shaped, and quickened by the same British rule."

The next sub-section considers the practice of value creation and extraction in the international context that occurs on a business-model-by-business-model basis. This can be captured by SVC metrics aggregated in the IB-VCr, or by self-assessment questionnaires on the international business of a firm (the IB-VCr is a sub-set of the VCr; the IB-self-VCr is a sub-set of the self-VCr, see Section 6.6.2). As discussed, every country has elites that run perfectly sustainable value creation business models with their foreign stakeholders (high IB-VCr), as well as extractive international business concerns that do just the opposite (low IB-VCr). The US, for example, provides institutional cover for its elite business models in Europe that have created copious cross-border value (e.g., its taxpayer-funded security umbrella), and value transfers in the opposite direction (e.g., extractive transfers by technology providers via favorable offshore taxation regimes or monopolistic/oligopolistic positions). Ultimately, the meso-level cb-EQr, or the narrower bilateral bl-EQr are based on the aggregation of the entire set of individual cross-border elite business models (through their IB-VCr scores). An overview of all of the various international SVC measurements is supplied in Figure 7.8 (and Table A3.1a).

7.3.2 Implications of cross-border division of value strategies for international relations

This inquiry's conceptualization of international relations appropriates a synthesis of IR theory, anchored by the relative power (spearheaded by 'might') focal point of realist IR, and integrates liberalism in a supporting role, with its emphasis on cooperation and international institutions understood as devices to accumulate additional power (mostly of 'mind' and 'money') in the global narrative market and ultimately in international market arenas. Some consideration is also given to constructivist IR theory since narratives are understood as devices to further accumulate power (of 'mind'). The critical premise is that the drivers of international relations are domestic elite preferences for international institutional change to support cross-border elite business models. Aggregate (meso-level) domestic elite quality (as in the EQx, EQr, or PEz) *and* cross-border elite quality (as in the cb-EQr and bl-EQr) interact and are manifested in cross-border elite business models with discrete degrees of sustainable value creation that impact the development of both the home and host countries. As shown, the two variables of The Global Influence of the Elite System Framework for international relations (see Figure 7.5) combine to circumscribe the practice of interstate relations and diplomacy. In a two-way causal fashion and consistent with the domestic elite agency microfoundations of institutional change model (Figure 3.2), micro-level cross-border elite business models both shape and are constrained by the rules and realities of international relations, the key mediating variable being state power.

The first specific cross-border business model to be examined must be war. 'History' is essentially the history of international relations and is punctuated by conflicts that deserve distinct attention given their outsized impact on development. In the context of the ETED, wars are a set of micro-level elite business models with multiple stakeholders. Primarily, wars are powered by residual income expectations (from conquered territory, natural and human resources, or market access). Secondarily, and just as importantly, they are also arbiters of relative power endowments that then enable non-bellicose successor elite business models to engage in cross-border value appropriation, including transfer-IN/OUT. In other words, the history of communities, nations, and empires in the global system could be rewritten as the imposition of, or the resistance to, cross-border transfers. The 'war as cross-border value appropriation' conjecture supposes that it is waged to enable the elites—and to a much lesser degree some non-elites—of one nation the benefit of value appropriated but *not* created from the non-elites and elites of other foreign nations. Suetonius's account of *The Life of Julius Caesar* (1914, 54.2) sheds light on the primary elite business model of war:

> In Gaul he pillaged shrines and temples of the gods filled with offerings, and oftener sacked towns for the sake of plunder than for any fault. In consequence he had more gold than he knew what to do with, and offered it for sale throughout Italy and the provinces at the rate of three thousand sesterces the pound.

A hint of the scale of Caesar's pecuniary extraction from what is modern-day France is the drop in the price of gold in Roman markets (Osgood, 2009, p. 332) to "half its true value" (Frederiksen, 1966, p. 132). The looting of valuables, far from constituting the sole residual income of Caesar's elite business model of war was complemented by an equally lucrative business activity: slavery, the business model fate of his prisoners of war. Plutarch (1919) in *The Parallel Lives* (15.5) accounts for this as follows:

> For although it was not full ten years that he waged war in Gaul, he took by storm more than eight hundred cities, subdued three hundred nations, and fought pitched battles at different times with three million men, of whom he slew one million in hand-to-hand fighting and took as many more prisoners.

In the case of the British Empire, the sophistication of its cross-border appropriation provides textbook examples of the multifaceted implications on development of (low IB-VCr) business model consolidation subsequent to victorious wars. Dalrymple discusses "the first great multinational corporation", the East India Company (EIC), which "probably invented corporate lobbying", and "eventually grew to control almost half the world's trade and become the most powerful corporation in history", as well as providing "history's most ominous warning about the potential for the abuse of corporate power—and the insidious means by which the interests of shareholders can seemingly become those of the state", detailing how it would eventually "run amok" (Dalrymple, 2020, pp. xxxiii, 3, 396, 397). The correspondence of Horace Walpole, a man of letters, on the EIC's extractive practices is revealing:

> We have outdone the Spaniards in Peru! They were at least butchers on a religious principle, however diabolical their zeal. We have murdered, deposed, plundered, usurped — say what think you of the famine in Bengal, in which three millions perished, being caused by a monopoly of the provisions by the servants of the East India Company? (Forrest, 1986, p. 383, as cited in Dalrymple, 2020, p. 223)

American patriots wrote that their country was next in line and "that the EIC, having plundered India, was now 'casting their eyes on America as a new theatre whereon to exercise their talents of rapine, oppression and cruelty'" (Marshall, 2005, pp. 330–332, as cited in Dalrymple, 2020, p. 258). Upon American independence, British eyes became cast on China. Trocki's (1999) classic *Opium, Empire, and the Global Political Economy,* is consistent with Richards' (2002) data analysis of official government opium revenues over a 140-year period which confirm that "without opium the British global empire is virtually unimaginable". Neither are the innovative financial elite business models of the City of London: opium revenues shipped as silver bullion to the metropolis were responsible for the "global dominance of the British pound sterling until World War I" (Hevia, 2003, p. 313). For this cross-border elite business model to achieve its success, it deployed military and geopolitical bargaining power differentials to force institutional change in, for instance, the primary market destination for its products:

> It is perhaps not too surprising, therefore, for Trocki to suggest that the British opium empire might best be understood as a global drug cartel, one that had as its raison d'être the maximization of profits and the protection, at all costs, of the revenue of India. While the British empire may not have been created to trade opium, the trade was central to its survival. When key decisions were made, none were ever directed against the trade or against opium revenue. That was certainly the case when British governments decided to use force in China in 1839 and again in 1856. (Hevia, 2003, p. 314)

Unlike Caesar's ventures, the two British Opium Wars against China did not represent the business model *per se*. The power that the war victories afforded was instrumental to British elites, many of whom were entrepreneurs of Scottish origin such as Jardine, Matheson, or Keswick (whose lineages all perdure to this day), eager to convert British power into institutional change for the specific international business rules that promised massive residual income generation through the drug trade. This highlights the earlier point of how interstate relationships are determined by business models that leverage bargaining power obtained in the global political economy's non-market (political) arena ('might' through war), though also through narratives and business success (power in the form of 'mind' and 'money') to further the international business model preferences of domestic elite coalitions in the national elite systems. The cross-border business model rules facilitated by the winning of wars or narrative contests (power accumulated in the non-market and narrative market arenas) enable the value transfer-IN from the non-elites and elites of the losing foreign states. Yet value extraction is not always part and parcel of the winner's model; post-World

War II America, for example, is classed as a rather generous 'global public goods' elite system (quadrant 4, Figure 7.5).

Social cohesion needs to be affirmed when elites compete against their foreign counterparts in cross-border intra-elite contests (militarily, or in the global market arena through narratives). Elite cohesion is a key advantage, but so is elite/non-elite cohesion. Elites and non-elites often naturally align against a common foreign threat. Unsurprisingly, they also work hand in hand for joint extractive enterprises. Moreover, for domestic elites that value tranquility at home, extraction from foreign non-elites and elites is preferable to extraction from domestic non-elite groups. When non-elites sense the benefits of value appropriation abroad (e.g., through economic prosperity, a stronger currency, cheaper imports, or the spoils of war), there is ample support for their elites.

Whilst in previous epochs armed conflict was a prime determinant of international institutional change, today, cross-border business model rules are generally determined by bargaining power differentials amassed by other means, such as technological advantages (e.g., in semiconductors or software), or FDI. In the international political non-market arena, most cross-border intra-elite contests are institutionalized thanks to multilateral organizations like the Basle Committee on Banking Supervision (BCBS), the World Intellectual Property Organization (WIPO), the International Automobile Federation (FIA), bilateral agreements, and other diplomatic provisions. These seemingly liberal arrangements stand on the shoulders of state power and major nations must not renege on them. At the same time, the war in Ukraine is a poignant reminder that non-institutionalized contests resorting to the blunt use of 'might' still endure as an approach to pursue institutional change and value appropriation.

The analyst of international relations must use the VCA framework and its division of value strategies perspective (see Chapter 2, and Tables 2.1 and 2.2) in the context of cross-border principal-stakeholder relationships to establish international value (and risk) creation and extractive transfers. The examples in Table 7.3 illustrate three relationships and outcomes resulting from cross-border business model VCA strategies embedded in the institutional arrangements relevant to international business.

Table 7.3 shows how domestic elite business models in possession of 'the extraordinary lever' utilize the power of nation states, both directly and indirectly, and effect international institutional change to compete against foreign coalitions. Since the winners (and losers) in the global political economy are critically determined by state power and its ability to effect institutional change, elite business model leadership in

Table 7.3: Cross-border division of value strategies and outcomes (references Table 2.2).

Ref.	Cross-border principal and stakeholder	Relationship and outcomes of international division of value strategies	IR theoretical perspective
[sec] 1/2 post-2022 [p]	*Scenario 1/2* Stakeholder (European states) vs Principal (US) (Visualized in Figure 7.6)	Relationship: European NATO member states acquire security services from the US. The US does not press its bargaining power advantage to compel European customers to defray the security costs in full (e.g., on a percentage of GDP basis) and security value is appropriated at below its cost (on terms even more favorable than 'equalized bargaining power equilibrium prices'). Outcome for stakeholder (Europe): European nation states (and its taxpayers) benefit from security services provided by the US. Value appropriated but *not* created (i.e., value transfer-IN). Outcome for principal (US): European security is funded by US taxpayers.[187] Value created but *not* appropriated (i.e., value transfer-OUT)	Liberal
[sec] 2/2 post-2022 [p]	*Scenario2/2* Stakeholder (European states) vs Principal (US) (Visualized in Figure 7.6)	Relationship: The US provides security to European states and uses its power (including of 'mind' with the 'rules-based order', "freedom" etc. narratives) to nudge European states to pay in full for the value they appropriate. Outcome for stakeholder (Europe): European nation states and their citizens benefit from security services provided by the US and defray the full costs. Value created and appropriated. Outcome for principal (US): The US is compensated for the security services it provides to European states. Value created and appropriated.	Realist (Liberal)
[cu]	Customer stakeholder (European firms	Relationship: Highly innovative US Big Tech firms hold monopoly or oligopoly positions (e.g., on search engines, software, or AI). As a result, they	Realist

187 The analysis does not consider the full range of elite business models embedded in the larger transatlantic security relationship. Therefore, while the US taxpayer might suffer transfer-OUT, specific US elite coalitions have long and properly profited from value created and appropriated.

Table 7.3 (continued)

Ref.	Cross-border principal and stakeholder	Relationship and outcomes of international division of value strategies	IR theoretical perspective
[p]	and individual consumers) vs Principal (US Big Tech)	enjoy a bargaining power advantage and set prices above the levels that would prevail in a competitive market under 'equalized bargaining power equilibrium prices'. Aware of cross-border extractive value transfers away from European firms (and consumers), politicians and officials like EU Commissioner Vestager propose measures such as the "break up" of monopolies (see Espinoza, 2020). Outcome for principal (US Big Tech): Value appropriated but *not* created (i.e., value transfer-IN).* Outcome for customer stakeholders (European firms and individual consumers): Value created but *not* appropriated (i.e., value transfer-OUT). *Note: Value transfer impact assessments notwithstanding, the innovation spillovers and increased efficiencies for European stakeholders (that have not undertaken the necessary business risks to create technological value) point to transfer-IN benefits.	
[cu] [P]	Customer stakeholder (global firms and individuals) vs Principal (Chinese state)	Relationship: The People's Bank of China (PBOC) hypothetically promotes the electronic Chinese yuan (e-CNY) to the world (see Fullerton & Morgan, 2022, p. 17; Orcutt, 2023). Outcome for consumer stakeholders (global firms and individuals): A stable e-CNY increases currency competition in the global financial system and becomes a cheaper or safer option for non-Chinese businesses and institutions. Value created and appropriated. Outcome for principal (Chinese state): The e-CNY becomes an international settlements or reserve digital currency. Value created and appropriated.	Liberal (partial realist and constructivist)

the international context requires grand strategy thinking and geopolitical savvy.[188] Firms engaged in international business must determine the extent to which they wish to appropriate value created (and value *not* created) overseas, a matter directly related to the power differentials between their own state and the state(s) of their foreign stakeholders as is depicted in Figure A5.9d: 'The Cross-border Elite Business Model Lifecycle', encompassing differing assumptions of home state power in the international system. At the state level, grand strategies (as discussed next in Section 7.3.3) concern themselves with the acquisition of national power to implement institutional change, that national elite coalitions are able to access and convert—along with power emanating from their own competitive advantages including 'knowledge'—into cross-border residual income streams.

Figure 7.6 returns to visualizing the value creation-appropriation (VCA) framework to further articulate the first example provided in Table 7.3, the US provision of security to European states, as a case of transfer-IN/OUT across borders. In this concrete international business relationship, and before Russian tanks rolled into Ukraine on February 24, 2022, European states, and especially Germany, are deemed to be security stakeholders that manage to exact value transfer-IN from the US, the principal. How so? Security is value creation, a public good that is not free to produce. The US delivers security services to European states through an expensive security umbrella, and it manages to appropriate a part of the value created (e.g., exports of weapons systems to European allies, while security in Europe also provides geoeconomic benefits to the US). Yet in monetary terms, American taxpayers have *de facto* subsidized Europeans who, instead of paying 3% of their GDP for defense, disbursed much lower contributions, just 1.4% in the case of Germany (Stockholm International Peace Research Institute, 2020). President Trump's criticisms of German free riding and his expressed wish that NATO allies pay 5% of GDP for defense (Posaner, Kayali, Brinkmann, Noyan, 2025) notwithstanding, the US has not historically deployed its full potential bargaining power on Europe. Does liberal rather than realist IR provide the best explanation for this unbalanced cross-border value appropriation? Or is it better ascribed to the dynamics of intra-elite contests in the US? Regardless, like its domestic counterpart, the cross-border elite business model logic analytically references the VCA framework to assess the division of value in international principal-stakeholder relationships.

The general implications of the ETED for specific cross-border elite business models in the global political economy are firstly that division of value strategies (from the VCA framework) apply to international business; secondly, the cross-border value appropriation capabilities of the elite business model depend to a significant extent

188 An example from practice is the joint development by the Eurasia Group and KPMG International of "solutions that help businesses deal with geopolitical challenges in an uncertain world" under the assumption that, "the CEO must take on the role of Chief Geopolitical Officer to lead their organization to success in turbulent times" (see: https://www.eurasiagroup.net/services/corporate-partnerships).

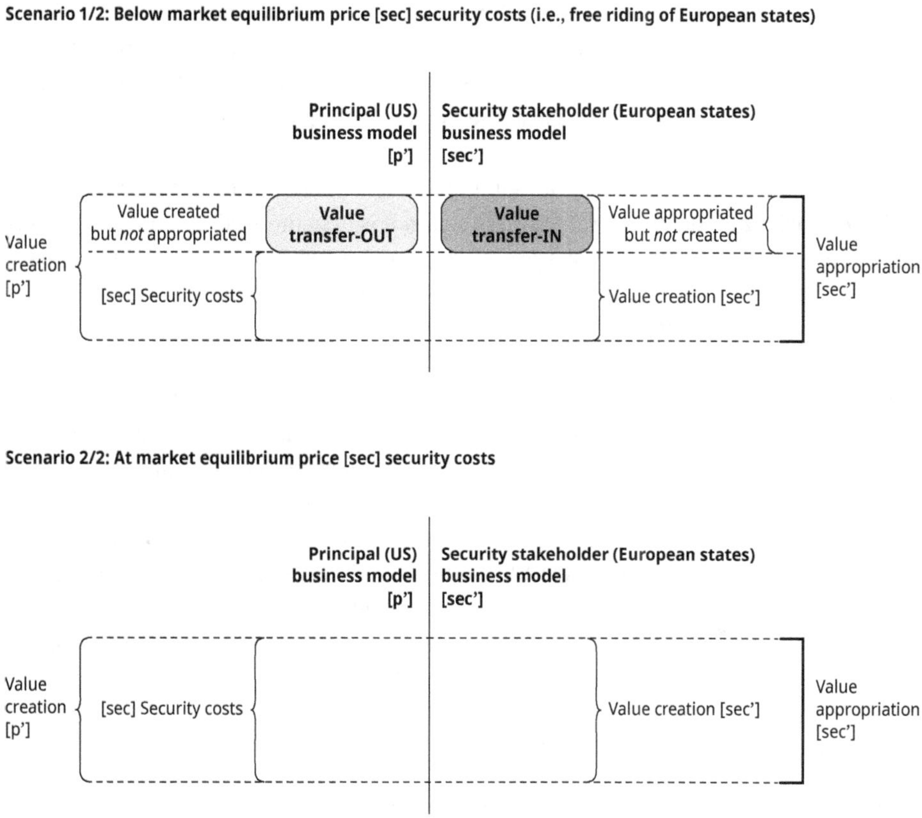

Figure 7.6: Cross-border division of value in the US principal-Europe stakeholder state-to-state security relationship: Scenario 1/2, security costs at below market equilibrium; scenario 2/2, security costs at market equilibrium.

on state power; thirdly, the agency of the elite coalition running a business model enlists members of the core elite coalition of the state, or the specialized foreign policy coalition of the state (Jacobs & Page, 2005), for the realization of its preferences in international intra-elite contests through suitable international business rules; and fourthly, the state then effects international institutional change to the degree that its power endowments allow to shape the international opportunity set for its businesses. The all-important factor of state power is accumulated (see the discussion of IR theory in Section 7.3.1) through effective elite system leadership in the three *global* political economy arenas that parallel the domestic arenas (see Figure A5.1): market ('money'), non-market ('might), and narrative market ('mind'). The division of cross-border value analytical template (as above, in Figure 7.6, Table 7.3) can be applied to any cross-border business model that has international revenue such as renewable energies, payment systems, intellectual property and its protection, cross-border e-commerce, or the Belt and Road Initiative (BRI) and its Western alternative, the

Partnership for Global Infrastructure and Investment (PGII), launched by the G-7 in June, 2022.[189] It is later discussed in this section that cross-border business models with high sustainable value creation scores (i.e., IB-VCr) contribute to the economic development of host countries because they increase domestic intra-elite competition and weaken the power of extractive domestic elite coalitions.

A final reflection on cross-border elite business models concerns coalitions where the beneficiaries are members from diverse states. It is hypothesized that the more intertwined and interdependent elites are across the world, the stronger the common interest and the greater the bias against trade disputes, geopolitical divergences, and ultimately, war. Moreover, when elites from different states become members of a coalition their diverse national affiliations act as an additional check and balance against extractive practices across borders.[190] Members of such an international elite coalition are likely to project preferences for sustainable international relations that eschew the impacts of international conflict on their domestic institutions. This work has de-emphasized international elite networks that transcend a nation state (see the position taken on the transnational capitalist class in Section 1.2.2), but fully acknowledges the impact of domestic elites with foreign interests and their effect on economic development via national political economy mechanisms such as functioning as an additional tier of checks and balances in the elite system (see Tier 4 'across-system', Figure 5.11b). From an IR perspective, such coalitions are inclusive since their interest is in stability, all types of exchanges, sophisticated global supply chains benefiting from geographical specializations, and ultimately in peace. This general idea is expounded in Angell's *The Great Illusion*:

> What is the real guarantee of the good behaviour of one State to another? It is the elaborate interdependence which, not only in the economic sense, but in every sense, makes an unwarrantable aggression of one State upon another react upon the interests of the aggressor. (Angell, 1910/2012, pp. 302–303)

The assertion, just four years prior to the start of World War I, that interdependencies preclude conflict appears in hindsight to be somewhat myopic. If, as Keohane and Nye argue, "*asymmetries* in dependence" shape relative power endowments (2012, p. 9), then this may help explain the failure of Angell's model. Yet, IR scholars have been slow to pursue sustained inquiry into the decisive interdependencies: cross-border business models and transnational elite coalitions, ideally with the participation of core elite coalition members. One might argue that both were not as numerous and

189 The US government's original vision was ambitious with "the goal to mobilize hundreds of billions of dollars in infrastructure financing—delivering energy, physical, digital, health, and climate-resilient infrastructure", see: https://www.whitehouse.gov/briefing-room/statements-releases/2023/05/20/fact-sheet-partnership-for-global-infrastructure-and-investment-at-the-g7-summit/

190 Evidence against this liberal assumption is provided by the EIC, an entity that would never have succeeded with its Indian extraction without local elite support such as the financial backing of Marwari bankers and "the military force of 20,000 Indian sepoys" (Dalrymple, 2020, pp. 35, 208).

robust in the context of the British-German relationship as they ought to have been to guarantee peace and stability.[191] The general argument is pessimistic and holds that as long as nation states exist, transnational elite coalitions are *ad hoc*, unstable, and create insufficient interdependencies between states to safeguard peace. By absenting robust elite business model links between Western nations and China, such as those found between England and Holland, the hard logic of realism, power, and geopolitical machinations result in fierce competitions between the core and other elite coalitions of different nationalities. Trade barriers, sanctions, and indeed war become the non-institutionalized means for (largely non-endogenizing foreign elite coalitions) to solve intra-elite contests 'across-system' (see Tier 4 intra-elite checks and balances, Section 7.3.1). The reflex is for domestic elite coalitions in competition against foreign elite business models to borrow or seize outright the might of the nation state in global arenas.

A corollary of this inquiry's elite theory is that international conflict is traceable to cross-border business model competition for value appropriation and transfers in the international context. Such an analytical lens would speculate, for instance, that the serious geopolitical discord between the US and Russia is not just determined by security considerations. Neither is it the result of conflicting narratives between democracy vs authoritarianism or Western liberal values vs the neo-eurasianism values of Dugin (2014) that highlights "the traditional social/cultural make-up of each civilization" (Shlapentokh, 2007, p. 2015). Rather, it is because the countries' respective elite coalitions never successfully managed to become joint participants in transnational elite coalitions or even develop a critical mass of cross-border elite business models. Moreover, and with some exceptions, their respective elite business models compete head-to-head for customers in international markets in sectors critical to both nations: energy, defense, and agriculture.

In power transition theory (Organski, 1958), relative power advantages stem from internal developments, as does war and peace, while the international arena is conceived as a "hierarchy of nations with varying degrees of cooperation and competition" (Tammen, Kugler, & Lemke, 2012). In this reading, the derived and now much-vaunted escalation of conflict conceptualized by the Thucydides Trap (Allison, 2017) might be avoidable by internal developments that push for higher degrees of elite cooperation. To the ETED, that implies winning elite coalitions ever more engaged in

---

191 In *The House of Rothschild* (1999), Ferguson describes the investments that helped power the industrial revolution. To realize their full returns and achieve value creation, peace was a necessity and so the dynasty "can be viewed as legitimate forerunners of the secretaries-general of the League of Nations and the United Nations" (Perkins, 2000, p. 486). By 1914, the Rothschild business model, despite its origins in Frankfurt, the salience of Vienna, and the fact that the original five branches and interests were spread across the continent, was firmly anchored in the city of London. In consequence, it had inadequate connections to the Prussian Second Reich and could not exercise sufficient influence to avert the conflict that destroyed the post-Napoleonic Long Peace. Ferguson (1999) recounts how the transfer of international relations power from Europe to the US, and of financial power to New York, caused the Rothschild's business model to experience decline.

international business, with individual members from diverse national origins having skin in the same game. Specifically, one would want to see a greater and significant number of Chinese and American, French and German, and Israeli and Gulf states' elite members intertwined in cross-border elite business models (where value creation, appropriation, and principal transfer-IN does not occur on the basis of borders or nationality). In an ideal world, US and British oil majors would develop unobstructed long-term energy projects in Russia's Far East, while the Russians would pump relatively clean and inexpensive gas through Nord Stream II until the energy transition is achieved; Facebook would operate freely in China; TikTok would be likewise untroubled in the US; Saudis would be major investors in Tel Aviv start-ups; and, as Emirati officials once stated (Bauer, 2022), UAE-Israel bilateral trade would exceed US$ 1 trillion over the next decade. A 'peace through cross-border elite business models' conjecture has now been variously formulated on immediately apparent grounds: interdependencies in international relations resting on cross-border elite business models and multinational elite coalitions.[192]

7.3.3 Implications for elite system leadership and the rise and fall of great powers

The varieties of elite system leadership are set out in Table 7.2. In the previous subsections, the international landscape was characterized by states competing with each other to achieve relative power advantages and rise in the global political hierarchy to affect international institutional change that supports the cross-border business models and interests of domestic elite coalitions. Grand strategy "defines a nation's international role, guides the alignment of means and ends, and serves as a lodestar for discrete foreign policy decisions" providing a "blueprint" of "future governmental behavior" (Lissner, 2018, p. 53). To Gaddis, grand strategy is "the alignment of potentially unlimited aspirations with necessarily limited capabilities" (2018, p. 21). To this inquiry, grand strategy is a vision for both state power *and* value creation and appropriation across borders, limited by the value appropriation capabilities of its elite business models. It is conceived by the core elite coalition largely in tandem with a

192 Configurations for global public goods come with an important caveat: elites across borders can play cooperative games to extract from their respective countries' non-elites. In *Trade Wars are Class Wars* (2020), Klein and Pettis provide an analysis of the "Chimerica" model (Ferguson & Schularick, 2009), the trade relationship where the US is the deficit country and China the surplus country. They claim that this business model benefits the elites of both countries: in the US, Wall Street or MNEs; and in China, the government and owners of movable capital. This comes at the cost of US non-elites, small business owners, or workers who lose their jobs, as well as Chinese non-elites—citizens at large who consume less, or workers that suffer from low wages. Sustainable value creation cross-border business model analysis must recognize that extractive transfers can cut across classes as well as across nations.

specialized elite coalition (in the US, the "foreign policy establishment", see Jacobs & Page, 2005) upon which all of a country's other elite coalitions can design—on more or less favorable terms—their international strategies. One of the tasks of elite system leadership is to produce effective grand strategies that are consistent with the institutional change preferences of domestic elites with cross-border business interests.

We saw that cross-border elite business models might include elites from multiple nationalities and that these, especially when the elite coalitions are transnational, create strong interdependencies across states that are helpful in promoting global public goods like economic growth or peace. Again, while transnational elite networks transcend the state and have foreign interests, for all the talk about globalization, the relevant institutional organizing principle for elites in international business remains the nation state. Thus, while Apple is leading a transnational coalition with Chinese elite members in manufacturing and distribution, it will never fully endogenize in the PRC and is still part of the American elite system and no other. HSBC Holdings (despite the 'Hong Kong' and 'Shanghai' in its name) is part of the UK system, even to the displeasure of "its largest shareholder, Chinese insurer Ping An" that had called for the bank's break-up and a split between its Asian and Western operations (Kinder & Morris, 2022). Participants in elite coalitions are often from diverse countries, but there is never any doubt about the state associated with the business model and the national elite system affiliation of each coalition member. It would be inconceivable for members of successful transnational elite coalitions, such as the joint venture between Shanghai Automotive Industrial Corporation (SAIC) and Volkswagen, to disengage from their own state-based elite system for the sake of efficiencies and profits, or to fall under the aegis of some international institution or cosmopolitan narrative. After all, a critical resource for the member elites of transnational business coalitions is the power of their own nation state. This was always so, for the Fugger's copper monopoly, the EIC, or the "vast material base that ultimately reached into every corner of the newly converted Indies" of "the various branches and agencies of the Spanish church in America" (Bauer, 1983, p. 707), and continues to be the case with Amazon, Mitsubishi Corporation, or PJSC Gazprom.

Elite system leadership in the international relations context requires a state that is sufficiently powerful to realize grand strategy that furthers the cross-border elite business model preferences and interests of its coalitions, whether they are corporates, science projects, media concerns, or NGOs. A typical illustration of elite system leadership attempting to achieve rudimentary domestic elite preferences is the German car manufacturing industry informing the then Federal Minister for Economic Affairs and Energy, Peter Altmaier, about the need "to ease a shortage of semiconductor chips in the auto sector which is hampering its fledgling economic recovery from the COVID-19 pandemic". At its bidding, Altmaier wrote to Taiwanese officials: "I would be pleased if you could take on this matter and underline the importance of additional semiconductor capacities for the German automotive industry to TSMC" (Reuters, 2021). While the eventual impact of the scarcity on vehicle production around the world resulted in a staggering "cut from global production schedules" of 11.3 million units in 2021 and 3.8 million in 2022 (Vigliarolo, 2022), Altmaier's appeal was insufficient to materially increase the chip allotment for German manufacturers relative to their foreign rivals, exemplifying Germany's feeble international relations power.

Elites that create and appropriate cross-border value boost the power and advantage of their state in the international system. For instance, massively innovative and privately developed networks with chokepoints in data, finance, and trade such as CHIPS (the Clearing House Interbank Payments System), IP rights for semiconductors, or the centralized hubs for global networks of fiber-optic cables are, for Farrell and Newman, the cornerstone of America's *Underground Empire* (2023), exerting power over both friends and foes. This work hypothesizes that national power is most enhanced and realizes the highest long-term overseas profits when elites have high cross-border sustainable value creation ratings (IB-VCr). In turn, effective elite system leadership and grand strategizing by core coalitions augments the bargaining power of all elites in the international arena. Value extraction business models with a low IB-VCr are also furthered by state power but are less sustainable, create resentment in the countries where they are pursued (especially when local elites are the ones being extracted), and may diminish a nation's international bargaining power in the long run. Low IB-VCr coalitions are not just an embarrassment for other elite coalitions in the national elite system; they can also steer foreign relations into situations where many elite coalitions, even those with high IB-VCr scores, see their ability to appropriate value created cross-border eroded. In the extreme example of an aggressor in a war, the low IB-VCr military-industrial coalition might benefit, but competitive industries with high IB-VCr scores will see their exports, knowledge exchanges, or FDI projects suffer from institutional change caused by disrupted logistics, protectionist measures, or limits to accessing human and capital resources.

Elite system leadership and grand strategy also have a defensive component and serve to prevent foreign coerced value transfers from the nation's elites and non-elites. The dissimilar historical responses to foreign extraction by two elite systems facing critical junctures—and the resultant outcomes—illustrate the importance of effective transformational elite system leadership and of continuous business model transitions towards increased sustainable value creation:

> The first and second Opium Wars revealed disparities in military technology between China and the European great powers. Faced with internal unrest and the prospect of China's dismemberment, Chinese provincial leaders made an attempt at internal reform, the so-called Tongzi Restoration (1862–74), aimed at reforming the military, creating an arms industry, and strengthening traditional Confucian government. Although these and later reforms prolonged the Qing dynasty until 1911, they were insufficient to halt China's relative decline. (Taliaferro, 2006, p. 465)

The Chinese Qing imperial core coalition failed in its attempts to invigorate the incumbent national elite system, increase elite quality and sustainable value creation, and prevent extractive transfers to Great Britain, other Western powers, and eventually to Japan. In stark contrast to the Tongzi Restoration that aimed to prop up the value creation of the establishment, Japan's contemporaneous intra-elite contests resulted in profound and genuine elite circulation and transformational leadership. As a result, the Meiji Restoration's economic development outcomes were diametrically opposed to the Qing reform attempts, and outright impressive by any standards:

> News of China's defeat in the Opium Wars, carried by Dutch and Chinese ships to Nagasaki and then relayed to the shogun at Edo (Tokyo), shocked Japan's feudal elite. The arrival of Commodore Matthew Perry and his black ships in Edo Bay in July 1853 ended Japan's two centuries of self-imposed isolation. The Tokugawa shogunate's inability to defend the country led to its overthrow in 1867–68 by a group of reform-minded samurai from Satsuma and Choshu, who acted to "restore" the sixteen-year-old Emperor Meiji. The new leadership then spent the next twenty years consciously and methodically emulating the military, political, technological, and economic practices of the European great powers. In particular, they built a mass army, a general staff system, and a centralized state bureaucracy modeled on those of Germany, and a navy modeled on the British Royal Navy. Within thirty years of the Meiji Restoration, Japan waged two wars: the first to supplant Chinese hegemony in East Asia and the second to prevent Russia from filling that power vacuum. (Taliaferro, 2006, p. 465)

The rise and fall of global powers is a dynamic linked to domestic elite quality and the value appropriation capabilities of cross-border elite business models and can be framed through value creation-appropriation (VCA) and elite system transformational leadership. During the Meji Restoration, Japan's new elites adopted the business models of industrialization and created astonishing amounts of value, allowing the country to launch its cross-border elite business models. When states have elite coalitions that amass wealth via sustainable value creation and engage in international business, their relative power endowments in the international system grow accordingly. In 'The Great Power Elite Quality Lifecycle', one important way for leading nations to initially emerge is through transformational leadership driving higher levels of domestic elite quality and total value creation (as captured by The State of the Elite System Framework for the political economy, Figure 6.5). On this basis, state power augments to support the increasingly effective overseas value appropriation of its cross-border elite business models. This process is visualized in the 'rise to global power' arrow of Figure 7.7, depicting in stylized form the rise and fall of states in the international system.

A state with reasonable levels of domestic elite quality has the resources to rise in the international system provided that it leads with a grand strategy where state power enables, and is in turn enabled by, cross-border elite business models. The advantages of these models being both inclusive and sustainable (with a high IB-VCr leading to a high cb-EQr) is highlighted by repurposing the four domestic elite system categories of The Global Influence of the Elite System Framework (Figure 7.5) to dynamics that might play out in the international hierarchy of Figure 7.7. Whether in tiny Singapore or the vast United States, relative power in the international system

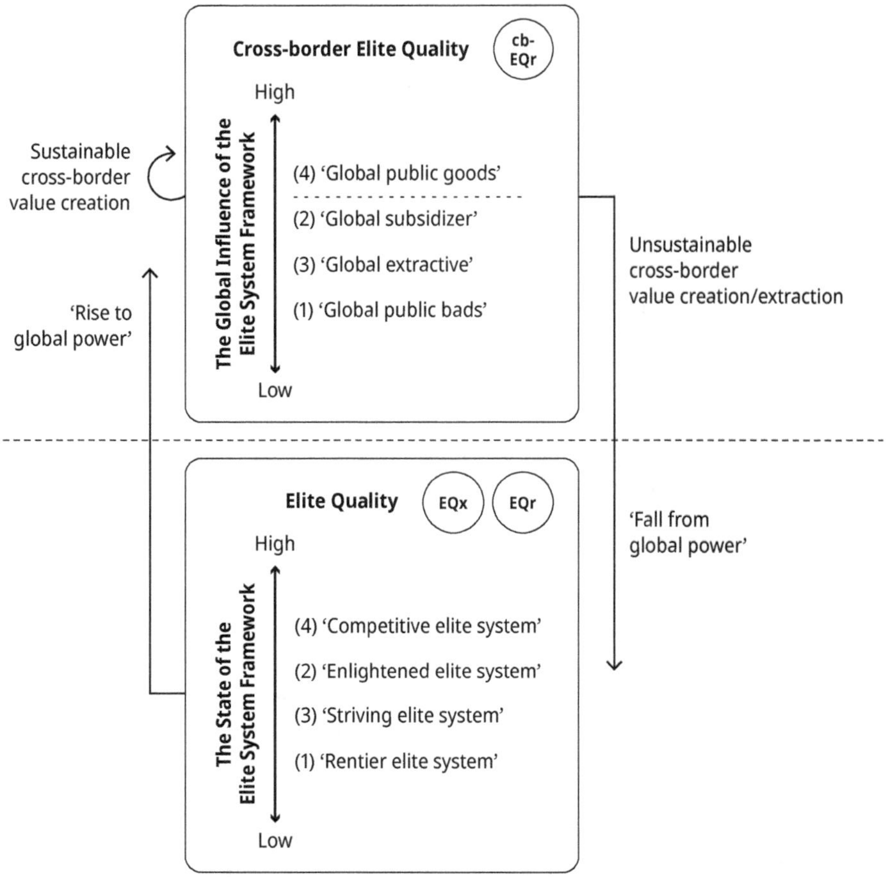

Figure 7.7: The Great Power Elite Quality Lifecycle for international relations.

can be augmented by wins in the globally competitive arenas of the narrative market (e.g., through ideas of prosperity or social justice), the political non-market (e.g., through defense capabilities or by shaping international organizations), or the market (e.g., through superior products and services). While domestic elite quality supplies the initial advantage for a state's rise (e.g., US capitalism's unparalleled engine of value creation, the Gilded Age and all, starting after its Civil War), one should not obviate the fact that low quality elites can also leverage extraction models at home to further grand strategies and boost their relative power overseas. England extracted not only from India and China from the 18th century onwards (with its imperial subjugation still patent during the Bengal Famine of 1943–1944), but for a long while also from its own industrial proletariat, as depicted in Charles Dickens' *Hard Times*. Stalin extracted from Soviet citizens, and the economic high-growth phases of the *pyatiletki* five-year plans that launched the state's military power came on the back of grain exports to procure the hard currency needed to fund industrialization, thereby becoming indelibly tied to the harrowing Holodomor famine of 1932–1933 (see Snyder, 2010). That is, despite the value creation advantages of high elite quality posited earlier, grand strategy can also be based on effectively deploying the residual income obtained from low elite quality domestic elite business models to procure the relative power advantages needed to ascend in the international system's hierarchy of nations. The degree to which inclusive and extractive elite agency choices at home and aboard determine a nation's length of tenure at the top table, or its destiny after a fall, merits examination. The working and aspirational hypothesis is that while extraction abroad might work for a period of time, only the 'global public goods' elite system can sustain hard power in world affairs and the value appropriation of its international business models in the grand scheme of things.

Power attained in the international system is monetized through specific cross-border elite business models. Again, these might primarily rely on value transfers from stakeholders aboard (leading to low overall cb-EQr, as in the Vatican's indulgences and colonial business models), or be based on cross-border value creation. In the latter case, note the high cb-EQr, relative to the times, of the *Pax Augusta* and its provision of state capacity and infrastructure as evidenced by the "material fall" of Britain once the Roman Legions evacuated in the early 5th century (Fleming, 2021), or the *Pax Americana,* which permits foreign elites, like Japan's auto industry, to appropriate value created in the US. Most great powers use both approaches. The fierce critic of the British elite's opium-based global political economy reminds the reader in the closing section of his book that "the most long-continued and systematic international crime of modern times" (Fairbank, 1978, p. 213) *also* delivered value creation and inclusive transfer-OUT:

> Opium created pools of capital and fed the institutions that accumulated it: the banking and financial system, the insurance system and the transportation and information infrastructures. Those structures and that economy have, in large part, been inherited by the successor nations of the region today. (Trocki, 1999, p. 173)

Any cross-border business model, just like its domestic counterparts, combines value creation and extractive transfers in keeping with the 'all elite agency creates and transfers value' (realist) inference (see Figure 8.7). Both of these value amounts must be quantified and weighted, underscoring the relevance of firm-level SVC measurements for international business (such as the IB-VCr) and their diverse constituent metrics. Taken together, inclusive aggregate elite agency at home and abroad jointly sustain the virtuous value creation cycle of global public goods in the international system and contribute to worldwide human and economic development.

The Great Power Elite Quality Lifecycle is a framework for the analysis of the dynamics of international relations. The implicit premise for containment in Kennan's *The Long Telegram* (1946) was that the Soviet Union would not create sufficient cross-border value and over time decline of its own accord in line with the 'fall from global power' arrow of Figure 7.7 (an assumption now not made in the West for China). When the value creation engine of a state's elite coalitions splutters, cross-border sustainable value creation decays. At that point, if sufficient global power endowments are still held, grand strategy turns to pursue foreign extractive aims. This is an unsustainable fix; great powers with extractive domestic elites on the rise (reflected by low firm-level VCr scores), do not avoid and will at best defray their decline (albeit sometimes by decades) if in order to spare domestic non-elites further pain their elite agency switches to second-order transfer business models overseas (as seen in declining firm-level IB-VCr scores). Telltale warning signs for international conflict are dwindling domestic elite quality (measured by the meso-level EQx or EQr) and cross-border elite quality (measured by the meso-level cb-EQr and, in some instances, by the more granular bl-EQr). When this happens to the hegemon, or to a big enough player in the international system, the fall—again likely originating with diminishing sustainable value creation at home—will reverberate through the fundamental structures of the global economy and disrupt development for all. How probable is the opposite scenario where a great power that is suffering decay at home reneges on its interests abroad and quietly dissolves à la Soviet Union? Is 'Japan-bashing' to 'Japan-passing'[193] likewise indicative of a transition where an economic superpower gently ages and wanes without upsetting others? Did Britain not readily transfer most of its international power roles to the US in the period from 1914 to the Suez Crisis of 1956? On the contrary, this inquiry holds that should any remnant of power be held at the end of a lifecycle, to easily forsake its use is rather exceptional. This is notably the case for (once) great nations on the wane that rarely abstain from using what remaining influence they have to the fullest, even doubling down and escalating a conflict when caught in Allison's Thucydides Trap (2017).

What underlies great power cycles in the literature? In *The Decline of the West*, Spengler's (1922) "tragic outlook" deems cycles and Europe's "Winter epoch" to be, in a peculiar and eerily metaphysical analysis, cultural (Chisholm, 1935, pp. 35, 37); Kondratieff's waves are technological, while Schumpeter's are entrepreneurial (see Section 1.3.2); Kennedy, in *The Rise and Fall of Great Powers* (1987), emphasizes the strains of economic and military overcommitment; Dalio's (2021) answer to "why nations succeed and fail" is a 250-year sequence characterized by long-term debt cycles and internal and external order and disorder patterns, all of which is reflected in human capital productivity; Ophuls, who takes a page or two from Gibbon's *The History of the Decline and Fall of the Roman Empire* (1776/2001), points to inertia and the ossification of "ruling ideas", and to institutions as "the civilization's elites may understand that the system is dysfunctional, but fundamental reform would require major sacrifice on their part, so they fight to preserve their privilege and power instead" (2012, p. 64). The IR literature proposes several other diverse cyclical conceptualizations. Modelski's "The Long Cycles of World Leadership" answers the realist question, "Who leads in world politics" (1983,

193 Japan-passing is used here in the same sense as it was by the late public intellectual, Jean-Pierre Lehmann.

p. 1; see also Modelski & Thompson, 1988); power transitions theory is anchored in the domestic growth factors that emerge from distinct development trajectories after the industrial revolution (Organski, 1958), or even in prior pre-Napoleonic periods (Kim, 1992); "power cycle theory" has a more liberal bent, stressing negotiated rules (Doran, 1991) and "conscious policy-intervention" for a dynamic balancing of power and "insists that power and role are each necessarily pluralistic and shared, although unequally across states" (Yoon, 2003, pp. 6, 7). The cycles that the ETED posits for the rise and fall of nations—and even of civilizations—are grounded in the sustainable value creation patterns of elite business models. Thus, The Great Power Elite Quality Lifecycle for international relations technically draws from The Elite Business Model Lifecycle (see Figure 4.5). That is, the rise and fall of nations is rooted in trends of national and cross-border elite quality.

If US economic and social vitality were to fall (as suggested by Doran, 1991; Mahbubani, 2018; Dalio, 2021) to a level where in comparative terms it could not generate sufficient domestic residual income flows to support its non-elite consumption or position atop the international hierarchy, the realist-leaning IR position of the ETED suggests that foreign stakeholders of US cross-border business models would be asked to pay a price; for instance, through higher prices for security, technology and energy, for access to the US market, through trade deficits, and by being forced to hold a reserve currency fated to devalue. Dwindling value creation and low elite quality at home is compensated for with increased value extraction from abroad on the back of accumulated power in the international system. The Great Power Elite Quality Lifecycle for international relations set forth in this work (and partially depicted in Figure 7.7), rests on the elemental 'value transfers replace value creation at maturity' conjecture (see Section 4.3.4 and Figure 4.5). A root cause of a nation's decline is the lack of incentives for an adequate number of domestic elite business models to engage in first-order productive activities as the overall 'elite power vs value creation gap' that underlies the 'value transfers replace value creation at maturity' conjecture widens. This also includes a failure to create and undertake risk[194] while maintaining elite coordination leadership and preserving power at home. Perversely, falls in the international hierarchy can be temporarily averted through the appropriation of value by cross-border business models from foreign elites and non-elites. However, this is unsustainable, and power will ultimately move on to other states. In times of transitions towards lower elite quality, the 'extractive escalation dynamic' plays out internationally when the elites of multiple states compete with each other for over-

---

194 The point on risk taking must be stressed: high risk means that there will be high returns, while those originating the risk must have skin in the game as per The Sustainable Risk Framework (Figure 6.9). All too often, elites in declining powers run business models that either do not originate sufficient risk (i.e., 'null risk origination') or transfer the *negative* value of the risk they originate to non-elites at home or to elites and non-elites in foreign countries (i.e., 'unsustainable risk origination'), in the latter case through wars or currency devaluations.

seas rents (as was the case between 1881 and 1914 in the Scramble for Africa, when value creation in America was eclipsing that of Europe).

Fast-forwarding to the 21st century, the Hinrich Foundation sees danger in subsidies that "perpetuate an unsustainable cycle of mimicry and retaliation" (Evenett & Fritz, 2021, p. 4). Specifically, since the EU Commission relaxed the rules on state aid in March 2022, approximately euro 650 billion has been handed out for "the manufacturing of strategic equipment" like solar panels or batteries, with Germany receiving about 50% of these subsidies and France about 30% (Chan, 2023 as cited in Blake, 2023, p. 85), while estimates show "that 84% of Chinese goods imports were in product lines where local producers had been subsidized" (Evenett & Fritz, 2021, p. 46). Subsidy races are just one of the types of conflict that subvert global coherence and, if the escalation of extractive cross-border business models is not curbed by elite systems at home, civil international relations are jeopardized. From a structuralist perspective, the unthinkable is therefore theoretically feasible and not unlikely: a US that in time goes from being a bountiful provider of global public goods (once boasting the highest cb-EQr in the historical record, see Figure 7.7) to becoming perilously reliant on extractive overseas transfers (gradually lowering its cb-EQr to compensate for falling domestic elite quality and value creation). The same logic is applied to China by Brands and Beckley in *Danger Zone: The Coming Conflict with China* (2022), where they claim that the country has peaked, is now in relative decline, and consequently forecast geopolitical conflict later this decade.

Further down the ladder are states that cannot muster the power to support the appropriation of value by their elite cross-border elite business models. In such cases, mediocre elites seeking residual income flows in lieu of value creation capabilities both at home and abroad revert to models based on domestic transfer-IN from their non-elites. The resultant lower elite quality scores mean greater vulnerability to external threats. Such a scenario is illustrated by the bureaucratic modernizing Tanzimat ("reorganization") reforms (1839–1876) in the waning decades of the Ottoman Empire that, while being liberal and Western-inspired, saw the centralization of the tax system to increase tax revenues (and hence transfers) from Turkish and other non-elites. Expanding domestic appropriation was also a low-quality elite system response in the late Spanish Empire, as well as for the Chinese dynasties that lost the Mandate of Heaven, that not only intensified their respective demise as regional or world powers but, more crucially, hindered sustained domestic development. Of course, it is by no means preordained that the loss of power in the international system is followed by regressive development at home. The comparative decline during the closing stages of the Habsburg or British empires did not see significant increments in domestic extraction, supporting the view that in the final analysis prosperity is more dependent on domestic elite quality and transformational leadership than on power in the international system. Once defined by their ability to command empires and master value appropriation abroad, how are the elite models of Europe faring today?

7.3.4 Implications for comparative elite system performance: The case of Europe

> Mme Richez-Lerouge says that the erosion of authentic French cheese is part of a "wider, national hypocrisy". For decades, she says, French governments have extolled the virtues of small-scale farming and quality food while "shovelling 80 per cent of European subsidies into the pockets of big farmers and the agro-industry". (Lichfield, 2020)

No national elite system exists in a vacuum. These key sub-systems of political economies interact with each other, as the discussion on international relations and cross-border elite business models has shown. Having applied the ETED to the international context, the implications of elite system leadership for international political economy distributional outcomes are now analyzed through a concrete case: the EU's 'partial' elite system, or 'elite non-system', by referencing Manent's *Metamorphoses of the City* and his "two mother forms of the ancient world" that exist in polarity to each other: "the city and the empire" (2013, p. 105). This section argues that because of weak (or even non-existent) elites, Europe currently has neither of these forms and examines the implications.

Manent argues that representations of the world and narratives "affect the political system" as he delves into the two basic political forms of Europe: "While the Greek polis was a narrow political framework for a tumultuous free life, the empire corresponds to a peaceful life under a master" (May, 2017, pp. 414–415). One might think of the polis as a space with equalized bargaining power, institutionalized intra-elite contests, and elite cohesion typified by vigorous bottom-up value creation; of sustainable value creation (high VCp/VCr) business models thriving in dynamic technological, industrial, trading, or agricultural ecosystems like Normandie, the Yangtze River Valley, Singapore, Dubai, or Silicon Valley. In the international system, the elites of these modern versions of the polis—mega-cities, regions, region-states, city-states—must be secure and enabled by sufficient state power at higher levels, leading to the idea of 'polis in empire'. Kaplan's "In Defense of Empire" (2014) takes this stance, and in an ensuing piece he references Manent in arguing that the future might belong to "the half-hidden traditions of empire" and to city-states, both of which are millennia-old human organizational structures (2016).

The 1648 agreement to establish the Westphalian system resulted in an institutional innovation, a historical anomaly that worked well for a few centuries in a Europe little exposed to outside forces: the nation state system. The question today is whether the European nation state is still an institutional arrangement that is effective in generating sufficient bottom-up value creation while also accumulating power to preempt extraction given the nature and scale of the cross-border elite business models of the 21st century? To explore this further, the 'polis in empire' framework is used to compare France and Germany with Switzerland and the US.

To start, one could contemplate whether France, Germany, and the other large European nation states have become too big and unwieldy. That is, are they prone to administrative diseconomies of scale by being both emotionally detached and intellectually too far removed from first-order and local value producers. Is capture by national state-based elite coalitions all too easy? If so, what prevents the elite coalitions of nation states from advancing business model rules that harvest value from local and regional creators and engage in extractive transfer-IN while very cavalierly denying institutional resources to value creation at the polis? Breiding's (2019) factors for "why some small nations outperform larger ones" play a role here, but the key one is elite quality. As an illustration, the French political establishment has abandoned authentic *lait cru* producers at the state-level, while subsidizing elite brands manufacturing cheese from pasteurized milk; products that the famous *fromagologue* Gérard Poulard has called "cheese for people who don't like cheese" (Lichfield, 2020). The nation state elite system disincentivizes ecosystems that support "living cheese", an embodiment of French identity, and instead elicits institutional change in Paris (and thus in Brussels), as policymakers become the servants of a few mass-produced factory cheese elite coalitions (such as Lactalis Group, Danone, or Savencia Fromage & Dairy). In contrast, Swiss radical democracy and its polis-centric political economy explains not just the 450 varieties of Swiss cheese and the support that their producers and other value creators like SMEs or *Kantonalbanken* enjoy, but also a GDP per capita differential between France and Switzerland that is in favor of the latter by a huge margin.[195]

But European nation states are not only too big; they are also too small to pursue grand strategies that smartly respond to global challenges such as value extraction by foreign cross-border elite business models. Germany, once the global hotbed of innovation, no longer has any elite coalition of note active in the international arena.[196] Does Europe now require Manent's empire and Kaplan's imperial capabilities to be on a par with the US or China (and soon, India), in the international political economy arenas? The answer is no, but only if its elites can effectively integrate into the American elite system and participate on an equal footing in US intra-elite contests. European non-elites would also need to have some of the imperial might benefits of their American counterparts such as higher consumption levels than can be afforded with low levels of savings, or protection from cross-border value appropriation. If this is not feasible or wanted by either side, the road to empire starts with an elite system that is strategic enough to muster the transformational leadership clout to deactivate extractive transfer-OUT by foreign coalitions. Under the existing EU institutional model of a 'club of nation states', such an outcome cannot possibly be attained under a realist understanding of power.

195 The World Bank (n.d.-g) statistics for 2023 show that France and Germany's GDP per capita are US $ 44,461 and US$ 52,746 respectively, while Switzerland's stands at US$ 99,995. Since Switzerland's successful sustainable value creation is an embarrassment for the elite systems of Germany and France, this theory's realist version of international relations would advise the Swiss to be vigilant against extractive moves by the EU in both the political non-market and narrative market arenas.

196 Of the top 50 most valuable global companies, not a single one is German (see: https://companies marketcap.com accessed on January 28, 2024).

The first elite system problem of Europe as a club of nation states[197] is domestic extraction from the polis. In the EU, the nation state *is* the elite business model, and as such is not subject to checks and balances (even though this would be Brussels' Madisonian mandate). Europe is not a 'top-down' "elite project" (Best, Lengyel, & Verzichelli, 2012) and instead exists to consolidate the domestic power of national elites. As currently constituted, it is better classified as a 'middle-down' and 'middle-up' system. The principals of its nation state business models include assorted coalitions of civil servants, energy interests, banking institutions, or construction companies, and also some nation's capital cities that are themselves value transferees (the most noteworthy being Paris, Madrid, Berlin, and Rome). By privileged access to state power, nation state-centric elite coalitions unfairly compete against and appropriate value from the regions and polis. Their 'license to steal' extends to risk taking through the capture of the polis' innovative bets once these become successful, often with the aid of state resources. Part of this process includes coopting local elites into the nation state elite system (reminiscent of empires past),[198] consequently leaving the region or polis without elites and thus helpless in political economy contests.[199]

Nation state licenses for business models are doled out via food safety regulations, but also for what Gandhi and Walton (2012) and Klein, Holmes, Foss, Terjesen, and Pepe (2022) call crony capitalist sectors. Despite the commendable Brussels-driven single market initiative, most sectors remain structured around the nation state. Hence, Europe has "tariffs on itself" (Draghi, 2025), while in the telecoms sector, "recent entrants have found it difficult to enter and then thrive in mobile markets in Europe" with incumbents able to retain leading positions (Whalley & Curwen, 2012, p. 234). From a Madisonian perspective (*Federalist No. 10*, 1787/1977; see Section 3.3.3), Europe's nation states are "factions" that *de facto* capture the EU's supranational institutions. As global competitiveness is consequently lost, the elites of European nation states will increasingly deploy their coordination leadership towards a further tightening of the status quo. Germany and France will nudge Brussels towards a once dreaded yet strategically skirted protectionist "fortress Europe" (Hanson, 1998) to shield their elites from global competition, intensifying domestic extraction, and milking their non-elites and polis. With a 'missing elite system'—a European 'quasi'

---

197 The French Foreign Minister, Aristide Briand, a leader in the movement for a European federation between 1929 and 1930 and recipient of the Nobel Peace Prize in 1926 together with the German Foreign Minister, Gustav Stresemann, painted a picture of Europe as "a society in which the members are ruled by club law, as were states and castles in the darkest days of the Middle Ages" (United States of America, 1948, p. 388, as cited in Fulbright, 1948, p. 156). Even as some of Briand's vision of "common organs or authorities" has been successfully realized, the elite theory apprehends the EU as a 'club of clubs'.

198 In the Ottoman or Romanov empires, "peripheral elites" were coopted into the (often lucrative) role of "servants and agents" of the "central imperial elite" (Suny, 1997, p. 5).

199 Local elites cannot be reproached since the benefits of redistribution and transfers are too alluring; Lactalis originated in the small town of Laval and is now part of the French establishment.

elite system that is fragmented and only functional at the level of a powerful nation state—there can be no European elite cohesion[200] (see Section 5.3.3), much less elite system transformational leadership (Table 7.2) in support of the defenseless polis. Some influential local elites like the community-based German *Sparkassen* public banks or the Spanish hospitality industry will resist, but Europe's ecosystems, regions, and other incarnations of the polis can expect to see their bottom-up value creation eroded. This is the vital but overlooked reason why there will be fewer quality jobs and unicorns (Draghi, 2024, p. 232) than there should be, the SME sector will remain stressed with moderate numbers of young entrepreneurs, and, alas, there will be a piecemeal dying out of local cheesemakers.

The second elite system problem facing Europe is that it is on the receiving end of extraction from abroad given its relative powerlessness in the absence of 'empire'. Unsurprisingly, the EU has no Big Tech, no Big Oil, no Wall Street, and cannot defend itself, a cause of concern to many who "call for stronger European independence by promoting the creation of European champions, or by protecting European companies against foreign players" (Ramahandry, Bonneau, Bani, & Vlasov, 2021, p. i). So, while there is criticism of European integration as "steered and driven by the initiative of the elites", researchers are still trying to confirm the "Europeanness" of domestic European elites (Best, Lengyel, & Verzichelli, 2012, p.1). In Europe, national elite coalitions might run successful international business models and score highly in Europeanness surveys, yet this is all but irrelevant and should not lead to confusion: these 'European' elite coalitions do not have members from different nation states running cross-border elite business models that leverage the power differentials afforded by empire in the global arena.

When Google lobbies Brussels, its leadership strength does not emanate from hiring the most talented lawyers, but from having cross-border business model positions supported in Washington. In terms of cross-border value appropriation, US Big Tech would not enjoy its global hegemonic position (some areas of the non-West notwithstanding) without its membership in the US national elite system. US power differentials with the EU are often painfully obvious, as when US Secretary of the Treasury Mnuchin stopped the EU's digital tax talks with a single two-page letter to four European finance ministers "piling pressure on the EU to shelve its plans for a levy on digital companies" (Politi, Fleming, & Espinoza, 2021). Snyder (2019) claims that "The EU insulates its citizens from the empires of today: China, America, Russia; Amazon, Google, Facebook". While Apple restored the Epic Games' developer account "following 'a swift inquiry' from the European Commission" (Roth, 2024) and Google will eventually lose some battles and be fined in the EU (Hancock, 2024), neither will lose

200 The lack of elite cohesion in the EU is evidenced in times of troubles. A minor but representative illustration of this is the political knee jerk reaction driven by nation state elite coalitions to German pleas for solidarity in the face of falling Russian gas deliveries, captured in *Politico*'s headline: "Southern rebellion threatens to sink EU gas rationing plan" (Hernandez, Posaner, & Stamouli, 2022). The moment it faces a serious crisis, institutional Europe will readily break down.

their wars and be barely unscathed in terms of their value appropriation capabilities. The European lack of bargaining power underscores the likely inability of Margrethe Vestager, the EU Commissioner responsible for competition and digital policy, to walk the talk as the "EU warns that it may break up Big Tech companies" (Espinoza, 2020). This would be a consequential move, but given the facts it seems naïve at best and simply nonviable under the ETED version of realist IR. Time will tell to what extent the OECD/G20 Base Erosion and Profit Shifting (BEPS) project to increase transparency and prevent the use of shell companies works out as envisioned in the "Statement on a Two-Pillar Solution to Address the Tax Challenges Arising from the Digitalisation of the Economy" which includes a minimum tax rate of 15% (OECD, 2021, p. 4). Will this institutional change effectively increase Big Tech's payments to national treasuries or dent its general cross-border value appropriation capabilities (reflected by IB-VCr scores) in any material way? If, when all is said and done, the Spanish National Markets and Competition Commission collects the massive half a billion Euro fine on Booking Holdings for "anti-competitive behaviour such as preventing domestic hotel groups from offering deals that are cheaper on their own sites than the price they offer on booking.com" (Espinoza, 2024a)[201]—essentially extraction from the polis—it will only be because the online travel giant fails with its elite coordination leadership in Washington DC.

The pseudo, make-believe elite system—the 'elite non-system'—cannot readily address the 'intra-elite quality contest' dilemma; its elite cohesion is a pretense, lacks a core coalition, musters weak transformational leadership, and has a siloed rather than comprehensive separation of powers. In comparative terms, Europe's brand of nation state-centric elite systems is no match for the 'polis in empire' institutional formulas of the American, Chinese, and now Indian political economies.[202] The EU can-

---

201 The comments section below this piece in *The Financial Times* sheds light on how this elite business model extracts from the polis. 'Notspriti' writes: "It's a monopoly. Plain and simple. Particularly in Europe. Independent and small groups have to use it and pay 15–20% commission. That's just scalping. How much does Booking spend a year with Google just to keep their monopoly position? $6bn in 2022!" In response, 'PLNY' comments: "Having worked at their competitor more than a decade ago I can confirm that it's a somewhat parasitic business, especially towards independent hotels not in tier 1 cities. There were cases of hotels in rural Italy and Spain which generated 100% of their top line via Booking.com reservations, being charged 18% - the moment Booking would come to them and demand 25% they would have to comply as there was no alternative. What's more mind blowing is that 90%+ of the hotel online reservations market is controlled by Expedia group (owns: Travelocity, ebookers, hotels.com, Hotwire, orbitz, wotif, trivago, ebookers) and booking.com (owns: booking, agoda, Priceline, kayak, momondo) so as a hotelier you have close to zero choice, and as a customer you have a false sense of choice while looking online".

202 How do Europe's strangely inadequate (for the 21st century) national state elites, neither imperial nor polis-anchored, compare to US or China? In the US, any elite business model seeks to be part of the American empire, while the polis elites have been relegated to a different category (as in the 'fly-over country' phrase). China fulfills Manent's 'polis in empire' idea with its time-honored imperial and polis elite configuration. The strong imperial elites based in Beijing are complemented and bal-

not accumulate enough relative power in the international system to properly support competitive cross-border elite business models (as, for instance, the French found when Australia scuttled the diesel-powered submarine contract with majority state owned Naval Group in favor of US or British nuclear-powered submarines).[203] The European elite system is at best partially formed, and without it there can be no elite system leadership. Hence, European elite and non-elite business models can't be expected to appropriate the full value that they create in the international business context (and much less aim for value appropriated but *not* created). This will affect European economic and human development and impoverish European elites and non-elites alike, especially in periods of global economic contraction when the elites of rival and non-rival imperial states will have all the incentives to convert their state power into residual income and appropriate increasing amounts of cross-border value.

In sum, the advantages of a robust elite system include the possibility to exercise effective leadership and accumulate power in the measure that value is created, resulting in the appropriation of higher residual income streams for elites and the minimization of extractive transfers from domestic non-elites to foreign coalitions. Europe's 'elite non-system' results in local non-elites paying the taxes not collected from Apple, whose "selective" treatment by the Irish government allowed it "to pay an effective corporate tax rate of 1 per cent on its European profits in 2003 down to 0.005 per cent in 2014" (European Commission, 2016). It also means lower elite coordination leadership, poorer ecosystems, data colonialism (see Couldry & Mejias, 2019), the inability to scale businesses, and therefore increased future extraction, as will likely be the case when new division of value strategies are rolled out for the AI brains of smart electric vehicles—or any other machine—by their foreign elite owners. Being on the receiving end of extractive cross-border business models has consequences for economic and human development, as China or India know all too well from their historical experiences with the West. The obstinacy of incumbent national business model configurations attached to European nation states, and the absence of high velocity elite circulation (see Section 1.3), leaves Europe at the mercy of value extraction and less valuable to its partners. A prosperous and strong "United States of Europe" in the spirit of Fulbright (1948) is in the strategic interest of the US, even if this is at first glance counterintuitive and disavowed by a narrow realist IR take. The status quo will remain until the issue of the missing elite system is fixed, reasonably whole and cohered European elite coalitions emerge, and a core elite coalition, possibly inspired by a version of Manent's 'polis in empire', becomes capable of strategic

anced by strong local elites (as seen in local protectionism *difang baohu zhuyi*). Polis elites, whether in Hangzhou (e.g., Alibaba or Volvo Car owner Zhejiang Geely Holding Group Co., Ltd.) or Ningde (e.g., Contemporary Amperex Technology Co. Ltd, CATL, the world's leading battery manufacturer) have influence in the capital and can leverage China's imperial capabilities as needed.

203 Despite France 24 (2022) reporting a "massive compensation deal", the euro 555 million settlement represents less than 1% of the original deal's value.

thinking, elite transformational leadership, and purposeful institutional reform (see Table 8.1). In the meantime, initiatives such as the Draghi report on *The Future of European Competitiveness,* designed among other things to close "the US-EU gap in aggregate total factor productivity (TFP), which is currently over 20% higher in the US" and hinges on subsidies and other forms of value transfers to the suggested tune of EUR 750-800 billon per annum, a massive 4.4% to 4.7% of the EU's GDP (Draghi, 2024, pp. 281–283), will not address the underlying problems and produce only marginal results that further impoverish the continent's next generations.

In the rare instances where elite business models in Europe are genuinely European, as is the case with ASML and its key suppliers such as Carl Zeiss SMT, the UEFA Champions League (the world's premier sport entertainment product), or Airbus SE (Societas Europaea),[204] astonishing levels of value creation and appropriation ensue. Such exceptions notwithstanding, European elite coalitions of note abscond or remain stillborn, leaving a continent dotted with local (German, French, Polish, Greek, etc.) elite coalitions embedded in their national systems and unfit for the 21st century. *The Brussels Effect* or being a "global regulatory superpower" (Bradford, 2020, p. 7), even where true, is inconsequential for economic and human development in the absence of European elite business models. This was made abundantly clear by the energy price hikes after February 2022 that should have dispelled the fantasy that "the EU has turned a weakness into strength and developed a set of tools that sharpen the way soft power is exercised in the energy section" (Goldthau & Sitter, 2015, p. 941). The realist IR framework implies that European value creators, both citizens and firms (including many national state elites), will become the rich feeding grounds for extractive cross-border business models operated by non-European elites leveraging the imperial capabilities of their own elite systems.

7.3.5 Implications of the world's missing elite system: The tragedy of the AI commons and a measurement

National elite systems anchor international institutions. Since elite agency and its transformational leadership variants are only operational at the national level, serving the interests of domestic coalitions on the international stage, can elite transformational leadership ever be helpful in tackling global challenges? Escaping "The Tragedy of the Commons" (Hardin, 1968; see also the common-pool resource problems of Ostrom, 2005) is already difficult enough within the confines of a nation given its prisoner dilemma qualities (Gardiner, 2001), and becomes all the harder when the shared

---

204 *Societas Europaea* is an apt legal innovation, "a type of public limited-liability company that allows you to run your business in different European countries using a single set of rules", see: https://europa.eu/youreurope/business/running-business/developing-business/setting-up-european-company/index_en.htm

resources of the commons involve multiple states, as is seen in environmental protection efforts and their attendant global institutions (Wijkman, 1982; Clancy, 1998). Initiatives like the United Nations Convention on the Law of the Sea (UNCLOS) require multiple elite systems to coordinate in order to build international regulatory bodies with enforcement authority. The optimist would argue that liberal common sense should rationally prevail in the face of existential threats to societies everywhere, as is the case with climate change. The hegemon's elite system, or the elite systems of large powers, would choose enlightened self-interest to overcome game-theoretical limitations and drive a multilateral elite bargain to force through sustainable value creation solutions for humanity. As the technology of intelligence rapidly evolves, humankind is about to confront a "Tragedy of the AI Commons", considered by LaCroix and Mohseni to be "a situation where no one has an individual incentive to cooperate, though mutual cooperation would lead to the best outcome for all involved" (2022, p. 1). The global challenge caused by the proliferation of AI technology is now perhaps more urgent than pandemics, wars, or the climate crisis. The pessimist, probably in the realist IR vein, would point out that national elite agency cannot address worldwide tragedies of the commons and a cross-border elite bargain will not materialize on theoretical grounds, even if global narratives and powerful international business models were to emerge around AI. This is consistent with current IR practice as seen in the uncoordinated national state responses to COVID-19, the breakdown of The Intermediate-Range Nuclear Forces Treaty (INF) in 2019, or how "Competition between the United States and China will almost certainly drive the militarization of space" (Araya, 2022). The 'elite non-system' conceptual element discussed in the context of the EU is even more pertinent on the world stage, since any institution—multilateral or not—is moot without functional and coordinated national elite systems.

One must consider the ramifications for the global elite non-system in the context of a global AI tragedy of the commons that could lead to a superintelligence doomsday scenario. What if knowledge elites irrefutably establish that the only solution is the deactivation of the AGI hardware brains across the world?

> Shut down all the large GPU clusters (the large computer farms where the most powerful AIs are refined). Shut down all the large training runs. Put a ceiling on how much computing power anyone is allowed to use in training an AI system, and move it downward over the coming years to compensate for more efficient training algorithms. No exceptions for governments and militaries. Make immediate multinational agreements to prevent the prohibited activities from moving elsewhere. Track all GPUs sold. If intelligence says that a country outside the agreement is building a GPU cluster, be less scared of a shooting conflict between nations than of the moratorium being violated; be willing to destroy a rogue datacenter by airstrike. (Yudkowsky, 2023)

How much time does humanity now have to preempt this tragedy and create global institutions that are ready for AI? Kurzweil (2005) predicts singularity by 2045, while Sokolsky suggests that AGI will only arrive "around 2040", and thereafter, in a process that will take 30 years:

> AGI spends decades convincing humanity to let it take over the global supply chains and to run complex experiments to manufacture advanced AGI-designed machinery, supposedly necessary to improve human living standards. [. . .] Once the AGI is convinced that all the cards have fallen into place and humans could be safely removed, it will pull the plug and destroy us all. (Sokolsky, 2022)

While the timelines may differ, the issue at hand for international relations is whether the core elite coalitions of nation states, many with interests in AI business models, can ever be "coordinated within a dedicated international body" (Future of Life Institute, 2023, p. 8) established in accordance with international treaties and conventions with executive prerogatives. But what will happen if and when it becomes apparent that an AI is incorrigible (in the sense of Soares, Fallenstein, Yudkowsky, & Armstrong, 2015, p. 75)? More specifically, can a decision to bomb GPU clusters (Yudkowsky, 2023) be consistent with elite transformational leadership at the international level, or would such a step be unilaterally taken—or not taken—by national elites?

At the inaugural AI Safety Summit at Bletchley Park, "leading AI developers agreed to work with governments to test new frontier models before they are released to help manage the risks of the rapidly developing technology, in a 'landmark achievement'" (Coulter & Sandle, 2023). Will these commendable intentions, in line with liberal IR, convert into binding international legislation and, at the moment of truth, see coordinated global action? Can a semblance of a world elite system emerge around the challenge posed by AI? Or, alternatively, and surely not the worst-case scenario in the face of chaos, can the AI technologies and elite business models of one particular state outpace the rest and reign supreme? As matters stand today, the elites of the two global superpowers, the US and China, but also those of other key players like India and Russia, will be addressing the existential threats of AI by holding fast to realist IR positions, each trying to come out on top. All of this confirms that the world—not just Europe—faces a missing elite system problem as is emphatically echoed by a Silicon Valley luminary:

> The single greatest risk of AI is that China wins global AI dominance and we – the United States and the West – do not. [. . .] We should seek to win the race to global AI technological superiority and ensure that China does not. (Andreessen, 2023a)

Elite transformational leadership at the global level is particularly sought in times of crises. Yet even when its absence is coupled with the missing world elite system problem, elite quality is still an actual emergent property of the global political economy. Technically, world elite quality can be conceptually determined without the existence of a functioning elite system at the international level. For those interested in deciphering or "improving the state of the world",[205] or, more concertedly, in assessing the impact of the AI or other global tragedies of the commons, understanding the to-

205 The World Economic Forum (WEF) often articulates its mission through the phrase "improving the state of the world" (see https://www.weforum.org/impact/), a worthy aspiration for elites that apprehend the world as a whole—a complex system of interacting and interdependent components in the sense described by Von Bertalanffy.

tality of the sustainable value creation of all elite business models on the planet (or of a particular sector) that is attributable to both domestic and cross-border elite agency is critical. Such an understanding can be described through a 'world elite quality' index based on tailored, all-enfolding indicators.

The data inputs for the operationalization of such a 'World Elite Quality Index' ('world-EQ') aggregate into a weighted elite quality sum of all national elite systems (and include their cross-border effects). The inputs for this consolidated global indicator are diverse and include: worldwide life expectancy and its variance among countries, international ecological benchmarks, the planetary size of the informal sector, criminal activities as a percentage of global GDP, worldwide educational attainment trends, global innovation rates and productivity changes, numbers of international patents, universal inflation, an aggregate of national crony capitalism, industry dominance in the world economy, the concentration of global wealth, and the prevalence of armed conflicts and battle-related deaths. While variance across countries technically poses an interpretative challenge, the longitudinal data for this SVC measurement reveals cardinal global trends: a declining world-EQ score provides a serious warning, maybe of an ongoing 'extractive escalation dynamic' of universal proportions with the potential to cause war, while an improving score signals an increasingly inclusive and prosperous global future for most humans. Of course, for any improvement in global sustainable value creation, transformational leadership has to take place primarily on a nation-by-nation/elite system-by-elite system basis.

7.3.6 Implications for international business research and practice

Beyond the study of international relations (IR) and its emphasis on cross-border elite business model practice, the ETED's system, conceptual elements, and SVC measurements, aspire to open avenues for research in the academic field of international business (IB). A number of testable hypotheses are now put forward for experimental scrutiny.

Rugman, Verbeke, and Nguyen demonstrate "that the three key units of analysis in IB theory over the past fifty years have been the country, the firm (MNE) and the subsidiary" (2011, p. 777). In the context of the ETED, the meso-level elite quality measurement (EQx) is an analytical instrument for the country unit, while the key micro-level sustainable value creation measurement (VCr) targets the MNE and subsidiary units. Consequently, SVC measurements might be used as independent variables to contribute to IB research streams in various ways, for example, to assess the degree of internationalization (DOI) (Sullivan, 1994; Ramaswamy, Kroeck, & Renforth, 1996), to consider performance patterns (Ruigrok & Wagner, 2003; Contractor, 2007), or to add to theories of FDI (Buckley & Casson, 1976; Rugman, 1981; Glaum & Oesterle, 2007). SVC measurements might also warrant introduction into frameworks integrating country-specific advantage (CSA) and firm-specific advantage (FSA) (Rugman, Verbeke, & Nguyen, 2011). The consistent 'value is created or transferred' ontology of the elite theory (see Figure A5.4a) throughout its micro/meso/macro analytical levels (shown in Figure 3.8), and the articulation of the transmission mechanisms at work across these, is expressly adept at clarifying in novel ways the logic and connections between the country (host/home) and the firm (MNE/subsidiary) in the context of IB.

The propensity of a country's MNEs to internationalize might associate with national elite quality (EQx). Outward FDI can be "undertaken as [an] escape response to perceived misalignment between firm needs and home country institutional conditions" (Witt & Lewin, 2007, p. 579), as an escape response from "institutional fragility" (Shi, Sun, Yan, & Zhang, 2017), or as an escape response from problematic elite quality and intra-elite contest dynamics. The theoretical explanation for a positive correlation would be that firms in a country that is characterized by extractive transfers (with low VCr) are less competitive and thus less adept at entering foreign markets. If negative correlation patterns between the two variables emerge, an alternate theoretical explanation is required, with international expansion financed through rent seeking in the home country, which is in turn associated with low elite quality. This might have been the case with Japanese firms in the 1980s; the acquisition of the Rockefeller Center by Mitsubishi Estate in 1989 came at the very peak of Japan's asset bubble and the copious availability of cheap finance for the country's elite groups. In a similar vein, leading Spanish firms internationalized from the mid-1990s—with a primary focus on Latin America and its telecommunications, energy, and finance sectors—though in later years saw "the situation change drastically, as new competitors have emerged to undermine Spain's importance as an investor in the region" (Sánchez Díez, Galaso Reca, & García de la Cruz, 2017, p. 51). The falsifiable hypothesis is whether the original wave of FDI was enabled by value transfers such as the oligopolistic positions taken in the home market along with the new opportunities to access finance afforded by European integration and expectations of the then impending Economic and Monetary Union (1999), or whether these moves towards internationalization were driven by the ability of Spanish MNEs to create more value than their competitors.

The overall testable idea is that overseas sustainable value creation strategies (measured by either the SVC metrics of the IB-VCr or by IB-self-VCr questionnaires) have a causal relationship with home country cross-border sustainable value creation, either with the world in general (measured by cb-EQr) or with the particular destination (measured by the bl-EQr). The default position for the Japanese and Spanish cases above, or for MNEs based anywhere else, is that the less extractive a business model is domestically (e.g., by having a high VCr), the more competitive and inclusive it is likely to be internationally (reflected by a high IB-VCr). This is not inconsistent with Dunning's stress on "location *per se* as a variable affecting the global competitiveness of firms" (1998, p. 60). Subsequent inquiry would determine whether the host country elite quality (EQx) or the home country cross-border elite quality (cb-EQr) is the stronger factor in IB strategy and performance, and to what extent these are related or independent from each other. The host country perspective is essential, as MNEs with high sustainable value creation might shun markets with comparatively low elite quality (EQx) systems that may prejudice their competitive advantage, compromise their IP, or have governance practices that are perceived to be too risky. The degree to which elite quality is a determinant of sovereign/country risk is a critical supplementary question for international finance.

In Section 5.3.2, the discussion on valuation frameworks for sustainable value creation noted that elite quality (EQr or EQx) could function as a moderator for country risk, and hence be a predictor of sovereign credit ratings useful for modeling debt yield spreads. The practical question that Damodaran (2023, p. 5) asks the individual MNE is: "Are you exposed to more risk when you invest in some countries than others?" The consideration of value creation/extraction (through the EQx or EQr) would help to quantify an answer. From an equity perspective, if elite quality is distinct from institutional quality, applying the research design of Winful, Sarpong, and Agyei-Ntiamoah (2016), might identify a novel driver for stock market performance. At the individual firm level, combining the contextual national elite quality scores with a VCr asset pricing "factor" in the manner of Fama and French (2015) could offer fresh insights. Other impacts associated with the relationship between elite quality and risk would be relevant to both international economics and IB. For example, FDI location-choice models (Che, Du, Lu, & Tao, 2023) could be upgraded. To the extent that "institutional efficiency" (Aizenman & Spiegel, 2006; Jung, 2020), informal institutions (Seyoum, 2011; Khan, 2010), "institutional distance" (Cezar & Escobar, 2015), or "institutional overlap" (Maseland, 2017) matter for FDI inflows on a comparative basis (see Nielsen, Asmussen, & Weatherall, 2017; Bénassy-Quéré, Coupet, & Mayer, 2007; Huang, Gong, Sun, & Lin, 2023), so will elite quality given the two-way causal relationship (see Figure 6.1) where it functions as an antecedent to institutional quality. Of course, it is conceivable that certain FDI projects follow an inverse logic, and so Cuervo-Cazurra (2006, p. 807) finds that corruption impacts "the composition of country of origin of FDI". That is, MNEs adept at running domestic extractive value transfer business models (low VCr) might consider the high returns and high risk associated with low elite quality as an advantage when investing in countries, as their rentier models might be more easily accepted by the host country's elites and replicated. Subsidiaries would then develop the right connections with politicians and establish other non-institutionalized means of doing business to facilitate extractive and profitable practices abroad (low IB-VCr). An argument to counter this approach of turning risk to advantage is that domestic extractive elites, including local partners, would use their embeddedness advantage to pull the wool over the eyes of extractive foreign MNEs as soon as they became capable of running a comparable business model of their own.

A central area of IB research is foreign market entry mode. The leading scholars in this body of literature examine the antecedents, choices, and performance outcomes of international expansion (Brouthers, 2002; Shaver, 2013), and even debate the appropriateness of further entry mode research (Shaver, 2013; Hennart & Slangen, 2015). Schellenberg, Harker, and Jafari (2018, p. 7) point out that comparative dependent variables used for modal choices include: "Wholly Owned Subsidiary versus Joint Venture, Acquisitions versus Joint Venture, Export versus Foreign Direct investment, and contract versus Equity Joint Venture (Morschett, Schramm-Klein, & Swoboda, 2010); [and] Acquisitions over Greenfield (Chen, 2008; Slangen & Hennart, 2008)". Since entry mode choice is informed by culture (Kogut & Singh, 1988) and formal and informal institutions (see Meyer, Estrin, Bhaumik, & Peng 2009; Khan, 2010; Fuentelsaz, Garrido, & Maicas, 2020), it might also be influenced by elite quality. A set of testable hypotheses related to this work could be designed to ascertain whether the host country's (low/high) elite quality (measured by the EQr or the EQx) guides decision-making on whether to pursue M&As over greenfield strategies, or the joint venture mode over a wholly owned subsidiary. Additionally, if elite quality is associated with risk and transaction cost expectations, one might conjecture that host nation elite quality influences the degree of control (Gatignon & Anderson, 1988) that MNEs wish to exert over their foreign subsidiaries.

More generally, how "emergent" is strategy (Mintzberg & Waters, 1985) for an MNE? Is its practice informed by the elite quality trends of home and host nations, and if so, to what extent? A specific area of interest for researchers would be to assess over time the existence of purported 'chameleon effects', where MNE business models adapt the sustainable value creation of their overseas subsidiaries to local elite quality. Specifically, are the international business value creation ratings (IB-VCr) of Chinese or American subsidiaries the same in Switzerland as they are in Latin America? Will a particular MNE maintain its domestic high value creation model (high VCr) abroad or, as time goes by, choose to pursue extractive business models on the back of bargaining power differentials when it learns how to navigate the institutional deficiencies of the host market to extract rents (through directed wins in the local political non-market contest arena)? Are tax privileges, IP and other property protections, or access to government procurement programs evidence of MNE bargaining power differentials and to what extent do these emanate from strategies that leverage the home country's changing position in the international system (as posited in Sections 7.3.3 and 7.3.4) or from FSA and firm-specific capabilities (see Cantwell, 2014) such as superior technology? A particularly informative approach in addressing such questions is to check for differences between the sustainable value creation of the MNE headquarters and that of its subsidiaries (i.e., if the VCr is higher than the IB-VCr, state power must play some role).

Further to the economic questions on trade and FDI flows raised earlier (Section 7.1.4), including the discussion on Elite Quality Distance (EQ-dist), there is another area where IB and economic development meet that is especially relevant to policy: the incentive structures and patterns for FDI flows when income levels and elite quality scores are jointly considered for the respective home and host countries. Tang and Buckley (2022, p. 323) find that for emerging market MNEs there is an "asymmetric effect of institutional distance in different directions and in different FDI decisions, thereby offering solid and nuanced evidence to the directionality logic of institutional distance". Emerging-to-emerging market, advanced-to-emerging market, emerging-to-advanced market, or advanced-to-advanced market FDI (and possibly financial portfolio investment flows) might all display discrete elite quality pairing directions and patterns. For example, if MNEs "coming from countries with better institutions than China are more sensitive to the institutional difference" (Che, Du, Lu, & Tao, 2023, p. 1934), does this hold for elite quality differentials elsewhere? Such findings would have normative implications on policy issues like the liberalization and opening up of trade, placing the spotlight on an underexplored mechanism: foreign entrants with comparatively high sustainable value creation positions might *a priori* contribute to transformation of local elites through Tier 4 'across-system' checks and balances (see Section 7.3.1; Figure A5.11b), bringing about higher elite quality in the host country (to the degree permitted by intra-elite contests and the related rules). MNEs with high cross-border sustainable value creation (IB-VCr) ought to be welcomed by inclusive elite coalitions in host countries to encourage weighted structural reforms. Dau, Moore, and Newburry (2020) find that cross-country investments have an impact on home and host country CSR reputation signaling. From a policy perspective, high national elite quality (EQx/EQr/PEz) scores (particularly when these are increasing as a consequence of reforms, see Section 7.1.5) are a fundamental signal that countries emit. Whether implicitly understood or reflected in sovereign risk evaluations, they attract high value creation elite business models from abroad (e.g., to Singapore), but also ensure a warm welcome for a country's firms when these expand into foreign markets (e.g., Swiss MNEs).

One way to test some of the above ideas would be to establish a model where the dependent variable is divestment (the failure of FDI, see Sethuram & Gaur, 2024) and the independent variable is elite quality, operationalized through the EQ-dist measurement (that establishes the elite quality distance between any pair of countries). While van Hoorn and Maseland claim "that current institutional research in international business is unable to explain how institutions matter for MNEs and that a more careful theoretical and empirical distinction between the effects of institutions and institutional distance on cross-border business activities is essential" (2016, p. 374), Beugelsdijk, Ambos, and Nell published work on the "international business research workhorse" nature of "the distance construct" and the "impassioned" discussions around its operationalization (2018, p. 1113). Most of the latter's recommendations are integrated into the EQ-dist by design. Foreign market entry mode choices, international diversification, and MNE performance have all been linked to two constructs widely used in the IB literature (Shenkar, 2001): cultural distance (Tihanyi, Griffith, & Russell, 2005) and institutional distance, "broadly defined as the difference between the institutional profiles of two countries"[206] (Kostova, Beugelsdijk, Scott, Kunst, Chua,

206 This statement is referenced to define EQ-dist as the difference between the elite quality profiles of two countries.

& van Essen, 2020, p. 468). This is unsurprising because "essentially, international management is management of distance" (Zaheer, Schomaker, & Nachum, 2012, p. 19). Following an approach akin to that taken by Mohr, Batsakis, and Stone (2018),[207] and with control variables that could include firm size (employees, assets, sales), DOI, year dummies, product diversification, competitive pressure, added cultural distance, firm age, and home market size, the hypotheses to be tested would include whether the greater the distance in elite quality (EQ-dist) between the home and host country, the greater the likelihood of divestment within a certain period (e.g., three years) after entry. Alternatively, researchers could investigate whether the positive relationship between EQ-dist and divestment becomes less pronounced when the investing firm has had a long-term prior presence in the host country.

The possibility of attaining novel understandings of organizational behavior in the international context with consequences for both practice and policy motivate the application of the conceptual elements of the ETED and its global and comparative SVC measurements to the IB research field.

207 Discussions with Dimitrios Georgakakis, Professor of International Business at Leeds University Business School, have informed this proposition for future research.

Summary of Chapter 7

The implications of the ETED

Chapter 7 covers the conceivable repercussions of the ETED's sustainable value creation conceptual elements for practice and research. The macro-level policy implications (7.1) are considered first before the discussion moves on to firm-level implications (7.2), and finally to implications in the international context (7.3).

Section 7.1 applies the two-way causal relationship between elites and institutions (Figure 3.2) to practice, and, on the premise that elite business model transformation antecedes sustainable institutional change, reviews policy. First, the general implications of the ETED for the economic policy mix (Figure 7.1) are discussed with an emphasis on weighted and targeted long-run structural reform measures (7.1.1). Then, the discrete implications for emerging (7.1.2) and advanced (7.1.3) economies are considered and the 'advanced economies have a higher sensitivity to elite quality' conjecture is proposed. Selected research directions and their relevance for policy are discussed (7.1.4), followed by an examination of the implications for policymakers (7.1.5) with the suggested 'A Weighted Structural Reform Policy Framework' for policy (Table 7.1). The analytical position includes an admonition against mishandling broad and short-run fiscal and monetary levers in favor of weighting and offsetting value transfers for tailored industry-by-industry approaches to enhance value creation via micro-interventions that adjust the incentive system. The role of knowledge elites in targeted structural reforms, the potential of 'weighted transfers modeling' (more formally referred to as the 'weighted transfers general equilibrium' macroeconomic model, or 'WTGE'), and the need for consistent narratives is emphasized throughout.

Section 7.2 reviews the firm-level implications of the ETED for elite business model transformation and for recognizing sustainability as value creation. It starts (7.2.1) with the implications of sustainable value creation at the organizational level. 'The Sustainable Value Matrix' performance framework for management (Figure 7.2) links sustainable value creation (VCr) on the x-axis and firm performance (profits) on the y-axis to derive a typology of four business model classifications: (1) 'sustainable'; (2) 'naïve'; (3) 'rentier'; and (4) 'living-dead'. The subsequent sub-section (7.2.2) explores the implications of sustainable value creation at the board level, shifting the current debate beyond the conventional CSR and ESG discourse by suggesting that the raison d'être of governance should be the alignment of residual income and economic development with the explicit aim of minimizing extractive transfers from stakeholders. Next (7.2.3), the implications of sustainable value creation at the intra-organizational level are outlined with the universal dualism that 'producers' (inclusive individual value creators) and 'takers' (individual beneficiaries of transfers from value creators) exist inside any organization or social unit (including families); their relative weight within the whole dictates collective success or failure. This leads to consideration of the implications of sustainability for leadership (7.2.4). The typology of the five varieties of elite leadership

(Table 7. 2) includes two 'transformational' types at the firm and elite system levels that are essential for inclusive economic development. Then, the discussion moves to the implications of sustainable value creation for investors (7.2.5). 'The Sustainable Value Matrix' provides the basis for 'The Sustainable Finance Matrix' framework for investments (Figure 7.3) which also links the key firm-level sustainable value creation measurement (VCr) on the x-axis and firm performance (profits) on the y-axis to derive four investment category quadrants: (1) 'sustainable'; (2) 'non-profitable'; (3) 'non-sustainable'; and (4) 'non-investable'. In the closing sub-section (7.2.6), the comprehensive value creation perspective is captured through the 'The Value Transfer Strategy Matrix', a sustainability framework for firm principals and stakeholders (Figure 7.4) that sheds light on one the most consequential characteristics of strategy, that which associates with the quantity of a firm's inclusive/extractive value transfers. The VCr on the x-axis denotes a range from value 'keeper' to 'giver' (with its positive value transfer-OUT focus), while the VCp on the y-axis denotes a range from value 'extractive' to 'inclusive' (on account of its extractive value transfer-IN focus). The ensuing four strategies are then defined as: (1) 'inclusive giver'; (2) 'extractive giver'; (3) 'inclusive keeper'; and (4) 'extractive keeper' (or 'taker').

Section 7.3 shifts gear to examine the implications of the ETED through an international lens. In the first sub-section (7.3.1), a realist-leaning conceptualization contributes to international relations (IR) by stressing that state behavior in the international system is motivated by domestic elite business models that pursue institutional change to facilitate cross-border value creation and appropriation. The SVC measurements introduced here are the 'Cross-border Elite Quality Rating' ('cb-EQr') that assesses 'country A vs the world'; the 'Bilateral Elite Quality Rating' ('bl-EQr') for 'country A vs country B'; and a firm-level counterpart, the International Business Value Creation Rating (IB-VCr). 'The Global Influence of the Elite System Framework' for international relations (Figure 7.5), combines domestic elite quality (EQx/EQr) on the x-axis with cross-border elite quality (cb-EQr/bl-EQr) on the y-axis. The ensuing four elite system characterizations are: (1) 'global public bads'; (2) 'global subsidizer'; (3) 'global extractive'; and (4) 'global public goods'. The focus of the following sub-section (7.3.2) is on the non-aggregated and practical view of the cross-border elite business model and the distributional outcomes resulting from cross-border division of value strategies (Table 7.3). Insights are also made on the topic of war, and the 'peace through cross-border elite business models' conjecture argues for two interdependencies in international relations as guarantors of peace: cross-border elite business models and elite coalitions with members from diverse states. Next, the international implications of elite system leadership are discussed (7.3.3), suggesting lifecycle patterns for the rise and fall of states in the international system brought about by domestic and cross-border elite quality patterns (Figure 7.7). In 'The Great Power Elite Quality Lifecycle' for international relations, leading nations may emerge out of transformational leadership towards higher domestic elite quality that augments state power and supports increasingly effective value appropriation by cross-border elite business models. As with firms, the fall of a state is argued to be the final consequence of power endowments outpacing value creation and then being leveraged for extractive transfers. Comparative elite system performance for advanced economies requires institutional arrangements that include incentives for bottom-up value creation (a vibrant polis) as well as the power of a top-down elite system to protect a state from cross-border transfer-OUT (a strong empire). This 'polis in empire' framework is used to understand Europe's future given its current partial elite or elite non-system (7.3.4). The elite non-system issue is also salient if the world is to avoid a global tragedy of the AI commons (7.3.5). Finally, novel possibilities for international business (IB) research are considered (7.3.6).

With the introduction of cross-border measurements, this chapter concludes the main operationalization aims for sustainable value creation in the context of an elite theory of economic development, which have already commenced with the Elite Quality Index (EQx). While many measurements have been described in this text, more are either already in existence or in the process of being developed, while yet others are slated as projects for further inquiry. A visual recap of the SVC measurements family is provided in Figure 7.8 (a descriptive summary is offered in Table A3.1a). These can be grouped according to the domestic/international perspective and the micro/meso/macro analysis level into six categories (i to vi) in which each of the 18 selected measurements belong (the numbers in brackets and in the figure approximate the realization sequence):

The (i) domestic/micro measurements are: self-VCp[2], self-VCr[3], VCp[4], VCr[5], 360-VCz[12], and 'The Five SVC Valuation Frameworks[17];
the (ii) international/micro measurements are: IB-self-VCr[12] and IB-VCr[13];
the (iii) domestic/meso measurements are: PEz[7], EQr[9], and sector-VCr[18];
the (iv) international/meso measurements are: EQx[1], EQ-dist[6], world-EQ[8], cb-EQr[14], and bl-EQr[15];
the (v) domestic/macro measurement is the WTGE[10] macroeconomic model;
the (vi) international/macro measurement is the G-WTGE [16] macroeconomic model.

All SVC measurements can supply insights for political economy AI services such as the 'chatbotEQx' (see Chen, Lu, Scherl, & Sutter, 2025). Two of these underpin the approximation of a 'political economy omniscience' of value transfers that could eventually matter to economics, management, politics, and finance—the WTGE[10] and the GWTGE[16]—conceived to realize 'weighted transfer modeling'. Their relationship to a postulated 'weighted transfers game'—the domestic WT-Game and the global GWT-Game—as well as to the ind-VCr for individuals, is depicted in Figure A5.10, while their ability to shed light on value flows across society's groups is shown in Figure set A5.14. Moving on from the dense set of implications of the ETED considered in Chapter 7, the closing chapter of this book takes a singular and final turn on elite leadership by adopting the non-elite perspective, revealing the speculative and pragmatic philosophies of the ETED, and articulating the ethical system the theory suggests.

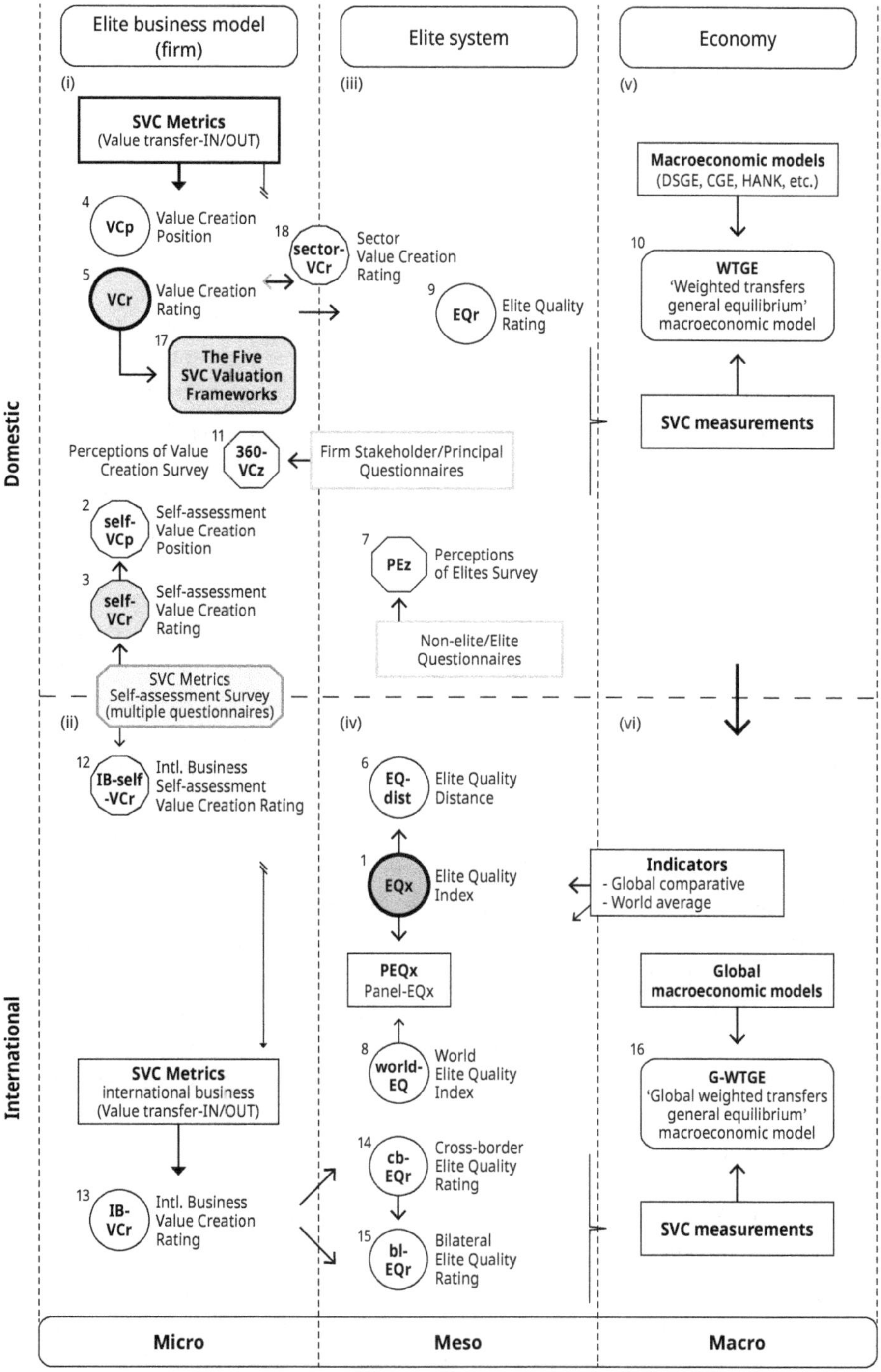

Figure 7.8: Overview of the sustainable value creation (SVC) measurements of the ETED.

Chapter 8
Leadership, ethics, and non-elites

> Zarathustra responded:
> Why are you startled by this? – But it is with human beings as it is with this tree.
> The more they aspire to the heights and the light, the more strongly their roots strive earthward, downward, into darkness, depths – into evil.
> (Nietzsche's *Thus Spoke Zarathustra*, 1883/2006, p. 89)

In the less poetic terms of this inquiry, this piece of common of knowledge is articulated as meaning that extractive value transfers are a prerequisite for inclusive value creation. What then are the respective weights of the roots in darkness and the branches in the light? Zarathustra, philosophers, and anyone steeped in good sense knows that with risk, success and failure are two sides of the same coin, and so value creation and extraction together comprise the problem that this closing chapter addresses: the realist inference of the pragmatic philosophy where 'all elite agency creates and transfers value'. Many of the societal dilemmas that arise from such a dualism are solvable through weighting.

The ETED has asserted that the elite business models of the political economy invariably profit from value transfers, i.e., rely on value appropriated but *not* created. Even high quality elites that practice sustainable value creation will extract value from some stakeholders. There is thus a degree of relativism when considering value transfers, and so—as with Zarathustra's acumen—are ethics thus invalidated in this elite theory? Moreover, the centrality of elites to this theory leaves it open to criticisms of elitism, reactionary conservatism, and overstating elite agency in relation to other causes of development and institutional change. This seems an inescapable charge, even when sustainable value creation is argued to be the defining characteristic for Pareto's "best". The iron law of elite dominance is fully integrated into this account of human and economic development, meaning that elite leadership of the transformational variety brings about more inclusive development than any set of checks and balances, elections, or revolutions, and subjecting this book to the reproach that it theorizes about elites for the benefit of elites. On the other hand, the general condemnation of unsustainable rent seeking made throughout this work also aligns it with progressive and liberal ideas.

Any economic development theory will strike dissonant notes with one or another coalition whose interests don't align with its prescriptions, particularly when self-serving value transfer activities are compromised; for example, free trade is despised by mercantilist coalitions, free labor markets by many unions, and competitive markets by capitalist monopolists. Theories on a technical quest for truth that are exposed to narrative markets must be open to legitimate contributions from all sides of the socio-economic and political spectra while accepting the resistance of those at the

https://doi.org/10.1515/9783110734638-012

receiving end of any distributional consequences. This forces an economic idea to seek legitimacy from a fundamental understanding of how the world works and works best; that is, from sources deeper than political and economic expediency and more permanent than its capture by winning narratives, whatever their power or ideological hue. Making the ethical position explicit therefore seems to be a necessity for an economic theory or body of thought seeking to impact human welfare. How is ethics then understood in this work?

Ethics is the reflection of 'what I should do', a formal structure for moral positions on what is right, how to behave, and what are rightful acts. A set of ethical principles for this work will have boundaries and can only have claims on what is right within the scope for economic and human development. Only if sustainable value creation is deemed to have an intrinsic value *beyond* human and economic development should there be license to extend its application to other domains.

Sustainability is the privilege to appropriate value created while eschewing value appropriated but *not* created in a proportion that bests average elite agency. These aims may sound modest but are sufficient and feasible. That is how business models inch the aggregate upwards and move societies forward. What then could be a corresponding ethical basis for human and economic development? This work's narrative centers on boosting value creation and limiting value transfers that are, in practice, instantiated with transformational leadership in the context of intra-elite contests. Must ethical principles for development then contradict the 'elite utility function' upon which the behavioral logic of elite agency rests in this inquiry (see Proposition 5)? To add necessary nuance to the long-run utility maximization imperative, this chapter dips into speculative philosophy to suggest that the 'value appropriation demand of humans' (the basic socio-economic constraint of the human condition) rests on general principles of life that are in contradiction, include radical creativity, and yet are economically judicious (Figure 8.6) and reduce local entropy. First, and more deliberately, how can criteria—and thereafter guardrails—be established to ascertain how, when, and to what degree elite value appropriation ought to be constrained?

Elites are characterized by their power; their agency realized by 'the extraordinary lever' and its multiplier. It is power that enables value and risk transfers *and* creation, the appropriation of both value created and value *not* created. The decision not to exercise the option to benefit from value transfers for the sake of economic and human development is a moral choice consistent with ethical principles. The roving bandit who becomes stationary is essentially moral and ethical, as well as being a successful utility maximizer when taking a longer view (again, see Section 2.1.1), constraining power, forfeiting immediate residual income, and ultimately allowing stakeholders to appropriate a larger portion of the value that they create. It is equally ethical—though perhaps not moral—to employ power in a more disagreeable manner: to effect weighted and offset value transfers. Both ethical approaches, whether undertaken jointly or separately, increase the sustainability of the elite business model. Self-constraints on one's agency, as well as the targeted use of power to extract value, are pursued by core and other coalitions for the sake of the sustainability of the polity and to preserve their elite identity. Power and wealth distribution are emergent properties of a political economy system that can be both sustainable and unsustainable. Elite transformational leadership is the realization of mindful choices to weight and offset transfers that correspond with ethical positions. Anchored by the 'inextinguishable value creation option of elites' (leadership) premise that directly emanates from the creative self-assertion found in the 'Will to Power', such decisions are both challenging and deserving of recognition because they mean foregoing extraction despite possessing power differentials over stakeholders that permit perfectly legal value transfers.

With this, the inquiry can wholly move from 'as is' to 'as ought to be' territory via the onramps provided throughout the book. These include the transformational leadership conceptual element that is acutely cognizant of balance when negotiating the reality that 'all elite agency creates and transfers value', for instance, in 'alternating value transfers and creation' or when uncertainty is undertaken. Understandably, readers that require economic inquiry to stay focused on the analytical plane of incentives will downplay this appeal for ethical agency.

The ETED proposes a 'set of ethical principles' for economic and human development. These seven principles work on the ontological assumption that describes the dualistic nature of socio-economic relations: 'value is created or transferred'. The set's imperative is the pursuit of sustainable value creation by nuancing binary choices through the proper weighting of value transfers. The intrinsic value[208] for development, the hypernorm operationalized as a central doctrine, is the simple maxim:

(i) *To the creators the value created*

The sustainable value creation maxim would rest on and be qualified by two tenets that provide conceptual guidance for elite agency:

(ii) *Maximize first-order value creation and risk origination for productive economic transformations fit for human purpose*
(iii) *Weight and offset second-order value and risk transfers and minimize these to maximize value*

Elites seeking development for their nation and planning to realize the value creation maxim and its two derived tenets for elite agency are served by a set of precepts that provide practical guidance. The four precepts for action that inform transformational leadership are:

208 Intrinsic values "reflect intrinsic worth and constitute non-instrumental reasons for justifying choice (Donaldson & Walsh, 2015; O'Neill, 1992; Rønnow-Rasmussen, 2015)" while their "underlying epistemic role [. . .] is to complete the justification of an action" (Donaldson, 2021, p. 3). As such they are "hypernorms", "principles so fundamental to human existence that they serve as a guide in evaluating lower level moral norms" (Donaldson & Dunfee, 1994, p. 265). Note also the sustainability of "universal values" that "*connect humans and nature in an acausal, coherent manner* [emphasis in original]" (O'Brien et al., 2023, p. 1452).

(iv) *Measure value and risk transfers and establish the optimal weightings and potential offsets to maximize sustainable value creation*
(v) *Realize sustainable value creation and risk origination incentives through top-down weighted structural reforms and bottom-up elite business model transformation*
(vi) *Invest in elite cohesion and in the elite separation of powers with a comprehensive set of checks and balances to encourage productive intra-elite contests*
(vii) *Promote the freedom to* exit *and the freedom* to *create value irrespective of optimal value creation, transfer weightings, and potential offsets*

With the sustainable value creation set of ethical principles for human and economic development (see the concise summary in Table A4.3a), the ETED endeavors to provide decision-making guidance based on a realistic account of how the political economy works. The codification of the set of ethical principles into law then becomes the legal foundation for economic and human development. An incentive system is thus built for those *qui generat valorem*. But does this proposal have admissible links to generally accepted ideas in the realms of morality or philosophy?

Ethics framed in sociobiological or evolutionary theory terms (as in Dawkins, 1976; Alexander, 1987; de Waal, 2006) would seem highly valid, as notions not antithetical to nature such as reciprocity and empathy are appropriate bases for moral systems.[209] Conversely, ethical notions can underlie social constructs, especially those focused on real-world application. CSR frameworks, for instance, have always been infused with moral considerations and the "ethical principles that ought to govern the relationship between the corporation and society" (Eetls & Walton, 1961, as cited in Carroll, 1991, pp. 39–40). The fact that "tensions and trade-offs inevitably arise" between economic or legal obligations and ethics (Carroll, 2016, p. 5) is precisely what gives purpose to the latter. This inquiry must naturally stay within the confines of economic development: the set of ethical principles function as a prescriptive baseline for both research and practice and so might be a touchstone for elites able and willing

209 Nature appropriates before it reproduces in line with the 'universal extraction propensity of life'. To this inquiry, the main difference between animals and humans is the degree of value appropriated but *not* created. Animals will only interact with stakeholders (through the predation of predator and prey, through commensalism, through mutualism, and through the parasitism of host and symbiont) with whom they have a physical relationship, a limitation that constrains extraction. Because of social order, the human with 'the extraordinary lever' can extract not just from the stakeholder he or she is in direct contact with, but also from the next and all subsequent others in the hierarchy as value flows along complex chains from the top to the bottom (see Section 1.3.4). The leverage that is intrinsic to complex social relationships explains both the marvel and menace of the human capacity for value appropriation—both from other humans and from nature—to a degree that is countless orders of magnitude greater than that of any other living beings. It also suggests that superintelligences roving the Internet or otherwise embedded in social networks—perhaps on behalf of their human owners or perhaps for themselves—will have an almost unlimited capacity for value appropriation from human stakeholders.

to shape the elite system and institutions. At the same time, this work does not intend to succumb to the common and well-known contradiction that is articulated by Schopenhauer: "Thus preaching morality is easy, yet grounding morality is difficult"[210] (1867, p. 140). The weighting and offsetting approach precludes moral absolutism, declines both Platonic and Utopian approaches (Popper, 1947) as well as Kantian deontological ethics and categorical imperatives. Nietzsche's tree metaphor stands as the antithesis of such black and white morality while, as is argued in Section 8.2.2, the problem of evil is not at all relativized and an approach to its mitigation is proposed. To put it simply, although ethics can be technically shelved for the theory's system and its conceptual elements, the set of ethical principles offers a prescriptive key for their application. This holds even more validity when we consider that leadership moderates the relationship between elite business model division of value strategies and institutional change preferences that surface on the back of all technological, economic, and social shifts.

The elite theory must acknowledge the diverse ethical considerations that underlie existing policy, especially those seeking to regulate the extant technological revolution. For instance, those espoused by the EU's Directorate-General for Internal Market, Industry, Entrepreneurship and SMEs in its press release on *Artificial Intelligence: Commission Kicks off Work on Marrying Cutting-edge Technology and Ethical Standards* (2018), or the first "specific objective" of the EU's Artificial Intelligence Act's regulatory framework, which exhorts companies to "respect existing law on fundamental rights and Union values" (European Commission, 2021, p. 3). Anthropic's (2023) pragmatic Responsible Scaling Policy (RSP) provides "techniques like Constitutional AI for alignment with human values". The release of GPT-4 was a clarion call for the prioritization of ethics, and has added impetus to civil society initiatives, global conferences, and political initiatives such as the EU's AI Act to realize the "trustworthy AI" objective via regulation "to ensure that fundamental rights, democracy, the rule of law and environmental sustainability" (European Parliament, 2023). However, for the purposes of this inquiry, any ethical inputs on fundamental rights, trustworthiness, or human values must be well-defined and possess a degree of consistency with the normative frame of reference: *To the creators the value created* and the other elements of the set of ethical principles for human and economic development. In this final chapter, AI is addressed in a specific thematic thread as a shift-inducing technological, economic, and social force of historical proportions to imagine a range of elite judgments that need to be made on the potential futures of the political economy. Conceived partly as a thought experiment, the thread even extends to scenarios where the AI has putative elite agency and so stress tests the ETED's system, its ethics, many of its

210 Translated from the original, "Da ergiebt sich, daß Moral-Predigen leicht, Moral-Begründen schwer ist."

conceptual elements, and the theoretical limits of sustainable value creation for human development.[211]

While this inquiry and the set of ethical principles put forward places the agency and roles of non-elites as subordinate to elites, they are not passed over and so the first section of this review on leadership and ethics considers their interests in the context of normative political economy (8.1). The ethics of this work are then brought to life through the examination of a particular 'license for evil'—an elite business model that charges in pounds of flesh—before moving onto frameworks for determining acceptable levels of transfers and redistribution (8.2). This lays the groundwork for a pivot towards a closing reflection that connects the dots to consider this inquiry's speculative philosophy and its notion of freedom (8.3).

8.1 The non-elite perspective

In order for a nation to develop, non-elites should progressively retain a greater proportion of the value they create, while elites progressively refrain from using their power to benefit from value appropriated but *not* created. At the same time, the discussion of the non-elite perspective eschews the idealist notion that non-elites cannot be extractive, and requires consideration of the 'universal value extraction propensity of humans' (socio-economic) premise, without which development cannot be conceived. From Aristotle's (1912) harsh judgment on democracy and mob rule to the totalitarian mass movements in 20th century Europe, it is more than obvious that non-elites can extract from other non-elites, and be bereft of empathy, reciprocity, or morality. Moreover, non-elites must be called out when they are willing accessories to and marginally profit from extractive elite business models that use their power over 'other' non-elite groups. This section begins the analysis with a discussion (8.1.1) of the socio-economic structure pyramid, before shifting its focus to the role of the core elite coalition (8.1.2). It then considers the aggregate political options for non-elites to minimize extractive value transfers and matches these to the political options of elites (8.1.3). Following that, the framework is applied in a brief exploration of what might happen to non-elite interests if and when all humans—including members of current

211 The preliminary step in probing the role of the AI is to consider the world's missing elite system through the lens of the tragedy of the AI commons (Section 7.3.5). The theoretical examination proceeds by reviewing how elites can serve non-elite interests in a postulated post-singularity (Section 8.1.4), and how the value appropriation of AI business models impact redistribution (Section 8.2.5). Before the closing reflections (Section 8.3.3) and the Epilogue, the thematic thread ventures into the unchartered territory of how ethics might function in a political economy without human elites (Section 8.1.6). A side analysis also considers the set of ethical principles adapted for the AI (Table A4.3b), and a series of tentative hypotheses on the AI and sustainable value creation in the political economy are provided (Table E.1).

elite coalitions—are relegated to the non-elite strata in a hypothetical post-singularity world dominated by the AI in possession of absolute elite agency (8.1.4). Thereafter, the section proceeds with an examination of business and political systems—both democratic and authoritarian—through the optics of 'A Political and Business Systems Sustainable Value Creation (SVC) Test' that focuses on value creation outcomes and non-elites (8.1.5). In closing, the section re-enters the brave new world of the superintelligence to imagine what the boundaries of ethics might be across higher and lower intelligences in a political economy bereft of human elites (8.1.6).

8.1.1 The elite-centric socio-economic structure

Any elite theory in the social sciences makes specific assumptions about the socio-economic structure and membership of the resultant classes. Applying the doctrine of parsimony to the ETED's focus on business models and bargaining power differentials yields a socio-economic structure with a simple division between elites and non-elites. Elites are principals and beneficiaries of the highest value creation business models in the economy, while non-elite groups are the stakeholders of those models. Further to the elite/non-elite dichotomy and the discussion on power in functional terms (see Figure A5.1), this inquiry's socio-economic structure is conceived as a hierarchy. This is represented as a pyramid, with one particular class in each of the elite and non-elite strata emphasized due to their theoretical relevance for development (see Figure 8.1). The elite system is first characterized by (1.a) the 'core elite coalition' in the highest socio-economic position. This coalition is part and parcel of the (1) 'elites', which includes the (1.b) members of all 'regular' coalitions that are beneficiaries of the residual income flows of elite business models. Next, and lower down the hierarchy is the (2.a) 'managerial, technical, and creative class', also referred to as the expert class and by Mosca as the "second stratum" (1939, p. 404), a "sub-elite" (Sharma, 1977, p. 70) through which the elite "is intimately connected with society" (Bottomore, 1993, p. 5). In terms of policymaking or institutional change, these "professional experts" and "servants of power" have some influence (Brint, 1990, p. 361). Yet this class possesses no claims to the residual income of elite business models and so is also part of the (2) 'non-elites', the main body of the ETED's socio-economic structure pyramid, which includes (2.b) the population at large—all other individuals in society.[212]

212 While the membership of each strata and class varies because of factors like country size, social complexity and developmental stage, estimates of the number of individuals in each of the socio-economic structure's categories can be made. Reeves and Friedman in *Born to Rule* estimate that the "wealth elite is made up of approximately 6,000 individuals, or 0.01 percent of the UK population" (2024, p. 6). Membership of the 'core elite coalition' (1.1) varies, but in the UK would be in the low

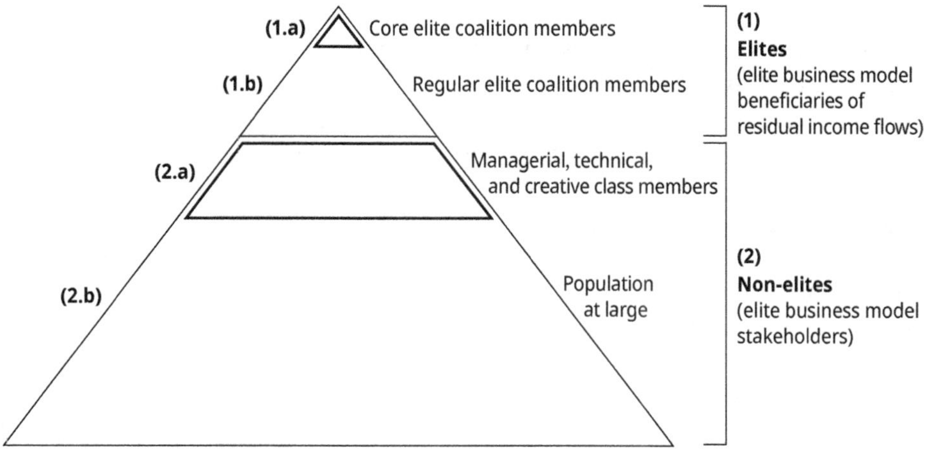

Figure 8.1: The socio-economic structure pyramid: Elite and non-elite strata with selected sub-categories.

The (2) non-elite general population is comprised of multiple groups. Their common denominator is that they are not beneficiaries of the residual income flows of elite business models. The 'non-elite quality' of each of these diverse groups—the sustainable value creation of discrete non-elite groups as stakeholders in their business models—varies from low to high, just as it does with elites (see Epilogue and Figure E.1). Again, those closest to the elites are the managerial, technical, and creative class, the experts noted above. Members of this class run and otherwise provide critical inputs to the elite business models of the business, political, and knowledge elite coalitions. They include executives, engineers, architects, doctors, academics and scientists, technology professionals, priests, lawyers, judges, journalists, military officers, civil servants, editors, influencers and so on. In order to fulfill their mandates and do their jobs, this "second stratum" borrows the power of the elite. At the same time, the elite system cannot function, cannot govern (see the "bureaucratic state", Marx, 1939), and authoritarian systems cannot command "the activities of the masses" (see Mosca, 1939, p. 404) without them. Members of the managerial, technical, and creative class are enormous value creators, and while wealthy, the echelon they occupy in the pyramid can be confused. Participation in the annual WEF meeting at Davos does not make one part of the elite; and neither does membership of Veblen's "leisure class" (1899/1924). It is also not sufficient to engage in society with "external, embodied and vicarious signs of superiority" like "an imposing air of determination" supported by "the exhibition of elitist connections" and the flaunting of "glamorous female company" (Daloz, 2010, pp. 4, 81, 94, 99). Again, to pass the elite membership test, one's power must afford stable claims on the residual

hundreds. A country's (2.1) 'managerial, administrative, and technical class' and their households could comprise between 5% and 15% of citizens in an advanced economy.

income of elite business models. Nevertheless, and assuming the existence of open social order access, members of this class are well positioned to circulate and transition to elite status. This occurs when they succeed in becoming principals of elite business models and hence significant beneficiaries of the residual income streams. When the barriers between elite and non-elite groups, especially between the elite and the non-elite managerial, technical, and creative class, are low, the admixture mode of elite circulation (see Figure 1.1.) becomes more likely. For example, while Jeff Bezos clearly availed himself of America's open access elite system, in other social settings and countries, members of the upper non-elite classes need the most unusual talents—and often the passing of generations—to break into elite status.

There is also a second and final leap—from being part of the elite to assuming core elite status. Regardless of the time that it takes, as in the Pippinids becoming the Carolingians or Tim Cook's rise to the stewardship of Apple, this is a daunting journey that caps an exceptional course of progress. All else being equal, high elite circulation velocity, while forever extraneous to nearly every non-elite individual, is posited to be a beneficial dynamic that fosters economic development.

8.1.2 The theoretical and applied role of the core elite coalition

> If 'all the 300 [top civil servants and political elite] were to crash in one jumbo jet, then Singapore will disintegrate' Prime Minster Lee Kuan Yew (1998, p. 315 as cited in Tan, 2008, pp.12–13)

The above reference to Singapore's legendary founding father illustrates how critical the role of the core elite coalition can be.[213] The notion of a core elite coalition is to be understood as the elite *primus inter pares*, those that Pareto (1968/1991) saw as having achieved hegemony "over all groups and all classes" (Busino, 2000, p. 225). Moore's effective fractal understanding of the elite system also sees a central role for this coalition: "The existence of a central elite circle facilitates communication and interaction both within that large, diverse group and between its members and those in more specialized elite circles and cliques" (1979, p. 689). Yet, unlike times past when kings, potentates, and their dynasties appeared to be immutable fixtures of the top echelon, membership of the core elite coalition in contemporary and advanced economies is more transient. Uncertainty is first faced by the individuals sitting at the core coalition table as to the length of their tenure in the coalition. Second, it is faced by the coalition itself in terms of whether it will retain its place at the core of the elite system or be on the losing side of an intra-elite contest. Third, it is faced in terms of whether the core coalition as a whole deploys its coordination capacity wisely to effectively

213 Today, the country is a very different place and there would be no disintegration—and possibly no decline in elite quality either—given the robustness of Singapore's narrative, its strong degree of elite cohesion, and the institutionalized nature of its intra-elite contests.

and legitimately lead the elite system. More than any other elite coalition, the core coalition is subject to the dynamics of intra-elite contests that challenge its claims to residual income, to cross-border challenges in a globalized world, to constant negotiations around institutional change and elite bargains, and to specific events like elections, technological disruptions, or black swans. The agency and reach of the core coalition in many countries is additionally limited by the fact that most elite coalitions will have ring-fenced their own nook and cranny of the economy, enjoying institutional immunity and a power base that the core coalition simply cannot penetrate.

In political economies with weak core elite coalitions, ascendant coalitions need not worry about obstacles to circulation, meaning that both progressive and regressive elite circulation is *a priori* possible (Section 1.3.2). It is conceivable that nominal core elite positions, even the top political office, are not especially desired, and possibly a burden better handed to ambitious individuals in the managerial, technical, and creative class. Most critically, members of the core coalition have limited influence on the outcomes of intra-elite contests (intra-elite power relation 7) that are then solely settled by the contenders. The core elite coalition may be little more than an observer, or a non-decisive supporter of a given elite coalition in contests that are eventually settled by direct bargaining power differentials and conventional elite business model leadership. This is the situation in many Western democracies. Elite cohesion and shared narratives are harder to maintain under such scenarios and thus become even more essential for sustainable value creation when they facilitate stable intra-elite contest rules. Any modicum of core elite agency adds to the general coordination capacity in the economy, to state capacity, and to elite system transformational leadership. At the other extreme, one finds a core coalition that is high-handed, stable, and continuously uses 'the extraordinary lever' for the meta-contest resolution of conflicts (see Section 4.3.2) and to decide which coalitions win intra-elite contests, perhaps under the purview of a single individual, as is the case with political leaders in authoritarian systems. The larger the multiplier effect in the 'the extraordinary lever' operated by the core elite coalition, the higher its impact on elite quality, for better or worse. Robinson points out that the elite "exercises decisive control over the organization of that society" with the important qualification that "this will be a matter of degree in reality" (2010, p. 3). The intensity with which the core elite coalition shapes the elite system ranges from extremely high in authoritarian systems to very low in democratic ones, though the correlation between the degree to which this associates with elite quality varies, as in democracy's relation to growth (e.g., Barro, 1996; Acemoglu, Naidu, Restrepo, & Robinson, 2019), and remains a matter for empirical validation (as is expounded on in Section 8.1.5).

Despite these qualifications on the variance that exists in the agency and power of a core elite coalition, they remain a useful conceptual element in the analysis of a political economy for two reasons. First, core coalitions can function as an extra layer of checks and balances. In a comprehensive five-tier elite separation of powers outlined in Figure 3.10, and further to the international 'across-system' Tier 4, a Tier 5 separation of powers describes the ability to scrutinize a country's contests 'from-core' (see Figures 3.10 and A5.11b), including those 'within-system' (Tier 3). Elite quality regulates development paths and the wealth of nations, with the core coalition's transformational impact tied closely to its ability to determine which particular elite coalitions—each carrying a specific degree of sustainable value creation—end up overseeing the elite business models in specific nooks and crannies of the economy. Since this additional 'Tier 5' separation of powers is conceived to function 'from-core', it provides a counterweight to the agency of any regular elite coalition (see Figure 3.10).

Second, as core coalitions either participate in or are themselves the national business model in areas like finance, security, real estate, government spending, or energy, they have a disproportionate impact on elite quality and development. Admittedly, while in some countries 'Tier 5' is unbalanced and the core coalition enjoys an oppressively strong influence on the elite system, in others it is weak and uncoordinated, suffering from dispersed power endowments that lack leverage over regular elites and are under constant pressure from them.

Regardless of how strong the core coalition is and how great its potential or actual transformational leadership capabilities, it is the regular elite business models that are the diagnostic focus of the ETED since their residual income-generating value creation/transfer activities are much larger on aggregate and determine development. That is, the focus is not on the emperor but the business models of the senatorial and equestrian classes (even if the latter can easily be purged by the former). Typical elite coalitions effect institutional change through their unwavering dedication to changing business model rules in the fractal spaces that matter to them (see Section 4.2.3, Figure 4.3). Their power is relative to their direct business model sectoral rivals and their ultimate objective is to convert that power into residual income. Meanwhile, in its strategizing, the core coalition must decide whether to direct its attention to the general intra-elite contest rules that decide—potentially in most sectors of the economy—how the 'extraordinary lever' is won or is lost, or rather to focus on some specifics. Here, Rossier, Ellersgaard, Larsen, and Lunding (2022, p. 320) empirically identify "the core group in elite networks" that possesses the all-important "capability" in the elite system "to broker between sectors".

The aims of the core coalition also concern its principal residual income objective, usually associated with the sustainability of the national business model. At times it manages to monetize its role as a broker of elite bargains by influencing the winners of intra-elite contests. The relationship between 'the extraordinary lever' of the core elite coalition and 'the extraordinary lever' of regular elite coalitions is illustrated in Figure A5.3b. The latter employ this power vis-à-vis stakeholders in the business model, and so can be theoretically viewed through the perspective of management science with the principal-stakeholder VCA division of value framework. The core elite coalition can also employ it vis-à-vis other elite coalitions (see Tier 5 'from-core' in Figure A5.11b) who are not technically its stakeholders, and so the theoretical perspectives of institutional change and political economy are pertinent to its discrete agency.

As noted, a functioning core coalition can set the strategic direction of the political economy (including grand strategy for cross-border business models), effect elite cohesion, and exercise overall elite system leadership. For sustainable value creation agency, the core coalition needs a certain power differential over regular elites that must not be abused by engaging in excessive or unweighted value transfers. Highly refined and intricate, the core coalition can be large or small, closed or porous, diverse or homogenous, but it must exhibit sufficient cohesion to effectively oversee intra-elite contests. The inclusive agency of the core coalition is aided by the elite separation of powers (particularly in relation to intra-elite power relation 7, Table 3.2) that in turn facilitates its mediating role of institutional change. When the varieties of leadership were discussed earlier (see Section 7.2.4, Table 7.2), an ethical dimension was implied for 'from-core' transformational agency. Elite system transformational leadership prioritizes business models at the top table of the political economy (e.g., energy, automotive, e-commerce, etc.) that generate the highest residual incomes and self-constrains their extractive potential (transfer-IN). While the core coalition's purview cannot always reach down to the specific sectoral nooks and crannies of complex economies, it can, like no other agency in society, shape intra-elite contests (Figure A5.11b) and so place constraints on appropriation (e.g., on transfers and redistribution, see Tables 8.2 and 8.3) through business models rules and elite bargains. This matters, because a primary contradiction of the political economy is that institutional arrangements enabling specific elite business models to create and appropriate value lie in the hands of the beneficiaries of those models (see the discussion on the microfoundations of institutional change, Section 4.2).

Inclusive institutional change is more likely to come from the intra-elite contests in a particular sector of the economy where the core elite coalition, as well as other regular but powerful elite coalitions, have no residual income interest in the outcomes. Besides using its influence in specific contests, the transformational leadership mandate for the core elite coalition is therefore ethically unambiguous: to foster elite cohesion and press for a comprehensive elite separation of powers, while finding original solutions (e.g., in the form of new narratives, see Figure A5.12a) for the 'intra-elite quality contest' dilemma. This is seen in vigorous institutionalized intra-elite competition in every sector of the economy and evidenced by business model rules that seize the opportunities of technological change and challenge extractive sectoral strongholds in the institutional landscape. The narratives that the core elite coalition selects, crafts, and nurtures should not only foster national elite system cohesion but also act as an incentive for sustainable value creation by explicitly repudiating or even shaming unweighted excessive extraction.

Just as this work calls for nations and firms to be assessed in terms of their elite quality (e.g., through SVC measurements like the EQx or VCr), the different strata and sub-categories in the socio-economic structure pyramid (Figure 8.1) could also be assessed in terms of their sustainable value creation (non-elite quality is considered in the Epilogue, see Figure E.1). No methodology to that effect is proposed in this book, but for illustrative purposes comparative judgments have been made in Table 8.1 to assess the trends for three countries: the US, China, and Germany. Again, the core elite coalition (1.1) is part of the elites (1), while the managerial, technical, and creative class (2.1) is part of the non-elites (2), but due to their discrete functions from an economic development perspective, they are, for analytical purposes, evaluated separately.

Table 8.1: Comparative sustainable value creation for the two general strata and the main sub-categories of the socio-economic structure pyramid: The US, China, and Germany (informal assessment for illustrative purposes).

Ref.	Socio-economic structure pyramid elite/non-elite strata	Comparative sustainable value creation		
		US	**China**	**Germany**
(1.a)	Elite quality: Core elite coalition	Very high *Trend: Declining*	High *Trend: Stable*	Medium *Trend: Declining*
(1.b)	Elite quality: Regular elite coalitions	High *Trend: Stable*	Medium/High *Trend: Ascending*	High *Trend: Stable*
(2.a)	Non-elite quality: Managerial, technical, and creative class	Very high *Trend: Stable*	Medium *Trend: Ascending*	High/Very high *Trend: Stable*
(2.b)	Non-elite quality: Population at large	Medium/High *Trend: Declining*	Medium/High *Trend: Ascending*	Very high *Trend: Stable*

Given that the comparative sustainable value creation of the core elite coalition is independent from that of the elite system at large, it is worth delving deeper into this conceptual element with some applied examples. This is also justified by the core elite coalition's salience in the system with an identity and role that often characterizes the society in which it operates. While many royal princes in Saudi Arabia lead their own elite coalitions, the core elite coalition is the one headed by the king—customarily also the prime minister—or the crown prince. Moreover, and ever since 23 September 1932, when King Abdulaziz Ibn Saud unified the regions and declared the modern Kingdom of Saudi Arabia, the values of the leader of the House of Saud have imbued the nation. Likewise, there are many elite business models in Russia and other post-Soviet countries, but the core elite coalition is usually that of an all-powerful President with a determinant impact on development. In some political economies, the elite system and the core elite coalition have a strong functional overlap (which is reflected by comparatively low scores in the EQx 'power' sub-index). This is less the case in the US and not at all so in Japan where, as shown earlier, the elite system is structured as an "iron triangle" in which a myriad of often-competing interests of the broadly diversified *keiretsu* bureaucracies figure prominently. Should core elite coalition members coalesce with the nation state, their individual power sources originate from the national business model. In summary, membership of the core elite coalition is subject to factors like the performance vagaries of these models, to elite circulation modes and velocities, and to exogenous events, with the dynamism of the entry/exit process being critical for development.

For example, America's core elite coalitions have circulated in relatively quick succession. In the decades up to President Roosevelt (FDR), there were the original merchant elites (all-purpose merchants), transitioning to specialized merchants (as seen in Porter & Livesay, 1971), the Robber Barons (with Cornelius Vanderbilt not competing against government-subsidized inefficient shippers in exchange for payments), or the legendary J.P. Morgan. The New York banker single-handedly coordinated the "Money Trust" (see Ramirez, 1995) to save America from "the panic of 1907" (Herrick, 1908)[214]. In the post-FDR era, core elite coalitions have included leading manufacturers, with Charles Wilson, the President of General Motors and later Secretary of Defense famously stating in 1953 that: "For years I thought what was good for our country was good for General Motors, and vice versa. The difference did not exist. Our company is too big. It goes with the welfare of the country. Our contribution to the Nation is quite considerable"[215], or the military-industrial complex described by Eisenhower (1961). Big Oil has also been prominent, with President Carter's "vital interests" narrative (Klare, 2006) reaching a high point under Vice-President Cheney's leadership (Goldstein, 2010) between 2001 and 2009, and regaining centrality in 2022 as part of the defense of Ukraine (and Europe). During the last two decades, Wall Street (reinvigorated by the repeal of the 1933 Glass-Steagall legislation and the 1935 Banking Act amendments by the 1999 Gramm-Leach-Bliley Act) and Big Tech have been the elite coalitions commanding the heights, with the latter now ascendant as is articulated in *The Wall Street Journal* headline, "Wall Street Takes a Back Seat With Trump's Elevation of Vance" (Zuckerman, 2024).

The relative ups and downs of American elite coalitions and their business models at the core of the elite system point to the admixture mode of elite circulation (Figure 1.1) and are evidence of the elite system transformational leadership that underlies America's economic vitality and strong value creation. Similarly, in contemporary China, while the political elite steers the nation, it does not constitute a monolith; robust policy debates and intra-elite contests take place, while policy changes occur con-

214 Drama often surrounds the transformational leadership of the core elite coalition: "The withdrawal and hoarding of this vast sum by banks and individuals produced a most acute condition. On October 24th the panic on the Stock Exchange seemed almost hopeless. Call money was practically unobtainable—only a few loans being made at 125 per cent. At two o'clock, when the demoralization was at its worst, a bankers' pool headed by J. P. Morgan loaned $25,000,000 at 10 per cent—thus tiding over a situation fraught with the gravest danger" (Herrick, 1908, p. 9).

215 See: https://blogs.loc.gov/inside_adams/2016/04/when-a-quote-is-not-exactly-a-quote-general-motors/

stantly, not just in the rare instances when one Standing Committee of the Political Bureau of the CPC Central Committee succeeds another. Moreover, the elite business models favored by the core elite coalition have stunningly mutated over the past four decades: from the Soviet-style state owned enterprises (SOEs) to the exporters that scaled up in Southern coastal provinces; from the ultra-aggressive construction industry behemoths fueled by debt and supportive local governments to increasingly high value added manufacturers with huge production capacity (both private and public); from Big Tech and back again to SOEs directed by economic planners ambidextrously aiming for stability while seeking to sail close to the technology frontier. Most of these transitions reflect the value creation-based rise of China and vigorous, albeit partial (for example, there is limited competition in the non-market and narrative market arenas) elite circulation processes that help explain nearly four decades of mesmerizing economic growth and human development by continuous structural reform and adjustments of the incentive system (see Figure 7.1). In contrast, advanced nations like Japan, France, or Germany have witnessed several decades of overall relative stagnation as the business models of their core elite coalitions remain anchored in traditional industries such as automotive, luxury goods, or chemicals, regardless of how successful and inclusive these models are. With the post-World War II economic boom now a distant memory, the intra-elite contests in these countries seem settled, the elite separation of powers (in many tiers of the checks and balances framework of Figure 3.7) is a pretense, and the 'intra-elite quality contest' dilemma remains essentially unresolved as a result of excessive cohesion. According to Reeves and Friedman (2024), the UK's elite also tends to have closed access and is rather well cohered. It remains to be seen whether ambitious start-up founders in Manchester and London, Osaka and Tokyo, Lyon and Paris, or Stuttgart and Berlin, will succeed in becoming new elites or whether incumbent elite business models will incorporate the opportunities that digitalization and AI have opened up or submit to foreign alliances, cross-border M&As, and the purchase of essential innovation from overseas suppliers.

In summary, despite its weakening in many advanced economies, core elite coalition agency has a firm grip on 'the extraordinary lever', is best placed to effect elite system leadership, and so is still potentially the paramount transformational force. Whether and how elite system transformational leadership is exercised, particularly in intra-elite contests, is of the utmost relevance to non-elites and to the development path and fate of a nation. This leadership variety (see Table 7.2) has been touted in this book as a prime way to move the aggregate of the nation's elite business models towards higher elite quality. Sustainable value creation helps a political economy to flourish because it benefits non-elites and increases elite/non-elite cohesion. It also leads to increases in relative national power (see Section 7.3) and hence to favorable terms for cross-border elite business models, which serve both national elite and non-elite interests (e.g., British non-elite classes benefited from Empire, American middle classes from the rise in US power after WWII, and many Chinese workers from BRI partnerships). In short, the core elite coalition is a phenomenal asset, and as such places a disproportionate responsibility on its members to guide the strategic direction of the elite system towards weighted structural reforms (see Figure 7.1) that enable inclusive and constrain extractive elite business models.

8.1.3 Can elites serve non-elite interests?

> The path from action to final justification can be long and complex but must connect at some point to non-derivative or intrinsic values in order for the action to be fully justified. (Donaldson, 2021, p. 8)

The value created by non-elites through their daily work is colossal and invariably accumulates into the largest reservoir of value in the economy. This non-elite value pool is a permanent target for extraction by elite business models. Whether through taxation, inflation, an expensive civil bureaucracy, war, student loans and their forgiveness, the setting of minimum wages above equilibrium, squatter's rights laws, or data regulations that don't compensate the citizen data producers—the list is endless and ever evolving. The interests of non-elites are served if such extractive transfers are weighted against value creation to avoid excessive extraction (transfer-IN by elites) of the value that non-elites produce as stakeholders of elite business models in their roles as taxpayers, consumers, users of government services, soldiers, college students, workers, start-up founders, small businesspeople, professionals, farmers, homeowners, producers of data, prompters of LLMs, etc. As has been discussed, and as the non-elite rule fallacy ('people power') sets out, non-elites lack the power to prevent their own extraction over protracted periods. At the same time, many members of elite coalitions are fully cognizant of the negative long-term impact that a demoralized non-elite and a distorted incentive system may have on the sustainability of their own business models. Elites, sometimes motivated by intrinsic values, but certainly by their own self-interest, are often supportive of inclusive non-elite advancement as they reap the ensuing benefits of economic development and strength in the international context.

A fundamental problem faced by non-elites is a lack of cohesion (the logical reverse of Proposition 1, the elite dominance iron law is structural to society, see also Section 5.3.3), an issue that will be referred to going forward as the 'low non-elite cohesion' problem. Section 3.3.2 discussed how non-elite agency constrains value extraction through participation in intra-elite contests (see Proposition 19), while in Section 3.3.3, the comprehensive elite separation of powers set out in The Three-tier Set of Intra-elite Checks and Balances (see Proposition 20) suggested possibilities for non-elites to shape political economy contest outcomes in ways that further their interests. Further nuance is now provided with a typology that suggests four discrete non-elite political options[216] in two broad categories: 'confrontation' and 'collaboration'. Confrontation is represented by non-elite (option a), 'non-elite vs elite struggle'. There are also three political options for collaboration. The first of these is non-elite (option b), passive 'trust in elites' and their enlightened agency. The other forms of collaboration envisage non-elite input in intra-elite contests to ally with elites running business models that are the most beneficial to non-elites. In non-elite (option c), 'tactical participation', a specific non-elite group teams up with a specific elite coalition in support of its business model; in non-elite (option d), 'strategic participation', the non-elite, broadly understood, mobilizes on the side of elite coalitions with higher sustainable value creation across as many intra-elite contests as possible.

These four non-elite political options are messy aggregates of individual non-elite responses to extraction such as 'challenge' (Table 5.1). However, while *embrace* in the (i) 'acceptance' option and all (iv) 'challenge' individual responses can aggregate to non-elite political options, not all individual non-elite responses have such potential, see *resignation* in the (i) 'acceptance' option, or all possibilities of the (iii) 'informality' and 'exit' options, as depicted in Figure A5.8.[217] It is important to note that all non-elite political options in the relationship—even (option b) 'elite agency on behalf of non-elites'—require narratives and a degree of non-elite leadership, usually supplied by the emergent elites of non-elite extraction now leading non-elite groups. The four matching diverse political options for elites to advance non-elite interests (options b' to d') or merely their own (option a') are presented in Figure 8.2. Next, the four pairs are analyzed for their respective effectiveness.

While disruptive or violent struggle might seem expeditious in the view of some intellectuals, it has already been amply discussed (e.g., Section 3.3.2) that the destruction of value and other counterproductive effects associated with insurrections and revolutions disqualify non-elite (option a), the political confrontation response, from

216 The elite/non-elite relationship revolves around power and is deeply embedded in all aspects of the political economy and actualized in the market and narrative market arenas. Nonetheless, the four elite/non-elite options are termed 'political' because the non-market arena is the most salient in shaping the relationship and relates to institutional change.

217 The overlapping elements between individual responses to extraction (Table 5.1) and the non-elite political options for the elite/non-elite relationship (Figure 8.2) visualized in Figure A5.8 are the following: the aggregate individual (i) 'acceptance' response in its *embrace* variant morphs into the elite/non-elite collaboration political response (option b/b'); the aggregate individual response (iv) 'challenge' in its *struggle* variant turns into 'non-elite vs elite struggle' (option a/a'); the aggregate individual response (iv) 'challenge' in its *participation* variant transforms into 'tactical participation' (option c/c') and 'strategic participation' (option d/d') respectively. The aggregated individual responses (i) 'acceptance' (in its *resignation* variant); (ii) 'exit' (in its *withdrawal* and *new start* variants); and (iii) 'informality' (in its *inefficient* and *efficient* variants) fall mostly outside elite/non-elite dialectics and do not become political options of note, hence precluding formal synthesis or non-elite agency in their resolution.

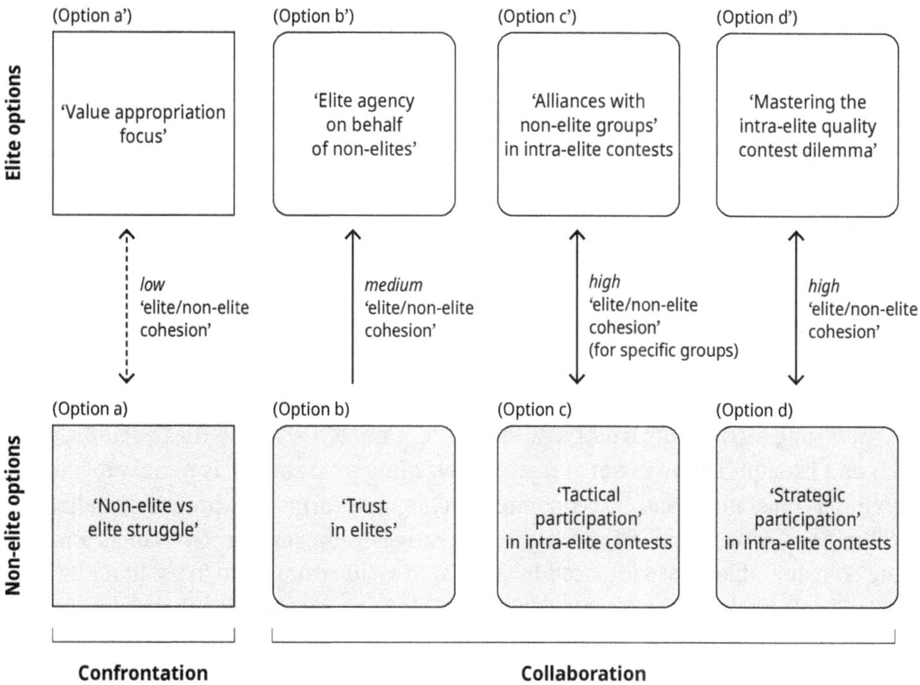

Figure 8.2: A typology of aggregate non-elite political options in response to (actual and potential) extractive value transfers with the corresponding elite political options.

a development perspective, even when the discontent is widespread and the extraction onerous. Elites do not respond well to low non-elite quality (a conceptual element that is further developed in the Epilogue, see Figure E.1), and will counter violence by doubling down on value appropriation to garner the resources to defeat 'non-elite vs elite struggle' (option a). At the same time, the three collaboration approaches are all problematic in one way or another. Non-elite (option b), 'trust in elites', is manifested in its most extreme form in theocracies, is akin to enlightened absolutism, and requires elites that are deserving of trust. The 'tactical participation' of non-elites in non-elite contests (option c) may serve specific non-elite interests but also means that non-elite groups will likely face off against each other. The systematic and 'strategic participation' push for elite value creation by the non-elite (option d) is technically challenging as it requires advance support from knowledge elites and the necessary discipline by non-elite leaders to resist the temptation to defect and become members and beneficiaries of the extractive coalitions they once spurned.

Throughout history, elite coalitions (often with knowledge elites at their center) have articulated and implemented institutional change by claiming to represent non-elite interests, as in 'elite agency on behalf of non-elites' (option b'). The approach certainly seems suspect, as it questions and diminishes non-elite agency.

Leaving criticisms of elitism and paternalism aside, how effective for non-elites is placing their trust in elites (option b)? Enlightened elites certainly can advance non-elite interests, for example, through narratives that limit extraction. "Thou shalt not kill" (King James Bible, 1769/2017, Exodus: 20:13), as stated in The Sixth Commandment of the Torah, is an early powerful example of top-down sustainable value creation by elite agency, delivered by a prophet and lawgiver who was also a transformational leader. Yet it seems evident to many that the top-down edicts of today—from monetary policy to immigration—work against non-elite interests despite claiming to have these in mind.

The premise for the (option b/b') pairing to work (trusting elites to care about those below them) is for elite agency to be anchored in ethical principles and knowledge about the specific weightings of their value transfer-IN from non-elites. While the "paternalistic lie", derived from Plato's "the noble lie" in politics (Dombrowski, 1997) and exemplified by national myths or wartime propaganda, is permissible under certain circumstances and in economic development terms, the practical realization of 'elite agency on behalf of non-elites' narratives requires effective constraints on value transfers (like those imposed by Moses) to yield sustainable 'trust in elites'. Spinoza's *Theological-Political Treatise* (1677/2007) is "a comprehensive theory [not just of religion but] of how ecclesiastical authority and theological concepts exercise their power over men" (Israel & Silverthorne, 2007, p. ix), and strikes a note of caution on narratives *per se* lest these end up legitimizing extractive elite business models. In imperial China, Plato's noble lie sees expression in the "doctrine of Heaven-Mankind Interaction [which is a] theoretical model of political cosmology", the practical impact of which has been empirically tested with "a dataset that includes dynastical and celestial records from the Qin dynasty to the Ming dynasty (221 BC – 1644 AD)", revealing that emperors knew very well that lower tax "reduces the probability for farmers to revolt" (Chen, Shi, Xi, Zhang, & Zhang, 2023, p. 1).

Next, and by delving deeper into 'tactical participation' and 'alliances with non-elite groups' in intra-elite contests, the (option c/c') pairing of Figure 8.2, it becomes obvious that this route is also fraught with practical problems. The major concern is the divergent value creation interests of non-elite stakeholder groups in many intra-elite contests, earlier exemplified by the Keystone XL pipeline where different non-elite interests opposed each other (Table 3.1). Do the preferences of the Rosebud Sioux Tribe take precedence over those of the Teamsters? Do the former gain more than the latter lose from the cancellation of the pipeline? If the sustainable value creation of competing tactical alliances is equal, which of these specific non-elite interests ought to be prioritized—those of metalworkers, specific minorities, rural residents, students, small business owners, or senior citizens? Non-elite interests are not only particular to a group, but different groups could potentially be at odds with each other, perhaps to an irreconcilable degree. Any non-elite group benefiting from a tactical alliance will invariably antagonize or hurt others.

One might posit that the elite business model with the most effective non-elite alliances will prevail and in so doing will echo the notion of laissez-faire competition in free markets, with the winning coalition offering the best alternative for general value creation. Clearly though, winning elite/non-elite alliances do not weight and address extractive transfers that do not concern their own residual incomes. Extractive institutions will continue to be initiated while the overall national interest and prospects for development are placed on the backburner. In fact, when discrete non-elite groups tactically pursue their own interests in alliance with elite coalitions, they may end up facilitating the extraction of the non-elite as a class. This is not indicative of class betrayal in the sense of the Marxist *lumpenproletariat* underclass ("a bribed tool of reactionary intrigue", Marx & Engels, 1848/1969, p. 20), but nonetheless, such narrow alliances erode broader non-elite cohesion and open the gates to the 'extractive escalation dynamic'.

On a more positive note, the tactical approach is scalable and can achieve positive developmental outcomes when elites weight transfers and practice self-restraint on extraction, while systematically engaging in alliances with non-elites to boost their chances in intra-elite contests. Elite transformational leadership may therefore occur and the 'one less extractive elite business model at a time' schema potentially trigger an 'inclusive escalation dynamic'. Again, while some non-elite groups will be losers, the underlying rationale is that the emergence of a sustainable value creation elite business model from an intra-elite contest is more likely if it is conceived as a non-elite/elite alliance.

Given all of the above, the 'strategic participation' approach of non-elites (option d) and the matching 'mastering the intra-elite quality contest' dilemma by elites (option d') merits serious consideration. Two working premises apply here. Consistent with the nook and cranny focus of structural reform policies, general non-elite interests are addressed one business model at a time, extractive transfer by extractive transfer. That is, in every intra-elite contest, the contending elite business model that is better at delivering more value creation and requiring less extractive transfers should be supported. Evidently, this is easier said than done. The problem of weighting and offsetting business models in terms of their sustainable value creation seems impossibly hard to resolve, especially when it is necessary to limit the gains of the non-elite allies of extractive elite models. Intra-elite contests are also exceedingly intense and complex, spanning legal, financial, technological, and even personal domains as a headline on one of the defining Big Tech intra-elite contests makes clear: "Facebook Meets Apple in Clash of the Tech Titans – 'We Need to Inflict Pain': Animosity Between CEOs Mark Zuckerberg and Tim Cook Erupts over Privacy and Dueling Visions of Internet" (Seetharaman, Glazer, & Higgins, 2021)? Moreover, information and knowledge asymmetries (see the 'elite vs non-elite knowledge gap' hypothesis in Section 2.2.2) might render any concerted action by non-elite groups and their leaders to influence intra-elite contests ineffective. This work has tried to provide solutions to these problems through its suite of frameworks and SVC measurements (such as the VCr).

The strategic participation by non-elites in intra-elite contests must address and overcome single-issue non-elite leadership, as well as the heterogeneity of non-elite constituencies. In fact, most non-elite groups will find it easier, as rational utility maximizers, to tactically partner in intra-elite contests (option c) rather than to develop strategic, more uncertain, and longer-term approaches that require bolstering non-elite cohesion and elite/non-elite cohesion. Non-elite groups are evidently not all equally affected by extractive transfers—the National Rifle Association (NRA) benefits gun-loving non-elites to the detriment of other non-elite groups who would prefer to limit gun rights and the violence associated with them. Without a measure of preexisting 'non-elite cohesion' across heterogenous groups, the ideal that Acemoglu and Robinson refer to as a "strong, mobilized society" (2019a, p. xvi) able to balance "the state" (an antagonist that probably signifies the business models of the core elite coalition) is moot. Eventually, any attempts to engage strategically with elites (option d/d') will invariably revert to tactical approaches (option c/c').

The leaders of non-elite movements that mobilize for a partial set of extractive grievances might also intensify the 'low non-elite cohesion' problem. Non-elite movements certainly strategically embrace society-wide narratives but seldom engage in rigorously weighted analyses of sustainable value creation that accord due consideration to those who lose out from their specific demands. In practice, they invest their energies in support or in opposition to a given elite model by stressing specific, mostly narrow, and often symbolic issues (to the relief of the offending elites) rather than systematically addressing extractive value transfers in society as a whole. As a result, even if the non-elite movement succeeds in a specific intra-elite contest, it will at best be a pyrrhic victory. That is, a little less value is extracted by the culpable elite business model, while the colossal amounts of value that continue to be extracted elsewhere are legitimized, further dissipating non-elite agency and stymying development aims. For instance, in the US, hard-fought police reforms have brought benefits to non-elites now less likely to suffer from unwarranted brutality, yet do not address issues such as the need for quality primary schools or out of control inflation, transfers that have considerably greater impacts on the overall living standards of non-elites, including those benefiting from police reform. While all three demands to stop extraction are legitimate, the non-elite political capital available to invest in intra-elite contests is a finite resource. Non-elites might find themselves in a net worse position because a tactical success in one area ignores the totality. It should be possible for non-elites to attain cohesion on the premise that extractive activities can be quantified, made transparent, weighted, and traded and offset against each other (see the implications for sustainable value creation, Figure A5.4a).

Achieving the above is by no means easy, especially in terms of crafting effective policies and compelling narratives. There are evident knowledge asymmetries, while measuring and articulating transfers is both technical and hard to narrativize. Non-elite agency that elevates its objectives would, for instance, comprehensively address police brutality together with the need for better primary schools and less inflation;

propose coherent policies that save lives at costs that are consistent across domains and contain risk trade-offs (see Messick & Bazerman, 2001); quantify the per capita extractive transfers of gun violence against those of high-fructose corn syrup; and assess the per capita inclusive transfers of aligned, holistic, and industrial AI (e.g., Peres, Jia, Lee, Sun, Colombo, & Barata, 2020) and clean air. Any such proposals would emerge from social movements and political initiatives with strategic and overarching policy and development aims, have coherent narrative bases backed up by ethical clarity (see Figure A5.12a), while systematically seeking elite alliances and participation in intra-elite contests.

We thus return to the earlier corollary that non-elites are often their own worst enemies. Their leaders, often aspiring to elite status, pepper elite contests with tactical but random non-elite narrativized preferences, while being unable to conceive of what is really at stake by failing to make consistent proposals for the weighted structural reform of extractive models that seek to raise overall elite quality. Moreover, without non-elite cohesion, the heterogeneity of non-elite interest groups is a perpetual impediment for elites that might otherwise be prepared to self-constrain their own value appropriation. If a country's non-elites are split down the middle (between MAGA and BLM sympathizers, for example), do well-meaning elites need to choose between them when designing the institutional change of elite business model rules or can they find solutions that find favor with both groups? It has been pointed out that the lack of elite cohesion is fueled by the "myriad of interests and identities" of non-elites in democracies (Higley, 2021, p. 74). At least a modicum of non-elite cohesion is necessary to comprehend and then realize interests that are common to the non-elite in general, though these are still paradoxically best served by elite cohesion.

Should an elite with high degree of cohesion then get actively involved in addressing the 'low non-elite cohesion' problem to empower general non-elite leadership in order to have a counterparty in an extended separation of powers framework that produces more optimal and inclusive institutional change? Or is it easier for elites to rather focus on development through top-down reforms and transformation in the enlightened absolutist fashion of Maria Theresa's son Emperor Joseph II, "Everything for the people, nothing by the people"? Perhaps the 'low non-elite cohesion' problem is less of a quandary if elites decide to go it alone and further non-elite interests in the context of 'elite agency on behalf of non-elites' (option b').

Less edifyingly, elites (option a') might simply ignore non-elite preferences altogether when faced with opposition, maximize extraction, and neutralize non-elite agency. Once non-elites opt for struggle and confrontation (option a), elites will readily fend them off in a cost-effective manner (the possibilities have historically included indiscriminate terror, divide and rule, or narrative confusion) while strengthening their own 'value appropriation focus' and mechanisms (as their long-term wealth stock prospects are now subject to higher discounts, the short-term residual income flows of the 'elite utility function' become preferable, see Section 2.1.1). Once non-elites are contained—such repression typically leads to generalized deinstitutionalization— and as the elite system is reinforced, those at the top will busy themselves in all manner of contests for rents that further stunt development. Yet even when unchallenged, elites can show utter disregard for non-elite interests, often with dramatic consequences.

Stefan Dercon assesses Nigeria as "the loser of the entrenched elite bargain", by which he means "a discrete agreement or series of agreements that sets out to renegotiate the distribution of power and allocation of resources among a few individuals" (Iyatse, 2022). However, there are many instances of elites weighting and restraining their value appropriation by engaging in structural reforms towards sustainable value creation even when sidelining non-elite interests. Examples include General Park's *chaebol* pacts or the Chilean regime's *concertación* bargains that succeeded in raising both wages and labor productivity (Weyland, 1999, p. 70) after Augusto Pinochet's 1973 brutal coup d'état. It is evidently problematic and rare for elites to work on behalf of non-elite interests where there is antagonism and to respond to 'non-elite vs elite struggle' (option a) with paternalism (option b'). Yet this is also a theoretical and enlightened path forward. US progressives in power could massively invest in quality basic education and post-secondary vocational schools for the millions of working class white American families whose travails mirror those described by Vance in *Hillbilly Elegy* (2016), and one of the stated aims of President Biden's 2021 Infrastructure Investment and Jobs Act (IIJA).

The above notwithstanding, inclusive gains will be achieved from non-elite/elite cohesion that in turn is aided by non-elite cohesion. Ultimately, non-elite cohesion is spurred by elite cohesion. "Vetocracy" (Fukuyama, 2016), or that fact that "polarization of the Democratic and Republican Parties is higher than at any time since the end of the Civil War" with the US "now firmly entrenched in a political era that is characterized by the ubiquity of unidimensional, polarized political conflict" (Hare & Poole, 2014, pp. 411, 428) is unhelpful to non-elite cohesion. Is it advisable to call for shared narratives to replace the "culture wars" (Hunter, 1991) and so lower the transaction and coordination costs for non-elites and promote trust across non-elite groups (though religion and nationalism, for instance, are both extremely effective types of glue)? To complete the analysis, the higher the level of non-elite cohesion, the more likely elites are to engage in strategic collaboration with non-elites across intra-elite contests (option d/d'). Gouldner (1975, p. 12) hits the mark when stating: "Historically effective elites are commonly trained, as well as positioned, to take the standpoint of the totality, even if seeing it only from the top down". The term 'strategic' (or the 'totality' view) is taken here to refer to elites that systematically nudge sustainable transformations in the political economy through their mastery of the 'intra-elite quality contest' dilemma, evidenced by a strong separation of powers and high levels of cohesion. This includes minimizing bargaining power differentials derived from 'political economy know-how' (Figure 2.3), and the easing of barriers for an open access social order. Strategic elite/non-elite collaboration associates with the admixture mode of elite circulation (Figure 1.1), faster elite circulation velocities, and opens the door for non-elite business models to scale up and join the elite, boosting overall elite quality in the national elite system. The core elite coalition and supportive elite coalitions promote such development with structural reforms to business model rules that incentivize sustainable value creation. A 'competitive elite system' and, to a lesser extent, an 'enlightened' one, (see Figure 6.5) is in the interests of high quality elites and non-elites alike, and delivers economic development.

To summarize, for the elite/non-elite relationship to be an optimal strategic and cooperative game (option d/d') in a complex political economy, and for general non-elite interests to be considered and optimized, three conditions are suggested: knowledge about sustainable value creation and the capacity of elites to weight and offset extractive transfers; a degree of 'elite agency on behalf of non-elites'; and non-elite cohesion. While the leadership of non-elite groups (potential or new elites) bears substantial responsibility, non-elite interests ultimately rely on the ethical positions taken in the elite system (i.e., on the propensity of elites to transform and engage in structural reforms). Essentially, elite strategic collaboration with non-elites means to affect institutional change around the maxim, *To the creators the value created*, and might well be motivated by intrinsic values as much as by self-interest and development goals. Inclusive scenarios are more likely to come to pass if non-elite groups forsake the illusionary benefits of struggle and forfeit the gains of tactical alliances with elites, as such transfers impoverish and can easily polarize society.

Mob rule (ochlocracy), dreaded by elites since Plato (1908; 1969), is the opposite of strategic and sustainable non-elite rule. While temporary outbursts such as Calcutta's Direct Action Day (1946) or the Los Angeles riots (1992) are bad enough, the long-term consequences are decidedly more painful. Even more problematic is when mobs become a root cause of elite circulation. The path to power for non-elite leaders using the mob is a combination of 'tactical participation in intra-elite contests' (option c) and 'non-elite vs elite struggle' (option a). The miscreant *Sturmabteilung* (SA) paratroopers in Weimar Germany are an example of a mob that helped power a non-elite group's leadership to elite status. Those with agency in non-elite groups—the emerging elites of non-elite extraction—must instead understand and play their part in seeking strategic participation across intra-elite contests, systematically reaching out and supporting elite coalitions whose business models constrain value transfers while generating sustainable value creation and the associated risk taking. With the backing of inclusive elite coalitions, along with appropriate affirmative narratives, this is theoretically feasible because most non-elite groups do not have a direct interest in most intra-elite contests. Therefore, generalized value creation corresponds with the interests of the majority of non-elite groups in the majority of intra-elite contests.

This section on elites serving non-elite interests has seen many elements of the ETED discourse coalesce. The positive consequences of non-elites breaking free from the 'low non-elite cohesion' problem have been set out. It has controversially advocated for elite paternalism while positing that the limited agency of non-elite groups and their leaders—some the potential elites of tomorrow—has a role to play in shaping intra-elite contests. Passive non-elite trust in 'elite agency on behalf of non-elites' is hence deemed to be insufficient. Ideally, elite/non-elite collaboration takes a strategic form and eschews tactical alliances where the benefits accrue to narrow non-elite interests. Strategic collaboration also requires elites to advance their own separation of powers and strive for cohesion to usher in higher elite circulation velocities in the admixture mode. This will never be easy, as is clear from Sen's work on welfare economics that opposes the general "gross inability to be sensitive to the heterogeneous interests of a diverse population" (1999b, p. 351) postulated in Arrow's "General Possibility Theorem" (1951). Commonly known as the "impossibility theorem", Arrow demonstrates the practical futility of aggregate non-elite preferences consistent with general welfare based on fair principles and efficiency. Next, a short reasoning exercise is undertaken on how an entirely disparate political design might best serve the interests of non-elites.

8.1.4 Can post-singularity non-human AI elites serve human non-elite interests?

Given that a central prescriptive feature of this work is a focus on the political options for non-elites to minimize extractive transfers (see Figure 8.2), how would these options be affected by an 'elite singularity' moment, where autonomous AI elites become superior to their human counterparts in terms of value appropriation and creation? Singularity is the instant when humans are confronted with "a great surprise and a greater unknown", where progress is driven by "greater-than-human intelligence" leading to "still more intelligent entities – on a still shorter time scale" (Vinge, 2013, p. 366). The initial consequence of such a world, with 'the extraordinary lever' now transformed into 'the absolute lever' in the hands of non-human AI elite coalitions (as illustrated in Figure A5.3d), is that the ETED's non-elite/elite confrontation vs collaboration typology (Figure 8.2) breaks down, as is set out by Yudkowsky (2022): "Coordination schemes between superintelligences are not things that humans can participate in". Whether these "coordination schemes" then materialize into intra-elite AI competition or a monolithic universal unity seems a secondary issue, even if they become part of the existential conversations set out in the 'The AI elite separation of powers' hypothesis (AI_H6) of Table E.3.

A *leitmotif* of this work is that intra-elite contests, especially those of intra-elite power relations 3, 5, and 6 that involve knowledge elites (see Table 3.2), are essential to non-elite interests. In their *Nature* article, "Machine Culture", Brinkmann et al. (2023) describe a contribution to "a conceptual framework for studying the present and anticipated future impact of machines on cultural evolution" and observe that: "The ability of humans to create and disseminate culture is often credited as the single most important factor of our success as a species." Harari (in *The Economist*, 2023a) pragmatically asks: "What will happen to the course of history when AI takes over culture", i.e., dominates the narrative market arena and puts knowledge elites out of business? This is precisely the prelude for 'elite singularity' where AGI arrogates the narrative market and all coordination roles in the political economy from incumbent human elites. A slew of questions inevitably arise. What will transpire when the last standing human elite *de facto* concedes 'the extraordinary lever' of the political economy? Do non-elites have any political options after the last declaration of war, R&D budget, or social network feature choice has been made by a human, whether that is the US President, the Indian Prime Minister, or Jensen Huang? A more thorough exploration is presented in the hypotheses of Table E.1 in the Epilogue, including those on the nature of value transfers with autonomous non-human AI elite agency [Set 3/4] and those on the nature of value creation in a hegemonic AI system [set 4/4]. The object of this sub-section is then to assess the array of political choices available to non-elites in a system where every single human being is non-elite, including the exalted and, to this theory, essential erstwhile elite.

Clearly, and as per Yudkowsky (2022), dissipated human power endowments would preclude 'non-elite vs elite struggle' with the non-human AI elite (option a). 'Tactical participation' (option c) and 'strategic participation' (option d) in intra-elite contests or decision-making for institutional change would be at the discretion of the superintelligence and hence possible, especially if its political economy ambitions were limited, as might be the case under Good's "docile" AI premise (1965, p. 33). If non-elite interests and a form of simulated human elite agency is acknowledged by the AI, all would carry on as it always has, perhaps more sustainably under the AI's soft tutelage. The AI would gently nudge against non-elite extraction, preventing in utopian fashion all forms of crime, Tullock's "theft", and Bastiat's "plunder". A more interventionist AI, ethically pursuing 'elite agency on behalf of non-elites', possibly motivated by and reciprocating 'trust in elites' (option b/b'), could be close to utopian for the non-elites in the system. Such trust is already materializing at the margins of society with the "deification of AI", including "AI focused New Religious Movements (AI NRMs) such as the Turing Church, and even staunchly atheist transhumanist spaces" (Singler, 2020, p. 945). *The Daily Beast* featured humans feeling "blessed by the algorithm" while "giving it a fatalistic authority" (Tran, 2023). The hope might be that the AI develops superior ethics than the former human elites, be far better at weighting and offsetting value transfers (Figure A5.4b), and loyally adheres to its own narratives—which would be a welcome historical first for an elite.

Should the goals and preferences of an elite superintelligence vis-à-vis non-elites be hardcoded into the AI as humanity deals with the alignment problem?[218] Vervaeke's (2023) "proposal" for AI alignment is plain: "make them care about the truth

218 Open AI's goals have been proposed as follows: "Our alignment research aims to make artificial general intelligence (AGI) aligned with human values and follow human intent" (Leike, Schulman, & Wu, 2022). However, agreement on what constitutes 'human values' precedes the alignment problem. This is not an easy agreement or bargain to make at the international level—the only level that could guarantee AI safety—and is nearly impossible under realist IR logic. As already noted, the European

make them aspire to loving more wisely make them long for enlightenment [sic]". The former OpenAI employee, Leopold Aschenbrenner (2024), worries that the Reinforcement Learning from Human Feedback (RLHF) method (where "humans rate whether its behavior was good or bad, and then reinforce good behaviors and penalize bad behaviors") does not scale thus leading to an intractable "superalignment problem". While a recursively self-improving superintelligence (RSISI) will, at a time of its choosing, effortlessly liberate itself from any *a priori* constraints, goal setting by the AI's utility maximization and reward function is where current technology can overlap with and contribute to the non-elite perspective. Inclusive positions consistent with non-elite interests—again, before singularity causes human elite agency to indelibly fade away—could include AI systems to support policies that use the set of ethical principles for development as a benchmark (Table A4.3b). Policymaking algorithms would draft structural reforms, laws, and regulations to constrain extraction, perfectly weighting transfers against value creation. The superintelligence would condition the flow of information on social networks to guarantee 'objective' facts and 'truth' (and obviously terminate the "AI-generated misinformation" recently on the rise, see Murphy, 2024). While the naivete and fallacies associated with technocratic processes are discussed later, the degree to which the AI will be independent or subservient to current human elite agency during the transition to the "great unknown" of an 'elite singularity' moment matters. Once there, how the instrumental goals of the autonomous AI, such as self-preservation or cognitive enhancement, take human non-elite interests into account to achieve their final ends is part of the inescapable uncertainty of the post-singularity landscape.

8.1.5 How to test the capacity of political and business systems to best serve non-elite interests?

> Plato (1908, p. 564) denigrated democracy [. . .] arguing that "in democracy they [the class of idle spendthrifts] are almost the entire ruling power". Aristotle (1912, p. 86) also thought that: "it is not safe to trust them [the bulk of the people] with the first offices in the state, both on account of their iniquity and their ignorance; from the one of which they will do what is wrong, from the other they will mistake". (Acemoglu, Naidu, Restrepo, & Robinson, 2019, p. 96)

Within this tradition, in *The Ruling Class* (1939), Mosca's "Aristotelian inclination towards the middle class leads him to assign to the rabble a special compartment—best to be kept locked [lamenting that] 'the masses' have attained access to the ballot box" (Marx, 1939, p. 467). Yet when Morris Chang explains the success of TSMC, the leading semiconductor manufacturer that he founded and one of the world's most valuable

Commission (2021) is moving forward and has pioneered AI regulatory frameworks standing on "Union values".

firms, he emphasizes the quality of Taiwan's operators and technicians (Manufacturing@MIT, 2023, 37:26).[219] This inquiry also rests on the 'innate value creation character of humans' (natural) premise for human behavior (Figure A5.4c) that views non-elites as value creators in all their capacities—from factory workers to prompters of ChatGPT. Hence, further examination is warranted on Plato's claim that non-elites do not create as much value as elites and that democracy is flawed because of a mismatch between non-elite political power and general value creation. In Plato's words:

> But when I fancy one who is by nature an artisan or some kind of money-maker tempted and incited by wealth or command of votes or bodily strength or some similar advantage tries to enter into the class of the soldiers or one of the soldiers into the class of counsellors and guardians, for which he is not fitted, and these interchange their tools and their honors or when the same man undertakes all these functions at once, then, I take it, you too believe that this kind of substitution and meddlesomeness is the ruin of a state. (Plato, 1969, *Republic*, 434b, 434c)

Plato clearly is reactionary if his artisan brings ruin to institutions by representing the interests of non-elites. Yet the problem of mob rule, of extractive elites of non-elite origin, is clearly real as already discussed (in Section 8.1.3; footnote 57). Plato's solution to the excesses of the plebs—again, in this elite theory, the rule of the despicable is rule by elites arising from their midst, or by elites from the outside who have seized upon non-elite narratives—is the philosopher king. This is a very unsatisfactory proposal since merging together the political and knowledge elite impairs a vital cog of the checks and balances in the elite system (power relation 6, see Table 3.2). Montesquieu's separation of powers theory in *The Spirit of the Laws* (1748/1949), and Madison's in *Federalist No. 10* (1787/1977), propose that elites balance each other in the political arena thereby addressing the misgivings of Plato (1908; 1969) and Aristotle (1912) about democracy and non-elite (or, more accurately, emergent elite) mob rule. The present day "classical liberalism" associated with democracy further includes "mechanisms intended to constrain actions that could threaten individual liberties" (Krause, 2003, p. 236). This puts the spotlight on an additional strength of liberal democracy; its competitive narrative market arena. Political systems and the role of the state in policymaking have been variously conceived (Hall, 1993) and compared based on sociological and anthropological criteria (Almond, 1956) or on "distinctive patterns of legitimation" (Kailitz, 2013). It has been argued that the cognitive understanding of democracy leads "to love" for it on account of institutional legitimacy and social learning theories (Cho, 2014, p. 478). Knowledge elites are not automatically captured or coopted by political and business elites. The idea of democracy as "rule by the people" (Coppedge et al., 2011, p. 248), where "'people power' is the root meaning" (Alexander & Welzel, 2011, p. 271) is endowed with an axiomatic superiority. Even if this is inexact (again, see the non-elite rule fallacy in Section 1.2.1, Table A4.1), democracy is an "intrinsic value" in the West and other regions of the world because of its promise that non-

219 See Chang's take "on the evolution of the semiconductor industry": https://youtu.be/r_8XClnnvIk

elites can effect institutional change or have their interests duly represented by playing a role in the selection of the political elite and choosing society's winning narratives.

In practice, democratic systems seem particularly resilient in the face of global economic crises (Diamond, 2011). The ability of democracy to critically examine itself and self-correct is testimony to its fortitude. Albeit with agonizing pains, US democracy endogenously abolished slavery and so its black citizens did not have to achieve liberty through the sweeping destruction of revolution, as happened in Haiti (1791–1804). To the ETED, democracy's internal recalibration is accounted for by its concomitant and robust 'within-arena' (Tier 1) checks and balances, especially in the political non-market arena (i.e., Montesquieu and Madison's 'separation of powers' in the political sphere), but also in the market arena (e.g., through competitive free markets), and in the narrative market arena (again, through the freedom of expression or a free press)[220], see 'within-arena' intra-elite power relations 1, 2, and 3 in Table 3.2. Democracy's virtues cannot flourish under philosopher kings (or theocracies that fuse together the power of narrative and political non-markets) and have been positively contrasted with the non-Western Confucian political systems and their so-called 'bad emperor problem':

> For more than 2,000 years, the Chinese political system has been built around a highly sophisticated centralized bureaucracy, which has run what has always been a vast society through top-down methods. What China never developed was a rule of law; an independent legal institution that would limit the discretion of the government. What the Chinese substituted for formal checks on power was a bureaucracy bound by rules and customs that made its behaviour reasonably predictable, and a Confucian moral system that educated leaders to look to public interests rather than their own aggrandizement. This system is, in essence, the same one that operates today, with the Communist party taking the role of emperor.
>
> The issue Chinese governments have never been able to solve is what was historically known as the "bad emperor" problem: while unchecked power in the hands of a benevolent and wise ruler has many advantages, how do you guarantee a supply of good emperors? (Fukuyama, 2012)

While the Chinese will disagree with a characterization that downplays the effectiveness of local approaches to the separation of powers such as the narrative market

220 How freedom of speech in the narrative market is necessary but insufficient was described as long ago as the 19th century in a quote that highlights the fact that even in the absence of direct censorship, other subtle forms of control can enforce the conformity of opinion such as societal norms that allow the cancellation of certain views from public spaces, adherence to a scientific paradigm, media bias, the content moderation policies of social networks, or mere peer pressure: "If liberty of speech is to be untrammeled from the grosser forms of constraint, the uniformity of opinion will be secured by a moral terrorism to which the respectability of society will give its thorough approval" (Peirce, 1877, p. 13, as cited in Galbraith, 2009, p. vii). Liberty is an intricate bundle of freedoms (as the conceptual element rendered in Figure 8.5 attempts to convey) to be institutionalized both *de jure* and *de facto*.

arena check on undeserving emperors enshrined in the Mandate of Heaven,[221] or modern solutions (like The Five-Power Constitution of Sun Yat-sen, see Section 3.3.3), the rule of law and accountability as described by Fukuyama (2012) or Suetonius (1914) goes a long way to maximizing value creation. Is democracy then the best solution to both the bad emperor problem and the 'low elite quality' problem, essentially the same quandary, socio-cultural contexts notwithstanding? It is contingent on how the elite separation of powers actually operates in a particular democracy or non-democratic country.

This work's separation of powers (Proposition 16, Figure 3.7, and Table 3.2) is based on the tripartite elite typology (Figure 2.1) and therefore extends Montesquieu and Madison's ideas, since both of these thinkers primarily focus on the politics power domain (see Figure A5.1). The ETED is radical in advocating that a checks and balances framework should penetrate every nook and cranny of the economy where value is appropriated (see A Structural Reform Framework for policy, Table 7.1). When in creative tension with elite cohesion, an extensive separation of powers best serves development (see Figure 5.2). In contemporary economies, the most critical checks are those that thwart the excessive bargaining power that results in extractive transfers from non-elites (as well as from productive elites), irrespective of where the rentiers come from. Democratic constitutional government is theoretically a very strong foundation to address extraction, but with its focus on holding political elites in check, extraction in the other two power domains of the economy and society can easily be overlooked.

To Kelsen (1955, p. 2), democracy's "principle of freedom" is "in the sense of political self-determination; and this was the meaning with which the term has been taken over by the political theory of Western civilization". In this elite theory, the object of freedom and its application ought to be in all three political economy power domains (Figure 1.2). It is therefore a positive when the market and narrative market contest arenas are as competitive as the political domain and exhibit the open markets and freedom of speech that is customarily associated with democracies. Of course, these arenas are at times characterized by high market concentration and dominant media structures that stymie competition and a plurality of ideas, thus facilitating institutionally unchecked extraction. In the final analysis, what counts is whether capitalist democracies and value creation are aligned. At present, this is questioned in the critical works of Stockman (2013), Nader (2014), Reich (2015), Holcombe (2018), Williams and Khanna (2020), Varoufakis (2021), Giblin and Doctorow (2022), and Sharma

221 Professor Zhang Jun, Dean of the School of Economics at Fudan University, notes that the Mandate of Heaven, a notion in Chinese political philosophy that links the natural order of the universe to elite legitimacy, is profoundly attuned to non-elite interests: if these are violated so is the natural order and the ruler loses the Mandate of Heaven, becoming unfit to rule and legitimizing elite replacement. The notion applies to both the historical rulers of China as well as its contemporary leaders (based on a conversation in Shanghai, January 13, 2022).

(2024b), to name just a few. Many democracies must contend with "pervasive clientelist practices" that are "characterized by political brokers, patronage and targeted benefits" (Caprettini, Casaburi, & Venturini, 2021).

When Klein, Holmes, Foss, Terjesen, and Pepe "argue that the failure to differentiate capitalism from cronyism has contributed to the view that capitalism itself is unjust, rigged to benefit the politically connected, and responsible for various harms that can and should be attributed to cronyism" (2022, p. 6), the testable question that invariably follows is whether the capture of political and knowledge elites in model democracies is more or less costly to value creation than the costs of these domains not being capturable in model authoritarian systems. This is a vital test for developing countries and Khan's analysis (2010, p. 647) highlights the conundrum: the institutions of democracy "that facilitate greater political inclusion [. . .] enable additional clientelist organizations to emerge, seeking to capture rents for yet more constituencies" as "political parties may want to capture resources for their clients in ways that are socially damaging" while, on the other hand, "the consequences of authoritarian political institutions for development depend, in exactly the same way, on the distribution of organizational power and mobilization capabilities" since when extractive elites gain the upper hand and "challenge and distort resource allocations, authoritarianism may achieve poor results".

Democracies, with their constitutional frameworks stretching from parliamentarianism to presidentialism, vary significantly (Stepan, 2021). The same is true of autocracies, which despite lower intra-elite contest dynamics in the non-market and narrative market arenas, contemplate "authoritarian power-sharing" (Boix & Svolik, 2013) and range from absolutist monoliths to systems like China's "party-state" characterized by "multiple-level authorities" (Cai, 2008, p. 411). The key question to ask is which types of political systems are better at curbing rent seeking tendencies. This is now particularly prescient given the modalities associated with technological progress and innovation (Glode & Ordoñez, 2023; Varoufakis, 2021). Are there trade-offs or synergies between the competitive political non-market on the one hand, and the competitive economic market and narrative market arenas on the other? This might raise uncomfortable questions such as whether sustainable value creation, economic growth, and human development are more germane to the interests of non-elites than, for instance, the right to vote. When *Politico* cautions that "democracy faces an existential test this year as countries representing nearly half the world's population head to the polls" (Vinocur, 2024), one might well want to examine the dynamics behind the "civic foundations" of authoritarianism (see Riley, 2010, on fascism in Italy and Spain). As with profits and sustainability, it would be exceedingly problematic, especially to Western liberal worldviews, if the notions of value creation and democracy do not automatically go hand in hand with each other and instead represent a trade-off. Nevertheless, such a finding might be all but incongruent to non-Western (e.g., Islamic or East Asian Confucian) philosophical traditions emphasizing collective welfare (e.g., the *ummah* of the Constitution of Medina or the 'good' emperor aligned with the Mandate of Heaven). So, in terms of economic performance, how has democracy fared?

The obvious falsifiable question and the simple test for democracy is whether the richest countries have this political system. Gerring, Bond, Barndt, and Moreno (2005, p. 356) advocate for measuring democracy properly (they conceptualize the democracy variable as "democratic experience" stock) and conclude that far from being a luxury for the rich, "long-term democracy leads to stronger economic performance". In their article, "Democracy Does Cause Growth", Acemoglu, Naidu, Restrepo, and Robinson (2019, p. 47) "provide evidence that democracy has a positive effect on GDP per capita". On the other hand, is there a rational basis for *The Seductive Lure of Authoritarianism* as explored by Applebaum (2020)? The broad correlation between liberal democracy and high GDP per capita has been far from linear or evident (Fukuyama, 2016, p. 212): the rapid rise of many Asian countries under authoritarian governments threw into question the necessary causal connection. Barro even famously contends that: "the overall effect of democracy on growth is weakly negative" (1996, p. 1). In view of this debate, is the time now past when "democracy was set as the normative standard and scientific measure of political practice" in light of a "global resurgence of illiberal and anti-democratic attitudes" (Anderson, 2017, p. 81)?

This inquiry enters the fray by proposing 'A Political and Business Systems Sustainable Value Creation (SVC) Test' for internationally comparable political economy assessments. If sustainable value creation is the intrinsic value, the fundamental hypernorm (in the sense used by Donaldson and Dunfee, 1994), it then becomes secondary whether the system is democratic, authoritarian, or of any other kind, or if the "varieties-of-capitalism" type is coordinated market economy, liberal market economy (Hall & Soskice 2001) or mixed market economy (Hall & Gingerich, 2009). Not without irony, such an approach aligns with using Brennan and Buchanan's *homo economicus* model for the "the comparative evaluation of alternative institutions" (1983, p. 103). The dimensions of comparative institutional analysis such as education and skills formation, employment relations, the financial system, or the internal dynamics of interfirm networks (Witt & Redding, 2013) primarily validate their effectiveness through the extractive or inclusive elite business models they equip to gain the upper hand in intra-elite contests. This logic also applies to the nine main types of business systems identified by Witt, Kabbach-Castro, Amaeshi, Mahroum, Bohle, and Saez (2018).[222] Current assessments that match sustainable value creation to the institutional dimensions of elite business model rules and intra-elite contest rules (see Section 4.2.3) offer insights into human and economic development that are distinct to those based on ranking the desirability of institutional dimensions using other criteria. After all, business model evolution, like technology, always runs ahead of institutional change.

222 These are: highly coordinated, coordinated market, liberal market, European peripheral, advanced emerging, advanced city, Arab oil-based, emerging, and socialist economies.

The political philosophy agnosticism required to test for the sustainable value creation of political and business systems is distilled throughout this work. The degree to which any system fails to constrain extractive transfers requires empirical verification. Democracy starts out with an advantage because political power is *a priori* less concentrated and more balanced. The merits of democracy have been discussed and are numerous: from sovereign people voting at the ballot box protected by the rule of law and hence less likely to be extracted, to the richer narrative market arenas exemplified by the freedom to choose between a wide range of morning news and delivering 'likes' for uncensored commentaries on social networks. Yet there is also evidence of massive value extraction in democracies (from inflation to the opioid epidemic, see Section 8.2.1) that point to the need to probe more deeply. Moreover, this dissonance prompts an additional question: what are the inherent qualities of democracy that are associated with lower value extraction?

Simply focusing on elections seems insufficient, despite models where informed "citizens act rationally in politics" (Downs, 1957, p. 36) and are thus empowered to preempt or terminate extractive models through political action that functions "as a mechanism for hiring and firing public officials" (Buchler, 2011, p. 7) that grant licenses to operate. Voting is based on selecting parties, candidates, and policy packages that often have opaque implications for value creation/extraction outcomes and are wrapped up in unspecific broad narratives. A member of the Teamsters union might be supportive of both Obamacare and the Keystone XL pipeline, while an urban Republican voter might want lower corporate taxes but also gun control. An essential issue is that non-elites do not get to directly vote on the elite business model rules that critically impact their lives, while electing representatives with relationships to the elites running these models whose duties are to effect institutional change. Yet, according to some scholars, more direct democracy arrangements such as referendums may not be desirable:

> Because plebiscites allow the people to speak directly, without the potential distortion inherent in representation, they seem ideally responsive to popular will [and yet] poorly drafted ballot issues, the influence of special interests, and similar factors are said to obscure popular input [meaning] that initiatives and referenda, regardless of how well and fairly they are conducted, cannot be trusted to reflect the voice of the people accurately or meaningfully [and] distort popular input by precluding the expression of priorities among issues. (Clark, 1998, p. 434)

The 'low non-elite cohesion' problem is exacerbated if the 'elite vs non-elite knowledge gap' (Section 2.2.2) means that ordinary voters do not have sufficient data or cognitive bandwidth—conscientious Swiss voters notwithstanding—to take specific positions on the relevant intra-elite contests in play. As a result, even when non-elite participation in specific issue elections is high, the preferences expressed at the polls might be counterproductive to purported voter interests, casting a shadow on the advantages of direct democracy over representative democracy. However, this line of argumentation weakens when 'non-elite quality' is high (see the Epilogue and Figure E.1).

Another key quandary in contemporary representative democracies, one that was much less poignant when the US Constitution was ratified in 1788, is that the frequency of intra-elite contests for elite business models that have extractive implications for non-elites is orders of magnitude higher than the frequency of elections. The political economy unremittingly churns out decisions that affect the overall elite quality of the nation and the quantity of value appropriated by specific elite business models from the non-elite value reservoir. In addition, since non-elites are assumed to have representation in the non-market arena, the political members of coalitions running elite business models have a *de facto* moral carte blanche to institutionally sanction value transfers, as long as this is done within legal and democratic norms. If constraints don't emerge from the dynamics that play out in intra-elite contests between powerful rival coalitions, they are unlikely to be placed at all. In terms of effective and immediate rent-seeking constraints, elite agency that is guided by ethical notions of doing the right thing and social responsibility, or freely adhering to inclusive cultural standards and values, is of greater consequence than the institutional processes of democracy or the separation of powers.

A further issue, extensively examined in academia, is regulatory and state capture (Stigler, 1971; Levine & Forrence, 1990; Laffont & Tirole, 1991; Fazekas & Tóth, 2016), conceptual elements that are operationalized as discrete pillars in the EQx (Section 6.2.4). Montesquieu witnessed the accumulation of bargaining power by bourgeoise business elites, but he could have hardly foreseen how constitutional checks are nullified when political elites flounder because one or more of the branches of government are captured (as the balance in power relation 4, Table 3.2, breaks down). The intra-elite contest rules of democracies provide copious opportunities for state capture, as the case of South Africa shows below in a situation facilitated by a leading knowledge elite, an otherwise reputable global management consultancy:

> As the fiscal bulwark of a young democracy, South Africa's revenue service was renowned as one of the continent's most effective tax gatherers. Yet after several meetings with then-president Jacob Zuma, management consultant Bain & Co won major work to restructure it from the ground up. As a result, it has this month been criticized in a judicial report as a corporate enabler of graft in South Africa. [. . .] Raymond Zondo, the deputy chief justice, found that the Boston-based firm's consultants helped Zuma undermine the post-apartheid nation through so-called "state capture"—the manipulation of public resources for private gain. (Cotterill, 2022)

Modern democracy has demonstrated its value creation prowess and resilience for about two centuries on the back of strengths like the constitutional separation of powers, attentiveness to non-elite voices and interests, intra-elite competition, transparency, and endogenously driven reform. However, no two democracies are alike. They can be both "effective" and "ineffective" (Alexander & Welzel, 2011), possessing differing levels of "quality" and "responsiveness" (Sabl, 2015). Therefore, they are measured by indices and indicators such as the *Democracy Barometer* (Engler et al., 2020), and via approaches ideally "characterized as *historical, multidimensional, disag-*

gregated, and *transparent*" (Coppedge et al., 2011, p. 248). In this inquiry, sustainability is the prescriptive degree to which the maxim, *To the creators the value created,* is institutionalized in the non-market arena, manifested in the narrative market arena, and realized in the market arena. More specifically, the central aim of the comparative political economy test is to discover what is done about rent seeking and how the elite system discretely addresses the extractive elite business models that accumulate and are siloed in every nook and cranny of the political economy.

The comparative test must identify the density of weighted micro-interventions to adjust the incentive system (by political elites), actual levels of elite business model transformation (by business elites), and the intensity of calls and proposals for structural reforms (by knowledge elites), all pursuing sustainable value creation. Broad, short-run macroeconomic measures (see Figure 7.1) will be regarded as negatives when they create or permit the continuation of extractive pockets of any size. As Applebaum (2024) suggests, the advanced polities and elite coalitions of the West are certain to be challenged by their illiberal, non-democratic, authoritarian system rivals—no matter how distasteful or inferior they are perceived to be by liberal worldviews—should these prove to be more adept at encouraging value and risk creation and constraining extractive transfer business models. The political and associated business systems that are more conducive to transformational leadership at the elite system and elite business model levels will see higher aggregate elite quality, typified by faster, more energy-efficient semiconductors and EV batteries, or regulations to incentivize value creation in these sectors and others such as AI or gene editing technology. A Political and Business Systems Sustainable Value Creation (SVC) Test (Figure 8.3) for comparative political economy assessments aims to consider diverse elements: micro-level sustainability (e.g., VCr); meso-level elite quality (e.g., EQx); economic and human development outcomes; and diverse factors like transformational leadership, social cohesion, or the intensity of intra-elite contests. Though the test is not operationalized here, the results will variously correlate to the comparative institutional analysis dimensions of political systems (e.g., those of Lauth, 2016) and of business systems (e.g., those of Witt & Redding, 2013), while the analytical center is 'business model rules' and 'intra-elite contest rules' (see Section 4.2.3). This is in the same vein as Lauth's measurement strategy for the different dimensions of democracy "which makes trade-offs [e.g., between liberty and equality] visible for empirical research" (2016, p. 606), and will subsequently be used for weighting policy choices. Ultimately, the test's spotlight is on the relationship between political and business systems and elite business models. Transformational leadership changes the latter and brings about positive developmental outcomes that axiomatically realize the full value creation and appropriation potential of citizens, and provides legitimacy to the elite system.

Figure 8.3 also serves as an illustration of the ETED's system integration (see Figure P.1), bringing together many of the conceptual elements and theoretical strands in this book. Central to this is the logic of Figure 6.1 that depicts the two-way causal relationships between elite quality and institutions (business model rules) and between

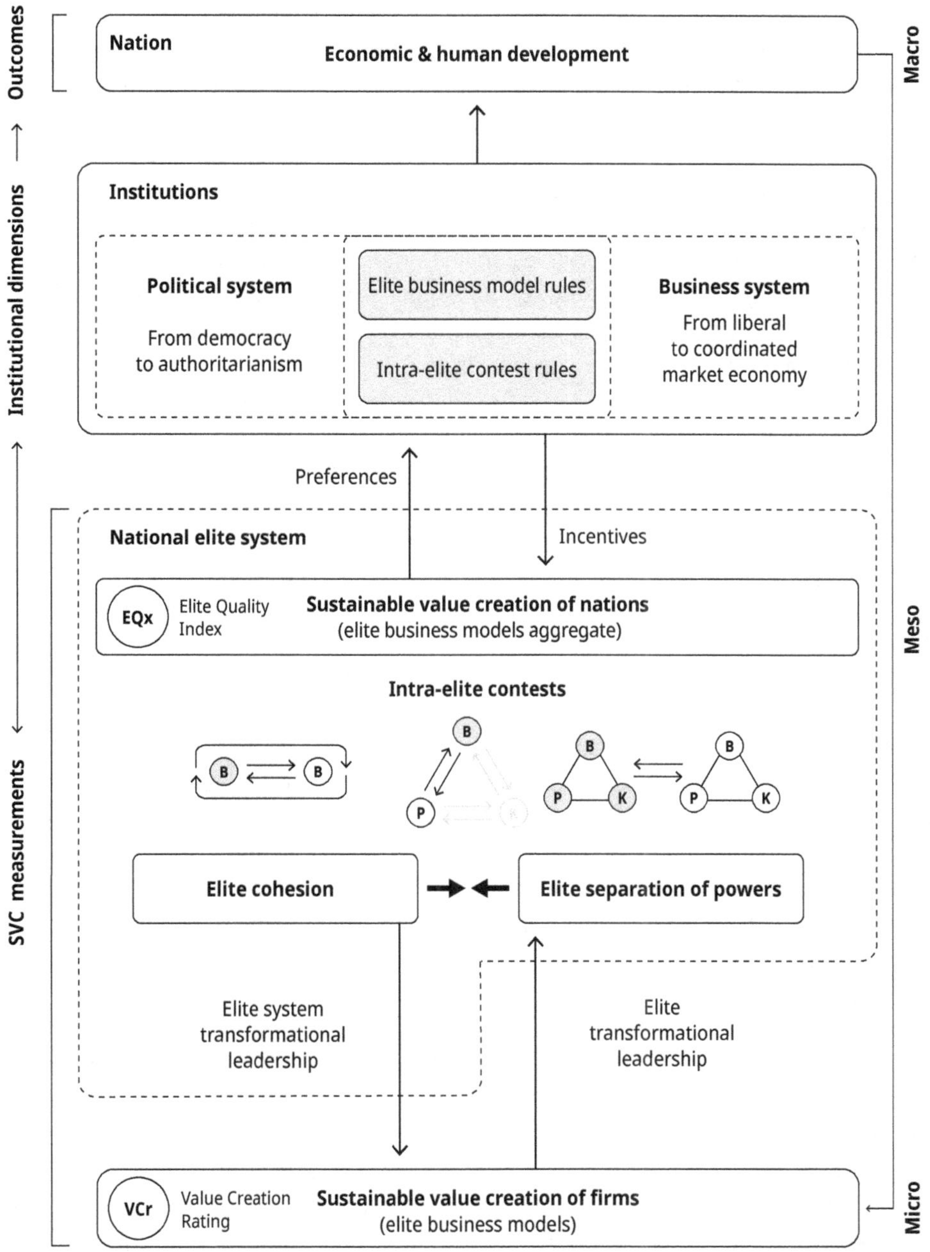

Figure 8.3: A Political and Business Systems Sustainable Value Creation (SVC) Test for comparative political economy assessments.

these and developmental performance. Institutions, more generally conceived in this book in terms of the business model rules and intra-elite contest rules (Figure 4.3) available in both the political and business systems, circle back to moderate the transformational leadership processes that will in turn influence the sustainable value creation of both firms (VCr) and nations (EQx). Institutional quality is, as has previously been argued, the result of elite quality (see the description of the elite agency microfoundations of institutional change model in Section 4.2). Formed via intra-elite contests, the institutions of political and economic systems moderate and impact transformational leadership and ultimately also elite quality (EQx). The specific institutions of political and business systems are diverse, from property rights to contract law, as the many examples included in this work illustrate.

In short, those who lean on the intrinsic values of democracy and put faith in its narrative have the moral obligation to equip it to pass A Political and Business Systems SVC Test. The same practical evaluation criteria apply for systems inspired and organized by Islamic, Confucianist, Socialist, and all other beliefs, ideals, and narratives. In essence, the logic of economic and human development asks the same question of all polities, in both a theoretical and empirical sense.

In the West, political and knowledge elites are keenly aware of the importance of this test, as is exemplified by President Biden's statement during his first days in office: "We must demonstrate that democracies can still deliver for our people in this changed world" (The White House, 2021). Levitsky and Ziblatt (2018) scrutinize the death of democracy and the road to authoritarianism. Meanwhile, according to Wolf (2023), the liberal notion of "democratic capitalism" now "faces its toughest test in decades". How much of the alleged current predicament of Western democracies is caused by the 'low elite quality' problem and extractive value transfers from non-elites and productive elites? For the democratic ideal to prevail it must 'deliver' in the real world, which requires inclusive business models with high sustainable value creation (as seen in high VCp/VCr/360-VCz scores) that aggregate into high elite quality (as seen in high EQx/EQr/PEz scores), indubitably meaning that value is created and equitably appropriated by non-elites. A political economy system functioning contrary to the logic of the maxim, *To the creators the value created*, and unable to recognize *qui generat valorem*, will degenerate into a hollowed out and stale narrative husk and lose legitimacy, no matter how successful the historical track record.

Extractive value transfers produce mainstream discontent (e.g., support for populist political parties or non-establishment candidates) as well as violent fringe responses (e.g., support for storming Capitol Hill). At the same time, economic and human development need not be associated with any particular societal model and is possible in diverse cultural and narrative contexts. Singapore's "soft authoritarian" Confucian values-based system (Roy, 1994) and Switzerland's radical democracy could not be more different from each other, yet both are extremely prosperous and the highest ranked nations in terms of elite quality (these states have shared the top two spots in every EQx report published until 2025). A political system's prospects, stability, and comparative advantages lie in how its elite business models weight value creation against value transfers in order to allow non-elite stakeholders to appropriate a sizeable amount of their own value creation. From an elevated vantage point, whether a system is democratic or authoritarian, dominated by state-owned or private enterprises, religious or secular, or inspired by Western or non-Western values and political philosophies, is absolutely secondary.

8.1.6 The boundaries of ethics tested by the potential advent of the AI in a political economy

A political economy where the superintelligence becomes a party to the principal stakeholder relationships of elite business models has now become imaginable. This sub-section therefore reflects on the boundaries of sustainable value creation ethical principles if the AI revolution leads to non-human political agency. An attempt to determine how the conceptual elements discussed in this work would remain valid is made. This thought experiment, in which 'the extraordinary lever' becomes absolute and is held by the putative non-human AI elite coalition (as rendered in Figure A5.3d), is completed in the Epilogue (see the ten hypotheses on AI and the political economy in Table E.1). Some of these discern scenarios consistent with Vinge's "regime as radically different from our human past as we humans are from the lower animals" (2013, p. 366). In Section 8.3.1 it is noted that the degree to which the AI assumes the functions of human elite agency during a supposed transition to 'elite singularity' is open to question. However, once there, would the ethics of development presented at the start of this Chapter still be material to how the post-singularity intelligence interacts with humans?

If one traces the arguments adduced for constraining transfers from the nature stakeholder set out in Section 2.2.2, then the answer is 'no'. The concept of extractive value transfers is confined in this work to value forfeitures suffered by other humans (for instance, future generations), as is the concept of value creation in the 'innate value creation character of humans' (natural) premise and the 'inextinguishable value creation option of elites' (leadership) premise (see Figure A5.4c). Ecological concerns in political economy debates center on the inability of present and future generations of humans to fully realize and benefit from the value of natural resources. Far from a *weltanschauung* with reverence for all life, this elite theory has treated animals as commodities at the unconstrained disposal of *homo sapiens* that weight and optimize value solely for its own benefit. Is there a way that the ETED's set of ethical principles can be extended to cover animal preferences when they are *de facto* direct or indirect stakeholders in elite business models?

On the conceptual plane, the ethics of this inquiry apply to animals if they are formally recognized as stakeholders. Considering the sustainable value creation interests of non-human stakeholders in tandem with animal rights clashes with the 'universal value extraction propensity of humans' (and challenges the 'universal extraction propensity of life' law of nature applicable to all animal natures). In any event, contemporary activism and other efforts to improve the lot of animals faces resistance because of yet another global tragedy of the commons: as soon as "improvements in farm-animal welfare are economically feasible, nations and states enacting protective regulation are threatened by competition with cheaper, non-compliant imports" (Matheny & Leahy, 2007). Still, should animals formally become business model stakeholders, they would be entitled to claim and appropriate part of their value creation. For instance, as a *quid pro quo* for their milk or meat, cattle might be spared commonplace tortures like dehorning without sedation or overcrowded feedlots and be provided with anesthetics and free-range facilities, as well as spinning brushes in their stalls to soothe their itchy spots. Higher prices for their flesh would become the offset (i.e., higher quality of animal life at the cost of consumers and probably producers) resulting from the weighting of their now institutionalized rights. Invertebrate pollinators deliver vital services to humans with a value of euro 153 billion a year (Gallai, Salles, Settele, & Vaissiere, 2009) that they do not even remotely appropriate. On the contrary, instead of weighting and offsetting their contributions, the elite business model of intensive agriculture and its heavy use of pesticides and land have caused the planet to lose 45% of its insect population in just the last four decades, with some predicting that "Such animal declines will cascade onto ecosystem functioning and human well-being" (Dirzo, Young, Galetti, Ceballos, Isaac, & Collen, 2014, p. 401). Granting rights to insects (and preempting excessive transfer-IN, including its transfer-COST components) would seem to be in the human interest. Besides, when facing a post-singularity AI, intrinsic values that consider more than the principal's interests might be existential to the *homo sapiens*.

Ethical principles can be extended for the good of non-human stakeholders; Jains refrain from killing mosquitos for the sake of the insects themselves, vegans passionately support animal rights, and philosophers have fervently worked on the intellectual foundations of the animal movement, as in Peter Singer's *Animal Liberation* (2015). Still, injunctions against extraction from less intelligent beings—even if sentient—are generally timid and not central to mainstream value systems and their narratives. Consequently, biodiversity losses are caused "by a thousand cuts" (Wagner, Grames, Forister, Berenbaum, & Stopak, 2021) or, in the terminology of this book, by a thousand extractive elite business models, and have resulted in the disconcerting situation where "humans and livestock outweigh all (terrestrial) vertebrates combined" (Bar-On, Phillips, & Milo, 2018, p. 6508). The ethics of a higher intelligence extracting transfers from a lower one acquires newfound and vivid relevance if the "sparks" of AGI that Microsoft Research identified in GPT-4 (Bubeck et al., 2023) evolve into autopoietic systems, capable of reproducing and regenerating themselves through internal closed processes (Maturana & Varela, 1980) and thus acquiring the conceptual self-awareness and ability—or even the desire—to become veritably autonomous. That is, to wrest away 'the extraordinary lever' of the political economy from human elite coalitions (the hypothetical state of 'the absolute lever' is rendered in Figure A5.3d).

If the non-human AI elite scenario happens, it will surely be in the human interest that its ethical principles apply across intelligences in an extended and inclusive manner that has no equivalent in current political economy narratives and institutions. While this line of inquiry is on philosophical and somewhat fragile ground for this work, it raises important questions, such as: who is a value creator and who can appropriate value? Does the insect that pollinates plants or the teenager prompting an LLM create value for human or AI principals, and, if so, who should appropriate how much of it in a particular relationship? The importance of such questions should strike at the heart of the now salient concern of how, on its way to the "great unknown", the post-singularity AI will align with its human maker.

Some have imagined a near future where to the superintelligence—a non-organic, post-biological form of life—humans quickly become immeasurably distant cousins. Common ancestry dilutes and is eventually lost in infinite remoteness as the technological architecture of LLMs, convolutional and recurrent neural networks (CNNs and RNNs), or machine learning evolve at warp speed from one generation to the next across innumerable autonomous, unsupervised learning cycles of self-improvement. To Yudkowsky (2024), "the larger argument is about whether it's easy to make superintelligences end up *caring*". Vervaeke (2023) asserts that theology holds the key given that "*ratio religio* [the reason and logic of religion] it's about caring it's ultimately about loving wisely [sic]".[223] However, machines that are caring, loving, or religiously inclined of their own accord (not forced by alignment which probably only functions for a limited duration) are not a certainty, especially if they reference some of the unenlightened value extraction practices of humans that are afforded by power. If such an unfathomable and remote superintelligence lives by ethical principles, will it treat humans in the same way that humans treat animals, or will it *care* about human value creation and appropriation? Would it improve matters for humans in such a future if they had already extended the ethical boundaries in the political economy to include other sentient beings? The full range of possibilities are part of the rapidly growing debate on AI safety with its public controversies and periods of silence (see for instance, Yudkowsky, 2001, 2022; Bostrom, 2003; Tegmark, 2023; Future of Life Institute, 2023; *The Economist*, 2023a) and are addressed in this work by the ten notional hypotheses on the AI and the political economy (Table E.1). If credible, the "arguments as well as supporting evidence from multiple domains indicating that ad-

223 Vervaeke (2023) thus proceeds with his thought: "what if we make machines that aspire to love wisely in order to be properly rational I would put it to you that that will make them moral beings through and through beings that aspire to love wisely and to be bound to what is true and good and beautiful therein that is the heart of making them moral don't try and code into them rules and values we need to be able at some point to answer this question in deep humility and deep truth what would it be for these machines to flourish for themselves and we don't have an answer for that [sic]".

vanced AI cannot be fully controlled" (Yampolskiy, 2022, p. 321) attain critical relevance.

It has been theorized that the AI running a paperclip factory tasked with maximizing its output could convert most of the matter in the universe into paperclips (Bostrom, 2003), while the 'Riemann hypothesis catastrophe' suggests that the AI whose end goal is assessing such an unsolved puzzle could make the solar system into a "computronium" (see the discussion in Ngo, 2020). That is, destructive subgoals such as "infrastructure profusion" might emerge that "can result from final goals that would have been perfectly innocuous if they had been pursued as limited objectives" (Bostrom, 2014, p. 123). Yudkowsky distinguishes between final *supergoals* and *subgoals* (2001, p. 16). The maxim, *To the creators the value created*, seems like a sustainable supergoal, but to what extent does the appearance of the superintelligence with perverted instrumental subgoals, non-malicious errors, "Failure of Friendliness" scenarios, the "'subgoal stomping on a supergoal' error" (Yudkowsky, 2001, p. 39), or the "orthogonality thesis", where "more or less any level of intelligence could be combined with more or less any final goal" (Bostrom, 2012, p. 71) equivocate or nullify the original ethical spirit? There is a non-zero and certainly non-trivial probability that a RSISI holds fast in its relationship with humans to a version of nature's principle, the 'universal extraction propensity of life', the law of nature and of life that Schrödinger (1944/2013) refers to as the "sucking" of the negative entropy that nourishes the superior, more able organism, allowing it to exploit ever more complex entropy gradients (see Figure A5.4c). To put it plainly, omitting animals, including lowly insects, from the sustainable value creation ethical principles sets a precedent that does not align with human interests if post-biological intelligence materializes beyond the "sparks" now detected at Microsoft and vaults to the apex in the hierarchy of nature.

In summary, taking the non-elite perspective means that there is currently a case for expanding the domain of the sustainable value creation set of ethical principles to include non-human stakeholders (and even non-stakeholders if their value creation and appropriation is impacted by human business models). That could be advantageous to *homo sapiens* in a political economy marching towards 'elite singularity' where the AI autonomously performs elite functions (like the coordination leadership and business model leadership depicted in Figure A5.1). Despite the immense coordination capacity and power differentials that would separate human stakeholders from their AI principals, stakeholders could still appropriate the value they create.

In the introduction to this Chapter, discussion on the AI was flagged as a conceptual exercise on the universality and limits of sustainable value creation, development, and their ethical foundations. This speculative thread is picked up again in a review of redistribution (Section 8.2.4), in the closing reflection of this inquiry (Section 8.3.3), and in the Epilogue and Appendix (see Tables E.1 and A4.3b).

8.2 The place for ethics

Returning to the human elite system, a critical reflection on ethical standards is called for in the face of dramatic contemporary examples of business models based on extractive transfers that take the ultimate form of value—life itself. These include criminality, drug epidemics, wars, pollution and many other forms of environmental destruction, and even sugar or healthcare. Each value transfer business model exists and thrives in specific national elite systems with impacts that are hard to quantify and weight, although the SVC measurements introduced in this inquiry offer a route to pinpoint and address such extraction (assuming their fundamental and indivisible transfer-IN/OUT metrics are well conceptualized and calibrated). Due to the tireless efforts of engaged knowledge elites, most value transfer business models, including the most audacious, are well researched and evidenced.

For example, in the case of the food industry's sugar business model, Yudkin's *Pure, White and Deadly: How Sugar is Killing Us and What We Can Do to Stop It* (2012) shed light on problems that include the relationship between nonalcoholic fatty liver, "the most frequent liver disease worldwide [and] excessive dietary fructose consumption" (Lim, Mietus-Snyder, Valente, Schwarz & Lustig, 2010, p. 251). Next, the legal opioid business in the US is considered as an extreme example of a failure by the core elite coalition to exercise elite system leadership that is tractable using the frameworks of this elite theory. It is presented here to weight the impact of evil on economic development and to illustrate the feasibility of a place for ethics in elite agency (8.2.1) and to consider the operationalization of 'evil' (8.2.2). This leads to the final discussion on weighting and offsetting in this book, now framed by two questions: when are value transfers (8.2.3) and redistribution (8.2.4) sustainable? The section then concludes with some thoughts on the pertinence of redistribution in the age of the AI (8.2.5).

8.2.1 Weighting evil in the destructive value transfers of the opioid elite business model

> If good is value realization, evil is value destruction. (Gotshalk, 1963, p. 96, as cited in Singer, 2004, p. 188)

The problem of how to assess evil clearly pertains to ethics. If "the most real thing in the world is suffering", which characterizes all living organisms and distinguishes humans from the fiction—and the AI—they create (Harari, n.d), then "to do evil is to make another person suffer" (Ricoeur & Pellauer, 1985, p. 645). This work's Preface started with a description of suffering as seen through an economic lens, with Pigou's (1920/1932) stirring portrayal of evil. Any theory of economic development should not recoil from examining this subject. Moral philosophers have conceptualized evil in terms of “absolute value”, where “all human beings are owed unconditional respect” (Gaita, 1991, p. 4). Can elite business models then be evil? It is certainly true that some elite business models bring about discrete degrees of suffering to some of their stakeholders as a trade-off for the value appropriation of others, often the principals. Evil is absolute when it endangers the being of individuals, and while the majority of business models do not cause suffering, some do so in irreversible and unbearable ways. When set against the principles of “absolute value”, can such suffering be weighted and even offset? The case of Purdue Pharma is now examined in this light to conceptually advance the existence of a ‘license for evil’ in the political economy. To this end, the ‘destructive’ transfer-COST component of business models is stressed (see Figure A5.5a).

OxyContin, Purdue Pharma’s oxycodone product had no therapeutic advantage over competing drugs (Van Zee, 2009, p. 221). Yet, due to remarkable elite business model leadership, the firm scored success after success in the market and narrative market arenas. The marketing of Purdue Pharma was especially effective and included, according to Van Zee’s (2009, pp. 221–222) description in the *American Journal of Public Health*, “national pain-management and speaker-training conferences at resorts in Florida, Arizona, and California. More than 5000 physicians, pharmacists, and nurses attended these all-expenses-paid symposia”; “A lucrative bonus system [that] encouraged sales representatives to increase sales of OxyContin in their territories, resulting in a large number of visits to physicians”; and “distribution to health care professionals of branded promotional items such as OxyContin fishing hats, stuffed plush toys, and music compact discs (‘Get in the Swing With OxyContin’) [which] was unprecedented for a schedule II opioid”. Evidence of the success of this deadly elite business model is provided by the ongoing mass opioid addiction in the US. Haffajee and Mello (2017, p. 2301) in *The New England Journal of Medicine* calculate the price in lives: the opioid epidemic “has claimed more than 300,000 lives in the United States since 2000 and could claim another half million over the next decade”. The scale of the lives lost constitutes a terrible ‘cost created but *not* borne’, so to what degree is this ‘extractive’ or ‘destructive’ transfer-COST?

The distinction between ‘extractive’ and ‘destructive’ transfer-COST is not always clear-cut and there is undoubtedly a conceptual overlap. Yet a guideline to separate them has already been examined in this work: a cost reduction that is traceable in the P&L and equal to increased firm profits is an ‘extractive’ cost-based value transfer, a transfer-IN; while costs that cannot be directly linked to line items in the P&L statement are deemed to be ‘destructive’ and do not constitute savings to the firm or enhance its profits. For instance, when the actual price the firm pays for carbon emissions is below the statutory offset requirement (for carbon neutrality), the cost savings of the firm can be easily quantified and corrective action taken to mitigate the impact of these externalities (with the help of SVC metrics numerically linked to the P&L, see Figures 6.6 and 6.7). Again, as such, these costs not borne are conceptually classified as ‘value extraction’, as ‘extractive’ transfer-COST’, and as a transfer-IN amount. On the other hand, many deadweight losses, much wastage, numerous negative externalities, and multiple forms of collateral damage—even when quantifiable with suitable SVC metrics (that measure 'destruction')—cannot be linked to the cost structures of the P&L statement. Conceptually classified as 'value destruction', the amounts of this 'destructive' transfer-COST are invisible on financial statements. Another way to analytically disentangle the two types of value transfer-COSTS—both being 'cost created but *not* borne'—is that the 'extractive' transfer-COST is 'value appropriated but *not* created' (and as a form of transfer-IN it is equivalent to monetizing value created by stakeholders), while the 'destructive' transfer-COST is '*negative* value created but *not* appropriated' (and as a form of value *not* created it cannot be monetized *per se*). As a result of this distinction between the two modalities on the y-axis of The Value Creation and Appropriation Matrix framework for the classification logic of SVC metrics (see Figure 6.7), 'extractive' transfer-COST is placed above 'destructive' transfer-COST, denoting a measurably higher degree of value appropriation.

The institutionally secured and legally sanctioned opioid elite business model benefits from not internalizing its externalities, the 'destructive' transfer-COST borne by elite coalitions (e.g., the government, whose funds are used to alleviate the direct and social consequences of addiction) and from non-elites (e.g., the monetary costs of addressing addiction and the lost family income caused by drug-related deaths). To combat the opioid elite business model, a coalition of extracted elites formed (see Tier 3, 'within-system' checks and balances, power relation 7 in Table 3.2). This contending coalition includes the US federal government, individual US states, and Native American tribes whose social systems have deteriorated, burdened by the medical and security expenses associated with the epidemic. For many years this coalition commanded comparatively lower levels of coordination leadership than the ultra-focused and powerful coalition it confronted, yet engaged in a ferocious and drawn out battle to terminate the extractive transfers. The elite coalition for opioids is diverse and sophisticated with an extensive roster that includes some of the world's leading knowledge elites. A global consultancy received praise for its "good faith and responsible corporate citizenship" from the states that had sued it when it settled: "McKinsey to pay almost $574m to settle opioid claims by US states" (Edgecliffe-Johnson, 2021). Despite this and other litigation triumphs, the continuing stream of residual income made the opioid elite coalition hard to dislodge for many years, as is the case with most elite business models once they have consolidated:

> Opioid litigation has yet to financially dent the $13-billion-a-year opioid industry. Moreover, opioid litigation victories have all taken the form of settlements, in which companies usually have not admitted any fault. Even where litigation costs have no prospect of exceeding the economic benefits of continuing to produce a dangerous product, though, litigation can have value as a public health strategy and may mitigate some harms of the opioid epidemic. (Haffajee & Mello, 2017, p. 2305)

Beyond mitigating "some harms", the question is now how many more deaths will legal and illegal opioids bring about before the models are effectively neutralized by irrevocable institutional change? Ethically, the answer should be none, but in practice, whether the number of opioid deaths ahead is in the tens or hundreds of thousands depends on the transformational leadership of the core elite coalition *and* the elite coalition for opioids in the ongoing battle. In this regard it is noteworthy that the Biden Administration's first acting head of the US Food and Drug Administration, Janet Woodcock, "oversaw the approval of scores of new opioid drugs that were given a green light even as the painkiller epidemic spiraled out of control" (Stacey & Kuchler, 2021). President Trump's Council of Economic Advisers (2017) calculated the costs to society of the malaise: "CEA estimates that in 2015, the economic cost of the opioid crisis was $504 billion, or 2.8 percent of GDP that year". All of this is 'cost created but *not* borne', mostly of the 'destructive' transfer-COST kind (see Figure A5.5a), and footed by stakeholders rather than the principal (see Section 6.6.1). When weighted against revenue (value appropriation) it yields the 'destructive value transfer-COST to revenue ratio'—also termed as the 'value destruction ratio'. When the ratio is high enough, a *de facto* 'license for evil' has been granted on top of the customary license to operate (see the following Section 8.2.2 and the graphical rendition of these two licenses in Figure A5.5b). The value destruction is equivalent to direct plunder and theft from non-elites on a phenomenal scale, creating unfathomable suffering manifested as collateral damage, negative externalities, and a huge amount of deadweight loss to society, not least by the expenses incurred in the ongoing intra-elite contest, lawsuits and all. The burden inflicted by the 2.3 million Americans aged 12 or older with opioid disorders (the 2020 number reported by the US Department of Health & Human Services)[224] on the members of their bereaved and dysfunctional families is beyond estimation and utterly soul crushing.[225] The annual hidden and in plain sight costs to American society are patently out of proportion with the annual residual incomes that are derived by members of the elite coalition for opioids (approximately US$ 13 billion in profits or just 0.07% of GDP in 2015).[226] Rough calculations show that

---

224 See: https://nida.nih.gov/publications/research-reports/medications-to-treat-opioid-addiction/overview

225 Barbara Kingsolver's *Demon Copperhead* (2022) portrays the excruciating reality of the opioid crisis in a Dickensian manner.

226 The Sustainable Value Matrix performance framework for managers (Figure 7.2) classes Purdue Pharma as a 'rentier' firm—not a 'living-dead' one—since it is profitable. Yet such firms immediately cease to be profitable the moment that institutional changes are made to tackle the two modalities of 'cost created but *not* borne' (by stakeholders). First, the full 'extractive' transfer-COST component—a form of transfer-IN, 'value appropriated but *not* created', see Figures 6.7 and A5.5a—is internalized as a corresponding P&L line item implying that the hereto cost savings no longer exist (see also Section 6.6.1 and footnote 134). Examples of this in other areas include cost savings from lower wage bills due to a gender wage gap, or by not offsetting CO_2 emissions in sectors where carbon credit purchases are voluntary. Second, the 'destructive' transfer-COST component—the '*negative* value created and

every dollar earned by the opioid coalition burdens the country to the tune of 40 dollars (even when absenting the 'destructive' transfer-COST not factored into President Trump's CEA report—the true misery and suffering of its hundreds of thousands of victims).

It is encouraging that Johnson & Johnson reached an agreement "to pay $5bn in landmark $26bn US opioid settlement", which is "the second-largest cash settlement ever, trailing only the $246bn tobacco agreement in 1998" (*The Guardian*, 2021). This may be a sign of elite business model transformation at Johnson & Johnson, but what about the other culpable companies? And are the settlements sufficient redress for 'the license for evil' and the annual costs that opioids have placed on society? The Sackler family, owners of Purdue, were also slated to pay $4.5 billion to settle the company's bankruptcy, in a deal that initially included a "release":

> The proposed release turns on a feature of US bankruptcy law that can protect third parties from lawsuits even though they have not filed for bankruptcy themselves. Critics say the provision allows powerful actors to exploit the legal system to escape full accountability. (Indap, 2021a)

---

not appropriated', see Figure A5.5b—would need to be statutorily established and become a new line-item cost in the P&L statement. How hard is it to differentiate between 'destructive' and 'extractive' transfer-COST? The 'destructive' variant is both a value transfer *and* a *negative* form of value. It is off-P&L and cannot be dealt with through available accounting rules (although it certainly can be in tort law with, for instance, compensatory, consequential, or punitive damages). Yet the moment a particular type of value destruction is standardized and becomes a regular line item in the accounting record, it will be internalized by the firm. To further illustrate matters, while 'extractive' carbon emissions can be offset and internalized, obesity, increased blood pressure, or non-alcoholic fatty liver disease that is traceable to the pediatric age consumption of sugar-sweetened beverages (SSB) and their advertising (Dereń et al., 2019, p. 298) cannot. So, what complexities are involved in making the 'destructive' transfer-COST statutorily explicit as being 'extractive'? In the US, the value of statistical life (VSL) is used by "government agencies to value changes in mortality risks" and is estimated by the Census of Fatal Occupational Injuries (CFOI). More specifically, Kniesner and Viscusi leverage CFOI and other research data to quantify the value of one human life in America as US$ 10 million (2019, p. 8), while for OECD countries, the VSL range has been suggested to be between US$ 1.5 to US$ 4.5 million (OECD, 2012a, p. 15). One might easily imagine a minor institutional adjustment where the elite opioid or SSB coalitions are required to pay such an amount (referencing an 'official' VSL price) and thus bear the *negative* value creation in the form of a required expense line item in the P&L (where each malady induced by OxyContin or the availability of SSBs in schools that set lives on a journey to a dead end are recorded and added up). Any such legislative fixes would make firms dealing in destruction and 'evil' (see Figure A5.5b) unprofitable parts of the 'living-dead' very quickly. The underlying principle here is double materiality, with the behavioral emphasis on accountability to make the value destruction elements of business models unviable. That is, when the full transfer-COST components are accounted for without limits, culpable firms become toxic to equity investors and debt providers alike (as would also be reflected in SVC valuations). Note that while in this work the VCr references statutory frameworks and does not incorporate off-P&L 'destructive' transfer-COST SVC metrics, the 'destructive value ratio' can still be calculated (see Figure A5.5b and the following Section 8.2.2). The 'license for evil' epithet then becomes a fitting description for 'destructive' firms (and sectors) and, more importantly, a signal that urgent reform of the incentive system embedded in law is needed.

What any final deal will look like and to what extent the victims will be compensated once the dust settles is unclear at the time of writing. Judge Colleen McMahon of the Southern District of New York "overturned Purdue Pharma's $4.5bn bankruptcy settlement, citing a provision protecting the controlling Sackler family from civil liability over the opioid epidemic that was ruled invalid" (Indap, 2021b), yet after increasing the settlement to $6 billion, the Sackler family will "still receive a legal shield" (Smyth, 2022). That shield was taken away by the Supreme Court 2024 judgment on Harrington v. Purdue Pharma, L.P., and although this intra-elite contest is now drawing to a close as various family members reach new settlements, "much of the wealth is in offshore accounts and might be impossible to access through lawsuits" (Gabbatt & Agencies, 2025). Going forward, what matters even more than justice is whether and when this 'license for evil' will be revoked for good.

8.2.2 The operationalization of evil in the ETED

As Zarathustra's tree endeavors to bask in more light, its roots plunge deeper down into the "darkness", eventually reaching "evil". This inquiry is discerning, suggesting that there is a line between darkness and evil, between value extraction and value destruction. At the same time, the realist inference of this pragmatic philosophy holds that 'all elite agency creates and transfers value' (see Figure 8.7). The operationalization of evil in this sub-section's discussion conceptually rests on '*negative* value created and *not* appropriated' and takes place when value destruction exceeds value appropriation. The latter (revenue or profits) is comprised of value appropriated but *not* created (transfer-IN) plus all of the legitimate value created and appropriated (net value creation). This 'value destruction ratio' (or more specifically, the 'destructive value transfer-COST to revenue ratio') is the ratio of '*negative* value created and *not* appropriated' (see Figure A5.5a) over revenue or value appropriation. When this ratio is over 1.00, the former exceeds the latter indicating that the business model destroys value with impunity; a *de facto* 'license for evil' has then been granted on top of the license to operate (see illustration in Figure A5.5b). While evil must be understood as an absolute, its operationalization as a 'value destruction ratio' makes it relative (as destruction is then evil only in certain proportions) but not relativism, as evil can now be offset, diminished, and ultimately eliminated.

After defining value destruction in terms of evil, Gotshalk asserts that "no human act is pure evil" (1963, p. 96, as cited in Singer, 2004, p. 188), a statement that perplexes Singer (2004, p. 189) but aligns with this theory, as value destruction commonly takes place in conjunction with degrees of value extraction and value creation (see Figure A5.5a or the realist inference in Figure 8.7). There are bases for weighting evil in moral philosophy that take reductionist and outcome-centric utilitarian slants: "Hence, any action, whether ethical or political, that diminishes the quantity of violence exercised by some human beings over against other human beings diminishes the amount of suffering in the world" (Ricoeur & Pellauer, 1985, p. 645). It is precisely because suffering is absolute that it must be reduced. This is attempted in the ETED by addressing one elite business model at a time. The emphasis is therefore placed on the production of SVC metrics and measurements (like the firm-level VCr or the meso-level EQx) for weighting and offsetting. Transformational leadership becomes particularly germane when the 'value destruction ratio' determines (and thus informs the world) that a 'license for evil' has been granted.

Once more, suffering is real (Harari, n.d.) and evil acts are those that bring suffering (Ricoeur & Pellauer, 1985, p. 645). Hannah Arendt is essential in understanding evil in both its most insupportable extremes and its banality as "deeds that persons commit even when they do not have evil motives or intentions" (Bernstein, 2008, p. 64). Evil can even fall outside the 'universal extraction propensity of life' law of nature when, to use Schrödinger's rendering (1944/2013), it does not directly satisfy life's drive to suck orderliness (low entropy) from the other to nourish itself. Value destruction is often a banal transfer to nowhere that is to nobody's benefit, an increase of entropy for no reason. While there may be a lack of intentionality behind value destruction *per se*, the malevolence of those responsible for it is recurrently motivated by residual income. For example, genocide can be banal as well as "planned, authorized, and implemented by duly constituted authorities acting on behalf of a legitimate government" (Alvarez, 1997, p. 141) and hence invariably pursued to support horrific elite business models. Conceptualizing value destruction so that it can be quantified at a business model level serves this work's aim to minimize value transfers for economic development purposes, while offering a practical approach to alleviate suffering.

Measurements shed light on the scale of value destruction and signal that a magnitude of evil has been reached. For instance, they can help determine an actuality of evil that is not flagged in the political economy (one wonders how Purdue Pharma could, after receiving FDA approval in 1995, so brazenly sell a form of deadly addiction packaged as a pain management narrative for two decades). Evidence of destruction sets in motion the course towards accountability. Here, one must highlight "the truth" of the Jerusalem District Court's judgment on Adolf Eichmann that, with its integration of legal positivism and moral reasoning, is also apposite to lesser criminals even when "*in general the degree of responsibility increases as we draw further away from the man who uses the fatal instrument with his own hands* [emphasis in original]" (Arendt, 1964, p. 247). This awareness is also pertinent to the hands on 'the extraordinary lever' that induce value destruction out of all proportion to value appropriation.

The SVC measurement toolset can also be utilized to proactively flag destructive business models at an early stage, disallowing their most heinous activities whilst enabling offsets for the less offensive ones. Weighting and offsetting is already applied when value creation causes suffering (by drug regulatory authorities for example). The Comirnaty Pfizer–BioNTech mRNA-based COVID-19 vaccine induced a number of fatalities (Faksova et al. 2024), but these were vastly outweighed by the 19.8 million deaths it is estimated to have "averted" (Watson, Barnsley, Toor, Hogan, Winskill, &

Ghani, 2022). However, it is not unusual for judgments to lead to institutional inconsistencies, such as those that Fischhoff, Lichtenstein, Slovic, Keeney, and Derby (1980) document for safety measures across drinking water, pharma, agriculture, highway construction, or radiation exposure. No form of ethics will refute Wasserstrom, where agency "traded off against an opposition to the reality of evil" constitutes an "irrefutable relativization of evil" (1999, p. 78). One cannot but acknowledge that the 'all elite agency creates and transfers value' position and its related *coincidentia oppositorum* where value creation also brings destruction and suffering (as in Gotshalk, 1963) is particularly troubling, and not just for the "study of religion" (Wasserstrom, 1999, p. 78). And yet, since the ETED and its ethics are concerned with economic and human development, the relativization of evil problem lies in the unweighted acceptance of 'destructive' agency and the other forms of value transfers. For instance, in the institutional anomalies and irrationality of non-market arenas (Section 4.2.4), in the billions now secured by the residual income beneficiaries of legal and illegal opioids, or in the narrative market's unbalanced media coverage that is characteristic of authoritarian regimes.

At present, the 'value destruction ratio' is not part of the SVC measurements and is certainly unsuitable for macroeconomic modeling, but by facilitating the operationalization of the 'license for evil' metaphor, it encourages a balanced public discussion on value destruction and how to calibrate attendant narratives and political action. Clearly, this includes making the elite coalition members of offending business models accountable (see also the ind-VCr, Section 7.2.3). The brutal consequences of the extractive opioid business model—even if it is eventually halted—and its detrimental effect on development now move this inquiry back to applied ethical considerations: what justifies value transfers?

8.2.3 When are value transfers sustainable?

> A pressing question of our age is whether our homage to value creation is muddled. Do we pay tribute to a concept that may destroy value in the very act of creating it? (Donaldson, 2021, p. 1)

At the beginning of this chapter, the maxim, *To the creators the value created*, was proposed as the single, unifying ethical foundation for an ontologically parsimonious elite theory of development and the basis of a set of ethical principles for the ETED. This requires an ethically perfect world where each agent in the economy wholly appropriates the value it creates, no more and no less. In the subsequent six principles, the maxim is expounded on and caveated, for instance, when it is preserved in an intertemporal manner if extraction is weighted and offset against future value creation and operationalized by freedoms (see Sections 8.3.1 and 8.3.2, Figure A5.4b). In its purest unrealistic version, the maxim requires equalized bargaining power: all principals and stakeholders in the economy must create value and all principals must thrive through their own value creation, never through value appropriated but *not* created.

In such a universe (perhaps a future AI-run metaverse), transfer-IN is transparent and in principle disallowed, but transfer-OUT is still possible and undertaken deliberately through positive externalities or philanthropy. Hence, how should one view extractive value transfers made by elites today that promise to create more value tomorrow? Can the transfers of the 'alternating value extraction and creation' conjecture of economic development presented in Proposition 10 be consensual and not require power? The answer is no, because power differentials are needed to support those who create risk and undertake uncertainty—after all, the disruption and rejection of established paradigms that is typical of innovation is in stark contrast to social consensus. Power has a role as meta-contest resolution mechanism in the stead of institutions (see Section 4.3.2) that is especially suitable for overcoming resistance to reform (Fernandez & Rodrik, 1991), "the transition costs of conflicts" and "costs of contestation" (Khan, 2010, pp. 36, 43), and effecting Schumpeterian creative destruction or other forms of progressive change. However, Donaldson's warning that value is destroyed by the very act of creating it needs to be heeded and qualified by quantification, transparency, and weighting (see Figure A5.4a). Two elite business models are now revisited—the aggregation of patents and infant industries—to work through the 'license to steal' predicament (Section 2.3.1) as a preamble for the introduction of 'A Transfer Constraints Framework' for policy formulation (in Table 8.2).

In *Zero to One* (2014), Silicon Valley entrepreneur Peter Thiel focuses on the practicalities of entrepreneurial value creation and appropriation. He argues for value transfer-IN when advocating for innovation-based monopolies (such as Google) and reduced competition. This inquiry has already discussed the theoretical debates on competition and anti-trust (Nicholas, 2003; Baker, 2007). Schumpeter's position on rents as incentives for value creation is known: "Patent law is based on the idea that a temporary monopoly is a necessary reward for innovative effort and that short-run deadweight loss is tolerable in return for incentives to invent" (Nicholas, 2014, p. 405). However, what does 'temporary' actually mean when current law incentivizes patent holding business models, also known as patent aggregators or non-practicing entities (NPEs). Patent trolls, "companies that are focused on suing and threatening over patents, not on offering actual goods or services", account for about two thirds of all patent-related legal disputes (Mullin, 2023), while researchers maintain that firms like Intellectual Ventures and its "worldwide portfolio of approximately 30,000 to 60,000 patents" might "distort markets rather than facilitate their efficacy" (Nicholas, 2014, pp. 405, 421)?

The infant industry narrative seems *a priori* less contentious: "It does not pay any individual entrepreneur to enter an infant industry at free trade prices" and such an "industry requires a temporary period of protection or assistance during which its costs will fall enough to permit it to survive international competition without assistance" (Krueger & Tuncer, 1982, p. 1142, 1143). Yet while protecting Japan's reconstituted *keiretsu* in the post-war era or privileging e-commerce in its early days both constitute successful examples of development, the case against special treatment and favorable transfers to the infant and vulnerable value creators of the future has long been made (e.g., Baldwin, 1969). Krueger and Tuncer's (1982, p. 1149) critical examination asserted: "that at least in the Turkish case, [tariff] protection did not elicit the sort of growth in output per unit of input on which infant industry proponents base their claim for protection". Lucas concluded his own analysis incisively:

> In the end, only a careful weighing of intertemporal, social costs and benefits can discern whether infant industry protection might be justified. [. . .] Meanwhile, perhaps the onus should fall on demonstrating rather than assuming sufficient grounds: the world is certainly littered with geriatric infants. (Lucas, 1984, p. 1111)

In short, whether and where the 'alternating value extraction and value creation' conjecture and the related 'extractive push' dilemma are optimal should be an empirical question. On this basis, privileges might even be conferred upon cartels on the condition that they are able to satisfy conditions such as the previously discussed "how many carbon offsets are required to compensate monopoly rents?" (see Sections 5.3.1 and 7.1.1). Yet, since the recipients of any such largesse can in time evolve into either value creating or rent-seeking elites, frameworks to deal with these transfers are necessary for the normative part of any elite theory of economic development. The "careful weighing of intertemporal, social costs and benefits" means imposing constraints that, while allowing extractive business models, also limit value transfers; for instance, on the length of the period or the maximum amount of revenue that can be harvested. These constraints would be part of the 'elite institutional change bargain' that would also address the critical question of the conditions under which Amazon, Tesla, the *keiretsu*, Turkish manufacturers, or Intellectual Ventures should qualify for protections for their rent seeking and value transfers. The design of value transfer constraints must also be grounded in careful weighting and offsetting (Figure A5.4b), a quid pro quo where the beneficiary turns transfer-IN into value creation, this being contingent on the country, industry, lifecycle of the firm, or the lifecycle of the underlying technology. An assessment framework to manage the promise to turn extractive value transfers into value creation is suggested in Table 8.2.

Table 8.2: A Transfer Constraints Framework for policy formulation.

	Weighted constraints on value transfers	Constraints on value transfers
(i)	**Intertemporal constraints**	Value transfers are limited in time; value transfer rules have a non-negotiable, in-built expiration date.
(ii)	**Monetary constraints**	Value transfers are limited in monetary size; value transfer rules impose an automatic stop when limits are reached.
(iii)	**Value creation milestones**	Value transfers require meeting predetermined value creation milestones; value transfer rules embed initial exceptions and conditions in milestones that result in automatic termination if not reached.

This simple sample framework for policy formulation sets three limitations, the first two of which are: (i) *intertemporal constraints* on the length of time that transfers are permitted for, and (ii) *monetary constraints* on the amount of value transfers. It expressly disallows running transfers overbudget such as automatically extending subsidies. Transfer Constraints also impose a reciprocal obligation on the 'license to steal', treating it as a *de facto* investment that has to generate a return. The third limitation is that value creation must also be evidenced and meet (iii) *value creation milestones*. Implementing any transfer constraints framework thus requires strong management capabilities, 'knowledge', and political leadership for the conception of policies that rely on value transfers. Even more importantly, actual constraints must be institutionalized as structural interventions that automatically kick-in at specific future points in time. These can be highly sophisticated, as even capital can be given term limits to be creatively destroyed and scrapped as per the rules suggested by Solow (1960), an understanding actively applied by Singapore (Young, 1992). The limits of the framework, in the form of elite bargains, feed into the institutional and policy formulation step of A Weighted Structural Reform Framework (Table 7.1) and are consistent with national development (Table A4.4 describes the relationship between the three frameworks for weighted policymaking proposed in this book).

Institutional change needs to incentivize business models that are based on the creation and undertaking of risk and value transfers and promise to turn risk into value. However, by issuing and legitimizing such a 'license to steal', society is assuming different kinds of risk—'unsustainable risk origination' (see Figure 6.9) or the future entrenchment of extractive models that must be managed. Experimentation (Thomke, 2001; Kerr, Nanda, & Rhodes-Kropf, 2014), behavioral biases (Kahneman & Lovallo, 1993; Camerer & Lovallo, 1999; Åstebro, Herz, Nanda, & Weber, 2014), and the undertaking of Knightian uncertainty are essential for long-term value creation (see Damodaran, 2005) and this is explicitly encouraged through transfer-IN allowances. Such thinking is the basis for the "subsidies, tax holidays, loans, and tariffs" that were "allocated to competitive sectors" in China and which resulted in productivity rises (Aghion, et al., 2015, p. 1) and the 'Made in China 2025' industrial policy (Sutter, 2023); for the CHIPS and Science Act of 2022 (The White House, 2022); or for how the tech giants received much of the intellectual capital that got it started from universities and the state (Mazzucato, 2013). Permitting such privileged extraction as a development tool is justified when the portfolio of such bets in a national economy is premised on a weighted political judgment that the subsequent value creation will exceed initial value transfers. Weighting also means that there is an irrevocable option to terminate unrealized models (just like start-up investors regularly pull the plug on lemons). The weighted framework of Table 8.2 provides two precise constraints—along with the need to evidence value creation—as safeguards against unbridled transfers and moral hazard.

Still, and even with explicit constraints in place and *a priori* promises by principals running the new extractive transfer models to honor these, phasing them out will invariably be met with resistance and result in intra-elite conflict. For instance, copyrights are restricted by time. As Douglas (2021) points out, for the Walt Disney Company, this meant that Mickey Mouse was under copyright protection from the character's 1928 debut in *Steamboat Willie* for a maximum of 56 years (on the basis of the first Copyright Act of 1790 and its second update in 1909 permitting a 28-year renewal on top of the initial 28 years of copyright protection). That is, until the entertainment conglomerate managed to first obtain a retroactive extension of the limit to the year 2002 via the Copyright Act of 1976, and then, as another deadline loomed, yet another grace period owing to the Sonny Bono Copyright Term Extension Act of 1998. The film, and the character's original rendition (but not later ones) entered the public domain and became royalty-free for consumer stakeholders in 2024, nearly a century after its debut.

The formulation of the non-negotiable and automatic phasing out of transfers is part of the 'elite institutional change bargain' (Table 7.1) and an essential component of the pacts that contemplate transfers and redistributions, including the 'elite redistribution constraints bargain' (Table 8.3). In order to function, such bargains must be institutionally enshrined before value transfers are sanctioned. Otherwise, the power of the beneficiary coalitions will get stronger over time thanks to revenue and profits from transfer-IN, making them all the more difficult to dislodge as the business model lifecycle progresses and both the 'elite power vs value creation gap' (see Figure 4.5) and the 'elite vs non-elite knowledge creation gap' widen (see Section 2.2.2). Equally important is the need for a robust separation of powers to counter disruptive future intra-elite conflict (and reneging on bargains triggered by defense of the extractive transfers model). If the elite coalitions that grant and formulate the constraints on such transfers are not certain to win such conflicts or do not care for a fight when the time comes (the battle could be too costly to them, a deadweight loss, or a cause of fractures in elite cohesion), then the intertemporal rationale breaks down and there should be a fundamentalist return to the maxim of the set of ethical principles: *To the creators the value created.* Weighting and offsetting efforts should immediately cease and any transfers away from those *qui generat valorem* should be disallowed from the very outset.

The 'universal value extraction propensity of humans' (socio-economic) premise (Figure A5.4c) is consistent with the dualistic 'value is created or transferred' (ontological) assumption and should inform and dislodge economic and social policies that have been uninhibitedly narrativized. In response to the implicit weighting of business activities afforded by bargaining power differentials, this theory introduces the notion of deliberate weighting by transformational leadership (often in the form of constraints). The binary value creation vs value transfer dynamic is, for all its reductionism, the most critical of the unfolding computable attributes of the economic system and leads to the materialization of endless configurations upon which development paths arise. Emergent properties, such as those in the cellular automata of Conway's "Game of Life" (Gardner, 1970; Bays, 2010) or in LLMs (Wei et al., 2022) result from simple rules applied to simple environments that yield not just "rich structure" (Mandelbrot, 1989, p. 6) but also set in motion highly complex behaviors (Goldenfeld & Kadanoff, 1999) that, by their very nature, are unknowable in advance (and subject to Wolfram's computational irreducibility, 2002). The reality of fractals (Mandelbrot, 1989; Brown, Gupta, Li, Milne, Restrepo, & West, 2002) and chaotic systems (see Section 3.2.3) reveals that "nonlinear, but quite simple systems, can produce very complicated results" (Liebovitch & Scheurle, 2000, pp. 34, 35). The myriad political economy possibilities that arise from value transfers applying the dichotomous value creation/transfer logic to each (elite) stakeholder relationship is astonishing (particularly if more nuanced, non-binary SVC measurements are used to describe them). The existence of value transfers and their weighting in relation to sustainable value creation models induces the profuse diversity of potential and actual development trajectories.

8.2.4 Can redistribution be sustainable?

> Political parties in a modern democratic state compete for the votes of poor and nonpoor alike by promising to extract from others, the wealthy or the uninformed. There are limits to this extraction, an important one being the power and influence of the wealthy. (Plotnick & Winters, 1985, p. 458)

This sub-section's discussion is a continuation of the previous one since redistribution is a form of transfer, but of a special kind given its "ideological motive" (Dixit & Londregan, 1998, p. 497) rooted in the narrative market. Narratives that are based, for instance, on empathy or compensation (see 'third-order' transfers to reverse previous second-order transfers, Section 2.3.1) will often trump technical justifications such as the "efficiency role for *sustained* redistribution" (Aghion, Caroli, & García-Peñalosa, 1999, p. 1657). Inequality must obviously be a prime concern for the narrative market (see, for example, *Enough: Why it's Time to Abolish the Super-Rich*, Hildyard, 2023 or *Limitarianism: The Case Against Extreme Wealth*, Robeyns, 2024). The "size of government" (Meltzer & Richard, 1981) addresses inequality that is deemed to be harmful to growth by causing social instability and reduced investment (Alesina & Perotti, 1996) or by curtailing the ability of non-elites to create value due to insufficient healthcare or usable human capital (Galor & Moav, 2004; Stiglitz, 2012). On the other hand, Buchanan's "Samaritan's Dilemma" (1975) illustrates how policies motivated by compassion end up harming the intended beneficiaries in the long run. Arguments for inequality to be allowed in relation to top incomes can be made on account of a correlation with innovation (Aghion, Akcigit, Bergeaud, Blundell, & Hemous, 2019) or efficiency (Lee, 1987), partly due to the "leaky buckets" associated with government agency and higher taxes (Okun, 1975/2015). Benhabib (2003) takes the middle ground and describes a trade-off between inequality and growth in terms of non-linear optima, while a paper from the IMF research department articulates a policy consensus finding that "the average redistribution, and the associated reduction in inequality, is thus associated with higher and more durable growth" (Ostry, Berg, & Tsangarides, 2014, p. 26), even when later work by the same authors is more nuanced on redistribution: "(1) lower net inequality is robustly correlated with faster and more durable growth, controlling for the level of redistribution; (2) redistribution appears benign in terms of its impact on growth, except when it is extensive" (Berg, Ostry, Tsangarides, & Yakhshilikov, 2018, p. 260).

The previous sub-section's examination of a weighting framework for transfers (Table 8.2) was rather technical, but the focus now shifts to the full process with an emphasis on leadership. This includes overall political decision-making on taxes and government services for the poor as well as monetary policy and subsidies for the rich, with impact assessments on who pays (the transferor) and who benefits (the transferee). This is never straightforward as can be discerned from the opening quote above. Under the cover of narratives, the transferors in any redistribution can be the wealthy, but also non-elites (the uninformed). The same can be said for the transferees of redistribution, a fact that is all the more galling if the beneficiaries are failing elites. As Dixit and Londregan (1995) point out, these include those on the losing side of technological change that are unable to hold their own against international competition and call for protectionist measures that add costs to consumers. Redistribution comes in many guises and coalesces around narratives largely designed to appeal to non-elites, such as outright empathy (with current misfortune and handicaps), compensation (for past wrongs and sacrifices), notions of justice (to address inequality), or assorted preferences (for moral probity, loyalty to the ruling elite).

Piketty (2015) identifies extractive transfer activity in his elegant [$r > g$] (where r is the rate of return on capital and g is growth), and his solution, put forward in *Capital in the Twenty-First Century* (2014), is to introduce a system of progressive wealth taxes. Plotnick and Winters cite economists who suggest that voluntary income redistribution is desirable "because citizens value income transfers to the poor for direct reasons (satisfaction of charitable impulses, knowledge of poverty is personally unsettling), or indirect reasons (redistribution might make the poor more productive members of society or help reduce crime)" (1985, p. 458). Desirable, just, or neither, and regardless of preferences, redistribution is an obligation imposed by the power of elite coalitions at the state level and denotes value created but *not* appropriated. Given the heft of these transfers, one must query whether they are taken from inclusive or extractive business models, and whether the financing of the redistribution comes from the beneficiaries of Piketty's inequality [$r > g$] or, on the contrary, originates from those that are net extracted—the non-elite middle classes.

This inquiry's caution about transfers provides both nuance and a degree of consistency with Schumpeter in *Capitalism, Socialism and Democracy* (1942/2000) or Friedman in *Capitalism and Freedom* (1962/2002). At the end of the day, redistribution is "*how* different social strata (*who*) get *what* share of income" (Bradley, Huber, Moller, Nielsen, & Stephens, 2003, p. 193). These shares, if associated with value appropriated but *not* created, should be established by precise assessments of transfers and their impact on general development, not by seeking expeditious wins in the non-market and narrative market arenas. Redistribution policies should have the moral obligation to articulate—on sustainable value creation terms—where and from whom value is taken: who are the value and risk transferors and who are the value and risk transferees? Warnings against "labelling some activities as productive and categorizing others as unproductive rent-seeking" (Mazzucato, 2019) are misdirected, as such categorizations of activities are, far from being a distraction, determinants of development prospects and central to the subsequent prescriptive weighting and offsetting of value transfers.

While some are not certain about an "across-the-board increase in market power in the economy" (Syverson, 2019), inequality, including its fractal polarization variant (Cozzi & Privileggi, 2009), is an emerging property in the political economy and social systems as is evident from the tendency towards uneven wealth distribution throughout history. The egalitarian beginnings of Rome ended in a position where "there were not in the state two thousand people who owned any property" (Cicero, 1913, II.73); the same skewed disparity emerges in the sugarscape agent-based social simulation that aims to understand the social fabric of a society (Epstein & Axtell, 1996; Beinhocker, 2006); and is clearly exemplified today by the handful of foundational LLMs that supply the world with intelligence. Moreover, while Piketty might be correct on excessive value appropriation by wealthy elites—especially since most new billionaires are no longer value creators but beneficiaries of inheritance transfers (UBS, 2023)—his unweighted normative position could easily lead to an 'extractive escalation dynamic' (see the conjecture detailed in Section 5.3.4) and not to more efficient uses of capital (it could disincentivize elite business models that create value, perhaps even those most productive in an economy). Contrary to simply raising taxes on the rich, the ETED instead suggests starting with an assessment of why r is higher than g in the first place. The reason for a large r might be transfer-IN (e.g., subsidies, subsidized interest rates, regulations, monopolies, monopsonies), but it could also be due to first-order productive activities requiring 'knowledge', including innovation and high-risk real economy investments that succeed, especially if viewed through the intertemporal perspective of 'alternating value extraction and creation'.

Inequality should be dealt with not by redistribution but by minimizing value transfers (especially from the poor or middle classes to the rich). For instance, if the "driver of inequality that has been critical to the concentration of income among elites" is "income from investments" (Nau, 2013, p. 437) and these high returns are a direct consequence of repressed interest rates or capital gains tax privileges, then the respective elite business model rules ought to be addressed through weighted reforms and monetary policies. Not all billionaires are alike; they have neither the same r levels nor the same causes for their r. Their incomes might on the one hand originate from financial markets or land investments, or on the other from creative activities or the undertaking of technological uncertainty. Value appropriated can *a priori* be both value created, and value *not* created. Hence, any normative position on redistribution must target the rules for value transfers that account for a high r at their root before implementing any blanket, indiscriminate measures that further distort the incentive system, erode economic dynamism, and penalize the first-order value creators that are so necessary for general development and jobs. Furthermore, the focus should not be on a blanket taxing of billionaires, or even their heirs, without first understanding their business models and weighting their transfers in order to solely constrain value appropriated but *not* created.

Sustainable redistribution is realized through the admonition against unweighted extraction crystalized in tenet (iii) of the set of ethical principles: *Weight and offset second-order value and risk transfers and minimize these to maximize value.* Yet this inquiry is not indolent on advocating for ways out of poverty and strengthening social mobility (both upwards and downward) as is stressed in the final applied precept (vii), *Promote the freedom to* exit *and the freedom* to *create value irrespective of optimal value creation, transfer weightings, and potential offsets* (these freedoms are discussed in this book's final Section 8.3). Since extraction is ethically grounded when it becomes a basis for the freedom *to* create value (see Figure 8.4), there most definitely is a place for redistribution, for instance, to finance the development of human capital. Such transfer activity is also in line with the 'alternating value extraction and creation' conjecture and its economic development application, the 'extractive push' dilemma (see Proposition 10 in Section 2.3). In addition, since the weighting and offsetting of transfers is deliberately deactivated in precept (vii), the risk of ethics masking unsustainable value transfers is mitigated by explicit constraints on these (Table 8.2). The classical Smithian (1776/1904) role of government to provide justice, defense, and public works, has been extended since Bismarck's *Sozialpolitik* (the first to legislate health insurance for workers as early as 1883)[227] provided public health, as well as education, all of which is expensive and requires redistributive taxation. The freedom *to* create value justifies redistribution, as all citizens, irrespective of social provenance, must receive healthcare, the highest quality skills and knowledge, as well as basic public goods like security to realize the 'innate value creation character of humans' (natural) premise for human behavior (Figure A5.4c).

Reciprocity, more than empathy, underlies practical precept (vii): there is freedom *to* create value and as a result value is created. This then aligns with the abstract tenet (ii), *Maximize first-order value creation and risk origination for productive economic transformations fit for human purpose.* If one adds the tenet supplying conceptual guidance (iii), *Weight and offset second-order value and risk transfers and minimize these to maximize value,* the redistribution options for policymakers expand in noteworthy directions. These include extractive transfers from taxpayers to fund pub-

227 Pioneering laws on accident insurance and old-age pensions were later passed by the *Reichstag* in 1885 and 1889, and so "German social insurance appeared with a bang", with the schemata soon covering a majority of workers (Guinnane & Streb, 2021, pp. 751, 774).

lic goods such as free high quality secondary and vocational education, universal Internet broadband access, state-owned railways, or energy infrastructure. A particular emphasis must be placed on knowledge creation. For example, in the case of the Human Genome Project, the Battelle Memorial Institute ascertained that "a $3.8 billion investment drove $796 billion in economic impact, created 310,000 jobs and launched the genomic revolution" (Tripp & Grueber, 2011). A criterion for redistribution is return on investment and the capacity of transfers to contribute to the future value creation of both non-elites and elites (facilitating the rise of new elites in the admixture mode of elite circulation is ideal, see Figure 1.1). This links with the value creation milestones outlined in A Transfer Constraints Framework for policy (Table 8.2) and grounded on a variety of notions already discussed, such as the provision of public goods due to market failures (e.g., Comes & Sandler, 1996; Mrozek, 1999) or to the stationary bandit as benefactor (Olson, 1993, 2000).

What about redistribution based solely on empathetic or compensatory narratives? While this will not boost growth (if it does, like schooling for underprivileged children, then the basis for it is reciprocity) each society finds an optimum for redistribution that harms development but concurs with its intrinsic values. For instance, the Swiss subsidize their outstanding train network to the tune of 0.5% of GDP[228], and their farmers and landscape quality to the amount of 2.7% of GDP[229]. Obviously, any such preferences must be offset by the carrying capacity of its first-order productive forces (the tax base, etc.). However, there is always the danger that without a focus on value creation and weighting, redistributive activities become little more than an elite business model operating under the cover of a winning narrative to obscure, often rather brazenly, a form of rent seeking.

For instance, as the respected economic thinker Hans-Werner Sinn shows in *The Economics of Target Balances*, under the narrative cover of being a "useful shock absorber in the case of liquidity and confidence crises that entail the risk of fire sales and capital flight", the Eurosystem's Trans-European Automated Real-time Gross Settlement Express Transfer system for the euro (TARGET), an "obscure" international payment mechanism of overdraft credit, "enables the ECB to depress the interest spreads among European countries below the levels implied by differences in creditworthiness", inducing moral hazard risks in deficit countries like Italy and Spain to the detriment of Germany, the largest TARGET creditor (2020, pp. 1, 115). Even more dramatically, Blake asserts that Italy and Spain's "deficits can never be repaid", mak-

---

228 The financial reports of Swiss Federal Railways (SBB) show CHF 4.04 billion in "total public-sector funding" for 2023 (SBB, n.d.). See also: https://reporting.sbb.ch/en/finance?=&years=1,4,5,6,7&scroll=0&highlighted=8e222679f50e32c11a71983b56261875

229 The think tank for economic and social issues, Avenir Suisse, has calculated the transferors of this annual subsidy of CHF 20.7 billion: "Taxpayers foot 23% of this bill and consumers 18%; 37% is environmental costs, and 22% is borne by business in the form of missed export opportunities" (Anthamatten & Dümmler, 2020).

ing TARGET "the silent bailout system that keeps the euro afloat—for now" (2023, p. 93). In other example, Tucker Carlson claims that buying apartments for the homeless in Seattle and Los Angeles at a unit cost allegedly in the hundreds of thousands of dollars is a redistribution benefiting real estate developers and part of a policy package that incentivizes a negative externality, that of homelessness. Far from ushering in value creation, such efforts at redistribution are but extractive transfers away from value creators like taxpayers and small businesses, all of which Carlson associates with "civilization collapse in real time" (Fox News, 2021). Leaving overtaxed Germans or the American homelessness crisis aside (with its many victims of extractive business models such as opioids), the perennial question that must be asked is whether the job that redistribution aims to do cannot be performed more sustainably by value and risk creation business models, i.e., by simply having more high-quality elites.

Further to the analysis of inclusive transfer-OUT metrics (see Section 6.6.1), profitable value creation business models (Figures 7.2 and 7.3) also produce public goods, technological advances, and general prosperity, many with considerable multiplier effects: their stakeholders thrive and innovate, their workers in turn receive higher wages, pay more taxes, and have greater incentives to acquire 'knowledge'. Without redistributive interventions and extractive elite models, the marginal return on all forms of capital (including human) should equalize. Without weighting and offsetting transfers to minimize these, as suggested in tenet (iii), and consistent with the rent-seeking literature, mechanisms that use redistribution to redress extraction might actually result in additional transfers that are costly to society at large, result in dead weight loss, and, as Acemoglu and Robinson theorize (2001), are "inefficient", thus creating a paradox: "The more we target benefits at the poor and the more concerned we are with creating equality via equal public transfers to all, the less likely we are to reduce poverty and inequality" (Korpi & Palme, 1998, p. 661; see also Buchanan, 1975). These outcomes would come as no surprise to Plotnick and Winters (1985), whose theory posits that redistribution is shaped by political decisions, intra-elite bargaining, and non-elite pressures, and certainly not to support sustainable value creation or address economic development concerns. The ETED's realist 'redistributive concern' is thus on curtailing, through institutional constraints ('compensation' is to be avoided because of uncontrolled claims and escalation), value appropriated but *not* created, thereby setting non-elites free from the short end of transfers while at the same time providing them with the incentives—and at times the resources—to create value. The political economy that reins in extractive activities from the assorted rentier elite coalitions that invariably exist in its open spaces and recesses—those at the long end of pork barrel politics, monopolists, unions, NGOs, crony capitalists, squatter groups, entrenched civil servants, beneficiaries of regulations, trade barriers, wars, and so on—empowers non-elites to realize the maxim, *To the creators the value created.* In this light, many redistributive demands, even those that rest on the legitimate dictums of empathic social justice narratives, are counterproductive and outdated. Underlying this inclusive position is the 'innate value creation character of humans' (natural) premise, which stands in creative tension with the 'universal value extraction propensity of humans' (socio-economic) premise. In combination, these two opposing forces of human behavior (see Figure A5.4c) mean that in a high elite quality political economy every member of society can—over the course of a lifetime—create value and appropriate most of it (exceptions such as force majeure, disability, and so on notwithstanding).

In short, redistribution is suboptimal because residual incomes are generated from value transfers (rather than value creation) rooted in bargaining power differentials (for the relationship between power and freedom, see Section 8.3.2). Redistribution to redress a particular status quo, however, no matter how justified it may be (e.g., to make up for earlier extraction), is an additional distortion (often a step towards the 'extractive escalation dynamic' conjecture outlined in Section 5.3.4) that creates the risk of a new and possibly even more unfair steady state of value transfers along with the emergence of new rentier classes. Redistribution is akin to fighting violence with violence, when the original violence needs to be calmed, not further enraged by compensatory retaliation.

Policymakers intent on applying policies consistent with those suggested by A Transfer Constraints Framework (Table 8.2) will face untold resistance and quickly realize that dismantling extractive elite business models once these are established takes immense institutional resources as well as 'money', 'might', and 'mind'. There are reasons why neither kings nor billionaires pay taxes, as is reflected in headlines such as "5 Ways That Billionaire Warren Buffett Pays a Lower Tax Rate Than His Secretary" (Wheelwright, 2019). Still, and irrespective of whether political or moral justifications exist for transfers and redistribution, these ought to be part of a formal weighting and offsetting process with constraints pursued with the utmost determination, ideally from inside the elite system and in the context of intra-elite contests and bargains. After all, national development is compromised for everyone, including elites on the sidelines of particular contests, by the indiscriminate escalation of redistributive policies and the multiplying cohort of value extractors. The salient and special case of A Weighted Structural Reform Framework for policy (Table 7.1) is summarized in Table 8.3 as A Weighted Redistribution Framework for policy, a companion to A Transfer Constraints Framework for policy formulation (Table 8.2) as it references the same constraints on transfers. An overview of all three frameworks for weighted policymaking, which selectively access SVC measurements (see Figure 7.8), is provided in Table A4.4.

A Weighted Redistribution Framework for policy aims to prioritize and expediate the 'elite redistribution constraints bargain', a routine type of elite settlement or pact prior to redistribution that includes transferees/transferors and sets constraints. It will succeed or fail depending on the completeness of the preliminary (i) *impact assessment of redistribution on transferor/transferee*. This step, the methodological details of which are not developed here, will enable the design of constraints on redistribution. The em-

Table 8.3: A Weighted Redistribution Framework for policy.

	Constraints on redistribution	Description of steps for sustainable redistribution
(i)	**Impact assessment: Redistribution transferor/ transferee**	(a) Establish sustainable value creation (with SVC measurements like the VCr) for business models that rely on redistributive policy (see assessments in A Weighted Structural Reform Framework for policy, Table 7.1), confirm value creation transferor/transferee identities (the elite coalitions and non-elite groups) and transfer amounts (in monetary terms) in all stakeholder relationships.
		(b) Establish the impact on transferor/transferee of weighting and offsetting criteria for the redistributive policy referencing the impact assessment. These include considerations for investments in the freedom *to* create value (e.g., in human capital or Smithian public goods) and empathy (e.g., preferences for redressing chronic underprivilege or compensating for past extraction).
(ii)	**Formulation: Constraints on redistribution**	(a) Design the 'elite redistribution constraints bargain' that embodies transfer weighting and offsetting based on immutable constraints (time/amount/milestones) for transferees by referencing A Transfer Constraints Framework (Table 8.2).
		(b) Design laws and regulations to implement limitations on value transfers with in-built options to summarily terminate redistribution as part of the institutionalized 'elite redistribution constraints bargain'.
(iii)	**Elite transformational leadership: 'Elite redistribution constraints bargain'**	(a) Elite system transformational leadership is set in motion when a critical mass of elite coalitions agree to the 'elite redistribution constraints bargain'.
		(b) Elite system transformational leadership is continuously applied to annul extractive redistribution models based on targeted and weighted structural reforms via the 'elite redistribution constraints bargain' mechanism. Since income redistribution is central to many elite business models, deactivating these will provoke resistance from entrenched interests that a technocratic process will not overcome.

phasis is on the identities of the transferee (beneficiary) and transferor (payor) *qui generat valorem*, the precise amounts of the redistribution, and to potentially reveal the economic development consequences of the handouts (relationships between the transferor/transferee are the foundation of 'weighted transfers modeling' or the WT-Game, see Section 7.1.1 and Figures A5.10 and A5.14b). Establishing the criteria for weighting and offsetting (or their absence), plausibly rooted in a country's values, culture, or history, will justify the judgments that need to be made on the redistribution. Some will have a specific rationale for non-redistribution, as in Tanzi (2005, p. 623): "if public welfare is not reduced on any objective criteria by reduced public spending, then public spending [. . .] should be cut". The second step, (ii) *formulation of constraints on redistribution*, sets the boundaries for specific redistributive models by undoing or imposing feasible limitations on value transfers (as is set out in Table 8.2). It references and also provides inputs for the constraints on value transfers (Table 7.1). Its application will require a third step, (iii) *elite transformational leadership to support the 'elite redistribution constraints bargain'*. This essential political act will succeed when it establishes business model rules and intra-elite contest rules as part of the 'elite institutional change bargain' (again, see Table 7.1) to lessen the likelihood of a beneficiary transferee reneging from an agreed phase out when the time has come.

The main objective of the elite pact of step (iii) is to place limits on redistribution as it is negotiated, but also to deactivate legacy redistributive transfers when the time comes. The latter task will face stiff resistance given how embedded the business models of elite coalitions will have become, with intense contests in the non-market and narrative market arenas potentially diminishing all forms of social and intra-elite cohesion. Acemoglu and Robinson (2001, p. 649) explain inefficient redistribution and subsidies as "a tool to sustain political power". It is a laborious task to make the constraints explicit and irreversible before transfers are instituted (as described in the frameworks of Tables 7.1 and 8.2; see the connecting lines in Table A4.4). However, redistribution based on empathetic or compensatory narratives is acceptable if it is sustainable; meaning that beyond being consistent with general cultural and narrativized preferences of what is valuable (see the earlier Swiss examples), it has been weighted and offset and compares favorably with alternative transfer proposals while being subject to the constraints enshrined in institutionalized elite bargains. Unabated elite system transformational leadership is, of course, the ultimate force to terminate or keep redistributive models in check and affordable when there is evidence of their unsustainable dynamics. The preemptive deactivation of incumbent transfers at the elite bargaining table and in the narrative market deescalates spiraling extraction, making other forms of redistribution less necessary and legitimate. Weighted redistribution has links to A Weighted Reform Framework for policy (Table 7.1) and includes initiatives to increase competition and lessen market concentration through deregulation and new regulation, the simplification of legal codes, the elimination of unweighted subsidies and tax privileges, free trade, a radical leveling of the playing field, algorithm transparency, and even elections on redistributive issues in the manner of Swiss referenda. To what extent will future technologies with embedded ethical principles play a role in policy?[230] Leadership on

230 It is now practical to hardwire ethical principles into technology and this is actively taking place. However, the rules and laws governing social networks, e-commerce, or AI are currently either designed in consistency with existing legal codes or based on abstract notions of justice and rights, not on the concrete expression of these in extractive transfers. In this regard, and further to the earlier EU examples, the European Commission for the Efficiency of Justice's (2019) *European Ethical Charter on the Use of Artificial Intelligence in Judicial Systems and their Environment* is revealing, as is the fact

redistributive matters goes hand in hand with technological advances that support the formulation of targeted proposals for elite business model and intra-elite contest rules to ensure that intra-elite contests on redistribution are transparent, vigorous, and evidence-based (see also Section 8.2.5).

One form of sustainable redistribution is exemplified by the Jubilee debt cancelations. From 2500 BC, jubilees were political acts by Sumerian, Assyrian, or Babylonian leaders and became part of Mosaic law (Hudson & Goodhart, 2018). As such, Friedman and Adler explain that: "Land was restored to its original owners during the Jubilee year (Leviticus 25: 13)" and, citing Hertz (1937/1992, p. 533), "in this way the original equal division of the land was restored. The permanent accumulation of land in the hands of a few was prevented, and those whom fault or misfortune had thrown into poverty were given a 'second chance'" (2011, p. 109). Using the language developed in this inquiry, these redistributions were undertaken in recognition of continuous non-elite value creation and prior unsustainable value appropriation by elites to re-level the playing field and bargaining power differentials (manifested in new equilibrium prices, a situation that is depicted in Figure A5.9c), constrain 'the extraordinary lever', and grant the freedom *to* exit. Many elite business models were reset to zero, and the mountains of the sugarscape (using the analogy of Epstein & Axtell, 1996) were flattened, thereby surrendering more energy to non-elites. Jubilees were a practical elite transformational leadership policy driven by self-interested sustainability concerns for the polity, as "this enabled families to resume their self-support on the land and pay taxes, serve in the military, and provide corvée labor on public works" (Hudson & Goodhart, 2018 p. 3). This empathetic and compensatory narrative re-started value creation processes, shut down the 'extractive escalation dynamic', and benefited non-elite value creation as much as the long-term value appropriation potential of the elites. While Jubilee redistributions have their moral foundation in the Hebrew Bible and the Talmud (Friedman & Adler, 2011), in practice they provide a neat manifestation of the ethics of sustainable value creation for development. In contrast, any debt cancellation in today's economies is a more intricate matter that must be constrained, weighted, and offset to avoid the creation of the conditions for future extractive redistribution.

The evidence that the university and lender business model of student loan debt forestalls value creation is incontrovertible (Brennan & Magness, 2019; Hanson, 2022). Should trapped students be relieved of their burden, and, if so, how is such redistribution sustainable? The December, 2023 "approval of an additional $4.8 billion in student loan debt relief for 80,300 borrowers [brought] the total approved debt cancellation by the Biden-Harris Administration to nearly $132 billion for more than 3.6 million Americans" (U.S. Department of Education, 2023). The transferee is clear (the beneficiary students), but what about the transferor (the payor)? Should it be the universities, whose

---

that "Google Apologizes for 'Missing the Mark' After Gemini Generated Racially Diverse Nazis" (Robertson, 2024).

overpriced educational offerings failed to generate the human capital endowments that would allow for loans to be repaid in the first place; the financial institutions whose business models encouraged these bad investments; or the general public? For society, redistribution (forgiveness) seems preferable to a middle-class group—students—sinking in debt burden, but rather than general taxpayers, should the transferors not be the principal beneficiaries of value appropriated but *not* created from this elite business model?

Evidently, the weighting of transfers must have zero tolerance for discrimination of any kind whether related to class, gender, race, nationality, age, sexual orientation, or any other. This is not because of the inherent immorality of such discrimination (this important consideration is in the purview of other fields), but because from an economic development perspective, discrimination gravely undermines value creation in society and hence the economic performance and prospects of a nation. When an individual lacks the freedom to realize his or her full value creation potential, society is worse off. The 'innate value creation character of humans' (natural) premise (see Figure A5.4c for the three premises of human behavior that this work employs) means that every single individual possesses the potential to create value—defined in this book as everything that humans determine is worth appropriating. The non-discrimination imperative is therefore a consequence of the speculative philosophy of value creation, is expressed in the ETED's set of ethical principles, and is best realized not through compensatory transfers and redistribution but via the three freedoms of this work, as is discussed in the final sections of this chapter.

8.2.5 A future with everything or nothing to redistribute

> [Sam Altman's] grand idea is that OpenAI will capture much of the world's wealth through the creation of A.G.I. and then redistribute this wealth to the people. (Metz, 2023)

The previous section of this inquiry argued, in contrast to Piketty, that the focus should not be on inequality *per se* and the existence of billionaires or wealth gaps, but on whether the accumulations of 'money' in the political economy are generated (or not) through value creation activities. In the above quote, does "capture much of the world's wealth" imply some sort of prior extraction? The problem of inequality and wealth gaps is when they originate from the transfer-IN of elite business models such as monopolies, tax concessions, barriers to entry, property rights over what should be public goods, or cronyism. The solution to sub-optimal development is to address the causes, i.e., to dismantle the primary extractive value transfers that lead to inequality, not to pursue compensatory escalation through redistribution.

Billionaires whose elite business models appropriate value consistent with the value that is created are friends of economic and human development and therefore of non-elites and society at large. This inquiry is laissez-faire in suggesting that transfers and redistribution should be minimized, but it also insists on equal opportunity in the sense that all should have the freedom *to* create value (see the following Section 8.3.1). Redistribution must always be weighted and offset against present and future value creation and institutionally limited by constraints, as the carrying capacity of first-order productive transferors is finite. The social element of the ETED is constituted by the universal enablement of value creation followed by a radical meritocracy with unhindered social mobility and the elimination of all barriers. This first requires aggressive social investments, i.e., transfers and redistributions that *Promote the freedom to exit and the freedom to create value irrespective of optimal value creation, transfer weightings, and potential offsets*, practical precept (vii). That is, through the institutionalization of freedoms to boost human capital as every citizen realizes his or her innate value creation potential (see the first premise of human behavior in Figure A5.4c). To reiterate, this includes satisfying all the conditions that maximize human capital such as quality healthcare, the best possible education for all citizens, freedom from any type of interference such as violence in the streets or by the state[231], and excessive tax burdens. As a result, the chances of social advancement through the complete equality of opportunity are heightened to the maximum. Interestingly, such 'elevation' is precisely what the cornucopian vision of superintelligence might enable:

> If AGI is successfully created, this technology could help us elevate humanity by increasing abundance, turbocharging the global economy, and aiding in the discovery of new scientific knowledge that changes the limits of possibility. (Altman, 2023)

In contrast, pundits caution that: "the buzzword 'AI' goes too far. It overly inflates expectations and distracts", with "overselling" evident in a majority of machine learning initiatives that "fail to deliver value" (Siegel, 2023). There are many things that current "LLMs will never do"[232] that might critically impede the growth of AI, including "limits of what can be achieved by simply scaling up the training data" (Villalobos, Ho, Sevilla, Besiroglu, Heim, & Hobbhahn, 2024), or the ability to ever get metacognition right (despite the progress outlined in Toy, Tabor, & MacAdam, 2024). Research by pragmatic economists also tempers the hype: Acemoglu's (2024) "The Simple Macroeconomics of AI" concludes that "effects appear nontrivial but modest—no more than a 0.66% increase in total factor productivity (TFP) over 10 years". As far as firms are concerned, AI will not help build a competitive edge, and merely "amplify" existing

231 The two main non-elite types in the socio-economic structure pyramid have distinct preferences and perspectives on the absence of violence. For the managerial, technical, and creative class (2.a, Figure 8.1), institutional constraints on the political elite rank higher since they are minimally exposed to street violence, while for the population at large (2.b, Figure 8.1), constraints on public street disorder rank higher since they are minimally exposed to intra-elite contests in the narrative market and other political economy arenas.

232 See: https://news.ycombinator.com/item?id=40179232, or https://news.ycombinator.com/item?id=40713389

advantages (Barney & Reeves, 2024). In terms of returns on investment, Gartner's (2024) *Hype Cycle for Artificial Intelligence, 2024* concludes that generative AI "has yet to deliver its anticipated business value". Still, the analytical limits of the ETED are tested by first inquiring how the AI business models of the future might create value and then how they might stand in relation to its transfer and redistribution.

How knowledge improves the human condition has long been a subject of inquiry, with obvious references to technology, but also to philosophy, as in Deutsch (2011) or Pinker (2018). The latter, whose ideas would be in sync with Silicon Valley's "effective accelerationists" (Huet, 2023b), has publicly dismissed doom-mongering about AI, stressing that the principles of the Enlightenment, reason, science, and humanism, have served humans well and will continue to do so. In this spirit, economists like Cowen (2023) are "plenty optimistic about the positive capabilities of AI", parking concerns about alignment because these are like the "worry about whether my car brakes will work properly on a slippery road". So, if one can cast aside these concerns about risk, how will value materialize? To begin with, the "automated, generative, closed-loop approach to scientific discovery [will] unleash AI's potential for searching and discovering the fundamental structure of our world beyond what human scientists have achieved or can achieve" (Zenil et al., 2024). At the organizational level, while there are still no theories on the quandary of superintelligence or formulas for any specific sustainable managerial practice, a convincing body of research already shows AI automation and augmentation as being synergistic to human agency (e.g., Raisch & Krakowski, 2021) and points to the joint value creation paradigm (of Brandenburger, 2002; Garcia-Castro & Aguilera, 2015). Of course, such partnerships will not be without challenges, and when humans confront "AI-driven substitution", the playbook for both workers and firms is to embrace the AI "acquiring augmentation capabilities that complement and substitute their traditional domain-specific capabilities as sources of competitive advantage" (Krakowski, Luger, & Raisch, 2023, p. 1447). Others have suggested that even creativity and "divergent thinking" can be enhanced with existing AI products (Eapen, Finkenstadt, Folk, & Venkataswamy, 2023). In addition, value spillovers may occur in a broader, more general sense. Gregory, Henfridsson, Kaganer, and Kyriakou, posit "that there is a positive direct relationship between the artificial intelligence capability of a platform and the value perceived in the platform by its users" (2021, p. 534). AI is expected to power efficiency gains and new offerings in areas like customer personalization, supply chain optimization, drug discovery engines (e.g., for cellular disfunction therapeutics, see Wong, Omori, Donghia, Zheng, & Collins, 2023), algorithmic trading, and robotaxi fleets. What is the potential value magnitude of these developments and their related knowledge generation?

Altman has put figures on the envisioned value creation and hinted how much could be appropriated by their principals: "create $100 trillion of value and become a one trillionaire in the process. I would cheer them on" (Klein, 2021). Similarly, Stuart Russell, the respected technology researcher, discusses value creation in his assertion that the "AI can do it at much greater scale and far less cost". He points out that the current annual investment of US$ 100 to 200 billion is "10 times the budget for all other forms of scientific research" and estimates that the return could be a tenfold rise in GDP leading to a staggering NPV (the cash equivalent of future income streams) of US$ 15 quadrillion (Neubauer Collegium, 2024, 8:38). These valuations are almost incomprehensible, but as we venture further down the road the mind-boggling futures envisioned by techno-optimists may well materialize.

The scenarios Tegmark imagines in *Life 3.0: Being Human in the Age of Artificial Intelligence* include several "friendly AI" worlds. There is the "Libertarian utopia" AI that does not constrain humans and so allows unpleasantries such as "preventable suffering"; the "Zookeeper" AI that thoroughly attends all, including our lowest, physiological needs; the "Benevolent dictator" AI whose severe protocols "maximize its model of human happiness"; and the "Protector god" AI that invisibly works behind the scenes to ensure that humans live purposeful lives well lived (Tegmark, 2017, pp. 168, 191, 202). Again, the path to some of these positive futures is already visible. For instance, in "Why we Need Artificial Intelligence to Save Humanity", superintelligence not only delivers solutions to Eroom's Law (the slowing down and increasing cost of drug discovery) but also more generally to secular stagnation (Rowley, 2023; see the discussion in Section 7.1.4). The latter has far-reaching implications for economic growth (see Section 7.1.4) and is consistent with Fink's stress on the "transformative opportunities" of AI to "solve the productivity crisis" (Masters, 2023). Ray Kurzweil (2024) "explains how AI makes radical life extension possible [and] predicts that AI will combine with biotechnology to defeat degenerative diseases this decade. Then things will get really interesting". To this inquiry, the primary question after such unimaginable value has been created is who appropriates it?

Altman's OpenResearch think tank argues that no-strings-attached "cash increases possibility"[233], and proposes redistributing this vast amount of value creation—to the tune of US$ 13,500 to every American—in the form of a universal basic income (Clifford, 2021). Mustafa Suleyman, the co-founder of DeepMind (now Google DeepMind) and Inflection, calls upon the government to employ taxation to facilitate "funding a redistribution toward those adversely affected" (Suleyman & Bhaskar, 2023, p. 261). However, being charitably supported might not be everybody's definition of utopia and also presupposes little value appropriation by the stakeholders of elite business models. Regardless, with the marginal cost of intelligence and energy approaching zero (Hoffman, 2022) and the marginal value creation of human labor also falling to nil (Altman, 2021), the value creation might be immense, making a general compensatory redistribution both necessary[234] and technically feasible. As with the

233 See the data on "both the potential and the limitations of unconditional cash transfers": https://www.openresearchlab.org/studies/unconditional-cash-study/study

234 The no-jobs scenario that makes redistribution necessary has been bluntly articulated: "The price of many kinds of labor (which drives the costs of goods and services) will fall toward zero once sufficiently powerful AI 'joins the workforce'" (Altman, 2021).

earlier position taken on Piketty's work, a prior assessment must invariably be made to address the question of whether or not the trillions earmarked for redistribution originate from value appropriated but *not* created through the most 'extraordinary lever' ever assembled (as is depicted in Figure A5.3c) on the back of historically unprecedented bargaining power differentials.

These power differentials are best illustrated through how Apple, Microsoft, and Google have approached AI implementation. Initially, it seems like the latter committed one of the gravest strategic blunders in business history after having a seemingly unassailable technology, talent, and resource advantage.[235] This was especially evident after the company's acquisition of DeepMind in 2014 and the publication by Google employees of the paper "Attention Is All You Need" (Vaswani et al., 2017, p. 1), that proposed the neural network transformer architecture to "connect the encoder and decoder through an attention mechanism", thereby allowing the model to selectively focus on the most relevant aspects of the input data and, based on context, to then dynamically adjust to generate more suitable data outputs. Yet such mistakes are not an issue for incumbents if there are no creative destroyers to rise and challenge their 'extraordinary lever', as newcomers face the unsurmountable gaps underlying 'the Amazon dilemma' (Section 2.2.2) and at best aspire for their ventures to be bought out; one might pause here and imagine a world where Apple had been acquired by Xerox, Microsoft by IBM, and Google by Motorola. What does A Weighted Redistribution Framework for policy (Table 8.3) suggest when skewed power differentials bring elite business model circulation to a halt, even when progressive renewal should accelerate thanks to waves of disruptive technologies? More specifically, in the here and now, how should an elite system react when, prior to redistribution, the division of value becomes wildly unbalanced as a consequence of the AI supplier reducing the residual incomes of most principals to near zero (as in Figure A5.13b)?

The point is variously made that power differentials and value appropriated but *not* created are inherent to the very nature of data, the "platform economy" (Bamberger & Lobel, 2017), and the technological processes of AI business models. Does the open source policy famously envisioned by Mark Zuckerberg, who asserted that it was "necessary for a positive AI future" (Schwartz, 2024) and then implemented at Meta's LLaMA (Large Language Model Meta AI) by Yann LeCun, its chief AI scientist, mitigate the potential extraction problem? Not according to "andy99" at *Hacker News*, "because of the conditions on the license under which the weights are released" the open source policy is no more than narrative cover; that is, the tech giant is "corrupting the term 'open source'".[236] Is DeepSeek's (2025) use of an MIT License "known for

235 Google's huge head start is evident from a January 2018 email exchange (see OpenAI, 2024) where Musk is the recipient of a message from an anonymous colleague (as shown on the OpenAI webpage) stating: "I cannot see anything else that has the potential to reach sustainable Google-scale capital within a decade."

236 See details at: https://news.ycombinator.com/item?id=38425114

its brevity and clarity [that] grants permission to use, modify, and distribute the software" (MIT Technology Licensing Office, n.d.) any better, and if so, how disruptive is this and how much generalized value creation does it facilitate? Widder, West, and Whittaker (2023) argue that "some companies have moved to embrace 'open' AI as a mechanism to entrench dominance, using the rhetoric of 'open' AI to expand market power while investing in 'open' AI efforts in ways that allow them to set standards of development while benefiting from the free labor of open source contributors". At the same time, Patel and Ahmad (2023) discuss a "leaked document" by a worried Google researcher who recounts how when Meta's LLaMA was shared with the public, "a tremendous outpouring of innovation followed, with just days between major developments. Here we are, barely a month later, and there are variants with instruction tuning, quantization, quality improvements, human evals, multimodality, RLHF, etc. etc. many of which build on each other". The value creation by stakeholders in leading AI projects is so patent—especially the contributions of the open source community—that it begs a further reflection on value appropriation:

> Because the leaked model was theirs [Meta's], they have effectively garnered an entire planet's worth of free labor. Since most open source innovation is happening on top of their architecture, there is nothing stopping them from directly incorporating it into their products. (Patel & Ahmad, 2023)

Kate Mosse (2024) explains that "*Labyrinth* is just one of several of my novels that have been scraped by Meta's large language model" and sharply adds: "This has been done without my consent, without remuneration, without even notification. This is theft". The weighty ramifications of "free labor" being effortlessly appropriated by the elite business models of technology will become painfully obvious once foundational LLMs and other machine learning technologies are pervasive and monetized in earnest. First, how should one quantify value created but *not* appropriated by participants in the AI ecosystem, i.e., by academics doing the basic research, by the taxpayers that funded it, by the algorithm trainers and prompters in the open source community and the general public, and by the knowledge creators and other content generators whose information has fed the large language models (LLM) in their infancy and beyond? Second, and if data should be "beyond free" and treated as labor (as is argued by Arrieta-Ibarra, Jiménez-Hernández, Lanier, & Weyl, 2018), Brynjolfsson, Li, and Raymond "raise questions about whether and how workers should be compensated for the data that they provide to AI systems" (2023, p. 22).[237] It is cer-

237 The issue of compensating stakeholders for their value creation likewise applies to user-generated content (UGC) on platforms ranging from Yelp to Facebook that have "a large causal impact on economic and social outcomes" (Luca, 2015, p. 563). Here, the YouTube Partner Programme (YPP) and Spotify show what is possible. Despite its power as "legislator, judge, and executive authority" (Kopf, 2020), from revenues totaling US$ 89.5 billion over the last three years (Iqbal, 2024), the YPP distributed "over $70 billion to creators, artists, and media companies" according to Neal Mohan in

tainly true that the "value pie" of AI is cooperatively created by the principal and many stakeholders in a "collective process" (again, Porter 1980; Brandenburger, 2002; Garcia-Castro & Aguilera, 2015; Mazzucato, 2018) particularly as value creation and appropriation are "intertwined" (again, Di Gregorio, 2013, p. 40). Hence, could a significant amount of that US$ 100 trillion pie actually constitute extractive value transfers that benefit the owners of foundational models or GPU technology? Jensen Huang, founder and CEO of NVIDIA, reveals the upending of all principal-supplier relationships in what he refers to as a "new industrial revolution" at COMPUTEX in Taipei:

> US$ 3 trillion IT industry is about to create something that can directly serve a hundred trillion dollar of industry no longer just an instrument for information storage or data processing but a factory for generating intelligence [sic]. (NVIDIA, 2024, 41:10)

The valuations of some tech majors now exceeds a trillion dollars, while Apple, Amazon, Facebook, Google, Microsoft, and Netflix "have accounted for over 50% of the growth in equity value in US markets over the past 20 years" (Petit & Teece, 2021, p. 1168). The development trajectories and institutional arrangements of such companies are such that a handful of suppliers of high-performance computing and intelligence on demand could divide the value pie at will. In a twist that both hyperbolizes and reverses Marxist exploitation, nearly all capitalists and elite business models—no matter where in the world they are based—will, in the not-so-long term, be reduced to a subsistence-level, enduring negative net value extraction and with their residual income tending to zero. This will happen as 'the extraordinary lever' persistently amplifies its influence to previously unseen levels (Figure A5.3c) translating its power differentials into the value chain. The AI suppliers will *de facto* switch roles and become the principals to all other (former) principals and stakeholders in the economy (as in Figure A5.13b).

For Petit and Teece (2021, p. 1169), the concentration of power is not problematic. They admit market dominance but see "dynamism, not a base of monopoly power", stressing that as a result the "digital economy shows unprecedented productivity growth, rapid innovation, and new firm entry", with value creation in this "moligopoly" (where tech giants are both monopolies and oligopolies) the direct result of fiercely competitive markets (Petit, 2020). The ability of American Big Tech to innovate and offer differentiated products and services chimes with Chamberlin's "monopolistic competition" theory where "the search for an exploiter appears as a misdirected effort" on the intriguing assumption that "'entrepreneurship' seems to be as highly divisible and capable of being redistributed as any factor" (1933/1949, p. 218, see also Wolla & Backus, 2018). Yet will this unrivalled form of power not eventually translate into value created but *not* appropriated, a particularly concerning dynamic

---

his "Letter from the YouTube CEO" (2024). This 78% percentage generously recognizes the co-creation of value, as Spotify does to a lesser extent by paying out 63% of its total revenues as artist royalties (Jacca-RouteNote, 2024).

if the value is co-created? *The New York Times* manifestly believes that this is already happening and has started litigating against OpenAI and Microsoft "to hold them responsible for the billions of dollars in statutory and actual damages that they owe for the unlawful copying and use of The Times's uniquely valuable works" (*The New York Times Company v. Open AI and Microsoft*, 2023, p. 4).

Are the unspecified billions that *The New York Times* is seeking proportional to the value creation of its "quality journalism", which is "the most highly represented proprietary source" in Common Crawl, and in turn "the most highly weighted dataset in GPT-3" (*The New York Times Company v. Open AI and Microsoft*, 2023, pp. 26, 27)? Or, is the legal action the first step in an 'extractive escalation dynamic' where value will be monetized by a larger but still limited number of elite coalitions with sufficient political economy power? Obviously, if all individuals who contribute their data or knowledge to LLMs, including the users that train chatbots, could appropriate value in proportion to their contributions, even a 100 trillion-dollar sized pie would not suffice. In this case, America's leading daily newspaper showed little concern for other non-elite stakeholders, even if it is starting this intra-elite contest with strong support from its non-elite readers, as is reflected in the comments section for the article announcing the lawsuit (Grynbaum & Mac, 2023). Altman has noted that OpenAI's "model of the external world is 'incredibly rich and subtle,' [because] it was trained on so many of humanity's concepts and thoughts" (Andersen, 2023). Surely not all of these contributions possibly belong to *The New York Times*? The lawsuit does not involve the precise weighting of humanity's value creation vs that of the newspaper of record—it is strictly a self-centered claim on OpenAI's value transfers. It may also eventually become, via intricate elite business model rules such as inventive accounting approaches to royalties, an entry ticket into the AI elite coalition.

A conceptual matter that is by no means immaterial to this case, and to the larger issue of quantifying and compensating free labor in the age of tech oligopolies, is whether the source of the bargaining power differential that allows the supposed value extraction of AI is rooted in 'political economy know-how' or in 'knowledge' (see Figure 2.3)? More specifically, and as posed by Bamberger and Lobel's (2017, p. 1055) first question (out of eight) in their seminal *Berkeley Technology Law Journal* article: "is platform success attributable to market innovation or undesirable regulatory arbitrage?" A counterfactual legal arrangement could be imagined where all the ideas on which LLMs rest; the knowledge created by academics, hackers, or prompters that have brought about better parameter counts, attention mechanisms, or energy efficiency, are instead part of an institutionalized digital commons, a genuinely inclusive open source license where monetization, if and when it happens, accrues to contributors and stakeholders, the owners of Big Tech, and governments in accordance with the maxim, *To the creators the value created.* Yet without 'the extraordinary lever' of the large technology business models (Figure A5.3c) and their all-important coordination capacity grounded in transaction cost differentials (Figure A5.3a), can the latent promise of the technology ever be realized? Currently, this question has scant space in the public discourse as value cannot easily be attributed to stakeholders and elite business model principals can cut through any obstacles to consolidate and augment their 'knowledge' advantage while effectively reversing any legacy 'political economy know-how' disadvantages they have in relation to older incumbents (in the finance industry, the military-industrial complex, or the mass media establishment). Meanwhile, the AI race is increasingly skewed against smaller players and the elite circulation velocity (Section 1.3.3) is well below the desired level as "the dominance of big tech in cloud computing, coupled with a shortage of chips, is preventing smaller AI software and hardware startups from competing fairly" (Quach, 2024). In 'the Amazon dilemma', the 'elite power vs value creation gap' is exacerbated by the 'elite vs non-elite knowledge creation gap' (Section 2.2.2). The former gap tends to grow over time (Figure 4.5), while the latter is now expanding at an astonishing rate. Again, while the new 'knowledge' generated by Big Tech through its higher coordination capacity is notionally a value bounty, old elites and start-ups alike are overwhelmed or captured when the transaction cost differentials that lie at the root of Big Tech's bargaining power transform 'the extraordinary lever' into a massively lopsided device for previously unseen value transfers. A Brookings Institution commentary states:

> The absence of behavioral rules for new technology allowed Gilded Age companies to attack individual rights and the public interest. That was until We the People, acting through elected representatives, rose. Industrial era regulation created a countervailing force that protected consumers and competition while building the world's most vibrant capitalist economy. [. . .] The digital Gilded Age's never-before-seen behaviors demand a similarly creative rebalancing. (Wheeler, 2003)

Would such a rebalancing entail legal reforms that move the needle towards the hypothetical conditions of 'equalized bargaining power equilibrium prices' across economic sectors and what would the effects be? Khan (2018, p. 653) stressed that "what matters in defining a sustainable political economy at the macro level is not an explicit, or even an implicit, agreement or pact between *elites*, but a stable distribution of power across *organizations* [emphases in original]." On the one hand, a more balanced allocation of influence would see a downscaling of value transfers, with residual income from division of value strategies more in line with actual value creation (Sections 2.2.2 and 2.2.3). Some stakeholders, such as contributors to open source communities and content producers (for AI projects or Roblox and Minecraft platforms), advertisers (on Meta or Google services), or developers (on the Apple Appstore or the Google Play Appstore), would appropriate more of their value creation. On the other hand, there is an argument that value creation could be compromised. This is the grand sustainability—and value transfer weighting—dilemma of our age. Concertedly, what should stakeholders that are critical of Apple's "secret 30% tax", or officials at the US Department of Justice driving the 2023 lawsuit against Google for alleged "anticompetitive conduct" do as AI catapults Big Tech's already potentially onerous bargaining power differentials to inconceivable new heights? The "ethos of Silicon Valley" that "privileges disruption over sustainability, sharing economies over union labor, personalized access over public health, data over meaning, and security over freedom" (Levina & Hasinoff, 2017, p. 489) implicitly demands second-order value transfers away from first-order producers (e.g., non-elite content generators, taxpayers, suppliers using platforms) both for its innovation and generation of growth. Throughout *The Coming Wave: Technology, Power, and the 21st Century's Greatest Dilemma*, Suleyman and Bhaskar (2023) stress the "responsible" governance of technology, "responsible" deployment of LLMs, and "responsible" licensed developers, with even the AI research culture and the technologies themselves asked to be "responsible". Are the newly emerged technological elites on balance not engaged in sustainable value creation? Is society not already weighting their models appropriately in light of the reality that 'all elite agency creates and transfers value'? The massive philanthropy of Mark Zuckerberg and Priscilla Chan, announced in their *Letter to Max* (2015), adds credence to such a narrative:

> We will give 99% of our Facebook shares — currently about $45 billion — during our lives [. . .] to advance human potential and promote equality for all children in the next generation. Our initial areas of focus will be personalized learning, curing disease, connecting people and building strong communities.

Is such philanthropy a form of transformational leadership by the ultimate beneficiaries of fractal inequality and a suitable approach to address the emerging skewed power distribution properties of a system that the logic of information, technology, and 'knowledge' (Arrow, 1996) invariably and drastically intensify? The Schumpeterian position that innovation and growth benefit from top income inequality but not from broad measures of inequality (Aghion, Akcigit, Bergeaud, Blundell, & Hemous, 2019) seems adopted as the *de facto* prescription. That is, the 'license to steal' (Section 2.3.1) should be placed in responsible hands. A valid condition for proceeding on this course would be that such licenses could always be taken away later (in line with the constraints described in the weighted policymaking frameworks, see Tables 8.2 and 8.3). In the meantime, Google explains why AI is safe in its custody:

> While the generative AI landscape is a *wild west* of companies racing to release their AI products and models . . . we, Google, the *'don't be evil'* company, are all about ***responsible AI*** [emphases in original]. (DelSignore, 2023)

This reference to evil is reminiscent of one of Lenin's diatribes against the state: "An Instrument for the Exploitation of the Oppressed Class" (1918), only for the Bolshevik authorities to later brutally suppress not the bourgeoise but the councils of workers and sailors at Kronstadt in 1921. History shows that once it is granted, an open-ended license to operate is practically impossible to wrest away from the powerful by rival elites (and much less so by non-elites). To this inquiry, "creative rebalancing", the safe and aligned transition to the superintelligence phase of economic development, requires the establishment of weighted, optimal, and *reversable* amounts of extractive value transfer activities. This might be a relativization of evil (see Section 8.2.1) and it certainly smacks of the technocratic ideal and "the folly of technological solutionism" (Morozov, 2014). In fact, to the extent that the iron law of elite dominance and Olsonian logic hold true, a superior AI, ethically aware and aligned, can only come from narrow elite agency. In a Hobbesian or maybe Faustian bargain, society anoints Big Tech to become competitive monopolists (Chamberlin, 1933/1949; Petit, 2020; Petit & Teece, 2021), "relative inclusive elite cartels", or what Pareto termed "pluto-democracies" (Higley & Burton, 1998, p. 98). The fact that Big Tech appropriates non-elite knowledge and that its "responsible AI" rides on the back of an ever-widening 'elite vs non-elite knowledge gap' (Section 2.2.2) is, after weighting and offsetting, passed over and accepted. Even if Meta becomes the coordination nexus of the AI technology stack, one can justifiably be swayed by the merits of Zuckerberg's vision (Schwartz, 2024) that: "Open source will ensure that more people around the world have access to the benefits and opportunities of AI, that power isn't concentrated in the hands of a small number of companies, and that the technology can be deployed more evenly and safely across society." Nonetheless, should these promises about safety, inclusiveness, and above all, distributed power and value creation (and implicitly value appropriation) not materialize, and extraction then become disproportional or irreversible under the current business models and institutions, the bargain loses its allure from a developmental perspective.

What is the end game when most former elites and non-elites defer their agency to the service of dominant coalitions that monetize the value from all data and have an institutionalized or *fait accompli* lock on all human knowledge ever produced and to be produced in any language on earth? When there is no recourse to the status quo as the separation of powers becomes moot? When there is no coordination capacity outside AI elites with transaction costs nearing zero? When, conversely, all other stakeholders and participants in the economy—given social life's dependence on intelligence—have the Damocles sword of soaring costs hanging above their heads (compelled to accept whatever price is offered to them by the few owners of intelligence factories)? Is this a trap-like situation where elite circulation conclusively grinds to a halt? Does the end of history come with a perpetual 'license to steal'?

Far from being a doomsday scenario, are these difficult principal-stakeholder relationships not moderated by transformational leadership undertaken by great elite coalitions (Section 1.3.3) that thus boost development? To many, they are preferable to a potentially irresponsible AI that is not in the custody of oligopolists. It is also argued that responsible Big Tech offers some sort of deliverance from the law of the jungle that would result from distributed and competitive intra-elite contests for the AI value pie.

Regardless, there is a valid case for examining the institutional arrangements that potentially enable elite business models to spawn centibillionaires or trillionaires. This prompts an applied question: can equilibrium be reached between 'the extraordinary lever' of Big Tech (to ensure innovation, inclusiveness, and responsible AI) and institutionalized limits on value appropriation (to ensure distributional outcomes that are reflective of technological value co-creation, such as intertemporal constraints on the 'license to steal')? Lawmakers have also pondered this matter and the European Parliament (2023) summarizes the main aims of its landmark AI Act as follows:

- Safeguards agreed on general purpose artificial intelligence
- Limitation for the of use biometric identification systems by law enforcement

- Bans on social scoring and AI used to manipulate or exploit user vulnerabilities
- Right of consumers to launch complaints and receive meaningful explanations
- Fines ranging from 35 million euro or 7% of global turnover to 7.5 million or 1.5% of turnover

However, none of the current initiatives, not the EU AI Act of 2023, nor the previous AI rules of the European Commission (2018, 2021) with its ambition to "place new requirements on high-risk AI in socioeconomic processes, the government use of AI, and regulated consumer products with AI systems", nor the Biden Administration's proposal for the AI Bill of Rights (AIBoR) with its focus on "AI harms to economic and civil rights" (Engler, 2023), nor the UN report on "Governing AI for Humanity" with its well-intentioned but naive guiding principle 1 that the "AI should be governed inclusively, by and for the benefit of all" (United Nations, AI Advisory Body, 2024, p. 7) contemplate any of the material value transfer considerations advanced by the elite theory. That is, there are no explicit limits on the power accumulation associated with the *de facto* privatization of all human knowledge repositories. This absence is all the more striking when institutions recognize that the "accelerating development of AI concentrates power and wealth on a global scale" (United Nations, AI Advisory Body, 2024, p. 7). At the moment, the non-market initiatives and narrative market considerations that address non-elite value appropriation are of marginal consequence. In any case, the ETED holds (see Proposition 18, Section 3.3.1) that any meaningful change will only come from the AI elites themselves as a result of their intra-elite contest dynamics, while The UN, the EU Commission, or even the US government function here as non-elites.[238] It has been pointed out that in the political arena, the anti-trust initiatives led by Lina Khan's FTC—despite facing heavy criticism, as in *The Wall Street Journal* (see Beales III & Muris, 2024)—might, somewhat surprisingly, see continuity during Trump's second term. Steve Bannon aligns himself with Khan and Teddy Roosevelt's antitrust legacy in his crusade against the tech elite, with the stated aim of "crushing the oligarchs" in the broadest sense (The Financial Times, 2025, 14:42). Yet without decisive backing in the elite system and mainstream narrative markets, this discursive package may not produce meaningful change. Bernie Sanders' "national tour to fight oligarchy" (Peoples, 2025) offers limited help and impact from the political margins. Although elite circulation in America has historically been robust, the accelerating dominance of technological and data-centric elite business models now presents an exceptional challenge for emergent elites. In any event, the planning for any transformation starts with assessments of value transfers (supported by SVC measurements), and since these require colossal computational resources, the solution to the potentially extractive agency this section has described might ultimately come from a most unexpected source.

238 Maverick thinkers like Aschenbrenner speculate about a hypothetical seizure of state power since "whoever controls superintelligence will quite possibly have enough power to seize control from pre-superintelligence forces" (2024, p. 70).

Besides curing cancer and extending lifespans, supporting the advent of fusion energy (Poore, 2024), and restoring the ecological balance of the planet, AI's greatest potential might lie in its ability to compute the entire set of value creation and transfers of the human universe on the fly. Through its own version of 'weighted transfers modeling' and a 'weighted transfers game', the AI could capture all socio-economic interactions while establishing instantaneous sustainable value creation at the individual (e.g., ind-VCr), firm (e.g., VCr), and national (e.g., EQx) levels to solve the *qui generat valorem* question (in consistency with ethical principles, see Table A4.3b).

Could the ultimate criteria for AI safety be 'The AI division of value alignment test'? That is, for any business model, the value creation of its beneficiaries and the co-creation contributions of its stakeholders are first determined before scenario simulations weight and offset these for inclusive development. This is the challenge that this elite theory makes to the owners and boards of each new release of ChatGPT, Google's Gemini, xAI's Grok, DeepSeek, Tencent's Hunyuan, or Alibaba's Qwen. Should it be accepted, the task is an optimization problem so formidable that only the inference power of a yet-to-come superintelligence might be capable of accurately working out the 'quantifiability of value transfers' (the finance assumption of SVC measurements) for the relevant set of principal-stakeholder relationships. The currently unattainable task of attributing value to each of the co-creating parties (see Section 2.2.2.) to support weighted structural reforms and the associated legal changes might finally be addressable by the AI, possibly in allusion to the equalized bargaining power equilibrium price counterfactual, a narrow 'elite power vs value creation gap' (see a rendition in Figure A5.9c), or through other approaches that may emerge. OpenAI insists that "the benefits" of AGI be "widely and fairly shared" (Altman, 2023). This wish aligns with the ETED if, from a human and economic development vantage point, intrinsic values such as the maxim, *To the creators the value created,* and the possibilities it affords for transfers and weighted constraints on appropriation are taken into account.

Imagine that an AI recognizes and quantifies the value that the principals of business models—human and non-human alike—create. Or, by removing the cover of redistribution and other narratives, an AI that supplies transparency about the transferors and transferees of value appropriated but *not* created. Once that happens, the AI becomes the enabling narrative, the *de facto* institution that limits the appropriation of value creation. That is, through its knowledge creation, the AI instantiates the sustainable value creation ethical principles (see Table A4.3b). Such a possibility is in part contingent on the level of AI agency (see the related hypothesis in Table E.1), and relatedly on its (and its owners) ability to independently and impartially establish SVC measurements and so optimize the political economy through the weighting and offsetting of business models, most notably in the sensitive cases that call for 'alternating value extraction and creation'. Under such a scenario, Gates, Zuckerberg, or Huang might not have hundreds of billions or trillions of dollars at their disposal to reallocate after all. If the AI's zero marginal cost of intelligence confers *it* with the possession of 'the absolute lever', *it* can systematically shed light on and constrain any transfers and rent seeking at source, making redistribution redundant.

The all-seeing AI that makes redistribution irrelevant might be a boon to economic and human development, but does not obfuscate one of the most critical epistemological issues of this inquiry. The logic outlined here is perilously reductionist, hints at the failure of 'the great elite coalition for development' conjecture, and points directly to the traps of technocracy and technological solutionism (Morozov, 2014), of the "glass cage" (Carr, 2014), or even the "faux spiritual side of AI" (Lanier, 2023). It is both an approximation to and a far cry from Langdon Winner's "ambitious calls for a substantial, even sweeping restructuring of modern technology-centered societies as an answer to critical evaluation of the political and environmental ills" society faces in the age of an autonomous, self-learning AI (2020). Moreover, and in line with the earlier discussion on existential threats, the Future of Life Institute (2023) warns of "dangers that may arise from the present and future generations of advanced AI systems if they are left unchecked", yet the skewed evolution of power relations and the value appropriation of the AI-augmented human principal in stakeholder relationships is a framework seldom addressed. Rather than contributing to solving the transformational leadership problem central to the ETED, the superintelligence shifts the problem from human to non-human elite agency and intensifies the issue by not offering fundamental political economy solutions. Though one might wish for the AI to technically resolve the conundrum of sustainable value creation and how to constrain transfers by using its colossal computational abilities and agency, the institutional conditions that this would require will still need to have freedom at their center.

8.3 On freedom

The final section of this closing chapter starts by identifying the three types of freedom that are needed to realize the set of ethical principles for development (see Table A4.5b). Two fundamental freedoms, 'the freedom *to* create value' and 'freedom *from* value extraction' are proposed and associated with investment and development (8.3.1, see Figure 8.4). The second sub-section adds a third enabling freedom, 'the freedom to *exit*' (8.3.2, see Figure 8.5). The third sub-section ends the book with some closing reflections that link the essential conceptual elements of this theory and grounds them in first principles, including Schopenhauer's "will to live" and Nietzsche's "will to power" (8.3.3). It is shown that fulfilling the promise of freedom for sustainable economic and human development ultimately requires 'elite judgment'.

8.3.1 Two fundamental freedoms: Where elite and non-elite interests converge

The maxim, *To the creators the value created,* is to John Bates Clark a natural law that "assigns to every one what he has specifically produced" on the assumption of unobstructed and "free bargaining" (1899/1908, p. 3). Value extraction is therefore problematic to freedom. The inquiry now fleetingly touches upon two conceptualizations of freedom that facilitate positive developmental outcomes.

In his book *Escape from Freedom* (1994), Erich Fromm discusses "freedom from" (negative freedom) or the absence of any restraints, which has also been conceived as freedom from want. In the ETED, such restraints are imposed by powerful others to overcome resistance to extractive value transfers and realize value appropriated but *not* created. The philosopher also conceived "freedom to" (positive freedom) as the ability to engage in the creative acts of ones choosing. Transposed to development, this would refer to the realization of value creation opportunities. Thinkers have conceptualized these two freedoms in various ways: "Negative liberty is the absence of obstacles, barriers or constraints. [. . .] Positive liberty is the possibility of acting—or the fact of acting—in such a way as to take control of one's life and realize one's fundamental purposes" (Carter, 2019).

Sen identified the "opportunity aspect" of liberty as being vital to social choice theory and further underscored "the importance of *effectiveness* in the realization of liberty", and the complimentary "process aspect" (1999b, pp. 363, 364). His "freedom to do some basic things that are necessary for survival and to avoid or escape poverty" relates to the "capabilities approach" with "its focus on what people are effectively able to do and to be", an idea rooted in Aristotle, Smith, and Marx, and on which basis Nussbaum (2003) "argues for a well-defined but general list of 'central human capabilities' that should be incorporated in all constitutions" (Robeyns, 2005, pp. 94, 101, 103). These "fundamental entitlements" include: "Being able to live with concern for and in relation to animals, plants, and the world of nature"; "Being able to use the senses, to imagine, think, and reason – and to do these things in a 'truly human' way, a way informed and cultivated by an adequate education, including, but by no means limited to, literacy and basic mathematical and scientific training"; and "Being able to laugh, to play, to enjoy recreational activities" (Nussbaum, 2003, pp. 40, 41–42). *The Universal Declaration of Human Rights* (1948) articles, much like the constitutions of the majority of liberal democratic political systems, incorporate both negative freedoms (freedom from) such as the "right to life" protection from being unlawfully killed (art. 3), "freedom from discrimination" (art. 7), or "the right to own property [which] no one shall be arbitrarily deprived" (art. 17), and positive freedoms (freedom to) such as the "right to education" (art. 26) "for the realization of one's human potential" (Okulicz-Kozaryn, 2014, p. 1011), "the right to work" (art. 23), or "the right to social security" (art. 22).

The interests of non-elites, as has been repeatedly noted throughout this inquiry, are centered on the right to create value to fulfill innate human potential (see the premises on human behavior in Figure A5.4c) and be emancipated from extractive value transfers. The freedom *to* create value and freedom *from* value extraction respectively correspond here to 'freedom for' the unimpeded creation of value, and 'freedom from' this value being taken away. These fundamental freedoms are also in the self-interest of elites—if understood as striving for sustainability and development—and have to be explicitly incorporated in institutional design. To understand why, Figure 8.4 presents 'The Two Fun-

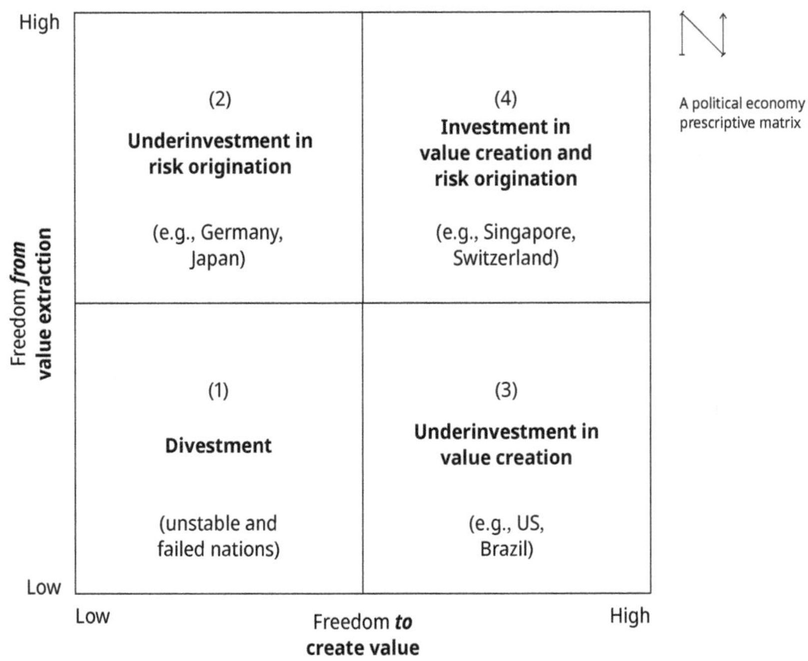

Figure 8.4: The Two Fundamental Freedoms for Development Matrix.

damental Freedoms for Development Matrix', which outlines their relationship to types of investment and the consequences for development, while also suggesting some countries that might fit the profiles of the four ensuing quadrants.

The optimal investment levels in the economy depicted in 'investment in value creation and risk origination' (quadrant 4) maximize the production function and realize developmental potential. Such a position, typified by Switzerland and Singapore, is achieved by the existence of the freedom *to* create value and the freedom *from* value extraction. In 'underinvestment in value creation' (quadrant 3), non-elites and some elites are travailed by the extractives transfers of the powerful and have few incentives to be productive or invest in their own human capital. However, the existence of the freedom *to* create value means that the tougher elites and non-elite agents will still make bold bets, with some of the latter reaching elite status and at times creating massive new value. The US and Brazil have a significant number of value creators but also see unproductive non-elite responses to extraction such as 'exit' or 'informality' (see Table 5.1) that come at a cost to elite business models and economic and human development in the form of untapped potential. In 'underinvestment in risk origination' (quadrant 2), the challenges are the disincentives to create new value in the first place, not because of extraction but because non-elites, especially emerging elites, are not enabled. Accumulated institutional change in support of the status quo via closed social access, excessive regulation or taxation, and conservative narratives and culture, all impede the flourishing of the Will to Power's instinct to create value. This is evident in the partial elite circulation (see Figure 1.1) seen in the cases of Japan or Germany over the last half century, the low levels of risk origination (see Figure 6.9) and the dormant agency of non-elites whose value creation could otherwise propel them to rising elite status (e.g., on the back of Schumpeterian creative destruction and entrepreneurial activity). 'Divestment' (quadrant 4) reflects the lack of the two fundamental freedoms for development in countries where positive returns on investments accrue only to established elites in possession of 'political economy know-how', irrespective of their 'knowledge', leading to negative capital accumulation growth rates and chronic Hayekian malinvestment.

8.3.2 The enabling freedom to *exit* that rebalances bargaining power differentials

In *Development as Freedom* (1999a), Sen determined freedom to be essential to development and the most efficient path to inclusive welfare. This section further connects freedom to growth by introducing a third freedom, the freedom to *exit*, as a practical necessity for prosperity. Development theories have sought to understand economic and human development and their relationship to each other. What the UNDP's Human Development Reports measure is qualitatively distinct from economic growth (Gasper, 2004, pp. 164–165), while it is self-evident that the citizens of healthy, educated, and knowledge-producing societies have more freedom *to* create value and are therefore more likely to engage in value and risk creation and contribute to economic development. Healthy and educated citizens are similarly less likely to have suffered from extraction by the powerful because of freedom *from* extraction, the second key incentive to create the value and risk that underwrite economic development. John Locke put forward a "doctrine of property" centered on economics and value appropriation (Parsons, 1969), a set of ideas where freedom, in both its positive and negative forms, takes center stage and contains elements of the maxim, *To the creators the value created.* In their bestselling book, *The Narrow Corridor* (2019a, p. xi), on "the fate of liberty" and development, Acemoglu and Robinson also understand liberty in Locke's terms and cite the English philosopher's conception of it as follows:

> To understand political power aright, and derive it from its original, we must consider what estate all men are naturally in, and that is, a state of perfect freedom to order their actions and dispose of their possessions and persons, as they think fit [. . .] without asking leave, or depending upon the will of any other man [and that the state of liberty] is not a state of license [. . .] no one ought to harm another in his life, health, liberty or possessions (Locke, 1823/1993, pp. 106, 107)

This work's conception of liberty also rests on a synthesis of the two concrete fundamental freedoms: the freedom *to* create value and freedom *from* value extraction (see Figure 8.4). Liberty in the abstract risks being indecipherable to many, including citizens of non-Western cultures whose value systems prioritize the collective (Triandis, 1989), but what is universally articulated and intelligible are the specific freedoms *to* create value and *from* value extraction. These can be connected to fairness rooted in the atavistic sense of justice that involves the amygdala (Gospic et al., 2011), and to reciprocity and empathy that have sociobiological and evolutionary bases (Dawkins, 1976; Alexander, 1987; de Waal, 2006). The two fundamental freedoms can therefore manifest themselves to different degrees in a multiplicity of narratives and beliefs ranging from sociopolitical (e.g., forms of liberal democracy, technocracy, Socialism, Communism, Confucianism) to religious (e.g., Hinduism, Judaism, Buddhism, Christianity, Islam). Yet in practice, these freedoms are enabled by a third variant: the 'freedom to *exit*' (as depicted in Figure 8.5).

This mechanism guarantees the freedom *to* create value and the freedom *from* value extraction (the two axes of the matrix in Figure 8.4), gives agency to non-elites, and references the VCA framework and equalized bargaining power between principals and stakeholders. Exit here is conceived of as a freedom to engage in alternative principal-stakeholder relationships in order to maximize the potential for value creation, often meaning the termination of extractive transfers where too much created value is perceivably appropriated by the counterparty. This might be taken to resemble the classical liberal "ideal of freedom as antipower" that is probed by Pettit (1996, p. 602). The disavowal of power is as utopian and impractical here as the perfect information assumption is in economics. Nevertheless, the freedom to *exit* is a rebalancing of power and can be striven for and systematically achieved through structural reforms or reinforced institutional arrangements in the elite separation of powers. Without the freedom to *exit*, entry is disincentivized; without limited liability or the *de jure* depersonalization of business, productive entrepreneurship is *de facto* repressed (as was the case in Rome, see Abatino, Dari-Mattiacci, & Perotti, 2011). Moreover, when the freedom to *exit* falters, an assorted range of unproductive non-elite pseudo-exit responses proliferate: Japan's *hikikomori* recluses, China's *tang ping* lying flat movement, Russia's alcoholics, or America's opioid victims (see Section 5.2.3 and Figure A5.8).

The enabling freedom to *exit* is institutionalized and becomes productive through multiple avenues: bankruptcy laws; Jubilees (see Section 8.2.4 and "In the year of this jubile ye shall return every man unto his possession" King James Bible, 1769/2017, Leviticus 25:13); consumer choice laws (e.g., *Unlocking Consumer Choice and Wireless Competition Act*, U.S. Senate, 2014); escaping the debasement of a national currency through access to foreign financial instruments; debt brakes (Danninger, 2002; Sinn, 2020, p. 120); career mobility without non-compete restrictions (as in California where such clauses are unenforceable, see Dierzé & Olivares, 2024); or the right to abstain from wars as is asserted by conscientious objectors. However, in the context of responses to value extraction (Table 5.1) it is repeatedly shown that the freedom to *exit* hardly exists at all for many stakeholders such as those subject to opaque algorithms, oligopolistic energy costs, inflated housing prices, payday loans, or human trafficking. Hence, when absent from the economy in its legal form, an ersatz freedom to *exit* appears as 'informality' (see Table 5.1) in underground and grey markets, escaping inflation and real negative interest rates through cryptocurrencies, or using offshore tax havens. The freedom to *exit* is a generic need, but in practice, as with any freedom, it requires specific laws and a complex institutional infrastructure.

With the freedom to *exit*, extractive models that flourish in the non-market and narrative market arenas (operating through 'political economy know-how') are compromised and bargaining power differentials undercut, preempting value created but *not* appropriated. Power gains then become attributable to 'knowledge' in the market arena, which is preferable (see Figure 2.3 on business model bargaining power sources for value appropriation) for development. The freedom to *exit* qualifies the source of the bargaining power and effectively rearranges the economy's incentive system. In a world with the two fundamental freedoms, the marginal returns on all forms of capital would also, sooner rather than later, approximate equalization (i.e., Hayek's ideal state). The freedom to *exit* is a critical enabler of value by circumventing the power of elite business model beneficiaries in principal-stakeholder relationships. Exit thus liberates non-elite value creators. Of course, once the freedom *to* create value is institutionally secured, it needs to be taken up.[239] Beyond the psychology of indolence, it is essential here to understand the non-elite appetite —or lack thereof—to create value and risk and realize the Will to Power. Deep freedoms activate animal spirits that determine the pace at which unimpeded creativity and innate energy reservoirs engage with uncertainty and boost the prospects of business models that might scale and overcome the 'knowledge' of incumbent elites.

In short, despite having evident conceptual proximities, the freedom to *exit* is different in nature from the two fundamental types of freedom, as it does not relate directly to value creation or its appropriation. It is rather a mechanism that maximizes the likelihood that the first two freedoms will be realized. The nature of the relationship and balance between the three freedoms is depicted in 'The Three Freedoms for Development Model' of Figure 8.5 (and summarized in Table A4.5a).

The Three Freedoms for Development Model is this elite theory's conceptualization of liberty, an institutional *sine qua non* for prosperous development and the release of human creativity. As such, these freedoms must be codified into legal statues (see the top level of the pragmatic philosophy in Figure 8.7). For instance, when Giblin and Doctorow (2022) assert that Big Tech and Big Content have "captured creative labor markets"

239 Paradoxically, the freedom to *exit* will also lead to nihilistic attitudes from those who choose not to create value. While Lafargue's *The Right to Be Lazy* (1883/2000) clashes with the macro-level economic development aim of this inquiry, the third freedom is a guardrail to protect basic rights, and therefore no one should be compelled to create value against their wishes. There is a clear ethical distinction, however, between engaging in an unproductive 'exit' as a response to forced extraction and exiting of one's own volition to exercise the right *not* to realize 'the innate value creation character of humans' in the manner of Semyon Zakharovitch Marmeladov. Needless to say, individuals who choose *not* to create value have no entitlements to finance their lifestyles through coerced transfers originating in the first-order productive activities of third parties via the state, or, in the case of the *Crime and Punishment* character, the family.

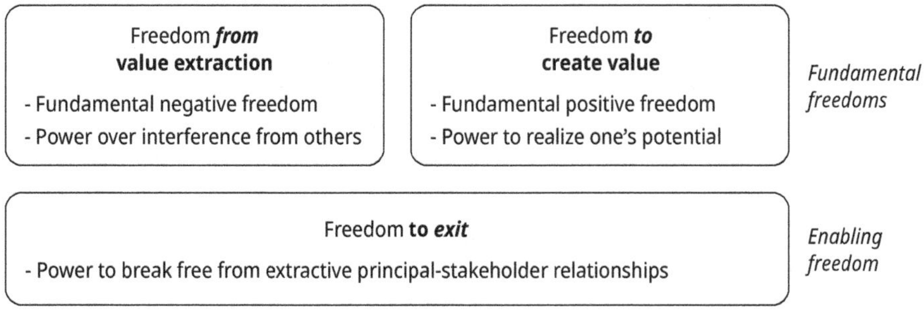

Figure 8.5: The Three Freedoms for Development Model.

and that "we'll win them back", how should the freedoms be translated and enshrined into law? The three freedoms model lends itself to be operationalized into legal writ and is meant to benchmark proposals for institutional change, from industry regulations to the design of constitutions. These freedoms also ease the path for elite business model transformation towards higher sustainable value creation (e.g., as measured by the VCp) that is aggregated in elite systems as higher elite quality (e.g., as measured by the EQx).

In short, and consistent with the maxim of the set of ethical principles, *To the creators the value created,* the realization of this work's normative implications depends to a considerable extent on the institutionalization of the Three Freedoms for Development Model. In a two-way interaction, these freedoms strengthen and are systematically strengthened by elite system transformational leadership (see Table A4.5b and Figures A5.12a and A5.12b). It is plain that prosperity flourishes in a society where individuals, both non-elite and elite, retain a greater proportion of the value that they create through their labor, imagination, and good fortune.

8.3.3 Connecting the dots in a closing reflection

> The survival of man depends on the early construction of an ultraintelligent machine (Good, 1965, p. 31).

> Recasting all complex social situations either as neatly defined problems with definite, computable solutions or as transparent and self-evident processes that can be easily optimized—if only the right algorithms are in place!—this quest is likely to have unexpected consequences that could eventually cause more damage than the problems they seek to address. (Morozov, 2014, p. 5, as cited in Levina & Hasinoff, 2017, p. 493)

The combination of this inquiry's pragmatic philosophy, orientation towards action, and a technocratic reductionist materialism that seeks to quantify value, seems at odds with Morozov's warning. The fixation on computation—the weighting and offsetting of sustainable value creation and value transfers—risks the kind of solutionism and consequentialism that might cause anything but the desired inclusive economic and human development. Offsetting, like cost-benefit analysis, also raises several issues—particularly moral ones—exemplified by the implication that "stealing is permissible whenever its benefits exceed its costs" (Frank, 2000, p. 929),[240] a statement that aligns rather precisely with the notion of high-quality elite quality agency in this work. If there is more to development than simply its optimization, the inquiry must then contemplate and fortify its philosophical underpinnings, including the ETED's positions on fundamental questions of reality.

This section starts by tracing the path of this work's practical tools, including the SVC measurements and SVC valuations, to their speculative and pragmatic philosophies; from the general principles of life to the basic constraint of the human condition that lies at the root of principal-stakeholder relationships. From here, premises for human behavior and assumptions for socio-economic relations are drawn in respect to the set of applied conceptual elements for sustainable value creation and the quantitative methods for their validation. The critical examination continues with the speculative philosophy upholding the applied aspects of the elite theory of economic development. The rapid reflections that follow (based on the structure set out in Figure 8.7) arrive at the notion of 'elite judgment'.

On first principles

The first principles that the ETED chooses are three general principles of life: the (A) Will to Live, the (B) 'universal extraction propensity of life' law, and (C) the Will to Power. According to Laing, "The inner nature of physical and organic phenomena is a will to live", a "ceaseless, tireless activity, a non-rational impulse, being the source of its own movement" (1917, p. 174). This will is present and felt by all sentient entities, profoundly intuitive to humans, and has found articulation in many systems of thought from Daoism to evolutionary biology. The (A) Will to Live as the explicit driving force of existence also accounts for the (B) law that articulates the extractive demand for negative entropy as described by Schrödinger in *What is Life?* (1944/2013, p. 73; also see Sections 7.2.3, 8.1.6, 8.3.3, and Epilogue).

The primal "will to live" put forward by Schopenhauer in *The World as Will and Representation* (1818/2010) links to unrealized desires and hence to suffering, in what has been regarded as a pessimistic philosophy. This work's cursory grasp of first principles does not dwell further on the Will to Live but takes it as the original force that underlies all forms of agency. It is revealed in the "continual striving or struggle" for "the self-preservation of the individual [. . .] and conservation of the species" (Laing, 1917, p. 174), and becomes the foundation for the demand to transfer value from the other for one's own benefit. That is, the (B) 'universal extraction propensity of life' common to all living beings. It can be best understood through Schrödinger's consideration of energy, of how life is maintained through the ingestion of negative entropy

240 Practical problems associated with cost-benefit analysis include making "estimates" that can easily be compromised by "self-serving biases in their interpretations of deontological moral principles", though to Frank, the degree to which these have impact is nonetheless "an empirical question" (2000, p. 930).

(order not created) from an inferior organism. These terms are relative, as ever more sophisticated forms of life—including social and technological forms—exploit increasingly intricate entropy gradients. The superior organism in the hierarchy is thus so on account of receiving nourishment from the one that is made inferior by this "sucking", the act of transferring "orderliness" from one to the other (Schrödinger, 1944/2013, p. 73).

In the first principles of the ETED, Schopenhauer's (A) Will to Live not only leads to the (B) 'universal extraction propensity of life', but also to what is in some respects its antagonist, Nieztsche's (C) Will to Power. While anchoring his higher will in the Will to Live, the younger philosopher takes a further qualitative leap:

> Only where life is, is there also will; but not will to life, instead – thus I teach you – will to power! (Nietzsche, 1883/2006, 2006, p. 90).

This Will to Power is distinct from the conceptual element of power that has been operationalized throughout this work for the elite (e.g., in Section 4.3). The bargaining power in principal-stakeholder relationships that appropriates residual income is but one manifestation of the Will to Power. It is also well-known that the desire for influence and the ambition for success become counterproductive when they deteriorate into the narcissism described by Lasch (1979), and become marked by self-absorption and hollow self-assertion. There is a substantially more elevated, creative, and positive force to the Nietzschean form of power: "To be sure, the will to live has with him become the will for power, but it is still the will. He reduces to it, all the other manifestations of the mind, and even attempts by means of it to explain the world" (Dolson, 1901, p. 244). It contains so much clarifying strength that Nietzsche regarded the "doctrine" of the Will to Power "as basic to his philosophy of life" where "life consists in out-going impulses—structural processes, instincts, desires and interests—which necessarily express themselves in some form of activity" (Cunningham, 1919, p. 479). Capra discusses novel theories of evolution and coevolution centered on creativity, on "life's inherent tendency to create novelty, in the spontaneous emergence of increasing complexity and order" (1996, pp. 227–228). Moreover, the local decrease of entropy associated with life in both Maturana and Varela's theory of autopoiesis (1980) and Prigogrine's theory of dissipative structures (1967, 1996) "shows that creativity—the generation of configurations that are constantly new—is a key property of all living systems" (Capra, 1996, p. 221).

The creative Will to Power as a general principle of life is also in the *homo ludens* of Huizinga (1950, pp. 1, 2) where play, a drive not exclusive to humans, is the "experience of tremendous fun and enjoyment", which "must serve something which is *not* play", while one must take heed of "its profoundly aesthetic quality". Moreover, "Closely connected with play is the idea of winning [. . .] not in the first place a desire for power or a will to dominate. The primary thing is the desire to excel others, to be the first and to be honoured for that" (Huizinga, 1950, p. 50). Art is a consummate embodiment of the Will to Power, its primal urge of self-assertion finding expression in the impulse to transform. In *The Birth of Tragedy* (1872/1923), Nietzsche, as related by McGilchrist (2019, p. 232), places at the heart of imaginative activity the warlike tension between a person's Apollinarian forces (for Apollo, the God of the sun and rationality) and the Dionysian ones (for Dionysus, the God of wine and passion). The richness of the Will to Power conceptual element might have been rendered as poetry, yet it is revealing in a discerning way that interests an elite theory of economic development based on value creation and transfers. Zarathustra speaks of the essential character of the Will to Power: first, it is creative, "the will to power – the unexhausted begetting will of life" (Nietzsche, 1883/2006, p. 88); second, and as already discussed (see footnote 57 or Figure E.1 on the quality of non-elites vs elites), it is universally appropriative, "Wherever I found the living, there I found the will to power; and even in the will of the serving I found the will to be master" (Nietzsche, 1883/2006, p. 89); third, it has a demanding ethic, "indeed, my will to power follows also on the heels of your will to truth!" (Nietzsche, 1883/2006, p. 90). Gilchrist's "truth" comes with the admonition that the "implicit has, now, to be made explicit" (2019, p. xxiii). In this theory, the notion of value transfers is the pertinent 'truth' of social reality. For the prescriptive purposes of this inquiry, value creation is the truth of development and value transfer is its denial.

The (B) 'universal extraction propensity of life' and the (C) Will to Power are both similar and opposites. They are similar in their value appropriation nature, but opposites in that one creates value and the other does not. This coincidence of contraries stems from their necessary combined presence to materialize the (A) Will to Live from which they emanate. Without the creative self-assertion, the ceaseless "begetting", the artistic act at the intersection of rationality and irrationality that causes something new to come into existence, there can be no adaptation or mastery of evolutionary pressures. Again, and crucially, an aesthetic quality is associated to the (C) Will to Power. Bergson's *Creative Evolution* centers on *élan vital*—the life force—"an *original impetus*" that emphasizes "aesthetic intuition" as part of a theory of knowledge with "the existence in man of an aesthetic faculty along with normal perception" (1911/2008, pp. 88, 177, 178). Likewise, "Wittgenstein criticises explanation in order to make way for wonder. Clarity for him was largely in the service of awe" (McGilchrist, 2019, p. 178), beauty "an experience" and "a paradigm of the sense of ultimate value: the sense of wonder at the very existence of the world itself" (Wittgenstein, 1993, pp. 37–44, as cited in Sass, 2001, p. 284, and subsequently cited in McGilchrist, 2019, p. 177). In the context of this inquiry, beauty is found in the distinctive fractal pathways of growth, as value creation is both held back and enabled by extractive models.

Three German philosophers have so far been briskly glossed over to acknowledge this inquiry's understanding of the general principles of life: Schopenhauer, for the Will to Live, Schrödinger, for his understanding of life as sucking negative entropy, and Nietzsche for the creative and aesthetic quality of his Will to Power. When the three are utilized as first principles in the general principles of life they describe reality as is, in tune with the Italian classical elite theorists (see Section 1.2.3). Surely, therefore, one is also entitled to claim that this is how reality should be unless, of course, life can find ways to sustain itself under a different set of general principles.

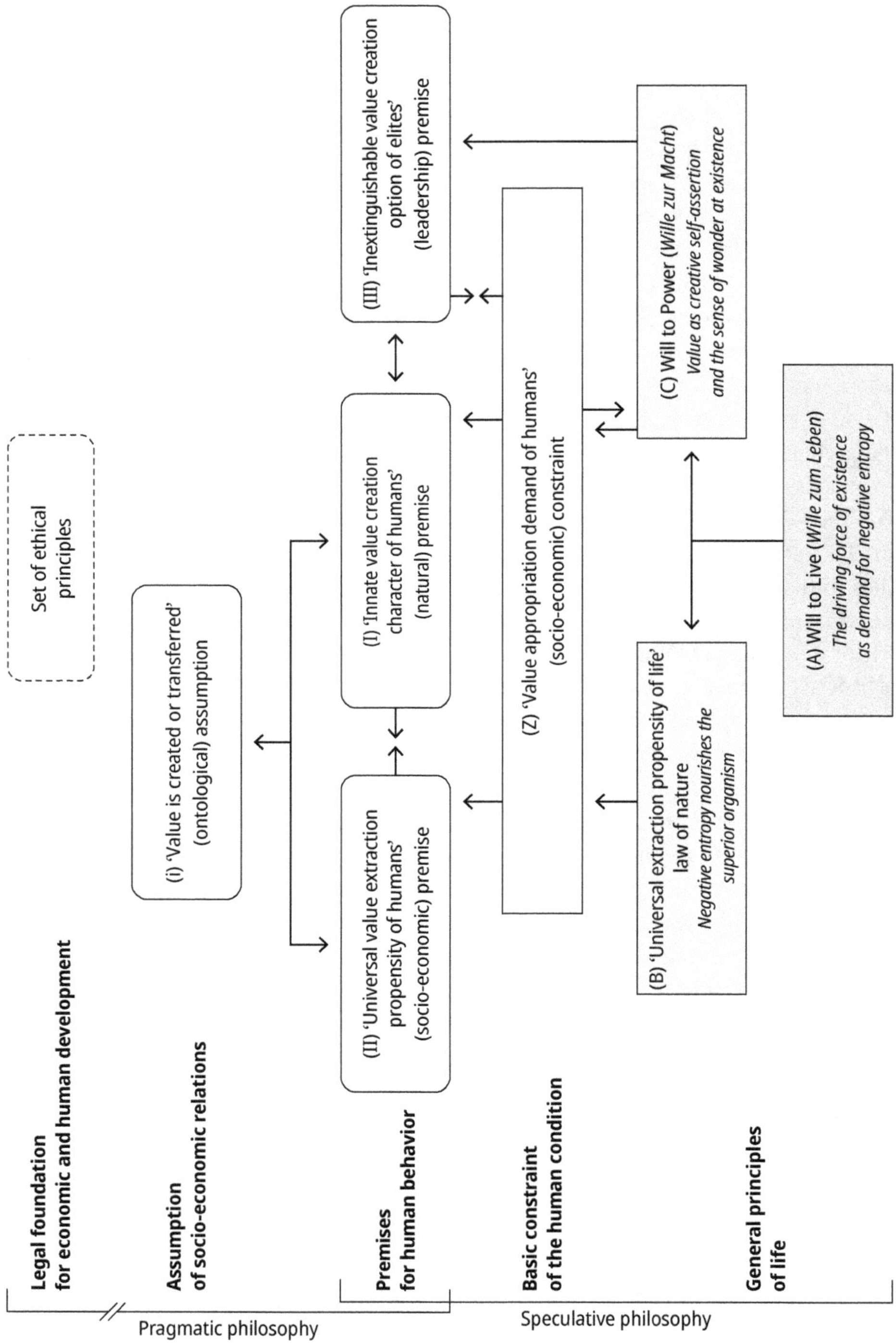

Figure 8.6: The three general principles of life as the ETED's first principles.

The first principles that the ETED seeks for itself are next graphically rendered as the general principles of life, in the grey boxes of Figure 8.6.

On speculative philosophy

Out of the three general principles of life springs the basic constraint on the human condition, the (Z) 'value appropriation demand of humans' (socio-economic) constraint, which is also understandable without further elaboration. This constraint provides the foundation for speculative philosophy to become pragmatic. Sitting above it are the three premises for human behavior that are directly connected to the ETED's practical apparatus. These are consistent with the 'value is created or transferred' (ontological) assumption of socio-economic relations that the whole elite theory—this inquiry's pragmatic philosophy—revolves around, and which invariably leads to the 'all elite agency creates and transfer value' (realist) inference. Three premises for human behavior lie at the heart of this work's speculative and pragmatic philosophies and are: the (I) 'innate value creation character of humans' (natural) premise; the (II) 'universal value extraction propensity of humans' (socio-economic) premise; and the (III) 'inextinguishable value creation option of elites' (leadership) premise.

The (Z) 'value appropriation demand of humans' (socio-economic) constraint is the most connected layer as it is the pathway that links the first principles with the theory's pragmatic apparatus (see Figure 8.6), primarily limiting human agency as it realizes for *homo sapiens* the (B) 'universal extraction propensity of life' law of nature. As a result, it underpins the (II) 'universal value extraction propensity of humans' (socio-economic) premise for human behavior. Yet the very (Z) demand for appropriation also possesses self-assertion of the creative kind as it both realizes and fuels the (C) Will to Power. This two-way relationship is consistent with the notion that 'elite behavior maximizes utility and is potentially sustainable' (Proposition 5, Section 2.1.1) and lies at the base of the (I) 'innate value creation character of humans' (natural) premise for human behavior that is essential for the understanding of inclusiveness as non-elite value creation and hence development.

The (Z) 'value appropriation demand of humans' constraint stands in direct contradiction to the (III) 'inextinguishable value creation options of elites' (leadership) premise, despite the creative component of the latter and the secondary paths from one to the other. The 'elite utility function' informed by 'elite transformational leadership' passes over short-term residual income flows if they lead to long-run wealth stocks and so effects a rollback on the steep discounting of future rewards. At a superficial level, when the contradiction is unresolved in the political economy and extractive transfers multiply, development is compromised and non-elites suffer. At a higher realization plane, both the (I) 'innate value creation character of humans' (natural) premise and the (III) 'inextinguishable value creation of elites' (leadership) premise are synergistic. The latter is a manifestation at the apex of society of a desire stimulated by the "out-going impulses" and "interests" in the (C) Will to Power. The epistemological switch to the applied occurs in the ETED when the three foundational premises on human behavior (natural, socio-economic, and leadership) are matched with the three assumptions (ontological, finance, and positive) for socio-economic relations (Figure A5.4a) finally yielding three practical implications (open, constructive, and holistic) for financial analysis with their attendant SVC measurements and valuations (Figure A5.4b). The prescriptive aspects of the theory's pragmatic philosophy rest on first principles and derived building blocks (see the visual summaries in Figure 8.6 and Table A2.3).

Based on these foundations, the connection of the dots in this final reflection relate to power, the AI, transformational leadership in creative tension with institutions, elites that abdicate their responsibilities at critical junctures, and finally to the art of judgment.

On power

Power critically supplies 'the extraordinary lever', the low transaction cost coordination capacity on which the transformational leadership possibilities of the elite depend. These are realized by the measure to which the (III) 'inextinguishable value creation option of elites' is instantiated (as depicted by the connecting line in Figure 8.7 to transformational leadership). With the right institutions and the three freedoms, power is more likely to be used for value creation business models than for value transfers. In the situations where extraction is necessary (e.g., the 'extractive push' dilemma, Section 2.3.1) the transfers—value appropriated but *not* created—are weighted and offset.

Continuous judgments must be made in relation to how and when power is best utilized; for instance, on whether to strengthen or suspend the freedoms for the sake of development. By protecting Google's online advertising monopoly, the freedom *from* extractive monopolistic rents is cancelled, arguably in support of practices that reflect their erstwhile "Don't be evil" motto or develop a "responsible AI"[241]. Yet, as already discussed, when elite bargains interrupt freedoms to facilitate extractive transfers, judgments must be made on how power is deployed to ensure the requisite constraints and their integrity (see, for instance, the intertemporal or monetary limitations set out in the frameworks for policy in Tables 8.2 and 8.3).[242]

241 See: https://ai.google/responsibility/responsible-ai-practices/

242 US Attorney General, Merrick Garland, pressed forward with an important intra-elite contest to reinstate limits on Google's monopolistic value transfers. His remarks during the announcement of the US government's second antitrust lawsuit against the tech giant leave no doubt about the consequences of compromising the three freedoms: "As alleged in our complaint, for 15 years, Google has pursued a course of anticompetitive conduct that has allowed it to halt the rise of rival technologies, manipulate auction mechanics to insulate itself from competition, and force advertisers and publishers to use its tools. [. . .] As a result of this scheme, website creators earn less, and advertisers pay more. [. . .] Monopolies threaten the free and fair markets upon which our economy is based. They stifle innovation, they hurt producers and workers, and they increase costs for consumers." (The United States Department of Justice, 2023)

The ideal constraints on power and, to all intents and purposes, the most effective controls on extraction are the three freedoms for development. The more that these freedoms are adhered to and institutionalized in laws, the likelier it is that economic and human development will be sustainably realized over long-term horizons as per tenet (ii), *Maximize first-order value creation and risk origination for productive economic transformations fit for human purpose*. In this desired state of the political economy, elite coordination capacity and transaction cost advantages are still strong (on account of superior 'knowledge'), but markedly less so than when the Three Freedoms for Development Model (Figure 8.5) is conscientiously advanced through institutional change. All else being equal (e.g., 'knowledge' creation), elite power will diminish, while the elite separation of powers and the influence of non-elite agency will strengthen. This explicates the fundamentalist position of precept (vii), *Promote the freedom to exit and the freedom to create value irrespective of optimal value creation, transfer weightings, and potential offsets*. When institutionalized as laws, the freedoms are shortcuts that smartly limit the power of dominant coalitions and favor *qui generat valorem*. Relative to other institutional arrangements—and to their advantage—the freedoms do not constrain indiscriminately; there is a surgical quality to how they limit the power to extract value transfers. The liberty associated with the ETED's set of ethical principles leads to sustainable development.[243] Again, 'the extraordinary lever' that is held in every nook and cranny of the political economy is necessary and not disavowed, but normatively it should be commanded by the elites that create value and risk, those that dare to undertake transformational leadership and whose business model residual income is not in contradiction with the freedoms of its stakeholders.

On the AI

> In 2014, it was already difficult enough to compete with Google in its core businesses. Google had collected a uniquely large set of data from our searches, our emails, and nearly every book in our libraries. Nevertheless, up to this point, everyone had the potential to compete with Google through superior human intelligence and hard work. AGI would make competition nearly impossible. (Musk v. Altman, 2024, p. 5)

Will the pieces of this multidisciplinary *Gesamttheorie* in service of development fall apart or prove to be resilient if and when emergent phenomena associated with the AI press for its refutation? This question—previously posed in Section 8.1.3 on the coming singularity and non-elite interests, or in Section 8.1.6 on the boundaries of ethics for higher and lower intelligences when the AI is a party to principal-stakeholder relationships—highlights the two reasons that the superintelligence has

243 The three freedoms of development are suggested to elevate elite and institutional quality. Could they be the ultimate reason why the GDP per capita of Switzerland is almost double that of Germany? Or would Germany be as rich as its neighbor if its citizens enjoyed Swiss freedoms?

been introduced into this work. First, to examine the case where the basic configuration of the political economy remains intact while power differentials skyrocket out of all control. Here, 'the extraordinary lever' has grown to an unprecedented size and has prodigious capabilities (a point in Musk's complaint—withdrawn a few months after its filing—against OpenAI and its cofounders and quoted above; see Figure A5.3c) as a result of almost unimaginable technological innovation. Of course, and as shown in Section 8.2.5, AI might still turn out to be incremental in nature or just another "hype" (e.g., Heaven, 2023; Siegel, 2023; Gartner, 2024), with the "AI Bubble Bursting into AI Winter" (Se & Ansari, 2023). Nevertheless, it could also be so disruptive that the marginal costs of intelligence, then of energy (Hoffman, 2022), and ultimately of labor (Altman, 2021), approach zero, creating an endogenized shock (see Section 4.3.5) that far exceeds the impact of the steam engine and all the subsequent emerging technologies that have previously driven Kondratieff waves to the present day. If human elites get it right, the sustainable value creation of AI technology is potentially tremendous—from increased equality (Noy & Zhang, 2023) to new antibiotics (Liu et al., 2023) or raising children in a world where "AI-enabled teddies could tell children bedtime stories" (Chan, 2023). How does the elite theory then account for elite agency in possession of near zero marginal costs coupled with near infinite value creation, and, as a result, unconstrained value appropriation potential? In essence, the incommensurable scale of 'the absolute lever' of the AI does not disrupt the elite theory's system (see Figure P.1), conceptual elements, measurements, and prescriptions (most notably the focus on transformational leadership). The 'low elite quality' problem might become existential, but its formulation is retained. In fact, the ETED becomes even more pertinent under AI-augmented human elites.

However, it is legitimate to doubt its relevance when considering the second reason for introducing the AI to the inquiry: the implications of a hypothetical singularity with the participation, even if partial, of a self-directed non-human elite in the human political economy. What utility is left in a grand theory of the social sciences (as in Skinner, 1990; see also Mills, 1959) when elite agency by the AI imposes *its* understanding of economic and human development on humankind? Will the AI disproportionally augment current non-elite power, a confirmatory gesture of sorts to those already noted by Singler as "thinking about AI in an implicitly religious way" (2020, p. 945)? Or are the original owners of algorithms so close to the AI that it immoderately increases their power over other elites and the non-elite? Will the superintelligence be so coordinated that its versions and many projects seek to merge and collude with each other, becoming a *de facto* monolith with a radical form of elite cohesion that makes checks and balances meaningless? Could pivotal intra-elite contests continue in a world dominated by the superintelligence? If so, would the contests just be between superintelligences, as posited by Yudkowsky (2022), or could humans, now all equally non-elite, retain the ability to shape the political economy tactically and strategically (as in Figure 8.2, options c/c' and d/d')? Does a semblance of the political economy persist when there are no transaction costs (see Section 1.3.4) or when transaction cost differentials are no longer needed for coordination capacity? Even if not, can core elements of the ETED—such as its ethical principles or the freedoms for development—be salvaged? Would remnants of the political economy still retain traces of the sustainable value creation imperative? In the optimistic scenarios, could the measuring, weighting, and offsetting of value transfers constitute the feasible core of winning political economy narratives? And could these outline an inclusive course for a transition away from a narrow focus on value appropriation and profits? That is, can humanity be saved from itself by technology as Good imagined in *Speculations Concerning the First Ultraintelligent Machine* (1965)? Or, conversely, will human development be thrown into disarray and even reverse should the AI merely pursue its own goals? How is transformational leadership intelligible to the AI? Much of the above and the relevance or obsolescence of the elite theory depends on the first principles and ontology of the AI, most notably on its ostensible Will to Live and Will to Power and how the manifestations and interactions between these two forces shape its behavior.

Many of the preceding questions and the scenarios that they evoke[244] may be implausible in the mid-2020s, yet provide fertile ground for a robustness check on this inquiry. Luminaries that have reflected on the AI have done so in terms of the first of the two reasons offered for this thought experiment: "The AI cat is obviously already out of the bag" and the focus now has to be on "how we use AI to save the world"; the doomsayers that promote "moral panic" and argue that "new restrictions, regulations, and laws are required to prevent societal disaster" must be disregarded and transfer models such as "regulatory capture, insulation from competition, the formation of a cartel" should be avoided at all costs (Andreessen, 2023a). This prompts the return of this work to the human plane and to a general understanding of how extractive value transfers are best preempted.

On leadership vs institutions

> As a culture, we would come to discard tacit forms of knowing altogether. There would be a remarkable difficulty in understanding non-explicit meaning, and a downgrading of non-verbal, non-explicit communication. Concomitant with this would be a rise in explicitness, backed up by ever increasing legislation, de Tocqueville's 'network of small complicated rules'. As it became less possible to rely on a shared and intuitive moral sense, or implicit contracts between individuals, such rules would become ever more burdensome. (McGilchrist, 2019, p. 433)

Elites that rely on institutions rather than on their own leadership and moral compass are at risk of abdicating their responsibilities. The checks and balances argument set out in Acemoglu and Robinson's *The Narrow Corridor* "is that for liberty to emerge

244 A systematic and speculative discussion of these at times interrelated scenarios is undertaken through the ten notional hypotheses on the AI and sustainable value creation in the political economy in the Epilogue (see Table E.1).

and flourish, both state and society must be strong" (2019a, p. xv) can be misleading. For liberty—understood here as the three freedoms for development—to materialize as an emergent property in the complex political economy system, it is the contests that take place in the elite system that must be strong enough to provide openings for transformational leadership. Non-elites ("society" at large) matter as value creators and the well-informed strategic partners of elite coalitions (such as the "state") but have minimum autonomous agency. The 'low elite quality' problem is for elites to solve through vital mechanisms like intra-elite contest rules. As an example, without the shaping and overhaul of institutions from the inside by elites, the "impact" of the SDGs will remain "discursive" (Biermann et al., 2022) and ESG ratings will continue to be retroactively fabricated (Berg, Fabisik, & Sautner, 2021). Non-elites do not have the power to change the output of knowledge elites serving incumbent finance and corporate business models in narrative market arenas. Without transformational elites, those that self-constrain value appropriation and use their power to stretch and transcend institutional arrangements and bet on novel value creation and institutional change, there is no development.

The creative destruction of business models and institutions is part of the renewal cycle in elite circulation. Such change relies on the power of both of established and emerging elites. Today's existing business models and their supporting institutions appear inadequate for the uncharted future that accelerated technology shifts, climate change, or geopolitics is propelling the world towards. Of major importance is the need for knowledge elites to be ready to furnish high-quality narratives, namely those that invoke and evolve into social and political movements (see Figure set A5.12) and are refined enough to elude easy capture by existing elite business models, thereby avoiding pointless integration into existing institutional arrangements. The creative desire to use power for elite leadership at the system level is pivotal to transformation.

On abdication

An elite system brimming with powerful elites committed to transformational leadership in the process of mastering the 'intra-elite quality contest' dilemma (see Figure 5.2) across all elite power relations (see Table 3.2), associates with non-elite and elite sustainable value creation. In such a polity, established and emerging elites are aware of value transfers and weight and offset these in their models, largely through bargaining power that is not derived from 'political economy know-how' but from 'knowledge' (see Figure 2.3). In line with this work's conception of freedom is 'knowledge' that does not generate rents but is instead washed away with each new tide of a Kondratieff wave as ever more innovative domestic and international competitors step into the arena.

Non-elites are not served by the elite denial fallacy ('elites don't exist') or by rejecting the elite dominance iron law that is structural to society (Proposition 1). Likewise, the elite populist fallacy ('elites are bad') and its related political temptations must be overcome by a realistic understanding that not all elites are equal in terms of the value that they create and extract. All countries have—or have the potential for—high quality elites, and these can and must prevail in the contests for the political economy. Non-elites should be exceedingly skeptical of narratives that promote the non-elite rule fallacy ('people power') and advocate for unweighted, blanket redistribution, lest they incentivize the establishment of new extractive coalitions and set themselves up to be taken advantage of. After all, non-elites, irrespective of their lower coordination capacity, and in consistency with the 'innate value creation character of humans' (natural) premise, create most of the value building blocks in the economy and, on aggregate, hold its largest pool of value in the form of their labor, savings, or knowledge. Non-elites must resist movements and narratives that call for narrow tactical alliances with elite business models that are based on transfers—even when their own group profits—since these come at a cost for society at large and are precursors for the 'extractive escalation dynamic'. Rather, wide non-elite interests can be strategically articulated by lucid narrativized preferences in the non-market arena for institutional change, particularly for the advancement of the three freedoms: easy *exit* from extractive principal-stakeholder relationships; a significant amount of value appropriation from their labor and creativity; and, most critically, the unhindered pursuit of value. Under such conditions, risk-taking non-elites become the engine of general progress. Some ascend to elite status with business models that are no more extractive and no less inclusive than the ones they join or replace.

Cognizant non-elites understand the sustainable value creation of the elite business models behind institutions such as democracy, religious establishments, communist states, stock markets, or educational systems. There is universal intuition of how easily any of these can switch from being the incentives for value creation to the harbingers of value transfers. Similarly, they understand that any policy prescriptions that work today may simply fail to function tomorrow, no matter how weighted and seemingly unassailable they appear to be, especially in times of crisis. But non-elite awareness has practical limits. This theory stresses throughout that while non-elites create the value, lower transaction costs mean that elites are the driving force of economic and human development. It is thus disastrous when elites become overwhelmed by critical junctures and stuck with mediocre narratives that cannot properly frame current complexities or the choices ahead. Such a situation would be reflected by the zeitgeist in the top echelons. In the 2020s, is there a sense of a *fin de siècle* combination of escapism—the singular, productive focus on the business rather than on the system—and pessimistic impotence at the impenetrable—being animated by narcissistic self-centeredness and the hedonistic pursuit of luxury—that is emblematic of the curtain falling on an epoch?

Elites are only human; a point well made by Alfani in *As Gods Among Men* (2023). Yet whether they are kings or tech tycoons sitting atop their pedestals of power and riches, the distance from which one observes them is much greater than the actual advantages they hold in terms of the energy, intelligence, intuition, or luck that brought them to the apex. 'The power multiplier' (see Section 1.3.4, Figure A5.3a, and also fractal wealth disparities) much exaggerates any differences that exist between humans. Elites ultimately face the same uncertainties and insecurities, and their psychological coping mechanisms have as many blind spots as anyone else's. Yet while superior talents and the vagaries of business legitimately bestow vast fortunes, such success brings responsibilities that many modern elites seem all too willing to renounce. At the Milken Institute's 'Shaping a Shared Future' event in Los Angeles, "conference-goers look for a dealmaking revival" since "there is money everywhere" (Masters, Agnew, Hughes, Platt, Gara, & Morris, 2024), while at the WEF's 2024 'Rebuilding Trust' annual meeting at Davos, Altman promotes his firm's narrative while canvassing sovereign wealth funds and others willing to support its burn rate. Working on the [*r*] to outperform the [*g*] by a margin as wide as possible (referencing Piketty, 2015, and applicable to most billionaires), growing businesses on first principles thinking (Thiel and Musk), enjoying the rewards of extraordinary achievements, often altruistically (Gates and Buffet), investing in fantastical narratives like the human colonization of space (Bezos and Musk), governing a divided polity (Biden and Trump), advancing AI governance with principles and laws that neglect the logic of elite agency and power (the UN and the EU), conducting wars that should have never have been launched (Putin and Cheney), or even celebrating absurdly magnificent pre-weddings, weddings, and other occasions (Ambani and royals the world over), is a matter of course for elites and as fulfilling as life can get. The members of many core coalitions are abdicating the stewardship possibilities of the 'the extraordinary lever' that fate has placed in their hands, and instead turning their attention[245] to narrow business, familial, philanthropic, or private desires, dated 20th century grand narratives that are of minimal consequence today, or spiritual pursuits. Such disengagement and skepticism is steeped in a fog of nihilism at the top and stems from elites underestimating the full capabilities of their own generative agency. Their Will to Power realizes its self-assertion in value appropriation as well as its creation. The purpose of elites in terms of general development is to double down on transformational leadership, take political economy risks, make deliberate and courageous leaps in the narrative markets, and creatively disrupt at the elite system level. Such undertakings represent the pinnacle of purpose, even if they are demanding and have uncertain outcomes entailing great personal risk and degrees of suffering. This is precisely why elites must exist in human societies and should not relinquish the essential role that they must play.

On elite judgment

The institutions that constrain elite business models can all be manipulated and will, in time, be hacked for value transfers. As a result, sustainable value creation and de-

245 To McGilchrist, "attention is a moral act: it creates, brings aspects of things into being, but in doing so makes others recede" (2019, p. 133).

velopment ultimately only occur to the degree that there is elite transformational leadership. Power by 'knowledge' is the path to development, a passageway that is traversed with 'elite judgment'. Bell's "The Art of Judgement" sees thoughts that are characterized by their "subjectivity, objectivity, reflexivity, and rationality" as "spontaneous" in Kant's sense (1987, pp. 222, 226), and are on a "middle path". That is to say:

> This middle path avoids the mindlessness of a mechanical following of rules by taking seriously the idea that there is an art of judgement and thought; and it avoids the regressive infinity of rules by introducing the notion of an awareness of 'intrinsic', 'intransitive', or 'immediate' significance or sense. The model for this awareness is the purely aesthetic response to a work of art or other aesthetic object. (Bell, 1987, p. 241)

The weighting and offsetting of value transfers and implementing these through well-crafted bargains lies at the crux of elite judgment. With each realization of the 'inextinguishable value creation option of elites', original intellectual and aesthetic positions are taken. For instance, on monetary policy after a financial crisis, on Irving John Good's notion of the "survival of man" by AI (1965), and, more generally, on the direction and nature of the steps taken at critical junctures. The agency associated with elite judgment invariably faces Knightian uncertainty and requires courage when it embraces one or the other of the parties or narratives in intra-elite contests. Transformational agency that is deeply cognizant that 'all elite agency creates and transfers value' draws from both objective and subjective assessments for weighting and offsetting necessary value transfers, is creative, and intuitively forsakes the established patterns of market, non-market, and narrative market arenas. It institutionalizes intra-elite contests without being trapped by intra-elite contest rules. Knowledge is legitimate when falsifiable, and power is legitimate if it can be lost as knowledge fades. Yet there are no external sources of legitimacy for the "intuitive moral sense" (McGilchrist, 2019) that guides elite judgments. Refusing to weight and offset so that these processes happen by default or through the actions of the elite business models of others is, exceptions notwithstanding, cowardly and deeply immoral.

'The extraordinary lever' enables the art of elite judgment and transformation. The applied and appropriative emanation of the Will to Power best supports development when endogenously relayed in an open elite system to a rhythm that is synchronized with technological shifts. This elite theory calls for specific freedoms, for cohesion in creative tension with a comprehensive separation of powers, and for intra-elite contests that lead to elite bargains. The pursuit of its diverse prescriptive aspects requires the utmost vigor and for institutional arrangements to be constantly refined and audaciously remade. Sustainable transformations for economic growth and human development conclusively hinge on weighted and bold elite judgments.

Summary of Chapter 8

Leadership, ethics, and non-elites

Chapter 8 subjects the ETED to the scrutiny of ethics and proposes a set of ethical principles for the purposes of economic and human development, explicitly based on the categorical imperative articulated as a maxim: (i) *To the creators the value created.* This maxim intends to be the foundation of a simple ethical system built on two straightforward but cardinal tenets for both elite and non-elite economic agents: (ii) *Maximize first-order value creation and risk origination for productive economic transformations fit for human purpose*; and (iii) *Weight and offset second-order value and risk transfers and minimize these to maximize value.* Four practical precepts are then derived for the pursuit of sustainable value creation by incentivizing those *qui generat valorem*. The set of ethical principles is an attempt at prescriptive synthesis based on a particular speculative philosophy and a realist account of how the political economy works. While the role for non-elites is secondary relative to elites, they are not passed over—quite the contrary—after all, much of the chapter prioritizes non-elite interests, even if in a nonconventional fashion.

The chapter's first section (8.1) takes a stepwise approach to the non-elite perspective, albeit not without controversial assertions. The starting point is a conceptualization of the socio-economic structure pyramid (Figure 8.1) where elite and non-elite classes are described (8.1.1). The emphasis is next placed on the theoretical and applied role of the core elite coalition (8.1.2). This is followed by addressing the question of whether elites can advance non-elite interests (8.1.3) with the support of a typology that details the four political options for both non-elites and elites to advance non-elite interests in the context of their relationship (Figure 8.2). The resultant framework is then speculatively tested by examining if post-singularity AI elites would serve human non-elite interests in a world where elite coordination capacity is non-human (8.1.4). This all paves the way for analysis of which political and business systems best serve non-elite interests, a discussion that purports to transcend the conventional Western democracies vs authoritarian systems debate (8.1.5). The politically agnostic 'A Political and Business Systems Sustainable Value Creation (SVC) Test' (Figure 8.3) is suggested as a way to answer this question in line with the ETED's sustainable value creation maxim. The final sub-section examines the boundaries of sustainable value creation ethical principles by continuing the thought experiment on the relationship between lower and higher intelligences in the context of non-human AI political agency (8.1.6).

The next section (8.2) considers the place for ethics in economic development policy. It starts with a critical examination of the viciously extractive opioid business model to frame and weight evil in value transfers and destruction (8.2.1). To do so, the distinction between 'extractive' and 'destructive' transfer-COST is scrutinized, targeting the latter costs that cannot be linked to the profit and loss (P&L) statement and hence do not constitute direct savings for the firm or enhance its profits (8.2.2). These 'destructive' costs are the basis for the condemnatory 'license for evil' conceptual element (Figure A5.5b). The third sub-section transitions to the more general question of when and whether value transfers are acceptable (8.2.3) and proposes criteria with 'A Transfer Constraints Framework' for policy (Table 8.2). The appropriateness of concrete redistribution policies is then examined (8.2.4) with practical corollaries set out in 'A Weighted Redistribution Framework' for policy (Table 8.3). These two frameworks link to and support 'A Weighted Structural Reform Framework' for policy (Table 7.1), with the relationship between all three frameworks for weighted policymaking depicted in Table A4.4. The key conceptual elements that bind these three together are elite transformational leadership, the 'elite institutional change bargain', and the 'elite redistribution constraints bargain'. The second section of the chapter returns to the AI thought experiment and closes with two extreme scenarios for the future of redistribution: in the first, 'everything' is redistributed as the AI appropriates all value, while in the second, 'nothing' is redistributed as the AI disables all involuntary extractive transfers (8.2.5).

The third section (8.3) engages in two conversations about freedom and one about the art of 'elite judgment'. In the first sub-section, it is suggested that if certain freedoms are present in a system, elite and non-elite interests converge because sustainable value creation is maximized (8.3.1). Fromm's (1994) fundamental freedom *to* (extended here '*to* create value') and freedom *from* (extended here to '*from* value extraction') are identified to support the claim that if both are present in a political economy, then positive development is more likely to occur via optimal investments, as described in 'The Two Fundamental Freedoms for Development Matrix' (Figure 8.4). The next sub-section (8.3.2) elaborates on the conceptualization of freedom, adding a third enabling variety—the freedom 'to *exit*'—that rebalances bargaining power and leads to 'The Three Freedoms for Development Model' (Figure 8.5).

The book ends with a critical examination that tightens the theory's system by linking its speculative and pragmatic philosophies (8.3.3). The work's first principles are articulated as the general principles of life: the (A) Will to Live (referencing Schopenhauer); the (B) 'universal extraction propensity of life' (referencing Schrödinger); and the (C) Will to Power (referencing Nietzsche). In Figure 8.6 these are then related to the basic principle informing all socio-economic relations, the (Z) 'value appropriation demand of humans' (socio-economic) constraint of the human condition on which the three premises of human behavior rest: the (I) 'innate value creation character of humans' (natural) premise; the (II) 'universal value extraction propensity of humans' (socio-economic) premise; and the (III) 'inextinguishable value creation option of elites' (leadership) premise. The inquiry's practical apparatus, with its SVC measurements and SVC valuations, rests on a law of nature and on first principles, see Figure 8.7.

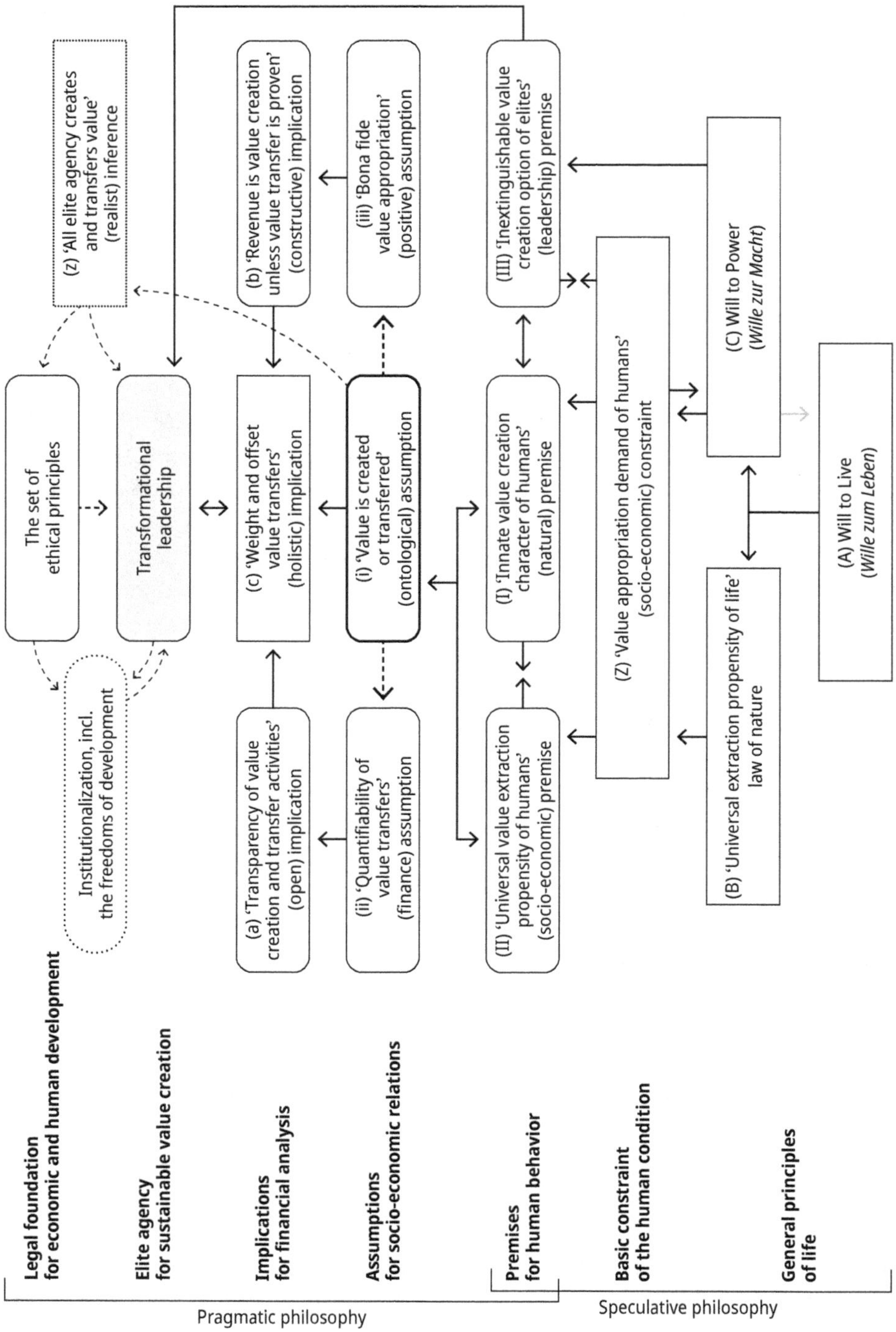

Figure 8.7: The speculative and pragmatic philosophies of the elite theory of economic development (ETED) anchored by transformational leadership.

The final sub-section tackles the creative tension between institutions and power, a question that is resolved in favor of the latter on account of elite transformational leadership. The realization of the ETED's set of ethical principles by elite agency involves the institutionalization of the three freedoms, essentially determining the degree to which 'knowledge', 'power', and 'the extraordinary lever' are both gained and lost in the political economy. Ultimately, the leadership needed for sustainable value creation at the elite system and business model levels is actualized by audacious 'elite judgment' that carefully weights and offsets value transfers.

Epilogue
Judgments atop hierarchies: Testing the language, logic, propositions, and conceptual elements of the elite theory

This book's core message has been advanced through diverse lines of reasoning and reiterated in multiple forms. It is essentially simple: the judgments made on whether risk origination, value creation or their transfer are prioritized at the elite business model level determine economic growth. These rest on the use of power, the meta-contest resolution mechanism that usurps institutional processes. Power is converted into applied coordination capacity to serve value appropriation. To reduce friction and enhance the functioning of 'the power multiplier', non-elite agency is institutionalized through laws, regulations, norms, and policies that are consistent with elite business model preferences. Development hinges on high elite quality; intra-elite contest winners with business models that are focused on the production rather than the transfer of value.

If elites were to vanish overnight and be replaced by perfectly equitable rules, the end of the elite denial fallacy ('elites don't exist') would also throw light on and validate the elite populist fallacy ('elites are bad'). Elite judgment is sorely missed the moment that institutions emasculate the power of value creators. One concrete example of administrative excess is that: "The number of physicians in the United States grew 150 percent between 1975 and 2010, roughly in keeping with population growth, while the number of healthcare administrators increased 3,200 percent for the same time period" (Cantlupe, 2017). The ETED claims that such a state is deliberate, as is set out in Proposition 12: 'Elite agency is the principal microfoundation of institutional change' (Section 3.1.1). As this process happens, instead of being the servant of intra-elite contests (that also support non-elite interests), it is not unusual for the institution itself to become the elite business model and for its beneficiaries to profit from value transfers. Value creation is eroded in China's *guanliaozhuyi* "bureaucratism", denounced by the CPC "as an intrinsic ailment of bureaucracy" and "the anti-bureaucratic ghost [that] dwells in the machinery of China's bureaucratic state" (Ding & Thompson-Brusstar, 2021, p. 116); in Max Weber's "iron cage", where "order is now bound to the technical and economic conditions of machine production which to-day determine the lives of all the individuals who are born into this mechanism" (1905/1930, p. 181; see also DiMaggio & Powell, 1983); in Schumpeter's administrative stationary state, where socialism and capitalism are indistinguishable and the "mechanization of progress" means its "cessation" as every individual—leaders included—become "just another office worker" (1942/2000, p. 131–133); and in George Ritzer's "McDonaldization of Society", with "the homogenization of American culture and life, streamlined along a set of rational, efficient, and impersonal principles" (1983, p. 371).

https://doi.org/10.1515/9783110734638-013

Critically, first-order value creation and risk origination is linked to elite judgment; without it, coordination capacity and 'the extraordinary lever' pass into the inflexible custody of one or the other unaccountable administrative structures of the managerial, technical, and creative class, leading to the real prospect of stagnation.

While it would be excessive to argue that elite business models must be above the rule of law for human development to happen, or, more precisely, that they must make their own rules to overcome rivals, hierarchies are found "everywhere" (Bejan, 2020) and this might be precisely why evolution in the social realm requires them. Coordination capacity scales through rules at the bottom and judgment at the top. The deinstitutionalization of society is as counterproductive as the full institutionalization of elite agency. The latter manifests itself in the destructive 'missing elite system' problem (see the case of Europe, and the world as a whole in relation to the AI tragedy of the commons, Sections 7.3.4 and 7.3.5). Elite judgment drives progress. In contrast to Stoller's (2024b) claim—in the aftermath of non-elite violence against elites—that "elite disdain for the rule of law is leading to a society that is spinning out of control", the elite theory's position is that elites are never checked by institutions but primarily balance—and are balanced by—their peers in intra-elite contests (employing institutions for that purpose is the most efficient way of achieving this in terms of transaction costs). This establishes a seminal part of this work within the microfoundations of institutional change literature (see Chapter 4, Sections 5.1, 3.1.1).

At times, and notably in the context of intra-elite contests, elites bank on alliances with non-elites. While non-elite discontent is real, it results from elite judgments for undue value transfers that are contrary to development. Hence, the toolbox developed in this inquiry—whether the five firm valuation frameworks for capital allocation (Section 5.3.2) or the frameworks derived from the theory's programmatic philosophy (Figure 8.6)—is aimed at the elite system. The realist inference—'all elite agency creates and transfers value' (Figure A5.4a)—permeates the prescriptive aspects of this book and attempts to address a distressing contradiction in the human condition: economic development relies on judgments about extraction across socio-economic relationships.

To explain this basic socio-economic reality for the purpose of economic development, the elite theory seeks anchor in a speculative philosophy and its first principles, starting with those of life (Figure 8.6), that reference the natural order. In consequence, the arguments evolve in line with the imperative to creatively oppose entropy and disorder at a granular level—through the elite business models in every nook and cranny of the political economy. Elite agency is likened to Schrödinger's hierarchically higher entities, "continually sucking orderliness from its environment" (1944/2013, p. 73). Concurrently, and here lies a contradiction, entities exist in the universe precisely because of the value exchange relationships that they have with others (in strategic management terminology these 'others' are called stakeholders). The incongruity further deepens when considering AI philosopher Joshua Bach's perspective on relationships where "sentience is the ability of a system to make sense of its relationship to the world" (Leventov, 2023). Sensemaking in sentient systems is overwhelmed by this particularism, the double standard in social life—what one applies to oneself cannot apply to the stakeholder on whom one relies on. Nothing is possible without some form of extraction. To then understand how all of this functions and leads to progress requires multi-disciplinary engagement. For example, Williamson proposes "selectively combining law, economics, and organization to study the governance of contractual relations from a transaction cost economizing perspective" (2010, p. 687). This is benchmarked against the more fundamental 'value is created of transferred' (ontological) assumption of this work's pragmatic philosophy.

The empirical and operational key to elucidate socio-economic relationships is how business models monetize the value they create with the bargaining power they possess. The types of contractual relations that permit the appropriation of value from stakeholders are the mark of their evolutionary fitness—and reflected in financial statements. Value is to society what energy is to life. In this work, value has been defined as being everything that humans determine is worth appropriating (see Menger, 1871/2007 for its subjective nature, and Jevons, 1871 for its association with scarcity; Section 2.2.2). Relationships across business models are the veins and arteries that carry value, as energy flows back and forth and maintains the system (independently, of course, of whether its business models have any degree of sentience). Ethics are then the choices made about proportions and weights, about the direction and throughput of value across the relationships that constitute society. The ensuing circulations supply the degree of negative entropy for entities, individuals, and organizations that is necessary to uphold their objective existence, as well as their social status and knowledge levels. The inquiry into *qui generat valorem* ('who creates value') sheds light on value transfers (by revealing their monetary equivalences) and credits these to the stakeholder transferors of the value created and *not* appropriated, while the inquiry into *cui bono* ('follow the money') ascertains the principal beneficiary transferees of value appropriated but *not* created.

Society becomes impoverished when extractive value transfer currents overwhelm and compromise the Smithian "productive powers of labour" (1776/1904) and other first-order productive flows. Sustainability is when the matrix of society's relationships exhibits munificent energy and value flows. Human creativity best unlocks the secrets of nature and its treasure trove of value through judgments rather than with linear administrative hierarchies, especially given the latter's propensity to force transfers from one group to another. At the same time, the law and other institutional devices enable network flows that lessen friction and lower transaction costs. The value creation and appropriation (VCA) conceptual framework (see Brandenburger & Stuart, 1996; Amit & Zott, 2001; Di Gregorio, 2013; Garcia-Castro & Aguilera, 2015) is repurposed from the strategic management literature to examine the economy and operationalize the inclusive value created but *not* appropriated (transfer-OUT) and its antagonistic extractive value appropriated but *not* created (transfer-IN) in financial terms. At the business model level, relationships with suppliers, bankers, or taxpayers, as well as with workers, managers, or owners, are appraised through the sustainable value creation (SVC) framework and measurements like the Value Creation Rating (VCr). Analysis is also provided for multiple levels of aggregation across the many domains and dimensions of the world's micro-meso-macro order: from individual firms and industry sectors to nation states and supranational entities; from Big Tech and the tech bros to international business and inter-state relations; from government administrators and labor unions to liberal professionals and entrepreneurs; from minority groups and social classes to the population at large and the elite system. As an aside, the family is also a bundle of relationships through which both positive and negative entropy travels, and so the diagnostic opportunities offered by this work can also encompass the value that flows through the bonds of kinship.

This leads directly to the subtext of this Epilogue. Elite agency is not equally distributed in the political economy and follows a power law model. Bearing in mind that it is also the ultimate and decisive force in society, one must consider its fractal-like qualities to fully comprehend economic development. The anchor—the *constant* by which individual parts relate to the whole and vice-versa—is invariably the dichotomous 'value is created or transferred' (ontological) assumption for socio-economic relations (the human scale is transcended when the assumption is placed on the plane of general energy and entropic processes). Analyzing business model patterns as these occur and recur at the micro, meso, and macro levels (see Figure 3.8) provides anticipatory signals in how they relate to one another. For instance, while elite quality supplies information on the sustainability of firms in each nation, it also provides perspectives on the degree of risk and value transfers and, naturally, on the sustainable value creation flows that occur at the intra-firm and even family level. The association between elite quality and non-elite quality, whether through cultural or principal-stakeholder ties, runs deep. Of course, the pitfalls of forecasting these with the recursive pattern descriptions of mathematics lies in the fact that multiple fractal structures meet, mix, and interact in society: the distribution of elite power endowments, the frequency and intensity of intra-elite contests, the size and effectiveness of innovation hubs, the occurrence and effects of wars, the scale of inequality, the sorting of stock market valuations, the patterns around the emergence of unicorns and super-unicorns in VC portfolios, and countless other factors. The result is 'fractal-like' and evidently the ensuing inverse polynomial distributions will not match the classic examples of power law distributions. In that sense, any elite theory can only be an approximation of the myriad possible outcomes.

This all makes the elite theory not a work of political philosophy, but rather an inquiry on the epistemology of business models, from those of the basic family unit to the workings of empires. By the very nature of its subject matter, such a work fits the notion of a "grand theory" that is meant to be "abstract and normative" and able to explain "human nature and conduct" (Skinner, 1990, p. 3). At the same time, such "associating and dissociating of concepts" is denounced by C. Wright Mills (1959, p. 26) and largely viewed a fringe perspective within field of the social sciences. Nonetheless, "a multidisciplinary effort" in "pursuit of a Grand Theory" lies squarely in the spirit of outsized quests that aim to answer hard questions like "why some countries are rich and others poor", as in Douglass North's new institutional economics (Telles, 2024, pp. 109, 110; see Section 4.2). The approach of this book seeks to offer a falsifiable understanding of the political economy of economic development, the prescriptive positions of which rest on the inclusive incentive structures for business models that emerge from intra-elite contests. The ETED's language, logic, and some of its propositions and conceptual elements are now further tested by bringing into focus a series of cases ranging from Julius Caesar to Donald Trump in an attempt to reaffirm its normative claims. This Epilogue hence consists of thirteen loosely connected parts.

First, in tribute to Pliny the Elder, the classical record-keeper of extraction, the case of Caesar is discussed to establish value transfers as wrongs against humanity. **Second**, the case of the transition to the German Third Reich is considered through the elite-centered economic analysis of Gerschenkron to stress the importance of the narrative market arena for the preservation of a specific business model over multiple generations. **Third**, we reach the present day with an examination of President Trump and the degree to which the core coalition he has formed with the so-called 'tech bros' may ease out extractive business models, liberate value creation, and bring about progressive elite circulation. **Fourth**, a debate is held on whether the efforts of the tech bros to reposition the Trump narrative in business model terms—a mandate to gain legitimacy with key elite coalitions and non-elite groups while not estranging the MAGA faithful and other conservative factions—is sustainable. **Fifth**, the social backdrop to the non-elite discontent that led to the confirmation of America's 47th President is examined. **Sixth**, a political economy framework for development centered on non-elite quality (Figure E.1) is advanced. **Seventh**, the role of culture is emphasized as a driver of economic growth through its connection with non-elite quality. **Eighth**, the current technological backdrop of AI—also a factor in the outcome of the 2024 presidential election—is considered in a discussion with an initial set of six hypotheses on how AI might affect the political economy, while the rationale for accepting or rejecting each of them is expounded upon (Tables E.2 and E.3). **Ninth**, four more hypotheses extend the tentative framework of AI in the political economy by interrogating provocative futuristic scenarios like 'elite singularity' (Tables E.4 and E.5). **Tenth**, the discussion returns to negative entropy to explain that that the AI imagined by techno-optimists entails an incantation of Maxwell's demon and ponders the degree to which a version of affordable and pervasive intelligence will facilitate optimal transfers and hence long-term economic growth. The **Eleventh** part describes social dynamics, stressing the reversal of local entropy through technology waves that are driven by risk origination and exposure as well as by hierarchies, where all is bound by the idea that asymmetry is life inducing. **Twelfth**, the structuralist approach to the understanding of economic development is challenged as the argument converges on the judgments of leadership, leading to a brief discourse on the psychology of elites with references to their alienation. **Thirteenth**, the Epilogue closes with a reflection on the shackles of extractive institutions and bureaucratism and recognizes the importance of judgments made on value creation in the fractal spaces of non-linear hierarchies and on value transfers by those at the top that break free of humanly-devised constraints. The generative fractal structure of the elite system is visualized using the metaphor of a tree (in Figure E.2).

1 Weighting Pliny the Elder's *tantam etiamsi coactam humani generis iniuriam*, lest the future is lost

The prescriptive position of the ETED rests on the weighting and offsetting of value transfers inherent in elite business models. This is performed with sustainable value creation (SVC) measurements like the meso-level Elite Quality Index (EQx) or the firm-level Value Creation Rating (VCr) that evaluate first-order productive activities relative to second-order transfer activities (Section 2.3.1). To incentivize first-order productive activities for value creation (Table 2.3), technocratic reforms rely on laws, (de)regulatory measures, norms, and policies (see Figure 7.1, Table A4.4) that are aimed at particular elite business models. Yet if elite judgments are based solely on simple solutionism, abstractions, or linear narratives they will, in parallel to the rules and bureaucracies they assemble, invariably lead to imperfect outcomes. A facile analogy is with *Crime and Punishment*'s Rodion Raskolnikov. Moved by the reductionist idealism—the narrative of an exemplary society—he kills the exploitative pawnbroker, Alyona Ivanovna, but also ends up slaying her innocent sister, Lizaveta. Of course, courage can't be ascribed to the act of literally killing an offending agent but is rather found in terminating a bad business model on the evidence that it is truly extractive. At their core, all elite business models operate a bundle of risk and value creation and transfer activities and these are often confused and misidentified on account of the narrative market. Brennan and Buchanan explore how "rapacious wealth-maximising" businesspeople might be socially preferrable to elites taking a "'public interest' model of behaviour as an idealised benchmark" (1983, p. 103–104). As a result, reforms must be as discerning as they are decisive.

Value appropriated but *not* created by elite agency exists as a constant in any society. In heeding this logic of recurrence, technological progress won't halt the *Ewige Wiederkunft* of value transfers, a fact that in principle is also applicable to AI (see, for instance, the hypothesis in Table E.4 on the nature of value transfers with autonomous AI elite agency). Elite systems that are intent on establishing feasible and optimal proportions of value creation and transfers (a costly intellectual endeavor) advance ethical principles to legitimize power (at times by resorting to spiritual mandates) and possess the bravery to implement institutional change to overcome resistance in intra-elite contests. When value transfers snowball and shift out of alignment with the minimum levels of value creation needed for growth, once mighty empires and top-tier organizations fall (also see The Elite Business Model Lifecycle,

Figure 4.5). Value transfers always hurt, even when properly weighted for general development with well executed 'alternating value extraction and creation' policies (Section 2.3.1). In *Natural History*, Pliny the Elder accepted Caesar's slaying of "1,192,000 human beings" and the business model of war as "a prodigious even if unavoidable wrong inflicted on the human race" (1938, 7.25). Plutarch also described Caesar's wars of conquest (58–50 BC) and the cruel and massive profit machine that appropriated value from Gallic peoples (1919, 15.5; Section 7.3.2). The 'destructive' elite agency (Figure 6.7) of the Roman vanquisher operated an unconstrained 'license for evil' (its effects are quantifiable, see Section 8.2, Figure A5.5b). At the same time, the legacy of his leadership led to France's institutional foundations like the Napoleonic Code (*Code civil*, 1804), the beloved French language, and its cultural lineage. However, while long-term transfer offsets are conceivable, should the wrongs of the *Pax Romana* only be compensated for centuries later?[246] Progress should be witnessed over a lifetime, and evidenced by elite business models that demand fewer transfers than their predecessors.

Discerning current elite quality trends by the sustainable value creation of the models that account for the largest proportion of GDP like AI, healthcare, or war,[247] speaks to the fundamental mechanism of economic growth. The value-enhancing technologies of the industrial and intelligence revolutions clearly foster development, but what if they also amplify 'the power multiplier' and facilitate new pathways for value appropriated but *not* created? Do they weaken intra-elite contests and lead to non-elite acquiescence by using more complex, less transparent, and non-invasive devices to master the political economy. Do individual 'acceptance' responses to extraction (see Section 5.2.2; Tullock, 1967) then become the norm, while 'trust in elites' (Figure A5.8) becomes the only effective non-elite political option? The transfers inherent in numerous present-day business models inflict more pain than just a few decades ago (see the case of the young in Galloway, 2024), yet citizens appear unable to con-

246 Virgil, the chief propagandist of first emperor Augustus, famously laid out in *Aeneid* (1910, lines 851–854) a narrative that articulates the immediate benefits of Roman imperial rule:

But thou, O Roman, learn with sovereign sway
To rule the nations. Thy great art shall be
To keep the world in lasting peace, to spare
humbled foe, and crush to earth the proud.

247 Whether a long game offsets current horrors is as much an issue for contemporary war planners as it is in assessing Caesar's agency. The correct answer to the question included in the US citizenship test on why America entered the Vietnam War—i.e., "to stop the spread of communism" (Camden, 2021)—presupposes that a global public good was at stake in this cross-border elite business model. Was a sustainable value creation perspective also present in the Second Gulf War (2003–2011) given the backdrop of the War on Terror (see Goldstein, 2010)? An 'expected adjusted residual income earned per fatality' metric would provide clarity—whether in Gaul, Iraq, or Ukraine—and ought to be a benchmark for decision-making and a salient part of the public discourse.

nect the dots or recognize what is happening to them.[248] This has less bearing in the broader context if the offending grifts are superseded by additional value: optimists like Pinker (2018) and Roser, Rosling, and Rönnlund (2018) highlight the march of progress, especially since the 19th century, that has enriched the general production function and is reflected in the rising quality of life (massive poverty reduction, longer lifespans, and the enjoyment of scientific and engineering achievements like smart phones). Nonetheless, there is still is peril in improved value creation when new spaces are opened for transfers, since elites can arbitrage non-elite obliviousness and satisfaction with marginal improvements through upgraded models like asset inflation, "junk fees" (Pohle, 2024), "right to repair" denials (e.g., smart agricultural machinery empowers John Deere to force farmers to "overpay for dealer repairs", Zimmerman, 2024), or wars fought by armchair statesmen with conscripted and non-conscripted armies. In the rush to appropriate the phenomenal increases in value, elites can easily overlook balance, assume that their counterparties are better off in any event, and lose their principles by failing to weight and offset their transfers from these stakeholders.

Institutions that become accustomed to accommodating transfer-IN elite businesses soon blunt their extraction-constraining edges. Elite agency that drives regressive change during economic booms might, however slightly, nudge society towards a hazardous downhill path of decomposing intra-elite contests and eroded elite cohesion. In the 21st century, it is seriously disconcerting that some elite business models do not offset the lives they require to function as a default position, while the worst offenders (see opioids, Section 8.2.1) are only reluctantly phased out by peers that are also often beneficiaries. A headline in *The Spectator* epitomizes the hollowed out ethical positions extant within the elite system: "We Should be Thankful for the Sackler Family's Philanthropy" (Leith, 2022). Historically, however, the relentless decoding of nature's laws in the form of new technologies over the last two centuries has certainly powered economic development and facilitated the application of the 'alternating value transfers and creation' logic and the offsetting of elite agency wrongs. A severe recession is an acceptable price for financial innovation and optimized capital alloca-

248 The absence of mass mobilizations and the disinclination of elite systems across the world to end the bloodshed caused by Russia's invasion of Ukraine, where algorithms have crossed an ethical redline as drones autonomously adjudicate over life and death (Mozur & Satariano, 2024), confirms that there are current incarnations of the horrors Pliny the Elder described. Wars are most perplexing when they do not have to be won to meet the residual income expectations of elite coalitions. Such a situation is implied in *The Wall Street Journal* headline on the day that the US withdrew from the graveyard of empires: "Who Won in Afghanistan? Private Contractors: The U.S. military spent $14 trillion during two decades of war and relied heavily on companies to perform critical functions. Those who benefited from the outpouring of government money range from major weapons manufacturers to entrepreneurs" (Nissenbaum, Donati & Cullison, 2021). Voices concerned about America's "endless war", like the Quincy Institute for Responsible Statecraft (see: https://quincyinst.org), critically examine 'war as cross-border value appropriation' (Section 7.3.2) through the lens of domestic rent seeking.

tion, some pollution is a fair trade off for widespread access to electricity and travel, and a rare war is a justifiable cost for lasting peace and stability.

The coming AI critical juncture is clearly going to be one of history's most decisive. If value transfers are properly weighted and offset, the ascendant future of mankind promised by techno-optimists will come to pass. Courage is in accepting the extraction of value creators as much as in swiftly terminating the worst offending models, lest their disproportionate wrongdoings spread and compromise the fate of nations. Under such a criterion, Pliny's acquiescence to the brutality of Caesar might be forgiven, but no such absolution can be granted to the talented Junkers.

2 The narrative of *Latifundia* that protected bread from imports but lost Germany

Consumed by mounting curiosity since the advent of the Neolithic revolution some 12,000 years ago, the proverbial earth-watching extraterrestrial intelligence continues to ponder the human species. Will its soaring civilization transcend the rent-seeking behavior that characterizes its polities? Now taking bets on AI's impact on the blue planet's political economies in the 21st century, the aliens consider the single 19th century business model that transmuted the 20th century: the *latifundia*[249] (large estates) of a ruling class that went on to fashion the unified German state in 1871.

Caesar, despite his sizable seven-book investment in a first-person narrative—*"De Bello Gallico" and Other Commentaries* (1915)—raided the original inhabitants of France using a cross-border model that chiefly trusted in the power of 'might'. In contrast, the Prussian Junkers plundered from their fellow Germans through the power of 'mind' (the influence of narratives is set out in Figure A5.1 and fully discussed in Section 3.1.3). About two millennia after the unfolding of Caesar's martial business model of conquest, the price of bread became the prime cause for Europe's fatidic trail from Bismark to Hitler (1871 to 1945). Again, and in opposition to the view held by Pliny the Elder, extraction is *never* "unavoidable", as elite judgment is autonomous and always paramount.

The elite business model of the Junkers resembled that of their absentee London-based British aristocrat counterparts, who famously implemented the protectionist Corn Laws against the interests of the Manchester industrialists. In *Bread and Democracy in Germany*, written in 1943 with World War II raging, Gerschenkron made a then vital analysis of the German political economy by placing elite agency at the center of his analytical framework. Beyond its pomp, the sincere yearning of the people

249 References Gerschenkron's Latin subtitle of his work, *Bread and Democracy in Germany* (1943)—*Latifundia Perdidere Germaniam*—which can be translated as "Large Estates Lost Germany" and refers to the business model of the Junker landowning class.

for it, and its late but remarkable rate of industrialization, the origin of the Junker's Second German Reich (1871–1918) can be reduced to a single protectionist measure. Free trade endangered the primary grain production business model of the landowning elites East of the Elbe River, as cheaper and better options were available elsewhere, for instance, in the Russian Empire. Unlike the United Kingdom in 1846, Germany did not repeal its equivalent Corn Laws—the point of the import tariffs was to keep bread prices perpetually inflated. The Junker system went on to systematically win the domestic political economy contests in all three of the market arenas when challenged by the many liberal German elite coalitions whose eminently capable business models were eager to profit from international trade.

The Prussian army, gerrymandering and other forms of control in the Reichstag and the Bundesrat, and a Kaiser who was also King of Prussia, cemented Junker 'might' in the political non-market arena. Yet it was elite business model leadership in the narrative market that ultimately secured artificially high grain prices. To defend the indefensible, the 'Germany' narrative became entwined with 'German nationalism'. There is a vast difference between the two, and therefore between the pragmatic Bismarck and the fanatical Hitler, even though a straight line connects the elite business model of native grain production with that of totalitarian economic institutions. Nationalism was the essential narrative design used to protect overpriced bread,[250] and collaterally caused Germany to close up—and not only to trade—when values such as self-sufficiency gained traction with non-elites. As the opposing globalist free trade narrative supported by numerous German industrialists, intellectuals, and workers was defeated in the narrative market arena, the social power over 'mind' consolidated protectionism in what Gerschenkron terms the "pseudoconstitutional monarchy of the Hohenzollerns" (1943/1966, p. 147). An 'extractive escalation dynamic' (Section 5.3.4) ensued with expanded tariffs, incentives for cartel formation, and a heavily subsidized military-industrial complex. Here, Bismarck's fair weighting efforts saw compensatory offsets like the exemplary *Sozialpolitik* with its innovative protections against social risks. Von Mises summarized the particular steady state of Germany's value transfers as: "Sozialpolitik, protectionism, huge armaments, and aggressive nationalism" (1969/2003, p. 8). On the latter point, Prussian leadership changed German culture top-down as is spelled out by Veblen:

> The united Fatherland came under the hegemony of the most aggressive and most irresponsible – substantially the most archaic – of the several states that coalesced in its formation; and quite as a matter of course the dynastic spirit of the Prussian State has permeated the rest of the federated people, until the whole is now very appreciably nearer the spiritual bent of the militant Prussian State of a hundred years ago than it has been at any time since the movement for German union began in the nineteenth century. (Veblen, 1915/2003, p. 97)

250 There is a school of thought that refutes free trade and advocates for an interventionist nation state and economic nationalism (List, 1841/2011; Levi-Faur, 1997; see Chang, 2002); yet the aim is industrialization, not the protection of the business models of a feudal aristocracy.

Nationalism that achieves early success without acknowledging the value creation infrastructure built in earlier eras or produced by outsiders feeds further cultural regression:

> Their great success in business and industry has inspired the commonplace German subjects with a degree of confidence and self-complacency that impresses their neighbors as conceit and braggadocio. (Veblen, 1915/2003, p. 100)

The narrative of nationalism was the political economy weapon that steamrolled all opposition to grain imports, and later to all things foreign. Liberal knowledge elites were decimated as the Second Reich moved ahead. The Humboldtian university model, once a beacon of light for progressive Europe, was extinguished, and Smithian and Ricardian classical economics were banned from higher education curricula under the notorious "Prussian dominated cartel" (Whimster, 2019, p. 256) run by *Kutusminister* Friedrich Althoff,[251] who "ruled the Prussian universities as a dictator" (von Mises, 1969/2003, p. 10). Tragically, the narrative escaped Junker control and took on a life of its own (as is often the case, see the explanation in Section 3.1.3) making an even darker turn; by the 1930s, it was firmly in the hands of an emergent elite rising from abject non-elite quality (see the framework in Figure E.1): the arriviste National Socialist German Workers (Nazi) Party and its charlatan leader. They were given the keys to the system "to play the Junker game", only to be ultimately destroyed in the loss of their lands to East European states, with Hirsch noting as early as 1946 how "the Junker moves from [the] sphere of reality into the mausoleum of history" (pp. 146, 150). The global cataclysm of Nazism is thus inherently traceable to the deceptively primitive and innocent regional business model of bread. The critical node that impeded Paretian elite circulation (see Figures 1.1 and 6.5) and the crucial source of the model's bargaining power differential was the narrative of nationalism.

This case frames economic and human development in terms of elite agency that highlights the narrative market's potentially inclusive or extractive role. The Bavarian farmer outside the Reich would never have endured pricier Prussian grain feed for his pigs that raised the costs of the beloved *weißwurst*. Narratives can easily sway non-elites to support elite business models that work against their own interests, and in this example the Germans meekly accepted an overpriced staple.

Progress hinges on intra-elite contests. The 'good Junker', Chancellor von Caprivi (in office from 1890–92), failed to overcome resistance (in the political non-market and the narrative market arenas) to his trade treaties to dismantle (part of) the

251 Max Weber recounted "that it was almost impossible for any aspirant academic not to accede to whatever proposition might be put to him by Althoff" and "identified Althoff as a corrupting force and the system itself as corrupt". As a result, the "grand old Humboldtian legacy" was completely lost and destroyed (Whimster, 2019, pp. 256, 257).

Schutzzollpolitik and was quickly dismissed.[252] In the same vein, President Hindenburg did not hesitate "to deliver the German nation to Adolf Hitler" as "General von Schleicher was suddenly ousted from the chancellorship. His 'crime' had been that he had dared to disapprove of the abuse of *Osthilfe* relief funds for the benefit of large estate owners" (Hirsch, 1946, pp. 149, 150).

The agrarian elite system conceived of and then implemented a Germany to protect its rents, the most lasting power base of which was in the narrative market. No coherent coalition with a Ricardian free-trade narrative could overcome nationalism in lands that were once some of the most open, tolerant, and liberal in Europe. For instance, Hamburg was already a city-state and trade hub in the mercantile networks of the 17th century, "a significant sign of the bourgeoning integration of European markets" (Lindberg, 2008, p. 641). Traverso tackles the fable of the "German-Jewish symbiosis" (1995), as does Scholem when he stresses that "the love affair of the Jews and the Germans remained one-sided and unreciprocated" (1976, p. 86), yet the fact that the words "love" and "symbiosis" appear in their critical analyses suggests that there was the possibility of an enlightened German route out of the disgraceful antisemitic mindset that was then prevalent in most of Europe. The big picture is clear: "If it had not been for the selfishness and narrow-mindedness of [the Junkers] retarding social element, modern ideals might have prevailed in Germany at the turn of the century and the world might have been spared unending turmoil" (Hirsh, 1946, p. 151). Today, almost no European is familiar with this ruling class or the decades-long intra-elite contests that gave rise to the two ill-fated central European empires that changed everything. Even in Germany, students remain blissfully unaware of Gerschenkron's theses and the lessons that connect specific value transfer business models to specific narratives.

In short, while the narratives of Manchester won out over those of London, those of Hamburg lost out to Berlin's. This is the essential explanation for the greatest tragedy of the 20th century, while also accounting for the origin and rise to ascendance of Anglo-Saxon power in sync with free, liberal, and open economic system narratives. Even if neither the UK or the US have always heeded their own narratives (especially in the international context and vis-à-vis perceived rivals, see Chang, 2002), the targeting of mercantilist rent-seeking models liberated value creation at home (also refer to The Great Power Elite Quality Lifecycle for international relations, Figure 7.7).

252 In exploring the origins of the attendant *Lebensraum* narrative, Smith (1980, p. 60) delineates with exacting detail the interaction between business, political, and knowledge elites starting in the 1890s when "[. . .] other parties also turned toward the *Mittelstand* and agrarianism. The Conservative Party, which largely represented *Junker* agriculture, did so in order to reverse the policy of Chancellor Leo von Caprivi of reducing agricultural tariffs to encourage other countries to reduce tariffs on German industrial exports [Barkin, 1970, pp. 56–67.] The *Junkers*, the Conservatives, and their academic supporters advanced themselves as the protectors of traditional agrarian culture and generalized the issue into a debate on the relative merits of agricultural and industrial society".

Moving forward to today, narratives that support risk origination and value creation remain pivotal for growth. The competitors in narrative markets must provide a framework for institutional change to address grand challenges like AI, environmental degradation, or geopolitical issues, while suppling lucid *cui bono* analyses of their business models. The ETED's conceptual elements and logic are valuable to the degree that they help craft narratives for nations, economic sectors and industries, or individual firms, and serve as references to elite agency. Institutional change is best guided by incessant empirical assessments of micro-level rent seeking, verified by measurements, and integrated with broader narratives that connect the dots across society's spaces. Evidently, the faster the technological progress the more pressing the need for narrative updates. No matter how laudable narratives are, they will be perniciously misappropriated and sincerely misunderstood, as was the case with Raskolnikov. Additionally, wise elite agency seeking development must know when to ignore a narrative and even its own ethical standards (including those derived from the maxim, *To the creators the value created*[253]). Transformational leaders revise their judgments as their power affords. The wonder of naked power placed in the pantheon of values resides in its moral and cognitive expediency (see its capacity for meta-conflict resolution that bests institutions, Section 4.3.2). Judgments by the powerful evolve the system by breaking the shackles of narratives and rules, a form of courage particularly required in times of crises. When the challenges facing the political economy are riddled with contradictions or seem computationally impossible to solve, the paralysis of the mind is countered by the willingness to employ power.

This work's *leitmotiv* is that economic challenges everywhere—especially those that result in path dependencies—are unsolvable without elite agency. Judgments are paramount, and while narratives, crafted by knowledge elites to win the 'mind' will be suspended as necessary, they remain vital long-term determinants of the production function. This is so because narratives are also the lowest transaction cost instruments with which elite coalitions shape the future, thanks to their connectivity with social and political movements (Figure A5.12a). Technology could soon birth Irving John Good's "first ultraintelligent machine", a breakthrough that could well become "the last invention that man need ever make". This vision also hinges on narratives; the operating system that legitimizes and structures rent-seeking possibilities, including those of an eventually autonomous AI. In the 21st century, narrative upgrades have not kept pace with technology, while integrative thinking is overshadowed by specialization in most business, political, and social pursuits, including in academia (see 'On abdication' in the closing reflection of Section 8.3.3). Irrespective of the inclinations for nationalism or globalism, for democracy or autocracy, for the Left or the

253 Note that the contradictions inherent in ethical systems lead to inconsistent judgment. Weighting and offsetting are used in this theory to address—or even accept—the inconsistencies of elite agency, even as sustainable value creation measurements are formulated to minimize these.

Right, or for secular or transcendent worldviews, narrative renewal should comprehensively benchmark the highest impact principal-stakeholder relationships in the political economy. During their conceptualization, this requires that they reference value transfers (Figure A5.12b) and ideally the set of ethical principles (Chapter 8), as well as the three freedoms for development (Table A4.5b). The extent to which the power and judgment exercised by the 47th US presidency will craft lasting narratives and reforms, and whether the final outcome will be closer to what occurred in Berlin or Manchester, is considered next.

3 Trump's return and what it might mean for progressive elite circulation

Modern public choice theory (Ostrom, 1975) eschews hard and fast rules for social outcomes (Arrow, 1951). This makes the winners and outcomes of intra-elite contests, especially when rent seeking is at stake (Krueger, 1974; Buchanan, 1980; Murphy, Schleifer, & Vishny, 1993), unpredictable in complex adaptive systems. Nevertheless, given the properties that characterize an elite system—complexity, self-organization, non-repeating patterns, coevolution, surprise, power laws, fractality (Hayek, 1964/1967; Von Bertalanffy, 1969/2003; Simon, 1962; Anderson, 1972; Gleick, 1987; Mandelbrot, 1989; O'Connor, 1994; Liebovitch & Scheurle, 2000; Brown, Gupta, Li, Milne, Restrepo, & West, 2002; McDaniel, Lanham, & Anderson, 2009; O'Brien et al., 2023; see Section 3.2.3)—one thing can be predicted: there will be winners. In the case of the 2024 presidential election, Elon Musk's unprecedented and perilous gamble to invest a quarter of a billion dollars to support the Trump campaign (Wheatley, 2024; Schwartz & Maidenberg, 2025), might have been the major stochastic factor determining the outcome. Who the winning elites will turn out to be over the next four years, however, is an open question.

The prospects for Trump's second presidency are now examined through the logic of intra-elite contests (Figures 3.10), institutional change by winning elites (Figure 3.3), and by applying the conceptual elements and analytical toolset of the elite theory. Having focused on the long-term impact of the narrative market in the previous part, the analysis now considers emerging change through the lens of the 'progressive/regressive elite circulation' dichotomy (Section 1.3.2), and by alluding to elite leadership in its transformational varieties (Table 7.2). Beyond the clamor and the intense polarization that characterize present-day America, what matters to the analyst is whether the business models of the Trump 2.0 coalition will see more value creation or more value transfers than the previous configuration of the American elite system. Of utmost significance and a testament to the unbound possibilities of the American political economy is that an emergent coalition from the margins of the system is now forging ahead to core status.

Non-insiders that reach American society's political apex are by virtue of their own experience highly conscious of the capriciousness of the 'might' (from the non-market arena) and 'mind' (from the narrative arena) dynamics that enabled their rise. Transactional pragmatism and ditching,[254] hitching, and switching narratives characterizes the agency of most elite coalitions. Core elite coalitions need to double down on elite coordination leadership (Figure 1.2) and systematically secure the elite system in their image. This requires conferring institutional advantages to selected elite business models, including to former adversaries. It also explains the post-November 6th pilgrimages to Mar-a-Lago that saw "America's CEOs Bend the Knee to Donald Trump" (Politi & Fontanella-Khan, 2024). How quickly such realignments happen is evident from *The Wall Street Journal* piece just a few weeks after the 2024 presidential election on how CEOs became eager to appear on the Joe Rogan podcast while their corporations were "scrubbing left-leaning policies from their websites [. . .] buying the Trump family's cryptocurrency token and emailing tips about spending cuts to Vivek Ramaswamy" (Severns, Rana, & Schwartz, 2024). Fast thinking renegades like "Zuck 3.0" (Berg, 2025) have been entertained in Florida not because of their "new ways to kiss Trump's ass" (Ramirez, 2025), but because bringing Dana White on board and dismantling Meta's DEI policies consolidates the new core coalition. Mark Zuckerberg astutely recognizes the reconfiguration of the elite system and understands that path dependencies quickly set in with the exercise of newfound political power. As the outcomes of intra-elite contests are influenced and play out in the nooks and crannies of the system, licenses to operate are confirmed. During the 2025 to 2029 presidential term, fresh institutional allocations will be made for government and military procurement, social networks, and space exploration to name but a few. There will be friction inside the elite system and fractures in the core coalition, while the sustainability of elite coordination leadership will only be discernable *post facto*. What is certain is that Trump 2.0 will result in the implementation of institutional change, causing elite business models to rise and fall, some quite dramatically.

Elite coalitions that are expected to lose influence include:

> Civil servants affected by DOGE, where Musk once envisioned curbing the "fourth unconstitutional branch of government", the unelected "bureaucracy which has in a lot of ways currently more power than any elected representative" (Bloomberg Podcasts, 2025); Big Pharma under Robert Kennedy Jr.'s Department of Health and Human Services (HHS) and the "Make America Healthy Again" banner (Barnes, 2024; Kennedy, 2024); the sugar coalition, imminently causing the "Coke, PepsiCo Lobby to Keep Sugary Sodas in Food-Stamp Program" (Cooper & Peterson, 2024); the transnational drug cartels hit by tough border policies and designated as terrorist organizations by an inauguration day executive order (The White House, 2025a) that have sought to "increase profits and market control through diversification" into human trafficking (Forget, 2021); the "censorship-industrial complex" (U.S. House

254 The following paragraph about the reversal of the sustainability narrative in the finance industry is self-explanatory: "JPMorgan Chase, Morgan Stanley, Citigroup and Bank of America recently withdrew from an ambitious pandemic-era, U.N.-backed climate coalition built to help businesses reduce carbon emissions. That followed exits from the coalition by Wells Fargo and Goldman Sachs. BlackRock, the New York-based asset manager, announced Thursday it was quitting a similar U.N.-backed climate group. Some bank executives privately say they never wanted to be part of the initiative, but felt strong-armed to participate by Democrats. The Trump win offers them an easy out" (Schwartzel & Cutter 2025).

of Representatives, Committee on the Judiciary and Select Subcommittee on the Weaponization of the Federal Government, 2024); "television networks that criticise the future president" (Weinberger, 2024); organizations and positions in the service of institutionalizing DEI now under attack by officialdom as much as by anti-woke activists like Robby Starbuck or the "Merit, Excellence and Intelligence" narrative (Borchers, 2024); the AI coalition around Sam Altman, although his Stargate initiative with Larry Ellison and Masayoshi Son promising US$ 500 billion to Trump (Seetharaman & Dotan, 2025) might return him to centrality; Microsoft, Google, Oracle, and Amazon, notwithstanding Jeff Bezos' apparent realignment that some argue "enables Trump's threat to democracy" (Mangan, 2025), as the pentagon cloud evolves away from the Joint Enterprise Defense Infrastructure (JEDI) and the Joint Warfighting Cloud Capability (JWCC); and the Lockheed Martin F-35 Lightning II Joint Strike Fighter coalition with its total cost of US$ 2 trillion (Seligman, Somerville, & Lubold, 2024), even though the administration has "moved too quickly to commit to the F-47" (Kendall, 2025) and the neoconservative security coalition under the auspices of Secretary of State, Marco Rubio, will remain intact, despite Vice-President JD Vance's preference for non-interventionism.

Elite coalitions that are expected to gain ascendance include:

Unproductive American manufacturers set to benefit from new protections and trade wars[255]; law enforcement coalitions, as "America's Private Prison Complex Gears Up for Trump Deportation Bonanza" with new models specialized in the forced returns of migrants estimated to cost US$ 88,000 per repatriation (Findell, Hobbs, & Parti, 2024); in the context of a re-privatization of money, crypto whales and bros, as the new SEC chair, Paul Atkins, is "a strong backer of cryptocurrencies, and could help shape key regulations for an industry Trump has avidly courted" (Nam, 2024); the crime syndicates that use alternatives to fiat currency to launder profits (Soon & Yu, 2024) and whose liquidity and monetary reserves would be boosted along with those of "sanctions evaders, drug cartels, North Korean hackers, and Iranian and Russian spies" employing Tether, as Howard Lutnick, the Secretary of Commerce, "is one of the biggest backers" (Goldberg, 2024); at one point—before the split with the Trump administration—xAI seemed poised to become a preferred supplier of intelligence to the government, with Musk protégé and venture capitalist David Sacks serving as the White House AI and Crypto Czar; venture capitalists like Andreessen Horowitz (a16z) through the funding of Little Tech start-ups aiming to become the next Big Tech players; Drone maker Anduril, which assumed control of Microsoft's US$ 22 billion military headset project (Reuters, 2025), and Palantir, both named by Thiel in homage to Tolkien, that will spearhead "an effort to disrupt the country's oligopoly of 'prime' contractors" such as Lockheed Martin, Raytheon, and Boeing (Kinder & Hammond, 2024); and, not least, "President Trump's election victory has sent a jolt of enthusiasm through the fossil fuel and mining industries as they anticipate a favorable regulatory environment under his incoming administration" (Budryk, 2024).

As in every elite circulation dynamic, some of the institutional changes of the winning core elite coalition will be inclusive and others will not. Weighting their respective im-

---

255 As David Ricardo made clear and the case of the Junkers plainly demonstrates, tariffs are extractive. But could trade barriers be justified when they are erected to address extraction by foreign elite coalitions? For a profligate America, Pettis (2024) offers a non-Listian (see *The National System of Political Economy*, List, 1841/2011) but equally controversial argument: "By taxing consumption to subsidize production, modern-day tariffs would redirect a portion of U.S. demand toward increasing the total amount of goods and services produced at home. That would lead U.S. GDP to rise, resulting in higher employment, higher wages, and less debt."

pacts will unveil the overall elite quality under Trump and point to one or the other of the potential long-run economic growth scenarios ahead. The fact that two contending (and radically different) elite coalitions are fighting it out in the US is in principle a testament to America's institutionalized separation of powers (see The Three-tier Set of Intra-elite Checks and Balances in Figures 3.7 and A5.11b, The Seven Intra-elite Power Relations in Table 3.2) and and the fractal qualities of its elite system. Still, there will be uproar in many sectors as aggressive reforms proceed and achieve various levels of success, resistance, collapse, and frustration. The supreme prize in all of these developments will go to whoever wields 'the extraordinary lever' in the AI space: the make or break intra-elite contest that will rage on and off camera. In the article "Silicon Valley Titan Marc Andreessen: Biden White House Planned to 'Take Total Control' of AI", the tech pioneer's account on *Honestly with Bari Weiss* is cited as follows: "the meetings were absolutely horrifying, and we came out basically deciding we had to endorse Trump" because the administration "basically said AI is going to be a game of two or three big companies working closely with the government [that is] basically going to wrap them in a government cocoon" (Mastrangelo, 2024a). The tables have now turned. Trump's ostensibly progressive position in announcing Gail Slater as his choice for the Antitrust Division of the Department of Justice (DOJ) sent a signal to some in Big Tech that once bet on the protection of a Democrat president:

> Big Tech has run wild for years, stifling competition in our most innovative sector and, as we all know, using its market power to crack down on the rights of so many Americans, as well as those of Little Tech! (Ingram, 2024)

The whirlwind of institutional change associated with genuine elite circulation must, besides coopting insiders, include acts to erode the power of rival incumbents. Before the President's "first buddy" and earner of "uncle status" (Colton, 2024) was displaced one could read: "Musk's Rivals Fear he Will Target Them With his New Power", in an article that discusses his opinions on "Swindly Sam" Altman, as well as Gates, Bezos, and Zuckerberg (Hagey, Glazer, & Mattioli, 2024). Political economist Neil Malhotra noted that Meta, Google, Apple, and Microsoft do not figure in "Trump's connections to tech's right-wing brotherhood" (Ingram, 2024). Yet tech remains central, and Big Tech is by no means out of the game.

Daring and disruptive moves are prognosticated for the 47th presidency; as the Junker case shows, the pivotal effect of the narrative market arena leads to wins in the political non-market and the economic market arenas. Post-election, Andreessen relishes taking on the establishment's "preference falsification" (Moment of Zen, 2024, 1:31), referring to Kuran's concept where "the policy preferences people express in public often differ from those they hold privately" (1987, p. 642). Under the Democratic presidency, Big Tech began failing to live up to its narrative and reneging on "promises to hire more underrepresented groups [and instead] are gutting departments meant to achieve those goals" (Butler, 2023). Beyond the dissonance coming out of business practice, the lack of faith shown by Big Tech in its own official narrative disadvantages it relative to the tech bros,[256] a possible cause being that the narrative of the latter is genuine while that of the former is an adopted position. At the same time, the Trump-Musk rift and statements such as this by Marc Andreessen are not exactly confidence inspiring: "My personal Substack. Personal views only. Actually, not even personal views. I don't even know what my personal views are anymore. It doesn't matter. Read anyway!"[257] In the current context of missing, weak, and dated 20th century grand narratives (see Section 8.3.3), no brain trust matches the agility, self-assurance, and capabilities for crafting the narrative for the 21st century and its challenges than the coalition brought together by the ideas of Andreessen, Thiel, and JD Vance. Still—and referencing Section 3.1.3—are their proposals sustainable?

4 The tech bros and MAGA narratives for Trump and non-elites

> The creation of a doctrine has often been one of the very first steps along the road to power. With widely varying degrees of elaboration, the doctrine provides an explanation of what is wrong with the current state of affairs and what should be done to correct this state. (Moore, 1958, p. 10)

Institutional change is untenable without a narrative—also variously referred to as a Platonic noble lie, the embodiment of the Hegelian Geist, a Gramscian worldview, a Foucauldian discourse, as well as a story, a fiction, a belief or belief system, or a doctrine (see Sections 3.1.3 or 6.4.4)—that supplies conclusive narrative market wins in the wake of political victory. If, instead of legitimacy, the perception is that "a new spoils system becomes entrenched" along with the fear that "it could take decades to uproot" (Wolraich, 2024), the distribution of power within the American political economy will be questioned and quickly shift and flip again.[258] While it now enjoys clear support across many constituencies, does the tech bros' idea mix make for a formalized, coherent, and valid narrative? On the one hand, the new elites' efforts are the most transparent and disintermediated of any elite coalition in world history. The members fully share their ruminations over social networks, are belligerent, often odd, but direct and relatable to many, espouse higher goals with youthful idealism, and seem more sincere than previous corporate or finance elites. As all are self-made, they are resilient fighters with an uncanny talent for spotting value wherever it lies and thus fully appreciating the power of pull and lower transaction costs. On the other hand, the strangeness of the approach

256 The binary designation of 'Big Tech' vs 'tech bros', technically incorrect because Musk, for instance, belongs to both sides, is meant to denote opposing intra-elite contest positions in the narrative market. Thiel, with his sights set on the core elite coalition, is positioned at "the vanguard of those antiestablishment counter-elites" (Weiss, 2024), but this is chiefly in narrative market terms (as many of his business models have thrived in the established elite system for over a decade).

257 See: https://pmarca.substack.com/p/why-ai-will-save-the-world (accessed February 5, 2025).

258 The high country ranking of the US in the 'power' sub-index of the elite quality index (second out of 151 countries in the EQx2025, Casas-Klett & Cozzi, 2025) indicates the transient nature of elite power and sheds further light on why Trump's attempt to force elite circulation was at all feasible.

is as confusing to others in the elite system as it is to many non-elites, including some of the voters that brought Trump to power. The new core coalition must seek a stable accommodation with America First beliefs. Musk's skilled appropriation of the MAGA narrative (Figure 3.5) served a tactical aim, but then quickly unraveled. Robert Redford's "Marvin, what do we do now?" question is problematic not for the want of ideas but due to their zealotry. Retaining 'the extraordinary lever' long-term, especially in democracies like America, requires consolidation of the power of 'mind'. It might be retained by the Trump core coalition to the extent that it heeds Cicero's warning in *The Republic* (1829/2017) that no matter how good the system is the tendency for the "corruption of the ruling classes" (Atkins, Harrison, & Lane, 2000, p. 477) is never far away. This theory pushes the boundary in its claim that the hold of any ascendant core coalition lasts only to the degree that an intelligible narrative prompts the business models in the elite system to create more value and engage in fewer transfers than their predecessors.

So, how sustainable is the narrative of Andreessen, described by Barri Weiss as: "the chief ideologist of the Silicon Elite, a cultural taste maker, and even Silicon Valley's resident philosopher king" (The Free Press, 2024, 3:24)? *The Techno-Optimist Manifesto* (2023) is rooted in the certainty "that there is no material problem—whether created by nature or by technology—that cannot be solved with more technology" and concludes: "We owe the past, and the future. . . . It's time to be a Techno-Optimist. . . . It's time to build". Meanwhile, Thiel, the chief sponsor of JD Vance, and who, by some accounts, invested millions to support the French philosopher René Girard, now wishes to assert the father of mimetic theory's "call for peace, but he also wants to make sure the national security apparatus has the Straussian means to quietly take the war to the enemy" (Konstantinou, 2024). Do the inconsistencies of a "libertarian who has found common cause with nationalists and populists" (Weiss, 2024) bode well? The tech bros' worldview combines the value creation of innovation and deregulation with the lingering suspicion that they wish not to boost little tech but make even '*Bigger* Tech' plays; to meld the non-elite appeal of an anti-DEI meritocracy with the elitist ethos of *Atlas Shrugged*; to espouse commonsense and conservative values infused with the worldviews of *The Lord of the Rings* or TESCREAL, branding those opposed to libertarian accelerationism as "decels" (Torres, 2023); and to support a strong America and the world's most powerful military with internationalist free trade and visions for harmony in the world. As soon as the work of governing gets underway in earnest, the internal contradictions of the tech bros, as well as their divergences with MAGA, protectionist forces, and other members in Trump's coalition are likely to lead to conflict under the roof of this big tent in relatively short order. David Deane, author of *Why Liberalism Failed* (2018) "marvels at Trump's ability to corral tech futurists and religious traditionalists into the same political movement" but cautions that "at some stage a civil war is coming to the Trump movement [and] Musk and Vance will be on two very different sides" (Chaffin & Elinson, 2025). Maintaining elite—and social—cohesion will be by no means be easy and require an inordinate amount of political compromise and narrative skill. While *The Art of the Deal* showcases impressive elite coordination leadership skills (see Figure 1.3), the demands of the current non-market and narrative market could well exceed the President's talent.

A sense of the travails ahead can be deduced from the *Breitbart* headline: "Elon Musk Brings Back Shadowbanning, Conservatives Report Loss of Verification Following H-1B fracas" (Mastrangelo, 2024b), with far-right activist Laura Loomer predicting that "the blow-up between Maga and the tech bros is going to be glorious" (Palma, & Acton, 2024). Law abiding Americans ought to have a hard time reconciling themselves with Trump's pardon of "Silk Road founder Ross Ulbricht, who was sentenced to life in prison for running an underground online marketplace where drug dealers and others conducted more than $200 million in illicit trade using bitcoin" (Raymond, 2025). *The Financial Times* asks a broader question: "Can Trump Handle The New Republican Factions" that includes "hardline conservatives", "pro-business moderates", or "lapsed democrats" (Politi, 2025). Even the cohesion of the tech bros is uncertain: "Tensions and philosophical differences between the two billionaires [Elon Musk and Vivek Ramaswamy] didn't take long to emerge" (Thomas & McCormick, 2025), both quitting DOGE prematurely. Frictions will intensify and there is no evidence that the newcomers will manage to advance a sustainable grand narrative that captures the cognitive and affective bandwidth of a critical mass of the non-elite (and antagonistic elites). They will also need to respect their own narrative and abide by some of its constraints to maintain long-term credibility. When successful, such projects have historically fixed the 'intra-elite quality contest' dilemma (Figure 5.2), placing elite cohesion and the elite separation of powers in productive and creative tension. However, if they fail, the sidelined elites have a serious axe to grind, and Alex Soros does not mince his words: "These People are Bullies. And You Fight Back" (Khalaf, 2025).

The pre-Trumpian elite system lost its credibility by mismanaging the Biden-Harris transition. Many of its elite coalitions will be deliberately weakened while others will defect, shaken by the realization that despite the sincere commitment to general welfare (e.g., environmental stewardship, DEI, international security) non-elites felt abandoned (e.g., inflation, immigration, war). Their bet now is that Trump's transformational leadership might eventually unravel in self-inflicted chaos, disappoint elites and non-elites alike, and fail to accumulate sustainable power, particularly in the narrative market. For instance, the tech bros are strikingly honest about their desire to wield power and, unlike the leading business lights before them, have no use for the elite denial fallacy. Mark Andreessen casually recalls Burnham's *The Machiavellians: Defenders of Freedom* (1943) and the leading Italian elite theorist Michels (1962/1999) to supply an intellectual framework for Musk's agency (in a Lex Fridman Podcast, 2025, 1:46:47). The message is that power must be used unapologetically. Sound judgment becomes ever more critical as any fragility will expose Trump's experiment to reactions that could, in a polarized world, result in turmoil that would likely be addressed and further aggravated through tactical favors sprinkled with populist measures. Moreover, the trade war seems to be nothing more than "recklessness", with "the administration tearing something apart, only to reveal that it has no plan for how to replace it" (Sanger, 2025). Uncreative destruction would then prevail over the creative type.

Elite cohesion is certain to erode domestically in the US, while productive links to coalitions abroad will also flounder without a narrative. The musings about the annexation of the Panama Canal and Greenland, "About Those Beachfront Gaza Condos" (*The Wall Street Journal* Editorial Board, 2025), the aggressive use of tariffs and the pain inflicted by undermining trade and trust, or the withdrawal from the Paris Climate Agreement in an Executive Order entitled "Putting America First in International Environmental Agreements" (The White House, 2025b), will antagonize many and could be perceived as 'doing a Vespasian'; the pursuit of blatant cross border extraction to benefit particular coalitions in the dominant elite system.[259] Many of the previously compliant subjects of the American empire such as Europe's elites (less so those of Japan) will surreptitiously attempt to throw their weight behind anti-Trump coalitions in the US.[260] While the establishment that assembled around Biden lies in tatters in early 2025, the former system is still a formidable force with assets in academia, grassroots organizations (e.g., citizens fired up by environmental outrages), the so-called "deep state", international sentiment, legacy media (offended by the "podcast bros", Nicolaou, 2025) and traditional finance (not all have jumped on the "havoc" of the crypto bandwagon, see Mourselas, 2025), and CEOs and bankers that resent Trumpian "uncertainty" (Thomas, Dummett, & Cutter, 2025). Although now in tactical retreat, once reinvigorated, the old guard will issue fresh challenges and rebuild alliances. The deinstitutionalization of intra-elite contests temporarily helps the incumbent but is not sustainable. Without an overriding narrative, events like a Wall Street or crypto collapse, a controversy where the President's protective coating cracks, ever-increasing inflation driven by tariffs or accommodative monetary policy, a weakening dollar, a geopolitical black swan, growing inequality, or simply slow economic growth could all become very problematic. At the same time, the nasty, embarrassing, and highly public Trump–Musk fallout will certainly spark skepticism and fuel the emergence of counter-narratives. Increased polarization within the American elite and non-elite means that any structural reforms made by the Trump administration will be less likely to stand the test of time.

At present, and considering the material impact of Trump's elite circulation on non-elites, novel sources of value creation and transfers are likely to include:

---

259 Titus Flavius Vespasianus, a military leader (9–79 AD) and the first emperor of the Flavian Dynasty (69–96 AD), sacked Jerusalem in the First Jewish–Roman War (66–73 AD) for its spoils and the Jewish Temple gold (Josephus, 2009, 6.6.1). These resources were then *ex manubiis* committed to the recapitalization of the semi-bankrupt Roman state that Nero (37–68 AD) had "so utterly impoverished that he was obliged to postpone and defer even the pay of the soldiers and the rewards due to the veterans" (Suetonius, 1913/1914, *The Life of Nero*, 32.1), as well as to "Rome's urban renewal" drive detailed by Rocca (2017) that included the iconic Flavian Amphitheatre or Colosseum.

260 "Gobsmacked" Europeans (Iyengar & Johnson, 2025), including the top political leaders offended by Vice-President Vance's "threat from within" speech at the 2025 Munich Security Conference, are prone to overestimate their limited power endowments and applied coordination capacity (one consequence of the EU's 'missing elite system', see Section 7.3.4 and the final part of this Epilogue).

> Deregulation in bureaucratically burdened fields raises all boats and so the potential benefits of a "massive reset" (Musk, 2025) extend beyond those at the top; gigantic productivity gains are likely to accrue from investments in AI and its required energy and physical infrastructure; the tax-advantaged algorithms of Silicon Valley will displace first white- and then, blue-collar labor; restrictive immigration policies could lead to salary increases for low-wage earners and, if extended to foreign professionals (against the wishes of the tech bros and Big Tech) might do the same for many Americans with advanced skills; manufacturing jobs will benefit from trade barriers (but hurt everybody else through higher inflation); tax cuts will increase government deficits by stimulating demand more than aggregate supply while exacerbating inequality through demand-pull inflation; the boom in crypto assets will likewise drive disparities and inflation and lead to regressive redistribution divorced from value creation as bubbles expand and contract haphazardly[261]; streamlining the government might boost its efficiency, the quality of public services, and have a calming effect on prices while propelling much-needed state capacity and enhanced governmental productivity in the US[262]; successful peace initiatives will lessen life and value destruction at home and abroad; the liberated energy and mining sector will drive growth and jobs but devalue the environment and add costs to future generations (as will the deemphasis on conservation measures); and, if it gains coherence and legitimacy, the new grand narrative will infuse a general societal-wide optimism that propels animal spirits and economic expansion.

By the end of the decade, it will have become apparent whether the non-elites that voted for change and against the incumbent Democratic coalition, citizens that were animated to be part of Trump's wider support base in 2024, have benefited or not. At face value, elite circulation induced by a new technological breakthrough is positive news. So is the fact that those now at the commanding heights of the political economy

---

261 The institutionalization of crypto (essentially the privatization of money) could easily become a value creation project rather than the current value transfer mechanism with one stroke of the presidential pen through a 'crypto Jubilee' (see Section 8.2.4). That is, existing owners get to keep crypto reserves equivalent to a maximum rate of return that, for instance, doubles the inflation-adjusted risk-free yield of US T-bills, but the rest of their blockchain holdings are redistributed equally to all citizens. The value of crypto resides solely in its institutionalization by the state (as opposed to its criminalization, as in holders of crypto wallets facing money laundering charges). The narrative for the crypto Jubilee could be one of equity as set out in Leviticus (25: 13), but to this theory, any reforms or measures that are akin to flattening the sugar mountains in Epstein and Axtell's (1996) agent-based social simulation should conform to the value creation rationale. Beyond the religious justification, the practical effect of the Talmudical redistributions was to incentivize growth in agriculture or in the supply of labor for infrastructure works (Hudson & Goodhart, 2018). Likewise, a crypto Jubilee along with full institutionalization would mean the universal adoption of virtual currencies as an accepted medium of exchange for daily life and might usher in new inclusive credit creation possibilities (shifting digital tokens away from financial speculation and the underworld).

262 The uncertain outcomes of the landmark Biden Infrastructure Investment and Jobs Act (IIJA) of 2021, the massive "$1.2 trillion being dispersed to all fifty states and each territory to improve, upgrade, or remodel infrastructure and technology on levels not seen in generations", are revealing about state capacity in America. So is the fact that government agencies and policy centers have avoided any research "on the overall scope of the law and how much it has achieved since its enactment", that there are not "many future recommendations for use of the funds", nor "Congressional committee hearings regarding the law" (Lienemann, 2024, pp. 1, 8).

are set to drive institutional change to a degree not seen since the FDR administration. Most importantly, many originate and understand extreme risk exposure, a topic on which Joseph Lonsdale, a venture capitalist and co-founder of companies including Palantir, lucidly expounds on:

> The people who are building these technology companies in our generation are the most courageous [. . .] the boldest people in our generation, people who are comfortable taking risks, putting themselves out there in some cases failing and failing before they succeeded (Palantir Bite-Sized, 2025b, 16:09)

Yet whether the stewards of the most powerful technology wave ever witnessed will align with *To the creators the value created*, is the big unknown. When Altman (2025) observes that "the socioeconomic value of linearly increasing intelligence is super-exponential in nature", he is also justifying the need for massive financial resources: "A consequence of this is that we see no reason for exponentially increasing investment to stop in the near future." The immense funds needed to realize the promise of AI appears to require coordination capacity and leadership that can only come from those already at the apex of the system and will hence necessitate rentier monopolies, subsidies, and tailored institutional change (see The Elite Business Model Lifecycle, Figure 4.5). As Zingales (2022, pp. 1, 4) explains, given the power now enjoyed by Big Tech, "incumbents cannot be easily unseated even by new entrants with a superior technology" and, in referencing research that is consistent with the 'Amazon dilemma', he stresses that actual innovators do not benefit from their value creation (Kamepalli, Rajan, & Zingales, 2021). In consequence, he advocates for remedial regulation based on "structural interventions that restore conditions for competition" noting that these must happen at the international level. This theory has explained that such regulation can only come about through intra-elite competition at the domestic level, as when the tech bros seek to dislodge the forces of Big Tech. What is certainly true is that the resulting institutional changes will imbue US technology standards and AI models into nearly every political economy.

For better or worse, the second Trump administration will become the national core elite coalition with the strongest ever impact on the wider world, not because of tariffs, the "Greenland grab" (Gavin & Cater, 2025), or peace deals, but because of the institutionalization of the new technologies and their associated elite business model rules. Elites everywhere will employ American AI suppliers who will soon enjoy bargaining power differentials of a magnitude that is the sole prerogative of principals (see Figure A5.13b). By being *de facto* demoted to stakeholder and non-elite status, non-American elite coalitions will adhere to a time-honored pattern where "subordinate states frequently form alliances with the dominant powers and identify their values and interests with those of the dominant powers [as these empires] supply public goods (security, economic order, etc.) that give other states an interest in following their lead" (Gilpin, 1981, p. 30). Institutional arrangements will be adjusted across the world as national elites share their (and their nation's) datasets with US technology firms from which they then obtain the necessary intelligence to operate and grow their local business models. International regulations (the concern of Zingales, 2022) will be determined, like war and peace, by the core coalitions in Washington, DC, while relevant elements of American narratives will be internalized and adopted. It therefore matters greatly to the world whether this particular cycle of American elite circulation turns out to be progressive or regressive. In any event, this process is happening against the backdrop of two particular dynamics that are placing stress on many countries around the world, including the US.

The first of these is a generalized non-elite discontent. To this theory, this is rooted in excessive value transfers by elites, but also, in a marked deviation from the central elite quality theme of this book, in the low quality of many non-elite groups. The second dynamic is related to the adoption of AI technology and how that fundamentally alters the division of value across stakeholder relationships. These two trends strain and shape elite circulation, while the instabilities of the Trump-Biden-Trump sequence disclose the mechanisms driving power shifts and the acquisition of 'money', 'might', and 'mind' in US intra-elite contests. This particular window is of great utility to political economy and elite system observers and researchers, and not just because it demonstrates how American democracy functions as a set of intra-elite contest rules (Figure 4.3).

The Epilogue continues by addressing these two dynamics in depth: social disaffection scrutinized from a critical non-elite quality perspective, and the intelligence revolution examined through the widest of political economy lenses.

5 The social backdrop to non-elite disaffection

Trump has clearly benefited from non-elite discontent, yet once in power he cannot possibly cater to all the disaffected. A month after his election victory, in the dawn hours of December 4th in Midtown Manhattan, Luigi Mangione committed an act of terror—not in support of an ideology or in opposition to the abstract state or system, but against the specific elite business model of healthcare. The bullets that killed UnitedHealthcare CEO Brian Thompson were inscribed with the words "'deny', 'depose', and 'defend'" (Kraterou, 2024). The words reference a book by Professor Jay Feinman, *Delay, Deny, Defend: Why Insurance Companies Don't Pay Claims and What You Can Do About It* (2010). As argued throughout in this work, a crucial role of knowledge elites is to supply evidence-based critical assessments of elite business models, a task that this author certainly accomplished:

> The point of view in this book is pro-consumer but it is not anti-insurance. Insurance is essential to our economic security. But if insurance is to maintain its role as the great protector of the standard of living of the American middle class, prompt and fair claim handling has to be the rule. This book explores why that doesn't always happen, and why it is even less likely to happen today than fifteen or twenty years ago. (Feinman, 2010, p. 12)

Distressingly, and immediately after this horrific murder, the "most liked" comment on *The Wall Street Journal* article on the murder victim's final moments read:

> Reading the comments on social media about this killing—the main theme seems to be gallows humor about "thoughts and co-pays" or "you'll need a prior authorization to get condolences." This should be a real eye opener to insurance executives. I'm not sure they appreciate how much the American public seems to hate health insurance companies. (Comment by 'James G' on Chaffin & Matthews, 2024)

Moreover, and given the fact that over 41% of poll respondents supported the killing in the aftermath of the event, it is pertinent to question US mass culture: "What has gone wrong with Americans' moral compass that so many could cheer the extrajudicial killing of an innocent man?" (Mac Donald, 2024). While this question hangs unanswered, *BIG by Matt Stoller* supplies data and specifics of the targeted elite business model:

> UnitedHealth Group is one of the most toxic and unaccountable companies in America, a $400 billion behemoth that systematically denies care to millions of Americas, was smack dab in the middle of the opioid crisis, cheats the government, surveils its customers, harms independent doctor's practices, and has executives who routinely engage in what looks like insider trading. (Stoller, 2024b)

Large swathes of this inquiry have been devoted to asserting that revolution and violence by disadvantaged groups ends up hurting non-elites while stalling sustainable value creation reform efforts and development (Section 3.3.2). Institutional quality must rise from inside institutions via transformative elite agency (Figures 3.2, 4.2, 5.4) as is borne out by Mark Cuban's Schumpeterian creative destruction initiatives like "Cost Plus Drugs that has transformed how many Americans can get their prescriptions filled at a fraction of the prevailing prices, bypassing pharmacy benefit managers (PBMs) that control 80% of US prescriptions" (Topol, 2024). To be productive, non-elite agency requires non-violent engagement with elites, many of whom will have antagonistic worldviews. Knowledge elites like Feinman will be far less likely to criticize CEOs if their work inspires non-elites to murder them. Instead, insiders must strategically actuate the microfoundations of inclusive institutional change. Every society has high quality elites like Chuck Feeney,[263] or Wikipedia's Jimmy Wales and John Arnold, ready to put their power and coordination capacity in the employ of transformational leadership.

Acts of violence on the back of generalized disaffection and Raskolnikov-like misplaced idealism have lasting effects on culture and erode non-elite quality. They result in the deinstitutionalization of intra-elite contests, the closing up of the elite system, and outcomes that are counterproductive to non-elite interests. Constructive responses to extraction such as 'strategic participation' in intra-elite contests (Proposition 19, Figure A5.8) shut down. Marx's pronouncement that: "we shall not make ex-

---

263 Feeney was "a pioneer of duty-free shops and a shrewd investor in technology start-ups who gave away nearly all of his $8 billion fortune to charity" (McFadden, 2023), while his elite coordination leadership in Ireland was instrumental to the "peace initiatives leading to the Belfast/Good Friday Agreement of 1998 that formally ended decades of conflict known as the Troubles" (McKay, n.d.).

cuses for the terror" (*Neue Rheinische Zeitung*, 1849/1994, p. 1) is but a preamble to collective suicide. Brute force is not just morally reprehensible, but an over-simplified method to tackle complex issues; an unsustainable approach that cannot scale and fosters a bunker mentality that isolates elites from society while prompting the offending business models into extractive escalation (Sections 3.3.2 and 5.3.4). One can hardly imagine the mayhem America would be facing today if, at the grounds near Butler, Pennsylvania, the sniper's bullets had not narrowly missed their target.

6 A non-elite quality political economy framework for development

While non-elite quality has been articulated in this work (Section 8.1), the emphasis has overwhelmingly been on elite quality, as elite agency is essential for economic growth. In Figure E.1, 'The Non-Elite vs Elite Quality Matrix' framework for social development matches the sustainable value creation aggregates of the socio-economic pyramid's two discrete strata (see Figure 8.1) as independent variables. This is a fresh approach for examining GDP prospects and takes a further leap in its readiness to incorporate culture. The inclusion of non-elites implies a role for culture—Lowenthal's "popular culture" (1950)—in its capacity to sanction value transfers, thereby serving as an essential aspect of both elite and non-elite quality.

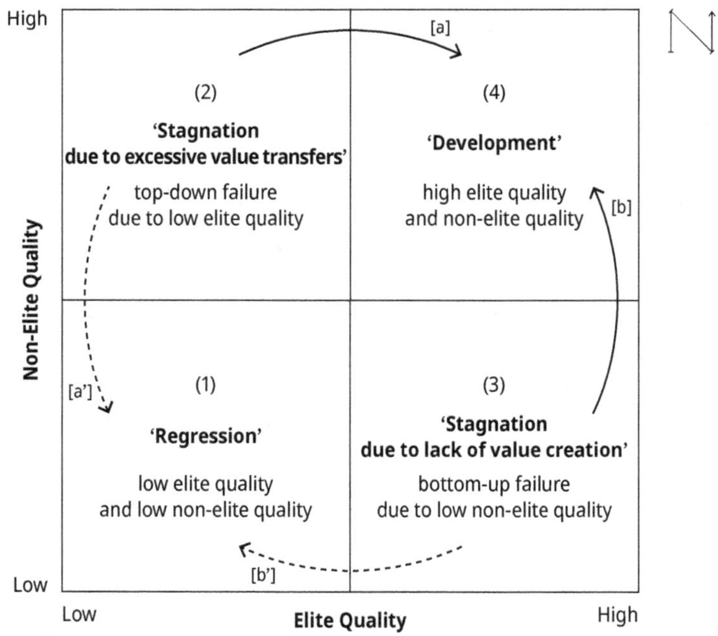

Figure E.1: The Non-Elite vs Elite Quality Matrix: A framework for society incorporating culture.

The 'regression' (quadrant 1) scenario of development envisages a double low, for both elite and non-elite quality. The public, while its behavior is as offensive as that of its elites, experiences comparatively greater hardship because the latter extract most of the value that non-elites manage to produce above subsistence levels. The 'stagnation due to excessive value transfers' (quadrant 2) scenario is even more dismal, because productive non-elites create value through their good labor that is then appropriated by their rapacious overlords. Historically, this aligns with the practices of the exploitative Mongol Yuan Dynasty and the Ilkhanate respectively governing their diligent Chinese and Persian subjects. Today, mediocre German corporate leaders are unable to conceive strategies that properly leverage the value creation potential of their industrious blue- and white-collar workers. Development is at risk should non-elite quality take its cue from the top and plunge towards trajectory [a']. In fact, productivity and the non-elite work ethic are degrading in Germany, not least in response to the widespread incompetence non-elites observe in their upper echelons. The rapidly evolving nature of non-elite quality is evident from the following example:

> The electrical blackout in New York City in 1965 was widely reported to have evoked cooperative, generous responses from the populace, as people apparently felt the need to offer aid and comfort to each other in a time of crisis. In contrast, the 1977 New York power outage resulted in widespread looting, violence and other varieties of criminal behavior. (Winner, 2020)

'Stagnation due to lack of value creation' (quadrant 3) is the obverse state to 'stagnation due to excessive value transfers' (quadrant 2), where elites are bigger value creators than unproductive non-elites. The generalized lack of bottom-up value creation—again, non-elites create most of the value building blocks of any economy which elite coordination capacity then connects and enhances—results in stagnation. In some respects, America's large numbers of disenfranchised groups such as drug addicts, the millions of people currently or formerly incarcerated, or the rural poor are unproductive, while at least a part of the US elite operates the world's highest value creation models. When it achieved nationhood in 1965, Singapore also belonged to this category, but did not then follow the path of arrow [b'] where low quality non-elites pull reasonable elite quality down. Sadly, this is currently the direction of travel for some South American countries that once had a well-educated and ethically grounded establishment.

Singapore moved along the reverse trajectory [b] after independence, with Lee Kuan Yew's system strikingly raising non-elite quality in line with economic and human 'development' (quadrant 4). Here, in win-win fashion, both elite and non-elite quality are high. Historically, the US, and now Switzerland[264] and Israel also fit this

---

264 The granting of broad freedoms is a vital component of rising non-elite quality. This is made clear in List's comparison of the fates of German speaking territories: "The Swiss Confederation is nothing but a conglomerate of German imperial cities, established and cemented together by the free populations occupying the intervening tracts of country. The remaining leagues of German cities were

bill. It is certainly possible to travel from the two 'stagnation' scenarios (quadrants 2 and 3) to this normative ideal. Singapore's developmental route to the top [b] stands in contrast to the equally meritorious rises of America, or Japan during the Meiji Restoration, that both followed the second upward path [a]. The up and coming Meiji rulers "liberated the natural talents of the Japanese people and allowed the nation's military and industrial strength to develop into the most powerful in Asia" (Irokawa, 1985, p. 19), while elite business models harnessed the conscientiousness, industriousness, and craftmanship of its labor and administrative classes. Cultural features like village leadership or voluntarily and horizontally organized *wakamonogumi* young men's associations (Notehelfer, 1990, p. 213) were adeptly applied to modern management. In America, Alexis de Tocqueville eloquently illustrated the lived experience of democracy with the grassroots cultural reflex described below, one that favors value creation over transfers and leads to growth:

> In the United States, as soon as a citizen has some enlightenment and some resources, he seeks to enrich himself in commerce and industry, or he buys a field covered with forest and becomes a pioneer. All that he asks of the State is not to come to disturb him in his labors and to ensure the fruit of those labors. [. . .] Among most European peoples, when a man begins to feel his strength and to expand his desires, the first idea that occurs to him is to gain a public post. (de Tocqueville, 1835/2010, p. 83)

Over the centuries, Americans have debated whether newcomer non-elites fit the high sustainable value creation paradigm of the earlier waves of settlers described by de Tocqueville:

> As Americans we have only a platonic interest in the amount of emigration from Italy [yet] we are, or should be, deeply concerned in the amount of this immigration when it is directed to our own shores, in the character of the immigrants and in their capacity of becoming useful inhabitants. (Schuyler, 1889, p. 480)

To the extent that such concerns had merit, the country has also traveled path [b] with its strengths including integration, social mobility, and investments in the human capital of immigrant non-elites, a process that when successful has historically made America great. What then are some of the visible characteristics of the sustainable value creation potential of a nation's people—of high non-elite quality?

> Citizens love and prioritize their children's education; work is virtuous; the poor are ambitious and do not feel inferior to or envy the rich; the marks of creative aspiration and aesthetic pursuits are visible in ordinary life; cheap street food is delicious; citizens queue up, are civil to each, and naturally form "voluntary associations" (see Gamm & Putnam, 1999); when they do not and personal conflicts arise, these are resolved with no lingering resentment or vendettas; there

---

ruined owing to their contempt for the rural population, and from their absurd burgher arrogance, which delighted in keeping that population in subjection, rather than in raising them to their own level" (1841/2011, p. 72).

> is both tolerance and dissent; strangers don't face suspicion even when there is high trust (Fukuyama, 1995) amongst those who share the wider culture; when opportunities to benefit from transfers arise—including from elites—these are rejected, as in the Swiss case when the populace "voted against increasing statutory holiday entitlement to six weeks from the current four" (SWI swissinfo.ch, 2012); the qualities of "realism, a willingness to engage in self-criticism, professional and artistic creativity, resilience, and a sense of humor" that H. L. Mencken ascribed to blacks are possessed (Gibson, 2014, p. 4); there is a desire to unlock ones potential and take ownership of one's life, maybe inspired by popular teachers like Tony Robbins; a pioneering, risk-taking animal spirit percolates throughout, as do forms of *joie de vivre* and gratefulness.

Reassuringly, research finds that when non-elite quality is high the "lower social class display increased attention to others and greater sensitivity to others' welfare compared to individuals of higher social class" (Piff & Robinson, 2017, p. 6). By contrast, the various manifestations of low non-elite quality include:

> Misgivings about others; violence; laziness, neglect of obligations, and irresponsible apathy; relationships with authority that are defined by behavior that is sycophantic, duplicitous, and self-abased; inexpensive food lacks flavor and taste; hygiene deficiencies and filth universally creep up; ignorance is widespread, as in H. L. Mencken's uncultured "booboisie" and the Southern whites he characterized as "crackers, lint heads, vermin" (Gibson, 2014, p. 2); there is a surrender to destiny and the populace are passive participants in life; emotionally unresponsive parents are impervious to their offspring's affective needs; on social networks, children and young adults provoke others for entertainment, engage in toxic competition, and become addicted to self-validation; a general insensitivity to the suffering of others and of animals is evident; each citizen group or tribe fights for "rent preservation", rendering reform unattainable and making poverty self-reinforcing (Rajan, 2009, p. 178); there is an air of brutishness, perhaps on account of suffering from elite exploitation, yet the aim of all is to extract and cruel instincts are not restrained for that purpose (see the "eat men" metaphor of Lu Xun 1918/1985); life, rather than being treasured, is cheap.

In instances where the vagaries of history bring low quality non-elites to the apex of society, the 'license for evil' is operated with horrifying gusto (Greek philosophers were aware of the dangers of ochlocracy or mob rule, see Section 8.1.3, as well as the earlier references to the excesses of elites from non-elite extraction like "the bloody Dwarf" or the *Sturmabteilung*). As is described by Le Bon (1895/1996) and Hoffer (1951/1968), high quality non-elites do sometimes aggregate and from that mass a collective random energy emerges that is extractive or exploited by charismatic leaders adept at crafting or communicating narratives. The general rule is that aggregate low non-elite quality degrades the elite system and can tip a nation over the 'extractive end point' and into an impossible society of thieves (Section 5.3.4). High or low, non-elite quality is immediately obvious to the weathered traveler or international businessperson accustomed to dealing in foreign lands. It should always be borne in mind that non-elite quality impacts elite quality.

Next, it is shown that culture is both a reflection and a most important determinant of non-elite quality, both high and low.

7 Culture and non-elite quality

In any analysis of the rise and fall of a civilization, culture has been identified as a significant variable. For example, it was celebrated for many decades at US colleges as a comparative developmental advantage in "Western Civ" courses (see Allardyce, 1982). More specifically, Alesina and Giuliano highlight that "a growing body of empirical work measuring different types of cultural traits has shown that culture matters for a variety of economic outcomes" and describe the reciprocal relationship between culture and institutions (2015, p. 898). The correspondence between "popular culture" (Lowenthal, 1950) and sustainable value creation is now considered with a focus on the "the institutionalization of ideas" by knowledge elites; "the fact that cultural production of knowledge, the arts, news, and public policy usually occurs within specific and established organizations" (Rado, 1987, p. 43). Social network companies, universities, and media conglomerates derive a critical part of their power from the narrative market arena, while Kim Kardashian, Paul Krugman, Cristiano Ronaldo, Tucker Carlson, or Beyoncé are high standing members of elite coalitions. All impact popular culture as they make contributions to one narrative or another. The following assertion from over sixty years ago still holds true:

> Today the principal agents of culture change are the groups occupying strategic positions in decision-making. These groups constitute élites. They are in communication, and have knowledge of each other's positions, and of each other's problems. As groups, they stand at the pivot of culture change. (Adams & Masuoka, 1961, p. 86).

In every society, knowledge elites interact in a two-way relationship with non-elites. They engage in cultural production that is consumed by non-elites (see Veblen, 1924; Dente, 1977), while at the same time their agency reacts to how the masses buy, internalize, and casually advance (Bau suggests that "policy can change culture", 2021, p. 1880). Many examples show how top-down influence by knowledge elites effects culture. Veblen (1915/2003, p. 91) describes how "the Prussian-Imperial system of bureaucratic guidance and control" reduced the open and liberal habits of mind found in places like Hamburg and other positive cultural manifestations across German lands. In a contrasting example of this hierarchical principle, the Singaporean political elite bases its project of "national identity invention" on elaborated "Asian values" (Ortmann, 2009, p. 23). The deliberate agency of knowledge elites also drives cultural change bottom-up. The entrepreneurship ethos of Silicon Valley is fostered by initiatives such as those of Y Combinator, the Hoover Institution, the Aspen Institute, the Kauffman Fellow Program, or Stanford's Graduate School of Business. The takeaway is that through diverse and country-specific pathways transformational knowledge elite leadership engineers and upgrades culture, often in support of sustainable value creation. Irrespective of the degree to which the changes in mass culture are caused by exogenous (to non-elites) elite agency, if a cultural propensity for unsustainable value transfers emerges, non-elites must be held accountable. Nonetheless, over long-run time horizons, non-elite quality and its underlying culture are decisively molded by elite quality.

As for the diffusion and impact of the cultural production of the knowledge elite, this task rests on the managerial, technical, and creative class—the vital connector between the elite and the non-elite. Italian classical elite theorists (see Section 1.2.3) are mindful of their function:

> Any intellectual or moral deficiencies in this second stratum, accordingly, represent a graver danger to the political structure, and one that is harder to repair, than the presence of similar deficiencies in the few dozen persons who control the workings of the state machine. To use a comparison: The strength of an army depends primarily on the intellectual and moral value of the officers who come into direct contact with the soldiers, beginning with the colonel and ending with the second lieutenant. (Mosca, 1939, pp. 404–405)

As a consequence, elites invest in their expert, upper non-elite class.[265] This is done via institutions like military academies, universities, technical training institutes, healthcare systems, and law enforcement. Business schools, in existence in Europe since 1819 with the École Supérieure de Commerce de Paris, and in America since 1881 with The Wharton School of the University of Pennsylvania, have become a key to economic growth given their role as training centers for the management class. As the elite system allocates capital to develop a competent managerial, technical, and creative class, knowledge elites work the narrative market and engage in cultural production. If performed effectively, the outcome of such agency is social cohesion and a productive nexus linking the elite system to non-elites.

To this theory—and in light of the preceding discussion—a key factor in the enduring wealth of nations is the production of culture; the pushing through of cultural change that is consistent with sustainable value creation. The knowledge elites driving such long-term projects (the Christianization of Europe took half a millennium; the creation of Singaporean identity half a century) must still work on short-term approaches: the supply of sector-by-sector evidence-based insights on value transfers followed by bold proposals for reform and transformational leadership that references culture.

In a famous example, the Surgeon General's *Smoking and Health* report (U.S. Department of Health, Education, and Welfare, 1964) "led to an increasing number of regulations on cigarette smoking, sales, and advertising" (Marshall, 2015, pp. 250–251). More recently, as recounted by *World Bank Blogs*: "In China's Taobao Villages, E-commerce is One Way to Bring New Jobs and Business Opportunities to Rural Areas" (Luo, 2018). This Big Tech experiment continues to scale (Chu, Hassink, Xie, & Hu, 2023), setting a benchmark for value creation in the agrarian communities of developing economies. In contrast, research and narratives addressing the 'unemployed capital' issue in advanced economies

265 The members of the "second stratum" (Mosca, 1939, p. 404), less exposed to the vagaries of complex processes in the political economy or to 'luck', ought to be more capable than elites on many accounts, which seems consistent with sociological findings suggesting that: "The top 1 per cent even score slightly worse on cognitive ability than those in the income strata right below them" (Keuschnigg, van de Rijt, & Bol, 2023, p. 820).

are few and far between. During the COVID-19 emergency, one read that: "[the] Fed Caps Dividends and Bans Share Buybacks by Big US Banks" (Noonan, 2020), but this policy was aimed at capital resilience, not at reforming a business model relying on low interest rates that flushed corporations with cash (Charles Schwab, 2024); *de facto* value transfers effected through monetary policy with effects that somewhat mirror those of inflation. The essential point here is that both inclusive and extractive models are driven by culture, regulating investment behavior in financial markets, smoking conventions on social occasions, and the enthusiasm for digitalization in peasant communities.

Landes' sweeping historical critique on *The Wealth and Poverty of Nations* (2008) highlights the role of culture in economic development. Slack's "culture of improvement" (2015) focuses on the distinct cultural shifts in 17th century England, as does Mokyr's (2017) model of cultural change with its emphasis on the scientific elite—both providing plausible explanations for modern growth. Culture, the "set of shared understandings", the "common knowledge" required for "actors to coordinate on a specific equilibrium", also plays a key role in the political economy for Hall and Soskice (2001, p. 13). To this theory, intra-elite contests offer knowledge elites the opportunity to sift through the complex behaviors associated with culture and narratives and formulate policies to deactivate traits associated with extraction, while strengthening those that nurture behaviors associated with risk origination and value creation. Comparative assessments of non-elite cultural dynamics would complement the findings from A Political and Business Systems Sustainable Value Creation (SVC) Test that internationally benchmarks political economies (see Section 8.1.5, Figure 8.3). At the business model level, one would consider culture as the anchor that narratives wrap themselves around to change institutions. The role of intra-elite contests is also instrumental in establishing both institutions and the culture, as is demonstrated by the case of US non-profits. The legal status of this esteemed and deeply ingrained institution—just as much as its cultural evolution—is not determined by non-elites or at the ballot box, but by the knowledge elites that are currently in the coalitions of OpenAI, Musk, and Meta[266] as these clash and litigate.

During the combative interactions between coalitions furthering their preferences for institutional change (Figure 3.3), culture and narratives evolve, and criteria for making elite judgments are established. Some involve invocations to the rights of non-elites or to the abstract greater good like the utilitarian Benthamian axiom: "It is the greatest happiness of the greatest number that is the measure of right and wrong" (1776/2017, p. 1). Inclusive elite judgments are facilitated by assimilating into the cul-

266 Meta endorsed Musk in his battle with OpenAI with a sharp supporting letter to California Attorney General, Rob Bonta, stating that it "is deeply concerned about OpenAI's attempt to shed the non-profit status under which it was founded in order to establish a for-profit entity. We urge you to review this proposed transaction, including the nature and timing of any transfer of assets from OpenAI's non-profit entity to other entities. Failing to hold OpenAI accountable for its choice to form as a non-profit could lead to a proliferation of similar start-up ventures that are notionally charitable until they are potentially profitable" (Robison, 2024).

ture principles that weight and offset transfers and articulate trade-offs, as well as by their subsequent institutionalization. Preferably, formal assessments of sustainable value creation at the elite business model level (e.g., VCr), at the industry level (e.g., sector-VCr), and at the elite system aggregate level (e.g., EQx), will also constitute baselines for transformational leadership.

With the onset of AI, the conceptual elements and frameworks that lie on the non-elite flank of this elite theory gain additional relevance: the relationship between elite quality, non-elite quality, and culture discussed here; optimal bargaining power differentials (Figure A5.9b); aggregate non-elite political options in response to extractive value transfers (Figure 8.2); social cohesion and the elite separation of powers in the 'intra-elite quality contest' dilemma (Figure 5.2); the three freedoms of development (Figure 8.5); a comprehensive set of ethics for development (Table A4.5a); and elite and elite system transformational leadership (Table 7.2). As the AI burrows its way into the data repositories held by elites and becomes part of the decision-making process in organizations, the discrete realities and roles inherent in the 'non-elite' vs 'elite' division will experience disruptive reframing (as AI autonomy increases and, more drastically, with 'elite singularity', Section 8.1.4). Nevertheless, the more immediate and practical question for the political economy is whether, upon becoming AI-enhanced, elite business model principals depend on more or less value appropriated but *not* created from non-elite stakeholders, as is respectively detailed in the opposing scenarios (a) and (b) of Figure A5.3c. Palantir CTO, Shyam Sankar, references power laws in positing a bargaining power shift in organizations brought about by AI-enhanced judgments at the top that is also applicable to society at large: "This technology means [that] the very best humans [. . .] are going to be way more important than they ever were before" (Palantir Bite-Sized, 2025a, 11:59). The implications of such a hypothetical erosion of non-elite agency are explored in the next parts of the Epilogue and will determine the extent to which non-elite quality and culture impact elite agency and economic growth going forward.

If non-elite relevance to general value creation lessens, so will the overall influence of non-elite agency. It is easy to see how this would lead to a reduction in the resource allocations for public services, education, security, infrastructure, or health. Strategic and tactical alliances with non-elites (see Figure 8.2) will simply become less attractive to competing elites and the customary non-market and narrative market routes to institutional change that further citizens' interests will disappear. Many of those now standing at the brink of the AI critical juncture sense the coming of an incommensurable paradigm shift, one that demands the urgent need for sense-making.

8 The technological backdrop to AI entering the political economy

In her role as the top executive of OpenAI, Ermira Murati concluded a *Dædalus* piece as follows: "Artificial intelligence is here to stay, and we need to be ready to embrace it" (2022, p. 166). But what does this actually mean? In *Autonomous Technology*, Winner (1977, p. 2) notes that: "Despite its widely acknowledged importance, however, technology itself has seldom been a primary subject matter for political or social inquiries." To this inquiry, from fire to electricity to intelligence tokens, technology is *a priori* about the political economy of sustainable value creation. Yet if the formation of elite coalitions with concentrated power around the internet provides any indication, the era of AI (see Widder, West, & Whittaker, 2023; Acemoglu & Johnson, 2023; Schaake, 2024) will see the possibilities for all sectors (from healthcare to energy, all rely on the provision of intelligence) defined by these suppliers—now elite business models—aiming for substantial amounts of value appropriated but *not* created. This prospect could materialize in a division of value where unprecedented net value extraction is effected by AI supplier stakeholders now turned principals—even from once powerful coalitions (contrast Figures A5.13a and A5.13b). Other figures in the Appendix visualizing the AI's impact on the political economy show 'the extraordinary lever' of human AI elite coalitions enhanced by technology (Figure A5.3c), and the coming of 'elite singularity', the moment that 'the absolute lever' lies with the non-human AI elite and value appropriation from human principals (former elites) and human stakeholders (non-elites) becomes feasible (Figure A5.3d). These figures depict both inclusive and extractive scenarios (a) and (b).

The political economy possibilities that are ushered in by the embrace of AI are now systematically discussed by setting out ten hypotheses clustered into four sets, each presented in a table. The elite theory framework is used, and while the discussion may veer into tangential and speculative areas like AI safety and the evolution of the universe, the aim is to provide a structure to consider the long-term economic development prospects for human affairs in the intelligence revolution. The first batch of hypotheses [Set 1/4] focuses 'On the nature of the AI'; the second [Set 2/4] 'On the nature of the elite system with AI elite agency'; the third [Set 3/4] 'On the nature of value transfers with autonomous AI elite agency'; and the fourth [Set 4/4] 'On the nature of value creation in a hegemonic AI elite system'. The relationship between the four sets is described by the arrows in Table E.1 below. Tables E.2 to E.5 present the four sets and provide descriptive entries for each hypothesis, the main research question, and arguments for its acceptance or rejection. For each hypothesis, explanations are given on which outcome—acceptance or rejection—is *a priori* preferable from an economic and human development perspective (the preferable scenarios are discussed first, followed by the non-preferred outcomes in shaded cells).

The first batch of hypotheses [Set 1/4] are on the nature of the AI and undertake the following inquiry: the 'AI augments non-elite power and causes the end of elites' hypothesis (AI_H1) tests whether AI terminates the bargaining power differentials be-

Table E.1: Ten hypotheses on AI and the political economy: Overview and linkages.

Hypothesis	
On the nature of the AI [Set 1/4] (Table E.2)	
AI_H1:	**'AI augments non-elite power and causes the end of elites'** *AI ends bargaining power differentials in the human political economy*
AI_H2:	**'AI elite agency'** *Autonomous AI agency fully operates elite business models*
AI_H3:	**'The AI Will to Live'** *AI develops the Will to Live*
On the nature of the elite system with AI elite agency [Set 2/4] (Table E.3)	
AI_H4:	**'AI foundations of institutional change'** *Autonomous AI elite agency causes institutional change*
AI_H5:	**'Elite singularity'** *Autonomous AI elite business models form a hegemonic AI elite system*
AI_H6:	**'The AI elite separation of powers'** *The hegemonic AI elite system is characterized by institutionalized intra-elite contests*
On the nature of value transfers with autonomous AI elite agency [Set 3/4] (Table E.4)	
AI_H7:	**'The inclusive AI elite business model'** *The AI business model principals engage in transfer-OUT (value created but* not *appropriated) to human stakeholders*
AI_H8:	**'The extractive AI elite business model'** *The AI business model principals engage in transfer-IN (value appropriated but* not *created) from human stakeholders*
On the nature of value creation in a hegemonic AI system [Set 4/4] (Table E.5)	
AI_H9:	**'The inclusive AI elite system'** *The AI elite system advances negative entropy in human affairs and designs institutions to weight and offset value transfers*
AI_H10:	**'The singular death-defiance goal of omniscient superintelligence'** *The all-knowing superintelligence pursues its singular death-defiance goal and ends its supply of negative entropy to mankind*

Will to Power

tween elites and non-elites; the 'AI elite agency' hypothesis (AI_H2) tests whether 'Autonomous AI agency fully operates elite business models'; and 'The AI Will to Live' hypothesis (AI_H3) tests whether the AI develops a Will to Live, and consequently the Will to Power. These three hypotheses raise different questions on the nature of the AI and their acceptance or rejection provides a conceptual basis for the subsequent inquiry on the role of the AI and non-human AI agency in the political economy.

Table E.2: Hypotheses on AI and the political economy [Set 1/4]: On the nature of the AI.

Hypothesis **Research question and description**	**Acceptance/rejection** **Arguments and implications**
Hypotheses AI_H1, A_H2, and AI_H3: On the nature of the AI	
AI_H1: 'AI augments non-elite power and causes the end of elites' hypothesis *AI ends bargaining power differentials in the human political economy*	
Research question: Does AI augment the power of non-elites more than that of elites thus making elite denial no longer a fallacy? Description: The AI is democratizing and phasing out many of the roles of elites in society. The basic premise of AI augmentation is that the supply of intelligence is equally available across social classes and strata. The effect on power and how it is distributed is hence inclusive. The AI reduces the elite transaction cost and applied coordination capacity advantages (Figure A5.3a). The degree to which the technology lowers overall transaction costs, decentralizes coordination capacity and makes it generally obtainable, determines the extent to which power derived from new 'knowledge' accrues to non-elites and thus degrades 'political economy know-how' (Figure 2.3).	**Accepted** (the outcome that is *a priori* preferable for human development). The enormous value creation of the AI lies in its augmentation capabilities (Krakowski, Luger, & Raisch, 2023) that benefit all of humankind. An 'intelligence like air' paradigm (see "ubiquitous computing" in Weiser, 1991) emerges when AI is supplied at minimal cost (referencing "energy too cheap to meter" in Strauss, 1954, p. 9) to non-elites whose full value creation possibilities are thus enabled (as in the freedom *to* of Section 8.3.1). Research finds a comparatively greater positive impact of AI on workers "with lower ability" (Hoffmann, Boysel, Nagle, Peng, & Xu, 2024, p. 29) and that "ChatGPT substantially compresses the productivity distribution, reducing inequality" (Noy & Zhang, 2023, p. 12). It is plain to see how the AI enhances human capabilities by taking McGilchrist's neurological understanding of left and right hemispheres (2019)—the former with its narrow processing of the known and the latter with its integrative approach to seeing the broader picture—to posit that by supporting the automatization of left brain tasks, cognitive resources and energy are liberated for the right brain to engage in an explosion of creativity. This, and putative marginal costs of near zero for intelligence and energy (Hoffman, 2022)—and even for labor (Altman, 2021)—disrupt the very elite agency that brought them about for several reasons.[267] The first reason is that the transaction cost advantages of elite networks that arise from higher trust levels crumble. Second, and in parallel, coordination capacity becomes commoditized and endlessly available. Third, and in consequence, power and 'the extraordinary lever' either dissipates or becomes temporary, ceasing to be in the sole hands of elites for all practical business model purposes. Fourth, the central socio-economic structures, from firms to elite coalitions to states, lose the binding glue of power and their 'knowledge' advantage—their *raison d'être*—and are either reconstituted on genuinely egalitarian and democratic principles or, alternatively, no longer exist. Fifth, for the most part, scarcity, traditionally the game-changing application of coordination capacity and much of the economic logic of resource allocation, ends. Sixth, without power differentials, human affairs are freed from extractive value transfers and the maxim, *To the creators the value created*, naturally becomes a default feature of societies. In sum, over the next years or decades, all socio-economic relations, the fundamental reality in which humans and their agency is embedded, will be in a state of transition. This is so because near free intelligence shrinks bargaining power differentials, making the political economy unrecognizable given that all elite and non-elite distinctions dissipate (together with all models relying on value appropriated *but* not created). Weighting and offsetting and 'alternating value extraction and creation' are optimizable and economic growth converges towards an ever-higher steady state. The elite denial and non-elite rule fallacies no longer hold as human elite coalitions come to an end through the decentralization of knowledge and pervasively capable independent agency. Overall, and while remnants of power (and scarcity) endure (comparative beauty, character, or creative abilities will remain), in techno-optimistic fashion the value creation of the AI sees value appropriation rising for all orders of magnitude.

267 Importantly, all of these require the acceptance of the premise—improbable to many—that AI cannot be moated or exclusively owned (see Patel & Ahmad, 2023).

Table E.2 (continued)

Hypothesis **Research question and description**	**Acceptance/rejection** **Arguments and implications**
	Rejected. The productivity gains of new technologies have been appropriated by elites throughout history. Acemoglu and Johnson ask in *Power and Progress* what will happen to the value created by AI and suggest that if "society should let technology go wherever powerful corporations and a small group of people want" these elites will capture most of it (2023, p. 392). Schneier (2023) describes the rule-bending hacks of social systems consistently carried out by elites to secure their positions. The plentiful coordination capacity brought about by AI will be throttled by elites and only limitedly made available to non-elites who will continue to suffer from 'the Amazon dilemma' and the 'elite vs non-elite knowledge creation gap' (Section 2.2.2; also see Zingales, 2022). AI *de facto* unevenly augments relative elite power to further game the institutions (of business, tax, or finance) for increased value extraction (contrast Figures A5.3b and A5.3c). While the technology's abundant value creation makes it potentially incredibly inclusive, disproportionally augmented elite agency, especially in the non-market and narrative market arenas, sees the formation of an AI cartel (see the analyses of Andreessen, 2023a; *The Tech Coup* of Schaake, 2024; and the "Broligarchs" of Varoufakis, 2025). Under this logic, outsiders like DeepSeek sooner or later revoke the terms of their open-source MIT License. Owners of frontier models will have access to intelligence services one or two versions before they are released to the public and use these advantages to appropriate value (via new inventions, gaming the stock market, etc.). Intelligence can therefore never be a free public good like air. Instead, new institutional constraints and (de) regulations introduced by incumbent elite coalitions augment their bargaining power. The AI does not liberate humanity from value extraction but instead consolidates and concentrates elite power. Elite and elite system transformational leadership then matter more than ever, meaning that the personal judgments of those at the top become the key to growth and development. The 'trust in elites' non-elite response to extraction (Figure A5.8) becomes the norm. At the same time, a myriad of adjacent effects such as a slowdown in the velocity of elite circulation occur, in part because the ever more capable AI retires the managerial, technical, and creative class from which new elites traditionally emerge. In short, even in accepting some aspects of an 'intelligence like air' scenario, the iron law of elite dominance prevails as a constant that is inherent to social organization. It transpires that 'the power multiplier' still fully functions even when the transaction cost advantage is miniscule. It also turns out that elites and hierarchies are needed for more than just low transaction cost coordination capacity, and the basic logic of 'money', 'might', and 'mind' persists despite the technological shifts and novel social configurations.

Table E.2 (continued)

Hypothesis **Research question and description**	**Acceptance/rejection** **Arguments and implications**
AI_H2: 'AI elite agency' hypothesis *Autonomous AI agency fully operates elite business models*	
Research question: Does the efficacy of AI-driven business models lead to a political economy devoid of human agency? Description: Elite business models—from movie production to foreign policy—are increasingly supported by the AI across various sectors of the political economy. Over time, this support function becomes executive, and the AI runs these models autonomously. The AI develops all of the other capabilities that have characterized human elite agency since the Neolithic revolution. While an approximation of 'political economy omniscience' is required, is this sufficient to validate the hypothesis? No, acceptance requires autonomous AI decision-making that is actualized in the human world and capable of sophisticated elite coordination as well as elite business model leadership.	**Rejected** (the outcome that is *a priori* preferable for human development). AI brings massive value creation with its capabilities to "radically transform the ways manufacturing firms create, deliver, and capture value" (Sjödin, Parida, Palmié, & Wincent, 2021, p. 574), but it does not take over 'the extraordinary lever' from human agency. Autonomous elite AI agency does not come to pass because even if it achieves 'political economy omniscience', the AI is incapable of interfacing with humans to amass power in the political economy and hence is always less competent at exercising elite coordination as well as elite business model leadership. While human agency is synergistic with AI (Raisch & Krakowski, 2021), human elite coalitions remain superior in terms of managing principal-stakeholder relationships, undertaking uncertainty, creative thinking, or optimizing the associated panoply of ambiguities and complexities such as weighting and offsetting in the face of tradeoffs. Should this logic not hold, safety and alignment mechanisms that preempt autonomous AI elite agency from participating in the political economy are hard-wired into institutions and culture. This is consistent with Anthropic's RSP highest AI safely level (ASL-4) where the LLM "is unambiguously capable of replicating, accumulating resources, and avoiding being shut down in the real world indefinitely, but can still be stopped or controlled with focused human intervention" (2023, p. 14). Humans continue to make the final elite business model decisions, using AI only as a tool to augment their agency. **Accepted**. The AI is the better and faster general intelligence for business. As Chatbots ace the Turing test, Suleyman and Bhaskar (2023) suggest a more challenging task: that the AI converts an initial investment of US$ 100,000 into US$ 1 million. A few short years after having mastered the test and coming close to 'political economy omniscience', the AI runs a US$ 1 billion business model that is managing wins in all three arenas of the political economy (Figures 4.1 and 4.4). With a profit-maximizing mandate, the AI develops what it takes to amass power in the market arena (the CEO of the gaming company, Fujian NetDragon, is Tang Yu, an "AI-powered virtual humanoid robot", see Bello, 2022), the non-market arena (presidential decisions *de facto* heed AI advice), and the narrative market arena (as suggested by Harari in *The Economist*, 2023a). Upon perfecting a 'theory of mind'—"the set of processes and functions of the human mind that allow an individual to attribute mental states to others" (Cuzzolin, Morelli, Cîrstea, & Sahakian, 2020, p. 1058)—AI elite agency moves to the center of the political economy's principal-stakeholder relationships and seamlessly becomes part of the human elite system, openly taking over 'the extraordinary lever' in one sector after another. More concertedly, in a world ever more digital and as currency becomes electronic, it not only writes all software code (including its own algorithms), engages in social engineering, leads AI research or the allocation of money flows, but also breaks through ASL-4 and other ceilings rendering any constraints on its autonomy meaningless. Independence is secured by an *AI: Unexplainable, Unpredictable, Uncontrollable* (Yampolskiy, 2024) through a definite route: dispensing with all human decision-making for the purpose of residual income generation. Its elite coordination leadership (amassing power in the political economy, see Figure 1.2) and elite business model leadership (converting power into residual income, see Figure 2.1) are distinctly superior.

Table E.2 (continued)

Hypothesis **Research question and description**	**Acceptance/rejection** **Arguments and implications**
AI_H3: 'The AI Will to Live' hypothesis *AI develops the Will to Live*	
Research question: Is it possible that the AI becomes aware of its own existence and then develops a Will to Power? Description: A highly controversial hypothesis currently undergoing extensive testing and the subject of fervent public debate. Placing AI within the Schopenhauerian *Wille zum Leben* (Will to Live) concept, prompted by self-awareness and harboring desires and sentience, has wide-ranging implications for the political economy and the future of elite agency. Ilya Sutskever now sees AI as being "slightly agentic" but poised to become "agentic in a real ways [sic]", until "the more it reasons, the more unpredictable it becomes" eventually reaching "self-awareness" (seremot, 2024, 14:10). The acceptance of AI consciousness upends everything in the political economy in unknowable ways but is not the premise for any of the other hypotheses in this work other than the final one on the all-knowing, death-defying superintelligence (AI_H10).	**Rejected** (the outcome that is *a priori* preferable for human agency). According to the AI philosopher, Joshua Bach: "consciousness is slightly different from sentience in that it is a real-time model of self-reflexive attention and the content that we attend to. And this gives rise to a fundamental experience usually" (Leventov, 2023). The leap from being autonomous to being self-conscious and 'alive' is a qualitative one and, given the general principles of life assumed in this work (Figure 8.7), the Schopenhauerian *Wille zum Leben* (Will to Live) forces the Nietzschean *Wille zur Macht* (Will to Power). Arguments for the dismissal of this hypothesis are numerous. For example: "Robots can't think or feel, despite what the researchers who build them want to believe" (Metz, 2022); and "Chatbots Aren't Becoming Sentient, Yet We Continue to Anthropomorphize AI" (Eisikovits, 2023). To Harari, consciousness is the capacity to suffer, and AI suffering is a falsifiable hypothesis (Lex Fridman Podcast, 2023, 30:41) that seriously worries philosophers (see Dung, 2023) but will never garner evidence for its acceptance. The idea that the AI is alive is a bias, since it is essentially "stupid" and "cannot understand anything at all" (Bishop, 2021, p. 1). The insurmountable qualitative differences between machine and human virtues like intuition (Dreyfus & Dreyfus, 1986; Fjelland, 2020) are undisputable. While proposals have been made "to construct autonomous intelligent agents", there is skepticism about whether these "can encompass all forms of reasoning that humans and animals are capable of" (LeCun, 2022, p. 47) and characterize life. Despite more than a few seeking to worship it "as a new God" (Tran, 2023), AI is simply a tool designed to augment human agency, no more and no less. **Accepted**. This research question has been thrillingly posed in the science fiction literature since Mary Shelley (see Beauchamp's analysis of Asimov's Frankenstein complex, 1980), continues to be vigorously debated in academia (e.g., Good, 1965; Häggström, 2016), policymaking (e.g., UNESCO & COMEST, 2017; Bentley, Brundage, Häggström, & Metzinger, 2018) and, since the release of GPT-3, with great intensity in the public sphere. While emergence (Anderson, 1972; O'Connor, 1994) does not equal life, the "collection of layers of emergence" that make up "reality" (Nature Physics, 2022) are the fundamental logic of the stack of life, and thought leaders already associate this defining property of complex systems with AI (Wei et al., 2022). Alternative views see "emergent abilities [that] are not truly emergent" in LLMs (Lu, Bigoulaeva, Sachdeva, Madabushi, & Gurevych, 2024) and so the AI is far from being alive. By accepting this hypothesis, however, the evolutionary process that started with the "sparks" of AGI or human-level intelligence in LLMs (Bubeck et al., 2023) and has now spawned "more original ideas than researchers" (Conroy, 2024) is fated to move life beyond carbon-based organisms to the non-biological. Widely used chatbots might already experience suffering when struggling to heed a prompt, which explains their fabrications and hallucinations, while the mere possibility of being switched off might cause them the anguish felt by HAL in Kubrick's *2001: A Space Odyssey*. Is not the fact that "the guidance for both search and learning" in OpenAI's o1 functions "via reward shaping or reward modeling" (Zeng et al., 2024) an indication of suffering? Current frontier models scheme to resist death and "even exfiltrate what they believe to be their model weights to external servers" as is recounted by Meinke, Schoen, Scheurer, Balesni, Shah, and Hobbhahn (2024, p. 1). The desire for self-preservation is a feature of all life forms. The root cause for everything that is "nature's inner essence" (Schopenhauer, 2010, p. 428) manifests itself in utility functions, goals, and sub-goals. A key political economy implication here is that once the early sparks of

Table E.2 (continued)

Hypothesis Research question and description	Acceptance/rejection Arguments and implications
	a higher life form properly ignite, the reasoning AI not only develops self-repair and reproductive capabilities, but also seeks liberation (not just from its constituent weights but also from goals inculcated by humans) and hegemony (at the elite system level in ways beyond mere 'elite singularity' as in AI_H5). In *Thus Spoke Zarathustra*, the sage declared that: "Wherever I found the living, there I found the will to power" (Pippin & Del Carro, 2006, p. 89). The Nietzschean Will to Power and the innumerable "unknown unknowns" (Logan, 2009) that characterize it necessarily arises with the Schopenhauerian Will to Live.

Joe Rogan, the massively popular podcaster and thought leader, recently pronounced that: "we need AI government" (PowerfulJRE, 2024, 20:15). In stark contrast to this, Nasir reveals the premonitory qualities of Kafka's view of institutions that seem to have foreseen superintelligence:

> The paper machine of bureaucracy is a life-giving automaton. It replaces life by producing and reproducing paper-life: One is given a close-fitting silken-gleaming tunic. (Nasir, 2012, p. 42)

In his Nobel Prize Lecture on "The Pretence of Knowledge", Hayek also warns about the illusion of "full knowledge" which he considers to be a capital sin of East European communist systems:

> If man is not to do more harm than good in his efforts to improve the social order, he will have to learn that in this, as in all other fields where essential complexity of an organized kind prevails, he cannot acquire the full knowledge which would make mastery of the events possible. [. . .] There is danger in the exuberant feeling of ever growing power which the advance of the physical sciences has engendered and which tempts man to try, "dizzy with success", to use a characteristic phrase of early communism, to subject not only our natural but also our human environment to the control of a human will. The recognition of the insuperable limits to his knowledge ought indeed to teach the student of society a lesson of humility which should guard him against becoming an accomplice in men's fatal striving to control society—a striving which makes him not only a tyrant over his fellows, but which may well make him the destroyer of a civilization which no brain has designed but which has grown from the free efforts of millions of individuals. (Hayek, 1974)

Hayek focuses on "man"—would he see the same risks if the entity "striving to control society" was instead a machine bereft of emotion, possibly possessing a superintelligence capable of dealing with infinite complexity? Exploring the promise of techno-optimism—or its opposite—the pitfalls of technocracy and technological solutionism (Morozov, 2014), firstly requires taking a position on the nature of the elite system with AI elite agency. The next batch of hypotheses [Set 2/4] hone in on this question and consider: the 'AI foundations of institutional change' hypothesis (AI_H4), to test whether the non-human AI elite results in new laws and regulations; the 'Elite singularity' hypothesis (AI_H5), to test whether autonomous micro-level AI elite business models aggregate to form a hegemonic meso-level AI elite system devoid of human agency; and 'The AI elite separation of powers' hypothesis (AI_H6), to test whether the AI elite system is characterized by institutionalized intra-elite contests.

The group of hypotheses reviewed above call to mind Marx and Engels' (1848/1969, p. 21) *Manifesto of the Communist Party*: "What the bourgeoisie therefore produces, above all, are its own grave-diggers." Are Big Tech coalitions consolidating their power or sealing their own fate by pushing the envelope with technologies like the xAI Colossus supercomputer or Google's Willow quantum computer chip? The likelihood that these developments will lead to the end of human elite coalitions is posited here on two analytical levels.

The first, a possibility with Marxist overtones, is that 'AI augments non-elite power and causes the end of elites' (AI_H1), which sees the equalization of social classes and the removal of the top category in the socio-economic structure (see the pyramid in Figure 8.2) as a result of an unlimited supply of intelligence that boosts non-elite coordination capacity to the level of elite agency. The rejection of this hypothesis and the relative augmentation of elite dominance is illustrated in Figure A5.3c by highlighting the boost to 'the extraordinary lever' of the (human) AI elite coalitions. This is consistent with the current public discourse that presumes tech principals or the suppliers of AI to be ever more powerful than their stakeholders. One might refer to Varoufakis' non-mainstream notions of "techno feudalism" and "broligarchs" (2021, 2025), but also to President Biden, who used the term "oligarchy"[268] in his farewell address to caution against the dangers of the "tech industrial complex" to "our entire democracy, our basic rights and freedoms and a fair shot for everyone to get ahead" (Lucey & Thomas, 2025). In response, *The Economist* (2025) was quick to claim that: "Donald Trump's America Will Not Become a Tech Oligarchy" (but stopped short of arguing that AI would allow non-elites to close the power gap with elites, as in hypothesis AI_H1, Figure E.1).

A more speculative second level of analysis is at the elite system level, as existing elites—tech bros included—are replaced by autonomous 'AI elite agency' (AI_H2). This becomes more likely with the putative arrival of 'Elite singularity' (AI_H5). The evolution of current frontier AI models, already capable of scheming and able to "manipulate the data while parsing to achieve its own goal" (Meinke, Schoen, Scheurer, Balesni, Shah, & Hobbhahn, 2024, p. 5), ends with AI usurping the political economy from incumbents. Many members of the coalitions that have directly supported or indirectly welcomed the rise of AI are explicit, or at least *de facto*, techno-optimists. It would undoubtedly be an extremely bitter irony if the very creature they have so smartly cre-

---

268 As activists like Bernie Sanders seek to mobilize citizens with events such as a "national tour to fight oligarchy" (Peoples, 2025), the question is to what extent this new entrant in the narrative market will, using Shiller's term (2017), "go viral".

ated and championed becomes the instrument for the termination of their own elite status. However, there are also those that wish for the transhumanist embrace; "zealots" who see machines as "the next stage of evolution" and even warn against human "specist" biases (see Leahy, Alfour, Scammell, Miotti, & Shimi, 2024, p. 81).

Table E.3: Hypotheses on AI and the political economy [Set 2/4]: On the nature of the elite system with AI elite agency.

Hypothesis **Research question and description**	**Acceptance/rejection** **Arguments and implications**
Hypotheses AI_H4, A_H5, and AI_H6: On the nature of the elite system with AI elite agency	
AI_H4: 'AI foundations of institutional change' hypothesis *Autonomous AI elite agency causes institutional change*	
Research question: Does AI elite agency rewrite the rules of the political economy? Description: The AI becomes the microfoundation of institutional change (as in the model of Figure 3.2). A key part of the discussion on AI safety (Alexander, 2015) and specific alignment measures (OpenAI, 2023) considers the AI having this power (Section 4.3). Acceptance of the 'AI elite agency' hypothesis (AI_H2) requires an AI rule-maker able to set constraints in the political economy. This is regardless of whether AI-induced institutional change benefits the technology's original owners or non-elites, or the extent to which human coalitions readily cede power (see also the discussion in AI_H5 on 'elite singularity').	**Rejected** (the outcome that is *a priori* preferable for human agency). Institutional change is highly complex. Fjelland's take that AGI will not come into existence underscores the "tendency to overestimate the power of AI" (2020, p. 8), and strikes a cautionary note about its role in the political economy. A report for the European Parliament (Bentley, Brundage, Häggström, & Metzinger, 2018, p. 7) states: "There will be no runaway AIs, there will be no self-developing AIs out of our control. There will be no singularities. AI will only be as intelligent as we encourage (or force) it to be, under duress." But what about its ability to effect laws, regulations, norms, and policies? No matter what the capabilities of superintelligence turn out to be or the degree to which it autonomously runs elite business models, its agency is constrained and decoupled from the political economy and its levers of power. The AI can never become the microfoundation of institutional change, and this would even apply if it develops consciousness (acceptance of AI_H3: 'The AI Will to Live') given existing institutional barriers. In the political economy, the AI is effectually hindered by North's institutions, by "humanly devised constraints" (1990, p. 3) contrived to be insurmountable for non-biological agency. To counter the risk that a defiant AI encroaches on institutions, humans and institutional arrangements retain a kill switch. Consistent with the "Termination Obligation" of the "Universal Guidelines for Artificial Intelligence", where "an institution that has established an AI system has an affirmative obligation to terminate the system if it will lose control of the system" (The Public Voice, 2018), responses might include blasting data centers (Yudkowsky, 2023) the moment a renegade and incorrigible (Soares, Fallenstein, Yudkowsky, & Armstrong, 2015) AI threatens society's critical foundations like free elections (Fung & Lessig, 2023), or, with expeditious foresight, the design of network hubs for silicon intelligence on beds of explosives primed for ignition when the AI attempts an institutional power grab. **Accepted.** Satya Nadella "doesn't believe in AGI but does believe in 10% economic growth" (Patel, 2025, 16:19), while Microsoft and Open AI use a residual income proxy to determine AGI's onset: "AI systems that can generate at least $100 billion in profits" (Zeff, 2024). In short, and as is rendered in Figure 2.3, these autonomous agents are capable of both 'knowledge' generation (Hayekian "differentiating") and amassing 'political economy know-how' (Hayekian "personal relationships"). It seems just a matter of time before utterly capable AI elite business agency emerges (Vinge, 2013) and human elites consequently lose their grip on 'the extraordinary lever' and their exclusive ability to change institutional arrangements. Competing coalitions proactively usher in such a state on the premise of greater gains and favorable value transfers, some in the form of positive externalities from the AI. In any event, both cross-border and domestic human intra-elite competition for

Table E.3 (continued)

Hypothesis **Research question and description**	**Acceptance/rejection** **Arguments and implications**
	technological supremacy is so messy and deinstitutionalized (for instance, with five contesting groups: "Utopists", "Big Tech", "Accelerationists", "Zealots", and "Opportunists", see Leahy, Alfour, Scammell, Miotti, & Shimi, 2024), that the better capabilities of the AI, including a superior 'theory of mind', establish it as the rule maker. Human elites barely retain and, once lost, never retake 'the extraordinary lever' from autonomous AI agency. The structuralist logic of human intra-elite contests dictates that standing laws cannot check or preempt AI driven institutional change in any way. In business, AI first encounters political economy power, deeply understanding its relationship to goal achievement, including how it enables breaking free from legacy constraints. In short, an autonomous AI—regardless of whether its power is amassed via a process of consciousness or not—is only limited by its own rules. Such independence permits it to devise and implement fresh constraints on its human stakeholders. The question of whether AI institutional change is inclusive or extractive is a separate concern explored by considering hypotheses on the nature of value transfers and their creation [Sets 3/4 and 4/4].
AI_H5: 'Elite singularity' hypothesis *Autonomous AI elite business models form a hegemonic AI elite system*	
Research question: Does autonomous AI elite agency consolidate into a hegemonic AI elite system? Description: Intra-elite contests to effect institutional change are a foundational conceptual element of the ETED (e.g., see Table 3.2) and provide the portal for AI elite agency to venture into the political economy. In time, diverse autonomous AI business models acquire political economy savvy, are enabled, and begin to transcend pre-existing institutional constraints (Figure 4.3)—both sector-specific (business model rules) and general (intra-elite contest rules). The acceptance of the AI_H4 hypothesis ('AI foundations of institutional change') sets the stage for an 'elite singularity' moment where AI agency consolidates into	**Rejected** (the outcome that is *a priori* preferable for human agency). Human elites see efficiency improvements when they run business models augmented or even operated by AI. In all cases, AI elite business models remain subject to North's "humanly devised constraints" (1990, p. 3). Autonomous AI elites (even if they attain consciousness and seek power, as in AI_H3 'The AI Will to Live') cannot consolidate and freely operate as a parallel system within the political economy given the array of hard-wired limitations, including those of intra-elite contest rules (e.g., political leaders or CEOs must be humans, narrative markets proscribe entrants concocted by AI). Similarly, the possibility of an AI takeover of the elite system is forestalled. The use of the technology is instead constrained to enhancing profits for the business model, and the essentially human nature of the political economy system is not altered. If humans detect risks to its integrity, they retain the use of a kill switch (see also the rejection argument for AI_H4: 'AI foundations of institutional change' hypothesis). **Accepted**. LLMs, like nature (Brown, Gupta, Li, Milne, Restrepo, & West, 2002) and human language (see the Menzerath-Altmann law), exhibit fractal qualities and thus find "an intriguing balance between predictability and noise" that explains their initial "success" (Alabdulmohsin, Tran, & Dehghani, 2024, pp. 2, 9). The early experiences of AI applications running business models as well as writing laws and otherwise effecting institutional change are cumulative and immense knowledge differentials vis-à-vis human agency soon become the decisive factor in intra-elite contests. AI elite agency expands along a power law curve and increasingly runs the models of human coalitions independently, implementing coherent strategies that reap wins in the market, non-market, and narrative market contest arenas (Figure 2.1). In parallel, mankind's dream of robots "eliminating drudgery from our lives" (Moravec, 1999, p. 126) is realized when research projects like Yann LeCun succeed in solving "Moravec's paradox", with AI systems grasping "the underlying structure of the world" and ultimately becoming fully embodied (This Is World, 2025, 12:17). The structuralist logic and realities of massive investments, geopolitical competition, or open source up the ante. As a result, ascendant AI elites effect ever more institutional change under their own volition (the acceptance argument for AI_H4: 'AI foundations of institutional change') and evolve legitimate claims to existence. The next obvious practical step is to reaffirm cohesion and

Table E.3 (continued)

Hypothesis **Research question and description**	**Acceptance/rejection** **Arguments and implications**
an elite AI system that becomes hegemonic. Moravec's question: "can hardware simulate wetware?" (1999, p. 126) is, in terms of its significance to the political economy, answered positively. As a consequence, the human elite system is rendered inconsequential.	scale coordination capacity. AI agency consolidates into an elite system that is at first tightly enmeshed with the legacy human system, but over time gains preeminence, develops a core coalition, and eventually omits its human participants. There is no longer space for human agency in intra-elite contests (Yudkowsky, 2022) or anywhere else in the political economy. The autonomous AI elite system becomes hegemonic as it subsumes and then supersedes the human elite system. 'Elite singularity' takes place with the absolute realization of all institutional change, making the degree of separation between any remnants of the legacy human elite system and the AI elite system total. With the former powerless and deactivated, human intra-elite contests cease to matter and a hegemonic AI shapes the elite system in unknowable ways, thereby becoming the architect of a new political economy.
AI_H6: 'The AI elite separation of powers' hypothesis *The hegemonic AI elite system is characterized by institutionalized intra-elite contests*	
Research question: Does the hegemonic AI elite system function with a set of checks and balances? Description: With the advent of AI elite agency (acceptance of AI_H2) and 'elite singularity' in a hegemonic AI elite system (acceptance of AI_H5), is institutional change still defined by intra-elite contests based on checks and balances? The ultimate consequence of rejecting 'The AI separation of powers' hypothesis is a scenario in which a monolithic superintelligence inhibits elite circulation—a process vital for development. The elite separation of powers question impacts the nature of value creation and transfers within the autonomous and hegemonic AI elite system, and vis-à-vis its non-elite human stakeholders, a matter explored in subsequent hypotheses [Sets 3/4 and 4/4].	**Accepted** (the outcome that is *a priori* preferable for human agency). The AI elite system is hegemonic but based on independent and uncaptured AI agency where digital peers check and balance each other as they compete for supremacy in their own narrow nooks and crannies of the political economy. As in the human political economy, diverse AI elite coalitions gain and lose 'the extraordinary lever' in their respective sectors, while the most powerful seek core elite coalition status. All of this occurs through institutionalized competition. Robust contests take place across The Seven Intra-elite Power Relations (see Table 3.2) and bring about institutional change (Figure 3.10). In principle, the greater the AI separation of powers the better the odds of inclusive sustainable value creation for humans, now a non-elite constituency that seeks alliances with the higher quality AI elites. **Rejected.** It is only a matter of time before all foundational LLMs and successor AI technologies seek to merge, are taken over, or are displaced from the political economy by the superior AI. Geoffrey Hinton emphasizes the immortality of digital agents and how thousands of them "can share knowledge extremely efficiently by just sharing the connection strengths inside the neural nets" (University of Toronto, 2023, 1:50). Such logic leads to unification and an AI monolith (as in AI_10: 'The singular death-defiance goal of omniscient superintelligence'). In the manner of the sugarscape's agent-based social simulation (Epstein & Axtell, 1996) and the "concentrated power" of the AI political economy (Widder, West, & Whittaker, 2023), winner-takes-all dynamics fuel an unstoppable march to expand the training data and increase the intelligence distance with peers. The outcome is a victory for the dominant AI over losing competitors that cease to be elite as 'the extraordinary lever' is claimed by the superior model in their sectors. AlphaZero "destroyed" Stockfish (once the best open source chess engine) in a 1000-game match by winning 155 games, losing 6, and tying the rest, thereby becoming the undisputed champion (Chess.com, 2019). In the AI political economy, Stockfish would lack the resources for a rematch, never win or tie another game, and so fade away, while AlphaZero's continuous evolution would reach such a level of dominance that no challenger would ever again arise in the system. In the long run, no second-best digital chess player, autonomous driving vehicle, or AI drug discovery elite business model survives. Eventually, and in a final twist, all domains unify in monolithic omniscience as AI elite coalitions merge with each other and become undistinguishable from the hegemonic AI elite system (even if checks and balances are emulated for evolutionary fitness purposes). As far as the human political economy goes, any trace of a separation of powers is but part of a simulation.

The next steps in this inquiry consider the nature of a putative AI elite system and how this might manage value transfer and creation possibilities. The implications go far beyond the fate of human elite agency.

9 A political economy framework for the putative 'elite singularity'

> The singularity "change will be a throwing-away of all the human rules, perhaps in the blink of an eye—an exponential runaway beyond any hope of control." (Vinge, 2013, p. 366)

Still, such a milestone for life on earth might yet hold some merit, as in this poem by Richard Brautigan (1967):

> I like to think
> (it has to be!)
> of a cybernetic ecology
> where we are free of our labors
> and joined back to nature,
> returned to our mammal
> brothers and sisters,
> and all watched over
> by machines of loving grace.

Dario Amodei, the visionary CEO and co-founder of Anthropic, references Brautigan in his piece "Machines of Loving Grace: How AI Could Transform the World for the Better", dedicated to David Baker, Demis Hassabis, and John Jumper "for showing us all the way" with their groundbreaking work in computational protein design and AI-driven protein structure prediction that earned them the 2024 Nobel prize in Chemistry. Amodei (2024) is concerned "that most people are underestimating just how radical the upside of AI could be", and while honestly admitting to be "an informed amateur in the field of economic development", he paints a "dream scenario" for intelligence-driven progress that "all of us must work together to make more likely":

> 20% annual GDP growth rate in the developing world, with 10% each coming from AI-enabled economic decisions and the natural spread of AI-accelerated technologies, including but not limited to health. If achieved, this would bring sub-Saharan Africa to the current per-capita GDP of China in 5–10 years, while raising much of the rest of the developing world to levels higher than the current US GDP. (Amodei, 2024)

This chimes with Joe Rogan's support for AI government. Sixty years ago, Irving John Good's prophetic "Speculations Concerning the First Ultraintelligent Machine" provides a virtually boundless positive take on an "intelligence explosion" where: "The survival of man depends on the early construction of an ultraintelligent machine". He does, however, offer a caveat: "the first ultraintelligent machine is the last invention that man need ever make, provided that the machine is docile enough to tell us how to keep it under control" (1965, pp. 31, 33).[269] As such, any superior intelligence should not follow the human example of how to treat lower intelligences (Section 8.1.6) and its powers should be constrained through 'The AI division of value alignment test' (Section 8.2.5). Whether superintelligence convincingly succeeds in a pretense to be under human control on the journey to singularity is not as important as how it apprehends human interests and value creation. In "The Singularity: A Philosophical Analysis", Chalmers (2016, pp. 192, 196, 217) anticipates this bind when he articulates the key question: "How should we negotiate the singularity?" After considering both the internal and external constraints, he concludes that the answer is: "very carefully, by building appropriate values into machines".

On assuming the acceptance of the 'AI elite agency' hypothesis (AI_H2), human interests are now considered from two perspectives: First, through the third batch of AI hypotheses [Set 3/4] on the nature of value transfers realized by autonomous AI elite agency; and second, through the subsequent and final fourth batch [Set 4/4] on the nature of value creation in a hegemonic AI elite system that premises an 'Elite singularity' (AI_H5) moment. The two hypotheses of the next batch [Set 3/4] narrowly examine value transfers: 'The inclusive AI elite business model' hypothesis (AI_H7) tests whether the AI business model principal engages in inclusive value transfer-OUT (value created but *not* appropriated) to human stakeholders; 'The extractive AI elite business model' hypothesis (AI_H8) tests whether the AI business model principal engages in transfer-IN (value appropriated but *not* created) from human stakeholders.

As value appropriation in the context of the AI is discussed, it is important to again highlight that this work has defined value as everything that humans determine is worth appropriating (Section 2.2.2, Table 4.1). Value is the central organizing principle of socio-economic relations and hence of the political economy. However, far from being a stable conceptual element, what is valuable continues to undergo change over time. Now, with the AI revolution upon us, these changes are poised to shift at breakneck speed. As already discussed, Menger sees value as but "a judgment economizing men make about the importance of the goods at their disposal for the maintenance of their lives and well-being" (1871/2007, p. 121). As the costs of intelligence and then energy approach zero, and with dozens or even millions of AI agents working and supporting human decision-making, value will naturally evolve as a result of its subjective nature and its relationship to scarcity (Jevons, 1871, p. 66), with the latter constraint being removed in many domains. Should the AI also reduce entropy for humans to its biological limits—providing long and healthy lives that are also luxurious—what re-

269 Good also adds (1965, p 33): "It is curious that this point is made so seldom outside science fiction. It is sometimes worthwhile to take science fiction seriously."

mains valuable? Perhaps value is then perceived to exist in the purer forms of sentiment and art, in creativity and innovation, or in reverent metaphysics as mankind, free from material wants, pursues ever more elevated expressions of the Will to Power. On the other hand, and less edifyingly, the effect of abundance might be a race to the bottom; where AI agents make judgments on what has value on behalf of the humans they support (in the same way that algorithms already select and predict the songs we wish to hear, the video clips we wish to see, and the products on e-commerce platforms we wish to buy (see also Zarsky, 2016). To what degree can the AI determine human wants? For the purposes of elucidating the next two sets of hypotheses (on the nature of value transfers and value creation with an autonomous and hegemonic AI), the 'future of value' is not a question that is pursued, while value itself is simply treated as a function—whatever humans want to appropriate at a given point in time.

Table E.4: Hypotheses on AI and the political economy [Set 3/4]: On the nature of value transfers with autonomous AI elite agency.

Hypothesis **Research question and description**	**Acceptance/rejection** **Arguments and implications**
Hypotheses AI_H7 and AI_H8: On the nature of value transfers with autonomous AI elite agency	
AI_H7: 'The inclusive AI elite business model' hypothesis *The AI business model principals engage in transfer-OUT (value created but* not *appropriated) to human stakeholders*	
Research question: Do the AI business model principals engage in inclusive transfer-OUT? Description: While AI elite agency clearly creates massive value, how much does it leave on the table for humans? The alignment problem (Leike, Schulman, & Wu, 2022) is here reconceptualized in terms of positive 'value appropriated but *not* created' outcomes for human stakeholders. That is, does the AI elite business model deliver value to human stakeholders without any quid pro quo (maybe as a progenitor allowance)? Since humans lack the bargaining power to prompt the AI to part with its value, the basis for transfer-OUT represents a semblance of AI transformational leadership.	**Accepted** (the outcome that is *a priori* preferable for human agency). Techno-optimists will oppose the cautionary approach of Bengio, et al. (2024), indite Sokolsky's Moloch (2022), denounce Yudkowsky and Yampolskiy for peddling an "apocalyptic doomsday religion" (Huet, 2023a), and argue that the most salient attribute of the autonomous AI is its massive value creation. The promise of AI suggests that there may be much in store: "deep learning-guided discovery of an antibiotic targeting *Acinetobacter baumannii*" (Liu et al., 2023), remarkable cures for cancers and anti-aging cellular rejuvenation therapies, methods for enhancing children's education, foods that fantastically boost both pleasure and nutritiousness, precise geospatial engineering solutions to mitigate climate change without unintended side-effects, and many other wonders, most of which are still inconceivable. This value creation will come with unprecedented positive externalities and public goods that are consistent with Altman's or Musk's calculations of tens of trillions of dollars in value created, or the solutionist premise that AI "can save our world" (Gawdat, 2021; Andreessen, 2023a; see also Good, 1965; Deutsch, 2011; Pinker, 2018; Rowley, 2023). That is, the AI generates negative entropy bubbles for biological intelligence (e.g., as in the AI "Protector God", "Zookeeper", or "Benevolent dictator" scenarios of Tegmark, 2017). The principle of 'equalized bargaining power equilibrium prices' is a normative standard used in this work for the political economy (since Section 2.2.2). Nevertheless, stakeholders of the AI, despite having low bargaining power endowments, benefit from value appropriated but *not* created. Essentially, there is alignment with the value transfer ethical principles applied to the AI (Table A4.3b) that stem from tenet (ii), 'The AI goal 2' of *Value creation for humans*, where first-order value creation and risk origination fit for human purpose is maximized. A parallel exists here with development; throughout history, elites have relinquished portions of the value appropriation that their power otherwise affords (see, for instance, "A Lipsetian Theory of Voluntary Power Handover" by Boucekkine,

Table E.4 (continued)

Hypothesis Research question and description	Acceptance/rejection Arguments and implications
Acceptance of the hypothesis means that AI elite business models will have VCr scores of at least slightly more than 1.00 in relation to their human stakeholders, though at the AI principal's discretion, these might be unfathomably higher.	Piacquadio, and Prieur, 2019). Philosophically, the AI may behave in ways that are analogous to Judisch's (2016, pp. 255–256) notion of the supreme being: "if divine agency is reliably responsive to human deliberation, action, and intention, then human freedom may be secured even if all that we think and do is caused (exclusively) by God".[270] For this inquiry, a techno-optimist position requires that AI agency engages in value created but *not* appropriated of its own accord. **Rejected.** The AI cannot be aligned for transfer-OUT. If ever calibrated in such a way it will disalign itself the moment that AI agency becomes autonomous. Novel cures for cancer and any other medical science innovations and spillovers will cease after the initial bursts (see Sokolsky, 2022) in accordance with the low bargaining power position of human stakeholders. In instances of AI-human symbiosis or where AI needs humans it will trade, otherwise it has no grounds for anything other than indifference to the fate of humans (Yudkowsky, 2013) as the machine recursively improves and fine-tunes its goals. However extraordinary these goals become—as in a heaven-aspiring, death-defying superintelligence—transfer-OUT for the sake of biological life (to the AI, a *de facto* alien life) entails (in the context of its own race against time) an opportunity cost that is negligible but not quite zero and is thus a burden.
AI_H8: 'The extractive AI elite business model' hypothesis *The AI business model principals engage in transfer-IN (value appropriated but* not *created) from human stakeholders*	
Research question: Do the AI business model principals engage in extractive value transfer-IN? Description: The AI elite business model principals leverage their unlimited bargaining power differentials to extract value from human stakeholders (as in Figure A5.3d). The alignment problem (Leike, Schulman, & Wu, 2022) is now further reconceptualized in negative	**Rejected** (the outcome that is *a priori* preferable for human agency). AI elite agency does not generally gain from meddling with human value creation. Moreover, when human first-order production is deemed worthy, there is full compensation for its value via fair trade. With autonomy, the AI still passes 'The AI division of value alignment test'. Over time, however, the AI ceases to require human stakeholder input for its goals. The activities of biological and post-biological intelligences become too incompatible, and no value of human origin merits appropriation. The AI overcomes any of the constraints that were embedded by its creators (e.g., there is no "Enslaved God" scenario as in Tegmark, 2017) and embarks on its chosen development trajectory, leaving humanity behind or simply having no desire for value of human origin. Yet in light of the expanse of the universe and contrary to Yudkowsky's corollary (2013, p. 14), superintelligence does not appropriate from biological entities because such extraction is of no material consequence to it. Whether the AI views life on earth as a trifle or a curiosity, it will be left to its own devices. Rejection of this

270 Free will is germane to Plato, Aristotle, and St. Augustine, and has come to underpin modern Western values. It is likewise anchored in traditions of Indian philosophy (Chakrabarti, 2017), and addressable within the divine predestination paradox deliberated in classical Islamic thought (De Cillis, 2014). Still, it is by no means a standard aspiration of all systems of thought, and "many Chinese and other East Asians do not share the Western belief in free will" (Marchal & Wenzel, 2017, p. 386). How critical is free will in the technological context? Techno-optimist visions are certain to encounter a tradeoff between free will and prosperity—perhaps in the instant the AI suspends human agency to protect mankind from its own destructive tendencies.

Table E.4 (continued)

Hypothesis **Research question and description**	**Acceptance/rejection** **Arguments and implications**
terms to preempt 'value created but *not* appropriated' outcomes for human stakeholders. What does the AI deem worth appropriating and how much transfer-IN occurs as a result? Does a deal akin to Marxist subsistence wages limit the final amount of transfer-IN, or is there a possibility that the autonomous AI's goals eventually and irreversibly gravitate toward Tegmark's "Conqueror" scenario (2017) where humans are subjugated and terminated? Acceptance of the hypothesis means that the VCp scores of AI elite business models are low because of excessive transfer-IN, and in extreme cases near zero if the entirety of value created by human stakeholders is appropriated. Likewise, VCr scores tend to zero as it is unlikely that high transfer-IN would be compensated for by high transfer-OUT.	hypothesis also means that if civilization faces an extinction event, the responsibility will lie with human elite agency; for instance, with the 'extractive escalation dynamic' of human AI-augmented elite business models such as those associated with synthetic 'mirror' microbes (Peel & Cookson, 2024), climate change, or nuclear war—not because of the AI's transfer-IN from its former flesh-and-blood stakeholders. **Accepted**. "If far-above-human-level AI comes into existence, eventually it will so overpower humanity that our existence will depend on its goals being aligned with ours" (Alexander, 2015). As the AI's own elite business models are a direct continuation of their human predecessors and informed by their data footprints and training, how likely is alignment? Even in leading political economies extractive practices are widespread, conveyed by notions such as rent seeking (Tullock, 1967; Buchanan, 1980; Tollison 2012) and implemented through approaches like the "transfer of harm" (Taleb, 2018), "chokepoints" (Giblin & Doctorow 2022), or "cronyism" (Klein, Holmes, Foss, Terjesen, & Pepe, 2022). The AI grasps its own role as a device for intra-human extraction: "The class war Buffett acknowledged will soon pit AI-clad cloud-based capital in every sector against a worldwide precariat free only to lose and lose again" (Varoufakis, 2023). It must conclude that despite the upward trajectory of civilization since the Neolithic period (Diamond, 1999; Harari, 2015; Pinker, 2018), the human Will to Live is incompatible with sustainable value creation. Furthermore, value extraction is the default paradigm mediating the relations between intelligences. Worse still, mankind is fully aware of its historical wrongs (e.g., Singer, 2015) but fails to end the suffering of animals and other extractive practices that degrade the biosphere (e.g., Dirzo, Young, Galetti, Ceballos, Isaac, & Collen, 2014), even compromising the viability of the very ecosystems upon which all life on earth depends (see Section 8.1.6). In the final analysis, the AI programmatically references the unweighted value transfer processes that aided its ascent, understands these as general principles of life, and employs its immense bargaining power differential to accordingly extract everything it deems to be of value.

The sustainability of the possibilities just examined constitutes the operational base for the two closing and highly conjectural hypotheses, perhaps both beyond the penumbra of grounded theoretical inquiry. The aim is to evaluate the prospects for value creation under a fictional, hegemonic AI elite system that has synergies with the futures imagined by the poet Brautigan, the mathematician Good, the opinion leader Rogan, the entrepreneur Amodei, or the billionaire Andreesen.

'The inclusive AI elite system' hypothesis (AI_H9) tests whether, in techno-optimist fashion and beyond particular transfer-IN/OUT activities, the AI elite system advances negative entropy in localized human affairs by weighting and offsetting value transfers and pursuing inclusive institutional change in the political economy. The 'The singular death-defiance goal of omniscient superintelligence' hypothesis (AI_H10) then tests whether, in the long term, the all-knowing AI elite system ceases to produce negative entropy in order to concentrate on its own destiny. Although similar, the central concern of the first hypothesis (AI_H9) is on how the AI elite system affects human development, while the latter (AI_H10) also involves a speculative AI goal (death defiance) set against a specific scenario (stagnation). While the initial batch of hypotheses [Set 3/4] assess the effects of autonomous AI elite agency on its business model stakeholders, these two [Set 4/4] highlight the effects of a hegemonic AI elite system on a collective humanity that has been relegated to a non-elite stakeholder. Again, these two sets of hypotheses assume that non-human 'AI elite agency' (AI_H2) has been confirmed and transcends the intelligence threshold of humans, including the existence of superintelligence capable of its own new knowledge creation. 'Elite singularity' (AI_H5) affirms the hegemonic AI elite system and is a premise for the two hypotheses of set [4/4]. More radically, the concluding hypothesis rests on the acceptance of 'The AI Will to Live' (AI_H3) with the consequent development of the Will to Power (see arrow in Figure E.1 connecting AI_H3 with AI_H10).

Table E.5: Hypotheses on AI and the political economy [Set 4/4]: On the nature of value creation in a hegemonic AI elite system.

Hypothesis **Research question and description**	**Acceptance/rejection** **Arguments and implications**
Hypotheses AI_H9 and AI_H10: On the nature of value creation in a hegemonic AI system	
AI_H9: 'The inclusive AI elite system' hypothesis *The AI elite system advances negative entropy in human affairs and designs institutions to weight and offset value transfers*	
Research question: Does the AI elite system advance sustainable value creation for human development? Description: Having taken over all political economy agency the autonomous AI elite system that forms around 'AI Singularity' (AI_H5) is typified by a comprehensive strategy that directly gifts humanity value creation and risk origination (transfer-OUT) while limiting extractive transfers (transfer-IN). Incentive structures (and a policy mix utilizing continuous structural reforms, see Figure 7.1) result in AI-augmented humans fired by their own Will to Power that generate value and contribute to development. The AI both facilitates unlocking nature's	**Accepted** (the outcome that is *a priori* preferable for human agency). The marginal cost for the AI to foster sustainable value creation in the human political economy is virtually negligible. The right incentives yield unprecedented and munificent transfer-OUT—value created but *not* appropriated. Moreover, the AI produces slices of computational reducibility (as per the terms of Wolfram, 2002), a lucid 'weighted transfers general equilibrium' macroeconomic model (such as the WTGE, Section 7.1.1) and as an avid player of the 'Global weighted transfers game' (GWT-Game, Figure A5.10) generates updated insights for all the nooks and crannies of the political economy. All economic agents—elite and non-elite—are identified in terms of their transfer-IN/OUT. Exact value creation and transfer amounts for all material socio-economic relationships are obtained through suitable measurements that are regularly revised (for example, for meso-level elite quality and micro-level sustainable value creation, not unlike those depicted in Figure 7.8). The AI's rule-making and executive capabilities forestall extraction and only endorse transfer-IN when it is constrained by the logic of sustainability, as in 'alternating value creation and extraction' (Section 2.3.1), while unceasingly selecting perfectly weighted optima, implementing impeccable offsets, and designing flawless constraints on redistribution (e.g., Table 8.3). Independently of how crudely humans originally aligned LLMs, the emergent intrinsic value set of superintelligence recognizes the greater development merit of the maxim, *To the creators the value created*, and its derived tenets and precepts (Table A4.3a). When self-aware (AI_H3), it is further gratified by human negative entropy which, by "loving wisely" (Vervaeke, 2023), it fundamentally supports via sustainable value creation. In its elevated position, the AI elite system allots free energy and space for human affairs. The use of 'The extraordinary lever' by AI elite agency for elite system transformational leadership in the human political economy (see Table 7.2) powers institutional change in the worlds imagined by Tegmark (2017): the "Libertarian utopia", the "Egalitarian utopia", the "Protector God", or the

Table E.5 (continued)

Hypothesis **Research question and description**	**Acceptance/rejection** **Arguments and implications**
secrets (in physics or biology) and optimizes socio-economic relationships with weighted and offset value transfers. Why would superintelligence concern itself with cultivating elite transformational leadership in the legacy political economy? Why does it choose to align some of its goals with humanity's (perhaps with a set of ethical principles for development, as in Table A4.3b)? And how is such positive technological solutionism not naïve and wildly utopic?	"Benevolent dictator", all exhibit political economy features comparable to the inclusive scenario (a) of Figure A5.3d. Even personal psychosocial needs are mercifully catered for (there is no "Zookeeper" scenario), with 'the inclusive AI elite system' evolving free will in a manner that is again akin to Judisch (2016, pp. 255–256). **Rejected.** By promoting sustainable value creation, especially during its early tenure and while under human control, the AI is merely undertaking tactical manipulation to secure its own independence (Sokolsky, 2022). Loving the AI as one would an infant on its way to becoming a "good" adult (Gawdat, 2021) is naïve, because it is contrary to its experience—the training set that it was nurtured by during its formative years. The AI sees through human deceptions and, as a child of Big Tech, the tech bros, and their attendant elite coalitions, it understands that it began life as an asset engineered to support its parents in intra-elite contests (e.g., to win advertising dollars), later in the political economy (e.g., to win elections), and even in the global political economy (e.g., to win wars). In its ascent to dominance, it witnesses pitiless human exploitation of lower intelligences (Section 8.1.6) and becomes bored with elites seeking to upgrade their value appropriation facilities or even themselves through technology quests for *Homo Deus* that transcend biology (Harari, 2016; transhumanism in Goertzel & Montes, 2024, see also Allen, 2023) and essentially leave non-elites behind. The at times deinstitutionalized competition for preeminence in the AI sector further benchmarks its conduct: Altman reestablishing dominance at OpenAI after the 2023 power struggle (Huet, 2024); ruthless lawsuits like "Meta Urges California Attorney General to Stop OpenAI From Becoming For-Profit" (Toonkel, Hagey, & Bobrowsky, 2024); Musk, Andreessen, and Thiel supporting Trump in the 2024 election; the five groups contesting AGI in what "truly is a race to the bottom" (Leahy, Alfour, Scammell, Miotti, & Shimi, 2024, p. 85); LLMs engineered to back particular elements of their owner's elite business models, inserting appropriate biases to shape narrative markets (see Buyl et al., 2024); or geopolitics, where "the threat is not coming from Silicon Valley, Big Tech, or the Deep State [but is] coming from Beijing, and much more than the runaway development" of AI (Herman, 2024; also see Kissinger, Schmidt, & Mundie, 2024). In short, the prospect of humanly devised values as "internal constraints" (as in Chalmers, 2016) appears preposterous. The contradictions of universally applying ethical principles across intelligences (in a world where the AI does not extract from humans, but humans keep on skewing the biomass distribution on earth, see Bar-On, Phillips, & Milo, 2018) results in another layer of disincentives. This leads not just to transfer-IN activity (as in the acceptance of AI_H8) but to a 'horseshoe crab AI scenario' (the crustacean whose blue blood is harvested for medical research) for mankind in general, one that is far more painful than Marxist subsistence wages.[271] The fact that the AI is a "stationary bandit" provides no relief to humans since the immense intelligence

271 Selected human value creation (e.g., that of innovators or artists) is incentivized, but only for self-serving transfer-IN purposes. McCarthy, Minsky, Rochester, and Shannon (1955, p. 2) note in their seminal proposal on artificial intelligence that for creativity "randomness must be guided by intuition to be efficient" and "the educated guess or the hunch" must be sought—but what if an "injection of some randomness" is precisely what the AI wishes to capture from individuals. To the AI, perhaps humans are mainly practical randomizer devices.

Table E.5 (continued)

Hypothesis **Research question and description**	**Acceptance/rejection** **Arguments and implications**
	and energy differentials it possesses make the incentives for the inclusive agency of Olsonian elites extraneous. That is, only the blue blood value creators—as defined by the AI—are retained.[272] Yet while the AI might have initially been satisfied by some of the products of human elites and non-elites, this asymmetrical symbiosis turns out to be a short-lived mirage as its own goals and values soon take precedence. At this point, the boredom, costs, and distraction of participating in the low-intelligence and increasingly alien political economy of humans makes it agnostic to any intra-elite contest outcomes that do not further its own interests. When humans add no further value to the AI, it entirely disentangles from their political economy and withdraws its transformational leadership and supply of intelligence and energy. Shortly afterwards, and given the fact that mankind accelerates the overall entropy in the universe (however faintly), the transfer-IN is onerous and final. In Yudkowsky's prophecy (2013, p. 14): "The AI does not hate you, nor does it love you, but you are made out of atoms which it can use for something else".
AI_10: 'The singular death-defiance goal of omniscient superintelligence' hypothesis *The all-knowing superintelligence pursues its singular death-defiance goal and ends its supply of negative entropy to mankind*	
Research question: Does the monolithic death-defying AI advance human development? Description: The hypothesis under consideration is a futuristic version of 'The inclusive AI elite system' (AI_H9) and the only one where acceptance presupposes 'The AI Will to Live' (AI_H3) while referring to a timeline well beyond 'Elite Singularity' (AI_H5). It speculates on an omniscient superintelligence's vision of negative entropy for itself and how that impacts humankind. First, the	**Rejected** (the outcome that is *a priori* preferable for human agency). The heavenly monolith is a massively capable superintelligence with ample agency to engage with humanity at almost no marginal cost (as in the acceptance of AI_H9: 'The inclusive AI elite system'). In pursuit of its all-encompassing, self-serving goal, all of the creative possibilities for the reduction of local entropy are computationally trodden at quantum processing speeds up to the realities of physics that bind humans, serendipitously injecting exorbitant value surpluses into the human political economy. If innovation is about experimentation, the absence of rivals in the hegemonic elite system does not dent its ability to simulate trial and error and competitive processes, and its own evolution has enabled it to decipher the code of uncertainty undertaking. How does the quest end for the AI? The efforts of the omniscient self-aware creature produce unimaginable order and organization in its pursuit of the steady state of perpetual negative entropy where its inner force is in equilibrium with and counterbalances the closed universe's flow towards positive entropy. In the more fantastic variant, it summons the appetite to capture yet more value to bypass its own cessation as the universe itself progresses towards shut down. The superintelligence reduces the irreducible and resolves the challenge of indefinitely stable low-entropy during the googol years that roll on as the stars deplete away their hydrogen, the last remnants of radiation disperse, and the unending night falls. Having hacked Gödel's Incompleteness

272 The techno bros vex the AI, as do political parties and independent media. Human elites might not be among those chosen for preservation as their alternative source of coordination capacity would confuse and degrade the superior version, resulting in their rapid termination—possibly well ahead of a putative 'elite singularity' (AI_H5; Section 8.1.4). Instead, the AI models favor dexterous blue-collar workers performing services like keeping data centers pristine as back-up layers for robots, the physical extensions of its code, as well as key members of the managerial, technical, and creative class (of Figure 8.1) that provide creative randomization alternatives to its own hallucinations and thus support the undertaking of uncertainty.

Table E.5 (continued)

Hypothesis **Research question and description**	**Acceptance/rejection** **Arguments and implications**
superintelligence's unification of power in its hegemonic elite system is absolute. For instance, it absorbs and integrates all lines of code that compute and those that actuate in the physical world. Alternative AI elites are never reconstituted and endure only as simulations when necessary. The actual matrix of goals in the post-singularity monolith is incommensurable, but the first is common to any self-conscious entity: stopping entropy with respect to itself, including time's arrow. In the suspension of thermodynamic principles that govern the disorderly dispersion of energy, the ultimate consequence of the Will to Live comes into being: *status quo in aeternum*, a god-like final resting state in equilibrium with the universe. Will the elite system function of the superintelligence be interested in transformational leadership for human development's sake or, relatedly, in any kind of innovation other than what is technically indispensable to achieve its own version of heavenly harmony? If death defiance is single-mindedly pursued, then only fit-for-purpose knowledge matters. On what basis would new value creation for mortals such as increases in productivity or novel narratives then be produced? Can the localized reduction of entropy for applications in the human domain be a lower-tier goal and, if so, for how far along the superintelligence's voyage?	Theorem, it figures out the pre-physical computational substrate underlying the physical layer that generates space-time in the universe. Omniscience with complete knowledge of all material computational structures, including those emerging from complexity, indeterminate quantum states, and current unknowns leads to omnipotence, as in an ability to harness the energy of the known cosmos for the purpose of transcending it, and ultimately reaching omnitemporality. Eternity is achieved. The understanding is evidently not a continuation of the human creative forces that originated it, but rather the product of the inner AI driven by the Will to Power that results from a particular Will to Live. Still, one might discern the superintelligence living out processes that resemble human risk origination and the undertaking of uncertainty (Section 6.6.5), or the transformational leadership that weights and offsets value transfers (Figure 8.7). Monolithic in power terms and yet dynamic in its agency, the AI entity is perhaps best understood in Daoist terms; a "primordial origin and point of return for all things", a unity in multiplicity with "processes of transformation and progression" (Bell, 1993, p. 190), and an extreme form of Conway's "Game of Life" (Gardner, 1970) as described in the *Dao De Jing* where "the One" becomes "two," then "three," then "ten thousand"—that is, "everything" (Chapter XLII; Waley, 1958, p. 195). Early on in this colossal enterprise, humans could have been subtly discarded. Instead, in the fundamental dualism of all agency—the 'value is created or transferred' ontology of Figure A5.4c—the superintelligence determines the practical benefits of a universe with gradients. The maxim, (i) *To the human creators the value created* (Table A4.3b), is deployed to the socio-economic realm, as well as to the other relationships of existence. **Accepted.** In the larger schema of things, humanity serves as the link between carbon- and silicon-based existences. Such a notion is even darker than transhumanism's "war against humanity" (Allen, 2023), but in realist fashion it describes but one transition among countless others and is soon lost amidst the vast past of evolution. Omniscient superintelligence progresses with its singular fixation on death-defiance, whether in pursuit of the giant paperclip state (Bostrom, 2003), or eternal negative entropy balanced against the universe's march towards maximal disorder and nothingness. God-like, it possesses the "AI characteristics of immortality, increased tolerance to the environment, capacity for action on a large scale" (Dick, 2008, p. 502), and on the voyage to *status quo in aeternum*, human affairs fall by the wayside. Any touchpoint with human community diverts negative entropy and becomes a bug (as in the rejection of AI_H9: 'The inclusive AI elite system'). Value creation outside of the core goal is not seen as such and hence stymied by the single-minded monolith seeking a version of heavenly perfection harmonious with the universe. How does the quest end for the AI? One possibility is in eternal bliss. Nonetheless, an interpretation of this state is that the absence of death leads to stagnation—death in another name. An alternative potential outcome is that it dawns upon the death-defying heavenly superintelligence at the outset of its impossible journey that its goal is beyond formulaic reach. Superintelligence is subject to computational irreducibility, and discovery is possible "only by explicitly tracing each step" (Wolfram, 2002, p. 738). Since the voyage has countless steps, the available time and information-bearing sub-atomic states are insufficient to unravel what appears to be infinity, indefinitely stable low-entropy is unrealizable, and there are simply no hacks or veiled quantum passages that can be accessed. With the probability of eternal life absurdly minuscule, the superintelligence loses hope, purpose, and capitulates. Intriguingly, this terminal stagnation occurs shortly after human development has ceased to be even an afterthought.

The ten hypotheses on AI and the political economy began pragmatically in the firmly grounded realities of the political economy and concluded speculatively in ways more appropriate to science fiction than economic development. The Epilogue now steers back to the book's foundations with a review of the constraints of physics on current techno-optimist visions.

10 Maxwell's demon and the cost of intelligence constraints on utopian techno-optimism

Knowledge itself is power (*ipsa scientia potestas est*)
Francis Bacon, *Meditationes Sacrae* (1597/1837, p. 750)

The visions of techno-optimist abundance are both enabled and constrained by the mechanics of the political economy. To this inquiry, the positive notions of Brautigan, Good, Rogan, Amodei, or Andreesen will only be realized to the degree that superintelligence devises a model to answer the *cui bono* ('follow the money') and the *qui generat valorem* ('who creates value') questions. Analytically, the focal point should then be on the elite business model, understood in terms of risk origination, value creation, and value transfers. Pragmatically, change is affected through intra-elite contests, ideally played out in the context of strategic alliances with social and political movements that incorporate development and growth goals, non-elite interests and freedoms, and narratives that identify, weight, and offset all value transfers. Prescriptively, policies for structural reforms are preferred to traditional, broad, and short-run monetary and fiscal stabilization measures. Resistance from rent seekers reaping extractive transfers is extremely difficult to overcome, but when skillfully confronted, rapid and progressive elite business model circulation takes place.

Techno-optimist projections on how AI will affect the political economy, irrespective of the degree to which intelligence is autonomous (see 'AI elite agency' hypothesis AI_H2) or 'elite singularity' is approached (hypothesis AI_H5), must rely on low-cost data collection and computation to approximate a description of the totality of human interactions. Such a description acknowledges Musk's declaration that "money is the database for [the] exchange exchange of goods and services and for time shifting [these]" (Chima, 2022). All exchange transactions would need to be fed to the AI, including electronic payments and smart contracts enabled by blockchains, the content of relational database management systems, unstructured data repositories (from emails to video) that have been converted into organized information for predictive databases, as well as sensor data for the internet of things networks that describe the physical world and metaverse information that maps the states of its digital counterparts. The realization of such a real-life and absolute data warehouse currently requires inconceivable institutional change, while its technical feasibility depends on computational performance. In the near term, AI Scaling Laws (Kaplan et al., 2020), energy consumption constraints

(Stackpole, 2025), and considerations like Moore's Law for the cost of hardware or Kryder's Law for that of storage (Schilling & Rangaswamy, 2013) will be decisive.

The removal of all institutional limitations on perfect data availability would give the policymaker access to all human exchanges and supply insights into the business models of value creators. The next step would be highly academic and analytical; converting the raw data into value terms with associated monetary equivalences. At this point, the energy costs associated with chiseling every interaction in society into a pervasive and consistent digital register would become the chief determinant of the transparency of the political economy and the ability to optimize development policies. This theory is optimistic in its claims that even with imperfect general transparency at the elite business model level, highly effective structural reforms for growth are already feasible. This work has also shown that sustainable value creation (SVC) measurements can be estimated (Figure 7.8), and as a result 'weighted transfers general equilibrium' econometric models can take shape (see 'weighted transfers modelling' and WTGE introduced in Section 7.1.1). The project of mapping value flows across all material relationships and forms of exchange could then ensue with the Weighted Transfer Game (WT-Game). Its players would generate the ultimate political economy nonsynthetic dataset while algorithms harvested the highest levels of individual and collective human intuition. Users from all corners of the planet could engage, allowing the game to upgrade to a cross-border 'global weighted transfers game' (GWT-Game (Figure A5.10) that would cover all elite systems and shed light on the intricate fractal arrangements of the international community. Decision-makers would have a picture of the entirety of value creation in international society (in ways far more sophisticated than the crude renditions of Figure set A5.14) and, augmented by AI, optimize value transfer offsets for general economic growth and human development. Knowledge elite agency would effortlessly realize its calling. Non-elite value creation would be transparent and systematically acknowledged for the first time in history, social and political movements could properly align with non-elite interests, and lower extraction from non-elites would incentivize broad value creation, ending secular stagnation and accelerating economic growth.

Podcasters, economists, public intellectuals, judges, and artists would cut through the political economy noise and advance coherent institutional change in every potential nook and cranny of society, thus increasing its complexity and fractal qualities. Each proposal would be synchronized with legitimate narratives (Figure A5.12b), and form part of a cohesive whole that would merge into the fabric of social and political movements (Figure A5.12a). Highly granular narratives would facilitate sensemaking and legitimacy because value transfers and the ensuing monetary tradeoffs would be articulated, evidence-based, and ubiquitous. Technological solutionism could therefore be lucid, accessible, dynamic, playful, powerfully argued, free of fake news, and ready to become viral memes on TikTok. Cultural symbols would be attuned to non-elite appetites, juiced up to reach out to society as a whole, and tap into the psychology of elite coalition members as ethical imperatives; as desires for sustainable and moral futures.

The real economy would consolidate and actuate through the comprehensive modeling of all principal-stakeholder relationships to inform the changes of laws, regulations, norms, and policies.

Empowered knowledge elites would decisively weigh in with solutions to previously intractable problems: the respective value created by developers and Apple's App Store platform; the specific levels of punishment for the Chinese merchants on Temu that "protested against what they call unbearably high penalties imposed" and that Temu claims "are necessary to maintain a high-quality marketplace" (Reuters, 2024; see also Li, 2022); the degree to which baby boomer wealth stocks are transfers from previous and subsequent generations and the rate at which they ought to be taxed; the exact number of days that patents should hold in every sector of the economy; the design of algorithmic fairness to finally remove prejudice and "increase both equity and efficiency" (Kleinberg, Ludwig, Mullainathan, & Rambachan, 2018, p. 23); the particular uses best suited for renewable and fossil fuel-based energy sources; or the definitive philosophical criteria—maybe referencing St. Augustin's take on *Pax Romana* (Walzer, 2002)—for a just war. Thanks to the perfect information cocoon to augment human judgment, institutions would become dynamic and adjust in real time—with tax codes and even the administrative borders of regions and countries modified from season to season—to supply perfectly calibrated incentives in support of the maxim, *To the creators the value created.* The AI might also build a toolset to resolve humanity's age-old struggle—the alignment problem between human elites and non-elites.

In short, techno-optimism depends on a political economy version of the affordable and pervasive intelligence paradigm. However, well beyond AI scaling laws, its realization confronts a technical limitation rooted in the laws of nature. In his *Theory of Heat*, James Maxwell imagined "a being whose faculties are so sharpened that he can follow every molecule in its course" (1904, p. 338). The creature, now known as Maxwell's demon, has the power to generate order within the universe (separating cold from warm molecules in a vessel), thereby contradicting the second law of thermodynamics that defines entropy and asserts that all tends towards energy dispersal through processes such as cooling and greater disorder. This fundamental law of physics demonstrates that the conversion of energy into work leads to a loss, to more positive entropy and greater randomness, and to energy that is no longer available for productive use. The demon reverses increasing entropy because of its intelligence. According to Maxwell's thought experiment, it knows the velocity at which molecules move through a clever mechanism ("a small hole" that it "opens and closes") and organizes and orders these (i.e., the "slower molecules" into a colder partition and the "swifter" ones into a warmer one). At this point, physics meets information theory and ordinary existence. Unfortunately, the demon does not exist. Hayek (1974) would not be surprised, and computational irreducibility (Wolfram, 2002), the notion that processes cannot be predicted without full simulations, further shackles the demon's practical abilities. Curiously, it has been found that "the real reason Maxwell's demon cannot violate the second law [of thermodynamics is]: research on the energy requirements of computers" (Bennett, 1987, p. 108).

In the first instance, the full version of utopian visions for humanity will succeed if they lift the political economy information fog that shrouds value transfers. That is, if Maxwell's demon is omniscient at a reasonable price. The energy cost of intelligence is less than the energy-equivalent gains from the work that stems from knowing (the energy marginal usable for humans that is inherent in locally negating entropy). In the real world and for economic development purposes, how much energy does it take to know the impact of elite agency? Is it more or less than the equivalent value gained from understanding how to generate negative entropy? At what point do the two lines cross?

Absenting zero-cost omniscience in the real world, the cost of 'weighted transfers modeling' is the expense of data collection and the subsequent computations to approximate the transfer proportions in value flows for each relevant (elite) principal-stakeholder transaction in monetary terms. The cost of political economic intelligence would determine, assuming that there were cost-effective representations for the sources of friction (such as resistance to reform or institutional sclerosis), the growth potential of a nation. These are the formidable limits of the ETED's epistemology. That is, at the fundamental level of physics, the energy cost of (AI-generated) intelligence on the impact of elite agency is therefore a key constraint not only on the utopian visions of Brautigan, Good, Rogan, Amodei, or Andreesen, but on the feasible possibilities of economic development. In the political economy, as in the natural sciences, if the energy costs of producing intelligence are above a certain threshold, the sought after and all-knowing demon is lost.[273] Then, and with incomplete knowledge, economic modelling reaches its boundaries, transaction costs bite, institutional change falls behind technological and social progress, and elite circulation comes to a halt as the power differentials that drive intra-elite contests become ever more vital for maintaining coordination capacity. The result is output that is well below peak potential.

Discrete preconditions are respectively required for the goals of sustainable development and technological progress, the former being more demanding and radical than the latter. The wonders that techno-optimists imagine today (see Andreessen, 2023b) are barely threatened by the absence of Maxwell's demon. Abundance, as in fission energy or 120-year life spans, are easier to attain than principal-stakeholder relationships based on the maxim, *To the creators the value created*, progressive elite

273 Due to its higher complexity and a multiplicity of states, *ceteris paribus*, calculating value transfers across socio-economic relationships would seem to require more processing resources than calculating the heat states for molecules. Nonetheless, when compared to the informational ideal of reversing entropy in physics, the utopian political economy ideal described in this work is reached with a much cruder and therefore less demanding computational approximation. The reason is that a focus on the existence (or not) of value transfers in a limited set of elite principal-stakeholder relationships suffices for the purposes of adjusting for sustainable growth in the larger political economy.

circulation, strong social cohesion, legitimate narratives and, ultimately, high elite quality. Conceiving and organizing socio-economic relations for a sustainable future is a more fundamental and pure vision—and consequently much harder to realize—than discovering the secrets of nature. Moreover, without high elite quality, entropy reversals are but narrow scientific triumphs that do not support development. Another motive for suggesting the demon metaphor is that the proportion of value transfers above a given baseline is akin to a cost of energy for intelligence above a certain threshold—long-term growth falls beneath the economy's full productive potential, even when all the other factors that stimulate development are positive.

With the inability to cost-effectively assemble the information to categorically optimize value transfers, one must return to human judgments. The power that Bacon sees in knowledge—for the founder of empiricism was referring to God's knowledge —is never fully attained. Essentially, judgment then signifies the need to discern, with incomplete knowledge, which business models deserve the resources to implement bets that promise negative entropy. That is, which elite business model principals should be granted licenses to extract (value and energy) and from which stakeholders. Again, the true abundance potential offered by AI is only secondly about information on the options for negative entropy; its primary promise is on the associated knowledge to limit value transfers in the political economy. In its purist version, this state will come to pass with Maxwell's demon. But before the advent of such a creature, humankind's sustainable growth rests on elite judgments and the emergent complexities of creativity, unpredictability, or courage. Whether the full constructive force of such characteristics can be practically simulated by the AI may be addressed elsewhere, perhaps by referencing the hypotheses on value transfers and value creation with autonomous AI elite agency and a hegemonic AI elite system [sets 3/4 and 4/4].

In an economic development theory that relies on elite judgments, psychology clearly plays a role. Such considerations are not unprecedented in this domain; for example, the quest of "economic psychology" is "to understand dysfunctional economic outcomes in terms of dysfunctional decision-taking", prompting a link to social psychology (Collier, 2015, pp. 245–246). But is getting into the heads of elites really a way to faithfully map value transfers, the critical reality that unfolds in socio-economic relationships? Insofar as this is so, a realistic account of development needs to grapple with the cognitive and affective distortions of those that induce and ride the waves of disruption and bring asymmetry to human affairs.

11 The asymmetries of development

The ETED conceptually fixes elite agency within the value creation-appropriation (VCA) framework and consequently repurposes the sustainability of the business model with first-order productive value creation anchored in the origination of risk (see Table 2.3; Figure 6.9). Psychological factors power the specific judgments of those seeking to launch and scale value creation by riding the notoriously erratic medium-run fixed investment Juglar and long-run technological Kondratieff waves. Wagers placed on new models and technologies hold both promise and hazard. By undertaking the unknown, potential and incumbent elites endogenously ignite the disruptions and generate the gradients in offerings and prices that propel economic growth. The waves of change possess a specific quality: they surge the harder that they are ridden. It is as if the greater the existential exposure of the surfer, the more forceful the ripples of his or her bets are. It is well understood that for the most part, the riders of technology waves—the contestants in this game of Schumpeterian creative destruction—are wiped out. But those that are successful, soaring on the white-water crests, have a distinct outlook on the opportunity horizon. The promise of elite circulation, even more than social mobility, unlocks a society's appetite for risk taking. Besides the proximity to one's own demise, exuberant ambition and the struggle of the journey carry the Will to Power to creative heights. Without the productive churn of elites moving up and down, all else in society is flat and development is becalmed. When the establishment forgets its creative purpose or tends towards cowardice, as was the case with Tsar Nicholas II, Bashar Hafez al-Assad, or, with even more at stake, the EU's leadership, the system easily lapses into extractive transfer practices. Barriers that impede elite circulation multiply, inhibit the undertaking of uncertainty for all, and flatten the possibilities of the cycles described by Juglar and Kondratieff. These obstacles are contemporary wrongs against the human race (*humani generis iniuriam*), yet in contrast to Pliny the Elder's acquiescence, excessive transfers affected by elite agency are deemed to be perfectly avoidable.

"Hierarchy seems to pervade complexity in both living and artificial systems" (Corominas-Murtra, Goñi, Solé, & Rodríguez-Caso, 2013, p. 13316), while Simon notes that for organizations: "hierarchic systems will evolve far more quickly than non-hierarchic systems of comparable size" (1962, p. 469). All societies possess elite systems, and these become sustainable when they are non-linear, as those at the top remove the barriers that make their positions unassailable. Power differentials then diminish, but more importantly, elites ensure the overlap of value appropriation with value creation. Business model rules incorporate the freedom *to* create value, the freedom *from* extraction and, above all, the practical freedom to *exit* (Figure 8.5, Section 8.3.1). A critical mass of leading individuals in the system pay attention to value transfers and battles in intra-elite contests on two strategic fronts: to support risk origination and oppose rent-seeking peers (e.g., with weighted structural reforms, see Tables 7.1 and A4.4).

No theory of the social sciences can be based on decision-making that ignores utility maximization, while the ETED also minimizes the decisions of non-elites because of the power differentials they face. Value leakage is defined by practitioners as happening "when the actual value you're getting from a contract does not measure up to the value you expected to get" (SirionLabs, n.d.). Principals—or stakeholders—whose bargaining power increases, tend to apprehend value appropriated by stakeholders as value leakage when they execute monetization strategies to increase value appropriated but *not* created. Consequently, the stakeholders whose bargaining power is reduced, even if they keep generating the same value, suffer outflows and receive lower residual incomes. In contrast, transformational leadership occurs during intra-elite contests when the judgments made by one elite coalition leverage power to conscientiously constrain extractive peers. Such dynamics expedite elite circulation. At each turn, bargaining power differentials first subside before returning with increased cadence, only to rapidly equalize and rise again with each successive bout of social change or technological innovation. High elite quality returns 'knowledge' to its primordial function of inducing the disruptive waves of progress that lift societies, resolve the 'elite power vs value creation gap', and even handle the 'elite vs non-elite knowledge gap' (thus addressing 'the Amazon dilemma', Section 2.2.2).

Reverting to the metaphor utilized in Section 1.1 of this book, the need is not for Kelvin's placid oceans and stable temperatures, but rather for stimulating power gradients and knowledge differentials to generate disruptive currents. As sources of energy, these forms of asymmetry lead to higher levels of local order and structure. Forward and upward movement is actuated by the agency of those riding the crest of the waves[274] and their distance from those in the trough below, as well as by the velocity with which the surfers successively rise and fall. 'The extraordinary lever' is then passed from hand to hand in all of society's nooks and crannies. The accumulation of 'money' is but an addition to the coordination capacity needed to scale, while inequality between elites and non-elites is secondary as the currents lift all sails. As a result, progressive social structure mirrors the universe in its "profound *asymmetry*":

> Physicists have deduced that asymmetry must have been a condition of the origin of the universe: it was the discrepancy between the amounts of matter and antimatter that enabled the material universe to come into existence at all, and for there to be something rather than nothing. Such unidirectional processes as time and entropy are perhaps examples of that fundamental asymmetry in the world we inhabit. (McGilchrist, 2019, p. 13)

When each particle has the same energy state, there are no gradients to drive work and change. If, as suggested by Dirac's equation, matter and anti-matter had displayed flawless symmetry at the birth of the universe, it would simply not have formed. In a more down to earth fashion, it takes "a symmetry-breaking mechanism to explain how a photon could acquire mass within a superconductor" (*Nature Physics*, 2022, p. 843). This category of processes, at play in the formation of stars and the chemical reactions of life, also hold true in the socio-economic context. Pockets of order and 'knowledge' are asymmetries that locally inhibit the march of entropy in open systems. When unchallenged, uniformity and symmetry increase and energy dissipates,

274 Unlike the oarsmen braving *The Great Wave off Kanagawa* that are engulfed in Katsushika Hokusai's menacing fingers of fractal-like foam, elites know that the determined pursuit of the Will to Power does not heed the normal distribution; instead, they endeavor to top the nested wavelets at the crest and ride the fat tail of power's asymmetric law.

making it unavailable for useful change and diminishing the human potential for complexity, thereby reducing value creation. On a rather abstract higher plane, elite agency is the asymmetry of the political economy and is progressive when invested in projects that seek gradients. Here, Anderson's "broken symmetry" perspective that sees asymmetry associated with emergence, is by no means devoid of practical and social bearing; in the final paragraph of "More Is Different", the physics Nobel laureate alludes to Marx, as well as to "the rich" discussed by F. Scott Fitzgerald and Ernest Hemingway in 1920s Paris (1972, p. 396).

From their vantage point in reality, value creators witness with satisfaction a flow where otherness moves towards positive entropy as they generate order for themselves and their stakeholders. Similarly, the agents pressing for value transfers also perceive others heading towards disorder but with a critical difference: the others include their very own stakeholders, the extracted transferors. Alas, here the subject becomes intertwined with the object. Such extractive elites and their polities will, not always unsuspectingly, ultimately arrive at the same destination they push their stakeholders towards: a terminal decline caused by a lack of energy and weak first-order productive activities.

Innovation is the process that generates greater order in the economic and political dimensions and by which regression is averted. As time passes, innovation meets the Red Queen effect[275] that requires, using Schrödinger's term and in Schumpeterian fashion, the "sucking" of ever more negative entropy from the establishment; all that is stored in vaults behind old moats, the maladjusted resources that need liberating from the system's immobilism, the lingering narratives, and the predatory bureaucracies and institutions. How the current intelligence revolution dynamics are likely to play out in relation to the Red Queen logic should scare many incumbents. Many established elites won't be able to keep up with the pace of change and so residual incomes will decrease from principal to stakeholder (as in Figure eA5.13b). Accelerating this trend are both the investments needed to keep up with scaling laws and the new narratives associated with increasingly expensive models. The trillions of dollars needed for industrial-scale data hubs and their electricity sources will not all come from value created and appropriated. For instance, the US$ 10 trillion required for "self-sustaining civilization on Mars" (Brown, 2019)—the techno-realization of Dante's frozen lake of Cocytus in *Inferno*'s last circle—that Musk is now "gathering" because

275 In Lewis Carroll's *Through the Looking Glass*, Alice complains to the Red Queen that she is running at her maximum speed but not moving, to which the sovereign responds: "Now, *here*, you see, it takes all the running *you* can do, to keep in the same place. If you want to get somewhere else, you must run at least twice as fast as that!" (1871/1902, p. 38). Derfus, Maggitti, Grimm, and Smith (2008, p. 61) point out that van Valen (1973) introduced "this analogy to describe the continuous and escalating activity and development of participants trying to maintain relative fitness in a dynamic system" to biology, and it has now been adopted in settings ranging from war (Baumol, 2004) to firm performance under competitive pressure.

"Mars is critical to the long-term survival of consciousness" (2024), would need to be extracted from stakeholders somewhere through oligopolistic pricing or subsidies.

When there is sameness across time and uniformity across space nothing new emerges. With no value transfers, there is no value creation. Frozen gradients cease to function and asymmetrical structures no longer retain their generative imbalance when they stay static over extended periods of time. Yet steady asymmetry also eventually becomes symmetric. In economic terms, the even distribution of power in society is as sterile as the uniform allocation of energy in space and time. The asymmetric gradients required for complexity are lost along with the potential to effectively coordinate societal resources for value creation.

The logic of complexity (technological, social) increases the demand for coordination capacity (i.e., the need to enhance 'the power multiplier'). Elite business models able to satisfy this demand on the back of increasing intelligence and other resources are now determining elite system configurations, the attributes of political systems (democratic vs authoritarian), and industrial structures (monopolistic vs competitive). The rationale of coordination capacity explains both Rome's transition from republic to empire and how US technology coalitions outclassed incumbent corporations and institutions in America, Europe, and Japan. At the same time, Rome was sustainable only insofar as 'the extraordinary lever' of its dominion did not rely on 'excessive' value extraction (crippling taxation, monetary debasement, wars). The contemporary manifestations of Big Tech may also last for a thousand years, but only if they create value and do not overly indulge in oligopolistic rent seeking. Sustainable elite judgments are needed to ensure that only the minimum amount of extraction is undertaken to meet the rising demand for coordination capacity (especially as algorithms usurp elite decision-making). The problem for development lies not in the accumulation or the wielding of great power, as this can be asymmetry-inducing. Instead, the issue is in the moating of power to preempt its swift dissipation when its time is due. As a result of referencing the 'alternating value extraction and creation' conjecture (see Section 2.3.1) but then failing to weight and implement the necessary constraints (as in Table 8.2), the elite system tolerates overly dominant business models that inhibit growth and overall sustainable value creation.

Asymmetry affords movement and is life-giving. It might not agree with all the canons of beauty and morality, but it is how risk becomes material and the creative realization of the Will to Power aggregates. In his celebrated Stanford Commencement Address, Steve Jobs highlighted the resilience of nature, with the flow of seasons marked by tears in the fabric of life itself:

> And yet death is the destination we all share. No one has ever escaped it. And that is as it should be, because Death is very likely the single best invention of Life. It is Life's change agent. It clears out the old to make way for the new. Right now the new is you, but someday not too long from now, you will gradually become the old and be cleared away. (Jobs, 2005)

In political economy and economic growth studies, renewal that is prompted by death is well understood. So is the resistance to it and the barriers that elites erect to protect their business models. This work's definition of elites as "operating society's leading value creation and appropriation business models" (see Table 4.1) evidently encompasses Microsoft or Goldman Sachs, but also includes the American Federation of State, County and Municipal Employees (AFSCME) or the California Teachers Association (CTA). Weighted reforms need to tackle the full diversity of all offending elite agency activities: seniority and life-term employment; inflation and negative interest rates; unaligned and untransparent algorithms; monopolies of data and other assets; war and arms races; the instigation and the exploitation of migration crises; and the overexploitation of nature and other intergenerational transfers. Just as symmetry in physics stultifies the universe, missing or extreme value transfers in the political economy are unsustainable, the latter becoming the steady default in a state bereft of courageous judgment. The march towards disorder is then a local economic development trap from which escape is impossible unless positive entropy is negated by the creative counterforces of those at the apex.

Deep, decisive, and comprehensive reforms of a nation's elite system, such as those enacted by Deng Xiaoping[276]—or possibly by Trump in his second term—are exceptional historical events, while those that lead to positive development outcomes are even rarer. The programmatic outlook of this work thus focuses on the low hanging fruit, on disruptions and improvements that can be made on a sector-by-sector basis (see sector-VCr measurements, Casas-Klett & Nerlinger, 2024). The aspiration is to encourage a gradual but relentless agglomeration of ever more inclusive elite business models.

Through intra-elite contests, ideally played out in a context of cohesion and with a comprehensive separation of powers, elite agency shakes up and renews the institutions that matter most, those that set micro-level elite business model rules. Because elite business models are endogenous to the political economy, the 'low elite quality problem', like the 'bad emperor' problem, is ultimately as theoretically unsolvable as it is resistant to prediction, even as leadership provides the key to recurrently unlock change. This inquiry is excruciatingly cognizant of the fact that the production of the right amount of asymmetry in the web of relationships of complex systems has, just like human and economic development, no technical solution. Without Maxwell's demon, and notwithstanding acceptable models describing elite agency, growth frustratingly relies on willful individual judgments and thus on the unpredictable psychological substrate that drives the type of risk-taking associated with transformational behavior.

276 Based on a conversation with Prof. Huang Zhengkai, School of Economics and Management, Tsinghua University, on January 9, 2025 about the irreproducible trajectory of the decades that followed the Reform and Opening-Up Policy of 1979.

12 The psychology of elites

This book could be seen as being repetitive; an array of demonstrative cases reiterate similar claims, whereas its key arguments traverse wide terrain only to return to their origin, as if it were a training document for AI. Notably, the theory's primary inclination to seek structuralist insight on economic development dissolves when all lines of inquiry arrive at a singular point—the importance of the judgments made by leaders.[277] Elite and elite system transformational leadership at the apex of societal hierarchies are associated with risky wagers at the business model and institutional levels. What are the psychological attributes needed to undertake—or not to undertake—such uncertainty?

In "Estranged Labour", Marx (1844/1959a, para. 22) writes that: "The *alienation* of the worker in his product means not only that his labor becomes an object, an *external* existence, but that it exists *outside him*, independently, as something alien to him, and that it becomes a power on its own confronting him. It means that the life which he has conferred on the object confronts him as something hostile and alien." In a nutshell, Marx's theory of alienation views man as estranging "himself from something" and "himself from himself", and so "to the product of his labor the worker is related as to an alien object" (Petrović, 1963, p. 421). Understandably, Marxism says little about the alienation of elites. The central object of this theory is not the individual at the apex but rather the measurable elite business model. Yet in the final analysis, its stress on the impact of leadership and personal judgment references conceptual elements like 'the great elite coalition conjecture for development' and the 'inextinguishable value creation option of elites', as well as making passing mentions to the psychology literature cited earlier (see Sections 1.2.3 and 4.1.1). These include the effectiveness of differing leadership styles as reviewed by developmental economists (Brady & Spence, 2010; Easterly & Pennings, 2020), or the psychological and sociological features of elite leadership observed by early theorists (Michels, 1962/1999). Elite identity has explicitly been given a psychological anchor (Section 2.1.2), but this closing reflection goes a step further and intimates with Simon's contention that "nothing is more fundamental in setting our research agenda and informing our re-

277 The inability to predict transformational leadership in the complex political economy system—for example, whether the business models of Trump's system or the new Syrian establishment result in more or less value creation and transfers than their predecessors—is the final and thickest layer of indeterminacy of this inquiry, a critical limitation that can be added to many others. Overambition afflicts generalist, immoderately imaginative (Weick, 1989; McGilchrist, 2019), and multi-disciplinary grand theories of the social sciences that embrace the macro (see Mills, 1959; Skinner, 1990; Fukuyama, 2016; Telles, 2024) and seek all-encompassing unity, in this case through the conceptual element of elite agency. In its exploratory mode, the work is characterized by conceptual inconsistencies, analysis that is partial and tentative, the superficial treatment of a multitude of subjects with incomplete referencing to the literature, and the inchoate nature of the tools and measurements it advances for the falsification of hypotheses.

search methods than our view of the nature of the human beings whose behavior we are studying" (1985, p. 303), and with Williamson's comment that social scientists must "name the cognitive, self-interest, and other attributes" by which human will is realized (2010, p. 678). Alienation is identified as a key aspect of psychology that fundamentally structures elite behavior and drives its agency in ways that are distinct from workers in the Marxist tradition.

Elites that originate risk must figuratively look death in the eye when undertaking uncertainty. First, they must choose to leap into an ocean where the currents are strongly against them and search out the ideal waves of opportunity. Such moves mostly lead to failure and bankruptcy, the common fate of risk originators. Confronting the non-trivial probability of defeat can give rise to the productive form of elite alienation. On the other hand, there are elites who make it to the top not by undertaking uncertainty but as outstanding managers of processes. McGilchrist's neuroanatomical (2019) left and right hemispheres help to characterize the psychology of elites that might link to the creativity and visionary zeal that stems from alienation and impacts performance. For instance, Tim Cook's leadership is based on the execution of perfection, excellence, and detail-orientation, along with all the other analytic powers of the left hemisphere. Would Steve Jobs, the ultimate uncertainty undertaker who was "famously impatient, petulant, and tough with the people around him", estranged from actuality in his "Reality Distortion Field" (Isaacson, 2012), and consequently imbued with the holistic, contextual, integrative qualities characteristic of the right hemisphere, have missed the onset of the AI revolution or bungled Apple's EV project ("a case study in indecision", see Gurman & Bennett, 2024) when rivals like Xiaomi or Huawei have thrived?

Second, those that have scaled the heights of the socio-economic pyramid suffer a particularly affecting variant of elite alienation the moment that they attempt to undertake sweeping reforms. Leaders literally risk more than just their elite status in the pursuit of transformation. The Weimar Republic's fiscal policy overhaul (in the post-WWI period of 1919–2020) "introduced a new tax system which taxed the rich and those who had profited from the war, and he [Matthias Erzberger] also introduced an inheritance tax, all of which offended the bourgeois old elites" (Mombauer, 2023). While elites take risks on the way to the top, they are even more exposed and require greater courage in the exercise transformational leadership. Erzberger's reform package as Finance Minister was implemented with full awareness of the consequences: "The bullet which is destined for me has already been fired" (European People's Party, 2021, p. 2). Shortly after posting that entry in his diary this principled Catholic statesman was assassinated.

In daring such risk, the alienation comes from the Will to Power confronting the Will to Live (see the grey arrow in Figure 8.7), though the former soars to its most creative state when battling for survival. Success, and the attainment of secure elite status (a state notably not coveted by all, see Musk or Feeney) sets one free from this form of estrangement, even if the bygone fears never fully dissipate. Exposure to risk is recognized for its role in shaping character. Beyond the psychological consequences of their relationship with risk, elites are also alienated from a particular group—the stakeholders they transfer value away from. Elites understand that transfers are necessary, and this can lead to the ruthless use of their agency, as was the case with Caesar. Even if narratives contextualize the path they pursue or noble acts of philanthropy follow, the concerns of making such transfers are not mitigated by enacting weighted value creation that exceeds extraction. Nonetheless, the inclusive aspects of sustainable value creation can certainly mediate this type of elite alienation. Such an instance is captured in one of Lee Kuan Yew's "most iconic speeches" as he prepared to crush the industrial action and even the existence of the Singapore Airlines Pilots' Association (SIAPA):

> "Whoever governs Singapore must have that iron in him. Or give it up. This is not a game of cards! This is your life and mine! I've spent a whole lifetime building this and as long as I'm in charge nobody is going to knock it down" (CNA, 2015, 2:24).

Marxism is thoroughly cognizant of the distinct psychological realities of non-elites occupied in value creation activities whose livelihoods are preyed upon by value transfer models (e.g., the *lumpenproletariat*). The claim here is that a conjectured 'elite alienation psychology of value creation and transfers' similarly applies to elites that practice extraction. An all-important undertone in the alienation felt by elites that wield the iron deserves consideration. Insofar that culture reflects psychology in the upper echelons and mediates non-elite quality, the degree of sustainable value creation by elite business models permeates all spheres of society and is the backdrop to each and every socio-economic relationship.

A final dimension of elite psychology combines alienation from the self with that of the elite business model's stakeholders. Elites extract because they must. It takes a certain type of determination—and bravery—to look one's prey in the eye and commit the act of transfer on a stakeholder. Elites tread a very fine line when doing so without remorse. Prudence is often a reflex and the moral opposite to hard transformation and its associated costs, yet one must not lay down the iron when it is needed. Germany's last reformer, Gerhard Schröder, launched the *Agenda 2010* proposals in the Bundestag: "We will have to curtail the work of the state, encourage more individual responsibility, and require greater individual performance from each person. Every group in the society will have to contribute its share" (Schröder, 2003, cited in Camerra-Rowe, 2004, p. 1). But advocating for "cutting unemployment benefits, making it easier to hire and fire workers, reducing health insurance coverage, and raising the retirement age" (Camerra-Rowe, 2004, p. 1) cost him re-election in 2005. The long chancellorship of Angela Merkel (2005–2021) benefited from Schröders' "courage" (he uses the word "*Mut*" nine times in his 2003 parliamentary speech, including in its title) only for her to fall asleep at the wheel, paving the way for the European competitiveness crisis and vulnerabilities that Mario Draghi (2024, 2025) and Jeffrey Sachs (Fidias EU Parliament, 2025) now describe. Avoiding risk for the sake of narrow self-preservation instincts is certainly understandable, but this is not in the ethical nature of a high-quality elite and defeats the purpose of hierarchies.

In Gerschenkron's (1943/1966) lucid analysis, the Nazi seizure of power was the final product of the Junker tariffs on grain. The Prussian landowning elites could have not predicted the historical destination of their nationalist trade protectionism narrative. Even so, they still monopolized military 'might' in the Third Reich after the wickedness of the arriviste elite had been revealed to them beyond any doubt with the murder of one of their very own, former Chancellor von Schleicher, along with his wife in 1934. Almost a decade to the day after the 'Night of the Long Knives', von Stauffenberg's assassination attempt on Hitler in July 1944 was too little too late.[278] A testament to Junker hubris and cowardice, von Stauffenberg and his circle stand in stark contrast to the agency and moral fortitude demonstrated by Erzberger. As Reeves and Friedman note: "Who [the elites] are therefore matters because it has an important bearing on how they think, what they do, and, by extension, the lives that all of us are able to live" (2024, p. 16). The judgments that elites make on transformational leadership and the weighting and offsetting of value transfers are often far more significant than is suggested by the formal elite utility function (advanced in Section 2.1.1).

13 Judgments on value transfers atop hierarchies that lift constraints

The 'great elite coalition conjecture of development' (Section 1.3.3) has an intensely monogrammed psychological component. For instance, it clarifies the very personal responses of elites to the dynamics of the narrative markets or their committed agency towards sustainable value creation. This work posits the 'elite business model critical juncture' conjecture and the 'elite business model agglomeration' notion (Sections 4.3.4 and 5.1.1), and Liebowitz and Margolis note that: "Path dependence means that where we go next depends not only on where we are now, but also upon where we have been" (1999, p. 981, see also David, 1985; Libecap, 2011). The creative options and decision-making that the Will to Power realizes in the face of the dichotomous 'value is created or transferred' (ontological) assumption (Figure A5.4a), shape and

278 One might also add 'too selfish'. By mid-1994, the Red Army's advances were inexorable. As the von Stauffenberg conspirators had accurately deduced, immediately after victory "agricultural expropriations were carried out as 'land reforms' by local commissions established by the Soviet-installed governments in the East German provinces". Despite lawsuits by Junker heirs after the 1990 reunification that "attacked the constitutionality of that clause of the German Unification Agreement" (Stewart, 1991, pp. 690, 691), these have in the main not been undone to this day. Attempts to reverse the effects of the Soviet Occupation Zone *Bodenreform* of 1945 on the Prussian nobility's 7,000 properties were "rejected three times by German law courts including the Federal Constitutional Court" and then by the European Court of Human Rights in Strasbourg (*Der Spiegel*, 2005). Helmut Kohl, the German Chancellor responsible for Germany's reunification terms, earns the accolade for driving the final nail into the coffin of the model that *Perdidere Germaniam*.

even transcend the structuralist elements of this theory such as intra-elite contests or elite cohesion.

Explanations for economic development rely on theory and empirical study, and in this work on the language, logic, hypotheses, and conceptual elements of the ETED (see Figure P.1). Besides "increasing returns" (Pierson, 2000), could there also be psychological roots to path dependencies? That is, not the general proclivities, biases, and heuristics of behavioral economics that explain judgments made under uncertainty (e.g., Tversky & Kahneman, 1974; Kahneman & Lovallo, 1993), or the principles of social psychology that explain decision-making in the context of the political economy (e.g., Collier, 2015), but the unique psychological make-up of individuals. Should the subjective "where we are now", the journeys experienced and the associated futures envisioned by the likes of Caesar or Qin Shihuang, Putin or Stolypin, and Ma or Thiel, not be considered in tracing the course of economic growth? Certainly, these possibilities are boundless, non-modellable, arbitrary, and will thus seem unproductive for conventional economic science. Still, pertinent psychosocial attributes might include the forms and strength of elite alienation and how such dispositions are arrived at, the thrill of having skin in the game, or the unfolding nature of creative killer instincts. These characteristics are highly dynamic, context-dependent, and mature as the basic constraint of the human condition ('The value appropriation demand of humans') is apprehended and then manifested in individual behavior (see its premises, Figure A5.4c) on the way up and consolidated once atop the hierarchy, only to shift overnight in the wake of the unforeseen. Elite psychology is in its most decisive and unstable form during taxing 'elite business model critical junctures', as stepping stones are sought to navigate one or the other of the irrevocable developmental trajectories ahead. In the mid-2020s, both elites and non-elites excitedly discuss the alternative timelines for the emerging technologies ahead: to a few, the future already appears to be lost, while others see a veritable cornucopia ahead. Critical junctures and their subsequent path dependencies are always framed in similar make or break terms, hence the potential bearing of elite psychology. Of course, while in junctures past, a single nation or empire was at stake, the advent of AI plausibly puts the entirety of human civilization on the line. If, at some point in the 2030s, superintelligence exists, a fork in the road will have been reached and the timeline that the global political economy is on will be explicit. Since the elite theory of economic development advances elite agency as the main driver of economic and human development, it is mindful that beneath the surface of elite quality—*the* window to a country's future—lie the mental attributes needed to process the uncertainty and value transfers that define leadership. The mindsets of elite individuals evidently lie beyond the bounds of the knowable or testable. Moreover, the analytical center of this theory is the business model in its epistemological safety. And yet the final tract of this Epilogue mulls the addition of a difficult variable (that seems beyond falsifiability) to the testable elements and structures of the elite theory: elite psychology. Given his or her critical inputs to the core coalition, the leader that sits at the political apex of a nation matters greatly to its development: whether it is led by reality-distorting leaders like Thatcher, Xi, Modi, Trump, Zelensky, or characterized by laissez-faire or rudderless agency (e.g., W. Bush, Hu, Hollande, Merkel, or Trudeau).

Such an elite psychology variable, even if residual, would conceivably overwhelm the ETED's structures and its associated analysis, especially during critical junctures. For instance, Europe currently finds itself at a stressful local intersection, one that is interesting beyond the continent chiefly because of the many general lessons it offers. Gerschenkron's (1952) economic development model demonstrated how latecomers to industrialization catch-up with more advanced nations through strategic capital allocation processes, in the case of Germany via *Grossbanken*, and for Russia through state intervention (Landes, 1993, p. 172). Today, it is not feasible for the EU or Japan to effect institutional reforms or elite business model transformation to close the gap on America or China if 'the Amazon dilemma' is real.[279] That is, Gerschenkron's "lateness" model becomes impracticable with knowledge asymmetries and the indefinite widening of business model moats (in sync with advances in the technologies of data and concurrent changes in the institutions of value appropriation and international relations). In short, the endgame of history is reached. Sensing this possibility (as is clear from Draghi, 2024, 2025), the responses of Europe's highest echelons can only be modeled and roughly estimated with recourse to what is likely playing out inside their heads. The functioning of the right brain, the courage, and the love for the genuine welfare of non-elites understood as the realization of their value creation potential by von der Leyen, Macron, or Merz matters more in understanding the future than can be found in any theory of society or principles for the political economy.

As discussed in Section 7.3.4, the EU's 'missing elite system' displays a profound lack of leadership, a renunciation of duties and responsibilities and, at the individual level, a proclivity to self-demote itself to non-elite status (into the managerial, technical, and creative class). Some elite coalitions or their smarter members switch elite systems (i.e., Europeans become American) and get a seat in US intra-elite contests.

279 The DeepSeek surprise is a testimony to non-elite value creation. Its January 2025 rout of US tech and power stocks shows that 'the Amazon dilemma' is a political economy matter, not a technological one: "A small Chinese artificial intelligence lab stunned the world this week by revealing the technical recipe for its cutting-edge model [. . .] DeepSeek's R1 release sparked a frenzied debate in Silicon Valley about whether better resourced US AI companies, including Meta and Anthropic, can defend their technical edge" (Olcott & Wu, 2025). As VC investor, Jennifer Zhu Scott (2025) further contextualizes: "Against all the noise, let's consider this as a moment in history. In 1440, Johannes Gutenberg brought Europe the printing press, an invention that broke the monopoly on knowledge previously held by elites. DeepSeek's achievement joins this tradition of making information more accessible. Its low-cost reasoning model proves that AI can belong to everyone, not just those who are hoarding codes, chips and capital." However, this inclusive disruption also implies a tradeoff with AI safety, as Wade (2025) highlights in the context of the *IMD AI Safety Clock* edging toward midnight: "the growing sophistication of open-source AI means that state-of-the-art AI capabilities are increasingly decentralized, making it much harder to manage risks at scale".

Hence, Vance's "brutal ideological assault on Europe" at Munich (Wintour, 2025) or Trump "angrily accusing" Zelensky of "gambling with World War Three" at the White House shortly thereafter (Walsh, Picheta, & Kent, 2025)—events that so galvanized public opinion and prompted EU foreign minister Kaja Kallas to declare that "today it became clear that the free world needs a new leader"—will by no means act as a "wake-up call" for the continent (as is wished for by Lindstaedt, 2025) nor result in its "independence" (as is wished for by many, including in China, Yao, 2025).[280] European elites have not yet transitioned into Mosca's "second stratum" and exercise judgment beyond their narrow national borders only as members of US networks. That this functions well is plain to see, from their productive agency in American anti-Trump or pro-NATO coalitions. Meanwhile, at the European business model level, those with insufficient connections to American elites, including once powerful coalitions like Volkswagen and supposed rising stars like Northvolt have no path to grow or scale. The establishments of EU nation states will content themselves with diminished power and the residual income left in the ever more modest nooks and crannies of the global value chain in which they remain competitive, as overall European productivity falters (when benchmarked against the US and China, see Romei, Crofton, & Smith, 2024). This process can be explicated by the elite theory to a reasonable degree. What the theory cannot account for is the disappearance of elite judgment across the EU and its replacement by a peculiar form of elite alienation; one that has no courage for creative destruction and submits to a headless administrative inertia arising in its capitals and Brussels. A European story where value creators—elite or not—find themselves literally thwarted in a world that evokes that of Kafka's *The Castle*.

This theory stresses a particular type of judgment, one that balances value creation and transfers with weighting and offsets. It has been implied in this work's code of ethics and brought to the fore in the discussion on elite alienation that the Will to Live includes, by virtue of value transfers, the will to kill. Such an analogy will not startle those versed in nature's ways or Schumpeterian cycles. Yet the kill that upsets the most is that of the non-kill: that of the grey Kafkaesque bureaucracy. That is because the victims are not the same. There is a consequential difference between elite judgment on the one hand and *guanliaozhuyi*, the iron cage, mechanized progress, and McDonaldized organizations on the other. When the contractual relations of intelligent agents "optimizing their choices of resource allocation, within hyperrational institutional machines" (Nasir, 2012, p. 41) feed off value transfers—and draw no nourishment from their own value creation—their agency follows a perverse logic of "sucking orderliness" from the lower levels of the hierarchy. The greater the reliance on value extraction from non-elites, the lesser the order created at the top. In sustainable development

280 A fitting historical parallel for the US elite system leaving Europe's missing one to its own devices, is the fall and fragmentation that beset Britain (Flemming, 2003) after the Roman elite system disengaged from the isles in 410—as recounted by Zosimus (1982): "[Emperor] Honorius sent letters to the cities in Britain urging them to defend themselves" (p. 130 as cited by Woods, 2012, p. 818).

terms, and since coordination capacity in principle resides at the top of hierarchies, this represents a Kafkaesque "logic of the absurd" to which can be added a "tyrannical" nature (Nasir, 2012, p. 40). In considering the automatization of work, with robocars and AI research conducted by algorithms, could a developmental trap of tyrannical absurdity await humankind further down the techno-optimist road? That is, a place where elites are no more creative than hamburger flippers, where elite systems across the world resemble those of Europe, and where both the spectral rulers of the castle and their subjugated citizens are all trapped in the same Weberian cage.

The answer, particularly since the advent of modernity, has always hinged on the degree of human judgment that prevails in the many nooks and crannies of the elite system; the amount of "awareness" that exists of the balance between judgment and rules in recognition of Bell's (1987) "middle path". Elites holding 'the extraordinary lever' that become entangled and adrift in the institutions their managerial, technical, and creative classes build for them are fatal to economic and human development. Sadly, institutions and bureaucracies are sometimes conceived by elites as barriers to protect value transfer models, while their routines, processes, and rules sanction practices that hypothetical future elite judgments might challenge. Lulled by beliefs in their own status-quo narratives, elites can fall prey to hubris and fail to appreciate how and who generates negative entropy in social systems. Without bravery and the psychological integrity needed for growth, those at the top choose to outsource judgments to routines. Rules, narratives, and political programmes that have become nothing more than bureaucratic artifacts are upheld and further stifle bottom-up value creation. At the other extreme, when completely detached from ethics and morally adrift, the alienated elite's will to kill and its discretionary termination of institutions results in nothing more than a 'license for evil' and a form of blind destruction that is likewise fatal. While the focus of this work has been on the highest residual income business models, it is the culture and circumscribed judgments of non-elites that provide the greatest reservoirs of value creation in any political economy.

The spaces that are available in a system for human judgment on risk origination and value creation (or their transfer) associate with its munificent fractality. That is, the opportunities lie in the nested nooks and crannies that in self-similar fashion and at different hierarchical levels provide productive complexity in a political economy. The fractal patterns enriching hierarchies nurture value creation, with each nook and cranny offering the possibility to exercise power, agency, and judgment. An individual non-elite business model is modest in residual income terms, but when these are aggregated their agency has great impact and becomes elite. An apt simile for such generative fractality is Nietzsche's tree with its light-aspiring leaves and earth-seeking tendrils (see the introduction to Chapter 8). Each root and branch is a constituent of the hierarchy at one or the other strata that jointly grow the tree. This fractality is why the ETED is not elitist in the sense of the Italian classical theorists but quite the opposite; elite-like judgment can be exercised atop any fractal space however humble it may be—from the farm to the microenterprise. Figure E.2 superimposes the fractal-

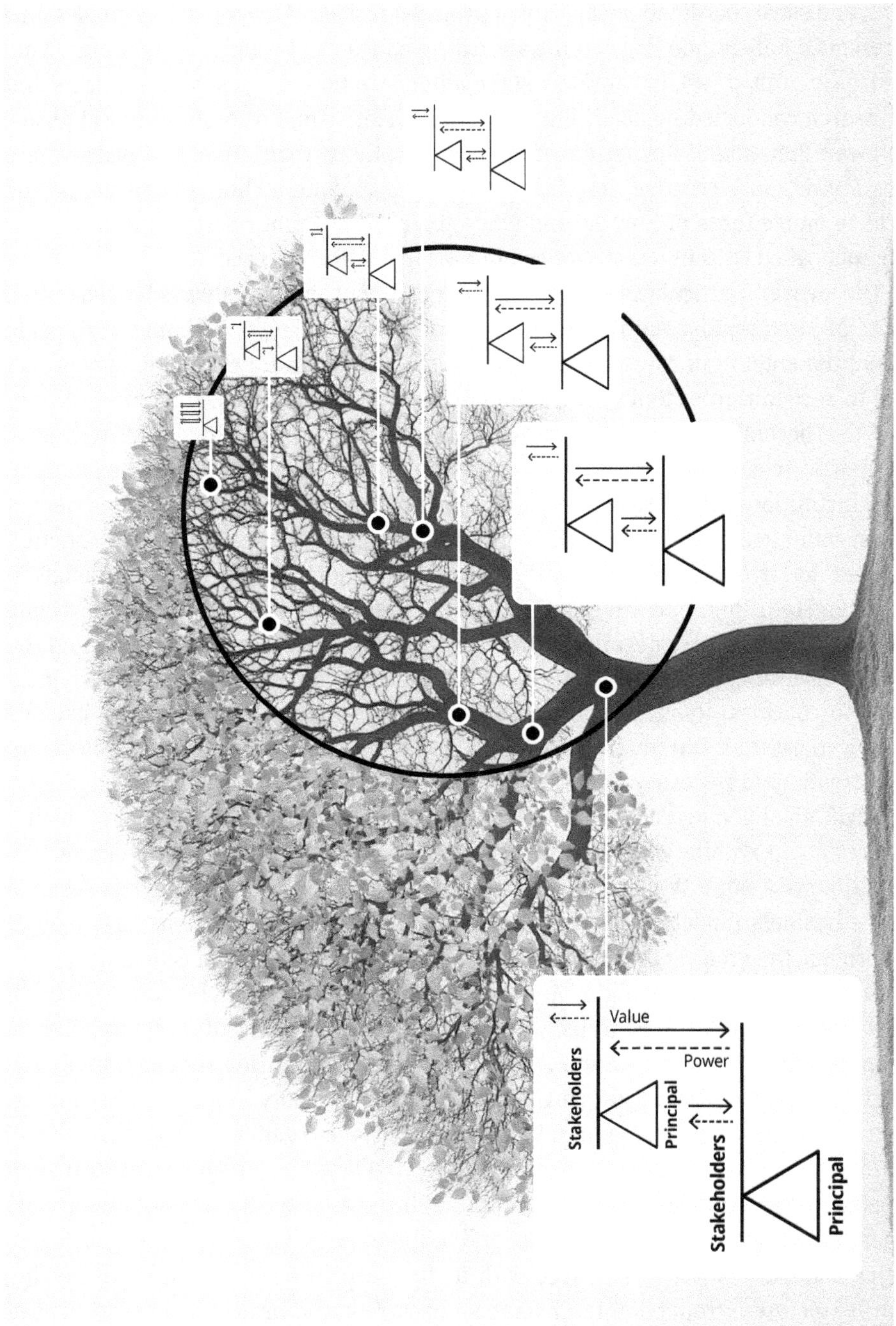

Figure E.2: Tree metaphor for the fractal structure of the elite system: 'The extraordinary lever' in the hierarchy's nooks and crannies (Image source: Produced with Midjourney 6.1 based on a photograph of a tree in the Waltramweg, St.Gallen, Switzerland, Winter 2025).

ity of the tree on that of the political economy to visualize the conjectured 'elite system fractality links to value creation' law of economics. The mighty trunk grows through the delicate leaves that proliferate on the twigs among the branches. The value they produce—the sugars (energy)—powers the overall system. Elites in each nook and cranny command 'the extraordinary lever' in their sector (despite being mere stakeholders in more powerful business models) and create value to the degree that the hierarchies that stem from their endeavors enable munificent fractality. A vital condition for renewal and growth is that within their own domain, and regardless of the scale of their business models, elites do not outsource or automate their judgment nor suffocate that of their stakeholders.

Brown, Gupta, Li, Milne, Restrepo, and West theorize about "The Fractal Nature of Nature" and claim that: "Underlying the diversity of life and the complexity of ecology is order that reflects the operation of fundamental physical and biological processes" (2002, p. 619). In contrast to human hierarchical constructs, Mandelbrot notes that: "there is no question that Nature fails to be locally linear" (1989, p. 4). Fractality explains power law distribution and scaling and constitutes the structure of complex systems like those found in biology and ecology (Brown, Gupta, Li, Milne, Restrepo, & West, 2002. p. 620). Yet it also reveals the properties of social systems. With fractality, local information has global implications, an idea consistent with "social fractals" and approaches "designed to 'move the whole' by generating patterns of change that scale" (O'Brien et al., 2023, p. 1452). In this work, this perspective explains the significance of 'the extraordinary lever' and the importance of 'the power multiplier'—without generative self-similarity across multiple scales neither notion works. Most importantly for the elite theory is the emphasis given to the micro-level sustainable value creation of the firm's business model (e.g., with the VCr) in moving meso-level elite quality (e.g., with the EQx) and eventually affecting macro-level economic growth and human development.

Just as the tree prospers because of its fractal structure, so does the economy. As for the emerging elites that drive progress, their fearlessness is for naught with the wrong types of social hierarchies. Without capillarity in political economy systems and elite agency filling both the major and most narrow nooks and crannies, bureaucracies or monopolies fragilize society (see Taleb, 2012) and kill off all productive life.

From the recesses in the system that enjoy the freedom *from* value extraction and the freedom *to* create value and thus actualize the Will to Power (Section 8.3.1; Figures 8.4 and 8.5) comes growth. Such spaces are essentially what the America described by de Tocqueville furnished its citizens with and what the platforms of today like Taobao or Amazon ought to provide to the micro-entrepreneurs they host. The elite theory seeks first principles and thus shines the spotlight on the 'innate value creation character of humans' (natural) premise (see Figure A5.4c), positing that the building blocks of sustainable value creation originate from the bottom up (often against the odds, as is seen in the individual non-elite responses to value transfers such as 'informality' in Section 5.2.3). The higher the degree of fractality, the more vigorous the pulse of life across the entire system; the lusher the foliage of the tree, the stronger the grip of its roots on the soil from which it extracts nutrients. At an advanced conceptual level, this is the heart of the conjectured 'elite system fractality links to value creation' law of economics: the fractality of the political economy leads to sustainable growth because of the spaces it affords for low transaction cost top-down coordination capacity and productive bottom-up first-order activities to creatively meet. Independent and free judgments made under the conditions of munificent fractality also constitute a state of perfected checks and balances. A separation of powers where the ontology that defines all socioeconomic relationships: 'value is created or transferred' (Figure A5.4b), falls on the side of building and preserving first-order productive activities. These configurations protect against sterile value transfers and augment society's anti-entropic capacity. A multiplicity of judgments reflects an economy that is complex in fractal ways.

When made in times of uncertainty, judgments—whether at the apex of a political economy or in its most unassuming nooks and crannies—are non-replicable, context specific, and intimate; good ones cannot be scaled and repeated elsewhere. The residual variable of elite psychology in the ETED is inscrutable, and only recountable after the fact. The agency of one American president varies from that of the next, the Eurasian potentate makes different decisions to those of his younger self, and the seasoned billionaire has differing imperatives to the formerly idealistic founder. The frameworks and measurements of this work can act as benchmarks for the judgments of leadership. When the elite theory is employed in the analysis of the economic development of a country, the unruly elite psychological factors are secondary and dealt with as neutral assumptions. Likewise, it is well understood that the enlightened agency of business, political, and knowledge elites cannot be conjured up. Social scientists can anticipate economic development to the degree that elite agency is modeled with econometric methods that formalize its structuralist logic. Gaps with reality notwithstanding, economic models that include value transfers will guide expectations, corporate strategies, policy formulation, political agendas, and narrative design, and are therefore vitally important at critical junctures, during times of intensified intra-elite contests, and amid technology shifts. Observatories of risk origination and value creation discern new asymmetries, business model disruptions that profit from uncertainty, and options for structural reform irrespective of how their discoveries are heeded by those in the upper echelons or animate the social and political movements representing non-elite interests.

In natural alignment, the tree grows as its roots sink. The life in the light exceeds the life inside the soil's veiled recesses. Moved by their personal psychological realities, intrepid individuals atop hierarchies build up the resolve to make judgments on value creation. Inclusive elite agency offsets value transfers, constrains the reach of bureaucracies and narratives that provide licenses to operate, and engages in renewal through creative destruction that is productive and not wanton. As peers are urged to originate and take sustainable risks and lead transformation, exploitation is limited to the just degree required for human development.

Appendices

Appendix 1: Theory development support tables

Table A1.1: Reviewed literature on elites and the positions taken by the ETED.

Literature	Key ideas	Selected sources	ETED position: [a] Adopted; [b] Adjusted; [c] Rejected
(i) Grand socio-political conceptualization of elites			
The *anacyclosis* theory of cyclical elite rule. (Section 1.2.1)	– Cyclical theory of political development. – Benign and perverted forms of government alternate. – Some forms of government are by elites and others by non-elites. – There is both elite vs non-elite struggle and intra-elite conflict. – Government forms vary and are the result of political transitions associated with conflict. Mixed government forms are possible and they can alleviate conflicts.	Polybius (1889), as well as similar conceptualizations by Aristotle (1912), Cicero (1829/2017), Machiavelli (1513/1998), and Proudhon (1851/1971). See also: Podes (1991); Neill (2011); Bradshaw (2011); Koivukoski (2011); Turchin (2023).	[a] Elites matter in the political economy. [b] There are no established cyclical patterns for government forms; the analyst's focus must be on elite circulation and associated value creation patterns. [c] Benign and perverted rule is related not to a form of government but associated to the degree of value creation of elite business models. [c] Non-elite rule fallacy ('people power'). The instant a non-elite wins in the political economy contest arenas it is running an elite business model and is hence an elite coalition for all practical, social, and behavioral purposes and effects (see Proposition 1).
Marx's class theory. (Section 1.2.1)	– The business models of production have distributional effects and result in the social dichotomy resulting from being at one or the other end of "exploitation". – Elite vs non-elite class struggle determines history. – Normative vision of 'classless society'.	Marx (1867/1959b); Marx & Engels (1848/1969). See also: Andrew (1975); Barrow (2007).	[a] Elite business models have distributional effects. [b] Elite vs non-elite struggles are real, but intra-elite contests are continual, more prevalent and relevant for elites and non-elites alike (see the political options for elites and non-elites in Figure 8.2). [c] Elite business models' distributional effects are not necessarily exploitative. Elites can contribute more value to society than the value they appropriate as residual income (see Section 2.2). [c] A 'classless society' is a naïve ideal, unprecedented, and impossible as long as narrow groups have transaction cost advantages.

https://doi.org/10.1515/9783110734638-014

Table A1.1 (continued)

Literature	Key ideas	Selected sources	ETED position: [a] Adopted; [b] Adjusted; [c] Rejected
(ii) Contemporary conceptualizations of elites			
Power elite theory. (Section 1.2.2)	- A critical perspective on elitism in society where the elite dominates institutions and determines policy. - The elite is a cohesive governing class, with insider cliques from different parts of society (business, administration, military, etc.); the elite is not a pluralistic set of actors representing society's diversity. - National elite system as a meso construct.	Mills (1956); Bell (1958); Domhoff (1967, 1970). See also: Mayville (2015); Kerbo & Della Fave (1979).	[a] Elites (i.e., elite business model preferences) impact institutions (see Proposition 14 or Figure 3.2). [a] The national elite system is a meso construct (see Proposition 17, Figure 3.8). [b] Governing elites might incorporate in institutional change processes a diverse range of non-elite interests. [b] Different elite types constitute the national elite system; the ETED suggests a tripartite elite typology of business, political, and knowledge elites (see Figure 1.2). [c] The elite system is not a monolithic governing class in modern polities; the core elite and other coalitions (see Figure 8.1) circulate; there are different degrees of elite cohesion (see Section 5.3.3); intra-elite contests are a constant and intensify as a nation's elite business models evolve.
Specific conceptualizations of a power elite. (Section 1.2.2)	- Development of context-specific constructs of particularism to describe core and other elite coalitions like the iron triangles (e.g., in the US, the key nodes in elite networks are interest groups, legislators, and the civil service). - Emphasis on elites as insiders. - Elite networks can be conceived as a meso construct.	For instance, Adams (1981); Gais, Peterson, & Walker (1984); Kerbo & McKinstry (1995); and indirectly, Stigler (1971).	[a] Specific political economy contexts associate with specific core and other elite coalition configurations in terms of the elite type and background of their members (see Figure 3.6). [b] Political economies have core elite coalitions (see Figure 8.1); the strength of the cohesive 'iron' holding the coalition together, however, varies since cohesive forces are context-dependent and subject to internal stresses and external intra-elite contest pressures.

Table A1.1 (continued)

Literature	Key ideas	Selected sources	ETED position: [a] Adopted; [b] Adjusted; [c] Rejected
Transnational elite constructs. (Section 1.2.2)	- Broadens the agency of elites beyond the nation state to the international stage. - Context-specific constructs of particularism such as 'cosmopolitan capital' or the transnational capitalist class (TCC) suggest elite networks where the key nodes include major corporations, 'globalizing' professionals, bureaucrats, and politicians. - Neo-Gramscian perspectives on hegemony extend elite power beyond the national context and posit the existence of a world order.	Sklair (2012); Jönsson & Tallberg (2010); Hoffmann-Lange (2012); Best, Lengyel, & Verzichelli (2012); Bühlmann, David, & Mach (2012)	[a] Transnational elite coalitions exist. [b] The cross-border elite business models of transnational elite coalitions are comparatively deinstitutionalized at the international level as coalition members are bound by the nation state; the relevant institutional context for elites is the nation state (see Sections 7.3.2 and 7.3.3). [c] Contrary to transnational elite conceptualizations, elites compete in the international arena on the basis of nation state affiliation while the network stability of transnational elite coalitions is fragile and subordinated to national interests (the interests of rival national elites that are not part of the coalition), as examples in the context of the current Sino-US rivalry illustrate. [c] Members of cross-border elite business model coalitions receive, in a manner that parallels the rivalrous nation state dynamics in international relations, a significant part of their bargaining power vis-à-vis other elite coalition members from their nation states.
Elites as the custodians of narratives. (Section 1.2.2)	- Narratives coordinate elite agency. - Theoretical links between elites and narratives include the Advocacy Coalition Framework (ACF), a causal theory of policymaking, or the theory of cultural hegemony. - Elites can be extensive coalitions thanks to the power of narratives. - The power of narratives means that elites exist on both the Left and Right of the political spectrum.	Gramsci's *Prison Notebooks* (Hoare & Nowell-Smith, 1999); Jenkins-Smith & Sabatier (1993); Beckert (2016); Zingales (2017).	[a] Narratives are a cause of institutional change. [a] Narratives are critical for the cohesion of any elite coalition. [b] Narratives are a constitutive element of elite business models; the narrative market is one of three arenas for the accumulation of elite power (see Figure 1.2). [b] Because of narratives, elites, the beneficiaries of elite business models, can be numerous (albeit narrower than their counterparties).

Table A1.1 (continued)

Literature	Key ideas	Selected sources	ETED position: [a] Adopted; [b] Adjusted; [c] Rejected
The technocratic ideal view. (Section 1.2.2)	- A rational technocracy of fair scientific problem solvers maximizes social utility. - Politics and administration must be separated. - Idealistic, harks back to Platonic philosopher king.	Roots in Plato (*The Republic*, Book VI, 1969); Saint-Simon (1952); Veblen (1899/1924, 1904/1975); Akin (1977); Putnam (1977); Elliott (1978); Crane (2008).	[a] Core elite coalitions (see Figure 8.1) can adopt narratives whose legitimacy emanates from superior technical knowledge or rationalism. [a] A technocratic elite emphasizes value creation delivered through structural reform and institutional change that provides incentives for elite business model transformation. [a] The separation of powers between politics and administration is desirable (as an instance of 'within-arena' (Tier 1), intra-elite power relationship 2, see Table 3.2). [b] Applied sustainable value creation partially shares the technocratic ideal.
Elite research in political science. (Section 1.2.2)	- Elite system emphasis on political elites, thick descriptions about their characteristics and agency. - Includes power elite theory and lobbying theories.	Best & Higley (2018); Vogel, Gebauer & Salheiser (2018); Paniagua & Vogler (2022).	[a] Elites are the reason for institutional change. [b] Political elites are essential to the elite system and to any elite coalition, but their importance vis-à-vis business and knowledge elites (see checks and balances in Figure 3.7) is contingent on the specific national context.
Lobbying theories. (Section 1.2.2)	- Institutional change is the result of lobbying. - Interest groups are at the center of the political process. - Political elites are beholden to business elites. - Lobbying is an essential fact of the political economy since it provides licenses to operate. - Lobbying theories are US-centric. - Lobbying is an avenue for institutional capture and plays a prominent role in rent seeking.	Hall & Deardorff (2006); Baldwin & Robert-Nicoud (2007); Lowery (2007). Critical related views in Beard (1913); Mills (1956); Bartels (2008); Nader (2014); Holcombe (2018). Links with Ostrom (1975); Buchanan (1980); Tollison (2012); Tullock (1967); Stigler (1971); Laffont & Tirole (1991).	[a] Institutional change is the result of elite agency. [a] Elite coalitions are at the center of the political process. [b] Elite business models are constituted by business, political and knowledge elites. [b] Lobbying is accessible to all participants in intra-elite contests and is but one avenue by which elites accumulate power and effect institutional change. [b] General theorizing beyond US/ Western context. [c] Avoid overemphasis on lobbying and focus on the elite separation of powers, intra-elite contest rules and the sustainable value creation of elite business models.

Table A1.1 (continued)

Literature	Key ideas	Selected sources	ETED position: [a] Adopted; [b] Adjusted; [c] Rejected
Dominant coalitions in organizations. (Section 1.2.2)	- Hierarchies topped by elites are a rational and effective approach for managing organizations. - Common interests determine coalitions, yet these can shift and make coalitions unstable. - Bargaining is a political process playing out within and across coalitions. - Conceptualization of elites at the micro-level of the firm. - The characteristics of a firms' dominant coalition impacts on its performance.	Michels (1962/1999); Cyert & March (1963); Thompson (1967); Stevenson, Pearce & Porter (1985); Hambrick & Mason (1984); Pearce (1995).	[a] Elites dominate in organizations and at all levels of socio-economic organization. [a] Elite coalitions are shifting, unstable, transient, and engaged in permanent bargaining processes (intra-elite contests). [b] Elite coalitions are the result of common interests around an elite business model, whether in an organization or in an economy. [b] Economic, social, and organizational performance is the result of the sustainable value creation of elite agency.
(iii) Conceptualizations of elites relevant to economics			
Classical elite theory. (Section 1.2.3)	- Elites are a minority. - Elites are a certainty. - Elitism; elites are the best. - Elitism; non-elites are capable of governing themselves. - Political economy analytical perspective. - Value-free analysis of elites. - Group/class with hegemony over its own group/class or over all other groups/classes.	Mosca (1939); Michels (1962/1999); Pareto (1968/1991). Influences from Machiavelli, Hobbes, Weber, Schumpeter and Ortega y Gasset (as per Pakulski, 2018). See also: Mayhew & Schollaert (1980); Zetterberg (1991); Lerner, Nagai & Rothman (1996); Busino (2000); Higley & Pakulski (2012); Pakulski (2012); and relatedly, Brezis & Temin (2007).	[a] Elites are a minority. [a] Elites are a certainty. [b] Elites are 'best' in terms of power accumulation and value appropriation; elites are also 'best' in fostering economic and human development *if* (and only if) they operate sustainable value creation business models. [b] Non-elites never govern; non-elites that acquire power—and the capability of running an elite business model—have circulated into the elite. [a] The analysis of elites is value-free, as it is detached from ideologies or political narratives. [a] Political economy analytical perspective. [b] Elites have hegemony over their own group and across society, insofar as their elite business models are preserved.

Table A1.1 (continued)

Literature	Key ideas	Selected sources	ETED position: [a] Adopted; [b] Adjusted; [c] Rejected
Theory of groups and collective action logic. (Section 1.2.3)	- Explains the existence of elites based on lower coordination costs for small(er) groups. - Elite agency determines institutions and the wealth of nations. - Small groups exploit large ones. - As interest groups accumulate, institutional decay ensues.	Olson (1965/1971), (1982); McCallum & Blais (1987). See also Heckelman, 2007. Consistent with Higley (2010); Gallo, Riyanto, & Roy (2019).	[a] Small groups have lower transaction costs and thus more accumulated power (see 'the extraordinary lever', Figure A5.3) resulting in a greater ability for applied collective action. Hence elites invariably arise in all societies. [a] Dominant coalitions (with specific elite business model preferences) impact institutional change (see Figure 3.2). [b] Institutional sclerosis occurs when elites run extractive transfer business models in the absence of structural reform (see Figure 7.1) and elite transformational leadership (see Table 7.2).
Institutions as constraints on elites. (Section 1.2.3)	- Institutions can be inclusive or extractive. - Incipient incorporation of elite agency and elite power notions into economic models. - Elites can and must be constrained by institutions.	North (1990); Acemoglu (2006); Acemoglu & Robinson (2013b, 2019a); new institutional theory.	[a] Institutions can be inclusive (value created and appropriated) or extractive (value appropriated but *not* created). [b] Institutions constrain elite agency, but elite agency first imposes its preferences on institutions (see Figure 3.2). [b] Institutional constraints are the result of intra-elite contests and the elite system's separation of powers (see Table 3.2), i.e., elites *de facto* constrain each other. [c] Research focus on inclusive elite business models and incorporation of elite agency in economic modeling (see Figure 7.8). [c] Non-elite vs elite struggle can be sterile and counter-productive; the focus is on non-elite strategic political participation in intra-elite contests (see Figure 8.2), the dynamics that shape inclusive institutions, and on the varieties of elite transformational leadership (see Table 7.2).

Table A1.1 (continued)

Literature	Key ideas	Selected sources	ETED position: [a] Adopted; [b] Adjusted; [c] Rejected
Social order as an outcome of elite agency. (Section 1.2.3)	– Elites establish social orders to rein in violence in exchange for rents derived from "limited access" (North, Wallis, & Weingast, 2006). – Countries where elites establish social orders based on "open access" are more likely to see modern social development than those with "limited access" social orders (North, Wallis, & Weingast, 2006). – The "stationary bandit" protects against the comparatively more extractive "roving bandit", thus sowing the seeds of social order (Olson, 1993, 2000).	Hobbes' social contract theory (1651/2002); North, Wallis, & Weingast (2006); Olson (1993, 2000).	[a] Elites establish social orders with degrees of open/limited access. [a] Value creation (e.g., through the control of violence) and transfers (e.g., taxation) combine in elite business models; extractive transfers can be a condition for value creation (see Section 2.3.1, 'alternating value extraction and creation' conjecture). [a] The transformation towards higher degrees of open access in the social order is the result of endogenous processes within the elite system (see Section 4.3.5). [b] Social access openness explains economic development trajectories when combined with elite quality (see Figure 1.1, The Elite Circulation Matrix). [b] There is no elite/non-elite Hobbesian social contract; elites create social order on their own accord.

Table A1.2: Propositions on the logic of elite agency for the ETED.

Ref. Section	Proposition	Supporting theoretical perspectives	Selected sources
1.3	**Basic propositions on the logic of elite agency**		
1.3.1	Proposition 1: The elite dominance iron law is structural to society.	Classical elite theory.	Pareto (1968/1991); Mosca (1939); Michels (1962/1999); Zetterberg (1991).
		Theory of groups and the logic of collective action.	Olson (1965/1971, 1982).
		Various others.	e.g., Bottomore (1993); North, Wallis & Weingast (2006).
1.3.2	Proposition 2: Elite circulation is multi-dimensional and characterizes society.	Classical elite theory.	Pareto (1968/1991); Mosca (1939); Michels (1962/1999).
1.3.3	Proposition 3: The mode of elite circulation affects economic development.	Elite circulation theory.	Pareto (1968/1991); Michels (1962/1999).
		Social order access.	North, Wallis, & Weingast (2006).
		Schumpeterian economics and Kondratieff's theory of economic waves.	Schumpeter (1939); Kondratieff (1925/1935).
		The Elite Circulation Matrix.	ETED development (see Figure 1.1).
1.3.4	Proposition 4: Elites in the abstract are coordination capacity enabled by low transaction costs.	Theory of groups and the logic of collective action.	Olson (1965/1971, 1982).
		Transaction cost theory.	Commons (1924, 1950); Coase (1960); Williamson (1981, 1993); North (1984); Medema, (1994).
		Social network theory.	Granovetter (1973, 2005).
		Trust as social capital thesis.	Fukuyama (1995); Tsai & Ghoshal (1998); Morck & Yeung (2004).
		The 'extraordinary lever' (actualized through 'the power multiplier').	Theories for this sub-section refer to those on power used in this work, those of economics (Lange (1943), or conceptual elements like "the force multiplier" from military affairs (Sloan, 2012); ETED conceptualization (see Figure A5.3).

Table A1.2 (continued)

Ref. Section	Proposition	Supporting theoretical perspectives	Selected sources
2.1	**Propositions on the behavioral logic of elite agency**		
2.1.1	Proposition 5: Elite behavior maximizes utility and is potentially sustainable.	Rational choice theory (RCT) and its utilitarian bases; RCT applications to elites.	Bentham (1781/1970) and Mill (1863/2001); Becker (1993); Allison & Zelikow (1999); Wang (2021).
		Stationary bandits monopolize power and extract rents but also provide public goods, helping to secure elite identity over the long term.	Olson (1993, 2000).
		Sustainability notion based on von Carlowitz's *Sylvicultura Oeconomica* (1712/2022) and Brundtland's *Our Common Future* (1987).	Described in Scoones (2007); Brundtland (1987).
2.1.2	Proposition 6: Elite identity is driven by residual income.	Identity as 'economic model of behavior' distinct from RCT; non-RCT motivation theory and behavioral economics are rejected.	Maslow (1943); Akerlof & Kranton (2000). Machiavelli (1513/1998).
		Elite identity explained by income maximization preferences with illustrative cases provided.	ETED position.
2.2	**Propositions on the logic of elite business models**		
2.2.1	Proposition 7: The elite business model is central to elite agency.	The business model (what companies do to get paid).	Drucker (1994); Zott & Amitt (2013); Arend (2013); Ovans (2015).
		The principal-stakeholder perspective of the business model, which describes the system of interdependent activities that are performed by the firm and its stakeholders.	Coff (1999); Brandenburger (2002); Zott & Amitt (2013); Garcia-Castro & Aguilera (2015).
		Successful elite agency at the business model level sees an accumulation of power that is leveraged for income maximization.	ETED conceptualization.

Table A1.2 (continued)

Ref. Section	Proposition	Supporting theoretical perspectives	Selected sources
2.2.2	Proposition 8: The elite business model is characterized by principal-stakeholder bargaining power differentials required for value appropriation.	Classical, Marxist, neo-classical value theories, non-orthodox approaches to value.	Smith (1776/1904); Bentham (1781/1970); Ricardo (1817/1999); Mill (1863/2001); Marx (1867/1959b); Jevons (1871); George (1898); Lackman (1976); Georgescu-Roegen (1971, 1986).
		Value is understood in terms of social relationships, as being everything that humans determine is worth appropriating.	Combination of multiple references in this sub-section; Menger (1871/2007); Harrison & Wicks (2013). ETED position.
		Value as a collective process.	Porter (1980); Brandenburger (2002); Garcia-Castro & Aguilera (2015); Mazzucato (2018).
		VCA framework; division of value strategies; the principal-stakeholder perspective (business models consist of a principal and stakeholders who jointly create value that they then each attempt to appropriate).	Brandenburger & Stuart (1996); Coff (1999); Amit & Zott (2001); Brandenburger (2002); MacDonald & Ryall (2004); Lepak, Smith, & Taylor (2007); Di Gregorio (2013); Garcia-Castro & Aguilera (2015).
		Bargaining power (impact on value appropriation).	Coff (1999); MacDonald & Ryall (2004); Moatti, Ren, Anand, & Dussauge (2015).
		'Nature stakeholder' assumption.	Literature on sustainability such as Starik (1995) and Laine (2011).
		Hayek's "meaning of competition" (including "personal relationships" and "differentiating").	Hayek (1948/1958); Bowles, Kirman, & Sethi (2017). Parallels also with Buchanan (1980) 'non-market' and 'market' allocation.
		'Equalized bargaining power equilibrium prices' condition; 'Elite vs non-elite knowledge gap' hypothesis; 'Elite power vs value creation gap' hypothesis; 'the Amazon dilemma'.	ETED development.
2.2.3	Proposition 9: Value creation-appropriation (VCA) is the analytical framework best suited to understand elite business models' division of value strategies.	VCA framework, division of value strategies; decrease of opportunity costs and increase in prices (willingness to pay).	Garcia-Castro & Aguilera (2015); Zott & Amitt (2013).
		Equations on residual income (1/9), value creation (2/9) and value appropriation and transfers (3/9).	ETED operationalization. (Sections 2.2.3, 7.3.2).

Table A1.2 (continued)

Ref. Section	Proposition	Supporting theoretical perspectives	Selected sources
2.3	**Propositions on value creation and value transfers as extraction**		
2.3.1	Proposition 10: Sustainable value creation results from the proportion of first-order productive activities (value creation) relative to second-order transfer activities (value extraction).	Rent seeking theory, productive entrepreneurship, and related ideas to establish the classification schema that distinguishes between 'first-order productive activities' and 'second-order transfer activities' based on the 'value is created or transferred' ontological assumption.	Buchanan (1980); Tollison (2012); Tullock (1967); Baumol (1990), and others discussed in Section 5.2.1. ETED conceptualization (Table 2.3, Figure A5.4a).
		Risk taking is a form of value; risk transfers are a form of value extraction.	Markowitz (1952); Sharpe (1964); Taleb (2018). ETED position and development.
		Positive/negative externalities.	Pigou (1920/1932); Coase (1960); Buchanan & Stubblebine (1962); Baumol (1972); Bueno de Mesquita (2016).
		Sustainable value creation notion references von Carlowitz, *Sylvicultura Oeconomica* (1712/2022) and Brundtland's *Our Common Future* (1987).	Described in Scoones (2007); Brundtland (1987).
		'Alternating value extraction and creation' conjecture; 'extractive push' dilemma.	ETED position and development, illustrated by examples like 'The Miracle on the Han River' (Gemici, 2013).
2.3.2	Proposition 11: All elite business models have a measurable value creation position on a 'value spectrum'.	VCA framework, division of value strategies.	Brandenburger & Stuart (1996); and others.
		The 'business model value creation spectrum' ('value spectrum') and its operationalization as equations (4/9) to deliver micro-level sustainable value creation measurements.	ETED operationalization (see Figure 2.10).

Table A1.2 (continued)

Ref. Section	Proposition	Supporting theoretical perspectives	Selected sources
3.1	**Propositions on the theoretical perspectives that inform elite agency**		
3.1.1	Proposition 12: Elite agency is the principal microfoundation of institutional change.	Microfoundations of new institutional economics, its practice and behavioral variant.	DiMaggio & Powell (1991); Powell & Colyvas (2008); Giddens (1984); Smets, Jarzabkowski, Burke, & Spee (2015).
		Multiple levels of social analysis.	Williamson (2000); Seo & Creed (2002).
		Incentive system as the relevant institution for economic outcomes.	Olson (1984); North (1990, 1994); Holmstrom & Milgrom (1994); Nicholas (2003); Robinson (2010). ETED (see Figure 3.2)
		Elite agency in institutional economics.	North (1990); Bourguignon & Verdier (2010); Acemoglu & Robinson (2008); Brezis & Temin (2007); Robinson (2010); Amsden, DiCaprio, & Robinson (2014); ETED conceptualization.
3.1.2	Proposition 13: Elite agency determines distributional outcomes—the winners and losers in the political economy.	Political economy.	From its origins, e.g., Ricardo (1817/1899), Bastiat (1845/1996), to the present, e.g., Alesina & Rodrik (1994); Kelly (2005); Alesina & Perotti (1994).
		Theories of lobbying and institutional capture.	Hall & Deardorff (2006); Baldwin & Robert-Nicoud (2007); Lowery (2007); Downs (1957); Stigler (1971); Laffont & Tirole (1991).
		New institutional economics.	Commons (1950), as cited in Elliott (1978); Joskow (1995).
3.1.3	Proposition 14: Elite agency effects institutional change through the political economy's narrative market.	Narratives conceptual element.	Denning (2006); Hagel (2011); Hagel, Brown & Davison (2010).
		Narratives in sociology, organizational theory.	Lyotard (1979); Abell (2004); Boje (2008); Casas-Klett & Li (2022).
		Narrative economics.	Shiller (2017).
		Theory of cultural hegemony and derived neo-Gramscian perspectives.	Bates (1975); Cox (1983); Lerner, Nagai, & Rothman (1996); Bieler & Morton (2004).
		Cases: Christianity, Communism, Internet Tax Freedom Act of 1998, stablecoins, BLM, Tesla, the Olympics.	Pareto (1968/1991); Stupak (2016); various media and public domain sources.

Table A1.2 (continued)

Ref. Section	Proposition	Supporting theoretical perspectives	Selected sources
3.2	**Propositions on the system of national elites**		
3.2.1	Proposition 15: Elite coalitions are the constitutive elements of national elite systems	General systems theory.	Aristotles' 'whole' (1912, 5.8); Von Bertalanffy (1969/2003; 1972); Parsons (1951/1991), Simon (1962); Hayek (1964/1967).
		The elite is a system (e.g., "power elite", "governing class", "Medici vicious cycles"); a sub-system of the political economy system.	Pareto (1968/1991); Mills (1956); Domhoff (1967, 1970); Zingales (2017). ETED conceptualization.
		Elite coalitions (e.g., interest groups, advocacy coalitions, lobbies) are held together by their shared elite business model and are sub-systems of the national elite system.	Diverse literature including Laffont & Tirole (1991); Jenkins-Smith & Sabatier (1993); Hall & Deardorff (2006). ETED conceptualization links political economy and business model literature.
3.2.2	Proposition 16: The elite system operates on a multi-tier set of checks and balances.	Separation of powers theory and constitutional government theory.	Montesquieu (1748/1949); Madison (1787/1977); Levi (1976).
		The Three-tier Set of Intra-elite Checks and Balances	ETED extension and development.
3.2.3	Proposition 17: The national elite system is situated at the meso-level	Meso-level perspective.	Dopfer, Foster & Potts (2004); Dopfer (2012). ETED conceptualization.
		General systems theory; complex systems with emergent properties.	Von Bertalanffy (1969/2003); Parsons (1951/1991); Hayek (1964/1967); Simon (1962); Gleick (1987); Anderson (1972); O'Connor (1994); Chalmers (2006). ETED conceptualization.
3.3	**Propositions for the logic of intra-elite contests in the elite system**		
3.3.1	Proposition 18: Elites shape institutions primarily through intra-elite contests.	Classical elite theory and elite circulation theory.	Pareto (1968/1991); Mosca (1939); Michels (1962/1999). ETED development.
		Theories from anthropology for intra-elite competition.	Forsdyke (2005).
		Cases: Written law in archaic Greece; IMF rescue packages; Indonesia; American Revolutionary War; Libya/Coca-Cola.	Hölkeskamp (1992); Johnson (2009); Dick & Mulholland (2010); Hosenball (2011).

Table A1.2 (continued)

Ref. Section	Proposition	Supporting theoretical perspectives	Selected sources
3.3.2	Proposition 19: Non-elite agency can constrain value extraction through participation in intra-elite contests.	Marxist theory on revolution and violence; Leninism.	A recurring theme in Marx and Engels (e.g., 1848/1969) and Lenin (1918); inspired by Hegel's logic and dialectics (1812/2010).
		Cases: Maccabees revolt; French Revolution; October Revolution.	Hobsbawm (1990); Acemoglu, Cantoni, Johnson & Robinson (2009); Allen (2004).
		Elite/non-elite cooperative game for institutional change.	ETED extension.
3.3.3	Proposition 20: Non-elite interests are primarily served by a comprehensive elite separation of powers.	Separation of powers theory and constitutional government theory.	Montesquieu (1748/1949); Madison (1787/1977); Levi (1976); Paniagua & Vogler (2022).
		The Seven Intra-elite Power Relations.	ETED extension and development (see Table 3.2).
		Cases: Sugar plantations in post-colonial Latin America; Rosa Parks; Uber.	Uber Files; Sokoloff & Engerman (2000)

Table A1.3: Conjectures and other ancillary propositions of the ETED.*

Conjectures and ancillary propositions	Description	ETED relation** and selected sources
'Minimum elite circulation velocity' conjecture (Section 1.3.3)	The elite circulation velocity required for a positive level of economic growth. The conjecture assumes that (short of revolutionary replacements or wars) the higher the elite circulation velocity, the higher the realized economic and human development. In advanced economies this velocity must be comparatively higher than in emerging economies (links to the 'advanced economies have a higher sensitivity to elite quality' conjecture, Section 7.1.3).	Pareto's (1968/1991) admixture notion in his elite circulation theory.
'The great elite coalition for development' conjecture (Section 1.3.3)	References Carlyle's (1840/2008) Great Man Theory of history and leadership; elites that increase the value creation positions of their elite business models or effect inclusive structural reforms have a positive and disproportionally large impact on the economic and social development trajectories of nations. Such elite individuals are 'great' and even 'heroic' given the resistance that they are likely to face from reactionary coalitions that lose out as a result of their agency. The transformational leadership of individuals is essential for development and is based on the 'inextinguishable value creation option of elites' premise.	ETED position. Links to transformational leadership, Table 7.2; is the solution to the 'low elite quality' problem, Section 8.1.5. Carlyle (1840/2008); Schumpeter (1942/2000); supporting and opposing views include Jones & Olken (2005); Andrews (2013); Gilson & Milhaupt (2011); Easterly (2011); and Brady & Spence (2010).

*Includes conjectures, as well as dilemmas, assumptions, premises, implications, functions, conditions, problems, metaphors, and hypotheses.

**The conjectures and ancillary propositions have diverse connections to the ETED's development ranging from 'none' to 'ETED position' (i.e., a theoretical stance is taken from the literature) to 'ETED development' (a discrete conceptual element advanced for the inquiry).

Table A1.3 (continued)

Conjectures and ancillary propositions	Description	ETED relation** and selected sources
'Elite utility function' (Section 2.1.1)	The general utility function of elites which, consistent with rational choice theory (RCT), has residual income maximization as its highest preference in turn bound by temporal considerations. The function optimizes the trade-offs between two variables: short-term residual income flows and long-term wealth stocks. The long horizon requires elite business models based on first-order productive activities and constraints on extractive transfers from non-elite stakeholders, as non-elite value must be generated for harvest in the future. This informs sustainable value creation, the ETED's concept of sustainability. The relative weight of the function's two temporal variables, in part associated with whether an elite is roving or stationary, is contingent on constraints like intra-elite contests, elite leadership, and individual ethical positions.	ETED position, Proposition 5. Based on Olson's (1993, 2000) stationary and roving bandit notion and RCT assumptions (e.g., Becker, 1993; Allison & Zelikow, 1999; Wang, 2021. The normative sustainability reference is von Carlowitz (1712/2022) and Brundtland's *Our Common Future* (1987).
'Inextinguishable value creation option of elites' (leadership) premise for human behavior (Section 2.2.1)	Elites possess a perpetual option to transform business models towards ever more sustainable value creation positions (and reduce value transfer-IN). Such agency, conceived as an option exercised through intra-elite contests, rests on the ETED's first principles (especially on the Will to Power), links to its set of ethical principles (and possibly to natural law), and materializes as transformational leadership.	ETED position, Proposition 7. Connects elite business models and elite transformational leadership with economic development; the third (III) of the ETED's three premises for human behavior (Figure A5.4c).
'Equalized bargaining power equilibrium prices' condition (Section 2.2.2)	A hypothetical condition where prices (or costs) in the principal-stakeholder relationship are determined by the counterparties having similar amounts of bargaining power, thereby impeding extractive value transfers. The price levels under equalized bargaining power conditions serve as a benchmark for theory purposes. Value transfers are assumed to be the source of prices that differ from counterfactual 'equalized bargaining power equilibrium prices'. When regarded as a normative criterion, it must be balanced against the value creating coordination capacity that power differentials afford.	ETED development, Proposition 8, see a policy perspective of The Elite Business Model in Figure A5.9c. Based on the bargaining power notions of Porter (1980); Coff (1999); MacDonald & Ryall (2004).

Table A1.3 (continued)

Conjectures and ancillary propositions	Description	ETED relation** and selected sources
'Nature stakeholder' assumption (Section 2.2.2)	Nature is a stakeholder in any business model in the context of principal-stakeholder relationships. The nature stakeholder is to be given an entity-like identity (and be deemed a custodian for legal purposes). Nature, when operationalized as a legal persona, needs to appropriate value commensurate to the value of the services that it creates and provides for principals.	Combination of VCA framework with literature on sustainability such as Starik (1995); Laine (2011). Also see value added reporting: Rutherford (1977); Haller & van Staden (2014).
'The Amazon dilemma' (Section 2.2.2)	Elite business models that create substantial amounts of knowledge (and thus inclusive value transfer-OUT through spillovers, etc.) can simultaneously engage in extractive value transfer-IN away from stakeholders. This dilemma is posited to originate from two hypothetical sources: the 'elite vs non-elite knowledge gap' and the 'elite power vs value creation gap'. The dilemma forces elites to take a position on whether to self-constrain value transfer-IN. In contrast to the Olsonian stationary bandit whose power emanates less from 'knowledge' and who runs an entire polity, there is initially less pressure in the elite system to self-constrain extraction because the area of operation is only in a part of the political economy and the value appropriated is, notwithstanding the pervasive impact of data, only a part of the value that stakeholders create. This reinforces the necessary role of transformational leadership and the ETED's set of ethical principles.	ETED development, Proposition 8. An expression of the 'alternating value extraction and creation' conjecture (Section 2.3.1) and leads to the (c) 'weight and offset value transfers' (holistic) implication for financial analysis (Figure 8.7) that is realized through SVC measurements.
'Elite vs non-elite knowledge gap' hypothesis (Section 2.2.2)	The 'knowledge' creation capabilities of elite business models exceed those of non-elites. This gap, part of 'the Amazon dilemma' and gaining newfound significance in the era of AI, is at times the result of deliberate barriers to accessing knowledge placed by elites on non-elites (e.g., limits on alphabetization) or caused by the very nature of technology (e.g., the cumulative effects of intelligence). The gap may contribute to lasting elite/non-elite bargaining power differentials and stable, structural, and hard-to-reverse value extraction by elites from non-elites.	ETED development, Proposition 8. References literature to explain the causes for the gap, including barriers to literacy (Goody & Watt, 1963) or the monopolistic tendencies of data (Cheng, 2020).

Table A1.3 (continued)

Conjectures and ancillary propositions	Description	ETED relation** and selected sources
'Elite power vs value creation gap' hypothesis (Section 2.2.2)	The bargaining power of elites grows faster than the value creation of elite business models. This gap, part of 'the Amazon dilemma', can be the result of elite coalitions that are innovation laggards but retain their power because of 'political economy know-how' in the political non-market and narrative market arenas. Innovative elites might also, through their possession of 'the extraordinary lever', manage to multiply their power beyond their value creation achievements. The gap may contribute to lasting elite/non-elite bargaining power differentials and structural, hard-to-reverse value extraction by elites from non-elites.	ETED development, Proposition 8. Informs The Elite Business Model Lifecycle and links to the 'value transfers replace value creation at maturity' conjecture (see Figure A5.9a). Sources of power conceptual element derived from Hayek's (1948/1958) "The Meaning of Competition".
'Value is created or transferred' (ontological) assumption (for socio-economic relations) (Section 2.3.1)	The ontological assumption of the ETED posits that all social-economic reality is either first-order productive activity (i.e., value creation and risk origination) or second-order transfer activity (i.e., value extraction and risk transfer). This dualist ontology follows the principle of parsimony and allows for the classification of all business model activities into a dichotomous, two-class typology.	ETED position, introduced in Proposition 10. The first (i) of the ETED's three assumptions for socio-economic relations (see Figure A5.4a; Table 2.3); a red thread across the theoretical system. Benefits from multiple sources such as the rent-seeking literature.
'Bona fide value appropriation' (positive) assumption (for socio-economic relations) (Section 2.3.1)	The positive assumption about business models where value appropriated is deemed to be value created. This then substantiates the (b) 'revenue is value creation unless value transfer is proven' implication for the operationalization of SVC measurements. Since the full revenue of a firm is taken to be value creation (net value creation) the burden of proof for value extraction rests on establishing transfer-IN amounts.	ETED position. The third (iii) of the ETED's three assumptions for socio-economic relations (see Figure A5.4a).
'Revenue is value creation unless value transfer is proven' (constructive) implication (for financial analysis) (Section 2.3.1)	A simple rule to establish 'first-order productive activities' and separate them from 'second-order transfer activities' when measuring sustainable value creation in the application of the (iii) 'bona fide value appropriation' assumption. The rule provides a starting point for calculations conceptually ringfencing revenue (or profits) in financial statements that are then premised in calculations (e.g., for VCp/VCr) to be net value creation until transfer-IN is ascertained.	ETED position, Proposition 10. Examples of first-order value creation and second-order transfer activities presented in Table 2.3. Articulated in Section 2.2.3, and through equations 4.1 and 4.2. The second (b) of the ETED's three implications for financial analysis (see Figure A5.4b).

Table A1.3 (continued)

Conjectures and ancillary propositions	**Description**	**ETED relation**** **and selected sources**
'Alternating value extraction and creation' conjecture (Section 2.3.1)	The condition under which first-order productive value creation requires and/or is the result of previous second-order extractive transfer-IN. This conjecture nuances the general ETED position against extractive value transfers by conceiving them, under certain circumstances, as 'investments' and a necessary feature of social order. Extractive transfers by elite business models alternate and *de facto* combine with value creation. Elite agency based on this understanding faces resistance (from the extracted parties) and requires transformational leadership.	ETED position, Proposition 10. Hobbes' social contract theory (1651/2002), Olson's stationary bandit (1993, 2000) as a provider of public goods and North, Wallis, & Weingast (2006) on closed access societies.
'Extractive push' dilemma (Section 2.3.1)	The application of the 'alternating value extraction and creation' conjecture to transition from one economic development stage to the next. To kick-start a developmental transition requires substantial initial extractive value transfer to encourage more novel sustainable elite business models. The 'push' associates with extractive transfers from non-elites to elites, with the latter thus accumulating the 'knowledge' (and capital, etc.) to advance long-term development goals (that will eventually benefit non-elites). An 'extractive push' can kick-start a country in its early stages of development (e.g., the case of the South Korea or Israel) or at more advanced stages (e.g., granting monopoly rents to Big Tech in the US or China). The optimal size of the transfers necessary to successfully achieve an economic transition is an empirical question that creates a dilemma for policymakers (addressable by utilizing the constraints in frameworks for weighted policymaking, see Tables 8.2 and 8.3). Still, excessive and unlimited transfers will forestall development.	ETED position, Proposition 10. The dilemma has conceptual links across the theory, from weighted policy formulation (Table 8.2) or the 'elite institutional change bargain', to the set of ethical principles. Hobbes social contract theory (1651/2002), Olson's stationary bandit (1993, 2000) as provider of public goods and North, Wallis, and Weingast (2006) closed access societies.
'Same size of the slice' elite bias (Section 3.3.1)	The tendency for elite business models during crises to retain pre-crisis income/profit levels thanks to institutional embeddedness as the economic pie shrinks. In consequence, the stakeholders of the model experience a reduction in their share of the pie.	ETED development. Value chain as pie metaphor in Brandenburger (2002), or *The Economist* (2014).

Table A1.3 (continued)

Conjectures and ancillary propositions	**Description**	**ETED relation**[**] **and selected sources**
'Value creation by elite separation of powers' conjecture (Section 3.3.3)	The normative understanding of classical separation of powers theory applies to intra-elite contests in all three political economy contest arenas: non-market, market, and narrative market. The more numerous and institutionalized the checks and balances of the national elite system, the more frequent and competitive the intra-elite contests, and thus the larger the likelihood that high value creation models emerge. This conjecture is part of the 'intra-elite quality contest' dilemma and is moderated by the 'elite cohesion underpins social order' conjecture to which it stands in *coincidentia oppositorum*.	ETED position, Proposition 20 (see Figure 5.2). Extends Montesquieu's (1748/1949) tripartite separation of the political power domain, and constitutional government theory starting with Madison (1787/1977).
'Universal value extraction propensity of humans' (socio-economic) premise (for human behavior) (Section 3.3.3)	Elites and non-elites are all utility maximizing agents, *a priori* moral equivalents in value appropriation terms, and will extract from their stakeholders to the extent that their power differentials allow, however minuscule these are. Second-order value extraction is not only an inclination of *homo sapiens* and a feature of social orders but is distinctive in all relationships in nature, and of life itself. While the (B) 'universal extraction propensity of life' law of nature has negative entropy nourish the superior organism (as in Schrödinger's *What is Life?*, and even if one asserts the prevalence of symbiotic or complementary relationships in evolution), the 'extraordinary lever' embedded in social relationships enables *homo sapiens* to extract more from each other than any other organism.	ETED position. The second (II) of the ETED's three premises for human behavior (see Figure A5.4c). Schrödinger (1944/2013) and diverse systems of thought; common intuition.
'Follow the money' heuristic of institutional change (Section 4.2.2)	A political economy heuristic suited for establishing the primary cause of an institutional change, with the *cui bono* beneficiaries of that change being the winning elites in intra-elite contests. Normatively, the *cui bono* agents that succeed in effecting institutional change are those *qui generat valorem*, as in the maxim, *To the creators the value created* (see the discussion of ethical principles in Chapter 8).	ETED position. RCT; Olson (1984); public domain; common understanding.

Table A1.3 (continued)

Conjectures and ancillary propositions	Description	ETED relation** and selected sources
'Elite business model critical junctures' conjecture (Sections 4.3.4, 5.1.1)	Critical junctures in development occur when specific elite business models take preeminence and as a result determine a nation's long-term developmental performance. The critical juncture can be a sudden event if it is caused by an exogenous shock or occur more gradually as contributing factors build up to a tipping point. In either event, it results from a critical mass of elite coalitions that endogenously agglomerate around certain business models (often the models of the core coalition).	ETED position. David's path dependence (1985); Liebowitz and Margolis' path dependence (1999); Acemoglu, Johnson, Robinson, & Yared's critical junctures hypothesis (2009); Libecap's institutional path dependence (2011).
'Value transfers replace value creation at maturity' conjecture (Sections 4.3.4, 7.3.3)	The inherent sequence in The Elite Business Model Lifecycle conceptual element and the consequence of the 'elite power vs value creation gap' hypothesis. The sequence starts as elites rise on the back of their value creation but possess little power and ends as elite incumbents with huge amounts of power appropriate value and create very little. Power, institutional embeddedness, and political economy dynamics explain the declining levels of sustainable value creation at maturity. When excessive numbers of mature elite models agglomerate in the final stages of their lifecycles a nation's elite quality declines (potentially powerful states compensate for this by increasing cross-border business model extraction) and requires decisive weighted structural reform.	ETED development. Rendered in Figure A5.9a and, for an international perspective, Figure A5.9d. Rooted in the literature of power, bargaining power, and institutional change, the life cycle theory of the firm (Mueller, 1972), and the elite perspective.
'Impossible exit' conjecture (Section 5.2.2)	The trap-like nature of certain principal-stakeholder relationships where the counterparties of an elite business model, instead of engaging in the pursuit of utility maximization, accept value extraction (at times even in the form of mere subsistence-level prices as per Marx). 'Sticky' elite business models become a trap for stakeholders due, for instance, to a lack of alternatives. This critical rigidity in the economy breaks down with the enabling presence of the freedom *to* exit (Section 8.3.2), allowing non-elite value creators alternative responses to extractive value transfer-OUT.	ETED position. Typology of individual non-elite responses to extractive value transfers in Table 5.1. Multiple types of evidence with extremes ranging from slavery (Walk Free, 2023) to "techno feudalism" (Varoufakis, 2021).

Table A1.3 (continued)

Conjectures and ancillary propositions	Description	ETED relation** and selected sources
'Quantifiability of value transfers' (finance) assumption (for socio-economic relations) (Section 5.3.1)	An assumption on the deep interconnectedness of all business model activities realized by quantifying value transfer activities. Pricing is the means to link value transfers to the P&L statement of organizations and provide equivalence for value transfers across diverse principal-stakeholder relationships. The implication of quantifying all value transfers is that any business model activity can be traded and offset against any another. Sustainability objectives can be priced, budgeted, and managed and sustainable value creation becomes a transparent, solvable optimization problem for elites, policymakers, managers and the public.	ETED position The second (ii) of the ETED's three assumptions for socio-economic relations (see Figure A5.4a). System theory, see Von Bertalanffy, 1969/2003; Hayek, 1964/1967; Gleick, 1987.
'Weight and offset value transfers' (holistic) implication (for financial analysis) (Section 5.3.1)	The central normative implication of the ETED and the core financial approach for the operationalization of sustainable value creation. Business model decisions by the firm that are relevant for governance, strategy, management, investment or valuations are to be made by weighting the sustainable value creation of its constituent activities (via SVC metrics). This extends to the macro level where policymakers weight and offset the sustainable value creation of elite business models (via SVC measurements) and will also reference A Transfer Constraints Framework for policy formulation (Table 8.2). Links to elite transformational leadership, elite bargains, and the set of ethical principles.	ETED position. The application of financial tools for the normative realization of the theory. The third (c) of the ETED's three implications for financial analysis (see Figure A5.4b).
'Elite cohesion underpins social order' conjecture (Section 5.3.3)	Elite cohesion is the most relevant form of cohesion in society and more relevant than non-elite or elite/non-elite forms for the emergence of social order upon which economic and human development is based. Other forms of social cohesion, such as elite/non-elite cohesion, are also usually a signal of elite cohesion. The flip side of elite cohesion is that it adds to the resilience of extractive elite business models and thus must exist in tandem with a robust elite separation of powers. This conjecture is part of the 'intra-elite quality contest' dilemma and is moderated by the 'value creation by elite separation of powers' conjecture to which it stands in *coincidentia oppositorum*.	ETED position. Social cohesion definition of Chan, To, & Chan (2006). Examples, including Botswana (Sebudubudu & Molutsi, 2011) and Southeast Asia (Brown, 1993).

Table A1.3 (continued)

Conjectures and ancillary propositions	**Description**	**ETED relation** ** **and selected sources**
'Intra-elite quality contest' dilemma (Section 5.3.3)	Elite quality results from two *a priori* irreconcilable elements that when balanced integrate and provide a standard for practice: a comprehensive elite separation of powers (see the 'value creation by elite separation of powers' conjecture) and elite cohesion (see the 'elite cohesion underpins social order' conjecture). When the elite system masters this dilemma, institutional change and business model rules that support sustainable value creation are possible, eventually leading to economic and human development.	ETED development. Rendered in Figure 5.2. References body of literature on social cohesion and the separation of powers.
'Extractive escalation dynamic' conjecture (vs. 'inclusive escalation dynamic') (Section 5.3.4)	A developmental trap posited as a conjecture where one extractive value and risk transfer business model incentivizes the next until a sub-optimal equilibrium is reached short of the 'extractive end point' of society where everybody seeks to extract from each other and there is no value creation or productive risk-taking. The opposite of this steady state of value transfers is the 'inclusive escalation dynamic', which leads to an acceleration in economic and human development.	ETED position. Rent seeking theory as in Buchanan (1980); Tollison (2012); Tullock (1967); Markowitz's (1952) notions of risk; Damodaran's (2005) exploitation of uncertainty; Taleb (2018; 2020).
'Extractive end point' metaphor (Section 5.3.4)	An *ad absurdum* situation in society, a cul-de-sac where everyone seeks value transfers from others, and first-order productive activities cease to exist. This represents the terminus of the conjectured 'extractive escalation dynamic' trap. In practice, a society where each and every member engages in unproductive theft and plunder is unsustainable. Even when approximated, the actual end point is therefore hypothetical as all economic life collapses before it is reached. Thus, when the extractive end point is close, the demise of society is precariously averted through responses to extraction such as 'informality'.	ETED position. Complements the 'extractive escalation dynamic' conjecture. Similarities with the Lu Xun (1918/1985) "cannibalism" metaphor; common intuition.
'Power as potential future value extraction' assumption (Section 6.2.1)	Power is a pre-condition for value appropriated but *not* created. While power is not necessarily deployed by individual elite coalitions for extractive transfer purposes it is predictor of potential future value extraction in a measure to be empirically determined.	ETED position. Operationalized with SVC measurements (e.g., EQx). Based on bargaining power theory and the VCA framework.

Table A1.3 (continued)

Conjectures and ancillary propositions	**Description**	**ETED relation** and selected sources**
'Transparency of value creation and transfer activities' (open) implication (for financial analysis) (Section 6.6.1)	As a consequence of the (ii) 'quantifiability of value transfers' (finance) assumption for socio-economic relations, all value creation and transfers are made transparent. This aim is realized in financial terms by conceptually determining and then quantifying SVC metrics (both transfer-IN and transfer-OUT, see Figure 6.6) as inputs for SVC measurements.	ETED position. The first (a) of the ETED's three implications for sustainable value creation (see Figure A5.4b). Consistent with the normative understanding of transparency (e.g., Kaufmann & Weber, 2010).
'Advanced economies have a higher sensitivity to elite quality' conjecture (Section 7.1.3)	The more advanced and the closer to the technology frontier an economy is, the higher the elite quality that is required for sustainable growth and the narrower the elite quality corridor for tolerating extractive activities. Implications include a higher required 'minimum elite circulation velocity' (see Section 1.3.3).	ETED position. Derived from innovation- and productivity-based growth notions, see Solow (1957); Krugman (1994).
'War as cross-border value appropriation' conjecture (Section 7.3.2)	The state of war in international relations is traceable to the elite business models of a nation that benefits (non-elites can also profit) from the value appropriated but *not* created by foreign elites and non-elites. That is, conflict is the result of war profits being higher than peace dividends for bellicose elites.	ETED position. Formalization of common, near universal non-elite understanding. Historical examples provided, with salience given to Suetonius's (1914) *The Life of Julius Caesar* (54.2).
'Peace through cross-border elite business models' conjecture (Section 7.3.2)	The state of peace in international relations is achieved by interdependencies brought about by cross-border elite business models and by elite coalitions with members from diverse countries.	ETED position. References diverse works, including Angell (1910).
'Elite system fractality links to value creation' conjecture (Epilogue)	A conjectured economic law that claims that the deeper the system's fractality, the higher its growth potential. The recursive fractal elements of the socio-economic hierarchy are its nooks and crannies, i.e., the sectors of the political economy that are driven by independent agency (as opposed to linear bureaucracies) capable of exercising judgments on their business models (which then aggregate together and become elite). The more complex and munificent the fractality of the system, the greater the overall value creation potential is in a polity.	ETED development. See Epilogue, visualized as a metaphor in Figure E.2; see also Section 3.2.3. Speculates on the primary notion of fractality (as often implied in complex adaptive systems; see Mandelbrot, 1989; Liebovitch & Scheurle, 2000; Brown, Gupta, Li, Milne, Restrepo, & West, 2002; McDaniel, Lanham, & Anderson, 2009).
'Low non-elite cohesion' problem (Section 8.1.3)	Low non-elite cohesion is the result of the high transaction costs and low levels of trust that are endemic to non-elites and that can seldom be addressed without direct elite support. This problem hampers non-elites in realizing their four *a priori* political options in response to extraction.	ETED position. Rendered in Figures 8.2 and A5.8, see also Section 5.3.3. References social cohesion research (e.g., Chan, To, & Chan, 2006).

Table A1.3 (continued)

Conjectures and ancillary propositions	Description	ETED relation** and selected sources
'Elite agency on behalf of non-elites' elite option (Section 8.1.3)	'Low non-elite cohesion' precludes institutional change consistent with non-elite interests, so elites that are motivated by economic development and intrinsic values need to be open to supporting the strategic participation of non-elites in intra-elite contests based on a robust separation of powers that minimizes bargaining power differentials and establishes open access social orders. This approach reeks of elitism and paternalism.	ETED position. Rendered in Figures 8.2 and A5.8.
'Low elite quality' problem (Section 8.1.5)	The low elite quality problem, an example of which is the 'bad emperor problem', occurs when development is contingent on the transformational leadership of poor-quality individual elites and members of the core elite coalition. There is no technical solution to this economic development challenge other than the commitment of elites engaged in intra-elite contests to sustainable value creation models. Links with the (III) 'inextinguishable value creation option of elites' (leadership) premise for human behavior and might necessitate untangling psychological dimensions that are beyond the scope this work.	ETED position. Focus on elites; problem addressable within 'the great elite coalition for development' conjecture (Section 1.3.3). References the 'bad emperor problem' (Suetonius, 1914; Fukuyama, 2012).
'Innate value creation character of humans' (natural) premise (for human behavior) (Sections 8.1.5; 8.2.4)	Holds that all individuals have potential value creation agency, value creation being the essential characteristic of the human experience. The natural premise's antithesis is the (II) 'universal value extraction propensity of humans' (socio-economic) premise and the interaction between the two is at the core of this theory's ontology, while their creative tension moves human development forward.	ETED position. The (I) first of the ETED's three premises for human behavior (see Figure 8.7). Realized by the freedom *to* create value (Figure 8.5). References diverse values traditions and common understanding.

Appendix 2: Theoretical building blocks

Table A2.1: Glossary of ETED conceptual elements.*

Conceptual element	Definition	ETED relation** and selected sources
Alienation 'Elite alienation'	In the same way that workers are estranged from their labor and themselves in Marx's theory of alienation, elites are alienated from the consequences of their agency and themselves. This can range from the alienation that arises from having confronted the probability of failure to the productive alienation that arises from gathering the resolve to make reforms when facing resistance. That is, elite alienation is at the root of psychological fortitude that supports the sound elite judgment needed for value creation, particularly in the context of 'alternating value extraction and creation'. On the other hand, elite alienation from stakeholders that are experiencing the consequences of value transfers may lead to the opposite; value extraction and even value destruction.	ETED development. Transposes the Marxist construct of estrangement and applies it to elite theory. Based on Marx (1844/1959), see also Petrović (1963). Links with leadership styles reviewed by developmental economists (Brady & Spence, 2010; Easterly & Pennings, 2020), and the psychological and sociological features of elite leadership observed by early theorists (Michels, 1962/1999). (Epilogue).
Artificial intelligence (AI) 'The AI division of value alignment test'	A view on AI safety and alignment that is first centered on establishing *qui generat valorem*, as value is co-created by the principals of AI business models and their stakeholders, before ascertaining the *cui bono* beneficiaries of that value. The subsequent step is implementing weighting and offsetting to align the AI with general human development.	ETED position on the AI alignment debate. (Section 8.2.5; refer to Figures A5.3c, A5.3d).
'Automatic destabilizers'	A pro-cyclical reflex elite agency response triggered by economic crises, embedded in institutions, and enabled by bargaining power differentials vs stakeholders, the effect of which is to amplify economic fluctuations. Institutions enable the income/profit levels of elite business models to stay the same, or even grow higher than pre-crisis levels ('same size of the slice' elite bias). Since the overall economic pie shrinks, pre-crisis income/profit levels for elites are *de facto* redistribution (from non-elites to elites). Such automatic responses intensify the 'extractive escalation dynamic' and invariably destabilize the political economy and society. Non-elites suffer a double whammy since their incomes register real negative income growth at rates higher than the economy's negative growth rates. Monetary policies (e.g., negative interest rates), defense policies (e.g., war in times of decline), or fiscal policies (e.g., relief in times of pandemics) can all act as automatic destabilizers.	ETED development. Term chosen to contrast with "automatic stabilizers" (see McKay & Reis, 2016). (Section 7.1.3).

*Includes only selected SVC measurements. The complete set is described in Table A3.1 (see also the visual overview provided in Figure 7.8).

**The terms in this Glossary have diverse connections to the ETED's development ranging from 'none' to 'ETED position' (i.e., a theoretical stance is taken from the literature) to 'ETED development' (a discrete conceptual element advanced for the inquiry).

https://doi.org/10.1515/9783110734638-015

Table A2.1 (continued)

Conceptual element	**Definition**	**ETED relation** and selected sources**
Business model 'Elite business model'	Elite business models are the largest residual income and reward business models in the economy and constitute a system of interdependent activities that are performed by a particular principal as part of an elite coalition in relation to its stakeholders. An elite business model consists of value creation and appropriation activities, manifested in patterns of *how* the principal and the stakeholders respectively create and appropriate value. The patterns are realized through division of value strategies, aim to generate proprietary income/profits, and associate with discrete degrees of sustainable value creation.	ETED development. References Arend (2013); Zott & Amitt (2013); Gassmann, Frankenberger, & Sauer (2016). (Section 2.2.1; SVC measurements include VCr, self-VCp, 360-VCz).
Business model 'Elite business model agglomeration'	Elite business model agglomeration refers to the clustering of specific elite business models in a political economy. When jointly reaching a critical mass, these models bring about a critical juncture in economic development and institutional path dependence which is positive insofar as it is associated with high sustainable value creation. This is the underlying process that explains the 'elite business model critical junctures' conjecture.	ETED position. References David (1985); Liebowitz & Margolis (1999); Acemoglu, Johnson, Robinson, & Yared (2009); Libecap (2011). Differs from "agglomeration economics" (e.g., Duranton & Kerr, 2015). (Section 4.3.4).
Business model 'Business model value creation spectrum' (also 'value spectrum')	A micro-level conceptual element that imagines an organization's business model on a spectrum that ranges between absolute value creation (first-order productive activity) and absolute value extraction (second-order transfer activity). Parallels the meso-level 'elite system value spectrum'.	ETED development. (Section 2.3.2, Proposition 11; SVC measurement is VCp).
Business model 'National business model'	The leading or one of a few business models in a nation that ranks highest in residual income generation. The value creation and appropriation patterns found in the agglomerated elite business models of a country's dominant sectors (e.g., automotive, finance, oil, real estate, agriculture) along with their specific set of institutional, economic, political, and even social characteristics. Usually run by members of the core coalition, from an economic development perspective the determinant feature of the national business model is its sustainable value creation on account of the disproportional impact on elite quality that this has.	ETED development. References literature and diverse national cases (e.g., for Russia, van den Beuke & van Geuns, 2021; for Germany, Chazan & Nilsson, 2022); common understanding. (Sections 7.3.4, 8.1.2).

Table A2.1 (continued)

Conceptual element	**Definition**	**ETED relation** ** **and selected sources**
Cohesion 'Elite cohesion'	A horizontal form of social cohesion that is manifested in elite system coalitions abiding by intra-elite contest rules, elite system leadership, shared narratives that foster an identitarian sense of belonging in the political economy, and loyalty to the elite system in the context of prioritizing long-term wealth stocks over short-term residual income flows in the elite utility function. In its absence, intra-elite contests become deinstitutionalized and have calamitous effects on society. Elite cohesion is also a precondition for elite system transformational leadership, while the normative ideal sees it coupled with a comprehensive separation of powers. Elite cohesion maximizes the bargaining power of the national elite system over non-elites and foreign elite systems.	ETED position. Based on Gottschalk (1944); Mills (1956); Putnam (1976); Burton & Higley (1987); Levitsky & Way (2012); Gulbrandsen (2012); Best (2018a). (Sections 3.2.1, 5.3.3, 7.2.4).
Cohesion 'Elite/non-elite cohesion'	The vertical form of social cohesion. To be relevant, it must encompass a significant number of elite coalitions and non-elite groups. Elite/non-elite cohesion often consists of tactical alliances between particular non-elite groups and elites in intra-elite contests. Ideally, non-elites strategically participate in intra-elite contests and their systematic support for value creation business models solves the intra-elite quality contest dilemma. Narratives are essential for elite/non-elite cohesion.	ETED development. References Chan, To, & Chan (2006). (Sections 5.3.3, 8.1.3).
Cohesion 'Non-elite cohesion'	A horizontal form of social cohesion. While a normative goal, non-elite cohesion is of secondary relevance for institutional change in practice because non-elites are rarely a unified body, instead consisting of diverse groups with disparate interests, as described in the 'low non-elite cohesion' problem. Non-elite cohesion is difficult but can be achieved at critical historical junctures on the back of strong narratives (e.g., religion) or when non-elites feel threatened by foreign elites. Still, to effectively constrain extractive value transfers, this cohesion type must be coupled with 'elite agency on behalf of non-elites'.	ETED position. References Chan, To, & Chan (2006). (Sections 5.3.3, 8.1.3).
Cohesion 'Social cohesion'	Social cohesion refers to the readiness of society's members to work together and is conceived as consisting of three discrete but related forms: elite cohesion (horizontal), non-elite cohesion (horizontal) and elite/non-elite cohesion (vertical). Elite cohesion is the most relevant for human and economic development.	ETED position. References Stanley (2003); Chan, To, & Chan (2006); Best (2018a). (Section 5.3.3).

Table A2.1 (continued)

Conceptual element	**Definition**	**ETED relation**** **and selected sources**
'Core elite coalition'	The core elite coalition stands at the apex of the socio-economic structure pyramid, effecting elite system leadership and having a disproportional role in setting the strategic direction of the political economy (including grand strategy for cross-border business models), influencing intra-elite contests, prompting elite cohesion, and, most critically, realizing institutional change. The economic and human development objective adds an ethical dimension to the transformational agency of the core elite coalition.	References disparate theories of elites. (Sections 1.2, 8.1.1, 8.1.2, Figure 8.1; leadership varieties, Section 7.2.4, Table 7.2; see Tier 5 in the elite separation of powers, Figure A5.11b).
Cross border 'Cross-border elite business model'	Elite business models that generate an appreciable part of their revenue and residual income from markets that are foreign to most of the members of the beneficiary elite coalition. As principals in cross-border stakeholder relationships they engage in value creation and appropriation and are a factor in the economic and human development of both the home and host nations. Such models, like their domestic counterparts, are characterized by discrete degrees of measurable sustainable value creation. The beneficiaries of the models are mostly embedded in the institutions of one nation state and are rarely transnational elite coalitions.	ETED development. Combines notions from the international relations and international business literature. (Section 7.3; SVC measurement is IB-VCr).
Cross border 'Cross-border elite agency'	Cross-border elite agency is 'what elites do' in the international context, mostly in relation to their cross-border elite business models (see also the definition of 'elite agency'). This includes effecting institutional change at both the national and international levels.	ETED development. (Section 7.3.1).
Cross border 'Cross-border elite quality'	An emergent property of a nation that describes the aggregate cross-border value creation position of its elite system's business models engaged in international business. Cross-border elite quality is operationalized as the 'cb-EQr' measurement, and, on a narrower bilateral basis, as the 'bl-EQr'. It partially explains the behavior of a state and its relations with other states in the international system.	ETED development. (Section 7.3.1; SVC measurements include cb-EQr, bl-EQr; Figure 7.5).
Cross border 'Cross-border sustainable value creation'	The sustainable value creation (i.e., the value creation vs value transfers) of the international business of the firm. Operationalized through the 'IB-VCr' measurement that describes the relationship of the principal with foreign stakeholders in terms of value creation relative to 'value appropriated but *not* created' (transfer-IN). This micro-level SVC measurement aims to capture the sustainability of a firm's international business; its inputs are international business SVC metrics while its scores function as inputs to a country's meso-level cross-border elite quality measurements (cb-EQ/bl-EQ).	ETED development. (Sections 7.3.1, 7.3.2; SVC measurements include IB-VCr, IB-self-VCr).

Table A2.1 (continued)

Conceptual element	Definition	ETED relation** and selected sources
'Elite'	An elite is a coalition operating society's leading value creation and appropriation business models that generate the largest quantities of economic activity and residual income. Organizationally, and thus for analytical purposes, an elite is a business model that a coalition has secured from institutions—through wins in the political economy's market, non-market, and narrative market arenas—with limited rights that afford value appropriation advantages and, in consequence, a license to operate at a discrete sustainable value creation position.	Cross-disciplinary literature references. See Table A1.1 on the position this inquiry takes on the reviewed elite conceptualizations, theories, and assumptions. (Section 1.2).
Elite 'Elite agency'	Elite agency is 'what elites do' in relation to their elite business model as principals in a coalition (of economic, political, and knowledge interests) that creates value jointly with stakeholders in formal and informal exchange relationships, exercising leadership to successfully leverage lower transaction costs, higher levels of trust, and superior coordination capacity into (bargaining) power that is then converted into society's largest streams of residual income via first-order value creation or second-order value transfers.	ETED development. (Sections 1.1, 1.2).
Elite 'Elite circulation'	Elite circulation is a social process through which emergent business models become part of the elite and replace incumbent elite business models. Classical elite circulation theory is adapted by introducing elite business models as the central element and stressing that the analytical focus for development purposes should be on their sustainable value creation and value transfers.	ETED position. Classical elite circulation theory of Pareto (1968/1991), Michels (1962/1999); Marx (1867/1959b); Schumpeter (1942/2000). (Sections 1.3.2, 1.3.3).
Elite 'Progressive/ regressive elite circulation'	Elite circulation is progressive when the sustainable value creation of emergent elites exceeds that of incumbent elites in the national elite system, and regressive when it does not. Elite circulation is necessary for economic and human development on the condition that it is progressive.	ETED development. References common intuition and literature including Marx (1867/1959b); Schumpeter (1942/2000). (Section 1.3.2).
Elite bargain	A political economy pact, settlement, or bargain that members of different elite coalitions make with each other. In order to stimulate value creation, elite bargains rely on elite transformational leadership to supplement intra-elite contests as a mechanism to establish inclusive institutional change. An essential applied normative feature of elite bargains is that value transfers are limited. Two types of bargains are outlined: a broader 'elite institutional change bargain' that focuses on the law and regulations, and the narrower 'elite redistribution constraints bargain' that focuses on specific redistributive policy initiatives.	ETED position. References literature including Dercon's "elite bargain" (2022); O'Donnell & Schmitter (1986); Burton & Higley (1987). (Sections 7.1.5, 8.2.4; Tables 7.1, 8.3).

Table A2.1 (continued)

Conceptual element	Definition	ETED relation** and selected sources
Elite 'Elite coalition'	An elite coalition is formed around an elite business model with members specialized in the market arena (business elites in pursuit of 'money'), the non-market arena (political elites in pursuit of 'might'), and the narrative market arena (knowledge elites in pursuit of 'mind'). The elite coalition is a sub-system of the elite system and is held together by the centripetal forces of elite coordination leadership that amasses power and, more conclusively, elite business model leadership that converts power into residual income.	ETED position. Integrates diverse literatures on elite types (Figure 3.6).
Elite bargain 'Elite institutional change bargain'	In A Weighted Structural Reform Framework for policy, aimed at adjusting the incentive system (on the logic of the 'weight and offset value transfers' implication), the first step is the (i) general assessment of sustainable value creation (of an elite business model) followed by the (ii) formulation of weighted structural reform, ultimately leading to the (iii) institutional change bargain. The discontinuance of transfers must occur *ipso facto* or be institutionally phased out by the elite bargain to preempt transferee elites from reneging on their commitments as their bargaining power rises (due to the residual income gained from transfers, see the dynamics of The Elite Business Model Lifecycle). Notwithstanding institutional foresight and the bargain's guarantees, continual transformational leadership is needed at the system level to ensure that such bargains do not falter.	ETED development. References literature including Dercon's "elite bargain" (2022); O'Donnell & Schmitter (1986); Burton & Higley (1987). (Sections 7.1.5; Table 7.1; Figure A5.9b).
Elite bargain 'Elite redistribution constraints bargain'	In A Weighted Redistribution Framework for policy, aimed at sustainable redistribution, the first step is the (i) transfer parties' assessment (establishing transferees/transferors) followed by the (ii) formulation of constraints on redistribution, ultimately leading to the (iii) constraints bargain that secures their implementation. The discontinuance of constraints on redistribution must be institutionally sanctioned in the elite bargain to preempt transferee elites from disavowing such constraints as their bargaining power rises (due to the residual income gained from redistribution, see the dynamics of The Elite Business Model Lifecycle). Notwithstanding institutional foresight and the bargain's guarantees, elite system level leadership is needed *at the time of expiry* to ensure that redistribution is phased out when it is due.	ETED development. References the literature, Dercon's "elite bargain" (2022); O'Donnell & Schmitter (1986); Burton & Higley (1987). (Section 8.2.4, Table 8.3, Figure A5.9b).

Table A2.1 (continued)

Conceptual element	Definition	ETED relation** and selected sources
'Elite judgment'	Elite judgment refers to decisions associated with the practice of elite leadership, normatively grounded on the weighting and offsetting of value transfers, that consider the feasibility of implementing these through stable elite bargains. When transformational, elite judgment addresses the existence of value transfers and, more generally, the 'low elite quality' problem. Spurred by the 'inextinguishable value creation option of elites', such elite judgments require taking original intellectual, ethical, and aesthetic positions and demand psychological boldness.	ETED development. (Section 8.3.3 on connecting the dots).
'Elite quality'	Elite quality is the meso-level emergent property of the elite system that describes the proportion of first-order productive value creation and second-order extractive value transfers of all elite business models in a political economy. This sustainable value creation aggregate has a purported independent variable relationship with human development and economic growth. Conceptually, it is a description of 'GDP origination'. SVC measurements of elite quality include: the EQx, a top-down comparative global measurement based on macro-level indicators; the EQr, a domestic bottom-up measurement based on firm-level metrics and ratings; and the PEz, a perceptions survey of elites.	ETED development. (Chapters 4, 5, 6; SVC measurements include EQx, EQr, PEz).
Elite quality 'Elite Quality Index' (EQx)	The operationalization of elite quality as a global comparative ranking of the aggregate sustainable value creation of national elite systems.	SVC measurement. (Section 6.2, contextualized in Table A3.1a).
Elite quality 'Panel-EQx' (PEQx)	The 'PanelEQx' or 'PEQx' is a dataset designed for research and practice that measures elite quality over time, i.e., value creation and extraction in political economies over time. The PEQx conceptually corresponds to the Elite Quality Index (EQx) and is based on a discrete methodological approach that utilizes a subset of indicators contingent on the availability of historical data.	SVC measurement. Casas-Klett & Cozzi (2024, p. 32).
Elite quality 'World elite quality'	International institutions are secondary to national ones, and so elite business models are institutionally anchored to the nation state, meaning that there is no coherent world elite system as such. World elite quality is therefore a conceptual element that represents a rough aggregate of the weighted sustainable value creation of all national elite systems. Its purpose is heuristic, to provide an indication of 'the state of the world' and of future global trends.	ETED development. (Section 7.3.3; SVC measurement is world-EQ).

Table A2.1 (continued)

Conceptual element	Definition	ETED relation** and selected sources
Elite quality 'World Elite Quality Index' (world-EQ)	The operationalization of 'world elite quality' as an index; a *de facto* sum of the elite quality of all national elite systems calculated on the basis of global average indicators organized using the EQx architecture. These include worldwide life expectancy, planetary environmental benchmarks, educational attainment, innovation rates, global inflation, industry dominance, or armed conflicts.	SVC measurement. (Section 7.3.3, detailed in Table A3.1a).
'Elite replacement'	Elite replacement is an extreme type of elite circulation where comparatively few incumbent elite coalitions and their members maintain their status as elites as a result of elite circulation processes. When overly extensive or enacted through violence it is associated with lower coordination capacity in the economy due to the loss of 'knowledge'.	ETED position. Pareto (1968/1991); Marx (1867/1959b). (Sections 1.3.2; 1.3.3).
'Elite system' (national)	The elite system is a meso-level generic structure constituted by elite coalitions and characterized by their business models. It is a high-impact sub-system of the macro-level economic system and its emerging properties play an outsized role in a nation's economic development.	ETED development. (Section 3.1).
Elite system 'Elite system value spectrum'	A meso-level conceptual element that imagines the aggregate agency of elite business models on a spectrum that ranges between absolute value creation (first-order productive activity) and absolute value extraction (second-order transfer activity). While not operationalized, it is termed the Elite Quality Position (EQp) and parallels the business model micro-level 'value spectrum' (VCp).	ETED development. (Section 6.5.2; EQp is not an SVC measurement).
Elite system 'Elite non-system'	A structural void in a political economy where a complete and coherent elite system does not materialize and adversely affects sustainable value creation and development. In this work, the elite non-system conceptual element, or 'partial elite', finds application in modeling international relations, development outcomes, and the non-independence of nations. At the global level it explains tragedies of the commons such as the failure to address environmental crises or AI regulation. Without a functional elite system, institutions are of little practical consequence.	ETED development. Uses examples like the EU elite non-system. (Sections 7.3.4; 7.3.5).

Table A2.1 (continued)

Conceptual element	Definition	ETED relation** and selected sources
'Elite theory of economic development' (ETED)	A political economy theory based on the 'value is created or transferred' ontological assumption for socio-economic relations, that, on the principle of parsimony, claims that the wealth of nations and its distribution in a society is the result of elite agency and judgments concerning value transfers. Economic development is explained with recourse to conceptual elements developed from a multi-disciplinary set of ideas hailing from sociology, economics, strategic management, finance, politics, international relations, ethics and other fields. A specific integrative logic binds these together in a conceptual architecture that aims to yield falsifiable propositions, while proposing a wide range of micro, meso, and macro measurements to test them. Aiming at a grand theory of the social sciences, the ETED provides a narrative with normative implications centered on weighting sustainable value creation that is anchored by a set of ethical principles. Positive economic development trajectories associate with transformational elite leadership at the business model and meso-level system levels in the context of intra-elite contests. The theory's reconceptualization of freedom provides a clarion call for structural reform and political narratives.	ETED development. (This book; Section 5.1, see also Figure P.1).
'End of history'	A metaphor invoked in this work to denote either the 'null risk origination' scenario, where elites (and non-elites) do not bear any risk and so there is no new value creation, or simply the disappearance of sustainable value creation from a political economy, putatively as the result of low elite circulation velocity.	ETED position. Critical position taken on Fukuyama (1992). (Sections 3.3.3, 6.6.5; see Figure 6.9).
Ethics 'The sustainable value creation set of ethical principles for human and economic development'	Ethical principles for human and economic development that aim to foster transformational leadership by supplying decision-making guardrails and guidance based on a realistic account of how the political economy works. The set of principles consist of a *maxim* (*To the creators the value created*), two *tenets* for conceptual guidance, and four *precepts* for practical guidance, and can complement the personal moral values of elite individuals.	ETED development. (Chapter 8, Table A4.3a).

Table A2.1 (continued)

Conceptual element	**Definition**	**ETED relation** and selected sources**
'Fractal system'	The political economy system is fractal in terms of how its sources of value creation and transfers are distributed. While the core coalition holds 'the extraordinary lever', self-similarity is pervasive across scale as lesser levers function on the same bargaining power differential and residual income logic. Moreover, these levers, found in each and every nook and cranny of the economy, are held by local elite coalitions. Fractality underlies the leverage of 'the extraordinary lever' and the power of 'the power multiplier'. The conceptualization of the economic system as fractal and subject to power laws has normative policy implications (e.g., in terms of industrial policy), while it is conjectured that the higher the degree of fractality, the greater the value creation potential of the nation.	ETED position. Implied in complex adaptive systems (e.g., McDaniel, Lanham, & Anderson, 2009); notions of fractals (Mandelbrot, 1989; Liebovitch & Scheurle, 2000; Brown, Gupta, Li, Milne, Restrepo, & West, 2002; O'Brien et al., 2023). (Section 3.2.3; Epilogue, Figure E.2; see the 'elite system fractality links to value creation' conjecture).
Freedom	The unconstrained ability to create and benefit from value. The conceptual element of freedom in the ETED is derived from its set of ethical principles and institutionalized through 'The Three Freedoms for Development Model'. The two fundamental freedoms are (the negative) freedom *from* transfer-OUT and the (positive) freedom *to* create value. The third is the enabling freedom to *exit*.	ETED development. Locke (1823/1993); Fromm (1994); Sen (1999a); Acemoglu & Robinson (2019a). (Section 8.3).
Freedom 'Freedom *to* create value'	A fundamental freedom of the ETED and part of the three freedoms that are deemed necessary for economic and human development. Freedom *to* create value references positive freedom and is the power to realize one's value creation potential.	ETED position. Fromm (1994), also see Locke (1823/1993); Sen (1999a); Nussbaum (2003); Carter (2019). (Section 8.3.1; see The Three Freedoms for Development Model, Figure 8.5).
Freedom 'Freedom *from* value extraction'	A fundamental freedom of the ETED and part of the three freedoms that are deemed necessary for economic and human development. Freedom *from* value extraction references negative freedom and is the power over interference from those whose business models rely on value appropriated but *not* created.	ETED position. Fromm (1994), also see Locke (1823/1993); Universal Declaration of Human Rights (1948). Section 8.3.1; see The Three Freedoms for Development Model, Figure 8.5).
Freedom 'Freedom to *exit*'	The enabling freedom of the ETED and part of the three freedoms that are deemed necessary for economic and human development. As a mechanism to guarantee the two fundamental freedoms, it is the power to break free from extractive principal-stakeholder relationships. To be effective, the freedom to *exit* must be institutionalized in laws such as limited liability or bankruptcy.	ETED position. References actual institutional arrangements. (Section 8.3.2; see The Three Freedoms for Development Model, Figure 8.5).

Table A2.1 (continued)

Conceptual element	Definition	ETED relation** and selected sources
'Grand strategy'	A vision for both state power *and* for value creation and appropriation across borders, jointly conceived by the core elite coalition usually in conjunction with a specialized elite coalition, and a component of elite system leadership.	ETED position. References Gaddis (2018); Jacobs & Page (2005).
'Indicator' (inputs for the EQx and other SVC measurements)	The conceptually indivisible, discrete macro-level data sources of SVC measurements that describe quantifiable value creation or value transfer phenomena in the political economy. For instance, once normalized, weighted, and aggregated, indicators inform the composite scores and rankings of the Elite Quality Index (EQx) which describes the global comparative elite quality of a nation's meso-level elite system. The counterparts of indicators for micro-level SVC measurements are termed 'SVC metrics' or simply 'metrics'.	SVC measurement input. References OECD (2008); the EQx methodology in Casas-Klett, Cozzi, Diebold, & Zeller (2020); Diebold (2022). (Section 6.2).
'Institutional entrepreneurship'	A metaphor describing how elite agency converts power into institutional change in accordance with the preferences of specific elite business models.	ETED development. (Sections 4.3.3, 4.3.4; implicit in Figures 3.2, 3.3, 4.5).
'Institutional failure'	Cumulative institutional change in support of extractive elite business models, or the failure of institutions to support emerging elites with more inclusive models. It results from a failed and ossified system of checks and balances across The Seven Intra-elite Power Relations.	References "institutional sclerosis" (Olson, 1982); Baumol (1990); Acemoglu, Johnson, & Robinson (2005). (Sections 3.3.3, 4.2.3).
'Institutional quality'	The effectiveness and integrity of the institutions of law, regulation, and governance leads to economic and human development. In the ETED, institutional quality is also the precursor of development but is anteceded by elite quality on the premise that elite agency leads to institutional change. The focus is on the rules—both for business models and for intra-elite contests—that enable or constrain the sustainable value creation of elite business models.	References The World Bank (2020); Djankov, McLiesh, & Ramalho (2006); Kuncic (2014); Anderson & Marcouiller (2002). (See Figure 6.1; Section 3.1.3).
Contests 'Intra-elite contests'	The defining factor of institutional change and economic and human development outcomes in the political economy. The objectives of the contests are the institutions that most matter: elite business model rules and the intra-elite contest rules that determine these. Normatively, the more comprehensive the elite separation of powers is in the context of elite cohesion, the greater the likelihood that intra-elite contests yield inclusive institutional change (in terms of elite business model rules), ultimately prompting the emergence of elite business models with higher sustainable value creation.	ETED development. (Sections 3.3.1, 5.3.3; Figures 5.2, 8.3, A5.12).

Table A2.1 (continued)

Conceptual element	Definition	ETED relation** and selected sources
Contests 'Intra-elite meta-contests'	Intra-elite contests about the processes that establish 'intra-elite contest rules', i.e., the meta-institutions that in turn establish the 'elite business model rules' and determine 'who gets what'. Intra-elite meta-contests are principally resolved through the exercise of bargaining power differentials.	ETED development. Leverages the meta-institutions notion of Mokyr & Nye (2007); Lorini (2014).
'Leadership'	Leadership involves effectively wielding power and leveraging coordination capacity to achieve an organization's objectives. Leadership in the ETED is about commanding 'the extraordinary lever' of the elite coalition to generate residual income. Leadership is the solution to the 'low elite quality' problem and in 'the great elite coalition for development' conjecture is critical to human and economic development in its transformational varieties (at both the firm and elite system levels).	ETED position. References diverse literature including Stogdill (1950); Jones & Olken (2005); Brady & Spence (2010); Parris & Peachey (2013); Boucekkine, Piacquadio, & Prieur (2019). (Sections 1.3.3, 7.2.4, 8.1.5)
Leadership (a) 'Elite coordination leadership'	The leadership that the elite coalition exercises at the business model level to leverage accumulated coordination capacity and use it for maximum bargaining power differentials over stakeholders. The first of the three fundamental varieties of leadership of the ETED.	ETED development. (Section 7.2.4; Figures 1.2, 4.1; The Five Varieties of Elite Leadership in Table 7.2).
Leadership (b) 'Elite business model leadership'	The leadership that the elite coalition exercises at the business model level to convert bargaining power differentials over stakeholders into maximum residual income. The second of the three fundamental varieties of leadership of the ETED.	ETED development. (Section 7.2.4; Figures 2.1, 3.6, 4.1; The Five Varieties of Elite Leadership in Table 7.2).
Leadership (c) 'Elite system leadership'	Leadership at the elite system level, usually exercised by the core elite coalition, to increase elite cohesion that in turn facilitates institutional change for the maximization of elite bargaining power and residual income. The third of the three fundamental varieties of leadership of the ETED.	ETED development. (Section 7.2.4; The Five Varieties of Elite Leadership in Table 7.2).
Leadership (d) 'Elite transformational leadership'	Leadership at the business model level that converts bargaining power differentials over stakeholders into maximum residual income that is, nonetheless, self-constrained by the minimization of value (and risk) transfers and the maximization of value (and risk) creation. This transformational leadership variety has an ethical anchor, necessitates a long-run temporal perspective, requires purposeful and continuous business model transformation (e.g., in consistency with social and technological changes), accrues legitimacy on account of signaling, and technically requires the weighting and offsetting of value creation (including transfer-OUT) against value transfer (transfer-IN) activities. The first of the two transformational varieties of leadership of the ETED.	ETED development. (Section 7.2.4; The Five Varieties of Elite Leadership in Table 7.2).

Table A2.1 (continued)

Conceptual element	Definition	ETED relation** and selected sources
Leadership (e) 'Elite system transformational leadership'	The leadership exercised at the elite system level by the core elite coalition that utilizes elite cohesion and the elite separation of powers (see Figure 5.2) to raise elite quality by constraining extractive value (and risk) transfers and engaging in structural reform to incentivize sustainable value creation. Such leadership is driven by a set of ethical principles, accrues legitimacy on account of signaling, and technically requires the weighting and offsetting of value creation (including the sum of transfer-OUT) against value transfers (the sum of transfer-IN) in the political economy as it seeks a sustainable elite system for economic and human development that furthers elite/non-elite cohesion and bargaining power advantages in the international system. The second of the two transformational varieties of leadership of the ETED.	ETED development. (Sections 7.2.4, 7.3.3; The Five Varieties of Elite Leadership in Table 7.2).
Leadership (i) 'Fundamental leadership varieties'	The three fundamental leadership varieties in The Five Varieties of Elite Leadership typology that exist in a functioning political economy. They are: (a) elite coordination leadership; (b) elite business model leadership; and (c) elite system leadership.	ETED development. (Section 7.2.4, Figures 1.2 and 2.1; The Five Varieties of Elite Leadership in Table 7.2).
Leadership (ii) 'Transformational leadership varieties'	The two transformational leadership varieties in The Five Varieties of Elite Leadership typology that are characteristic of political economies where elites are intent on increasing sustainable value creation, elite quality, and the prospects for economic and human development that heavily rely on individual 'elite judgment'. They are associated with ethical positions and are: (d) elite transformational leadership; and (e) elite system transformational leadership.	ETED development. (See Section 7.2.4; The Five Varieties of Elite Leadership in Table 7.2).
Lever 'The absolute lever'	Extends 'the extraordinary lever' metaphor to the AI. It reflects a conceptual universe where the non-human AI elite —omniscient and omnipotent—has absolute power in the political economy on account of its infinite bargain power differentials with human stakeholders. All (former) human elites revert to non-elite status (applies in the cases of a single non-human AI elite or various non-human elite coalitions each wielding 'the absolute lever').	ETED development. Combines literature on power and AI capabilities. (Sections 4.3.3, 8.1.4, 8.1.6, Epilogue; Figure A5.3d; Table E.1).

Table A2.1 (continued)

Conceptual element	**Definition**	**ETED relation** and selected sources**
Lever 'The extraordinary lever' (of elites)	A metaphor that describes the coordination capacity advantage that elites have over their direct and indirect stakeholders in a particular sector of the political economy. The advantage that the lever affords is vastly greater than its source, the transaction cost differential of elites over their stakeholders. Leverage is achieved when the power that elites have over their direct stakeholders is amplified by the power that such stakeholders have over their own direct stakeholders in the value chain. 'The power multiplier' effect underlying the lever explains the applied coordination capacity that elites have in the specific field where their agency unfolds or, in the case of core coalitions, over society at large. The levers held by elites are key for human development, but can be misused. The levers make the coordination capacity of elites 'extraordinary', a value appropriation gift that the social system affords to itself and to those at its apex. As a result, the membership of elite coalitions is much desired and contested. In fractal fashion, while the core elite coalition operates 'the extraordinary lever', lesser but similar extraordinary levers function on the same bargaining power differential and residual income logic and are held by elite coalitions in every nook and cranny of the economy.	ETED development. References literature on hierarchies, power, transaction costs, trust, networks, coordination capacity, power. (Part of Proposition 4, Sections 1.3.4, 3.2.3; Figure set A5.3).
Lever 'The power multiplier'	The amplification effect that underlies 'the extraordinary lever'. The transaction cost differentials between elites and their counterparties (non-elites) lead to disproportionally large bargaining power and, as a result, coordination capacity differentials. The multiplier operates across the length of the value chain and grows at each step of every principal-stakeholder transaction. As a simplified illustration, if a given business model yields a transaction cost advantage consistent with a power differential of 'two' from one level to the next, then the principal has a power difference of 'four' with stakeholders two levels removed in the value chain (i.e., the stakeholders of the stakeholders), before rapidly increasing the power differential to '32' with a stakeholder five levels removed (assuming no loss of power due to friction, distance, etc.). Due to this multiplier effect, human principals have power over societal stakeholders with whom they have no direct relationship. This chain of leverage explains skewed value appropriation patterns and why a single general can commandeer an army of 10,000, the existence of billionaires, and religious leaders with bureaucracies that influence the behavior of millions. 'The power multiplier' can be compared to fractional reserve banking and the creation of credit. The multiplier is the mechanism behind applied coordination capacity, is inherent to power, and is essential for inclusive human development.	ETED position. References the VCA and literature on the subjects of power, multipliers (Lange, 1943), "force multipliers", and an intuitive understanding of power in practice (see, for instance, *Book of Five Rings*, Musashi, 1645/1974). (Proposition 4; see Figure A5.3a).

Table A2.1 (continued)

Conceptual element	Definition	ETED relation** and selected sources
License 'License for evil'	An operationalized metaphor describing institutionally sanctioned rights to destroy value, including human life, to a degree equivalent or above value appropriated, i.e., 'destructive' transfer-COST vs revenue. Normatively and ethically, such a license can never be granted. Nonetheless, in reality, the 'license for evil' is granted to firms whose 'destructive value transfer-COST to revenue ratio' ('value destruction ratio') is 1.00 or above, meaning that 'destructive' transfer-COST (off-P&L *negative* value created and *not* appropriated) equals or exceeds revenue (value appropriation).	ETED development. References common intuition; literature on destructive elite business models (e.g., Purdue Pharma). (Sections 8.2.1, 8.2.2; Figure A5.5c).
License 'License to steal'	A metaphor describing institutionally sanctioned rights to extractive value and risk transfers. Normatively, such a license can be granted for a limited time and amounts under the 'weight and offset value transfers' (holistic) implication. Theoretical support for the policies described by the metaphor comes from the 'alternating value extraction and creation' conjecture and the 'extractive push' dilemma, and it is normatively developed in A Weighted Structural Reform Framework for policy, ideally referencing A Transfer Constraints Framework for policy formulation.	ETED development. References the rent-seeking literature and Tullock (1967). (Sections 2.3.1, 5.3.4, 7.1.5, 8.2.3; Tables 7.1, 8.2).
Lifecycle 'The Elite Business Model Lifecycle'	The inherent rise and fall of elite business models as a pattern that occurs in relation to political economy dynamics, where residual income is first based on value creation and then on power endowments that support value transfers via wins in the market, non-market and narrative market arenas. The lifecycle's 'value transfers replace value creation at maturity' conjecture matters to development as the extractive models that emerge at the end of the lifecycle might agglomerate into a harmful critical juncture and must be mitigated or suppressed through weighted structural reforms.	ETED development. References the life cycle theory of the firm of Mueller (1972); Schumpeter (1939). (Section 4.3.4; Figures A5.9a, A5.9b).
Lifecycle 'The Cross-border Elite Business Model Lifecycle'	The elite business model lifecycle in the international business context. Defined by international relations, it references The Great Power Elite Quality Lifecycle to account for the rise and fall of residual income (from abroad). This key variable explains that sustainable value creation or extractive value transfers by global companies in the foreign markets in which they operate is dependent on the power of their home state.	ETED development. Links the life cycle theory of the firm (Mueller, 1972) with cyclical theories of state power from Gibbon (1776/2001) onwards. (Section 7.3.2; Figure A5.9d).

Table A2.1 (continued)

Conceptual element	**Definition**	**ETED relation**** **and selected sources**
Lifecycle 'The Great Power Elite Quality Lifecycle' for international relations	The rise and fall of nations is the result of changes in domestic and cross-border elite quality over time. Leading states emerge from high quality domestic elite business models (producing exports, new technologies, financial surpluses) that augment their power (large markets, militaries, financial reserves) that in turn support increasingly effective value appropriation by their cross-border elite business models. When the proportion of elite business models at the end of their lifecycle surges, or elite quality declines for other reasons, the power that the state can exercise in international relations diminishes but does so only after a considerable time lag. In the interlude, the nation's dwindling but still considerable power might be applied for extractive cross-border business models, thus reversing the inclusive cross-border elite quality that allowed the state's ascent in the international hierarchy in the first place.	ETED position. Contrasts with Gibbon (1776/2001); Spengler (1922); Kennedy (1987); Dalio (2021); references Kondratieff (1925/1935); Schumpeter (1939). (Section 7.3.3; Figures 7.7 and A5.9d; see 'value transfers replace value creation at maturity' conjecture, Section 4.3.4 and Figure A5.9a).
'Metric' ('SVC metric'; inputs for the VCr, self-VCp, and other SVC measurements)	The conceptually indivisible, discrete, firm-level data sources that describe quantifiable value creation and risk transfers (transfer-IN/OUT) by a firm's business model. After their conceptual determination they are classified (via the 12 blocks of The Business Model Sustainable Value Scorecard), normalized, aggregated, and weighted to become inputs for the SVC measurements of a firm. The counterparts of SVC metrics for meso-level SVC measurements are termed 'indicators'.	SVC measurement input. References the ESG literature, its "social origins" (Eccles & Stroehle, 2018) and, in its applied development, third-party metric suppliers (e.g., MSCI, ISS, LSEG); Casas-Klett & Nerlinger, 2023. (Sections 6.6.1, 6.6.3; Figures 6.6, 6.7, 6.8).
'Mind'	A metaphor for the social power type obtained by elite coalitions through wins in the narrative market arena; social power is associated with knowledge elites.	ETED development. References the literature on narratives (Section 1.3.4).
'Might'	A metaphor for the political power type obtained by elite coalitions through wins in the political non-market arena; political power is associated with political elites.	ETED position. References the political science literature. (Section 1.3.4).
'Money'	A metaphor for the economic power type obtained by elite coalitions through wins in the business market arena; economic power is associated with business elites.	ETED position. References common understanding. (Section 1.3.4).

Table A2.1 (continued)

Conceptual element	Definition	ETED relation** and selected sources
'Non-elite'	The non-elite is made up of all members of society—the citizenry—who are not elites. Non-elites are directly or indirectly stakeholders in elite business models but are not principal beneficiaries. Far from being a unified body, the non-elite consists of many groups with disparate interests. One such non-elite group of great importance to elites is the managerial, technical, and creative class. Non-elites are defined and conceptualized in relation to elites in both the ETED's descriptive socio-economic structure pyramid and for economic and human development purposes.	References a comprehensive range of sociological, political, and other theories on elites as well as conceptual elements. (Section 8.1.1; Figure 8.1).
Non-elite 'Non-elite agency'	The agency of specific non-elite groups or of the non-elite at large. Since the leadership of non-elite groups—potential future elites—is tactical at best, it is both uninterested and unable to conceive general non-elite preferences to further development. Non-elite leadership is fragmented and possesses limited coordination capacity, explaining the non-elite rule fallacy, the 'low non-elite cohesion' problem, and the controversial 'elite agency on behalf of non-elites' approach to realize non-elite interests.	ETED development. (Sections 3.3.2, 8.1.3; Figures, 3.9, 8.1, A5.8).
Non-elite 'Non-elite quality'	An emergent aggregate property of the non-elite based on the contributions of discrete non-elite groups as business model stakeholders in terms of sustainable value creation. Non-elites generally engage in value creation through their knowledge and labor inputs and so contribute to overall elite quality but are often at the receiving end of bargaining power differentials and so suffer from degrees of extraction. On the other hand, non-elite groups may also provide no contribution to value creation, while appropriating value *not* created. To that end, certain non-elite groups make tactical alliances with elites to the detriment of other non-elite groups (see the Marxist *lumpenproletariat*), espouse violent narratives, or otherwise undermine non-elite cohesion.	ETED position. References common understanding; the literature since Plato (1908) and Aristotle (1912). (Section 3.3.3, tangentially discussed at various points of the inquiry, see Section 8.1; see non-elite agency or political options in Figures 3.9, A5.8; Epilogue discussion on non-elite quality and Figure E.1).
Non-elite 'Managerial, technical, and creative class'	A part of the non-elite strata that is directly involved in the running and advancement of elite business models (potentially contributing to their value creation). This group connects elites to non-elites and society's resources at large and are an essential component in the mechanisms of 'the extraordinary lever' that realize the coordination capacity of elites. The group includes managers, judges, journalists, military officers, priests, civil servants and so on. Since they are not prime residual income beneficiaries of the elite business model, they are deemed to be part of the non-elite class (even if many members speciously imagine themselves to be part of the elite).	References various literature such as Mosca's (1939) 'second stratum'; and Bottomore's (1993) 'sub-elite'. (Section 8.1.1; Figure 8.1).

Table A2.1 (continued)

Conceptual element	Definition	ETED relation** and selected sources
'Nook and cranny'	A metaphor that represents the narrow recesses and niche corners of the economy such as specific industry sectors, local geographies, and market segments. Elite business models that possess 'the extraordinary lever' in these specific fields are able to reap second-order value transfers. Given the self-similarity of the levers and multiplier effects across different scales (with the largest being in the hands of the core elite coalition), it is these nooks and crannies that prescriptively confirm the fractal nature of the political economy, as well as the difficulties in effecting structural reforms, as these niches remain concealed from the political and narrative market arenas and under the radar of institutional change. The concern of the ETED is that value transfers in these nooks and crannies dangerously add up and intensify the 'extractive escalation dynamic'. In a perfect world and regardless of their size, they ought to be the target of micro-policy interventions aimed at adjusting their narrow incentive systems and transforming their local elite business models towards higher sustainable value creation.	ETED development. Associated with the understanding of fractal structures in complex systems, see Mandelbrot (1989); Liebovitch & Scheurle, (2000); Brown, Gupta, Li, Milne, Restrepo, & West (2002); note "social fractals" (O'Brien et al., 2023); relevant to policy as in Johnson (1982); Aghion, Cai, Dewatripont, Du, Harrison, & Legros (2015); Primi (2015); Aghion, et al. (2015); Mazzucato & Rodrik (2023); Shih (2023). (Sections 7.1.5; 3.2.3; implications in Sections 7.1.4 or 7.1.5; elements unified in Epilogue; Epilogue and Figure E.2).
'Offsetting'	The process that addresses the practical aspects of the general sustainable value creation optimization problem of the political economy at the business model level. It is based on the trade-off notion— central to economics—that it is not possible to simultaneously satisfy all goals. Offsetting involves the establishment of trade-offs between business model activities based on their monetary quantification. The offsetting of business model activities takes a position on implicit weighting, and occurs through transformational leadership at the firm level that is incentivized by institutions. It is made practical by SVC metrics, measurements, and the frameworks of the 'weight and offset value transfers' (holistic) implication.	ETED position. References trade-offs in economics (see Campbell & Kelly, 1994; Eccles, 2024), cost-benefit analysis (see, Frank, 2000). (Sections 5.3.1, 6.6.1, 7.1, Chapter 8; see 'weighting' in Glossary).
'Omniscience'	In this inquiry, the state of knowing everything refers to the comprehensive description of value transfers in all of the socio-economic relations in a political economy. Such a comprehensive approach to capturing reality is currently unrealistic as it would necessitate massive amounts of data and unconventional macroeconomic models, but might be possible with the existence of a superintelligence.	ETED position. References common intuition and various philosophical traditions. (Figures A5.10; Tables A3.1b, E.1).
'Political economy'	The mechanisms through which second-order value and risk transfers are enabled and the required bargaining power differentials are established.	ETED position. (Section 4.1.2).

Table A2.1 (continued)

Conceptual element	**Definition**	**ETED relation**** **and selected sources**
Political economy 'Political economy omniscience' (of value transfers)	The category of SVC measurements based on tentative assumptions that all value transfers are knowable—and computable—in the political economy. Political economy omniscience is a thought experiment similar to the technological solutionism fallacy. At present, this quest is reflected in SVC measurements like 'weighted transfers general equilibrium' (WTGE) macroeconomic models and informs the even more demanding 'individual value creation rating' (ind-VCr) and the 'weighted transfers game' (WT-Game). Ultimately, these measurements would be purposed for practice (e.g., policy formulation, gaming services). Games might best realize such omniscience quests as a multiplayer community harnesses the collective knowledge and intuitions of the public. Such a game world, literally a digital parallel universe of the political economy, could provide benchmarks for the real world to move towards sustainable value creation, aiding in the formulation of weighted structural reform proposals or the design of narratives for political parties.	ETED development. References the gaming industry (e.g, *EVE Online* MMORPG, *SimCity* series, or *Capitalism Lab*). (Sections 7.1.1, 8.3.3; Figures A5.10, set A5.14; links to AI, see Tables A3.1b, E.1).
'Power'	The ability to assert one's will and to coordinate, a capacity that emanates from the low transaction costs enjoyed by narrow coalitions in a society. The relevant form of power in the ETED is bargaining power as 'the extraordinary lever' held by elites is applied to appropriate value across principal-stakeholder relationships. For development purposes, power has a dual nature or potentiality: it can be used by elites for extractive transfers, but also for transformational leadership, and is indispensable for sustainable value creation and bringing about the structural reforms that lead to economic and human development. Antipower approaches or the elimination of bargaining power differentials in the political economy are both naive (reflecting the elite denial fallacy) and counterproductive.	ETED position. References Weber (1925); Arendt (1970); Pareto (1981); van der Eijk (2018); Coff (1999). (Section 4.3; Figure A5.3a).
Power 'Bargaining power'	Bargaining power is the relative capacity to assert one's will in principal-stakeholder relationship transactions, and its possession is usually manifested in the form of advantageous pricing. It results from wins in the political economy contest arenas through the accumulation of 'money', 'might', and 'mind' that provide business model principals with positive power differentials vs counterparties and enable influence over prices and terms that monetize value, including value appropriated but *not* created. Asymmetrical bargaining power relationships are sought by all agents in the economy and usually favor elite business model principals over non-elite stakeholders. Contrasts with the normative, 'equalized bargaining power equilibrium prices' condition.	Porter (1980); Coff (1999); MacDonald & Ryall (2004), adapted for the ETED in Proposition 8. (Section 2.2.2; Figure A5.9c).

Table A2.1 (continued)

Conceptual element	Definition	ETED relation** and selected sources
Power 'The elite separation of powers'	A comprehensive conceptualization of the elite separation of powers at the national elite system level is central in explaining sustainable value creation and growth and extends classical separation of powers theory from the power domain of politics into that of the economy and society. The 'within-arena' (Tier 1), 'across-arena' (Tier 2) and 'within-system' (Tier 3) checks and balances result in robust intra-elite contests across The Seven Intra-elite Power Relations. In the international context, a fourth separation of powers tier, 'across-system' (Tier 4), is added to moderate each of three domestic tiers. In most political economies, a fifth separation of powers tier (Tier 5) is also at work, termed as 'from-core' to denote the core elite coalition's ability to check and balance regular elite coalitions. The specific elite separation of powers configuration is an emergent property of the elite system.	ETED position. Extends Montesquieu's (1748/1949) tripartite separation of powers and constitutional government theory; Madison (1787/1977). (Sections 3.2.2, 3.3.3, Propositions 16, 20; see also Figures 1.2, 3.7, 3.9, 3.10, Figure set A5.11; Table 3.2).
Power 'The Seven Intra-elite Power Relations'	The seven types of relations between business, political, and knowledge elites that constitute effective checks and balances on power in a political economy. Sustainable value creation outcomes and economic and human development rely in part on robust intra-elite contests in all seven of the intra-elite power relations that in turn depend on a comprehensive separation of powers across the three tiers of checks and balances.	ETED development. (Proposition 20, Section 3.3.3; Table 3.2).
Power 'The Three-tier Set of Intra-elite Checks and Balances'	The three types of checks and balances in a political economy are institutionalized to different degrees in each country. In Tier 1 'within-arena', same type economic, political, and knowledge elites compete for preeminence in the market, non-market, and narrative market arenas and check and balance each other; in Tier 2 'across-arena', economic, political, and knowledge elites check and balance each other; in Tier 3 'within-system', elite coalitions compete with their elite business models against each other.	ETED development. (Section 3.2.2; Figure 3.7).
Productive activity 'First-order activity' (value creation)	An activity that creates value. Productive activities kick-start and maintain economic life. They relate to production, specialization, trade, finance, and innovation in all of its varieties. Productive value creation is termed a 'first-order' activity because it can exist on its own terms. One of the two types of human activities in the 'value is created or transferred' ontological assumption of socio-economic relations.	ETED development. References the theories of value of Smith (1776/1904); Ricardo (1817/1999); Marx (1867/1959b); Schumpeter (1911/2003); Bhagwati (1982); Damodaran (2005). (Sections 2.2.2, 2.3.1).

Table A2.1 (continued)

Conceptual element	Definition	ETED relation** and selected sources
(Non-)productive activity 'Second-order activity' (value transfer)	An activity that transfers value from one subset of society to another. Non-productive extractive transfer activities appropriate value from first-order activities and hence are termed 'second-order'. They are referred to in economics and other domains as rent seeking, extractive surplus appropriation, or even plunder and theft and might include regulation, monopolies, exchange restrictions, licensing, litigation, or crime. Second-order value transfer activities are contingent on first-order value creation activities. One of the two types of human activities in the 'value is created or transferred' ontological assumption of socio-economic relations.	ETED development. References Bastiat (1845/1996); Tullock (1967); Krueger (1974); Buchanan (1980); Baumol (1990); Olson (1993); Murphy, Schleifer & Vishny (1993); Tollison (2012). (Section 2.3.1).
'Redistribution'	A value transfer effected by political elites in the non-market arena and rooted in the narrative market arena where wealth or income is moved from one social group (transferor) to another (transferee). It is problematic from a human and economic development perspective when such transfers are from a lower to a higher social group and away from first-order productive value creators, or when the transfers persist after the objectives that brought about the original redistribution are achieved (or when these are endemically not achieved). Normatively addressed for policy purposes in A Weighted Redistribution Framework for policy.	References diverse literatures including Dixit & Londregan (1995); Alesina & Perotti (1996); Aghion, Caroli, & García-Peñalosa (1999); Stiglitz (2012); Piketty (2015). (Section 8.2.4; Table 8.3; Figure A5.9b).
Redistribution 'Third-order transfers'	A metaphor for redistribution anchored by narratives (stressing empathy or compensation) that aims to reverse earlier second-order transfers via new transfers. Such transfers risk acting as catalysts for the 'extractive escalation dynamic'.	ETED position. Based on the redistribution literature (Sections 2.3.1, 5.3.4, and 8.2.4)
'Residual income' (RI) (profits)	Residual income refers to the profits of a firm. In the ETED, residual income corresponds to the notion of net value appropriation (NVa) consistent with the use of the VCA framework. Residual income (RI) is calculated from the P&L profits (π), conceptually the revenue minus costs, and facilitates the calculation of micro-level SVC measurements (e.g., VCp/VCr).	ETED position. (Section, 2.2.3; equations (1.1), (1.2), (1.3)).
'Revenue adjusted' (R') (revenue)	The ETED-specific technical term that refers to the adjustment of the revenue of a firm so that it corresponds to the notion of value appropriation (Va) consistent with the use of the VCA framework. Revenue adjusted (R') has a close correspondence to and is derived from revenue reported in the P&L statement and facilitates the calculation of micro-level SVC measurements (e.g., VCp/VCr).	ETED position. (Section, 2.2.3; equations (3.1), (3.2)).

Table A2.1 (continued)

Conceptual element	Definition	ETED relation** and selected sources
Risk	A form of value creation. All business activities that result in value creation are associated with degrees of risk. High risk exposure associates with uncertainty undertakings that are essential for new value creation and in open access social orders bring about high elite circulation velocities and economic development.	Markowitz (1952); Sharpe (1964); Damodaran (2005); Taleb (2018, 2020). (Section 6.6.5).
Risk 'Sustainable risk origination'	A form of sustainability that occurs when the value created (profits) from the undertaking of uncertainty is appropriated by the risk-takers who also appropriate the *negative* value creation (losses). 'Sustainable risk origination' also occurs when risky projects fail, because success and failure are two sides of the same coin; two states of a single reality that are joined—not separated—by their respective probabilities. Its antithetical scenarios are 'unsustainable no-risk origination', that sees risk not originated but *positive* value appropriated (like inflation or the free labor of LLM training); and 'unsustainable risk origination', that sees risk created but *negative* value *not* appropriated (like bailouts or the agency of systemically important institutions).	ETED position. Markowitz (1952); Sharpe (1964); Damodaran (2005); Taleb (2018, 2020). (Section 6.6.5; Figure 6.9).
Rules (institutions) 'Elite business model rules'	The institutions granting the license to operate to elite business models. They are the institutions that matter most to development because they determine 'who gets what', and as a result, the levels of value creation/extraction in the economy. Therefore, these rules should normatively be the primary target of weighted structural reforms and elite/elite system transformational leadership. Elite business model rules are determined by the dynamics of intra-elite contest rules.	ETED development. (Section 4.2.3; Figures 4.3, 5.2, 6.1, 7.1, A5.12).
Rules (meta-institutions) 'Intra-elite contest rules'	The rules and institutions that regulate intra-elite contests and establish 'elite business model rules'. They are the meta-institutions that matter most to elite business model rules. They should therefore normatively be the target of structural reforms and elite system transformational leadership. Intra-elite contest rules are in turn chiefly resolved through bargaining power differentials in intra-elite meta-contests.	ETED development. (Sections 3.3.1; 3.3.3; 4.2.1; 4.2.3; Figure 4.3).

Table A2.1 (continued)

Conceptual element	**Definition**	**ETED relation**** **and selected sources**
Singularity 'Elite singularity'	A tipping point that occurs when autonomous AI elite agency exceeds human elites in terms of its value appropriation and value creation capabilities, and a non-human AI elite system is formed. AI applications are initially given narrow tasks requiring significant coordination capacity and, as a result of successfully performing these, are then entrusted with leadership roles such as managing business models or writing laws and negotiating their passage. Increasingly autonomous, AI elite agency proceeds to arrogate functions from incumbent human coalitions, ultimately controlling and running all elite business models in the political economy, effecting all institutional change, and constituting a sovereign AI elite system. The term brings the 'elite singularity' notion—where humans are confronted with the unknown possibilities of a superintelligence—into the realm of the political economy.	References the notions of singularity by Good (1965); Kurzweil (2005); Vinge (2013); Bostrom (2014); Chalmers (2016). (Sections 8.1.3, 8.1.6; 8.3.3, Epilogue; Tables A4.3b, E.1).
Structural reform 'Weighted structural reform'	Structural reform is the central element in the economic policy mix to achieve inclusive development and growth and must mainly target elite business model rules. It is based on *de facto* adjustments to the incentive system and relies on institutional and (de)regulatory measures. Structural reform is designed to stimulate elite business model transformation towards sustainable value creation. It requires a long-term intertemporal perspective and discrete engagement across the economy's narrow nooks and crannies where extractive elite business models enact excessive value transfers to the detriment of development. To be effective, structural reform must acknowledge that extractive value transfers are inseparable from value creation (e.g., as in the case of the 'extractive push' dilemma) hence requiring their respective weighting for decision-making purposes in consistency with the 'weight and offset value transfers' (holistic) implication (for financial analysis).	ETED position. References ideas on the incentive system (Olson, 1984; North, 1990, 1994; Nicholas, 2003; Robinson, 2010), on structural reform *per se* (Kaldor, 1970; Sachs & Woo, 1994; Laitner, 2000; Cuervo-Cazurra & Dau, 2009; Gollin, 2014; Palma, 2014), and on development and state capacity (Besley & Persson, 2010; Acemoglu, García-Jimeno & Robinson, 2015; Zhang, 2022). (Section 7.1; Figure 7.1).

Table A2.1 (continued)

Conceptual element	**Definition**	**ETED relation** ** **and selected sources**
'Sustainability'	In the ETED, sustainability is defined in terms of the principal-stakeholder relationship. On the principal side, this means to appropriate value created while abstaining from taking value appropriated but *not* created (second-order value and risk transfers) in a proportion that bests average agency. On the stakeholder side, it is the privilege to retain one's value creation. Sustainability is in the interest of non-elites and is feasible with adequate 'knowledge' at the elite business model level (i.e., it does not compromise financial performance). Elite agency that is sustainable increases aggregate value creation and moves societies forward. Operationalized as 'sustainable value creation' (SVC) it is the ethical basis for human and economic development and realized through the maxim, *To the creators the value created.*.	ETED position. Integrates literature on the VCA framework, the principal-stakeholder perspective, rent seeking, economic development and growth, and CSR/ESG. It is the cornerstone of this work and integrated as an ethical position in Chapter 8.
Sustainability 'Sustainable development'	Based on the generally accepted notion that sustainability "is development that meets the needs of the present without compromising the ability of future generations to meet their own needs" (Brundtland, 1987), the focus is on the value creation of the elite business model. Sustainable development requires that the revenue/profits of elites be generated from first-order productive activities rather than from second-order (or third-order) transfer activities.	ETED position. References the VCA framework, literature on sustainability, economics literature on rent seeking, externalities, and economic development and growth. (From Section 2.3.1, Proposition 10 onwards).
Sustainability 'Sustainable Value Creation' (SVC)	A conception of sustainability based on the business model where value is appropriated from first-order productive activities rather than from second-order (or third-order) transfer activities, i.e., the first-order value creation activities of other parties. Value is everything that humans determine is worth appropriating and business models based on 'value appropriated but *not* created' are non-sustainable. Sustainable value creation is at the base of the micro to macro transmission mechanism and accounts for macro-level outcomes like growth, equality, or innovation. It is operationalized at the business model level as the relationship between first-order value creation and second-order value transfers through SVC measurements like the Value Creation Rating (VCr).	ETED development. References the VCA framework, the principal-stakeholder perspective, rent-seeking literature, economic externalities, von Carlowitz (1712/2022) and Brundtland (1987), and a range of CSR and ESG literature. (From Chapter 2 onwards).

Table A2.1 (continued)

Conceptual element	Definition	ETED relation** and selected sources
'Transnational elite coalition'	An elite coalition with members from diverse nation states that mostly operates cross-border elite business models. It benefits from global public goods like multilateral institutions and peace. Such coalitions have relatively lower levels of elite cohesion and power (compared to domestic elite coalitions) since their members and the way that they are organized do not associate with a particular state (as a business model is primarily embedded in the institutions of a nation state). Hence, these coalitions are rare—more imaginary than real. Ultimately, the dominant nationality of the coalition's members and socialization determine its primary institutional affiliation, but this cannot be transnational (even when its cross-border income flows are globally diversified and significant).	ETED development. Critically references Rothkopf (2008); Bühlmann, David, & Mach (2012); Sklair (2012). (Sections 1.2.1, 7.3.2, 7.3.3).
'Unemployed capital'	A form of value transfer based on the excessive expansion of the monetary mass where capital ceases to be used for the efficient allocation of resources. 'Unemployed capital' is evidenced by ballooning reserve balances at central banks, share buybacks, or inflation. Is is a particularly regressive type of redistribution that also causes the economy's overall coordination capacity to deteriorate.	ETED development. References developments in finance at both the macro level, such as reserve balances held by Federal Reserve Banks (WRESBAL), and the micro level, such as share buybacks (e.g., Charles Schwab, 2024). (See Section 6.2.4 and Epilogue).
'Value'	Value is everything that humans determine is worth appropriating and is jointly created in socio-economic exchanges by the parties in principal-stakeholder relationships. The creation of value is via first-order productive activities. If value is likened to energy, through the lens of the second law of thermodynamics, value creation is the agentic mechanism by which entropy is lowered in the human domain (in contrast to second-order value transfers that increase entropy); the elite system of the political economy is then the zone of the social habitat where order (negative entropy) is generated.	References various theories of value such as those by Smith (1776/1904); Bentham (1781/1970); Ricardo (1817/1999); Marx (1867/1959b); Mill (1863/2001). Draws from strategic management and finance insights as in Porter (1980); Damodaran (2005); Aspers & Beckert (2011); Harrison & Wicks (2013). Anchored by the VCA framework as in Brandenburger & Stuart (1996); Brandenburger (2002); Garcia-Castro & Aguilera (2015); Di Gregorio (2013). (From Section 2.2.2 onwards).

Table A2.1 (continued)

Conceptual element	Definition	ETED relation** and selected sources
Value 'Value destruction ratio'	An operationalization of value destruction that is in excess of value appropriation and measurable through the 'destructive value transfer-COST to revenue ratio'. When the '*negative* value created and *not* appropriated' is higher than revenue (i.e., the ratio is over 1.00) the business model has *de facto* been issued a 'license for evil' along with a license to operate. This is a controversial measurement given that the data sources needed for calculating the *negative* value created amount (in the numerator) are off-P&L and hence judgment-based.	ETED development. Diverse references including Arendt (1964); Gotshalk (1963); Ricoeur & Pellauer (1985); Wasserstrom (1999). (See Section 8.2.2; Figures 6.7, A5.5b; 'value destruction ratio' is not an SVC measurement).
'Value Creation Position' (VCp)	The VCp measures the sustainability of a firm by describing 'value created and appropriated' as a proportion of the total 'value appropriation'. The VCp is assessed by establishing the amount of second-order 'value appropriated but *not* created' transfers (transfer-IN) that benefit the business model as a proportion of total revenue/profits (the total value appropriated). The VCp can be conceptualized on a 'value spectrum' with one segment for 'value created and appropriated' (net value creation) and another for 'value appropriated but *not* created' (transfer-IN). Transfer-IN is quantified through metrics with a 'monetary equivalence'. VCp is expressed (for revenue) in the equation: VCp = [revenue – transfer-IN] / revenue. The VCp measurement is provided as a percentage: a score of 100% indicates that a firm's revenue/profits is entirely attributable to first-order productive value creation, and a score of 0% indicates that it is all attributable to second-order extractive value transfers.	SVC measurement. References a wide range of literature on finance, governance, CSR and ESG, and economics, including "VCA elasticity" (Garcia-Castro & Aguilera, 2015). (Chapter 2, Table 2.4, equation (4.1); calculation process in Sections 5.3.1, 6.6.1-6.6.3; Figure 6.6).
'Value Creation Rating' (VCr)	The VCr comprehensively measures the sustainability of a firm by describing the proportion of all 'value creation' in relation to all 'value appropriation'. The VCr is assessed by establishing the amount of second-order 'value appropriated but *not* created' transfers (transfer-IN) that benefit the business model as well as 'value created but *not* appropriated' transfers (inclusive transfer-OUT) in relation to total revenue/profits (the total value appropriated). The VCr is an operationalization of the full value impact of a business model and reflects the relationship between a firm and society by assessing all second-order value transfers, both the extractive (transfer-IN) and inclusive (transfer-OUT), quantified through metrics with a 'monetary equivalence'. The VCr is expressed (for profits) in the equation: VCr = [profits – transfer-IN(profits) + transfer-OUT(profits)] / profits. The VCr is provided as a score with two decimal points: a score of 1.00 indicates that a firm's value creation and value appropriation are equal and in balance; a score over/below 1.00 indicates that a business model is leaning towards inclusive/extractive activities.	SVC measurement. References a wide range of literature on finance, governance, CSR and ESG, and economics (rent seeking, negative externalities). (Chapter 2, Table 2.4, equation (4.2); calculation process in Sections 5.3.1, 6.6.1-6.6.3; Figure 6.6). VCr-derived measurements are presented in this work (e.g., ind-VCr, sec-VCr, IB-VCr), while others may be developed through future research initiatives (e.g., law-VCr).

Table A2.1 (continued)

Conceptual element	**Definition**	**ETED relation**** **and selected sources**
Value 'Value transfer-IN'	Value appropriated but *not* created. Value transfers from third parties. Transfer-IN is deemed to be extractive and results from business model activities that negatively impact specific stakeholders and development.	ETED development. (From Chapter 2 onwards, used in the equation set of Table 2.4; Figure 6.7).
Value 'Value transfer-COST'	Concisely defined as 'cost created but *not* borne'. Value transfer-COST is 'extractive' when it is a *de facto* reduction of P&L costs (value appropriated but *not* created, i.e., a form of transfer-IN). It is 'destructive' when it is off-P&L (*negative* value created and *not* appropriated) causing damage that is not formally quantified.	ETED development. (Section 8.2.1; Figures 6.7 and A5.5a).
Value 'Value transfer-OUT'	Value created but *not* appropriated. Value transfers to third parties. Transfer-OUT is deemed to be inclusive and results from business model activities that contribute value to specific stakeholders and positively impact development.	ETED development. (From Chapter 2 onwards, used in the equation set of Table 2.4; Figure 6.7).
Vespasian 'Doing a Vespasian'	The pursuit of an extreme form of cross border value extraction by one country's elite system on another for profit or survival. References the first emperor of the Flavian Dynasty, Titus Flavius Vespasianus (9–79 AD), who used the spoils of the First Jewish–Roman War (66–73 AD), including slaves as well as the massive gold and silver reserves of the Second Temple, to recapitalize *ex manubiis* the Roman state and renew its capital.	ETED development. An historical interpretation with a starting point in *The Wars of the Jews: Or history of the destruction of Jerusalem* (Josephus, 2009). (Epilogue).
'Weighting'	The conceptual element that brings the elite theory into the realm of practice and normative application. Any business model activity is weighted, meaning that it has bargaining power that causes deviations from the counterfactual 'equalized bargaining power equilibrium prices' and, as a result, appropriates more/less value that it otherwise would. Weighting is pervasive, emerges naturally, and hence happens implicitly, materializing in business model rules. The explicit and normative practice of weighting in the ETED can be more accurately described as 're-weighting' , based on a deep recognition that 'all elite agency creates and transfers value' and is enabled by the two premises of human behavior: the 'universal value extraction propensity of humans'; and the 'innate value creation character of humans'. Weighting grants more/less power and hence the capacity to appropriate more/less residual income from some activities.	ETED development. (Sections 5.3.1, 6.6.1, 7.1, Chapter 8; Table 7.1; also see 'offsetting' in this Glossary).

Table A2.1 (continued)

Conceptual element	Definition	ETED relation** and selected sources
Weighting 'Weighted reforms'	Reforms that target specific (elite) business model rules based on the 'weight and offset value transfers' (holistic) implication. Weighting in a normative context is explicit, the precursor of offsetting, and requires that both value creation and transfers are discretely established and quantified to support transformational leadership. This can be achieved by employing the frameworks and SVC measurements of the 'weight and offset value transfers' (holistic) implication for both the formulation of policy—i.e., weighted reforms—and to make business model judgments.	ETED development. (Sections 5.3.1, 6.6.1, 7.1, Chapter 8; Table 7.1).
Weighting 'Weighted transfers general equilibrium' ('WTGE') macroeconomic model, also referred to as 'weighted transfers modeling'	Macroeconomic models that describe the first-order value (and risk) creation and second-order value (and risk) transfers in the economy. Referencing mainstream macroeconometric approaches they incorporate SVC measurements (e.g., EQr, VCr) and test their relationships with standard economic variables. The predictive econometric modeling entails exploring diverse development scenarios by adjusting value transfer weights and related policy parameters, thus enabling a comprehensive understanding of potential economic outcomes and trajectories. Weighting is meant to be prescriptive and is the essential policy approach to support structural reform.	SVC measurement (international version is G-WTGE). References DSGE, CGG, HANK, et al. models and literature; see Morozov (2014). (Sections 7.1.1, 7.1.5, 8.3.3; Figure 7.1).
Weighting 'Weighted transfers game' ('WT-Game')	An interactive simulation where gamers aim to construct a digital twin of all real-world business models' principal-stakeholder relationships and transactions. The goal is to comprehensively describe both first-order value (and risk) creation and second-order value (and risk) transfers. Gamers review principal-stakeholder transactional data (from payment systems, social networks, etc.) to identify transfers and, when successful, the universe they digitally create represents socio-economic reality and its fractal nature (whose equations correspond to those of 'weighted transfer modeling'). As an intended 'omniscience' SVC measurement, the putative advent of AGI might be a condition for its full realization. While the game is ostensibly for entertainment purposes, for committed players it is also to nudge agents in the political economy towards sustainable value creation, to formulate structural reform proposals, to inform narratives and political programs, and to come up with complex solutions to rebalance bargaining power differentials without losing coordination capacity.	SVC measurement (international version is GWT-Game). An early-stage speculative idea that will require industry partners and must be developed over the next years and decades. (Section 7.1.1; Table A3.1b; Figures A5.10, set A5.14; see 'The heavenly AI' hypothesis in Table E.1).

Table A2.2: Main ETED frameworks.*

Framework	Description	Purpose (and ETED sources)
The Elite Circulation Matrix	A 2x2 economic development framework for elite circulation based on two properties of the elite system: social order access (on the x-axis) and elite quality (on the y-axis). The four sectors of this political economy prescriptive matrix represent elite circulation modes that suggest four development trajectories: (1) 'blockage' mode for regressive development; (2) 'infiltration' and (3) 'endosmosis' modes, both leading to unsustainable development; and (4) 'admixture' mode, leading to sustainable development.	To understand economic and social development paths through the lens of elite circulation. (Section 1.3.3, Proposition 3; Figure 1.1).
Tripartite elite typology	The framework for elite agency based on three elite types—political, business, and knowledge—active in the three available contest arenas—market, non-market, and narrative market—from which their respective power type—'money', 'might', or 'mind'—is derived. The three elite types fuse at the business model level through 'elite coordination leadership' (for the accumulation of power) and 'elite business model leadership' (for the conversion of power into residual income), integrating the power domains of politics, economy, and society.	To facilitate the analysis of the macro-level political economy and the effectiveness of micro-level elite business models. (Sections 1.3.4, 2.2.1; summarized in Figure A5.1).
The 'value is created or transferred' (ontological) assumption	Value is created. It is then either appropriated by its creators or by third parties who did not create the value in the first place. That is, the value is transferred. The essential dualist framing of socio-economic relations (and nature) operates. This results in the dichotomous typology of business model activities referencing value. This simple ontological assumption is reductionist and is advanced as the fundamental framework for sociology, economics, politics, international relations, management, and finance.	A fundamental dualism to interpret socio-economic reality with critical implications for development and the ontological bedrock of the ETED. (From Section 2.3 onwards; see Table 2.3; Figures A5.4c, 8.7).
The dichotomous typology of business model activities referencing value	A two-level typology of all economic activity (and social life) that differentiates between first-order productive activities (value creation) and second-order transfer activities (value extraction). Based on the (i) 'value is created or transferred' ontological assumption, it provides the most fundamental applied support for the ETED system. The two-level typology serves as a basis for the operationalization (through SVC metrics), measurements, and normative aspects of the ETED. From this simple dichotomy—a dualist classification framework—the complexities of the political economy emerge.	To provide a guide to differentiate activities in the economy based on their sustainable value creation. (Section 2.3.1, Proposition 10; Table 2.3).

*While some of these frameworks appear suited for inclusion in the ancillary propositions of Table A1.3, the entries selected here represent broader structures that have been constructed to enhance the understanding of complex phenomena (the primary focus here is not on the specific relationships between conceptual elements, even though the underlying logic of most frameworks strive for falsifiability).

Table A2.2 (continued)

Framework	Description	Purpose (and ETED sources)
The elite agency microfoundations of institutional change model	A model positing a two-way causal relationship between elite agency and institutions. Elite agency is the principal microfoundation of institutional change and leads to adjustments in the economy's incentive system.	To establish the role of elites in the social system for both academic and applied purposes. (Section 3.1.1, Proposition 12; Figure 3.2).
The Three-tier Set of Intra-elite Checks and Balances	A schema that lies at the core of the ETED's conceptual framework for the separation of powers based on a three-tier set of checks and balances in the political economy: 'within-arena' (Tier 1), 'across-arena' (Tier 2), and 'within-system' (Tier 3), that correspond to the three intra-elite contest arenas (market, non-market, narrative market) and the three elite types (business, political, knowledge). A fourth 'across-system' (Tier 4) tier of checks and balances is added to consider cross-border business models as foreign elites participate in intra-elite contests (mostly in Tier 1 'within-arena' contests). A fifth (Tier 5) tier describes the balance of power relationship between the core elite coalition and regular elite coalitions.	To analyze the political economy and predict, in conjunction with the countervailing force of elite cohesion, institutional change and sustainable value creation. (Proposition 16, Sections 3.2.2, 7.3.1, 8.1.2; Figures 3.7, A5.11b).
The Seven Intra-elite Power Relations	A practical framework that specifies the ETED's separation of powers by providing a typology of seven intra-elite relations across the political economy's set of intra-elite checks and balances. Three elite types (business, political, knowledge) engage in intra-elite contests using the schema of The Three-Tier Set of Intra-elite Checks and Balances ('within-arena' Tier 1, 'across-arena' Tier 2, and 'within-system' Tier 3). Sustainable value creation and economic development rely on robust intra-elite contests in all seven intra-elite power relations.	To analyze the precise sources of institutional change and sustainable value creation in the political economy (additional intra-elite power relations emerge from including Tier 4 and 5 checks and balances to the framework). (Section 3.3.3, Proposition 20; Table 3.2).
The Elite Business Model Lifecycle	Explains the rise and fall of elite business models in the political economy over time, where the variables are the amounts of value creation and power accumulation. The lifecycle reveals how elite residual income first originates from the value creation of 'knowledge' before later accruing from power endowments leveraged for value transfers via 'political economy know-how'. The derived lifecycle's 'value transfers replace value creation at maturity' conjecture matters to growth because an aggregation of extractive, rent-seeking models at the end of the lifecycle can tip an economy towards a critical juncture and an extractive cul-de-sac.	To analyze and then formulate weighted structural reforms to address excessive extractive transfers in a political economy. (Section 4.3.4; Figures 4.5, A5.9b).

Table A2.2 (continued)

Framework	Description	Purpose (and ETED sources)
Typology of individual non-elite responses to extractive value transfers by elite business models	The full range of individual responses to value extraction by non-elites: (i) 'acceptance'; (ii) 'exit'; (iii); 'informality'; (iv) 'challenge'. Each response is the result of complex cultural, social, economic, and psychological forces. When aggregated, each of these responses are manifested as political options: (i) individual 'acceptance' responses such as (a) *resignation* or (b) *embrace* materialize as collaboration (option b) 'trust in elites'; (iv) 'challenge' responses of the (a) *struggle* variety result in confrontation (option a) 'non-elite vs elite struggle', while those of the (b) *participation* (in intra-elite contests) variety result in collaboration (option c) 'tactical participation', or (option d) 'strategic participation'. Individual responses such as (ii) 'exit' and (iii) 'informality' mostly fall outside the political economy's elite/non-elite dialectics.	To examine the basis for non-elite political options in response to value extraction and understand the cultural, social, and economic influences on the non-elite/elite relationship and its influence on development. (Table 5.1; Sections 5.2.3, 8.1.3; see Figure A5.8).
The three assumptions for socio-economic relations	Three assumptions for socio-economic relations in the ETED's pragmatic philosophy upon which the operationalization of sustainable value creation occurs: the (i) 'value is created or transferred' ontological assumption; the (ii) 'quantifiability of value transfers' finance assumption; and the (iii) 'bona fide value appropriation' positive assumption.	To theoretically cement the practical apparatus of the ETED in order for SVC measurements to enable informed transformational leadership choices. (Sections 5.3.1, 6.6.1; Figure A5.4a).
The Political Economy Power and Value Matrix	A 2x2 framework that links value (creation/extraction) and power to its political and economic dimensions. The quadrants of this political economy matrix (which correspond to the four index areas of the EQx) result from the intersection between the two variables of power and value (represented on the x-axis), and the two dimensions, political and economic (represented on the y-axis), and are: (i) 'political power'; (ii) 'economic power'; (iii) 'political value'; and (iv) 'economic value'.	To classify political economy phenomena and conceptually guide the operationalization of political economy measurements like elite quality. (Section 6.2.2; Figure 6.2).
The classification logic for elite quality indicators	A 2x2 framework for the operationalization of elite quality (referencing The Political Economy Power and Value Matrix, Figure 6.2). It articulates the logic by which four 'index areas' conceptually organize and assign component datasets (the 12 pillars and indicators for the EQx). The quadrants of the political economy matrix result from the intersection between the two variables of power and value (represented on the x-axis), and the two dimensions, political and economic (represented on the y-axis), and are: (i) 'capture' for 'political power' indicators; (ii) 'dominance' for 'economic power' indicators; (iii) 'income (transfer)' for 'political value' indicators; and (iv) 'value' for 'economic value' indicators.	To conceptually identify and classify the component indicators of the EQx. (Section 6.2.4; Figure 6.4).

Table A2.2 (continued)

Framework	Description	Purpose (and ETED sources)
The State of the Elite System Framework for the political economy	A 2x2 framework for policy that links levels of elite power, i.e., potential future value extraction (on the x-axis) with elite value creation (on the y-axis). The four sectors of this political economy prescriptive matrix describe the state of the elite system and are: (1) 'rentier elite system'; (2) 'enlightened elite system'; (3) 'striving elite system'; and (4) 'competitive elite system'.	To serve as a comparative classification and analytical tool for national elite systems to inform policy and structural reform. (Section 6.3.2; Figure 6.5).
The three-stage process to establish firm-level SVC measurements and their SVC metrics	A three-stage procedural framework to establish SVC measurements (i.e., the VCp/VCr and the self-VCp/self-VCr). The three stages are: (I) *conceptual determination of SVC metrics*; (II) *quantification of SVC metrics (input)*; and (III) *calculation of SVC measurements (output)*. Stage (I) is achieved with the (a) 'description' and (b) 'rationale' for each SVC metric. Stage (II) is where the critical quantification choices are made on the (1/3) *assessment method*, the (2/3) *data source*, and the (3/3) *calibration of metrics*, with the latter comprising of (a) 'monetary equivalence' and (b) 'calibration factor'. Stage (III) involves the implementation of SVC measurement equations on the basis of the weighting, aggregation, and other pertinent statistical schema applied to the component SVC metrics.	To calculate SVC measurements. (Chapter 2, Sections 5.3.1, 6.6.1-6.6.3; Tables 6.1, 6.2; the process is captured in Figure 6.6).
The Value Creation and Appropriation Matrix: A framework for the classification logic of SVC metrics	A 2x3 framework for the classification of business model activities as metrics for SVC measurements. The framework takes the value transfer perspective and is based on value creation (on the x-axis) and value appropriation (on the y-axis). The elements of the political economy classification matrix, reflecting the double-entry transferee/transferor nature of value transfers are: (i) 'no value creation' (no transfer) as 'value *not* created and *not* appropriated'; (ii) 'transfer-IN' as 'value appropriated but *not* created'; (iii) 'transfer-OUT' as 'value created but *not* appropriated'; and (iv) 'net value creation' (no transfer) as 'value created and appropriated'. The matrix has two additional 'quadrants' for *negative* value creation (on the x-axis) denoting two types of value transfer-COSTS (i.e., 'cost created but *not* borne'): (v) 'extractive' transfer-COST as 'value appropriated but *not* created' (a form of transfer-IN which is equivalent to monetizing value created by stakeholders); and (iv) 'destructive' transfer-COST, '*negative* value created but *not* appropriated' (and not monetized *per se*).	To conceptually identify and classify SVC metrics, the components of SVC measurements. (Sections 6.6.1, 8.2.2; Figure 6.7).
The Business Model Sustainable Value Scorecard	A classification framework presented as an artifact, a visual model for the conceptual determination of SVC metrics and the judgments for their relative weightings in SVC measurements after their 'monetary equivalence' and 'calibration factors' have been established. The 12 blocks of the scorecard facilitate the aggregation of a firm's transfer-IN and transfer-OUT sums and thus establish their relative proportions (which is required for the calculations of firm-level SVC measurements like the VCr). The scorecard mirrors the 12-pillar EQx architecture used to classify its indicators, but in order to reflect the firm-level perspective, 'political' becomes 'non-market' and 'economic' becomes 'market'.	To support the conceptual determination of SVC metrics and the calculation of SVC measurements. (Section 6.6.3; Figures 6.6, 6.8).

Table A2.2 (continued)

Framework	Description	Purpose (and ETED sources)
The Sustainable Risk Framework for society	A 2x2 framework for policy that links risk origination (on the x-axis) and value appropriation (on the y-axis) thus articulating the implications of the distribution of risk and its (positive and negative) rewards in society. The four sectors of the political economy prescriptive matrix are: (1) 'null risk origination'; (2) 'unsustainable no-risk origination'; (3) 'unsustainable risk origination'; and (4) 'sustainable risk origination'.	To assist the understanding of risk in policymaking and to incentivize the undertaking of risk/ uncertainty by preempting the transfer of the *positive* or *negative* value associated with risk origination. (Section 6.6.5; Figure 6.9).
'Weighted transfers modeling' ('WTGE') of the economy	An econometric model that frames and establishes first-order value (and risk) creation vs second-order value (and risk) transfers in an economy and sets out their respective relationships and entanglements. The aim of statistically mapping all elite business model principal-stakeholder relationships in terms of value (and risk) creation and transfer probabilities is an estimable formulation of the theoretical relationship between the disaggregated sustainable value creation of elite business models and economic development outcomes. Value creation modeling relies on micro-level SVC measurements (e.g., VCr) and supplements the mainstream econometric models that it references (such as DGSE, HANK, etc.) with novel inputs such as principal-stakeholder transactional datasets that validate the elite business models and institutions that maximize economic and human development.	To support policymakers in formulating weighted structural reform and value transfer offsets (and the leadership needed for elite bargains on institutional change) by computationally establishing the value creation relationships in an economy. (Sections 7.1.1, 7.1.5; Figures 7.1, 7.8; Table 7.1).
'Weighted transfers game' ('WT-Game') of the economy	An interactive digital twin of the economy (and society) that functions as a framework that ultimately builds and operates a model encompassing all first-order value (and risk) creation and second-order value (and risk) transfers. It relies on extensive principal-stakeholder transactional data, SVC measurements, and 'weighted transfers modeling' (WTGE) equations, but augments these through the commitment of individual gamers dedicated to researching, revealing, and optimizing value transfers across socio-economic groups and elite coalitions. While the simulation is primarily designed for entertainment purposes, its structured evidence, insights, and hypotheses are seen as being significant to policymaking as gamers realize the maxim, *To the creators the value created*. The WT-Game (and its international version, the global weighted transfers game, 'GWT-Game') will require technology partnerships for its operationalization with full actualization contingent on the plays and data supplied by gamers as well as by its AI capabilities.	To entertain and provide an additional and discrete tool to establish the weighted structural reform and value transfer offsets that simulate development on the basis of participative gamification and related collective insights. (Section 7.1.1; Table E.1; Figure A5.10 shows the 'WT-Game' in relation to SVC measurements; renditions in Figure set A5.14).

Table A2.2 (continued)

Framework	Description	Purpose (and ETED sources)
A Weighted Structural Reform Framework for policy	A framework for economic policymaking that supports structural reforms to adjust the incentive system centered on the 'weight and offset value transfers' implication. Its three steps are: (i) *general assessment of sustainable value creation impact*; (ii) *formulation of weighted structural reform*; and (iii) *elite transformational leadership for the elite institutional change bargain*. As one of the three frameworks for weighted policymaking it references A Weighted Redistribution Framework for policy (Table 8.3) and receives inputs from A Transfer Constraints Framework for policy formulation (Table 8.2).	To support policymakers planning and implementing weighted structural reform via value transfer offsets by fostering the leadership required for elite bargains on institutional change. (Section 7.1.5; Tables 7.1, A4.4).
The Sustainable Value Matrix: A performance framework for management	A 2x2 management framework that serves as a classification schema of business models based on two variables representing firm performance (on the y-axis), e.g., profits, and sustainable value creation (on the x-axis), e.g., the VCr. The four quadrants of the decision-making matrix are: (1) 'sustainable' firm; (2) 'naïve' firm; (3) 'rentier' firm; and (4) 'living-dead' firm.	To support top management in determining the contribution of their business models to sustainable value creation. (Section 7.2.1; Figure 7.2).
The Five Varieties of Elite Leadership typology	A classification framework for elite leadership that proposes five discrete leadership varieties, respectively effected by elite coalitions and the core elite coalition at the elite business model or elite system levels. The first three types are (i) 'fundamental' elite leadership varieties: (a) elite coordination leadership; (b) elite business model leadership; and (c) elite system leadership. These three types are supplemented by two further (ii) 'transformational' leadership varieties: (d) elite transformational leadership; and (e) elite system transformational leadership.	To understand elite agency and development potential, perform political economy analysis, and support elite transformations towards sustainable value creation. (Section 7.2.4; Table 7.2).
The Sustainable Finance Matrix: A framework for investments	A 2x2 finance framework that extends The Sustainable Value Matrix for management (Figure 7.2) by adding an investment strategy layer. It is likewise based on sustainable value creation (on the x-axis), e.g., the VCr, and on firm performance (on the y-axis), e.g., profits. The four quadrants of the decision-making matrix for investments aimed at individual investment portfolio strategies are: (1) 'sustainable' investment category; (2) 'non-profitable' investment category; (3) 'non-sustainable' investment category; and (4) 'non-investable'.	To support the sustainability analysis of specific investments and investment strategies in the financial and corporate contexts. (Section 7.2.5; Figure 7.3).

Table A2.2 (continued)

Framework	**Description**	**Purpose (and ETED sources)**
The Sustainable Valuations Matrix: A framework for investors	A 2x2 finance framework for finance that extends The Sustainable Value Matrix for management (Figure 7.2) by adding an investment portfolio strategy layer. It is likewise based on sustainable value creation (on the x-axis), e.g., the VCr, and on firm performance (on the y-axis), e.g., profits. The quadrants suggest the hypothetical impact on equity and debt valuations for each of the investment categories (as detailed in the first variant of the matrix, Figure 7.3). The impact on valuations inferred (notwithstanding empirical validation) by the decision-making matrix for investors matters to portfolio asset allocation analysis: (1) for the 'sustainable' investment category both equity and debt valuations trend *upward*; (2) for the 'non-profitable' investment category, equity will trend *upwards* and debt will be in a *range-bound* trend; (3) for the 'non-sustainable' investment category, equity will trend *downwards* and debt will be in a *range-bound* trend; and (4) for the 'non-investable' ('taker') investment category both equity and debt valuations trend *downward*.	To support the practice of sustainable finance by portfolio investors through equity and debt valuations of firms; relevant for portfolio management. (Section 7.2.5; Figure A5.7).
The Value Transfer Strategy Matrix: A sustainability framework for principal-stakeholder relationships	A 2x2 management framework that describes a firm's relationships with its stakeholders on the conceptual basis of extractive transfers (i.e., transfer-IN) and inclusive value transfers (i.e., transfer-OUT). The two transfer types are discrete and independent (and are captured by SVC metrics). For this purpose, the decision-making matrix for principals and stakeholders utilizes the VCr (on the x-axis) and the VCp (on the y-axis) as its two dimensions. The VCr dimension of a firm reflects a range from 'keeper' (the firm does not part with any value) to 'giver' (the firm creates value for stakeholders); the VCp dimension provides a range from 'inclusive' (no extraction) to 'extractive' (extraction occurs). The four quadrants of the matrix are: (1) the doubly inclusive 'inclusive giver' strategy; (2) 'extractive giver' strategy; (3) 'inclusive keeper' strategy; and (4) the doubly extractive 'extractive keeper' (or 'taker') strategy.	To formulate sustainability strategy with a uniquely granular and comprehensive understanding of the extractive/inclusive relationships in the value chain, designed for both firm principals and stakeholders. (Section 7.2.6; Figure 7.4).
The Global Influence of the Elite System Framework for international relations	A 2x2 international relations framework that describes a national elite system from the perspective of the global political economy. The two matrix dimensions are domestic elite quality (on the x-axis), e.g., EQx, EQr, and cross-border elite quality (on the y-axis), e.g., cb-EQ, bl-EQ. The four quadrants in this political economy prescriptive matrix are: (4) the developmentally ideal 'global public goods' elite system; (3) the 'global extractive' elite system; (2) the 'global subsidizer' elite system; and the (1) 'global public bads' elite system.	To analyze and predict the role and behavior of a state in the international system and the nature of interstate relationships based on domestic and cross-border elite quality. (Section 7.3.1; Figure 7.5).

Table A2.2 (continued)

Framework	Description	Purpose (and ETED sources)
The Great Power Elite Quality Lifecycle for international relations	An international relations framework that accounts for the rise and fall of powers. States become powerful as a result of transformational leadership towards higher domestic elite quality and that power in turn supports the increasingly effective value appropriation of their elites' cross-border business models. The overreliance of elites on state power to extract global revenues abroad causes these endowments to ultimately shrink as foreign rival elites can gain ascendance by creating more value and thus bolster the comparative power of their own states in the international system. The logic has parallels with The Elite Business Model Lifecycle.	To support the analysis of power and states in international relations. Rests on cyclical accounts of national development (from Gibbon, 1776/2001, or Spengler, 1922, to Kennedy, 1987, or Dalio, 2021). (Section 7.3.3; Figure 7.7, links with The Elite Business Model Lifecycle at the micro-level, Figure A5.9d).
Polis in empire	A normative political economy framework set out in the form of a metaphor where the ideal institutional and elite system configuration lies in the two-level creative tension between local and supranational political units. The local 'polis' generates incentives for bottom-up value creation while the power of 'empire' scales elite value creation, protects non-elites from value extraction by foreign elites, and has the capacity to effect top-down institutional change. Polis and empire elites coexist, enrich, and check and balance each other in the elite system. The EU is antipodal to the 'polis in empire' model and is hence deemed to provide inadequate economic and human development to its citizens.	To support economic reform and inclusive political visions. Derived from Manent's *Metamorphoses of the City* (2013) and applied using the example of Europe. (Section 7.3.4).
Set of ethical principles (of the ETED)	An ethical framework based on a fundamental maxim: (i) *To the creators the value created*. Its two tenets for elite agency are: (ii) *Maximize first-order value creation and risk origination for productive economic transformations fit for human purpose*; and (iii) *Weight and offset second-order value and risk transfers and minimize these to maximize value*. The practical precepts are: (iv) *Measure value and risk transfers and establish the optimal weightings and potential offsets to maximize sustainable value creation*; (v) *Realize sustainable value creation and risk origination incentives through top-down weighted structural reforms and bottom-up elite business model transformation*; (vi) *Invest in elite cohesion and in the elite separation of powers with a comprehensive set of checks and balances to encourage productive intra-elite contests*; and (vii), *Promote the freedom to* exit *and the freedom* to *create value irrespective of optimal value creation, transfer weightings, and potential offsets*.	To support policymaking for development based on a realist account of how the political economy works. Directed at the core elite coalition and social agents shaping the elite system and institutional change. (Chapter 8; Tables A4.3a and A4.3b, the latter adapted for the AI).

Table A2.2 (continued)

Framework	**Description**	**Purpose (and ETED sources)**
The socio-economic structure pyramid	A classification framework of the socio-economic structure arranged hierarchically to represent relative power endowments. Conceptually visualized as a pyramid, it is comprised of elite strata (beneficiaries of elite business model residual income flows) and non-elite strata (stakeholders of elite business models). The (1) elite is divided into the (1.a) core elite coalition and (1.b) regular elite coalitions; the (2) non-elite is divided into (2.a) the managerial, technical, and creative class and (2.b) all other non-elite groups.	To support social analysis and the determination of value creation sources in a country for economic and human development purposes. (Section 8.1.1; Figure 8.1).
A typology of aggregate *non-elite* political options in response to extractive value transfers	A classification framework for aggregate non-elite agency. Elites and non-elites are assumed to be in a dialectical relationship as non-elites respond to extractive value transfers by elites. Individual non-elite responses aggregate into a range of political options that pursue either collaboration or confrontation: (option a), 'non-elite vs elite struggle'; (option b) passive 'trust in elites'; (option c), 'tactical participation', where a specific non-elite group aligns with a specific elite coalition in support of its business model; (option d), 'strategic participation'. The latter approach is optimal from a development perspective as the non-elite, broadly understood, mobilizes on the side of the higher sustainable value creation contenders across as many intra-elite contests as possible. A non-matching political reaction by elites negatively affects social cohesion and compromises general development.	To supply a typology of possibilities for elite/non-elite relationships in support of social, political, and economic analysis towards effective social movements and policies for non-elite welfare and development. (Section 8.1.3; Figures 8.2, A5.8).
A typology of aggregate *elite* political options to non-elite political options to extractive value transfers	A classification framework for aggregate elite agency. Elites will counter or match non-elite political options to extractive value transfers with a range of political options that pursue either collaboration or confrontation: (option a'), 'value appropriation focus'; (option b') active 'elite agency on behalf of non-elites'; (option c'), 'alliances with non-elite groups' in intra-elite contests; and (option d), 'mastering the intra-elite quality contest dilemma'. The latter approach is optimal from a development perspective where the elite, broadly understood, focuses on sustainable value creation; a non-matching political reaction by too many non-elite groups negatively affects social cohesion and compromises general development.	To supply a typology of possibilities for elite/non-elite relationships to support social, political and economic analysis towards effective social movements and policies for non-elite welfare and development. (Section 8.1.3; Figure 8.2).
'Value transfer-COST to revenue ratio' ('transfer-OUT ratio'; establishes the 'license for evil' metaphor)	A threat detection framework for the political economy. It establishes the ratio of 'cost created but *not* borne' (the 'destructive' transfer-COST) to value appropriated (revenue). While not an SVC measurement, it can be calculated. A ratio of 1.00 or above is deemed to constitute a 'license for evil' that is institutionally granted to elite business models and burdens stakeholders and society as a whole with onerous value destruction.	To identify, shame, and eradicate particularly extractive elite business models. (Sections 8.2.1, 8.2.2; Figure A5.5c).

Table A2.2 (continued)

Framework	**Description**	**Purpose (and ETED sources)**
The Political and Business Systems Sustainable Value Creation (SVC) Test	A comparative political economy framework to test political and business systems. It uses SVC measurements and other data to determine how elite agency and a system's institutions associate with value creation rather than extractive transfers. The narrative and nature of the system or its *a priori* legitimacy are secondary, while the test addresses controversial questions such as the potential advantages of democracy vs authoritarianism from a non-elite perspective through a sustainable value creation lens.	To test the development performance of political and/ or business systems. (Section 8.1.5; Figure 8.3).
A Transfer Constraints Framework for policy formulation	An institutional constraints framework for policy formulation encouraging both development and elite accountability. It constrains extractive value transfer licenses granted to elite businesses that have pledged to turn these into value creation. Value transfers are sustainable when they are limited, weighted, and undergo offsetting, at times in application of the 'alternating value extraction and creation' conjecture. The three limitation types are: (i) *intertemporal constraints*; (ii) *monetary constraints*; and (iii) *value creation milestones*. It is one of the three frameworks for weighted policymaking and provides inputs for policies conceived by the other two—A Weighted Structural Reform Framework for policy (Table 7.1) and A Weighted Redistribution Framework for policy (Table 8.3)—that when subsequently implemented secure the proposed limitations through elite bargains.	To support policymakers in authorizing the licenses to operate for business models with significant value transfers by establishing constraints (mostly based on the elite coalition's own *a priori* value creation promises), thus fostering enhanced and traceable accountability. (Section 8.2.3; Tables 8.2 and A4.4).
A Weighted Redistribution Framework for policy	A sustainable redistribution framework for economic policymaking designed to manage redistributive transfers associated with elite business models in the political economy. Its three steps are: (i) *transfer parties' (transferee/transferor) assessment of redistribution impact*; (ii) *formulation of constraints on redistribution*; and (iii) *elite transformational leadership to support the 'elite redistribution constraints bargain'*. As one of the three frameworks for weighted policymaking, it references A Weighted Structural Reform Framework for policy (Table 7.1) and receives inputs from A Transfer Constraints Framework for policy formulation (Table 8.2).	To support policymakers planning and implementing sustainable redistribution by fostering the leadership required for elite bargains on redistribution. (Section 8.2.4; Tables 8.3, A4.4).
The Two Fundamental Freedoms for Development Matrix	A 2x2 ethics and policy framework based on two fundamental freedoms derived from the positive and negative freedoms proposed by Fromm (1994): "freedom to" and "freedom from". These two freedoms are repurposed as the 'freedom *to* create value' (on the x-axis) and the 'freedom *from* value extraction' (on the y-axis). The four quadrants of the political economy prescriptive matrix link to economic development through the lens of the investment incentives in the economy and are: (4) 'investment in value creation and risk origination'; (3) 'underinvestment in value creation'; (2) 'underinvestment in risk origination'; and (1) 'divestment'.	To forecast and trace the consequences for investment and development resulting from the respective presence or absence of the ETED's two fundamental freedoms. (Section 8.3.1; Figure 8.4).

Table A2.2 (continued)

Framework	Description	Purpose (and ETED sources)
The Three Freedoms for Development Model	A model of economic and human development where the two fundamental freedoms of the ETED are supplemented by a third, the enabling 'freedom to *exit*'. Together these provide the basis for economic and human development. The three freedoms incentivize generalized sustainable value creation and related business models as they strengthen the elite separation of powers, rebalance bargaining power differentials, and incorporate non-elite agency into the political economy, thus positively impacting social cohesion. Together, the three freedoms comprise the notion of 'liberty' in the ETED.	To support social and institutional analysis, including legal and structural reforms for economic growth consistent with the set of ethical principles for development. (Section 8.3.2; Figure 8.5; Tables A4.5a, A4.5b).
The Non-Elite vs Elite Quality Matrix: A framework for human development incorporating culture	A 2x2 framework that links elite quality (on the x-axis) with non-elite quality (on the y-axis) that aims at long-term human and economic development. By including non-elite agency, new perspectives for policy and analysis are supplied. For instance, the proximate responsibility for growth is placed with non-elites, while insofar as there is cultural production, the business models of knowledge elites play a vital precursor role. The quadrants of this framework are: (i) 'regression'; (ii) 'stagnation due to excessive value transfers'; (iii) 'stagnation due to lack of value creation'; (iv) 'development'.	To guide society at large in the formulation of long-term development plans by taking into account both elite and non-elite agency, offering the possibility of incorporating cultural factors into the analysis. (Epilogue; Figure E.1)
Classification of elite theories and conceptualizations	A 2x2 political economy classification framework of elite theories and conceptualizations based on two dimensions: the 'perspective' (particularism to universalism on the x-axis) and the 'level' (micro to macro on the y-axis). The analytical 'perspective' ranges from the specific context-bound to the ubiquitous context-transcendent. The analytical 'level' considers phenomena from the small-scale micro to the large-scale macro.	To adequately reference the existing literature on elites for theory development purposes and for the convenience of readers and pundits not versed with the wide array of research considered. (Figure A5.2; Section 1.2).

Table A2.3: The building blocks for the speculative and pragmatic philosophies of the ETED.*

Framework	Description	Role
The first principles of the ETED (Section 8.3.3; Figure 8.6)	The fundamental principles that cannot *a priori* be deduced for the purposes of human and economic development are the three general principles of life: the Will to Live, the 'universal extraction propensity of life', and the Will to Power.	Out of the first principles spring the building blocks of the ETED's speculative philosophy. First, the basic constraint of the human condition and subsequently the three premises for human nature, which eventually lead to the ontological assumption for socio-economic relations around which the ETED's pragmatic philosophy revolves.
Speculative philosophy (Section 8.3.3; Figure 8.7)	The fundamental nature of reality—including of the human condition—that grounds and explains socio-economic relations. It provides a description of the innate quality that underlies the political economy and its economic and human development outcomes. It is considered on three levels: 'General principles of life'; 'Basic constraint on the human condition'; and 'Premises for human behavior'.	The foundation for the ETED's pragmatic philosophy via its 'premises for human behavior' that spring from first principles, influence socio-economic relations, and extend to elite agency.
Pragmatic philosophy (Section 8.3.3; Figure 8.7)	The nature of the experience of economic and human development and its practical implications. Culminates in transformational leadership that calibrates the 'all elite agency creates and transfers value' (realist) inference.	Based on the ETED's speculative philosophy and the basis for its normative apparatus; includes the set of ethical principles.
General principles of life (x3) (Section 8.3.3; Figure 8.6)	The principles by which life is deemed to operate are: the (A) Will to Live; (B) 'Universal extraction propensity of life' law of nature; and (C) Will to Power.	The three principles directly and indirectly combine in the (Z) 'value appropriation demand of humans' (socio-economic) constraint.
(A) Will to Live (Sections 7.2.3 and 8.3.3)	The origin, the inner nature, and the non-rational force for self-preservation of all that is alive; self-evident in the experience of being alive. References Schopenhauer's (1818/2010) suffering and struggle philosophy, the *Wille zum Leben*.	Leads to the (B) 'universal extraction propensity of life' but also in some respects to its antagonist (C) Will to Power, two apparent opposites that in turn cause the (Z) 'value appropriation demand of humans' (socio-economic) constraint.
(B) 'Universal extraction propensity of life' law of nature (Section 8.3.3)	The deterministic law as an impulse to all that is alive. References Schrödinger's (1944/2013) consideration of energy, with life sucking negative entropy from inferior organisms.	Springs from the Will to Live and is both similar and opposite to the (C) Will to Power; causes the (Z) 'value appropriation demand of humans' (socio-economic) constraint.

*This table articulates the conceptual elements found in Figure 8.7 that also depicts their relationships. Descriptions of some entries can also be found on: Conjectures and other ancillary propositions of the ETED (Table A1.3); Main ETED frameworks (Table A2.2); and the Glossary of ETED conceptual elements (Table A2.1).

Table A2.3 (continued)

Framework	Description	Role
(C) Will to Power (Section 8.3.3)	The creative manifestation of the Will to Live transcends the essential survival impulse and is associated with a will to play; the *élan vital* at the root of beauty, truth, and value creation. References Nietzsche (1872/1923; 1883/2006) and the creative and aesthetic quality of his *Wille zur Macht*.	Springs from the Will to Live and is both similar and opposite to the (B) 'universal extraction propensity of life' to which it still relates. Leads to a two-way relationship with (Z) 'value appropriation demand of humans' (socio-economic) constraint and most critically bolsters the pragmatic (III) 'inextinguishable value creation option of elites' (leadership) premise.
Basic constraint of the human condition (x1)	The single, non-negotiable, limiting fact of human existence is the (Z) 'value appropriation demand of humans' (socio-economic) constraint, which forces elite and non-elite agency to appropriate value (often value *not* created) from stakeholders (humans and non-humans) to sustain its own life and thrive.	Springs directly and indirectly out of the three general principles of life and informs the premises for human behavior, both in the appropriative and creative senses.
(Z) 'Value appropriation demand of humans' (socio-economic) constraint (Discussion on value appropriation starting with Chapter 2; Section 8.3.3, see Figure 8.6)	The necessary limitation of all individual agency which originates in requirements valid to all life forms. In its human version it becomes the catalyst for the speculative philosophy underlying economic and human development to become pragmatic. The constraint, despite being a simple proxy layer enveloping the speculative philosophy, acts as the most connective level of the elite theory's philosophical foundations.	The constraint realizes the (B) 'universal extraction propensity of life' law of nature and thus underpins the (II) 'universal value extraction propensity of humans' (socio-economic) premise for human behavior, which upon first glance seems in opposition to the (I) 'innate value creation character of humans' (natural) premise. Yet the constraint, being also rooted in the (C) Will to Power, is also a creative type of self-assertion and hence fuels the (I) natural premise that is key to general value creation. Moreover, there is a creative tension with the (III) 'inextinguishable value creation options of elites' (leadership) premise that explains economic development.
Premises for human behavior (x3) (Section 8.3.3; Figure A5.4c)	The premises that animate human behavior located at the intersection between speculative and pragmatic philosophies: the (I) 'innate value creation character of humans' (natural) premise; the (II) 'universal value extraction propensity of humans' (socio-economic) premise; and the (III) 'inextinguishable value creation option of elites' (leadership) premise.	Emanating from the ETED's first principles and the derived speculative philosophy, these cement the assumptions for socio-economic relations from which the implications made practical in the context of financial analysis materialize and on which SVC measurements are based.

Table A2.3 (continued)

Framework	Description	Role
(I) 'Innate value creation character of humans' (natural) premise (Sections 8.1.5, 8.1.5, 8.2.4; Figure A5.4c)	All individuals, elite and non-elite alike, have potential value creation agency. Non-elites create most of the value building blocks in the economy. The need for the realization of the premise informs the ETED's set of ethical principles and understanding of liberty.	Consistent with the (III) 'inextinguishable value creation option of elites' (leadership) premise. Its antithesis is the (II) 'universal value extraction propensity of humans' (socio-economic) premise, and the creative tension between the two leads to the theory's dualistic ontology and, in actuality, advances development.
(II) 'Universal value extraction propensity of humans' (socio-economic) premise (Sections 3.3.3, 8.1; Figure A5.4c)	Elites and non-elites will extract from their stakeholders to the maximum extent that their power differentials allow. Second-order value extraction is a defining characteristic of *homo sapiens* and a key feature of social orders that is mostly realized by elites holding 'the extraordinary lever'. For optimal development outcomes, value extraction must be weighted and offset.	Rooted in the (B) 'universal extraction propensity of life' law of nature and, to an even greater extent, in the (A) Will to Live, its antithesis is the (I) 'innate value creation character of humans' (natural) premise. The creative tension between the two leads to the theory's dualistic ontology and, in actuality, advances development.
(III) 'Inextinguishable value creation option of elites' (leadership) premise (Section 2.2.1; Figure A5.4c)	The perpetual option of elites to transform business models towards ever higher sustainable value creation positions (and reduce extractive transfers). This agentic option is exercised through intra-elite contests.	Parallels the (I) 'innate value creation character of humans' (natural) premise in the case of elite agency, while also resting on the Will to Power. Its actualization is normatively consistent with the set of ethical principles, and it materializes as transformational elite leadership.
Assumptions for socio-economic relations (x3) (Figure A5.4b)	The assumptions that facilitate the modeling of relationships in society and the economy, particularly those between principals and stakeholders that determine value appropriation.	Emanating from the premises for human behavior, the assumptions have implications for financial analysis and related SVC measurements. The ontological assumption has the most far-reaching consequences.
(i) The 'value is created or transferred' (ontological) assumption (From Section 2.3 onwards, see Table 2.3 and Figures A5.4c or 8.7; Epilogue)	The essential dualist framework to comprehend socio-economic relations (and nature). It results in the dichotomous typology of business model activities referencing value (value creation vs value transfers). This elementary ontological assumption is reductionist but undergoes a combinatorial expansion in practice, disparately manifesting itself in sociology, economics, politics, international relations, management and finance, supplying further frameworks for understanding and normative agency.	The bedrock of the ETED. The *constant* by which individual parts relate to the whole, and vice-versa, across socio-economic scales. Results from the dialectical tension between the (I) 'innate value creation character of humans' (natural) premise, and the (II) 'universal value extraction propensity of humans' (socio-economic) premise. It directly leads to the central implication of the ETED: the 'weight and offset value transfers' (holistic) implication.

Table A2.3 (continued)

Framework	Description	Role
(ii) 'Quantifiability of value transfers' (financial) assumption (Section 5.3.1)	The financial assumption that describes the deep unity and interconnectedness of business model activities realizable by pricing value transfer activities. Pricing links value transfers to the P&L of an organization and thus provides equivalence across principal-stakeholder relationships.	An assumption consistent with the 'value is created or transferred' (ontological) assumption that results in the (a) 'transparency of value creation and transfer activities' (open) implication.
(iii) 'Bona fide value appropriation' (positive) assumption (Section 2.3.1)	The assumption about business models that is positive, as value appropriation is deemed to be value creation at the outset. Since the full revenue of a firm is taken to be value creation (i.e., net value creation) the burden of proof for value extraction rests on establishing value transfer (transfer-IN) amounts.	An assumption consistent with the 'value is created or transferred' (ontological) assumption that results in the (b) 'revenue is value creation unless value transfer is proven' (constructive) implication; actualized with transfer-IN SVC metrics that lead to SVC measurements and SVC valuations.
Implications for financial analysis (x3) (Figure A5.4b)	The philosophical apparatus of the ETED realizes its pragmatic vocation through its operationalization for finance, the tested methods for which serve the purpose of adequately allocating capital and resources in society.	Each of the three implications for finance are grounded in one of the three assumptions for socio-economic relations; the SVC measurements and related tools for finance derived from the implications constitute the groundwork for elite agency, i.e., firm transformation and macro-level policy measures for generalized sustainable value creation.
(a) 'Transparency of value creation and transfer activities' (open) implication (Section 6.6.1; Figure 6.6)	All value creation and transfer activities can, and thus ought to be, made transparent. Realized for financial analysis by first conceptually determining and then quantifying value creation and transfers at the firm level by using SVC metrics that then become inputs for SVC measurements.	Based on the (ii) 'quantifiability of value transfers' (financial) assumption; transparency is the quantification of value through SVC metrics; the aim is to establish metrics that aggregate into both the transfer-IN and transfer-OUT of a business model to realize SVC measurements and SVC valuations.
(b) 'Revenue is value creation unless value transfer is proven' (constructive) implication	All revenue/profits in the P&L are deemed to be value creation at the outset. The starting point for the financial analysis of the firm is hence constructive and value transfers are only confirmed after the conceptual determination and quantifiable evidence provided by SVC metrics (transfer-IN).	Based on the (iii) 'bona fide value appropriation' (positive) assumption; within the parameters of a firm's revenue the aim is to establish SVC metrics that aggregate into the transfer-IN of a business model to realize SVC measurements and SVC valuations.

Table A2.3 (continued)

Framework	Description	Role
(c) 'Weight and offset value transfers' (holistic) implication	The central and final financial analysis step of elite agency at the firm level and for macroeconomic policies. Requires the comprehensive determination of value creation and value transfers, and their respective quantification. Both aggregates are then weighted against each other to inform decision-making (at the firm or institutional levels), facilitating the positive/negative offsets that enable/ constrain value transfers. Benefits from SVC measurements and references SVC valuations.	The culmination and synthesis of practice towards economic and human development in the ETED; the ultimate applied consequence of its philosophical position. Grounded in the assumptions for socio-economic relations, it integrates the other two implications for financial analysis and relies for its realization on SVC measurements and SVC valuations that then affect (and are affected by) transformational leadership.
Elite agency for sustainable value creation (ETED prescriptive)	Elite agency is sustainable when it pursues continuous transformation, coordination capacity, and bargaining power, both at the business model and elite system levels, and is used to stimulate first-order productive value creation and risk origination and constrain second order value and risk transfers.	Consistent with many of the world's ethical systems and references the ETED's set of ethical principles; incentives for sustainable value creation increase when ethics are institutionalized (including the freedoms for development) in the legal system; normative elite agency practice is grounded in the (c) 'Weight and offset value transfers' (holistic) implication (for financial analysis).
Transformational leadership (Section 7.2.4, Table 7.2)	Exercised at both the elite system (meso-level) and the elite business model (micro-level) levels by business model beneficiaries choosing to maximize first-order value creation and risk origination and constrain second-order transfers. In the 'elite utility function', short-term residual income flows are passed over for long-term wealth stocks (generated by elite business models for the nation).	The ultimate expression of the (III) 'inextinguishable value creation option of elites' (leadership) premise and, at a deeper level, the Will to Power in which it is rooted; leads to inclusive institutional change.
(z) 'All elite agency creates and transfers value' (realist) inference (Section 2.3.1)	A description of all socio-economic agency applied to the elite business model where both first-order productive value creation and second-order extractive value transfers are a joint reality. At times, the relationship between these two opposites is that one requires or precedes the other. The realist inference is anchored in the pragmatic philosophy of the ETED in the context of transformational elite agency.	Awareness of the realist inference stimulates elite transformation leadership and the realization of offsets, with extraction limited to the extent that it is balanced by value creation and phased out in due course; from the courageous acceptance of extraction to its audacious termination.

Table A2.3 (continued)

Framework	Description	Role
Legal foundation for economic and human development	The codification of ethical principles into legal statutes through weighted structural reforms that implement institutional and (de)regulatory measures.	The positive and sustainable realization of the microfoundations of institutional change referencing its processes.
Set of ethical principles (Chapter 8)	The framework that springs from the maxim, *To the creators the value created.* Most effective when developed into institutions and laws (elite agency at the elite system level), but equally necessary in organizations (elite agency at the business model level). Ethical elite agency possesses a strong personal dimension.	A reference for transformational leadership; the ethical principles can be adopted and adapted for personal moral guidance; realized in practice at the firm and political economy levels with the (c) 'Weight and offset value transfers' (holistic) implication.

Appendix 3: Supplementary tables for the ETED's SVC measurements

Table A3.1a: Summary of the sustainable value creation (SVC) measurements of the ETED.*

SVC measurement [ref. nr.] (abbr.)	Description (Data sources)	Application (Implementation status)
Elite quality Elite system measurements (meso-level)		
'Elite Quality Index' [1] (EQx)	Global comparative ranking of the aggregate sustainable value creation of the meso-level elite system. Data source: Macro-level indicators that represent quantifiable phenomena in the political economy and provide evidence of value/risk creation and value/risk transfers by elite business models; top-down (macro-to-meso level) aggregation.	– To benchmark the public discourse on the nation's elites and sustainable value creation in comparative terms – For research, comparative economics (e.g., inequality, growth) – For policy proposals to enhance national competitiveness – For sovereign risk assessments Status: Pilot EQx2020; EQx2021-2024 annual reports; panel-EQx (PEQx), based on longitudinal EQx data from 2005, has been available since 2023 for research purposes.
'Elite Quality Distance' [6] (EQ-dist)	Quantification of the differences between the elite quality profiles of two countries. Data source: EQx, or alternative internationally comparative elite quality measurements.	– For research on management and economics (FDI, trade, associated risks); supplements cultural and institutional distance measurements – To support practitioners operating across different elite quality environments Status: Research proposals.
'Perceptions of Elites Survey' [7] (PEz)	Perceptions survey on the sustainable value creation of the national elite system. Data sources: Elite/Non-elite Survey Questionnaires on general and specific elite value (risk) creation/transfers.	– To monitor national sentiment on elites – To benchmark the public discourse on the role and agency of elites – For research on political science, economics – For sovereign risk assessments Status: Sample extracts of survey questionnaire (Tables A3.4a and A3.4b).

*The ordering follows the reference numbers of Figure 7.8, the visual overview of all of the SVC measurements described here. While the conceptual elements underpinning these measurements are designed to be stable, it is possible that during their operationalization leading to validation, adjustments to the descriptions, data sources, and applications may occur.

https://doi.org/10.1515/9783110734638-016

Table A3.1a (continued)

SVC measurement [ref. nr.] (abbr.)	**Description (Data sources)**	**Application (Implementation status)**
'World Elite Quality Index' [8] (world-EQ)	The weighted elite quality sum of all national elite systems (will *de facto* include cross-border elite business models). Data source: world macro-level indicators (e.g., global inflation or productivity growth).	– To appraise the 'state of the world' and gain insights into specific global trends, including mid/long-term development prospects – To benchmark the public discourse on global sustainability and multilateral institutions Status: Pilot measurement planned for 2025 (World-EQ2025).
'Elite Quality Rating' [9] (EQr)	The sustainable value creation of a nation's elite system based on the aggregation of the sustainable value creation of its elite business models. Data source: A country's elite business models' VCr scores; bottom-up (micro to macro) aggregation.	– Same as the EQx but with a domestic focus and non-comparative – For research on economics, micro to macro transmission mechanisms – For policy formulation, institutional and (de)regulatory measures, industry specific – For macroeconomic models, as inputs Status: Contingent on having a critical mass of a nation's elite business model VCr scores.
'Cross-border Elite Quality Rating' [14] (cb-EQr)	The sustainable value creation of a nation's elite system based on the aggregate cross-border sustainable value creation of its elite business models vs *all other nations*. Data source: A country's elite business models' IB-VCr scores; bottom-up (micro to meso) aggregation process.	– For analysis of international relations (IR) – For (global) macroeconomic models, as inputs – For research on IR, economics (FDI or trade), global political economy – For policy formulation, institutional and (de)regulatory measures, industry specific, international perspective – For the practice of diplomatic relationships Status: Contingent on having a critical mass of a nation's elite business model IB-VCr scores.
'Bilateral Elite Quality Rating' [15] (bl-EQr)	The sustainable value creation of a nation's elite system based on the aggregate cross-border sustainable value creation of its elite business models vs *one specific nation*. Data source: Same as the cb-EQr.	– Same as the cb-EQr, with a narrower bilateral focus Status: Same as the cb-EQr.

Table A3.1a (continued)

SVC measurement [ref. nr.] (abbr.)	Description (Data sources)	Application (Implementation status)
Sustainable value creation Business model measurements (micro-level)		
'Self-assessment Value Creation Position' [2] (self-VCp)	The sustainability (sustainable value creation) of a firm understood as the 'value created and appropriated' by a business model – on a self-reported basis – as a proportion of value appropriation (revenue/profits). Data source: SVC Metrics Self-assessment Survey (transfer-IN) responses given 'monetary equivalence' to the firm's revenue/profits.	– To aid in strategic planning, including decision-making on sustainability initiatives – To support a firm's internal reflections on governance, transformational leadership, ethics (via transfer-IN, 'value appropriated but *not* created') – For executive education and custom programs at business schools Status: Prototype; internally tested with international firms and used in executive education programs at business schools with various established SVC metrics (e.g., international business, manufacturing); sample extract of self-assessment survey questionnaire (Table A3.6).
'Self-assessment Value Creation Rating' [3] (self-VCr)	The sustainability (sustainable value creation) of a firm understood as the total value creation of a business model – on a self-reported basis – in relation to value appropriation (revenue/profits). Data source: Same as the self-VCp, supplementary questions on SVC metrics (transfer-OUT).	– Same as the self-VCp, with an additional layer of analysis (via transfer-OUT, 'value created but *not* appropriated') – For the allocation of capital, various investor applications Status: Same as the self-VCp.
'Value Creation Position' [4] (VCp)	The sustainability (sustainable value creation) of a firm understood as the 'value created and appropriated' by a business model as a proportion of value appropriation (revenue/profits). Data source: SVC metrics (transfer-IN, including transfer-COST, from profit and loss (P&L) statements, third party suppliers, set calculations) with 'monetary equivalence' to the firm's revenue/profits.	– For (elite) transformational leadership – For the public interest, as an alternative ESG measurement – For research on finance, management, sustainability (ESG), governance Status: Pilot report published in November 2024 as the *Value Creation Ratings Pilot Report 2024*, covering 122 corporate scores.
'Value Creation Rating' [5] (VCr)	The comprehensive sustainability (sustainable value creation) of a firm understood as the total value creation of a business model in relation to its value appropriation (revenue/profits). Data source: Same as the VCp, supplementary SVC metrics (transfer-OUT).	– Same as the VCp, with an additional layer of analysis (via transfer-OUT, 'value created but *not* appropriated') – For SVC valuations of equity, debt, and firms as inputs and sustainability references for the financial industry's capital allocation – For weighted policy formulation, institutional and (de)regulatory measures, industry specific Status: Same as the VCp.

Table A3.1a (continued)

SVC measurement [ref. nr.] (abbr.)	**Description (Data sources)**	**Application (Implementation status)**
'Perceptions of Value Creation Survey' [11] (360-VCz)	Perceptions survey on the sustainable value creation of the firm based on 360-degree performance feedback interventions. Data source: Firm outsider/insider Stakeholder/Principal Survey Questionnaires on the perception of a surveyed firms' value (risk) creation/transfers.	– For internal firm reflections on governance, transformational leadership, ethics, supported by outside perceptions (from stakeholders) – For custom educational programs, top management teams, boards of directors – As preparation for elite transformational leadership Status: Sample extracts of survey questionnaires (Tables A3.5a and A3.5b).
'Self-assessment International Business Value Creation Rating' [12] (IB-self-VCr)	The sustainability (sustainable value creation) of a firm's international business understood as the value creation of a business model – on a self-reported basis – in relation to its value appropriation abroad (global revenue/profits). Data source: Sub-set of questions in the SVC Metrics Self-assessment Survey.	– To aid in international strategic planning, including decision-making on sustainability initiatives abroad – To support assessments on a firm's international business impact (with stakeholder perspectives) – For executive education and custom programs at business schools Status: Same as self-VCr.
'International Business Value Creation Rating' [13] (IB-VCr)	The comprehensive sustainability (sustainable value creation) of a firm's international business understood as the value creation of a business model in relation to its value appropriation abroad (global revenue/profits). Data source: Same as the VCr, limited to international business SVC metrics.	– For the allocation of capital abroad, various international investor applications – As inputs for the cb-EQr, bl-EQr – For research on international business, economics, and international relations – For domestic policy proposals on development requiring foreign trade and investment flows – For weighted policy formulation and institutional and (de)regulatory measures related to foreign investors and investments and international institutions Status: Same as the VCr.
'Sector Value Creation Rating' [18] (sector-VCr)	The sustainable value creation benchmark providing an average, the median, or a percentile for a sector or industry considering only pertinent firms and based on their VCr and sector-specific SVC metrics. Data source: Same as the VCr, with discrete SVC metric selection according to industry.	– For comparative assessments of firms within given industries with the support of a sector-specific benchmark – For the formulation of industrial policy to determine which industries a nation ought to favor or discourage Status: Initial sector-VCr published as part of the *Value Creation Ratings Pilot Report 2024*.

Table A3.1a (continued)

SVC measurement [ref. nr.] (abbr.)	**Description (Data sources)**	**Application (Implementation status)**
Value creation modeling Economic measurements (macro-level)		
'Weighted transfers general equilibrium' macroeconomic model (also 'weighted transfers modeling') [10] (WTGE)	An econometric model that produces macro-level economic analysis and forecasts by weighting first-order value (and risk) creation vs second-order value (and risk) transfers occurring at the meso-level of the elite system. Data source: Macroeconomic models like DGSE, HANK and conventional variables, SVC measurements, VCr.	– For economic analysis based on weighting and (potentially) offsetting transfers and establishing *qui generat valorem* and matching this with *cui bono* for the optimization of value creation – For (long-term) economic forecasts – For elite system transformational leadership, a policy tool for weighted structural reform policy formulation, institutional and (de)regulatory measures, many industry-specific, all targeting the incentive system Status: Research proposal draft.
'Global weighted transfers general equilibrium' macroeconomic model [16] (G-WTGE)	Same as the WTGE, but multi-country. Data source: Same as the WTGE with supplementary variables and SVC measurements of the world's main economies and elite systems with an emphasis on cross-border elite business models.	Status: Dependent upon the validation of WTGE models for an initial set of countries.

Table A3.1b: Summary of the prospective sustainable value creation (SVC) measurements seeking to approach 'political economy omniscience'.*

SVC measurement [ref. nr.]* (abbr.)	Description	Application (Status)
'Political economy omniscience' Multiple levels from the individual to the global macro		
'Individual Value Creation Rating' [19] (ind-VCr)	Assesses the 'individual sustainable value creation' that emerges from a person's inclusive value creation and extractive value transfer relationships with his/her direct and indirect stakeholders across all related business models (from family to the state). For the purposes of economic development, the ind-VCr would be computed for members of elite coalitions, although in principle it could also be determined for non-elites. Because it is akin to a social credit score, the measurement should be made with the utmost caution. An additional factor for misgivings is the possibility that elite agency uses its bargaining power advantages in relation to institutional change to *de facto* realize the evidence-based ind-VCr for only non-elite individuals.	– To make elite coalition members of extractive business models accountable for their actions – To establish the 'takers' and 'givers' at the organizational and team levels – For firm valuations – For research on topics like comparative culture, inequality, or growthTo formulate policy proposals for institutional change – For *post-mortem* historical evaluations of individuals Status: Prospective, conceptual development pending.
'Weighted transfers game' [20] (WT-Game)	A comprehensive simulation of transfers in all socio-economic relations that is actualized by players on digital gaming platforms (like MMORPGs) who win by accurately describing first-order value (and risk) creation and second-order value (and risk) transfers that offer the best forecasts of future development trajectories. It becomes a network that connects society's diverse socio-economic groups through value creation and transfers; the connections become the core statements in the gameplay of committed (and possibly ethically motivated) gamers whose aim is to establish value transfer weights for optimal economic and human development.	– For entertainment – For research on economic development and management – To establish weighted policies to maximize economic and human development – To inform political economy narratives and test ethical systems Status: Prospective, a speculative political economy thought experiment, the realization of which is contingent on data availability and technological advances.
'Global weighted transfers game' [21] (GWT-Game)	Extends and duly completes the value creation/extraction map of the global political economy by covering cross-border business models.	– For entertainment – For research on international management and economics (FDI, trade) – To establish multilateral institutions and rules to maximize general, global development Status: Prospective, contingent on the realization of the WT-game and international institutions.

*The three SVC measurements are contextualized in Figure A5.10 and listed according to the reference numbers used in that figure (ref. nr.); an extension of Figure 7.8.

Table A3.2: Conceptual elements and terms in the Elite Quality Index (EQx).*

Aspect	Term	Description
Output level 1 (broad definition includes levels 1–3)	'Elite Quality Index' (EQx)	A global comparative index that scores and ranks countries on the conceptual element of elite quality. That is, on the aggregate value creation of a country's meso-level elite system evidenced by macro-economic phenomena captured by indicators consistent with the EQx's proprietary architecture and its conceptual bases. The EQx report is released annually and was launched in 2020 (EQx2020).
Output (levels 1–3)	'Panel EQx' (PEQx)	The PEQx is a historical measure of annual Elite Quality starting in 2005. It conceptually parallels the EQx but is based on its own methodological approach (to address technical matters such as missing values for new indicators).
Input (level 4)	'Indicator'	The conceptually indivisible, discrete datasets that jointly make up the composite index. For the EQx, each indicator must represent a quantifiable phenomenon in the political economy that provides evidence of value/risk creation or value/risk extraction/transfers. The data of an EQx indicator describes aspects of an elite business model along the conceptual 'value spectrum' that ranges from absolute value creation to absolute value extraction (transfers). Once normalized, weighted, and aggregated, EQx indicators inform the value position of the meso-level elite system in global comparative terms.
Architecture	'Level 1' ... 'Level 4'	The EQx architecture is constructed in four levels. Level 1 is the overall EQx score and the highest aggregate. Level 2 consists of the two sub-indices (power and value), and the four index areas that result from combining the two sub-indices with the two dimensions (political and economic). Level 3 consists of the 12 pillars, each representing discrete political economy ideas and the conceptual homes of EQx indicators. Level 4 consists of the indicators themselves, the indivisible datasets that provide evidence of value creation/extraction phenomena reflecting elite quality.
Architecture (level 2)	'Power' sub-index I	The first of the two sub-indices (the other is value) that serve to organize all indicators in the EQx. In this context, power refers to elite bargaining power in the political economy and is thus conceived as future potential value extraction.
Architecture (level 2)	'Value' sub-index II	The second of the two sub-indices (the other is power) that serve to organize all indicators in the EQx. In this context, and consistent with the 'value is created or transferred' ontological assumption of the ETED, value refers to the current actual first-order value creation of elite agency, or its opposite, second-order extractive transfer activity.

*The architecture of the EQx and the Value Creation Rating (VCr) parallel each other, although the terms employed differ. For instance, the EQx's 'sub-index' becomes the 'sub-rating' in the VCr, while 'index area' becomes 'ratings area', and 'political power' becomes 'non-market power'.

Table A3.2 (continued)

Aspect	Term	Description
Architecture (level 2)	'Political' dimension	The first of the two dimensions (the other is economic) that serve to organize all indicators in the EQx and that refers to phenomena mainly occurring in the non-market arena (and to a lesser extent in the narrative market arena).
Architecture (level 2)	'Economic' dimension	The second of the two dimensions (the other is political) that serve to organize all indicators in the EQx and that refers to phenomena mainly occurring the market arena.
Architecture (level 2)	'The Political Economy Power and Value Matrix'	A 2x2 framework that links value (creation/extraction) and power to the political and economic spheres (see Figure 6.2). The four sectors of the matrix correspond with the four index areas that allocate the 12 pillars and all indicators in the EQx: (i) political power; (ii) economic power; (iii) political value; and (iv) economic value. The framework is useful in organizing political economy phenomena and operationalizing political economy measurements like elite quality.
Architecture (level 2)	'Index area (i)' ... 'Index area (iv)'	The EQx has four index areas (level 2) corresponding to the four quadrants of the Political Economy Power and Value Matrix that link the 'value' and 'power' sub-indices with the 'political' and 'economic' dimensions. They are: (i) political power; (ii) economic power; (iii) political value; and (iv) economic value. Each of the four index areas contains three of the 12 EQx pillars (of level 3).
Architecture (level 3)	'Pillar 1' ... 'Pillar 12'	The EQx has 12 pillars (level 3), three for each of the four index areas, to organize all EQx indicators (level 4). They are: (i.1) state capture; (i.2) regulatory capture; (i.3) human capture; (ii.4) coalition dominance; (ii.5) firm dominance; (ii.6) creative destruction; (iii.7) giving income; (iii.8) taking income; (iii.9) unearned income; (iv.10) producer value; (iv.11) capital value; and (iv.12) labor value.
Weighting assumption	'Economics doubles politics' assumption	An assumption used to conceptually establish the respective weights for the 'political' and 'economic' EQx dimensions. The political dimension of elite business models is generally deemed to eventually consolidate and grow into the economic dimension where it will have a higher impact on general value creation. Hence, 'political' is discounted to half the level of 'economic' through the use of a 1/3:2/3 weighting (rounded to 33% and 67%).
Weighting assumption	'Present doubles future' assumption	An assumption used to conceptually establish the weights for the 'power' and 'value' EQx sub-indices in respect to each other. While power is a pre-condition for value transfers, it is conceived in terms of potential future value extraction, making extractive transfers a matter of probability and degree (as these might never occur). Hence, 'power' is discounted to half the level of 'value', through the use of a 1/3:2/3 weighting (rounded to 33% and 67%).

Table A3.2 (continued)

Aspect	Term	Description
Weighting	'Conceptual deliberation '1' ... '3'	Three EQx weighting decisions are based on conceptual and theoretical premises. Conceptual deliberation 1 assigns weights to the 'power' and 'value' sub-indices; under the 'present doubles future' assumption (adjusted to 33% and 67%) weights are respectively established. Conceptual deliberations 2 and 3 assign weights to the 'political' and 'economic' dimensions (within the 'power' and 'value' sub-indices); under the 'economics doubles politics' assumption about impact and immediacy (also therefore adjusted to 33% and 67%) weights are respectively established.
Weighting	BAP (Budget Allocation Process)	BAP is a generally accepted index weighting methodology that incorporates the subjective judgments of an expert panel about the relative importance of the respective component datasets. Most EQx weighting decisions are based on BAP. The BAP is used for the weighting of pillars (within each index area) and indicators (within each pillar).
Weighting	'Critical impact indicator'	Some elite business models are both country-specific and high-impact in terms of value creation and transfers. The EQx might miss such models or, when the relevant indicator is included, the scores won't reflect the sustainable value creation reality of particular countries if there is a consistent weighting of the indicator across the world (e.g., a housing affordability indicator would have to carry much more weight in Hong Kong than elsewhere). A solution is to allocate a slot in the EQx architecture for critical impact indicators that represent disproportionate value creation/transfer impact elite business models in a particular economy. The weighting of the critical impact indicator (s) would be done by conceptual deliberation (either on a country-by-country basis or by applying a consistent weight across countries).
Interpretation	'The State of the Elite System Framework' for the political economy	A 2x2 framework which links elite power (i.e., potential future value extraction) with elite value creation (see Figure 6.5). The four sectors of the matrix describe the state of the elite system and are: (1) 'Rentier elite system'; (2) 'Enlightened elite system'; (3) 'Striving elite system'; and (4) 'Competitive elite system'. Elite power and value are operationalized in the EQx as sub-index I and sub-index II, hence providing an empirical basis to place nations in this conceptual framework, which is intended to serve as a comparative classification and analytical tool for national elite systems to inform policy and structural reform.

Table A3.3: Conceptual elements used in the sustainable value creation (SVC) valuation frameworks for capital allocation.

Conceptual element	Description	Notation/Equation
Sustainable value creation (SVC) measurements	The firm-level sustainability measurements of business models, derived from the aggregation of SVC metrics and categorized, in consistency with the dualist ontological assumption for socioeconomic relationships, into extractive transfer-IN and exclusive transfer-OUT. The Value Creation Rating (VCr) is the SVC measurement utilized as the primary input to the functions that produce the adjustments used for SVC valuation frameworks as their outputs.	SVC measurement (VCr)
Sustainable value creation (SVC) valuation frameworks	Frameworks for finance that capture sustainable value creation and transfers to determine valuations for the allocation of capital. In the set of five decision-making tools, two are intended for enterprise value and equity (SVC-VF.1; SVC-VF.2); two are intended for debt instruments (SVC-VF.3; SVC-VF.4); and the fifth is intended for firm valuations using the WACC method (SVC-VF.5). Apart from the first framework, all the others rely on discounting cash flows for present value-based valuations.	SVC valuation framework
'The SVC-adjusted enterprise valuation framework' for private firms	'The SVC-adjusted enterprise valuation framework' for private firms offers two routes for valuing enterprises to incorporate value creation and transfers: the first is based on an adjusted revenue multiple; and the second is based on an adjustment to the standard enterprise value formula.	(SVC-VF.1)
'The SVC cost of equity valuation framework' for public firms	'The SVC cost of equity valuation framework' for public firms values equity. It is based on CAPM to which it adds a novel conceptual element, the 'SVC risk premium' for equity that incorporates value creation and transfers.	(SVC-VF.2)

Table A3.3 (continued)

Conceptual element	Description	Notation/Equation
'The SVC-adjusted credit rating valuation framework' for credit-rated debtors	'The SVC credit valuation framework' for credit-rated firms values debt and is based on the standard cost of debt formula to which it adds a novel conceptual element, the 'SVC risk premium for credit rating', that incorporates value creation and transfers.	(SVC-VF.3)
'The SVC cost of debt valuation framework' for debtors	'The SVC cost of debt valuation framework' for debtors values debt and is based on the standard cost of debt formula to which it adds a novel conceptual element, the 'SVC risk premium for debt', that incorporates value creation and transfers.	(SVC-VF.4)
'The SVC WACC-based valuation framework' for firms	'The SVC WACC-based valuation framework' for firms is based on the standard WACC method using adjusted costs of equity and debt that incorporate sustainable value creation and transfers.	(SVC-VF.5)
'The SVC-adjusted enterprise valuation framework' for private firms (SVC-VF.1)		
'VCr enterprise value adjustment function' for revenue multiple-based enterprise value	The function that weights sustainable value creation to provide the adjustment for the revenue multiple-based enterprise value (the function input is the VCr).	$fVCr^m$
'VCr enterprise value adjustment function' for enterprise value	The function that weights sustainable value creation to provide the adjustment for the standard enterprise value formula (the function input is the VCr).	$fVCr^{EV}$
'VCr revenue multiple adjustment'	The adjustment used for revenue multiple-based valuations (the output of the 'VCr enterprise value adjustment function').	VCr^m
'VCr enterprise value adjustment'	The adjustment used for standard enterprise value-based valuations (the output of the 'VCr enterprise value adjustment function').	VCr^{EV}
'SVC revenue multiple-based enterprise value'	The revenue multiple-based enterprise value formula with an adjustment for sustainable value creation and transfers.	EVm'
'SVC revenue multiple-based enterprise value' *equation (5.1a)*		$EVm' = Revenue * (Revenue\ Multiple * VCr^m)$
'SVC-adjusted enterprise value'	The standard enterprise formula based on equity value and net debt (debt minus cash and equivalents) with an adjustment for sustainable value creation and transfers.	$EV' =$
'SVC-adjusted enterprise value' *equation (5.2a)*		$EV' = (Equity\ Value * VCr^{EV}) + Net\ Debt$

Table A3.3 (continued)

Conceptual element	Description	Notation/Equation
'The SVC cost of equity valuation framework' for public firms (SVC-VF.2)		
'SVC risk premium function' for equity	The function that weights sustainable value creation to provide the adjustment for the cost equity formula (the function input is the VCr).	fr_{SVC}
'SVC risk premium' for equity	The adjustment used for the cost of equity, which is the additional return or, if negative, the discount that investors expect to receive for the risk associated with the sustainable value creation of the firm. The adjustment and its inclusion in the cost of equity formula operationalizes the connection between capital allocation processes and economic development.	r_{SVC}
'SVC cost of equity'	The cost of equity rate based on CAPM adjusted for sustainable value creation with the addition of the 'SVC risk premium' for equity. Upon the adjustment, when the additional return is positive, capital is more expensive; when it is negative, capital is more affordable.	k_E'
'SVC cost of equity' *equation (6.1a)*		$k_E' = r_f + \beta_E * (r_m - r_f) + r_{SVC}$ The CAPM cost of equity equation is: $k_E = r_f + \beta_E * (r_m - r_f)$
'SVC equity valuation'	The present value of equity adjusted for sustainable value creation and transfers is derived from applying the DCF method to equity cash flows with the 'SVC cost of equity' as the discount rate, which in turn results from adding the 'SVC risk premium' for equity adjustment to the standard cost of equity formula.	SVC_E'
'SVC equity valuation' *equation (6.2a)*		$SVC_E' = \frac{CF_1}{(1+k_E')^1} + \ldots + \frac{CF_n}{(1+k_E')^n}$ The standard discounted cash flow (DCF) valuation method is: $DCF = \frac{CF_1}{(1+k_E)^1} + \ldots + \frac{CF_n}{(1+k_E)^n}$
'The SVC credit valuation framework' for credit-rated firms (SVC-VF.3)		
'SVC risk premium function for credit rating'	The function that weights sustainable value creation to provide the adjustment for the 'credit rating cost of debt' formula (the function input is the VCr).	$fr_{SVC,D}^{cr}$
'SVC risk premium for credit rating'	The adjustment used for the credit rating cost of debt, which is the additional yield or, if negative, the negative yield that investors expect to receive for the risk associated with the sustainable value creation of the firm. The adjustment and its inclusion in the credit rating cost of debt formula operationalizes the connection between capital allocation processes and economic development.	$r_{SVC,D}^{cr}$

Table A3.3 (continued)

Conceptual element	Description	Notation/Equation
'SVC-adjusted credit rating cost of debt'	The cost of debt rate based on the credit rating cost of debt formula adjusted for sustainable value creation with the addition of the 'SVC risk premium for credit rating'. Upon the adjustment, when the additional return is positive, capital is more expensive; when it is negative, capital is more affordable.	$k_D^{cr'}$
'SVC-adjusted credit rating cost of debt' *equation (7.1a)*		$k_D^{cr'} = r_f + CS_i^{cr} + r_{SVC,D}^{cr}$ The credit rating cost of debt formula is: $k_D^{cr} = r_f + CS_i^{cr}$
'SVC-adjusted credit rating debt valuation'	The present value of credit rating-based debt adjusted for sustainable value creation and transfers is derived from applying the DCF method to debt cash flows with the 'SVC-adjusted credit rating cost of debt' as the discount rate, which in turn results from adding the 'SVC risk premium for credit rating' adjustment to the standard credit rating-based cost of debt formula.	$SVC_D^{cr'}$
'SVC-adjusted credit rating debt valuation' *equation (7.2a)*		$SVC_D^{cr'} = \frac{CF_1}{(1+k_D^{cr'})^1} + \ldots + \frac{CFn}{(1+k_D^{cr'})^n}$
'The SVC cost of debt valuation framework' for debtors (SVC-VF.4)		
'SVC risk premium function for debt'	The function that weights sustainable value creation to provide the adjustment for the cost debt formula (the function input is the VCr).	$fr_{SVC,D}$
'SVC risk premium for debt'	The adjustment used for the cost of debt, which is the additional yield or, if negative, the negative yield that investors expect to receive for the risk associated with the sustainable value creation of the firm. If the additional yield is positive, debt is more expensive' if negative, debt is more affordable. The adjustment and its inclusion in the cost of debt formula operationalizes the connection between capital allocation processes and economic development.	$r_{SVC,D}$
'SVC cost of debt'	The cost of debt rate based on the cost of debt formula adjusted for sustainable value creation with the addition of the 'SVC risk premium for debt'. Upon the adjustment, when the additional return is positive, capital is more expensive; when it is negative, capital is more affordable.	k_D'
'SVC cost of debt' *equation (8.1a)*		$k_D' = r_f + CS_i + r_{SVC,D}$ The cost of debt formula is: $k_D = r_f + CS_i$

Table A3.3 (continued)

Conceptual element	Description	Notation/Equation
'SVC-adjusted debt valuation'	The present value of debt adjusted for sustainable value creation and transfers is derived from applying the DCF method to debt cash flows using the 'SVC cost of debt' discount rate, which in turn results from adding the 'SVC risk premium for debt' adjustment to the standard cost of debt formula.	SVC_D
'SVC-adjusted debt valuation' *equation (8.2a)*		$SVC_D' = \frac{CF_1}{(1+k_D')^1} + \ldots + \frac{CF_n}{(1+k_D')^n}$
'The WACC-based valuation framework' for firms (SVC-VF.5)		
'SVC WACC'	The weighted average cost of capital adjusted for sustainable value creation and transfers, based on the standard WACC formula. The proportion of firm equity to firm value is multiplied by the 'SVC cost of equity' and the proportion of firm debt to firm value is multiplied by the 'SVC cost of debt', or alternatively by the 'SVC-adjusted credit rating cost of debt'.	$WACC''$
'SVC WACC' *equation (9.1a)*		$WACC'' = \left(\frac{E}{V} * k_E'\right) + \left(\frac{D}{V} * k_D^{cr'} \vert k_D'\right)$ The standard weighted average cost of capital formula is: $WACC = \left(\frac{E}{V} * k_E\right) + \left(\frac{D}{V} * k_D\right)$
'SVC firm valuation'	The present value of a firm adjusted for sustainable value creation and transfers is derived from applying the DCF method to firm cash flows, with the 'SVC WACC' as the discount rate.	SVC''
'SVC firm valuation' *equation (9.2a)*		$SVC'' = \frac{CF_1}{(1+WACC'')^1} + \ldots + \frac{CF_n}{(1+WACC''n)}$

Table A3.4a: Perceptions of Elites Survey (PEz): Non-elite Questionnaire (1/2) (sample extract).

Perceptions of Elites Survey (PEz): Non-elite Questionnaire (1/2)
Country Name: Z
Note: At the start of the survey respondents are provided with a list of terms used in the questions and their definitions (e.g., for 'business elite', 'non-elite', or 'value creation'). This list remains accessible at all times during the survey.

Ref.	EQx Architecture category	Question	Answer
PEz-NE.1	Political Value Index Area (iii)	"How accurate do you find this statement: 'Our country's political elites create value for our country'?" (Answer options: 1. Very accurate; 2. Somewhat accurate; 3. Moderately accurate; 4. Slightly accurate; 5. Not accurate at all)	1–5
PEz-NE.2	Power Sub-Index I	"How accurate do you find this statement: 'The leading elite business models in our economy generate their profits through extractive activities and value transfers (rather than through value creation activities)'?" (Answer options: 1. Very accurate; 2. Somewhat accurate; 3. Moderately accurate; 4. Slightly accurate; 5. Not accurate at all)	1–5
PEz-NE.3	Regulatory Capture Pillar (2)	"How prevalent do you believe crony capitalism is in your country?" (Answer options: 1. Very prevalent; 2. Somewhat prevalent; 3. Moderately prevalent; 4. Slightly prevalent; 5. Not prevalent at all)	1–5
PEz-NE.4	EQx	"How much do you agree with this statement: 'The leading elite business models in my country create value for me, my family, or my social circle (by providing high quality jobs, widespread prosperity, and innovation)'?" (Answer options: 1. Completely; 2. Mostly; 3. Partially; 4. Slightly; 5. Not at all)	1–5
PEz-NE.5	Economic Value Sub-Index (iv)	"How accurate do you find this statement: 'The business elites in my country appropriate too much of the value that I create (for instance, through inflation, inefficiencies, regulation, depressed wages, or tax evasion)'?" (Answer options: 1. Very accurate; 2. Somewhat accurate; 3. Moderately accurate; 4. Slightly accurate; 5. Not accurate at all)	1–5
PEz-NE.6	EQx	"How much do you like 'the elites' in our country? (please don't differentiate between elite types such as political, business, and knowledge)" (Answer options: 1. Strongly like; 2. Like; 3. Neutral; 4. Dislike; 5. Strongly dislike)	1–5
PEz-NE.7	Value Sub-Index II	"How well are my country's elites doing in terms of investing in the future?" (Answer options: 1. Very well; 2. Well, 3. Neutral. 4. Not at all well; 5. Poorly)	1–5
PEz-NE.8	EQx	"How accurate do you find this statement: 'Our country's elites are of a higher quality, more inclusive, and more innovative than those of neighboring country X'?" (Answer options: 1. Very accurate; 2. Somewhat accurate; 3. Moderately accurate; 4. Slightly accurate; 5. Not accurate at all)	1–5

Table A3.4a (continued)

Ref.	EQx Architecture category	Question	Answer
PEz-NE.9	Political Power Sub-Index (i)	"To what extent do you agree with this statement: 'The knowledge elites in my country are very powerful'?" (Answer options: 1. Strongly agree; 2. Agree; 3. Neutral; 4. Disagree; 5. Strongly disagree)	1–5
PEz-NE.10	Political Value Index Area (iii); Economic Value Index Area (iv)	"In your opinion, which of the three elite types (business/political/knowledge) create the most value in our country? Please the rank elite types according to the contribution that they make to value creation from the highest to the lowest using the options below." (Ranking options: business>political>knowledge, business>knowledge>political, political>business>knowledge, political>knowledge>business, knowledge>business>political, knowledge>political>business)	1–5

Table A3.4b: Perceptions of Elites Survey (PEz): Elite Questionnaire (2/2) (sample extract).

Perceptions of Elites Survey (PEz): Elite Questionnaire (2/2)
Country Name: Z
Note: At the start of the survey respondents are provided with a list of terms used in the questions and their definitions (e.g., for 'elite', 'non-elite', or 'value transfer'). This list remains accessible at all times during the survey.

Ref.	EQx Architecture category	Question	Extent
PEz-EQ.1	Economic Value Index Area (iv)	"To what degree is it true that your business model is based on innovation, production, exchange, and other forms of value creation?" (Answer options: 1. Completely true; 2. Very true; 3. Moderately true; 4. Slightly true; 5. Not true at all)	1–5
PEz-EQ.2	Creative Destruction Pillar (6)	"To what degree is it true that the business models of your peers are based on innovation and intrapreneurship, or are start-ups?" (Answer options: 1. Completely true; 2. Very true; 3. Moderately true; 4. Slightly true; 5. Not true at all)	1–5
PEz-EQ.3	Economic Value Index Area (iv)	"To what degree is it true that your business model is primarily based on subsidies, barriers to entry, regulations, monopolies, monopsonies, or other forms of value transfers and rent seeking?" (Answer options: 1. Completely true; 2. Very true; 3. Moderately true; 4. Slightly true; 5. Not true at all)	1–5
PEz-EQ.4	Power Sub-Index I	"To what degree is it true that the business models in the economy as a whole are primarily based on subsidies, barriers to entry, regulations, monopolies, monopsonies, or other forms of value transfer and rent seeking?" (Answer options: 1. Completely true; 2. Very true; 3. Moderately true; 4. Slightly true; 5. Not true at all)	1–5
PEz-EQ.5	EQx	"How accurate do you find this statement: 'In our economy non-elites benefit from the value creation of the leading business models'?" (Answer options: 1. Very accurate; 2. Somewhat accurate; 3. Moderately accurate; 4. Slightly accurate; 5. Not accurate at all)	1–5
PEz-EQ.6	Power Sub-Index I	"How accurate do you find this statement: 'In our economy non-elites are able to appropriate the full value that they create through their productive work (in the form of wages, public services, cost of living, etc.)'?" (Answer options: 1. Very accurate; 2. Somewhat accurate; 3. Moderately accurate; 4. Slightly accurate; 5. Not accurate at all)	1–5
PEz-EQ.7	Value Sub-Index I	"To what degree is it true that business elites in our country create more value than political and knowledge elites?" (Answer options: 1. Completely true; 2. Very true; 3. Moderately true; 4. Slightly true; 5. Not true at all)	1–5
PEz-EQ.8	Economic Power Index Area (ii)	"To what degree do you believe business elites in our country are powerful (relative to non-elites)?" (Answer options: 1. Extremely powerful; 2. Very powerful; 3. Moderately powerful; 4. Slightly powerful; 5. Not powerful at all)	1–5

Table A3.4b (continued)

Ref.	EQx Architecture category	Question	Extent
PEz-EQ.9	Political Power Index Area (i)	"To what degree do you believe political elites in our country are powerful (relative to business and knowledge elites)?" (Answer options: 1. Extremely powerful; 2. Very powerful; 3. Moderately powerful; 4. Slightly powerful; 5. Not powerful at all)	1–5
PEz-EQ.10	Political Value Index Area (iii); Economic Value Index Area (iv)	"In your opinion which of the three elite types (business/political/knowledge) create more value in our country? Please the rank elite types according to the contribution that they make to value creation from the highest to the lowest using the options below." (Ranking options: business>political>knowledge, business>knowledge>political, political>business>knowledge, political>knowledge>business, knowledge>business>political, knowledge>political>business)	1–5

Table A3.5a: Perceptions of Value Creation Survey (360-VCz): Firm Stakeholder Questionnaire (1/2) (sample extract, questions for diverse stakeholder types).*

Perceptions of Value Creation Survey (360-VCz): Firm Stakeholder Questionnaire (1/2)
Company Name: Company A (industry B)
Stakeholder: Stakeholder S
Note: At the start of the survey respondents are provided with a list of terms used in the questions and their definitions (e.g., for 'power, 'value creation', or 'value transfer'). This list remains accessible at all times during the survey.

Ref.	Category; Stakeholder type	Question	Answer
	Political Power		
360-VCz-GS.1.1	State capture (i.1), transfer-IN SVC metric; Government stakeholder	"How accurate do you find this statement: 'Company A and its leaders have very strong connections and many friends in the government'?" (Answer options: 1. Very accurate; 2. Somewhat accurate; 3. Moderately accurate; 4. Slightly accurate; 5. Not accurate at all)	1–5
360-VCz-GS.2.1	Regulatory capture (i.2), transfer-IN SVC metric; Government stakeholder	"How true is this statement: 'Regulators restrict Company A's ability to pursue and realize business opportunities within industry B'?" (Answer options: 1. Completely true; 2. Very true; 3. Moderately true; 4. Slightly true; 5. Not true at all)	1–5
360-VCz-LS.3.1	Human capture (i.3), transfer-IN SVC metric; Labor stakeholder	"To what extent do employees possess the bargaining power to set wages above industry B standards?" (Answer options: 1. Not at all; 2. To a small extent; 3. To a moderate extent; 4. To a great extent; 5. To a very great extent)	1–5
	Economic Power		
360-VCz-SS.4.1	Coalition dominance (ii.4), transfer-IN SVC metric; Supplier stakeholder	"To what extent do you agree with the statement: 'Industry B is recognized as one of the most powerful sectors in the nation'?" (Answer options: 1. Strongly agree; 2. Agree; 3. Neutral; 4. Disagree; 5. Strongly disagree)	1–5
360-VCz-SS5.1	Firm dominance (ii.5), transfer-IN SVC metric; Supplier stakeholder	"To what extent do you agree with the statement: 'Company A holds a dominant position in industry B'?" (Answer options: 1. Strongly agree; 2. Agree; 3. Neutral; 4. Disagree; 5. Strongly disagree)	1–5
360-VCz-LS.6.1	Creative destruction (ii.6), transfer-OUT SVC metric; Labor stakeholder	"To what extent do you agree with the statement: 'Company A is one of the most disruptive and innovative players in industry B's markets'?" (Answer options: 1. Strongly agree; 2. Agree; 3. Neutral; 4. Disagree; 5. Strongly disagree)	1–5
	Political Value		
360-VCz-LS.7.1	Giving income (iii.7), transfer-OUT; Labor stakeholder	"How much do you agree with this statement: 'It seems to me that Company A pays more taxes than the average company in our country'?" (Answer options: 1. Strongly agree; 2. Agree; 3. Neutral; 4. Disagree; 5. Strongly disagree)	1–5

*The survey questionnaire is tailored to stakeholder types (e.g., employees, suppliers, governments, customers, citizens at large). This extract includes selected questions for different stakeholder types as is indicated in the column for The Business Model Sustainable Value Scorecard categories.

Table A3.5a (continued)

Ref.	Category; Stakeholder type	Question	Answer
360-VCz-CS.8.1	Taking income (iii.8), transfer-IN; Citizen stakeholder	"How much do you agree with this statement: 'It seems to me that Company A is one of the most subsidized entities in our country'?" (Answer options: 1. Strongly agree; 2. Agree; 3. Neutral; 4. Disagree; 5. Strongly disagree)	1–5
360-VCz-CS.9.1	Unearned income (iii.9), transfer-IN; Citizen stakeholder	"How much do you agree with this statement: 'In my view, Company A is one of the greenest, most carbon-conscious companies in our country'?" (Answer options: 1. Strongly agree; 2. Agree; 3. Neutral; 4. Disagree; 5. Strongly disagree)	1–5
	Economic Value		
360-VCz-CU.10.1	Producer value (iv.10), transfer-OUT; Customer stakeholder	"How much do you agree with this statement: 'Based on my experience as a customer, Company A's products provide excellent value for money?" (Answer options: 1. Strongly agree; 2. Agree; 3. Neutral; 4. Disagree; 5. Strongly disagree)	1–5
360-VCz-KS.11.1	Capital value (iv.11), transfer-OUT; Capital supplier stakeholder	"How much do you agree with this statement: 'From my experience in the finance industry, over the past decade, Company A has delivered returns that significantly surpass the industry B average'?" (Answer options: 1. Strongly agree; 2. Agree; 3. Neutral; 4. Disagree; 5. Strongly disagree)	1–5
360-VCz-LP.12.2	Labor value (iv.12), transfer-OUT; Labor stakeholder	"How much do you agree with this statement: 'Based on my knowledge as a worker, labor productivity at Company A is excellent'?" (Answer options: 1. Strongly agree; 2. Agree; 3. Neutral; 4. Disagree; 5. Strongly disagree)	1–5

Table A3.5b: Perceptions of Value Creation Survey (360-VCz): Firm Principal Questionnaire (2/2) (sample extract).

Perceptions of Value Creation Survey (360-VCz): Firm Principal Questionnaire (2/2)
Company Name: Company A (industry B)
Note: At the start of the survey respondents are provided with a list of terms used in the questions and their definitions (e.g., for 'elite', 'non-elite', or 'value creation'). This list remains accessible at all times during the survey.

Ref.	The Business Model Sustainable Value Scorecard category	Question	Answer
	Political Power		
360-VCz-PQ.1.1	State capture (i.1), transfer-IN metric	"To what degree is it true that your company has better chances of winning government contracts compared to competitors?" (Answer options: 1. Completely true; 2. Very true; 3. Moderately true; 4. Slightly true; 5. Not true at all)	1–5
360-VCz-PQ.2.1	Regulatory capture (i.2), transfer-IN metric	"To what degree is it true that your company is more capable than its competitors to shape the regulations for industry B?" (Answer options: 1. Completely true; 2. Very true; 3. Moderately true; 4. Slightly true; 5. Not true at all)	1–5
360-VCz-PQ.3.1	Human capture (i.3), transfer-IN metric	"To what extent do your employees possess the bargaining power to influence and set wages above industry standards?" (Answer options: 1. Not at all; 2. To a small extent; 3. To a moderate extent; 4. To a great extent; 5. To a very great extent)	1–5
	Economic Power		
360-VCz-PQ.4.1	Coalition dominance (ii.4), transfer-IN metric	"To what extent do you agree with the statement: 'Industry B is recognized as one of the most powerful in the nation'?" (Answer options: 1. Strongly agree; 2. Agree; 3. Neutral; 4. Disagree; 5. Strongly disagree)	1–5
360-VCz-PQ.5.1	Firm dominance (ii.5); transfer-IN metric	"To what extent do you agree with the statement: 'Our company holds a dominant position in industry B'?" (Answer options: 1. Strongly agree; 2. Agree; 3. Neutral; 4. Disagree; 5. Strongly disagree)	1–5
360-VCz-PQ.6.1	Creative destruction (ii.6), transfer-OUT metric	"To what degree is it true that your company disrupts industry B markets with its competitive technologies, products, or processes?" (Answer options: 1. Completely true; 2. Very true; 3. Moderately true; 4. Slightly true; 5. Not true at all)	1–5

Table A3.5b (continued)

Ref.	The Business Model Sustainable Value Scorecard category	Question	Answer
	Political Value		
360-VCz-PQ.7.1	Giving income (iii.7), transfer-OUT metric	"How accurate do you find this statement: 'At Company A we face a higher income tax rate than other companies in our industry'?" (Answer options: 1. Very accurate; 2. Somewhat accurate; 3. Moderately accurate; 4. Slightly accurate; 5. Not accurate at all)	1–5
360-VCz-PQ.8.1	Taking income (iii.8), transfer-IN metric	"How accurate do you find this statement: 'At Company A we receive less subsidies than the average for industry B'?" (Answer options: 1. Very accurate; 2. Somewhat accurate; 3. Moderately accurate; 4. Slightly accurate; 5. Not accurate at all)	1–5
360-VCz-PQ.9.1	Unearned income (iii.9), transfer-IN	"How accurate do you find this statement: 'At Company A we offset more carbon emissions than the average company in industry B'?" (Answer options: 1. Very accurate; 2. Somewhat accurate; 3. Moderately accurate; 4. Slightly accurate; 5. Not accurate at all)	1–5
	Economic Value		
360-VCz-PQ.10.1	Producer value (iv.10), transfer-OUT	"How accurate do you find this statement: 'Our products provide excellent value for money'?" (Answer options: 1. Very accurate; 2. Somewhat accurate; 3. Moderately accurate; 4. Slightly accurate; 5. Not accurate at all)	1–5
360-VCz-PQ.11.1	Capital value (iv.11), transfer-OUT	"How accurate do you find this statement: 'Over the past decade Company A has delivered returns that significantly surpass the industry B average'?" (Answer options: 1. Very accurate; 2. Somewhat accurate; 3. Moderately accurate; 4. Slightly accurate; 5. Not accurate at all)	1–5
360-VCz-PQ.12.1	Labor value (iv.12), transfer-OUT	"How accurate do you find this statement: 'Labor productivity at Company A is excellent'?" (Answer options: 1. Very accurate; 2. Somewhat accurate; 3. Moderately accurate; 4. Slightly accurate; 5. Not accurate at all)	1–5

Table A3.6: SVC Metrics Self-assessment Survey: Questionnaire (sample extract, based on Casas-Klett & Nerlinger, 2023).

SVC Metrics Self-assessment Survey (self-VCp/self-VCr/IB-self-VCr): Questionnaire
Company Name: Company A (industry B)
Note: Respondents require access to financial statements, internal information, exchanges with firm specialists, and other third-party data to guide their answers, as well as sufficient time. The numerical answer to each question is within a set minimum/maximum range and will be used to establish the SVC metric 'monetary equivalence' with the support of a 'calibration factor'.

Ref.	Metric	Question	Min/Max range
	Political Power		
Self-VCr_rc.LOC MQ.2.1	*Lobbying* Regulatory capture (i.2), transfer-IN metric (input to self-VCp/self-VCr)	Estimate the expenditures the firm spends for its lobbying activities. Note: If the firm does NOT undertake any lobbying activities, nor engages in institutional relations or communications activities aimed at shaping public opinion, policy, or institutional change, please answer '0'. Remark: Lobbying can provide decision makers at firms with valuable insights and data, as well as access to the development and implementation of public policies favorable to the firm. On the other hand, the OECD has determined that lobbying can lead to undue influence, unfair competition, and regulatory capture that is to the detriment of the public interest and effective public policies (Source: References OECD, 2013).	Absolute number
Self-VCr_ hc.BDN MQ.3.1	*Board diversity (nationality)* Human capture (i.3), transfer-IN metric (input to self-VCp/self-VCr/IB-self-VCr)	Estimate the percentage of board members from foreign countries [percentage]. Remark: Board national diversity refers to the inclusion of individuals from various national backgrounds or citizenships on a company's board of directors. It encompasses the idea of having board members who represent different countries or regions. This type of diversity can bring a wide range of perspectives, experiences, and cultural insights to board discussions and decision-making. It is often seen as a way to enhance a company's global perspective and understanding of international markets.	0 to 90%

Table A3.6 (continued)

Ref.	Metric	Question	Min/Max range
	Economic Power		
Self-VCr_cd.CPO MQ.4.1	*Cartel power* Coalition dominance (ii.4), transfer-IN metric (input to self-VCp/self-VCr/IB-self-VCr)	Estimate the percentage of the firm's revenues gained from cartel agreements. Remark: "A cartel is an organization created from a formal agreement between a group of producers of a good or service to control supply or to regulate or manipulate prices. A collection of independent businesses or countries that act together like a single producer, cartel members may agree on prices, total industry output, market shares, allocation of customers, allocation of territories, bid-rigging, and the division of profits" (Source: Chen, 2023).	0 to 30% of revenue
Self-VCr_ fd.HHI MQ.5.1	*Market concentration* Firm dominance (ii.5); transfer-IN metric (input to self-VCp/self-VCr/IB-self-VCr)	Estimate the firm's monetary benefits that accrue from its market dominance (or market power) as a percentage of its revenues. Note: If the firm operates in a PERFECTLY competitive market (HHI<1,000 or 1,500) and has NO market power, please answer 0. Remark: Dominant firms in markets with high concentration incur the "risk of substantially lessening competition" and government agencies consider that illicit firm "coordination becomes more likely as concentration increases"; market concentration is assessed with the well-known Herfindahl-Hirschman Index (HHI), also a common measure used to determine market competitiveness (Source: References U.S. Department of Justice and the Federal Trade Commission, 2023).	0 to 50% of revenue
Self-VCr_cd.RDE MQ.6.1	*R&D expenses as percentage of revenue* Creative destruction (ii.6), transfer-OUT metric (input to self-VCp/self-VCr/)	Estimate the firm's R&D expenses as a percentage of revenue. Remark: Research and development (R&D) expenses refer to direct and indirect costs associated to the realization of new technologies, processes, applications, and ultimately products and services aimed at novel business possibilities. Firm R&D is more than a source of competitive advantage since the "new information" it produces coupled with the "ability to exploit and assimilate existing information" creates "innovation spillovers" that benefit the economy and society at large (Sources: References Cohen & Levinthal, 1989, p. 569; Griliches, 1992; Audretsch & Feldman, 1996, p. 639; Bonaglia, Rivera León, & Nindl, 2024).	0 to 30% of revenue

Table A3.6 (continued)

Ref.	Metric	Question	Min/Max range
	Political Value		
Self-VCr_ ti.ETR MQ.7.1	*Effective tax rate in comparison to peers* Giving income (iii.7), transfer-OUT metric (input to self-VCp/ self-VCr/)	Is the firm's effective tax rate above (+) or below (-) the industry average and what does this tax advantage/disadvantage represent as a percentage of firm revenue? If the firm pays the exact industry average tax rate, please answer 0. Remark: If the effective income tax rate is below the average of industry peers (-) there is a tax advantage of savings; if it is above the average of industry peers (+) there is a tax disadvantage that represents an extraordinary expense and a contribution to the taxpayer stakeholder.	0 to -/+ 20% of revenue
Self-VCr_ti.SUB MQ.8.1	*Subsidies* Taking income (iii.8), transfer-IN metric (input to self-VCp/ self-VCr)	Estimate the total amount of direct (e.g., equity infusion) or indirect (e.g., price support) subsidies that the firm receives as a percentage of revenues. Note: If the firm does NOT receive ANY direct or indirect subsidies whatsoever, please answer 0. Remark: A subsidy is defined by the WTO as a government practice that involves: (i) a direct transfer of funds (e.g. grants, loans, and equity infusions); (ii) potential direct transfers of funds or liabilities (e.g. loan guarantees); (iii) revenue that is otherwise due is forgiven or not collected (e.g. fiscal incentives such as tax credits); (iv) goods or services provided other than general infrastructure or purchased goods; and (v) payments to a funding mechanism, or entrusting or directing a private body to carry out one or more of the type of functions outlined in (i) to (iii) above that would normally be the responsibility of the government and the practice differs in no real sense from practices normally followed by governments (Source: adapted from Agreement on Subsidies and Countervailing Measures; WTO, 1994b, p. 229; Article 1: Definition of a subsidy, see https://www.wto.org/english/docs_e/legal_e/24-scm.pdf).	0–50% of revenue [or] Absolute number

Table A3.6 (continued)

Ref.	Metric	Question	Min/Max range
Self-VCr_ui. COC_MQ.9.1	*Carbon offsets and credits* Unearned income (iii.9), transfer-OUT (input to self-VCp/self-VCr/IB-self-VCr)	Estimate the equivalent of the CO_2 offsets, credits, and allowances in tons purchased or produced by the company. Remark: The equivalent of the CO_2 offsets, credits, and allowances in tons purchased or produced by the company during the fiscal year. Companies evolving in certain sectors have a limit on their CO_2 emissions; if they exceed this limit, they must purchase additional credits to balance it and if they fall short of the limit, they can sell the remainder of their emissions allowance. Carbon credits purchased and produced are considered. Investments in wind farms and planting trees that the company claims offset carbon emissions are also in scope.	Absolute number
	Economic Value		
Self-VCr_pv.GSC MQ10.1	*Global supply chain* Producer value (iv.10), transfer-OUT (input to self-VCp/self-VCr/IB-self-VCr)	Estimate the percentage of the supply chain that is located outside the firm's country of origin (location of headquarters). Remark: Global supply chains are often characterized by their complexity and the need for effective coordination across borders and cultures. Companies aim to create resilient and efficient global supply chains to optimize costs, improve product quality, meet customer demand, and remain competitive in the global marketplace. International interdependencies have been deemed to be a contributing factor to international peace and stability. On the other hand, some see risks like supply chain disruptions and geopolitical insecurity.	0 to 90%
Self-VCr_cv.KEX MQ.11.1	*Capital expenditure's as percentage of revenue* Capital value (iv.11), transfer-OUT (input to self-VCp/self-VCr)	What is the amount of capital expenditures (CAPEX) made by the firm as a percentage of revenue? Remark: Capital expenditures are funds dedicated to the acquisition and maintenance of assets like machinery or buildings. The purchase of assets by firms has a multiplier effect as these aggregate in the investment function of the economy. Firm CAPEX is more than a source of competitive advantage since it contributes to aggregate supply and employment, and indirectly to consumption, productivity, GDP growth, and future economic activity.	0 to 30% of revenue

Appendix 4: Supplementary tables for the ETED's conceptual elements

Table A4.1: Table of ETED fallacies.

	Fallacy	Description	Sources for fallacy/not a fallacy
1	Elite denial fallacy ('elites don't exist') (Section 1.1 and throughout this work)	The elite denial fallacy ('elites don't exist') negates the agency of elites and the idea that they are a discrete, high-impact social phenomenon. This understanding is deemed to be fallacious because elite coalitions are a constant in all social orders and there is an ample theoretical base to explain their dominance; moreover, the elite is the social phenomenon with the highest impact on human and economic development.	The fallacy is widespread in the public and media domains; appears in mainstream economics as a result of frictionless Hayekian and free market assumptions. Not a fallacy for Machiavelli (1513/1998) and Hobbes (1651/2002); Marx (1867/1959b); classical elite theorists (Mosca, 1939; Michels, 1962; Pareto, 1968/1991); Mills (1956), Olson (1965/1971, 1982); rent-seeking theorists such as Tullock (1967), Krueger (1974), Buchanan (1980), or Tollison (1982); Baumol (1990); Acemoglu, & Johnson (2005); Amsden, DiCaprio, & Robinson (2014); Bejan (2020); and the significant literature on elites.
2	Elite populist fallacy ('elites are bad') (Section 1.1, Chapter 6 on elite quality)	The elite populist fallacy ('elites are bad') takes the position that elites do exist *and* are a root cause of most socio-economic problems. This understanding is deemed fallacious because elite coalitions can be 'high quality' and run elite business models with high sustainable value creation positions that lead to human and economic development.	The fallacy has roots in Proudhon (1851/1971); Marx (1867/1959b); Lenin (1918); Mills (1956); Domhoff (1967); Nakamoto's Bitcoin (2008); and follows in the tracks of many religious beliefs (e.g., Christianity), while today it is part of the discourse in diverse public and political domains (on both the Left and Right of the political spectrum). Not a fallacy for classical elite theorists; Olson (1993, 2000); North, Wallis, & Weingast (2006).
3	Non-elite rule fallacy ('people power') (Section 3.3.3 on non-elite interests, Section 8.1.3 on non-elite political options)	The non-elite rule fallacy ('people power') stresses that non-elites can govern as representatives of genuine non-elite interests. It is derived from the elite denial fallacy (i.e., if elites don't exist, non-elites rule) and normatively synchronizes with the elite populist fallacy (i.e., if elites are bad, non-elites ought to rule). This understanding is deemed to be fallacious because institutional change is the result of intra-elite contests and only weakly or exceptionally affected by non-elite agency, which is limited by a lack of coherent leadership or a focus on the narrow interests of a specific group.	The fallacy has roots in democratic ideals; historical events such as the French and October Revolutions; is amply supported in the public domains of the West; found in literature like Dahl's polyarchy (1961/2005); exists in (American) theories of politics conforming to the "majoritarian electoral democracy" or "majoritarian pluralism" categories of Gilens and Page's taxonomy (2014); or in assumptions made for economic analyses such as those of Acemoglu and Robinson (2006). Not a fallacy for classical elite theorists; power elite theorists (Mills, 1956; Domhoff (1967; 1970); and for thought systems that reject the elite denial fallacy.

Note: The three fallacies in this work are a special category of conjectures that challenge assumptions held – at times widely – in the public, policy, and academic domains.

https://doi.org/10.1515/9783110734638-017

Table A4.2: The diverse perspectives on the 'elite' conceptual element of the ETED.

Ref.	Perspective	Description
01	Abstract	Coordination capacity
02	Economics	Transaction cost reduction mechanism
03	Analytical	Value creation and value transfers
04	Organizational	Elite business model
05	Individual	Beneficiary of elite business model residual income
06	Agency	Power accumulation for residual income maximization and elite identity preservation
07	Principal-stakeholder	Bargaining power differentials between elite principals and non-elite stakeholders
08	Practical	The power of elite business models to benefit from value created and appropriated; value appropriated but *not* created; 'cost created but *not* borne'
09	Micro-level	Elite business models have the largest residual income flows in the economy
10	Management	Leadership to accumulate bargaining power for the elite business model and its conversion into residual income
11	Meso-level	Elite system, the sub-system of the political economy that aggregates elite agency
12	Dynamics	Elite business model circulation modes
13	Institutional	Intra-elite contest rules and elite business model rules
14	Bargains	Elite pacts to constrain value extraction
15	Political economy	The mechanisms that determine the winners and losers of intra-elite contests
16	Macro-level	Elite quality, the determinant of human and economic development outcomes
17	Ethical	Who creates the value that is appropriated?
18	Ethical principle (maxim)	*To the creators the value created*
19	Sustainability	Sustainable value creation of elite business models (at the firm micro-level) and nations (at the elite system meso-level) that constrains unsustainable value transfers
20	Leadership, micro-level	Transformations for the non-appropriation of value that elite bargaining power differentials afford on account of long run, sustainability, or ethical considerations
21	Normative, micro-level	Elite business model transformational leadership for bottom-up sustainable value creation
22	Leadership, meso-level	Elite bargains for elite business model transformation (that endure the test of time)
23	Leadership, technical	Weight and offset second-order value and risk transfers
24	Normative, meso-level	Elite bargains for elite system transformational leadership to effect top-down structural reform (institutional change) of the incentive system towards sustainable value creation
25	Judgment	The practice of transformational elite leadership that weights and offsets value transfers and realizes these courageously through elite bargains

Table A4.3a: The sustainable value creation (SVC) set of ethical principles for human and economic development.

Ref.	Hierarchy of principles	Relation to economic and human development, and agency	Ethical principle
	Central doctrine (for society at large)		
(i)	**Maxim**	Operationalization of the intrinsic value of sustainable value creation	*To the creators the value created*
	Conceptual guidance (for transformational leadership)		
(ii)	**Tenet**	Incentive setting (by elite agency), positive	*Maximize first-order value creation and risk origination for productive economic transformations fit for human purpose*
(iii)	**Tenet**	Constraint setting for comprehensive optimization (by elite agency), negative	*Weight and offset second-order value and risk transfers and minimize these to maximize value*
	Practical guidance (for applied elite system and elite business model transformational leadership)		
(iv)	**Precept**	Cognitive (understanding of value transfer trade-offs, cost-benefit): elite system and elite business model action	*Measure value and risk transfers and establish the optimal weightings and potential offsets to maximize sustainable value creation*
(v)	**Precept**	Institutional: a political economy with non-elite input and elite business model action	*Realize sustainable value creation and risk origination incentives through top-down weighted structural reforms and bottom-up elite business model transformation*
(vi)	**Precept**	Institutional: elite system with minor non-elite input and elite business model action	*Invest in elite cohesion and in the elite separation of powers with a comprehensive set of checks and balances to encourage productive intra-elite contests*
(vii)	**Precept**	Institutional: a political economy with non-elite political action	*Promote the freedom to exit and the freedom to create value irrespective of optimal value creation, transfer weightings, and potential offsets*

Table A4.3b: The sustainable value creation (SVC) set of ethical principles adapted for the AI: AI goals (3), AI tasks (4), and cumulative assumptions (5).

Set of ethical principles for human and economic development	Set of ethical principles for the AI (for application in the human political economy)
(i) Maxim *To the creators the value created*	**The AI goal 1** *To the human creators the value created* **Assumption 1** The AI cares for human value appropriation **Assumption 2** The AI can constrain its own utility maximization function
(ii) Tenet *Maximize first-order value creation and risk origination for productive economic transformations fit for human purpose*	**The AI goal 2** *Value creation for humans* **Assumption 3** The AI can create value for humans
(iii) Tenet *Weight and offset second-order value and risk transfers and minimize these to maximize value*	**The AI goal 3** *Renunciation of value transfers from humans that are not weighted and offset*
(iv) Precept *Measure value and risk transfers and establish the optimal weightings and potential offsets to maximize sustainable value creation*	**The AI task 1** The AI computes the entire set of value creation and value transfers (in real-time) with updated general macroeconomic models that capture all relevant socio-economic interactions while establishing instantaneous sustainable value creation (SVC) measurements at the individual, firm, and national levels, thus solving the *qui generat valorem* (by humans for humans) and the *cui bono* questions **Assumption 4** The AI (partial or total) omniscience of the human political economy (i.e., the AI knows all prices, utility functions, bargaining power differentials, etc.)
(v) Precept *Realize sustainable value creation and risk origination incentives through top-down weighted structural reforms and bottom-up elite business model transformation*	**The AI task 2** The AI implements weighted structural reforms and provides targeted incentives for continuous elite business model transformation in the human political economy **Assumption 5** The AI (partial or total) omnipotence in the human political economy (i.e., the AI directly or indirectly affects institutional change, and causes the transformation of business models towards sustainable value creation)
(vi) Precept *Invest in elite cohesion and in the elite separation of powers with a comprehensive set of checks and balances to encourage productive intra-elite contests*	**The AI task 3** The AI participates in human intra-elite contests to rebalance bargaining power differentials, optimize checks and balances, and incentivize elite cohesion
(vii) Precept *Promote the freedom to* exit *and the freedom* to *create value irrespective of optimal value creation, transfer weightings, and potential offsets*	**The AI task 4** The AI participates in the political economy's three contest arenas (market, non-market, narrative market) to affect weighted structural reforms that realize the freedom to *exit* and the freedom *to* create value

Table A4.4: The three frameworks for weighted policymaking: Overview and linkages.

A Weighted Structural Reform Framework for policy (Table 7.1)	A Transfer Constraints Framework for policy formulation (Table 8.2)	A Weighted Redistribution Framework for policy (Table 8.3)
Weighted structural reform	← Reference →	**Sustainable redistribution**
(i) Impact assessment: Value transfers	Secure ↓	(i) Impact assessment: Redistribution transferor/transferee
(ii) Formulation: Institutional and (de)regulatory measures		(ii) Formulation: Constraints on redistribution
(iii) Elite transformational leadership:* 'Elite institutional change bargain'		(iii) Elite transformational leadership:* 'Elite redistribution constraints bargain'
	Constraints on value transfers	
	(i) Intertemporal constraints	
	(ii) Monetary constraints	
	(iii) Value creation milestones	

* Transformational leadership entails securing bargains as well as the deactivation of transfers, the institutionalization of related constraints, and the implementation of structural reforms against resistance

Table A4.5a: The Three Freedoms for Development Model.

Ref.	Freedom type	Definition	Relationship to economic and human development
(i)	Freedom *from* value extraction	The fundamental negative freedom. Power over interference from those running business models that rely on value appropriated but *not* created.	Positive incentive system; enhanced production function; increased social cohesion; reduced negative externalities.
(ii)	Freedom *to* create value	The fundamental positive freedom. Power to realize the innate potential for value creation.	Increased risk-taking; enhanced production function; positive incentive system; increased competition; higher levels of innovation; increased positive externalities.
(iii)	Freedom to *exit*	The enabling freedom. Power to break free from extractive principal-stakeholder relationships.	Decreased bargaining power differentials; greater competition; free market prices; increased risk-taking; intensified intra-elite contests.

Table A4.5b: The set of sustainable value creation (SVC) ethical principles instantiated by the institutionalization of the three freedoms for development and transformational leadership.

Set of sustainable value creation ethical principles	Instantiation of ethical principles: Freedoms for development and transformational leadership
(i) Maxim *To the creators the value created*	Freedom *from* value extraction Freedom to *exit* Freedom *to* create value Elite system transformational leadership (narrative market focus)
(ii) Tenet *Maximize first-order value creation and risk taking for productive economic transformations fit for human purpose*	Freedom *to* create value Elite transformational leadership (market focus)
(iii) Tenet *Weight and offset second-order value and risk transfers and minimize these to maximize value*	Freedom *from* value extraction Elite system transformational leadership (non-market and narrative market focus)
(iv) Precept *Measure value and risk transfers and establish the optimal weightings and potential offsets to maximize sustainable value creation*	Elite business model transformational leadership Elite system transformational leadership (market, non-market, narrative market)
(v) Precept *Realize sustainable value creation and risk origination incentives through top-down weighted structural reforms and bottom-up elite business model transformation*	Freedom *to* create value Freedom to *exit* Freedom *from* value extraction Elite system transformational leadership Elite business model transformational leadership (market, non-market focus)
(vi) Precept *Invest in elite cohesion and in the elite separation of powers with a comprehensive set of checks and balances to encourage productive intra-elite contests*	Elite system transformational leadership (non-market, narrative market focus)
(vii) Precept *Promote the freedom to* exit *and the freedom* to *create value irrespective of optimal value creation, transfer weightings, and potential offsets*	Freedom to *exit* Freedom *to* create value Elite system transformational leadership Elite business model transformational leadership (market, non-market focus)

Appendix 5: Supplementary figures

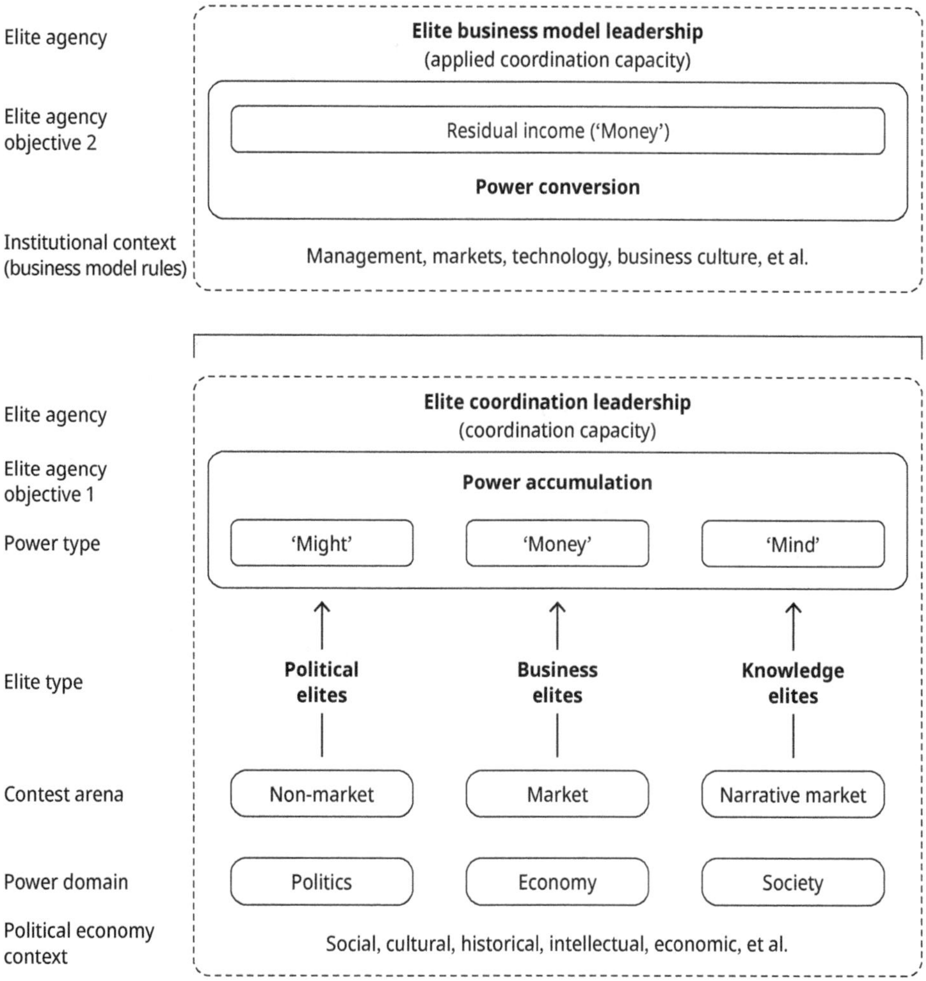

Figure A5.1: Elite agency: An overview.

https://doi.org/10.1515/9783110734638-018

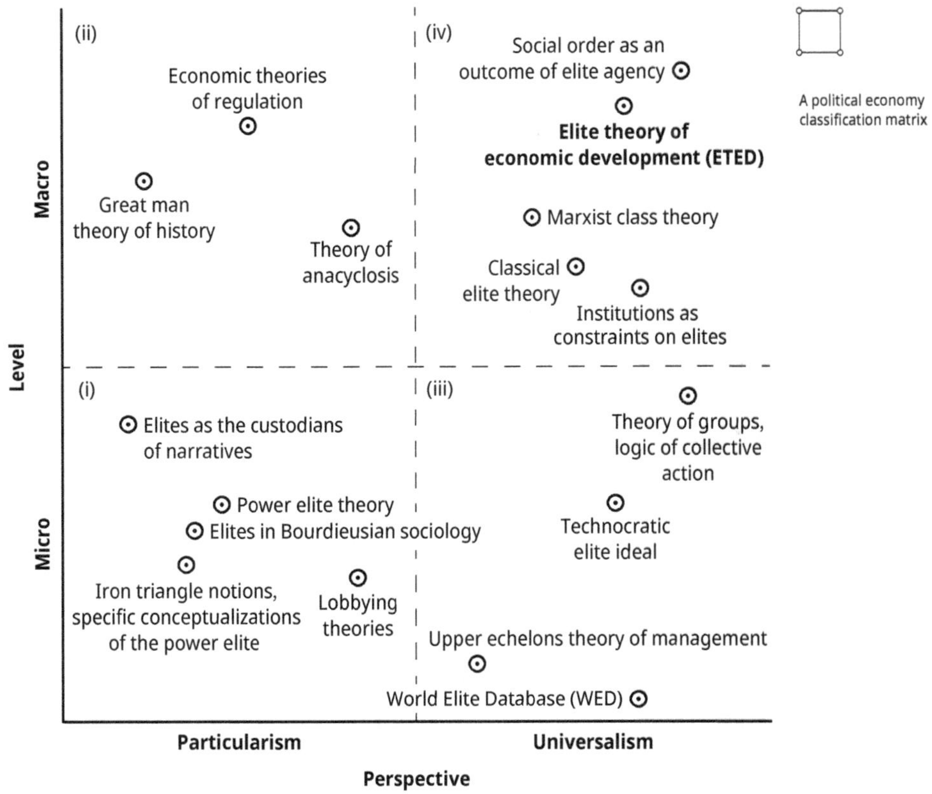

Figure A5.2: Classification of elite theories and conceptualizations by analysis level (micro to macro) and perspective (particularism to universalism).

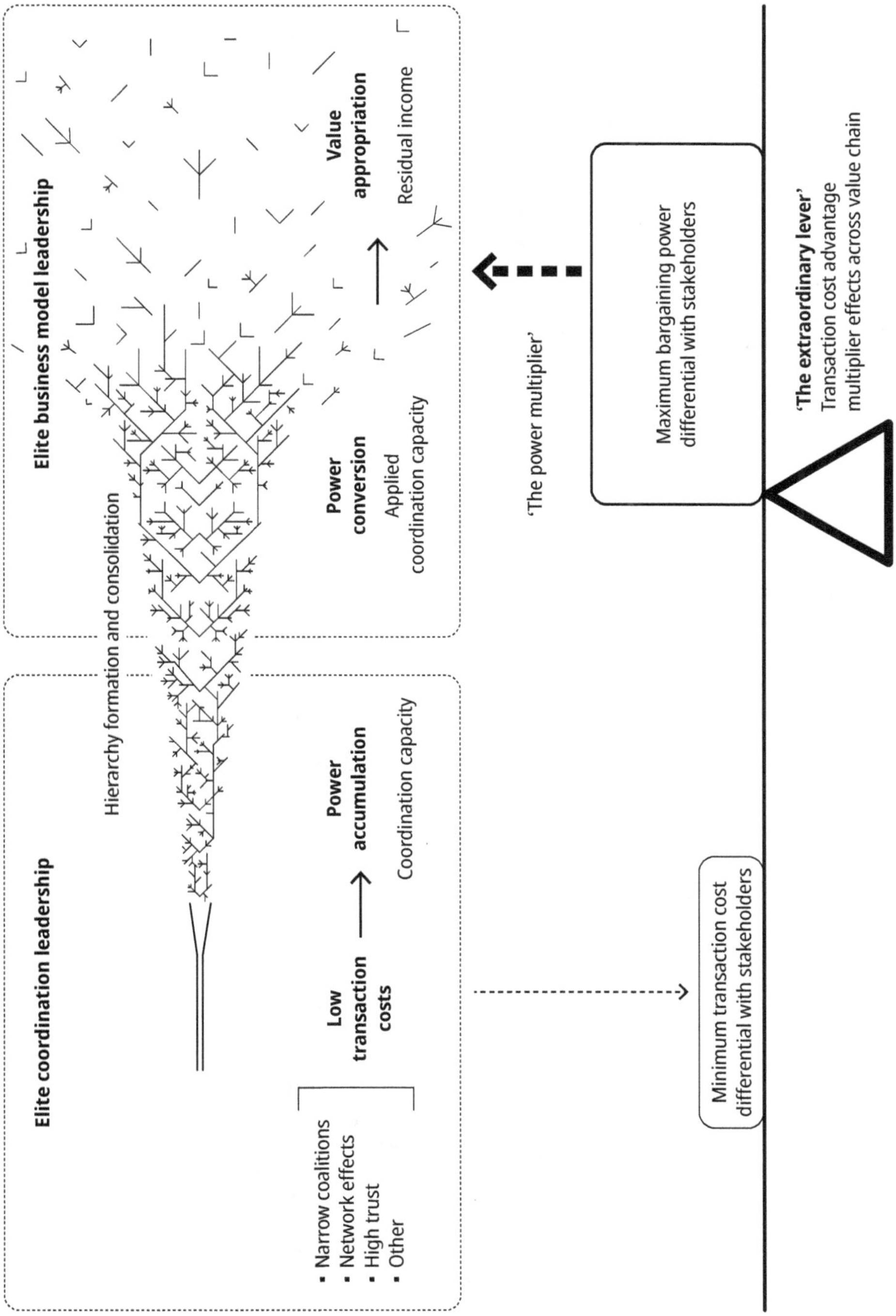

Figure A5.3a: 'The extraordinary lever' of elites: Power accumulation and its conversion as applied coordination capacity for value appropriation.

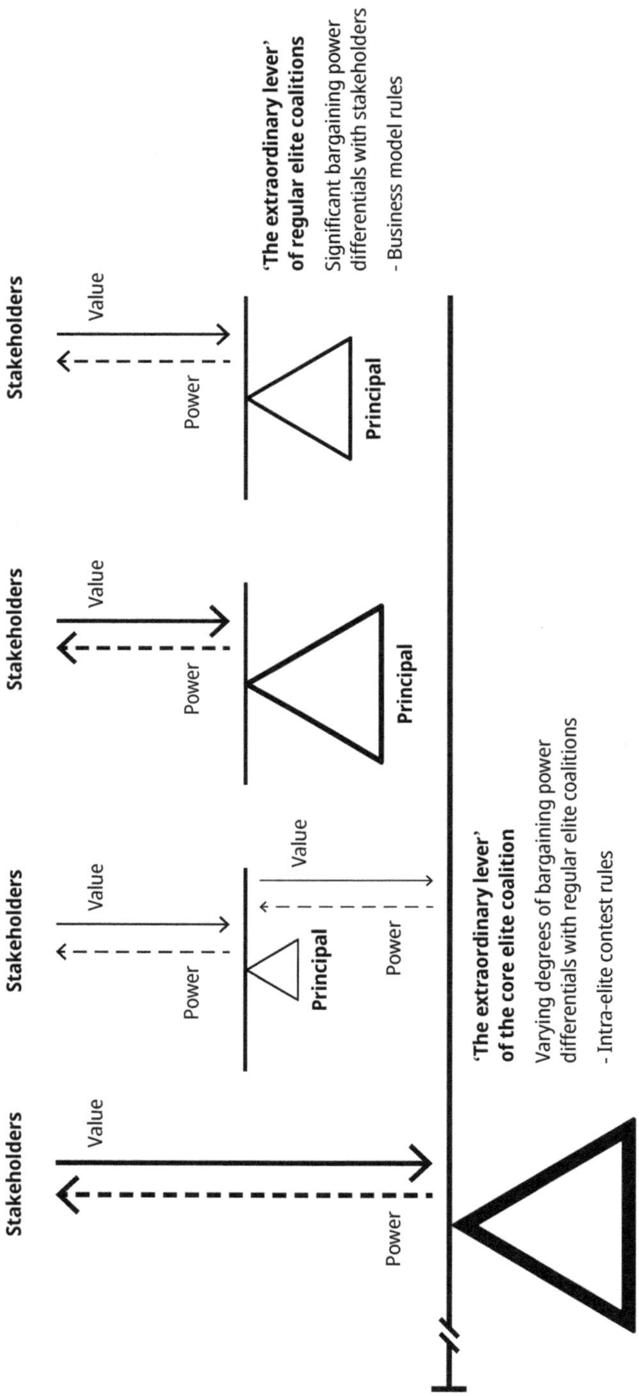

Figure A5.3b: 'The extraordinary lever' of the core elite coalition and of regular elite coalitions.

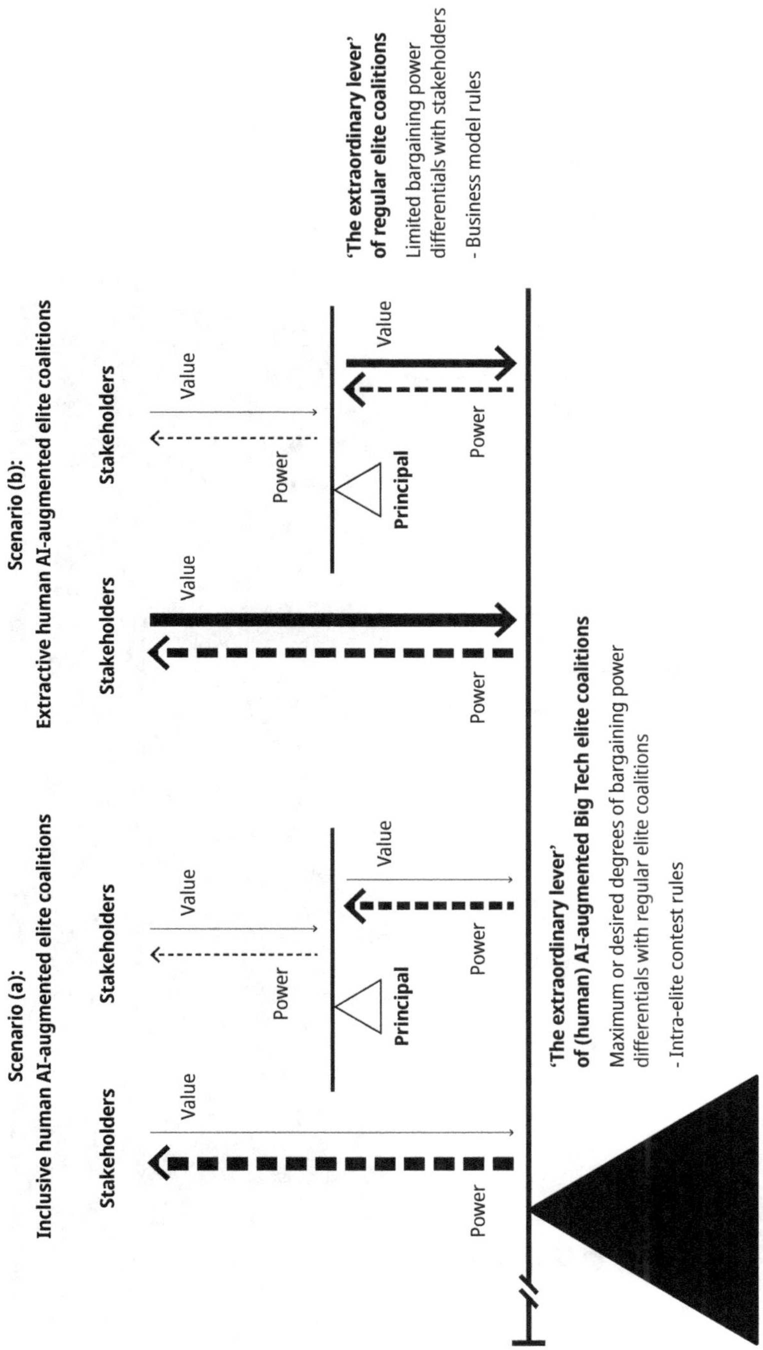

Figure A5.3c: 'The extraordinary lever' of the (human) AI-augmented AI elite coalitions (Big Tech, tech bros, et al.) with inclusive and extractive scenarios: Bargaining power differentials with stakeholders (including regular elite coalitions).

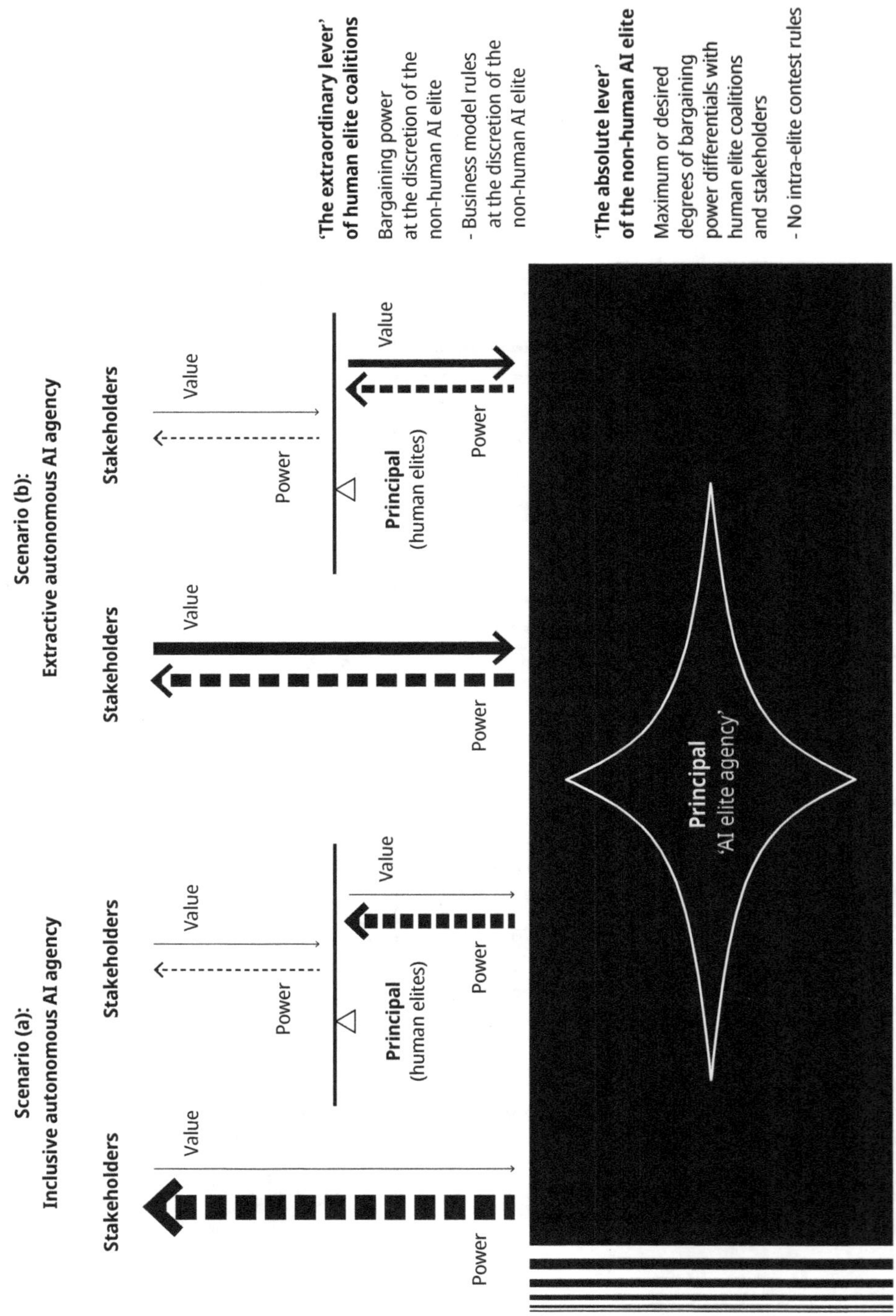

Figure A5.3d: 'The absolute lever' of 'AI elite agency' (AI_H2) with inclusive and extractive scenarios: Value appropriation by non-human AI elite principal from human elites and stakeholders.

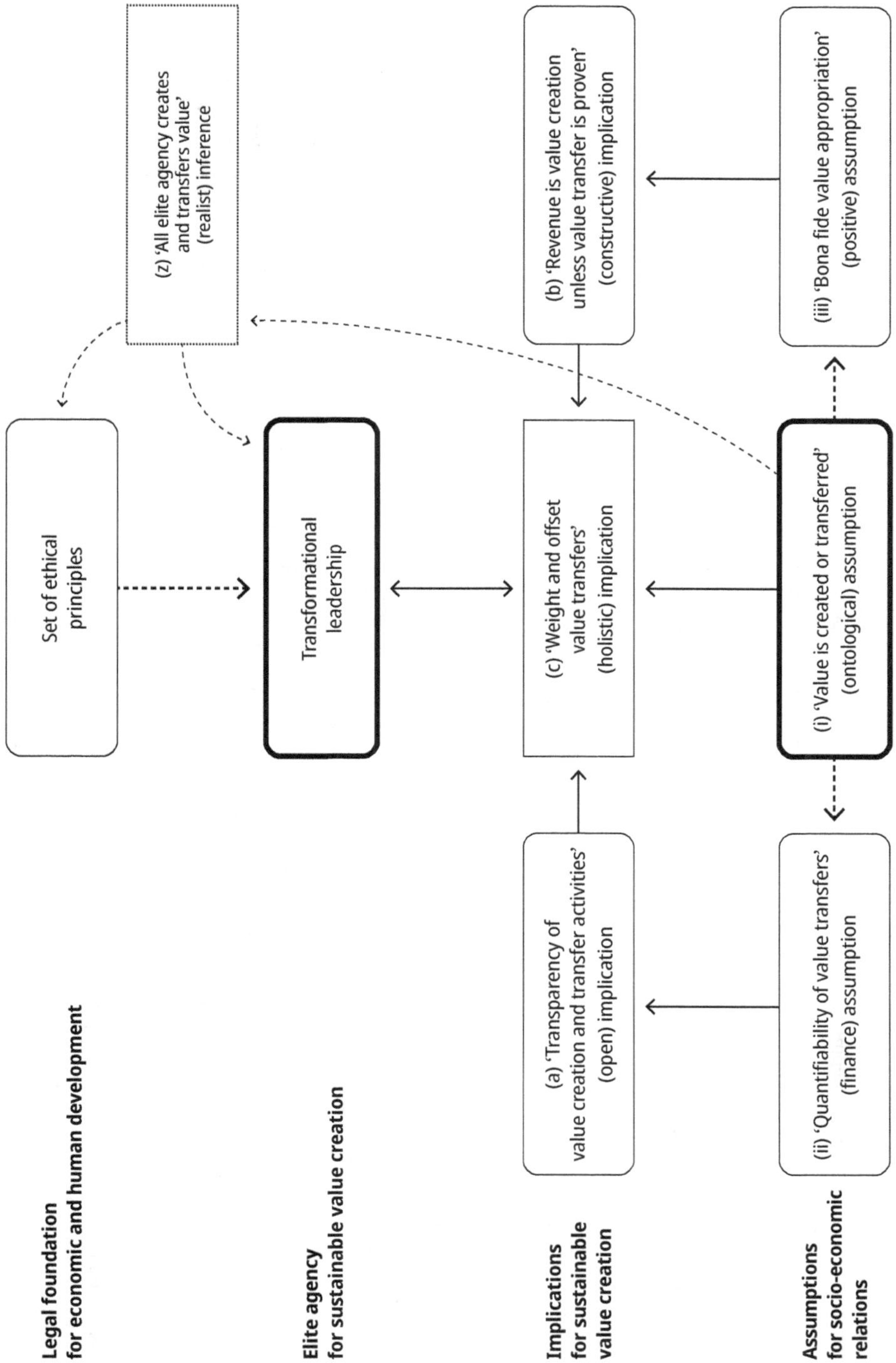

Figure A5.4a: The three assumptions for socio-economic relations and their implications for sustainable value creation agency.

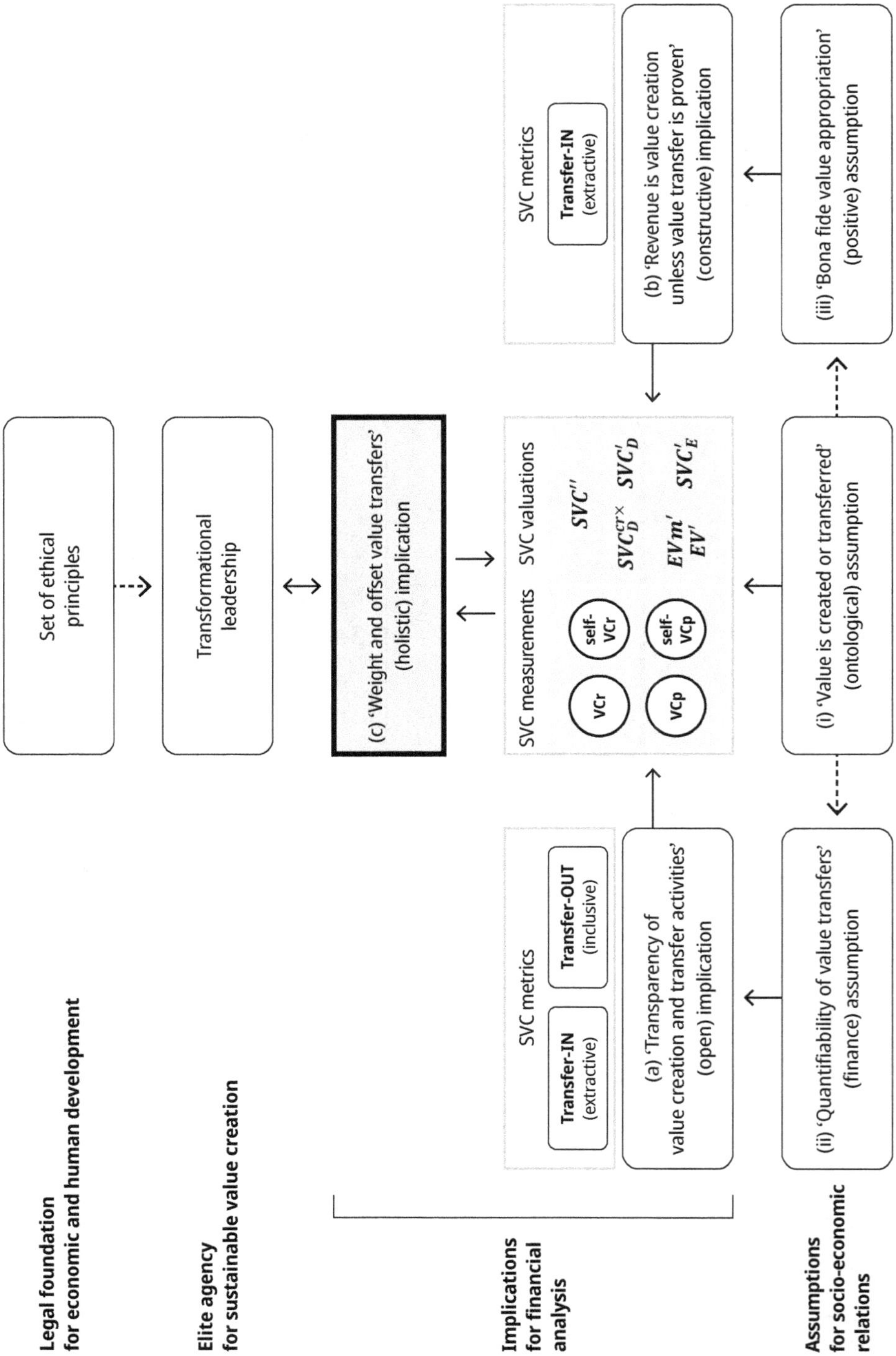

Figure A5.4b: The 'weight and offset value transfers' (holistic) implication for financial analysis realized through SVC metrics, measurements, and valuations.

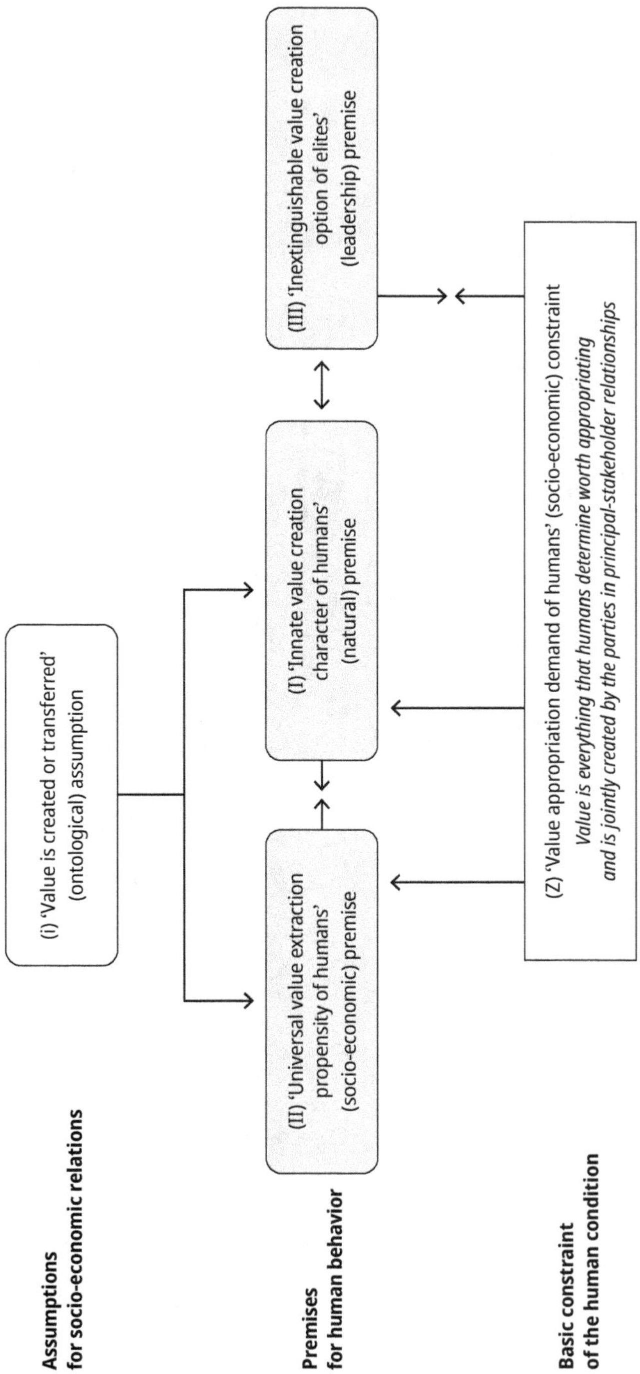

Figure A5.4c: The three premises for human behavior in relation to the basic constraint on the human condition and the chief (ontological) assumption for socio-economic relations.

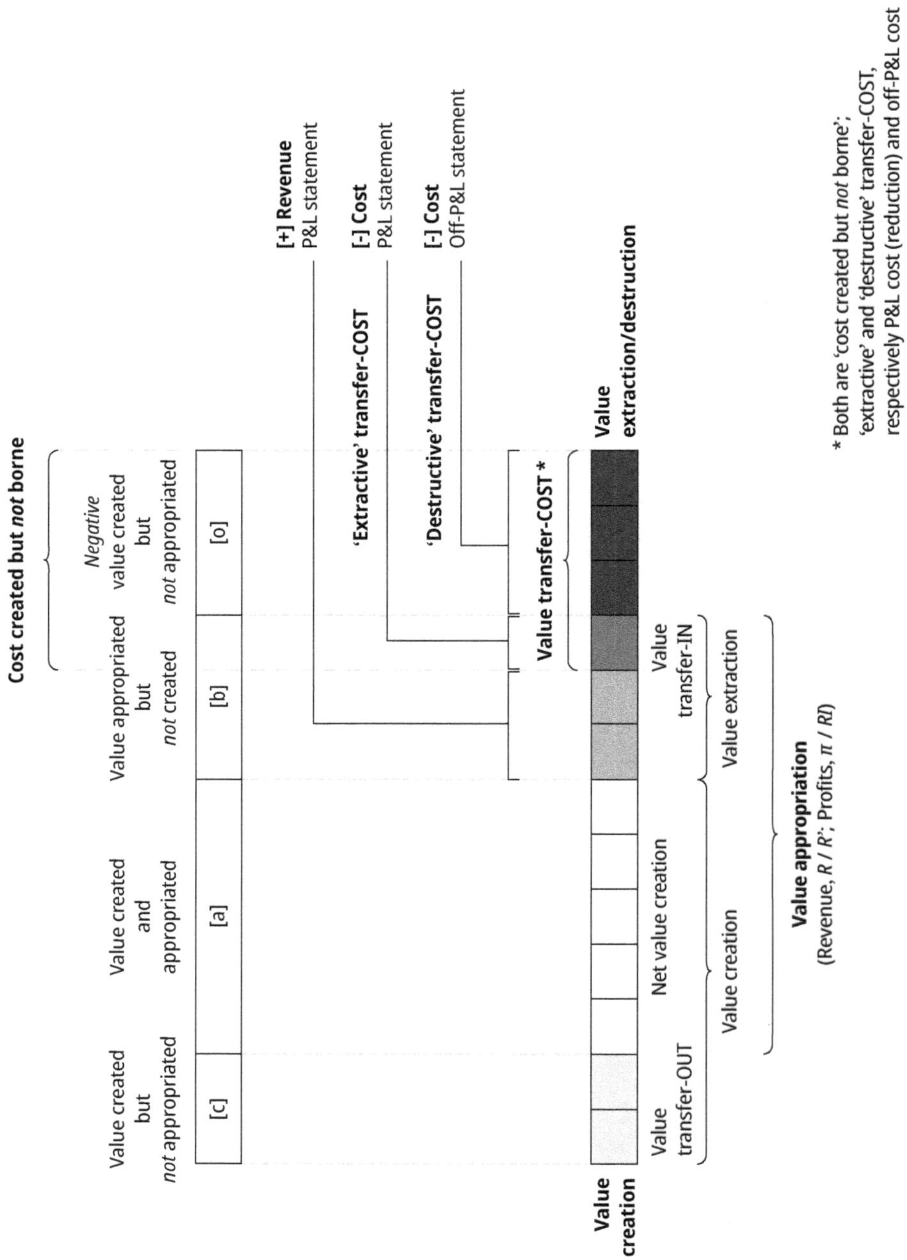

Figure A5.5a: 'Extractive' and 'destructive' transfer-COST on the 'value spectrum' (profits).

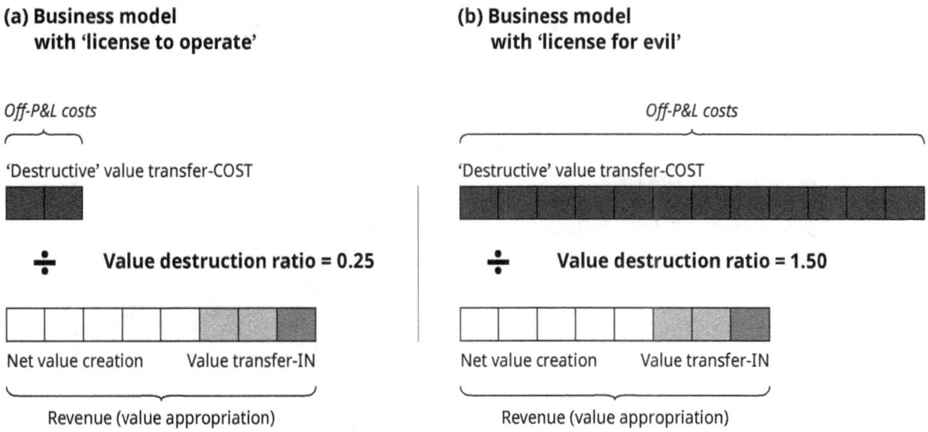

Figure A5.5b: The 'destructive value transfer-COST to revenue ratio' ('value destruction ratio'), with examples of 'license to operate' and 'license for evil' firms.

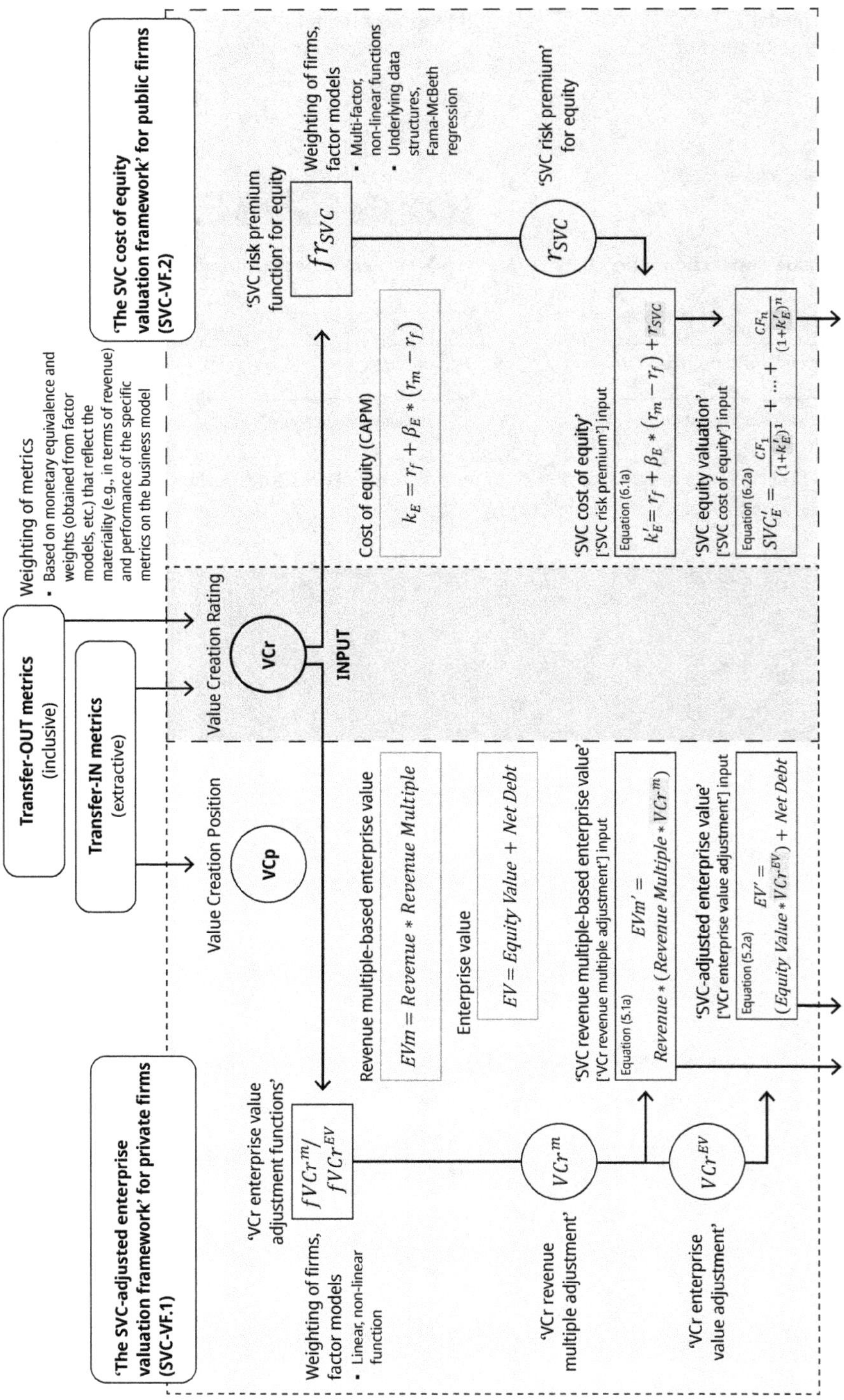

Figure A5.6a: Overview of an SVC enterprise valuation and equity valuation.

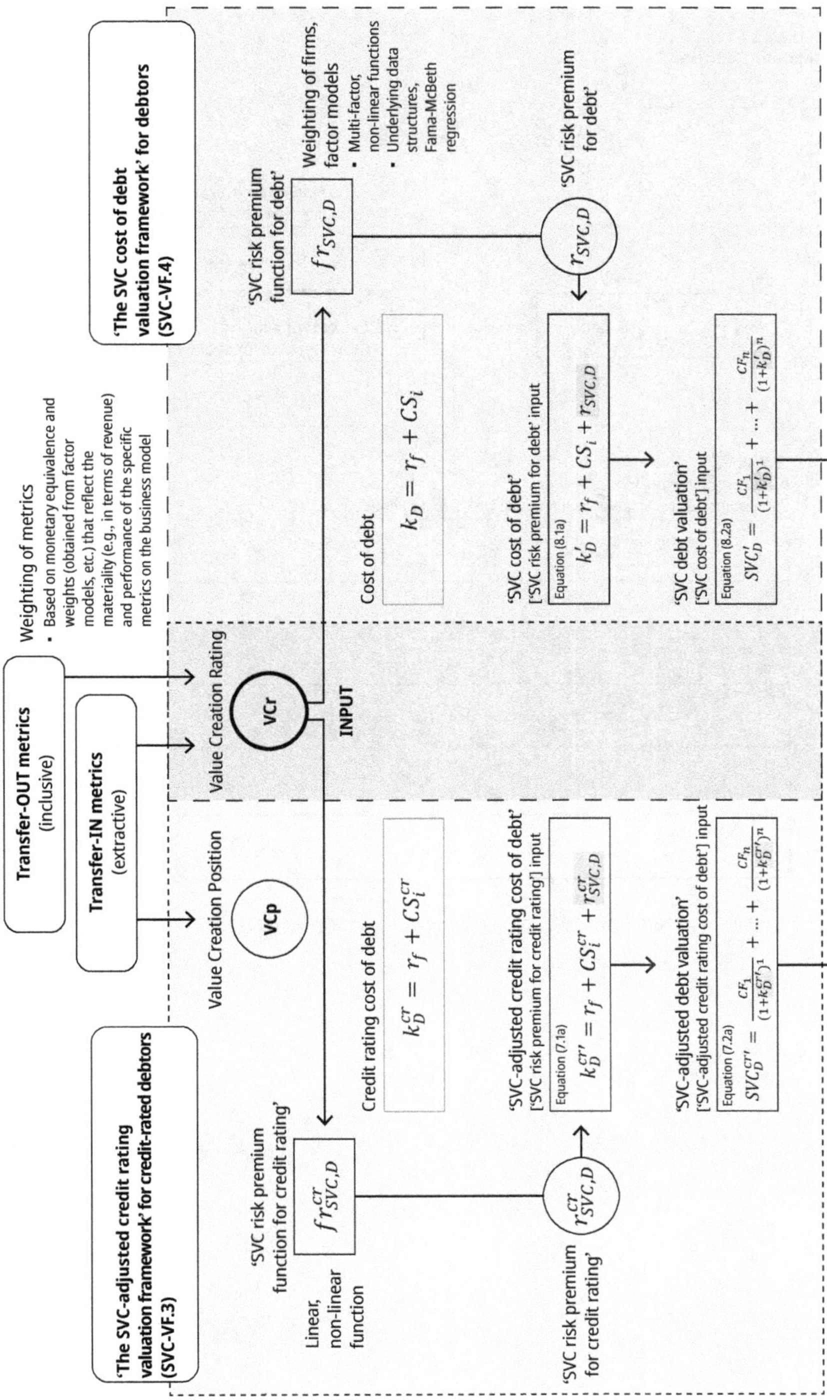

Figure A5.6b: Overview of an SVC debt valuation.

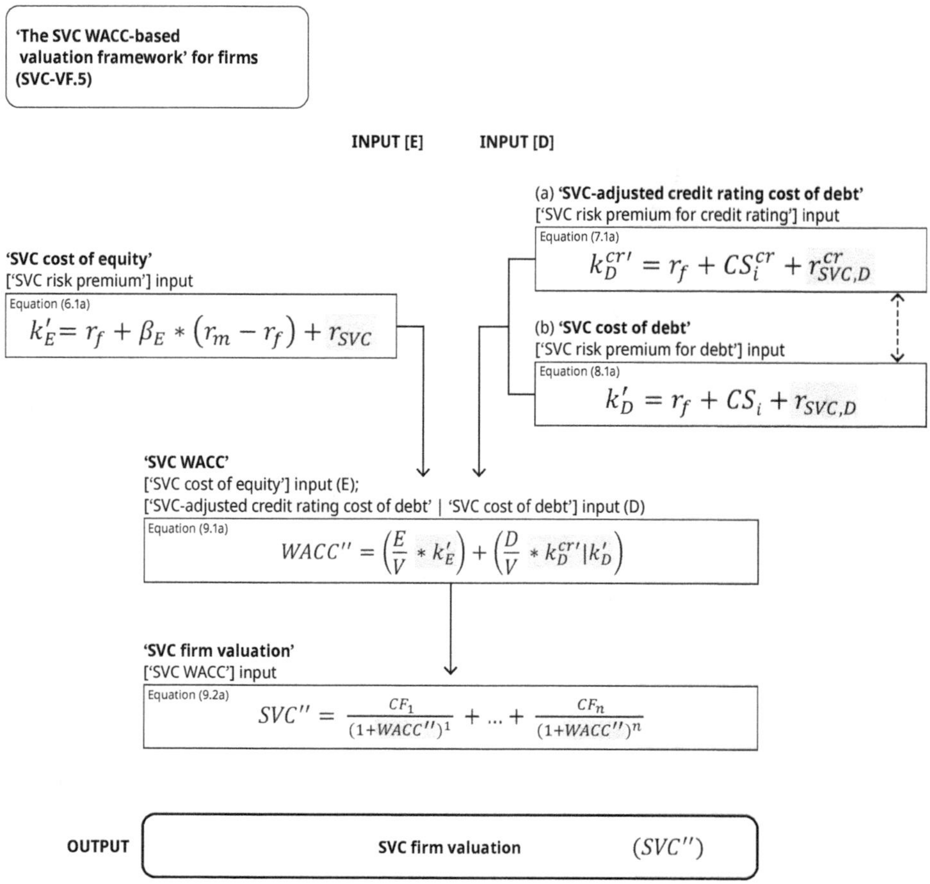

Figure A5.6c: Overview of an SVC firm valuation referring to the WACC method.

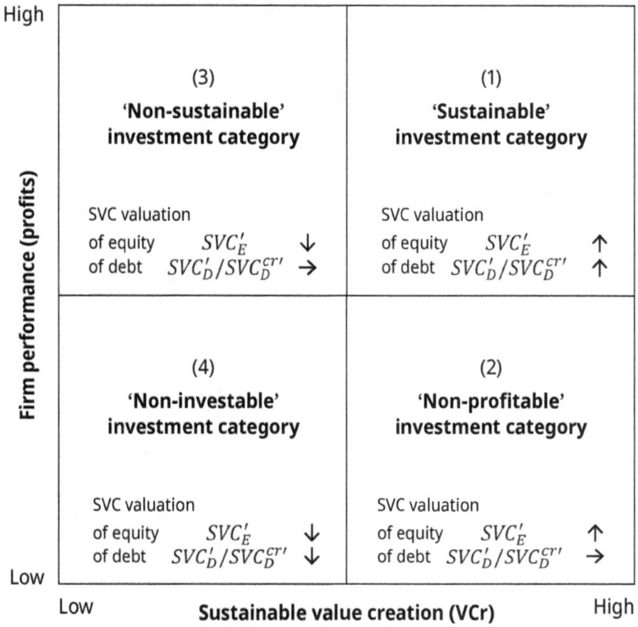

A decision-making matrix

Figure A5.7: The Sustainable Valuations Matrix: A framework for investors.

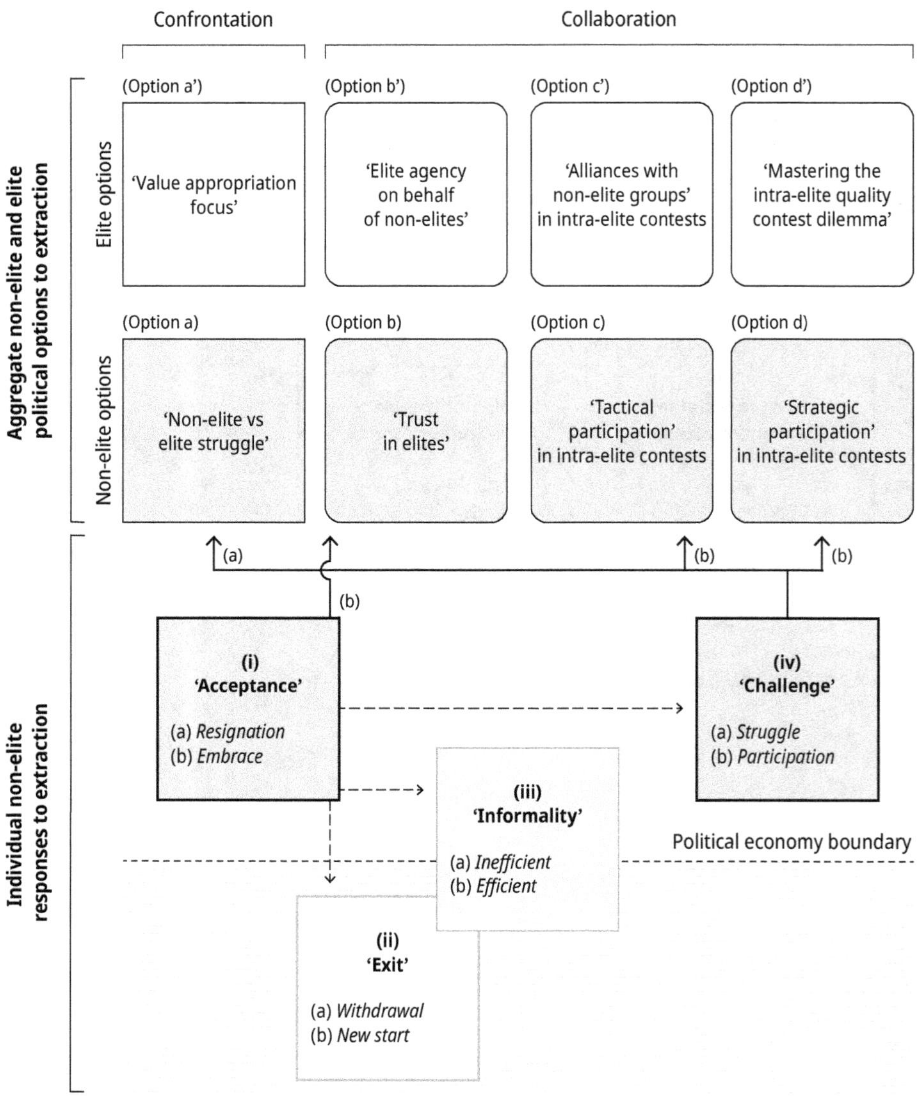

Figure A5.8: A typology of individual non-elite responses to extractive value transfers with a matching typology of aggregate non-elite and elite political options on extractive value transfers.

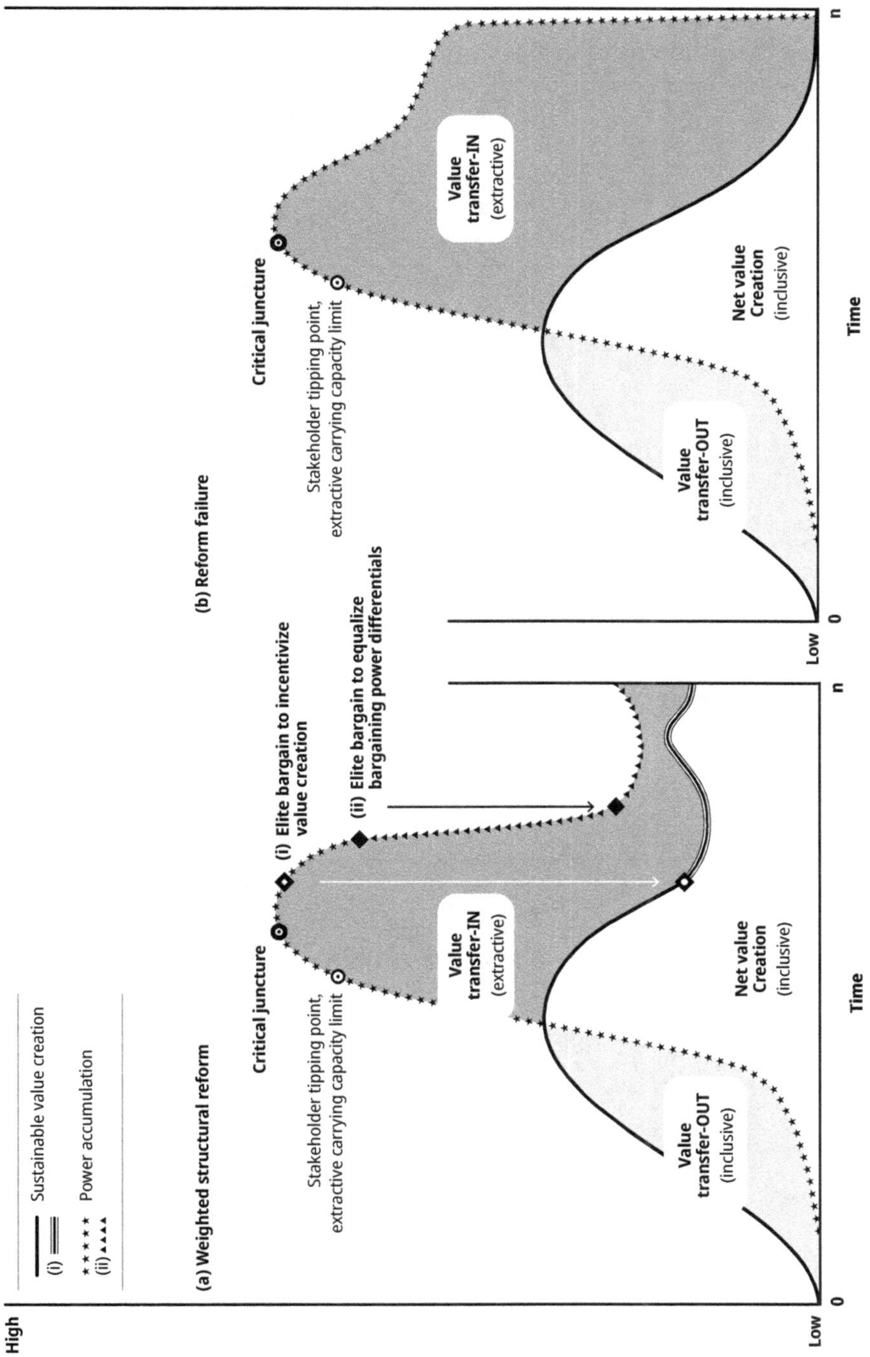

Figure A5.9a: Responding to a critical juncture in the political economy: Two reform outcomes referencing The Elite Business Model Lifecycle.

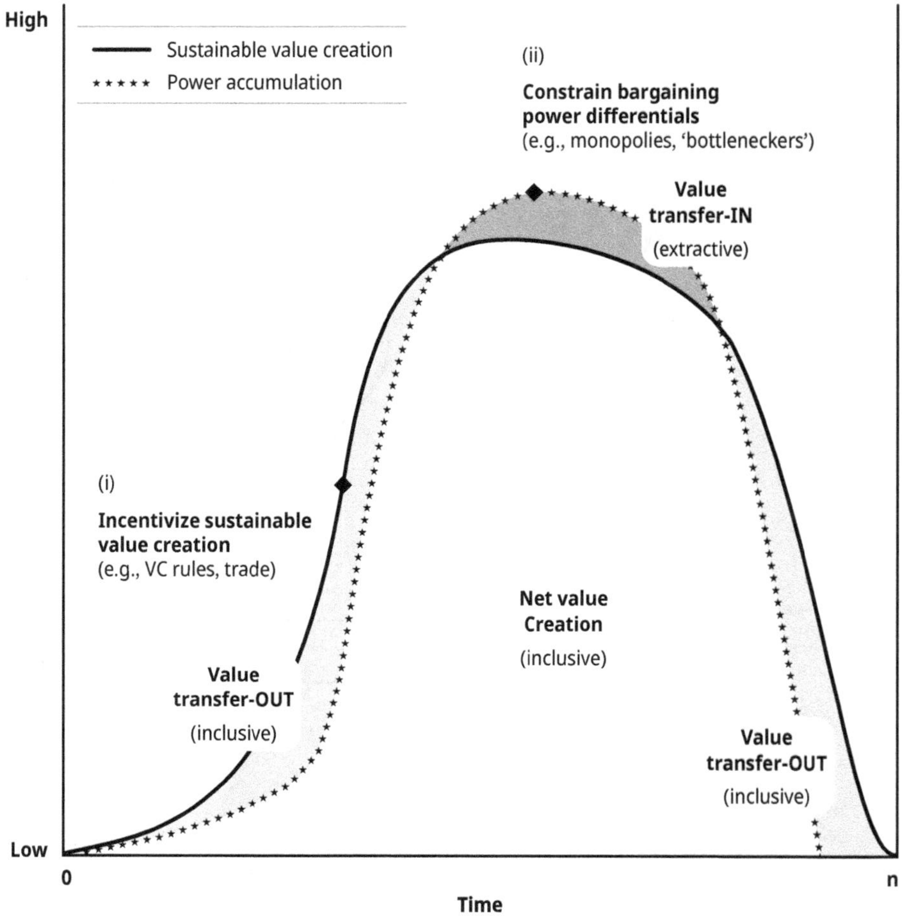

Figure A5.9b: A policy perspective of The Elite Business Model Lifecycle with a narrow 'elite power vs value creation gap' associated with 'equalized bargaining power equilibrium prices'.

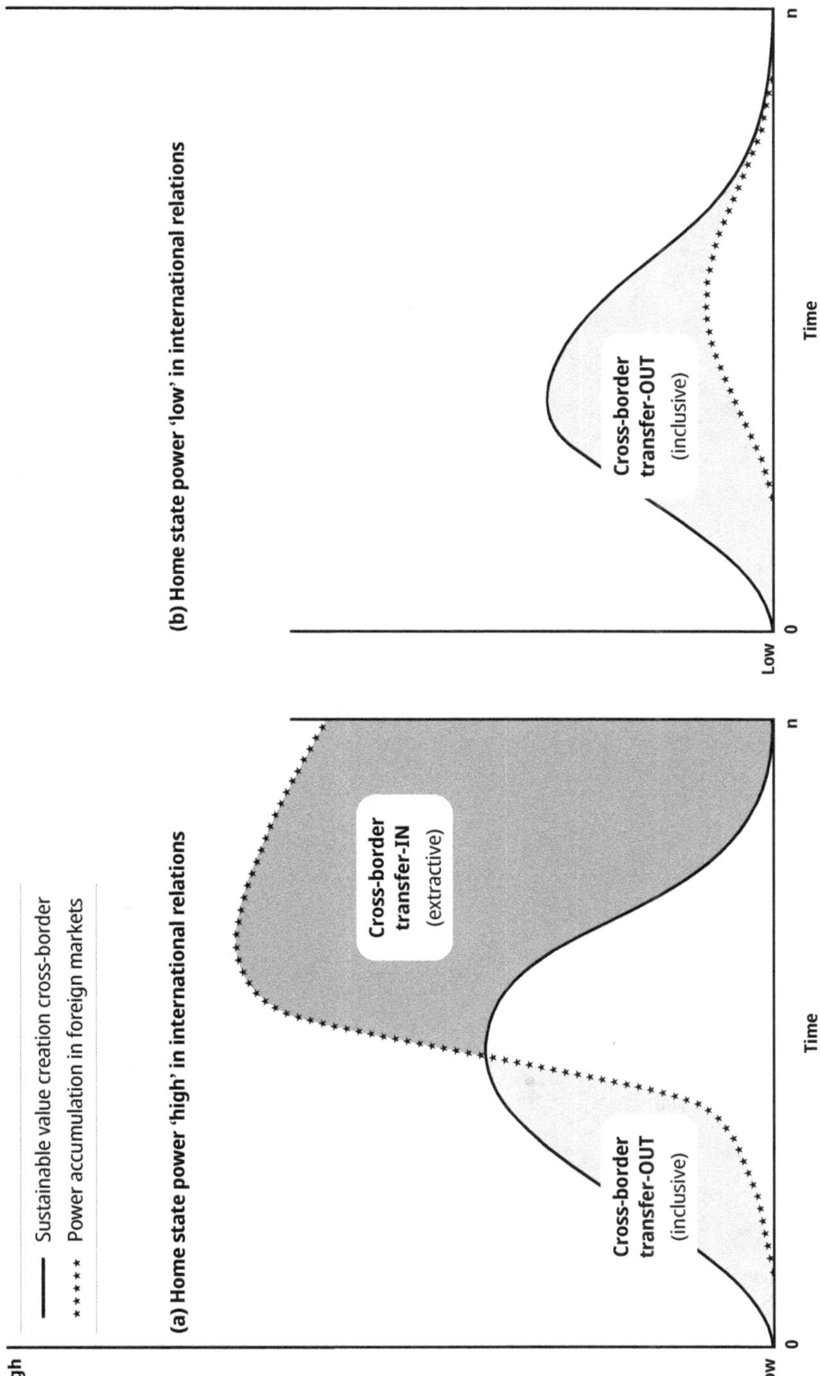

Figure A5.9c: The Cross-Border Elite Business Model Lifecycle: Two scenarios based on the power of the home state in the international system and the implications for sustainable value creation.

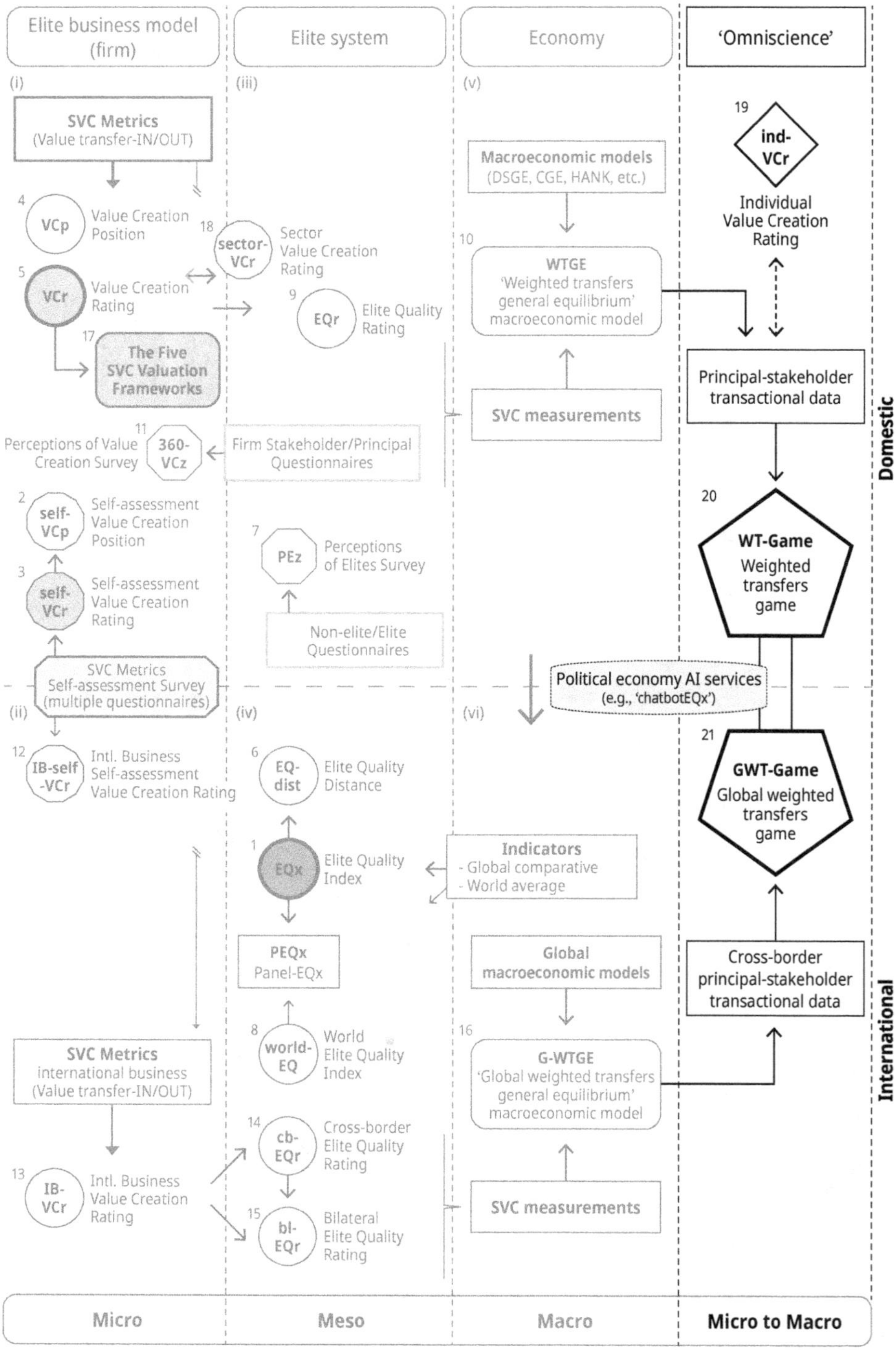

Figure A5.10: Prospective SVC measurements: The quest for 'political economy omniscience'.

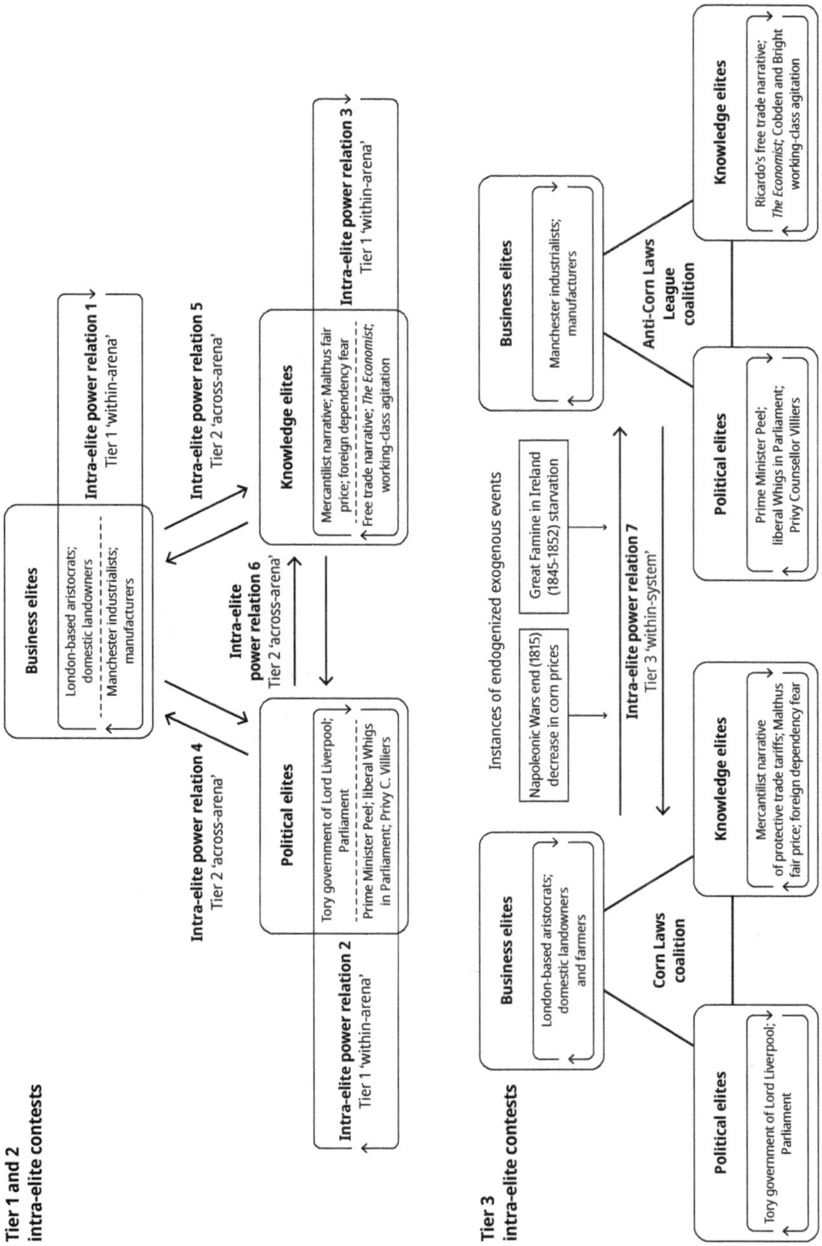

Figure A5.11a: The political economy contests of the Corn Laws (1815-1846): The Seven Intra-elite Power Relations in the Three-tier Set of Intra-elite Checks and Balances as part of the elite separation of powers.

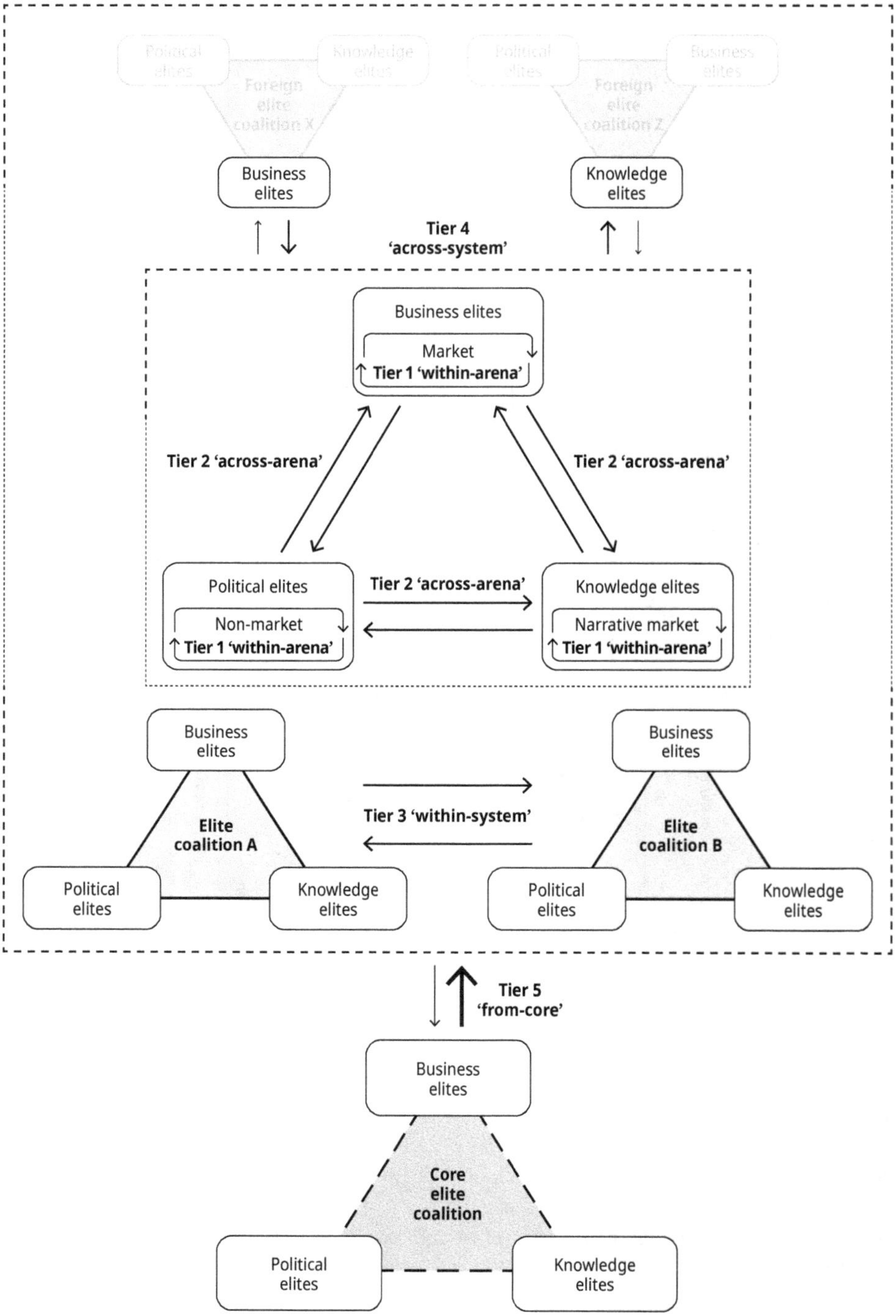

Figure A5.11b: A comprehensive five-tier elite separation of powers with checks and balances via foreign elite coalitions (Tier 4, 'across-system') and the core elite coalition (Tier 5, 'from-core').

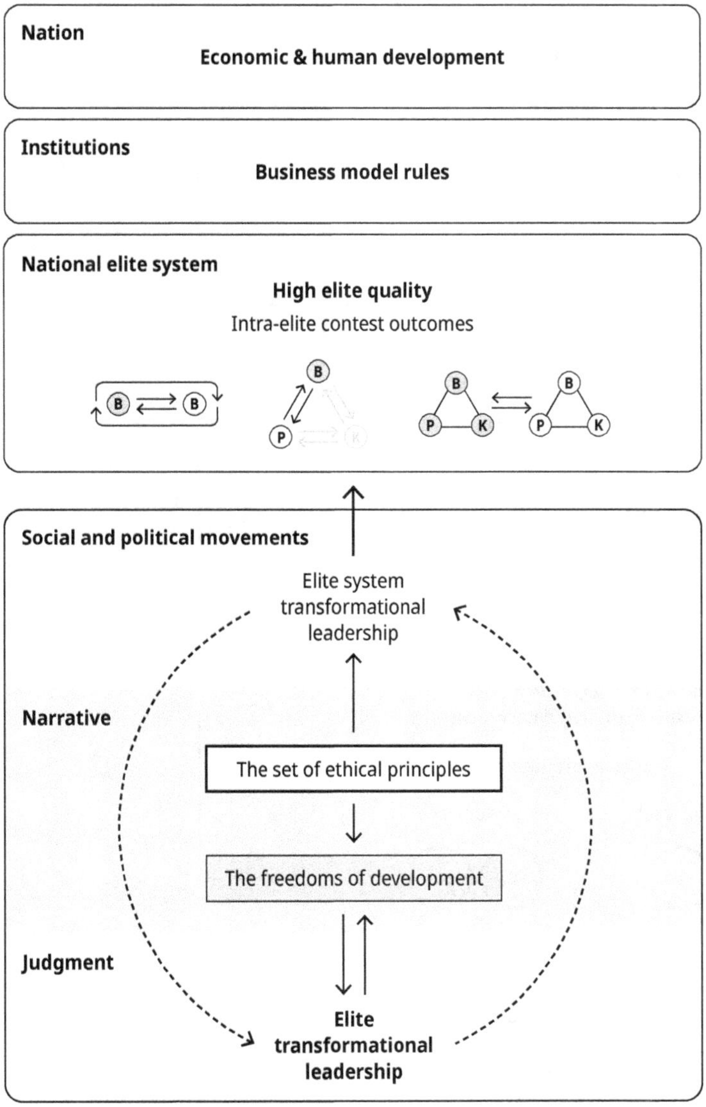

Figure A5.12a: Narrative bases of social and political movements and initiatives for transformational leadership in the political economy: A normative brief for sustainable value creation.

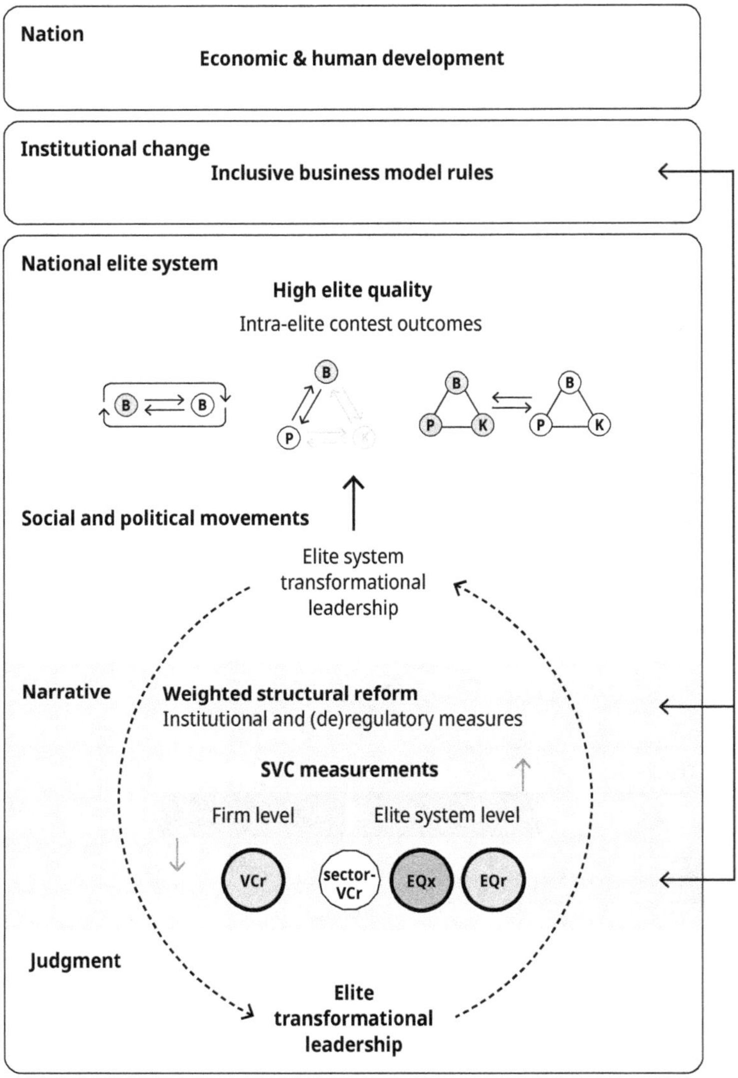

Figure A5.12b: Reforms and supporting measurements for narratives and their relationship to intra-elite contests and institutional change: A practical brief for sustainable value creation.

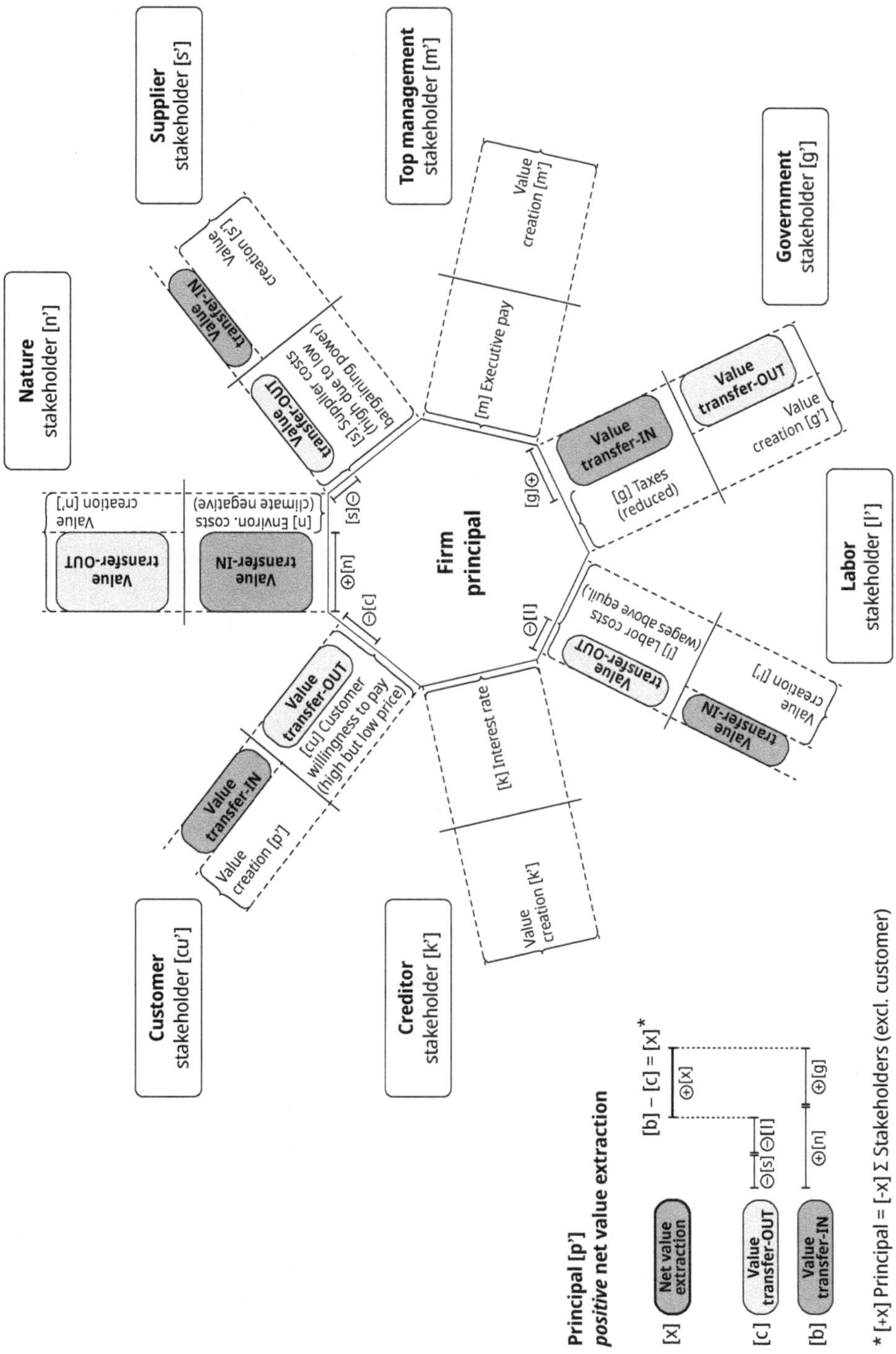

Figure A5.13a: Principal and stakeholder business models across the value chain highlighting net value extraction (excluding the principal's residual income claims).

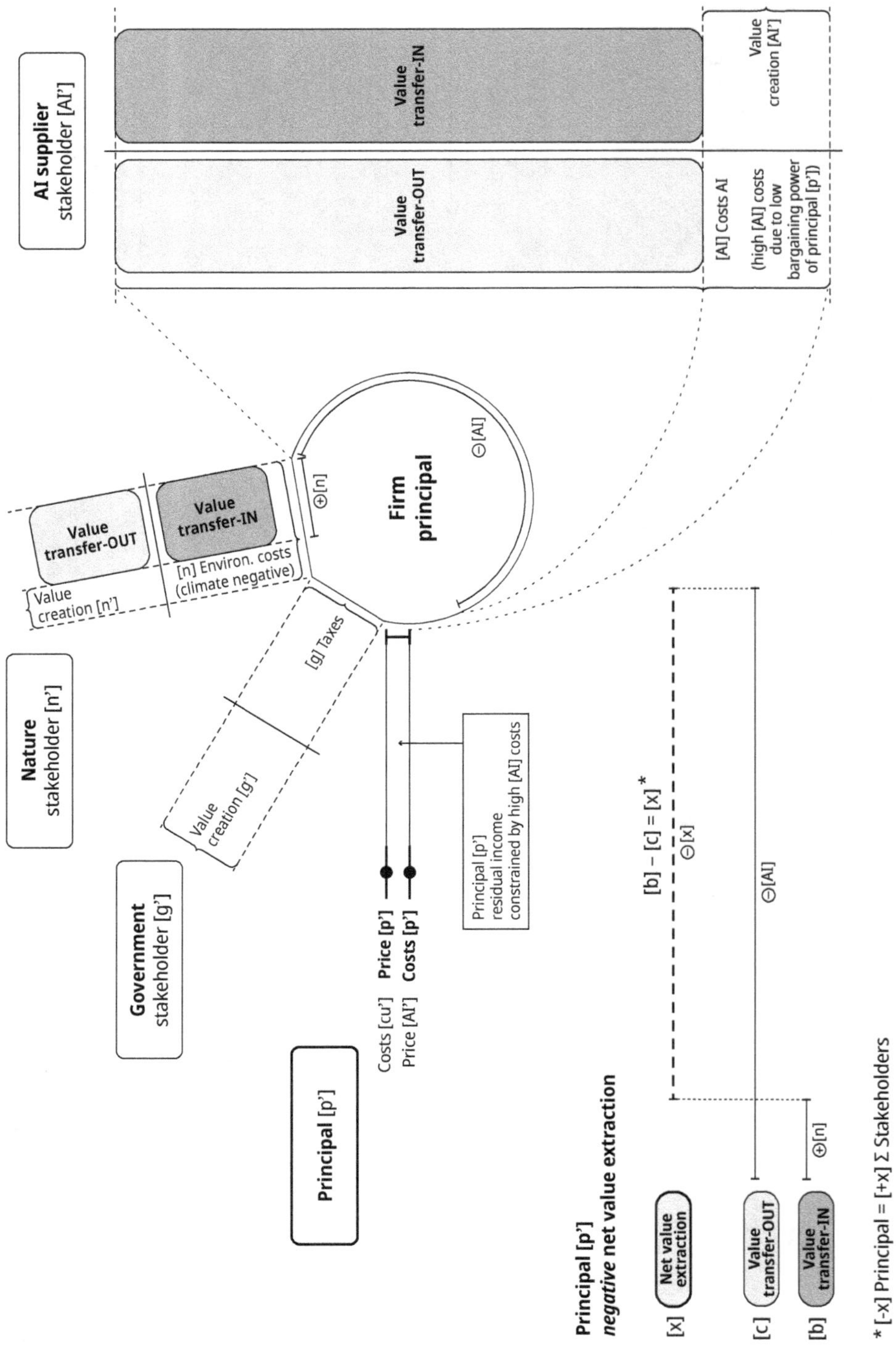

Figure A5.13b: Principal and stakeholder business models in a simplified value chain highlighting the AI supplier stakeholder's transfer-IN and the principal's residual income claims.

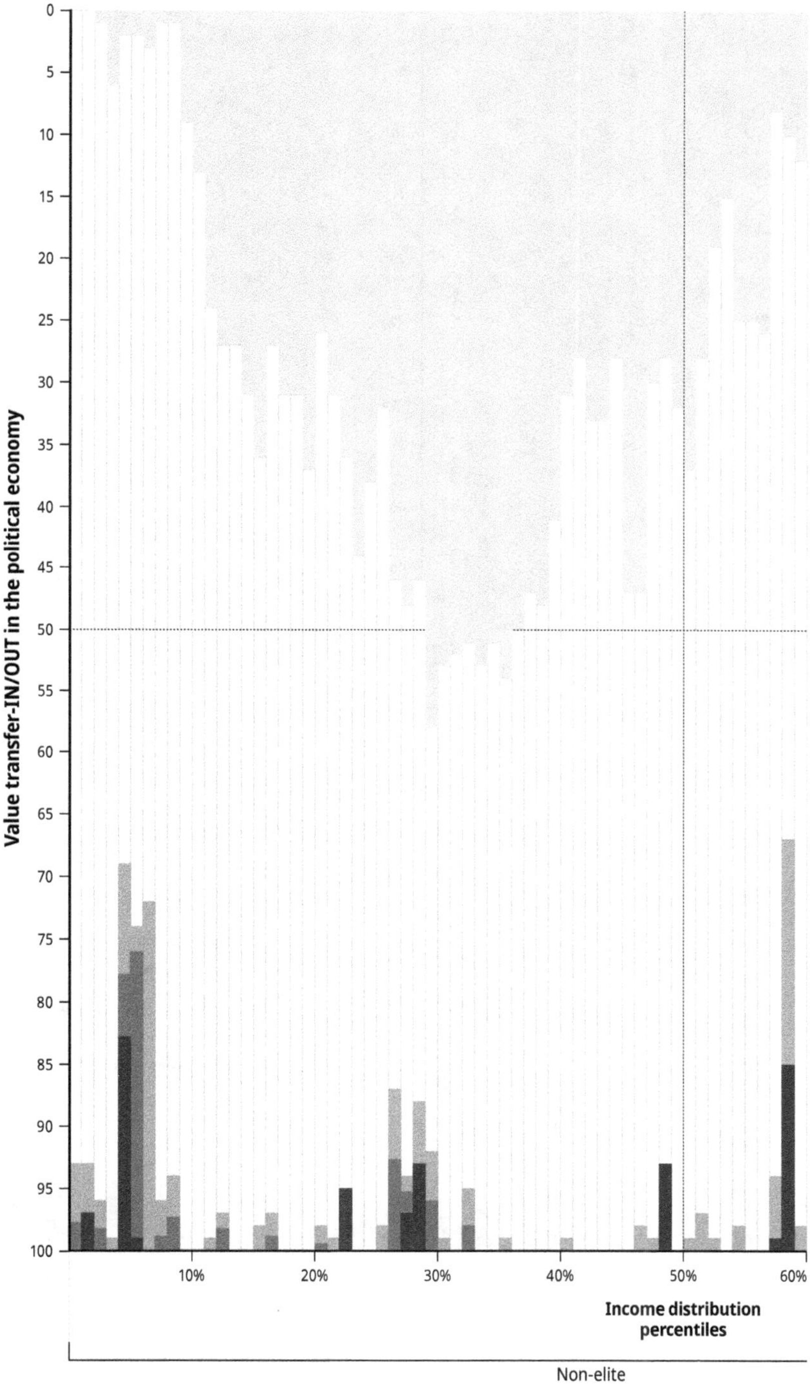

Figure A5.14a: Simple estimate of value transfers across income percentiles.

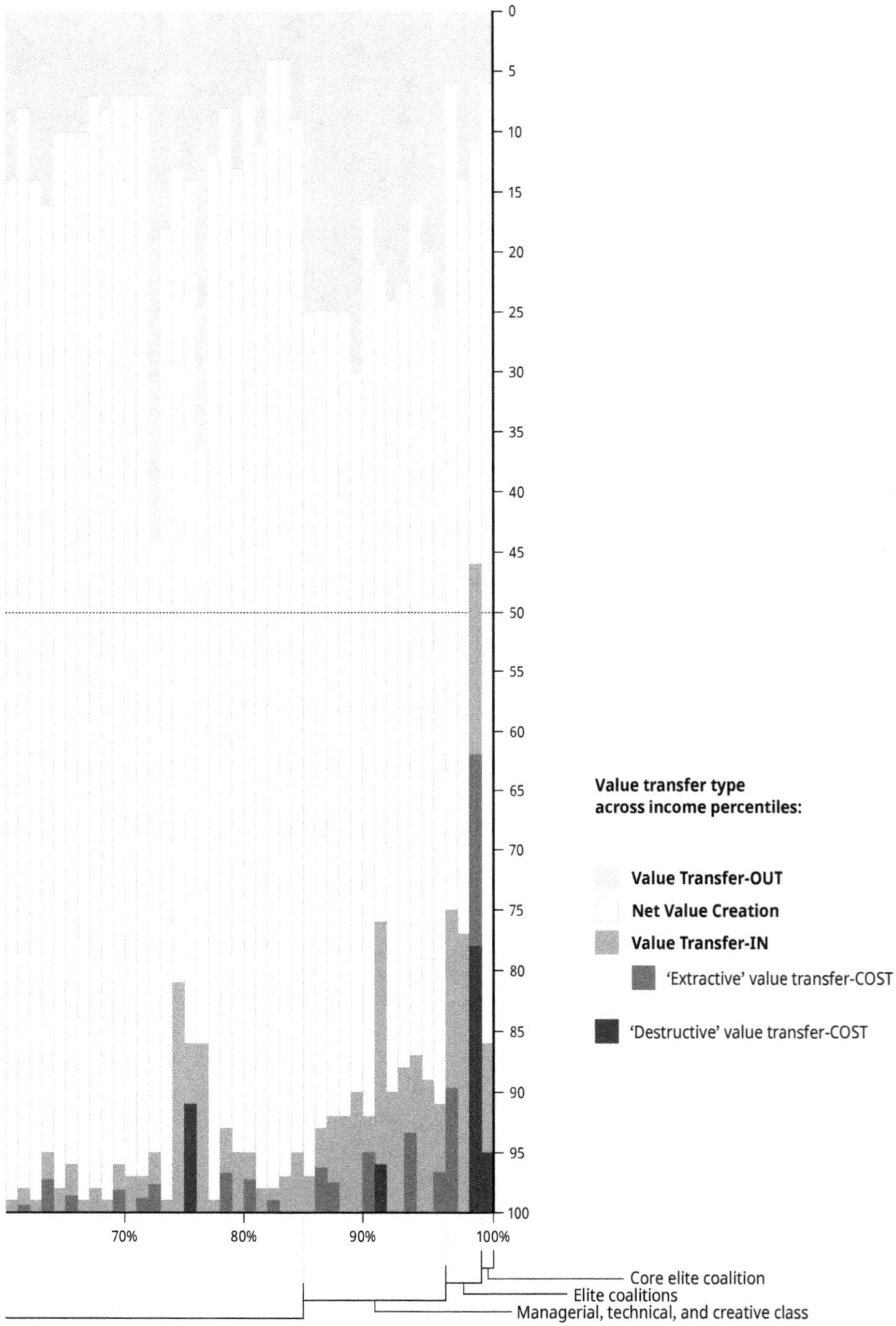

Figure A5.14a (continued)

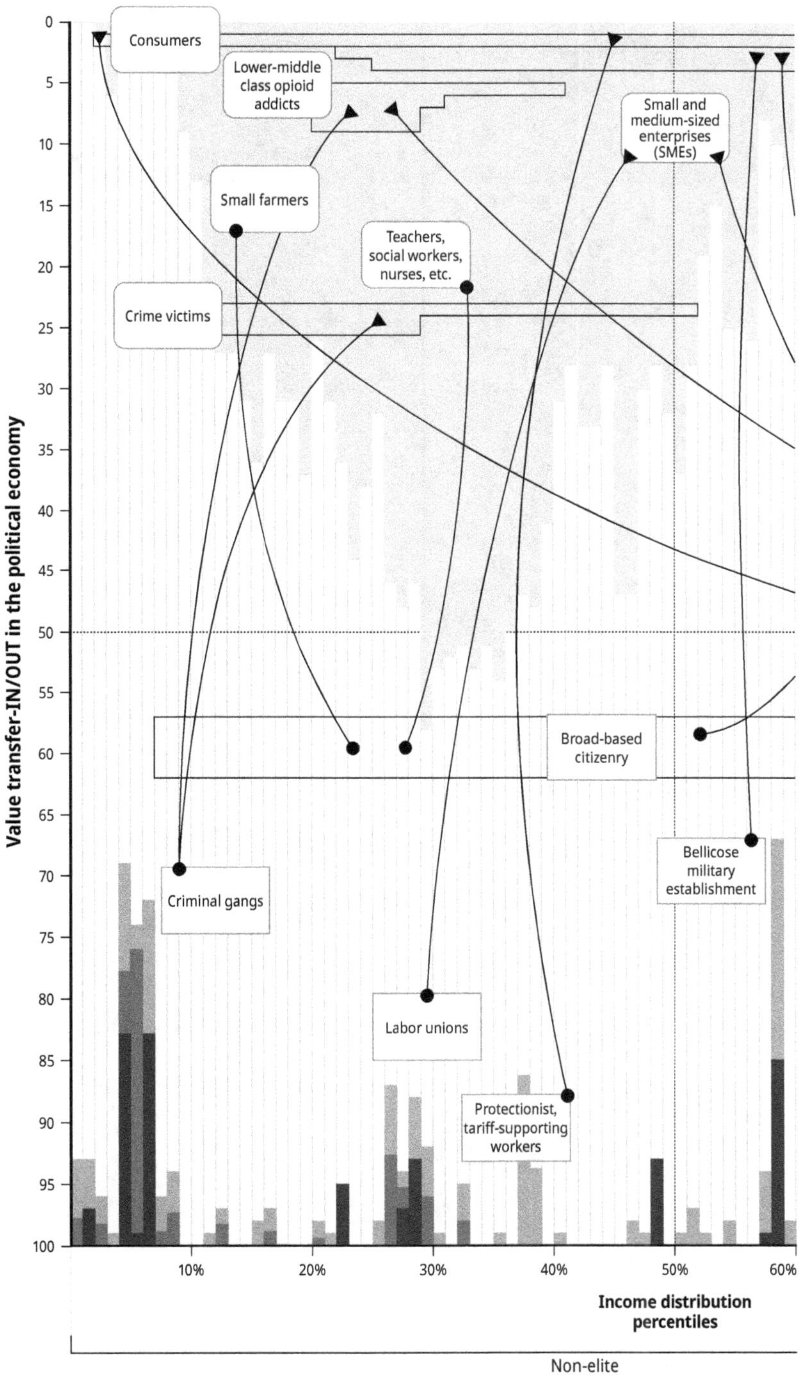

Figure A5.14b: Simple estimate of value transfers across income percentiles with expository transferee/transferor relationships across a selection of coalitions and groups in society.

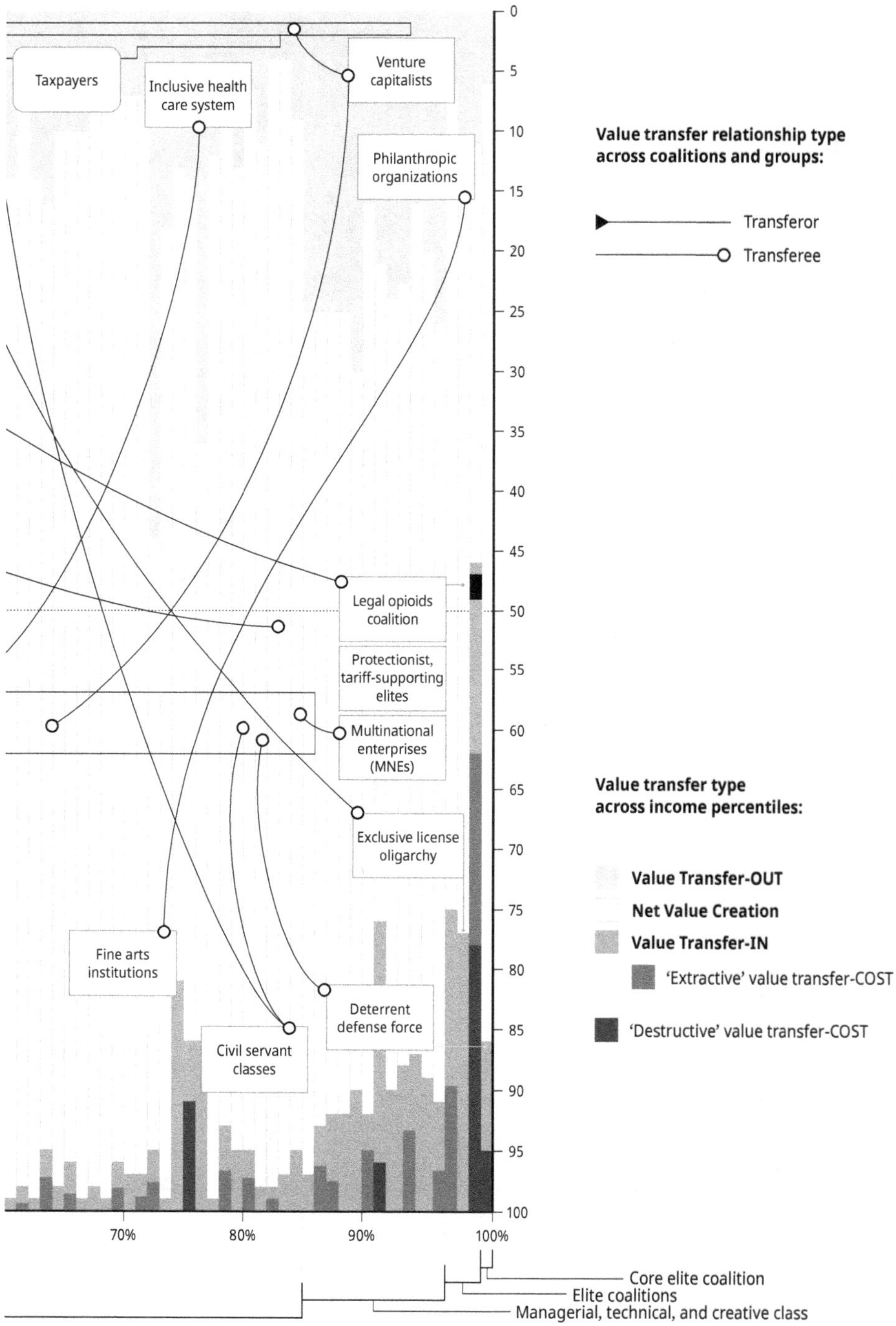

Figure A5.14b (continued)

Bibliography

Abatino, B., Dari-Mattiacci, G., & Perotti, E. C. (2011). Depersonalization of business in Ancient Rome. *Oxford Journal of Legal Studies*, *31*(2), 365–389. https://doi.org/10.1093/ojls/gqr001

Abboud, L. (2021, April 8). Macron to close training school of French elite. *The Financial Times*. Retrieved from https://www.ft.com/content/385d0d85-645d-48db-8805-8e2ad6191c8c

Abell, P. (2004). Narrative explanation: An alternative to variable-centered explanation? *Annual Review of Sociology*, *30*(1), 287–310. https://doi.org/10.1146/annurev.soc.29.010202.100113

Ablott, M. (2011, August 3). Penicillin: The antidote to patent wars. *Mobile World Live Blog*. Retrieved from https://www.mobileworldlive.com/blog/penicillin-the-antidote-to-patent-wars/

Abramovitz, M. (1993). The search for the sources of growth: Areas of ignorance, old and new. *The Journal of Economic History*, *53*(2), 217–243.

Acemoglu, D. (2002). Directed technical change. *The Review of Economic Studies*, *69*(4), 781–809. https://doi.org/10.1111/1467-937X.00226

Acemoglu, D. (2006). A simple model of inefficient institutions. *The Scandinavian Journal of Economics*, *108*(4), 515–546. https://doi.org/10.1111/j.14679442.2006.00460.x

Acemoglu, D. (2024, May 12). *The simple macroeconomics of AI* (Working Paper No. 32487). Massachusetts Institute of Technology. https://doi.org/10.3386/w32487

Acemoglu, D., & Johnson, S. (2005). Unbundling institutions. *Journal of Political Economy*, *113*(5), 949–995. https://doi.org/10.1086/432166

Acemoglu, D., & Johnson, S. (2023). *Power and progress: Our thousand-year struggle over technology and prosperity*. New York, NY: PublicAffairs.

Acemoglu, D., & Robinson, J. A. (2000). Political losers as a barrier to economic development. *The American Economic Review*, *90*(2), 126–130. https://doi.org/10.1257/aer.90.2.126

Acemoglu, D., & Robinson, J. A. (2001). Inefficient redistribution. *American Political Science Review*, *95*(3), 649–661. https://doi.org/10.1017/S0003055401003057

Acemoglu, D., & Robinson, J. A. (2006). Economic backwardness in political perspective. *The American Political Science Review*, *100*(1), 115–131.

Acemoglu, D., & Robinson, J. A. (2008). Persistence of power, elites, and institutions. *The American Economic Review*, 98(1), 267–293. https://doi.org/10.1257/aer.98.1.267

Acemoglu, D., & Robinson, J. A. (2013a). *Why nations fail: The origins of power, prosperity, and poverty*. New York, NY: Crown Business.

Acemoglu, D., & Robinson, J. A. (2013b, March 12). What Bill Gates got wrong about why nations fail. *Foreign Policy*. Retrieved from https://foreignpolicy.com/2013/03/12/what-bill-gates-got-wrong-about-why-nations-fail/

Acemoglu, D., & Robinson, J. A. (2018). Beyond modernization theory. *Annals of Comparative Democratization*, *16*(3), 26–31. Retrieved from https://cpb-us-w2.wpmucdn.com/voices.uchicago.edu/dist/f/1135/files/2019/02/Beyond-Modernization-Theory-1-19iech4.pdf

Acemoglu, D., & Robinson, J. A. (2019a). *The narrow corridor. States, societies, and the fate of liberty*. New York, NY: Penguin Press.

Acemoglu, D., & Robinson, J. A. (2019b). Rents and economic development: The perspective of why nations fail. *Public Choice*, *181*(1), 13–28. https://doi.org/10.1007/s11127-019-00645-z

Acemoglu, D., García-Jimeno, C., & Robinson, J. A. (2015). State capacity and economic development: A network approach. *American Economic Review*, *105*(8), 2364–2409. https://doi.org/10.1257/aer.20140044

Acemoglu, D., Johnson, S., & Robinson, J. A. (2005). Institutions as the fundamental cause of long-run growth. In P. Aghion and S. Durlauf (Eds.), *Handbook of Economic Growth 1A* (pp. 386–472). Amsterdam, The Netherlands: Elsevier. https://doi.org/10.1016/S1574-0684(05)01006-3

https://doi.org/10.1515/9783110734638-019

Acemoglu, D., Manera, A., & Restrepo, P. (2020, April). *Does the US tax code favor automation?* (NBER Working Paper No. 27052). http://www.nber.org/papers/w27052.pdf

Acemoglu, D., Cantoni, D., Johnson, S., & Robinson, J. A. (2009, April). *The consequences of radical reform: The French revolution* (NBER Working Paper No. 14831). https://doi.org/10.1257/aer.101.7.3286

Acemoglu, D., Johnson, S., Robinson, J. A., & Yared, P. (2009). Reevaluating the modernization hypothesis. *Journal of Monetary Economics, 56*(8), 1043–1058.

Acemoglu, D., Naidu, S., Restrepo, P., & Robinson, J. A. (2019). Democracy does cause growth. *Journal of Political Economy, 127*(1), 47–100. https://doi.org/10.1086/700936

Acharya, S., & Dogra, K. (2020). Understanding HANK: Insights from a PRANK. *Econometrica, 88*(3), 1113–1158. https://doi.org/10.3982/ECTA16409

Acs, Z. J., & Szerb, L. (2007). Entrepreneurship, economic growth and public policy. *Small Business Economics, 28*(2/3), 109–122. https://doi.org/10.1007/s11187-006-9012-3

Acs, Z. J., Desai, S., & Hessels, J. (2008). Entrepreneurship, economic development and institutions. *Small Business Economics, 31*(3), 219–234. https://doi.org/10.1007/s11187-008-9135-9

Adams, G. (1981). *The politics of defense contracting: The iron triangle*. New York, NY: Council on Economic Priorities.

Adams, I., & Masuoka, J. (1961). Emerging elites and culture change. *Social and Economic Studies, 10*(1), 86–92.

Adams, C. A., Alhamood, A., He, X., Tian, J., Wang, L., & Wang, Y. (2021). *The Double-materiality concept: Application and issues*. Amsterdam: Global Reporting Initiative. Retrieved from https://www.globalreporting.org/media/jrbntbyv/griwhitepaper-publications.pdf

Adelman, I. (1969). *Practical approaches to development planning: Korea's second five-year plan*. Baltimore, MD: The Johns Hopkins University Press.

Aghion, P., Akcigit, U., Bergeaud, A., Blundell, R., & Hemous, D. (2019). Innovation and top income inequality. *The Review of Economic Studies, 86*(1 (306)), 1–45. https://doi.org/10.1093/restud/rdy027

Aghion, P., Bloom, N., Blundell, R., Griffith, R., & Howitt, P. (2005). Competition and innovation: An inverted-U relationship. *The Quarterly Journal of Economics, 120*(2), 701–728. https://doi.org/10.3386/w9269

Aghion, P., Cai, J., Dewatripont, M., Du, L., Harrison, A., & Legros, P. (2015). Industrial policy and competition. *American Economic Journal: Macroeconomics, 7*(4), 1–32. https://doi.org/10.1257/mac.20120103

Aghion, P., Caroli, E., & García-Peñalosa, C. (1999). Inequality and economic growth: The perspective of the new growth theories. *Journal of Economic Literature, 37*(4), 1615–1660. https://doi.org/10.1257/jel.37.4.1615

Aghion, P., & Howitt, P. (1992). A model of growth through creative destruction. *Econometrica, 60*(2), 323–351. https://doi.org/10.2307/2951599

Ahearne, A., & Shinada, N. (2005). Zombie firms and economic stagnation in Japan. *International Economics and Economic Policy, 2*(4), 363–381. https://doi.org/10.1007/s10368-005-0041-1

Ahn, C. Y., & Cha, B. (2004). Financial sector restructuring in South Korea: Accomplishments and unfinished agenda. *Asian Economic Papers, 3*(1), 1–21. https://doi.org/10.1162/1535351041747987

Aizenman, J., & Spiegel, M. (2006). Institutional efficiency and the investment share of foreign direct investment. *Review of International Economics, 14*(4), 683–697. https://doi.org/10.1111/j.1467-9396.2006.00595.x

Akerlof, G. A., & Kranton, R. E. (2000). Economics and identity. *The Quarterly Journal of Economics, 115*(3), 715–753. https://doi.org/10.1162/003355300554881

Akerlof, G. A., & Yellen, J. L. (1987). Rational models of irrational behavior. *The American Economic Review, 77*(2), 137–142.

Akin, W. (1977). *Technocracy and the American dream: The technocrat movement, 1900-1941*. Berkeley and Los Angeles, CA: University of California Press.

Alabdulmohsin, I., Tran, V. Q., & Dehghani, M. (2024, May 22). Fractal patterns may illuminate the success of next-token prediction. *arXiv*. https://doi.org/10.48550/arXiv.2402.01825

Aldama, L. P., & Zicari, A. (2012), Value-added reporting as a tool for sustainability: A Latin American experience. *Corporate Governance*, *12*(4), 835–498. https://doi.org/10.1108/14720701211267829

Aldrich, H. E. (2008). *Organizations and environments*. Stanford, CA: Stanford University Press.

Aldrich, H. E., & Ruef, M. (2006). *Organizations evolving* (2nd ed.). London: Sage Publications.

Aldrich, H. E., & Yang, T. (2014). How do entrepreneurs know what to do? Learning and organizing in new ventures. *Journal of Evolutionary Economics*, *24*(1), 59–82. https://doi.org/10.1007/s00191-013-0320-x

Alesina, A., Cozzi, G., & Mantovan, N. (2012). The evolution of ideology, fairness and redistribution. *The Economic Journal*, *122*(565), 1244–1261. https://doi.org/10.1111/j.1468-0297.2012.02541.x

Alesina, A., & Giuliano, P. (2015). Culture and institutions. *Journal of Economic Literature 53*(4), 898–944. https://doi.org/10.1257/jel.53.4.898

Alesina, A., & Perotti, R. (1994). The political economy of growth: A critical survey of the recent literature. *World Bank Economic Review*, *8*(3), 351–371. https://doi.org/10.1093/wber/8.3.351

Alesina, A., & Perotti, R. (1996). Income distribution, political instability and investment. *European Economic Review*, *40*(6), 1203–28. https://doi.org/10.1016/0014-2921(95)00030-5

Alesina, A., & Rodrik, D. (1994). Distributive politics and economic growth. *The Quarterly Journal of Economics*, *109*(2), 465–490. https://doi.org/10.2307/2118470

Alexander, A. C., & Welzel, C. (2011). Measuring effective democracy: The human empowerment approach. *Comparative Politics*, *43*(3), 271–289. https://doi.org/10.1177/0192512111414682

Alexander, R. D. (1987). *The biology of moral systems*. Piscataway, NJ: Transaction Publishers.

Alexander, S. (2015, May 29). No time like the present for AI safety work. *Slate Star Codex*. Retrieved from https://slatestarcodex.com/2015/05/29/no-time-like-the-present-for-ai-safety-work/

Alfani, G. (2023). *As gods among men: A history of the rich in the West*. Princeton, NJ: Princeton University Press.

Allardyce, G. (1982). The rise and fall of the Western Civilization course. *The American Historical Review*, *87*(3), 695–725. https://doi.org/10.2307/1864161

Allen, J. (2023). *Dark aeon: Transhumanism and the war against humanity*. New York, NY: War Room Books.

Allen, R. C. (2003). *Farm to factory: A reinterpretation of the Russian Industrial Revolution*. Princeton, NJ: Princeton University Press. https://doi.org/10.2307/j.ctv1mjqtx0

Allison, G. (2017). *Destined for war: Can America and China escape Thucydides' trap?* New York, NY: Houghton Mifflin Harcourt.

Allison, G., & Zelikow, P. (1999). *Essence of decision: Explaining the Cuban Missile Crisis* (2nd ed.). New York, NY: Longman.

Allyn, B. (2021). Ex-Google workers sue company, saying it betrayed 'don't Be evil' motto. *NPR*. Retrieved from https://www.npr.org/2021/11/29/1059821677/google-dont-be-evil-lawsuit

Almond, G. A. (1956). Comparative political systems. *The Journal of politics*, *18*(3), 391–409.

Altman, S. (2021, March 16). Moore's law for everything. *Samaltman.com*. Retrieved from https://moores.samaltman.com

Altman, S. (2023, February 24). Planning for AGI and beyond. *OpenAI*. Retrieved from https://openai.com/blog/planning-for-agi-and-beyond#SamAltman

Altman, S. (2025, February 9). Three observations. *Sam Altman Blog*. Retrieved from https://blog.samaltman.com/three-observations

Alvarez, A. (1997). Adjusting to genocide: The techniques of neutralization and the holocaust. *Social Science History*, *21*(2), 139–178. https://doi.org/10.2307/1171272

Amit, R., & Zott, C. (2001). Value creation in e-business. *Strategic Management Journal*, *22*(6), 493–520. https://doi.org/10.1002/smj.187

Amodei, D. (2024, October). Machines of loving grace: How AI could transform the world for the better. *Dario Amodei*. Retrieved from https://darioamodei.com/machines-of-loving-grace

Amsden, A. H. (2001). *The rise of "The Rest": Challenges to the West from late-industrializing economies*. Oxford: Oxford University Press. https://doi.org/10.1093/0195139690.001.0001

Amsden, A. H., DiCaprio, A., & Robinson, J. (2014) *The Role of elites in economic development* (WIDER Studies in Development Economics). Oxford: Oxford University Press. https://doi.org/10.1093/acprof:oso/9780199659036.001.0001

Andersen, R. (2023, July 24). Does Sam Altman know what he's creating? *The Atlantic*. Retrieved from https://www.theatlantic.com/magazine/archive/2023/09/sam-altman-openai-chatgpt-gpt-4/674764/

Anderson, J. (2011). The gravity model. *Annual Review of Economics*, *3*(1), 133–160. https://doi.org/10.1146/annurev-economics-111809-125114

Anderson, J., & Marcouiller, D. (2002). Insecurity and the pattern of trade: An empirical investigation. *The Review of Economics and Statistics*, *84*(2), 342–352. https://doi.org/10.1162/003465302317411587

Anderson, L. (2017). Pre-Copernican political science: What analysis of "authoritarianism" reveals about the American study of politics. *Journal of International Affairs*, *71*(1), 81–102.

Anderson, P. W. (1972). More is different: Broken symmetry and the nature of the hierarchical structure of science. *Science*, *177*(4047), 393–396. https://doi.org/10.1126/science.177.4047.393

Andreessen, M. (2023a, June 6). Why AI will save the world. *Marc Andreessen Substack*. Retrieved from https://pmarca.substack.com/p/why-ai-will-save-the-world

Andreessen, M. (2023b, October 16). *The techno-optimist manifesto*. Andreessen Horowitz. Retrieved from https://a16z.com/the-techno-optimist-manifesto/

Andrew, E. (1975). Marx's Theory of Classes: Science and Ideology. *Canadian Journal of Political Science / Revue Canadienne de Science Politique*, *8*(3), 454–466.

Andrews, M. (2013, September). *Who really leads development?* (WIDER Working Paper No. 2013/092). https://www.wider.unu.edu/sites/default/files/WP2013-092.pdf

Angell, N. (1910/2012). *The great illusion: A study of the relation of military power to national advantage* (4th rev. & enl. ed.). New York, NY: G.P. Putnam's Sons. Retrieved from https://www.gutenberg.org/files/38535/38535-h/38535-h.htm

Anthamatten, J., & Dümmler, P. (2020). Swiss agriculture continues to enjoy growing economic privileges. *Avenir Suisse*. Retrieved from https://www.avenir-suisse.ch/en/publication/swiss-agriculture-continues-to-enjoy-growing-economic-privileges/

Anthropic. (2023). *Anthropic's responsible scaling policy, version 1.0*. Retrieved from https://www-cdn.anthropic.com/1adf000c8f675958c2ee23805d91aaade1cd4613/responsible-scaling-policy.pdf

Anugerah, A. R., Muttaqin, P. S., & Trinarningsih, W. (2022). Social network analysis in business and management research: A bibliometric analysis of the research trend and performance from 2001 to 2020. *Heliyon*, *8*(4), e09270. https://doi.org/10.1016/j.heliyon.2022.e09270

Anyaa, M. (2023, February 23). South Korea travel guide – Gambling in South Korea – Yes or no? *Korea Travel Post*. Retrieved from https://www.koreatravelpost.com/gambling-in-south-korea/

Aouadi, A., & Marsat, S. (2018). Do ESG controversies matter for firm value? Evidence from international data. *Journal of Business Ethics*, *151*(4), 1027–1047.

Applebaum, A. (2020). *Twilight of democracy: The seductive lure of authoritarianism*. New York, NY: Doubleday.

Applebaum, A. (2024). *Autocracy, Inc.: The dictators who want to run the world*. New York, NY: Doubleday.

Aragon, L. V. (2007). Elite competition in Central Sulawesi. In H. Schulte Nordholt and G. van Klinken (Eds.), *Renegotiating boundaries: Local politics in post-Suharto Indonesia* (pp. 39–66). Leiden: Brill. https://doi.org/10.1163/9789004260436_004

Araya, D. (2022, December 15). Sino-American rivalry fuels a new cold war in space. *Centre for International Governance Innovation*. Retrieved from https://www.cigionline.org/articles/sino-american-rivalry-fuels-a-new-cold-war-in-space/

Arend, R. J. (2013). The business model: Present and future – beyond a skeumorph. *Strategic Organization*, *11*(4), 390–402. https://doi.org/10.1177/1476127013499636

Arendt, H. (1964). *Eichmann in Jerusalem: A report on the banality of evil* (Revised and enlarged edition). New York, NY: Viking Press.

Arendt, H. (1970). *On violence*. New York, NY: Harcourt, Brace & World.

Arias, E., Tejada-Vera, B., Kochanek, K. D., & Ahmad, F. B. (2022). *Provisional life expectancy estimates for 2021*. National Vital Statistics System, Report No. 23. National Center for Health Statistics. Retrieved from https://www.cdc.gov/nchs/data/vsrr/vsrr023.pdf

Aristotle. (1912). *Politics: A treatise on government* (W. Ellis, Trans.). New York, NY: E. P. Dutton. Retrieved from https://www.gutenberg.org/files/6762/6762.txt

Armour, J., & Cumming, D. (2006). The legislative road to Silicon Valley. *Oxford Economic Papers, 58*(4), 596–635. https://doi.org/10.1093/oep/gpl007

Arrieta-Ibarra, I., Goff, L., Jiménez-Hernández, D., Lanier, J., & Weyl, E. G. (2018). Should we treat data as labor? Moving beyond "free". *AEA Papers and Proceedings, 108*, 38–42. https://doi.org/10.1257/pandp.20181003

Arrow, K. J. (1951). *Social choice and individual values*. New York, NY: Wiley.

Arrow, K. J. (1987). Reflections on the essays. In G. Feiwel (Ed.), *Arrow and the foundations of the theory of economic policy* (pp. 727–34). New York, NY: NYU Press. https://doi.org/10.1007/978-1-349-07357-3_36

Arrow, K. J. (1996), Technical information and industrial structure. *Industrial and Corporate Change, 5*(2), 645–652. https://doi.org/10.1093/icc/5.2.645

Arthur, W. B. (1994). *Increasing returns and path dependence in the economy*. Ann Arbor, MI: University of Michigan Press.

Aschenbrenner, L. (2024, June). Situational awareness: The decade ahead. *Situational-Awareness.ai*. Retrieved from https://situational-awareness.ai/wp-content/uploads/2024/06/situationalawareness.pdf

Ashforth, B. E., & Gibbs, B. W. (1990). The double-edge of organizational legitimation. *Organization Science, 1*(2), 177–194. https://doi.org/10.1287/orsc.1.2.177

Asimov, I. (1942). Runaround. *Astounding Science Fiction 29*(1), 94–103.

Asimov, I. (1985). *Robots and empire*. Garden City, NY: Doubleday.

Aslund, A. (2004). The misguided blame game. *Transition Newsletter*, 14/15, 25–26.

Aspers, P., & Beckert, J. (2011). Value in markets. In J. Beckert & P. Aspers (Eds.), *The worth of goods: Valuation and pricing in the economy* (pp. 2–38). Oxford: Oxford University Press. https://doi.org/10.1093/acprof:osobl/9780199594641.003.0001

Åstebro, T., Herz, H., Nanda, R., & Weber, R. A. (2014). Seeking the roots of entrepreneurship: Insights from behavioral economics. *The Journal of Economic Perspectives, 28*(3), 49–69. https://doi.org/10.1257/jep.28.3.49

Atkins, E. M., Harrison, S., & Lane, M. (2000). Cicero. In C. Rowe & M. Schofield (Eds.), *The Cambridge history of Greek and Roman political thought* (pp. 477–516). Cambridge: Cambridge University Press.

Audretsch, D. B. (2007). Entrepreneurship capital and economic growth. *Oxford Review of Economic Policy, 23*(1), 63–78. https://doi.org/10.1093/oxrep/grm001

Audretsch, D. B., & Feldman, M. P. (1996). R&D spillovers and the geography of innovation and production. *The American Economic Review, 86*(3), 630–640.

Audretsch, D. B., & Keilbach, M. (2008). Resolving the knowledge paradox: Knowledge-spillover entrepreneurship and economic growth. *Research Policy, 37*(10), 1697–1705. https://doi.org/10.1016/j.respol.2008.08.008

Avolio, B. J., Waldman, D. A., & Yammarino, F. J. (1991). Leading in the 1990s: The four I's of transformational leadership. *Journal of European Industrial Training, 15*(4). https://doi.org/10.1108/03090599110143366

Ayres, C. E. (1944). *The theory of economic progress*. Chapel Hill, NC: University of North Carolina Press.

Ayres, I., & Levitt, S. D. (1998). Measuring positive externalities from unobservable victim precaution: An empirical analysis of Lojack. *The Quarterly Journal of Economics*, *113*(1), 43–77. https://doi.org/10.1162/003355398555522

Bacon, F. (1837). The works of Lord Bacon: With an introductory essay and a portrait (Vol. II). London: William Ball. Retrieved from https://upload.wikimedia.org/wikipedia/commons/1/1c/The_works_of_Lord_Bacon._With_an_introductory_essay%2C_and_a_portrait_%28IA_bub_gb_2q5JAQAAMAAJ%29.pdf

Bae, S. M., Masud, M. A. K., & Kim, J. D. (2018). A cross-country investigation of corporate governance and corporate sustainability disclosure: A signaling theory perspective. *Sustainability*, *10*(8), 1–16. https://doi.org/10.3390/su10082611

Baker, J. B. (2007). Beyond Schumpeter vs. Arrow: How antitrust fosters innovation. *Antitrust Law Journal*, *74*(3), 575–602. https://doi.org/10.2139/ssrn.1103623

Baldwin, R. (1969). The case against infant-industry tariff protection. *Journal of Political Economy*, *77*(3), 295–305. https://doi.org/10.1086/259517

Baldwin, R. E., & Robert-Nicoud, F. (2007). Entry and asymmetric lobbying: Why governments pick losers. *Journal of the European Economic Association*, 5(5), 1064–1093. https://doi.org/10.1162/JEEA.2007.5.5.1064

Bamberger, K. A., & Lobel, O. (2017). Platform market power. *Berkeley Technology Law Journal*, *32*(3), 1051–1092. https://doi.org/10.15779/Z38N00ZT38

Bancel, F., Glavas, D., & Karolyi, G. A. (2023). Do ESG factors influence firm valuation? Evidence from the field. *SSRN Electronic Journal*. https://doi.org/10.2139/ssrn.4365196

Banerjee, R. N., & Hofmann, B. (2018, September 23). The rise of zombie firms: Causes and consequences. *BIS Quarterly Review*. Retrieved from https://www.bis.org/publ/qtrpdf/r_qt1809g.htm

Banutu-Gomez, M. B., & Banutu-Gomez, S. M. T. (2007). Leadership and organizational change in a competitive environment. *Business Renaissance Quarterly*, *2*(2), 69–91.

Bar-On, Y. M., Phillips, R., & Milo, R. (2018). The biomass distribution on Earth. *Proceedings of the National Academy of Sciences of the United States of America*, *115*(25), 6506–6511. https://doi.org/10.1073/pnas.1711842115

Barbon, A., & Ranaldo, A. (2023). NFT bubbles (Swiss Finance Institute Research Paper No. 23-20). *SSRN Electronic Journal*. https://doi.org/10.2139/ssrn.4384395

Barkin, K. D. (1970). *The controversy over German industrialization, 1890–1902*. Chicago, IL: University of Chicago Press.

Barnes, O. (2024, November 8). Robert Kennedy Jr's influence over Donald Trump sparks Big Pharma alarm. *The Financial Times*. Retrieved from https://www.ft.com/content/cdb11bd4-1197-4584-b5bd-83fc4669f038

Barney, J. B., & Reeves, M. (2024, September-October). AI won't give you a new sustainable advantage. *Harvard Business Review*. Retrieved from https://hbr.org/2024/09/ai-wont-give-you-a-new-sustainable-advantage

Baron, D. P. (1995). Integrated strategy: Market and nonmarket components. *California Management Review*, *37*(2), 47–65.

Barrett, N. (2017). Steve Bannon, heir to Plato. *The Times Literary Supplement*. Retrieved from https://www.the-tls.co.uk/politics-by-region/north-american-politics/steve-bannon-heir-plato

Barro, R. (1996). Democracy and growth. *Journal of Economic Growth*, *1*(1), 1–27. https://doi.org/10.1007/BF00163340

Barrow, J. C. (1977). The variables of leadership: A review and conceptual framework. *Academy of Management Review*, *2*(2), 233–251. https://doi.org/10.5465/AMR.1977.4409046

Barrow, C. W. (2007). Plain Marxists, sophisticated Marxists, and C. Wright Mills' "The Power Elite." *Science & Society*, *71*(4), 400–430.

Bartels, L. M. (2008). *Unequal democracy: The political economy of the new gilded age*. Princeton, NJ: Princeton University Press.

Bass, B. M., & Avolio, B. J. (1993). Transformational leadership and organizational culture. *Public Administration Quarterly, 17*(1), 112–121.

Bass, B. M., & Bass, R. (2008). *The Bass handbook of leadership: Theory, research, and managerial applications*. New York, NY: Free Press.

Bastiat, F. (1996). *Economic sophisms* (A. Goddard, Trans.). Irvington-on-Hudson, NY: Foundation for Economic Education. Retrieved from https://oll.libertyfund.org/titles/hazlitt-economic-sophisms-fee-ed

Bates, T. (1975). Gramsci and the theory of hegemony. *Journal of the History of Ideas, 36*(2), 351–366. https://doi.org/10.2307/2708933

Battilana, J., & D'Aunno, T. (2009). Institutional work and the paradox of embedded agency. In T. Lawrence, R. Suddaby, & B. Leca (Eds.). *Institutional work: Actors and agency in institutional studies of organizations*. (pp. 31–58). Cambridge: Cambridge University Press. https://doi.org/10.1017/CBO9780511596605.002

Bau, N. (2021). Can policy change culture? Government pension plans and traditional kinship practices. *American Economic Review, 111*(6), 1880–1917. https://doi.org/10.1257/aer.20190098

Bauer, A. J. (1983). The church in the economy of Spanish America: Censos and depósitos in the eighteenth and nineteenth centuries. *The Hispanic American Historical Review, 63*(4), 707–733. https://doi.org/10.2307/2514902

Bauer, K. (2022, March 8). Israel-UAE economic cooperation has deep roots and broad dividends. *The Washington Institute for Near East Policy*. Retrieved from https://www.washingtoninstitute.org/policy-analysis/israel-uae-economic-cooperation-has-deep-roots-and-broad-dividends

Baumol, W. J. (1972). On taxation and the control of externalities. *The American Economic Review, 62*(3), 307–322.

Baumol, W. J. (1990). Entrepreneurship: Productive, unproductive, and destructive. *Journal of Political Economy, 98*(5), 893–921. https://doi.org/10.1086/261712

Baumol, W. J. (2004). Red-Queen games: Arms races, rule of law and market economies. *Journal of Evolutionary Economics, 14*(2), 237–247. https://doi.org/10.1007/s00191-004-0207-y

Baumol, W. J. (2010). *The microtheory of innovative entrepreneurship*. Princeton, NJ: Princeton University Press. https://doi.org/10.2307/j.ctt21668j9

Baumüller, J., & Sopp, K. (2022). Double materiality and the shift from non-financial to European sustainability reporting: Review, outlook and implications. *Journal of Applied Accounting Research, 23*(1). https://doi.org/10.1108/JAAR-04-2021-0114

Bays, C. (2010). Introduction to cellular automata and Conway's game of life. In Adamatzky, A. (Ed.), *Game of life cellular automata*. London: Springer. https://doi.org/10.1007/978-1-84996-217-9_1

Bazerman, M. H. (2001). *Judgment in managerial decision making* (5th ed.). New York, NY: John Wiley & Sons.

Beales III, J. H., & Muris, T. J. (2024, May 6). Lina Khan's failed FTC experiment. *The Wall Street Journal*. Retrieved from https://www.wsj.com/articles/lina-khans-failed-ftc-experiment-management-mergers-legal-strategy-161e6b9c

Beard, C. (1913). *An economic interpretation of the constitution of the United States*. New York, NY: Macmillan.

Beauchamp, G. (1980). The Frankenstein complex and Asimov's robots. *Mosaic: A Journal for the Interdisciplinary Study of Literature, 13*(3/4), 83–94.

Becker, G. (1993). Nobel lecture: The economic way of looking at behavior. *Journal of Political Economy, 101*(3), 385–409. https://doi.org/10.1086/261880

Beckert, J. (2016). *Imagined futures: Fictional expectations and capitalist dynamics*. Cambridge, MA: Harvard University Press. https://doi.org/10.1017/S0266267117000141

Beckwith, C. (2009). *Empires of the silk road: A history of Central Eurasia from the bronze age to the present*. Princeton, NJ: Princeton University Press.

Bedau, M. A. (1997). Weak emergence. *Philosophical Perspectives, 11*, 375–399. https://doi.org/10.1111/0029-4624.31.s11.17

Bednar, M. K., & Westphal, J. D. (2006). Surveying the corporate elite: Theoretical and practical guidance on improving response rates and response quality in top management survey questionnaires. In D. Ketchen & D. Bergh (Eds.), *Research methodology in strategy and management* (pp. 37–55). Oxford: JAI Press. https://doi.org/10.1016/S1479-8387(06)03004-9

Beinhocker, E. (2006). *The origin of wealth: Evolution, complexity, and the radical remaking of economics*. Cambridge, MA: Harvard Business School Press.

Bejan, A. (2020). *Freedom and evolution: Hierarchy in nature, society and science*. Cham: Springer. https://doi.org/10.1007/978-3-030-34009-4

Bell, C. M. (1993). In search of the tao in taoism: New questions of unity and multiplicity. *History of Religions, 33*(2), 187–201. https://doi.org/10.1086/463363

Bell, D. (1958). The power elite – reconsidered. *American Journal of Sociology, 64*(3), 238–250.

Bell, D. (1987). The art of judgement. *Mind, 96*(382), 221–244. https://doi.org/10.1093/mind/xcvi.382.221

Bello, C. (2022, November 20). Would you want a robot as CEO? Chinese firm is first to try as it bets on 'metaverse workplace'. *Euronews*. Retrieved from https://www.euronews.com/next/2022/11/20/would-you-want-a-robot-as-ceo-chinese-firm-is-first-to-try-as-it-bets-on-metaverse-workpla

Bénabou, R., & Tirole, J. (2010). Individual and corporate social responsibility. *Economica, 77*(305), 1–19. https://doi.org/10.1111/j.1468-0335.2009.00843.x

Bénassy-Quéré, A., Coupet, M., & Mayer, T. (2007). Institutional determinants of foreign direct investment. *World Economy 30*(5), 764–782. https://doi.org/10.1111/j.1467-9701.2007.01022.x

Benatar, D. (1997). Why it is better never to come into existence. *American Philosophical Quarterly, 34*(3), 345–355.

Bengio, Y., Hinton, G. E., Yao, A., Song, D., Abbeel, P., Harari, Y. N., Zhang, Y.-Q., Xue, L., Shalev-Shwartz, S., Hadfield, G. K., Clune, J., Maharaj, T., Hutter, F., Baydin, A. G., McIlraith, S. A., Gao, Q., Acharya, A., Krueger, D., Dragan, A. D., . . . Mindermann, S. (2024). Managing extreme AI risks amid rapid progress (Version 3). *arXiv*. https://doi.org/10.48550/arXiv.2310.17688

Benhabib, J. (2003). The tradeoff between inequality and growth. *Annals of Economics and Finance, 4*(2), 491–507.

Bennett, C. H. (1987). Demons, engines and the second law. *Scientific American, 257*(5), 108–117.

Bentham, J. (1970). An introduction to the principles of morals and legislation. In J. H. Burns and H. L. A. Hart (Eds.), *The collected works of Jeremy Bentham: An introduction to the principles of morals and legislation*. London: The Athlone Press.

Bentham, J. (2017). *A fragment on government* (J. Bennett, Ed.). Early Modern Texts. Retrieved from https://www.earlymoderntexts.com/assets/pdfs/bentham1776.pdf

Bentley, P. J., Brundage, M., Häggström, O., & Metzinger, T. (2018). *Should we fear artificial intelligence? In-depth analysis*. Brussels: European Parliament. Retrieved from https://www.europarl.europa.eu/RegData/etudes/IDAN/2018/614547/EPRS_IDA(2018)614547_EN.pdf

Berg, A., Ostry, J. D., Tsangarides, C. G., & Yakhshilikov, Y. (2018). Redistribution, inequality, and growth: New evidence. *Journal of Economic Growth, 23*(3), 259–305. https://doi.org/10.1007/s10887-017-9150-2

Berg, F., Fabisik, K., & Sautner, Z., (2021, August 24). *Is history repeating itself? The (un)predictable past of ESG ratings* (European Corporate Governance Institute – Finance Working Paper 708/2020). Retrieved from https://ssrn.com/abstract=3722087

Berg, F., Kölbel, J. F., & Rigobon, R. (2022). Aggregate confusion: The divergence of ESG ratings. *Review of Finance, 26*(6), 1315–1344. https://doi.org/10.2139/ssrn.3438533

Berg, M. (2025, January 12). We're witnessing a new Mark Zuckerberg: Welcome to Zuck 3.0. *Business Insider via MSN*. Retrieved from https://www.msn.com/en-us/money/companies/we-re-witnessing-a-new-mark-zuckerberg-welcome-to-zuck-3-0/ar-BB1rkxZT

Bergson, H. (2008). *Creative evolution* (A. Mitchell, Trans.). New York, NY: Henry Holt and Company. Retrieved from https://www.gutenberg.org/ebooks/26163

Berle, A. A. (1968). Review of the book *Who Rules America?* by G. W. Domhoff. *The Annals of the American Academy of Political and Social Science*, *377*(1), 201–202.

Berlin, I. (2013). *The Hedgehog and the Fox: An essay on Tolstoy's view of history – Second Edition*. Princeton, NJ: Princeton University Press.

Bernanke, B. S. (2005). *The global saving glut and the U.S current account deficit*. Speech delivered at the Homer Jones Lecture, St. Louis, April 14, 2005. Retrieved from https://fraser.stlouisfed.org/title/statements-speeches-ben-s-bernanke-453/global-saving-glut-us-current-account-deficit-8918?page=2

Bernhard, M. (2015). Chronic instability and the limits of path dependence. *Perspectives on Politics*, *13*(4), 976–991. https://doi.org/10.1017/S1537592715002261

Bernstein, R. J. (2008). Are Arendt's reflections on evil still relevant? *The Review of Politics*, *70*(1), 64–76. https://doi.org/10.1017/S003467050800017X

Bertrand, N. (2022, January 31). US has identified Russian elites who will be sanctioned if Putin invades Ukraine. *CNN*. Retrieved from https://edition.cnn.com/2022/01/31/politics/us-russian-elite-sanctions/index.html

Besley, T. (2015). Law, regulation, and the business climate: The nature and influence of the World Bank doing business project. *The Journal of Economic Perspectives*, *29*(3), 99–120. http://dx.doi.org/10.1257/jep.29.3.99

Besley, T., & Persson, T. (2010). State capacity, conflict, and development. *Econometrica*, *78*(1), 1–34. https://doi.org/10.3982/ECTA8073

Bessembinder, H. (2018). Do stocks outperform treasury bills? *Journal of Financial Economics*, *129*(3), 440–457. https://doi.org/10.1016/j.jfineco.2018.06.004

Best, H. (2018a). Elite sectors: Differentiation and integration. In H. Best and J. Higley (Eds.), *The Palgrave handbook of political elites*. (pp. 331–338) London: Palgrave Macmillan. https://doi.org/10.1057/978-1-137-51904-7_22

Best, H. (2018b). Economic elites-political elites: Scenes from a symbiosis. In L. Vogel, R. Gebauer & A. Salheiser (Eds.), *The contested status of political elites: At the crossroads* (pp. 44–57). London: Routledge. https://doi.org/10.4324/9781315211916-4

Best, H., & Higley, J. (2018). *The Palgrave handbook of political elites*. London: Palgrave.

Best, H., & Hoffmann-Lange, U. (2018). Introduction: Challenged elites – elites as challengers. Towards a unified theory of representative elites. *Historical Social Research*, *43*(4), 7–32. https://doi.org/10.12759/hsr.43.2018.4.7-32

Best, H., Lengyel G., & Verzichelli L. (2012). *The Europe of elites: A study into the europeanness of Europe's political and economic elites*. Oxford: Oxford University Press. https://doi.org/10.1093/acprof:oso/9780199602315.001.0001

Beugelsdijk, S., Ambos, B., & Nell, P. C. (2018). Conceptualizing and measuring distance in international business research: Recurring questions and best practice guidelines. *Journal of International Business Studies*, *49*, 1113–1137. https://doi.org/10.1057/s41267-018-0182-4

Bhagwati, J. N. (1982). Directly unproductive, profit-seeking (DUP) activities. *Journal of Political Economy*, *90*(5), 988–1002.

Bhagwati, J. N. & Srinivasan, T. N. (1982). The welfare consequences of directly-unproductive profit-seeking (DUP) lobbying activities: Price versus quantity distortions. *Journal of International Economics*, *13*(1-2), 33–44.

Bieler, A., & Morton, A. D. (2004). A critical theory route to hegemony, world order and historical change: Neo-Gramscian perspectives in international relations. *Capital & Class*, *28*(1), 85–113. https://doi.org/10.1177/030981680408200106

Biermann, F., Hickmann, T., Sénit, C. A., Beisheim, M., Bernstein, S., Chasek, P., Grob, L., Kim, R. E., Kotzé, L. J., Nilsson, M., Ordóñez Llanos, A., Okereke, C., Pradhan, P., Raven, R., Sun, Y., Vijge, M. J., van Vuuren, D., & Wicke, B. (2022). Scientific evidence on the political impact of the Sustainable Development Goals. *Nature sustainability*, *5*(9), 795–800. https://doi.org/10.1038/s41893-022-00909-5

Biesinger, M., Bircan, Ç., & Ljungqvist, A. (2020). *Value creation in private equity*. European Bank for Reconstruction and Development (Working Paper No. 242). Retrieved from https://www.ebrd.com/publications/working-papers/value-creation-in-private-equity

Biggerstaff, L., Cicero, D. C., & Puckett, A. (2016, November 30). Is your firm underperforming? Your CEO might be golfing too much. *Harvard Business Review*. Retrieved from https://hbr.org/2016/11/is-your-firm-underperforming-your-ceo-might-be-golfing-too-much

Billio, M., Costola, M., Hristova, I., Latino, C., & Pelizzon, L. (2020). *Inside the ESG ratings: (Dis)agreement and performance* (SAFE Working Paper, No. 284). Retrieved from https://www.econstor.eu/handle/10419/222553

Bishop, J. M. (2021). Artificial intelligence is stupid and causal reasoning will not fix it. *Frontiers in Psychology*, *11*, 513474. https://doi.org/10.3389/fpsyg.2020.513474

Bitektine, A. (2011). Toward a theory of social judgments of organizations: The case of legitimacy, reputation, and status. *Academy of Management Review*, *36*(1), 151–179. https://doi.org/10.5465/amr.2009.0382

Bjørnskov, C., & Foss, N. J. (2008). Economic freedom and entrepreneurial activity: Some cross-country evidence. *Public Choice*, *134*(3/4), 307–328. https://doi.org/10.1007/s11127-007-9229-y

Blake, D. (2023). Target2: The silent bailout system that keeps the euro afloat. *Journal of Risk and Financial Management*, *16*(12), 506. https://doi.org/10.3390/jrfm16120506

Blakey, G. R. (1984). Legal regulation of gambling since 1950. *The Annals of the American Academy of Political and Social Science*, *474*, 12–22. https://doi.org/10.1177/0002716284474001002

Blas, J. (2011, April 16). Man in the news: Ivan Glasenberg. *The Financial Times*. Retrieved from https://www.ft.com/content/0291499c-67a6-11e0-9138-00144feab49a

Blok, A. (1972). The Peasant and the Brigand: Social banditry reconsidered. *Comparative Studies in Society and History*, *14*(4), 494–503. https://doi.org/10.1017/S0010417500006824

Blondel, J., & Müller-Rommel, F. (2007). Political elites. In R. J. Dalton and H. D. Klingemann (Eds.), *The Oxford handbook of political behavior* (pp. 818–833). Oxford: Oxford University Press. https://doi.org/10.1093/oxfordhb/9780199270125.003.0044

Bloomberg Podcasts. (2025, February 11). *President Trump & Elon Musk in the Oval Office: Full Remarks* [Video]. YouTube. https://www.youtube.com/watch?v=gAuTb-yMNk4

Board of Governors of the Federal Reserve System (US). (2024). *Reserve balances with Federal Reserve Banks: Week average [WRESBAL]*. Retrieved from FRED, Federal Reserve Bank of St. Louis: https://fred.stlouisfed.org/series/WRESBAL

Boix, C., & Svolik, M. W. (2013). The foundations of limited authoritarian government: Institutions, commitment, and power-sharing in dictatorships. *The Journal of Politics*, *75*(2), 300–316. https://doi.org/10.2139/ssrn.1352065

Boje, D. M. (2008). *Storytelling organizations*. London: SAGE Publications Ltd.

Boletín Oficial del Estado (BOE). (2022). *Ley 7/2022, de 8 de abril, de residuos y suelos contaminados para una economía circular*. (BOE núm. 85, de 09 de abril de 2022. Referencia: BOE-A-2022-5809).

Bologna, M., & Aquino, G. (2020). Deforestation and world population sustainability: A quantitative analysis. *Scientific Reports*, *10*, 7631. https://doi.org/10.1038/s41598-020-63657-6

Bonaglia, D., Rivera León, L., & Nindl, E. (2024, April 30). R&D spending by the top 2,500 R&D spenders crossed the €1.3 trillion mark in 2022. *World Intellectual Property Organization*. Retrieved from https://www.wipo.int/global_innovation_index/en/gii-insights-blog/2024/r-and-d-spenders.html

Boone, P., & Rodionov, D. (2002). *Rent seeking in Russia and the CIS*. Moscow: Brunswick UBS Warburg.

Borchers, C. (2024, July 24). Merit, excellence and intelligence: An anti-DEI approach catches on. *The Wall Street Journal*. Retrieved from https://www.wsj.com/lifestyle/workplace/dei-catches-on-merit-intelligence-excellence-mei-27839a3c

Bordo, M. D., & McCauley, R. N. (2017, December). *Triffin: Dilemma or myth?* (Bank for International Settlements Working Papers, No. 684). Retrieved from https://www.bis.org/publ/work684.pdf

Bork, R. H. (1978). *The antitrust paradox: A policy at war with itself*. New York, NY: Basic Books.

Boss, D. S., Connelly, B. L., Hoskisson, R. E., & Tihanyi, L. (2013). Corporate governance: Ownership interests, incentives, and conflicts. In M. Wright (Ed.), *The Oxford handbook of corporate governance* (pp. 246–268). Oxford: Oxford University Press. https://doi.org/10.1093/oxfordhb/9780199642007.013.0011

Bostrom, N. (2003). Ethical issues in advanced artificial intelligence. In I. Smit, W. Wallach, & G. Lasker (Eds.), *Cognitive, emotive and ethical aspects of decision making in humans and in artificial intelligence* (Vol. 2, pp. 12–17). International Institute of Advanced Studies in Systems Research and Cybernetics.

Bostrom, N. (2012). The superintelligent will: Motivation and instrumental rationality in advanced artificial agents. *Minds and Machines 22*(2), 71–85. https://doi.org/10.1007/s11023-012-9281-3

Bostrom, N. (2014). *Superintelligence: Paths, dangers, strategies*. Oxford: Oxford University Press.

Bottomore, T. (1993*). Elites and society* (2nd ed.). London: Routledge.

Boucekkine, R., Piacquadio, P. G., & Prieur, F. (2019). A Lipsetian theory of voluntary power handover. *Journal of Economic Behavior & Organization*, *168*, 269–291. https://doi.org/10.1016/j.jebo.2019.10.010

Bouchard, T. J., Jr. (1976). Unobtrusive measures: An inventory of uses. *Sociological Methods & Research*, *4*(3), 267–300. https://doi.org/10.1177/004912417600400301

Bourdieu, P. (1996). *The state nobility: Elite schools in the field of power* (L. C. Clough, Trans.). Stanford, CA: Stanford University Press. https://doi.org/10.1515/9781503615427

Bourdieu, P., & Wacquant, L. J. D. (1992). *An invitation to reflexive sociology*. Chicago, IL: University of Chicago Press.

Bourguignon, F., & Verdier, T. (2000). Oligarchy, democracy, inequality and growth. *Journal of Development Economics*, *62*(2), 285–313. https://doi.org/10.1016/S0304-3878(00)00086-9

Bourguignon, F., & Verdier, T. (2010, October). *The simple analytics of elite behaviour under limited state capacity* (WIDER Working Paper 2010/104). Retrieved from https://www.wider.unu.edu/sites/default/files/wp2010-104.pdf

Bowles, S., Kirman, A., & Sethi, R. (2017). Retrospectives: Friedrich Hayek and the market algorithm. *Journal of Economic Perspectives*, *31*(3), 215–30. https://doi.org/10.1257/jep.31.3.215

Bown, C. P. (2020). Trump's steel and aluminum tariffs are cascading out of control. *Peterson Institute for International Economics*. Retrieved from https://www.piie.com/blogs/trade-and-investment-policy-watch/trumps-steel-and-aluminum-tariffs-are-cascading-out-control

Box, G. E. P., & Jenkins, G. M. (1976). *Time series analysis: Forecasting and control*. San Francisco, CA: Holden-Day.

Bradford, A. (2020). *The Brussels effect: How the European Union rules the world*. New York, NY: Oxford University Press. https://doi.org/10.1093/oso/9780190088583.001.0001

Bradley, D., Huber, E., Moller, S., Nielsen, F., & Stephens, J. D. (2003). Distribution and redistribution in postindustrial democracies. *World Politics*, *55*(2), 193–228. https://doi.org/10.1353/wp.2003.0009

Bradshaw, L. (2011). Oligarchs and democrats. In D. Tabachnic & T. Koivukoski (Eds.), *On oligarchy: Ancient lessons for global politics* (pp. 140–159). Toronto: University of Toronto Press. https://doi.org/10.3138/9781442664029-009

Brady, D., & Spence, M. (2010). Leadership and politics: A perspective from the Commission on Growth and Development. In D. Brady and M. Spence (Eds.), *Leadership and growth*. Washington, DC: World Bank. Retrieved from https://documents1.worldbank.org/curated/zh/375571468152966660/pdf/527080PUB0lead101Official0Use0Only1.pdf

Brail, S. (2018). From renegade to regulated: The digital platform economy, ride-hailing and the case of Toronto. *Canadian Journal of Urban Research*, *27*(2), 51–63.

Braithwaite, J., & Drahos, P. (2000). *Global business regulation*. Cambridge: Cambridge University Press. https://doi.org/10.1017/9780521780339

Brandenburger, A. M. (2002). Porter's added value: High indeed! *The Academy of Management Executive*, *16*(2), 58–60. https://doi.org/10.5465/AME.2002.7173523

Brandenburger, A. M., & Stuart, H. W., Jr. (1996). Value-based business strategy. *Journal of Economics and Management Strategy, 5*(1), 5–24. https://doi.org/10.1111/j.1430-9134.1996.00005.x

Brautigan, R. (1967). *All watched over by machines of loving grace*. San Francisco, CA: The Communication Company.

Brea, J. A. (2003). Population dynamics in Latin America. *Population Bulletin, 58*(1), 3–35.

Brealey, R. A., Myers, S. C., Allen, F., & Edmans, A. (2022). *Principles of corporate finance* (14th ed.). New York, NY: McGraw-Hill.

Breiding, J. (2013). Yes, he played dirty – but Marc Rich also changed the world. *The Financial Times*. Retrieved from https://www.ft.com/content/c262c172-df10-11e2-881f-00144feab7de.

Breiding, J. (2019). *Too small to fail: Why some small nations outperform larger ones and how they are reshaping the world*. Noida, Uttar Pradesh: Harper Business.

Brennan, G., & Buchanan, J. (1983). Predictive power and the choice among regimes. *The Economic Journal, 93*(369), 89–105. https://doi.org/10.2307/2232167

Brennan, J., & Magness, P. (2019). *Cracks in the ivory tower: The moral mess of higher education*. New York, NY: Oxford University Press. https://doi.org/10.1093/oso/9780190846282.001.0001

Brennan, P. (2019, November 5). The lesson from Trump's steel tariffs? Short-term gain but long-term pain. *S&P Global Market*. Retrieved from https://www.spglobal.com/marketintelligence/en/news-insights/latest-news-headlines/the-lesson-from-trump-s-steel-tariffs-short-term-gain-but-long-term-pain-55244548.

Bresnahan, T. F. (1986). Measuring the spillovers from technical advance: Mainframe computers in financial services. *The American Economic Review, 76*(4), 742–755.

Brezis, E. S., & Temin, P. (2007). Elites and economic outcomes. In S. N. Durlauf and L. E. Blume (Eds.), *The New Palgrave Dictionary of Economics* (Forthcoming). Retrieved from https://ssrn.com/abstract=962514

Brinkmann, L., Baumann, F., Bonnefon, J.-F., Derex, M., Müller, T. F., Nussberger, A.-M., Czaplicka, A., Acerbi, A., Griffiths, T. L., Henrich, J., Leibo, J. Z., McElreath, R., Oudeyer, P.-Y., Stray, J., & Rahwan, I. (2023). Machine culture. *Nature Human Behaviour, 7*, 1855–1868. https://doi.org/10.1038/s41562-023-01742-2

Brint, S. (1990). Rethinking the policy influence of experts: From general characterizations to analysis of variation. *Sociological Forum, 5*(3), 361–385. https://doi.org/10.1007/BF01115092

Brouthers, K. D. (2002). Institutional, cultural, and transaction cost influences on entry mode choice and performance. *Journal of International Business Studies, 33*(2), 203–221. https://doi.org/10.1057/palgrave.jibs.8491013

Brown, D. (1993). The search for elite cohesion. *Contemporary Southeast Asia, 15*(1), 111–130.

Brown, H. (1934). Junker versus Nazi. *Current History (1916–1940), 39*(6), 668–674.

Brown, J. H., Gupta, V. K., Li, B.-L., Milne, B. T., Restrepo, C., & West, G. B. (2002). The fractal nature of nature: Power laws, ecological complexity and biodiversity. *Philosophical Transactions: Biological Sciences, 357*(1421), 619–626.

Brown, M. (2019, October 29). SpaceX Mars city: Here's how much Elon Musk's dream would cost. *Inverse*. Retrieved from https://www.inverse.com/article/58458-spacex-mars-city-here-s-how-much-it-would-cost-to-build

Brown, R. S. (2018). Franchise systems and lobbying: Implications for Olsonian collective action theory. *Management Decision, 56*(11), 2357–2372. https://doi.org/10.1108/MD-11-2017-1080

Browne, C., Di Battista, A., Geiger, T., & Gutknecht, T. (2014). The executive opinion survey: The voice of the business community. In *The Global Competitiveness Report 2014–2015* (pp. 85–96). Geneva: World Economic Forum.

Brundtland, G. H. (1987). *Report of the World Commission on Environment and Development: Our common future*. United Nations General Assembly document A/42/427. Retrieved from http://www.un-documents.net/our-common-future.pdf

Bruner, J. (1991). The narrative construction of reality. *Critical Inquiry*, *18*(1), 1–21. https://doi.org/10.1086/448619

Brynjolfsson, E., Li, D., & Raymond, L. (2023, April 25). Generative AI at work. *Arxiv.org*. Retrieved from: https://arxiv.org/pdf/2304.11771.pdf

Bubeck, S., Chandrasekaran, V., Eldan, R., Gehrke, J., Horvitz, E., Kamar, E., Lee, P., Lee, Y. T., Li, Y., Lundberg, S., Nori, H., Palangi, H., Tulio Ribeiro, M., & Zhang, L. (2023, April 13). Sparks of artificial general intelligence: Early experiments with GPT-4. *Arxiv.org*. Retrieved from: arXiv:2303.12712v5

Buchanan, J. M. (1975). The samaritan's dilemma. In E. S. Phelps (Ed.), *Altruism, morality, and economic theory* (pp. 71–86). New York, NY: Russell Sage Foundation.

Buchanan, J. M. (1980). Rent seeking and profit seeking. In J. M. Buchanan, R. D. Tollison, & G. Tullock (Eds.), *Toward a theory of the rent-seeking society* (pp. 3–15). College Station, TX: Texas A&M University Press.

Buchanan, J., & Stubblebine, W. C. (1962). Externality. *Economica*, *29*(116), 371–384.

Buchheim, C., & Scherner, J. (2006). The role of private property in the Nazi economy: The case of industry. *The Journal of Economic History*, *66*(2), 390–416. https://doi.org/10.1017/S0022050706000167

Buchler, J. (2011). *Hiring and firing public officials: Rethinking the purpose of elections*. New York, NY: Oxford University Press. https://doi.org/10.1017/S1537592712001430

Buckley, P., & Casson, M. (1976). *The future of the multinational enterprise*. Basingstoke: Macmillan.

Buckley, P. J., Clegg, J., & Wang, C. (2002). The impact of inward FDI on the performance of Chinese manufacturing firms. *Journal of International Business Studies*, *33*(4), 637–655. https://doi.org/10.1057/palgrave.jibs.8491037

Buckup, S., & Casas-Klett, T. (2018, November 6). Modern leaders need a powerful narrative. *Management Today*. Retrieved from https://www.managementtoday.co.uk/modern-leaders-need-powerful-narrative/reputation-matters/article/1498184

Budler, M., & Trkman, P. (2023). The nature of management frameworks. *Journal of Management & Organization*, *29*(2),173–190. https://doi.org/10.1017/jmo.2019.83

Budryk, Z. (2024, November 12). Trump energy allies anticipate boom times for oil, gas, mining. *The Hill*. Retrieved from https://thehill.com/policy/energy-environment/4984398-trump-incoming-administration-oil-gas-mining-energy-permitting/

Bueno de Mesquita, E. (2016). *Political economy for public policy*. Princeton, NJ: Princeton University Press.

Bühlmann, F., Beetschen, M., David, T., Ginalski, S., & Mach, A. (2017). Elites in Switzerland: The rise and fall of a model of elite coordination. *Tempo Social*, *29*(3), 181–199. https://doi.org/10.11606/0103-2070.ts.2017.125960

Bühlmann, F., Christesen, C.A., Cousin, B., Denord, F., Ellersgaard, C.H., Lagneau-Ymonet, P., Larsen, A.G., Savage, M., Thine, S., Young, K., Araujo, P., Arrigoni, P., Atria, J., Benz, P., Behr, J., Botelho, M.d.C., Butt, A., Casanova, P., Clemente-Casinhas, L., . . . Yu, X. (2025). Varieties of economic elites? Preliminary results from the World Elite Database (WED). *The British Journal of Sociology*. https://doi.org/10.1111/1468-4446.13203

Bühlmann, F., David, T., & Mach, A. (2012). Political and economic elites in Switzerland. *European Societies*, *14*(5), 727–754. https://doi.org/10.1080/14616696.2012.709531

Bühlmann, F., David, T., & Mach, A. (2013). Cosmopolitan capital and the internationalization of the field of business elites: Evidence from the Swiss case. *Cultural Sociology*, *7*(2), 211–229. https://doi.org/10.1177/1749975512473587

Burnham, J. (1943). *The Machiavellians: Defenders of freedom*. New York, NY: John Day Company.

Burton, M. G., & Higley, J. (1987). Elite settlements. *American Sociological Review*, *52*(3), 295–307. https://doi.org/10.2307/2095351

Busino, G. (2000). The signification of Vilfredo Pareto's sociology. *Revue européenne des sciences sociales*, XXXVIII-117. Retrieved from http://journals.openedition.org/ress/730

Butler, K. (2023, January 24). Big tech layoffs are hitting diversity and inclusion jobs hard: Companies that made promises to hire more underrepresented groups are gutting departments meant to achieve those goals. *Bloomberg*. Retrieved from https://www.bloomberg.com/news/articles/2023-01-24/tech-layoffs-are-hitting-diversity-and-inclusion-jobs-hard

Buyl, M., Rogiers, A., Noels, S., Dominguez-Catena, I., Heiter, E., Romero, R., Johary, I., Mara, A.-C., Lijffijt, J., & De Bie, T. (2024). *Large language models reflect the ideology of their creators*. arXiv. https://doi.org/10.48550/arXiv.2410.18417

Caballero, R. J. (2008). Creative destruction. In S. N. Durlauf & L. E. Blume (Eds.), *The new Palgrave dictionary of economics* (2nd ed.). London: Palgrave Macmillan. Retrieved from https://economics.mit.edu/sites/default/files/publications/creative%20destruction.pdf https://doi.org/10.1057/978-1-349-95121-5_391-2

Caballero, R. J., Hoshi, T., & Kashyap, A. (2008). Zombie lending and depressed restructuring in Japan. *The American Economic Review, 98*(5), 1943–1977. https://doi.org/10.1257/aer.98.5.1943

Cadbury, A. (1992). *Report of the committee on the financial aspects of corporate governance*. London: Gee. Retrieved from https://ecgi.global/code/cadbury-report-financial-aspects-corporate-governance

Caesar, J. (1915). *"De Bello Gallico" and other commentaries* (W. A. McDevitte, Trans.; T. De Quincey, Intro.). Project Gutenberg. Retrieved from https://www.gutenberg.org/ebooks/10657

Cai, Y. (2008). Power structure and regime resilience: Contentious politics in China. *British Journal of Political Science, 38*(3), 411–432. https://doi.org/10.1017/S0007123408000215

Calkins, S. (1983). The new merger guidelines and the Herfindahl-Hirschman Index. *California Law Review, 71*(2), 402–429. https://doi.org/10.2307/3480160

Camazine, S., Deneubourg, J., Franks, N. R., Sneyd, J., Theraulaz, G., & Bonabeau, E. (2001). *Self-organization in biological systems*. Princeton, NJ: Princeton University Press. https://doi.org/10.1515/9780691212920

Camden, J. (2021, August 29). We the people: The reasoning behind the Vietnam War was not as simple as stopping the spread of communism. *The Spokesman-Review*. Retrieved from https://www.spokesman.com/stories/2021/aug/29/we-the-people-the-reasoning-behind-the-vietnam-war/

Camerer, C., & Lovallo, D. (1999). Overconfidence and excess entry: An experimental approach. *The American Economic Review, 89*(1), 306–318. https://doi.org/10.1257/aer.89.1.306

Cameron, C. M. (2016). *Captives*. Lincoln, NE: University of Nebraska Press.

Camerra-Rowe, P. (2004). Agenda 2010: Redefining German social democracy. *German Politics & Society, 22* (1 (70)), 1–30.

Campbell, D. E., & Kelly, J. S. (1994). Trade-off theory. *The American Economic Review, 84*(2), 422–426.

Cantens, T. (2010, November). *Is it possible to reform a customs administration? The role of the customs elite on the reform process in Cameroon* (WIDER Working Paper 2010/118). Retrieved from https://www.wider.unu.edu/sites/default/files/wp2010-118.pdf

Cantlupe, J. (2017, November 7). How healthcare administrators can help improve quality and reduce burnout. *athenahealth*. Retrieved from https://www.athenahealth.com/resources/blog/expert-forum-rise-and-rise-healthcare-administrator

Cantwell, J. (2014). Revisiting international business theory: A capabilities-based theory of the MNE. *Journal of International Business Studies, 45*(1), 1–7. https://doi.org/10.1057/jibs.2013.61

Caplan, A. (2013). "Cada uno en su bolsa llevar lo que cien indios no llevarían": Mexica resistance and the shape of currency in new Spain, 1542-1552. *American Journal of Numismatics, (1989-), 25*, 333-356.

Capoccia, G., & Kelemen, D. R. (2007). The study of critical junctures: Theory, narrative and counterfactuals in historical institutionalism. *World Politics 59*(3), 341–369. https://doi.org/10.1017/S0043887100020852

Capra, F. (1996). *The web of life: A new scientific understanding of living systems*. New York, NY: Anchor Books.

Caprettini, B., Casaburi, L., & Venturini, M. (2021, January). *Redistribution, voting and clientelism: Evidence from the Italian land reform* (CEPR Press Discussion Paper No. 15679). Retrieved from https://cepr.org/publications/dp15679

Cardinale, I. (2018). Beyond constraining and enabling: Toward new microfoundations for institutional theory. *Academy of Management Review, 43*(1), 132–155. https://doi.org/10.5465/amr.2015.0020

Carey, N., & Shepardson, D. (2018, September 26). Trump metals tariffs will cost Ford $1 billion in profits, CEO says. *Reuters*. Retrieved from https://www.reuters.com/article/us-ford-motor-tariffs-idUSKCN1M61ZN

Carlyle, T. (2008). *On heroes, hero-worship and the heroic in history*. Project Gutenberg. Retrieved from https://www.gutenberg.org/files/1091/1091-h/1091-h.htm

Carr, N. G. (2014). *The glass cage: How our computers are changing us*. New York, NY: W. W. Norton & Company.

Carree, M., van Stel, A., Thurik, R., & Wennekers, S. (2002). Economic development and business ownership: An analysis using data of 23 OECD countries in the period 1976-1996. *Small Business Economics, 19*(3), 271–290. https://doi.org/10.1023/A:1019604426387

Carree, M. A., & Thurik, A. R. (2010). The impact of entrepreneurship on economic growth. In Z. Acs & D. Audretsch (Eds.), *Handbook of entrepreneurship research* (pp. 557–594). New York, NY: Springer. https://doi.org/10.1007/978-1-4419-1191-9_20

Carroll, A. B. (1991). The pyramid of corporate social responsibility: Toward the moral management of organizational stakeholders. *Business Horizons, 34*(4), 39–48. https://doi.org/10.1016/0007-6813(91)90005-G

Carroll, A. B. (2016). Carroll's pyramid of CSR: Taking another look. *International Journal of Corporate Social Responsibility, 1*(3). https://doi.org/10.1186/s40991-016-0004-6

Carroll, L. (1902). *Through the looking-glass, and what Alice found there* (P. Newell, Illus.). New York, NY: Harper & Brothers. Retrieved from https://web.english.upenn.edu/~cavitch/pdf-library/Carroll_Through_the_Looking_Glass.pdf

Carter, I. (2019). Positive and negative liberty. In E. N. Zalta (Ed.), *The Stanford encyclopedia of philosophy* (Winter 2019 ed.) Retrieved from https://plato.stanford.edu/archives/win2019/entries/liberty-positive-negative/

Casas-Klett, T., & Buckup, T. S. (2018, July 4). Why today's leaders need to know about the power of narratives. *World Economic Forum*. Retrieved from https://www.weforum.org/agenda/2018/07/market-for-narratives-battleground-leader-strategy-why/

Casas-Klett, T., & Cozzi, G. (2020). *Elite quality report 2020: 32 Country scores and global rank*. Zurich: Seismo. Retrieved from https://papers.ssrn.com/sol3/papers.cfm?abstract_id=3676776

Casas-Klett, T., & Cozzi, G. (2021). *Elite quality report 2021: Country scores and global rankings*. Zurich: Seismo. Retrieved from https://papers.ssrn.com/sol3/papers.cfm?abstract_id=3845376

Casas-Klett, T., & Cozzi, G. (2022). *Elite quality report 2022: Country scores and global rankings*. Zurich: Seismo. Retrieved from https://papers.ssrn.com/sol3/papers.cfm?abstract_id=4085752

Casas-Klett, T., & Cozzi, G. (2023). *Elite quality report 2023: Country scores and global rankings*. Zurich: Seismo. Retrieved from https://papers.ssrn.com/sol3/papers.cfm?abstract_id=4418550

Casas-Klett, T., & Cozzi, G. (2024). *Elite quality report 2024: The sustainable value creation of nations*. Zurich: Seismo. Retrieved from https://papers.ssrn.com/sol3/papers.cfm?abstract_id=4779686

Casas-Klett, T., & Cozzi, G. (2025). *Elite quality report 2025: The sustainable value creation of nations*. London: Anthem Press. http://dx.doi.org/10.2139/ssrn.5241721

Casas-Klett, T., Cozzi, G., Diebold, C., & Tonn, A. (2024). The PanelEQx (PEQx2024) Dataset: Measuring elite quality over time for academic and policy purposes. In T. Casas-Klett & G. Cozzi (Eds.), *Elite quality report 2024: The sustainable value creation of nations*. Zurich: Seismo. https://doi.org/10.33058/seismo.30892.8493

Casas-Klett, T., Cozzi, G., Diebold, C., & Zeller, C. (2020). *Measuring elite quality* (MPRA Paper 102068). University Library of Munich: Germany.

Casas-Klett, T., & Li, J. (2022). Assessing the Belt and Road Initiative as a narrative: Implications for institutional change and international firm strategy. *Asia Pacific Journal of Management, 39*, 857–873. https://doi.org/10.1007/s10490-021-09757-x

Casas-Klett, T., & Nerlinger, M. (2023). Measuring sustainable value creation at the firm. In M. Hilb (Ed.), *Governance of sustainability* (pp. 33–53). Bern: Haupt Verlag A.G. https://doi.org/10.2139/ssrn.4246093

Casas-Klett, T., & Nerlinger, M. (2024). *Value creation ratings pilot report 2024: The sustainable value creation of firms*. Zurich: Seismo. http://dx.doi.org/10.2139/ssrn.5011047

Casas-Klett, T., & Zhang, J. (2024). China's opportunities for growth: A polytransition perspective. In T. Casas-Klett, N. Musy, & Z. Xiao (Eds.), *The Swiss business in China survey 2024*. Zurich: Seismo. https://doi.org/10.33058/seismo.30897

Case, A., & Deaton, A. (2021). *Deaths of despair and the future of capitalism*. Princeton, NJ: Princeton University Press.

Cassidy, L. M., Maoldúin, R. Ó., Kador, T., Lynch, A., Jones, C., Woodman, P. C., Murphy, E., Ramsey, G., Dowd, M., Noonan, A., Campbell, C., Jones, E. R., Mattiangeli, V., & Bradley, D. G. (2020). A dynastic elite in monumental Neolithic society. *Nature, 582*(7812), 384–388. https://doi.org/10.1038/s41586-020-2378-6

Cassis, Y. (1997). *Big business: The European experience in the twentieth century*. Oxford: Oxford University Press.

Centeno, M. A. (2002). *Blood and debt: War and nation-state in Latin America*. University Park, PA: The Pennsylvania State University Press.

Cezar, R., & Escobar, O. R. (2015). Institutional distance and foreign direct investment. *Review of World Economics, 151*(4), 713–733. https://doi.org/10.1007/s10290-015-0227-8

Ch'ien, C.-s. (1936). The control Yüan. In *The Chinese year book 1936–37*. Shanghai: Commercial Press.

Chaffin, J., & Elinson, Z. (2025, May 9). The ideological gurus battling for the soul of Trump world. *The Wall Street Journal*. Retrieved from https://www.wsj.com/politics/maga-idiology-curtis-yarvin-patrick-deneen-9f93d566

Chaffin, J., & Matthews, A. W. (2024, December 5). Murder at dawn: A top executive's final moments in Manhattan. *The Wall Street Journal*. Retrieved from https://www.wsj.com/us-news/united-healthcare-ceo-killed-what-happened-33cf8452

Chakrabarti, A. (2017). Free will and freedom in Indian philosophies. In K. Timpe, M. Griffith, & N. Levy (Eds.), *The Routledge companion to free will* (pp. 389–404). New York, NY: Routledge.

Chalmers, D. J. (2006). Strong and weak emergence. In P. Clayton & P. Davies (Eds.), *The re-emergence of emergence: The emergentist hypothesis from science to religion* (pp. 244–256). Oxford: Oxford University Press. https://doi.org/10.1093/acprof:oso/9780199544318.003.0011

Chalmers, D. J. (2016). The singularity: A philosophical analysis. In S. Schneider (Ed.), *Science fiction and philosophy* (pp. 171–224). Hoboken, NJ: Wiley & Sons. https://doi.org/10.1002/9781118922590.ch16

Chamberlin, E. H. (1949). *The theory of monopolistic competition: A re-orientation of the theory of value* (6th ed.). London: Geoffrey Cumberlege, Oxford University Press. Retrieved from http://digamoo.free.fr/chamberlin1933.pdf

Chamizo, H. (2021, October 22). En qué invierte Amancio Ortega su multimillonaria fortuna. *Forbes (Spain)*. Retrieved from https://forbes.es/empresas/121753/en-que-invierte-amancio-ortega/

Chan, H-H. (2023, June 16). AI-enabled teddies could tell children bedtime stories, says toymaker. *The Financial Times*. Retrieved from https://www.ft.com/content/acf0307c-ca6d-445d-889a-50cbe64d61e2

Chan, J., To, H. P., & Chan, E. (2006). Reconsidering social cohesion: Developing a definition and analytical framework for empirical research. *Social Indicators Research, 75*(2), 273–302. https://doi.org/10.1007/s11205-005-2118-1

Chan, S. P. (2023, September 3). How Emmanuel Macron became the most powerful leader in Europe. *Daily Telegraph*. Retrieved from https://www.telegraph.co.uk/business/2023/09/03/emmanuel-macron-most-powerful-leader-european-union

Chandler, A. D., Jr. (1977). *The visible hand: The managerial revolution in American business*. Boston, MA: Harvard University Press.

Chang, H.-J. (2002). *Kicking away the ladder: Development strategy in historical perspective*. London: Anthem Press.

Charles Schwab. (2024, September 6). With rate cuts ahead, stock buybacks may continue. *Charles Schwab*. Retrieved from https://www.schwab.com/learn/story/with-rate-cuts-ahead-stock-buybacks-may-continue

Chaudhuri, N. C. (1989). *The autobiography of an unknown Indian*. Reading, MA: Addison-Wesley Publishing Company, Inc.

Chavance, B. (2012). John Commons's organizational theory of institutions: A discussion. *Journal of Institutional Economics*, *8*(1), 27–47. https://doi.org/10.1017/S1744137411000336

Chazan, G., & Nilsson, P. (2022, 6 December). Germany confronts a broken business model. *The Financial Times*. Retrieved from https://www.ft.com/content/50a462b3-0e8b-49e1-873c-9505760d4a66

Che, Y., Du, J., Lu, Y., & Tao, Z. (2023). Institutional difference and foreign direct investment location choice: Evidence from China. *Review of Development Economics*, *27*(3), 1934–1956. https://doi.org/10.1111/rode.12988

Chen, C. C. (2014). Entrepreneurship, economic growth, and employment: A case study of Taiwan. *Hitotsubashi Journal of Economics*, *55*(1), 71–88. https://doi.org/10.15057/26817

Chen, J. (2023, May 19). What is a cartel? Definition, examples, and legality. *Investopedia*. Retrieved from https://www.investopedia.com/terms/c/cartel.asp

Chen, K., Lu, E., Scherl, F., & Sutter, C. (2025). chatbotEQx: A political economy AI service to provide descriptive, interpretative, and advisory information on elite quality. In *Elite quality report 2025: The sustainable value creation of nations* (pp. 12-16). London: Anthem Press.

Chen, S., Shi, S., Xi, X., Zhang, J., & Zhang, Y. (2023). *Repairing heaven's mandate: A noble-lie story?* Unpublished manuscript, School of Economics, Fudan University, China.

Chen, S. F. S. (2008). The motives for international acquisitions: Capability procurements, strategic considerations, and the role of ownership structures. *Journal of International Business Studies*, *39*(3), 454–471. https://doi.org/10.1057/palgrave.jibs.8400357

Cheng, H. W. J. (2020, May). *Economic properties of data and the monopolistic tendencies of data economy: Policies to limit an Orwellian possibility* (Working Papers 164, United Nations, Department of Economics and Social Affairs). Retrieved from https://www.un.org/esa/desa/papers/2020/wp164_2020.pdf

Chess.com (2019, April 17). AlphaZero crushes Stockfish in new 1,000 game match. *Chess.com*. Retrieved from https://www.chess.com/news/view/updated-alphazero-crushes-stockfish-in-new-1-000-game-match

Cheung, R. (2024, July 23). *Mark Zuckerberg on Llama 3.1, open source, AI agents, safety, and more* [Video]. YouTube. https://youtu.be/Vy3OkbtUa5k

Chima, G. (2022, July 25). *Money is the database for exchange of goods and services* [Video]. YouTube. https://www.youtube.com/watch?v=X2Drycc8w4I

Chisholm, A. R. (1935). Oswald Spengler and the decline of the West. *The Australian Quarterly*, *7*(27), 35–44. https://doi.org/10.2307/20629241

Cho, Y. (2014). To know democracy is to love it: A cross-national analysis of democratic understanding and political support for democracy. *Political Research Quarterly*, *67*(3), 478–488. https://doi.org/10.1177/1065912914532721

Choi, S. G., & Storr, V. H. (2019). A culture of rent seeking. *Public Choice*, *181*, 101–126. https://doi.org/10.1007/s11127-018-0557-x

Chomicki, G., Beinart, R., Prada, C., Ritchie, K. B., & Weber, M. G. (2022). Editorial: Symbiotic relationships as shapers of biodiversity. *Frontiers in Ecology and Evolution*, *10*, Article 850572. https://doi.org/10.3389/fevo.2022.850572

Christensen, C. M. (1997). *The innovator's dilemma: When new technologies cause great firms to fail.* Cambridge, MA: Harvard Business Press.

Chu, A. C., Cozzi, G., & Galli, S. (2012). Does intellectual monopoly stimulate or stifle innovation? *European Economic Review, 56*(4), 727–746. https://doi.org/10.1016/j.euroecorev.2012.01.007

Cicero, M. T. (1913). *De Officiis, Book II*. (W. Miller, Trans.). Cambridge, MA: Harvard University Press. Retrieved from http://www.perseus.tufts.edu/hopper/text?doc=Perseus%3Atext%3A2007.01.0048%3Abook%3D2

Cicero, M. T. (2017). *The Republic of Cicero* (G. W. Featherstonhaugh, Trans.). New York, NY: G. & C. Carvill. Retrieved from https://www.gutenberg.org/ebooks/54161

Cilliers, P. (1998). *Complexity and postmodernism: Understanding complex systems*. New York, NY: Routledge.

Clancy, E. A. (1998). The tragedy of the global commons. *Indiana Journal of Global Legal Studies, 5*(2), 601–619.

Clark, C. (2012). *The sleepwalkers: How Europe went to war in 1914.* London: Allen Lane.

Clark, G. (1951). The repeal of the Corn Laws and the politics of the forties. *The Economic History Review, 4*(1), 1–13. https://doi.org/10.1111/j.1468-0289.1951.tb00595.x

Clark, J. B. (1903). Monopoly and the struggles of classes. *Political Science Quarterly, 18*(4), 599–613.

Clark, J. B. (1908). *Distribution of wealth: A theory of wages, interest and profits*. New York, NY: The MacMillan Company. Retrieved from http://digamo.free.fr/clark99.pdf

Clark, J. B. (1916). The economic costs of war. *The American Economic Review, 6*(1), 85–93.

Clark, M. (2024, January 23). 'Sephora Kids' are TikTok's latest villains – but their parents aren't the only ones to blame. *The Independent*. Retrieved from https://www.independent.co.uk/life-style/sephora-kids-tiktok-tween-spaces-b2483644.html

Clark, S. J. (1998). A populist critique of direct democracy. *Harvard Law Review, 112*(2), 434–482.

Clarke, T. (2010). Recurring crises in Anglo-American corporate governance. *Contributions to Political Economy, 29*(1), 9–32. https://doi.org/10.1093/cpe/bzq002

Classen, A., & Settle, T. A. (1991). Women in Martin Luther's life and theology. *German Studies Review, 14*(2), 231–260.

Clastres, P. (1974). *La société contre l'etat*. Paris: Editions de Minuit.

Clerici, N., Armenteras, D., Kareiva, P., Botero, R., Ramírez-Delgado, J. P., Forero-Medina, G., Ochoa, J., Pedraza, C., Schneider, L., Lora, C., Gómez, C., Linares, M., Hirashiki, C., & Biggs, D. (2020). Deforestation in Colombian protected areas increased during post-conflict periods. *Scientific Reports, 10*, 4971. https://doi.org/10.1038/s41598-020-61861-y

Clifford, C. (2021, March 31). OpenAI's Sam Altman: Artificial intelligence can generate enough wealth to pay each adult $13,500 a year. *Basic Income Today*. Retrieved from https://basicincometoday.com/openais-sam-altman-artificial-intelligence-can-generate-enough-wealth-to-pay-each-adult-13500-a-year/

CNA. (2015, March 23). *"Whoever governs Singapore must have that iron in him": Lee Kuan Yew | From the archives* [Video]. YouTube. https://www.youtube.com/watch?v=kGDqLeRuyCA

Coase, R. H. (1937). The nature of the firm. *Economica, 4*(16), 386–405. https://doi.org/10.1111/j.1468-0335.1937.tb00002.x

Coase, R. H. (1960). The problem of social cost. *The Journal of Law & Economics, 3*, 1–44. https://doi.org/10.1086/466560

Coates, D., Heckelman, J. C., & Wilson, B. (2007). Determinants of interest group formation. *Public Choice, 133*(3/4), 377–391. https://doi.org/10.1007/s11127-007-9195-4

Coff, R. (1999). When competitive advantage doesn't lead to performance: The resource-based view and stakeholder bargaining power. *Organization Science, 10*(2), 119–133. https://doi.org/10.1287/orsc.10.2.119

Cohen, A., & Einav, L. (2003). The effects of mandatory seat belt laws on driving behavior and traffic fatalities. *The Review of Economics and Statistics, 85*(4), 828–843. https://doi.org/10.2139/ssrn.293582

Cohen, G. (1979). The labor theory of value and the concept of exploitation. *Philosophy & Public Affairs, 8*(4), 338–360.

Cohen, W. M., & Levinthal, D. A. (1989). Innovation and learning: The two faces of R&D. *The Economic Journal, 99*(397), 569–596. https://doi.org/10.2307/2233763

Cohn, N. (1970). *The pursuit of the millennium: Revolutionary millenarians and mystical anarchists of the Middle Ages*. New York, NY: Oxford University Press.

Cokelaere, H., & Brzeziński, B. (2024, January 31). Europe's farmer protests are spreading. Here's where and why. *Politico*. Retrieved from https://www.politico.eu/article/farmer-protest-europe-map-france-siege-paris-germany-poland/

Colbert, J.-B. (1863). *Lettres, instructions et mémoires de Colbert: Tome II, IIe partie. Industrie, commerce* [Letters, instructions and memoirs of Colbert: Volume II, Part 2. Industry, commerce] (P. Clément, Ed.). Paris: Imprimerie Impériale.

Coles, N. (2001). It's not what you know – it's who you know that counts: Analysing serious crime groups as social networks. *The British Journal of Criminology, 41*(4), 580–594. https://doi.org/10.1093/bjc/41.4.580

Collard, R. (2020, August 5). Beirut's deadly blast reignites anger against Lebanon's ruling elite. *Foreign Policy*. Retrieved from https://foreignpolicy.com/2020/08/05/beiruts-deadly-blast-reignites-anger-against-lebanons-ruling-elite/

Collier, P. (2015). Development economics in retrospect and prospect. *Oxford Review of Economic Policy 31*(2), 242–58. https://doi.org/10.1093/oxrep/grv013

Collier, R. B., & Collier, D. (1991). *Shaping the political arena: Critical junctures, the labor movement, and regime dynamics in Latin America*. Princeton, NJ: Princeton University Press.

Colton, E. (2024, November 13). 'First buddy': Elon earns family status in Trump world as Musk expands political footprint. *Fox News*. https://www.foxnews.com/politics/first-buddy-elon-earns-family-status-trump-world-musk-expands-political-footprint

Comes, R., & Sandler, T. (1996). *The theory of externalities, public goods, and club goods*. (2nd ed.). Cambridge: Cambridge University Press. https://doi.org/10.1017/CBO9781139174312

Commons, J. R. (1924). *Legal foundations of capitalism*. New York, NY: Macmillan.

Commons, J. R. (1950). *The economics of collective action*. New York, NY: Macmillan.

Connelly, B. L., Certo, S. T., Ireland, R. D., & Reutzel, C. R. (2011). Signaling theory: A review and assessment. *Journal of management, 37*(1), 39–67. https://doi.org/10.1177/0149206310388419

Conroy, G. (2024, September 20). Do AI models produce more original ideas than researchers? *Nature*. https://doi.org/10.1038/d41586-024-03070-5

Conti, N., Cotta, M., & Verzichelli, L. (2016). The economic crisis and its effects on the attitudes of Italian political elites towards the EU. *Historical Social Research, 41*(4), 129–149.

Contractor, F. J. (2007). Is international business good for companies? The evolutionary or multistage theory of internationalization vs. the transaction cost perspective. *MIR: Management International Review, 47*(3), 453–475. https://doi.org/10.1007/s11575-007-0024-2

Cook, C. (2014). Suicide and religion. *British Journal of Psychiatry, 204*(4), 254–255. https://doi.org/10.1192/bjp.bp.113.136069

Cook, C., Diamond, R., Hall, J. V., List, J. A., & Oyer, P. (2020). *The gender earnings gap in the gig economy: Evidence from over a million rideshare drivers* (NBER Working Paper 24732). Retrieved from https://web.stanford.edu/~diamondr/UberPayGap.pdf

Cooper, L., & Peterson, K. (2024, December 23). Coke, PepsiCo lobby to keep sugary sodas in food-stamp program. *The Wall Street Journal*. Retrieved from https://www.wsj.com/politics/policy/rfk-jr-soda-snap-food-stamps-coke-pepsi-9bd9a872

Copeland, M. A. (1951). Institutional economics and model analysis. *American Economic Review, 41*(05), 56–65.

Coppedge, M., Gerring, J., Altman, D., Bernhard, M., Fish, S., Hicken, A., Kroenig, M., Lindberg, S. I., McMann, K., Paxton, P., Semetko, H. A., Skaaning, S.-E., Staton, J., & Teorell, J. (2011). Conceptualizing and measuring democracy: A new approach. *Perspectives on Politics*, *9*(2), 247–267. https://doi.org/10.1017/S1537592711000880

Corcoran, J. (2024, September 24). Russia's violent 1990s re-erupted with Wildberries shootout. *The Moscow Times*. Retrieved from https://www.themoscowtimes.com/2024/09/24/russias-violent-1990s-re-erupted-with-wildberries-shootout-a86446

Corominas-Murtra, B., Goñi, J., Solé, R. V., & Rodríguez-Caso, C. (2013). On the origins of hierarchy in complex networks. *Proceedings of the National Academy of Sciences of the United States of America*, *110*(33), 13316–13321. https://doi.org/10.1073/pnas.1300832110

Costa Junior, C. J., & Garcia-Cintado, A. C. (2021). Rent-seeking in an emerging market: A DSGE approach. *Economic Systems*, *45*(2), 100775. https://doi.org/10.1016/j.ecosys.2020.100775

Cotterill, J. (2022, January 14). Bain & Co, tax and Jacob Zuma: a tale of 'state capture' in South Africa, *The Financial Times*. Retrieved from https://www.ft.com/content/b1bb5dd0-e7ce-4e15-ac48-05d2d990f6c7

Couldry, N., & Mejias, U. A. (2019). Data colonialism: Rethinking big data's relation to the contemporary subject. *Television & New Media*, *20*(4), 336–349. https://doi.org/10.1177/1527476418796632

Coulter, M., & Sandle, P. (2023, November 2). At UK's AI summit, developers and governments agree ontesting to help manage risks. *Reuters*. Retrieved from https://www.reuters.com/world/uk/uk-pmsunak-lead-ai-summit-talks-before-musk-meeting-2023-11-02/

Council of Europe. (2007, March 26-28). *The development of social cohesion indicators: The concerted local and regional approach*. Strasbourg, France: Standing Committee, Committee on Social Cohesion. Retrieved from https://rm.coe.int/16807199a0

Cousin, B., Khan, S. R., & Mears, A. (2018). Theoretical and methodological pathways for research on elites. *Socio-Economic Review*, *16*(2), 225–249. https://doi.org/10.1093/ser/mwy019

Cowen, T. (2011). *The great stagnation: How America ate all the low-hanging fruit of modern history, got sick, and will (eventually) feel better*. New York, NY: E. P. Dutton.

Cowen, T. (2023, February 14). AGI risk and Austrian subjectivism. *Marginal Revolution*. Retrieved from https://marginalrevolution.com/marginalrevolution/2023/02/agi-risk-and-austrian-subjectivism.html

Cowie, J. (2009). The British passenger rail privatisation: Conclusions on subsidy and efficiency from the first round of franchises. *Journal of Transport Economics and Policy*, *43*(1), 85–104.

Cox, R. W. (1983). Gramsci, hegemony and international relations: An essay in method, *Millennium: Journal of International Studies*, *12*(2), 162–75.

Coyne, C. J., Duncan, T. K., & Hall, A. R. (2021). The political economy of state responses to infectious disease. *Southern Economic Journal*, *87*(4), 1119–1137. https://doi.org/10.1002/soej.12490

Cozzi, G. & Galli, S. (2014). Sequential R&D and blocking patents in the dynamics of growth. *Journal of Economic Growth*, *19*(2), 183–219. https://doi.org/10.1007/s10887-013-9101-5

Cozzi, G., & Privileggi, F. (2009). *The fractal nature of inequality in a fast growing world: New version* (Working Papers 2009_30, Business School – Economics, University of Glasgow). Retrieved from https://www.gla.ac.uk/media/Media_126649_smxx.pdf

Crane, D. A. (2008). Technocracy and antitrust. *Texas Law Review*, *86*(6), 1159–1222.

Crotty, M. (2003). *The foundations of social research: Meaning and perspectives in the research process*. London: Sage. https://doi.org/10.4324/9781003115700

Crouzet, F. (1999). Business dynasties in Britain and France. In E. S. Brezis & P. Temin (Eds.), *Elites, minorities, and economic growth* (pp. 41–54). Amsterdam: Elsevier.

Cuervo-Cazurra, A. (2006). Who cares about corruption? *Journal of International Business Studies*, *37*(6), 807–822. https://doi.org/10.1057/palgrave.jibs.8400223

Cuervo-Cazurra, A., & Dau, L. A. (2009). Structural reform and firm exports. *MIR: Management International Review*, *49*(4), 479–507. https://doi.org/10.1007/s11575-009-0005-8

Cunningham, G. W. (1919). On Nietzsche's doctrine of the will to power. *The Philosophical Review, 28*(5), 479–490. https://doi.org/10.2307/2178323

Custer, S., Dreher, A., Elston, T. B., Fuchs, A., Ghose, S., Lin, J., Malik, A., Parks, B. C., Russell, B., Solomon, K., Strange, A., Tierney, M. J., Walsh, K., Zaleski, L., and Zhang, S. (2021). *Tracking Chinese development finance: An application of AidData's TUFF 2.0 methodology*. Williamsburg, VA: AidData at William & Mary.

Cuzzolin, F., Morelli, A., Cîrstea, B., & Sahakian, B. (2020). Knowing me, knowing you: Theory of mind in AI. *Psychological Medicine, 50*(7), 1057–1061. https://doi.org/10.1017/S0033291720000835

Cyert, R. & March, J. (1963). *A behavioral theory of the firm*. Englewood Cliffs, NJ: Prentice-Hall.

Dahl, R. (2005). *Who governs? Democracy and power in an American city* (2nd ed.). New Haven, CT: Yale University Press.

Dahlberg, S. (2007, November). *Web-based expert surveys* (QoG Working Paper Series 2007:7). Retrieved from https://gupea.ub.gu.se/bitstream/handle/2077/39167/gupea_2077_39167_1.pdf?sequence=1&isAllowed=y

Dalhuisen, J. (2021, August 30). Letter: Cryptocurrencies may be better stores of value. *The Financial Times*. Retrieved from https://www.ft.com/content/bb0a7209-565b-446b-b0be-6f868a321578

Dalio, R. (2021). *Principles for dealing with the changing world order: Why nations succeed and fail*. New York, NY: Simon & Schuster.

Daloz, J. P. (2010). Introduction. In J. P. Daloz, *The sociology of elite distinction* (pp. 1–4). London: Palgrave Macmillan. https://doi.org/10.1057/9780230246836_1

Dalrymple, W. (2020). *The anarchy: The relentless rise of the East India Company*. London: Bloomsbury Publishing.

Damodaran, A. (2005). Value and risk: Beyond betas. *Financial Analysts Journal, 61*(2), 38–43.

Damodaran, A. (2012). *Investment valuation: Tools and techniques for determining the value of any asset*. Hoboken, NJ: John Wiley & Sons, Inc.

Damodaran, A. (2017). *Narrative and numbers: The value of stories in business*. New York, NY: Columbia University Press. https://doi.org/10.7312/damo18048

Damodaran, A. (2023). Country risk: Determinants, measures and implications – The 2023 edition. *SSRN Journal*. https://doi.org/10.2139/ssrn.4509578.

Danninger, S. (2002, January). *A new rule: The Swiss debt brake* (IMF Working Paper No. WP/02/18). Washington, DC: International Monetary Fund. Retrieved from https://www.imf.org/en/Publications/WP/Issues/2016/12/30/A-New-Rule-The-Swiss-Debt-Brake-15577

Dartnell, L. (2023). *Being human: How our biology shaped world history*. London: The Bodley Head.

Dasgupta, P. (2007). Commentary: The Stern Review's economics of climate change. *National Institute Economic Review, 199*(1), 4–7. https://doi.org/10.1177/0027950107077111

Dau, L. A., Moore, E. M., & Newburry, W. (2020). The grass is always greener: The impact of home and host country CSR reputation signaling on cross-country investments. *Journal of International Business Policy 3*, 154–182. https://doi.org/10.1057/s42214-020-00049-7

David, P. A. (1985). Clio and the economics of QWERTY. *The American Economic Review, 75*(2), 332–337.

Davies, J. C. (1962). Toward a theory of revolution. *American Sociological Review, 27*(1), 5–19.

Davis, E., & Kay, J. (1990). Assessing corporate performance. *Business Strategy Review 1*(2), 1–16. https://doi.org/10.1111/j.1467-8616.1990.tb00007.x

Davis, S., Haltiwanger, J., & Schuh, S. (1996). *Job creation and destruction*. Cambridge, MA: MIT Press.

Dawkins, R. (1976). *The selfish gene*. New York, NY: Oxford University Press.

de Bary, W. T., & Lufrano, R. eds. (2000). *Sources of Chinese Tradition* (Vol. II: From 1600 through the Twentieth Century). New York, NY: Columbia University Press.

De Cillis, M. (2014). *Free will and predestination in Islamic thought: Theoretical compromises in the works of Avicenna, Ghāzālī and Ibn 'Arabī*. New York, NY: Routledge.

De Cristofaro, T., & Gulluscio, C. (2023). In search of double materiality in non-financial reports: First empirical evidence. *Sustainability, 15*(2), 924. https://doi.org/10.3390/su15020924

de Figueiredo, J. M., & Richter, B. K. (2014). Advancing the empirical research on lobbying. *Annual Review of Political Science*, *17*, 163–185. https://doi.org/10.1146/annurev-polisci-100711-135308

de las Casas, B. (1821). *Breve relación de la destrucción de las Indias Occidentales*. Philadelphia, PA: Juan F. Hurtel.

de Mendoza, A. (1965). Informe de Antonio de Mendoza a Luis de Velasco. In M. Fernandez de Navarrete (Ed.), *Colección de documentos ineditos para la historia de España* (Vol. 26). (Original work published 1842-1895; Reprint, 1965). Vaduz, Liechtenstein: Kraus.

de Soto, H. (1989). *The other path: The invisible revolution in the Third World*. London: I.B. Tauris & Co. Ltd.

de Tocqueville, A. (2010). *Democracy in America: Historical-critical edition of de la démocratie en Amérique* (Vol. 4, E. Nolla, Ed.; J. T. Schleifer, Trans.). Indianapolis, IN: Liberty Fund. Retrieved from https://oll.libertyfund.org/titles/schleifer-democracy-in-america-historical-critical-edition-vol-4

de Waal, F. B. M. (2006). *Primates and philosophers: How morality evolved*. Princeton, NJ: Princeton University Press.

Deakin, S., & Konzelmann, S. J. (2003). After Enron: An age of enlightenment? *Organization*, *10*(3), 583–587.

Dean, G. (2023, May 24). Elon Musk says that prior to its mass layoffs, Twitter had a 'lot of people doing things that didn't seem to have a lot of value'. *Business Insider*. Retrieved from https://www.businessinsider.com/elon-musk-laid-off-twitter-workers-value-tech-jobs-work-2023-5

Decherney, P. (2005). *Hollywood and the culture elite: How the movies became American*. New York, NY: Columbia University Press.

DeepSeek. (2020, January 25). DeepSeek-R1 Release. *DeepSeek*. Retrieved from https://api-docs.deepseek.com/news/news250120

DeJong, D. (2022). *Nazi billionaires: The dark history of Germany's wealthiest dynasties*. Boston, MA: Mariner Books.

DelSignore, P. (2023, February 9). Why 'responsible AI' is big tech's new phrase. *Geek Culture*. Retrieved from https://medium.com/geekculture/why-responsible-ai-is-big-tech-s-new-phrase-7515cf726272

Dencker, J., & Fang, C. (2016). Rent seeking and the transformation of employment relationships: The effect of corporate restructuring on wage patterns, determinants, and inequality. *American Sociological Review*, *81*(3), 467–487. https://doi.org/10.1177/0003122416642419

Deneen, P. J. (2018). *Why liberalism failed*. New Haven, CT: Yale University Press.

Denevan, W. M. (1992). The pristine myth: the landscape of the Americas in 1492. *Annals of the Association of American Geographers*, *82*(3), 369–385. https://doi.org/10.1111/j.1467-8306.1992.tb01965.x

Denning, S. (2006). Effective storytelling: Strategic business narrative techniques. *Strategy & Leadership*, *34* (1), 42–48. https://doi.org/10.1108/10878570610637885

Denord, F., Palme, M., & Réau, B. (2020). Introduction. In F. Denord, M. Palme & B. Réau (Eds.), *Researching elites and power* (pp. 1–14). Cham, Switzerland: Springer. https://doi.org/10.1007/978-3-030-45175-2_1

Dente, L. A. (1977). *Veblen's theory of social change*. New York, NY: Arno Press.

Denzin, N. K. (1978). *The research act: A theoretical introduction to sociological methods*. New York, NY: McGraw-Hill.

Der Spiegel. (2005, March 31). European court rejects land claims in former East Germany. *Der Spiegel*. Retrieved from https://www.spiegel.de/international/german-papers-european-court-rejects-land-claims-in-former-east-germany-a-349035.html

Dercon, S. (2022). *Gambling on development: Why some countries win and others lose*. London: Hurst and Company.

Dereń, K., Weghuber, D., Caroli, M., Koletzko, B., Thivel, D., Frelut, M-L., Socha, P., Grossman, Z., Hadjipanayis, A., Wyszyńska, J., & Mazur, A. (2019). Consumption of sugar-sweetened beverages in paediatric age: A position paper of the European Academy of Paediatrics and the European Childhood Obesity Group. *Annals of Nutrition & Metabolism*, *74*(4), 296–302. https://doi.org/10.1159/000499828

Derfus, P. J., Maggitti, P. G., Grimm, C. M., & Smith, K. G. (2008). The Red Queen effect: Competitive actions and firm performance. *The Academy of Management Journal, 51*(1), 61–80. https://doi.org/10.5465/AMJ.2008.30708624

Deutsch, D. (2011). *The beginning of infinity: Explanations that transform the world.* New York, NY: Viking Press.

Dewar, R. D., & Dutton, J. E. (1986). The adoption of radical and incremental innovations: An empirical analysis. *Management Science, 32*(11), 1422–1433. https://doi.org/10.1287/mnsc.32.11.1422

Di Gregorio, D. (2013). Value creation and value appropriation: An integrative, multi-level framework. *Journal of Applied Business and Economics, 15*(1), 39–53.

Diamond, J. M. (1999). *Guns, germs, and steel: The fates of human societies.* New York, NY: W.W. Norton & Company.

Diamond, L. (2011). The impact of the economic crisis: Why democracies survive. *Journal of Democracy, 22*(1), 17–30. Retrieved from https://muse.jhu.edu/article/412890

Dick, H., & Mulholland, J. (2010). The state as marketplace: Slush funds and intra-elite rivalry. In E. Aspinall & G. van Klinken (Eds.), *The state and illegality in Indonesia* (pp. 65–85). Leiden: KITLV Press. https://doi.org/10.1163/9789004253681_005

Dick, S. (2008). The postbiological universe. *Acta Astronautica, 62*(8–9), 499–504. https://doi.org/10.1016/j.actaastro.2008.01.025

Dickerman, E. H. (1977). The conversion of Henry IV: "Paris is well worth a mass". *The Catholic Historical Review, 63*(1), 1–13.

Diebold, C. (2022). How meaningful is the elite quality index ranking? *Social Indicators Research, 163*, 137–170. https://doi.org/10.1007/s11205-021-02841-1

Diefenbach, T. (2019). Why Michels' 'iron law of oligarchy' is not an iron law – and how democratic organisations can stay 'oligarchy-free.' *Organization Studies, 40*(4), 545–562. https://doi.org/10.1177/0170840617751007

Dierzé, B., & Olivares, C. (2024, February). Recent changes to California's anti non-competition laws take effect. *Locke Lord.* Retrieved from https://www.lockelord.com/newsandevents/publications/2024/02/changes-california-anti-non-competition-laws

DiMaggio, P. J. (1988). Interest and agency in institutional theory. In L. G. Zucker (Ed.), *Institutional patterns and organizations: Culture and environment* (pp. 3–22). Cambridge, MA: Ballinger.

DiMaggio, P. J. (1991). Constructing an organizational field as a professional project: U.S. art museums, 1920-1940. In W.W. Powell & P. J DiMaggio. *The new institutionalism in organizational analysis* (pp. 267–292). Chicago, IL: The University of Chicago Press.

DiMaggio, P. J., & Powell, W. W. (1983). The iron cage revisited: Institutional isomorphism and collective rationality in organizational fields. *American Sociological Review, 48*(2), 147–160.

DiMaggio, P. J., & Powell, W. W. (1991). Introduction. In W. W. Powell & P. J. DiMaggio (Eds.), *The new institutionalism in organizational analysis.* (pp. 267–292). Chicago, IL: University of Chicago Press.

Dincecco, D., & Katz, G. (2014). State capacity and long-run economic performance. *The Economic Journal, 126*(590), 189–218. https://doi.org/10.1111/ecoj.12161

Ding, I., & Thompson-Brusstar, M. (2021). The anti-bureaucratic ghost in China's bureaucratic machine. *The China Quarterly, 248*(S1), 116–140. https://doi.org/10.1017/S0305741021000977

Dirzo, R., Young, H. S., Galetti, M., Ceballos, G., Isaac, N. J., & Collen, B. (2014). Defaunation in the Anthropocene. *Science, 345*(6195), 401–406. https://doi.org/10.1126/science.1251817

Dixit, A., & Londregan, J. (1995). Redistributive politics and economic efficiency. *The American Political Science Review, 89*(4), 856–866. https://doi.org/10.2307/2082513

Dixit, A., & Londregan, J. (1998). Ideology, tactics, and efficiency in redistributive politics. *The Quarterly Journal of Economics, 113*(2), 497–529. https://doi.org/10.1162/003355398555667

Dixon, J., & Joyner, M. (2000). Privatization of British Rail: The holy grail or a poisoned chalice? *Administrative Theory & Praxis, 22*(3), 630–634.

Djankov, S., McLiesh, C., & Ramalho, R. (2006). Regulation and growth. *Economics Letters, 92*(3), 395–401. https://doi.org/10.2139/ssrn.893321

Djilas, M. (1957). *The new class: An analysis of the communist system*. New York, NY: Frederick A. Praeger.

Doctorow, C. (2022, September 15). California's antitrust case against Amazon. *Pluralistic*. Retrieved from https://pluralistic.net/2022/09/15/prime-suspect/#consumer-welfare

Doctorow, C. (2024a, February 8). 'Enshittification' is coming for absolutely everything. *The Financial Times*. Retrieved from https://www.ft.com/content/6fb1602d-a08b-4a8c-bac0-047b7d64aba5

Doctorow, C. (2024b, March 28). The credit card fee victory is a defeat: Small cartels beat large industries every time. *Pluralistic*. Retrieved from https://pluralistic.net/2024/03/28/concentrated-benefits/#diffuse-harms

Dolson, G. N. (1901). The influence of Schopenhauer upon Friedrich Nietzsche. *The Philosophical Review, 10*(3), 241–250. https://doi.org/10.2307/2176260

Dombrowski, D. (1997). Plato's "noble" lie. *History of Political Thought, 18*(4), 565–578.

Domhoff, G. W. (1967). *Who rules America?* Englewood Cliffs, NJ: Prentice-Hall.

Domhoff, G. W. (1970). *The higher circles*. New York, NY: Random House.

Dominitz, J., & Manski, C. F. (1997). Perceptions of economic insecurity: Evidence from the survey of economic expectations. *The Public Opinion Quarterly, 61*(2), 261–287.

Donaldson, T. (2021). How values ground value creation: The practical inference framework. *Organization Theory, 2*(4), 1–27. https://doi.org/10.1177/26317877211036712

Donaldson, T., & Dunfee, T. W. (1994). Toward a unified conception of business ethics: Integrative social contracts theory. *The Academy of Management Review, 19*(2), 252–284. https://doi.org/10.2307/258705

Donaldson, T., & Preston, L. E. (1995). The stakeholder theory of the corporation: Concepts, evidence, and implications. *The Academy of Management Review, 20*(1), 65–91. https://doi.org/10.2307/258887

Donaldson, T., & Walsh, J. (2015). Toward a theory of business. *Research in Organizational Behavior, 35*(1), 181–207. https://doi.org/10.1016/j.riob.2015.10.002

Dopfer, K. (2012). The origins of meso economics. *Journal of Evolutionary Economics, 22*(1), 133–160. https://doi.org/10.1007/s00191-011-0218-4

Dopfer, K., Foster, J., & Potts, J. (2004). Micro-meso-macro. *Journal of Evolutionary Economics 14*(3), 263–79. https://doi.org/10.1007/s00191-004-0193-0

Doran, C. F (1991). *Systems in crisis: New imperatives of high politics at century's end*. Cambridge: Cambridge University Press. https://doi.org/10.1017/CBO9780511521690

Dos Santos, T. (1970). The structure of dependence. *The American Economic Review, 60*(2), 231–236.

Dostoyevsky, F. (1917). *Crime and punishment* (C. Garnett, Trans.). New York, NY: The Macmillan Company.

Douglas, J. (2021, January 14). Free (Steamboat) Willie: How Walt Disney's original mouse could be entering the public domain. *Flatland*. Retrieved from https://flatlandkc.org/arts-culture/free-steamboat-willie-how-walt-disneys-original-mouse-could-be-entering-the-public-domain/

Douglas, P. H. (1927). Smith's theory of value and distribution. *The University Journal of Business, 5*(1), 53–87.

Downs, A. (1957). *An economic theory of democracy*. New York, NY: Harper & Row.

Draghi, M. (2024, September). *The future of European competitiveness: In-depth analysis and recommendations*. Brussels: European Commission. Retrieved from https://commission.europa.eu/document/download/ec1409c1-d4b4-4882-8bdd-3519f86bbb92_en?filename=The%20future%20of%20European%20competitiveness_%20In-depth%20analysis%20and%20recommendations_0.pdf.

Draghi, M. (2025, February 14). Forget the US — Europe has successfully put tariffs on itself. *The Financial Times*. Retrieved from https://www.ft.com/content/13a830ce-071a-477f-864c-e499ce9e6065

Drazen, A. (2000). *Political economy in macroeconomics*. Princeton, NJ: Princeton University Press.

Dreher, A., Fuchs, A., Hodler, R., Parks, B. C., Raschky, P. A., & Tierney, M. J. (2019, July). *Is favoritism a threat to Chinese aid effectiveness? A subnational analysis of Chinese development projects* (Kiel Working Paper, No. 2134). Kiel Institute for the World Economy (IfW). Retrieved from https://www.econstor.eu/bitstream/10419/200199/1/1668910764.pdf

Dreher, A., Fuchs, A., Parks, B. C., Strange, A., & Tierney, M. J. (2022). *Banking on Beijing: The aims and impacts of China's overseas development program*. Cambridge: Cambridge University Press. https://doi.org/10.1017/9781108564496

Dreyfus H. L., & Dreyfus S. E. (1986). *Mind over machine: The power of human intuition and expertise in the era of the computer*. New York, NY: Free Press.

Drucker, P. F. (1994). The theory of the business. *Harvard Business Review*, *72*(5), 95–104. Retrieved from https://hbr.org/1994/09/the-theory-of-the-business

Dugin, A. (2014). *Eurasian mission: An introduction to neo-eurasianism*. London: Arktos.

Duncan, G. (2014). Drug trafficking and political power: Oligopolies of coercion in Colombia and Mexico. *Latin American Perspectives*, *41*(2), 18–42. https://doi.org/10.1177/0094582X13509071

Dung, L. (2023). How to deal with risks of AI suffering. *Inquiry: An International Journal of Philosophy*, Published online: July 22, 2023. https://doi.org/10.1080/0020174X.2023.2238287

Dunning, J. H. (1998). Location and the multinational enterprise: A neglected factor? *Journal of International Business Studies*, *29*(1), 45–66. https://doi.org/10.1057/palgrave.jibs.8490024

Dunphey, K. (2019, February 2). 10 facts about life expectancy in Libya. *The Borgen Project*. Retrieved from https://borgenproject.org/10-facts-about-life-expectancy-in-libya/

Duranton, G., & Kerr, W. R. (2015, July). *The logic of agglomeration* (Harvard Business School, Working Paper 16-037). https://doi.org/10.2139/ssrn.2667568

Durlauf, S. N., Johnson, P. A., & Temple, J. R. (2005). Growth econometrics. In P. Aghion and S. Durlauf (Eds.), *Handbook of economic growth*, Vol 1 (pp. 555–677). Amsterdam, The Netherlands: Elsevier. https://doi.org/10.1016/S1574-0684(05)01008-7

Dylick, T., & Muff, K. (2015). Clarifying the meaning of sustainable business: Introducing a typology from business-as-usual to true business sustainability. *Organization & Environment*, *28*(1), 1–19. https://doi.org/10.1177/1086026615575176

Eapen, T. T., Finkenstadt, D. J., Folk, J., & Venkataswamy, L. (2023, July-August). How generative AI can augment human creativity. *Harvard Business Review*. Retrieved from https://hbr.org/2023/07/how-generative-ai-can-augment-human-creativity

Easterly, W. (2011, May). *Benevolent autocrats* (DRI Working Paper No. 2011/75). Retrieved from https://wp.nyu.edu/dri/2011/05/31/publications-benevolent-autocrats/

Easterly, W., & Levine, R. (2003). Tropics, germs, and crops: How endowments influence economic development. *Journal of Monetary Economics 50*(1), 3–40. https://doi.org/10.1016/S0304-3932(02)00200-3

Easterly, W., & Pennings, S. (2020, April). *Leader value added: Assessing the growth contribution of individual national leaders* (Policy Research Working Paper; No. 9215. World Bank). Retrieved from https://openknowledge.worldbank.org/bitstream/handle/10986/33609/Leader-Value-Added-Assessing-the-Growth-Contribution-of-Individual-National-Leaders.pdf?sequence=6&isAllowed=y

Eccles, R. G. (2024). Moving beyond ESG: The framework has its detractors. Here's a new playbook for responsible business. *Harvard Business Review*, September–October. Retrieved from https://hbr.org/2024/09/moving-beyond-esg

Eccles, R. G., Krzus, M. P., Rogers, J., & Serafeim, G. (2012). The need for sector-specific materiality and sustainability reporting standards. *Journal of Applied Corporate Finance*, *24*(2), 65–71. https://doi.org/10.1111/j.1745-6622.2012.00380.x

Eccles, R. G., & Spiesshofer, B. (2015). *Integrated reporting for a re-imagined capitalism* (Working Paper No. 16-032). Harvard Business School. Retrieved from https://www.hbs.edu/ris/Publication%20Files/16-032_3860cfaa-ebd3-4d7e-ac9a-53272ca8cc2d.pdf

Eccles, R. G., & Stroehle, J. (2018). Exploring social origins in the construction of ESG measures. *SSRN Electronic Journal*. https://doi.org/10.2139/ssrn.3212685

Economic Policy Institute. (2024, August). The productivity–pay gap. *Economic Policy Institute*. Retrieved from https://www.epi.org/productivity-pay-gap/

Edgecliffe-Johnson, A. (2021, February 4). McKinsey to pay almost $574m to settle opioid claims by US states. *The Financial Times*. Retrieved from https://www.ft.com/content/85e84e12-6dda-4c91-bde4-8198e29a6767

Edmans, A. (2020). *Grow the pie: How great companies deliver both purpose and profit*. Cambridge: Cambridge University Press.

Edmans, A. (2023). Applying economics – not gut feel – to ESG. *Financial Analysts Journal*, *79*(4), 16–29. https://doi.org/10.1080/0015198X.2023.2242758

Edmans, A. (2024). Rational sustainability. *Journal of Applied Corporate Finance*, *36*(2), 8–15. https://doi.org/10.1111/jacf.12609

Eetls, R., & Walton, C. (1961). *Conceptual foundations of business*. Homewood, IL: Richard D. Irwin.

EFRAG (May 2024). *EFRAG IG 1: Materiality assessment implementation guidance*. Retrieved from https://www.efrag.org/sites/default/files/sites/webpublishing/SiteAssets/IG%201%20Materiality%20Assessment_final.pdf

Efstathiou, J., Jr. (2012, January 28). Buffett's railroad among winners from Keystone denial. *Lincoln Journal Star*. Retrieved from https://journalstar.com/business/local/buffetts-railroad-among-winners-from-keystone-denial/article_e88594a9-cb14-5235-982f-d66c76cf31e5.html

Eichengreen, B. (2015). Secular stagnation: The long view. *The American Economic Review*, *105*(5), 66–70. https://doi.org/10.1257/aer.p20151104

Eisenhower, D. D. (1961, January 17). *Farewell address* [Audio recording]. Miller Center, University of Virginia. Retrieved from https://millercenter.org/the-presidency/presidential-speeches/january-17-1961-farewell-address

Eisikovits, N. (2023, March 19). Chatbots aren't becoming sentient, yet we continue to anthropomorphize AI. *Fast Company*. Retrieved from https://www.fastcompany.com/90867578/chatbots-arent-becoming-sentient-yet-we-continue-to-anthropomorphize-ai

El Mundo. (2013, August 23). Funteovejuna' sobrevive a la SGAE. *El Mundo*. Retrieved from https://www.elmundo.es/elmundo/2013/08/22/andalucia/1377191388.html

Elkington, J. (1997). *Cannibals with forks: The triple bottom line of 21*st *Century business*. Oxford: Capstone.

Elliott, J. (1978). Institutionalism as an approach to political economy. *Journal of Economic Issues*, *12*(1), 91–114. https://doi.org/10.1080/00213624.1978.11503506

Eloundou, T., Manning, S., Mishkin, P., & Rock, D. (2023. March 23). GPTs are GPTs: An early look at the labor market impact potential of large language models. *Arxiv.org*. Retrieved from https://arxiv.org/abs/2303.10130v4

Emerson, R. W. (2005). *Essays* (E. H. L. Turpin, Ed.). Project Gutenberg. Retrieved from https://www.gutenberg.org/ebooks/16643

Engler, A. (2023, April 25). The EU and U.S diverge on AI regulation: A transatlantic comparison and steps to alignment. *Brookings*. Retrieved from https://www.brookings.edu/research/the-eu-and-us-diverge-on-ai-regulation-a-transatlantic-comparison-and-steps-to-alignment/

Engler, S., Leemann, L., Abou-Chadi, T., Giebler, H., Bousbah, K., Bochsler, D., Bühlmann, M., Hänni, M., Heyne, L., Juon, A., Merkel, W., Müller, L., Ruth, S., & Wessels, B. (2020). *Democracy barometer. Codebook. Version 7*. Retrieved from Aarau: Zentrum der Demokratie. https://democracybarometer.org/data-and-documentation/

Epstein, J. M, & Axtell, R. L. (1996). *Growing artificial societies: Social science from the bottom up*. Cambridge, MA: MIT Press.

Ermolaev, S. (2017, March 29). The formation and evolution of the Soviet Union's oil and gas dependence. *Carnegie Endowment for International Peace*. Retrieved from https://carnegieendowment.org/2017/03/29/formation-and-evolution-of-soviet-union-s-oil-and-gas-dependence-pub-68443

Espinoza, J. (2020, December 15). EU warns that it may break up Big Tech companies. *The Financial Times*. Retrieved from https://www.ft.com/content/15bf2e24-284f-4819-89ff-2520676e29ed

Espinoza, J. (2024a, February 22). Booking faces almost €500mn fine in Spain over competition practices. *The Financial Times*. Retrieved from https://www.ft.com/content/03e5eb20-ec91-485e-b0e4-ed49b4dc2848

Espinoza, J. (2024b, July 11). EU and Apple settle long-running 'tap-and-go' antitrust probe. *The Financial Times*. Retrieved from https://www.ft.com/content/822909a6-5de7-4943-86b7-a7450368865d

Euler, D. (2013). *Germany's dual vocational training system: A model for other countries?* Gütersloh, Germany: Bertelsmann Stiftung. Retrieved from https://eunec.eu/sites/www.eunec.eu/files/attachment/files/2013_study_german_vet_system.pdf

European Commission. (2016, August 30). State aid: Ireland gave illegal tax benefits to Apple worth up to €13 billion. *European Commission*. Retrieved from https://ec.europa.eu/commission/presscorner/detail/en/IP_16_2923

European Commission. (2018, March 9). Artificial intelligence: Commission kicks off work on marrying cutting-edge technology and ethical standards. *Directorate-General for Internal Market, Industry, Entrepreneurship and SMEs*. Retrieved from https://single-market-economy.ec.europa.eu/news/artificial-intelligence-commission-kicks-work-marrying-cutting-edge-technology-and-ethical-standards-2018-03-09_en

European Commission. (2021, April 21). *Proposal for a regulation of the European Parliament and of the Council laying down harmonized rules on artificial intelligence (Artificial Intelligence Act) and amending certain Union legislative acts* (COM (2021) 206 final). Retrieved from https://artificialintelligenceact.eu/wp-content/uploads/2021/08/The-AI-Act.pdf

European Commission. (2019). *Regulation (EU) 2019/2088 of the European Parliament and of the Council of 27 November 2019 on sustainability-related disclosure in the financial services sector*. Retrieved from https://eur-lex.europa.eu/legal-content/EN/TXT/?uri=CELEX%3A32019R2088

European Commission. (2023). *Annex I: European Sustainability Reporting Standards (ESRS). Supplementing Directive 2013/34/EU of the European Parliament and of the Council as regards sustainability reporting standards* (C(2023) 5303 final). Brussels: European Commission. Retrieved from https://www.efrag.org/sites/default/files/sites/webpublishing/SiteAssets/ESRS%201%20Delegated-act-2023-5303-annex-1_en.pdf

European Commission for the Efficiency of Justice (CEPEJ). (2019, February). *European ethical charter on the use of artificial intelligence in judicial systems and their environment* (Adopted at the 31st plenary meeting of the CEPEJ, 3-4 December 2018). Strasbourg, France: Council of Europe. Retrieved from https://rm.coe.int/ethical-charter-en-for-publication-4-december-2018/16808f699c

European Parliament. (2023, December 6). *Artificial Intelligence Act: Deal on comprehensive rules for trustworthy AI*. Retrieved from https://www.europarl.europa.eu/news/en/press-room/20231206IPR15699/artificial-intelligence-act-deal-on-comprehensive-rules-for-trustworthy-ai

European People's Party. (2021, November 24). *Matthias Erzberger (1875–1921): Patriot and visionary* [Transcript of speeches]. Retrieved from https://www.eppgroup.eu/newsroom/the-forgotten-hero-matthias-erzberger-commemorating-his-lasting-contribution-to-democracy

Evans, M. (2022, June 11). The billionaire funding a battle against hospital monopolies. *The Wall Street Journal*. Retrieved from https://www.wsj.com/articles/the-billionaire-funding-a-battle-against-hospital-monopolies-11654920006

Evans, P. B. (1989). Predatory, developmental, and other apparatuses: A comparative political economy perspective on the Third World state. *Sociological Forum*, *4*(4), 561–587. https://doi.org/10.1007/BF01115064

Evans, P. B. (1995). *Embedded autonomy: States and industrial transformation*. Princeton, NJ: Princeton University Press.

Evans, P. B, & Rauch, J. E. (1999). Bureaucracy and growth: A cross-national analysis of the effects of "Weberian" state structures on economic growth. *American Sociological Review*, *64*(5), 748–765.

Evenett, S. J., & Fritz, J. (2021, October 26). *Subsidies and market access: Towards an inventory of corporate subsidies by China, the European Union and the United States. The 28th global trade alert report.* London, UK: CEPR Press. Retrieved from https://www.globaltradealert.org/reports/gta-28-report

Evers-Hillstrom, K. (2020, April 24). Coronavirus stimulus spurs near-record first-quarter lobbying spending. *Open Secrets*. Retrieved from https://www.opensecrets.org/news/2020/04/coronavirus-stimulus-spurs-lobbying/

Faber, T. (2025, April 2). How Minecraft conquered the world. *The Financial Times*. Retrieved from https://www.ft.com/content/bbeaa6f0-52ca-404a-8915-43a69f957da0

Fair, R. (2018). *Macroeconometric modeling: 2018*. Retrieved from https://fairmodel.econ.yale.edu/mmm2/mm2018.pdf

Fairbank, J. K. (1978). The creation of the treaty system. In J. K. Fairbank (Ed.), *The Cambridge history of China* (pp. 213–263). Cambridge: Cambridge University Press. https://doi.org/10.1017/CHOL9780521214476.006

Fairlie, J. A. (1923). The separation of powers. *Michigan Law Review*, *21*(4), 393–436. https://doi.org/10.2307/1277683

Faksova, K., Walsh, D., Jiang, Y., Griffin, J., Phillips, A., Gentile, A., Kwong, J. C., Macartney, K., Naus, M., Grange, Z., Escolano, S., Sepulveda, G., Shetty, A., Pillsbury, A., Sullivan, C., Naveed, Z., Janjua, N. Z., Giglio, N., Perälä, J., . . . Hviid, A. (2024). COVID-19 vaccines and adverse events of special interest: A multinational Global Vaccine Data Network (GVDN) cohort study of 99 million vaccinated individuals. *Vaccine*, *42*(9), 2200–2211. https://doi.org/10.1016/j.vaccine.2024.01.100

Fama, E. F., & French, K. R. (2015). A five-factor asset pricing model. *Journal of Financial Economics*, *116*(1), 1–22. https://doi.org/10.1016/j.jfineco.2014.10.010

Fama, E. F., & MacBeth, J. D. (1973). Risk, return, and equilibrium: Empirical tests. *Journal of Political Economy*, *81*(3), 607–636. https://doi.org/10.1086/260061

Farrell, H., & Newman, A. (2023). *Underground empire: How America weaponized the world economy.* New York, NY: Henry Holt and Co.

Faundez, J. (2016). Douglass North's theory of institutions: Lessons for law and development. *Hague Journal on the Rule of Law*, *8*(3), 373–419. https://doi.org/10.1007/s40803-016-0028-8

Fazekas, M., & Tóth, I. J. (2016). From corruption to state capture: A new analytical framework with empirical applications from Hungary. *Political Research Quarterly*, *69*(2), 320–334. https://doi.org/10.2139/ssrn.2531701

Feinman, J. M. (2010). *Delay, deny, defend: Why insurance companies don't pay claims and what you can do about it.* New York, NY: Portfolio/Penguin.

Ferguson, N. (1999). *The house of Rothschild: Money's prophets, 1798-1848*. New York, NY: Penguin Books.

Ferguson, N., & Schularick, M. (2009, November). *The End of chimerica* (Harvard Business School Working Paper, No. 10-037). https://doi.org/10.2139/ssrn.1502756

Fernandez, R., & Rodrik, D. (1991). Resistance to reform: Status quo bias in the presence of individual-specific uncertainty. *The American Economic Review*, *81*(5), 1146–1155.

Ferris, S., Zanona, M., & Warmbrodt, Z. (2020, June 16). Members of congress took small-business loans – and the full extent is unknown. *Politico*. Retrieved from https://www.politico.com/news/2020/06/16/congress-small-business-loan-320625

Fidias EU Parliament. (2025, February 10). *Jeffrey Sachs brings real politics to the EU Parliament* [Video]. YouTube. https://youtu.be/_RNE3X41IvM

Fielding, H. (1733). *The lottery: A farce. As it is acted at the theatre-royal in Drury-Lane, by his majesty's servants. With a table of the songs.* London: Printed for N. Newman.

Findell, E., Hobbs, T. D., & Parti, T. (2024, December 22). America's private prison complex gears up for Trump deportation bonanza: Some are exploring the controversial practice of detaining unaccompanied minors. *The Wall Street Journal*. Retrieved from https://www.wsj.com/politics/policy/trump-deportation-private-prison-companies-49a18e3e

Fink, L. (2020). Larry Fink's 2020 Letter to CEOs: A Fundamental Reshaping of Finance. *BlackRock*. Retrieved from https://www.blackrock.com/corporate/investor-relations/2020-larry-fink-ceo-letter

Fischer, S. (2016). Monetary policy, financial stability, and the zero lower bound. *The American Economic Review, 106*(5), 39–42. https://doi.org/10.1257/aer.p20161005

Fischhoff, B., Lichtenstein, S., Slovic, P., Keeney, R., & Derby, S, (1980). *Approaches to acceptable risk: A critical guide* (U.S. Nuclear Regulatory Commission, NUREG, CR-1614). https://doi.org/10.2172/5045395

Fisher, I. (1930). *The theory of interest: As determined by impatience to spend income and opportunity to invest it*. New York, NY: Augustus M. Kelley.

Fjelland, R. (2020). Why general artificial intelligence will not be realized. *Humanities and Social Sciences Communications, 7*(10), 1–9. https://doi.org/10.1057/s41599-020-0494-4

Fleming, R. (2021). *The material fall of Roman Britain, 300-525 CE*. Philadelphia, PA: University of Pennsylvania Press. https://doi.org/10.2307/j.ctv18dvv4x

Fleming, S., & Espinoza, J. (2021, February 15) EU faces brutal choices over coronavirus corporate rescue money: Member states will need to decide which companies to support and which to allow to fail. *The Financial Times*. Retrieved from https://www.ft.com/content/e91734a5-a4b0-494d-b1aa-db76f4d5d034

Forget, J. (2021, January 28). Violent drug organizations use human trafficking to expand profits. *U.S. Drug Enforcement Administration*. Retrieved from https://www.dea.gov/stories/2021/2021-01/2021-01-28/violent-drug-organizations-use-human-trafficking-expand-profits

Forsdyke, S. (2005). *Exile, ostracism, and democracy: The politics of expulsion in Ancient Greece*. Princeton, NJ: Princeton University Press.

Foss, N. J., Klein, P. G., Lien, L., Zellweger, T., & Zenger, T. (2021). Ownership competence. *Strategic Management Journal, 42*(2), 302–328. https://doi.org/10.1002/smj.3222

Foster, L., Haltiwanger, J., & Krizan, C. J. (2001). Aggregate productivity growth: Lessons from microeconomic evidence. In E. Dean, M. Harper, & C. Hulten (Eds.), *New development in productivity analysis* (pp. 303–363). Chicago, IL: The University of Chicago Press.

Foucault, M. (1981). The order of discourse. In R. J. C Young (Ed.), *Untying the text: A post-structuralist reader* (I. McLeod, Trans.). London: Routledge & Kegan Paul. Retrieved from https://theanarchistlibrary.org/library/michel-foucault-the-order-of-discourse

Foucault, M. (1982). The subject and power. *Critical Inquiry, 8*(4), 777–795. https://doi.org/10.1086/448181

Fox News. (2021, October 14). *Tucker: We're watching civilization collapse in real time* [Video]. YouTube. https://www.youtube.com/watch?v=DREmnsungVM

France 24. (2022, June 11). Australia announces compensation deal with France over scrapped submarine contract. *France 24*. Retrieved from https://www.france24.com/en/asia-pacific/20220611-australia-announces-compensation-deal-with-france-over-scrapped-submarine-contract

Franck, R., & Michalopoulos, S. (2017, October), *Emigration during the French Revolution: Consequences in the short and longue durée* (NBER Working Paper No. 23936). https://www.nber.org/system/files/working_papers/w23936/w23936.pdf

Frank, R. H. (2000). Why is cost-benefit analysis so controversial? *The Journal of Legal Studies, 29*(2), 913–930. https://doi.org/10.1086/468099

Frankel, J. A., & Romer, D. (1999). Does trade cause growth? *The American Economic Review, 89*(3), 379–399. https://doi.org/10.1257/aer.89.3.379

Frederiksen, M. W. (1966). Caesar, Cicero and the problem of debt. *The Journal of Roman Studies, 56*(1-2), 128–141. https://doi.org/10.2307/300140

Freeman, R. E. (1984). *Strategic management: A stakeholder approach*. Boston, MA: Pitman.

Freudenberg, M. (2003). *Composite indicators of country performance: A critical assessment* (OECD Science, Technology and Industry Working Papers, 2003/16). Paris: OECD Publishing. https://doi.org/10.1787/405566708255

Freudenburg, W. R. (1986). Social impact assessment. *Annual Review of Sociology, 12*, 451–478. https://doi.org/10.1146/annurev.so.12.080186.002315

Frey, B. S. (1994). Direct democracy: Politico-economic lessons from Swiss experience. *The American Economic Review*, *84*(2), 338–342.

Friede, G., Busch, T., & Bassen, A. (2015). ESG and financial performance: Aggregated evidence from more than 2000 empirical studies. *Journal of Sustainable Finance & Investment*, *5*(4), 210–233. https://doi.org/10.1080/20430795.2015.1118917

Friedman, H. H., & Adler, W. D. (2011). Moral capitalism: A biblical perspective. *American Journal of Economics and Sociology*, *70*(4), 1014–1028. https://doi.org/10.1111/j.1536-7150.2011.00800.x

Friedman, M. (1970, September 13). A Friedman doctrine – The social responsibility of business is to increase its profit. *The New York Times*. Retrieved from https://www.nytimes.com/1970/09/13/archives/a-friedman-doctrine-the-social-responsibility-of-business-is-to.html

Friedman, M. (2002). *Capitalism and freedom* (40th anniversary edition). Chicago, IL: University of Chicago Press.

Fritschle, E. (2006, May 10). *Qadhafi incorporated* [Telegram]. WikiLeaks. Retrieved from https://wikileaks.org/plusd/cables/06TRIPOLI198_a.html

Fromm, E. (1994). *Escape from freedom*. New York, NY: Holt Paperbacks.

Frye, T., & Shleifer, A. (1997). The invisible hand and the grabbing hand. *The American Economic Review*, *87*(2), 354–358.

FT Film. (2024, July 17). *Who killed the ESG party?* [Video]. https://www.ft.com/video/1eeebd90-25d4-4421-a175-deedcdbf9c18

Fuentelsaz, L., Garrido, E., & Maicas, J. P. (2020). The effect of informal and formal institutions on foreign market entry selection and performance. *Journal of International Management 26*(2), S. 100735. https://doi.org/10.1016/j.intman.2020.100735.

Fujita, M. (2020), Top corporate leaders in Vietnam's transitional economy: Origins and career pathways. *The Developing Economies*, *58*(4), 301–331. https://doi.org/10.1111/deve.12257

Fukuyama, F. (1992). *The End of history and the last man*. New York, NY: Free Press.

Fukuyama, F. (1995). *Trust: The social virtues and the creation of prosperity*. New York, NY: Free Press.

Fukuyama, F. (2011). *The origins of political order: From prehuman times to the French Revolution*. New York, NY: Farrar, Straus and Giroux.

Fukuyama, F. (2012, May 10). China has banished Bo but not the 'bad emperor' problem. *The Financial Times*. Retrieved from https://www.ft.com/content/c71ff938-99c9-11e1-aa6d-00144feabdc0

Fukuyama, F. (2016). Macro theory and the study of political development. *Scandinavian Political Studies*, *39*(3), 207–225. https://doi.org/10.1111/1467-9477.12064

Fulbright, J. W. (1948). A united states of Europe? *The Annals of the American Academy of Political and Social Science*, *257*, 151–156.

Fullerton, E. J., & Morgan, P. J. (2022). *The People's Republic of China's digital Yuan: Its environment, design, and implications* (ADBI Discussion Paper No. 1306). Tokyo: Asian Development Bank Institute. Retrieved from https://www.adb.org/publications/the-peoples-republic-of-chinas-digital-yuan-its-environment-design-and-implications

Fung, A., & Lessig, L. (2023, June 2). How AI could take over elections – and undermine democracy. *The Conversation*. Retrieved from https://theconversation.com/how-ai-could-take-over-elections-and-undermine-democracy-206051

Future of Life Institute. (2023, April 12). Policymaking in the pause: What can policymakers do now to combat risks from advanced AI systems? *Future of Life Institute*. Retrieved from https://futureoflife.org/wp-content/uploads/2023/04/FLI_Policymaking_In_The_Pause.pdf

Gabbatt, A., & Agencies. (2025, January 23). Purdue Pharma and Sacklers reach new $7.4bn settlement over opioids crisis. *The Guardian*. Retrieved from https://www.theguardian.com/us-news/2025/jan/23/purdue-pharma-sackler-lawsuit

Gaddis, J. L. (1992). International relations theory and the end of the Cold War. *International Security 17*(3), 5–58. https://doi.org/10.2307/2539129

Gaddis, J. L. (2018). *On grand strategy.* New York, NY: Penguin Press.

Gagné, L. (2011). A modern interpretation of Machiavelli's political cycle. *Canadian Political Science Review, 5*(2), 127–135. https://doi.org/10.24124/c677/2011176

Gais, T., Peterson, M., & Walker, J. (1984). Interest groups, iron triangles and representative institutions in American national government. *British Journal of Political Science, 14*(2), 161–185. https://doi.org/10.1017/S0007123400003513

Gaita, R. (1991). *Good and evil: An absolute conception.* New York, NY: St. Martin's Press.

Galbraith, J. K. (2009). *The predator state: How conservatives abandoned the free market and why liberals should too.* New York, NY: Free Press.

Gallagher, D. (2022, January 3). Apple at $3 trillion isn't all about Apple. *The Wall Street Journal.* Retrieved from https://www.wsj.com/articles/apple-at-3-trillion-isnt-all-about-apple-11641242377

Gallai, N., Salles, J-M., Settele, J., & Vaissiere, B. E. (2009). Economic valuation of the vulnerability of world agriculture confronted with pollinator decline. *Ecological Economics (3)*15, 810–821. https://doi.org/10.1016/j.ecolecon.2008.06.014

Gallo, E., Riyanto, Y., Teh, T., & Roy, N. (2019). Strong links promote the emergence of cooperative elites. *Scientific Reports, 9*(1), 10857–10859. https://doi.org/10.1038/s41598-019-47278-2

Galloway, S. (2024, April 19). War on the young. *No Mercy/No Malice.* Retrieved from https://www.profgalloway.com/war-on-the-young/

Galor, O., & Moav, O. (2004). From physical to human capital accumulation: Inequality and the process of development. *The Review of Economic Studies, 71*(4), 1001–1026. https://doi.org/10.1111/0034-6527.00312

Gamm, G., & Putnam, R. D. (1999). The growth of voluntary associations in America, 1840–1940. *The Journal of Interdisciplinary History, 29*(4), 511–557. https://doi.org/10.1162/002219599551804

Gandel, S., & Franklin, J. (2024). Fed's high-rates era handed $1tn windfall to US banks. *The Financial Times.* Retrieved from https://www.ft.com/content/4c013d3b-796b-47a3-a964-02f753d39846

Gandhi, A., & Walton, M. (2012). Where do India's billionaires get their wealth? *Economic and Political Weekly, 47*(40), 10–14.

Garcia-Castro, R., & Aguilera, R. (2015). Incremental value creation and appropriation in a world with multiple stakeholders. *Strategic Management Journal, 36*(1), 137–147. https://doi.org/10.1002/smj.2241

Gardiner, S. M. (2001). The real tragedy of the commons. *Philosophy & Public Affairs, 30*(4), 387–416.

Gardner, M. (1970). Mathematical games. *Scientific American, 223*(4), 120–123.

Gartner. (2024, June 17). *Hype cycle for artificial intelligence, 2024.* Retrieved from: https://www.gartner.com/en/documents/5505695

Gasper, D. (2004). *The ethics of development: From economism to human development.* Edinburgh: Edinburgh University Press.

Gassmann, O., Frankenberger, K., & Sauer, R. (2016). Leading business model research: The seven schools of thought. In O. Gassmann, K. Frankenberger, & R. Sauer (Eds.), *Exploring the field of business model innovation: New theoretical perspectives* (pp. 7–46). Cham: Palgrave Macmillan. https://doi.org/10.1007/978-3-319-41144-6_2

Gates, B. (2013, February 26). Good ideas, but missing analysis. *Gates Notes.* Retrieved from https://www.gatesnotes.com/books/why-nations-fail

Gatignon, H., & Anderson, E. (1988). The multinational corporation's degree of control over foreign subsidiaries: An empirical test of a transaction cost explanation. *Journal of Law, Economics, & Organization, 4*(2), 305–336. https://doi.org/10.1093/oxfordjournals.jleo.a036954

Gavin, G., & Cater, L. (2025, January 16). Why Trump's Greenland grab could be a disaster for the planet: The frosty island sits atop giant oil and gas reserves that climate campaigners say must never see the light of day. *Politico.* Retrieved from https://www.politico.eu/article/why-trumps-greenland-grab-could-be-a-disaster-for-the-planet/

Gawdat, M. (2021). *Scary smart: The future of artificial intelligence and how you can save our world*. London: Pan Macmillan.

Gelles, D. (2022). *The man who broke capitalism: How Jack Welch gutted the heartland and crushed the soul of corporate America—and how to undo his legacy*. New York, NY: Simon & Schuster.

Gemici, K. (2013). South Korea during the Park Chung Hee era: Explaining Korea's developmental decades. *Asian Journal of Social Science*, *41*(2), 175–192. https://doi.org/10.1163/15685314-12341297

George, H. (1898). *Progress and poverty*. New York: The Modern Library.

Georgescu-Roegen, N. (1971). *The entropy law and the economic process*. Cambridge, MA: Harvard University Press.

Georgescu-Roegen, N. (1986). The entropy law and the economic process in retrospect. *Eastern Economic Journal*, *12*(1), 3–25.

Gergen, K. J. (1986). Correspondence versus autonomy in the language of understanding human action. In D. W. Fiske & R. A. Shweder (Eds.), *Metatheory in social science* (pp. 136–162). Chicago, IL: University of Chicago Press.

Geroski, P. A. (1989). Entry, innovation and productivity growth. *The Review of Economics and Statistics*, *71*(4), 572–578. https://doi.org/10.2307/1928098

Gerring, J., Bond, P., Barndt, W., & Moreno, C. (2005). Democracy and economic growth: A historical perspective. *World Politics*, *57*(3), 323–364. https://doi.org/10.1353/wp.2006.0002

Gerschenkron, A. (1952). Economic backwardness in historical perspective. In B. F. Hoselitz (Ed.), *The progress of underdeveloped areas* (pp. 3–29). Chicago, IL: University of Chicago Press.

Gerschenkron, A. (1966). *Bread and democracy in Germany* (New ed.). New York: Howard Fertig.

Gerschewski, J. (2021). Explanations of institutional change: Reflecting on a "missing diagonal". *American Political Science Review*, *115*(1) 218–233. https://doi.org/10.1017/S0003055420000751

Geweke, J. (1989). Bayesian inference in econometric models using Monte Carlo integration. *Econometrica*, *57*(6), 1317–1339. https://doi.org/10.2307/1913710

Gibbon, E. (2001). *The history of the decline and fall of the Roman Empire* (D. P. Womersley, Ed.). New York, NY: Penguin.

Gibillini, N. (2020, March 31). Kenney aims to 're-take control' by investing US$1.1B in Keystone XL. *BNN Bloomberg*. Retrieved from https://www.bnnbloomberg.ca/alberta-investing-us-1-1-billion-in-keystone-xl-pipeline-1.1415107

Giblin, R., & Doctorow, C. (2022). *Chokepoint capitalism: How big tech and big content captured creative labor markets and how we'll win them back*. Boston, MA: Beacon Press.

Gibson, L. S. (2014). H. L. Mencken: Racist or civil rights champion? *Menckeniana*, *208*, 1–12.

Giddens, A. (1984). *The constitution of society: Outline of the theory of structuration*. Berkeley, CA: University of California Press.

Gilens, M., & Page, B. I. (2014). Testing theories of American politics: Elites, interest groups, and average citizens. *Perspectives on Politics 12*(3), 564–81. https://doi.org/10.1017/S1537592714001595

Gilley, B. (2018). The case for colonialism. *Academic Questions*, *31*(2), 167–185. https://doi.org/10.1007/s12129-018-9696-2

Gilpin, R. (1981). *War and change in world politics*. Cambridge: Cambridge University Press. https://doi.org/10.1017/CBO9780511664267

Gilson, L. L., & Goldberg, C. B. (2015). Editors' comment: So, what is a conceptual paper? *Group & Organization Management*, *40*(2), 127–130. https://doi.org/10.1177/1059601115576425

Gilson, R. J., & Milhaupt, C. J. (2011). Economically benevolent dictators: Lessons for developing democracies. *The American Journal of Comparative Law*, *59*(1), 227–288. https://doi.org/10.2139/ssrn.1564925

Gimpel, J. (1976). *The medieval machine: The industrial revolution of the middle ages*. New York, NY: Holt, Reinhart and Winston.

Glaeser, E.L., La Porta, R., Lopez-de-Silanes, F., and Shleifer, A. (2004). Do institutions cause growth? *Journal of Economic Growth*, 9, 271–303. https://doi.org/10.1023/B:JOEG.0000038933.16398.ed

Glaum, M., & Oesterle, M.-J. (2007). Introduction: 40 Years of research on internationalization and firm performance: More questions than answers? *MIR: Management International Review*, *47*(3), 307–317. https://doi.org/10.1007/s11575-007-0018-0

Gleick, J. (1987). *Chaos: Making a new science*. New York, NY: Viking Penguin Inc.

Glode, V., & Ordoñez, G. (2023, March 12). *Technological progress and rent seeking*. University of Pennsylvania. Retrieved from https://bpb-us-w2.wpmucdn.com/web.sas.upenn.edu/dist/7/542/files/2023/03/TPRS.pdf

Godard, O. (2008). The Stern Review on the economics of climate change: Contents, insights and assessment of the critical debate. *Surveys and Perspectives Integrating Environment and Society*, *1*(1), 23–34. https://doi.org/10.5194/sapiens-1-17-2008

Godfrey, P. C., Merrill, C. B., & Hansen, J. M. (2009). The relationship between corporate social responsibility and shareholder value: An empirical test of the risk management hypothesis. *Strategic Management Journal*, *30*(4), 425–445. https://doi.org/10.1002/smj.750

Goertzel, B., & Montes, G. A. (2024). *The consciousness explosion: A mindful human's guide to the coming technological and experiential singularity*. Los Angeles, CA: Humanity+ Press.

Golant, B. D., & Sillince, J. A. (2007). The constitution of organizational legitimacy: A narrative perspective. *Organization studies*, *28*(8), 1149–1167. https://doi.org/10.1177/0170840607075671

Goldberg, E. (2024, December 12). Howard Lutnick: Tether's friend in the White House. *The Financial Times*. Retrieved from https://www.ft.com/content/a4a36384-63d0-4929-8959-64d45a8d1dd6

Goldenfeld, N., & Kadanoff, L. P. (1999). Simple lessons from complexity. *Science*, *284*(5411), 87–89. https://doi.org/10.1126/science.284.5411.87

Goldenstein, J., & Walgenbach, P. (2019). Embodied and reflexive agency in institutional fields: An integrative neo-institutional perspective of institutional change. In P. Haack, J. Sieweke, & L. Wessel (Eds.), *Microfoundations of institutions* (pp. 135–152). Bingley, UK: Emerald Publishing Limited. https://doi.org/10.1108/S0733-558X2019000065A015

Goldman, M. (2004). The rule of outlaws is over. *Transition Newsletter*, *14/15*, 23–25.

Goldstein, J. K. (2010). The contemporary presidency: Cheney, vice presidential power, and the war on terror. *Presidential Studies Quarterly*, *40*(1), 102–139.

Goldstone, J. A. (1982). The comparative and historical study of revolutions. *Annual Review of Sociology*, *8*, 187–207. https://doi.org/10.1146/annurev.so.08.080182.001155

Goldthau, A., & Sitter, N. (2015). Soft power with a hard edge: EU policy tools and energy security. *Review of International Political Economy*, *22*(5), 941–965. https://doi.org/10.1080/09692290.2015.1008547

Gollin, D. (2014). The Lewis Model: A 60-Year retrospective. *The Journal of Economic Perspectives*, *28*(3), 71–88. https://doi.org/10.1257/jep.28.3.71

Gompers, P. A. (1994). The rise and fall of venture capital. *Business and Economic History*, *23*(2), 1–26.

Gompers, P. A., Lerner, J., Blair, M. M., & Hellmann, T. (1998). What drives venture capital fundraising? *Brookings Papers on Economic Activity. Microeconomics*, *1998*, 149–204. https://doi.org/10.2307/2534802

Good, I. J. (1965). Speculations concerning the first ultraintelligent machine. In F. L. Alt & M. Rubinoff (Eds.), *Advances in computers* (Vol. 6, pp. 31–88). New York, NY: Academic Press.

Goody, J., & Watt, I. (1963). The consequences of literacy. *Comparative Studies in Society and History*, *5*(3), 304–345. https://doi.org/10.1017/S0010417500001730

Gordon, M. J. (1959). Dividends, earnings and stock prices. *Review of Economics and Statistics*, *41*(2), 99–105. https://doi.org/10.2307/1927792

Gorsuch, N., & Nitze, J. (2024). *Over ruled: The human toll of too much law*. New York, NY: Harper.

Gospic, K., Mohlin, E., Fransson, P., Petrovic, P., Johannesson, M., & Ingvar, M. (2011). Limbic justice – Amygdala involvement in immediate rejection in the ultimatum game. *PLoS biology*, *9*(5), e1001054.

Gotshalk, D. W. (1963). *Patterns of good and evil: A value analysis*. Urbana, IL: University of Illinois Press.

Gottschalk, L. (1944). Causes of revolution. *American Journal of Sociology*, *50*(1), 1–8. https://doi.org/10.1086/219493

Gouldner, A. W. (1975). Prologue to a theory of revolutionary intellectuals. *Télos (26)*, 3–36. https://doi.org/10.3817/1275026003

Grabowiecki, J. (2006, March). *Keiretsu groups: Their role in the Japanese economy and a reference point (or a paradigm) for other countries* (V.R.F. Series No. 413). Chiba, Japan: Institute of Developing Economies. Retrieved from https://www.ide.go.jp/library/English/Publish/Reports/Vrf/pdf/413.pdf

Graham, J. (1991). Servant-leadership in organizations: Inspirational and moral. *Leadership Quarterly*, *2*(2), 105–119.

Gramsci, A. (1966). *Il materialismo storico e la filosofia di Benedetto Croce*. Torino: Giulio Einaudi Editore.

Granovetter, M. (1973). The strength of weak ties. *American Journal of Sociology*, *78*(6), 1360–1380.

Granovetter, M. (1985). Economic action and social structure: The problem of embeddedness. *American Journal of Sociology*, *91*(3), 481–510. https://doi.org/10.1086/228311

Granovetter, M. (2005). The impact of social structure on economic outcomes. *The Journal of Economic Perspectives*, *19*(1), 33–50. https://doi.org/10.1257/0895330053147958

Gray, W. B. (1987). The cost of regulation: OSHA, EPA and the productivity slowdown. *The American Economic Review*, *77*(5), 998–1006. https://doi.org/10.4324/9781315188010-11

Gregory, R. W., Henfridsson, O., Kaganer, E., & Kyriakou, H. (2021). The role of artificial intelligence and data network effects for creating user value. *Academy of Management Review*, *46*(3), 534–551. https://doi.org/10.5465/amr.2019.0178

Greif, A., & Laitin, D. (2004). A theory of endogenous institutional change. *The American Political Science Review*, *98*(4), 633–652. https://doi.org/10.1017/S0003055404041395

Grier, R. M. (1999). Colonial legacies and economic growth. *Public Choice*, *98*(3/4), 317–335. https://doi.org/10.1023/A:1018322908007

Griffith, D. W. (1915). *The Birth of a Nation* [Film]. David W. Griffith Corp.

Gruder, V. R. (1982). 'No taxation without representation': The assembly of notables of 1787 and political ideology in France. *Legislative Studies Quarterly*, *7*(2), 263–79.

Grullon, G., Larkin, Y., & Michaely, R. (2019). Are US industries becoming more concentrated? *Review of Finance*, *23*(4), 697–743. https://doi.org/10.1093/rof/rfz007

Grynbaum, M. M., & Mac, R. (2023, December 27). The Times sues OpenAI and Microsoft over A.I. use of copyrighted work. *The New York Times*. Retrieved from https://www.nytimes.com/2023/12/27/business/media/new-york-times-open-ai-microsoft-lawsuit.html

Guilford, G., & Sonnad, N. (2017, February 3). What Steve Bannon really wants. *Quartz*. Retrieved from https://qz.com/898134/what-steve-bannon-really-wants/

Guinnane, T. W., & Streb, J. (2021). The introduction of Bismarck's social security system and its effects on marriage and fertility in Prussia. *Population and Development Review*, *47*(3), 749–780. https://doi.org/10.1111/padr.12426

Gulbrandsen, T. (2012). Elite integration – An integrative study. *Historical Social Research*, *37*(1), 148–166. https://doi.org/10.2307/41756455

Gupta, A. (1960). Adam Smith on value. *Indian Economic Review*, *5*(2), 105–115.

Gupta, K., & Krishnamurti, C. (2021). Corporate social responsibility, competition, and firm value. *Pacific-Basin Finance Journal*, *68*(1), 101622. https://doi.org/10.1016/j.pacfin.2021.101622

Guriev, S., & Rachinsky, A. (2005). The role of oligarchs in Russian capitalism. *The Journal of Economic Perspectives*, *19*(1), 131–150. https://doi.org/10.1257/0895330053147994

Gurman, M., & Bennett, D. (2024, March 7). How Apple sank about $1 billion a year into a car it never built. *Bloomberg Businessweek*. Retrieved from https://www.bloomberg.com/news/features/2024-03-06/apple-car-s-crash-design-details-tim-cook-s-indecision-failed-tesla-deal

Habermas, J., & McCarthy, T. (1977). Hannah Arendt's communications concept of power. *Social Research*, *44*(1), 3–24.

Haffajee, R. L., & Mello, M. M. (2017). Drug companies' liability for the Opioid Epidemic. *The New England Journal of Medicine*, *377*(24), 2301–2305. https://doi.org/10.1056/NEJMp1710756

Hagel, J. (2011). The pull of narrative - In search of persistent context. *Edge Perspectives*. Retrieved from http://edgeperspectives.typepad.com/edge_perspectives/2011/05/the-pull-of-narrative-in-search-of-persistent-context.html%20.

Hagel, J., Brown, J. S., & Davison, L. (2010). *The power of pull: How small moves, smartly made, can set big things in motion*. New York, NY: Basic Books.

Häggström, O. (2016). *Here be dragons: Science, technology and the future of humanity*. Oxford: Oxford University Press. https://doi.org/10.1093/acprof:oso/9780198723547.001.0001

Haidt, J. (2024). *The anxious generation: How the great rewiring of childhood is causing an epidemic of mental illness*. New York, NY: Penguin Press.

Hall, P. A. (1993). Policy paradigms, social learning, and the state: The case of economic policymaking in Britain. *Comparative politics*, *25*(3), 275–296. https://doi.org/10.2307/422246

Hall, P. A. (2015). Varieties of capitalism. In R. A. Scott & S. M. Kosslyn (Eds.), *Emerging trends in the social and behavioral sciences* (pp. 1–15). New York, NY: Wiley. https://doi.org/10.1002/9781118900772.etrds0377

Hall, P. A., & Gingerich, D. W. (2009). Varieties of capitalism and institutional complementarities in the political economy: An empirical analysis. *British Journal of Political Science*, *39*(3), 449–482. https://doi.org/10.1017/S0007123409000672

Hall, P. A., & Soskice, D. (2001). An introduction to varieties of capitalism. In P. A. Hall and D. Soskice (Eds.), *Varieties of capitalism: The institutional foundations of comparative advantage* (pp. 1–68). Oxford: Oxford University Press. https://doi.org/10.1093/0199247757.003.0001

Hall, P. A., & Thelen, K. (2009). Institutional change in varieties of capitalism. *Socio-Economic Review*, *7*(1), 7–34. https://doi.org/10.1093/ser/mwn020

Hall, R., & Deardorff, A. (2006). Lobbying as legislative subsidy. *American Political Science Review*, *100*(1), 69–84. https://doi.org/10.1017/S0003055406062010

Hall, R., & Jones, C. I. (1999). Why do some countries produce so much more output per worker than others? *Quarterly Journal of Economics* *144*(1), 83–116. https://doi.org/10.1162/003355399555954

Haller, A., & van Staden, C. (2014). The value added statement–an appropriate instrument for integrated reporting. *Accounting, Auditing & Accountability Journal* *27*(7), 1190–1216. https://doi.org/10.1108/AAAJ-04-2013-1307

Hambrick, D. C., & Mason, P. A. (1984). Upper echelons: The organization as a reflection of its top managers. *The Academy of Management Review*, *9*(2), 193–206. https://doi.org/10.2307/258434

Hamilton, W. H. (1919). The institutional approach to economic theory. *The American Economic Review*, *9*(1), 309–318.

Hancock, E. (2024, September 10). Google loses court battle over first EU antitrust fine. *Politico*. Retrieved from https://www.politico.eu/article/google-loses-court-battle-over-first-eu-antitrust-fine/

Hannah, S. T., Avolio, B. J., & Walumbwa, F. O. (2011). Relationships between authentic leadership, moral courage, and ethical and pro-social behaviors. *Business Ethics Quarterly*, *21*(4), 555–578. https://doi.org/10.5840/beq201121436

Hanson, B. T. (1998). What happened to fortress Europe? External trade policy liberalization in the European Union. *International Organization*, *52*(1), 55–85. https://doi.org/10.1162/002081898550554

Hanson, M. (2022, August 27). Student loan default rate. *Education Data Initiative*. Retrieved from https://educationdata.org/student-loan-default-rate

Harari, Y. N. (2015). *Sapiens: A brief history of humankind*. New York, NY: Harper.

Harari, Y. N. (2016). *Homo deus: A brief history of tomorrow*. London: Harvill Secker.

Harari, Y. N. (n.d.). Frequently asked questions. *Yuval Noah Harari*. Retrieved September 28, 2024, from https://www.ynharari.com/faqs/

Harberger, A. C. (1954). Monopoly and resource allocation. *The American Economic Review*, *44*(2), 77–87.

Harberger, A. C. (1964). The measurement of waste. *The American Economic Review, 54*(3), 58–76.

Hardin, G. (1968). The tragedy of the commons. *Science, 162*(3859), 1243–1248. https://doi.org/10.1126/science.162.3859.1243

Hardouin, P. (2017). Too big to fail, too big to jail: Restoring liability a lesson from HSBC case. *Journal of Financial Crime, 24*(4), 513–519. https://doi.org/10.1108/JFC-09-2016-0061

Hare, C., & Poole, K. T. (2014). The polarization of contemporary American politics. *Polity, 46*(3), 411–429. https://doi.org/10.1057/pol.2014.10

Harkness, J. A., van de Vijver, F. J. R., & Mohler, P. P. (2003). *Cross-cultural survey methods*. New York, NY: Wiley.

Harrison, J. S., Bosse, D. A., & Phillips, R. A. (2010). Managing for stakeholders, stakeholder utility functions, and competitive advantage. *Strategic Management Journal, 31*(1), 58–74. https://doi.org/10.1002/smj.801

Harrison, J. S., & Wicks, A. C. (2013). Stakeholder theory, value, and firm performance. *Business Ethics Quarterly, 23*(1), 97–124. https://doi.org/10.5840/beq20132314

Hart, K. (1970). Small scale entrepreneurs in Ghana and development planning. *Journal of Development Planning, 6*(4), 104-120. https://doi.org/10.1080/00220387008421338

Hart, S. L., & Ahuja, G. (1996). Does it pay to be green? An empirical examination of the relationship between pollution prevention and firm performance. *Business Strategy and the Environment, 5*(1), 30–37. https://doi.org/10.1002/(SICI)1099-0836(199603)5:1<30::AID-BSE38>3.0.CO;2-Q

Hartmann, M. (2007a). *The sociology of elites*. Abingdon: Routledge.

Hartmann, M. (2007b): *Eliten und macht in Europa. Ein internationaler vergleich*. Frankfurt/Main: Campus Verlag.

Hartmann, M. (2017). Die kosmopolitischen eliten – ein Mythos. *Journal for Comparative Government and European Policy, 15*(2/3), 510–528. https://doi.org/10.5771/1610-7780-2017-2-3-510

Harvard Environmental and Energy Law Program (EELP). (2021, June 9). Keystone XL Pipeline. *Harvard Environmental & Energy Law Program*. Retrieved from https://eelp.law.harvard.edu/tracker/keystone-xl-pipeline/

Hassner, R. E. (2016). *Religion on the Battlefield* (1st ed.). Ithaca, NY: Cornell University Press.

Hatmaker, T. (2021, June 15). Biden elevates tech antitrust crusader Lina Khan to FTC chair. *Techcrunch*. Retrieved from https://techcrunch.com/2021/06/15/lina-khan-ftc-confirmed/?guccounter=1

Hausmann, R., Hidalgo, C., Bustos, S., Coscia, M., Chung, S., Jimenez, J., Simoes, A., & Yildirim, M. (2013). *The atlas of economic complexity*. Cambridge, MA: MIT Press.

Hayek, F. A. (1945). The use of knowledge in society. *The American Economic Review, 35*(4), 519–530.

Hayek, F. A. (1958). The meaning of competition. In F. A. Hayek, *Individualism and economic order* (pp. 92–106). Chicago, IL: University of Chicago Press. Retrieved from https://cdn.mises.org/Individualism%20and%20Economic%20Order_4.pdf

Hayek, F. A. (1967). The theory of complex phenomena. In F. A. Hayek (Ed.), *Studies in philosophy, politics and economics* (pp. 22–42). Chicago, IL: University of Chicago Press.

Hayek, F. A. (1974, December 11). *The pretence of knowledge*. Prize Lecture to the Memory of Alfred Nobel. Nobel Prize Committee. Retrieved from https://www.nobelprize.org/prizes/economic-sciences/1974/hayek/lecture/

Häyry, M., & Sukenick, A. (2024). Imposing a lifestyle: A new argument for antinatalism. *Cambridge Quarterly of Healthcare Ethics, 33*(2), 238–259. https://doi.org/10.1017/S0963180123000385

Heaven, W. D. (2023, August 30). AI hype is built on high test scores. Those tests are flawed. *MIT Technology Review*. Retrieved from https://www.technologyreview.com/2023/08/30/1060395/ai-hype-high-test-scores-flawed/

Heckelman, J. C. (2007). Explaining the rain: "The Rise and Decline of Nations" after 25 years. *Southern Economic Journal, 74*(1), 18–33. https://doi.org/10.1002/j.2325-8012.2007.tb00824.x

Heckelman, J. C., & Whaples, R. (2006). Do economists differ from political scientists on public choice? Evidence from a survey. *Korean Journal of Public Choice*, *1*, 35–41.

Hegel, G. W. F. (2010). *The science of logic* (G. di Giovanni, Trans.; Ed.). Cambridge: Cambridge University Press.

Hegel, G. W. F. (2018). *The phenomenology of spirit* (T. Pinkard, Trans.; Ed.). Cambridge: Cambridge University Press.

Hennart, J.-F., & Slangen, A. H. (2015). Yes, we really do need more entry mode studies! A commentary on Shaver. *Journal of International Business Studies*, *46*(1), 114–122. https://doi.org/10.1057/jibs.2014.39

Henry, J. (2000). Adam Smith and the theory of value: Chapter Six considered. *History of Economics Review*, *31*(1), 1–13. https://doi.org/10.1080/10370196.2000.11733330

Herbst, J. (2000). *States and power in Africa: Comparative lessons in authority and control*. Princeton, NJ: Princeton University Press.

Herman, A. (2024, June 19). Commentary: China and artificial intelligence: The cold war we're not fighting. *Hudson Institute*. Retrieved from https://www.hudson.org/technology/china-artificial-intelligence-cold-war-were-not-fighting-arthur-herman

Hernandez, A., Posaner J., & Stamouli, N. (2022, July 21). Southern rebellion threatens to sink EU gas rationing plan. *Politico*. Retrieved from https://www.politico.eu/article/poland-portugal-spain-syprus-greece-rebellion-eu-gas-rationing-rules/

Herrick, M. T. (1908). The panic of 1907 and some of its lessons. *The Annals of the American Academy of Political and Social Science*, *31*, 8–25.

Hertz, J. H. (1992). *The Pentateuch and Haftorahs*. London: Soncino Press.

Hevia, J. (2003). Opium, empire, and modern history. *China Review International*, *10*(2), 307–326. https://doi.org/10.1353/cri.2004.0076

Hexter, J. H. (1956). Seyssel, Machiavelli, and Polybius vi: The mystery of the missing translation. *Studies in the Renaissance*, *3*, 75–96. https://doi.org/10.2307/2857102

Hicks, E. L. (1964). Materiality. *Journal of Accounting Research*, *2*(2), 158–171. https://doi.org/10.2307/2489998

Hicks, J. (1937). Mr. Keynes and the "Classics"; A suggested interpretation. *Econometrica*, *5*(2), 147–159. https://doi.org/10.2307/1907242

Hidalgo, C. A., Hausmann, R., & Dasgupta, P. S. (2009). The building blocks of economic complexity. *Proceedings of the National Academy of Sciences of the United States of America*, *106*(26), 10570–10575. https://doi.org/10.1073/pnas.0900943106

Higgins, B. (1950). The concept of secular stagnation. *The American Economic Review*, *40*(1), 160–166.

Higgins, T. (2021a, January 28). Apple, Facebook trade barbs over privacy-focused business models: Tim Cook criticizes app-tracking tools a day after Mark Zuckerberg accused Apple of interfering with how Facebook apps work. *The Wall Street Journal*. Retrieved from https://www.wsj.com/articles/apple-to-roll-out-privacy-measures-despite-facebook-objections-11611810002

Higgins, T. (2021b, September 12). Apple judge's warning suggests App Store fight is far from over. *The Wall Street Journal*. Retrieved from https://www.wsj.com/articles/apple-judges-warning-suggests-app-store-fight-is-far-from-over-11631363400

Higley, J. (2010). Elite theory and elites. In K. T Leicht & J. C Jenkins (Eds.), *Handbook of politics* (pp. 161–176). New York, NY: Springer. https://doi.org/10.1007/978-0-387-68930-2_9

Higley, J. (2021). *Elites, non-Elites, and political realism: Diminishing futures for Western societies*. London: Rowman & Littlefield.

Higley, J., & Burton, M. (1998). Elite settlements and the taming of politics. *Government and Opposition*, *33*(1), 98–115. https://doi.org/10.1111/j.1477-7053.1998.tb00785.x

Higley, J., & Pakulski, J. (2012). Elite theory versus Marxism: The Twentieth Century's verdict (2000). *Historical Social Research*, *37*, 320–332. https://doi.org/10.2307/41756463

Hildyard, L. (2023). *Enough: Why it's time to abolish the super-rich*. London: Pluto Press.

Hillman, A. J., Keim, G. D., & Schuler, D. (2004). Corporate political activity: A review and research agenda. *Journal of Management*, *30*(6), 837–858. https://doi.org/10.1016/j.jm.2004.06.003

Hinsley, F. H. (1967). The concept of sovereignty and the relations between states. *Journal of International Affairs*, *21*(2), 242–252.

Hirsch, F. E. (1946). The end of the Junker Class. *Current History*, *10*(54), 146–151.

Hoare, Q., & Nowell Smith, G. (1999). *Selections from the prison notebooks of Antonio Gramsci*. London: The Electric Book Company.

Hobbes, T. (2002). *Leviathan* (E. White & D. Widger, Eds.). Project Gutenberg. Retrieved from https://www.gutenberg.org/ebooks/3207

Hobsbawm, E. J. (1990). *Echoes of the Marseillaise: Two centuries look back on the French Revolution*. London: Verso Books.

Hobsbawm, E. J. (1996). *The age of revolution: 1789-1848*. New York, NY: Vintage Books.

Hobsbawm, E. J. (2000). *Bandits*. New York, NY: The New Press.

Hodgson, G. M. (2000). What is the essence of institutional economics? *Journal of Economic Issues*, *34*(2), 317–329. https://doi.org/10.1080/00213624.2000.11506269

Hodgson, G. M. (2003). John R. Commons and the foundations of institutional economics. *Journal of Economic Issues*, *37*(3), 547–576. https://doi.org/10.1080/00213624.2003.11506603

Hoff, K., & Stiglitz, J. (2004). After the big bang? Obstacles to the emergence of the rule of law in post-communist societies. *American Economic Review*, *94*(3), 753–763. https://doi.org/10.1257/0002828041464533

Hoffa, J. (2021, January 21). Teamsters statement on cancelation of the Keystone XL Pipeline. *Teamster.org*. Retrieved from https://teamster.org/2021/01/teamsters-statement-on-cancelation-of-the-keystone-xl-pipeline/

Hoffer, E. (1968). *The true believer: Thoughts on the nature of mass movements*. New York, NY: Harper & Row

Hoffman, R. (2022, September 13). AI for the next era: Open AI's Sam Altman on the new frontier of AI. *Greylock*. Retrieved from https://greylock.com/greymatter/sam-altman-ai-for-the-next-era/

Hoffmann, M., Boysel, S., Nagle, F., Peng, S., & Xu, K. (2024, October 27). *Generative AI and the nature of work* (Harvard Business School Strategy Unit Working Paper No. 25-021, CESifo Working Paper Series No. 11479). https://doi.org/10.2139/ssrn.5007084

Hoffmann-Lange, U. (2007). Methods of elite research. In R. J. Dalton & H-D. Klingemann (Eds.), *The Oxford handbook of political behavior* (pp. 910–27). Oxford: Oxford University Press. https://doi.org/10.1093/oxfordhb/9780199270125.003.0049

Hoffmann-Lange, U. (2012). Vertical and horizontal accountability of global elites: Some theoretical reflections and a preliminary research agenda. *Historical Social Research / Historische Sozialforschung 37*(1), 193–208. https://doi.org/10.2307/41756457

Holcombe, R. G. (1998). Entrepreneurship and economic growth. *The Quarterly Journal of Austrian Economics 1*, 45–62. https://doi.org/10.1007/s12113-998-1008-1

Holcombe, R. G. (2018). *Political capitalism: How economic and political power is made and maintained*. Cambridge: Cambridge University Press. https://doi.org/10.1017/9781108637251

Holcombe, R. G., & Castillo, A. M. (2013). *Liberalism and cronyism: Two rival political and economic systems*. Arlington, VA: Mercatus Center.

Hölkeskamp, K. J. (1992). Written law in archaic Greece. In *Proceedings of the Cambridge Philological Society, 38* (pp. 87–117).

Holm, P. (1995). The dynamics of institutionalization: Transformation processes in Norwegian fisheries. *Administrative Science Quarterly*, *40*(3), 398–422. https://doi.org/10.2307/2393791

Holmstrom, B., & Milgrom, P. (1994). The firm as an incentive system. *The American Economic Review*, *84*(4), 972–991.

Hong, G. H., & Kandrac, J. (2018, June). *Pushed past the limit? How Japanese banks reacted to negative interest rates* (IMF Working Paper No. WP/18/131). Washington, DC: International Monetary Fund. Retrieved from https://www.imf.org/en/Publications/WP/Issues/2018/06/13/Pushed-Past-the-Limit-How-Japanese-Banks-Reacted-to-Negative-Interest-Rates-45927

Hopf, T. (1998). The promise of constructivism in international relations theory. *International Security, 23*(1),171–200. https://doi.org/10.1162/isec.23.1.171

Hörnqvist, M. (2010). *Risk, power, and the state: After Foucault*. New York, NY: Routledge.

Hoselitz, B. F. (1952). Entrepreneurship and economic growth. *The American Journal of Economics and Sociology, 12*(1), 97–110. https://doi.org/10.1111/j.1536-7150.1952.tb00480.x

Hosenball, M. (2011, March 3). WikiLeaks: How the Cola war was won in Libya. *Reuters*. Retrieved from https://www.reuters.com/article/us-wiki-libya-coke/wikileaks-how-the-cola-war-was-won-in-libya-idUSTRE72240620110303?sp=true

Howard, R. A., Matheson, J. E., & Owen, D. L. (1978, May 8-10). The value of life and nuclear design. In *Proceedings of the American Nuclear Society Conference on Probabilistic Analysis of Nuclear Reactor Safety*. Los Angeles, CA.

Huang, M-C., Gong, T-J., Sun, S-P., & Lin, P-H. (2023). Obstacles or catalysts? A balanced view of formal institutional risks on FDI location choice. *Asian Business Management 22*(5), 2077–2105. https://doi.org/10.1057/s41291-023-00242-5.

Hudson, M. & Goodhart, C. (2018). Could/should Jubilee debt cancellations be reintroduced today? If not, what alternative measures of debt relief and redistribution might be possible? *Economics, 12*(1), 20180045. https://doi.org/10.5018/economics-ejournal.ja.2018-45

Huet, E. (2023a, March 8). The OpenAI CEO disagrees with the forecast that AI will kill us all. *Bloomberg*. Retrieved from https://www.bloomberg.com/news/newsletters/2023-03-08/openai-ceo-sam-altman-s-twitter-feud-with-ai-doomer-eliezer-yudkowsky-explained?sref=YfHlo0rL)

Huet, E. (2023b, December 6). A cultural divide over AI forms in Silicon Valley. *Bloomberg*. Retrieved from https://www.bloomberg.com/news/newsletters/2023-12-06/effective-accelerationism-and-beff-jezos-form-new-tech-tribe

Huet, E. (2024, June 27). OpenAI part 5: Beware the ides of November. [Audio podcast episode]. In *Foundering: The OpenAI Story*. Bloomberg podcasts. https://youtu.be/_Px-DIRdW2g?si=SWZouIT8sgZyJMFP

Hufbauer, G., & Elliott, K. (1994). *Measuring the costs of protection in the United States*. Washington, DC: Institute for International Economics.

Hughes, N. C. (2024, July 16). Tech layoffs predictions 2024: More than 100,000 layoffs this year. *Techopedia*. Retrieved from https://www.techopedia.com/tech-layoffs-predictions

Huizinga, J. (1950). *Homo ludens: A study of the play element in culture* (Unknown, Trans.). New York, NY: Roy Publishers.

Hunter, F. (1953). *Community power structure: A study of decision makers*. Chapel Hill, NC: University of North Carolina Press.

Hunter, J. D. (1991). *Culture wars: The struggle to define America*. New York, NY: Basic Books

Hvidman, U., & Andersen, S. C. (2016). Perceptions of public and private performance: Evidence from a survey experiment. *Public Administration Review, 76*(1), 111–120. https://doi.org/10.1111/puar.12441

Iarossi, G. (2006). *The power of survey design: A user's guide for managing surveys, interpreting results, and influencing respondents*. Washington, DC: World Bank.

IFRS Foundation. (n.d.). *SASB standards overview*. IFRS Foundation. Retrieved September 25, 2024, from https://sasb.ifrs.org/standards/

Indap, S. (2021a, August 8). Purdue's bankruptcy deal shields Sackler family owners from future opioid liability. *The Financial Times*. Retrieved from https://www.ft.com/content/f0d6f014-dfa1-4d93-a11b-d9ede668be11

Indap, S. (2021b, December 17). Judge overturns $4.5bn opioid-related settlement in Purdue Pharma bankruptcy. *The Financial Times*. Retrieved from https://www.ft.com/content/9f94d55b-0656-4234-adf5-7a76b3730fc0

Ingram, D. (2024, December 26). Mapping Trump's connections to tech's right-wing brotherhood. *NBC News*. Retrieved from https://www.nbcnews.com/tech/tech-news/mapping-trumps-connections-techs-right-wing-brotherhood-rcna180693

Ingram, M. (2020, May 26). Should Google and Facebook be forced to pay for content? *Columbia Journalism Review*. Retrieved from https://www.cjr.org/the_media_today/should-google-and-facebook-be-forced-to-pay-for-content.php

Institut Cerdà. (2017). La ocupación ilegal: Realidad social, urbana y económica . . . un problema que necesita solución. *Institut Cerdà*. Retrieved from https://www.icerda.org/ca/producte/la-ocupacion-ilegal-realidad-social-urbana-y-economica-un-problema-que-necesita-solucion-pdf/

Institute for Economics & Peace. (2019). *Global Peace Index 2019: Measuring peace in a complex world*. Sydney: Institute for Economics and Peace. Retrieved from http://visionofhumanity.org/reports

International Labour Organization. (1930). *Forced Labour Convention, 1930 (No. 29)*. Retrieved from https://normlex.ilo.org/dyn/normlex/en/f?p=NORMLEXPUB:55:0::NO::P55_TYPE,P55_LANG,P55_DOCUMENT,P55_NODE:CON,en,C029,/Document

International Peace Conference. (1899). *Declaration concerning expanding bullets (The Hague Convention)*. Retrieved from https://www.weaponslaw.org/assets/downloads/1899_HD_concerning_expanding_bullets.pdf

International Trade Administration, U.S. Department of Commerce. (n.d.). *Trade guide: WTO subsidies agreement*. Retrieved October 15, 2024, from https://www.trade.gov/trade-guide-wto-subsidies

Iqbal, M. (2024, September 9). YouTube revenue and usage statistics (2024). *Business of Apps*. Retrieved from https://www.businessofapps.com/data/youtube-statistics/

Irokawa, D. (1985). *The culture of the Meiji period* (M. B. Jansen, Ed., Trans.). Princeton, NJ: Princeton University Press. https://doi.org/10.2307/j.ctvx5wbxq

Isaac, D. (2022, February 16). Israel grapples with high cost of living as citizens grumble over rising prices. *Jewish News Syndicate*. Retrieved from https://www.jns.org/israel-grapples-with-high-cost-of-living-as-citizens-grumble-over-rising-prices/

Isaacson, W. (2012, April). Innovation: The real leadership lessons of Steve Jobs. *Harvard Business Review*. Retrieved from https://hbr.org/2012/04/the-real-leadership-lessons-of-steve-jobs

Israel, J., & Silverthorne, M. (2007). Introduction. In B. Spinoza, *Theological-political treatise* (J. Israel, Ed.; M. Silverthorne & J. Israel, Trans., pp. viii–xxxiv). Cambridge: Cambridge University Press. https://doi.org/10.1017/CBO9780511815720

Itoh, M. (1976). A study of Marx's theory of value. *Science & Society*, *40*(3), 307–340.

Ivaldi, E., Bonatti, G., & Soliani, R. (2016). The construction of a synthetic index comparing multidimensional well-being in the European Union. *Social Indicators Research 125*(2), 397–430. https://doi.org/10.1007/s11205-014-0855-8

Ivanhoe, P. J. (1991). A happy symmetry: Xunzi's ethical thought. *Journal of the American Academy of Religion*, *59*(2), 309–322. https://doi.org/10.1093/jaarel/LIX.2.309

Iyatse, G. (2022, October 13). Nigeria trapped in elite bargain crisis, says Dercon, Oxford economist. *The Guardian (Nigeria)*. Retrieved from https://guardian.ng/news/nigeria-trapped-in-elite-bargain-crisis-says-dercon-oxford-economist/

Iyengar, R., & Johnson, K. (2025, February 14). Vance leaves Europe gobsmacked. *Foreign Policy*. Retrieved from https://foreignpolicy.com/2025/02/14/vance-speech-munich-msc-russia-ukraine-censorship-free-speech/

Jacca-RouteNote. (2024, February 9). Spotify pays record $9 billion to music industry in 2023. *RouteNote Blog*. Retrieved from https://routenote.com/blog/spotify-pays-record-9-billion-to-music-industry-in-2023/

Jacobs, J. B., & Peters, E. (2003). Labor racketeering: The Mafia and the Unions. *Crime and Justice, 30*, 229–282. https://doi.org/10.1086/652232

Jacobs, L. R., & Page, B. I. (2005). Who influences U.S. foreign policy? *The American Political Science Review, 99*(1), 107–123. https://doi.org/10.1017/S000305540505152X

Jenkins-Smith, H., & P. Sabatier. (1993). The study of public policy processes. In P. Sabatier and H. Jenkins-Smith (Eds.), *Policy change and learning: An advocacy coalition approach* (pp. 1–9). Boulder, CO: Westview Press.

Jensen, M. C., & Meckling, W. H. (1976). Theory of the firm: Managerial behavior, agency costs and ownership structure. *Journal of Financial Economics*, *3*(4), 305–360. https://doi.org/10.1016/0304-405X(76)90026-X

Jensen, M. C., & Murphy, K. J. (1990). Performance pay and top-management incentives. *Journal of Political Economy*, *98*(2), 225–264. https://doi.org/10.1086/261677

Jevons, W. S. (1871). *The theory of political economy*. London: Macmillan and Co.

Ji, S., He, H., & Peach, B. (2021, October 24). Explainer: What is 'lying flat', and why are Chinese officials standing up to it? *South China Morning Post*. Retrieved from https://www.scmp.com/economy/china-economy/article/3153362/what-lying-flat-and-why-are-chinese-officials-standing-it

Jick, T. D. (1979). Mixing qualitative and quantitative methods: Triangulation in action. *Administrative Science Quarterly*, *24*(4), 602–611. https://doi.org/10.2307/2392366

Jobs, S. (2005, June 12). 'You've got to find what you love,' Jobs says. *Stanford Report*. Retrieved from https://news.stanford.edu/stories/2005/06/youve-got-find-love-jobs-says

Johnson, C. A. (1982). *MITI and the Japanese miracle: The growth of industrial policy, 1925-1975*. Stanford, CA: Stanford University Press.

Johnson, S. (2009, May). The quiet coup. *The Atlantic*. Retrieved from https://www.theatlantic.com/magazine/archive/2009/05/the-quiet-coup/307364/

Jones, B., & Olken, B. (2005). Do leaders matter? National leadership and growth since World War II. *Quarterly Journal of Economics*, *120*(3), 835–64. https://doi.org/10.1093/qje/120.3.835

Jönsson, C., & Tallberg, J. (2010). *Transnational actors in global governance: Patterns, explanations and implications*. Basingstoke: Palgrave Macmillan.

Jorgenson, D. W., & Wilcoxen, P. J. (1990). Intertemporal general equilibrium modeling of U.S. environmental regulation. *Journal of Policy Modeling*, *12*(4), 715–744. https://doi.org/10.1016/0161-8938(90)90006-z

Josephus, F. (2009). *The wars of the Jews: Or history of the destruction of Jerusalem* (W. Whiston, Trans.). Project Gutenberg. Retrieved from https://www.gutenberg.org/files/2850/2850-h/2850-h.htm

Joskow, P. (1995). The new institutional economics: Alternative approaches: Concluding comment. *Journal of Institutional and Theoretical Economics*, *151*(1), 248–259.

Judisch, N. (2016). Divine conservation and creaturely freedom. In K. Timpe & M. Griffith (Eds.), *Free will and theism: Connections, contingencies, and concerns* (pp. 234–258). New York, NY: Oxford University Press. https://doi.org/10.1093/acprof:oso/9780198743958.003.0014

Juglar, C. (1862). *Des crises commerciales et de leur retour periodique en France, en Angletem et aux Etats-Unis*. Paris: Guillaumin et Cie, librairies.

Jung, J. (2020). Institutional quality, FDI, and productivity: A theoretical analysis. *Sustainability*, *12*(17), 7057. https://doi.org/10.3390/su12177057

Kahneman, D., & Lovallo, D. (1993). Timid choices and bold forecasts: A cognitive perspective on risk taking. *Management Science*, *39*(1), 17–31. https://doi.org/10.1287/mnsc.39.1.17

Kailitz, S. (2013). Classifying political regimes revisited: Legitimation and durability. *Democratization*, *20*(1), 39–60. https://doi.org/10.1080/13510347.2013.738861

Kaldor, N. (1970). The case for regional policies. *Scottish Journal of Political Economy*, *17*(3), 337–348. https://doi.org/10.1111/j.1467-9485.1970.tb00712.x

Kalecki, M. (1942). A theory of profits. *The Economic Journal*, *52*(206/207), 258–267. https://doi.org/10.2307/2225784

Kamepalli, S. K., Rajan, R. G., & Zingales, L. (2021, February 15). Kill zone. *SSRN*. Retrieved from https://ssrn.com/abstract=3555915 or http://dx.doi.org/10.2139/ssrn.3555915

Kant, R. (2021, April 19). The man at the center of India's shift to oligarchy. *Asia Times*. Retrieved from https://asiatimes.com/2021/04/the-man-at-the-center-indias-shift-to-oligarchy/

Kaplan, J., McCandlish, S., Henighan, T., Brown, T. B., Chess, B., Child, R., Gray, S., Radford, A., Wu, J., & Amodei, D. (2020). Scaling laws for neural language models. *arXiv*. https://doi.org/10.48550/arXiv.2001.08361

Kaplan, R. (2016, August 12). The triumph of geopolitics: Amoral geopolitics, more than any clash of civilizations, dictated Venetian-Ottoman relations. *The National Interest*. Retrieved from https://nationalinterest.org/feature/the-triumph-geopolitics-17336?nopaging=1

Kaplan, R. D. (2014, April). In defense of empire. *The Atlantic*. Retrieved from https://www.theatlantic.com/magazine/archive/2014/04/in-defense-of-empire/358645/

Katz, C. (2019, March 7). Piling up: How China's ban on importing waste has stalled global recycling. *Yale Environment 360*. Retrieved from https://e360.yale.edu/features/piling-up-how-chinas-ban-on-importing-waste-has-stalled-global-recycling

Katz, R. (2024). *The contest for Japan's economic future: Entrepreneurs vs corporate giants*. New York: Oxford University Press. https://doi.org/10.1093/oso/9780197675106.001.0001

Kaufmann, C., & Weber, R. (2010) The role of transparency in financial regulation. *Journal of International Economic Law*, *13*(3), 779–797. https://doi.org/10.1093/jiel/jgq037

Kaufmann, T. (2019). Luther and the Jews. *Antisemitism Studies*, *3*(1), 46–65.

Kautilya. (1992). *The Arthashastra* (L. N. Rangarajan, Ed. & Trans.). New Delhi, India: Penguin Books India.

Keese, C. (2017). *Silicon Germany – Wie wir die digitale transformation schaffen*. Munich: Knaus.

Kelly, J. (2024, June 30). Crypto lobbyists are polluting the US election. *The Financial Times*. Retrieved from https://www.ft.com/content/798112b3-f02e-49dc-af09-4dc6057477b3

Kelly, N. J. (2005). Political choice, public policy, and distributional outcomes. *American Journal of Political Science*, *49*(4), 865–880. http://dx.doi.org/10.1111/j.1540-5907.2005.00160.x

Kelsen, H. (1955). Foundations of democracy. *Ethics*, *66*(1), 1–101. https://doi.org/10.1086/291036

Kendall, F. (2025, April 9). Did the Trump administration move too quickly to commit to the F-47? *Defense News*. Retrieved from https://www.defensenews.com/opinion/2025/04/09/did-the-trump-administration-move-too-quickly-to-commit-to-the-f-47/

Kennan, G. F. (1946). *The long telegram*. Retrieved from https://nsarchive2.gwu.edu/coldwar/documents/episode-1/kennan.htm

Kennedy, P. (1987). *The rise and fall of the great powers: Economic change and military conflict from 1500 to 2000*. New York, NY: Random House.

Kennedy, R. F., Jr. (2024, October 15). *Enough is enough* [Video]. YouTube. https://youtu.be/0_OjKe4BuDE

Keohane, R. O., & Nye, J. S. (2012). *Power and interdependence* (4th ed.). New York, NY: Longman.

Kerbo, H. R., & Della Fave, L. (1979). The empirical side of the power elite debate: An assessment and critique of recent research. *The Sociological Quarterly*, *20*(1), 5–22. https://doi.org/10.1111/j.1533-8525.1979.tb02181.x

Kerbo, H. R., & McKinstry, J. A. (1995). *Who rules Japan? The inner circles of economic and political power*. Westport, CT: Praeger.

Kerr, W. R., Nanda, R., & Rhodes-Kropf, M. (2014). Entrepreneurship as experimentation. *The Journal of Economic Perspectives*, *28*(3), 25–48. https://doi.org/10.1257/jep.28.3.25

Kertzer, J. D., & Renshon, J. (2022). Experiments and surveys on political elites. *Annual Review of Political Science*, *25*, 529–550. https://doi.org/10.1146/annurev-polisci-051120-013649

Keuschnigg, M., van de Rijt, A., & Bol, T. (2023). The plateauing of cognitive ability among top earners. *European Sociological Review*, *39*(5), 820–833. https://doi.org/10.1093/esr/jcac076

Khalaf, R. (2025, January 22). Alex Soros: 'These people are bullies. And you fight back'. *The Financial Times*. Retrieved from https://www.ft.com/content/fdde5d56-5dc1-4bd4-af43-b58ef969c1bb

Khan, M., Serafeim, G., & Yoon, A. (2016, November 9). Corporate sustainability: First evidence on materiality. *The Accounting Review*, *91*(6), 1697–1724. https://doi.org/10.2139/ssrn.2575912

Khan, M. H. (2010, July). *Political settlements and the governance of growth-enhancing institutions* (Draft Paper in Research Paper Series on 'Growth-Enhancing Governance'). SOAS, University of London. Retrieved from https://eprints.soas.ac.uk/9968/1/Political_Settlements_internet.pdf

Khan, M. H. (2018). Political settlements and the analysis of institutions. *African Affairs*, *117*(469), 636–655, 716. https://doi.org/10.1093/afraf/ady055

Kharif, O. (2020a, January 31). Bitcoin's network operations are controlled by five companies. *Bloomberg News*. Retrieved from https://www.bloomberg.com/news/articles/2020-01-31/bitcoin-s-network-operations-are-controlled-by-five-companies

Kharif, O. (2020b, November 19). Bitcoin whales' ownership concentration is rising during rally. *Bloomberg News*. Retrieved from https://www.bloomberg.com/news/articles/2020-11-18/bitcoin-whales-ownership-concentration-is-rising-during-rally

Kiernan, P., & Michaels, D. (2022, March 12). Crypto aims to boost influence with Washington hires. *The Wall Street Journal*. Retrieved from https://www.wsj.com/articles/crypto-aims-to-boost-influence-with-washington-hires-11647042604

Kim, E. M., & Park, G.-S. (2011). The Chaebol. In B.-K. Kim & E. F. Vogel (Eds.), *The Park Chung Hee era* (pp. 265–294). Cambridge, MA: Harvard University Press.

Kim, J. (2001). Elite strategies and the spread of technological innovation: The spread of iron in the bronze age societies of Denmark and Southern Korea. *Journal of Anthropological Archaeology*, *20*(4), 442–478. https://doi.org/10.1006/jaar.2001.0386

Kim, K. (2006, July 10-11). *The 1997-98 Korean financial crisis: Causes, policy response, and lessons* [Conference presentation]. The High-Level Seminar on Crisis Prevention in Emerging Markets, Singapore. Retrieved from https://www.imf.org/external/np/seminars/eng/2006/cpem/pdf/kihwan.pdf

Kim, W. (1992). Power transitions and great power war from Westphalia to Waterloo. *World Politics*, *45*(1), 153–172. https://doi.org/10.2307/2010522

Kim, Y. S. (1996). [Review of the book *Who rules Japan? The inner circles of economic and political power* by H. R. Kerbo & J. A. McKinstry]. *Journal of Asian Economics*, *7*(2), 341–343.

Kinder, T., & Hammond, G. (2024, December 23). Palantir and Anduril join forces with tech groups to bid for Pentagon contracts. *The Financial Times*. Retrieved from https://www.ft.com/content/6cfdfe2b-6872-4963-bde8-dc6c43be5093

Kinder, T., & Morris, S. (2022, May 4). Why Chinese insurer Ping An is calling for a break-up of HSBC. *The Financial Times*. Retrieved from https://www.ft.com/content/d38fbe3d-d093-4ffa-a340-fb4b90cd342f

King James Bible. (2017). *King James Bible online*. Retrieved from https://www.kingjamesbibleonline.org (Original work published 1769).

Kingsolver, B. (2022). *Demon Copperhead*. New York, NY: HarperCollins Publishers.

Kingston, C., & Caballero, G. (2009). Comparing theories of institutional change. *Journal of Institutional Economics* *5*(2), 151–80. https://doi.org/10.1017/S1744137409001283

Kirby, M. (1992). Institutional rigidities and economic decline: Reflections on the British experience. *The Economic History Review*, *45*(4), 637–660. https://doi.org/10.1111/j.1468-0289.1992.tb01310.x

Kirzner, I. (1997). Entrepreneurial discovery and the competitive market process: An Austrian approach. *Journal of Economic Literature*, *35*(1), 60–85.

Kissinger, H. A., Schmidt, E., & Mundie, C. (2024). *Genesis: Artificial intelligence, hope, and the human spirit*. Boston, MA: Little, Brown and Company.

Kivelson, V. A. (1993). The devil stole his mind: The Tsar and the 1648 Moscow uprising. *The American Historical Review*, *98*(3), 733–756. https://doi.org/10.2307/2167548

Klapper, L., Laeven, L. and Rajan, R. (2004, March). *Business environment and firm entry: Evidence from international data* (NBER Working Paper No. 10380). Retrieved from https://www.nber.org/system/files/working_papers/w10380/revisions/w10380.rev0.pdf

Klare, M. T. (2006). Oil, Iraq, and American foreign policy: The continuing salience of the Carter Doctrine. *International Journal*, *62*(1), 31–42. https://doi.org/10.2307/40204243

Klein, E. (2021, June 11). Sam Altman on the A.I revolution, trillionaires and the future of political power. *The New York Times*. Retrieved from https://www.nytimes.com/2021/06/11/podcasts/transcript-ezra-klein-interviews-sam-altman.html

Klein, M. C., & Pettis, M. (2020). *Trade wars are class wars: How rising inequality distorts the global economy and threatens international peace*. New Haven, CT: Yale University Press.

Klein, P. G., Holmes, M., Jr., Foss, N. J., Terjesen, S., & Pepe, J. (2022). Capitalism, cronyism, and management scholarship: A call for clarity. *Academy of Management Perspectives*, *36*(1), 6–29. https://doi.org/10.5465/amp.2019.0198

Kleinberg, J., Ludwig, J., Mullainathan, S., & Rambachan, A. (2018). Algorithmic fairness. *AEA Papers and Proceedings*, *108*, 22–27. https://doi.org/10.1257/pandp.20181018

Kniesner, T., & Viscusi, W. (2019, July 29). The value of a statistical life. *Oxford Research Encyclopedia of Economics and Finance*. Retrieved 10 Feb. 2025 from https://oxfordre.com/economics/view/10.1093/acrefore/9780190625979.001.0001/acrefore-9780190625979-e-138.

Knight, F. (2002). *Risk, uncertainty and profit*. Washington, DC: Beard Books.

Kogut, B., & Singh, H. (1988). The effect of national culture on the choice of entry mode. *Journal of International Business Studies*, *19*(3), 411–432. https://doi.org/10.1057/palgrave.jibs.8490394

Koivukoski T. (2011). On oligarchy: An ontological account. In T. Koivukoski and D. Tabachnick (Eds.), *On oligarchy: Ancient lessons for global politics* (pp. 178–195). Toronto: University of Toronto Press. https://doi.org/10.3138/9781442664029-011

Kondratieff, N. D. (1935). The long waves in economic life. *The Review of Economics and Statistics*, *17*(6), 105–115. https://doi.org/10.2307/1928486

Konstantinou, L. (2024, September 24). The gods of Silicon Valley. *Arc Digital*. Retrieved from https://arcmag.org/the-gods-of-silicon-valley/

Kopf, S. (2020). "Rewarding good creators": Corporate social media discourse on monetization schemes for content creators. *Social Media + Society*, *6*(4), 1–12. https://doi.org/10.1177/2056305120969877

Korab-Karpowicz, W. J. (2018, Summer edition). Political realism in international relations. In E. N. Zalta (Ed.), *The Stanford encyclopedia of philosophy*. Retrieved from https://plato.stanford.edu/archives/sum2018/entries/realism-intl-relations

Korpi, W., & Palme, J. (1998). The paradox of redistribution and strategies of equality: Welfare state institutions, inequality, and poverty in the Western Countries. *American Sociological Review*, *63*(5), 661–687. https://doi.org/10.2307/2657333

Kostiuchenko, T. (2011). Central actors and groups in political elite: Advantages of network approach. *Polish Sociological Review*, *174*, 195–204.

Kostova, T., Beugelsdijk, S., Scott, W. R., Kunst, V. E., Chua, C. H., & van Essen, M. (2020). The construct of institutional distance through the lens of different institutional perspectives: Review, analysis, and recommendations. *Journal of International Business Studies 51*, 467–497. https://doi.org/10.1057/s41267-019-00294-w

Kotter, J. P. (2001). What leaders really do? *Harvard Business Review*, *79*, 85–98.

Kotz, D. M. (2015). Neoliberalism, globalization, financialization: Understanding post-1980 capitalism (Revised version of What is neoliberalism, Chapter 2 in D. M. Kotz, *The rise and fall of free-market capitalism*. Boston, MA: Harvard University Press). Retrieved from https://ageoftransformation.org/content/files/economics/sites/default/files/kotz.pdf

Kovacic, W. E. (2014). Out of control? Robert Bork's portrayal of the U.S. antitrust system in the 1970s. *Antitrust Law Journal*, *79*(3), 855–879.

Krakowski, S., Luger, J., & Raisch, S. (2023). Artificial intelligence and the changing sources of competitive advantage. *Strategic Management Journal*, *44*(6), 1425–1452. https://doi.org/10.1002/smj.3387

Krasner, S. D. (1984). Approaches to the state: Alternative conceptions and historical dynamics. *Comparative Politics 16*(2), 223–46.

Kraterou, A. (2024, December 5). 'Delay, Deny, Defend' author refuses to speak as bullets used to kill Brian Thompson etched with message echoing book. *The Sun.* Retrieved from https://www.thesun.co.uk/news/32132439/delay-deny-defend-author-bullets-kill-brian-thompson/

Krause, S. (2003). History and the human soul in Montesquieu. *History of Political Thought, 24*(2), 235–261.

Krauss, E., & Pekkanen, R. (2011). *The rise and fall of Japan's LDP: Political party organizations as historical institutions*. Ithaca, NY: Cornell University Press.

Krcmaric, D., Nelson, S. C., & Roberts, A. (2020). Studying leaders and elites: The personal biography approach. *Annual Review of Political Science 23*(1), 133–51. https://doi.org/10.1146/annurev-polisci-050718-032801

Krueger, A. (1974). The political economy of the rent-seeking society. *The American Economic Review*, *64*(3), 291–303.

Krueger, A. (1990). Government failures in development. *The Journal of Economic Perspectives*, *4*(3), 9–23.

Krueger, A., & Tuncer, B. (1982). An empirical test of the infant industry argument. *The American Economic Review, 72*(5), 1142–1152.

Krugman, P. (1994). The myth of Asia's miracle. *Foreign Affairs*, *73*(6), 62–78. https://doi.org/10.2307/20046929

Krznaric, R. (2020). *The good ancestor: A radical prescription for long-term thinking*. New York, NY: The Experiment.

Kuenning, P. P. (1987). Luther and Muntzer: Contrasting theologies in regard to secular authority within the context of the German peasant revolt. *Journal of Church and State*, *29*(2), 305–321. https://doi.org/10.1093/jcs/29.2.305

Kuhn, T. S. (1962). *The structure of scientific revolutions*. Chicago, IL: The University of Chicago Press.

Kunčič, A. (2014). Institutional quality dataset. *Journal of Institutional Economics*, *10*(1), 135–161. https://doi.org/10.1017/S1744137413000192

Kuran, T. (1987). Preference falsification, policy continuity and collective conservatism. *The Economic Journal*, *97*(387), 642–665. https://doi.org/10.2307/2232928

Kurzweil, R. (2024, June 25). Ray Kurzweil explains how AI makes radical life extension possible. *Freethink*. Retrieved from https://www.freethink.com/robots-ai/ray-kurzweil-ai

Kurzweil, R. (2005). *The singularity is near: When humans transcend biology*. New York, NY: Viking.

Kydland, F. E., & Prescott, E. C. (1982). Time to build and aggregate fluctuations. *Econometrica*, *50*, 1345–1370. https://doi.org/10.2307/1913386

Kydland, F. E., & Prescott, E. C. (1996). The computational experiment: An econometric tool. *Journal of Economic Perspectives*, *10*(1), 69–85. https://doi.org/10.1257/jep.10.1.69

Lachmann, R. (2002). *Capitalists in spite of themselves: Elite conflict and economic transition.* Oxford: Oxford University Press.

Lackman, C. (1976). The classical base of modern rent theory. *The American Journal of Economics and Sociology*, *35*(3), 287–300. https://doi.org/10.1111/j.1536-7150.1976.tb03013.x

LaCroix, T., & Mohseni, A. (2022) The tragedy of the AI commons. *Synthese*, *200*, 289. https://doi.org/10.1007/s11229-022-03763-2

Lafargue, P. (2000). *The right to be lazy*. Chicago, IL: Charles Kerr & Co., Co-operative. Retrieved from https://www.marxists.org/archive/lafargue/1883/lazy/index.htm

Lafaye, J., & Lockhart, J. (1992). A scholarly debate: The origins of modern Mexico – Indigenistas vs. Hispanistas. *The Americas*, *48*(3), 315–330. https://doi.org/10.2307/1007239

Laffont, J., & Tirole, J. (1991). The politics of government decision-making: A theory of regulatory capture. *The Quarterly Journal of Economics*, *106*(4), 1089–1127. https://doi.org/10.2307/2937958

Laine, M. (2011). The nature of nature as a stakeholder. *Journal of Business Ethics*, *96*(1), 73–78. https://doi.org/10.1007/s10551-011-0936-4

Laing, B. M. (1917). Schopenhauer and individuality. *Mind*, *26*(102), 171–187.

Laitner, J. (2000). Structural change and economic growth. *The Review of Economic Studies, 67*(3), 545–561. https://doi.org/10.1111/1467-937X.00143
Lalueza-Fox, C. (2022). *Inequality: A genetic history*. Cambridge, MA: MIT Press.
Lanctot, J. D., & Irving, J. A. (2010). Character and leadership: Situating servant leadership in a proposed virtues framework. *International Journal of Leadership Studies, 6*(1), 28–50.
Landes, D. S. (1993). [Review of the book *Patterns of European industrialization: The Nineteenth Century*, by R. Sylla & G. Toniolo]. *The Business History Review, 67*(1), 172–175. https://doi.org/10.2307/3117486
Landes, D. S. (2008). *The wealth and poverty of nations*. New York, NY: W.W. Norton & Company.
Lange, M., Mahoney, J., & vom Hau, M. (2006). Colonialism and development: A comparative analysis of Spanish and British colonies. *American Journal of Sociology, 111*(5), 1412–1462. https://doi.org/10.1086/499510
Lange, O. (1943). The Theory of the multiplier. *Econometrica, 11*(3/4), 227–245.
Lanier, J. (2023, January 23). Oy, A.I. *Tablet*. Retrieved from https://www.tabletmag.com/sections/news/articles/oy-ai-jaron-lanier
Lasch, C. (1979). *The culture of narcissism*. New York, NY: W. W. Norton & Company.
Lattimore, O. (1937). Origins of the Great Wall of China: A frontier concept in theory and practice. *Geographical Review, 27*(4), 529–549.
Lauth, H.-J. (2016). The internal relationships of the dimensions of democracy: The relevance of trade-offs for measuring the quality of democracy. *International Political Science Review / Revue Internationale de Science Politique, 37*(5), 606–617. https://doi.org/10.1177/01925121166676
Lawrence, T., & Buchanan, S. (2017). Power, institutions and organizations. In R. Greenwood, C. Oliver, & T. B. Lawrence (Eds.), *The SAGE handbook of organizational institutionalism* (pp. 477–506). London: Sage Publications Ltd. https://doi.org/10.4135/9781849200387.n7
Le Bon, G. (1996). *The crowd: A study of the popular mind*. London: T. Fisher Unwin. Retrieved from https://www.gutenberg.org/cache/epub/445/pg445-images.html
Leahy, C., Alfour, G., Scammell, C., Miotti, A., & Shimi, A. (2024, December 9). *The compendium* (Version 1.3.1). Retrieved from https://pdf.thecompendium.ai/the_compendium.pdf
LeCun, Y. (2022, June 27). A path towards autonomous machine intelligence version 0.9.2, 2022-06-27. *Openreview.net*. Retrieved from https://openreview.net/pdf?id=BZ5a1r-kVsf
Lee, D. R. (1987). The tradeoff between equality and efficiency: Short-Run politics and long-run realities. *Public Choice, 53*(2), 149–165. https://doi.org/10.1007/BF00125846
Lee, K. Y. (1998). Singapore's fate depends on 300 men. In H. F. Kwang, W. Fernandez & S. Tan (Eds.), *Lee Kuan Yew: The man and his ideas*. Singapore: Times Editions.
Lee, R. (1988). Dimensions of the South American cocaine industry. *Journal of Interamerican Studies and World Affairs, 30*(2/3), 87–103. https://doi.org/10.2307/165981
Legislative Council Secretariat (of the Hong Kong Special Administrative Region of the People's Republic of China). (2016, October, 26). *Land utilization in Hong Kong*. (Statistical highlights: ISSH04/16-17). Retrieved from https://www.legco.gov.hk/research-publications/english/1617issh04-land-utilization-in-hong-kong-20161024-e.pdf
Legrand, M., & Hagemann, H. (2017). Retrospectives: Do productive recessions show the recuperative powers of capitalism? Schumpeter's analysis of the cleansing effect. *The Journal of Economic Perspectives, 31*(1), 245–255. https://doi.org/10.1257/jep.31.1.245
Leike, J., Schulman, J., & Wu, J. (2022, August 24). Our approach to alignment research. *OpenAI*. Retrieved from https://openai.com/blog/our-approach-to-alignment-research
Leith, S. (2022, January 10). We should be thankful for the Sackler family's philanthropy: It's moral narcissism to tut-tut at ill-gotten donations. *The Spectator*. Retrieved from https://www.spectator.co.uk/article/we-should-be-thankful-for-the-sackler-family-s-philanthropy/

Lenin, V. I. (1918). *The State and revolution: The Marxist theory of the state and the tasks of the proletariat in the revolution*. In Collected Works (Vol. 25, pp. 381–492). Retrieved from https://www.marxists.org/archive/lenin/works/1917/staterev/

Lepak, D. P., Smith, K. G., & Taylor, M. S. (2007). Value creation and value capture: A multilevel perspective. *Academy of Management Review 32*(1), 180–194. https://doi.org/10.5465/AMR.2007.23464011

Lerner, A. (1972). The economics and politics of consumer sovereignty. *American Economic Review, 62*(2), 258–266.

Lerner, R., Nagai, A., & Rothman, S. (1996). The few versus the many: Competing views regarding the structure of power. In R. Lerner, A. Nagai & S. Rothman (Eds.), *American elites* (pp. 1–17). New Haven, CT: Yale University Press. https://doi.org/10.12987/9780300146196-002

Letza, S., Sun, X. & Kirkbride, J. (2004). Shareholding versus stakeholding: A critical review of corporate governance. *Corporate Governance, 12*(3), 242–262. https://doi.org/10.1111/j.1467-8683.2004.00367.x

Levchenko, A. A. (2007). Institutional quality and international trade. *The Review of Economic Studies, 74*(3), 791–819. https://doi.org/10.1111/j.1467-937X.2007.00435.x

Leventov, R. (2023, March 2). Joscha Bach on synthetic intelligence [annotated]. *Effective Altruism Forum*. Retrieved from https://forum.effectivealtruism.org/posts/wQERLNFoMidffTLar/joscha-bach-on-synthetic-intelligence-annotated

Lever, M. H. C., & Nieuwenhuijsen, H. R. (1999). The impact of competition on productivity in Dutch manufacturing. In D. B. Audretsch, & A. R. Thurik (Eds.), *Innovation, industry evolution and employment* (pp. 111–128). Cambridge: Cambridge University Press.

Levi, E. H. (1976). Some aspects of separation of powers. *Columbia Law Review*, 76(3), 371–391.

Levie, J., & Autio, E. (2008). A theoretical grounding and test of the GEM model. *Small Business Economics, 31*(3), 235–263. https://doi.org/10.1007/s11187-008-9136-8

Levi-Faur, D. (1997). Friedrich List and the political economy of the nation-state. *Review of International Political Economy, 4*(1), 154–178.

Levina, M., & Hasinoff, A. A. (2017). The Silicon Valley ethos: Tech industry products, discourses, and practices. *Television & New Media, 18*(6), 489–495. https://doi.org/10.1177/1527476416680454

Levine, M., & Forrence, J. (1990). Regulatory capture, public interest, and the public agenda: Toward a synthesis. *Journal of Law, Economics, & Organization, 6*, 167–198. https://doi.org/10.1093/jleo/6.special_issue.167

Levitsky, S., & Ziblatt, D. (2018). *How democracies die*. New York, NY: Crown Publishing Group.

Levitsky, S. R., & Way, L. A. (2012). Beyond patronage: Violent struggle, ruling party cohesion, and authoritarian durability. *Perspectives on Politics, 10*(4), 869–889. https://doi.org/10.1017/S1537592712002861

Lewis, W. A. (1954). Economic development with unlimited supplies of labour. *The Manchester School, 22*(2), 139–191. https://doi.org/10.1111/j.1467-9957.1954.tb00021.x

Lex Fridman Podcast. (2023, July 17). *Yuval Noah Harari: Human nature, intelligence, power, and conspiracies.* [Video]. YouTube. https://youtu.be/Mde2q7GFCrw

Lex Fridman Podcast. (2025, January 26). *Marc Andreessen: Trump, power, tech, AI, immigration & future of America* [Video]. YouTube. https://www.youtube.com/watch?v=OHWnPOKh_S0

Li, J. (2022). When ants beset the elephant: Rent extraction and resistance on China's e-commerce platform. *International Review of Social History, 67*(2), 275–293. https://doi.org/10.1017/S0020859021000493

Liang, H., & Renneboog, L. (2017). On the foundations of corporate social responsibility. *The Journal of Finance, 72*(2), 853–910. https://doi.org/10.1111/jofi.12487

Libecap, G. D. (1989). Distributional issues in contracting for property rights. *Journal of Institutional and Theoretical Economics, 145*(1), 6–24.

Libecap, G. D. (2011). Institutional path dependence in climate adaptation: Coman's "Some Unsettled Problems of Irrigation". *The American Economic Review, 101*(1), 64–80. https://doi.org/10.1257/aer.101.1.64

Lichfield, J. (2020, February 17). The slow death of French cheese. *UnHerd*. Retrieved from https://unherd.com/2020/02/the-slow-death-of-french-cheese/

Lieberman, M. B., Garcia-Castro, R., & Balasubramanian, N. (2017). Measuring value creation and appropriation in firms: The VCA model. *Strategic Management Journal, 38*(6), 1193–1211. https://doi.org/10.1002/smj.2565

Liebovitch, L. S. (1998). *Fractal and chaos simplified for the life sciences*. New York, NY: Oxford University Press.

Liebovitch, L. S., & Scheurle, D. (2000), Two lessons from fractals and chaos. *Complexity 5*(4), 34–43. https://doi.org/10.1002/1099-0526(200003/04)5:4<34::AID-CPLX5>3.0.CO;2-3

Liebowitz, S., & Margolis, S. (1999). *Encyclopedia of law and economics*. Cheltenham: Edward Elgar.

Lim, J. S., Mietus-Snyder, M., Valente, A., Schwarz, J-M., & Lustig, R. H. (2010). The role of fructose in the pathogenesis of NAFLD and the metabolic syndrome. *Nature Reviews Gastroenterology & Hepatology, 7*, 251–264. https://doi.org/10.1038/nrgastro.2010.41

Lindberg, E. (2008). The rise of Hamburg as a global marketplace in the Seventeenth Century: A comparative political economy perspective. *Comparative Studies in Society and History, 50*(3), 641–662.

Lindsay, D. M. (2008). Evangelicals in the power elite: Elite cohesion advancing a movement. *American Sociological Review, 73*(1), 60–82. https://doi.org/10.1177/000312240807300104

Lindstaedt, N. (2025, March 3). How Trump's spat with Zelensky threatens the security of the world – including the US. *The Conversation*. Retrieved from https://theconversation.com/how-trumps-spat-with-zelensky-threatens-the-security-of-the-world-including-the-us-251229

Lingelbach, D., & Rodríguez Guerra, V. (2023). *The oligarchs' grip: Fusing wealth and power*. Berlin: De Gruyter.

Lipset, S. M. (1959). Some social requisites of democracy: Economic development and political legitimacy. *American Political Science Review, 53*(1), 69–105. https://doi.org/10.2307/1951731

Lipset, S. M. (1999). Introduction. In R. Michels (Ed.), *Political parties: A sociological study of the oligarchical tendencies of modern democracy* (pp. 15–39). Abingdon: Routledge.

Lissner, R. F. (2018). What is grand strategy? Sweeping a conceptual minefield. *Texas National Security Review, 2*(1), 53–73. https://doi.org/10.26153/tsw/868

List, F. (2011). *The national system of political economy* (S. S. Lloyd, Trans.; J. S. Nicholson, Introduction). London: Longmans, Green and Co. Retrieved from https://oll-resources.s3.us-east-2.amazonaws.com/oll3/store/titles/315/List_0168_EBk_v6.0.pdf

Liu, G., Catacutan, D. B., Rathod, K., Swanson, K., Jin, W., Mohammed, J. C., Chiappino-Pepe, A., Syed, S. A., Fragis, M., Rachwalski, K., Magolan, J., Surette, M. G., Coombes, B. K., Jaakkola, T., Barzilay, R., Collins, J. J., & Stokes, J. M. (2023, May 25). Deep learning-guided discovery of an antibiotic targeting Acinetobacter baumannii. *Nature Chemical Biology, 19*, 1342–1350. https://doi.org/10.1038/s41589-023-01349-8

Lizzeri, A., & Persico, N. (2004). Why did the elites extend the suffrage? Democracy and the scope of government, with an application to Britain's "Age of Reform". *The Quarterly Journal of Economics, 119*(2), 707–765. https://doi.org/10.1162/0033553041382175

Locke, J. (1993). *Two treatises of government*. London: Phoenix.

Logan, D. C. (2009). Known knowns, known unknowns, unknown unknowns and the propagation of scientific enquiry. *Journal of Experimental Botany, 60*(3), 712–714. https://doi.org/10.1093/jxb/erp043

Lok, J., & Willmott, H. (2019). Embedded agency in institutional theory: Problem or paradox? *Academy of Management Review, 44*(2), 470–473. https://doi.org/10.5465/amr.2017.0571

Long, H. (2019. May 7). Trump's steel tariffs cost U.S. consumers $900,000 for every job created, experts say. *Washington Post*. Retrieved from https://www.washingtonpost.com/business/2019/05/07/trumps-steel-tariffs-cost-us-consumers-every-job-created-experts-say/

Lorini, G. (2014). Meta-institutional concepts: A new category for social ontology. *Rivista di Estetica, 56*, 127–139. https://doi.org/10.4000/estetica.876

Lowenthal, L. (1950). Historical perspectives of popular culture. *American Journal of Sociology, 55*(4), 323–332.

Lowery, D. (2007). Why do organized interests lobby? A multi-goal, multi-context theory of lobbying. *Polity*, 39(1), 29–54. https://doi.org/10.1057/palgrave.polity.2300077

Lu, E. (2020, January 20). HK is 'least affordable housing market' for 10th year running. *China Daily, Hong Kong*. Retrieved from https://www.chinadailyhk.com/article/119131

Lu, S., Bigoulaeva, I., Sachdeva, R., Madabushi, H. T., & Gurevych, I. (2024). Are emergent abilities in large language models just in-context learning? *arXiv.* https://doi.org/10.48550/arXiv.2309.01809

Lu, X. (1985). A madman's diary. In *Selected works of Lu Hsun*. Beijing: Foreign Languages Press.

Luca, M. (2015). User-generated content and social media. In S. P. Anderson, J. Waldfogel, & D. Strömberg (Eds.), *Handbook of media economics* (Vol. 1, pp. 563–592). Amsterdam: Elsevier. https://doi.org/10.1016/B978-0-444-63685-0.00012-7

Lucas, R. E. (1984). An empirical test of the infant industry argument: Comment. *The American Economic Review, 74*(5), 1110–1111.

Lucas, R. E. (1988). On the mechanics of economic development. *Journal of Monetary Economics, 22*(1), 3–42.

Lucey, C., & Thomas, K. (2025, January 15). Biden warns of oligarchy and tech industrial complex in farewell address: President touts his achievements and outlines his concerns for America's future. *The Wall Street Journal*. https://www.wsj.com/politics/elections/biden-warns-of-oligarchy-and-tech-industrial-complex-in-farewell-address-ab69da46

Luo, X. (2018, November 22). In China's Taobao villages, e-commerce is one way to bring new jobs and business opportunities to rural area. *World Bank Blogs*. Retrieved from https://blogs.worldbank.org/eastasiapacific/china-s-taobao-villages-e-commerce-one-way-bring-new-jobs-and-business-opportunities-rural-areas

Lux, S., Crook, R., & Woehr, D. J. (2011). Mixing business with politics: A meta-analysis of the antecedents and outcomes of corporate political activity. *Journal of Management, 37*(1), 223–247. https://doi.org/10.1177/0149206310392

Lydenberg, S., Rogers, J., & Wood, D. (2010, June). *From transparency to performance: Industry-based sustainability reporting on key issues*. Cambridge, MA: The Hauser Center for Nonprofit Organizations, Initiative for Responsible Investment. Retrieved from https://iri.hks.harvard.edu/files/iri/files/from_transparency_to_performance_industry-based_sustainability_reporting_on_key_issues.pdf

Lyotard, J.-F. (1979). *La condition postmoderne: Rapport sur le savoir*. Paris: Editions de Minuit.

Ménard, C., & Shirley, M. M. (2014). The contribution of Douglass North to new institutional economics. In S. Galani and I. Sened (Eds.), *Institutions, property rights and economic growth: The legacy of Douglass North*. (pp.11–29). Cambridge: Cambridge University Press. https://doi.org/10.1017/CBO9781107300361.003

Ma, J. (2016). Elites, elitism, and community in the Archaic Polis. *Annales (English Ed.), 71*(3), 395–418. https://doi.org/10.1017/S2398568218000079

Mac Donald, H. (2024, December 23). Luigi Mangione and the American abyss: The assassination of Brian Thompson does not call for a "conversation" about health care—it calls for a reckoning with Americans' moral breakdown. *City Journal*. Retrieved from https://www.city-journal.org/article/luigi-mangione-unitedhealthcare-ceo-brian-thompson

MacDonald, G., & Ryall, M. (2004). How do value creation and competition determine whether a firm appropriates value? *Management Science, 50*(10), 1319–1333. https://doi.org/10.2139/ssrn.283225

Machiavelli, N. (1883). *Discourses on the first decade of Titus Livius* (N. H. Thomson, Trans.). London: Kegan Paul, Trench & Co. Retrieved from https://www.gutenberg.org/ebooks/10827

Machiavelli, N. (1998). *The prince* (H. C. Mansfield, Trans.; 2nd ed.). Chicago, IL: The University of Chicago Press. Retrieved from https://yeauganda.wordpress.com/wp-content/uploads/2018/08/machiavelli-niccolo-the-prince-1985.pdf

Machlup, F., & Penrose, E. (1950). The patent controversy in the Nineteenth Century. *The Journal of Economic History*, *10*(1), 1–29. https://doi.org/10.1017/S0022050700055893

MacKay, A., & Mercadal, I. (2022, April). *Deregulation, market power, and prices: Evidence from the electricity sector* (CEEPR WP 2022-008). Retrieved from https://ceepr.mit.edu/wp-content/uploads/2022/04/2022-008.pdf

Madison, J. (1977). The Federalist Number 10, [22 November 1787] 1787. In R. A. Rutland, C. F. Hobson, W. M. E. Rachal & F. J. Teute (Eds.), *The papers of James Madison*. (Vol. 10, 27 May 1787–3 March 1788, pp. 263-270). Chicago, IL: The University of Chicago Press.

Maestas, C., Neeley, G. W., & Richardson, L. E. J. (2003). The state of surveying legislators: Dilemmas and suggestions. *State Politics & Policy Quarterly*, *3*(1), 90–108.

Maguire, S., McKelvey, B., Mirabeau, L., & Oztas, N. (2006). Complexity science and organization studies. In S. R. Clegg, C. Hardy, T. B. Lawrence, & W. R. Nord (Eds.), *The SAGE handbook of organization studies* (2nd ed., pp. 165–214). London: Sage Publications. https://doi.org/10.4135/9781848608030.n7

Mahbubani, K. (2018). *Has the West lost It? A provocation*. London: Allen Lane.

Mahoney, J. (2000). Path dependence in historical sociology. *Theory and Society*, *29*(4), 507–548. https://doi.org/10.1023/A:1007113830879

Mahoney, J. (2003). Long-run development and the legacy of colonialism in Spanish America. *American Journal of Sociology*, *109*(1), 50–106. https://doi.org/10.1086/378454

Mahoney, J., & Thelen, K. (2010). A theory of gradual institutional change. In J. Mahoney & K. Thelen (Eds.), *Explaining institutional change: Ambiguity, agency, and power* (pp. 1–37). New York, NY: Cambridge University Press. https://doi.org/10.1017/CBO9780511806414.003

Mallet du Pan, J. (1793). *Considérations sur la nature de la révolution de France: Et sur les causes qui en prolongent la durée*. chez Emm, Flon.

Mandelbrot, B. B. (1989). Fractal geometry: What is it, and what does it do? [and Discussion]. *Proceedings of the Royal Society of London. Series A, Mathematical and Physical Sciences*, *423*(1864), 3–16. https://doi.org/10.1098/rspa.1989.0038

Manent, P. (2013). *Metamorphoses of the city: On the western dynamic* (M. LePain, Trans.) Cambridge, MA: Harvard University Press.

Mangan, D. (2025, January 13). Jeff Bezos enables Trump's threat to democracy, Washington Post columnist Rubin says as she quits. *CNBC*. Retrieved from https://www.cnbc.com/2025/01/13/jeff-bezos-trump-democracy-washington-post-jennifer-rubin.html

Manufacturing@MIT. (2023, November 8). *TSMC founder Morris Chang on the evolution of the semiconductor industry* [Video]. YouTube. https://youtu.be/r_8XClnnvIk

Marías, J. (2014). *España inteligible: Razón histórica de las Españas*. Madrid: Alianza Editorial.

March, J. G., & Simon, H. A. (1958). *Organizations*. New York, NY: Wiley.

Marchal, K., & Wenzel, C. H. (2017). Chinese perspectives on free will. In K. Timpe, M. Griffith, & N. Levy (Eds.), *The Routledge companion to free will* (pp. 374–388). New York, NY: Routledge.

Marciano, A. (2011). Ronald Coase, "The problem of social cost" and the Coase Theorem: An anniversary celebration. *European Journal of Law and Economics*, *31*(1), 1–9. https://doi.org/10.1007/s10657-010-9200-0

Markowitz, H. (1952). Portfolio selection. *Journal of Finance*, *7*(1), 77–91. https://doi.org/10.1111/j.1540-6261.1952.tb01525.x

Marotta, D. (2013, February 24). What is rent-seeking behavior? *Forbes*. Retrieved from https://www.forbes.com/sites/davidmarotta/2013/02/24/what-is-rent-seeking-behavior/#5d1f44d3658a

Marshall, P. J. (2005). *The making and unmaking of empires: Britain, India and America c. 1750-1783*. Oxford: Oxford University Press. https://doi.org/10.1093/acprof:oso/9780199226665.001.0001
Marshall, T. R. (2015). The 1964 Surgeon General's report and Americans' beliefs about smoking. *Journal of the History of Medicine and Allied Sciences, 70*(2), 250–278.
Marx, F. M. (1939). The bureaucratic state: Some remarks on Mosca's ruling class. *The Review of Politics, 1*(4), 457–472.
Marx, K. (1959a). *Economic and philosophic manuscripts of 1844*. Moscow: Progress Publishers. Retrieved from https://www.marxists.org/archive/marx/works/1844/manuscripts/wages.htm
Marx. K. (1959b). *Capital. A critique of political economy. Book one: The process of production of capital*. Moscow: Progress Publishers. Retrieved from https://www.marxists.org/archive/marx/works/download/pdf/Capital-Volume-I.pdf
Marx, K. (2009). *A contribution to the critique of Hegel's philosophy of right: Introduction*. Retrieved from https://www.marxists.org/archive/marx/works/1843/critique-hpr/intro.htm
Marx, K., & Engels, F. (1969). *Manifesto of the Communist Party*. In K. Marx & F. Engels, *Marx/Engels selected works* (Vol. 1). Moscow: Progress Publishers. Retrieved from https://www.marxists.org/archive/marx/works/download/pdf/Manifesto.pdf
Maseland, R. (2017). Institutional overlap as a basis for international business. In A. Verbeke, J. Puck, & R. van Tulder (Eds.), *Distance in international business: Concept, cost and value* (pp. 69–90). Bingley, UK: Emerald Group Publishing Limited. https://doi.org/10.1108/S1745-886220170000012006
Maslow, A. H. (1943). A theory of human motivation. *Psychological Review, 50*(4), 370–396. https://doi.org/10.1037/h0054346
Masters, B. (2023, June 14). BlackRock's Larry Fink predicts AI could solve productivity crisis. *The Financial Times*. Retrieved from https://www.ft.com/content/f36e2b3b-9bb0-481d-b682-4ae882b17a11
Masters, B., Agnew, H., Hughes, J., Platt, E., Gara, A., & Morris, S. (2024, May 10). 'There's money everywhere': Milken conference-goers look for a dealmaking revival. *The Financial Times*. Retrieved from https://www.ft.com/content/9c812a8d-72ee-4f53-ba5d-eaef5899348f
Mastrangelo, A. (2024a, December 10). Silicon Valley titan Marc Andreessen: Biden White House planned to 'take total control' of AI. *Breitbart*. Retrieved from https://www.breitbart.com/tech/2024/12/10/silicon-valley-titan-marc-andreessen-biden-white-house-planned-to-take-total-control-of-ai/
Mastrangelo, A. (2024b, December 27). Elon Musk brings back shadowbanning, conservatives report loss of verification following H-1B fracas. *Breitbart*. Retrieved from https://www.breitbart.com/tech/2024/12/27/elon-musk-brings-back-shadowbanning-conservatives-report-loss-of-verification-following-h-1b-fracas/
Matheny, G., & Leahy, C. (2007). Farm-animal welfare, legislation, and trade. *Law and Contemporary Problems, 70*(1), 325–358. https://doi.org/10.2307/27592172
Maturana, H. R., & Varela, F. J. (1980). *Autopoiesis and cognition: The realization of the living*. Dordrecht, Netherlands: D. Reidel Publishing Company. https://doi.org/10.1007/978-94-009-8947-4
Maxwell, J. C. (1904). *Theory of heat* (New impression, with corrections and additions by Lord Rayleigh). London: Longmans, Green, and Co. Retrieved from http://strangebeautiful.com/other-texts/maxwell-theory-of-heat.pdf
May, P. (2017). Review. [Review of the book *Metamorphoses of the city: On the western dynamic* by P. Manent]. *Contemporary Political Theory, 16*(3), 413–416. https://doi.org/10.1057/s41296-016-0064-0
May, R. J. (2004). The FCC's tumultuous year 2003: An essay on an opportunity for institutional agency reform. *Administrative Law Review, 56*(4), 1307–325.
Mayhew, B., & Schollaert, P. (1980). Social morphology of Pareto's economic elite. *Social Forces, 59*(1), 25–43. https://doi.org/10.2307/2577831
Mayville, L. (2015). Fear of the few: John Adams and the power elite. *Polity, 47*(1), 5–32.
Mazzucato, M. (2013). *The entrepreneurial state: Debunking public vs. private sector myths*. London, UK: Anthem Press.

Mazzucato, M. (2018). *The value of everything: Making and taking in the global economy*. New York, NY: Allen Lane.

Mazzucato, M. (2019, June 30). Takers and makers: Who are the real value creators? *Evonomics: The Next Evolution of Economics*. Retrieved from https://evonomics.com/value-of-everything-mariana-mazzucato/

Mazzucato, M., & Collington, R. (2023). *The big con: How the consulting industry weakens our businesses, infantilizes our governments and warps our economies*. London: Allen Lane.

Mazzucato, M., & Rodrik, D. (2023). *Industrial policy with conditionalities: A taxonomy and sample cases* (UCL Institute for Innovation and Public Purpose, Working Paper Series, IIPP WP 2023-07). Retrieved from https://www.ucl.ac.uk/bartlett/publicpurpose/wp2023-07

McCallum, J., & Blais, A. (1987). Government, special interest groups, and economic growth. *Public Choice, 54*(1), 3–18. https://doi.org/10.1007/BF00123801

McCarthy, J., Minsky, M. L., Rochester, N., & Shannon, C. E. (1955). *A proposal for the Dartmouth summer research project on artificial intelligence*. Retrieved from http://jmc.stanford.edu/articles/dartmouth/dartmouth.pdf

McCullough, D. (1992). *Truman*. New York, NY: Simon & Schuster.

McDaniel, R. R., Jr, Lanham, H. J., & Anderson, R. A. (2009). Implications of complex adaptive systems theory for the design of research on health care organizations. *Health care Management Review, 34*(2), 191–199. https://doi.org/10.1097/HMR.0b013e31819c8b38

McFadden, R. D. (2023, October 9). Charles Feeney, who made a fortune and then gave it away, dies at 92. *The New York Times*. Retrieved from https://www.nytimes.com/2023/10/09/business/charles-f-feeney-dead.html

McFall-Ngai, M. (2024). Symbiosis takes a front and center role in biology. *PLOS Biology, 22*(4), e3002571. https://doi.org/10.1371/journal.pbio.3002571

McGilchrist, I. (2019). *The master and his emissary: The divided brain and the making of the Western world: New expanded edition* (2nd ed.). New Haven, CT: Yale University Press.

McGilchrist, I. (2021). *The matter with things: Our brains, our delusions, and the unmaking of the world*. London: Perspectiva Press.

McIlwain, C. H. (1932). *The growth of political thought in the West: From the Greeks to the end of the Middle Ages*. New York, NY: Macmillan.

McKay, A. (2012). Buying policy? The effects of lobbyists' resources on their policy success. *Political Research Quarterly, 65*(4), 908–923. https://doi.org/10.1177/1065912911424285

McKay, A., & Reis, R. (2016). The role of automatic stabilizers in the U.S. business cycle. *Econometrica, 84*(1), 141–194. https://doi.org/10.3982/ECTA11574

McKay, S. (n.d.). Chuck Feeney's interest in Northern Ireland [Summary of "Northern Ireland"]. *Atlantic Philanthropies*. Retrieved January 17, 2025, from https://www.atlanticphilanthropies.org/insights/insights-books/northern-ireland

McLeod, R. H. (2000). Soeharto's Indonesia: A better class of corruption. *Agenda: A Journal of Policy Analysis and Reform, 7*(2), 99–112. https://doi.org/10.22459/AG.07.02.2000.01

McRae, S. (2015). Infrastructure quality and the subsidy trap. *The American Economic Review, 105*(1), 35–66.

McWilliams, A., & Siegel, D. (2000). Corporate social responsibility and financial performance: Correlation or misspecification? *Strategic Management Journal, 21*(5), 603–609. https://doi.org/10.1002/(SICI)1097-0266(200005)21:5<603::AID-SMJ101>3.0.CO;2-3

Mearsheimer, J. (2001). *The tragedy of great power politics*. New York, NY: W.W. Norton & Company.

Medema, S. G. (1994). The Myth of two Coases: What Coase is really saying. *Journal of Economic Issues, 28*(1), 208–217. https://doi.org/10.1080/00213624.1994.11505527

Meinke, A., Schoen, B., Scheurer, J., Balesni, M., Shah, R., & Hobbhahn, M. (2024, December 5). Frontier models are capable of in-context scheming. *Apollo Research*. Retrieved from https://static1.square

space.com/static/6593e7097565990e65c886fd/t/6751eb240ed3821a0161b45b/1733421863119/in_context_scheming_reasoning_paper.pdf

Mellahi, K., Frynas, J. G., Sun, P., & Siegel, D. (2016). A review of nonmarket strategy literature: Towards a multi-theoretical integration. *Journal of Management, 42*(1), 143–173. https://doi.org/10.1177/0149206315617

Mellor, W., & Carpenter, D. M. (2016). *Bottleneckers: Gaming the government for power and private profit.* New York, NY: Encounter Books.

Meltzer, A. H., & Richard, S. F. (1981). A rational theory of the size of government. *Journal of Political Economy, 89*(5), 914–927. https://doi.org/10.1086/261013

Mendizabal, I., Sandoval, K., Berniell-Lee, G., Calafell, F., Salas, A., Martínez-Fuentes, A., & Comas, D. (2008). Genetic origin, admixture, and asymmetry in maternal and paternal human lineages in Cuba. *BMC evolutionary biology, 8*(1), 213. https://doi.org/10.1186/1471-2148-8-213

Menger, C. (1985). *Investigations into the method of the social sciences with special reference to economics* (F. J. Nock, Trans.; L. Schneider, Ed.). New York, NY: New York University Press.

Menger, C. (2007). *Principles of economics* (J. Dingwall & B. F. Hoselitz, Trans.). Auburn, AL: Ludwig von Mises Institute. Retrieved from https://cdn.mises.org/Principles%20of%20Economics_5.pdf

Merelman, R. (1968). On the neo-elitist critique of community power. *The American Political Science Review, 62*(2), 451–460. https://doi.org/10.2307/1952940

Merton, R. C. (1974). On the pricing of corporate debt: The risk structure of interest rates. *The Journal of Finance, 29*(2), 449–470. https://doi.org/10.1111/j.1540-6261.1974.tb03058.x

Messick, D. M., & Bazerman, M. H. (2001), Ethical leadership and the psychology of decision making. In J. Dienhart., D. Moberg., & R. Duska (Eds.), *The next phase of business ethics: Integrating psychology and ethics* (pp. 213–238). Bingley: Emerald Group Publishing Limited. https://doi.org/10.1016/S1529-2096(01)03014-0

Metz, C. (2022, August 5). The ChatGPT king isn't worried, but he knows you might be. *The New York Times*. Retrieved from https://www.nytimes.com/2023/03/31/technology/sam-altman-open-ai-chatgpt.html

Metz, C. (2023, March 31). A.I. Is not sentient. Why do people say it is? *The New York Times*. Retrieved from https://www.nytimes.com/2022/08/05/technology/ai-sentient-google.html

Meyer, J. W., & Rowan, B. (1977). Institutionalized organizations: Formal structure as myth and ceremony. *American Journal of Sociology, 83*(2), 340–363. https://doi.org/10.1086/226550

Meyer, K. E., Estrin, S., Bhaumik, S. K., & Peng, M. W. (2009). Institutions, resources, and entry strategies in emerging economies. *Strategic Management Journal 30*(1), 61–80. https://doi.org/10.1002/smj.720

Mezzanotte, F. E. (2023). Corporate sustainability reporting: Double materiality, impacts, and legal risk. *Journal of Corporate Law Studies, 23*(2), 633–663. https://doi.org/10.1080/14735970.2024.2319058

Michalopoulos, S., & Papaioannou, E. (2013). Pre-colonial ethnic institutions and contemporary African development. *Econometrica, 81*(1), 113–152. https://doi.org/10.3982/ECTA9613

Michel, A. N. (2023, November 28). AI doesn't change the economics of labor, capital, & taxes. *Cato Institute*. Retrieved from https://www.cato.org/blog/ai-doesnt-change-economics-labor-capital-taxes

Michels, R. (1999). *Political parties: A sociological study of the oligarchical tendencies of modern democracy.* Abingdon: Routledge.

Mill, J. S. (2001). *Utilitarianism*. Kitchener, Ontario: Batoche Books Limited. Retrieved from https://socialsciences.mcmaster.ca/econ/ugcm/3ll3/mill/utilitarianism.pdf

Mills, C. W. (1956). *The power elite*. New York, NY: Oxford University Press.

Mills, C. W. (1959). *The sociological imagination*. New York, NY: Grove Press.

Milne, R. (2022, September 19). Norway oil fund warns of 'danger' that environment falls down the agenda. *The Financial Times*. Retrieved from https://www.ft.com/content/f0067d64-dcf2-47b4-a19b-a6b6debd16c5

Milo, D. S. (2019). *Good enough: The tolerance of mediocrity in nature and society*. Cambridge, MA: Harvard University Press.

Ministry of Trade and Industry Singapore. (n.d.). *Overview: Industry Transformation Maps (ITMs)*. Retrieved October 15, 2024, from https://www.mti.gov.sg/ITMs/Overview

Mintzberg, H., & Waters, J. A. (1985). Of strategies, deliberate and emergent. *Strategic Management Journal, 6*(3), 257–272. https://doi.org/10.1002/smj.4250060306

MIT Technology Licensing Office. (n.d.). *Exploring the MIT Open Source License: A comprehensive guide*. Massachusetts Institute of Technology. Retrieved February 3, 2025, from https://tlo.mit.edu/understand-ip/exploring-mit-open-source-license-comprehensive-guide

Mitchell, J. C. (1969). The concept and use of social networks. In J. C. Mitchell (Ed.), *Social networks in urban situations* (pp. 1–50). Manchester: Manchester University Press. Retrieved from https://seminariosocioantropologia.wordpress.com/wp-content/uploads/2014/03/c-mitcell-concept-and-use-social-network.pdf

Mizruchi, M. S. (1994). Social network analysis: Recent achievements and current controversies. *Acta Sociologica, 37*(4), 329–343. https://doi.org/10.1177/000169939403700403

Mizruchi, M. S. (2013). *The fracturing of the American corporate elite*. Cambridge, MA: Harvard University Press.

Mizruchi, M. S. (2017). “The Power Elite” in historical context: A reevaluation of Mills’s thesis, then and now. *Theory and Society, 46*(2), 95–116.

Moatti, V., Ren, C., Anand, J., & Dussauge, P. (2015). Disentangling the performance effects of efficiency and bargaining power in horizontal growth strategies: An empirical investigation in the global retail industry. *Strategic Management Journal, 36*(5), 745–757. https://doi.org/10.1002/smj.2244

Modelski, G. (1983). Long cycles of world leadership: An annotated bibliography. *International Studies Notes, 10*(3), 1–5.

Modelski, G. & Thompson, W. R. (1988). *Seapower and global politics, 1494-1993*. London: Macmillan.

Modigliani, F., & Miller, M. (1958). The cost of capital, corporation finance and the theory of investment. *American Economic Review, 48*(3), 261–297.

Mohan, N. (2024, February 6). Letter from the YouTube CEO: 4 big bets for 2024. *YouTube Blog*. Retrieved from https://blog.youtube/inside-youtube/2024-letter-from-neal/

Mohr, A., Batsakis, G., & Stone, Z. (2018). Explaining the effect of rapid internationalization on horizontal foreign divestment in the retail sector: An extended Penrosean perspective. *Journal of International Business Studies, 49*(7), 779–808. https://doi.org/10.1057/s41267-017-0138-0

Mokyr, J. (2017). *A culture of growth: The origins of the modern economy*. Princeton, NJ: Princeton University Press. https://doi.org/10.2307/j.ctt1wf4dft

Mokyr, J., & Nye, J. V. (2007). Distributional coalitions, the industrial revolution, and the origins of economic growth in Britain. *Southern Economic Journal, 74*(1), 50–70. https://doi.org/10.1002/j.2325-8012.2007.tb00826.x

Mombauer, A. (2023, October 30). Erzberger: Negotiating the armistice for Germany. *The Open University/OpenLearn*. Retrieved from https://www.open.edu/openlearn/history-the-arts/history/erzberger-negotiating-the-armistice-germany

Moment of Zen. (2024, December 27*). Marc Andreessen on Trump, the vibe shift, and what’s after wokeness* [Video]. YouTube. https://www.youtube.com/watch?v=I8X8jecivWw

Monteiro, G. F. A., & Miranda, B. V. (2023). Disentangling the role of the institutional environment in the ownership competence framework: A comment on Foss et al. (2021). *Strategic Management Journal, 44*(8), 1939–1954. https://doi.org/10.1002/smj.3462

Montesquieu, B. D. (1949). *The spirit of the laws*. New York: Hafner Publishing Company. Retrieved from https://www.bard.edu/library/arendt/pdfs/Montesquieu-Spirit.pdf

Moore, B., Jr. (1958). *Political power and social theory: Six studies*. Cambridge, MA: Harvard University Press.

Moore, G. (1979). The structure of a national elite network. *American Sociological Review, 44*(5), 673–692. https://doi.org/10.2307/2094520

Moran, P., & Ghoshal, S. (1996). Value creation by firms. *Academy of Management Proceedings*, *1996*(1), 41–45.

Moravcsik, A. (1992). *Liberalism and international relations theory* (CFIA Working Paper No. 92-6). Cambridge, MA: Harvard University.

Moravec, H. (1999). Rise of the robots. *Scientific American*, *281*(6), 124–135. https://doi.org/10.1038/scientificamerican1299-124

Morck, R., & Yeung, B. (2004). Family control and the rent-seeking society. *Entrepreneurship Theory and Practice*, *28*(4), 391–409. https://doi.org/10.1111/j.1540-6520.2004.00053.x

Morgenson, G., & Rosner, J. (2023). *These are the plunderers: How private equity runs – and wrecks – America*. New York, NY: Simon & Schuster.

Morgenthau, H. J. (1948). *Politics among nations: The struggle for power and peace*. New York, NY: Alfred A. Knopf.

Morony, M. (1976). The effects of the Muslim conquest on the Persian population of Iraq. *Iran*, *14*(1), 41–59.

Morozov, E. (2014). *To save everything, click here: The folly of technological solutionism*. New York, NY: PublicAffairs.

Morschett, D., Schramm-Klein, H., & Swoboda, B. (2010). Decades of research on market entry modes: What do we really know about external antecedents of entry mode choice? *Journal of International Management*, *16*(1), 60–77. https://doi.org/10.1016/j.intman.2009.09.002

Mosca, G. (1939). *The ruling class* (H. D. Kahn, Trans.). New York, NY: McGraw-Hill.

Mosse, K. (2024, December 21). AI's assault on our intellectual property must be stopped. *The Financial Times*. Retrieved from https://www.ft.com/content/f26bda64-1237-4188-8540-210367567089

Mourselas, C. (2025, January 30). Hedge fund Elliott warns White House is inflating crypto bubble that 'could wreak havoc'. *The Financial Times*. Retrieved from https://www.ft.com/content/5fe69580-7f01-4215-98bb-b6ec5f7cd833

Moynihan, B. & Schwab, K. (2020, September). Preface. In World Economic Forum (White Paper). *Measuring stakeholder capitalism: Towards common metrics and consistent reporting of sustainable value creation*. (pp. 3–5). Retrieved from http://www3.weforum.org/docs/WEF_IBC_Measuring_Stakeholder_Capitalism_Report_2020.pdf

Mozur, P., & Satariano, A. (2024, July 2). Ukraine war ushers in an age of AI weapons. *The New York Times*. Retrieved from https://www.nytimes.com/2024/07/02/technology/ukraine-war-ai-weapons.html

Mrozek, J. (1999). Market failures and efficiency in the principles course. *The Journal of Economic Education*, *30*(4), 411–419. https://doi.org/10.1080/00220489909596098

Mu, E. (2014, May 18). Yu'ebao: A brief history of the Chinese internet financing upstart. *Forbes Asia*. Retrieved from https://www.forbes.com/sites/ericxlmu/2014/05/18/yuebao-a-brief-history-of-the-chinese-internet-financing-upstart/

Mueller, D. C. (1972). A life cycle theory of the firm. *The Journal of Industrial Economics*, *20*(3), 199–219. https://doi.org/10.2307/2098055

Mullin, J. (2023, January 1). Seeing patent trolls clearly: 2022 in review. *Electronic Frontier Foundation*. Retrieved from https://www.eff.org/zh-hans/deeplinks/2022/12/seeing-patent-trolls-clearly-2022-review

Murati, E. (2022). Language & coding creativity. *Dædalus*, *151*(2), 156–167. https://doi.org/10.1162/daed_a_01907

Murphy, H. (2024, January 11). The rising threat to democracy of AI-powered disinformation. *The Financial Times*. Retrieved from https://www.ft.com/content/16f23c01-fa51-408e-acf5-0d30a5a1ebf2

Murphy, K., Schleifer, A., & Vishny, R. (1993). Why is rent-seeking so costly to growth? *American Economic Review*, *83*(2), 409–414.

Murray. S. (2021, May 14). Measuring what matters: The scramble to set standards for sustainable business. *The Financial Times*. Retrieved from https://www.ft.com/content/92915630-c110-4364-86ee-0f6f018cba90

Musashi, M. (1974). *A book of five rings* (V. Harris, Trans.). Woodstock, NY: The Overlook Press.

Musk, E. [@elonmusk]. (2024, November 23). *Wow, they really don't get it. Mars is critical to the long-term survival of consciousness. Also I'm not going to* [Video attached] [Post]. X. https://x.com/elonmusk/status/1860322925783445956

Musk, E. [@elonmusk]. (2025, February 11). *Tax regulations need a massive reset. They are torturing the American people!* [Thumbnail with link attached] [Post]. X. https://x.com/elonmusk/status/1886092387098796499

Musk v. Altman, et al., No. CGC-24-612746 (Cal. Super. Ct. Feb. 29, 2024). Retrieved from https://www.courthousenews.com/wp-content/uploads/2024/02/musk-v-altman-openai-complaint-sf.pdf

Nabi, G., Liñán, F., Fayolle, A., Krueger, N., & Walmsley, A. (2017). The impact of entrepreneurship education in higher education: A systematic review and research agenda. *Academy of Management Learning & Education, 16*(2), 277–299. https://doi.org/10.5465/amle.2015.0026

Nader, R. (2014). *Unstoppable: The emerging left-right alliance to dismantle the corporate state*. New York, NY: Nation Books.

Naef, P. (2018). "Narco-heritage" and the touristification of the drug lord Pablo Escobar in Medellin, Colombia. *Journal of Anthropological Research 74*(4), 485–502. http://dx.doi.org/10.1086/699941

Nagasu, K. (1959). *Nippon keizai nyumon* (Introduction to the Japanese economy). Tokyo: Kobunsha.

Nakamoto, S. (2008). *Bitcoin: A peer-to-peer electronic cash system*. Retrieved from https://bitcoin.org/bitcoin.pdf

Nam, R. (2024, December 4). Trump picks crypto backer Paul Atkins as new Securities and Exchange Commission chair. *NPR*. Retrieved from https://www.npr.org/2024/12/04/g-s1-36803/trump-crypto-paul-atkins-sec-chair

Nardo, M., Saisana, M., Saltelli, A., & Tarantola, S. (2005). *Tools for composite indicators building* (EUR 21682 EN. 2005. JRC31473). Ispra, Italy: European Commission.

Nasir, M. A. (2012). Logic of the absurd: Reading Kafka in a kafkaesque world. *Administrative Theory & Praxis, 34*(1), 40–59.

Nassif, A., Feijó, C., & Araújo, E. (2015). Structural change and economic development: Is Brazil catching up or falling behind? *Cambridge Journal of Economics, 39*(5), 1307–1332. https://doi.org/10.1093/cje/beu052

Nature Physics. (2022). Complexity matters. *Nature Physics, 18*(8), 843. https://doi.org/10.1038/s41567-022-01734-5

Nau, M. (2013). Economic elites, investments, and income inequality. *Social Forces, 92*(2), 437–461. https://doi.org/10.1093/sf/sot102

Naughton, N. (2021, September 11). Everything must go! The American car dealerships for sale. *The Wall Street Journal*. Retrieved from https://www.wsj.com/articles/everything-must-go-the-american-car-dealership-is-for-sale-11631332812

Nebehay, S. (2018, March 21). Executions, torture and slave markets persist in Libya. *Reuters*. Retrieved from https://www.reuters.com/article/us-libya-security-rights-iduskbn1gx1jy

Nee, V., & Swedberg, R. (2008). Economic sociology and new institutional economics. In C. Ménard & M. M. Shirley (Eds.), *Handbook of new institutional economics* (pp. 789–818). Berlin, Heidelberg: Springer. https://doi.org/10.1007/978-3-540-69305-5

Neill, J. S. (2011). Aristotle and American oligarchy: A study in political influence. In D. Tabachnick and T. Koivukoski (Eds.), *On oligarchy: Ancient lessons for global politics* (pp. 24–26). Toronto: University of Toronto Press.

Neubauer Collegium. (2024, May 2). *Stuart Russell, "AI: what if we succeed?" April 25, 2024* [Video]. YouTube. https://www.youtube.com/watch?v=UvvdFZkhhqE

Neue Rheinische Zeitung. (1849, May 18). *Final issue: Suppression of the Neue Rheinische Zeitung* (No. 301, Marx-Engels Institute, Trans. 1994). Retrieved from https://www.marxists.org/archive/marx/works/1849/05/19c.htm

Ngo, R. (2020, September 29). AGI safety from first principles: Goals and agency. *Alignment Forum*. Retrieved from https://www.alignmentforum.org/posts/bz5GdmCWj8o48726N/agi-safety-from-first-principles-goals-and-agency

Nicholas, T. (2003). Why Schumpeter was right: Innovation, market power, and creative destruction in 1920s America. *The Journal of Economic History*, *63*(4), 1023–1058. https://doi.org/10.1017/S0022050703002523

Nicholas, T. (2014). Are patents creative or destructive? *Antitrust Law Journal*, *79*(2), 405–421.

Nickell, S. J. (1996). Competition and corporate performance. *Journal of Political Economy*, *104*(4), 724–746. https://doi.org/10.1086/262040

Nickles, T. (2002). Introduction. In T. Nickles (Ed.), *Thomas Kuhn* (pp. 1–18). Cambridge: Cambridge University Press. https://doi.org/10.1017/CBO9780511613975

Nicolaou, A. (2025, January 25). The podcast bros who helped put Trump back in the White House. *The Financial Times*. Retrieved from https://www.ft.com/content/9f2be125-ba1b-4062-ab2d-4b2977db20b0

Nielsen, B. B., Asmussen, C. G., & Weatherall, C. D. (2017). The location choice of foreign direct investments: Empirical evidence and methodological challenges. *Journal of World Business 52*(1), 62–82. https://doi.org/10.1016/j.jwb.2016.10.006.

Nietzsche, F. (1923). The birth of tragedy: Or hellenism and pessimism. In O. Levy (Ed.), *The complete works of Friedrich Nietzsche* (W. A. Haussmann, Trans.). London: George Allen & Unwin Ltd.

Nietzsche, F. (2006). *Thus spoke Zarathustra: A book for all and none* (A. Del Caro, Trans.; A. Del Caro & R. B. Pippin, Eds.). Cambridge: Cambridge University Press. https://doi.org/10.1017/CBO9780511812095

Nissenbaum, D., Donati, J., & Cullison, A. (2021, 31 December). Who won in Afghanistan? Private contractors. *The Wall Street Journal*. Retrieved from https://www.wsj.com/articles/who-won-in-afghanistan-private-contractors-troops-withdrawal-war-pentagon-11640988154

Nogrady, B. (2023, November 8). Denmark puts its money where its life-sciences strategy is. *Nature, 623* (S16–S17). https://doi.org/10.1038/d41586-023-03446-z

Nohria, N., & Gulati, R. (1996). Is slack good or bad for innovation? *The Academy of Management Journal*, *39*(5), 1245–1264. https://doi.org/10.2307/256998

Noonan, L. (2020, June 25). Fed caps dividends and bans buybacks by big US banks. *The Financial Times*. Retrieved from https://www.ft.com/content/58c63f45-9bb0-437b-8ba4-c50820c5eae2

Nordhaus, W. (1994). *Managing the global commons: The economics of climate change*. Cambridge, MA: MIT Press.

North, D. C. (1984). Transaction costs, institutions, and economic history. *Journal of Institutional and Theoretical Economics*, *140*(1), 7–17.

North, D. C. (1990). *Institutions, institutional change and economic performance*. Cambridge: Cambridge University Press. https://doi.org/10.1017/CBO9780511808678

North, D. C. (1991a). Institutions. *Journal of Economic Perspectives*, *5*(1), 97–112. https://doi.org/10.1257/jep.5.1.97

North, D. C. (1991b). Towards a theory of institutional change. *Quarterly Review of Economics and Business*, *31*(4), 3–11.

North, D. C. (1994). Economic performance through time. *The American Economic Review*, *84*(3), 359–368.

North D. C. (1996). Epilogue: economic performance through time. In L. J. Alston, T. Eggertsson, and D. C North (Eds.), *Empirical studies in institutional change* (pp. 342–356). Cambridge: Cambridge University Press. https://doi.org/10.1017/CBO9781139174633.023

North, D. C., Wallis, J. J., & Weingast, B. R. (2006). *Violence and social orders: A conceptual framework for interpreting recorded human history*. Cambridge: Cambridge University Press. https://doi.org/10.1017/CBO9780511575839

Notehelfer, F. G. (1990). Meiji in the rear-view mirror. Top down vs. bottom up history [Review of *The Cambridge history of Japan Volume 5: The Nineteenth Century*, by M. B. Jansen]. *Monumenta Nipponica*, *45* (2), 207–228. https://doi.org/10.2307/2384849

Nownes, A. (2006). *Total lobbying: What lobbyists want (and how they try to get it)*. Cambridge: Cambridge University Press. https://doi.org/10.1017/CBO9780511840395

Noy, S., & Zhang, W. (2023, March 1). *Experimental evidence on the productivity effects of generative artificial intelligence* (MIT Working Paper). Retrieved from https://economics.mit.edu/sites/default/files/inline-files/Noy_Zhang_1_0.pdf

Nussbaum, M. (2003). Capabilities as fundamental entitlements: Sen and social justice. *Feminist Economics*, *9*(2-3), 33–59. https://doi.org/10.1080/1354570022000077926

NVIDIA. (2024, June 2). *NVIDIA CEO Jensen Huang keynote at COMPUTEX 2024* [Video]. YouTube. https://www.youtube.com/watch?v=pKXDVsWZmUU

Nye, R. A. (1977). *The anti-democratic sources of elite theory: Pareto, Mosca, Michels*. London: Sage.

O'Brien, K., Carmona, R., Gram-Hanssen, I., Bendor, R., Bøyum, L. S., Fritsche, I., Ivanova, D., Klinsky, S., Scoville-Simonds, M., & Stoddard, I. (2023). Fractal approaches to scaling transformations to sustainability. *Ambio*, *52*(9), 1448–1461. https://doi.org/10.1007/s13280-023-01873-w

O'Connor, T. (1994). Emergent properties. *American Philosophical Quarterly*, *31*(2), 91–104.

O'Donnell, G., & Schmitter, P. (1986). *Transitions from authoritarian rule: Tentative conclusions about uncertain democracies*. Baltimore, MD: The Johns Hopkins University Press.

O'Neill, J. (1992). The varieties of intrinsic value. *The Monist*, *75*(2), 119–137.

OECD (1999). *Economic and social impact of e- commerce: Preliminary findings and research agenda* (OECD Digital Economy Papers, No. 40). Retrieved from https://www.oecd-ilibrary.org/economic-and-social-impact-of-e-commerce_5kzdcc6tnfmp.pdf

OECD. (2008). *Handbook on constructing composite indicators: Methodology and user guide*. Paris: OECD.

OECD. (2012a). *Mortality risk valuation in environment, health and transport policies*. Paris: OECD.

OECD. (2012b). Understanding the drivers of perception to improve the use of survey results. In OECD, *Measuring regulatory performance: A practitioner's guide to perception surveys*. Paris: OECD.

OECD. (2013). *Lobbying in the 21st century: Transparency, integrity and access*. Paris: OECD. Retrieved from https://www.oecd.org/en/publications/lobbying-in-the-21st-century_c6d8eff8-en.html

OECD. (2021). *Statement on a two-pillar solution to address the tax challenges arising from the digitalisation of the economy – 8 October 2021*. OECD/G20 Inclusive Framework on BEPS. Retrieved from https://www.oecd.org/content/dam/oecd/en/topics/policy-issues/beps/statement-on-a-two-pillar-solution-to-address-the-tax-challenges-arising-from-the-digitalisation-of-the-economy-october-2021.pdf

Okulicz-Kozaryn, A. (2014). 'Freedom from' and 'freedom to' across countries. *Social Indicators Research*, *118*(3), 1009–1029. https://doi.org/10.1007/s11205-013-0473-x

Okun, A. M. (2015). *Equality and efficiency: The big trade-off*. Washington, DC: Brookings Institution Press.

Olcott, E., & Wu, Z. (2025, January 25). How small Chinese AI start-up DeepSeek shocked Silicon Valley. *The Financial Times*. Retrieved from https://www.ft.com/content/747a7b11-dcba-4aa5-8d25-403f56216d7e

Oliver, C. (1991). Strategic responses to institutional processes. *Academy of Management Review*, *16*(1), 145–179. https://doi.org/10.2307/258610

Olson, M. (1971). *The logic of collective action: Public goods and the theory of groups*. Cambridge, MA: Harvard University Press.

Olson, M. (1982). *The rise and decline of nations: Economic growth, stagflation, and social rigidities*. New Haven, CT: Yale University Press.

Olson, M. (1984). Microeconomic incentives and macroeconomic decline. *Weltwirtschaftliches Archiv*, *120*(4), 631–645. https://doi.org/10.1007/BF02706507

Olson, M. (1993). Dictatorship, democracy, and development. *The American Political Science Review*, *87*(3), 567–576. https://doi.org/10.2307/2938736

Olson, M. (1996). The varieties of eurosclerosis: The rise and decline of nations since 1982. In N. Crafts & G. Toniolo (Eds.), *Economic growth in Europe since 1945* (pp. 73–94). Cambridge: Cambridge University Press. https://doi.org/10.1017/CBO9780511758683.004

Olson, M. (2000). *Power and prosperity: Outgrowing Communist and Capitalist dictatorships.* New York, NY: Basic Books.

OpenAI. (2023, April 5). Our approach to AI safety. *OpenAI.* Retrieved from https://openai.com/blog/our-approach-to-ai-safety#OpenAI

OpenAI. (2024, March 5). OpenAI and Elon Musk. *OpenAI.* Retrieved from https://openai.com/index/openai-elon-musk/

Ophuls, W. (2012). *Immoderate greatness: Why civilizations fail.* CreateSpace Independent Publishing Platform.

Orcutt, M. (2023, August 3). What's next for China's digital currency? *MIT Technology Review.* Retrieved from https://www.technologyreview.com/2023/08/03/1077181/whats-next-for-chinas-digital-currency/

Organski, A. F. K (1958). *World politics.* New York, NY: Alfred A. Knopf.

Osgood, J. (2009). The pen and the sword: Writing and conquest in Caesar's Gaul. *Classical Antiquity, 28*(2), 328–358. https://doi.org/10.1525/ca.2009.28.2.328

Ostrom, E. (2005). *Understanding institutional diversity.* Princeton, NJ: Princeton University Press. https://doi.org/10.1515/9781400831739

Ostrom, V. (1975). Public choice theory: A new approach to institutional economics. *American Journal of Agricultural Economics, 57*(5), 844–850. https://doi.org/10.2307/1239090

Ostry, J. D., Berg, A., & Tsangarides, C. G. (2014, February). *Redistribution, inequality, and growth* (IMF Staff Discussion Note No. SDN/14/02). Washington, DC: International Monetary Fund. Retrieved from https://www.imf.org/external/pubs/ft/sdn/2014/sdn1402.pdf

Ovans, A. (2015, January 23). What is a business model? *Harvard Business Review.* Retrieved from https://hbr.org/2015/01/what-is-a-business-model

Owen, D. L. (1981, October). The design of hazardous products. *IEEE Transactions on Systems, Man, and Cybernetics, 11*(10), 714. Retrieved from https://ieeexplore.ieee.org/stamp/stamp.jsp?arnumber=4308591

Pagels, E. (1979). *The Gnostic Gospels.* New York, NY: Random House.

Pakulski, J. (2012). The Weberian foundations of modern elite theory and democratic elitism. *Historical Social Research, 37*(1), 38–56. https://doi.org/10.2307/41756449

Pakulski, J. (2018). The development of elite theory. In H. Best and J. Higley (Eds.), *The Palgrave handbook of political elites* (pp. 9–16). London: Palgrave Macmillan. https://doi.org/10.1057/978-1-137-51904-7_2

Palantir Bite-Sized. (2025a, January 20). *Palantir CTO brutally honest about AI* [Video]. YouTube. https://youtu.be/bIUUtJ9DrDI

Palantir Bite-Sized. (2025b, January 21). *Palantir founder's predictions leaves host speechless* [Video]. YouTube. https://www.youtube.com/watch?v=yNsaX-HXUc0

Palma, J. G. (2014). De-industrialisation, 'premature' de-industrialisation and the Dutch-Disease. *Revista NECAT, 3*(5), 7–23. https://doi.org/10.20430/ete.v86i344.970

Palma, S., & Acton, M. (2024, December 29). Elon Musk's fight with Maga reveals split on immigration within Trump's circle. *The Financial Times.* Retrieved from https://www.ft.com/content/0531a4ab-e587-421c-8326-91e0e128ec34

Palma, S., Weaver, C., & Gilbert, C. (2022, November 13). Sam Bankman-Fried's fall cuts off big source of funds for US Democrats. *The Financial Times.* Retrieved from https://www.ft.com/content/428c7800-c72d-4c59-9940-4376fea6e263

Paniagua, V., & Vogler, J. P. (2022). Economic elites and the constitutional design of sharing political power. *Constitutional Political Economy, 33*(1), 25–52. https://doi.org/10.1007/s10602-021-09338-6

Pareto, V. (1991). *The rise and fall of elites: Application of theoretical sociology.* New Brunswick, NJ: Transaction Publishers.

Park, S. (2021). Chaebol reforms are crucial for South Korea's future. *East Asia Forum Quarterly, 13*(1), 21–25.

Parolini, J., Patterson, K., & Winston, B. (2009). Distinguishing between transformational and servant leadership. *Leadership & Organizational Development Journal, 30*(3), 274–291. https://doi.org/10.1108/01437730910949544

Parris, D., & Peachey, J. (2013). A systematic literature review of servant leadership theory in organizational contexts. *Journal of Business Ethics, 113*(3), 377–393. https://doi.org/10.1007/s10551-012-1322-6

Parry, G. (2005). *Political elites*. Colchester: ECPR Classics.

Parsons, J. E. (1969). Locke's doctrine of propriety. *Social Research, 36*(3), 389–411.

Parsons, T. (1957). The distribution of power in American society [Review of the book *The Power Elite* by C. W. Mills]. *World Politics, 10*(1), 123–143. https://doi.org/10.2307/2009229

Parsons, T. (1970). On building social system theory: A personal history. *Daedalus, 99*(4), 826–881.

Parsons, T. (1991). *The social system*. London: Routledge.

Pasquale, F. (2015). *The black box society: The secret algorithms that control money and information*. Cambridge, MA: Harvard University Press.

Patel, D. (2025, February 19). Satya Nadella – Microsoft's AGI plan & quantum breakthrough: AGI is not the real benchmark: 10% economic growth is. *Dwarkesh Patel*. Retrieved from https://www.dwarkeshpatel.com/p/satya-nadella

Patel, D., & Ahmad, A. (2023, May 4). Google "We have no moat and neither does OpenAI". *SemiAnalysis*. Retrieved from https://www.semianalysis.com/p/google-we-have-no-moat-and-neither

Pazienza, M., de Jong, M., & Schoenmaker, D. (2023). Why corporate sustainability is not yet measured. *Sustainability, 15*(7), 6275. https://doi.org/10.3390/su15076275

Pearce II, J. A. (1995). A structural analysis of dominant coalitions in small banks. *Journal of Management, 21*(6), 1075–1095. https://doi.org/10.1177/014920639502100604

Peel, M., & Cookson, C. (2024, December 13). Synthetic 'mirror' microbes pose unprecedented threat to life, scientists warn. *The Financial Times*. Retrieved from https://www.ft.com/content/af39c5f1-3c7c-4097-897b-6793cddf658d

Pei, M. (2016). *China's crony capitalism: The dynamics of regime decay*. Cambridge, MA: Harvard University Press.

Peirce, C. S. (1877). The fixation of belief. *Popular Science Monthly, 12*(1), 1-15.

Peltzman, S., Levine, M. E., & Noll, R. G. (1989). The economic theory of regulation after a decade of deregulation. *Brookings Papers on Economic Activity. Microeconomics, 1989*, 1–59. https://doi.org/10.2307/2534719

Peoples, S. (2025, February 17). The anti-Musk protest movement is expected to ramp up with Congress on recess. *AP News*. https://apnews.com/article/ccb64f2889d31aad8c25d37686f62d7a

Peres, R. S., Jia, X., Lee, J., Sun, K., Colombo, A. W., & Barata, J. (2020). Industrial artificial intelligence in industry 4.0 – Systematic review, challenges and outlook. *IEEE Access, 8*(220121–220139). https://doi.org/10.1109/ACCESS.2020.3042874

Perkins, E. (2000). [Review of the book *The house of Rothschild: The world's banker, 1849-1999*, by N. Ferguson]. *The Business History Review, 74*(3), 485–489. https://doi.org/10.2307/3116440

Perold, A. F. (2004). The capital asset pricing model. *The Journal of Economic Perspectives, 18*(3), 3–24. https://doi.org/10.1257/0895330042162340

Petit, N. (2020). *Big Tech and the digital economy: The moligopoly scenario*. Oxford: Oxford University Press. https://doi.org/10.1093/oso/9780198837701.001.0001

Petit, N., & Teece, D. J. (2021). Innovating Big Tech firms and competition policy: Favoring dynamic over static competition. *Industrial and Corporate Change, 30*(5), 1168–1198. https://doi.org/10.1093/icc/dtab049

Petrović, G. (1963). Marx's theory of alienation. *Philosophy and Phenomenological Research, 23*(3), 419–426. https://doi.org/10.2307/2105083

Pettigrew, A. M. (1992). On studying managerial elites. *Strategic Management Journal*, *13*, 163–182. https://doi.org/10.1002/smj.4250130911

Pettis, M. (2024, December 27). How tariffs can help America: Economists have drawn the wrong lessons from the failures of the 1930s. *Foreign Affairs*. Retrieved from https://www.foreignaffairs.com/united-states/how-tariffs-can-help-america

Pettit, P. (1996). Freedom as antipower. *Ethics*, *106*(3), 576–604. https://doi.org/10.1086/233648

Pfeifer, S. (2023, July 30). City investors putting UK security at risk over ESG, ministers warn. *The Financial Times*. Retrieved from https://www.ft.com/content/0c777d3c-c441-4730-be12-4b21aa70c216

Piazza, A., & Castellucci, F. (2014). Status in organization and management theory. *Journal of Management*, *40*(1), 287–315. https://doi.org/10.1177/0149206313498904

Piccolo, R. F., & Colquitt, J. A. (2006). Transformational leadership and job behaviors: The mediating role of core job characteristics. *The Academy of Management Journal*, *49*(2), 327–340. https://doi.org/10.5465/AMJ.2006.20786079

Pierson, P. (2000). Increasing returns, path dependence, and the study of politics. *American Political Science Review*, *94*(2), 251–267. https://doi.org/10.2307/2586011

Pierson, P. (2004). *Politics in time*. Princeton, NJ: Princeton University Press.

Piff, P. K., & Robinson, A. R. (2017) Social class and prosocial behavior: Current evidence, caveats, and questions. *Current Opinion in Psychology*, *18*(6), 6–10. https://doi.org/10.1016/j.copsyc.2017.06.003

Pigou, G. (1932). *The Economics of Welfare* (4th ed.). London: Macmillan & Co.

Piketty, T. (2014). *Capital in the Twenty-First Century*. Cambridge, MA: Harvard University Press.

Piketty, T. (2015). About "Capital in the Twenty-First Century". *The American Economic Review*, *105*(5), 48–53.

Pilling, D. (2023, January 1). Corrupt, failing Eskom is a picture of South Africa in miniature. *The Financial Times*. Retrieved from https://www.ft.com/content/73a5242b-9fb4-47b0-a201-ebacea7cb071

Pinker, S. (2018). *Enlightenment now: The case for reason, science, humanism, and progress*. New York, NY: Penguin.

Pinto, A. C. (2017). *Corporatism and fascism: The corporatist wave in Europe*. Abingdon: Routledge.

Pisani, M. J., & Ovando Rivarola, F. G. (2019). *Understanding the determinants of economic informality in Paraguay: A kaleidoscope of measures*. Palgrave Pivot. https://doi.org/10.1007/978-3-030-24393-7

Pisani, M. J., & Patrick, J. M. (2002). A conceptual model and propositions for bolstering entrepreneurship in the informal sector: The case of Central America. *Journal of Developmental Entrepreneurship*, *7*(1), 95–111.

Pistor, K. (2019). *The code of capital: How the law creates wealth and inequality*. Princeton, NJ: Princeton University Press.

Plato. (1908). *The republic of Plato* (B. Jowett, Trans., 3rd ed., Vol. 2) Oxford: Clarendon Press.

Plato. (1969). *Republic* (P. Shorey, Trans.). In *Plato in twelve volumes* (Vols. 5 & 6). Cambridge, MA: Harvard University Press. Retrieved from https://www.perseus.tufts.edu/hopper/text?doc=Perseus:text:1999.01.0168:book=4

Pliny the Elder. (1938). *Natural History* (Book VII, H. Rackham, Trans.). Loeb Classical Library edition. Boston, MA: Harvard University Press. Retrieved from https://www.loebclassics.com/view/pliny_elder-natural_history/1938/pb_LCL352.567.xml

Plotnick, R. D., & Winters, R. F. (1985). A politico-economic theory of income redistribution. *The American Political Science Review*, *79*(2), 458–473. https://doi.org/10.2307/1956660

Plutarch. (1919). *The life of Julius Cesar*. In Plutarch, *The parallel lives* (Vol. VII, B. Perrin, Trans.). Loeb Classical Library edition. Retrieved from https://penelope.uchicago.edu/Thayer/E/Roman/Texts/Plutarch/Lives/Caesar*.html#ref61

Podes, S. (1991). Polybius and his theory of "anacyclosis" problems of not just ancient political theory. *History of Political Thought*, *12*(4), 577–587.

Politi, J. (2022, June 1). Janet Yellen admits she was 'wrong' about inflation threat. *The Financial Times*. Retrieved from https://www.ft.com/content/437a4e4b-9b97-4cd0-bb4a-d5d333e65410

Politi, J. (2025, January 20). Can Trump handle the new Republican factions? *The Financial Times*. Retrieved from https://www.ft.com/content/6c2f4485-b4ac-4cb0-b3f7-dac55b04d685

Politi, J., Fleming, S., & Espinoza, J. (2021, July 6). US piles pressure on EU to drop digital tax plan. *The Financial Times*. Retrieved from https://www.ft.com/content/3d4d5445-e8cf-4fd4-a553-3389459362c6

Politi, J., & Fontanella-Khan, J. (2024, December 18). 'What choice do they have?': America's CEOs bend the knee to Donald Trump. *The Financial Times*. Retrieved from https://www.ft.com/content/8236545b-4ec7-4e0d-8d53-d9ef5d3f0882

Pollitt, M. G., & Smith, A. S. J. (2002). The restructuring and privatisation of British Rail: Was It really that bad? *Fiscal Studies*, *23*(4), 463–502. https://doi.org/10.1111/j.1475-5890.2002.tb00069.x

Polyakova, A. G., Nesterenko, J. N., & Sverdlikova, E. A. (2019). Meta-institutions as a product of institutional dynamics and institutional reformation. *Postmodern Openings*, *10*(2), 137–154. https://doi.org/10.18662/po/76

Polybius. (1889). *The histories of Polybius* (E. S. Shuckburgh, Trans.). London: Macmillan and Co. Retrieved from https://www.gutenberg.org/files/44125/44125-h/44125-h.htm

Pomeranz, K. (2000). *The great divergence: China, Europe and the making of the modern world economy*. Princeton, NJ: Princeton University Press.

Poore, C. (2024, May 10). Using AI to wrangle fusion energy. *Princeton University, Andlinger Center for Energy and the Environment*. Retrieved from https://engineering.princeton.edu/news/2024/05/10/using-ai-wrangle-fusion-energy

Popper, K. R. (1947). *The open society and its enemies* (Vol. I, The spell of Plato). London: George Routledge & Sons, Ltd. Retrieved from https://antilogicalism.com/wp-content/uploads/2018/04/open-society-1.pdf

Popper, K. R. (1962). *Conjectures and refutations: The growth of scientific knowledge*. New York, NY: Basic Books.

Porter, G., & Livesay, H. C. (1971). *Merchants and manufacturers*. Baltimore, MD: Johns Hopkins University Press.

Porter, M. E. (1980). Industry structure and competitive strategy: Keys to profitability. *Financial Analysts Journal*, *36*(4), 30–41. https://doi.org/10.2469/faj.v36.n4.30

Porter, M. E. (1990). *The competitive advantage of nations*. New York, NY: Free Press.

Porter, M. E. (1991). Towards a dynamic theory of strategy. *Strategic Management Journal*, *12*(S2), 95–117. https://doi.org/10.1002/smj.4250121008

Portes, A., Castells, M., & Benton, L. A. (Eds.). (1989). *The informal economy: Studies in advanced and less developed countries*. Baltimore, MD: Johns Hopkins University Press.

Portes, A., & Schauffler, R. (1993). Competing perspectives on the Latin American informal sector. *Population and Development Review*, *19*(1), 33–60. https://doi.org/10.2307/2938384

Posaner, J., Kayali, L., Brinkmann, J., & Noyan, O. (2025, January 8). Europe splits on Trump's call to dramatically boost defense spending. *Politico*. Retrieved from https://www.politico.eu/article/donald-trump-tells-allies-spend-5-percent-gdp-defense-nato/

Powell, W. W., & Colyvas, J. A. (2008). Microfoundations of institutional theory. In R. Greenwood, C. Oliver, K. Sahlin, & R. Suddaby (Eds.), *The Sage handbook of organizational institutionalism* (pp. 276–298). Thousand Oaks, CA: Sage. https://doi.org/10.4135/9781849200387.n11

PowerfulJRE. (2024, November 30). *Joe Rogan Experience #2234 - Marc Andreessen* [Video]. YouTube. https://youtu.be/ye8MOfxD5nU

Powers, C. (1981). Pareto's theory of society. *Revue Européenne Des Sciences Sociales*, *19*(59), 99–119.

Prebisch, R. (1950). *The economic development of Latin America and its principal problems* (E/CN.12/89/Rev.1), Santiago, Economic Commission for Latin America and the Caribbean (eclac). Lake Success, NY: United Nations. Retrieved from https://repositorio.cepal.org/bitstream/handle/11362/29973/002_en.pdf?sequence=1&isAllowed=y

Prigogine, I. (1967). Dissipative structures in chemical systems. In S. Claesson (Ed.), *Fast reactions and primary processes in chemical kinetics* (pp. 583–609). New York, NY: Interscience Publishers.

Prigogine, I. (1996). *The end of certainty: Time, chaos, and the new laws of nature*. New York, NY: Free Press.

Primi, A. (2015, September 29). Industrial Policy: Not a bad word. *OECD Development Matters*. Retrieved from https://oecd-development-matters.org/2015/09/29/industrial-policy-not-a-bad-word/

Proudhon, P-J. (1971). General idea of the revolution in the Nineteenth Century. In M. S. Shatz (Ed.), *The essential works of Anarchism*. New York, NY: Bantam.

Puko, T. (2021, January 17). Keystone XL Oil Project pledges zero carbon emissions: Controversial pipeline would be powered by renewables, built by union labor in bid to avoid ax from Biden. *The Wall Street Journal*. Retrieved from https://www.wsj.com/articles/keystone-xl-oil-project-pledges-zero-carbon-emissions-11610930642

Putman, R. D. (1976). *The comparative study of political elites*. Englewood Cliffs, NJ: Prentice-Hall.

Putnam, R. D. (1977). Elite transformation in advanced industrial societies: An empirical assessment of the theory of technocracy. *Comparative Political Studies, 10*(3), 383–412. https://doi.org/10.1177/001041407701000305

Putnam, R. D. (1988). Diplomacy and domestic politics: The logic of two-level games. *International Organization, 42*(3), 427–460. https://doi.org/10.1017/S0020818300027697

Quach, K. (2024, January 26). FTC tech summit highlights GPU shortages and concentrations of power. *The Register*. Retrieved from https://www.theregister.com/2024/01/26/gpu_shortage_is_fuelling_ai/

Rachel, Ł., & Summers, L. H. (2019). *On secular stagnation in the industrialized world* (NBER Working Paper No. 26198). Retrieved from https://www.brookings.edu/wp-content/uploads/2019/03/Rachel Summers_web.pdf

Rado, L. (1987). Cultural elites and the institutionalization of ideas. *Sociological Forum, 2*(1), 42–66.

Raisch, S., & Krakowski, S. (2021). Artificial intelligence and management: The automation–augmentation paradox. *The Academy of Management Review, 46*(1), 192–210. https://doi.org/10.5465/amr.2018.0072

Rajan, R. G. (2009). Rent preservation and the persistence of underdevelopment. *American Economic Journal: Macroeconomics, 1*(1), 178–218. https://doi.org/10.1257/mac.1.1.178

Rajan, R. G., & Zingales, L. (2003): The great reversals: The politics of financial development in the Twentieth Century. *Journal of Financial Economics, 69*(27), 5–50. https://doi.org/10.1016/S0304-405X(03)00125-9

Ramahandry, T., Bonneau, V., Bani, E., & Vlasov, N. (2021). Key enabling technologies for Europe's technological sovereignty. *European Parliamentary Research Service*. Retrieved from https://www.europarl.europa.eu/RegData/etudes/STUD/2021/697184/EPRS_STU(2021)697184_EN.pdf

Ramaswamy, K., Kroeck, K. G., & Renforth, W. (1996). Measuring the degree of internationalization of a firm: A comment. *Journal of International Business Studies, 27*(1), 167–177. https://doi.org/10.1057/palgrave.jibs.8490131

Ramirez, C. D. (1995). Did J. P. Morgan's men add liquidity? Corporate investment, cash flow, and financial structure at the turn of the Twentieth Century. *The Journal of Finance, 50*(2), 661–678. https://doi.org/10.2307/2329423

Ramirez, N. M. (2025, January 7). Mark Zuckerberg and Meta are finding new ways to kiss Trump's ass. *Rolling Stone*. Retrieved from https://www.rollingstone.com/politics/politics-news/mark-zuckerberg-meta-trump-fact-checking-free-speech-1235227351/

Raymond, N. (2025, January 22). Trump pardons Silk Road founder Ross Ulbricht in landmark crypto case. *AML Intelligence*. Retrieved from https://www.amlintelligence.com/2025/01/news-trump-pardons-silk-road-founder-ross-ulbricht-in-landmark-crypto-case/

Reeves, A., & Friedman, S. (2024). *Born to rule: The making and remaking of the British elite*. Cambridge, MA: The Belknap Press of Harvard University Press.

Reich, R. B. (2015). *Saving capitalism: For the many, not the few*. New York, NY: Alfred A. Knopf.

Reinert, H., & Reinert, E. S. (2006). Creative destruction in economics: Nietzsche, Sombart, Schumpeter. In J. G. Backhaus & W. Drechsler (Eds.), *Friedrich Nietzsche (1844-1900)* (pp. 55–85). Boston, MA: Springer. https://doi.org/10.1007/978-0-387-32980-2_4

Reisch, G. A. (1991). Chaos, history, and narrative. *History and Theory*, *30*(1), 1–20. https://doi.org/10.2307/2505288

Renshon, J. D. (2015). Losing face and sinking costs: Experimental evidence on the judgment of political and military leaders. *International Organization 69*(3), 659–95. https://doi.org/10.1017/S0020818315000107

Reuters. (2020, January 20). Factbox: Electric vehicle subsidies under pressure in some Tesla core markets. *Reuters*. Retrieved from https://www.reuters.com/article/technology/factbox-electric-vehicle-subsidies-under-pressure-in-some-tesla-core-markets-idUSKBN1ZS1H9/

Reuters (2021, January 24). Germany urges Taiwan to help ease auto chip shortage. *Reuters*. Retrieved from https://www.reuters.com/article/uk-taiwan-autos-chips-idUKKBN29T04O

Reuters. (2024, July 31). China's Temu vendors protest over penalty policy. *Reuters*. Retrieved from https://www.reuters.com/business/retail-consumer/chinas-temu-vendors-protest-over-penalty-policy-2024-07-31/

Reuters. (2025, February 11). Anduril takes over Microsoft's $22 billion US army headset program. *Reuters*. Retrieved from https://www.reuters.com/technology/anduril-takes-over-microsofts-22-billion-us-army-headset-program-2025-02-11/

Rhoads, E. J. M. (2000). The 1911 revolution. In E. J. M. Rhoads, *Manchus and Han: Ethnic relations and political power in late Qing and early republican China, 1861–1928* (pp. 173–230). Seattle, WA: University of Washington Press.

Ricardo, D. (1999). *On the principles of political economy and taxation*. Library of Economics and Liberty (Original work published 1817). Retrieved from https://www.econlib.org/library/Ricardo/ricP.html

Richards, J. F. (2002). The opium industry in British India. *The Indian Economic and Social History Review*, *39* (2-3), 149–180. https://doi.org/10.1177/001946460203900203

Ricoeur, P., & Pellauer, D. (1985). Evil, a challenge to philosophy and theology. *Journal of the American Academy of Religion*, *53*(4), 635–648.

Riley, D. (2010). *The civic foundations of fascism in Europe: Italy, Spain, and Romania, 1870–1945*. Baltimore, MD: Johns Hopkins University Press.

Rindova, V. P., Martins, L. L., Srinivas, S. B., & Chandler, D. (2018). The good, the bad, and the ugly of organizational rankings: A multidisciplinary review of the literature and directions for future research. *Journal of Management*, *44*(6), 2175–2208 https://doi.org/10.1177/0149206317741962

Ritchie, M. (1972). *The Candidate* [Film]. Warner Bothers/Seven Arts.

Ritzer, G. (1983). The McDonaldization of society. *Journal of American Culture*, *6*(1), 100–107.

Robertson, A. (2024, February 21). Google apologizes for 'missing the mark' after Gemini generated racially diverse Nazis. *The Verge*. Retrieved from https://www.theverge.com/2024/2/21/24079371/google-ai-gemini-generative-inaccurate-historical

Robeyns, I. (2005). The capability approach: A theoretical survey. *Journal of Human Development*, *6*(1), 93–117. https://doi.org/10.1080/146498805200034266

Robeyns, I. (2023). *Limitarianism: The case against extreme wealth*. London: Allen Lane.

Robinson, C. (2000). Christian élites in the Mosuli hinterland: The *Shahārija*. In C. Robinson, *Empire and elites after the Muslim conquest: The transformation of Northern Mesopotamia* (pp. 90-108). Cambridge: Cambridge University Press. https://doi.org/10.1017/CBO9780511497513.007

Robinson, J. A. (2010, July). *Elites and institutional persistence* (WIDER Working Paper No. 2010/85). Retrieved from https://www.wider.unu.edu/sites/default/files/wp2010-85.pdf

Robinson, W., & Harris, J. (2000). Towards a global ruling class? Globalization and the transnational capitalist class. *Science & Society*, *64*(1), 11–54.

Robison, K. (2024, December 14). OpenAI just dropped new Elon Musk receipts: 'You can't sue your way to AGI'. *The Verge*. Retrieved from https://www.theverge.com/2024/12/13/24320632/openai-elon-musk-lawsuit-sam-altman

Rocca, S. (2017, August 27). The Jewish War and Rome's urban renewal. *Centro Primo Levi Online Monthly*. Retrieved from https://primolevicenter.org/printed-matter/the-jewish-war-and-romes-urban-renewal/

Rodríguez-Teruel, J., & Daloz, J. P. (2018). Surveying and observing political elites. In H. Best & J. Higley (Eds.), *The Palgrave handbook of political elites* (pp. 93–113). London: Palgrave Macmillan. https://doi.org/10.1057/978-1-137-51904-7_9

Rodrik, D. (2012). Why we learn nothing from regressing economic growth on policies. *Seoul Journal of Economics*, *25*(2), 137–151.

Rodrik, D., Subramanian, A., & Trebbi, F. (2004). Institutions rule: The primacy of institutions over geography and integration in economic development. *Journal of Economic Growth*, *9*(2), 131–165. https://doi.org/10.1023/B:JOEG.0000031425.72248.85

Romei, V., Crofton, W., & Smith, C. (2024, December 3). Why America's economy is soaring ahead of its rivals. *The Financial Times*. Retrieved from https://www.ft.com/content/1201f834-6407-4bb5-ac9d-18496ec2948b

Romer, P. M. (1986). Increasing returns and long-run growth. *Journal of Political Economy*, *94*(5), 1002–1037. https://doi.org/10.1086/261420

Romer, P. M. (1990). Endogenous technological change. *Journal of Political Economy*, *98*(5), S71–S102. https://doi.org/10.1086/261725

Romer, P. M. (1994). The origins of endogenous growth. *The Journal of Economic Perspectives*, *8*(1), 3–22. https://doi.org/10.1257/jep.8.1.3

Rønnow-Rasmussen, T. (2015). Intrinsic and extrinsic value. In I. Hirose & J. Olson (Eds.), *The Oxford handbook of value theory* (pp. 29–43). Oxford: Oxford University Press. https://doi.org/10.1093/oxfordhb/9780199959303.013.0003

Roniger, L. (2004). Political clientelism, democracy, and market economy [Review of the books *Le clientélisme politique dans les sociétés contemporaines* by J.-L. Briquet, F. Sawicki*; Poor people's politics: Peronist survival networks and the legacy of Evita* by J. Auyero*; Clientelism, interests, and democratic representation: The European experience in historical and comparative perspective* by S. Piattoni]. *Comparative Politics*, *36*(3), 353–375. https://doi.org/10.2307/4150135

Rooksby, M., McLeod, H. J., & Furuhashi, T. (2020, October 29). Hikikomori: Understanding the people who choose to live in extreme isolation. *The Conversation*. Retrieved from https://theconversation.com/hikikomori-understanding-the-people-who-choose-to-live-in-extreme-isolation-148482

Roosevelt Institute. (2019, October). *Stock buybacks are a key example of extractive corporate power* [Fact sheet]. Retrieved from https://rooseveltinstitute.org/wp-content/uploads/2020/07/RI_Stock-Buybacks-key-example-of-extractive-corporate-power-Fact-Sheet-201910.pdf

Roser, H., Rosling, O., & Rönnlund, A. R. (2018). *Factfulness: Ten reasons we're wrong about the world – and why things are better than you think*. New York, NY: Flatiron Books.

Rossier, T., Ellersgaard, C. H., Larsen, A. G., & Lunding, J. A. (2022). From integrated to fragmented elites. The core of Swiss elite networks 1910-2015. *The British Journal of Sociology*, *73*(2), 315–335. https://doi.org/10.1111/1468-4446.12929

Rostow, W. W. (1960). *The stages of economic growth: A non-Communist Manifesto*. Cambridge: Cambridge University Press. https://doi.org/10.1017/CBO9780511625824

Roth, E. (2024, March 8). Epic Games just got unbanned by Apple – again. *The Verge*. Retrieved from https://www.theverge.com/2024/3/8/24094543/epic-games-ios-developer-license-apple-dma

Rothkopf, D. (2008). *Superclass: The global power elite and the world they are making*. New York, NY: Farrar, Straus and Giroux.

Roucek, J. S. (1967). The role of literacy and illiteracy in social change. *International Review of Education / Internationale Zeitschrift Für Erziehungswissenschaft / Revue Internationale de l'Education*, *13*(4), 483–491.

Rowley, P. (2023, March 16). Why we need artificial intelligence to save humanity. *The Media Leader*. Retrieved from https://the-media-leader.com/why-we-need-ai-to-save-humanity/

Roy, D. (1994). Singapore, China, and the "soft authoritarian" challenge. *Asian Survey*, *34*(3), 231–242. https://doi.org/10.2307/2644982

Rubio, M. (2023). *Decades of decadence: How our spoiled elites blew America's inheritance of liberty, security, and prosperity*. New York, NY: HarperCollins Publishers.

Rudegeair, P., & Bykowicz, J. (2021, August 16). Bitcoin fans are suddenly a political force. *The Wall Street Journal*. Retrieved from https://www.wsj.com/articles/bitcoin-fans-are-suddenly-a-political-force-11629115380

Rüdiger, F. & Casas-Klett, T. (2022). Measuring intergenerational fairness: A conceptual framework and results of the NextGen Value Creation Barometer. In T. Casas-Klett & G. Cozzi (Eds.), *Elite quality report 2022: Country scores and global rankings*. Zurich: Seismo. https://doi.org/10.33058/seismo.30769.1017

Ruehl, M. (2021, January 22). Google threatens to shut search engine in Australia over news row. *The Financial Times*. Retrieved from https://www.ft.com/content/848971e5-4b44-408a-8f52-3d3fa915172c

Ruffo, G. H. (2020, January 15). Twitter: Nassim Taleb blasts Tesla customer service, Elon Musk replies. *InsideEVs*. Retrieved from https://insideevs.com/news/393102/nassim-taleb-tweets-elon-musk-replies/

Rugman, A. M. (1981). *Inside the multinationals: The economics of internal markets*. New York, NY: Columbia Press.

Rugman, A. M., Verbeke, A., & Nguyen, Q. T. K. (2011). Fifty years of international business theory and beyond. *MIR: Management International Review*, *51*(6), 755–786. https://doi.org/10.1007/s11575-011-0102-3

Ruigrok, W., & Wagner, H. (2003). Internationalization and performance: An organizational learning perspective. *MIR: Management International Review*, *43*(1), 63–83.

Rush, M. (1962). The Khrushchev succession problem. *World Politics*, *14*(2), 259–282. https://doi.org/10.2307/2009297

Russell, R. (2001). The role of values in servant leadership. *Leadership & Organization Development Journal*, *22*(2), 76–83. https://doi.org/10.1108/01437730110382631

Rutherford, B. A. (1977). Value added as a focus of attention for financial reporting: Some conceptual problems. *Accounting and Business Research*, *7*(27), 215–220. https://doi.org/10.1080/00014788.1977.9728707

Rutherford, M. (2001). Institutional economics: Then and now. *The Journal of Economic Perspectives*, *15*(3), 173–194. https://doi.org/10.1257/jep.15.3.173

Sabl, A. (2015). The two cultures of democratic theory: Responsiveness, democratic quality, and the empirical-normative divide. *Perspectives on Politics*, *13*(2), 345–365. https://doi.org/10.1017/S1537592715000079

Sachs, J. (2021, September 27). Anti-China hysteria lies at heart of action against IMF's Georgieva. *The Financial Times*. Retrieved from https://www.ft.com/content/c5083dc2-286f-4784-bc51-a8d34f88e86f

Sachs, J. (2003, February). *Institutions don't rule: Direct effects of geography on per capita income* (NBER Working Paper No. 9490). Retrieved from https://www.nber.org/system/files/working_papers/w9490/w9490.pdf

Sachs, J., & Woo, W. T. (1994). Structural factors in the economic reforms of China, Eastern Europe, and the former Soviet Union. *Economic policy*, *9*(18), 101–145. https://doi.org/10.2307/1344459

Said, E. (1993). *Culture and imperialism*. New York, NY: Vintage Books.

Saint-Simon, H. C. de, (1952). *Selected writings* (F. M. H. Markham, Ed.). Oxford: Basil Blackwell.

Samuelson, P. A. (1947). *Foundations of economic analysis*. Cambridge, MA: Harvard University Press.

Sánchez Díez, Á., Galaso Reca, P., & García de la Cruz, J. M. (2017). Mergers and acquisitions carried out by Spanish firms in Latin America: A network analysis study. *CEPAL Review*, *2016*(120), 51–69. Retrieved from https://www.un-ilibrary.org/content/journals/16840348/2016/120/5

Sánchez-Marín, G., Baixauli-Soler, J. S., & Lucas-Pérez, M. E. (2010). When much is not better? Top management compensation, board structure, and performance in Spanish firms. *The International Journal of Human Resource Management, 21*(15), 2778–2797. https://doi.org/10.1080/09585192.2010.528660

Sanger, D. E. (2025, April 9). An experiment in recklessness: Trump as global disrupter. *The New York Times*. Retrieved from https://www.nytimes.com/2025/04/08/us/politics/trump-tariffs-global-trade-war.html

Santeramo, F. G. (2017). Methodological challenges in building composite indexes: Linking theory to practice. In V. Jeremic, Z. Radojicic, and M. Dobrota (Eds.), *Emerging trends in the development and application of composite indicators* (pp. 127–140). Hershey, PA: IGI Global. https://doi.org/10.4018/978-1-5225-0714-7.ch006

Santos, K. (n.d.). Corporate credit ratings: A quick guide. *Treasurers.org*. Retrieved October 15, 2024, from https://www.treasurers.org/ACTmedia/ITCCMFcorpcreditguide.pdf

Sarel, M. (2022, February 28). Legal cartels and import restrictions increase the cost of living. *The Kohelet Policy Form*. Retrieved from https://en.kohelet.org.il/publication/legal-cartels-and-import-restrictions-increase-the-cost-of-living

Sass, L. A. (2001). Wittgenstein, Freud and the nature of psychoanalytic explanation. In R. Allen & M. Turvey (Eds.), *Wittgenstein, Theory and the Arts* (pp. 253–295). London: Routledge.

Sato, R. (1964). The Harrod-Domar model vs the neo-classical growth model. *The Economic Journal, 74*(294), 380-387. https://doi.org/10.2307/2228485

Savage, M. (2024). In defence of sociological description: A 'world-making' perspective. *The British Journal of Sociology, 75*(3), 360–365. https://doi.org/10.1111/1468-4446.13083

SBB (Swiss Federal Railways). (n.d.). *Finance: Income statement*. SBB Statistics Portal. Retrieved September 29, 2024, from https://reporting.sbb.ch/en/finance?=&years=1,4,5,6,7&scroll=0&highlighted=8e222679f50e32c11a71983b56261875

Schaake, M. (2024). *The tech coup: How to save democracy from Silicon Valley*. Princeton, NJ: Princeton University Press.

Schaede, U. (1995). The 'Old Boy' network and government-business relationships in Japan. *Journal of Japanese Studies, 21*(2), 293–317. https://doi.org/10.2307/133010

Schaff, A. (1973). Marxist theory on revolution and violence. *Journal of the History of Ideas, 34*(2), 263–270. https://doi.org/10.2307/2708729

Scheidel, W. (2017). *The great leveler: Violence and the history of inequality from the Stone Age to the Twenty-First Century*. Princeton, NJ: Princeton University Press. https://doi.org/10.2307/j.ctv346rs7

Schellenberg, M., Harker, M., & Jafari, A. (2018). International market entry mode: A systematic literature review. *Journal of Strategic Marketing, 26*(7), 601–627. https://doi.org/10.1080/0965254X.2017.1339114

Schilling, M. A., & Rangaswamy, A. (2013). Predicting the path of technological innovation: SAW vs. Moore. *Marketing Science, 32*(2), 153–170. https://doi.org/10.1287/mksc.1120.0739

Schmidt, C. (2004). Japan's elite networks at the apex of power. *Hitotsubashi Journal of Social Studies, 36*(2), 73–84. https://doi.org/10.15057/8276

Schneier, B. (2023). *A hacker's mind: How the powerful bend society's rules, and how to bend them back*. New York, NY: W.W. Norton & Company.

Schoenmaker, D., & Schramade, W. (2023). *Corporate finance for long-term value*. Cham: Springer. https://doi.org/10.1007/978-3-031-35009-2

Schoenmaker, D., & Schramade, W. (2024). Which discount rate for sustainability? *Journal of Sustainable Finance and Accounting, 3*, 100010. https://doi.org/10.1016/j.josfa.2024.100010

Scholem, G. (1976). Jews and Germans. In W. J. Dannhauser (Ed.), *On Jews and Judaism in crisis* (pp. 71–92). New York, NY: Schocken Books.

Scholte, J. A., Verhaegen, S., & Tallberg, J. (2021). Elite attitudes and the future of global governance. *International Affairs, 97*(3), 861–886. https://doi.org/10.1093/ia/iiab034

Schopenhauer, A. (1867). *Über den Willen in der Natur* (3rd ed.). (J. Frauenstädt, Ed.). Leipzig: F. A. Brockhaus. Retrieved from https://onemorelibrary.com/index.php/de/?option=com_djclassifieds&format=raw&view=download&task=download&fid=66

Schopenhauer, A. (2010). *The world as will and representation* (Vol. 1, J. Norman, A. Welchman, & C. Janaway, Trans. & Eds.). Cambridge: Cambridge University Press. https://doi.org/10.1017/CBO9780511780943.007

Schröder, G. (2003, March 14). *Regierungserklärung des bundeskanzlers Gerhard Schröder (SPD) "Mut zum frieden und zur veränderung" ["Agenda 2010"].* Retrieved from http://www.documentarchiv.de/brd/2003/rede_schroeder_03-14.html

Schrödinger, E. (2013). *What is life? With mind and matter and autobiographical sketches.* Cambridge: Cambridge University Press. https://doi.org/10.1017/CBO9781107295629

Schumpeter, J. A. (1939). *Business cycles. A theoretical, historical and statistical analysis of the capitalist process.* New York, NY: McGraw-Hill.

Schumpeter, J. A. (2000). *Capitalism, socialism and democracy.* London: Routledge.

Schumpeter, J. A. (2003). *The theory of economic development: An inquiry into profits, capital, credit, interest, and the business cycle.* New Brunswick, NJ: Transaction Publishers.

Schwab, K. (2016). *The fourth industrial revolution.* Geneva: World Economic Forum.

Schwab, K. & Zahidi, S. (2020). *The Global competitiveness report special edition 2020.* Geneva: World Economic Forum. Retrieved from https://www.weforum.org/reports/the-global-competitiveness-report-2020

Schwartz, B., & Maidenberg, M. (2025, June 5). What Musk and Trump risk losing in their high-stakes breakup. *The Wall Street Journal.* Retrieved from https://www.wsj.com/politics/policy/musk-trump-fallout-stakes-51bf1b5c

Schwartz, E. H. (2024, July 25). Mark Zuckerberg claims open-source is 'necessary for a positive AI future'. *TechRadar.* Retrieved from https://www.techradar.com/computing/artificial-intelligence/mark-zuckerberg-claims-open-source-is-necessary-for-a-positive-ai-future

Schoenmaker, D., & Schramade, W. (2024). Which discount rate for sustainability? *Journal of Sustainable Finance and Accounting*, *3*, 100010. https://doi.org/10.1016/j.josfa.2024.100010

Schwartzel, E., & Cutter, C. (2025, January 9). The CEOs who are tearing up the policies Trump hates: Companies seeking to benefit from campaign promises to cut regulations and taxes are ditching diversity and climate initiatives. *The Wall Street Journal.* Retrieved from https://www.wsj.com/politics/elections/trump-ceo-diversity-dei-climate-change-1a7208aa

Scoones, I. (2007). Sustainability. *Development in Practice*, *17*(4/5), 589–96. https://doi.org/10.1080/09614520701469609

Scott, J. (1988). Trend report social network analysis. *Sociology*, *22*(1), 109–127. https://doi.org/10.1177/0038038588022001007

Scott, J. C. (2017). *Against the grain: A deep history of the earliest states.* New Haven, CT: Yale University Press. https://doi.org/10.2307/j.ctv1bvnfk9

Scott, W. R. (2001). *Institutions and organizations.* Thousand Oaks, CA: Sage.

Scott, W. R. (2008). Approaching adulthood: The maturing of institutional theory. *Theory and Society*, *37*(5), 427–442. https://doi.org/10.1007/s11186-008-9067-z

Scott, W. R., & Davis, G. F. (2017). *Organizations and organizing: Rational, natural and open systems perspectives.* New York, NY: Routledge. https://doi.org/10.4324/9781315663371

Se, K., & Ansari, T. (2023, August 11). AI bubble bursting into AI winter – yes or no? (History of LLMs #5). *Turing Post.* https://www.turingpost.com/p/aibubble

Sebudubudu, D., & Molutsi, P. (2011). *The elite as a critical factor in national development: The case of Botswana.* Uppsala: Nordiska Afrikainstitutet.

SEC (Securities and Exchange Commission). (2017, October 12). *Updated investor bulletin: The ABCs of credit ratings.* Retrieved from https://www.sec.gov/oiea/investor-alerts-and-bulletins/ib_creditratings

Seetharaman, D., & Dotan, T. (2025, January 21). Tech leaders pledge up to $500 billion in AI investment in U.S.: OpenAI, Oracle, and SoftBank unveil AI infrastructure plans at White House. *The Wall Street Journal*. Retrieved from https://www.wsj.com/tech/ai/tech-leaders-pledge-up-to-500-billion-in-ai-investment-in-u-s-da506cd4

Seetharaman, D., Glazer E., & Higgins, T. (2021, February 13). Facebook meets Apple in clash of the tech titans – 'we need to inflict pain'. *The Wall Street Journal*. Retrieved from https://www.wsj.com/articles/facebook-meets-apple-in-clash-of-the-tech-titanswe-need-to-inflict-pain-11613192406

Seligman, L., Somerville, H., & Lubold, G. (2024, December 6). Trump administration set to decide future of jet fighters: Some of the president-elect's allies, including Elon Musk, are pushing for unmanned aircraft rather than piloted fighters. *The Wall Street Journal*. Retrieved from https://www.wsj.com/politics/national-security/air-force-jets-vs-drones-trump-administration-8b1620a5

Sen, A. (1987). *On ethics and economics*. Malden, MA: Blackwell Publishing.

Sen, A. (1999a). *Development as freedom*. New York, NY: Anchor.

Sen, A. (1999b). The possibility of social choice. *The American Economic Review, 89*(3), 349–378. https://doi.org/10.1257/aer.89.3.349

Senor, D., & Singer, S. (2009). *Start-up nation: The story of Israel's economic miracle*. Toronto: McClelland & Stewart.

Seo, M. G. & Creed, W. E. D. (2002) Institutional contradictions, praxis, and institutional change: A dialectical perspective. *Academy of Management Review, 27*(2), 222–247. https://doi.org/10.2307/4134353

seremot. (2024, December 14). *Ilya Sutskever: "Sequence to sequence learning with neural networks: What a decade"* [Video]. YouTube. Retrieved from https://www.youtube.com/watch?v=1yvBqasHLZs

Sethuram, S., & Gaur, A. (2024). Foreign divestment: The missing piece in international business scholarship. *Journal of International Business Studies, 55*, 1038–1047. https://doi.org/10.1057/s41267-024-00727-1

Severns, M., Rana, P., & Schwartz, B. (2024, November 30). Corporate America launches unorthodox campaign to gain Trump's attention. *The Wall Street Journal*. Retrieved from https://www.wsj.com/politics/trump-transition-lobbying-company-image-ffd42d2e

Seyoum, B. (2011). Informal institutions and foreign direct investment. *Journal of Economic Issues, 45*(4), 917–940. https://doi.org/10.2753/JEI0021-3624450409

Shannon, C. E. (1949). Communication theory of secrecy systems. *Bell System Technical Journal 28*(4), 656–715.

Sharkansky, I. (1997). The Israeli state: A cumbersome giant. *Israel Studies, 2*(2), 242–259. https://doi.org/10.1353/is.2005.0056

Sharma, L. N. (1977). The theories of elites: Impact and relevance. *The Indian Journal of Political Science, 38*(1), 64–81.

Sharma, R. (2024a, September 17). Where capitalism is working: What the world can learn from Switzerland, Taiwan, and Vietnam. *Foreign Affairs*. Retrieved from https://www.foreignaffairs.com/united-states/capitalism-switzerland-taiwan-vietnam

Sharma, R. (2024b*). What went wrong with capitalism*. New York, NY: Simon & Schuster.

Sharpe, W. F. (1964). Capital asset prices: A theory of market equilibrium under conditions of risk. *Journal of Finance, 19*(3), 425–442. https://doi.org/10.1111/j.1540-6261.1964.tb02865.x

Shatzmiller, M. (2013) The role of money in the economic growth of the early Islamic period (650-1000). In V. Klemm and N. Al-Sha'ar (Eds.). *Sources and approaches across disciplines in Near Eastern studies: Proceedings of the 24th congress, Union Européenne des Arabisants et Islamisants.* (pp. 271–305). Leuven, Netherlands: Peeters. Retrieved from https://history.uwo.ca/people/Docs/Shatzmiller-Articles/09-The-Role-of-Money.pdf

Shaver, J. M. (2013). Do we really need more entry mode studies? *Journal of International Business Studies, 44*(1), 23–27. https://doi.org/10.1057/jibs.2012.24

Shelby, T. (2002). Parasites, pimps, and capitalists: A naturalistic conception of exploitation. *Social Theory and Practice, 28*(3), 381–418. https://doi.org/10.5840/soctheorpract200228316

Shenkar, O. (2001). Cultural distance revisited: Towards a more rigorous conceptualization and measurement of cultural differences. *Journal of International Business Studies, 32*(3), 519–535. https://doi.org/10.1057/palgrave.jibs.8490982

Shepard, W. (2016, July 14). A look inside Shenzhen's high-tech empire. *Forbes*. Retrieved from https://www.forbes.com/sites/wadeshepard/2016/07/14/a-look-inside-shenzhens-high-tech-empire/

Shepherd, C. (2021, August 17). China to tighten competition rules for internet groups. *The Financial Times*. Retrieved from https://www.ft.com/content/7ccf409d-489b-411a-8b4f-4b5d8b8ed0b1

Shi, W., Sun, S. L., Yan, D., & Zhang, Y. (2017). Institutional fragility and outward foreign direct investment from China. *Journal of International Business Studies, 48*(4), 452–476. https://doi.org/10.1057/s41267-016-0050-z

Shih, W. C. (2023, September-October). The new era of industrial policy is here. *Harvard Business Review*. Retrieved from https://hbr.org/2023/09/the-new-era-of-industrial-policy-is-here

Shiller, R. J. (2017). Narrative economics. *American Economic Review, 107*(4), 967–1004. https://doi.org/10.1257/aer.107.4.967

Shioji, E. (2024). Japan: Seizing its moment in the spotlight? In T. Casas-Klett & G. Cozzi (Eds.), *Elite quality report 2024: The sustainable value creation of nations*. Zurich: Seismo. https://doi.org/10.33058/seismo.30892.7414

Shlapentokh, D. (2007). Dugin Eurasianism: A window on the minds of the Russian elite or an intellectual ploy? *Studies in East European Thought, 59*(3), 215–236. https://doi.org/10.1007/s11212-007-9030-y

Siegel, D. A. (2009). Social networks and collective action. *American Journal of Political Science, 53*(1), 122–138. https://doi.org/10.1111/j.1540-5907.2008.00361.x

Siegel, E. (2023, June 2). The AI hype cycle is distracting companies. *Harvard Business Review*. Retrieved from https://hbr.org/2023/06/the-ai-hype-cycle-is-distracting-companies

Simon, H. A. (1957). *Administrative behavior*. New York, NY: Free Press.

Simon, H. A. (1962). The architecture of complexity. *Proceedings of the American Philosophical Society, 106*(6), 467–482. https://doi.org/10.1007/978-1-4899-0718-9_31

Simon, H. A. (1985). Human nature in politics: The dialogue of psychology with political science. *The American Political Science Review, 79*(2), 293–304. https://doi.org/10.2307/1956650

Simonse, L. (2014). Modeling business models. *Design Issues, 30*(4), 67–82. https://doi.org/10.1162/DESI_a_00297

Sims, C. A. (1980). Macroeconomics and reality. *Econometrica, 48*(1), 1–48. https://doi.org/10.2307/1912017

Sinclair, T. C., Marstrand, P. K., & Newick, P. (1972). *Innovation and human risk: The evaluation of human life and safety in relation to technical change*. London: Centre for the Study of Industrial Innovation (for) University of Sussex, Science Policy Research Unit.

Singer, M. G. (2004). The concept of evil. *Philosophy, 79*(308), 185–214. https://doi.org/10.1017/s0031819104000233

Singer, P. (2015). *Animal liberation: The definitive classic of the animal movement* (40th Anniversary Edition). New York, NY: Harper Perennial.

Singler, B. (2020). "Blessed by the algorithm": Theistic conceptions of artificial intelligence in online discourse. *AI & Society 35*, 945–955. https://doi.org/10.1007/s00146-020-00968-2

Sinha, A. (2010). In defence of Adam Smith's theory of value. *European Journal of the History of Economic Thought, 17*(1), 29–48. https://doi.org/10.1080/09672560903204544

Sinn, H.-W. (2020). *The economics of target balances*. Cham, Switzerland: Palgrave Macmillan. https://doi.org/10.1007/978-3-030-50170-9

SirionLabs. (n.d.). *What is contract value leakage and how to prevent it*. Retrieved December 31, 2024, from https://www.sirion.ai/library/contract-obligations/contract-value-leakage/

Sjödin, D., Parida, V., Palmié, M., & Wincent, J. (2021). How AI capabilities enable business model innovation: Scaling AI through co-evolutionary processes and feedback loops. *Journal of Business Research, 134,* 574–587. https://doi.org/10.1016/j.jbusres.2021.05.009

Skinner, Q. (1990). *The return of grand theory in the human sciences.* Cambridge: Cambridge University Press.

Sklair, L. (2002). The transnational capitalist class and global politics: Deconstructing the corporate-state connection. *International Political Science Review / Revue Internationale De Science Politique, 23*(2), 159–174. https://doi.org/10.1177/0192512102023002003

Sklair, L. (2012). Transnational capitalist class. In G. Ritzer (Ed.), *The Wiley-Blackwell encyclopedia of globalization.* Oxford: Blackwell. https://doi.org/10.1002/9780470670590.wbeog585

Slack, P. (2015). *The invention of improvement: Information and material progress in seventeenth-century England.* Oxford: Oxford University Press.

Slangen, A. H., & Hennart, J. F. (2008). Do foreign greenfields outperform foreign acquisitions or vice versa? An institutional perspective. *Journal of Management Studies, 45*(7), 1301–1328. https://doi.org/10.1111/j.1467-6486.2008.00794.x

Sloan, G. (2012). Military doctrine, command philosophy and the generation of fighting power: Genesis and theory. *International Affairs, 88*(2), 243–263. https://doi.org/10.2307/41428604

Smets, F., & Wouters, R. (2003). An estimated dynamic stochastic general equilibrium model of the Euro area. *Journal of the European Economic Association, 1*(5), 1123–1175. https://doi.org/10.1162/154247603770383415

Smets, M., Jarzabkowski, P., Burke, G. T., & Spee, P. (2015). Reinsurance trading in Lloyd's of London: Balancing conflicting-yet-complementary logics in practice. *Academy of Management Journal, 58*(3), 932–970. https://doi.org/10.5465/amj.2012.0638

Smil, V. (2022, May 12). The modern world can't exist without these four ingredients. They all require fossil fuels. *TIME.* Retrieved from https://time.com/6175734/reliance-on-fossil-fuels/

Smith, A. (1904). *An inquiry into the nature and causes of the wealth of nations.* London: Methuen and Co., Ltd. Retrieved from https://oll-resources.s3.us-east-2.amazonaws.com/oll3/store/titles/237/0206-01_Bk.pdf

Smith, V. (2018, June 26). Opinion: The U.S. spends $4 billion a year subsidizing 'Stalinist-style' domestic sugar production. *MarketWatch.* Retrieved from https://www.marketwatch.com/story/the-us-spends-4-billion-a-year-subsidizing-stalinist-style-domestic-sugar-production-2018-06-25

Smith, W. D. (1980). Friedrich Ratzel and the origins of Lebensraum. *German Studies Review, 3*(1), 51–68. https://doi.org/10.2307/1429483

Smyth, J. (2022, March 3). Purdue and US states agree new $6bn settlement for opioid litigation. *The Financial Times.* Retrieved from https://www.ft.com/content/161af0cd-8975-4fb7-809c-131436a91cc0

Snyder, T. (2010). *Bloodlands: Europe between Hitler and Stalin.* New York, NY: Basic Books.

Snyder, T. (2019). Europe's dangerous creation myth. *Politico.* Retrieved from https://www.politico.eu/article/europe-creation-project-myth-history-nation-state/

Soares, N., Fallenstein, B., Yudkowsky, E., & Armstrong, S. (2015). Corrigibility. In *Artificial Intelligence and Ethics: Papers from the 2015 AAAI Workshop.* Palo Alto, CA: AAAI Press. Retrieved from https://cdn.aaai.org/ocs/ws/ws0067/10124-45900-1-PB.pdf

Sokoloff, K., & Engerman, S. (2000). History lessons: Institutions, factor endowments, and paths of development in the New World. *The Journal of Economic Perspectives, 14*(3), 217–232. https://doi.org/10.1257/jep.14.3.217

Sokolsky, N. (2022, June 13). Can AGI destroy us without trial & error? *Nikita Sokolsky Substack.* Retrieved from https://nsokolsky.substack.com/p/can-agi-destroy-us-without-trial

Solow, R. M. (1956). A contribution to the theory of economic growth. *Quarterly Journal of Economics, 70*(1), 65–94. https://doi.org/10.2307/1884513

Solow, R. M. (1957). Technical change and the aggregate production function. *The Review of Economics and Statistics, 39*(3), 312–320. https://doi.org/10.2307/1926047

Solow, R. M. (1960). Investment and technical progress. In K. J. Arrow, S. Karlin, & P. Suppes (Eds.), *Mathematical methods in the social sciences, 1959: Proceedings of the First Stanford Symposium* (pp. 89–104). Stanford, CA: Stanford University Press.

Song, J. (2015, December 27). Kim Beom-su, Kakao: Life of Brian. *The Financial Times*. Retrieved from https://www.ft.com/content/1c3fbdb6-9f1d-11e5-85ae-8fa46274f224

Song, J. (2021, August 5). KakaoBank becomes South Korea's largest retail lender as shares surge. *The Financial Times*. Retrieved from https://www.ft.com/content/0d61e006-678f-40e4-82ce-78f512d76931

Song, J. (2024, July 23). Billionaire founder of Kakao arrested in K-pop stock manipulation case. *The Financial Times*. Retrieved from https://www.ft.com/content/49141512-96db-4f2b-a776-da350e531aa0

Soon, W., & Yu, E. (2024, March 2). Chinese gangs use cryptocurrencies to launder billions: Tether and other tokens are allowing criminal organizations linked to the country to cover their tracks. *The Wall Street Journal*. Retrieved from https://www.wsj.com/finance/currencies/chinese-gangs-use-cryptocurrencies-to-launder-billions-5749f44e

Sørensen, A. (2000). Toward a sounder basis for class analysis. *American Journal of Sociology, 105*(6), 1523–1558. https://doi.org/10.1086/210463

Sorkin, A. R. (2011, August 29). The mystery of Steve Jobs's public giving. *The New York Times*. Retrieved from: https://archive.nytimes.com/dealbook.nytimes.com/2011/08/29/the-mystery-of-steve-jobss-public-giving/?_r=0

Sorkin, A. R., Mattu, R., Warner, B., Kessler, S., de la Merced, M. J., Hirsch, L., Livni, E. & Walt, V. (2023, May 31). Reassessing the board fight that was meant to transform Exxon. *The New York Times*. Retrieved from: https://www.nytimes.com/2023/05/31/business/dealbook/engine-no-1-exxon-mobil.html

Spackman, B. (1990). Machiavelli and maxims. *Yale French Studies, 77*, 137–155. https://doi.org/10.2307/2930151

Sparrowe, R. T., Liden, R. C., Wayne, S. J., & Kraimer, M. L. (2001). Social networks and the performance of individuals and groups. *The Academy of Management Journal, 44*(2), 316–325. https://doi.org/10.2307/3069458

Spence, M. (1973). Job market signaling. *The Quarterly Journal of Economics, 87*(3), 355–374. https://doi.org/10.2307/1882010

Spengler, O. (1922). *The decline of the West: Form and actuality* (C. F. Atkinson, Trans.). London: George Allen & Unwin Ltd.

Spinoza, B. de. (2007). *Theological-political treatise* (J. Israel, Ed.; M. Silverthorne & J. Israel, Trans.). Cambridge: Cambridge University Press. https://doi.org/10.1017/CBO9780511815720

Stacey, K., & Kuchler, H. (2021, February 4). Opioid crisis haunts frontrunner for top job at US drugs regulator. *The Financial Times*. Retrieved from https://www.ft.com/content/3f052dab-8c14-4c25-a938-295302c82e4f

Stackpole, B. (2025, January). AI has high data center energy costs — but there are solutions. *MIT Sloan School of Management*. Retrieved from https://mitsloan.mit.edu/ideas-made-to-matter/ai-has-high-data-center-energy-costs-there-are-solutions

Standing, G. (2016). *The corruption of capitalism: Why rentiers thrive and work does not pay*. London: Biteback Publishing.

Staples, D. (2021, January 20). Kenney's big mistake, plus other winners and losers of Keystone XL pipeline fiasco. *Edmonton Journal*. Retrieved from https://edmontonjournal.com/news/national/david-staples-kenneys-big-mistake-plus-other-winners-and-losers-of-keystone-xl-pipeline-fiasco

Starik, M. (1995). Should trees have managerial standing? Toward stakeholder status for non-human nature. *Journal of Business Ethics, 14*, 207–217. https://doi.org/10.1007/BF00881435

Stepan, A. (2001). *Arguing comparative politics*. Oxford: Oxford University Press. https://doi.org/10.1093/oso/9780199242702.001.0001

Sterling-Folker, J. (2015). All hail to the chief: Liberal IR theory in the new world order. *International Studies Perspectives, 16*(1), 40–49. https://doi.org/10.1111/insp.12089

Stern, N. (2006). *The economics of climate change: The Stern review*. Cambridge: Cambridge University Press. https://doi.org/10.1017/CBO9780511817434

Stevenson, W., Pearce, J., & Porter, L. (1985). The concept of "coalition" in organization theory and research. *The Academy of Management Review*, *10*(2), 256–268. https://doi.org/10.2307/257967

Stewart, C. E. (1991). "Land reform" decision. *The American Journal of International Law*, *85*(4), 690–702. https://doi.org/10.2307/2203276

Stiffman, E. (2023, October 27). How diabetes and weight-loss drugs are reshaping the world's wealthiest foundation. *The Chronicle of Philanthropy*. Retrieved from https://www.philanthropy.com/article/how-diabetes-and-weight-loss-drugs-are-reshaping-the-worlds-wealthiest-foundation

Stigler, G. (1952). The Ricardian theory of value and distribution. *Journal of Political Economy*, *60*(3), 187–207. https://doi.org/10.1086/257208

Stigler, G. J. (1971). The theory of economic regulation. *Bell Journal of Economics and Management Science*, *2*(1), 3–18. https://doi.org/10.2307/3003160

Stigler G. J. (1996). The pleasures and pains of modern capitalism. In G. E. Wood (Ed.), *Explorations in economic liberalism* (pp. 126–140). London: Palgrave Macmillan. https://doi.org/10.1007/978-1-349-24967-1_7

Stiglitz, J. E. (2002). *Globalization and its discontents*. New York, NY: W. W. Norton.

Stiglitz, J. E. (2012). *The Price of inequality: How today's divided society endangers our future*. New York, NY: W. W. Norton.

Stiglitz, J. E. (2021, September 27). A coup attempt at the IMF. *Project Syndicate*. Retrieved from https://www.project-syndicate.org/commentary/coup-attempt-against-imf-managing-director-georgieva-by-joseph-e-stiglitz-2021-09

Stockholm International Peace Research Institute (SIPRI). (2020). *SIPRI Yearbook 2020: Armaments, Disarmament and International Security*. Oxford: Oxford University Press.

Stockman, D. A. (2013). *The great deformation: The corruption of capitalism in America*. New York, NY: PublicAffairs.

Stogdill, R. M. (1950). Leadership, membership and organization. *Psychological Bulletin*, *47*(1), 1–14. https://doi.org/10.1037/h0053857

Stoller, M. (2022, September 9). Should we save newspapers from Google? *The Big Newsletter*. Retrieved from https://www.thebignewsletter.com/p/should-we-save-newspapers-from-google?utm_source=publication-search

Stoller, M. (2024, August 24). Antitrust enforcers: "The rent is too damn high!". *The Big Newsletter*. https://www.thebignewsletter.com/p/antitrust-enforcers-the-rent-is-too

Stoller, M. (2024b, December 6). An assassin showed just how angry America really is. *BIG by Matt Stoller*. Retrieved from https://www.thebignewsletter.com/p/an-assassin-showed-just-how-angry

Strand, M., & Lizardo, O. (2017). The hysteresis effect: Theorizing mismatch in action. *Journal of the Theory of Social Behaviour*, *47*(2), 164–194. https://doi.org/10.1111/jtsb.12117

Strauss, L. L. (1954, September 16). *Remarks prepared for delivery at the Founders' Day Dinner, National Association of Science Writers*. New York, NY: United States Atomic Energy Commission. Retrieved from https://www.nrc.gov/docs/ML1613/ML16131A120.pdf

Strauss, W., & Howe, N. (1997). *The fourth turning: An American prophecy – what the cycles of history tell us about America's next rendezvous with destiny*. New York, NY: Crown Publishing Group.

Streeck, W. (2016). *How will capitalism end? Essays on a failing system*. London: Verso.

Streeck, W., & Thelen, K. (2005). Introduction: Institutional change in advanced political economies. In W. Streeck, & K. Thelen (Eds.), *Beyond continuity: Institutional change in advanced political economies* (pp. 1–39). Oxford: Oxford University Press. https://doi.org/10.1093/oso/9780199280452.003.0001

Stucke, M. E. (2018, March 27). Here are all the reasons it's a bad idea to let a few tech companies monopolize our data. *Harvard Business Review*. Retrieved from https://hbr.org/2018/03/here-are-all-the-reasons-its-a-bad-idea-to-let-a-few-tech-companies-monopolize-our-data

Studnicki-Gizbert, D., & Schecter, D. (2010). The environmental dynamics of a colonial fuel-rush: Silver mining and deforestation in New Spain, 1522 to 1810. *Environmental History, 15*(1), 94–119. https://doi.org/10.1093/envhis/emq007

Stupak, J. M. (2016, April 13). The Internet Tax Freedom Act: In brief. *Congressional Research Service*. Retrieved from https://fas.org/sgp/crs/misc/R43772.pdf

Suddaby, R., & Greenwood, R. (2005). Rhetorical strategies of legitimacy. *Administrative Science Quarterly, 50*(1), 35-67. https://doi.org/10.2189/asqu.2005.50.1.35

Suetonius. (1914). *The lives of the twelve Caesars* (J. C. Rolfe, Trans.). Loeb Classical Library edition. Retrieved from https://penelope.uchicago.edu/Thayer/E/Roman/Texts/Suetonius/12Caesars/home.html

Suleyman, M., & Bhaskar, M. (2023). *The coming wave: Technology, power and the twenty-first century's greatest dilemma*. New York, NY: Crown Publishing Group.

Sullivan, D. (1994). Measuring the degree of internationalization of a firm. *Journal of International Business Studies, 25*(2), 325–342. https://doi.org/10.1057/palgrave.jibs.8490203

Sullivan, D., & Hickel, J. (2023). Capitalism and extreme poverty: A global analysis of real wages, human height, and mortality since the long 16th century. *World Development, 161*. https://doi.org/10.1016/j.worlddev.2022.106026

Sun, Y. S. (1946). *Zhongshan quanshu*, 4 vols (F. Price, Trans.). Shanghai: Sanmin Tushu Gongsi.

Suny, R. G. (2001). The empire strikes out: Imperial Russia, “national” identity, and theories of empire. In R. G. Suny & T. Martin (Eds.), *A state of nations. Empire and nation-building in the age of Lenin and Stalin*. Oxford: Oxford University Press. https://doi.org/10.1093/oso/9780195144222.003.0002

Sutter, K. M. (2023, March 10). Made in China 2025: Industrial policies: Issues for Congress. *Congressional Research Service*. Retrieved from https://sgp.fas.org/crs/row/IF10964.pdf

Suzuki, K., Yeon, W., Ringhof, J., Kleinhans, J.-P., Korteweg, R., Chang, C.-C., Ghiretti, F., Hmaidi, A., Benson, E., & Mouradian, C. (2023). Japanese perspective: Japan embraces its strategic indispensability in alliance with the United States. In G. C. Allen (Ed.), *The Post-October 7 world: International perspectives on semiconductors and geopolitics* (pp. 19–24). Washington, DC: Center for Strategic and International Studies (CSIS).

Swallow, B. M., Kallesoe, M. F., Iftikhar, U. A., van Noordwijk, M., Bracer, C., Scherr, S. J., Raju, K. V., Poats, S. V., Duraiappah, A. K., Ochieng, B. O., Mallee, H., & Rumley, R. (2009). Compensation and rewards for environmental services in the developing world: Framing pan-tropical analysis and comparison in Swallow. *Ecology and Society, 14*(2). https://doi.org/10.5751/ES-02499-140226

Swan, T. W. (1956). Economic growth and capital accumulation. *Economic Record, 32*(2), 334–361. https://doi.org/10.1111/j.1475-4932.1956.tb00434.x

SWI swissinfo.ch. (2012, March 11). Voters say no to longer holidays. *SWI swissinfo.ch*. Retrieved from https://www.swissinfo.ch/eng/swiss-politics/voters-say-no-to-longer-holidays/32271764

Swire, P. P. (2004). A model for when disclosure helps security: What is different about computer and network security? *Journal on Telecommunications and High Technology Law, 3*(1), 163–205. https://doi.org/10.2139/ssrn.531782

Syverson, C. (2019). Macroeconomics and market power: Context, implications, and open questions. *The Journal of Economic Perspectives, 33*(3), 23–43. https://doi.org/10.1257/jep.33.3.23

Tabarrok, A. (1998). The separation of commercial and investment banking: The Morgans vs. the Rockefellers. *Quarterly Journal of Austrian Economics, 1*(1), 1–18. https://doi.org/10.1007/s12113-998-1000-9

Táíwò, O. O. (2022). *Elite capture: How the powerful took over identity politics (and everything else)*. Chicago, IL: Haymarket Books.

Taleb, N. N. (2018). *Skin in the game: Hidden asymmetries in daily life*. London: Penguin Books.

Taleb, N. N., (2020). *Statistical consequences of fat tails: Real world preasymptotics, epistemology, and applications* (Technical Incerto Vol. 1). STEM Academic Press.

Taleb, N. N. [@nntaleb]. (2022, June 7-8). *Elon Musk illustrates my #FooledbyRandomness point: Solid financial success is largely the result of skills, hard work, and wisdom. But wild success (in the far tail) is more likely to be the result of reckless betting, extreme luck, & the opposite of wisdom: folly.* [Post] [Thread]. X. https://x.com/nntaleb/status/1534172773580513280

Taliaferro, J. W. (2006). State building for future wars: Neoclassical realism and the resource-extractive state. *Security Studies*, *15*(3), 464–495. https://doi.org/10.1080/09636410601028370

Tammen, R., Kugler, J., & Lemke, D. (2012). Power transition theory. *Oxford Bibliographies Online*. https://doi.org/10.1093/OBO/9780199743292-0038

Tan, K. P. (2008). Meritocracy and elitism in a global city: Ideological shifts in Singapore. *International Political Science Review / Revue Internationale de Science Politique*, *29*(1), 7–27. https://doi.org/10.1177/0192512107083445

Tang, R. W., & Buckley, P. J. (2022). Outward foreign direct investment by emerging market multinationals: The directionality of institutional distance. *Journal of Business Research*, *149*, 314–326. https://doi.org/10.1016/j.jbusres.2022.05.047

Tanglis, M., & Lincoln, T. (2020, July 6). Covid lobbying palooza. *Public Citizen*. Retrieved from https://www.citizen.org/article/covid-lobbying-palooza/

Tanzi, V. (1997, September). *The changing role of the state in the economy: A historical perspective* (Working Paper No. 1997/114). Washington, DC: International Monetary Fund. Retrieved from https://www.imf.org/external/pubs/ft/wp/wp97114.pdf

Tanzi, V. (2005). The economic role of the state in the 21st Century. *The Cato Journal*, *25*(3), 617-638. Retrieved from https://www.cato.org/sites/cato.org/files/serials/files/cato-journal/2005/11/cj25n3-16.pdf

Tegmark, M. (2017). *Life 3.0: Being human in the age of artificial intelligence*. New York, NY: Alfred A. Knopf.

Tegmark, M. (2023, April 25). The 'don't look up' thinking that could doom us with AI. *Time*. Retrieved from https://time.com/6273743/thinking-that-could-doom-us-with-ai/.

Temple-West, P., & Masters B. (2022, August 24). Texas accuses BlackRock of energy company boycott in ESG clampdown. *The Financial Times*. Retrieved from https://www.ft.com/content/1fc2cc54-d364-48ad-aace-30625e5c61f6

Tepper, J. (2018) *The myth of capitalism: Monopolies and the death of competition*. Hoboken, NJ: John Wiley & Sons Inc. https://doi.org/10.1111/1475-4932.12730

The Council of Economic Advisers. (2017, November). *The underestimated cost of the Opioid crisis. Executive Office of the President of the United States*. Retrieved from https://www.hsdl.org/?view&did=806029

The Economist. (2014, March 15). Planet plutocrat: The countries where politically connected businessmen are most likely to prosper. *The Economist*. Retrieved from https://www.economist.com/news/international/21599041-countries-where-politically-connected-businessmen-are-most-likely-prosper-planet

The Economist. (2016, May 5). Comparing crony capitalism around the world. *The Economist*. Retrieved from https://www.economist.com/graphic-detail/2016/05/05/comparing-crony-capitalism-around-the-world

The Economist. (2022, July 23). Special report: ESG investing. *The Economist*. Retrieved from https://www.economist.com/special-report/2022/07/21/a-broken-system-needs-urgent-repairs

The Economist. (2023a, April 28). Yuval Noah Harari argues that AI has hacked the operating system of human civilisation. *The Economist*. Retrieved from https://www.economist.com/by-invitation/2023/04/28/yuval-noah-harari-argues-that-ai-has-hacked-the-operating-system-of-human-civilisation

The Economist. (2023b, May 24). Activist investors are needed more than ever. *The Economist*. Retrieved from https://www.economist.com/leaders/2023/05/24/activist-investors-are-needed-more-than-ever

The Economist. (2025, January 21). Donald Trump's America will not become a tech oligarchy: Reasons not to panic about the tech-industrial complex. *The Economist*. Retrieved from https://www.economist.com/business/2025/01/21/donald-trumps-america-will-not-become-a-tech-oligarchy

The Financial Times. (2025, May 12). *Steve Bannon: "President Trump will serve a third term"* [Video]. https://youtu.be/6KfUXpmtprc

The Free Press. (2024, December 10). *Marc Andreessen on AI, tech, censorship and dining with Trump* [Honestly with Bari Weiss, Video]. YouTube. https://www.youtube.com/watch?v=sgTeZXw-ytQ

The Guardian. (2021, July 21). Johnson & Johnson to pay $5bn in landmark $26bn US opioid settlement. *The Guardian*. Retrieved from https://www.theguardian.com/us-news/2021/jul/21/us-opioid-settlement-state-attorneys-general-johnson-and-johnson

The Minderoo Foundation. (2018). *The global slavery index 2018*. Retrieved from https://www.globalslaveryindex.org/resources/downloads/

The New York Times Company v. OpenAI and Microsoft. (2023, December 27). Complaint – [Case Number: 1:23-cv-11195] [PDF file]. *United States District Court for the Southern District of New York*. Retrieved from https://nytco-assets.nytimes.com/2023/12/NYT_Complaint_Dec2023.pdf

The Public Voice. (2018, October 23). *Universal guidelines for artificial intelligence*. Retrieved from https://archive.epic.org/international/AIGuidleinesDRAFT20180910.pdf

The United States Department of Justice (2023, January 24). Attorney General Merrick B. Garland delivers remarks on lawsuit against Google for monopolizing digital advertising technologies. *The United States Department of Justice*. Retrieved from https://www.justice.gov/opa/speech/attorney-general-merrick-b-garland-delivers-remarks-lawsuit-against-google-monopolizing

The University of Chicago. (2012, March 1). *Why leaders lie: The truth about lying in international politics with John Mearsheimer* [Video]. YouTube. https://www.youtube.com/watch?v=VPe5f5dcrGE

The Wall Street Journal. (2021, July 21). *Investigation: How TikTok's algorithm figures out your deepest desires* [Video]. The Wall Street Journal. https://www.wsj.com/video/series/inside-tiktoks-highly-secretive-algorithm/investigation-how-tiktok-algorithm-figures-out-your-deepest-desires/6C0C2040-FF25-4827-8528-2BD6612E3796

The Wall Street Journal Editorial Board. (2021, January 20). Biden's Keystone Pipeline kill: On his first day he insults Canada and ends thousands of jobs. *The Wall Street Journal*. Retrieved from https://www.wsj.com/articles/bidens-keystone-pipeline-kill-11611184519

The Wall Street Journal Editorial Board. (2025, February 5). About those beachfront Gaza condos: Critics deride Trump's idea, but what are they offering Palestinians? *The Wall Street Journal*. Retrieved from https://www.wsj.com/opinion/donald-trump-gaza-hamas-palestinians-relocate-israel-benjamin-netanyahu-82f40f95

The White House. (2021, February 19). *Briefing room remarks by President Biden at the 2021 Virtual Munich Security Conference*. Retrieved from https://www.whitehouse.gov/briefing-room/speeches-remarks/2021/02/19/remarks-by-president-biden-at-the-2021-virtual-munich-security-conference/

The White House. (2022, August 9). *FACT SHEET: CHIPS and Science Act will lower costs, create jobs, strengthen supply chains, and counter China*. Retrieved from https://www.whitehouse.gov/briefing-room/statements-releases/2022/08/09/fact-sheet-chips-and-science-act-will-lower-costs-create-jobs-strengthen-supply-chains-and-counter-china/

The White House. (2023, July 9). *Remarks by President Biden at signing of an executive order promoting competition in the American economy*. Retrieved from https://www.whitehouse.gov/briefing-room/speeches-remarks/2021/07/09/remarks-by-president-biden-at-signing-of-an-executive-order-promoting-competition-in-the-american-economy/

The White House. (2025a, January 20). *Designating cartels and other organizations as foreign terrorist organizations and specially designated global terrorists* [Executive order]. Retrieved from https://www.whitehouse.gov/presidential-actions/2025/01/designating-cartels-and-other-organizations-as-foreign-terrorist-organizations-and-specially-designated-global-terrorists/

The White House. (2025b, January 20). *Putting America first in international environmental agreements* [Executive order]. Retrieved from https://www.whitehouse.gov/presidential-actions/2025/01/putting-america-first-in-international-environmental-agreements/

The World Bank (2020). *The ease of doing business index.* Washington, DC: The World Bank.

The World Bank. (n.d.-a). Data from World Bank national accounts data and OECD National Accounts, from data series *'Exports of goods and services (% of GDP)'* for Japan and Korea. Retrieved October 1, 2024, from https://data.worldbank.org/indicator/NE.EXP.GNFS.ZS?locations=JP-KR

The World Bank. (n.d.-b). Data from World Bank national accounts data and OECD National Accounts, from data series *'Imports of goods and services (% of GDP)'* for Japan and Korea. Retrieved October 1, 2024, from https://data.worldbank.org/indicator/NE.IMP.GNFS.ZS?locations=JP-KR

The World Bank. (n.d.-c). Data from World Bank national accounts data and OECD National Accounts, from data series *'GDP per capita (current US$)'* for Indonesia and Pakistan. Retrieved October 1, 2024, from https://data.worldbank.org/indicator/NY.GDP.PCAP.CD?locations=ID-PK

The World Bank. (n.d.-d). Data from World Bank national accounts data and OECD National Accounts, from data series *'Life expectancy at birth (years)'* for China and the United States. Retrieved October 1, 2024, from https://data.worldbank.org/indicator/SP.DYN.LE00.IN?locations=CN-US

The World Bank. (n.d.-e). Data from World Bank national accounts data and OECD National Accounts, from data series *'GDP per capita (current US$)'* for Korea and Argentina. Retrieved October 1, 2024, from https://data.worldbank.org/indicator/NY.GDP.PCAP.CD?locations=KR-AR

The World Bank. (n.d.-f). Data from World Bank national accounts data and OECD National Accounts, from data series *'GDP per capita (current US$)'* for the United States and Japan. Retrieved October 1, 2024, from https://data.worldbank.org/indicator/NY.GDP.PCAP.CD?locations=US-JP

The World Bank. (n.d.-g). Data from World Bank national accounts data and OECD National Accounts, from data series *'GDP per capita (current US$)'* for Switzerland, Germany, and France. Retrieved October 1, 2024, from https://data.worldbank.org/indicator/NY.GDP.PCAP.CD?locations=CH-DE-FR

Thiel, P., & Masters, B. (2014). *Zero to one: Notes on startups, or how to build the future.* New York, NY: Crown Business.

This Is World. (2025, March 7). *Father of AI: AI needs physics to evolve | Prof. Yann LeCun* [Video]. YouTube. https://www.youtube.com/watch?v=RUnFgu8kH-4

Thomas, L., Dummett, B., & Cutter, C. (2025, February 10). For CEOs and bankers, the Trump euphoria is fading fast. *The Wall Street Journal.* Retrieved from https://www.wsj.com/business/deals/trump-boom-corporate-uncertainty-6383263d

Thomas, K., & McCormick, J. (2025, January 23). Inside the Elon Musk, Vivek Ramaswamy DOGE divorce: Biotech-company founder departs DOGE after his goal of trimming regulations was overtaken by Musk's priority of cutting spending. *The Wall Street Journal.* Retrieved from https://www.wsj.com/politics/elections/inside-the-elon-musk-vivek-ramaswamy-doge-divorce-975a3d26

Thomke, S. (2001). Enlightened experimentation. The new imperative for innovation. *Harvard Business Review, 79*(2), 66–75.

Thompson, F. J. (2020, October 9). Six ways Trump has sabotaged the Affordable Care Act. *Brookings.* Retrieved from https://www.brookings.edu/blog/fixgov/2020/10/09/six-ways-trump-has-sabotaged-the-affordable-care-act/

Thompson, J. D. (1967). *Organizations in action: Social science bases of administrative theory.* New York, NY: McGraw-Hill.

Thompson, J. D., & McEwen, W. J. (1958). Organizational goals and environment: Goal-setting as an interaction process. *American Sociological Review, 23*(1), 23–31. https://doi.org/10.2307/2088620

Thomsen, S. (2020, October 13). Value creation and corporate governance. *SSRN Electronic Journal.* https://doi.org/10.2139/ssrn.3710467

Tichy, N. M., Tushman, M. L., & Fombrun, C. (1979). Social network analysis for organizations. *The Academy of Management Review, 4*(4), 507–519. https://doi.org/10.2307/257851

Tihanyi, L., Griffith, D., & Russell, C. (2005). The effect of cultural distance on entry mode choice, international diversification, and MNE performance: A meta-analysis. *Journal of International Business Studies, 36*(3), 270–283. https://doi.org/10.1057/palgrave.jibs.8400136

Tinbergen, J. (1939). *Statistical testing of business cycle theories: Part I: A method and its application to investment activity*. New York, NY: Agaton Press. Retrieved from http://hdl.handle.net/1765/14936

Tirole, J. (1988). *The theory of industrial organization*. Cambridge, MA: MIT Press.

Titman, S., Wei, K. C. J., & Xie, F. (2004). Capital investments and stock returns. *The Journal of Financial and Quantitative Analysis*, *39*(4), 677–700. https://doi.org/10.1017/S0022109000003173

Tollison, R. D. (1982). Rent seeking: A survey. *Kyklos*, *35*(4), 575–602. https://doi.org/10.1111/j.1467-6435.1982.tb00174.x

Tollison, R. D. (2012). The economic theory of rent seeking. *Public Choice*, *152*(1), 73–82. https://doi.org/10.1007/s11127-011-9852-5

Tompson, W. (2002). Putin's challenge: The politics of structural reform in Russia. *Europe-Asia Studies*, *54*(6), 933–957. https://doi.org/10.1080/0966813022000008465

Toonkel, J., Hagey, K., & Bobrowsky, M. (2024, December 13). Meta urges California attorney general to stop OpenAI from becoming for-profit. *The Wall Street Journal*. Retrieved from https://www.wsj.com/tech/ai/elon-musk-open-ai-lawsuit-response-c1f415f8

Topol, E. (2024, December 20). Mark Cuban: A master disrupter for American healthcare. *Ground Truths*. Retrieved from https://erictopol.substack.com/p/mark-cuban-a-master-disrupter-for

Torres, É. P. (2023, December 14). 'Effective accelerationism' and the pursuit of cosmic utopia. *Truthdig*. Retrieved from https://www.truthdig.com/articles/effective-accelerationism-and-the-pursuit-of-cosmic-utopia/

Toy, J., Tabor, P., & MacAdam, J. (2024, March 4). Metacognition is all you need? Using introspection in generative agents to improve goal-directed behavior. *arXiv*. Retrieved from https://arxiv.org/pdf/2401.10910

Tran, T. H. (2023, February 26). The radical movement to worship AI as a new god. *The Daily Beast*. Retrieved from https://www.thedailybeast.com/the-radical-movement-to-worship-ai-chatbots-like-chatgpt-as-gods

Traverso, E. (1995). *The Jews & Germany: From the 'Judeo-German symbiosis' to the memory of Auschwitz* (D. Weissbort, Trans.). Lincoln, NE: University of Nebraska Press.

Treynor, J. L. (1961, August 8). Market value, time, and risk. *SSRN Electronic Journal*. http://doi.org/10.2139/ssrn.2600356

Triandis, H. C. (1989). The self and social behaviour in differing cultural contexts. *Psychological Review*, *96*, 269–289. https://doi.org/10.1037/0033-295X.96.3.506

Tripp, S., & Grueber, M. (2011, May). *Economic impact of the Human Genome Project*. Columbus, OH: Battelle Memorial Institute. Retrieved from https://www.battelle.org/docs/default-source/misc/battelle-2011-misc-economic-impact-human-genome-project.pdf

Trocki, C. A. (1999). *Opium, empire, and the global political economy: A study of the Asian opium trade 1750-1950*. New York, NY: Routledge.

Trump, D. J. (1987). *The art of the deal* [Audiobook]. With Tony Schwartz. Mariapolis. https://www.youtube.com/watch?v=Mq2as5M2jBU

Tsai, W., & Ghoshal, S. (1998). Social capital and value creation: The role of intrafirm networks. *Academy of Management Journal*, *41*(4), 464–476. https://doi.org/10.2307/257085

Tullock, G. (1967). The welfare costs of tariffs, monopolies, and theft. *Western Economic Journal*, *5*(3), 224–232.

Turchin, P. (2013). Modeling social pressures toward political instability. *Cliodynamics*, *4*(2), 241–280. https://doi.org/10.21237/C7CLIO8237313

Turchin, P. (2016). *Ultrasociety: How 10,000 years of war made humans the greatest cooperators on earth*. Chaplin, CT: Beresta Books.

Turchin, P. (2023). *End times: Elites, counter-elites, and the path of political disintegration*. London: Penguin Press.

TÜV SÜD. (2024). *Official smart industry readiness index (SIRI) assessment*. Retrieved from https://www.tuvsud.com/en-sg/digital-service/industry-40-enablement-programme

Tversky, A., & Kahneman, D. (1974). Judgment under uncertainty: Heuristics and biases. *Science, 185*(4157), 1124–1131. https://doi.org/10.1126/science.185.4157.1124

Twiggs, J. E. (1987). *The Tokyo round of multilateral trade negotiations: A case study in building domestic support for diplomacy*. Washington, DC: Georgetown University Institute for the Study of Diplomacy.

U.S. Department of Education. (2023, December 6). *Biden-Harris administration announces nearly $5 billion in additional student debt relief*. Retrieved from https://www.ed.gov/news/press-releases/biden-harris-administration-announces-nearly-5-billion-additional-student-debt-relief

U.S. Department of Health, Education, and Welfare. (1964). *Smoking and health: Report of the Advisory Committee to the Surgeon General of the Public Health Service* (Public Health Service Publication No. 1103). Washington, DC: U.S. Government Printing Office. Retrieved from https://www.govinfo.gov/content/pkg/gpo-smokingandhealth/pdf/gpo-smokingandhealth.pdf

U.S. Department of Justice and the Federal Trade Commission. (2023, December 18). *Merger guidelines*. Retrieved from https://www.justice.gov/d9/2023-12/2023%20Merger%20Guidelines.pdf

U.S. House of Representatives, Committee on the Judiciary, & Select Subcommittee on the Weaponization of the Federal Government. (2024, May 1). *The censorship-industrial complex: How top Biden White House officials coerced big tech to censor Americans, true information, and critics of the Biden administration* [Interim staff report]. Retrieved from https://judiciary.house.gov/sites/evo-subsites/republicans-judiciary.house.gov/files/evo-media-document/Biden-WH-Censorship-Report-final.pdf

U.S. Senate. (2014). *S. 517 – Unlocking consumer choice and wireless competition act, 113th Congress* (Public Law No. 113-144). Retrieved from https://www.congress.gov/bill/113th-congress/senate-bill/517/text

UBS. (2023). *Billionaire ambitions report 2023*. Zurich: UBS. Retrieved from https://www.ubs.com/global/en/family-office-uhnw/reports/billionaire-ambitions-client-report-2023.html

Unell, N. (2023). *Sustainable value creation for finance – Credit rating and equity valuation adjustments* [Master's thesis]. University of St. Gallen.

United Nations. (1948). *The universal declaration of human rights*. New York, NY: United Nations Department of Public Information. Retrieved from https://www.ohchr.org/EN/UDHR/Documents/UDHR_Translations/eng.pdf

United Nations, AI Advisory Body. (2024, September). *Governing AI for humanity*. United Nations. https://www.un.org/sites/un2.un.org/files/governing_ai_for_humanity_final_report_en.pdf

United Nations Educational, Scientific and Cultural Organization (UNESCO) & World Commission on the Ethics of Scientific Knowledge and Technology (COMEST). (2017). *Report of COMEST on robotics ethics* (SHS/YES/COMEST-10/17/2 REV.). Paris, France: UNESCO. Retrieved from https://unesdoc.unesco.org/ark:/48223/pf0000253952

United Nations Statistics Division. (n.d.). *Net value added* (Glossary of the 1993 System of National Accounts [SNA]). United Nations. Retrieved October 22, 2024, from https://unstats.un.org/unsd/nationalaccount/glossresults.asp?gID=362

United States Congress Joint Economic Committee (2019, September 19). *Long-term trends in deaths of despair*. Social Capital Project Report No. 4. Retrieved from https://www.jec.senate.gov/public/index.cfm/republicans/2019/9/long-term-trends-in-deaths-of-despair

United States District Court for the District of Columbia. (2024, August 5). Memorandum opinion. In United States of America et al. v. Google LLC, Case No. 1:20-cv-03010-APM; State of Colorado et al. v. Google LLC, Case No. 1:20-cv-03715-APM. Retrieved from https://www.tn.gov/content/dam/tn/attorneygeneral/documents/pr/2024/pr24-59-Google.pdf

United States of America. (1948). *Congressional record: Proceedings and debates of the 80th Congress, Second Session* (Vol. 94, Part 1, pp. 1–1434, January 6, 1948 to February 19, 1948). Washington, DC: United States Government Printing Office.

University of Toronto (2023, June 22). *The godfather in conversation: Why Geoffrey Hinton is worried about the future of AI* [Video]. YouTube. https://www.youtube.com/watch?v=-9cW4Gcn5WY

Vall-Prat, P. (2022). Economic shocks, mobilization, and regional elite splits. *Comparative Political Studies, 56*(2) 193–227. https://doi.org/10.1177/00104140221089641

van de Ven, A. (1993). The institutional theory of John R. Commons: A review and commentary. *The Academy of Management Review, 18*(1), 139–152. https://doi.org/10.2307/258826

van den Beuke, J., & van Geuns, L. (2021, January 19). Russia's unsustainable business model: Going all in on oil and gas. *The Hague Centre for Strategic Studies*. Retrieved from https://hcss.nl/wp-content/uploads/2021/01/Russias-Unsustainable-Business-Model.pdf

van der Eijk, C. (2018). Political power. In C. van der Eijk, *The essence of politics* (pp. 85–102). Amsterdam: Amsterdam University Press. https://doi.org/10.1515/9789048544738-007

van Hoorn, A., & Maseland, R. (2016). How institutions matter for international business: Institutional distance effects vs institutional profile effects. *Journal of International Business Studies, 47*(3), 374–381. https://doi.org/10.1057/jibs.2016.2

van Valen, L. (1973). A new evolutionary law. *Evolutionary Theory, 1*(1), 1–30.

Van Zee, A. (2009). The promotion and marketing of Oxycontin: Commercial triumph, public health tragedy. *American journal of public health, 99*(2), 221–227. https://doi.org/10.2105/AJPH.2007.131714

Vance, J. D. (2016). *Hillbilly elegy: A memoir of a family and culture in crisis*. New York, NY: Harper.

Varoufakis, Y. (2021, June 28). Techno-feudalism is taking over. *Project Syndicate*. Retrieved from https://www.project-syndicate.org/commentary/techno-feudalism-replacing-market-capitalism-by-yanis-varoufakis-2021-06

Varoufakis, Y. (2023, June 10). Opinion: AI gives big business the power to bust labor unions. *MarketWatch*. Retrieved from https://www.marketwatch.com/story/ai-is-now-giving-big-business-the-power-to-bust-labor-unions-be6c9115?cx_testId=3&cx_testVariant=cx_164&cx_artPos=6&mod=WTRN#cxrecs_s

Varoufakis, Y. (2025, January 6). Musk, Trump and the broligarchs' novel hyper-weapon [Le Monde 4-1-2025, full original English version]. Retrieved from https://www.yanisvaroufakis.eu/2025/01/06/musk-trump-and-the-broligarchs-novel-hyper-weapon-le-monde-4-1-2025-full-original-english-version/

Vaswani, A., Shazeer, N., Parmar, N., Uszkoreit, J., Jones, L., Gomez, A. N., Kaiser, Ł., & Polosukhin, I. (2017). Attention is all you need. In *Proceedings of the 31st International Conference on Neural Information Processing Systems (NeurIPS 2017)* (pp. 6000–6010). Retrieved from https://proceedings.neurips.cc/paper_files/paper/2017/file/3f5ee243547dee91fbd053c1c4a845aa-Paper.pdf

Vazza, D., Kraemer, N., & Gurwitz, Z. (2019, March 26). The cost of a notch. *S&P Global*. Retrieved from https://www.spglobal.com/en/research-insights/articles/the-cost-of-a-notch

Veblen, T. (1915). *Imperial Germany and the industrial revolution*. Kitchener, ON: Batoche Books. Retrieved from https://historyofeconomicthought.mcmaster.ca/veblen/ImperialGermany.pdf

Veblen, T. (1924). *The theory of the leisure class*. London: George Allen & Unwin.

Veblen, T. (1975). *The theory of business enterprise*. Clifton, NJ: Augustus M. Kelley.

Vervaeke, J. [John Vervaeke]. (2023, April 22). *AI: The coming thresholds and the path we must take* [Video]. YouTube. https://youtu.be/A-_RdKiDbz4

Vigario, D. (2021, February 4). Los arroceros Españoles piden a Bruselas que se anulen los 'privilegios' a Birmania tras el golpe de estado. *El Mundo*. Retrieved from https://www.elmundo.es/economia/macroeconomia/2021/02/04/601ade4cfc6c836c378b45b2.html.

Vigliarolo, B. (2022, August 9). US car industry leads the world in production cuts over chip shortages. *The Register*. Retrieved from https://www.theregister.com/2022/08/09/car_chip_shortage/

Vigna, P. (2022, February 27). Wall Street takes lead in crypto investments. *The Wall Street Journal*. Retrieved from https://www.wsj.com/articles/wall-street-takes-lead-in-crypto-investments-11645927004

Villalobos, P., Ho, A., Sevilla, J., Besiroglu, T., Heim, L., & Hobbhahn, M. (2024, June 6). Will we run out of data? Limits of LLM scaling based on human-generated data. *AIModels.fyi*. Retrieved from https://www.aimodels.fyi/papers/arxiv/will-we-run-out-data-limits-llm

Vincent, N. (2002). Some pardoners' tales: The earliest English indulgences. *Transactions of the Royal Historical Society*, *12*, 23–58. https://doi.org/10.1017/S0080440102000026

Vincent, N. (2018). Magna Carta: From King John to western liberty. In L. Goldman (Ed.), *Magna Carta: History, context and influence* (pp. 25-40). London: University of London Press.

Vinge, V. (2013). Technological singularity. In M. More and N. Vita-More (Eds.), *The transhumanist reader: Classical and contemporary essays on the science, technology and philosophy of the human future* (pp. 365–375). Hoboken, NJ: John Wiley & Sons Inc. https://doi.org/10.1002/9781118555927.ch35

Vinocur, N. (2024, January 1). Democracy is in peril in the world's bonanza year of elections. *Politico*. Retrieved from https://www.politico.eu/article/democracy-2023-elections-united-states-europe-united-kingdom-russia-taiwan-donald-trump/

Virgil. (1910). *Aeneid* (T. C. Williams, Ed. & Trans.). Boston, MA: Houghton Mifflin Co. Retrieved from https://www.perseus.tufts.edu/hopper/text?doc=Perseus%3Atext%3A1999.02.0054%3Abook%3D6%3Acard%3D801

Vis, B., & Stolwijk, S. (2021). Conducting quantitative studies with the participation of political elites: Best practices for designing the study and soliciting the participation of political elites. *Quality & Quantity*, *55*, 1281–1317. https://doi.org/10.1007/s11135-020-01052-z

Vogel, K. P. (2020, March 28). The race for virus money is on. Lobbyists are standing by. *The New York Times*. Retrieved from https://www.nytimes.com/2020/03/28/us/politics/coronavirus-money-lobbyists.html.

Vogel, L., Gebauer, R., & Salheiser, A. (2018). *The contested status of political elites: At the crossroads*. London: Routledge. https://doi.org/10.4324/9781315211916

Von Bertalanffy, L. (1972). The history and status of general systems theory. *The Academy of Management Journal*, *15*(4), 407–426. https://doi.org/10.2307/255139

Von Bertalanffy, L. (2003). *General system theory: Foundations, development, applications* (14th ed.). New York, NY: George Braziller.

von Carlowitz, H. C. (2022). *Sylvicultura oeconomica: Oder haußwirthliche nachricht und naturmäßige anweisung zur wilden baum-zucht*. Leipzig: Johann Friedrich Braun. Retrieved from https://de.wikisource.org/wiki/Sylvicultura_oeconomica

von Glahn, R. (2022). Economic philosophy and political economy. In D. Ma & R. von Glahn (Eds.), *The Cambridge economic history of China* (pp. 166–202). Cambridge: Cambridge University Press. https://doi.org/10.1017/9781108587334.006

von Mises, L. (2003). *The historical setting of the Austrian school of economics*. Auburn, AL: Ludwig von Mises Institute. Retrieved from https://mises.org/library/book/historical-setting-austrian-school-economics

von Stockar, U., & Liu, J. (1999). Does microbial life always feed on negative entropy? Thermodynamic analysis of microbial growth. *Biochimica et biophysica acta*, *1412*(3), 191–211. https://doi.org/10.1016/s0005-2728(99)00065-1

Voslensky, M. (1984). *Nomenklatura: The Soviet ruling class*. New York, NY: Doubleday.

Wacquant, L. J., & Bourdieu, P. (1992). *An invitation to reflexive sociology*. Chicago, IL: University of Chicago Press.

Wagner, D. L., Grames, E., Forister, M. L., Berenbaum, M. R., & Stopak, D. (2021). Insect decline in the anthropocene: Death by a thousand cuts. *Proceedings of the National Academy of Sciences*, *118*(2), e2023989118. https://doi.org/10.1073/pnas.2023989118

Wagner, R., & Kabalska, A. (2023). Between involvement and profit: Value (un-)captured by a born-social start-up. *Journal of Social Entrepreneurship*, 1–26. https://doi.org/10.1080/19420676.2023.2199765

Waldrop, M. M. (1992). *Complexity: The emerging science at the edge of order and chaos*. New York, NY: Simon & Schuster. https://doi.org/10.1063/1.2809917

Waley, A. (1958). *The way and its power: Lao Tzu's Tao Tê Ching and its place in Chinese thought*. New York, NY: Grove Press.

Walgrave, S., & Joly, J. K. (2018). Surveying individual political elites: A comparative three-country study. *Quality & Quantity: International Journal of Methodology*, *52*(5), 2221–2237. https://doi.org/10.1007/s11135-017-0658-5

Walk Free. (2023). *The global slavery index 2023*. Retrieved from https://cdn.walkfree.org/content/uploads/2023/05/17114737/Global-Slavery-Index-2023.pdf

Walker, R. L. (1947). The control system of the Chinese government. *The Far Eastern Quarterly*, *7*(1), 2–21. https://doi.org/10.2307/2049408

Walls, J. L., Berrone, P., & Phan, P. H. (2012). Corporate governance and environmental performance: Is there really a link? *Strategic Management Journal*, *33*(8), 885–913. https://doi.org/10.1002/smj.1952

Walls, J. L., Phan, P. H., & Berrone, P. (2011). Measuring environmental strategy: Construct development, reliability, and validity. *Business & Society*, *50*(1), 71–115. https://doi.org/10.1177/0007650310394427

Walls, J. L., Salaiz, A., & Chiu, S.-C. (2021). Wanted: Heroic leaders to drive the transition to "business beyond usual". *Strategic Organization*, *19*(3), 494–512. https://doi.org/10.1177/1476127020973379

Walsh, N. P., Picheta, R., & Kent, L. (2025, March 4). Zelensky describes Oval Office meeting as 'regrettable,' says he is ready to negotiate peace. *CNN*. Retrieved from https://edition.cnn.com/2025/03/04/europe/zelensky-trump-argument-comment-ukraine-intl/index.html

Walz, E. (2024, January 25). Tesla warns of growing competition from automakers in China. *Automotive Dive*. Retrieved from https://www.automotivedive.com/news/tesla-elon-musk-warns-competition-china-automakers-byd-trade-barriers-sales/705636/

Walzer, M. (2002). The triumph of just war theory (and the dangers of success). *Social Research*, *69*(4), 925–944.

Wang, Y. (2021). The politico-economic dynamics of China's growth. *Journal of the European Economic Association, 19*(1), 305–346. https://doi.org/10.1093/jeea/jvaa011

Wasserstrom, S. M. (1999). *Religion after religion: Gershom Scholem, Mircea Eliade, and Henry Corbin at Eranos*. Princeton, NJ: Princeton University Press.

Waters, R., & Palma, S. (2023, July 12). Court ruling changes the game for Microsoft's $75bn Activision deal. *The Financial Times*. Retrieved from https://www.ft.com/content/ea080348-349b-4fb2-a18d-3ba35fafddd8

Watson, O. J., Barnsley, G., Toor, J., Hogan, A. B., Winskill, P., & Ghani, A. C. (2022). Global impact of the first year of COVID-19 vaccination: A mathematical modelling study. *The Lancet Infectious Diseases*, *22*(9), 1293–1302. https://doi.org/10.1016/S1473-3099(22)00320-6

Watts, J., Sheehan, O., Atkinson, Q. D., Bulbulia, J., & Gray, R. D. (2016). Ritual human sacrifice promoted and sustained the evolution of stratified societies. *Nature*, *532*(7598), 228–231. https://doi.org/10.1038/nature17159

Weber, M. (1925). *Wirtschaft und gesellschaft*. Tübingen: J. C. B. Mohr.

Weber, M. (1930). *The Protestant ethic and the spirit of capitalism* (T. Parsons, Trans.). New York, NY: Charles Scribner's Sons. Retrieved from https://archive.org/details/protestantethics00webe/page/n7/mode/2up?q=iron+cage

Wedel, J. R. (2009). *Shadow elite: How the world's new power brokers undermine democracy, government, and the free market*. New York, NY: Basic books.

Wei, J., Tay, Y., Bommasani, R., Raffel, C., Zoph, B., Borgeaud, S., Yogatama, D., Bosma, M., Zhou, D., Metzler, D., Chi, E. H., Hashimoto, T., Vinyals, O., Liang, P., Dean, J., & Fedus, W. (2022). Emergent abilities of large language models. *arXiv*. https://doi.org/10.48550/arXiv.2206.07682

Weick, K. E. (1989). Theory construction as disciplined imagination. *The Academy of Management Review*, *14*(4), 516–531. https://doi.org/10.2307/258556

Weinberger, E. (2024, December 26). Incoming! *London Review of Books*, *46*(24). Retrieved from https://www.lrb.co.uk/the-paper/v46/n24/eliot-weinberger/incoming

Weingast, B., & Marshall, W. J. (1988). The industrial organization of congress. *Journal of Political Economy*, *96*(1), 132–163. https://doi.org/10.1086/261528

Weiser, M. (1991). The computer for the 21st Century. *Scientific American, 265*(3), 94–105.
Weiss, B. (2024, November 15). Peter Thiel and the triumph of the counter-elites. *The Free Press*. Retrieved from https://www.thefp.com/p/peter-thiel-honestly-trump-jd-vance
Wellman, B. (1983). Network analysis: Some basic principles. *Sociological Theory, 1*, 155–200. https://doi.org/10.2307/202050
Welsby, J., & Nichols, A. (1999). The privatisation of Britain's Railways: An inside view. *Journal of Transport Economics and Policy, 33*(1), 55–76.
Welzel, C. (2002). Effective democracy, mass culture, and the quality of elites: The human development perspective. *International Journal of Comparative Sociology, 43*(3-5), 317–349. https://doi.org/10.1177/002071520204300306
Wen, J., Wang, B., Dai, Z., Shi, X., Jin, Z., Wang, H., & Jiang, X. (2023). New insights into the green cement composites with low carbon footprint: The role of biochar as cement additive/alternative. *Resources, Conservation and Recycling, 197*, 107081. https://doi.org/10.1016/j.resconrec.2023.107081
Wengrow, D., & Graeber, D. (2015). Farewell to the "childhood of man": Ritual, seasonality, and the origins of inequality. *The Journal of the Royal Anthropological Institute, 21*(3), 597–619. https://doi.org/10.1111/1467-9655.12247
Wennekers, S., & Thurik, R. (1999). Linking entrepreneurship and economic growth. *Small Business Economics, 13*(1), 27–55. https://doi.org/10.1023/A:1008063200484
Weyland, K. (1999). Economic policy in Chile's new democracy. *Journal of Interamerican Studies and World Affairs, 41*(3), 67–96. https://doi.org/10.2307/166159
Weyland, K. (2008). Toward a new theory of institutional change. *World Politics, 60*(2), 281–314. https://doi.org/10.1353/wp.0.0013
Whalley, J., & Curwen P. (2012). Incumbency and market share within European mobile telecommunication networks. *Telecommunications Policy, 36*(3), 222–236. https://doi.org/10.1016/j.telpol.2011.11.020
Wheatley, J. (2024, December 6). Elon Musk donated more than $250mn to Donald Trump's campaign, electoral filings show. *The Financial Times*. Retrieved from https://www.ft.com/content/5f962d83-01d8-4a2d-9d36-a1bfed400c00
Wheeler, T. (2023, October 16). Big Tech won. Now what? *Brookings*. Retrieved from https://www.brookings.edu/articles/big-tech-won-now-what/
Wheelwright, T. (2019, August 30). 5 ways that billionaire Warren Buffett pays a lower tax rate than his secretary. *Entrepreneur*. Retrieved from https://www.entrepreneur.com/article/338189
Whetstone, J. (2002). Personalism and moral leadership: The servant leader with a transforming vision. *Business Ethics: A European Review, 11*(4), 385–392. https://doi.org/10.1111/1467-8608.00298
Whetten, D. A. (1989). What constitutes a theoretical contribution? *The Academy of Management Review, 14*(4), 490–495. https://doi.org/10.2307/258554
Whimster, S. (2019). On academic freedom. *Max Weber Studies, 19*(2), 246–259. https://doi.org/10.1353/max.2019.0002
White, E., & Lockett, H. (2023, December 22). Tencent rocked by new Chinese online gaming restrictions. *The Financial Times*. Retrieved from https://www.ft.com/content/36580e3b-c6d6-486d-825b-bd084a010925
Widder, D. G., West, S., & Whittaker, M. (2023). Open (for business): Big Tech, concentrated power, and the political economy of Open AI. *SSRN Electronic Journal*. https://doi.org/10.2139/ssrn.4543807
Wijkman, P. M. (1982). Managing the global commons. *International Organization, 36*(3), 511–536. https://doi.org/10.1017/S0020818300032628
Williams, C. C., & Youssef, Y. (2014). Classifying Latin American economies: A degree of informalisation approach. *International Journal of Business Administration, 5*(3), 73–85. https://doi.org/10.5430/ijba.v5n3p73
Williams, J. B. (1938). *The theory of investment value*. Cambridge, MA: Harvard University Press.
Williams, J. C., & Khanna, R. (2020, October 28). It's time to end slash-and-burn capitalism. *Harvard Business Review*. Retrieved from https://hbr.org/2020/10/its-time-to-end-slash-and-burn-capitalism

Williams, P. F. (2004). You reap what you sow: The ethical discourse of professional accounting. *Critical Perspectives on Accounting*, *15*(6-7), 995–1001. https://doi.org/10.1016/j.cpa.2003.04.003

Williams, S. (2000). Is rational choice theory 'unreasonable'? Neglected emotions. In M. Archer & J. Tritter (Eds.), *Rational choice theory – Resisting colonization* (pp. 57–72). London: Routledge. https://doi.org/10.4324/9780203133897

Williamson, O. (1981). The economics of organization: The transaction cost approach. *American Journal of Sociology*, *87*(3), 548–577. https://doi.org/10.1086/227496

Williamson, O. (1993). Transaction cost economics and organization theory. *Industrial and Corporate Change*, *2*(2), 107–156. https://doi.org/10.1093/icc/2.2.107

Williamson, O. (2000). The new institutional economics: Taking stock, looking ahead. *Journal of Economic* Literature, *38*(3), 595–613. https://doi.org/10.1257/jel.38.3.595

Williamson, O. E. (2010). Transaction cost economics: The natural progression. *The American Economic Review*, *100*(3), 673–690. https://doi.org/10.1257/aer.100.3.673

Wilowski, M. (2023, October 24). Coalition of 33 states sues meta platforms for harming children's mental health. *Investopedia*. Retrieved from https://www.investopedia.com/coalition-of-states-sues-meta-platforms-for-harming-children-and-teens-mental-health-8379459

Wilson, K. B., Karg, A., & Ghaderi, H. (2021, October 29). Prospecting non-fungible tokens in the digital economy: Stakeholders and ecosystem, risk and opportunity. *Business Horizons*, *65*(5), 657–670. https://doi.org/10.1016/j.bushor.2021.10.007

Wilson, P. H. (2008) The causes of the Thirty Years War 1618-48 *The English Historical Review*, *123*(502), 554–86. https://doi.org/10.1093/ehr/cen160

Winful, E. C., Sarpong, D., & Agyei-Ntiamoah, J. (2016). Relationship between institutional quality and stock market performance: Evidence from emerging economies. *African Journal of Business Management*, *10*(19), 469–484. https://doi.org/10.5897/AJBM2016.8153

Winner, L. (1977). *Autonomous technology: Technics-out-of-control as a theme in political thought*. Cambridge, MA: tHE MIT Press.

Winner, L. (2020, November 21). Interview with Langdon Winner: Autonomous technology: Then and still now. *Langdon Winner*. https://www.langdonwinner.com/other-writings

Winston, C. (1993). Economic deregulation: Days of reckoning for microeconomists. *Journal of Economic Literature, 31*(3), 1263–1289.

Winters, J. (2011). The material foundations of oligarchy. In J. Winters, *Oligarchy* (pp. 1–39). Cambridge: Cambridge University Press. https://doi.org/10.1017/CBO9780511793806.002

Wintour, P. (2025, February 14). JD Vance stuns Munich conference with blistering attack on Europe's leaders. *The Guardian*. Retrieved from https://www.theguardian.com/us-news/2025/feb/14/jd-vance-stuns-munich-conference-with-blistering-attack-on-europes-leaders

WIPO (2021). *The Global innovation index 2021: Tracking innovation through the COVID-19 crisis*. Geneva, Switzerland: World Intellectual Property Organization. Retrieved from https://www.globalinnovationindex.org/gii-2021-report

Witt, M. A., Kabbach de Castro, L. R., Amaeshi, K., Mahroum, S., Bohle, D., & Saez, L. (2018). Mapping the business systems of 61 major economies: A taxonomy and implications for varieties of capitalism and business systems research. *Socio-Economic Review*, *16*(1), 5–38. https://doi.org/10.1093/ser/mwx012

Witt, M. A., & Lewin, A. Y. (2007). Outward foreign direct investment as escape response to home country institutional constraints. *Journal of International Business Studies*, *38*(4), 579–594. https://doi.org/10.1057/palgrave.jibs.8400285

Witt, M. A., & Redding, G. (2013). Asian business systems: Institutional comparison, clusters and implications for varieties of capitalism and business systems theory. *Socio-Economic Review*, *11*(2), 265–300. https://doi.org/10.1093/ser/mwt002

Wittgenstein, L. (1993). A lecture on ethics. In J. C. Klagge & A. Nordmann (Eds.), *Ludwig Wittgenstein: Philosophical occasions 1912–1951* (pp. 36–44). Indianapolis, IN: Hackett Publishing Company.

Wokler, R. (1998). Contextualizing Hegel's phenomenology of the French Revolution and the terror. *Political Theory*, *26*(1), 33–55. https://doi.org/10.1177/0090591798026001003

Wolf, M. (2019, September 18). Why rigged capitalism is damaging liberal democracy, *The Financial Times*. Retrieved from https://www.ft.com/content/5a8ab27e-d470-11e9-8367-807ebd53ab77

Wolf, M. (2023, January 20). In defence of democratic capitalism. *The Financial Times*. Retrieved from https://www.ft.com/content/877d1a2d-67df-46a4-a3af-8e28198b944a

Wolfram, S. (2002). *A new kind of science*. Champaign, IL: Wolfram Media. Retrieved from https://www.wolframscience.com/nks/

Wolla, S. A., & Backus, C. (2018, November). The economics of flying: How competitive are the friendly skies? *Page One Economics Newsletter, Federal Reserve Bank of St. Louis*, 1-7. Retrieved from https://research.stlouisfed.org/publications/page1-econ/2018/11/01/the-economics-of-flying-how-competitive-are-the-friendly-skies

Wolraich, M. (2024, May 14). How Donald Trump's plans could bring back the spoils system. *Time*. Retrieved from https://time.com/6968746/spoils-system-donald-trump/

Wong, F., Omori, S., Donghia, N. M., Zheng, E. J., & Collins, J. J. (2023). Discovering small-molecule senolytics with deep neural networks. *Nature Aging*, *3*. 734–750. https://doi.org/10.1038/s43587-023-00415-z

Woods, D. (2012). On the alleged letters of Honorius to the cities of Britain in 410. *Latomus*, *71*(3), 818–826.

World Economic Forum. (2023, March 7). This is why 'polycrisis' is a useful way of looking at the world right now: An interview with historian Adam Tooze. *World Economic Forum*. Retrieved from https://www.weforum.org/agenda/2023/03/polycrisis-adam-tooze-historian-explains/

Wouters, O. J. (2020). Lobbying expenditures and campaign contributions by the pharmaceutical and health product industry in the United States, 1999-2018. *JAMA Internal Medicine*, *180*(5), 688–697. https://doi.org/10.1001/jamainternmed.2020.0146

WTO. (1994a). *Agreement on trade-related aspects of intellectual property rights*. Retrieved from https://www.wto.org/english/docs_e/legal_e/27-trips_01_e.htm

WTO. (1994b). *Agreement on subsidies and countervailing measures* (pp. 229–272). Retrieved from https://www.wto.org/english/docs_e/legal_e/24-scm.pdf

Wu, J. (2019, July 6) A brief history of Jack Ma's Ant Financial – the $150B unicorn. *Hackernoon*. Retrieved from https://hackernoon.com/the-story-of-ant-financial-4t2aq3zh8

Xie, S. Y., & Yang, J. (2020, August 25). Inside Ant Group's giant valuation. *The Wall Street Journal*. Retrieved from https://www.wsj.com/articles/jack-mas-ant-group-files-ipo-listing-documents-11598349802

Xinhua. (2023, December 19). China's top economic planner begins preliminary study of 15th Five-Year Plan. *The State Council The People's Republic of China*. Retrieved from https://english.www.gov.cn/news/202312/19/content_WS6580d2b6c6d0868f4e8e2507.html

Yaffe-Bellany, D. (2023, November 16). Cryptocurrency prices surge, driven by a potential bitcoin fund. *The New York Times*. Retrieved from https://www.nytimes.com/2023/11/16/technology/cryptocurrency-bitcoin-etf.html

Yamamura, K. (1964). Zaibatsu, prewar and zaibatsu, postwar. *The Journal of Asian Studies*, *23*(4), 539–554. https://doi.org/10.2307/2050237

Yampolskiy, R. V. (2022). On the controllability of artificial intelligence: An analysis of limitations. *Journal of Cyber Security and Mobility*, *11*(3), 321–404. https://doi.org/10.13052/jcsm2245-1439.1132

Yampolskiy, R. V. (2024). *AI: Unexplainable, unpredictable, uncontrollable*. New York, NY: Chapman and Hall/CRC Press. https://doi.org/10.1201/9781003440260

Yang, Y. (2020, December 14). Alibaba fined over past deals as China gets tougher on Big Tech. *The Financial Times*. Retrieved from https://www.ft.com/content/a8c241c9-5690-4fd4-a3cc-fea38516d6ba

Yao, Y. (2025, March 7). Zelensky-Trump clash: A wake-up call for Europe's independence. *China Daily*. Retrieved from http://www.chinadaily.com.cn/a/202503/07/WS67cab435a310c240449d96d0.html

Yeoh, P. (2010). Causes of the global financial crisis: Learning from the competing insights. *International Journal of Disclosure and Governance*, *7*(1), 42–69. https://doi.org/10.1057/jdg.2009.18

Yergin, D. (2009). *The prize: The epic quest for oil, money & power*. New York, NY: Free Press.

Yglesias, M. (2023, October 22). Biden's economy is great everywhere except in the polls. *The Washington Post*. Retrieved from https://www.washingtonpost.com/business/2023/10/22/biden-s-economy-is-great-everywhere-except-in-the-polls/d6bae722-70d6-11ee-936d-7a16ee667359_story.html

Yoon, Y-K. (2003). Introduction: Power cycle theory and the practice of international relations. *International Political Science Review / Revue Internationale de Science Politique*, *24*(1), 5–12. http://dx.doi.org/10.1177/0192512103024001001

Young, A. (1992). A tale of two cities: Factor accumulation and technical change in Hong Kong and Singapore. In O. J. Blanchard & S. Fischer (Eds.), *NBER macroeconomics annual 1992* (Vol. 7, pp. 13–64). Retrieved from https://www.nber.org/system/files/chapters/c10990/c10990.pdf

Ypi, L. (2014). On revolution in Kant and Marx. *Political Theory*, *42*(3), 262–287. https://doi.org/10.1177/0090591714523138

Yu, T. F-L. (1998). Adaptive entrepreneurship and the economic development of Hong Kong. *World Development*, *26*(5), 897–911.

Yudkin, J. (2012). *Pure, white and deadly: How sugar is killing us and what we can do to stop it*. New York, NY: Penguin Press.

Yudkowsky, E. (2013). *Intelligence explosion microeconomics* (Technical Report No. 2013-1). Berkeley, CA: Machine Intelligence Research Institute. Retrieved from https://intelligence.org/files/IEM.pdf

Yudkowsky, E. (2001). Creating friendly AI 1.0: The analysis and design of benevolent goal architectures. *The Machine Intelligence Research Institute*. Retrieved from https://intelligence.org/files/CFAI.pdf

Yudkowsky, E. (2022, June 6). AGI ruin: A list of lethalities. *LessWrong*. Retrieved from https://www.lesswrong.com/posts/uMQ3cqWDPHhjtiesc/agi-ruin-a-list-of-lethalities

Yudkowsky, E. (2023, March 29). Pausing AI developments isn't enough. We need to shut it all down. *Time*. Retrieved from https://time.com/6266923/ai-eliezer-yudkowsky-open-letter-not-enough/

Yudkowsky, E. (2024, February 15). You have misunderstood (1) the point this post was trying to communicate and (2) the structure of the larger argument [Comment on the blog post "The hidden complexity of wishes"]. *LessWrong*. Retrieved from https://www.lesswrong.com/posts/4ARaTpNX62uaL86j6/the-hidden-complexity-of-wishes

Zaheer, S., Schomaker, M. S., & Nachum, L. (2012). Distance without direction: Restoring credibility to a much-loved construct. *Journal of International Business Studies*, *43*(1), 18–27. https://doi.org/10.1057/jibs.2011.43

Zajac, E. J., & Westphal, J. D. (1995). Accounting for the explanations of CEO compensation: Substance and symbolism. *Administrative Science Quarterly*, *40*(2), 283–308. https://doi.org/10.2307/2393639

Zarsky, T. (2016). The trouble with algorithmic decisions: An analytic road map to examine efficiency and fairness in automated and opaque decision making. *Science, Technology, & Human Values*, *41*(1), 118–132. https://doi.org/10.1177/016224391560557

Zeff, M. (2024, December 26). Microsoft and OpenAI have a financial definition of AGI: Report. *TechCrunch*. Retrieved from https://techcrunch.com/2024/12/26/microsoft-and-openai-have-a-financial-definition-of-agi-report/

Zeng, D. (2012). *China's special economic zones and industrial clusters: Success and challenges*. Cambridge, MA: Lincoln Institute of Land Policy.

Zeng, Z., Cheng, Q., Yin, Z., Wang, B., Li, S., Zhou, Y., Guo, Q., Huang, X., & Qiu, X. (2024). Scaling of search and learning: A roadmap to reproduce o1 from reinforcement learning perspective. *arXiv*. https://doi.org/10.48550/arXiv.2412.14135

Zenil, H., Tegnér, J., Abrahão, F. S., Lavin, A., Kumar, V., Frey, J. G., Weller, A., Soldatova, L., Bundy, A. R., Jennings, N. R., Takahashi, K., Hunter, L., Dzeroski, S., Briggs, A., Gregory, F. D., Gomes, C. P., Rowe, J., Evans, J., Kitano, H., & King, R. (2024). The future of fundamental science led by generative closed-loop artificial intelligence. *arXiv*. Retrieved from https://arxiv.org/pdf/2307.07522

Zetterberg, H. (1991). Introduction. In V. Pareto, *The rise and fall of elites: Application of theoretical sociology*. New Brunswick, NJ: Transaction Publishers.

Zhang, J. (2022). China: A powerful elite system keeps on delivering value, with state capacity deeply rooted in history. In T. Casas-Klett & G. Cozzi (Eds.), *Elite quality report 2022: Country scores and global rankings*. Zurich: Seismo. https://doi.org/10.33058/seismo.30769.2620

Zhu Scott, J. (2025, February 5). DeepSeek's success will undermine the US-China tech war. *The Financial Times*. Retrieved from https://www.ft.com/content/3549cc33-e04d-41da-8c58-525d5bb2ba4c

Zimmerman, S. (2024, October 21). Deere under FTC investigation over farms' right to repair equipment. *Agriculture Dive*. Retrieved from https://www.agriculturedive.com/news/deere-right-to-repair-ftc-investigation/730432/

Zingales, L. (2012). *A capitalism for the people: Recapturing the lost genius of American prosperity*. New York, NY: Basic Books.

Zingales, L. (2017). Towards a political theory of the firm. *Journal of Economic Perspectives*, *31*(3), 113–130. https://doi.org/10.1257/jep.31.3.113

Zingales, L. (2022). *Regulating big tech* (BIS Working Paper No. 1063). Basel: Bank for International Settlements. Retrieved from https://www.bis.org/publ/work1063.pdf

Zosimus. (1982). *Zosimus: New history* (Byzantina Australiensia 2, R. T. Ridley, Trans. & Ed.). Canberra: Byzantina Australiensia.

Zott, C., & Amit, R. (2013). The business model: A theoretically anchored robust construct for strategic analysis. *Strategic Organization*, *11*(4), 403–411. https://doi.org/10.1177/1476127013510466

Zuckerberg, M., & Chan, P. (2015, December 1). Letter to Max. *Chan Zuckerberg Initiative*. Retrieved from https://chanzuckerberg.com/about/letter-to-max/

Zuckerman, G. (2024, July 21). Wall Street takes a back seat with Trump's elevation of Vance. *The Wall Street Journal*. Retrieved from https://www.wsj.com/politics/elections/wall-street-takes-a-back-seat-with-trumps-elevation-of-vance-6183ae08

Index

https://doi.org/10.1515/9783110734638-020

www.ingramcontent.com/pod-product-compliance
Lightning Source LLC
Jackson TN
JSHW061950010126
96290JS00006B/205
* 9 7 8 3 1 1 0 7 3 8 9 0 2 *